Criminal Law

LONGMAN LAW SERIES

Providing you with the best possible
basis for critical legal study.

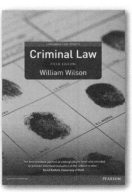

ALWAYS LEARNING

PEARSON

Criminal Law

Fifth edition

William Wilson

PEARSON

Harlow, England • London • New York • Boston • San Francisco • Toronto • Sydney
Auckland • Singapore • Hong Kong • Tokyo • Seoul • Taipei • New Delhi
Cape Town • São Paulo • Mexico City • Madrid • Amsterdam • Munich • Paris • Milan

Pearson Education Limited
Edinburgh Gate
Harlow CM20 2JE
United Kingdom
Tel: +44 (0)1279 623623
Web: www.pearson.com/uk

First published 1998 (print)
Second edition published 2003 (print and electronic)
Third edition published 2008 (print and electronic)
Fourth edition published 2011 (print and electronic)
Fifth edition published 2014 (print and electronic)

ISBN: 978-1-292-00194-4 (print)
      978-1-292-00198-2 (PDF)
      978-1-292-00199-9 (eText)

British Library Cataloguing-in-Publication Data
A catalogue record for the print edition is available from the British Library

Library of Congress Cataloging-in-Publication Data
Wilson, William.
  Criminal law / William Wilson. – Fifth edition.
    pages cm
  Includes bibliographical references and index.
  ISBN 978-1-292-00194-4 (pbk.)
  1. Criminal law–England.   2. Criminal law–Wales.   I. Title.
  KD7888.W55 2014
  345.42–dc23
                                          2014002917

ARP Impression 98
Printed in Great Britain by Clays Ltd, St Ives plc
Print edition typeset in 10/12pt Minion Pro by 35

NOTE THAT ANY PAGE CROSS REFERENCES REFER TO THE PRINT EDITION

Contents in brief

Contents

10
Defences (2): affirmative defences 245

Preface

This is the fifth edition of this book. As with previous editions this book aims to read more like a story of criminal law than a textbook. Again, a number of chapters have been substantially rewritten to take into account substantive changes in the law, reform proposals and other critical and evaluative commentaries.

Some of the 'highlights' are as follows: The first few cases on the new partial defences to murder have reached the courts. Some of the potential problems referred to in the previous edition have surfaced, including, in particular, the cogency of a blanket ban on raising evidence of sexual jealousy or possessiveness as a qualifying trigger for the defence of loss of self-control and the indeterminacy of the 'recognised medical condition' provision for diminished responsibility. *R* v *Asmelash* is important for the interplay of intoxication and the defence of loss of self-control whereas in *R* v *Coley*, *McGhee* and *Harris* the Court of Appeal sought to clarify where the line is drawn between the law of voluntary intoxication and the law of insanity and automatism.

Some interesting developments have occurred in relation to affirmative defences, including in *Pipe*, judicial recognition that a mortal emergency is not always necessary for those wishing to rely on necessity by contrast with duress of circumstances, for which see *Dao*. On the other hand a credible threat of rape was, in *R* v *A*, accepted *obiter* as capable of grounding the defence of duress. The recent changes to the law of self-defence in the context of householders introduced by the amended Section 76(5A) of the Criminal Justice and Immigration Act 2008 are also examined and subjected to critical scrutiny. The chapter on sexual offences has been rewritten to give greater prominence to policy implications and a number of interesting new cases on consent are examined. Again the major problems which have emerged concern apparent consent undermined by fraud. Other chapters benefiting from substantial rewrites include Chapters 7, 18 and 19.

On matters of structure, I am pleased that the standardised and slightly altered synoptic elements of each chapter have gone down well with reviewers. At the beginning there is a brief overview of the coverage of the chapter. The longer synopsis, which hitherto was placed at the beginning of the chapter, is now placed at the end. I think the reader will find the chapters, thus configured, easier to digest and to use as revision material.

Finally, I would like to express my grateful thanks to Cheryl Cheasley, Angela Hawksbee, Dhanya Ramesh and the rest of the team at Pearson for their patience and professionalism. I would also like to thank Carla Teteris for her invaluable help with the research for this book.

Table of cases

Note: Cases are listed under the name of the accused whenever the usual method of citation would cause them to be preceded by 'R v' signifying prosecution undertaken by the Crown.

Table of statutes

Table of statutory instruments

Table of United States legislation

Table of international conventions

Abbreviations

The following abbreviations are commonly used in the course of this book and are provided here for ease of reference.

M. Allen (2012) – M. Allen, *Textbook on Criminal Law* (2012)

A.J. Ashworth *PCL* (2006) – A.J. Ashworth, *Principles of Criminal Law* (2006); A.J. Ashworth and J. Horder, 7th edition (2013) also cited

Clarkson and Keating (2010) – C.M.V. Clarkson and H.M. Keating, *Criminal Law: Text and Materials* (2010)

J. Dressler (1987) – J. Dressler, *Understanding Criminal Law* (1987)

G. Fletcher (1978) – G. Fletcher, *Rethinking Criminal Law* (1978)

J. Gardner (2007) – J. Gardner, *Offences and Defences: Selected Essays in the Philosophy of Criminal Law* (2007)

P. Glazebrook (1978) – P.R. Glazebrook (ed.), *Reshaping the Criminal Law* (1978)

E. Griew (1995) – E. Griew, *The Theft Acts* (1995)

J. Hall (1960) – J. Hall, *General Principles of Criminal Law* (1960)

H.L.A. Hart (1968) – H.L.A. Hart, *Punishment and Responsibility: Essays in the Philosophy of Law* (1968); 2008 edition by J. Gardner also cited

(von) Hirsch and Simester (2006) – A. von Hirsch and A.P. Simester (eds), *Incivilities: Regulating Offensive Behaviour* (2006)

J. Horder – *Excusing Crime* (2004)

***Kenny's Outlines* (1966)** – Kenny's *Outlines of Criminal Law*, 19th edition (1966), ed. J.W.C. Turner; 18th edition (1962) also cited

N. Lacey (1988) – N. Lacey, *State Punishment* (1988)

Lacey and Wells (2003) – N. Lacey and C. Wells, *Reconstructing Criminal Law* (2003)

A. Norrie (1993) – A. Norrie, *Crime, Reason and History* (1993)

Perkins and Boyce (1982) – R. Perkins and R. Boyce, *Criminal Law* (1982)

Russell (1965) – *Russell on Crime*, 12th edition (1965)

Shute and Simester (2002) – S. Shute and A.P. Simester (eds), *Criminal Law Theory: Doctrines of the General Part* (2002)

S. Shute *et al.* (1993) – S. Shute, J. Gardner and J. Horder (eds), *Action and Value in Criminal Law* (1993)

Simester (2006) – A.P. Simester (ed.), *Appraising Strict Liability* (2006)

Simester and Sullivan – A. Simester, J. Spencer, G. Sullivan and G. Virgo, *Simester and Sullivan's Criminal Law: Theory and Doctrine*, 5th edition (2013)

A.T.H. Smith (1994) – A.T.H. Smith, *Property Offences* (1994)

J.C. Smith (2007) – D.C. Ormerod and D. Williams (eds), *Smith's Law of Theft* (2007)

Smith and Hogan (2011) – J.C. Smith and B. Hogan, *Criminal Law* (2011), D.C. Ormerod (ed.)

K.J.M. Smith (1991) – K.J.M. Smith, *A Modern Treatise on the Law of Criminal Complicity* (1991)

Tadros (2005) – V. Tadros, *Criminal Responsibility* (2005)

G. Williams *TCL* (1983) – Glanville Williams, *Textbook of Criminal Law* (1983); 1993 edition also cited

G. Williams *CLGP* (1961) – Glanville Williams, *Criminal Law: The General Part* (2nd edition 1961); 1st edition (1953) also cited

American MPC (1980) – American Law Institute, *Model Penal Code Proposed Official Draft* (1962); for preference see *Model Penal Code and Commentaries Part I: General Provisions* (1985); Part II: *Definitions of Specific Crimes* (1980)

CLRC 14th Report (1980) – Criminal Law Revision Committee, *14th Report Offences Against the Person* Cmnd 7844 (1980)

Draft Criminal Code (1989) – Law Commission (No. 177), *A Criminal Code for England and Wales Vol. 1* (1989)

Law Commission (No. 304) – *Murder, Manslaughter and Infanticide* (2006)

Legislating the Code (1993) – Law Commission (No. 218) *Legislating the Criminal Code: Offences Against the Person and General Principles* CM 2370 (1993)

Part I
Introduction

1 Understanding criminal law

1.1 INTRODUCTION

Proficiency in criminal law involves a number of different skills and competencies. It requires a knowledge of the rules wherein the elements of criminal offences are to be found. It requires a knowledge of the rules of evidence and procedure. It requires an ability to identify the rule(s) applicable to a fact situation and to apply them logically and coherently. Attaining these latter competencies is necessary to discharge effectively the day-to-day tasks of a criminal lawyer – solicitor, advocate or judge. However, true mastery requires something further. It requires also a critical and evaluative attitude. The criminal law in action is not just a matter of doctrine. Criminal law doctrine has as its purpose the delivery of criminal justice and criminal justice is a contingent outcome in which rule, process and context all play their part. It is not simply a logical description of what happens when rule meets (prohibited) event.

Understanding criminal law requires, therefore, an appreciation of the day-to-day workings and constitution of the criminal justice system. Moreover, it requires an understanding of the resources of the criminal law to produce substantive justice. If the mechanical application of a given rule to a fact situation acquits a dangerous or wicked person, or convicts someone neither dangerous nor blameworthy according to ordinary standards, the law may be considered not only 'an ass' but as confounding its own rationale. Understanding this rationale is also, therefore, a necessary preliminary to understanding the law itself since it will inform a realistic appreciation of what can be argued and what can not. At its most basic, to know what the law is may require an understanding of how to produce cogent and principled arguments for change.

This book seeks to examine the rules of criminal law in an evaluative context. It concerns itself with what makes a crime, both at a general theoretical level and at the level of individual offences. It addresses what the law is and, from the point of view of the ideas, principles and policies informing it, also what it ought to be. In Chapters 1–3 we will explore some general matters which will help to inform such an evaluative attitude. In Chapter 2 the principles and ideas informing decisions to criminalise will be considered. What is it, say, that renders incitement to racial hatred a criminal offence, incitement to sexual hatred a matter at most of personal morality, and sexual and racial discrimination a subject of redress only under the civil law? Chapter 3 examines punishment and the theories used to justify it. Although this is the subject-matter of its own discrete discipline, namely penology, some understanding is necessary for the student of criminal law. It provides a basis for subjecting the rules of criminal law to effective critical scrutiny. If we have a clear idea of why we punish, we are in a position to determine, for example, what fault elements should separate murder from manslaughter, or indeed whether they should be merged in a single offence. Without such an idea our opinions will, inevitably, issue from our prejudices rather than our understanding.

Individual offences themselves are covered in Chapters 11–17. The elements of these offences vary but they have certain things in common. In particular, they require proof of some proscribed deed on the part of the offender unaccompanied by any excusing or justifying condition, together with a designated mental attitude, commonly known as guilty mind. Since this model of liability (conduct–consequence–mental attitude–absence of defence) is fairly constant throughout the criminal law these separate elements and the ideas informing them will be explored in Chapters 4–10 before we meet the offences themselves, so as to avoid unnecessary duplication. Finally, in Chapters 18 and 19, we will examine how criminal liability may be incurred without personally executing a substantive offence, whether by participating in an offence perpetrated by another or by encouraging, assisting, attempting, or conspiring to commit a substantive offence.

Before tackling these issues we will, in this chapter, examine some general issues pertinent to understanding the criminal law and its operation, concentrating, in particular, upon the philosophy, workings and constitution of the criminal justice system.[1]

1.2 WHAT IS THE CRIMINAL LAW?

Crimes are characterised, and are distinguished from other acts or omissions which may give rise to legal proceedings, by the prospect of state punishment. It is this latter feature which distinguishes the criminal law from the civil law and other methods of social control such as institutional rules or community morality. The formal threshold at which the criminal law intervenes is when the conduct in question has a sufficiently deleterious social impact to oblige or permit the state, rather than simply any individual affected, taking on the ownership of the wrong.

1.3 WHAT ARE THE CONCERNS OF THE CRIMINAL LAW?

The identifying characteristic of the criminal law, generally, is its coercive, controlling nature and its function as society's formal method of social control. The criminal law sets boundaries both to our behaviour and to the power of the state to coerce and punish us. This affords no clue as to any essential internal characteristic of the act or omission which marks it as criminal. Indeed there are none. There is no requirement even that the proscribed conduct be immoral or anti-social. Parliament could enact that giving money to the poor or failing to brush one's dog was punishable and no argument of morality would prevent such conduct from being criminal.

In a sense, then, the rules of criminal law are contingent. The contingency may be the enduring and universal need to ensure that human beings treat each other as human beings rather than as objects. Or, from another perspective, it may be to secure the continuity of existing patterns of power. Often, however, the contingency is nothing more than historical accident, owing little to enduring themes of human depravity or class and much more to political expediency.[2]

Underlying the criminal law and its operation are, however, a number of ethical principles which seek to restrict its mandate. The American Model Penal Code provides what is probably the nearest thing we have to an uncontroversial statement of the proper purposes of the criminal law, namely:[3]

---

[1] See generally A. Marmor (ed.), *The Routledge Companion to Philosophy of Law*, London: Routledge (2012).
[2] J. Edwards, 'Coming Clean About the Criminal Law' (2011) 5(3) Criminal Law & Philosophy 315.
[3] Section 1.02(1).

(a) to forbid and prevent conduct that unjustifiably and inexcusably inflicts or threatens substantial harm to individual or public interests;
(b) to subject to public control persons whose conduct indicates that they are disposed to commit crimes;
(c) to safeguard conduct that is without fault from condemnation as criminal;
(d) to give fair warning of the nature of the conduct declared to be an offence;
(e) to differentiate on reasonable grounds between serious and minor offences.

These five propositions form the basic ethical building blocks of the criminal law and its operation. Without (d) the very **legality** of a criminal proscription is compromised.[4] Unless (a), (c) the relevant conduct discloses moral fault, a person should not be blamed (and suffer punishment) however serious the consequences.[5] Even (a) if fault is disclosed criminal consequences should only attend **substantial** interferences with or threats to public or private interests.[6] Severity of sentence should vary according to the seriousness of the offence (c).[7] Moral distinctions between different kinds of proscribed conduct should be reflected by the creation of different offences (e).[8]

It should be noted at this early stage, however, that this statement, principled and humane as it is, fails adequately to account for the majority of criminal laws in operation. A huge number of statutory offences, most notably those relating to traffic, environment and safety, are constituted without proof of fault. Where major public interests are at stake the operating principles underlying state coercion emphasise more our individual responsibility to act conscientiously rather than simply not to act selfishly or wickedly.

Paragraph (a) of the Model Penal Code is a convenient starting point for exploring the scope of the criminal law. It concerns itself with prohibiting and preventing conduct which harms or threatens harm to either public or private interests. It will be helpful to clarify the distinction between public and private interests since they are not coterminous. For example, the criminal law prohibits citizens from killing or even harming each other. It is contrary to the public interest that they should, and will usually be contrary also to the private interests for obvious reasons. Again, it is in the public interest that people pay their taxes. The economic and social structures of society depend on it. Yet no individual is affected by individual instances of tax evasion. State coercion is justified on the grounds of the public interests threatened rather than the victimisation of individuals. On the other side of the equation private interests will be offered support through the criminal law, but only where the protection of those interests is a matter of public interest. At the forefront of such interests is that of individual autonomy.[9] The crimes of rape, assault and theft are examples of offences where the defence of individual interests in autonomy is subsumed within the public interest obligating the state to take the side of the injured party.

The major concerns of the criminal law may be expressed, therefore, as follows.

---

[4] This is known as the principle of legality.
[5] The principle of responsibility.
[6] The principle of urgency or minimal criminalisation.
[7] The principle of proportionality.
[8] The principle of fair labelling. For an incisive analysis, see J. Chalmers and F. Leverick, 'Fair Labelling in Criminal Law' (2008) MLR 217; cf. V. Tadros, 'Fair Labelling and Social Solidarity' in L. Zedner and J.V. Roberts (eds), *Principles and Values in Criminal law and Criminal Justice: Essays in Honour of Andrew Ashworth*, Oxford: Oxford University Press (hereafter OUP) (2012) 67.
[9] This will be examined in Chapter 2.

A The support of public interests in –

(1) preventing physical injury. This accounts for the crimes of murder, manslaughter, arson and other crimes of violence; also certain road traffic offences, and those relating to public health and safety.

(2) proscribing personal immorality deemed injurious to society's well-being. This accounts for the criminalisation of bigamy, incest, sado-masochism, bestiality and obscenity, drug possession and supply.

(3) preventing the moral corruption of the young through crimes such as gross indecency with children and unlawful sexual intercourse.

(4) maintaining the integrity of the state and the administration of justice through crimes such as treason, perjury, perverting the course of justice, tax evasion.

(5) maintaining public order and security through offences such as riot, affray, breach of the peace, public drunkenness.

B The support of private interests in –

Remaining free from

(1) undesired physical interference through crimes such as rape, assault, indecent assault, false imprisonment, harassment;

(2) offence through crimes such as indecent exposure, indecency in public, solicitation;

(3) undesired interference with property through crimes such as theft, robbery, taking and driving away a road vehicle, fraud.

1.4 HOW ARE THE CRIMINAL LAW'S PURPOSES DISCHARGED?

A Law enforcement

The criminal law's purposes are discharged by law enforcement and the machinery of criminal justice generally.[10] This includes both the operational prevention of crime, typically via policing, and also by bringing offenders to justice. Procedures vary according to the nature of the offence committed. Criminal offences are classified according to whether they are arrestable or non-arrestable. The former, which includes more serious crimes, allows a suspect to be arrested without warrant.[11] The notion of arrestable and non-arrestable offences was introduced by the Criminal Justice Act 1967 and replaced the previous classification of offences into felonies and misdemeanours.

To understand properly the operation of the criminal justice system, it is important to be aware of the general context of criminal behaviour and law enforcement.[12] Only a tiny proportion of crimes result in criminal proceedings whether culminating in conviction or otherwise. Estimates of the number of offences committed which result in conviction are steady at between two and three per cent. One obvious reason why people may escape 'justice' in this way is that their offences are not detected. Few offences come to the attention of the police. The police are heavily dependent on public reporting of offences.

---

[10] See generally A.J. Ashworth and M. Redmayn, *The Criminal Process* (4th edn), Oxford: OUP (2010).

[11] Police and Criminal Evidence Act 1984, s. 24(1) and (2).

[12] For the misleading picture offered by statistics see: M. Maguire, 'Criminal Statistics and the Construction of Crime', in M. Maguire, R. Morgan and R. Reiner (eds), *The Oxford Handbook of Criminology* (5th edn), Oxford: OUP (2012) 206. See also http://www.homeoffice.gov.uk/rds/pdfs07/recorded-crime-2002-2007.xls.

Criminal offences may not be reported either because they do not come to the public's attention, as with many 'crimes of the powerful', or are not treated as worth police involvement.[13] For example victims are not disposed to report property crimes except to support an insurance claim, or if they have evidence as to who the culprit was. Research also shows that the victims of domestic violence are particularly loath to report acts of violence committed by a partner, parent or surrogate parent.[14]

The police also have a discretion as to how to react to crimes reported to them. The discretion extends to the decision whether to investigate, or even simply record a reported offence. Clearly the more serious the offence the more likely it will be taken seriously. It should be noted, however, that matters other than the grade of offence committed have a bearing on how serious it is perceived to be. For example, the decision whether or how to enforce the law is rarely neutral as to context. Research indicates that discretion is structured by bias, whether based on class, age, race or gender.[15] This has led to calls for discretion to be exercised in an open and regulated fashion. If criminal liability is so much of a lottery, it is doubly unfair that success in the outcome should be so heavily determined by cultural or economic status.[16] A more radical suggestion is for non-serious offences to be diverted altogether from the criminal courts.[17]

Some offences already 'bypass' the criminal justice system, for example minor traffic offences which carry fixed penalty notices. The Inland Revenue and Department of Social Security have the power to levy penalties rather than prosecute tax or social security fraud. This means that prosecutorial discretion has the power to structure offences according to, say, the economic status of the offender rather than the seriousness of the harm caused or his culpability. Evidence suggests that criminal justice agencies such as the police are increasingly relying on 'out of court disposals' such as fixed penalty notices and cautions, even for serious core crime. The lack of proper monitoring is such a concern that it has resulted in a review of such practices by the Office of Criminal Justice Reform.[18]

Another concerning development for the criminal justice system is the anti-social behaviour order (ASBO). This was introduced by the Crime and Disorder Act 1998 to enable communities to protect themselves from anti-social behaviour falling short of a criminal offence, by means of a civil order prohibiting certain forms of disruptive conduct

[13] C. Clarkson, A. Cretney, G. Davis and J. Shepherd, 'Assaults: the Relationship between Seriousness, Criminalisation and Punishment' [1994] Crim LR 4.

[14] For most recent statistics see ONS *Focus on: Violent Crime and Sexual Offences, 2011/12*: http://www.ons.gov .uk/ons/rel/crime-stats/crime-statistics/focus-on-violent-crime/stb-focus-on-violent-crime-and-sexual-offences-2011-12.html#tab-Types-of-violence-domestic-violence-sexual-offences-and-intimate-violence.

[15] For a good analysis of the historical perspective see J. Miller, 'Stop and Search in England: a Reformed Tactic or Business as Usual?' (2010) 50(5) Brit J Criminol 954; C. Phillips and B. Bowling, 'Ethnicities, Racisim, Crime and Criminal Justice,' in M. Maguire, R. Morgan and R. Reiner (eds), *The Oxford Handbook of Criminology* (5th edn), Oxford: OUP (2012) 370. The latest figures on gender differentiation with respect to cautioning shows this at its starkest: 'In Quarter 3 2012/2013 the percentage gender split for those who have received a conditional caution is 13.5% for women and 86.5% for men. In the comparison quarter these figures were 14.1% for women and 85.9% for men', https://www.cps.gov.uk/publications/performance/conditional_cautioning/conditional_cautioning_data_Q3_12_13.pdf.

[16] A.J. Ashworth and L. Zedner, 'Defending the Criminal Law: Reflections on the Changing Character of Crime, Procedure, and Sanctions' (2007) 2(1) Criminal Law and Philosophy 21–51; R. Cruft, 'Liberalism and the Changing Character of the Criminal Law: Response to Ashworth and Zedner' (2008) 2(1) Criminal Law and Philosophy 59.

[17] A. Sanders, 'The Limits of Diversion from Prosecution' (1988) 28(4) BJ Crim 513; A.J. Ashworth, 'Prosecution, Police and Public: A Guide to Good Gate-keeping?' (1984) 23 Howard JCJ 65; A. Sanders, 'Class Bias in Prosecutions' (1985) 24 Howard JCJ 176.

[18] Examples include *Gore and Maher* [2009] 1 WLR 2454 and *Hamer* [2010] EWCA Crim 2053. For a discussion of this issue see N. Padfield, 'Out-of-Court (Out of Sight) Disposals' [2010] Camb LJ 6.

in the community. Nominally a civil order, its breach, however, results in criminal penalty. This enables criminal penalties to attach to conduct which is not inherently criminal and although the rules of evidence and procedure characterising criminal trials are not complied with. Given that they are used most profitably in areas of urban deprivation to tackle various levels of disorder and bad behaviour in the youth,[19] the charge again is that this process facilitates the targeting for coercion of the young and disempowered in order to secure the security and autonomy of the majority, but at the price of compromising the human rights of the former.[20]

The stuff of academic criminal law ignores these various contexts but to understand how legal rules convert themselves into legal consequences it must be appreciated that, while it is a sufficient condition of being subject to state coercion that the accused satisfies a relevant offence definition, it is by no means a necessary one.

B Bringing proceedings

The Crown Prosecution Service has the overall responsibility for instituting proceedings, assessing the weight of evidence, charging and deciding, in the light of the evidence and the public interest, whether the prosecution should proceed.[21] Once again discretion, as much as the rules of criminal law, is influential but is now controlled by a Code for Crown Prosecutors.[22] A simple example of how discretion may defeat the logical application of 'paper rules' arises in connection with charging. Although official charging standards govern the exercise of discretion there is no necessary connection between the offence actually committed and that charged, beyond what is necessary to secure a conviction. Thus a person who has committed robbery may be charged only with theft; a person who has committed a wounding may be charged only with assault; a person who has committed murder may be charged only with manslaughter. Undercharging carries a number of benefits. First, it may have evidential advantages. It is easier to prove theft than robbery. Second, it may encourage a guilty plea. Third, it may enable the case to be heard summarily before lay magistrates rather than on indictment before a judge and jury. The advantage for the prosecution of summary trial is that it is less costly and more efficient. It is also thought to increase the chances of conviction. It has been estimated that only one per cent of criminal cases undergo trial by jury. This is particularly significant in the context of those serious offences triable either way, most of which are tried summarily. The neutral application of paper rules and disinterested fact-finding upon which criminal justice is premised does not come so easily in the magistrates' court. The fact that so little criminal wrongdoing is brought before courts of authority leads some to conclude that the substantive study of criminal law might be something of an esoteric pursuit.[23]

Offences are triable (a) summarily, that is, before magistrates, (b) on indictment, that is, in Crown Court before a judge and jury, or (c) either way, that is, either summarily or on

---

[19] A. Ashworth, J. Gardner, R. Morgan, A.T.H. Smith, A. von Hirsch and M. Wasik, 'Neighbouring on the Oppressive: The Government's "Anti-Social Behaviour Order" Proposals' (1998) 16(1) Criminal Justice 7.

[20] A. Crawford, 'Governing through Anti-Social Behaviour: Regulatory Challenges to Criminal Justice' (2009) 49(6) British Journal of Criminology 810–31.

[21] Criminal Justice Act 2003, section 29.

[22] Updated/revised version of Code for Crown Prosecutors in effect from January 2013: http://www.cps.gov.uk/publications/docs/code2013english_v2.pdf; J. Baldwin, 'Understanding Judge Ordered and Directed Acquittals' [1997] Crim LR 536.

[23] See P. Darbyshire, 'The Importance and Neglect of the Magistracy' [1997] Crim LR 627.

indictment. All defendants have a right to jury trial in respect of offences triable either way.[24] This right is increasingly questioned by commentators for a number of reasons, most notably the expense of jury trials, and the complexity of many trials, particularly concerning economic crime. A topical concern is the dangers of jurors being influenced by information from the internet. In a number of recent cases appeals against conviction have been lodged on the basis of evidence that a juror had engaged in internet research in the course of the trial.[25] Recent research, however, seems to confirm the opinion of the vast majority of the legal profession at least that the jury system works, and is generally an efficient, fair and effective mode of fact finding.[26]

In practice the vast majority of offences are heard by magistrates, who in addition to judging the case also act as fact finders. Whether heard summarily or on indictment the conduct of the trial is dictated to a greater or lesser extent by the rules of evidence and procedure. Some of these will be examined in outline now. To aid comprehension, they will be considered in the context of a jury trial of a typical offence, with the rider that such an offence (triable either way) will, however, rarely be tried there.

C Trial

The formal accusation made against a defendant is in the form of an indictment or, where the matter is tried summarily before magistrates, an information. This contains a statement of the offence and particulars of the offence charged. Thus an indictment for burglary will adopt the following form:

> John Smith is charged as follows:
> **Statement of Offence:** burglary contrary to section 9(1)(b) Theft Act 1968.
> **Particulars:** John Smith on the first of September 1998, having entered a building known as Buckingham Palace as a trespasser, stole therein one cushion.

1 Proving guilt

The job of the prosecution will be to prove all the elements of burglary as described in the particulars of the offence. These include the elements of theft comprehended by the word 'stole'. Theft is defined as 'the dishonest appropriation of property belonging to another with the intention of permanently depriving the other of it'. The purpose of the trial will be to establish that these elements are present. This involves both legal determinations (e.g. what does 'appropriation' mean?) and factual determinations (e.g. did John Smith do the appropriating?). The burden of proving all the elements of the offence lies with the prosecution. They will be required to prove that

---

[24] The Auld Report, *Review of the Criminal Courts of England and Wales*, http://www.criminal-courts-review.org.uk/, recommends the abolition of the defendant's right to elect jury trial in either way cases, at p. 200 ff. For discussion see M. Zander's *Response*, http://www.lse.ac.uk/collections/law/staff/zander/auld_response_web.pdf; G. Slapper, 'Opinion: The Desirable Dozen' (2012) 76 J Crim L 99.

[25] *Thompson and Others* [2010] EWCA Crim 1623; *McDonnell* [2010] EWCA Crim 2352; *Mpelenda and Another* [2011] EWCA Crim 1235. See K. Crosby, 'Controlling Devlin's Jury: What the Jury Thinks, and What the Jury Sees Online' [2012] Crim LR 15. A practice direction was issued in November 2012 to address these concerns (QBD: Crown Court: Jury Irregularities) [2013] 1 WLR 486; [2013] 1 Cr App R 22.

[26] C. Thomas, 'Are Juries Fair?' (2010) Ministry of Justice Research Series 1/10 February 2010. The report involved a two-year survey of more than 1,000 jurors at Crown Courts and a separate study of over 68,000 jury verdicts: http://www.justice.gov.uk/downloads/publications/research-and-analysis/moj-research/are-juries-fair-research.pdf.

(1) there was a taking (appropriation) of a cushion,
(2) the taking was by John Smith,
(3) the cushion belonged to someone other than John Smith,
(4) the taking was dishonest, and
(5) the taking was intended permanently to deprive the owner of it.

The burden of persuading the jury (or magistrates where tried summarily) of the accused's guilt extends beyond proving the elements of the offence to include the burden of **disproving** any defence for which the defendant adduces evidence. Included in the meaning of defence in this context are general defences such as duress, provocation or self-defence[27] and defences arising out of the structure of the offence charged. Thus if the defendant adduces evidence to the effect that he was coerced or thought the cushion was his own (and was therefore not dishonest) it is for the prosecution to persuade the jury that his story is untrue.

It should be noted that a defence can only be raised by the adducing of evidence by the defendant. It cannot be done simply by means of pleading. The prosecution does not have to disprove every cock-and-bull story the defendant might raise.[28] Thus, John Smith will have to do something more than claim that he thought the cushion was his own. If he does not do so the jury will be entitled to assume that he is simply trying it on and that the circumstantial evidence raised by the prosecution is strong enough for a conviction. This requires him to adduce some evidence sufficient to put a doubt in the jury's mind that he may have had this belief.[29] For example he might be able to raise evidence that he had brought a cushion with him and had mislaid it. If this evidence is credible – it does not have to be overwhelming – the judge must direct the jury that the prosecution will not prove the element of dishonesty unless it persuades them to disbelieve the accused's story.

2 Burdens of proof: evidential burden and burden of persuasion

The above account makes clear that there are two burdens on the parties in a criminal trial. The **evidential burden** is the initial requirement that the prosecution (always) and the defence (sometimes) must **raise sufficient evidence to substantiate the reasonable possibility that a particular element which they wish to rely on may be true**. If, at the close of the prosecution case, it fails to discharge this evidential burden in respect of any of the elements of the offence charged, the defence may submit that there is no case to answer. Success with such a submission means an acquittal without the need for the defence to raise evidence of its own. Thus if the prosecution is able to prove that John Smith entered the palace as a trespasser but can adduce no evidence to link him with the disappearance of the cushion save that it disappeared on the day of his entry, it will fail to discharge its evidential burden on this element. Being a trespasser in a house is hardly probative of theft of a cushion.[30] No evidential burden lies with the defence in relation to the elements of the offence. On a charge of murder, rape or theft on a not guilty plea the defence need raise no evidence at all but the prosecution must still prove all the elements of the offence beyond reasonable doubt to gain the conviction. An evidential burden does lie, however, with respect to defences. If the defence, say, wish to claim self defence in answer to a charge of assault some evidence must be forthcoming that this was a possibility. This is not an onerous burden. The defendant is not required to prove that he was acting in self-defence,

---

[27] *Lobell* [1957] 1 All ER 734; *Gill* [1963] 2 All ER 688.
[28] *Bratty* v *Attorney-General for Northern Ireland* [1963] AC 386.
[29] Cf. E. Griew *The Theft Acts*, London: Sweet & Maxwell (1995) 75.
[30] This is the effect of *Woolmington* v *DPP* [1935] AC 462.

only that he might have been. Once this evidential burden is discharged it is then for the prosecution to disprove the defence, as we shall see now.

The other burden is that of **persuading the jury of the truth of the matter relied upon**. This is commonly known as the legal burden of proof, or, more helpfully, 'the burden of persuasion' or 'persuasive burden'. In theory this burden lies, with very few exceptions,[31] upon the prosecution who must prove the elements of the offence and disprove any defence for which sufficient evidence is raised to justify consideration by the jury. The standard of proof is 'beyond reasonable doubt'.[32] In effect, this means that the jury should acquit if they are not sure the defendant is guilty even if they think he most probably is.[33] An acquittal means that guilt is not proven, not that the jury believe the defendant to be innocent.[34]

3 The presumption of innocence

The prosecution carries this latter burden as reflective of a fundamental premise underpinning the criminal law, namely that the accused is innocent until proven guilty.[35] It is enshrined in Article 6(2) of the European Convention on Human Rights which the Human Rights Act 1998 incorporates into domestic law. Research suggests that the presumption of innocence is much dishonoured in English criminal law.[36] Such an aberration is challenged not simply as an error of process, but as reflecting an absence of state respect for the autonomy, freedom and diversity of citizens and visitors.[37] It seems that an increasingly large proportion of offences triable in the Crown Court[38] include some form of derogation from the principle that it is for the prosecution to do the proving. The ways in which this is achieved is via explicit statutory reversals of the burden of proof, via statutory presumptions which have the same effect, or by incorporating in an otherwise strict liability offence a defence of 'due diligence' or 'no intention'.[39] Although there may no doubt sometimes be good reasons for such derogation, it would obviously serve justice if Parliament were required to place the burden of proof on the prosecution unless good reasons for reversal were explicitly considered and debated in the debating chamber.[40]

Challenges to reverse burdens can be made on the basis of the Human Rights Act 1998 for a violation of Article 6, which guarantees the right to a fair trial.[41] Such challenges are

---

[31] For example the burden of proving insanity or diminished responsibility is on the defendant if he wishes to rely on the defence.

[32] Where the legal burden lies with the defence, as where the defendant pleads insanity, the standard of proof is on a balance of probabilities.

[33] See *Majid* [2009] EWCA Crim 2563 for an example of the problems which can arise when the judge attempts to explain reasonable doubt to the jury. Also discussed by D. Wolchover and A. Heaton-Armstrong, 'Reasonable Doubt' (2010) 174(32) Criminal Law & Justice Weekly 484.

[34] In Scotland an acquittal can generate one of two verdicts – not guilty, and not proven.

[35] *Woolmington* v *DPP* [1935] AC 462: 'throughout the web of the English criminal law one golden thread is always to be seen, that it is the duty of the prosecution to prove the prisoner's guilt . . .' at 481 per Viscount Sankey LC.

[36] See generally A. Stumer, *The Presumption of Innocence*, London: Hart (2010); D. Hamer in OJLS 31 (2011) 417: 'A Dynamic Reconstruction of the Presumption of Innocence'; R. Lippke, 'The Prosecutor and the Presumption of Innocence' (March 2013) Criminal Law & Philosophy; I. Dennis, 'Reverse Onuses and the Presumption of Innocence' [2005] LR 901; A. Ashworth and M. Blake, 'The Presumption of Innocence in English Criminal Law' [1996] Crim LR 306.

[37] R.A. Duff, *Answering for Crime* (2007).

[38] Forty per cent on Ashworth and Blakes estimate.

[39] See generally R.A. Duff, 'Presuming Innocence' in L. Zedner and J.V. Roberts (eds), *Principles and Values in Criminal Law and Criminal Justice: Essays in Honour of Andrew Ashworth*, Oxford: OUP (2012) 51.

[40] A. Ashworth and M. Blake, ibid., at 316; a less radical proposal is to be found in the CLRC Report on Evidence Cmnd 4991 of 1972 paras 137–42.

[41] P. Lewis, 'The Human Rights Act 1998: Shifting the Burden' [2000] Crim LR 667.

rarely successful. If unsuccessful an application may be made to the European Court. The Court has declared that presumptions and statutory reversals of the burden of proof do not contravene Article 6 if confined within reasonable limits.[42] In *Kebilene* the Divisional Court ruled that reverse burdens of proof in relation to the possession of weapons under the Prevention of Terrorism Act 1989 were incompatible with Article 6, given that they undermined the presumption of innocence. On appeal, the House of Lords adopted a more cautious approach, holding that reverse burdens of proof are Convention compatible if they are capable of being interpreted as imposing an evidential rather than persuasive burden on the accused.[43] Otherwise, if they impose a persuasive burden,[44] compatibility depends upon matters such as the relative difficulty of proving the relevant matter for both prosecution and defence and the seriousness of the threat the provision is designed to combat.[45]

4 Judge and jury

As should be apparent from the foregoing discussion, judge and jury have separate roles in the conduct of the trial. The jury are the judges of fact. This means that it is for them ultimately to decide how much weight to ascribe to the various pieces of evidence adduced by prosecution and defence. They will not do this unsupervised. At the outset of the trial, the trial judge will instruct the jury to make its decision on the basis of the evidence presented in court and in no circumstances to explore or canvas external sources such as newspapers or the internet.[46] In the course of the trial the judge may refuse to admit certain evidence likely to be more prejudicial than probative. The judge may also tell the jury to ignore things said in the witness-box if such things are irrelevant to the proof of guilt of the defendant or, if relevant, less probative than prejudicial. After prosecution and then defence have presented their cases the judge will sum up and will review the facts for the jury. The idea behind this is that the jury members will need help in discriminating between those facts which are relevant to prove guilt and those which are not. Thus judges will pinpoint key issues for the jury to consider and will also highlight inconsistencies, weaknesses and strengths in either case. It is open to judges to make clear their view as to how credible a piece of evidence is as long as they leave the final determination to the jury. Ideally they should do all this in as simple and direct a fashion as possible and link it to the relevant legal issue. Returning to the case of John Smith, one of the legal issues is that of dishonesty. To make this determination as easy as possible for the jury, the judge will try to explain the relevance of any claim made by the defendant to that issue, bearing in mind the evidence adduced by prosecution and defence; and will remind them that the burden

---

[42] *Salabiaku* v *France* (1988) 13 EHRR 379; *Phillips* v *UK* [2001] Crim LR 217; *R* v *Williams* [2012] EWCA Crim 2162, CA.

[43] Cf. *R* v *Webster* [2010] EWCA Crim 2819, reverse burden of proof held incompatible with the presumption of innocence under the ECHR 1950 Art. 6(2). Cf. L. Madhloom, 'Court of Appeal: Corruption and a Reverse Burden of Proof' (2011) 75(2) J Crim L 96 53.

[44] An example is Criminal Justice and Police Act 2001, ss. 39(3) and 40(3).

[45] *R* v *DPP ex parte Kebilene* [1999] 4 All ER 801; cf. *Lambert, Ali and Jordan* [2001] 1 Cr App Rep 205 and *HM Advocate* v *Mcintosh* [2001] 3 WLR 10; *R* v *Williams* [2012] EWCA Crim 2162, CA; *R* v *Chargot Ltd (t/a Contract Services)* [2008] UKHL 73; [2009] 1 WLR 1 (HL) 7. For critical discussion see V. Tadros and S. Tierney, 'The Presumption of Innocence and the Human Rights Act' (2004) MLR 402.

[46] In recent years a number of appeals against conviction have been lodged on the basis of illicit internet research by jurors. A practice direction was issued in November 2012 to address these concerns (QBD: Crown Court: Jury Irregularities) [2013] 1 WLR 486; [2013] 1 Cr App R 22.

of persuasion is on the prosecution at all times and that the standard is beyond reasonable doubt. The summing up, on the issue of dishonesty, may take a form similar to the following in which legal, factual and evidential issues are knitted together:

> (Members of the jury), did you believe his story that he thought the cushion was his own? If you think that he may have done you must acquit since it would indicate his taking of the cushion may not have been dishonest. Remember it is not for the defendant to prove that he was not dishonest but for the prosecution to prove that he was. They must do this by removing any reasonable doubt from your mind that the defence he raised may have been true. Have they done this? Let me remind you of the evidence. The defendant said that he thought the cushion was his own – the one which he had brought with him and had then mislaid. But what was the defendant doing breaking into Buckingham Palace with a cushion? He gave evidence on oath that it was for comfort. But the prosecution said he found the cushion in a cupboard. How could he think it was his own cushion if he found it in a cupboard? And, why did the accused have the key to the cupboard in his hand? You may consider this fact conclusive. It would not be unreasonable. It is a matter for you.

The judge may not, then, direct the jury to convict but can highlight the logical deficiencies of the defendant's case.[47] On the other hand, if the prosecution has failed to adduce enough evidence to justify a conviction, a judge may direct them to acquit.

The satisfying picture painted by the above sample summing-up is of a judge who takes care of all things legal and evidential, and a jury which decides the factual issues necessary to establish guilt, each keeping politely to the appropriate function. This picture is not entirely accurate, however. Apart from the influence judges are able to exert over the fact-finding process, there are also ways in which the jury may participate in deciding essentially legal questions. This confusion is more marked in the magistrates' courts where magistrates are in effect judges of both law and fact.

In the Crown Court, legal and factual roles are particularly confused over the interpretation of words in common parlance.[48] For example, if a crime is defined by statute as including the mental element of 'intention', 'recklessness' or 'dishonesty', does the judge allow jurors to apply their own meaning of these words or do the words carry a technical meaning which the judge must convey to the jury? There are no hard and fast rules on the matter. A major problem posed by handing the interpretation of provisions to the jury is the inconsistency and consequent problems of justice this may engender.[49]

1.5 WHERE DO THE RULES OF CRIMINAL LAW COME FROM?

The rules of criminal law, like any other standards of behaviour, are the product of human minds. The traditional view holds that the essence of 'law' is the authoritative guidance of conduct by means of source-based rules. Murder or theft are crimes because the conduct described by these words has been designated criminal by an appropriate source. The three main sources of the criminal law are common law, legislation, both domestic and European, and the European Convention on Human Rights.[50]

---

[47] Nelson [1997] Crim LR 234.
[48] See generally G. Williams, *Textbook of Criminal Law* (hereafter *TCL*), London: Stevens (1993) 59–67.
[49] F. Stark, 'It's Only Words: On Meaning and *Mens Rea*' (2013) 72 CLJ 155.
[50] The House of Lords has confirmed that international law was not a source of criminal law. The House of Lords could not therefore rule that action taken by the armed forces was criminal by virtue of it being allegedly contrary to international law. *Jones et al.* [2006] UKHL 16.

A Common law

1 Historical perspective

Until the nineteenth century the criminal law was almost entirely common law, that is, judge-made.[51] Included amongst the inventory of common law crimes were murder, manslaughter, rape, assault and battery, burglary and larceny. Particularly influential upon the development of the common law were the works of commentators, notable amongst whom were Hale, Hawkins, Foster, and Blackstone. The commentaries reported important decisions in criminal cases and also attempted some form of rationalisation and systematisation. This latter process was important for the future development of the criminal law because the criminal law, in comparison with some other areas of substantive law (and equity), lacked secure doctrinal foundations.[52] To appreciate why, consider the kind of reasoning necessary to decide whether A owes B money, and that necessary to decide whether A is responsible for B's death. It is relatively easy to formulate coherent and internally consistent rules governing the creation and discharge of a debt. It is less easy to formulate coherent and consistent rules governing the imputation of criminal liability. We may know a villain when we see one but how do we capture the elements of villainy in the form of a rule capable of providing a consistent blueprint for the disposal of offenders? How do we decide what people may or may not do? How do we decide whether they are to blame for what they do such that they deserve punishment?

As an illustration of how these questions may provoke contradictory responses and a consequent need for doctrinal rationalisation, it may be worthwhile examining the crime of rape. Rape was constituted as a felony by judicial decision at a relatively early stage in the development of the common law. An enduring issue has been the status of coerced intercourse by husbands upon their wives. Is this a form of 'private violence' which, although deplorable, has no public dimension sufficient to warrant state coercion? Or is it just another variation on a consistent theme of non-consensual intercourse? Until a few years ago the former account dominated legal thinking. This was the outcome not of a judicial decision but of the general commentary on the law of rape given by Hale. He deemed this to be private violence lacking a public dimension on the ground that wives give irrevocable consent to intercourse with their husband as an incident of a marriage contract. It followed that, since absence of consent is of the essence of rape, husbands cannot practise it on their wives. The commentary added meaning to the rule and, in effect, became law for no better reason than that legal custom honoured it as such. Astonishingly perhaps, it was not until 1991 that the House of Lords felt able to consign the marital rape exemption, and the reasoning behind it, to the dustbin of legal history. This example should alert readers to the contextual nature of legal reasoning. No doubt Hale's proposition looks irrational. At the time he uttered it, however, it was entirely rational in the sense that it expressed accurately the reasoning of the age. That the criminal law has authoritative sources tells us nothing about the enduring wisdom of its utterances.

The general power of judges to invent crimes and their constituent elements was clearly attributable to the absence of any other effective legislature. The judges were the law-makers

---

[51] See generally R.M. Jackson, 'Common Law Misdemeanours' (1937) 6 Camb LJ 193 and G. Williams, *Criminal Law: The General Part* (1961) (hereafter *CLGP*) ch. 12 to which the discussion following is indebted.

[52] Cf. S.F. Milsom, *The Historical Foundations of the Common Law*, Oxford: OUP (1968) ch. 14.

to all intents and purposes and this power was for a long period relatively unfettered. Judges invented new crimes as the need arose, commonly justifying their creations as instances of a more general power to criminalise conduct which 'outraged public decency', corrupted 'public morals' or effected a public mischief.[53] Examples of such offences included blasphemy,[54] attempt,[55] conspiracy and incitement,[56] grave-snatching,[57] and public nudity. By the middle of the nineteenth century the power of the courts to create new crimes was questioned, not least by the judges themselves.[58] This phenomenon coincided with the emergence of Parliament as an effective instrument of legal and social reform and the general intellectual revolt against the idea of unelected judges legislating to restrict freedom. Recommendations were made to abolish common law crimes and replace them with a criminal code.[59] These calls were resisted in England although taken up in some other common law jurisdictions. Some substantial attempts have been made, from time to time, to put the criminal law on a statutory footing. The most notable of these include the consolidating Act of 1861 on Offences Against the Person and the Theft Acts of 1968 and 1978.

2 The modern perspective

From time to time in the twentieth century, judges have reasserted a residual power to create new crimes using the old umbrella terms of corrupting public morals, outraging public decency, perverting the course of justice and effecting a public mischief. Examples have included the making of a false accusation of robbery,[60] the publication of a magazine containing advertisements from prostitutes,[61] taking photographs up women's skirts,[62] and most recently deleting pornographic images from a partner's memory stick.[63] In none of these cases was the activity, when actually performed, a recognised criminal offence. It became so only as the result of a judicial decision to fill an empty doctrinal vessel (effecting a public mischief/corrupting public morals) with the substance of conduct of which they disapproved. Such cases suffered a great degree of criticism because, while inventing offences may address matters of genuine social need,[64] it is now expected that the proper forum for determining that need, and the measures required to satisfy it, is Parliament.[65] Always alert to the need to confound expectations a new and unwelcome development is the judicial exploitation of another of these common law offences of indeterminate scope, namely perverting the course of justice.[66]

---

[53] *Jones v Randall* 98 ER 706.
[54] *Taylor* (1676) 1 Vent 293.
[55] *Vaughan* (1769) 4 Burr 2494.
[56] *Higgins* (1801) 2 East 5.
[57] *Lynn* 168 ER 350 (1788).
[58] *R v Price* (1884) 12 QBD 247, per Stephen J.
[59] See generally R. Cross, 'Reports of the Criminal Law Commissioners (1833–49) and the Abortive Bills of 1853' in P. Glazebrook (ed.), *Reshaping the Criminal Law*, London: Stevens (1978), pp. 5–20.
[60] *Manley* [1933] 1 KB 529.
[61] *Shaw v DPP* [1962] AC 220.
[62] *Hamilton* [2007] EWCA Crim 2062.
[63] *R v T* [2011] EWCA Crim 729 CA and commentary by J. Richardson, 25 March Criminal Law Week Issue 15, 18 April 2011; A. Gillespie, 'Perverting the Course of Justice by Deleting Indecent Images' (case comment) (2012) 76(1) J Crim L 10.
[64] Such as unarguably appears in *Manley*.
[65] This has been recently re-emphasised by the Law Commission. Law Com. Consultation Paper No. 193 *Simplification of Criminal Law: Public Nuisance & Outraging Public Decency* (2010).
[66] See note 63.

(a) *Judicial creativity: the impact of precedent*

Such law-making power as remains issues from the system of precedent. The trial courts (Crown Courts and Magistrates' Courts) do not set precedents although, by convention, first instance decisions at Crown Court are of persuasive authority.[67] Therefore, no ruling made by the judge in the case of *R* v *John Smith* will take effect as law. The appellate courts, which are in reverse order of hierarchy the Queen's Bench Divisional Court, Court of Appeal (Criminal Division) and Supreme Court, which replaced the House of Lords as the final court of appeal in October 2009, have the power to set binding precedents on courts lower in the court hierarchy. With the exception of the Supreme Court, which is free to depart from previous decisions, appellate courts will also normally be bound by their own decisions. In theory, even courts of higher standing will respect the precedent of a lower court unless it is manifestly wrong. Outside this hierarchy, decisions of the European Court must be taken into account if relevant to the proceedings.[68] Privy Council decisions are also of highly persuasive authority, and decisions from other common law jurisdictions are treated with ever-increasing respect.[69]

In practice, judicial development of the law is a lot 'fuzzier' than the above scheme would appear to suggest.[70] Although judicial rule-following is overwhelmingly the norm, particularly in trial courts, judges (in accordance with their powers) sometimes overrule precedents, even those of long standing, and where they cannot or choose not to, they may refuse to follow a precedent or distinguish it. Although the occasions on which judges are now prepared to invent new offences have diminished almost to vanishing point[71] they still retain, then, power to adapt and develop the common law.[72] In effect, this power is legislative power and it can be used both to reduce and to extend the reach of the criminal sanction.[73] It would be reassuring to think that there are some ultimate rules governing the practice of judges in this respect but there are none which command general agreement and obedience. There are few judges of any standing who have not sometimes played 'fast and loose' with the system of precedent where it was thought desirable.[74]

Examining the case of marital rape is again instructive in this regard. In the leading case of *R* v *R*, Owen J, at first instance, accepted the authority of Hale's rule that a husband was generally exempt from punishment for rape.[75] He nevertheless ruled that the exemption did not apply where, as here, the parties had separated, extending earlier authority where married couples were separated by court order or its equivalent. In the same year in another case a different judge came to a different conclusion. He denied that there had ever been a legally binding rule. The exemption was simply the product of the musings of an antique commentator which nobody had seen fit to doubt.[76] Finally, the Court of Appeal and House of Lords in *R* v *R* stated, in effect, that the fiction of implied consent could not be supported in a society where the dominant ethic was one of equal rights, both economic and political. If there was a rule, it was overruled.

---

[67] A.J. Ashworth, 'The Binding Effect of Crown Court Decisions' [1980] Crim LR 402.
[68] Human Rights Act 1998, s. 2.
[69] In recent years the opinions of academic writers have also become more influential.
[70] See generally S. Shapiro, *Legality*, Cambridge: Harvard University Press (2010).
[71] See discussion at note 74.
[72] A significant recent example has been the development of the common law offence of assault.
[73] And in its latter tendency, since judge-made law operates retrospectively, may breach the fair warning principle.
[74] For a robust attack on the quality of the appeal system of England and Wales and indeed its judges see J. Richardson 'Is the Criminal Appeal System Fit for Purpose? A Reflection to Mark the 750th Issue of *Criminal Law Week* 1997–2013'. See A. Paterson, *The Law Lords*, London: Macmillan (1982).
[75] [1991] 4 All ER 481.
[76] Simon Brown J, *R* v *C* [1991] 1 All ER 755.

Three important insights can be drawn from these cases. The first is that a piece of doctrine which had stood unchallenged for centuries was dismissed as if it counted for nothing. The second is that no judge, of whatever standing in the court hierarchy, had any difficulty in refusing to follow it. One judge distinguished it, another denied its binding quality, another overruled it. All that matters, it seems, is that they did not like it. The third is that the effect of each decision was to extend the scope of criminal liability retrospectively to the husband. In effect, he was punished by a law which was not in existence at the time of action. At a moral level, there can have been few people who, on hearing of the decision, did not feel that the world was a better place for the judges' decision. But the case raised two fundamental issues of principle. The first is whether it is proper for unelected and unaccountable judges to try to make the world a better place in a Parliamentary democracy. The second is whether, in trying to make the world a better place, the historically legitimated expectations of individuals that they cannot be punished for what they do in a private domain may be ignored. So abstract is this latter sentiment and so concrete is the social evil represented by marital rape, that one might prefer to dismiss it as vacuous. It is noteworthy that the decision was affirmed by the European Court of Human Rights (ECHR) despite the fact that it apparently breached Article 7 of the European Convention proscribing retrospective criminalisation.[77] The story did not end there. In 2002 it was held not to be an abuse of process for D to face, in 2002, a count of raping his wife in 1970 even where the incident occurred before the decision of *R v R*. Such a conviction did not breach a defendant's rights under the ECHR.[78]

Whatever the rights and wrongs of these two cases, it must be remembered, however, that judicial power exercised for the obvious good of humankind can also be exercised for less worthy purposes. We might find it less acceptable, for instance, if judges, without the explicit authority of Parliament or the ECHR, legislated that spouses could not engage in consensual oral sex or sado-masochism for purposes of sexual stimulation, or that parents could not lawfully punish their children.[79]

A model of law-making which avoids some of these dangers has sought to refine the function of judges in hard cases such as *R v R* where rule contradicts morality. It emphasises the requirement that judges should balance competing legal principles as well as blindly following legal rules. Sometimes a rule which operates to give effect to one legal principle confounds another. In such circumstances it is thought the judge should weigh the relevant principles in the balance and give effect to the principle most valued by society.[80] Applied to the case of marital rape, the two most obvious competing principles were the rights of husbands not to be punished without fair warning of the criminality of their acts, and the rights of wives to have their autonomy and privacy respected. On this view it seems, then, that the judges found the latter more descriptive of society's overall values than the former. Although this may not have been obvious to the defendant, he must have known he was 'sailing close to the wind' and so could hardly complain if he was treated like every other 'rapist'.

---

[77] In *SW and CR* v *UK* (1995) 21 EHRR 363.

[78] *R* v *C* [2004] EWCA Crim 292 – I.

[79] Cf. *A* v *UK* (1998) Crim LR 892 where the ECHR ruled that the UK was in breach of Article 3 of the European Convention (proscribing inhuman and degrading treatment) for allowing too broad a defence of reasonable chastisement. The Children Act 2004 withdraws such a defence from those who punish with cruelty or causing actual bodily harm. Cf. also *R* v *Emmett*, *The Times*, 15 October 1999.

[80] The progenitor of this theory is Ronald Dworkin. See R. Dworkin, *Taking Rights Seriously*, London: Duckworth (1977), cf. P. Devlin, 'Judges and Law Makers' (1976) 39 MLR 1.

R v *R* by no means stands alone as an example of the occasional tendency of judges to eschew the principle that judges should neither create new offences nor expand the impact of existing ones.[81] In recent years the House of Lords has expanded the scope of the law of assault,[82] and the reach of both assault occasioning actual bodily harm and inflicting grievous bodily harm.[83] Lest it be thought that judicial law-making is all one-way traffic aiming to increase the number of villains who pay the penalty for wrongdoing it should be noted that the courts also have been known to expand the coverage of defences. An instructive example, which has coincided with the narrowing of the scope of duress by threats,[84] is the recognition of the defence of duress of circumstances and the gradual widening of the defence of necessity. Intriguingly, therefore, as the circumstances under which a person can escape liability for capitulating to a threat of injury from a third party are **decreasing**, so the circumstances are **increasing** where a person can escape liability for capitulating to the compulsion of circumstances. It is to be hoped that some sort of doctrinal equilibrium will soon be achieved.

(b) *The tensions underlying judicial decision-making*

It is difficult to discern any consistent framework to account for these divergent themes. Judicial behaviour, like weather, is not easily reducible to mechanistic laws. As with modern climatology, understanding judicial decision-making in the field of criminal law requires an acceptance that it is ultimately 'chaotic' but underscored by enduring patterns of behaviour. Unless we know what these patterns are it is difficult, if not impossible, for the student of criminal law to understand what at all is going on. Sometimes judges legislate. Usually they do not.[85] Sometimes they reserve to themselves a law-making function. Usually they deny such a function and implore Parliament to intervene. It is tempting to suppose that some judges are conservative and others radical and that patterns of judicial law-making are reducible to the ebb and flow of different currents of opinion. While this is undoubtedly true to a degree, it does not help us to understand why sometimes conservative judges legislate and radical judges hold back.

The enduring patterns of behaviour referred to derive from, at their most basic, the eternal tension between the social need for villains to be punished and the equally urgent requirement that non-villains escape punishment. Resolution of this tension requires a clear vision of what kind of people we wish to punish and why. The rules governing criminal liability are susceptible to judicial manipulation, not only to ensure that society's baddies are taken care of, but also to ensure that society's goodies are not prejudiced by the necessarily abstract nature of criminal prohibitions. The balancing exercise is not made easier by other tensions to be discovered, for example, the tension between the judge's rationalising instincts and the more usual cautious deference to the rule of law.[86] It must be appreciated that the impact of these tensions derives to a large degree from the absence of a codified criminal law. Where there is one, or at least a consolidating statute, the inevitable tendency will be for 'the judge (to) start his thinking about the law at the relevant

---

[81] Lord Reid in *Knuller*, above; M. Giles, 'Judicial Law-making in the Criminal Courts: the Case of Marital Rape' [1992] Crim LR 407; A.T.H. Smith, 'Judicial Law-Making in the Criminal Law' (1984) 100 LQR 46; W. Wilson, (1992), casenote in Journal of Social Welfare and Family Law 445.

[82] *R* v *Ireland* [1997] 4 All ER 225.

[83] *R* v *Burstow* [1997] 4 All ER 225.

[84] Which has been withdrawn from murder and attempted murder. See Chapter 10.

[85] Cf. *Clegg* [1995] 1 All ER 334; *Kingston* [1994] 3 All ER 353.

[86] See generally P. Alldridge, *Relocating Criminal Law*. Aldershot: Ashgate (2000).

section. (But when) the common law is in control there is no guarantee that judicial thought concerning a particular problem will always start in the same place'.[87] It goes without saying that the mere existence of common law offences poses a challenge to the legality principle, which has been heavily influential in the call for codifying the criminal law.[88]

The latest attempt to provide judicial guidelines for the orderly development of the common law, whether in expanding the coverage of existing offences or expanding the reach of defences occurred in *C v DPP*. A first instance decision to abolish the presumption that children under the age of fourteen are incapable of forming *mens rea* was reversed by the House of Lords. Although they were not disposed to disagree with the substance of the judge's reasons, they were also not prepared to abrogate a long-standing rule governing the scope of criminal responsibility in a 'classic case (requiring) Parliamentary investigation, deliberation and legislation'.[89] What distinguished this case from such as *R v R*, it was said, was the fact that abolishing the rule would be politically controversial and that recent Parliamentary consideration of the issue had not resulted in a change of the law. Lord Lowry set out the guidelines as follows:

(1) if the solution is doubtful the judges should beware imposing their own remedy;
(2) caution should prevail if Parliament has rejected opportunities of clearing up a known difficulty or has legislated while leaving the difficulty untouched;
(3) disputed matters of social policy are less suitable areas for judicial intervention than purely legal problems;
(4) fundamental legal doctrines should not lightly be set aside;
(5) judges should not make a change unless they can achieve finality and certainty.[90]

Lest it might be thought, however, that these guidelines would seriously restrict the power of judges to develop the rules of criminal responsibility it should be pointed out that very few of the more notable changes made by judges over the past 20 years[91] would be caught by them. Enactment of the Human Rights Act 1998 has created another tension, with a corresponding increase in judicial activity designed to reconcile domestic law with the perceived requirements of the ECHR. On the strength of it, Diane Pretty, who was suffering from motor neurone disease, sought a declaration that her husband could lawfully help her to commit suicide. Although ultimately unsuccessful it illustrates the potential of the ECHR to challenge fundamental features of domestic doctrine on the grounds that they are infringements of human rights.[92] In *R (Purdy) v DPP*, on similar facts, this potential was advanced. Although the House of Lords affirmed the illegality of assisting a person to commit suicide[93] it was a breach of human rights for the claimant not to know what assistance comprised as a matter of law. The Court held that the failure of the DPP to set out an offence-specific prosecution policy fell foul of the requirement that the law or rule

---

[87] R. Cross, in P. Glazebrook (ed.), *Reshaping the Criminal Law*, London: Stevens (1978) 11.
[88] Below; and see G. Fletcher, 'The Fall and Rise of Criminal Theory' [1998] 1 Buffalo Crim LR 276, 280–6.
[89] *C v DPP* [1995] 2 All ER 43 at 64 per Lord Lowry. The legal position has now changed. In *R v T* [2009] UKHL 20: HL held that section 34 Crime and Disorder Act 1998 abolished the defence of *doli incapax* altogether in the case of a child aged between 10 and 14 years. For criticism of this case see F. Bennion, '*Mens rea* and Defendants Below the Age of Discretion' [2009] Crim LR 757.
[90] At 52.
[91] Including changes to the definition of intention and recklessness, changes in the coverage of manslaughter and modifications to defences as mentioned above.
[92] *R (on the application of Pretty) v DPP* [2002] 1 All ER 1 HL, *R (Purdy) v DPP* [2009] UKHL 45, and see generally A. Ashworth, 'Criminal Proceedings After the Human Rights Act: The First Year' [2001] Crim LR 855.
[93] See more recently on this matter *R (Nicklinson) v Ministry of Justice; R (AM) v DPP and others* [2013] EWCA Civ 961.

in question should be sufficiently accessible to the affected individuals, or sufficiently precise, to enable them to understand its scope and foresee the consequences of their actions so that they could regulate their conduct without breaking the law.[94]

B Statute law

1 Interrelationship of statute and common law

Although the overall structure of the criminal law has been created by the common law, the majority of criminal offences are now statute based.[95] These offences may be the original creatures of statute or perhaps common law offences whose elements have been incorporated into statute. In the latter case such statutes will not always define the full common law offence. This will leave the common law with a significant role still to fulfil. It may be instructive to consider the interaction of common law and statute in such circumstances. Once again rape serves as a useful illustration. When the common law offence of rape was put on a statutory footing by the Sexual Offences Act of 1956 the elements of rape were left largely undefined. The common law continued to apply, therefore, in respect of these undefined elements. Many of these same elements were then incorporated into the Sexual Offences (Amendment) Act 1976. These included the requirement of an absence of consent, that the intercourse be *per vaginam* and be unlawful. This latter element was not itself defined. The common law rule continued to apply, therefore, that a husband could not rape his wife, since the common law deemed sexual intercourse between man and wife 'lawful' whatever the contingency. This latter rule was itself abrogated by the House of Lords in 1991 as we have seen. A later statutory amendment extends the scope of the offence to cover male, as well as female victims.[96] Finally by the Sexual Offences Act 2003 the concept of rape was extended to include anal and oral intercourse and the fault element was expanded to include absence of a reasonable belief in the victim's consent. The Act as a whole brought into existence for the first time a schematic approach to sexual offences generally.

2 The principle of legality

The basic ethical structure governing both the enactment and interpretation of criminal statutes is the principle of legality.[97] It is commonly represented by the maxim *nullum crimen sine lege, nulla poena sine lege* or 'no crime or punishment without law'. This is a matter of general legislative morality since it requires an individual to be given fair warning of what he or she may or may not do. Moreover, it discourages state use of the criminal law for political rather than social ends.[98] There are two key incidents of the legality principle. First, criminal laws should not be retroactive. In modern liberal democracies the

---

[94] Following the ruling the CPS issued new guidance – 'Policy for Prosecutors in Respect of Cases of Encouraging or Assisting Suicide' which took effect in February 2010: http://www.cps.gov.uk/publications/prosecution/assisted_suicide_policy.html.

[95] There are exceptions, notably murder and manslaughter.

[96] Criminal Justice and Public Order Act 1994, s. 142 substituting s. 1, Sexual Offences Act 1956.

[97] See generally G. Hallevy, *A Modern Treatise on the Principle of Legality in Criminal Law*, London: Springer (2010).

[98] A prime example is the violation of the principle of legality implemented by Nazi and Soviet systems. This principle is now enshrined in Article 7 of the European Convention.

enactment of criminal statutes having retrospective effect is utterly exceptional. Second, offence definitions should not be unduly vague. A citizen is not given fair warning of the criminality of his action if, using standard procedures for discovering the law,[99] a reasonably intelligent person would be left unsure as to whether the relevant conduct was proscribed or not.[100] The major impediment to the successful realisation of the fair warning ethic is the unavoidable vagueness of generalised or indeterminate criminal prohibitions and the resulting need for judicial interpretation or exercise of judgement.

3 Interpreting criminal statutes

The same premise governs approved approaches to statutory interpretation as the system of precedent, namely that a judge administer 'justice according to law'. Judges typically ascribe for themselves a far less dynamic role when engaging in statutory construction than when developing the common law. To focus readers' attention, I shall, in the pages following, examine this contention by reference to case decisions in one relatively narrow field, namely street offences. Any conclusions drawn will, of course, be of more general application.[101]

(a) The principle of strict construction

Adherence to the principle of legality has given rise to the principle of interpretation that criminal statutes should be interpreted strictly so as to minimise any penal effect. An example of a provision being construed strictly arose in *Darroch v DPP*.[102] The appellant was convicted of persistently soliciting women for the purposes of prostitution contrary to section 2(1), Sexual Offences Act 1985.[103] On more than one occasion he had been seen driving 'around and around' a red-light district and had been seen to communicate with prostitutes. Allowing the appeal, the court held that something more than driving round was necessary to show that this communication was 'persistent' solicitation.

(b) Purposive approaches to statutory interpretation

The principle of strict construction is increasingly disregarded throughout the criminal law.[104] Current orthodoxy holds that it should be observed only if it is not clear from either the provisions of the Act itself or the purpose for which the statute was enacted that the defendant's conduct is proscribed.[105] A further application is sometimes advanced. Where

---

[99] Such as the canons of statutory interpretation.

[100] The classic expression of the principle is that of Holmes J in *McBoyle v US* (1930) 283 US 25. The ECHR has declared that binding a person over not to act *contra bonos mores* is incompatible with the Convention since it leaves the applicant, here hunt saboteurs, unclear as to the limits of their responsibilities: *Hashman v UK* [2000] Crim LR 185.

[101] A topical area in which statutory indeterminacy has prompted much comment on the issue of interpretation is in the field of terrorism offences.

[102] [1990] Crim LR 814.

[103] This provision is now repealed.

[104] It was born at a time before the nineteenth century when there were literally hundreds of capital crimes and construing a statute strictly was an obvious way of mitigating the effect.

[105] For a recent example of an unsuccessful attempt to avoid conviction on the basis of the strict meaning of the statutory provision see *R v Edmondson, R v Weatherup, R v Brooks, R v Coulson, R v Kuttner* [2013] EWCA Crim 1026; [2013] WLR (D) 262. The appellants were charged with conspiring unlawfully to intercept communications in the course of their transmission without lawful authority. They argued that the intercept only occurred after the communication had been accessed by the recipient on their answer phone and so was not intercepted 'in the course of transmission'. Argument rejected.

it is clear that the relevant provision was **not** intended to criminalise the behaviour of the defendant, it will be construed accordingly even if his behaviour lies on the borderline of criminality and even if, on a literal interpretation, the behaviour is proscribed. With both these ideas in mind, judges are now expected to consult *Hansard* and Committee reports to discover what mischief the legislature intended to remedy so as to determine whether the defendant is within the intended coverage of the Act.[106]

By adverting to the purpose of an enactment, the scope of criminal liability may be both expanded and cut down. A classic illustration where the scope was expanded is that of *Smith* v *Hughes* where a prostitute was charged with 'soliciting *in* a street for the purpose of prostitution'.[107] It was held that the offence was committed even where the woman was not in a street but was soliciting from a balcony *above* the street. The provision was obviously interpreted neither literally nor strictly, but according to the purpose of the Act, namely to remove the nuisance and offence of solicitation.[108] In *Bull*, using the same purpose approach for the same provision, the scope was cut down.[109] B, a male prostitute, was charged under the Street Offences Act 1959 with loitering, as a common prostitute, in a street or public place for the purpose of prostitution, contrary to s. 1(1). The Divisional Court interpreted 'common prostitute' to refer only to the activities of female prostitutes since the purpose behind the originating Act was limited to proscribing such activities.[110]

4 Fair warning and social protection

The message emerging from the above discussion is that judicial development of the law does not necessarily mean that judges make the law up as they go along. Although there is flexibility in the system, judicial decision-making is controlled by canons of interpretation, most notably the purpose approach, which may either argue for or against the extension of liability. Today, more so than ever, judges must ensure that these canons are applied consistently in such a way as to ensure that social goals such as social protection do not override individual rights to fair treatment.[111]

Williams has argued, with reference to the one very narrow field of inquiry presently under consideration, namely street offences, that the canons are susceptible to manipulation for purposes of social protection. He describes the tendency in the following terms: '. . . the looser the defendant's conduct, the more loosely the judges construe the statute designed to control him . . . nothing short of the most powerful reasoning based on the wording of the statute is likely to dissuade the judges from holding that the statute applies to him'.[112]

It is possible to take another view of the interpretive stance of judges in this area, namely that it is infected by double standards. When it is the immorality of women which is at issue it is easy to agree with Williams. When it is male immorality under the interpretive microscope things are not quite so simple. By way of illustration consider the cases

---

[106] *Attorney-General's Reference (No. 1 of 1988)* (1989) 88 Cr App R 60. See discussion of *Bull*, below.

[107] [1960] 2 All ER 859.

[108] Compare *DPP* v *Fearon* [2010] EWHC 340 (Admin); [2010] Crim LR 646 – where it was held that a single act of soliciting a woman for prostitution within a recognised vice area by a male on foot could not amount to the common law offence of public nuisance; see also *Fellows and Arnold* [1997] 2 All ER 548.

[109] *DPP* v *Bull* [1994] 4 All ER 411. See A. Diduck and W. Wilson, 'Prostitutes and Persons' [1997] JLS 504.

[110] It should be noted that the view taken of the purpose of the Act (nuisance of **female** solicitation) was slightly narrower than that taken in the earlier case (nuisance of solicitation).

[111] See Art. 14 ECHR.

[112] *TCL* at 12; G. Williams, 'Statute Interpretation, Prostitution and the Rule of Law' in C. Tapper (ed.), *Crime, Proof and Punishment*, London: Butterworths (1981) 71; cf. A.T.H. Smith, 'Judicial Law-Making', above; A.J. Ashworth, 'Interpreting Criminal Statutes: a Crisis of Legality?' (1991) 107 LQR 419.

Williams mentions together with some others he did not. As we have seen, in *Smith v Hughes* a prostitute was held to be soliciting in the street even though her activities were conducted from a first-floor bedroom. In another case solicitation was held to be taking place even though no form of communication occurred, by a woman displaying herself motionless in a window.[113] In other cases women have been interpreted as engaging in prostitution whether they have intercourse or merely provide masturbatory relief or other acts of 'lewdness'.[114]

In *McFarlane*[115] the view taken of the purpose behind an enactment was a notably loose one. Here the provision to be interpreted was 'living on the earnings of prostitution'. A woman offered sexual services to would-be clients, received payment in advance and then absconded without ever providing any such services. The question for the court was whether the woman's partner would commit this offence if part of the benefit of the scam found its way to him. The Court of Appeal held that he would, even though the woman had done nothing in the slightest measure sexually immoral. It should be noted that this was not a case where, as in *Darroch*, the wording of the statute was vague or where the intended scope of the statute was unclear.[116] Although the purpose of the particular provision was to protect women from sexual exploitation,[117] the more general purpose relied upon was found in a different Act entirely, namely the Street Offences Act 1959. The purpose of this Act was to remove the nuisance of street solicitation and it was in support of this **extra-legislative**[118] aim that the provision's penal effect was extended retrospectively to cover living off the earnings of fraud.

These examples illustrate that as long as the general (social protection) purposes of the relevant Act are advanced by criminalising the relevant behaviour, it is no obstacle that the behaviour fell outside the explicit scope of the proscription. Indeed it may be enough that the purpose of some other Act is thereby advanced.[119] This may offend the principle of legality but it is not necessarily unfair. Both vagueness of statutory provision and laxity of construction may sometimes be necessary to combat determined efforts to avoid the penal consequences of behaviour known to be at the margins of criminality.[120] This principle of fairness is commonly known as the **thin ice principle**.[121] Those who skate at the margins of legality cannot complain if they are not given precise warning as to when they are about to fall in.

If, as Williams suggests, a preference for social protection over fair warning apparently holds good in the general field of street offences, how, then, do we explain *Bull* and *Darroch*? In a number of other cases the preference has also been reversed. In *Crook v*

---

[113] Section 1 Street Offences Act 1959 has now been amended. It is replaced by a non-gender specific offence of loitering or soliciting for purposes of prostitution. It also defines what is meant by street or public place. By section 1(2) '"street" includes any bridge, road, lane, footway, subway, square, court, alley or passage, whether a thoroughfare or not, which is for the time being open to the public; and the doorways and entrances of premises abutting on a street (as hereinbefore defined), and any ground adjoining and open to a street, shall be treated as forming part of the street.'

[114] *deMunck* [1918] 1 QB 635.

[115] [1994] 2 All ER 283.

[116] *deMunck* [1918] 1 QB 635; *R v Webb* [1963] 3 All ER 177; cf. *Fisher v Bell* [1961] 1 QB 394.

[117] See now Policing and Crime Act 2009: s. 14.

[118] 'Extra' that is to the enactment being interpreted.

[119] See discussion of *McFarlane* above.

[120] 'Overly precise statutes invite the criminally inclined to frustrate the intent of legislation by skirting the inflexibly precise language. As a result fairness only requires that a statute put law-abiding non-lawyers on reasonable notice that their intended conduct runs a reasonable risk of violating the statute.' J. Dressler, *Understanding Criminal Law*, New York: Matthew Bender (1987) (hereafter Dressler) 28.

[121] See generally A. Ashworth and J. Horder, *Principles of Criminal Law* (7th edn), Oxford: OUP (2013) (hereafter PCL) ch. 3.5.

Edmondson,[122] a male kerb-crawler was found not to be 'soliciting for sex', an offence interpreted, by reference to the purpose of the originators of the Act, to cover only the mischief offered by prostitutes and their pimps trawling the streets for custom. Again, in *R v Morris-Lowe*,[123] it was held that a man who attempted to dupe would-be masseuses into masturbating him was not guilty of the offence of attempting to procure a woman to become a common prostitute, since his action was intended to be a 'one-off' and not therefore intended to propel a woman into a career as a prostitute.[124]

The significant picture emerging is that implementing the same canons of statutory interpretation seems to operate inconsistently against different classes of defendant. Unlike the simple picture painted by Williams, judicial moralism does not always cut both ways. The defendants in *Crook, Bull, Darroch,* and *Morris-Lowe* were protected by the principle of fair warning but in *Smith, McFarlane,* and *de Munck* they were compromised by thin ice and in each case the purpose of the Act was relied upon. It might be assumed that this assertion must now be read in the light of Article 7 ECHR which protects against retrospective legislation. However, the European Court have affirmed the right of domestic courts to adapt criminal offences to ensure their ingredients reflect existing social conditions. The thin ice principle may be expected, therefore, to continue to play a role in the construction of criminal identities. Whether by accident or design (systemic or individual), the benefit of legislative ambiguity in street offences, at least, has until recently tended to favour men before women. The implicit message in the cases examined above is that the social defence purpose underpinning the various provisions is the control of female sexuality rather than, say, the protection of vulnerable women from manipulative (immoral) men.

Recent legislative trends have sought to remove the gendered approach to prostitution. Males and females are subject to the same restrictions on soliciting. Kerb-crawling and similar activities is an offence without the need to prove persistence.[125] And paying for sexual services is criminal if the prostitute concerned is the victim of sexual exploitation, whether or not the payer knew or ought to have known of this.[126] Victims of trafficking are protected from penalty for their actions.[127] Protection from sexual exploitation is the touchstone for most of these provisions. The trend is by no means all one way, however. Soliciting for sexual services is still an offence, albeit a degendered offence.[128] The burgeoning use of anti-social behaviour orders to address community anxieties about prostitution indicate that, as far as the courts, police and local authorities are concerned, the control of female sexuality in the public arena is still of key concern.

C European Union law

Apart from any residuary powers retained by the Courts, Parliament is historically sovereign on the question of what conduct can and what cannot be made the subject of

---

[122] [1996] 2 QB 81.
[123] [1985] 1 All ER 400.
[124] The position governing solicitation is now addressed by s. 51A Sexual Offences Act 2003.
[125] Section 19 of the Policing and Crime Act 2009 introduces s. 51A into the Sexual Offences Act 2003.
[126] Policing and Crime Act 2009 s. 14.
[127] The European Convention on Action against Trafficking in Human Beings 2005 Art. 2.6, now Article 8 of the EU Directive 2011/36/EU on human trafficking, provides for the non-prosecution or non-application of penalties on victims of trafficking in human beings for their involvement in criminal activities which they have been compelled to commit as a direct consequence of being subjected to any of the acts of trafficking referred to above. See *R v LM* [2010] EWCA Crim 2327; [2011] Crim LR 425.
[128] Section 1(1) of the Street Offences Act 1959 as amended by s. 16 of the Policing and Crime Act 2009.

a criminal offence. That sovereignty was reduced when the UK joined the European Union. The UK now accepts that domestic law must defer to EC law in cases of conflict and the process of legislation must ensure that all new criminal legislation and procedure must be EU compatible. This means that a defendant has the right to challenge the validity of an item of domestic criminal law if it is in conflict with EU law.

In recent years the potential power of the EU over the criminal law has been manifested in increased activity. In 2005 the European Commission outlined a number of offences which member states were required to implement. These included counterfeiting, credit card fraud, money laundering, people-trafficking, computer hacking and virus attacks, corruption and environmental protection. Although such legislation was already largely on the domestic statute book, Europe's influence as a source of criminal law seems set to increase substantially. A recent illustration is *Murphy* v *Media Protection Services Ltd*. The case concerned an English publican who used a Greek satellite company to screen matches in her pub rather than Sky with which the Premier League had an exclusivity agreement. The High Court quashed the conviction, following the ruling by the ECJ the previous year that such agreements were contrary to EU laws on free trade.[129]

D The European Convention on Human Rights[130]

The European Convention on Human Rights allows individual citizens of a member state to make complaint before the European Court of Human Rights that their Convention rights have been infringed.[131] Infringements may take the form of positive state violations of such rights. For example, in *Dudgeon* v *UK*, the Court held that a legislative provision criminalising homosexual activity between consenting adults in private in Northern Ireland was a breach of Article 8.[132] They may also take the form of state failures to provide protection of Convention rights due to, say, an ineffective system of criminal sanctions. In *A* v *UK*[133] the Court ruled that a common law defence of reasonable chastisement which had led to the acquittal of a man who had beaten his stepchild with a garden cane did not provide adequate protection for the latter's Article 3 rights.[134] In both cases Parliament acted quickly to eradicate the inconsistency.[135]

1 The Human Rights Act 1998

With the coming into force of the Human Rights Act 1998 Convention rights have an even greater impact than hitherto. They now form part of the domestic system's own basic resources for ensuring the delivery of criminal justice, substantive, procedural and evidential. In theory, therefore, the occasions will be reduced when citizens will need to petition

---

[129] [2011] EUECJ C-429/08 (04 October 2011).

[130] See E. Bates, 'British Sovereignty and the European Court of Human Rights' (2012) 128 LQR 382 for a discussion of the constitutional background to the surrender of sovereignty implicit in ratifying this convention.

[131] Article 25.

[132] See also *Sutherland* v *UK* (1998) 24 EHRLR 117.

[133] (1998) 27 EHRR 611.

[134] Namely the right to be protected from inhuman or degrading treatment. See, however, *R* v *H* [2002] Cr App R 59.

[135] B. Dickson, 'The Record of the House of Lords in Strasbourg' (2012) 128 LQR 354 tells the story of the decision-making of the European Commission of Human Rights and the European Court of Human Rights between 1966 and 2009 in response to applications challenging House of Lords judgments.

the European Court for infringement of rights. These will be taken into account in the interpretation of existing law and the development of new law.[136]

The manner in which Convention rights impinge on domestic law should be noted. Convention rights do not supplant domestic legislation, in the manner of European criminal law, such that the courts can strike down Convention-incompatible provisions.[137] Rather, the courts must, so far as possible, interpret legislation, whenever enacted, 'in a way which is compatible with Convention rights'.[138] Where such a compatibilist interpretation is not possible a declaration of incompatibility may be made[139] which sets in motion a legislative fast-track procedure for the amending statute.[140]

In developing and ensuring compatibility Government ministers are expected to respond to declarations of incompatibility from the courts, and to make a declaration of compatibility with respect to all new Bills brought before Parliament, thus generating a rights-sensitive process.[141] It has been argued that the operation of this process may be more form than substance since it has not had any discernible effect on the passage of legislation bearing significant implications for human rights.[142] Likewise judges, without being bound by the jurisprudence of the Court and the European Commission on Human Rights, are bound by section 2 to take their decisions into account.[143]

The Human Rights Act contains no specific procedure for dealing with incompatible common law offences and defences. Sir Richard Buxton has argued that judicial power in this respect cannot exceed that available in cases of legislative incompatibility.[144] On this view, it would not be proper, for example, for a Crown Court judge to amend the common law defence of parental chastisement in anticipation of amending legislation. Given that the common law rules are creatures of the judiciary, this view seems unduly restrictive.[145]

---

[136] Petitions are still made regularly, however. In *James* v *United Kingdom* 25119/09 (2013) 56 EHRR 12 (ECHR), for example, the ECHR ruled that the failure to provide prisoners serving sentences of imprisonment for public protection with rehabilitation schemes and an effective system of review breached Article 5(1) ECHR making their detention arbitrary and unlawful. In 2012, the European Court of Human Rights ruled that Abu Qatada could not be deported to Jordan as that would be a violation of his right to a fair trial under Article 6 of the European Convention on Human Rights: *Othman (Abu Qatada)* v *The United Kingdom* (Application no. 8139/09).

[137] As they can be incompatible with community law.

[138] It has been suggested that this may even include reading words into statutes so as to render an otherwise incompatible provision compatible, as well as more orthodox interpretive strategies: Mrs Justice Arden DBE, 'Criminal Law at the Crossroads' [1999] Crim LR 439 at 446–7. A.J. Ashworth, 'Criminal Proceedings after the Human Rights Act: the first year' [2001] Crim LR, Nov, 855–72. Cf. *Litster* v *Forth Dry Dock Co. Ltd* [1990] 1 AC 546.

[139] Section 4.

[140] The track is not always so fast however. See note 152.

[141] Section 19 HRA 1998. The Law Commission will also ensure that all law reform proposals are Convention compatible. See Arden, 'Criminal Law at the Crossroads' at 451–3.

[142] M. Wasik, 'Legislating in the Shadow of the Human Rights Act: The Criminal Justice and Police Act 2001' [2001] Crim LR 931. A recent example of legislative procrastination concerns the failure to amend the legislation imposing a blanket ban on voting in national and European elections for convicted prisoners in detention in the UK arising out of the decision in *Greens & MT* v *United Kingdom* (2010) ECHR (Applications nos. 60041/08 and 60054/08). The judgment became final on 11 April 2011. A number of deadlines have come and gone. The latest is September 2013.

[143] For a radical view of what this may entail see A.J. Ashworth, 'HRA 1998 and Substantive Criminal Law' [2000] Crim LR 564 at 566. Cf. C. Gearty, 'The HRA – an academic sceptic changes his mind but not his heart' (2010) 6 EHRLR 582.

[144] 'The Human Rights Act and Substantive Criminal Law' [2000] Crim LR 335. See B. Malkani, 'A Rights-specific Approach to Section 2 of the Human Rights Act' (2012) 5 EHRLR 516 for a discussion of some of the difficulties involved in dealing with incompatible common law offences and defences and the three approaches the domestic courts have adopted in taking account of such jurisprudence.

[145] A.J. Ashworth, 'HRA 1998 and Substantive Criminal Law' [1999] Crim LR 564, at 566. See now H, *The Times* 17 May 2001.

A plausible *via media* is that such changes should be effected only by an appellate court with the appropriate constitutional jurisdiction, and only then when such a change would be consistent with other Convention rights.[146]

When considering the scope for doctrinal development post enactment of the 1998 Act the major Convention rights likely to form the basis of legal challenges to domestic substantive law, or otherwise influence legal development, are as follows and include examples of how they have been or may be used. Article 2, which protects the right to life, has been referred to in a case assessing the legality of an operation to separate conjoined twins and other cases involving the legality of mercy killing.[147] In *Menson*, a case involving a racially motivated attack in London,[148] the European Court of Human Rights indicated that this may require States to enact special legislation to provide for vulnerable groups to deter the commission of offences against the person, backed up by law enforcement machinery for the prevention, suppression and punishment of breaches of such provisions.[149] It is also likely to have a future impact on the rules governing mistake and reasonable force in self-defence, effecting arrest and the prevention of crime, since domestic law affords a rather broader justification (reasonableness) for the use of deadly force than that envisaged by Article 2 (absolutely necessary and strictly proportionate).[150]

Article 3, which protects the right not to be subjected to torture or to inhuman or degrading treatment or punishment, was the basis for changes to the rules governing parental chastisement effected by the Children Act 2004. Article 3 also formed a major plank in the case brought by Diane Pretty who argued that the criminal law should permit her husband to help her take her life when she was in the final throes of motor neurone disease, to vindicate her right not to suffer unnecessarily.[151]

Article 5, which protects the right to liberty and security of the person, was the basis for a challenge in *Gillian and Quinton v UK* by reason of the applicants having been stopped and searched by police officers, pursuant to their powers under the Terrorism Act 2000 sections 44 to 47, whilst on the way to a demonstration.[152] It also has ramifications for the criminal law's definition of insanity, in particular the internal/external mental abnormality test of insanity and the court's powers to commit to hospital.[153]

Article 6, which guarantees a right to a fair and public hearing, was the basis for a challenge to the definition of 'drunkenness' for being unduly vague for the purpose of the offence of being drunk on an aircraft.[154] The joint enterprise rules in relation to convicting accessories for murder have been (unsuccessfully) challenged.[155] A number of cases have involved challenges to the use of strict liability and reverse burdens of proof.

---

[146] Notably Article 7, prohibiting retrospective criminalisation.

[147] *Re A (conjoined twins)* [2000] 4 All ER 961; *R (on the application of Pretty) v DPP* [2002] 1 All ER 1 HL; *R (Purdy) v DPP* [2009] UKHL 45; *R (Nicklinson) v Ministry of Justice*; *R (AM) v Director of Public Prosecutions and others* [2012] LS Gazette, 30 August 30, 17, DC.

[148] *Menson and others v United Kingdom* (App. 47916/99) Decision of Court (Second Section) as to admissibility, 6 May 2003.

[149] J.K. Goodall, 'Conceptualising "racism" in criminal law', (2012) Legal Studies.

[150] A.J. Ashworth, 'The European Convention and the Criminal Law' in *The Human Rights Act and the Criminal Justice and Regulatory Process*, Cambridge Centre for Public Law (1999).

[151] See previous note.

[152] [2010] Crim LR 415 (case comment).

[153] Sutherland and Gearty, 'Insanity and the European Court of Human Rights' [1992] Crim LR 418. See Chapter 9.

[154] *Tagg, The Times*, 14 June 2001.

[155] In *R v Concannon* the Court of Appeal, refusing leave to appeal against conviction, rejected the defendant's argument that the mismatch between the *mens rea* necessary to convict the principal and that necessary to convict an accessory was a breach of Article 6 ECHR.

Article 7 guarantees a right not to be convicted under retrospective laws. This is particularly relevant in cases where a jury decision is necessary to ensure whether the relevant criminal standard has been breached or not. Cheating and other offences of dishonesty pose potential problems of legality,[156] as do offences of public nuisance,[157] public mischief, corrupting public morals and outraging public decency, perverting the course of justice, and binding over.[158] It is also of particular significance in cases where the law has changed in the time between the commission of the offence and the time when final judgment is delivered.[159]

Article 8, which protects the right to respect for private and family life, has clear application in relation to the defence of consent in sexual offences.[160] A salutary example is *R v M*. The defendant took nude photographs, with her consent, of a girl of 17 with whom he was having a sexual relationship. He was charged under the Protection of Children Act 1978 s. 1A of making indecent photographs of a child. Although it was not unlawful for him to have had sexual relations with her, the 1978 Act makes it unlawful for him to have taken nude photographs, the age of consent for this crime being 18. It is a defence to that charge that the child was over 16, was reasonably believed to have consented to the photographs and was married to, in a civil partnership with or living with the defendant in an enduring family relationship.[161] His conviction was based upon the fact that he was not in such a relationship. It seems fairly clear that this sorry example of discriminatory criminalisation would not survive an application to the ECHR. Article 8 was used, again unsuccessfully, in *Pretty* on the basis that mercy killing of a consenting adult is a matter of conscience, not state concern.[162] In *Purdy*, on facts comparable with those of *Pretty*, it was the basis for a successful challenge before the House of Lords in that Art. 8(2) requires consideration of whether section 2 of the Suicide Act is sufficiently clear to enable a spouse to know what he could and could not do without committing the offence of assisting suicide.

Article 10 (right to freedom of expression) is important for challenges to laws based on obscenity, official secrets, binding over, racially or religiously aggravated offences and incitement. It is also of increasing importance in respect of blogging and communications sent via social media.[163] Article 11 sets out the right to free assembly and association. In

---

[156] In *R v Pattni, Dhunna, Soni and Poopalarajah* [2001] Crim LR 570 counts of 'cheating the revenue' were unsuccessfully attacked for failing to meet the test of reasonable certainty required by Article 7 ECHR. The problem posed by 'dishonesty' is even more acute following enactment of the Fraud Act and recent case decisions on theft which require no manifest wrongdoing. Similarly the notion of 'gross' in gross negligence manslaughter was unsuccessfully challenged in *Misra* [2005] 1 Cr App R 21 as being in contravention of Article 7.

[157] The problem posed by public nuisance has now been resolved. See *Rimmington and Goldstein* [2006] 1 AC 459: here the House of Lords defined public nuisance restrictively to impart certainty. As Lord Bingham remarked, 'the offence of public nuisance lacked the clarity and precision which both the law and the Convention require' at 466.

[158] *Hashman v UK* [2000] Crim LR 185. And see C. Murphy, 'The Principle of Legality in Criminal Law under the European Convention on Human Rights' (2010) 2 EHRLR 192.

[159] M. Bohlander considers the implications for English law in 'Retrospective Reductions in the Severity of Substantive Criminal Law – the *Lex mitior* Principle and the Impact of *Scoppola v Italy No. 2*' [2011] Crim LR 627 following the ECtHR ruling in *Scoppola v Italy* (10249/03). The ruling was that in such cases, the courts had to apply the law whose provisions were most favourable to the defendant.

[160] See *Laskey v UK* (1997) 24 EHRR 39.

[161] *R v M* [2011] EWCA Crim 2752; [2012] Crim LR 789 (case comment).

[162] Other Convention rights include Article 9 (right to freedom of thought, conscience and religion). It has obvious implications for the future of the offence of blasphemy.

[163] In December 2012 the CPS published 'Interim Guidelines on Prosecuting Cases Involving Communications Sent via Social Media', at: http://www.cps.gov.uk/consultations/social_media_consultation.html; and see D. McGoldrick, 'The Limits of Freedom of Expression on Facebook and Social Networking Sites: a UK Perspective' (2013) 13 Human Rights Law Review 125.

Steel v UK,[164] it was held that taking part in a demonstration was a protected right under Article 11 and, without more, conviction and punishment for breach of the peace was a disproportionate response.

1.6 LOGIC AND RATIONALITY IN THE CRIMINAL LAW

A system is rational if it is organised by rules and principles which require judges to defer to pre-existing law rather than legislate for 'what seems to them an ideally just society'.[165] If, on the other hand, a system has built into it politically satisfactory justifications for avoiding the implementation of binding rules,[166] it has no claim to be designated a rational system or even a semi-rational system.

The reader will no doubt appreciate, from his treatment of street offences, that Williams has no illusions that the criminal law is entirely rational. He clearly accepts that judges can and do decide cases on political rather than strictly legal grounds. Indeed, he explains the cases simply as an example of judges allowing their morals to get the better of them.[167] This is not the same, of course, as conceding that the system as a whole is irrational. The fault, in his view, lies with a bunch of incompetent and/or biased judges. If the benches were populated with Williams' clones, everything might run smoothly and rationally.[168]

Some theorists reject this latter possibility in its entirety, concluding that the idea that the criminal law is more or less rational is untenable.[169] Among the more subtle of such accounts Norrie, while recognising that rationality has a part to play in legal decision-making, sides with critical theorists in denying criminal law the scope to rid itself entirely of systemic irrationality.[170]

His general conclusion is that it is inevitable that the criminal law will reflect, in contradictory doctrine, the social contradictions besetting society at large. Most, but not all, of these reduce to the contradictory ambitions of different classes, sub-classes and groupings, the political compromises which these give rise to, and the patterns of power which these compromises reflect and sustain. This point is perhaps best understood, once again, from the point of view of street offences. The criminal law is located in a society which, as a whole, is organised on the assumption that males visiting prostitutes is a natural, if unfortunate, expression of their sexuality.[171] On the other hand, women acting as prostitutes is assumed not to be natural. Indeed, it is viewed as a dangerously subversive form of sexual behaviour, which society needs to control if ideal patterns of womanhood are to be sustained and men are not to be hostages to their own weaknesses. The contradiction, then, is society's urgent need to control the sexual autonomy of women, while being committed, in principle, to sexual autonomy for all.

On this view, it is not coincidental that following the same rule of interpretation has a differential effect on males and females, since the phenomenon of street offences is itself

---

[164] [1998] Crim LR 893.

[165] D.N. MacCormick, *Legal Reasoning and Legal Theory*, Oxford: Clarendon Press (1978) 107.

[166] That is, which allows judges to get away with it.

[167] A. Reeves, 'Judicial Practical Reason: Judges in Morally Imperfect Legal Orders' (2011) 30(3) Law & Philosophy 319.

[168] A. Norrie, *Crime, Reason and History*, Cambridge: Cambridge University Press (hereafter CUP) (2001) 11.

[169] M. Kelman, 'Interpretive Construction in the Substantive Criminal Law' (1980–81) 33 Stanford LR 591; M.J. Horowitz, 'The Historical Contingency of the Role of History' (1981) 90 Yale LJ 1057.

[170] Norrie, ibid. particularly ch. 1.

[171] N. Naffine, *Law and the Sexes*, Sydney: Allen and Unwin (1990); C. Smart, 'The Woman of Legal Discourse', 1 Social and Legal Studies (1992) 29; A. Diduck and W. Wilson, ibid.

contradictory. Rules designed to control female (without male) sexual autonomy, if neutrally interpreted, will reinforce this contradictory effect. The only alternative would be for judges to ignore the rules of precedent and interpretation and advance social justice (sexual autonomy for all) instead. But if they did so, this would require the law's inner logic (rule-following) to be ignored. One way or another the law has no built-in mechanism for reconciling public and private interests. It requires political choices to be made, not simply legal determinations.[172]

Norrie's account cannot be lightly dismissed. Reconciling public and private interests in a way which offers no systematic challenge to the rule of law is a challenge indeed. Nevertheless as an explanation of what is going on and as a predictor of what judges will do, it is perhaps a less persuasive model of law-making than those which treat rationality and legality as an achievement, that is something to be aimed for, and thus an evaluative yardstick,[173] rather than, as Norrie would have it, a dubious form of window dressing disguising the true nature of (criminal) legal doctrine.[174] Decisions of domestic courts involving issues of human rights indicate that judges are increasingly anxious to address explicitly the fairness of individuals shouldering the penal burden of community interests.[175] This is not to deny that criminal law allows social needs to 'trump' individual rights and that it may do so in a discriminatory way. Cases such as *C v DPP* and *A-G's Reference (No. 1 of 1988)* which seek to control the exercise of judicial discretion do little to inhibit the emergence and development of unfair and discriminatory rules. However, as *R v R* indicates and the Human Rights Act requires, ethical principles already at work in criminal law have the capacity to 'trump' unfair rules and to do so in a way which sustains rather than undermines the rule of law.[176] The main threat to rule of law values is posed by doctrinal vagueness and ambiguity. Here too the Human Rights Act has an important role to play.[177] However, the enactment of a comprehensive criminal code is also widely considered to be a major functional priority in ensuring criminal doctrine is an apt vehicle for the delivery of criminal justice.

1.7 CODIFICATION

The German theorist Max Weber loosely characterised legal systems according to the degree of systemic rationality they enjoy.[178] At one extreme, case decisions are arrived at as a result of a consideration of the contingent merits of the individual case. At the other, case decisions are compelled by the formal determination of a 'gapless' system of rules in the manner of a codified system. Somewhere between the two extremes lies the common law

---

[172] Driven by an increasing problem of sexual trafficking, such initiatives are being implemented by Government.

[173] Even where the critic despairs of the ability of the criminal justice system to live up to its name. See J. Richardson 'Is the Criminal Appeal System Fit for Purpose? A Reflection to Mark the 750th Issue of *Criminal Law Week* 1997–2013'.

[174] M. Weber, *On Law in Economy and Society*, Cambridge: Harvard University Press (1954). This is not to say that Norrie rejects the value of the rule of law. He recognises its value as a check to overweening state power, p. 16. See E.P. Thompson, *Whigs and Hunters: The Origins of the Black Acts*, London: Allen Lane (1975).

[175] See for example *R v K* [2001] Crim LR 133.

[176] An obvious example is the principle of neutrality which appears to have informed the decision in *R v R*. This principle holds that the penal effect of any rule should be visited neutrally on all persons irrespective of status in the absence of specific Parliamentary provision.

[177] See for example *R v Pattni, Dhunna, Soni and Poopalarajah* [2001] Crim LR 570 in which counts of 'cheating the revenue' were unsuccessfully attacked for failing to meet the test of reasonable certainty required by Article 7 ECHR. See also A.J. Ashworth [2001] at 863. And see P. Sales and R. Ekins, 'Rights-consistent Interpretation and the Human Rights Act 1998' (2011) 127 LQR 217.

[178] M. Weber, ibid. 62 ff.

system, where the gaps between rules may be filled by decisions dictated by ethical prin-ciples informing analogous cases or matters entirely extrinsic to the system such as social morality or public policy. It is commonly supposed that codification represents an advance on the common law system since it combines both rationality and justice. It is rational because case outcomes are the result of a legal rather than a political or moral determina-tion. It is just in the sphere of criminal law because people do not suffer the evil of punish-ment except for breach of a pre-existing penal norm, the existence and content of which the individual is given fair warning.

It may be appreciated that the principle of legality (fair warning) is breached, in theory, every time an offence of vague meaning or indeterminate scope is enacted, or an offence of determinate scope is extended beyond that scope, or a moribund statutory rule is dis-interred for reasons of penal convenience,[179] and every time a new common law offence is created or defence cut down.[180] Codification promises to reduce the occasions when this will occur. Accordingly, in many other jurisdictions the criminal law is to be found in a single criminal code.

Apart from efficiency of promulgation, the major formal purpose of codification remains that of clarification and simplification. In this respect its object is to replace an unwieldy, unstructured mess of statutory and common law provisions with a comprehen-sive, clear, and internally consistent code, including a well drafted set of crimes, defences and general rules of criminal responsibility.[181] The codifying aim of clarity and simplicity is not simply a matter of linguistic aesthetics. It is a functional priority in a system in which the vast majority of criminal cases are dealt with by lay magistrates dependent upon non-specialist court clerks for advice on the law.[182] It also guarantees the moral hygiene of any system of rules, the importance of which cannot be understated. In *Okosi*,[183] O, a minicab driver, drove off with H, a passenger, hanging onto the car following an altercation. H was injured. O was charged under s. 35, Offences Against the Person Act 1861 (OAPA) with causing bodily injury through wanton or furious driving. This was an antiquated offence first created in 1820 to deal with the contemporary mischief of stagecoach drivers who were making a dangerous nuisance of themselves on public roads. It was superseded by the Road Traffic Acts and is largely redundant, albeit still in force. Charging this offence was unnecessary given that O could have been charged under these Acts, or, if it were thought necessary, with an offence against the person such as unlawful wounding. It was also argu-ably unfair since the probative burden on the prosecution was slightly eased over what they would have had to prove to establish the latter offence. Perhaps the strongest argument against the deployment of the rule, however, is that criminal justice[184] demanded that O be punished for the same crime as everybody else who injures another while driving danger-ously. What did he do wrong to get lumbered with this old-fashioned thing? Under a codified system, any offence 'swallowed up', as this was, by another offence or offences would simply be removed.[185]

---

[179] G. McBain, 'Abolishing Obsolete Legislation on Crimes and Criminal Procedure' (2011) 31(1) Legal Studies 96.

[180] K. Stevenson and C. Harris, 'Breaking the Thrall of Ambiguity: Simplification (of the Criminal Law) as an Emerging Human Rights Imperative' (2010) 74(6) J Crim L 516.

[181] A.J. Ashworth, 'Ignorance of the Criminal Law and the Duties to Avoid it' (2011) 74 MLR 21.

[182] Law Commission (No. 177): *A Criminal Code for England and Wales, Vol. 1* (1989) London: HMSO (hereafter Draft Criminal Code, Law Com. No. 177) para. 2.5.

[183] [1996] Crim LR 666; upheld [1997] RTR 1 CA.

[184] The principle of justice relied upon is commonly known as the principle of fair labelling.

[185] Its abolition was recommended by the CLRC, 14th Report Cmnd 7844 (1980) at 65.

1.8 THE DRAFT CRIMINAL CODE

The legal system of England and Wales has not followed the line of codification.[186] Historically this was due in large part to the hostility of nineteenth-century judges to the codes proposed in 1878–80 towards what would constitute a 'diminution in their status and authority'.[187] In recent years attempts have been renewed to produce a codified criminal law. A draft Criminal Code was published by the Law Commission in 1989. The groundwork was that of a team of senior academics invited by the Law Commission to undertake the task. In general the Code seeks to restate the common law, including the elimination of inconsistencies, rather than reform it.[188] By creating such systemic clarity and coherence, codification promises to render the criminal justice system more efficient and limit the reach of the criminal penalty to those occasions explicitly provided for by the elected legislature. Judges would retain significant legislative power, however, through the interpretive function to develop existing common law doctrine not abrogated by the code, of particular significance in the field of criminal defences.[189] The substantive merit of the Code's provisions will be considered in due course. However, students desirous of an accurate, clear and concise statement of much of the law examined and discussed in the pages of this book are recommended to obtain a copy of the Report and the attached Draft Code.[190]

This time, the codification project has foundered on the rocks of Parliamentary indifference rather than judicial hostility. Parliament has taken little notice of the Draft Code, which stretches to 220 sections. Lest it be thought that this attitude has been prompted by pressure of Parliamentary time, no more notice has been taken of shorter efforts in the form of individual draft bills on areas of particular pressing concern.[191] Far more notice was taken in the United States of a similar initiative by the American Law Institute. Since its publication in 1962 the American Model Penal Code has been the model for the enactment of completely new criminal codes by a large majority of states in the union.[192] Other common law jurisdictions have adopted criminal codes, including Australia, New Zealand and Canada. Ireland is in the early stages of codifying its criminal law.[193]

Social commentators usually explain the general lack of political will to legislate a code as an example of the peculiarly English talent for recognising the political advantages accruing from a system with ambiguity and discretion built into it.[194] Though we may

---

[186] For an interesting addition to the literature see A. Braun, 'The English Codification Debate and the Role of Jurists in the Development of Legal Doctrines' in M. Lobban and J. Moses (eds), *The Impact of Ideas on Legal Development (series of Comparative Studies of the Development of Tort Law in Europe)*, Cambridge: CUP (2012).

[187] D.A. Thomas, 'Form and Function in Criminal Law' in P. Glazebrook (ed.), *Reshaping the Criminal Law*, London: Stevens (1978) 21 at 22.

[188] There are, in fact, many reform proposals within it, encompassing reform proposals of official bodies previously set up to scrutinise the law with a view to reform, notably the Criminal Law Revision Committee and the Butler Committee on Mentally Abnormal Offenders.

[189] Draft Code, para. 3.37.

[190] Clauses 55, 70, 71, 72 on offences against the person and 33–40 on mental disorder are reform proposals and so do not represent a restatement of the current law.

[191] A.T.H. Smith, 'Legislating the Criminal Code: the Law Commission's Proposals' [1992] Crim LR 396. P.H. Robinson and M. Dubber, 'The American Model Penal Code' (2007) New Crim LR 319–41.

[192] American Law Institute, *Model Penal Code and Commentaries* (Part I: General Provisions (1985); Part II: Definitions of Specific Crimes (1980) (hereafter *MPC*).

[193] For an excellent analysis of the parameters and pitfalls of codification projects see P. Ferguson, 'Constructing a Criminal Code' (2010) Criminal Law Reform 20(1) 139–61.

[194] R. Cross, 'Reports of the Criminal Law Commissioners', in P. Glazebrook (ed.), *Reshaping the Criminal Law*, London: Stevens (1978); for a more radical and less sanguine view see 'Property, Authority and the Criminal Law' by D. Hay in D. Hay *et al.*, *Albion's Fatal Tree*, London: Allen Lane (1975) 63; A. Norrie, *Punishment, Responsibility and Justice*, Oxford: Clarendon Press (2001) generally.

doubt whether such considerations still rank high with the modern legislator, Parliament, it seems, still desires something more of its law reform programme than the clarification, simplification and efficient promulgation of the rules governing criminal liability.[195] The enactment of the Human Rights Act 1998 should have given fresh impetus to the Code project but nothing came of it. Given the complexity and ambiguity of much of domestic law, challenges under the Convention are increasingly launched on grounds of certainty and retroactivity as well as more basic infringements of Convention Rights. While courts may find the clarification they seek in the European Convention and the various reports or consultation papers produced by the Law Commission, this is but a poor half-way house to a Code designed specifically with clarity, certainty, accessibility and substantive human rights in mind.[196] In 2008 the Law Commission finally conceded defeat, removing codification from its programme of reform.[197] The main explanation given was the inability of the project to keep pace with the speed and complexity of legislative change and its interpenetration with European law. True no doubt, but more likely a sad acknowledgement that hope had at last run out.

Further reading

Ashworth, A.J. *Positive Obligations in the Criminal Law*, Oxford: Hart Publishing (2013)

Ashworth, A.J. and Zedner, L. 'Defending the Criminal Law: Reflections on the Changing Character of Crime, Procedure and Sanctions' (2008) Criminal Law and Philosophy 21.

Chalmers, J. 'Tracking the Creation of Criminal Offences' (2013) Crim LR 543.

Chalmers, J. and Leverick, F. 'Fair Labelling in Criminal Law' (2008) 71 Modern Law Review 217.

Lamont, G., 'What is a Crime?' (2007) 27 Oxford Journal of Legal Studies 609–63.

Law Commission Consultation Paper No. 193, *Simplification of Criminal Law: Public Nuisance and Outraging Public Decency*, London: TSO (2010).

---

[195] *Legislating the Criminal Code: Offences Against the Person and General Principles*, Law Com. No. 218 (1993) London: HMSO.

[196] Mrs Justice Arden DBE, 'Criminal Law at the Crossroads' [1999] Crim LR 439, at 453–9. For a more sceptical view see R. Buxton, 'The Human Rights Act and Substantive Criminal Law' [1999] Crim LR 335.

[197] Law Com. No. 311, HC 605, *Tenth Programme of Law Reform* (2008). J. Lavery, 'Codification of the Criminal Law: an Attainable Ideal?' (2010) 74(6) J Crim L 557 for a discussion of why historical efforts to codify the English criminal law have failed, including the insights offered by the codification endeavours in other jurisdictions.

2 Decisions to criminalise

2.1 INTRODUCTION

Although it is hard to conceive of a society without criminal law, the existence of coercive rules backed up by state punishment is in fact problematic. In this chapter the limits, if any, on the power of the state to coerce our behaviour will be examined. A key concern is to consider what the criminal law does, which could not equally well be done by morality, regulation[1] or the civil law.[2] The parameters for discussion have been described in the following question: 'What are the facts, beliefs and principles which should underpin a political body's choice to proscribe certain sorts of behaviour by means of the criminal justice system?'[3] As a starting point we will consider some of the basic premises which generate the need for criminal law as opposed to other forms of social control, namely those of autonomy, social welfare and harm prevention.[4]

2.2 PRINCIPLES AND IDEAS INFORMING DECISIONS TO CRIMINALISE

A Autonomy

Underlying the operation of the criminal law is a fundamental, yet challengeable, premise.[5] It is that human beings are characterised by their ability to control their own destiny. Human action is conceived as the product of free, rational choices on the part of the individual.[6] This capacity for free and rational action taking effect in and on the natural and social world designates human beings as autonomous moral agents, that is as bearing responsibility for their actions whether good or bad.[7] It is this same capacity which, in liberal societies, coercive rules exist to support. The premise has, then, direct implications for the relationship of the individual and state because it provides a potential basis by which to justify and evaluate a system of coercive rules and punishment for breach. The coercive rules are justified by the fact that they act to promote human autonomy rather than restrict

---

[1] V. Tadros, 'Criminalization and Regulation' in R. Duff, L. Farmer, S. Marshall, M. Renzo and V. Tadros (eds), *The Boundaries of the Criminal Law*, Oxford: OUP (2010) 163.

[2] For incisive discussion of this point see A.J. Ashworth, 'Is the Criminal Law a Lost Cause?' (2000) 116 LQR 225 at 230–7.

[3] N. Lacey, *State Punishment*, London: Routledge (1988) (hereafter Lacey) 100. For a recent addition to the range of arguments supporting criminalisation see T. Hörnle, 'Criminalizing Behaviour to Protect Human Dignity' (2012) 6(3) Criminal Law & Philosophy 307.

[4] There is a growing body of work in this area. Indicative reading includes: J. Feinberg, *The Moral Limits of the Criminal Law. Vol. 1, Harm to Others*, New York: OUP (1984); J. Feinberg, *The Moral Limits of the Criminal Law. Vol. 2, Offense to Others*, New York: OUP (1985); A.P. Simester and A. Von Hirsch, *Crimes, Harms and Wrongs: On the Principles of Criminalisation*, London: Hart Publishing (2011); D.N. Husak, *Overcriminalization: The Limits of the Criminal Law*, Oxford: OUP (2008); R.A. Duff, L.L. Farmer, S.E. Marshall, M.M. Renzo, V. Tadros, *The Boundaries of the Criminal Law* (Criminalization Series), D. Baker, *The Right not to be Criminalised: Demarcating Criminal Law's Authority*, Aldershot: Ashgate (2011).

[5] The challenge is explored in Chapter 8.

[6] See generally H.J. Paton, *The Moral Law: Kant's Groundwork of the Metaphysic of Morals*, London: Hutchinson (1948).

[7] J. Raz, *From Normativity to Responsibility*, Oxford: OUP (2011).

it. Subjects, as rational, free human beings, have the choice whether to conform or not and are able, using rules as standards, to conduct their lives with the minimum risk of suffering interference. Punishment for breach can then be justified because, by offending, the individual (free and rational) is deemed to choose not only to offend but also the punishment 'price-tag' attached to his conduct.[8]

The premise also gives us a basis for evaluating the content of the coercive rules. Since the purpose of the rules is to facilitate human autonomy, that is to maximise a person's life-choices, a rational free individual is taken to consent to coercion only insofar as it is necessary for him to be able to lead an autonomous life consistent with the enjoyment of similar rights for others. Rules which are found wanting in this respect may be criticised as involving an unjustified interference with individual autonomy. It has a number of other important consequences which will inform later discussion. Most obviously it limits the scope of the criminal to the activities of human beings and, in theory at least, only then to the extent that they display the fundamental attributes necessary for effective 'rule-following', namely free choice and rationality. The principle gives us therefore a blueprint for a system of defences, namely that people should not be the subject of coercion unless they could have acted otherwise.

1 The harm principle

The notion of autonomy currently informing the bulk of criminal law proscriptions issues from J.S. Mill in his essay 'On Liberty':[9]

> The only purpose for which power can be rightfully exercised over any member of a civilised community against his will is to prevent harm to others. His own good, either physical or moral, is not a sufficient warrant. He cannot rightfully be compelled to do or forebear . . . because in the opinion of others to do so would be wise or even right.

The harm principle has both a negative and a positive thrust. Its negative thrust, which gives it its liberal appeal, is that the state has limited authority to coerce and punish. It may only do so to prevent harm to other people. Beyond this individuals should be allowed to do, say, think what they like. Harm to self is not enough, nor is upholding society's moral values. They may smoke, or drink themselves to death.[10] They may spend every waking day watching TV or looking at pornography. They may blaspheme, commit suicide, deny the existence of God, engage in any form of consensual sexual unorthodoxy. In short the 'harm principle' gives political priority to **individual freedom** from coercion rather than individual or collective goods such as morality or welfare.

Its positive thrust is to identify what justifies state coercion, namely harm prevention. Taken together the principle yields the following equation. Where freedom of action must be restricted in order to maintain the autonomy and security of citizens, it is proper to curtail it. Otherwise freedom takes priority. The crimes of theft and violence express this at its simplest.[11] People who punch or steal from us seek to be authors of our destiny as well as their own. It is right, therefore, to restrict their freedom to do so. The crime of dangerous driving reflects a further dimension. Driving a vehicle is lawful, albeit that it inevitably

[8] S. Garvey, 'Was Ellen Wronged?' (2013) 7(2) Criminal Law & Philosophy 185.

[9] J.S. Mill, 'On Liberty' in J. Gray (ed.), *On Liberty and Other Essays*, Oxford: OUP (1991).

[10] J. Wolff, *Ethics and Public Policy: A Philosophical Inquiry*, London: Routledge (2011).

[11] For a less obvious example of the kind of wrongful harmdoing which justifies the criminal penalty see B. Wardhaugh, 'A Normative Approach to the Criminalisation of Cartel Activity' (2012) 32(3) Legal Studies 369.

involves some risk of harm; however, freedom is curtailed to the extent that taking unjustified risks of causing harm while driving is subject to penalty.[12]

2 What is harm?[13]

In a restatement of Mill's harm principle, Joel Feinberg describes it as follows:

> (S)tate interference with a citizen's behaviour tends to be morally justified when it is reasonably necessary . . . to prevent harm or the unreasonable risk of harm to parties other than the person interfered with. More concisely, the need to prevent harm (private or public)[14] to parties other than the actor is always an appropriate *reason* for legal coercion.[15]

Three points should be noted about this quotation. Feinberg talks of both private and public harm. State coercion is thus justified to prevent theft (harm to the individual) and tax evasion (harm to the state). Second, the harm principle covers both harm and the threat of harm. Third, the quotation makes clear that these considerations are 'a reason for' criminalisation. It does not make the claim that it necessitates criminalisation.[16]

If harm or the threat of harm provides a reason for criminalisation, how is it to be defined? Does the playing of loud music 'harm' those subjected to it? Do fox hunting, public nudity, soliciting for sex in the street, begging, tax evasion, insider trading, harm anybody? Feinberg distinguishes between harm in the everyday sense of physical damage to persons, institutions, or their property and harm in a politico-legal sense. In a politico-legal sense harm refers to a wrongful set-back to some protected interest. Feinberg describes 'setting-back' an interest as invading an interest in such a way as to leave it 'in a worse condition than it otherwise would have been had the invasion not occurred at all'.[17] This definition is not entirely satisfactory. Does it cover, for example, the illustrations given above? Absent a meaningful definition of harm, the harm principle can be invoked in aid of any conduct which is hurtful, disliked or considered immoral or offensive to others – an anti-liberal conclusion. For this reason, as we shall see, all liberal accounts of criminalisation are informed by a general limiting principle, namely the principle of minimal criminalisation or the principle of restraint. In other words, the state should not criminalise and punish, although it may have reason to, unless it is unavoidable.[18]

To ensure 'harm' is not too all-embracing. Feinberg refines the harm principle somewhat by distinguishing 'harm', 'hurt' and offensiveness or 'offence'. It is against harm that the criminal law is primarily pitched. What is harmful to us is a reason to stop it wherever it takes place. What is offensive to us, however, is not, in itself, reason to stop it since liberal society is committed to tolerating things done or said which do not affect us directly.[19] If

---

[12] S. Cunningham, 'Taking "causing serious injury by dangerous driving" seriously' [2012] Crim LR 261.

[13] For a recent discussion see V. Tadros, 'Harm, Sovereignty, and Prohibition' (2011) 17 Legal Theory 35.

[14] A. Lee in 'Public Wrongs and the Criminal Law' (May 2013) Criminal Law & Philosophy [online article not assigned to an issue] makes the point that a public wrong is not one which necessarily 'harms' the public but rather one which the public via the state ought to punish. Cf. G. Lamond, 'What is a Crime?' (2007) 27 Oxford Journal of Legal Studies 609.

[15] *Harm to Others: The Moral Limits of the Criminal Law*, New York: OUP (1984) 11.

[16] Cf. A. von Hirsch, 'Harm and Wrongdoing in Criminalisation Theory' (Nov 2012) Criminal Law & Philosophy [online article not assigned to an issue]; E. Yankah, 'Legal Vices and Civic Virtue: Vice Crimes, Republicanism and the Corruption of Lawfulness' (2013) 7(1) Criminal Law & Philosophy 61; B. Malkani, 'Article 8 of the European Convention on Human Rights, and the Decision to Prosecute' [2011] Crim LR 943.

[17] Ibid. 34.

[18] 'The State must not only have good reason to restrict a person's freedom of action but also good reason to censure and punish people who, rightly or wrongly, reject that reason as a reason to comply with the law.' (Husak)

[19] A. Bailin, 'Criminalising Free Speech?' [2011] Crim LR 705.

we feel disgusted, indignant, ashamed or diminished by knowing what is going on next door, that may be a reason to remonstrate, demonstrate, or move house but is not a reason for state coercion. However, criminalisation of conduct causing offence may be justified, but subject to conditions and for different reasons. If such conduct is seriously offensive, is widely considered unacceptable, and takes place in public this does directly affect us. It affects our sense of well-being, our ability to feel comfortable in a public space, our sense that our values and the way we live our life is respected by others. So while punching some-one (harm) is a criminal offence whether it takes place in public or private, homosexual activity or soliciting for sex (no harm) is an offence only if it takes place in public.[20] This begs the question, of course, as to how to gauge the degree and extent of public offence caused by such activities and whether, in any event, disgust, indignation, anger and affront are a sufficient basis for state coercion.[21] It also begs the question as to the extent the liberal state in our increasingly heterogenous social culture owes a duty to minister to the preferences of sections of society other than the liberal majority.[22]

Noise, graffiti, begging,[23] smoking in public,[24] litter are all things capable of reducing our quality of life without individual instances having a sufficient impact to cause a measurable set-back to interests.[25] The problem of course with criminalising activities without a clear, measurable and politically neutral threshold for intervention is that it threatens to undo all the good work which the harm principle is thought to achieve. Indeed, the contemporary context has seen a drastic ratcheting up of control measures designed to curb any amount of behaviours typical of the homeless and the unemployed with no serious inquiry as to whether this is justified.[26] The use of anti-social behaviour orders, for example, has been criticised for its tendency to suck into the apparatus of state coercion those, particularly the young, who are rowdy, loud, and disruptive without, however, harming in any defined and substantial fashion the interests of others.[27] To address this problem we need to keep at the forefront of our thinking the need for criminalisation to be a technique of last resort and for the offensive conduct to be both wrongful and of a nature to justify state coercion rather than individual or civil action, that is, that it shows gross disrespect for values which we hold in common or if it does not, nevertheless has a profound impact on the quality of life of those who are subjected to it.[28]

---

[20] Section 1(1) SOA 1967.
[21] See on this C. Newman and P. Rackow, 'Undesirable Posters and Dubious Symbols: Anglo-German Legal Solutions to the Display of Right-wing Symbolism and Propaganda' (2011) 75(2) J Crim L 142.
[22] M. Pinto, 'What are Offences to Feelings Really About? A New Regulative Principle for the Multicultural Era' (2010) 30(4) OJLS 695.
[23] D. Baker 'Critical Evaluation of the Historical and Contemporary Justifications for Criminalising Begging' (2009) 73(3) J Crim L 212.
[24] P. Ferguson, '"Smoke gets in your eyes. . . ." The Criminalisation of Smoking in Enclosed Public Spaces, the Harm Principle and the Limits of the Criminal Sanction' (2011) 31(2) Legal Studies 259–78.
[25] Dennis J. Baker, 'The Moral Limits of Criminalising Remote Harms' (2007) 10(3) New Criminal Law Review 370–91.
[26] J. Mitchell, 'Crimes of Misery and Theories of Punishment' (2012) 15(4) New Criminal LR 465; D. Baker, 'Critical Evaluation of the Historical and Contemporary Justifications for Criminalising Begging' (2009) 73(3) J Crim L 212.
[27] For other examples of the (covert) overuse of the criminal sanction see J. Edwards, 'Coming Clean About the Criminal Law' (2011) 5(3) Criminal Law & Philosophy 315. See J. Cromby and others, 'Constructing Crime, Enacting Morality: Emotion, Crime and Anti-social Behaviour in an Inner-city Community' (2010) 50(5) Brit J Criminol 873 for research on the attitudes of the young in deprived areas towards crime and anti-social behaviour and community anxiety. For discussion of the distinction between hark and offence see Duff and Marshall, 'How Offensive Can you Get?' in A. von Hirsch and A.P. Simester (eds), *Incivilities: Regulating Offensive Behaviour*, Oxford: Hart (2006); cf. Hirsch and Simester, 'Penalising Offensive Behaviour' 115.
[28] Ibid. 78; cf. Hirsch and Simester, 'Penalising Offensive Behaviour' 115.

3 The harm principle: its influence on criminal doctrine

(a) *Welfare offences*

The harm principle seems to underpin much of the political rhetoric regarding criminalisation. Criminalisation is rarely justified on paternalistic grounds, that is to prevent harm to self as opposed to others, and where it does, as with seat-belt laws, serious public interests are at stake[29] and Parliament is invariably the legislator. Its influence, then, is seen not only with respect to core crimes involving moral wrongs committed against individuals but more obviously in the context of statutory public welfare offences such as traffic/building/food/ environmental protection regulation and state security. Such legislation is not designed, as core crimes are, to support the individual's dominion over his own life choices.[30] It is designed to allow the state to secure its own, and our, welfare interests – obviously a key function in the constitution of a civilised autonomy-respecting society. Public welfare is here deemed so crucial to society's general purposes that such offences are often constituted in violation of the principle of responsibility.[31] Punishing for speeding and many other traffic offences, for example, does not require proof of fault. Since such offences represent the subjugation of individual autonomy to collective welfare interests it is not coincidental that they issue from politically accountable legislators rather than unaccountable judges. Parliament, rather than judges, is best able to make the 'complex judgement about the acceptable level of risk of physical and mental harm, taking into account costs of enforcement, utility of traffic circulation . . . , the autonomy of citizens who choose to take certain risks, and so on'.[32]

(b) *Core crimes*

It is to be expected, given the avowed role of judge as defender of freedoms, that an autonomy-led approach defines much of the outer boundaries of judge-made criminal law. Focal crimes such as rape, assault, criminal damage, and so on are constituted only upon proof of absence of consent, since only then will any private interests be wrongfully 'set back'.[33] It is, then, more precisely, wrongdoing against which the criminal law is pitted, the main, but by no means sole, criterion for which is harm.[34] Correspondingly, it is no defence to criminal liability that the 'victim' of wrongdoing benefited from it if consent was nevertheless absent. Overriding a person's consent is a wrong. That he benefits from it does not make it right. As will be appreciated from this discussion, the centrality of 'harm' for criminalisation is probably overstated by the harm principle. On the one hand preventing harm or the threat of harm is the central justification for that vast body of criminal offences which seek to regulate our day-to-day activities on the roads, in the workplace, in manufacturing and so on. On the other hand, for core traditional crimes such as rape, assault, murder and so on it is not so much the 'set-back' to a person's interests which supports the criminal sanction but the wrongfulness of the conduct. The moral enormity of the

---

[29] Most obviously health service costs. See A. Ogus 'The Paradoxes of Legal Paternalism and How to Resolve Them' (2010) 30(1) Legal Studies 61.
[30] Brudner, loc. cit. 24–7.
[31] M. Jefferson, 'Regulation, businesses, and Criminal Liability' (2011) 75(1) J Crim L 37.
[32] Lacey (1988) 105.
[33] Feinberg, op. cit. 215.
[34] A. du Bois-Pedain, 'The Wrongfulness Constraint in Criminalisation' (Sep 2012) Criminal Law & Philosophy [online article not assigned to an issue].

crime of rape does not hinge upon the effect on the victim, which may vary enormously, but upon the fact that our society cherishes autonomy. [35,36]

4 Alternative notions of autonomy

A particular problem which has been identified in the harm principle is that it may be too narrow to serve the interests (autonomy/self-fulfilment) which the criminal law acts to defend.[37] In emphasising the morality of minimal state coercion and concentrating upon freedom from interference, it ignores the diverse ways in which individual interests in autonomy can be compromised. A true commitment to autonomy may 'yield duties which go far beyond the negative duties of non-interference which are the only ones recognised by (the harm principle)'.[38] Consider, for example, a leading harm theorist's description of primary harms: 'violations of interest in **retaining or maintaining what one is entitled to have**. Interests regarding life, liberty, property and physical wellbeing and security are the most general and the most important classes'.[39]

Thus, society criminalises theft because it is a violation of what one is entitled to keep. On the other hand, it does not, say, criminalise a failure to reward an employee in accordance with her value, the reason being that no such violation has occurred. But why not? Consider how individual self-fulfilment may be reduced by financial exploitation. It may produce a sense of inferiority and injustice. It may prevent the individual from finding satisfactory accommodation and enjoying a meaningful social life. It may engender frustration which interferes with the stability of the individual's home life and the happiness of her family. All these harms may be far more damaging to the individual than the 'set-back' caused by the theft of a packet of cigarettes. Restricting the scope of the criminal law to the prevention of direct harm-creating acts, on this argument, is a blueprint for legislation informed by political conservatism, rather than that which might be expected to advance general human flourishing. A society truly committed to the autonomy of its members would, one might suppose, be committed to a more radical set of 'do's' and 'don'ts' underwritten by the prospect of state coercion.

B Harm prevention and other welfare values

Even in the context of judge-made crimes there are limits to the moral priority accorded to autonomy. There are limits to what harms can be consented to, for example. The support of collective interests in harm prevention or social welfare must be prayed in aid of such doctrine. So, the principle of the sanctity of life outweighs the principle of autonomy to prevent consent being a defence to murder, at least by positive action. Similar values operate to render the consensual infliction of injury criminal unless, as when they issue from socially approved activities such as contact sports, counterbalancing values and interests can be called upon in support.[40]

---

[35] See S. Shute and J. Gardner, 'The Wrongness of Rape' in J. Horder (ed.), *Oxford Essays in Jurisprudence*, Oxford: Clarendon Press (2000).

[36] For some of the problems of application this may give rise to see R. Mullender, 'Involuntary Medical Treatment, Incapacity, and Respect' (2011) 127 LQR 167; see also J. Coggon and J. Miola, 'Autonomy, Liberty, and Medical Decision-making' (2011) 70(3) CLJ 523.

[37] See generally J. Raz, *Morality of Freedom*, Oxford: Clarendon Press (1986) ch. 11.

[38] Ibid. 408.

[39] H. Gross, *A Theory of Criminal Injustice*, New York: OUP (1979) 119.

[40] See generally Chapter 11.

The weight accorded these various principles and interests is not fixed. It may well be that at some stage in the future Parliament may wish to partially decriminalise voluntary euthanasia or the infliction of consensual injury.[41] The demand for extreme and unusual forms of entertainment currently popular in Japan may soon make this a priority if it catches on over here.[42] At present, however, it is clear that the principle of autonomy may sometimes be 'trumped' by other values, in the public interest. Of particular significance in this respect are those values least directly connected to the private interests of others, namely those connected with personal morality.

1 Enforcing morality

Law and morality have a number of things in common. Most particularly, they both serve to lay down standards of behaviour (norms) for the observance of society's members. Criminal law even tends to reflect the form in which moral injunctions are encountered, namely as prohibitions or 'thou shalt nots'. If we go beyond traditional crimes, such as murder and theft, the actual content of the criminal law is only marginally concerned with upholding and enforcing community values *per se*. As we have seen, for example, a large proportion of criminal law is concerned with protecting people's welfare interests rather than society's moral structure. Thus food and health regulations are put in place to ensure that strict standards of hygiene are observed in contexts where the public may be put at risk.[43] Coercion is justified here not because public morality is confounded when food manufacturers and preparers fall down on their standards – surely implausible – but because society deems it right to protect the public's (welfare) interests in this way. The criminal law is a clear, smart, efficient way of ensuring that people keep up to scratch. A society which supported only its key moral values through state coercion would leave the interests those values exist to support largely unprotected. With these considerations in mind, most modern accounts of the proper scope of the criminal law concentrate upon the interests, both private (physical integrity, property interests, sexual autonomy, etc.) and public (political security, public order, etc.) which moral values serve to protect rather than the values themselves.

This leaves open the separate question as to whether serious breaches of morality are a sufficient basis upon which to criminalise conduct that does not also directly threaten these latter interests. If, for example, a moral consensus within society finds the practice of fox-hunting or body-piercing extremely offensive, does this justify prohibiting the practice? Given that the life choices of a rational person (fox-hunter/body-piercer) are diminished without being paid for by protecting her own or the autonomy of another rational person, would it be wrong to criminalise the activities?[44] Or is it reasonable for society to decide that our individual and collective moral welfare (or the welfare of the fox) may trump individual autonomy? At the level of general principle it seems right that society should have this power.[45] We are all diminished by cruelty to animals, for example. This does not help

---

[41] See Law Commission Consultation Papers No. 134, *Consent and Offences Against the Person*, London: HMSO (1994), and No. 139, *Consent in the Criminal Law*, London: HMSO (1995).

[42] S. Cooper and M. James, 'Entertainment – the Painful Process of Rethinking Consent' [2012] Crim LR 188.

[43] For a recent example see *R v Crestdane Ltd* [2012] EWCA Crim 958.

[44] See generally J. Raz (1986) ch. 9 for a persuasive account of how all key moral values reduce to a concern for individual autonomy. The view taken here is less complex. A concern to develop the necessary conditions for the flourishing of individual autonomy characterises the majority of society's rules but clearly not all of them.

[45] See generally R.A. Duff, 'Harms and Wrongs' (2001) Buffalo Crim LR 13 at 27 ff.

us decide, however, how to strike the appropriate balance between individual freedom and state control where, as in these two examples, criminalisation may seriously restrict the scope of a person's cultural and, therefore, 'self' identity.

A helpful starting point is the work of the French theorist, Emile Durkheim. He sought to distinguish between the values which some people **may hold**, which are consistent with the continued strength and integrity of a given society, and the values which all people **must hold** for that same society to survive. He concluded that only the latter were an appropriate object of enforcement. Punishment, in Durkheim's view, was the response of an outraged community to an infraction of a value it holds dear to its 'collective conscience'.[46] The significance of such an approach is that it offers to say both what aspects of social morality should be enforced through the criminal sanction and also what should not. It is not enough that moral values have been flouted or that individual interests have been damaged or threatened, since morality or the civil law is designed precisely so as to meet such cases. For example, the law of contract is the correct forum for dealing with the problems arising out of promise-breaking. State coercion is reserved for activities which pose a serious threat to the integrity of society, such that it demands a public rather than private response.[47] Less than this and the conduct concerned must fall outside the scope of the criminal law even if, as with fox-hunting or body-piercing, the majority may disapprove of the conduct concerned.[48] In this way collective interests can be reconciled with respect for individual autonomy.

A modern version of this position surfaced in the 1960s when the authority of the state to enforce personal morality was called into question. The new champion was Lord Devlin who argued that the enforcement of morals was as much a proper task of government as the suppression of political subversion, since both threatened to destroy or damage the community; political subversion by threatening political freedom and safety; moral subversion by threatening to topple the building blocks of our social structure. In the context of one of the burning issues of the day, namely homosexuality, he argued that the practice should not be decriminalised, since to do so would be to damage the 'moral cement' holding the social structure together. Sexual freedom should give way to the broader claims of community which require key social institutions such as the family to be protected from the potentially subversive effect of a counter-sexual culture. Mirroring the approach of Durkheim, he argued that the sounds of a community at the point of breakdown are the sounds of the community voicing distress, indignation and disgust at minority behaviour deemed unacceptable. In common with the latter, however, he agreed that society may not criminalise an activity simply because the majority do not like it. Society is only entitled to introduce the criminal sanction if the activity offers a **serious threat** to the social structure, supposedly reflected in the degree of indignation and outrage the practice excites.

2 Liberal objections to the enforcement of morality

The liberal objection to this view was, and remains, that state coercion is only legitimate insofar as it promises to prevent harm, or the risk of harm, to the interests of other people. The state should not intervene, therefore, simply to enforce morality unless perhaps the individual concerned, by virtue of youth or mental incapacity, was in need of paternalist

---

[46] E. Durkheim, *The Division of Labour in Society*, London: Macmillan (1984).
[47] Cf. *Coney* (1882) 8 QBD 534 at 549, 'A man may by consent . . . compromise his own civil rights, but he cannot compromise the public interests', at 553 per Hawkins J.
[48] Lacey (1988) calls this the principle of urgency, 100.

protection. Lord Devlin was also criticised for basing the test for assessing the propriety of criminalisation upon the degree of social disgust and outrage provoked by the activity.[49] Disgust, by itself, is unable to differentiate the good from the bad, the 'injurious' from the innocuous. Some people are quite sanguine about the export of powdered baby milk and cigarettes to the developing world, or experiments on animals. Others are disgusted by inter-racial marriage or homosexuality. It seems illogical and dangerous for society's blueprint of politically acceptable conduct to be drawn by irrational criteria so obviously conducive to political oppression. The danger, then, is that we may be left with a society in which an irrational and unprincipled majority is given licence to impose their views of right conduct on a powerless minority.[50]

3 Is there a meaningful difference between legislating to enforce morality and legislating to prevent harm?

Despite widespread concern that the criminal law should not take sides on questions of personal morality, the House of Lords, in a landmark decision, affirmed, by a majority, the role of the criminal law in enforcing morality. In *R v Brown* the question to be decided was whether consensual sado-masochism was lawful by virtue of the participant's consent or unlawful upon the ground that it involved acts of gratuitous violence.[51]

The minority, implicitly espousing J.S. Mill, took the view that there was no basis for criminalisation. No obvious harm is suffered by society if only the consenting individuals concerned are affected. The criminal law should fulfil a minimalist role, that is, to intervene only if necessary to protect the interests of other members of the public, not simply to satisfy their moral preferences.

The majority took the view that, unlike homosexuality and prostitution and other practices pertaining to sexual autonomy, criminalisation was appropriate because sado-masochism involved inflicting pain and injury. This was not only wrong in itself, but society collectively had a stake in preventing the possible emergence of cults of violence which might over time lead cult members both to proselytise for sado-masochism and abandon the general moral premise that hurting people is wrong.[52] The basic point of distinction between majority and minority reduces to the way that 'harm' is conceptualised. The minority would accept that public interests can be harmed by consensual violence but only if they have a direct public impact. Such an impact might result from the fact that they take place in public and cause offence or breach public order. Alternatively, it might result from the fact that the injuries suffered were sufficiently serious to require medical treatment and thus the expenditure of public money. The majority would insist that the public interest is not exhausted by such concerns. 'Moral harms' can be committed as well as more direct harms. The only difference between them is that the former take more time to become apparent, by which time it may be too late for the state to do anything about it.[53] Accordingly, the potential 'moral harm' to individuals and/or the community involved in

---

[49] See for example H.L.A. Hart, *Law, Liberty and Morality*, London: OUP (1963); G. Hughes, 'Morals and the Criminal Law' (1962) 71 Yale LJ 662.

[50] E. Melissaris, 'Toward a Political Theory of Criminal Law' (2012) 15(1) New Criminal LR 122.

[51] [1993] 2 All ER 75.

[52] 'Society is entitled and bound to protect itself against a cult of violence. Pleasure derived from the infliction of pain is an evil thing. Cruelty is uncivilised', p. 84 per Lord Templeman.

[53] For a recent example of the muddy waters engulfing the liberal's and moralist's sense of what is properly criminalised see S. Ost, 'Criminalising Fabricated Images of Child Pornography: A Matter of Harm or Morality?' (2010) 30(2) Legal Studies 230.

consensual sado-masochism for sexual gratification 'trumped' the individual's presumptive right to (sexual) autonomy.[54] The criminalisation of the possession of extreme pornography, has more recently been justified in this way.[55]

4 Principled approaches to the enforcement of morals

Contemporary defenders of enforcing morality, accepting the premise that collective welfare interests can be damaged in the absence of direct harm to public or private interests, have tended to emphasise the importance of society exhibiting moral neutrality in the standards it enforces. The problem with Lord Devlin's approach, on this view, is not that he wishes to enforce morality, but that he wishes to enforce morality preferentially.[56] He wants to limit the benefits of living in a free society to people like him. In short, he wants his cake and also to eat it. A just society may favour either autonomy or the enforcement of morals. What it may not justly do is to favour one group with the fruits of autonomy at the expense of other less favoured groups. If, for example, sexual autonomy is thought desirable, all citizens, whether heterosexual or homosexual, should be entitled to it. Significantly, this would allow society to retain the option to proscribe sado-masochism. As long as everyone was subject to the same proscription society would show no disrespect of rights by supporting one moral value (hurting people is wrong) against another (sexual autonomy).[57]

Of course, when morality and other welfare values are recognised as a proper basis for restricting autonomy, it is but a short step to advocate further extending the scope of the criminal law so as to actively promote socially beneficial behaviour rather than simply inhibiting bad behaviour.[58] A radical proposal along these lines advocates that the state should respond to 'serious and direct threats to and violations of . . . fundamental interests through behaviour which expresses a rejection of, hostility or total indifference to, the basic framework values which the society acknowledges'.[59]

To understand the radicalism of this latter proposal one needs only to compare it with the above morality-led approach which conceives of morality only in terms of a list of (largely sexual) prohibitions rather than prescriptions. The approach under discussion is as alert to the desirability of society demanding positive, good standards of behaviour as demanding moral self-sacrifice for the collective good. A failure to shoulder the responsibilities of

---

[54] See on this point P. de Marneffe, 'Sexual Freedom and Impersonal Value' (March 2013) Criminal Law & Philosophy [online article not assigned to issue]; for an interesting slant on this viewpoint see R.A. Duff, 'Harms and Wrongs' (2001) Buffalo Crim LR 13.

[55] Section 63 Criminal Justice and Immigration Act 2008. Extreme pornography is defined as involving:

   (a) an act which threatens a person's life,
   (b) an act which results, or is likely to result, in serious injury to a person's anus, breasts or genitals,
   (c) an act which involves sexual intercourse with a human corpse, or
   (d) a person performing an act of intercourse or oral sex with an animal (whether dead or alive) and a reasonable person looking at the image would think that any such person or animal was real.

See C. McGlynn and E. Rackley, 'Criminalising Extreme Pornography: a Lost Opportunity' (2009) Criminal Law Review 245. E. Rackley and C. McGlynn, 'Prosecuting the Possession of Extreme Pornography: A Misunderstood and Mis-used Law' [2013] Crim LR 400; S. Easton, 'Criminalising the Possession of Extreme Pornography: Sword or Shield?' (2011) 75(5) J Crim Law 391.

[56] See R. Dworkin, *Taking Rights Seriously*, London: Duckworth (1977).

[57] On this view society still has an obligation to ensure consistency of preference. It would be wrong for example to allow autonomy to defeat welfare in all cases but sexual activity.

[58] Lacey (1988) 104–5.

[59] Lacey (1988) 120. Cf. J. Gardner, 'Prohibiting Immoralities' (2007) 28(6) Cardozo Law Review 2613; McGlynn and Rackle, *supra* note 55.

good citizenship would, on this view, signify indifference to a basic framework value of most societies, that is, respect for others. It could be used, for example, to extend the range of punishable omissions, perhaps beyond the realm necessary to ensure that autonomy generally is enhanced.[60] It could be used to expand the range of both public welfare and traditional crimes to include sexual harassment, anti-social behaviour falling short of criminality, financial exploitation,[61] trading in weapons and other immoral goods, and vivisection. In 2003 it was implicit in the decision to replace the present fault element in rape, namely recklessness as to the victim's consent, with the more onerous one of negligence.[62] The 2010 Bribery Act contains provisions which criminalises actions for their moral wrongfulness whether or not such actions are harmful.[63]

Although both morality-led positions stress the need for 'thresholds of seriousness' to be satisfied before criminalisation is appropriate, unless supported by a comprehensive Bill of Rights for the protection of key freedoms, each is capable of legitimating an authoritarian of law; one which not only encourages socially valued forms of conduct but crucially **defines enforces**.[64] Adapting the words of Joseph Raz, 'a balanced view of the shortcomings of governments (should) lead to much more extensive freedom from governmental action' than is entailed by a concern to uphold society's 'basic framework values'.[65]

C Practical criteria underpinning decisions to criminalise: thresholds of seriousness

1 Grading wrongs

As this last quotation suggests, a central concern for an autonomy-respecting society is to maintain proper thresholds of 'seriousness' below which criminalisation is inappropriate. As Joel Feinberg puts it:

> The harm principle must be made sufficiently precise to permit the formulation of a criterion of 'seriousness', and also, if possible, some way of grading types of harms in terms of their seriousness. Without these further specifications, the harm principle may be taken to invite state interference without limit, for virtually every kind of human conduct can affect the interests of others for better and worse to some degree, and thus would properly be the state's business.[66]

Appropriate thresholds, in theory at least, are constituted by the requirement that criminal liability should only attend culpable wrongdoing. All other things being equal, while causing harm is the paradigm of wrongdoing, only where wrongdoing is substantial is the criminal sanction appropriate. The harm/culpability equation allows thresholds of seriousness to vary according to both gravity of harm and fault. So causing death (very) negligently is presently a criminal offence whereas causing minor personal injury negligently is not, but will be if caused intentionally. Again, intention and subjective recklessness is a more culpable state

---

[60] For example by imposing a general duty of litter removal. See Chapter 3.

[61] G. Slapper, 'Moral Voices and Market Forces' (2012) 76(5) J Crim L 359.

[62] Sexual Offences Act 2003.

[63] J. Horder, 'Bribery as a Form of Criminal Wrongdoing' (2011) 127 LQR 37.

[64] Legal moralism has recently attracted some new adherents which seek to avoid the dangers of traditional accounts such as *Devlin*. For discussion see T. Søbirk Petersen, 'New Legal Moralism: Some Strengths and Challenges' (2010) 4(2) Criminal Law & Philosophy 215; and for criticism L. Zaibert, 'The Moralist Strikes Back' (2011) 14(1) New Criminal LR 139.

[65] J. Raz (1986) 428.

[66] J. Feinberg, op. cit. 12. Cf. D. Husak, 'The Criminal Law as Last Resort' (2004) OJLS 2007; P. Alldridge, 'The Moral Limits of the Crime of Money Laundering' (2001) Buffalo Crim LR 279.

of mind than negligence which therefore affects the seriousness of the actor's wrongdoing.[67] The not uncontroversial assumption is that the more serious the harm/culpability, the greater the wrong. Although the assumption is not controversial, the legislative outcome often is. A prime example is the Crime and Disorder Act 1998 which enacted that crimes of violence, criminal damage and other crimes were more serious when motivated by racial or religious hostility. Much ink has been spilt in argument about how violence motivated by religious or racial hatred is worse than violence motivated by, say, the love of causing pain and suffering for its own sake, or even violence motivated by nothing more than boredom. The jury is still out on this one and has led many to view the legislation as one of a kind with a raft of legislation enacted over the last few years designed to symbolise that Government has its heart in the right place and is tough on anti-social behaviour but otherwise not conforming to the ethics of criminalisation which we have been discussing.

Even if we accept that the criminal law should have a role to play in preventing physical injury, protecting property and conserving society's general welfare interests, this does not help us to decide when such interests are sufficiently compromised or threatened to justify state coercion. Assessing appropriate thresholds of harm whether for purposes of basic criminalisation or for purposes of grading offences is not straightforward, although at a basic level it is deceptively easy to produce thresholds of seriousness capable of differentiating both criminal and non-criminal wrongs and offences of different grades of seriousness. The seriousness of the 'set-back' allows us to account for the majority of core wrongs, for example, murder, theft and criminal damage. Joel Feinberg's method for assessing seriousness of harm centres upon the victim's loss of choice or opportunity. Theft justifies criminalisation whereas dishonest borrowing does not, because, *ceteris paribus*, the latter does not seriously diminish the victim's range of choices. This goes to explain why dishonest borrowing is criminalised only in the exceptional cases where collective interests are imperilled.[68] So also, we are able to account for the fact that murder is treated more seriously by the criminal justice system than criminal damage. In recent years a loss of choice approach has been exploited to justify the criminalisation of stalking. It is obvious that determined psychological harassment can fundamentally restrict the range of life choices available to the victim, even choices as basic as whether to answer the telephone or leave the house to go shopping. It is also obvious that stalking affects the quality of life in a way which bears comparison with crimes, such as assault, involving similar consequences.[69]

Beyond core crimes bearing, as do assault and harassment, a family resemblance, this approach is less helpful. How, for example, does the notion of loss of choice help order in terms of gravity harms as distinct as rape, fraud, and environmental pollution? Andrew von Hirsch and Nils Jareborg have suggested an alternative way of settling thresholds of seriousness appropriate for both determining the level at which criminalisation is first appropriate and, thereafter, as a means of grading different offences for purposes of setting appropriate punishments.[70] The mechanism turns our attention from what the victim loses in terms of choice to what he loses in terms of quality of life. This latter focus is closer to the manner in which, in everyday life, we differentiate crimes. It is why we say that torturing someone or robbing them is worse than stealing from them or smashing their window.

---

[67] See A.P. Simester, 'Can Negligence be Culpable?', in J. Horder (ed.), *Oxford Essays in Jurisprudence*, Oxford: OUP (2000).

[68] See ss. 11 and 12 Theft Act 1968.

[69] Cf. C. Wells, 'Stalking: The Criminal Law Response' [1997] Crim LR 463.

[70] See generally A. von Hirsch and N. Jareborg, 'Gauging Criminal Harms: a Living Standard Analysis' (1991) 11 OJLS 1; see also J. Feinberg, op. cit. ch. 5.

Harms, then, are graded according to the effect that they have on a person's standard of living assessed according to material criteria such as financial resources and shelter and wider aspects of a good quality of life such as health, dignity, physical amenity, privacy and so on. This approach, like Feinberg's, is possibly unhelpful in fixing appropriate criteria for criminalising quintessentially public wrongs such as revenue offences. On the other hand, unlike Feinberg's more rough and ready approach, it achieves success in allowing the gravity of wrongs as distinct as crimes of violence and environmental pollution to be assessed according to common criteria, thus ensuring some degree of proportionality in the distribution of punishment.

2 Remote harms and non-victimising crimes

It will be appreciated that the above analysis is primarily geared towards victimising crimes. We need some other measure of appropriateness for regulatory offences and offences involving remote harms. A remote harm, for this purpose, is a harm at one or more stages removed from a risk-creating activity. The activity does not itself create the risk but it sets in chain causal processes which may do so. Consider, for example, s. 58(1) Terrorism Act 2000. This criminalises the possession of documents or records 'of a kind likely to be useful to a person committing or preparing to commit an act of terrorism'. Notice that there is no requirement that the possessor has any intention to so use the materials nor even that the materials themselves are dangerous. In short, there is scant connection between such provision and traditional ethics of criminalisation.[71] More broadly, crimes of possession such as drugs and weapon possession are typically justified upon the basis that criminalising possession reduces their use, which in turn reduces the risk that they will be used to cause harm to public or private interests. While individual instances of possession may pose no threat to such interests, criminalisation is justified on a cumulative basis. A weapons culture such as that existing in the United States seems to make for greater weapons use in unlawful contexts. If a person has a gun or knife in his pocket he is obviously more likely to shoot or stab someone in anger than if he carries only a pocket handkerchief. In 2009 the possession of extreme pornography was made the subject of a criminal offence.[72] One of the many justifications, similar to that offered in *Brown*, was that extreme pornography may create a climate in which sexual violence is not taken seriously, with all that that entails.[73]

Feinberg's mechanism for determining an appropriate threshold for state intervention in the absence of any direct harm-causing activity takes the form of a practical equation weighing the gravity of the harm and the likelihood of its occurrence on the one hand, against the social value of the relevant conduct and the degree of interference with personal liberty on the other. The greater the risk of harm and the greater the magnitude of the harm which would occur if the risk materialised, the greater must be the value of the conduct and the implications for personal liberty to justify criminalisation.

To focus attention on the special problem posed by remote harms it may be useful to rehearse the well-publicised criminalisation debate concerning the possession of small

---

[71] For recent comment see A. du Bois-Pedain, 'Terrorist Possession of Offences: Curiosity Killed the Cat' [2010] Camb LJ 261; E. Cape, 'The Counter-terrorism Provisions of the Protection of Freedoms Act 2012: Preventing Misuse or a Case of Smoke and Mirrors?' [2013] Crim LR 385.

[72] By s. 63 Criminal Justice and Immigration Act 2008. For discussion see Clare McGlynn and Erika Rackley, 'Criminalising Extreme Pornography: a Lost Opportunity' (2009) Criminal Law Review 245.

[73] Another topical example is the nuisance posed by beggars, leading some to question whether giving money to them might meet for criminalisation. See Dennis J. Baker, 'The Moral Limits of Criminalizing Remote Harms' (2007) New Criminal Law Review 370–91. Cf. P. Alldridge. 'The Moral Limits of the Crime of Money Laundering' (2001) 5 Criminal L Rev 279.

hand-guns. Applied to this case Feinberg's standard harms analysis is initially quite plausible. An argument can be marshalled to the effect that for reasons both of social value and personal liberty the countervailing risks involved are insufficient to justify criminalisation. This is because, unlike weapons such as Armalite rifles, their mere possession can easily be dissociated from their harm-causing potential. The threat represented by bearing hand-guns (and most other weapons) begins to crystallise only when removed from the home or gun-club. Before this occurs they offer no more threat than cricket bats which, like guns, can also kill when used improperly. The ownership and possession of the former cannot be analysed in the same way. Just as the natural disposition of an acorn is to grow into an oak tree, so the natural disposition of Armalite rifles is, in the hands of their owners, to kill other people.

This analysis does not adequately address the basis upon which it is sought to criminalise the possession of hand-guns, however. The argument in favour of criminalisation is not that the defendant's conduct presents a particular source of danger. This in fact renders the standard harms analysis somewhat otiose. While clearly plausible in connection with activities, such as dangerous driving, which involve an actor who causes a set-back to interests and is culpable in so doing, no such causal link to or moral blame for any future criminal event need be established in the case of remote harms. Rather the argument is the less focused coercive claim that societies in which weapons or other potentially harmful products are freely available are societies in which such products are more likely to be used. By criminalising their possession this offers to shore up a potential slippery slope leading to the routine use of guns in the course of criminal activity, although potential defendants may play no part whatsoever in encouraging such activity. Similar (slippery slope) arguments can be marshalled to justify the criminalisation of other perceived anti-social activities such as drug-taking and consensual sado-masochism. This justification offers to destabilise the accepted basis upon which state coercion is legitimated, namely that criminal liability requires proof of some harmful occurrence attributable to some culpable action of the defendant.[74] It is this ethical premise, after all, which offers to protect the individual from the unfocused rights-defeating claims of utility and legal moralism,[75] and which ultimately lends the harm principle its intrinsic appeal.[76]

3 Practical limiting criteria

Even if we are able to create workable criteria of seriousness of harm, other practical considerations may militate against criminalisation. A statement of these considerations which are widely accepted as limiting criteria is provided by Husak. Like many other theorists[77] Husak's concern is that liberal society is suffering a crisis of overcriminalisation. If social problems emerge the instinctive response of legislators is to reach for the criminal law.[78]

---

[74] See generally A. von Hirsch, 'Extending the Harm Principle' in A. Simester and A.T.H. Smith (eds), *Harm and Culpability*, Oxford: Clarendon Press (1995).

[75] R.A. Duff, 'Towards a Modest Legal Moralism' (Oct 2012) Criminal Law & Philosophy [online article not assigned to an issue].

[76] A.J. Ashworth, 'The Unfairness of Risk Based Possession Offences' (2011) 5(3) Criminal Law & Philosophy 237.

[77] See most recently J.R. Spencer, 'Legislate in Haste. Repent at Leisure' [2010] Camb LJ 19.

[78] For an exploration of this problem see A.J. Ashworth 'Is the Criminal Law a Lost Cause?' [2000] Law Quarterly Review 116; A.J. Ashworth and L. Zedner, 'Defending the Criminal Law: Reflections on the Changing Character of Crime, Procedure, and Sanctions' (2007) 2(1) Criminal Law and Philosophy 21–51; R. Cruft, 'Liberalism and the Changing Character of the Criminal Law: Response to Ashworth and Zedner' (2008) 2(1) Criminal Law and Philosophy 59; A. Crawford, 'Governing through Anti-Social Behaviour: Regulatory Challenges to Criminal Justice' (2009) 49(6) British Journal of Criminology, 810–13; E. Yankah, 'Paradox in Overcriminalization' (2011) 14(1) New Criminal LR 1.

The contrary presumption should define the liberal state, namely, that the criminal law is an evil which should be used only *in extremis* and if all else fails.[79]

Prominent amongst the considerations governing the propriety of criminalisation is that:

(1) Since punishment expresses condemnation, only conduct worthy of condemnation should be criminalised.

(2) Criminal laws should not punish innocent conduct.

(3) Each criminal law must do more good than harm.

(4) Conduct should not be criminalised unless the state has a compelling interest in punishing those who engage in it. Non-criminal means must be used if this would be effective.

(5) The criminal law should be narrowly tailored to serve the state's compelling interest; criminal laws should be neither over-inclusive nor under-inclusive.

(6) Each criminal law must be designed to prevent a non-trivial harm or evil.

There is little doubt that such considerations should, and often do, inform criminal policy.[80] For example, it seems clear that conduct which is generally accepted as constituting a social threat is likely to remain uncriminalised if it is condoned. Until very recently this was the political justification for the non-criminalisation of smoking. In the first edition of this book it was suggested that criminalisation was unlikely to occur in the foreseeable future. How times change. After centuries in which neither the health of smokers nor those who are forced to share their company carried sufficient clout to counteract the argument for autonomy, the new question is how long it will be before smoking in private is criminalised. Not, one would assume, in the foreseeable future. What one does in one's own home is one's own affair, is it not? But watch this space.[81] This rhetorical question satirises the kind of untheorised values which tend to intrude into decisions to criminalise.[82] Although the support of interests is the criminal law's prime function, the scheme according to which it supports (or fails to support) those interests is structured by general social morality.[83] Whether it should be is quite a different question, as is how that morality is itself to be constructed.[84] How can the state justify censuring and punishing the possession of a few grams of cannabis for one's own use, while possessing a cellar full of wine for the consumption of the diners of Hertfordshire risks only the award of the Michelin rosette?[85]

The criminalisation of drug use reflects all the considerations Husak was concerned to identify as in need of consideration.[86] The best estimates suggest that the majority of government spending on responding to illegal drugs is devoted to enforcing drug laws, not

---

[79] See for example R.A. Duff, *Answering for Crime*, Oxford: Hart (2007), 145; generally D. Husak, *Overcriminalisation: The Limits of the Criminal Law*, New York: OUP (2008).

[80] Cf. A.J. Ashworth and L. Zedner, 'Criminalization: Justifications and Limits' (2012) 15(4) New Criminal LR 542.

[81] Pamela Ferguson, op. cit.

[82] Health Act 2003, ss. 2, 7, 8. D. Husak, 'Limitations on Criminalisation and the General Part of the Criminal Law' in Shute and Simester (2002) 13.

[83] S. Marshall and A. Duff, 'Criminalisation and Sharing Wrongs' (1998) XI Canadian Journal of Law and Jurisprudence 7.

[84] J. Howard 'Punishment, Socially Deprived Offenders, and Democratic Community' (2013) 7(1) Criminal Law & Philosophy 121.

[85] For an interesting take on this question see E. Yankah, 'Paradox in Overcriminalization' (2011) 14(1) New Criminal LR 1.

[86] Ibid.

prevention or treatment.[87] Commenting on a similar phenomenon in Canada, David Roy makes the following plea:

> ... it is *ethically* wrong to continue criminalizing approaches to the control of drug use when these strategies fail to achieve the goals for which they were designed; create evils equal to or greater than those they purport to prevent; intensify the marginalization of vulnerable people; and stimulate the rise to power of socially destructive and violent empires ... ignore the more immediately commanding urgency of reducing the suffering of drug users and assuring their survival, their health, and their growth into liberty and dignity.[88]

In this context, the arguments **against** criminalisation of hand-guns were also pretty comprehensive. Whatever view one takes on the seriousness of the threat offered by the possession of hand-guns, enforcement would be extremely difficult, as it is with any other possession offence where the possessing does not have to take place in public. In any event, the obvious way of dealing with this is to separate out those who are likely to use them unlawfully from those who are not. This can be done most easily by means of regulation. Those who want to use hand-guns for sporting purposes will be little affected in their range of choices if they are required to keep them under lock and key at gun-clubs. Finally, the obvious side-effect of criminalising will be to further develop the infrastructure of organised crime. Criminalising private possession and consumption can be expected to produce rule-avoidance and black markets, along with the various functionaries which staff and support them, and, moreover, encourage ordinary law-abiding people to consider breaking the law.

The examples of hand-guns and dangerous drugs show how it is not always the balance of principle and policy which dictates the scope of our political freedoms. In practice it may be nothing more grand than government's desire to ratchet up levels of state coercion or make political capital without significant attendant political cost.[89] History confirms that the legislature, which is composed of real people rather than penologists, is regrettably as likely to respond reactively to the instantaneous 'moral panics' of voters as to satisfy the ethical and utilitarian restrictions on the use of state coercion for public purposes.[90]

---

[87] The Government reply to the Third Report from the Home Affairs Committee Session 2001–2 HC 318, *The Government Drugs Policy: Is it Working?* 5573, July 2002. See D. Husak, 'Guns and Drugs' (2004) 23(5) Law and Philosophy 437.

[88] *Injection Drug Use and HIV/AIDS: Legal and Ethical Issues*, Canadian HIV/AIDS Legal Network, 24 November 1999; cf. *An Analysis of UK Drug Policy: A Monograph Prepared for the UK Drug Policy Commission by Peter and Alex Steven*, 2007. J Howard, 'Punishment, Socially Deprived Offenders, and Democratic Community' (2013) 7(1) Criminal Law & Philosophy 121.

[89] A.J. Ashworth 'Firearms and Justice' (editorial) [2013] Crim LR 447; J Edwards, 'Coming Clean About the Criminal Law' (2011) 5(3) Criminal Law & Philosophy 315.

[90] A recent example of criminalisation which falls foul of every one of Husak's principles is section 144 of the Legal Aid, Sentencing and Punishment of Offenders Act 2012, which criminalises squatting.

Further reading

Ashworth, A.J. *Positive Obligations in the Criminal Law*, Oxford: Hart Publishing (2013).

Baker, D.J., 'The Moral Limits of Consent as a Defense in the Criminal Law' (2009) 12(1) New Criminal Law Review 93–121.

Deigh, J. and Dolinko, D. (eds), *The Oxford Handbook of Philosophy of Criminal Law*, Oxford: OUP (2011). Esp. chapters on 'The Limits of the Criminal Law' and 'Criminalising Expression: Hate Speech and Obscenity'.

Duff, R.A., Farmer, L., Marshall, S.E., Renzo, M. and Tadros, V. (eds), *The Boundaries of the Criminal Law*, Oxford: OUP (2010).

Ferguson, P., McDiarmid, C., *Scots Criminal Law: A Critical Analysis*, Dundee: Dundee University Press (2009) chs 1–4.

Ferguson, P., '"Smoke gets in your eyes . . ." The Criminalisation of Smoking in Enclosed Public Spaces, the Harm Principle and the Limits of the Criminal Sanction', (2011) 31(2) Legal Studies 259–78.

Husak, D., *Overcriminalization: The Limits of the Criminal Law*, Oxford: OUP (2008).

LCCP Consultation Paper, *Criminal Liability in Regulatory Contexts* (CP No. 195, TSO, August 2010).

Marshall, S.E. and Duff, R.A., 'Criminalization and Sharing Wrongs' (1998) 11 Canadian Journal of Law and Jurisprudence 7.

McSherry, B., Norrie, A. and Bronitt, S. (eds), *Regulating Deviance: The Redirection of Criminalisation and the Features of Criminal Law*, London: Hart Publishing (2009).

Simester, A. and von Hirsch, A., 'Penalising Offensive Behaviour', in A. Simester and A. von Hirsch (eds), *Incivilities: Regulating Offensive Behaviour*, Oxford: Hart (2006).

Stewart, H., 'The Limits of the Harm Principle' (2009) Criminal Law and Philosophy.

Tadros, V., *The Ends of Harm: The Moral Foundations of the Criminal Law*, Oxford: OUP (2011).

Wilson, W., *Central Issues in Criminal Theory*, Oxford: Hart (2002) ch. 2.

3 Punishment

3.1 INTRODUCTION

A premise underlying the operation of the criminal justice system is that it is desirable and, within limits, possible to ensure that those punished for crimes are punished fairly in accordance with rules explicitly designed to satisfy society's purposes, most particularly that of social control.[1] Theories of punishment have developed with the aim of justifying this premise, and in this section their overall cogency will be examined. The insights generated by theories of punishment are central to understanding and evaluating the operation of the criminal justice system and its laws. If we have a clear idea of why we punish[2] and of the wider justification for punishment, we may be in a position to answer questions as various as what fault elements offences should carry, or indeed whether there should be **any** fault requirement; whether new defences should be developed or existing defences modified; whether criminal liability is appropriate for people who have not offended but manifest an intention or propensity to cause harm; whether accomplices should be treated any differently from principal offenders, and so on.

3.2 PUNISHMENT IN THE LIBERAL STATE

If we are to account for punishment it is necessary to have in mind what punishment is. This is important also because it is the prospect of punishment which differentiates criminal proceedings from other state-sponsored proceedings and which, therefore, dictates whether the rights implied in Article 6 of the European Convention must be honoured.[3] What distinguishes taxes from fines, for example?[4] Or public lynchings from executions? Or detention under the Mental Health Act from imprisonment.[5] Is it punishment if the offender's sentence is something which he wants? The core features conjured up by the notion of state punishment have been described as follows:

(1) the principled infliction by a state-constituted institution
(2) of what are generally regarded as unpleasant consequences
(3) on individuals or groups publicly adjudicated to have breached the law

---

[1] See generally A.J. Ashworth, *Sentencing and Criminal Justice* (5th edn), Cambridge: CUP (2010); S. Easton and C. Piper, *Sentencing and Punishment: The Quest for Justice* (3rd edn), Oxford: OUP (2012); M. Maguire, R. Morgan and R. Reiner (eds), *The Oxford Handbook of Criminology* (5th edn), Oxford: OUP (2012), part V.

[2] For useful discussion of these questions see 'Punishment' in R. Christopher (ed.), *George Fletcher's Essays on Criminal Law*, Oxford: OUP (2013) chs 4–7.

[3] See generally B. Emmerson and A. Ashworth, *Human Rights and Criminal Justice* (2001); J.D. Shepherd, 'A Human Right not to be Punished? Punishment as Derogation of Rights' (2012) 6(1) Criminal Law & Philosophy 31.

[4] For a useful critical evaluation see R.M. White, '"Civil penalties": Oxymoron, Chimera and Stealth Sanction' (2010) 126 LQR 593; See also *Han and Yau v Commissioners of Customs and Excise* 3 July 2001, cited in A.J. Ashworth, 'Criminal Proceedings after the Human Rights Act' [2001] Crim LR 855, at 856.

[5] See *R v Jenkin* [2012] EWCA Crim 2557. For critical comment, D. Thomas, '*R v Jenkin*: Sentencing – Mentally Disordered Offender – Choice between Hospital Order and Life Imprisonment' (case comment) [2013] Crim LR 246.

(4) as a response to that breach of the law, or with the motive of enforcing the law, and not intended solely as a means of compensation.[6]

As will be apparent, such a definition would not include taxes (core feature 3), or an award of damages (cf. 4), or a lynching (cf. 1), or a detention under the MHA (cf. 4), as a form of punishment. But it would be punishment to imprison a vagrant who offended so as to celebrate Christmas in style (cf. 2).[7] The key feature informing the scope of the definition is the kind of moral argument which must be marshalled to justify the practice. So, justifying taxes requires a different kind of argument than justifying fines.

Serious theoretical difficulties arise in attempting to square the state institution of punishment with the avowed primacy, in liberal society, of individual autonomy.[8] Clearly it cannot be justified, for reasons of such primacy, on grounds of paternalism or the relative power of the state *vis-à-vis* the individual. Since it involves harming another simply because their behaviour is unacceptable, the practice is, then, profoundly problematic. It requires a different kind of justification than for compensating a wronged victim – an uncontroversially reasonable outcome.[9]

The nature of authority under a political system is generally held to derive, similar to that subjugating sportspersons or professionals to their ruling bodies, from the consent or complicity of adult individuals in their subjection to the rule of law.[10] By agreeing to a system of enforceable norms, citizens are treated as consenting to punishment.[11]

This explanation does not, of course, tell us the nature of the justification offered for punishment, only that we are deemed to assent to it.[12] In this way, the need to justify the institution of punishment is conveniently side-stepped. Most theories of punishment offer to advance not merely instrumental reasons why punishment should follow wrongdoing but moral reasons, that is, they seek to claim that punishment is the 'right response' to wrongdoing. It is an ambitious claim since, on the face of it, all punishment does is to substitute two harms for one. This is often conceded in the case of severe punishment, for example, state execution:

> . . . the primary moral principle (is) that the state, even as it punishes, must treat its citizens in a manner consistent with their intrinsic worth as human beings – a punishment must not be so severe as to be degrading to human dignity . . . The fatal constitutional infirmity in the punishment of death is that it treats 'members of the human race' as nonhumans, as objects to be toyed with and discarded. It is thus inconsistent with (that moral principle) . . . Justice of this kind is obviously no less shocking than the crime itself, and the new 'official' murder, far from offering redress for the offence committed against society, adds instead a second defilement to the first.[13]

---

[6] Lacey (1988), pp. 7–8. This is not Lacey's completed definition but it has the merit of simplicity; cf. H.L.A. Hart, *Punishment and Responsibility*, Oxford: Clarendon Press (1968) (hereafter Hart (1968)) 4–5.

[7] For a less formalistic view of punishment see J.R. Lucas, *On Justice*, Oxford: Clarendon Press (1980) 125.

[8] N. Lacey, 'Punishment, (Neo)Liberalism and Social Democracy', in J. Simon and R. Sparks (eds), *The Sage Handbook of Punishment and Society*, London: Sage Publishing (2012) 260–80.

[9] This objection is less warranted in relation to restorative approaches to punishment where the offender, the victim and other interested parties are encouraged to work together to resolve matters arising from the crime.

[10] Of course, such consent is fictional. The existence of a social contract binding state and individual is a necessary premise for most liberal accounts of the state's authority to govern and punish.

[11] I. Kant, *The Metaphysical Elements of Justice*, Indianapolis: Bobbs-Merrill (1965) 33–7 and 105, and see the discussion in J.G. Murphy, 'Marxism and Retribution', in R.A. Duff and D. Garland (eds), *A Reader on Punishment*, Oxford: OUP (1994) (hereafter Duff and Garland) 44–67.

[12] For some general principles see M. Berman, 'The Justification of Punishment' in A. Marmor (ed.), *The Routledge Companion to Philosophy of Law*, London: Routledge (2012) 141; K. Murtagh, 'What is Inhuman Treatment?' (2012) 6(1) Criminal Law & Philosophy 21.

[13] Mr Justice Brennan in a dissenting judgment in the American case of *Gregg* v *Georgia* 428 US 153 (1976). See generally J. Waldron, 'How Law Protects Dignity' (2012) 71(1) CLJ 200.

In the case of lesser punishments the basic question remains. What makes state punishment for harm a morally preferable state of affairs to harm alone?[14] Why, if it is generally considered morally unjustifiable for one to punish, rather than merely censure, one's flatmate for a breach of (house) rules, is it justifiable if the state acts in similar fashion?

3.3 THEORIES OF PUNISHMENT

Liberal theory offers a number of theories of punishment, each of which places punishment within a general theory of the state.[15] Implicit in each is the conviction that state punishment is a necessary feature of a freedom-respecting society since it supports the rights and freedoms of individuals to pursue their life plan with the minimum of interference from others – that which every 'rational' person is deemed to want. This account requires, with the qualifications described earlier, state interference to be kept to a minimum so as not to confound those same expectations.

Theories of punishment fulfil a number of functions. First, they may explain how punishment is ever morally justified. This is an important question, which is not simply reducible to the issue of whether punishment is useful or has a point to it. We do not have to agree with punishment as an institution to understand that it offers to serve certain valuable social and political functions, for example deterrence and social protection. Second, they may set out the conditions governing responsibility in individual cases and the level of punishment. If we allow that punishment as a system is capable of justification, what makes an individual an appropriate subject of punishment?[16] Third, they may explain how to determine the appropriate amount of punishment for a given wrong, both in absolute terms and in relation to other crimes in the same system.[17] Fourth, as suggested above, they may enable us to subject the rules of criminal law to effective critical scrutiny. If we know why we punish and who we consider worthy of punishment, the cogency, consistency and fairness of criminal doctrine can be assessed according to objective criteria.

Historically, theories of punishment have fallen into one of two categories. These theories follow the basic organisational structure of orthodox moral philosophy. The first category holds that whether an action (e.g. punishment) is good or not can be decided by reference to its intrinsic worth, whatever the consequences. Thus moral reasoning within this tradition will hold that people should keep their promises because keeping promises is intrinsically a 'good thing'. The second holds that whether an action is good or not is not something which can be decided in isolation from the consequences (consequentialism). Thus keeping a promise is good if the consequences which will flow from keeping it are better than those which will result from breaking it. The primary consequentialist theory is utilitarianism. A utilitarian might argue for example that a promise to a dying man to hand over all his money to his son should be kept if the son was poor and would benefit from it but could and should be broken if more good could be done by giving it to his poverty-stricken daughter.

[14] G. Binder, 'Punishment Theory: Moral or Political?' (2002) Buffalo Crim LR 321.

[15] See generally Duff and Garland, op. cit; N. Lacey, *State Punishment*, London: Routledge (1988); T. Honderich, *Punishment: The Supposed Justifications*, Harmondsworth: Penguin (1984); S.P. Garvey, 'Was Ellen Wronged?' (2013) 7(2) Criminal Law & Philosophy 185.

[16] For recent discussion see V. Tadros, *The Ends of Harm: The Moral Foundations of Criminal Law*, Oxford: OUP (2011); cf. S. Uniacke, 'Punishment as Penalty' (March 2013) Criminal Law & Philosophy [online version not yet assigned to issue].

[17] H.L.A. Hart, *Punishment and Responsibility* (1968) 3.

The primary non-consequentialist theory of punishment is retributivism. While recognising that punishment may have useful functions/consequences such as deterrence, incapacitation and denunciation, the only possible justification for punishment is that it is the right, natural and logical response to wrongdoing. The credentials of each of these opposing views of punishment will now be examined.

A Retributive theories

1 In general

The philosophical manifesto of retributivism is that of Immanuel Kant:

> Judicial punishment can never be used merely as a means to promote some other good for the criminal himself or for civil society, but instead it must in all cases be imposed on him only on the ground that he has committed a crime . . . He must first be found to be deserving of punishment before any consideration is given to the utility of this punishment for himself or for his fellow citizens.[18]

Retributive theories of punishment hold, then, that punishment is either right or wrong in itself. It cannot be 'made right' by some good consequence which flows from the imposition of punishment or wrong by some bad consequence. Most versions of retributivism hold that there is a natural link between a person choosing to cause harm, and censure and punishment, in the same way that there is a natural link between choosing to do good and suffering praise or reward. That link is desert.[19] Punishing people for their crimes shows society's respect for the choices a person has made. By punishing, we treat him as a human being. To err is human. If, lacking divinity, we cannot forgive, we can at least punish with justice. In so doing we can facilitate the offender's return to the human fold as soon as the relevant retributive function is effected. At its least pure this will be when the public's blood lust is satisfied. At its purest this will be when the debt of wrongdoing is paid.

A general problem common to all desert-based approaches to punishment is that their overall cogency seems to depend upon accepting the assumption that all cases of rule-breaking are automatically cases of 'wrongdoing' sufficient to justify censure (and punishment).[20] This is clearly not the case. Breaking evil rules may itself be a matter of moral obligation in extreme circumstances such as would destroy any presumptive state 'right' to punish.[21] A recognition of the truth of this charge underpins a version of desert theory which holds that while desert is **necessary** for **punishment**, it does not **necessitate it**. It insists simply that punishment without blame cannot possibly be deserved – a sentiment most people would agree with.[22] While doing little to solve the problem of how punishment can ever be **deserved**, such an approach provides a welcome moral case for restraint in punishment.

---

[18] I. Kant, op. cit. 100.
[19] See for example M. Moore, *Placing Blame: A Theory of the Criminal Law*, Oxford: OUP (2010); L. Alexander and K. Ferzan, *Crime and Culpability: A Theory of Criminal Law*, Cambridge: CUP (2009).
[20] M. Zimmerman, *The Immorality of Punishment*, Broadview Press (2011); N. Levy, 'Zimmerman's *The Immorality of Punishment*: A Critical Essay' (March 2013) Criminal Law & Philosophy [online version not yet assigned to issue].
[21] W. Sadurski, 'Distributive Justice and the Theory of Punishment' (1985) OJLS 47; M. Matravers, 'Political Neutrality and Punishment' (2013) 7(2) Criminal Law & Philosophy 217.
[22] M.N. Berman, 'Rehabilitating Retributivism' (2013) 32(1) Law & Philosophy 83.

Taken to extremes a pure retributive approach carries consequences which may be morally counter-intuitive.

> **Case 1**
>
> Adam is a murderer on death row. He is diagnosed as having terminal cancer so far advanced that he will die within seven days. The day fixed for execution is tomorrow. The authorities thus have the choice whether to execute him for his past crime or allow death to occur through natural causes.[23]

> **Case 2**
>
> Adam was wrongly convicted of murder 25 years ago. Last week he had his appeal against conviction upheld when new evidence came to light. While he has been serving his sentence he has attempted escape three times which under the laws in force mean that he must serve a full life sentence.[24]

Here the retributive response (execution tomorrow/full life sentence) is problematic. Do we feel that punishment is a moral necessity such that social equilibrium could not be restored without it? Or is the moral response to say that there was no point to be gained by punishment or that we have no desire to cause the offender 'unnecessary suffering'? It should be noted that if our moral intuition favours either of the latter two responses a coherent commitment to retribution becomes difficult to sustain.[25]

2 Forms of retributive theory

The traditional form of retributive theory follows two basic precepts; that punishment may justly be imposed (only) upon a person who deserves to be punished; and that the **level** of punishment must also reflect his desert. A well-known version is the *lex talionis* of the Bible. This is generally credited to be a primitive form of retributivism based in the 'natural justice' of vengeance.[26] The *lex talionis* is a superficially plausible basis for determining an offender's desert since the offender loses what he has claimed – the eye for the eye, the tooth for the tooth. Ultimately, however, it is unhelpful since relatively few crimes can be paid for in this way – is the rapist raped? – and because it fails to explain why the harm suffered by the victim demands a penal rather than say a compensatory response. How is it morally preferable for two people to lose an eye, rather than just one person, when simply compensating the victim would do most to redress and repair the harm caused?[27]

Until fairly recently the most widely accepted basis for desert in punishment was the unfair advantage gained by rule-breakers over rule-followers. The idea is that since we all benefit from rule-following, when a rule is broken the rule-breaker obtains the benefit of

---

[23] An example suggested by M. Perlmutter, 'Punishment and Desert' in J. Arthur (ed.), *Morality and Moral Controversies*, New Jersey: Prentice Hall (1981) 427 at 433–4. A topical variation concerns the prosecution and conviction of elderly one-time celebrities for sexual assaults in their youth – see A. Dufner, 'Should the Late Stage Demented be Punished for Past Crimes?' (2013) 7(1) Criminal Law & Philosophy 137.

[24] This hypothetical example is based upon a case recently heard in the United States Supreme Court.

[25] Cf. Tadros, *The Ends of Harm* (2011); M.N. Berman, 'Rehabilitating Retributivism'.

[26] M. Radin, 'Cruel Punishment and Respect for Persons: Super Due Process for Death' (1980) 53 S. Cal L Rev 1143; J.S. Stannard, 'Retaliation, Catharsis and the Criminal Process' (2001) NILQ 162.

[27] B. Rosebury, 'Moore's Moral Facts and the Gap in the Retributive Theory' (2011) 5(3) Criminal Law & Philosophy 361.

others' self-restraint without bearing his own corresponding share of the burden. It is this unfair advantage which punishment offers to redress, thus restoring society's moral equilibrium.[28] An obvious advantage of this approach is that it affords a basis for holding punishment to be deserved even where the content of the rule may be objectionable.

The notion of punishment as a means of eradicating an unfairly won advantage can be illustrated by reference to the social rule of 'queueing'. People who 'push in' in, say, a cinema queue take a short cut to the satisfaction of their needs. In so doing they gain an unfair advantage over rule-followers. If there was a rule that all people who pushed in would be immediately taken out of the queue and placed at the end of the now much longer queue 'where they belonged', it could hardly be argued that such a response was morally unjustified. Indeed, in this pure form the response to the queue-jumper is so appropriate to the offence that it almost loses the character of punishment. It becomes simply the 'right thing to do' and would remain so even if everybody was in no way discomforted by what the latter did because it was a lovely, hot, sunny day.

Applied to cases of 'real crime', 'unfair advantage' theory is less plausible if we cast the analytical net beyond those crimes – speeding, illegal parking, tax evasion – which are quintessential examples of taking short cuts. It would surely be missing the point, for example, to base the justification for punishing a rapist or a murderer upon the fact that the offender has cut corners to personal satisfaction while the rest of us have exercised restraint. Surely desert must derive from the wickedness of the deed itself rather than some purely notional and hypothetical unfair advantage a person is thought to have obtained by rule-breaking.

Again, how does one quantify the amount of unfair advantage represented by an offence? With some offences, such as tax evasion and traffic violations, the fine is an apt method of restoring equilibrium through its indirect ability to redistribute benefits gained and burdens suffered. But for offences as various as rape, murder, dangerous driving and theft, the difficulties of systematic quantification would seem intractable. Moreover, even if we could solve that problem, what the offender would have to give up to restore the equilibrium might be more than justice demands. It is with an eye to the pertinence of such observations that desert theorists of all types have begun to espouse proportionality as the basis for assigning the proper level of punishment.[29] If it is not possible to say what the deserved level of punishment is for a given crime,[30] at least we can try to ensure that the general minimum and maximum levels of appropriate punishment are fixed and punishment for one type of offence is not disproportionate to that given for another.[31] Such a stance is at its most attractive when articulated in the context of a denunciatory account of desert in punishment.

3 Punishment as an expression of censure

Denunciation, or censure, is often presented as a justification for punishment separate from that of retribution or utilitarianism. Many denunciatory accounts do, in fact, reduce to a non-utilitarian consequentialist justification, earmarking its useful social purposes. The most influential of these holds that punishment affords a socially necessary mechanism for the channelling of public outrage. This may serve an educative and therefore reductive

---

[28] See generally H. Morris, 'Persons and Punishment' (1968) 52 The Monist 475; J.G. Murphy, 'Marxism and Retribution' in Duff and Garland (eds) (1994) 47.
[29] See generally A. von Hirsch, *Past or Future Crimes*, Manchester University Press (1985).
[30] Lacey (1988) 24–5.
[31] See for example von Hirsch, *Censure and Sanctions*, Oxford: Clarendon Press (1993) ch. 2.

function. It may also promote social cohesion by vindicating the stance of the law-abiding and helping them make sense of the world – one in which order and stability are seen as a good thing rather than to be traded off against personal goals.[32]

The most persuasive basis upon which to justify punishment as an offender's desert is that it serves to express our moral condemnation of his behaviour. Denouncing wrongdoing, as is seen in everyday practice, is an essential aspect of blaming, itself a natural response to wrongdoing.[33] It is this fact of censure which denotes fines, but not taxes, a form of punishment. On this view, the fact that wrongdoing suffers censure provides the offender with a moral reason not to offend. Through different forms and degrees of punishment blame may then be expressed proportionately according to the degree of wrongdoing.[34]

An obvious problem with this 'expressive' account is that while condemnation is easily seen as a natural and deserved response to wrongdoing, it is less easy to see how state punishment is necessary to convey this response. There are two facets to this objection. First, what justifies the state taking on this censuring role? To account for this it seems that other consequentialist reasoning must be relied upon[35] as, for instance, the social need to avoid informal mechanisms of expressing outrage such as lynching. Second, why should punishment be linked to the denunciatory purpose? One can censure without fining, imprisoning or imposing community service.[36] Why is hard treatment necessary?[37]

In the most influential account Andrew von Hirsch concedes the need to rely upon consequentialist reasons to justify such practices, namely the need to provide disincentives for those who might otherwise be tempted to resist acting upon this moral reason.[38] In his account, however, this is not a **competing** aim of punishment, as utilitarianism is, but a **complementary** one. Indeed, punishment may be welcomed by citizens for providing an extra (prudential) reason to do what is right. As a practical example, readers, particularly parents, will understand that drawing behavioural lines by (fair and consistent) punishment rather than mere censure is often appreciated by children since it helps to form and sustain an autonomy-enhancing morality of compliance.[39]

What is significant in this approach is that while punishment is acknowledged as having both an expressive and a preventive purpose, the account remains retributivist in character since both the occasion and the amount of punishment must always be fixed by reference to desert rather than prevention. It is not justifiable, on preventive grounds, to give more punishment than necessary to express society's condemnation.[40] Indeed, as a safeguard against this, all punishment should be anchored to a baseline of conventionally accepted rights-respecting expressive punishment.[41]

[32] E. Durkheim, *The Division of Labour in Society*, London: Macmillan (1984).

[33] A. von Hirsch (1993), op. cit. ch. 2.

[34] A. von Hirsch calls this the principle of ordinal proportionality: discussed in *Past or Future Crimes*, Manchester University Press (1985) ch. 4, and in *Censure and Sanctions*, Oxford: Clarendon Press (1993) ch. 2.

[35] Tadros, *The Ends of Harm*.

[36] See generally J. Feinberg, 'The Expressive Function of Punishment' in Duff and Garland (eds) 71–91.

[37] G. Roebuck and D. Wood, 'A Retributive Argument against Punishment' (2011) 5(1) Criminal Law & Philosophy 73. For an argument against desert-based punishment see N. Lacey and H. Pickard, 'From the Consulting Room to the Court Room? Taking the Clinical Model of Responsibility without Blame into the Legal Realm' (2013) 33(1) OJLS 1.

[38] See generally A. von Hirsch, *Censure and Sanction* (1993) 12–13. Chapter 2 is also in A. von Hirsch 'Censure and Proportionality' in Duff and Garland (eds) (1994) 115–31.

[39] E. Durkheim calls the absence of this clarity of moral direction 'anomie'. For a recent call for such an approach see Z. Hoskins, 'Fair Play, Political Obligation, and Punishment' (2011) 5(1) Criminal Law & Philosophy 53.

[40] Cf. P. Robinson, 'Hybrid Principles for the Distribution of Criminal Sanctions', (1987) 82 Northwestern Law Review 19.

[41] A. von Hirsch calls this cardinal proportionality, see note 38 above.

Even with this change of emphasis, censure as the sole determinant of quantum in punishment is problematic, however. If quantum is determined simply by what is necessary to express proportionate condemnation, symbolic and shaming punishments which do not involve the deprivation of liberty or financial penalty would appear to be an equally effective disincentive to wrongdoing.[42] Consider the following system for effectively expressing censure. The offender is tattooed with the insignia of his offence. So that proportionality is achieved, the seriousness of the offence is conveyed by the message on the insignia, its location and the length of time for which it must be borne.[43] What could be more logical from the denunciatory point of view?[44] Present penal practices go far beyond this and seem to express a different justificatory penal rationale.[45] Retributive condemnation does not seem to capture quite what state punishment is for. So how else can (hard) punishment be justified?

B Utilitarianism

1 In general

Utilitarianism is a unified political, economic and moral theory. In its simplest, classical form it holds that human action (whether individual or collective) is justified to the extent that it promises to maximise human happiness or welfare. Thus, individual action is justifiable if more units of happiness/welfare are produced by doing it than not doing it or doing something else. A political or economic act of government is justifiable if it would be of overall benefit to the community. When looked at in combination, political decisions to break manifesto pledges on taxation for economic reasons would only be unjustified if the loss of electoral trust which this would engender would cause more harm to society than could be paid for by the promised economic benefits. Public interest arguments in the legal forum are informed by utilitarian (that is political rather than strictly legal) considerations.

Applied to punishment, utilitarianism holds that punishment is justified to the extent that it promises to produce better consequences than a failure to punish. At the heart of the theory lies the premise that punishment, since it visits harm upon the punished, is a *prima facie* wrong which can only be justified if some benefit accrues from punishing which will outweigh the misery inflicted. This is clearly a contrary premise to that sustaining retributivism which holds that punishment for wrongdoing is a moral necessity.

In many ways utilitarianism appears to be an advance on retributivism. Although it might be thought that criminal justice requires people to be treated as they deserve, no more no less, the punishment of crime is a response which has more than a merely backward-looking moral dimension. It is above all a political act – an exercise of power.[46]

---

[42] For an argument that a greater emphasis on the shaming aspect of punishment could reduce the general public's desire to ratchet up custodial sentences see Dan Kahan, 'What do Alternative Sanctions Mean?' (1996) 63 U Chic LR 591. See also P. Cartwright, 'Publicity, Punishment and Protection: The Role(s) of Adverse Publicity in Consumer Policy' (2012) 32(2) Legal Studies 179.

[43] A proposal called to mind by a story of Franz Kafka: F. Kafka, 'In the Penal Colony' in *Metamorphosis and other Stories*, Harmondsworth: Penguin (1971) 169.

[44] For further discussion see below, Conclusion.

[45] A topical example is sex offending. See A. du Bois-Pedain, 'Once a Sex Offender, Always a Reoffending Risk?' (2010) 69(3) CLJ 428; T. Rice Lave, 'Controlling Sexually Violent Predators: Continued Incarceration at What Cost?' (2011) 14(2) New Criminal LR 213.

[46] For an incisive exploration of this aspect of state punishment see A. Brudner, *Punishment and Freedom: A Liberal Theory of Penal Justice*, Oxford: OUP (2012), and a special issue of the *New Criminal Law Review* devoted to its analysis: (2011) 14(3) New Criminal LR 427.

The justification for it must arguably, therefore, reflect the explanations offered to justify other political actions, namely that it serves society's purposes. Punishment, on this view, is merely the negative side of what government is in business to achieve. The positive side includes broader aspects of social policy including non-punitive regulation, education, welfare provision, job-creation and so on. In principle, therefore, a utilitarian will think of punishment as a response of last resort where other mechanisms designed to promote order and stability in society have failed. It is not, unlike retribution, a natural response to wrongdoing.

Utilitarianism not only explains why punishment is proper, but bases that account in a systematic treatment of what makes the coercive rules themselves politically supportable. This is a theoretical advance on retributivism which, it should be remembered, does not seek to give an account of why rule-following is good and so rule-infraction is bad.[47] For utilitarianism, on the other hand, the same measure (society's well-being) is used to justify:

(a) the existence of the rules,
(b) the following of the rules, and
(c) punishing the infraction of the rules.

2 Forms of utilitarian penal theory
The broad thrust of utilitarian penal philosophy is concerned with crime reduction – a necessary adjunct to the advancement of social welfare. It should be noted carefully that whether or not one holds to the retributive theory of punishment, it is a matter of significance that punishment may still fulfil this aim. Thus the very same punishment, say life for murder, which is the murderer's desert may also function to make society a better place by reducing crime.[48] Punishment, under utilitarianism, offers to reduce crime in a number of different ways:

(1) it may deter the individual offender (individual deterrence);
(2) it may deter others who might be minded to commit a similar offence (general deterrence);
(3) it may fulfil an educative function by reminding the public of the norms by which their society is organised;
(4) it may reform or rehabilitate the individual offender, where punishment takes the form of educating him to understand the positive reasons for good behaviour rather than the negative reasons against bad behaviour;
(5) by removing the offender from society and thus his capacity to commit crime, it may fulfil a protective role for society.

3 Criticisms

(a) *Objections of principle*
The major objection to utilitarianism is that a consequences-led penal policy may lead to injustice. All the various functions of punishment subjugate the autonomy of the offender to the interests of society. This is most obvious with general social deterrence where the disproportionate sentencing of individuals can be justified to encourage others

---

[47] And therefore worthy of punishment.
[48] For critique see B. Mitchell and J. Roberts, *Exploring the Mandatory Life Sentence for Murder*, Oxford: Hart Publishing (2012).

to be law-abiding.[49] Indeed, if good consequences were all that mattered we might expect punishment to be far more draconian than utilitarians are prepared to advocate. If our justification for punishing people is to make society a better place, it might justify deterrence, rehabilitation or physical incapacitation far in excess of what the offender deserves. Drunken drivers could lose their licence for life; thieves could have their hands cut off; company fraudsters could be sent to a monastery to learn morality and lose acquisitiveness; sex offenders could be castrated; transportation to the uninhabited islands off our coastline could be introduced. One could go further. If desert does not matter there is no obvious reason why society needs to find the real offender at all. Punishing a confirmed recidivist would be just as effective, if not more so. Such punishment protects society by incapacitating a dangerous person, perhaps far more dangerous than the actual offender. It educates society in the rewards for wrongdoing. It satisfies the blood lust of victims, their families and the wider community. It has a general deterrent effect. From a consequentialist perspective it is not even obvious why we need punish anybody. The above purposes could equally well be served by punishing nobody while the impression is created, by skilful use of the media and rumour, that all calumny is treated with unbending vigour and ferocity; thus keeping potentially reformable offenders away from the insidious influence of prison.

The standard response to these objections is that utilitarianism does not work like this. In the real world oppression is counter-productive and people find out about injustices. The social consequences of unjust victimisation can be immense and lasting.[50] If moral values were ignored in judging the correct response to crime enforcement, both the legitimacy of the system would be imperilled and the feeling of 'well-being' which crime control exerts itself to promote would be dissipated through the indignation and anxiety of the rule-breakers and law-abiding alike. Both potential consequences argue against unjust, inhumane punishment.[51]

While the response is persuasive it should be noted that it is, however, parasitic on the existence of moral values lying outside itself. Utilitarianism does not seem to work, in other words, unless it is informed by a value system which is itself not consequentialist. At the heart of this objection lies the intuition crystallised in desert theory that **only** actual offenders must be punished and that criminal justice demands recognition of the relevance of desert both in terms of the question who, and how much, to punish. This intuition is confirmed by the very structure of criminal law, evidence and procedure. How can desert not matter where we have procedural and evidential safeguards such as the presumption of innocence, the 'beyond reasonable doubt' standard of proof in criminal trials, the centrality of responsibility and fault within the criminal trial, and so on? A theory of punishment is seriously flawed if it is capable of justifying practices of punishment which are fundamentally inconsistent with the ethical constraints informing the operation of an actual criminal justice system.[52]

---

[49] D.M. Farrell 'Using Wrongdoers Rightly: Tadros on the Justification of General Deterrence' (December 2012) Criminal Law & Philosophy [online version not assigned to issue].

[50] As the unfortunate instances of Dreyfus and Saccho and Vanzetti demonstrate.

[51] Utilitarianism, it should be noted, was the major penal influence against capital punishment and transportation.

[52] However, not all of the practices within the criminal justice system are susceptible to this analysis. Strict liability offences, for example, can only be justified on grounds of utility but there is no suggestion that strict liability is a potential model for the future development of our system: H.L.A. Hart, *Punishment and Responsibility* (1968) 12; Lacey (1988) 44–6; cf. B. Wooton, *Crime and the Criminal Law*, London: Sweet & Maxwell (1981) 46–57; K.W. Simons, 'Is Strict Criminal Liability in the Grading of Offences Consistent with Retributive Desert?' (2012) 32(3) OJLS 445.

(b) *Practical objections: the efficacy of punishment*

Although utilitarianism is concerned more with the functions of, rather than the moral justifications for, punishment it must be understood that the theory does not 'collapse' into a description of punishment's functions. It is a normative rather than descriptive theory.[53] It says 'do not punish **unless** punishment functions to reduce crime' in one of the above ways. This leads to consideration of the efficacy of punishment. The revival of retributivism in recent years is largely attributable to the perceived inefficacy of punishment rather than its actual or potential disregard for justice.[54] Although there is evidence to suggest that the threat of imprisonment[55] has a general deterrent effect, there is little evidence to suggest it discourages individual offenders from reoffending.[56] Similarly, the rehabilitative ideal has been shown to be an empty one, even if it could be successfully married to the need to show individual offenders justice in punishment.[57] Indeed, statistics indicate that the more a defendant has been incarcerated, with whatever object in mind, the more likely it is that he will reoffend. Such statistical evidence[58] is supported by the intuitions gained from social scientific studies of prison life and general anecdotal evidence[59] that prison is a very effective training ground for villainy, both in its moral and ideological aspects and in its technical demands. What better way of creating a villain than removing him from the society of the law-abiding, placing him in the company of experts in, and apologists for, villainy[60] and effectively disabling him from securing meaningful employment on his release?[61]

The one obviously reductive function which seems immune from these objections is that of incapacitation. The simple idea informing general protectionist policies is that if an offender is incarcerated it means that he, at least, no longer constitutes a danger to society. It is most sustainable in the context of sex offences and crimes of violence, since the ability of such offenders to offend is thereby minimised and their disposition to offend may be reduced with the passing of years. With other offences, most notably property offences, such a function is less plausible. In the long term, the effect of incarceration may simply be to increase the disposition to commit offences on release.[62] Moreover, in the short and medium term, much criminal activity is simply removed to a different environment where 'offences' are, paradoxically, less likely to be acknowledged and recorded. The associated social harms, one would hazard, are no less burdensome for the fact that they occur outside the public gaze.

---

[53] H. Carvalho, 'Terrorism, Punishment, and Recognition' (2012) 15(3) New Criminal LR 345.

[54] See for example S.R. Brody, *The Effectiveness of Sentencing: A review of the literature* (Home Office Research Study No. 35, 1976).

[55] And other punishments.

[56] See for example J. Adenaes, 'The General Preventive Effects of Punishment' (1966) 114 U Pa LR 949; Duff and Garland 21–8; N. Hanna, 'Facing the Consequences' (April 2013) Criminal Law & Philosophy [online version not yet assigned to issue].

[57] See for example Francis A. Allen, *The Decline of the Rehabilitative Ideal: Penal Policy and Social Purpose*, New Haven: Yale University Press (1981); A.E. Bottoms, 'An Introduction to the Coming Crisis' in A.E. Bottoms and R.H. Preston, *The Coming Penal Crisis*, Edinburgh: Scottish Academic Press (1980); A. von Hirsch, *Doing Justice – The Choice of Punishments* (Report of the Committee for the Study of Incarceration) (1976); S.R. Brody, op. cit.; S. Sverdlik, 'Punishment and Reform' (April 2013) Criminal Law & Philosophy [online version not yet assigned to an issue].

[58] R. Martinson, '"What Works?" Questions and Answers about Prison Reform' (1974) 35 Public Interest 22–54.

[59] W. Young, 'The Effects of Imprisonment on Offending: A Judge's Perspective' [2010] Crim LR 3; I. Dennis, 'Sentencing, Rehabilitation and the Prison Population' [2010] Crim LR 591.

[60] This has always been understood. Early prisons typically forbade communication between prisoners even to the extent of providing jaw clamps to prevent talking: Walsingham Jail Museum archive.

[61] One of the (many) theories of the workhouse was the obviation of this problem.

[62] W. Young, 'The Effects of Imprisonment on Offending: a Judge's Perspective' 3–18.

Utilitarian penal policy is thus faced with the dilemma that while the threat of punishment may have a general reductive effect and the imposition of certain forms of punishment (e.g. fines) may have an individual deterrent effect, the major institution of punishment for serious crimes, namely imprisonment, may actually be ineffective or counter-productive.

It seems, then, that utilitarianism offers neither a practical nor a moral advance on retributivism. It has no theory of justice in the distribution of punishment and it does not seem to work in the way we might require it to work if the extravagance of the punishments routinely meted for mundane offences were to be justified on anything other than a desert-based criterion.

C Mixed theories

1 Hart's solution

Recognition of the limitations in both theories has resulted in the development of mixed theories of punishment which attempt to combine the best of both. Foremost amongst mixed theories is that of H.L.A. Hart. At its simplest, Hart attempts to separate the question as to what punishment is for, from the questions as to who shall be punished and how much. In his view the institutions of punishment can only be justified on utilitarian (reductionist) grounds. This is termed the general justifying aim of punishment. This does not settle the question of who shall be punished. The answer to this question is entirely retributivist. Hart maintains that 'a moral licence to punish is needed by society'. The moral principles involved here are the right not to be punished unless one has done wrong and the right not to be punished excessively. In short, this approach says that the **institutions** of punishment can only be justified on utilitarian grounds, but that **individual instances** of punishment can only be justified if the individual concerned deserves his sentence.[63] Hart's notion of desert confines punishment to those who have voluntarily broken the law. His general conclusions are that 'unless a man has the capacity and fair opportunity to adjust his behaviour to the law, its penalties ought not to be applied to him'.[64]

2 Criticisms of Hart

Hart's theory is not without its own difficulties. First, there is the rather open-ended notion of 'fair opportunity'. Is this a meaningful basis upon which to determine desert in punishment? This issue will be scrutinised in Chapter 9. Second, while as a matter of general principle it seems quite plausible that rules and their enforcement should be justified by utilitarian considerations but individual punishment by desert, our system departs quite markedly from this satisfying model. For example, we have an extensive system of public welfare crimes which allow state punishment of harm-threatening behaviour without proof of moral fault.[65] Punishment under such circumstances cannot be deserved in Hart's terms. Does this mean that the system is flawed and needs immediate attention? Or does Hart give insufficient attention to the unresolvable tension between what society needs and what individuals deserve?[66] As one commentator argues:

---

[63] For a recent revisionist version which puts less emphasis on blame and more on dangerousness see L. Bomann-Larsen, 'Revisionism and Desert' (2010) 4(1) Criminal Law & Philosophy 1.

[64] Hart (1968) 181.

[65] See Chapter 7.

[66] For another example of this tension see the later discussion on the 1991 Act which combines desert-based and reductive elements.

It seems implausible that we should always be willing to accept fairness as an absolute constraint upon the pursuit of utility . . . There do appear to be emergency cases and possibly even less exceptional ones in which we are willing to make some trade-off between justice and utility: for example, in the case of killing (perhaps through punishment) an innocent person in order to save a million lives . . . What Hart fails to tell us is when the principle ought to be sacrificed; when it is right to do a wrong in punishing an offender who is not fully responsible for her offence.[67]

This omission is becoming of key concern given the socio-political tensions unleashed by terrorism and the state response thereto.[68] It is also the case that Hart supplies cogent reasons why it is wrong for the state to punish people lacking fault but does not even attempt to explain why it is right to punish if fault is present.[69] In other words, he falls into the trap of most desert theorists in assuming that wrongdoing deserves punishment. A more penetrating insight, perhaps, is that Hart affords no clear basis upon which the authority of state punishment may be impugned. At an obvious level, much crime is created by the structure of opportunities offered by the punishing state. How can punishment be morally justified when people are imprisoned in crime-engendering contexts not of their making, particularly when the state could reduce such contexts by expanding the range of human choices (through social policy) rather than restricting them (through punishment)?

3.4 RATIONALITY AND POLITICS IN SENTENCING

The general charge implicit in the above criticisms is that fairness and utility cannot easily be united in a way which reconciles individual rights and social goals. If it is not possible to provide a systematic mechanism for effecting such a reconciliation, then we have no inbuilt mechanism for ensuring that punishment remains true to the liberal ideal – that the institution is conducive to the general flourishing of individual freedom. The inevitable danger is that the freedom of some may become sacrificed in an unprincipled way to the good of the many. On one level this may be a necessary evil. No institution is perfect, after all. A deeper problem, however, is that, lacking such a systematic mechanism, the institution of punishment may, in fact, only be conducive to the flourishing of those whose freedom the state is most anxious to preserve.

Theorists within the Marxist tradition are particularly critical of this hidden feature of state punishment. Such theorists, typically, accept retributivism as the only plausible moral justification for punishment since, uniquely, it seeks to explain why punishment is deserved rather than is simply a good idea.[70] However, by centring the justification on the notion of justice (just deserts) retributivism is charged with failing to deliver a satisfactory justification for punishment in actual societies.[71] Actual societies disarm the retributivist justification, since actual societies encourage the rational pursuit of self-interest but disable large sections of society from doing so in a legitimate way.[72]

Others have suggested, not inconsistently, that the state's bad faith on this matter can be understood by an investigation of liberal society's paradigm punishment, namely

---

[67] Lacey (1988) 49; see A. Brudner, loc. cit. for an attempt at a solution to this problem.

[68] H. Carvalho, 'Terrorism, Punishment, and Recognition'.

[69] For an interesting answer to this question see D. Husak, 'Why Punish Attempts at All? Yaffe on "The Transfer Principle"' (2012) 6(3) Criminal Law & Philosophy 399; Fletcher (1978) 419.

[70] See J.G. Murphy, 'Marxism and Retribution' in Duff and Garland (eds) 47–65.

[71] For a well-argued elaboration of this position and some radical solutions see A. Norrie, *Punishment, Responsibility and Justice*, Oxford: Clarendon Press (2001) chs 1–3, 9–10.

[72] Duff and Garland (1994) 44.

imprisonment. This is represented as a method of separating, not the 'goodies' from the 'baddies' but the disruptive victims of social inequality from the lucky ones for whom deterrence actually has reason to work.[73] Imprisonment, along with the detention of the insane, not only fulfils a symbolic function of constructing battlelines between normality and abnormality, it also rids society of the disruptive implications of those who 'play by different rules', by putting them in enforced 'quarantine'.[74] Conceived as deterrence only, punishment as a social institution tends to be directed in its most symbolic forms against those with most to lose by offending. But its (harm-laden) operation as punishment is largely directed against those with nothing to lose (or to give). It is no coincidence that the majority of inmates in our prisons, for example, are from the ranks of the unskilled working class and unemployed – those who have least material incentive to be good and whose consciences are more likely to be compromised by their own material conditions of existence.[75] What kind of deterrent is it that an unemployable living in squalid, dehumanising conditions will be sent to prison for stealing the compact disc player from a rich man's car? Again, Government policy concerning the misuse of drugs emphasises punishment rather than treatment. This raises the key question whether this is an appropriate response. Rather should we not acknowledge that responsibility for the tragic results of drug misuse is shared with the society, whose policy failures regarding drugs, social exclusion, poverty and education make drugs supply into the raging social problem it is? Addressing this undoubted social problem by punishing the victims smacks of bad faith. At the very least there are strong grounds for looking at desert in the round when deciding upon quantum and nature of punishment.[76]

On this view, 'those who are being punished and those who are deterred are primarily from two different but adjoining socio-economic groups'.[77] It does not matter, then, that the group punished are essentially undeterrable, given their life conditions, because the effect of their imprisonment deters the 'goodies' and the removal of the former group is a necessary price to be paid if the freedom of the rest is to be guaranteed.

The picture presented by these approaches is a gloomy one, since it effectively destroys the moral legitimacy of punishment, whether conceived as retributive or reductionist in nature. Desert is compromised because the central notion of choice which underpins it is loaded against those whose choice is determined by damaging life conditions. Choosing to commit crime is a rational decision for those with nothing to lose, an irrational decision for those with everything to lose. Under utilitarianism, although utility may not necessarily be compromised, the burden of punishment, similarly, falls upon those whose behaviour is unlikely to be touched by supposedly 'rational' considerations such as deterrence.[78] Acting rationally thus imprisons the poor, but leaves the rich untouched. Punishment becomes

---

[73] See generally M. Foucault, *Discipline and Punish: The Birth of the Prison*, Harmondsworth: Penguin (1976); A. Norrie (1993) ch. 10; J. Howard, 'Punishment, Socially Deprived Offenders, and Democratic Community' (2013) 7(1) Criminal Law & Philosophy 121.

[74] A. du Bois-Pedain, 'Once a Sex Offender, Always a Reoffending Risk?' [2010] CLJ 428.

[75] R.A. Duff, 'Blame, Moral Standing, and the Legitimacy of Criminal Trial' (2010) 23(2) Ratio 123–40; C. Muller and C. Wildeman, 'Punishment and Inequality'; J. Howard, 'Punishment, Socially Deprived Offenders, and Democratic Community'; P. Chau, 'Duff on the Legitimacy of Punishment of Socially Deprived Offenders' (2012) 6(2) Criminal Law & Philosophy 247; R. Gargarella, 'Penal Coercion in Contexts of Social Injustice' (2011) 5(1) Criminal Law & Philosophy 21.

[76] Ashworth and Von Hirsch (2005) 62 *et seq*; R. Lippke, 'Social Deprivation as Tempting Fate' (2011) 5(3) Criminal Law & Philosophy 277; J. Roberts (ed.), *Mitigation and Aggravation in Sentencing*, Cambridge: CUP (2011).

[77] A. Norrie (1993) 201–2.

[78] R. Henham, *Sentencing and the Legitimacy of Criminal Justice*, London: Routledge (2011).

simply a method of social control and the pious platitudes we advance to justify it serve only to confirm how much our unequal society needs it.

The above charge offers to destabilise criminal law doctrine by subverting its coherence. The view taken here is less radical. It will be summarised in brief before suffering elaboration.

3.5 CONCLUSION

Punishment has a point to it but it must be deserved. The amount of punishment due cannot be fixed by retributive criteria alone except by ensuring as far as possible that like cases are treated alike and that coherent criteria of proportionality are adopted based upon the seriousness of the harm caused and the mental element accompanying it. The precise level of punishment, therefore, must be responsive to utilitarian criteria such as deterrence and incapacitation. From probation and community service (rehabilitation) to fines (deterrence) to prison (incapacitation, deterrence and rehabilitation), institutions of punishment in liberal society show the indelible imprint of utilitarian philosophy.[79] From the state's point of view, punishment must have some objective to it and that objective, it must be assumed, is the same as underlies having the norm itself, namely to make society a better place. Society is faced with the unpleasant fact that such measures are largely ineffective. This does not, however, entirely remove the point of punishment. In the final analysis, punishment is a logical requirement of a coercive order. It is the signal that norms must be treated as obligatory. What society could survive without making this political statement?

These considerations combined seem to support restraint as a guiding principle in punishment. Given that failure is built into punishment it should not be meted out as if it did necessarily work. For example, if imprisonment for incorrigible small-time thieves is neither deserved nor any more effective as an individual deterrent than a different form of punishment, including symbolic punishment, thought should be given to reducing it to the minimum necessary to give effect to this aim.[80] The problem of reconciling public and private interests can be addressed by ensuring that penal forms are introduced which restrict ineffective and costly prison sentences to occasions where the public need protection. Otherwise the retributive function can be satisfied by combining penalties to ensure both penal efficacy, say fines, and desert, for example shaming punishments expressing moral condemnation.[81] Significantly the provisions in the Criminal Justice Act 1991 gave some indication that legislators were alert to the desirability of restraint in punishment. By ss. 1 and 2 punishment should be at the minimum level necessary to do justice to the seriousness of the offence and, where appropriate, address the dangerousness of the offender. This is done by requiring judges to consider whether a custodial sentence is necessary at all (section 1(2)) on grounds of seriousness and to determine the level of punishment by reference to seriousness alone.[82] Unfortunately, the political will to execute

---

[79] But not all societies: see M. Foucault, op. cit. ch. 2.

[80] The approach informing the Criminal Justice Act 1991. This argument is made persuasively by P.Q. Hirst in 'The Concept of Punishment' in Duff and Garland (eds) 264–79.

[81] See D. Kahan, 'Punishment Incommensurability' (1998) Buffalo Crim LR 691 at 704–8. More recently Kahan has resiled from this position, arguing that shaming should not over determine the nature of punishment, in 'What's Really Wrong with Shaming Sanctions' (2006) Yale Law School Public Law Working Paper No. 125.

[82] Not deterrence or rehabilitation. The exception, in the case of sex offences and crimes of violence, is dealt with above.

such a policy of restraint was always weak and has only been kept in check, it appears, by the fact of a growing prison population.[83] In 1997 mandatory life sentences were enacted to be the sentence for repeat offenders committing serious crimes of violence or sex offences, unless in exceptional circumstances.[84] Minimalism and proportionality has become a lower priority as successive governments act to appear tough on crime if not, regrettably, the causes of crime. The latest legislative initiative is the Criminal Justice Act 2003 which emphasises crime reduction as the main purpose of punishment.[85] For the first time the courts are explicitly directed towards the purposes of punishment in setting the appropriate sentence. Significantly, however, little guidance is given, beyond the need to bear in mind questions of harm and culpability and the recent commission of previous offences, as to how to determine the relative weight of the different functions.[86] These purposes are expressed as follows: (a) the punishment of offenders, (b) the reduction of crime (including its reduction by deterrence), (c) the reform and rehabilitation of offenders, (d) the protection of the public,[87] and (e) the making of reparation by offenders to persons affected by their offences.[88] Minimalism and proportionality of sentence retain significance – custodial sentences must only be passed if non-custodial options would be inappropriate and the term must be the minimum necessary to reflect the seriousness of the offence – but beyond this no further guidance is given. More significant in practice, perhaps, the Coroners and Justice Act 2009 set up the Sentencing Council, replacing the Sentencing Guidelines Council, by which the Council are given powers to set guidelines. Henceforth, when sentencing an offender for an offence, a court must follow any relevant sentencing guidelines, unless it is contrary to the interests of justice to do so.[89]

It should be a high priority to inform judgments of seriousness by objective criteria. There have been recent attempts to improve upon[90] Hart's 'commonsense scale of gravity' as a measure of proportionality.[91] The most promising approach adds substance to 'common sense' by incorporating a more scientific foundation, namely that of the 'typical impact of the conduct on the victim's living standards' in the light of the offender's 'degree of purposefulness or carelessness'.[92] Some such equation would do much to ensure that public goods such as crime reduction did not submerge justice for the individual offender.[93] A further important feature of the Criminal Justice Act 2003 is that explicit reference, in the form of reparation, is given to the need for justice to the victim. Contemporary

---

[83] 14/02 Projections of Long-term Trends in the Prison Population to 2009; 11/06 Home Office Statistical Bulletin on Prison Population Projections; A.J. Ashworth, 'Analysing the Rise in the Prison Population' (editorial) [2013] Crim LR 367.

[84] Crime Sentences Act 1997, now contained in Powers of Criminal Courts (Sentencing) Act 2000, s. 109.

[85] M. Picton 'The Effect of the Changes in Sentencing of Dangerous Offenders Brought About by the Legal Aid, Sentencing and Punishment of Offenders Act 2012 and the Mystery of Schedule 15B' [2013] Crim LR 406.

[86] Section 143.

[87] The 2003 Act contained a sentence provision permitting indeterminate sentences for certain classes of dangerous offender. This is now repealed – s. 123 Legal Aid, Sentencing and Punishment of Offenders Act 2012. For discussion of this and other contemporary trends see D.A. Thomas, 'The Legal Aid, Sentencing and Punishment of Offenders Act 2012: The Sentencing Provisions' [2012] Crim LR 572. For comment see M. Picton, op. cit.

[88] Section 142.

[89] Coroners and Justice Act 2009 Part 4. For discussion see A.J. Ashworth, 'CAJA 2009: Sentencing Guidelines and the Sentencing Council' [2010] Crim LR 389.

[90] A. von Hirsch, *Censure and Sanctions* (1993) chs 4, 5.

[91] Hart (1968) 25.

[92] A. von Hirsch, op. cit. 105.

[93] On this see J. Loveless, 'Women, Sentencing and the Drug Offences Definitive Guidelines' [2012] Crim LR 592.

debates within penal theory have sought to revive the significance of the victim's point of view, but only in its positive manifestation as the reverse side of the offender's struggle for forgiveness and atonement. It is the victim after all who, in later confronting his attacker, is best placed to stimulate in the latter a spiritually honest sense of shame and desire to atone – something which talk of deterrence, reform and incapacitation cannot do. Restorative approaches in which the interests of the victim are given voice[94] and shaming approaches[95] which allow censure to take centre stage should be further explored to ensure that the link between wrongdoing and punishment is as transparent as possible. Recent approaches seek to reconcile the restorative and retributive themes in punishment by making the case for censure based not simply upon its communicative function but upon its facility to provoke a desire to atone and in so doing regain self-respect by restoring relations with the victim and the community.[96] Indeed, recent research into the restorative approach suggests that bringing offender and victim together may reduce the inclination to reoffend.[97]

Returning to the more basic criticism that the very **institution** of punishment cannot be justified where the dice are loaded against certain sections of society, the obvious response is 'why not'?[98] As long as society exercises itself in good faith through social and economic policy to minimise the social vicissitudes which might loosen the bonds of self-restraint;[99] gives fair warning of the occasions when punishment will be meted out; ensures that those occasions meet general social needs; ensures that the substantive, procedural and evidential rules are as fair as practicable and consistent with the maintenance of an effective system of norm enforcement; affords defences for those whose actions, measured by objective standards, are consistent with what we expect of reasonable citizens or, for reasons outside their control, are not susceptible to normative control; and keeps punishment to a minimum, then effective penal justice is done.[100] That some people find it easier to follow rules than others is no reason to condemn the rule-enforcement system. An action is no less harmful and worthy of censure if it stems from grievance, cupidity or brutalisation than if it is the product of 'original sin'. It is rather a reason for adopting a minimalist response to rule infraction consistent with the integrity of the social system. Social justice demands sentencing restraint and, arguably, nothing more radical when those who cut corners do so because their journey is further than that of ordinary people.[101]

---

[94] On this see *R v Perkins (Robert)* [2013] Crim LR 533 and comment by D.A. Thomas. For a useful introduction see A.J. Ashworth and A. von Hirsch, *Principled Sentencing*, Oxford: Hart (2009) ch. 7.

[95] Dan Kahan, 'What do Alternative Sanctions Mean?' (1996) 63 U Chic LR 591. Kahan has recently essayed such an approach. See note 81.

[96] Christopher Bennett, *The Apology Ritual: A Philosophical Theory of Punishment*; T. Kirchengast, 'Proportionality in Sentencing and the Restorative Justice Paradigm: "Just Deserts" for Victims and Defendants Alike?' (2010) 4(2) Criminal Law & Philosophy 197; cf. N. Smith, 'Against Court-Ordered Apologies' (2013) 16 New Criminal LR 1.

[97] Joanna Shapland, Anne Atkinson, *et al.*, 'Does Restorative Justice Affect Reconviction?' Ministry of Justice Research Series 10/08, June 2008; C. Hoyle, 'Victims, Victimisation and Restorative Justice' in M. Maguire, R. Morgan and R. Reiner (eds), *The Oxford Handbook of Criminology*, Oxford: OUP (2012) 398.

[98] Cf. A. Norrie (1993) 208–9.

[99] See earlier discussion on state drugs policy.

[100] A.W. Dzur, 'Participatory Democracy and Criminal Justice' (2012) 6(2) Criminal Law & Philosophy 115.

[101] Cf. A. Norrie, *Punishment, Responsibility and Justice*, Oxford: Clarendon Press (2001) chs 9–10.

Further reading

Bennett, C, *The Apology Ritual: A Philosophical Theory of Punishment*, Cambridge: CUP (2008).

Ferguson, P. and McDiarmid, C., *Scots Criminal Law: A Critical Analysis*, Dundee: Dundee University Press (2009) ch. 2.

Zaibert, L., *Punishment and Retribution*, Aldershot: Ashgate (2006).

Part II
General principles of criminal liability

4 *Actus reus*

Overview

Criminal liability typically hangs upon the establishment of some prohibited conduct, usually an act but exceptionally an omission, together with an accompanying, and concurrent, mental attitude. Where the definition of the crime incorporates a result it must be shown that the relevant conduct caused that result.

4.1 INTRODUCTION

The traditional framework governing criminal liability limits liability to occasions where the accused has perpetrated a given social 'harm' in circumstances disclosing moral fault. Following this framework, the general model for criminal offence definitions is a statement of some prohibited conduct, normally but not exclusively an act, with or without some designated result, and an accompanying mental attitude. This combination of elements is traditionally summed up by the Latin maxim *actus non facitreum nisi mens sit rea*. This maxim is usually translated as 'an act is not criminal in the absence of a guilty mind'.

As explained earlier, it is not accidental that crimes are constituted in this way. At the root of this equation, and also the theories of punishment, lies an assumption about the nature of human beings and the part they play in the world of events. Implicit in each theory is the assumption of free will and that social harms can be morally attributed to the choices which people make.[1] If we discovered next week that we were all sophisticated robots created by an alien race for their amusement and whose every action was mapped out for us by our own individual genetic 'computer program', punishment would lose any moral justification it might otherwise have.[2]

4.2 ELEMENTS OF LIABILITY

The *actus reus* of any crime constitutes the package of behaviour which forms the substance of a criminal prohibition. At its simplest, although this will require some qualification, it consists of those elements left over when the mental element (*mens rea*) is subtracted from the definition as a whole.[3] Thus the crime of murder may be defined as an unlawful killing with malice aforethought. The mental element described here – that is, what the prosecution has to show was 'going on in the defendant's mind' at the time of acting is 'malice aforethought'. This is satisfied by proof of an intention to kill or cause serious injury. The *actus reus* is an unlawful killing. It should be noted that the *actus reus* and *mens rea* of murder, in common with other offences, can only be fully unpacked by identifying certain

---

[1] M. Moore, *Causation and Responsibility: An Essay in Law, Morals and Metaphysics*, Oxford: OUP (2010).

[2] It might still retain a limited utilitarian function. It still makes good utilitarian sense to remove dangerous 'people' from society.

[3] This is only partly true. See Paul H. Robinson, 'Should the Criminal Law Abandon the *Actus Reus–Mens Rea* Distinction?' in S. Shute, J. Gardner and J. Horder (eds), *Action and Value in Criminal Law*, Oxford: Clarendon Press (1993) 187 generally, and see below page 73.

enduring features within offence definitions. As far as the *actus reus* is concerned, those features include, typically, a statement of the conduct, circumstance and result elements of the offence. Here, an 'unlawful killing' requires proof of some form of (homicidal) conduct such as a stabbing, wounding, etc. This is termed the act requirement. It requires proof of a death. It requires proof of certain circumstances constitutive of the crime in question, namely that the killing be unlawful. More broadly, it requires proof of an uninterrupted causal sequence linking the defendant's act with the death. To illustrate the potential impact of all these elements, consider the following cases.

Case 1
Adam sees his deadly enemy, Eve, walking towards a cliff. Although he knows she is blind he does nothing to stop her, hoping that she will fall to her death, which she does.

Adam is not guilty of murder since the act requirement is not satisfied.

Case 2
As in Case 1 except that Adam gave her false directions to encourage her along that particular route.

Here the act requirement is satisfied by Adam giving false directions. Adam would be liable, Eve's death being intended and having resulted from his act.

Case 3
As in Case 2 except that Eve took no notice of his directions and fell to her death as a result of her own error.

Here the act requirement and mental element is satisfied but as Adam's act made no difference to what subsequently transpired the causation requirement is not satisfied. Adam may yet be guilty of attempted murder, which does not require proof of causation.[4]

Case 4
As in Case 2 except that Adam did not know Eve to be blind and gave her false directions simply to irritate her.

Here the act and causation elements are satisfied. Adam will not be liable for murder, however, because the mental element of murder is lacking.

Case 5
Adam, a public executioner, is given the task, under statutory authority, of executing Eve who has been convicted of murder. Adam knows that Eve is innocent because Adam himself is the real killer. He nevertheless goes ahead and performs the execution because Eve is his deadly enemy and he wishes her dead.

Adam is not guilty of the murder of Eve since, although the mental element, act and causation requirements are satisfied, the execution, taking place under statutory authority, is not 'unlawful'.

---

[4] For an interesting application of this principle – is A guilty of intentionally intimidating a witness if the witness is not intimidated? – see *R* v *ZN* [2013] EWCA Crim 989 (CACD).

4.3 INTERRELATIONSHIP OF *ACTUS REUS*, *MENS REA* AND DEFENCES

In theory, the *actus reus* and *mens rea* elements of criminal offences are doing different jobs. The **external** (*actus reus*) elements of the offence approximately reproduce the substance of a society's 'rules of conduct' – the rules which tell all of us what we can and cannot do. If life was a game of golf, the *actus reus* of criminal offences would be like the golfer's rule-book. Golf rules, it should be noted, contain no mental element. A golfer who innocently hits the wrong ball or signs for the wrong score breaks a rule regardless of his honest intention, and suffers penalty therefor. On this theory, the **mental** element in crime (*mens rea*) is something quite distinct from the relevant rule of conduct. It operates to filter those deserving punishment for their wrong from those who do not, and to grade liability according to their degree of fault.[5] Theory does not tell the full story, however.[6] A mental element may on occasions serve to define the wrong itself. A person commits no wrong by entering a shop. If he enters with the intention of stealing from it, however, he commits the crime of burglary.[7] It is a burglar's state of mind which makes him a burglar, converting what might otherwise be a lawful act into a criminal wrong.

The fluidity of offence elements is not exhausted by mental states forming part of the conduct element in crime. For example, it is usual in textbooks to include a requirement of voluntariness of action as a conduct element in criminal liability.[8] Thus a person who crashes his car as a result of suffering an unexpected heart attack or brake failure is treated as absolved from liability for dangerous driving, on the basis that there was no (voluntary) act of his and thus no *actus reus*. Many students and not a few academics find this treatment unconducive to clear thinking[9] since the driver's claim is at heart a denial of fault – in effect, an excuse like any other, with its own set of rules governing its operation. In this book, all circumstances or events which are treated as capable of compromising free choice so as to negate criminal liability are dealt with in the chapter on defences.

The third element in criminal liability is (the absence of) defences. Once again the nature and operation of defences is ambiguous. It is not universally accepted that criminal defences are an independent (third) element in the constitution of criminal liability. Some theorists argue that defences involve nothing more than a denial that the criminal offence has been committed. Some defences are easy to analyse in this way. For example, those defences described as **justifications** challenge the very wrongfulness of the act in question. Self-defence is an example of such a defence. Then again, some defences negate the mental element as represented in the definition. An example is mistake. A person, charged with assault, who claims that he mistakenly believed the other to be consenting, is denying *mens rea*.[10] Disproving this belief is part of the prosecution's general burden of proving that the

---

[5] Paul H. Robinson, 'Should the Criminal Law Abandon the *Actus Reus–Mens Rea* Distinction?' in S. Shute, J. Gardner, J. Horder (eds), *Action and Value in Criminal Law*, Oxford: Clarendon Press (1993) 187 at 206: Paul H. Robinson, 'Rules of Conduct and Principles of Adjudication' (1990) 57 Univ of Chicago LR 729.

[6] By s. 18, Offences Against the Person Act 1861 a (minor) wounding is aggravated by an intention to cause serious injury. See generally P.H. Robinson, *Structure and Function in Criminal Law*, Oxford: Clarendon Press (1998); J. Gardner, 'On the General Part of the Criminal Law' in R.A. Duff (ed.), *Philosophy and the Criminal Law*, Cambridge: CUP (1998).

[7] Section 9(1)(a) Theft Act 1968.

[8] G. Yaffe, 'The Voluntary Act Requirement' in A. Marmor (ed.), *The Routledge Companion to Philosophy of Law*, London: Routledge (2012) 174. For critique see V. Chiao, 'Action and Agency in the Criminal Law' (2009) 15(1) Legal Theory 1.

[9] Paul H. Robinson in S. Shute *et al.*, *Action and Value in Criminal Law* (1993) 187 generally.

[10] See S. Kadish, 'Excusing Crime' (1987) 75 Cal L Rev 257 at 261.

elements of the offence are satisfied. Not all defences operate in this way, however. Some, which we may wish to term 'true' defences, operate extra-definitionally and so appear to be superimposed onto the conditions of liability. Duress is an example of such a defence.[11] A person who robs a bank under threat of death if he desists, 'confesses' to the commission of robbery as represented in the definition, but seeks to 'avoid' liability by presenting an (independent) excuse. It should be understood that whether or not defences can be subsumed within the offence elements is not purely a matter of theoretical conjecture. It has implications for the burden of proof.[12] And it has potentially serious implications for a person wishing to avail himself of a defence.

Case 6

Adam has violent intercourse with Eve believing her not to be consenting. In fact she is an entirely willing participant.

It is uncontroversial that Adam is not guilty of rape. The *actus reus* of rape as represented in the definition is having intercourse with a person who does not consent. Since Eve consents, the substance of the crime cannot be substantiated.[13] His 'guilty mind' cannot make the lawful unlawful. The analytical problem arises where the relevant defence does not form part of the definition of the crime.

Case 7

Eve, wishing to kill Adam, arranges to meet him at the top of a cliff. Her plan is to push him off the cliff and claim she acted in self-defence. Adam, unknown to Eve, also has murder in mind. His plan is to shoot Eve dead with a gun concealed in his jacket. While walking on the top of the cliff, Adam, unnoticed by Eve, puts his hand in his jacket and begins to press the trigger. Before he has a chance to fire, Eve takes her chance and pushes Adam to his death.

Eve's liability, in theory, may depend upon whether she has committed the *actus reus* of murder or whether her claim to avoid conviction depends upon her being able to avail herself of a defence operating independently of the offence elements. If it is the former, and Case 7 is to be treated like Case 6, she escapes liability for murder. If it is the latter, it is open to the court to reject the defence on the obvious basis that no action is justified in self-defence unless the actor acted for the purpose of resisting an unlawful attack, which he would not be doing if ignorant of such.[14]

Such authority as there is supports the latter analysis. In *Dadson*[15] D was a constable who wounded P, an escaping poacher, with a shotgun. Unknown to D, P was an escaping felon and the law permitted the shooting of escaping felons. Despite this the court held that he was guilty of unlawful wounding. Some have criticised the decision on the basis that,

---

[11] See A. Simester, 'Mistakes in Defences' (1992) OJLS 295 at 296. Simester designates self-defence as such a 'supervening mistake', those which 'deny neither *actus reus* or *mens rea*, but rather seek to defend the commission of the prima facie offence'.

[12] See R.A. Duff (2007) ch. 2.

[13] Cf. *Deller* (1952) 36 Cr App R 184; *R v Cornelius (Benjamin Jason)* [2012] EWCA Crim 500 (CACD).

[14] G. Williams, *Criminal Law: The General Part*, London: Stevens (1953) (hereafter *CLGP*) 20; S. Kadish, 'The Decline of Innocence' (1968) 26 CLJ 273; cf. D. Lanham, '*Larsonneur* Revisited' [1976] Crim LR 276; A.T.H. Smith, 'On *Actus Reus* and *Mens Rea*' in P. Glazebrook (ed.), *Reshaping the Criminal Law*, London: Stevens (1978) 95–107; B. Hogan, 'The *Dadson* Principle' [1989] Crim LR 679.

[15] (1850) 2 Den 35. For a compelling analysis of the theoretical contradictions involved in analysing defences as a third element in the constitution of criminal liability see A. Norrie (2001) ch. 7.

like Adam in Case 6, Dadson had done nothing which the law proscribed. He had shot someone he was entitled to shoot.[16] To punish Dadson for unlawful wounding, and Eve for murder, therefore, would be to punish them for their (bad) thoughts alone. The proper approach in such cases on this view would be to punish both Dadson and Adam for the crime whose definitional elements these thoughts, together with the action taken, satisfy. In the case of Eve this would be attempted murder. In the case of Dadson, less satisfactorily, this would be attempted unlawful wounding.[17]

The criminal law, however, distinguishes the two cases. There is a difference between claiming one has done nothing which the law prohibits (Case 6) and claiming that one was justified in doing what the law prohibits (Case 7). Where an actor such as Dadson seeks to rely upon a justification he is laying claim to having a (specially privileged) reason for acting which overrides his usual obligation to resist acting for his own reasons (say to avenge himself on a wrongdoer) and to act instead always for the reasons embodied in a criminal prohibition. In short, it is incumbent upon the actor to show not merely that his action was justified, but that he believed it to be justified and acted for that reason.[18]

4.4 THE ACT REQUIREMENT

The term *actus reus* refers to the external elements of the offence. All offences have such external elements. They require proof of some form of (prohibited) conduct, which will usually be some form of act. This is termed the 'act requirement'. Even inchoate offences such as attempt and conspiracy require proof of some form of action taken by the defendant of some harm-threatening variety.[19] The requirement that the defendant should perform some act for criminal liability to be incurred is a mark of a free society's distaste at the idea of punishing people for their anti-social thoughts, desires or intentions, rather than for the execution of such intentions.[20] By way of illustration, the American Supreme Court has invalidated a state statute making it an offence to be 'addicted to narcotics'.[21] Punishing such an offence would be punishing the defendant for who he was (an addict) rather than what he had done (take drugs). A pretty thin distinction, one might think.[22]

4.5 EXCEPTIONS TO THE ACT REQUIREMENT

Exceptionally, criminal liability may be incurred in the absence of a positive and voluntary act.[23] Liability may be incurred, for example, simply for being in a prohibited situation or for being in possession of a prohibited object. More generally, liability may be incurred for an omission where that omission is in breach of a duty to act.

---

[16] G. Williams, *CLGP* 23; cf. Case 5.

[17] Since he had the intention to wound and performed acts in execution of this intention. Such reasoning would not of course avail the prosecution in Case 5.

[18] Cf. Smith and Hogan, *Criminal Law* (13th edn by D.C. Ormerod), London: Butterworths (2011) and A.T.H. Smith, 'On *Actus Reus*' 97–103; also footnote 12 above; J. Gardner, 'Justifications and Reasons' in A. Simester and A.T.H. Smith (eds), *Harm and Culpability* (1996) 103; W. Wilson, *Central Issues in Criminal Theory* ch. 9. For critique see A. Norrie (2001) 149–55.

[19] As we shall see, not all criminal attempts can be so analysed.

[20] Cf. S. Bedi, 'Why a Criminal Prohibition on Sex Selective Abortions Amounts to a Thought Crime' (2011) 5(3) Criminal Law & Philosophy 349.

[21] *Robinson* v *California* (1962) 370 US 660.

[22] See Dressler (1987) 73 ff.

[23] The requirement of voluntariness of action is explored more fully in the chapters on defences. Certain forms of involuntary conduct are legally recognised excuses.

A Situational liability

The *actus reus* of certain (statutory) offences requires proof not of some form of conduct but simply of the defendant being 'in a situation which the law forbids (the defendant) to be in, or . . . continue to be in'.[24] Being drunk in charge of a vehicle is a well-known instance of this form of (situational) liability, conviction for which does not depend upon any act of taking charge of the vehicle. It is enough that the person is in charge and is drunk. Situational liability is often presented as objectionable, allowing for criminal conviction in the absence of any voluntary wrongdoing. Two infamous examples are *Larsonneur*[25] and *Winzar v Chief Constable of Kent*.[26] In the former the defendant was a French woman who had been allowed entry into the United Kingdom. She was later subject to an immigration order requiring her to leave the next day, whereupon she set sail for Ireland whence she was deported back to England. On arrival in England she was charged and convicted with being 'an alien to whom leave to land in the United Kingdom has been refused, (and who) was found in the United Kingdom contrary to the . . . Aliens Order 1920'. Clearly her conviction occurred despite the fact that her arrival in England was due to no voluntary act of hers. Accordingly the decision is unpopular with most commentators,[27] who view it as an example of unprincipled collusion by the court in oppressive executive practices.

In *Winzar*, the defendant was brought to hospital on a stretcher. It was found that he was simply drunk and so he was asked to leave. The police were called when he was later found asleep on a hospital seat. The police took him outside to the road whereupon they arrested him for being drunk on the highway contrary to section 12 of the Licensing Act 1872. The Divisional Court upheld his conviction, reasoning that whether he left the hospital in response to a request to leave or in response to a forcible eviction upon failing or refusing to leave, the mischief of the offence would have been satisfied. This mischief was the desirability of having drunks off the street and in a place where they pose no threat to themselves, to others or to public order.

Although these decisions are difficult to defend, a strong case has been made that they are not contrary to principle.[28] As long as an offence sets a standard of behaviour to which subjects are capable of conforming by appropriate avoiding action, there is no ethical reason to limit the substance of such offences to acts. Given that *Winzar* was the 'author of his own misfortune', how can he complain if, having got himself into the situation where he was unable to look after himself in a responsible fashion, he should find himself in a place where he did not wish to go, thus rendering himself vulnerable to arrest. The real issue is whether the law prohibiting being drunk in a highway could be considered a standard capable of enabling Mr Winzar not to fall foul of the police.[29] Of course it could. All he had to do was do his drinking at home.

In similar vein, a legal adviser advising Miss Larsonneur before she took off for Ireland would, no doubt, have explained to her that her reasons for going to Ireland[30] would

---

[24] P.R. Glazebrook, 'Situational Liability' in P.R. Glazebrook (ed.), *Reshaping the Criminal Law* (hereafter Glazebrook), London: Stevens (1978) 108 at 109.

[25] (1933) 97 JP 206.

[26] *The Times*, 28 March 1983.

[27] G. Williams, *TCL* 158.

[28] See for example D. Lanham, '*Larsonneur* Revisited' [1976] Crim LR 276; A. Simester, 'On the So-called Requirement for Voluntary Action' (1998) Buffalo Criminal Law Review 403; cf. M. Moore, *Act and Crime* (1993).

[29] D. Lanham, '*Larsonneur* Revisited' [1976] Crim LR 276; H.L.A. Hart, *Punishment and Responsibility: Essays in the Philosophy of Law*, Oxford: Clarendon Press (1968); cf. Norrie (1993) 120–2.

[30] She wished to marry to avoid immigration regulations.

render her susceptible to being deported back to where she came from and thus to conviction under the Aliens Order. If Miss Larsonneur had been kidnapped and returned here by terrorists, no question surely would have arisen that she was in breach of the Aliens Order. But she was not, and, indeed,[31] must have known she was 'sailing close to the wind'. A comparison may be made with the defence of duress which may not be relied upon where the defendant voluntarily places herself in the situation where she will be vulnerable to unlawful coercion.

Further support for this admitted rationalisation of two troublesome cases is the American case of *Martin*.[32] In this case, otherwise similar to that of *Winzar*, police officers took the drunken defendant from his own home and subsequently arrested him for '(appearing) in a public place, (manifesting) a drunken condition . , .'. Deciding that the defendant was not guilty, Simpson J held that the statute implicitly presupposed a 'voluntary' appearance, which was excluded where the defendant had been forcibly carried there against his will. The objection to a conviction on these facts is that the provision concerned could not operate as a mechanism for enabling people to remain on the right side of the law if it could be invoked against people who conscientiously limited the occasions upon which they became intoxicated to when they were in their own homes. It would arguably have been different, therefore, if the police had removed the defendant, at the request of the householder, from a house where he had been invited but had refused to quit.

The defendant's responsibility for causing the conditions of his own vulnerability to prosecution was highlighted in *R v Elvin*. The defendant's pit bull terrier escaped from the latter's inadequately secured house and bit a person.[33] He was charged with and convicted of being the owner of a dog which was dangerously out of control in a public place and which whilst so out of control injured a person, contrary to section 3(1) of the Dangerous Dogs Act 1991. On appeal, his argument that Parliament must have intended that he should have caused or permitted, by some voluntary act or omission, the dog to be at large was rejected. Although it was conceded that problems might arise if the dog had been let loose by a stranger, it was sufficient to dispose of the case that a more conscientious attitude on the part of the defendant would have scotched any possibility of the dog being at large in a public place.[34]

In conclusion, the problem with situational liability is less the fact that it is objectionable *per se* it need not be – but rather that it may stray too far from the criminal law's paradigm of culpable wrongdoing and can be used for objectionable purposes. Some scandalous examples have issued from the United States, most notably (failed) attempts to criminalise addiction to narcotics[35] and membership of the communist party.[36] It is not difficult to see the value an authoritarian government might reap from such offences.

---

[31] See generally D. Lanham, '*Larsonneur* Revisited' [1976] Crim LR 276.

[32] *Martin* v *State* 31 Ala. App. 334.

[33] *R v Bezzina, R v Codling, R v Elvin* [1994] 1 WLR 1057.

[34] Such an argument did not avail the defendant in *Adam (Derek)* v *HM Advocate* [2013] HCJAC 14 [High Court of Justiciary Scotland] but it did avail the defendant in *R v Robinson-Pierre* (2014) 158(3) SJ 37 CA where the dog had been let loose by the very police officers who it subsequently attacked.

[35] *Robinson* v *California* (1962), see above; cf. *Powell* v *Texas* (1968) 392 US 514 and commentary in Dressier 73–7.

[36] *Scales* v *US* (1961) 367 US 203. In England it is an offence to be a member of certain terrorist organisations. For comment see L. Levanon, 'Criminal Prohibitions on Membership in Terrorist Organizations' (2012) 15(2) New Criminal LR 224.

B Possession offences

English law contains a number of offences concerned with the possession of prohibited objects and substances. Consistent with the general pattern of situational liability, the possession of, say, firearms or controlled drugs does not impose any requirement upon the prosecution to establish any act of (voluntarily) **taking possession**. It is enough simply that the accused is **in possession** of the proscribed thing. So, if A is sent, by mistake, a postal package containing cannabis and, instead of ridding himself of it, puts it out of harm's way intending to dispose of it later, A is nevertheless in 'possession' of the drugs for the purpose of liability under the Misuse of Drugs Act.[37] The argument in favour of conviction here is that whether or not possessing is acting, liability is properly incurred by voluntarily remaining in possession. Imposing liability in such a situation is no more objectionable than imposing liability upon a parent for failing to seek medical attention for her sick child. In both cases the issue of principle is whether it is appropriate to hold someone to be under a legal duty to undo a social harm which he himself is not responsible for initiating.[38] This issue will be considered at length in the section on omissions. The strong case for penalising possession is that, by failing to remedy the harmful situation, the defendant thereby 'adopts' it as his own. As long as the defendant is in a position to avoid falling foul of the proscription, no obvious injustice is done by requiring him to remedy the situation, even if the initial fault was not his.[39]

The leading case in the area is the House of Lords decision in *Warner*, which goes part way to expressing this ethic.[40] The defendant had been given two boxes. One of the boxes contained scent. The other contained controlled drugs. The defendant said that he thought both boxes contained scent. The question for decision was whether the fact of being in possession of the box meant the defendant was also in possession of the contents. At first instance, and on appeal, the response was affirmative. The House of Lords, in a confusing set of opinions, decided in effect that the strong presumption was that a person who was in possession of a container was also in possession of its contents even if they were quite different from what they were believed to be. However, this presumption could be rebutted where:

(a) the thing has been secreted into the recipient's bag or onto his person without his knowledge, or

(b) the defendant receives an article whether in a container or not and the thing is fundamentally different from what it is thought to be.

Later cases have construed these latter restrictions almost out of existence. In *Lewis* the tenant of a house was held to be in possession of drugs found there even though he was a rare visitor to the premises, on the dubious ground that his tenancy of the house gave him the opportunity to acquaint himself with its contents.[41] In *McNamara* a person in

---

[37] There is a special defence available under the Misuse of Drugs Act 1971 for those who take possession of drugs under such circumstances: s. 5(4)(b).

[38] A comparable analysis is invoked by Glazebrook (1978) 114–16.

[39] Cf. *Miller* [1983] 1 All ER 978; *Fagan* v *MPC* [1968] 3 All ER 442. In the case of downloaded computer pornography it has been held that the possessor of the PC is in possession of any image that is stored in a file or internet cache, including the recycle bin, but not of images which have been entirely deleted from the machine, albeit that such images can be recovered by a computer expert: *R* v *Porter* [2006] Crim LR 748 See also *R* v *Leonard* [2012] EWCA Crim 277.

[40] [1969] 2 AC 256.

[41] *R* v *Lewis* (1988) 87 Cr App R 270; cf. *Sweet* v *Parsley* [1970] AC 132.

possession of a cardboard box thought to contain pornography was held to be in possession of the true contents, which was cannabis resin.[42]

As will be appreciated from the above cases, doctrine applicable to offences of possession appears inconsistent with the act requirement. Possession is a state of affairs, not a way of behaving. As in the case of situational offences, however, this is not an argument against possession offences *per se*, only against stretching the net of responsibility too far. The cases discussed above raise questions as to how a principled approach to the issue of possession (and wider situational offences) can be constructed, reconciling punishment's protective function with maintaining a basic minimum responsibility for criminal liability to be incurred.[43] Society is entitled to expect citizens to be responsible about what they allow into their possession[44]. If a friend asks me to take a bag through customs for her, society is entitled to expect that I will reassure myself as to the contents of the suitcase. If I do not do so, my conduct poses a threat to society which it is reasonable to sanction. On the other hand, if she gives me a walking stick as a reward for looking after her cat during her foreign holiday, society is not entitled to expect that I will examine it to reassure myself that it is not an ingenious swordstick.[45] If the existence of dangerous substances and objects is a social threat, it makes sense for such a society to impose liability for possession even upon some who are unaware of what they possess. Lacking awareness is not the same as lacking the ability to conform to a criminal prohibition. In this context it may be reasonable, for example, to impose liability on a possessor for failing 'to take action which he realises a reasonable man in his position would have taken to prevent (the relevant) situation[46] arising or continuing' rather than criminalise the mere state of affairs.[47]

C Omissions

The *actus reus* of numerous statutory crimes consists of some form of failure or omission. Counterposed to such crimes of omission, a statutory or common law crime of commission may, exceptionally, be committed by omission. For this to be possible the following minimum requirements must be satisfied, namely:

(1) the conduct element of the crime in question must be capable of commission by omission;
(2) the circumstances must be such as to create a legal duty to act;
(3) the defendant's failure to act must be voluntary. It will be involuntary if he lacked the physical capacity or if, given his characteristics, it would be unreasonable to expect him to have acted otherwise.

It was seen in the previous sections that although criminal liability is paradigmatically associated with some positive conduct on the part of the defendant, occasionally a sanction may attach just for being in a 'prohibited situation'. Many other offences can be committed

---

[42] (1988) 87 Cr App R 246. See also *R v Zahid* [2010] EWCA Crim 2158, CACD where the prohibited item 'innocently possessed' was bullets.

[43] For analysis see M. Dubber, 'The Possession Paradigm: the Special Part and the Police Power Model of the Criminal Process' in R.A. Duff and S.P. Green (eds), *Defining Crimes*, Oxford: OUP (2005).

[44] *R v Williams* [2012] EWCA Crim 2162 (CACD).

[45] In *Deyemi* [2007] EWCA Crim 2060, this argument failed. The defendant was held strictly liable for possessing a stun gun, which he believed only to be a torch and which in fact had the appearance of a torch. *Deyemi* [2007] applied in *R v Zahid* [2010] EWCA Crim 2158 (CACD).

[46] Including the 'situation' of being in possession of a proscribed 'thing'.

[47] Glazebrook (1978) 117. See generally Ashworth (2013) ch. 6.

in the absence of an affirmative act.[48] The majority of such offences are statute-based. Typically, the words of a statute will expressly create a duty to act in a particular way. Obvious examples include failing to submit a tax return, failing to provide a specimen[49] and failing to report a road traffic accident.[50] It will be seen that the essence of these offences is a failure, in breach of duty, to behave in the required fashion. Such crimes are commonly designated crimes of omission; that is a crime in which the external elements of the offence take the form of the defendant **not doing something** which he is placed under a legal duty to perform. Central to the characteristics of such offences is that the social harm of which the defendant is accused is some form of inappropriate conduct rather than some harmful result.[51]

Distinguished from the above (statutory) crimes of omission criminal liability may also attach for crimes of **commission** in respect of an **omission**. For example by statute a parent maybe liable for wilful neglect of her child.[52] Failure to feed the child will render the parent liable for this offence. If the child dies as a result the parent may also be liable for murder or manslaughter, both crimes of commission, depending upon *mens rea*. Likewise by section 5 of the Domestic Violence, Crime and Victims Act 2004 it is an offence to cause or allow the death of, or serious injury to a child under the age of 16 or of a vulnerable adult. It is an offence applicable to all members of the same household as V who have regular contact with them.[53] Few commentators criticise such a state of affairs. Such laws are common and uncontroversial in the sense that virtually no commentators claim that they should not be part of the criminal law. But there are nevertheless a number of theoretical problems attached. Before we examine the law let us examine some of the issues of principle involved.

1 Is it appropriate to criminalise omissions?

The traditional objection to omissions-based liability questions the propriety of calling people to action in the service of collective or individual interests. Paradoxically, although the rules of criminal law may be understood as restricting our range of choices, controlling harmful affirmative action generally enhances our opportunities to be effective authors of our own destiny. When people punch us or steal from us they are seeking to be authors of our destiny as well as their own. It is right then to restrict their ability to do so. Punishing omissions, by contrast, seems to compromise rather than enhance human autonomy since it makes demands of us which may well require us to subjugate our own interests to those of others. Is this not inconsistent with the point of the criminal law?

An answer to this question requires two separate affirmative duties to be distinguished. The first are the routine social responsibilities which arise out of the structural claims of people living together in a modern community. Such communities need to organise themselves so that collective as well as individual needs are satisfied. Unbridled individualism is inconsistent with society's structural integrity and a strong social structure is a precondition of individual self-fulfilment. Without rules criminalising failures to submit tax returns or wear seat belts, the problems posed for society trickle down to compromise the very framework within which individual autonomy can be enjoyed. An autonomy-respecting

---

[48] Glazebrook (1978) 115.
[49] Section 4 Road Traffic Act 1988.
[50] Contrary to section 170(4) Road Traffic Act 1988.
[51] Fletcher, *Rethinking Criminal Law*, Boston: Little, Brown (1978) 421.
[52] CYPA 1933.
[53] As amended by The Domestic Violence, Crime and Victims (Amendment) Act 2012. See *R v Akinrele* [2010] EWCA Crim 2972.

society may then quite legitimately constitute itself through rules by which welfare routinely trumps autonomy. The only crucial limiting feature is that the proscribing rule operates as a standard capable of enabling the defendant to avoid state coercion and that the trade-off is morally justifiable on an all-things-considered basis. For this reason few are disposed to challenge the propriety of affirmative duties *per se*. The enforcement of such duties is necessary for society itself to run smoothly and therefore for society's members to flourish as individuals. In this respect they evince no basic dissimilarity with proscriptive rules designed to create the basic framework for communal living. If the requirement to tax one's car or wear a seat belt is an interference with freedom and autonomy it is no more so than the duty not to exceed the speed limit or not to park in a restricted area.[54]

It is another type of affirmative duty which poses the greatest challenge to the moral legitimacy of state coercion. Unlike prohibitions such as theft or murder, which leave the actor with a full range of options save the conduct prohibited, some affirmative duties fall due unpredictably and consequently may deprive the duty bearer of one of the fundamentals of the autonomous life, namely the right to choose what to do at any given time.[55] An example is that requiring drivers of motor vehicles to report a road accident. This duty demands action and action now. It prohibits keeping that doctor's appointment, attending that meeting, or posting that letter. No action will satisfy it other than making report. The difference, then, between such affirmative duties and traditional prohibitions is that the former are apt to stigmatise the very people which liberal society cherishes – those who go around minding their own business and whose destiny is to leave no kind of mark on society, let alone a bloody one.[56] There is no reason of principle, however, why such affirmative duties should not be subject to the same criteria of criminalisation as proscriptions. The justification for imposing such a duty in the eyes of its advocates is the same as for imposing any other duty, namely harm prevention. And harm can be prevented by requiring citizens not merely to refrain from active wrongdoing but also by protecting the vulnerable and putting right that which goes wrong. The real issue is whether it is reasonable to force citizens to do so, and the determination of this issue is not foreclosed by the fact that the harm-engendering conduct involves no positive intervention in the world of events. Rather, they counsel caution in ensuring that the usual conditions for criminalisation are met. In particular, since the burden on liberty is high the countervailing advantages justifying imposing that burden must be correspondingly high.[57] Taking parenthood as a benchmark, society would be prosecuting an unusual notion of autonomy if enforcing a duty of protection and care of infants was seen as compromising its realisation. Perhaps more significantly, however, the fact that enforcing the duty interferes with the parent's freedom of action does not strike one as any kind of reason for not doing so. Sometimes autonomy is not the point. Sometimes responsibility trumps autonomy. The question for the criminal law is to determine when.[58]

D Omission and crimes of commission

Criminalising omissions can pose problems of application, however. The major difficulty arises in connection with criminalising omissions in the case of result crimes, such as murder,

---

[54] J. Feinberg, *Harm to Others* 164; G. Fletcher, *Rethinking Criminal Law* 602 and 'On the Moral Irrelevance of Bodily Movements' (1994) 142 U Pa L Rev.

[55] A.J. Ashworth, 'The Scope of Criminal Liability for Omissions' (1989) 105 LQR 424 at 427.

[56] M. Moore (1993) 58–60.

[57] That is, criminalisation must be effective and necessary and not such as would provoke harmful social side-effects.

[58] See generally G. Fletcher, 'On the Moral Irrelevance of Bodily Movements' (1994) 142 U Pa L Rev 1443.

assault, criminal damage and theft, as it may run counter to the legality principle. This holds, it will be remembered, that people are not the appropriate object of criminal sanction unless their behaviour falls clearly and explicitly within the scope of a provision designed to proscribe such behaviour. Specifically, people should be punished for offending a legal rule, not simply because their conduct is immoral, injurious or offensive. After all, law can only work if people are given fair warning not only of what they must not do, but also of what they must do. If a rule instructs me in clear terms not to drop litter, why should I fear a prosecution for not providing litter bins in my park, or not stopping my friend from dropping his cigarette packet? These general concerns are aggravated by various doctrinal problems raised by omissions liability for crimes of commission. Consider the following variation of a classic example where it is uncontroversial that liability will not be incurred.

Case 8

A turns a corner to see B, her neighbour's baby, head down and drowning in a puddle of water. To save the child would take no time and involve no trouble or risk. A does not do so because the baby keeps her awake at night and she wants the baby dead. B drowns.

Criminal liability for homicide, say murder, requires proof of a killing accompanied by an intention to kill (or cause serious injury) and of a causal link between some conduct of the defendant and the event (death) such that it is appropriate to attribute the death to the defendant. On the question of the 'killing' two questions arise. First, can one 'kill' someone by doing nothing? This will be addressed below, but briefly it depends upon whether we can interpret 'kill' (which implies some form of active agency) as 'causing someone to die' (which does not). If we allow that we can, the question then arises as to whether A **has** caused B to die. Once again, we will explore what 'cause' means later. At this stage it suffices to remark that applying general principles of causation confounds no general moral expectations in the ordinary case of positive acts of wrongdoing. People who raise arms against other people and kill or injure them are, without any need for elaborate meta-physical argument, the (causal) agents of such death or injury. Here, however, the only thing linking A with the death of the baby is her chance arrival on the scene. Other than that, A is no more a cause of the baby's death than any other person. After all, if A had never lived B would still have drowned.[59] Is it appropriate, then, to treat her as a cause of death? If so, this would threaten to extend the net of criminal responsibility far wider than is presently recognised. How could our new social responsibility be kept in reasonable bounds? Should I be liable for refusing a homeless beggar a room and food on a cold winter's night if he dies that very night of hypothermia? If so, how is my causal contribution any different than that of the thousands of other people who 'pass by on the other side'? How can it be shown that it was I, who lived five miles away in a one-bedroomed flat, who caused the death rather than the owner of the large mansion who lived just round the corner? Or do we all cause the death of people whose life we might have saved?

On the question of 'criminal intent', despite being in any reasonable sense of the word 'wicked' and 'at fault' it would be difficult to establish A's intent as a matter of evidence. For this reason, even where a relationship of responsibility does exist, omissions causing death are rarely charged as murder but rather as manslaughter. Moreover, even if A

---

[59] L. Katz, *Bad Acts and Guilty Minds*, Chicago: University of Chicago Press (1987) 143; P. Smith, 'Legal Liability and Criminal Omissions' (2002) Buffalo Crim LR 69; cf. T. Elliot, 'Liability for Manslaughter by Omission: Don't Let the Baby Drown!' (2010) 74(2) J Crim L 163.

admitted her hatred, is wanting someone dead the same as intending to kill them? Would it be a conceptual error for the bystander to say 'Yes I wanted the baby dead, but I drew the line at killing her. It is wrong to kill someone. If I had intended to kill her I would have smothered her in her pram, but I did not want her dead that much.' Is not our bystander presenting herself, if not as the model citizen, then as the citizen respected and valued by the criminal law – the kind of person who goes around minding her own business **and desisting from acting upon her basest desires**?

It should be appreciated that the above analysis raises a question about whether it would be appropriate to find A guilty of murder. It does not argue against A incurring some form of liability for her deeply anti-social behaviour. But this would be a matter for Parliament to enact a special offence such as appear in some other jurisdictions, such as failing to help a person in peril. The common law has no obvious warrant to create new offences in this way.

1 Acts and omissions: what's the difference?

The distinction between acts and omissions usually draws a satisfactory line between conduct appropriate for criminal liability and where it would not be appropriate. Omissions are usually less heinous, because more excusable, than acts and rarely satisfy basic demands of causality. From a common sense point of view, holding a person liable for a result in the absence of a positive act is generally inappropriate because acts and omissions do not seem to exhibit 'moral equivalence'.

Case 9

A cuts B's throat. C comes upon the scene later to find B bleeding to death. He does nothing to help.

There appears to be an obvious moral difference between cutting someone's throat and doing nothing to prevent the victim from bleeding to death.[60] For this common-sense reason, liability for omissions tends to be the exception rather than the rule for crimes of 'commission'. A is the killer, not C. There is, however, another point of view, namely that there is no deep analytical difference and consequently no **necessary** moral (or legal) difference between acts and omissions.[61]

Case 10

Eve, a strong swimmer, while swimming at the local baths, notices that Adam is struggling in the water. She swims over to rescue him but upon realising that he is her deadly enemy releases her grip and leaves him to drown.

Eve's liability here requires consideration of whether her conduct in relation to Adam is an act – releasing her grip – or an omission – failing to complete the rescue – which causes Adam's death.[62] It is clearly of central importance, given that liability for murder may depend upon it, to know whether given conduct constitutes one rather than the other. On first blush it seems to be her act. Adam drowned via a sequence of events which included the kind of bodily movements which we readily associate with drowning

---

[60] Cf. G. Williams, *TCL* 149 ff.
[61] T. Elliott and D. Ormerod, 'Acts and Omissions: A Distinction without a Defense?' (2008) 39 Cambrian LR 40.
[62] M. Moore, op. cit. 27.

someone. On the other hand, omissions, unlike acts, can take any number of forms, including affirmative actions. Eating a sandwich which would save the life of a starving beggar or snatching the sole remaining life belt before it is secured by another drowning person are, at the same time, both acts and omissions. They are the acts of eating and snatching but equally, for purposes of moral evaluation, they are instances of omitting to provide succour to the victim. It follows that the analytical grounds for supposing that the cause of Adam's death was Eve's act are less secure. Her actions clearly form part of the sequence by which Adam met his death, but, unlike the latter hypotheticals, those **actions** have made no difference to the outcome. Adam has been left in no worse position than if Eve had done nothing, had taken a photograph of the stricken victim, had busied herself saving someone else's life, or had simply rubbed her hands in glee.[63] Our condemnation may be further stoked by the physical movements accompanying the abandonment of the rescue but ultimately it is not prompted by it.[64] Our starting point for subjecting Eve's conduct to moral scrutiny is what she has **not** done rather than what she has done. Because not going to rescue an enemy is not the subject matter of criminal homicide it seems to follow that neither is abandoning the attempt once it has begun unless, as we shall see, Eve's initial intervention imposes upon her an obligation to see the rescue through.

Such considerations informed the House of Lords decision in *Airedale NHST v Bland*.[65] The patient was suffering from a condition known as persistent vegetative state (PVS) following brain damage in the Hillsborough football disaster. PVS is an irreversible condition and has the effect of removing all sensory and other mental experience, rendering the victim a human 'vegetable'. The patient was being kept alive by means of a naso-gastric feeding tube. Would disconnecting the tube be lawful? A major factor was whether the disconnection was an act or an omission. If it was an act the disconnection would be unlawful and would subject the doctor concerned to liability for murder, just as if he had administered a lethal injection or smothered the patient with a pillow.[66] If it were an omission, on the other hand, the disconnection would be lawful since the **doctor's** duties of succour are not absolute. Where the patient is unable to give consent to treatment, the doctor's duty (and right) to intervene is limited to cases where the intervention serves some interest of the patient. To intervene 'futilely' is an assault on the patient's autonomy. Removing the tube, on this analysis, would be a successful performance of a duty '**not to act**' rather than a failed performance of a duty **to act**.

The conclusion reached by the House of Lords was that it was an omission. Even though the visual picture of the disconnection was that of an act, the true cause of the subsequent death would be the failure to provide life-sustaining treatment. It was thought that no distinction could be drawn between the case where the tube was not connected in the first place and the case where it was disconnected upon being found futile.[67]

The House of Lords was clearly exercised by the implications of their finding, and rightly so. The major analytical headache is that the same course of conduct would be a positive act if effected by a stranger, but an omission if perpetrated by the appropriate medical officer.[68]

---

[63] Ibid. 267.

[64] J. Thomson, 'A Defense of Abortion' (1971) I Phil and Pub Aff 47; *Airedale NHS Trust v Bland* [1993] AC 789.

[65] [1993] 1 All ER 821.

[66] See for example where the defendant was the deceased's mother. *R v Inglis* [2010] EWCA Crim 2637; *R (on the application of Nicklinson) v Ministry of Justice* [2012] EWHC 2381 (Admin); [2011] Crim LR 243 (CACD).

[67] For discussion see D. Price, 'Fairly Bland: An Alternative View' (2001) LS 618; J. Keown, 'Restoring the Sanctity of Life' (2006) LS 109; D. Price, 'My View of the Sanctity of Life: A Rebuttal of John Keown's critique' (2007) LS 549.

[68] Whoever that might be; see I. Kennedy, *Treat Me Right* (1988).

Moreover, there was little ethical difference between administering a lethal injection and, as here, removing life-sustaining therapy.[69] Yet one course of conduct was the *actus reus* of murder and the other was entirely lawful. If one course of conduct was morally acceptable and lawful, why was not the other? Indeed, it is arguable that the administration of the lethal injection is morally better since it allows a person to die with dignity rather than as a slow, drawn-out 'death by starvation'.[70]

More cogent perhaps is the view that the disconnection, in both cases, is an act causing death. In the analysis of Jonathan Bennett, the disconnection is an act insofar as it closes off opportunities for action (e.g. going to the movies, having a cup of tea) which would otherwise be present.[71] What is special about the former disconnection is that the context justifies the action taken because the nature of the **act**, being demanded by the very incidents of the doctor/patient relationship, is not a direct attack on the patient's life.[72] As Moore puts it: 'there is not a break in the causal chain between our flipping of the switch and the patient's death. We therefore kill the patient just as surely as does an intruder who does the same sort of action with the same result.'[73] However, such killings are 'less wrong' than other killings and can therefore be more easily justified by reference to the good consequences which result. In *Bland* the good consequence was the desirable death of the victim. In another case, say the transfer of a life support machine from one person to another, it may be the desirability of ensuring optimal benefits from scarce medical resources.[74] In *NHS Trust* v *L* to all intents and purposes it was to respect the moral futility of force-feeding a severely anorexic patient who was near to death.[75]

For this reason, some commentators believe, not least in the limited field of medicine, that the dubious analytical and attendant moral distinction between act and omission should be laid to rest.[76] Such differences as arise are created by context. Usually actions are more blameworthy/causal than omissions and should be punished as such. But equally, sometimes, an omission maybe more blameworthy/causal than an action. What is morally worse/causally more significant, shooting a child to prevent the agony of her burning to death in a flaming inferno one is powerless to prevent, or failing to save a similar child from a similar fate by the simple mechanism of unlocking the door behind which she is trapped?

Liability should hinge instead, on this view, on the reasonableness of expecting the defendant to come to a victim's aid. The only problem which the criminal law faces is whether a duty of intervention should be enforced and in what form. All that is required

[69] Declaration was refused in *Re M (Adult Patient) (Minimally Conscious State: Withdrawal of Treatment)* (Also known as: *W v M*) [2011] EWHC 2443 (Fam); [2012] 1 WLR 1653; (2011) 156 NLJ 1368 where the patient had minimal consciousness falling short of PVS.

[70] J. Rachels, 'Active and Passive Euthanasia' in J. Arthur (ed.), *Morality and Moral Controversies*, New Jersey: Prentice Hall (1986) 155. See further – The right to decide when or how to die was not excluded from Art. 8(1) – *R (on the application of Purdy)* v *DPP* [2009] UKHL 45; [2010] 1 AC 345 (HL).

[71] J. Bennett, *The Act Itself*, Oxford: Clarendon Press (1995).

[72] The decision in the Diane Pretty case is consistent with this analysis. While it would have been unlawful to take direct steps to help Diane Pretty to die, the patient could still have insisted on being withdrawn from life support as a vindication of her autonomy. *Pretty* v *DPP* [2002] 1 AC 800; *Pretty* v *UK* (2002) 35 EHRR 1. See Chapter 1 pp. 26–8.

[73] At 276. For critical discussion see A. McGee, 'Ending the Life of the Act/Omission Dispute: Causation in Withholding and Withdrawing Life-sustaining Measures' (2011) 31(3) Legal Studies 467.

[74] It is clear from at least two of the speeches in *Bland* – [1993] 1 All ER 821 – per Lord Browne-Wilkinson at 879 and Lord Mustill at 893 that resources might be a legitimate concern of the doctor.

[75] [2012] EWHC 2741 (COP).

[76] P. Singer, *Rethinking Life and Death*, Oxford: OUP (1995) 195–6; J. Bennett, *The Act Itself*, Oxford: Clarendon Press, (1995); for a useful review of this book see G.R. Sullivan, 'Ministering Death', (1997) 17(1) OJLS 123–36.

of A, in **Case 9**, is **not to wound B** – hardly onerous. What duty would it make moral and political sense to subject C to? A duty of taking reasonable steps to prevent loss of life? A duty to call an ambulance or report the crime? Both suggestions have been canvassed, along with others.[77] What should be noted is that whatever the scope of the duty concerned it is bound to be significantly more onerous than the negative duty inhibiting active wrongdoing. It should be for this latter reason, it is thought, rather than because there is a genuine analytical difference between acts and omissions, that we should limit the occasions upon which we punish omissions. Since imposing liability for omissions as well as acts would be too restrictive of human freedom it should be allowed only in the most morally uncontroversial circumstances.

2 Omissions: the common law approach

(a) *The offence must be capable of commission by omission*

The basic stance adopted in the criminal law is that criminal liability for omitting to act can be incurred if, as a matter of interpretation, the offence definition is consistent with such liability and if the defendant is placed under a duty to act. In *Ahmad*,[78] a person was held not liable for doing 'acts calculated to interfere with the peace or comfort of a residential occupier with intent to cause him to give up occupation of the premises'.[79] He had done the relevant acts, removing defective windows, without this intent and later, wishing to be rid of his tenant, failed to remedy the situation. Clearly this decision is correct as a matter of strict interpretation. He had done no 'acts' with the relevant intent. The case shows how dependent are the courts, and society's purposes, on effective Parliamentary drafting.[80]

Outside such clear cases, the majority of result crimes include formal external elements indicative of some form of positive action on the part of the accused. Crimes of violence, for example, are generally designated by the use of 'action words'. Although the crimes of murder and manslaughter are normally defined in terms which stress an act of killing, these offences have been construed as capable of issuing from an omission to act. In effect, then, 'to kill' has been construed to mean 'to cause death'. As long as the causation and fault elements are satisfied it is no answer to a charge of manslaughter or murder that one's deed was one of omission rather than commission. By extension, we must assume that causing grievous bodily harm with intent to cause grievous bodily harm contrary to section 18 Offences Against the Person Act 1861 is also capable of commission by omission. This poses a question about the alternative mode of committing this offence, namely wounding with intent to cause grievous bodily harm. Wounding, unlike 'causing', suggests some form of act. Can one 'wound' someone by doing nothing? What, also, of offences such as assault and the unlawful infliction of grievous bodily harm, with unequivocal action elements?[81] Assault, for example, is defined as 'a threat or hostile act committed towards a person'[82] and was once thought to be incapable of commission by omission. In *Fagan* the unanimous opinion was to this effect.[83] It might seem a matter of sheer linguistic pedantry to allow a person to be guilty of **causing** serious injury by omission, but denying liability in respect of crimes of lesser seriousness on the basis simply of an interpretation

---

[77] See below, p. 97.
[78] [1986] Crim LR 739.
[79] Contrary to s. 1(3), Protection from Eviction Act 1977.
[80] Cf. *Speck* [1977] 2 All ER 859.
[81] An offence under section 20 Offences Against the Person Act 1861.
[82] Lord Goddard CJ, *Rolfe* (1952) 36 Cr App R 4.
[83] *Fagan* v *MPC* [1968] 3 All ER 442.

of what it is to assault or inflict harm upon another?[84] Surely what is important is that the proscribed harm occurred and the defendant, being in a position to do so, **culpably** failed to prevent it. The most recent codifying initiatives of the Law Commission would facilitate such an approach by defining fatal and non-fatal offences against the person in terms of 'causing' the relevant harm rather than specifying a given act – kill, inflict, wound and so on.[85] Current trends in the appeal courts suggest that the judiciary are broadly supportive of this line of analysis.[86] As long as the definition of the crime does not specify a particular mode of commission it is no objection that the crime is defined in such a way as to imply an active mode of execution.[87] Accordingly, in *DPP v Santana-Bermudez*, the Divisional Court held that an assault would be committed where, by virtue of the rule in *Miller*, the defendant was placed under a duty to prevent a danger materialising, whose breach caused the victim harm. This is the wrong way to address the question, I would suggest. The most important consideration is to identify what it is in any harm-causing conduct which we consider wrong. It may well be, for example, that we think causing death by omission is just as wrong as killing by action, but even if we do this does not necessarily mean that they should be designated the same wrong. Labels matter.[88]

(b) A duty to prevent harm must be owed

The common law does not impose generalised liability for omissions. As Case 8 illustrates, the mere existence of a moral duty to act is insufficient to support a legal obligation. The common law approach is to impose obligations of action upon citizens to satisfy general **social expectations** rather than general **moral aspirations**. Those expectations are generally limited to cases where the defendant has failed to act in breach of a social responsibility which has been voluntarily assumed.

The reason for expectations to be limited in this way is that society evinces no consensus about the moral obligations other people should satisfy beyond those the latter are themselves prepared to acknowledge or assume. In other words, in a free society without such a moral consensus, we can only **expect** people to help us if they have promised to or, at least, as in the case of parents and children, there is an explicit relationship of dependence.[89] Such relationships impose special duties not least because they isolate the dependent person from other potential sources of support. So, we **expect** lifeguards to help us when we are drowning. We **hope** strong swimmers will do likewise. Society will survive quite nicely if the latter **hope** is generally confounded, but will disintegrate if social **expectations** such as the former are.[90] Our expectations that moral duties of succour are fulfilled

[84] J.C. Smith, 'Liability for Omissions in Criminal Law' (1984) 4 Legal Studies 88, agrees that liability for omissions requires offence definitions to admit such a mode of 'commission', but disagrees that words such as 'assault' require some form of act. Cf. G. Williams, *TCL* 172, 179.

[85] Draft Criminal Code LC no. 177, Offences Against the Person Bill 1998.

[86] Perhaps too supportive! In *R v Jenkins* [2013] RTR 288(21) CA the Court of Appeal held that it was no part of the prosecution's case on a charge of causing death by careless driving that the death of the victim was caused by the driving of the defendant's lorry. That he was badly parked was enough. For a similar decision see *R v Williams* [2010] EWCA Crim 2552; C. Crosby, 'Causing Death by Faultless Driving' (2011) 75(2) J Crim L 111 (case comment). And see generally S. Cunningham, 'Taking "Causing Serious Injury by Dangerous Driving" Seriously' [2012] Crim LR 261.

[87] *DPP v Santana-Bermudez* [2003] EWHC 2908. See for example *Speck* [1997] 2 All ER 859; *R v Ireland*; *R v Burstow* [1997] 4 All ER 225.

[88] See J. Gardner, 'Rationality and the Rule of Law in Offences Against the Person' [1994] 53 CLJ 50. See also J. Chalmers and F. Leverick, 'Fair Labelling in Criminal Law' (2008) MLR 217.

[89] See G. Mead, 'Contracting into Crime: A Theory of Criminal Omissions' (1991) 11 OJLS 147.

[90] See A. Leavens (1988), 'A Causation Approach to Criminal Omissions' 76 Calif LR 547.

are thus socially validated, rather than simply an expression of a potentially contentious moral etiquette.

3 Circumstances giving rise to a duty to act: duty situations

The ruling view is that enunciated in *Kenny's Outlines*, 'No-one is held criminally responsible, at common law, for the harmful consequence of his omission to act, whether that omission be careless or intentional, unless the prosecution can prove that he was under a legal obligation to take action in the particular circumstances in which he was placed.'[91] The general pattern of liability is that obligations of action are imposed upon citizens in the case of certain special relationships such as spouses and parents and children, or where the defendant has assumed a responsibility of care for the victim, whether informally or by contract or other legal duty. More recently an obligation to intervene to prevent a risk of injury materialising has been imposed upon the creator of such a risk. There is probably room for creation of further duty situations, as will be seen.

(a) *Special relationships*

The formal reason for legal obligations to be restricted in this way is that society evinces no consensus about the moral obligations **other people** should satisfy beyond those **the latter are themselves** prepared to acknowledge or assume, whether by agreement or operation of law.[92] So, a parent can be guilty of murder for starving his child to death,[93] and of manslaughter for failing to secure medical attention where it is dangerously ill.[94] Similar responsibilities attach in the case of spouses.[95] On the other hand a duty does not arise automatically in respect of informal relationships in the absence of a formal assumption of care. In *People* v *Beardsley*[96] the defendant was held not to be under any duty to his lover who had taken an overdose of morphine in his presence.

It is probably not, however, the fact of being a spouse/parent/carer which grounds the duty. Rather it is the fact that such persons have placed themselves in the frame (causal and moral) by their status/role/conduct and in so doing excite expectations, whether in the victim or the wider society, which render the victim vulnerable if those expectations are not fulfilled. Confounded expectations can cause harm.[97] On this analysis a person who assumes a life-saving role, say he promises the victim's wife that he will act as the latter's bodyguard, will be liable for the consequences of failure only if there is detrimental reliance[98] – if, for example, the wife or victim failed to engage another bodyguard on the strength of that promise or if the victim entered a dangerous situation he would not otherwise have entered.[99]

---

[91] Kenny, at 16.
[92] See G. Mead, 'Contracting into Crime: A Theory of Criminal Omissions' (1991) 11 OJLS 147.
[93] *Gibbins and Proctor* (1918) 13 Cr App R 134.
[94] *Downes* (1875) 13 Cox CC 111.
[95] *Bonnyman* (1942) 28 Cr App R 131.
[96] (1967) 113 NW 1128. Cf. *R* v *Evans*, *infra* note 124.
[97] See Glazebrook (1960); A. Leavens, 'A Causation Approach to Criminal Omissions' (1988) 76 Calif LR 547; W. Wilson, *Central Issues in Criminal Theory* (2002) ch. 3; L. Alexander, 'Criminal Liability for Omissions' in Shute and Simester (eds), *Criminal Law Theory: Doctrines of the General Part*, Oxford: OUP (2002).
[98] A similar view is voiced by Alexander, who emphasises the need for detrimental reliance for liability to be incurred.
[99] Likewise it seems probable that a person who has promised to alert the victim if her deadly enemy, bent on killing the victim, should arrive in the neighbourhood, and whose identity he alone knows, is not guilty of murder for the deliberate failure. This is not apparently the position in American law. See Alexander, note 98 above.

(b) *Contractual relationships*

A requirement of detrimental reliance accounts for the finding in *Pittwood*[100] that a contractual duty owed by P to B could form the basis of a duty of action in favour of C. It was held, in line with the earlier case of *Instan*,[101] that the defendant level crossing keeper who had failed to close the crossing was responsible for the death of the driver of a haycart struck while crossing the line. By acting as a level crossing keeper, he had undertaken to keep him and other road users safe. The expectation had developed, since railways had first arrived, that those engaged in managing them would, as a matter of routine, ensure that the public were given due warning of the arrival of trains. Once such expectation existed it followed that the moral obligation of warning should be enforced. It explains also the superficially inconsistent case of *Smith*, decided earlier at a time when no such expectation existed because the responsibility had not been publicised.[102] Here G, an employee of H, left his post against instructions and so was unable to give warning to pedestrians of the approach of trams crossing a turnpike. On an indictment for manslaughter of a pedestrian who was run over and killed by a tram it was held that G was the private servant of H and under no duty to the deceased.

(c) *Informal assumptions of duty*

The clearest example of the moral basis underlying the duty to act is where such a duty is imposed upon those who voluntarily assume the responsibility of caring for another. Such a duty was initially thought to be generated by some semblance of a contract existing between the carer and the person cared for. Thus in the important case of *Instan*, the defendant had neglected to feed and seek medical care for her aunt despite the fact that she knew that she was very sick. This resulted in the aunt's death. The defendant was convicted of manslaughter. The Court said that not every moral duty to provide succour and assistance imposed a corollary legal duty. They justified imposing such a duty here by reason of the fact that both the aunt and niece were fed from the aunt's money and 'that it was only through the instrumentality of the (niece) that the deceased could get the food'.

Later decisions have avoided emphasising this contractual pattern, stressing that the assumption of responsibility for another typically generates the kind of dependency which demands to be satisfied. On this view, it is not the provision of money *per se* which imposed the obligation in *Instan*. What attracted the obligation was the fact that the parties knew and understood, evidenced by the provision of money, that this was a relationship of dependence. Taking the money confirmed the reciprocal understanding[103] but more importantly, perhaps, discouraged the aunt from seeking help elsewhere.

Again, in *R* v *Stone and Dobinson* it was stated that where a couple assumed the duty of caring for an infirm relative, the very assumption of that duty imposed a legal obligation to satisfy it.[104] The importance of the duty being **voluntarily** assumed is that it allows a proper reconciliation to be effected between respect for individual autonomy and duties of good citizenship. It is proper to sanction breaches of the duty assumed, both because of the potentially 'dangerous' expectations such an assumption excites and also because, by taking on the responsibility, the defendant has thereby **chosen** to restrict his own freedom

---

[100] (1902) 19 TLR 37.
[101] *Instan* [1893] 1 QB 450.
[102] *Smith* (1869) 11 Cox CC 210.
[103] Cf. G. Fletcher, *Rethinking Criminal Law* (1978) 615.
[104] [1977] 2 All ER 341. The decision can be criticised for other reasons. See section on Non-medical contexts, below. For a recent example *R* v *Barrass* [2011] EWCA Crim 2629; [2012] Crim LR 147.

of action.[105] This accounts for the decision in *Gibbins and Proctor*. Here both parent and cohabitee were held responsible for the death of an infant – the former for failing in his duty as a parent, the latter for having assumed, and failed to discharge, the care of the infant.[106] Although there was no blood tie between cohabitee and infant and it was clear from the outset that the former hated the child, by contrast with the other children in their joint charge, the context constituted her as being the person with primary responsibility for the infant's welfare who was thus rendered vulnerable by the reliance placed in her if that responsibility was not discharged.

On this analysis informal relationships may well support duties of intervention if they are so constituted as to excite the reasonable expectation that assistance will be rendered if needed. *Beardsley* notwithstanding, this will presumably be a routine assumption in cases of cohabiting couples but is arguably not so limited. If I continually render my flatmate the service of removing spiders from her bath, is it not reasonable for her or society to expect that if she collapses in a coma I will call for help, if not take her in my car to the hospital? In similar vein Fletcher has argued that duties of intervention are owed where persons engage in hazardous enterprises for limited purposes and the nature of the relationship is constituted as one of support and dependence. Examples include the case of a ship's crew and its passengers and that of mountaineers or astronauts. The essence of such enterprises is that they are entered into in order to provide mutually beneficial expectations of assistance. Mountaineers do not climb together for mere conviviality but because their enterprise demands the sharing of tasks and the reducing of risks.[107] The corollary of this is that it is unlikely that status-based duties such as exist between spouses are sufficient in themselves to ground a duty of intervention. Whether a duty of intervention is owed, and its scope, must pay regard to the context and the understandings generated by that context.[108] In *Bonnyman*[109] the Court of Criminal Appeal dismissed an appeal of a husband against conviction for the manslaughter of his drug addict wife on the basis that she was helpless to help herself and thus dependent upon her husband to ensure that her health and other needs were satisfied. His status as a spouse was necessary to generate the duty but would not be sufficient in itself.

(d) *The duty to avert a dangerous situation caused by the defendant*

A recent addition to the categories of duty-situations arises where the defendant has created a dangerous situation. In the normal case where the defendant shows fault there is no need to establish a duty of intervention. For example, if the defendant drives his car recklessly, knocks over a pedestrian and then fails to render assistance, liability for manslaughter or causing death by dangerous driving does not depend upon establishing a duty to render assistance. It requires proof simply of a causal relationship between a blameworthy act and the eventual death. Where the dangerous situation is created by the defendant without fault being attributable to the defendant's act, however, as where the pedestrian was jaywalking and the accident was unavoidable, the question arises whether the driver is responsible only for failing to report the accident or whether he may be liable for the subsequent death or injury.

---

[105] Cf. Glazebrook, 'Criminal Omissions: the Duty Requirement in Offences Against the Person' (1960) 76 LQR 386 generally.
[106] Evidenced by taking money for its upkeep.
[107] Cf. *Khan*, below.
[108] *Smith* [1979] Crim LR 251.
[109] (1942) 28 Cr App R 131.

If liability is to follow in such cases it must be grounded in a specialised duty of inter-vention.[110] Such a duty has now been recognised in English law.[111] In *Miller* the defendant, who was squatting in another's house, fell asleep on the bed without stubbing his cigarette. He awoke to find his bed on fire and, instead of extinguishing the fire, he moved to another room. The house was damaged and the defendant was charged with arson contrary to s. 1(1) and (3) Criminal Damage Act 1971. He argued that arson was a crime of commission and that his wrong, if any, consisted of 'not acting' rather than 'committing' arson. This argument was rejected at first instance and on appeal. In the House of Lords the explana-tion given was that no distinction could be made, for the purposes of criminal damage, between positive conduct and 'conduct which consists of a failure to take measures that lie within one's power to counteract a danger that one has oneself created'. Under such cir-cumstances a 'responsibility'[112] arises to prevent or reduce the damage thus caused. The use of the word 'responsibility' rather than 'duty' is noteworthy. It reminds us that criminal liability arises out of our responsibilities towards society at large rather than arising simply out of a moral duty owed to an individual. Those who precipitate dangerous situations cannot simply walk away from them claiming it was not their fault. Society, conceived as a community of interdependent individuals, expects people to shoulder their responsibi-lities towards the continued safety and integrity of that society which necessarily must involve putting right what one has done.[113] After all, who else can we expect to do so?[114]

It should be noted that the rule in *Miller* only operates where the offence definition is not inconsistent with liability for non-action. By implication the House of Lords was con-ceding that a person can 'damage property' without the accused 'doing anything'. It will not apply where the offence definition pinpoints a particular kind of act.[115]

(e) Miller *and beyond*

The full scope of the *Miller* principle has not yet fully been worked out. In *Evans* it was affirmed that the duty only crystallises where the defendant knows or ought reasonably to know that the danger to be guarded against has materialised.[116] Lord Diplock's stated basis for constructing the duty was, alternatively, that the defendant had 'created the danger' or that a 'physical act' of his had 'start(ed) the fire'. In other words he must have caused the fire. This leaves unclear how substantial a cause the defendant's act must be. Assume the fire started when the vagrant turned on the light which, in turn, caused the damaged light-ing circuit to short-circuit. Does this mean that no duty would arise because the state of the wiring rather than he had 'created the danger' or that a duty would arise because a 'physical act of his had started the fire'? It has been suggested that the basis for a duty of intervention arising from the innocent creation of a dangerous situation is that activities which generate even slight risks, such as driving cars, entering bathrooms containing drawn baths, and loafing around the edges of swimming pools, 'are permissible only if (the risk-taker) is prepared to undertake at least an easy rescue in case those slight risks eventuate'.[117] So a person who accidentally knocks another into a swimming pool or bath,

---

[110] An alternative basis suggested by the Court of Appeal in *Miller* is that Miller adopted the original uninten-tional act as his own.
[111] *Miller* [1983] 1 All ER 978.
[112] Per Lord Diplock.
[113] A. Norrie (1993) 128.
[114] Cf. Mead, 'Contracting into Crime' (1991) 11 OJLS 147.
[115] As in *Ahmad*, above.
[116] *R v Evans (Gemma)* (2009) EWCA Crim 650. See below.
[117] *Commonwealth v Cali* (1923) 247 Mass 20, 141 NE 510 (1923); *R v Miller* [1983] 1 AC 161.

or knocks over a pedestrian while driving, is placed under a duty to minimise resulting harm irrespective of culpability so long as their conduct in some measurable sense has added to the risk of such occurrence.

There is obviously some cogency in this position but it generates more problems than it seeks to solve. For example, it would seem to follow that if the fire in *Miller* was caused by the vagrant innocently turning on a (dangerous and defective) light, no duty of intervention would arise (activity creates negligible risks at most) but if a fire was caused by an ordinary house guest's careful stoking of a fire (activity occasionally results in flying sparks) a duty would arise. There seems little reason to distinguish the two situations in this way. They should stand or fall together. If they fall it is because neither of the actors has behaved in the kind of way which would justify depriving them of their usual liberty to put personal before collective interests. If they stand, the view taken here, it is because society conceived as a community of interdependent individuals has a legitimate expectation that people shoulder their responsibilities towards the continued safety and integrity of that society, which necessarily must involve eradicating the chance perils generated by one's actions.[118] After all, who else can we expect to do so?[119]

The further one strays from culpable causation the less plausible the case for linking liability to causal contribution and the greater the impetus to identify an alternative foundation for a duty of intervention. In this context *Miller* is a relatively simple case. Even if we accept that he was an 'innocent' cause of the fire there is little substance in his claim that the fire and its aftermath were not his doing. After all, he had fallen asleep while smoking a cigarette, which he should not have done. There is no injustice in holding him to account for culpably sustaining and continuing a fire which his freely chosen conduct initiated. There are innocent causes and there are innocent causes. But what if the smouldering cigarette had been thrown on top of him by the vagrant's bed-partner, prompting him to jump up precipitating the cigarette onto the bedclothes, or had been dropped by the vagrant's bed-partner whom he had invited to the house? Is the vagrant not entitled to claim that although in each case he was causally implicated in the resulting fire nevertheless he bore no responsibility to remedy the danger as it was not his doing? Why, given that in both cases he is not the legal cause of the fire, should he be in any worse position than others present in the house but who were fortunate enough not to form part of the sequence of events which led to the fire? Severing the linkage between legal causation and a duty of intervention seems to strip doctrine of a plausible rationale for distinguishing duty-bearing omitters from other Bad Samaritans, and yet in each case reasonable expectations are surely excited that the vagrant shall put matters right.

In other contexts such expectations are generated by the fact of detrimental reliance, as has been explained. This rationale clearly does not operate to support the existence of a duty in either *Miller* or its related hypothetical. An alternative basis for grounding a duty of intervention other than causal responsibility must be based in some socially validated special reason for action. Such reasons are best uncovered on a casuistic or paradigmatic basis, with other analogous duty situations being used as stepping stones to bridge the gap between old and new. For example, the civil law designates the occupation of land as such a reason. This too can create legitimate expectations of intervention to remedy or pre-empt chance perils. In *Smith* v *Littlewoods*, for example, it was stated that hazards (e.g. a fire risk)

[118] Norrie (1993) 128.
[119] Cf. Mead at 171.

created by a trespasser lay within the responsibility of the occupier to abate so as not to present a danger to neighbours.[120] It should be noted that there is no requirement that the householder/occupier should be responsible in the first place for creating the dangerous situation. The judgment of Lord Mackay is particularly pertinent since it locates the duty to act within the context of the rights and duties of neighbours and the reciprocal expectations which these excite. Comparing the case of preventing the risk of burglary to a neighbour, he states:

> There is also a sense in which neighbouring proprietors can . . . take action to protect themselves against theft in a way that is not possible with fire. Once the fire had taken hold on (the defendants') buildings, the (plaintiffs) could not be expected to take reasonable steps to prevent the sparks being showered over on their property.

In other words, if house occupancy is to enjoy legal protection, **both** neighbours are entitled to the exercise of duties of good neighbourliness on the part of the other. Without such exercise, house occupancy would be a potential source of danger in our society, where privacy is so jealously protected, since persons endangered by hazards arising on other people's property have little opportunity of protecting themselves therefrom.[121] There seems every reason, in principle, why this approach should be applicable in the criminal law as well. Indeed it might properly be extended to impose duties of intervention on all those so placed, whether by conduct, status, or relationship, to remedy hazards arising out of the occupation of land in favour of all those within the risk of harm. Society, as well as individuals, is threatened when householders are not responsive to the basic minimum requirements of community. The rules governing the imposition of duties should not, in this respect, simply parrot the civil law whose function is limited to reconciling the rights and liabilities of individuals.[122]

Miller illustrates how new duty situations may develop incrementally, in order to reflect what are generally agreed to be the moral foundations of good citizenship but clearly, as the foregoing analysis suggests, it does not exhaust the range of inchoate duty situations. Such narrowly-defined duties as the duty of house occupants to prevent chance perils getting out of control and threatening other occupiers, visitors and neighbours are consistent with maintaining the integrity of a society based upon interdependence and self-interest by providing a cogent basis by which to ring-fence the range of culpable omitters. Moreover it restricts the range of duty situations to those which are lodged in public consciousness as involving special reasons for action, thus pre-empting to a certain extent legality-based objections. An example occurred in *Evans*. D supplied V, her half-sister, with heroin. Later D realised that V was suffering from an overdose but, fearful that she would get into trouble, failed to summon medical assistance. Upholding the conviction for gross negligence manslaughter the Court of Appeal, extending the scope of the rule in *Miller*, affirmed that when a person had contributed to the creation of a state of affairs which he knew, or ought to have known, had become life-threatening to another, a duty arose to take reasonable steps to prevent loss of life. Further, the existence or otherwise of

---

[120] [1987] 1 All ER 710.

[121] See most recently *Clark Fixing* v *Dudley MBC* [2001] EWCA Civ 1898 – local authority found liable for fire damage on neighbour's property. Fire started by third party but local authority knew or had means of knowledge that third party had created or was creating risk of fire and failed to take reasonable steps to prevent fire from damaging neighbouring properties.

[122] See J. Herring, 'The Duty of Care in Gross Negligence Manslaughter' (2007) Criminal Law Review 24–41; LC 304, *Murder, Manslaughter and Infanticide* (2006).

such a duty of care was a question of law for the judge,[123] whereas the question whether the facts established the existence of the duty was for the jury.[124] Another example from the civil law demonstrates how detached from traditional duty situations these special reasons for action maybe. In *Kirkham* an action in negligence was taken by the deceased's wife against the police who had delivered the deceased to prison authorities without warning them that he was a suicide risk. Despite the barest of relationships between the police and the deceased the Court of Appeal held that a duty of warning existed. This arose from their knowledge of his propensity which, in the light of their custodial role in the proceedings, was enough for the court to deem them to have assumed responsibility for his well-being. This custodial role formed the basis for the imposition of a duty to prevent suicide in *Reeves* v *Metropolitan Police Commissioner* where police were held liable for failing to take reasonable care to prevent the deceased committing suicide[125] as it was reasonably foreseeable that the deceased would try to hang himself. If this type of expectation-based analysis was transferred to the criminal setting a person might well be liable for murder in a *Miller*-type context, assuming the elements were present, whether that person was Miller himself or his non-smoking bed-mate who had awoken to find the bed alight and the other insensible and unable to help him or herself. In the Soham murder trial in which a child drowned in a bath while visiting the defendant, liability for murder would not necessarily then hang upon whether the child was first pushed or tripped by the defendant, innocently or otherwise. It would simply be on the basis of the expectation we have that those who invite others into their home will take reasonable care to ensure that such chance perils which arise and to which their visitors are subject will be eradicated or prevented.

4 Circumstances governing the scope of the duty

Criminal liability for crimes of commission requires, within certain limits, voluntariness of action. A person who did not freely choose to act in the way he did may, once again within limits, be able to avail himself of an excuse. Criminal omissions also need to be voluntary. What counts as voluntary in this context? The American Model Penal Code describes a voluntary omission as an omission to 'perform an act of which the defendant is physically capable'.[126] It is intended cover cases where, for example:

(a) a person is unable to perform the muscular contractions necessary to perform the relevant duty, say due to paralysis or coma,

(b) a person has been incarcerated,

(c) some external force, including that of a third party, operates to restrain the person from acting so as to discharge his duty.

This proposition is probably only partly an accurate statement of the position in English law. The notion of voluntariness of 'omission' seems disposed to extend significantly further than this and is widely thought to encompass an (omissions-specific) defence of

---

[123] It seems that defendants placed in comparable situations are routinely pleading guilty to the charge of gross negligence manslaughter although the scope of *Evans*, in the light of *Miller*, is by no means settled. See *R v Phillips* [2013] EWCA Crim 358 (CACD).

[124] *R v Evans (Gemma)* (2009) EWCA Crim 650; *Khan* [1998] Crim LR 830. No such duty exists between drug supplier and client in Australia *Burns v R* [2012] HCA 35; for discussion of the duties owed by drug dealers to their clients see C.S. Elliott and C. de Than, 'Prosecuting the Drug Dealer When a Drug User Dies' (2006) 69 Modern Law Review 986; Glenys Williams, 'Gross Negligence Manslaughter and the Duty of Care in Drugs Cases' [2009] Crim LR 631.

[125] [2000] 1 AC 360 House of Lords. They had negligently left open the flap of the cell door.

[126] 1 Section 2.01(1) and (2).

impossibility.[127] For example, what one is physically capable of doing must have some connection with what one feels oneself capable of doing. A parent is under no duty to rescue a drowning child if he himself cannot swim, because he lacks the ability to save the child. But what if the parent can swim, but his nerve fails him? Such a person is physically capable but is no more able to save the child than if he had not been. It seems to follow that if action is involuntary where the actor could not have prevented himself from acting otherwise if he had so willed, an omission is similarly involuntary if he could not have motivated himself to act if he had so willed. If this is true it means, for example, that duress, by contrast with the position regarding affirmative action, will also negate voluntariness in cases of omission.[128]

Generally speaking the level of obligation imposed by a duty to act has yet to be fully worked out. Such statements as there are indicate that a duty holder must take such steps as are reasonable in the circumstances to prevent the relevant consequence materialising.[129] As we shall see in the next section, the only area where the scope of the duty has received any sustained treatment lies in the field of medicine. Here, at least, there is some (ambiguous) guidance concerning what medical carers are entitled to do, what they must do and what they must not do.

(a) *Medical omissions: the scope of a doctor's duty*

As a general proposition a doctor will be acting lawfully, in the case of a competent patient, if he acts reasonably in accordance with his patient's wishes. The doctor's duty is not solely to serve the patient's best (medical) interests but more broadly to vindicate the patient's rights. This means that the duty to act only crystallises if

(1) the defendant consents to treatment, or
(2) the defendant is unable to consent to treatment and it is in his best interests for treatment to be given.[130]

Assuming such consent is forthcoming, the doctor's duty, at its simplest, is to act reasonably given the resources available to him. The duty to act reasonably refers both to the question 'who (whether) to treat' and also the question 'how to treat'. By and large, the duty of the doctor on the 'who to treat' question is a matter for health authorities on questions of general policy, and a matter for individual discretion on the level of the individual case.[131]

How that discretion should be exercised is also pertinent to the 'how to treat' question and will be dealt with now. The basic structure for the exercise of discretion is provided by the civil case of *Bolam* v *Friern Hospital Management Committee*.[132] Essentially a doctor satisfies his duty if he acts in a way which a responsible body of medical opinion would

---

[127] A. Smart, 'Criminal Responsibility for Failing to do the Impossible' (1987) 103 LQR 532.
[128] This possibility unearths an intriguing difference between murder by commission and murder by omission. Duress is not a defence to murder by positive act but it seems it may be to murder by omission. See 'Scope of the defence of duress' in Chapter 10.
[129] See *Evans (Gemma) supra*.
[130] *F* v *West Berkshire Health Authority* [1989] 2 All ER 545 at 551 per Lord Brandon.
[131] *Airedale NHS Trust* v *Bland* [1993] AC 789 at 857 per Hoffmann LJ; and cf. R. Newdick, 'Rights to NHS Resources after the 1990 Act' [1993] Med LR 53. John Keown, 'Restoring the Sanctity of Life and Replacing the Caricature: A Reply to David Price' (2006) Legal Studies 109; D. Price, 'What Shape to Euthanasia after Bland?' [2009] LQR 142.
[132] [1957] 1 WLR 582.

recommend. This does not require his action to be objectively reasonable as long as it has some significant following within the medical profession.[133]

Although the *Bolam* test might seem to authorise any conduct of a doctor as long as he could drum up some significant support for it from his colleagues, one constant building block in the framework of legally acceptable conduct concerns the distinction between acts and omissions. *Bolam* does not, and cannot, legitimate the giving of lethal injections but it does, to a large extent, control the currently authoritative line drawn between 'caring for the patient' and, for want of a better word, 'executing' him.[134] In this field, however, it is becoming increasingly apparent that the judges are becoming frustrated with the often hollow distinction between acts and omissions in determining criminal liability. In many cases it seems they decide questions of lawfulness by reference to the reasonableness of the doctor's conduct. If it is reasonable it is likely to be considered lawful even if it has all the hallmarks of positive death-accelerating action. Thus 'caring for the patient' may **require** doctors to do something (e.g. give painkilling drugs)[135] or not do something (e.g. not perform a life-saving operation),[136] either of which conduct may be effectively lethal. The legality of such conduct is, to a large extent then, determined by its consonance with general medical ethics rather than, for example, by its formal status as act or omission.

(b) *Non-medical contexts*

What general conclusions can we draw about the scope of the common law duty to act? Drawing on doctrine in the field of medicine, we must assume that the scope of the duty is variable and must be bounded by what is reasonable in the circumstances. In the case of doctors, what is reasonable is dictated largely by the content of their professional duties as circumscribed by the *Bolam* criteria. In the tort of negligence the scope of any duty to act is also determined by questions of reasonableness. The level of intervention required to prevent harm depends upon matters such as the relative seriousness of the harm threatened, the degree of risk, the skill of the defendant, the cost of intervention and so on.[137] In the criminal law the standard expected remains hazy. It is arguable that similar considerations should apply here also, with one qualification, namely that the standard to be fulfilled should be tailored to the individual circumstances and capacities of the defendant rather than that of the reasonable man.[138]

In most cases this might mean that the duty might properly be discharged (and terminated) simply by informing another person (or body), fixed with responsibility to prevent the relevant harm, of the facts necessary to remedy the situation. For example, in cases such as *Miller*, it seems reasonable that the defendant should have exercised himself to put out a minor fire, but anything beyond this would entitle him to transfer responsibility by the simple mechanism of a telephone call to the fire brigade.[139] More tricky is the case of *Stone and Dobinson*, since the facts suggest that the defendants, who were of weak intellect, may have become psychologically incompetent to satisfy whatever obligation they might have

---

[133] *Arthur* (1981) 12 BMLR 1.

[134] The injection of appetite suppressant drugs is deemed not to be a positive homicidal act; see *Arthur*, above.

[135] *Adams* [1957] Crim LR 365.

[136] *Arthur*, above; *Re C* [1993] 2 FLR 757.

[137] *Smith* v *Littlewoods* [1987] 1 All ER 710 HL per Lord Mackay; *Goldman* v *Hargrave* [1967] 1 AC 645 at 655 per Lord Wilberforce.

[138] See O. Kirchheimer, 'Criminal Omissions' (1942) 55 Harv LR 615; *US* v *Knowles* 26 Fed Cas 800 (ND Cal 1864). For further argument on this point see W. Wilson, 'Murder and the Structure of Homicide' in A.J. Ashworth and B. Mitchell (eds), *Rethinking English Homicide Law*, Oxford: OUP (2000) 21 at 49–52.

[139] Cf. *US* v *Knowles* 26 Fed Cas 801.

assumed.[140] In such circumstances it seemed oppressive to insist that they nevertheless fully discharge the obligation. The case is probably best interpreted, therefore, as authority for the very limited proposition that ignoring a problem in the hope that it will go away is no way of satisfying a duty of care. If they had simply informed the social services that they could not cope, there is little doubt that their responsibility would have been effectively discharged.

A question remains as to whether, like doctors, the responsibilities of ordinary members of the public are affected by a dependent person's request for privacy. It seems that this is only partially true. In the case of R v Smith a husband failed, on his wife's insistence, to seek medical attention for the latter when she became dangerously ill.[141] It was held that no criminal liability would attach for such a failure where it was prompted by a reasonable respect for his wife's autonomy.[142] It was also said that where she had become dangerously ill and incapable of making decisions it might be right to override her wishes. This seems contrary to principle. Either a duty to care overrides autonomy or it does not.[143] Why should an ordinary member of the public be in any worse position than a doctor, where to act would be contrary to the other's wishes?

5 Omissions: an alternative approach

Some commentators have argued that the approach adopted by the common law to omissions is unsatisfactory, based as it is on a notion of society as a collection of essentially isolated individuals whose social responsibilities are limited to 'keeping their heads down' and rendering succour only to those for whom they have assumed a particular obligation. The ties which bind us, it is argued, are more deep-seated than this and are evidenced in the way that modern society evinces concern for its members through the provision of welfare support. What kind of schizophrenic society is it which provides a complex set of interlocking mechanisms for ensuring that the moral, physical and intellectual development of its members are satisfied, yet baulks at ensuring that, as individuals, we fulfil our basic responsibilities as human beings to our fellow citizens? The common-law rules of omission were fashioned at a time when the grandparents of the architects of the welfare state had not been born. Should they not be consigned to the dustbin of history along with the *laissez-faire* ethics which inspired them?[144] If communitarian ethics now form the heart of our political morality, as it seems they do, such ethics should now also be inculcated in our hearts and be expected to characterise our behaviour.[145]

(a) A duty of easy rescue?

Against those who argue that such a development would be inconsistent with the 'freedom enhancing' rationale of Western liberal systems, the more sophisticated of such proposals emphasise that freedom from coercion is one value of many recognised in a liberal society. Other values include the sanctity of life, and of good community. As long as a proper

---

[140] The evidence supporting an assumption of duty was not strong, and see note 151.

[141] [1979] Crim LR 251.

[142] A similar decision was reached in *R (on the application of Jenkins)* v *HM Coroner for Portsmouth and South East Hampshire* [2009] EWHC 3229 (Admin).

[143] See discussion of *DH NHS Foundation Trust* v *PS* [2010] EWHC 1217 – R. Mullender, 'Involuntary Medical Treatment, Incapacity, and Respect' (2011) 127 LQR 167 in which a complicating factor was the patient's phobia of hospitals and needles. See also J. Coggon and J. Miola, 'Autonomy, Liberty, and Medical Decision-making' (2011) 70(3) CLJ 523.

[144] Cf. Lacey (1988).

[145] See generally Ashworth (2013) ch. 2.

balance is struck between such values[146] no significant objection can be raised. Thus Ashworth proposes that omissions liability can be extended yet further to include duties to report serious crime, or to effect easy rescue.[147] No serious loss of freedom would be involved since the duty would only arise in cases of life-threatening injury and the scope of the duty could easily be restricted to taking action which involved no unreasonable risk, cost or inconvenience.[148] Presumably this would not result in liability for the result of the breach. It is illegitimate to jump from the proposition that a person has a moral duty of easy rescue to the conclusion 'therefore they ought to be responsible for the consequences of failing to rescue as if they had brought it about by their own positive action'. Given that the question of moral equivalence between acts and omissions is by no means settled, it must be for Parliament to ensure that a failure to fulfil a moral duty of rescue attracts an equivalent degree of censure.[149] Failing to save someone from drowning is not the same as holding someone's head under water until they drown, however 'easy' the rescue might have been and however helpless the victim. The proper response is not to distort the common law offences so as to enable us to censure conduct Parliament has not seen fit to proscribe, but to create new statutory offences which reflect more precisely the defendant's wrong. Feinberg gives an example of such an offence from the American state of Vermont: 'a person who knows that another is exposed to grave physical harm shall, to the extent that the same can be rendered without danger or peril to himself . . . , give reasonable assistance to the exposed person'.[150]

An objection is that it may be difficult to ensure consistency in what we consider it is reasonable to expect the defendant to do. If the rules of criminal law are there to help us understand what we must do in order to avoid criminal sanction, is there not a danger that the jury's view of what it would be reasonable to expect the defendant to do is so out of line with the defendant's view that the defendant is effectively punished for a crime he had no reason to know he might be committing?[151] A more ominous objection is made by Norrie, namely that the imposition of duties to act based upon well-meaning communitarian ideals would threaten to subvert the liberal order. If the basis of individual criminal liability is to be reconstructed in terms of what the ties of community, as a matter of morality, require us to do, this will render people susceptible to sanction for behaving in the very way that Western capitalism encourages and requires for its survival, namely the rational pursuit of self-interest in a community of like-minded individuals.[152]

(b) *Incremental development of new duty situations*

Clearly the scope of any more developed duty would need to address this important objection. The obvious way of doing so would be to ensure that new duty situations developed incrementally, in order to reflect what are generally agreed to be the moral foundations

---

[146] See for example G. Hughes, 'Criminal Omissions' (1958) 67 Yale LJ 590; A.J. Ashworth, 'The Scope of Criminal Liability for Omissions', (1989) 105 LQR 424.

[147] Also a duty to take reasonable steps to assist law enforcement, Ashworth, op. cit. 458.

[148] As J. Feinberg proposes, *The Moral Limits of the Criminal Law Vol 1: Harm to Others*, Oxford: OUP (1984) 155.

[149] G. Williams, 'Criminal Omissions: The Conventional View' (1991) 107 LQR 86 at 94–5.

[150] Vt. Stat. Ann., s. 519 (1973); Feinberg, *Moral Limits of the Criminal Law*, at 127.

[151] If so, this would clearly be contrary to Article 7 of the European Convention. A.J. Ashworth, 'Ignorance of the Criminal Law, and Duties to Avoid It' (2011) 74(1) MLR 1.

[152] Cf. Norrie 130–1.

of good citizenship. An example already referred to is the duty of neighbours to prevent hazards affecting their property threatening others. Such narrowly-defined duties are consistent with maintaining the integrity of a society based upon interdependence and self-interest, where duties arise to satisfy social expectations rather than moral aspirations. The duty of easy rescue, morally persuasive as it is, could command no such assent and could constitute the thin end of an authoritarian wedge incapable, as the homeless beggar example demonstrates, of reconciling the contradictory moral demands of our system of production with the corresponding system of distribution.

One reasonable development might be to impose a half-way house, namely a specific duty of immediate warning upon those who encounter a social hazard.[153] Such duties already have a small toe-hold in the collective consciousness of good citizenship, for example within the duty to report a motor vehicle accident. This would be neither too onerous nor inconsistent with the 'fair warning principle' and would be consistent with a cogent (non-subversive) notion of good citizenship. It would not satisfy all the unmet moral needs of a society of 'haves' and 'have nots', but a free society cannot sensibly impose the burden of remedying society's structural unfairnesses on individual citizens. Or at least it cannot fairly punish them for ignoring that which society as a whole shows no urgency to remove.

Summary

The *actus reus* of an offence is structured by general doctrines governing liability. These include a requirement that there be prohibited conduct voluntarily undertaken. Voluntary in this context means that the defendant had the physical capacity to have acted otherwise if he had so wished. The prohibited conduct usually involves some form of act (the act requirement). An act is not always insisted upon, however, most notably in the case of omissions in breach of duty, but also in the case of possession, and kindred 'situational', offences. Duty situations capable of supporting criminal liability for the consequences of omitting to act include duties arising by virtue of the relationship, a contract, an assumption of a duty of care or rescue, and the creation of a dangerous situation which imperils the safety of the victim.

Further reading

Ashworth, A.J. *Positive Obligations in the Criminal Law*, Oxford: Hart Publishing (2013).

Alexander, L., 'Criminal Liability for Omissions' in Shute and Simester (eds), *Criminal Law Theory: Doctrines of the General Part*, Oxford: OUP (2001) 121.

Duff, A., *Answering for Crime: Responsibility and Liability in the Criminal Law*, Oxford: Hart Publishing (2009).

Green, S.P., 'Theft by Omission' (May 27, 2009). *Essays in Criminal Law in Honour of Sir Gerald Gordon*, Edinburgh: Edinburgh University Press (2010).

Keown, J., 'Restoring the Sanctity of Life' [2006] LS 109.

Price, D., 'My View of the Sanctity of Life' [2007] LS 549.

---

[153] Or, more controversially for our civil liberties, a duty to report crime.

Simester, A.P., 'Why Omissions are Special' (1995) 1 Legal Theory 311.

Smith, J.C., 'Liability for Omissions in the Criminal Law' [1984] Legal S 6.

Westen, P., 'Offences and Defences Again' (2008) 28(3) Oxford Journal of Legal Studies 563.

Williams, G., 'Gross Negligence Manslaughter and Duty of Care in "Drugs" Cases: *R v Evans*' [2009] Crim LR 631.

Wilson, W., 'Murder by Omission: Some Observations on a Mismatch between the General and Special Parts' (2010) New Crim LR 1.

5 Causation

Overview

All result crimes require proof of causation. In this chapter we examine how the criminal law determines whether a particular act or omission of the defendant has caused the prohibited result.[1] This is particularly important in those cases where something happens unexpectedly after the commission of the relevant act or omission, which puts this causal connection in doubt.

5.1 INTRODUCTION

Crimes can be divided into two discrete groups – those whose *actus reus* consists simply of the violation of some norm of conduct and those where it consists of bringing about some harmful consequence which society wishes to avoid. Crimes of the former class are often described as 'conduct' crimes and those of the latter class as 'result' crimes. Dangerous driving is an example of the former class, causing serious injury by dangerous driving[2] of the latter class. For result crimes criminal liability turns upon proof of an act or omission performed with the requisite mental attitude which is causally connected to the relevant harmful consequence. This burden must be discharged whether or not the definition of the crime explicitly incorporates a causal element. Thus it must be shown that the accused's act 'caused' the proscribed consequence whether the defendant is charged under section 18 Offences Against the Person Act 1861 (**causing** grievous bodily harm with intent) or under section 20 of the same Act (maliciously **inflicting** grievous bodily harm) since to 'inflict' harm requires at the very least causal agency. Crimes of homicide such as murder or manslaughter require the accused, by his act or omission, to have caused the death of the victim. For the crime of assault, it must be shown that the accused caused an undesired contact or the victim to apprehend one. Most of the discussion about causation in this chapter takes place in the context of crimes of homicide, particularly murder and manslaughter. It is important to remember, however, that the observations made are, by and large, applicable to all result crimes.

To understand the key role played by causation in the criminal law, it must be understood that the causal requirement is not simply a requirement that a criminal harm has occurred and that the accused acted with the necessary intention, recklessness or negligence demanded by the crime charged. The bare minimum which the prosecution must show is a link between a particular (wrongful) act of the accused and a criminal harm, such that it is appropriate for the individual accused, rather than, for example, some other person, to be held accountable. A simple example illustrates the type of link which must be made.

---

[1] See generally H.L.A. Hart and A.M. Honore, *Causation in the Law* (2nd edn), Oxford: Clarendon Press (1985); M. Moore, *Causation and Responsibility: An Essay in Law, Morals and Metaphysics*, Oxford: OUP (2010).
[2] Section 1A RTA 1988.

> **Case 1**
> A delivers a lethal dose of poison to B in the form of an adulterated chocolate. Having eaten the chocolate, but before the poison has time to work, B is shot dead by C (or dies in a car accident).

It can be appreciated that A is not, in the manner in which we are generally disposed to perceive relations of cause and effect, the cause of death. The cause of death, we would say (and the law would say), is the subsequent act of C (or the accident).[3]

5.2 CAUSATION IN CRIME AND TORT

Both the criminal law and the law of tort involve causal elements. Questions of causation are normally central in tort, less so in the sphere of crime. The reason for this is that most tortious harms occur as a result of inadvertence on the part of the defendant. Inadverted-to harms are less easy to attribute causally than purposed and foreseen harms – the stuff of which most criminal cases are made. If A deliberately burns down B's hotel, it takes no great effort of reasoning to attribute the resultant damage to A's action, since his action is literally 'end-orientated'. It is calculated to be causal. If, on the other hand, A stubbed his cigarette on a linoleum floor and then, just prior to it extinguishing, a wind blew, causing the stub to reignite and a clump of dust to make contact with the stub, it will clearly be a matter of key importance, and potential difficulty, for the plaintiff to attribute the resulting fire to A's initial act.[4]

A further point should be borne in mind. Although the language used in the two contexts is similar (causal relations are typically delimited by the use of words such as 'foreseeable' and 'natural and probable'), what that language is doing may differ. In the law of tort the law is aiming to ensure that the burden of loss falls fairly.[5] Somebody has to foot the bill for harms suffered – either the victim, or the insurance company, or the person whose action led to the harm concerned. The judgment of the court, therefore, is that it is fair that one party, rather than the other, bears this loss. This may entail a relatively loose link between the defendant's conduct and the plaintiff's harm, particularly where the defendant is a profit-making concern and the plaintiff is his employee.[6] In crime, on the other hand, the nature of the judgment is different. Part, at least, of this judgment is that the accused deserves censure and punishment for the social harm which has occurred. For this retributive aim to be fairly imposed, it may seem only right that a clear causal link be established.[7]

5.3 CAUSATION AND BLAMEWORTHINESS

In theory causation and fault are separate offence elements.[8] Causal responsibility may be assigned in the absence of a blameworthy actor[9] and those whom we might wish to blame for an event are not necessarily causally responsible.

---

[3] It is this common-sense notion of causation which Hart and Honore identify as informing legal notions of causation.

[4] P. Cane, *Responsibility in Law and Morality*, Oxford: Hart (2002) ch. 4.

[5] Medical cases where a number of different causes may be influential are a case in point. See K. Amirthalingam, 'Causation and the Medical Duty to Refer' (2012) 128 LQR 208.

[6] *McGhee v NCB* [1973] 1 WLR 1; *Bonnington Castings v Wardlaw* [1956] AC 613; cf. *Wilsher v Essex AHA* [1988] AC 1074.

[7] Cf. C. Crosby, 'Causing Death by Faultless Driving' (2011) 75(2) J Crim L 111 (case comment).

[8] Moore (2010) ch. 2.

[9] See for example *National Rivers Authority v Yorkshire Water Services* [1994] 4 All ER 274.

Case 2

A and B, two joy-riders, drive through an army roadblock. Although they present no threat to the soldiers manning the roadblock, the soldiers, against orders, fire into the retreating car. The gun of C, another soldier, asleep at his post, goes off accidentally when C is startled by the noise. The resulting shot kills A. The shots of the other soldiers miss their target.

C causes the death of A, despite not being blameworthy. The other soldiers, although blameworthy, are not causes of the death.[10]

It should be noted, however, that causal inquiries are often influenced by judgments of fault. In particular, the courts are disinclined to attribute causal responsibility to blameless actors, even where there is no question of criminal responsibility accruing.[11] On the other hand, there is a strong inclination to attach responsibility for ultimately sustained harm to a party who culpably generated the sequence of events culminating in such harm,[12] particularly where the end result corresponded with what the actor intended.[13]

Thus doctors who, by administering drugs for therapeutic purposes such as pain relief, accelerate the time of death, have been held **not** to be the legal cause of death.[14] Whereas, a defendant who used his girlfriend as a human shield while resisting arrest **was** held to be causally responsible when his girlfriend was shot dead by a police marksman.[15] In another case two members of the public who started a fight with two club bouncers were held accountable when one of the bouncers, who had not been hit, died of a heart attack due to the combination of shock and an unknown arterial weakness.[16] Such cases act as a reminder that attributing causal responsibility is not a scientific exercise, rather a moral one.

5.4 THE PURPOSE OF ESTABLISHING CAUSAL RESPONSIBILITY

It is sometimes questioned whether any point is served by a causal requirement in crime. In tort, establishing causal responsibility for a given harm is central to the function of the law of torts, namely to attribute the burden of loss and quantify that loss. Without harm there would be nothing to compensate. Without causation there would be nothing to link the defendant to the harm. With crime, on the other hand, given the various justifications for and purposes of punishment it is arguably less sensible to focus on the causing of an event rather than, say, the culpability or dangerousness of the defendant's conduct. To do so may place undue emphasis on the accidents of fate.[17]

---

[10] There may also arise questions of proof. If the prosecution cannot prove who fired the fatal shot, then causal responsibility will not arise.

[11] See Moore (2010) Part III.

[12] S. Cooper, 'Culpable Driving and Issues of Causation' (2012) 76(5) J Crim L 431.

[13] In *Michael*, A, intending to kill her child, V, delivered poison to the child's nurse in the form of medicine. The nurse placed it on a mantelpiece where it was picked up by B, another child. B then gave it to V with fatal results. Conviction for murder was affirmed (1840) 9 C & P 356.

[14] *Bodkin Adams* in H. Palmer, 'Dr Adams' Trial for Murder' (1957) Crim LR 365.

[15] *Bodkin Adams* in H. Palmer, 'Dr Adams' Trial for Murder' (1957) Crim LR 365; *Pagett* (1983) 76 Cr App R 279, below; cf. I. Dennis (1993) 46 CLP, 25 at 48–9.

[16] *R v M* [2012] EWCA Crim 2293; [2013] Crim LR 335.

[17] S.J. Schulhofer, 'Harm and Punishment: A Critique of Emphasis on the Results of Conduct in the Criminal Law' (1974) 122 University of Pennsylvania LR 1497; cf. Fletcher, *Rethinking Criminal Law* (1978) 361; H.L.A Hart, *Punishment and Responsibility* 129–31; A.J. Ashworth, 'Belief, Intent and Liability' in J. Eekelaar and J. Bell (eds), *Oxford Essays in Jurisprudence*, Oxford: Clarendon Press (1987).

Ashworth has argued that, since punishment is desert-based there is no moral basis for differentiating between killing and attempting to kill. What an actor deserves punishing for is what he tried to do. Accordingly, offences might properly be redefined so as to capture this moral similarity.[18]

Abandoning the causing of harm as a focus for criminal responsibility would, however, ignore a major retributive concern. Having a causal requirement allows us to put on record precisely how the victim has been wronged, and reflect the extent of the harm done in punishment.[19] Could we do without a crime of manslaughter, for example, to cope with cases where a person died as a result of a beating? Is it not the death, rather than the action of beating, for which we wish to hold the defendant to account through punishment?[20] Indeed, without the production of harm we might be unable to discern whether the defendant's action was to be approved or deplored. Would William Tell be as revered today if he had missed the apple and shot his son instead?[21]

5.5 CAUSATION: THE LEGAL POSITION

A deceptively simple restatement of the common law position is to be found in the Draft Criminal Code Bill (1989). Clause 17 reads as follows:

(1) A person causes a result when he/she
   (a) does an act which makes a more than merely negligible contribution to its occurrence or,
   (b) omits to do an act which might have prevented its occurrence and which she/he is under a duty to do according to the law relating to the offence.
(2) A person does not cause a result where, after he does such an act or makes such an omission, an act or event occurs which
   (a) is the immediate and sufficient cause of the result;
   (b) he did not foresee, and
   (c) could not in the circumstances reasonably have been foreseen.

In simple terms to be accountable for a result crime the defendant's acts or omissions must be shown to have contributed to the coming about of the relevant harmful result and, in addition, nothing abnormal should have happened subsequently to that act or omission so as to render it appropriate to ignore that contribution.

This statement of principle can be put more analytically – the defendant must be the factual and the legal cause of the harm in question.

A Factual cause

Perhaps the nearest thing to a firm rule existing in the field of causation is that if the defendant is not a factual cause of a criminal harm he cannot also be a legal cause.[22] At its simplest, if it cannot be shown that **but for** the defendant's action the consequence would

---

[18] A.J. Ashworth, 'Belief, Intent; "Criminal Attempts and the Role of Resulting Harm"' (1988) 19 Rutgers LJ 725; A.J. Ashworth, 'Taking the Consequences' in Shute *et al.*, *Action and Value in Criminal Law*, Oxford: Clarendon Press (1993) 107; cf. R.A. Duff, 'Acting, Trying and Criminal Liability', in ibid. 90. H. Wishart, 'Criminal Culpability, Criminal Attempts and the Erosion of Choice Theory' (2013) 77(1) J Crim L 78.
[19] R.A. Duff, 'The Role of Luck and Criminal Liability for Death' in C. Clarkson and S. Cunningham (eds), *Criminal Liability for Non-aggressive Death*, Aldershot: Ashgate (2008).
[20] Leo Katz, 'Why the Successful Assassin is More Wicked than the Unsuccessful One' (2000) 88 Calif LR 791.
[21] A question posed by J. Kaplan in the course of substantive observations on the harm and causation aspects of the revised Model Penal Code; cf. P. Westen, 'Why Criminal Harms Matter: Plato's Abiding Insight in the Laws' (2007) Crim Law and Philos 307.
[22] As in Case 1.

not have occurred as and when it did, causal responsibility cannot be established.[23] Put another way, if the consequence would have occurred anyway, or the defendant's conduct made no difference, he/she will not be a cause. So in *White* D poisoned his mother's drink. She died a heart attack before taking the poison. His conviction for murder was quashed on the basis that the poisoning had not caused the death. The answer would have been the same had she swallowed the poison but she had died of a heart attack before the poison had begun to work. In both cases D's action made no difference to the outcome and would have occurred anyway. Compare the situation where, in the latter case, the heart attack was prompted by the initial effects of the poison. In this latter case the heart attack is not **independent** of the initial act of the defendant and so forms the final link in the causal chain.

1 Omissions as factual causes

The same principle applies in relation to **omissions as factual causes**. Significantly, in homicide generally, standard factual causation is insisted upon. In *Morby*, for example, the conviction of M for manslaughter was overturned where he had failed, for religious reasons, to summon a doctor for his child stricken with smallpox as it could not be shown that the life of the child would 'beyond a reasonable doubt, have been saved if proper efforts to save him had been . . . made'.[24] This stricture seems perfectly justified in such cases. A finding of accountability, whether in a case of affirmative action or an omission, amounts, in most parts of the criminal law,[25] to a finding that the outcome is the agent's 'doing'. The mere fact that there is a breach of duty and that satisfaction of that duty might, with a prevailing wind, have prevented the fatal outcome does not, without more, make the death his 'doing'.[26] In the particular context, smallpox is a disease which, even now, is substantially resistant to medical cure and we could rarely be sure that success would have attended appropriate intervention. More generally, as a matter of basic justice, liability for the consequences of a failure to discharge a duty of care which may be attributable to a simple human weakness such as ignorance, weak intellect, or misjudgement is surely unsustainable, in the absence of the clearest evidence possible that appropriate action would have prevented that death.[27]

This approach is not, however, the one adopted in the Draft Code, which has no requirement that 'but for' the relevant failure of the duty-bearer to act the relevant consequence 'would' not have occurred. That it 'might not' have occurred is enough. Causal liability for omissions, on this test, could be imposed even where intervention might not have made a difference:[28] Such a 'might have' basis of causal responsibility arguably conduces to the political desirability of finding a suitable person to bear responsibility rather than the legal/moral concern to ensure that such person is fairly selected.[29] On the other hand, as Glanville Williams has complained, 'in respect of the quantum of proof required, it . . . create(s) a wider liability for crimes of omission than for crimes of commission'.

[23] Cf. *White* [1910] 2 KB 124.
[24] *Morby* (1882) 8 QBD 571, 575.
[25] For a counter example see discussion of accessoryship, below at note 54.
[26] David Ormerod reminds me that in the case of homicide by commission a 'doing' includes 'accelerating' the time when death would otherwise occur. In cases of omission failing to seek treatment, such as *Morby* causation would be more easily provable if a comparable test were used. That it is not reflects an understandable caution in holding agents accountable for omissions. For criticism of such caution see G. Hughes 'Criminal Omissions' (1958) 67 Yale LJ 590.
[27] Cf. *Stone and Dobinson*, for just such a case.
[28] Law Commission Report 177, Draft Criminal Code Bill Cl 17(1): 'A person causes a result which is an element of an offence when . . . he omits to do an act which might prevent its occurrence and which he is under a duty to do according to the law relating to the offence.'
[29] Cf. Model Penal Code Art. 2.03(1)(a) which requires the act or omission to be an antecedent but for which the result in question would not have occurred.

2 Causes and conditions contrasted

To fully understand what it is to cause a consequence, a distinction must be drawn between factual (real) causes and mere conditions.[30] The factual cause of an event must be selected from the range of everyday '**but for**' conditions. Hart and Honore have described a cause as 'something which interferes with, or intervenes in, the course of events which would normally take place.'[31] To be a cause, an event must be something extraordinary or abnormal and 'what is abnormal in this way "makes the difference" between the accident and things going on as usual'.[32] Thus the fact that most urban riots take place in the summer does not mean that hot weather is a cause, much less the cause of riots, even if the 'but for' test is satisfied.[33] Since hot weather is a normal condition of human existence, it cannot be said to 'make a difference' to the unfolding of human events. Again if A gives B a knife for his birthday and B kills V with it does not mean that A's act is a cause of V's death.[34] What makes a difference is the 'voluntary' decision by the various actors to cause a riot/stab V. It is they, and not the weather or B, who cause the riot/stab V.

3 Particular instances of factual causation

If we return to Case 1 above, therefore, we can see that A is not a factual cause because the consequence would still have occurred **but for** A's conduct. A's conduct made no difference. Contrast the case where the consequence would still have occurred, but not when it did, but for the defendant's conduct. Here factual causation is still present.

Case 3

A shoots B. He leaves him dying in the road. C, a driver who is not paying attention, runs over B, advancing the time of death a few minutes.

Both A and C are factual causes of death. An act causes death when it advances the time when death would otherwise occur. A is a factual cause because but for his act, B would not now be dead. C is a factual cause because but for his act, B's life would not have been further foreshortened.

The most taxing problems concerning factual causation are those least likely to arise in practice, namely those involving concurrent causes.[35] A commonly discussed example is where two (or more) individuals independently wound another, causing him to die immediately. Medical evidence shows that either wound would have been capable of causing his immediate demise. Both assailants are factual causes of death, even though, on the face of it, the prosecution would be unable to prove that but for the action of one of them the death would not have occurred.[36] A consideration of this case might lead one to suppose that the 'but for' test of factual causation is not wholly reliable.[37]

---

[30] Normal everyday events or circumstances which were a precondition but not the reason why the consequence happened at the time and in the manner it did.

[31] H.L.A. Hart and A.M. Honore, *Causation in the Law* (2nd edn 1985) 27.

[32] Ibid. 33.

[33] Hart and Honore, op. cit.; cf. J.A. McLaughlin, 'Proximate Cause' (1921) 39 Harv LR 149, 160.

[34] A may be liable as an accomplice but complicity does not require proof of causation. See Chapter 19.

[35] These are arguably best thought of as particular problems of legal or imputable causation, but are dealt with here for convenience.

[36] See the analysis of this case in Dressler (1987) 161.

[37] Another problem posed by the 'but for' rule is the status of omissions. This has been considered above; Ashworth, *PCL* (2006) 132–3.

B Legal cause

A number of different expressions are used to convey the idea that causal responsibility is something which we assign to the defendant rather than a matter of scientific fact. Many of these phrases are used coextensively in the law of tort. Thus causal responsibility will not accrue if consequences are too 'remote' from the accused's action. The legal cause is sometimes also termed the 'assignable', 'attributable', 'proximate', blameable, or 'imputable' cause. These expressions have no theoretical magic attached to them. Each in its own way expresses the requirement that it must be fair to select the defendant to bear responsibility[38] but no precise formula exists to sustain this requirement.[39] There are no 'hard and fast' rules of causation, despite the efforts of some theorists to provide them. As a rule of thumb, however, if the defendant's acts or omissions are a factual cause of a consequence it will usually be morally appropriate to hold him legally accountable since there will be a direct link between a wrongful act of the accused and the harm suffered by the victim. He will have shot, punched, wounded, poisoned, and so on, his victim. The harm the victim suffers will be unequivocally the defendant's 'doing'.[40] It will only be in exceptional cases, for example, where a third party or the victim himself may have interfered with the chain of causation that the analytical waters become muddied. In the following sections the principles governing the attribution of causal responsibility will be examined, together with a discussion of some typically hard cases.

1 The general framework for imputing cause

(a) Where a person suffers injury at the hands of another, the latter will only be the legal cause of that injury if the injury was attributable to the wrongfulness of the act rather than simply the fact of the act.

The purpose of causation is to hold someone to account for the consequences of doing wrong. It follows that only where a result is caused by a **wrongful** act that a finding of accountability is appropriate. So, on a charge of causing death by dangerous driving it is not enough to show that D caused V's death **while** driving dangerously. The prosecution must show that V's death was caused **by** D driving dangerously. Thus, in *Dalloway*[41] a driver of a horse and cart was driving without his hands on the reins. A child ran in front of the cart and was killed. The jury was told that the cart driver was only responsible for the death if death could have been avoided by proper use of the reins. If it could not, then although the defendant would be the factual cause of death, he would not be the 'blameable' cause.[42]

(b) To be a legal cause the defendant's contribution to the result must be substantial. It need not be the sole cause.

---

[38] Cf. Model Penal Code s. 2.03(2)(b); Perkins and Boyce, *Criminal Law*, New York: Foundation Press (1982) 776.
[39] S. Morse, 'The Moral Metaphysics of Causation and Results' (2000) 88 Calif LR 879, 886.
[40] See Wilson (2002) ch. 6.
[41] (1847) 2 Cox CC 273.
[42] An (unfortunate) statutory qualification of this principle is the Road Traffic Act 1988 s. 3ZB of causing death by driving without insurance and without a license. This does not require death to be attributable to the manner of driving. See *R v Williams* [2010] EWCA Crim 2552; see D.C. Ormerod, 'Causation: Causing Death by Driving when Unlicensed, Disqualified or Uninsured – Construction of "Cause"' [2011] Crim LR 471 (case comment).

This is the most important framework principle. A person is not deemed to be a cause of a consequence if their causal contribution is negligible. In *Adams*, a doctor prescribed a life-threatening dose of drugs, for the purpose of pain relief, to a terminally ill patient. One of the issues for the court was whether this act had caused the patient's death. Devlin J told the jury that causation was not established simply upon proof that the measures taken had the effect of accelerating the death, as long as the doctor was exercising himself to relieve pain and suffering. Although Devlin J did not make explicit the basis upon which he came to this conclusion, it may be that the doctor's contribution was too negligible to be causal. He did not abbreviate life, so much as the length of time it took to die.

On the other hand, the fact that other causes contributed to or could have prevented the result does not generally bear upon the issue of causal responsibility, unless the later cause is so overwhelming as to rid the initial act of causal significance.[43] So, in *Benge* (1865) 4 F and F 504, D, a foreman platelayer on a railway, failed to check the train timetable to ensure the men working for him were safe on the line. A train killed one of the workmen. D claimed that he was not the cause since the driver of the train could have prevented the deaths if he had kept a proper lookout. It was held that the contribution of the defendant, was substantial enough to justify attributing responsibility for the death to him. His contribution was too significant to be ignored. Again, in *Smith*[44] the defendant, who had stabbed his victim, appealed against his conviction for murder on the ground that the victim would have survived had he not been dropped several times on the way to receiving medical treatment and had been properly diagnosed and cared for by the medical team. The defendant's conviction for murder was upheld. The real issue was whether the defendant's contribution was substantial and still operating at the time of death, rather than whether there happened to be a significant contributory cause. The following important statement of principle was made in this case which neatly, if indeterminately, summarises this aspect of the law on causation:

> if at the time of death the original wound is still an operating and a substantial cause, then the death (is) the result of the wound albeit that some other cause is also operating. Only if it can be said that the original wound is merely the setting within which another cause operates can it be said that the death does not result from the wound . . . putting it another way only if the second cause is so overwhelming as to make the original wound merely part of the history can it be said that death does not flow from the wound.

(c) If, subsequent to an actor's 'but for' causal contribution, an independent voluntary act or abnormal event occurs sufficient in itself to cause the ensuing harm, the 'but for' cause of that harm will be ignored.

This is a qualification of B above. Sometimes a later intervening cause is too powerful to be ignored. When it is, causal responsibility will be reassigned. The principle generally applied, similar to that in tort, is that if the harm remains within the class of harms rendered foreseeable as a consequence of the accused's action, the accused will be causally responsible. Otherwise he will not. Another way of saying this is that A will be the cause of an unexpected event if it is within the risk created by his action.[45] Consider the following variations of Case 1.

---

[43] Such an intervening cause is known as a *novus actus interveniens*. For explanation and discussion see later.
[44] *Smith* [1959] 2 QB 35.
[45] See generally G. Williams, *TCL* (1983) 388–90.

> **Case 4**
>
> B, feeling giddy from the effects of the poison, falls out of his bedroom window, thus killing himself.

> **Case 5**
>
> B calls an ambulance. On the way to hospital he is killed along with the ambulance crew, in a car crash.

A will remain responsible in Case 4 since falling out of a window is within the risk of (made more likely to occur by) the initial poisoning. In Case 5 common sense tells us that, without A's initial act, B would not be lying dead. But common sense also tells us that the cause of B's death is the same as that of the ambulance crew, and if A is not the cause of the latter's death (surely beyond the bounds of common sense) he can hardly be deemed the cause of B's death. Death by car crash is not within the risk of (made more likely by) a poisoning. As we shall see, the authorities tend to avoid using the 'within the risk' formula in cases involving intervening events, preferring to apply less analytic tests such as whether the event was 'abnormal' or 'unforeseeable'.

In the case of intervening acts (as opposed to natural events) the principle generally thought to be applicable is that causal responsibility will only be deflected if the act is voluntary. Thus, A will not be responsible in Case 6 below as the terrorist's action is voluntary and independent of A's act.

> **Case 6**
>
> As Case 4 except that B is taken to hospital still alive where he is given an antidote which promotes a rapid recovery. He later dies in a terrorist bomb attack.

Outside obvious cases of sheer coincidences, such as Case 5 or 6, exactly what counts as a 'voluntary' act or an abnormal or unforeseeable event is not always so easy to determine. The tests used to determine these things are manipulable in accordance with varying notions of 'common sense', 'fairness' and penal policy.[46] To understand how causal responsibility is imputed, therefore, it is probably most helpful to examine the practice of judges in some of the more common situations which give rise to causal problems, to see how the above ideas are used to justify the type of decision made. Such situations involve either subsisting conditions or intervening causes.

5.6 PARTICULAR EXAMPLES OF CAUSAL SEQUENCES GIVING RISE TO CAUSATION PROBLEMS

A Subsisting conditions

The general rule, as we have seen, is that judges look for causes and exclude from consideration the fact that some condition was necessary to invest an act with its causal significance.

1 Medical conditions: the thin skull principle

Where the victim suffers from a **subsisting** medical condition which renders him particularly vulnerable to the injury inflicted, the principle applied is that the defendant must take the victim as he is or, misleadingly, 'as he finds him'. Thus, if the victim of the defendant's

---

[46] See M. Moore, 'Foreseeing Harm Opaquely' in Shute *et al.* (1993) 143–54.

violence suffers from haemophilia,[47] fragile health, or the eponymous thin skull,[48] the defendant will bear causal responsibility for whatever injury is sustained by consequence of that condition although that condition was unforeseeable. Thus, in *Dyson*, the defendant was held responsible for the death of a child from meningitis, where it ensued after a period of neglect and ill treatment, rendering him particularly vulnerable to the disease.[49]

The principle has been said to extend to encompassing causal responsibility for death by fright in those suffering from heart conditions. In *Murton*[50] the defendant was held responsible for the manslaughter of his wife when an undiagnosed medical condition affecting her caused her literally to die of fright ten days after he had assaulted and bruised her.[51] The jury were told that death could be caused by fright alone so long as the causal chain was begun by the unlawful attack.[52]

2 Other subsisting conditions

If the defendant must take the risk that the victim may be unusually susceptible, then he also takes the risk of other subsisting conditions which may have an impact upon the harm which the victim sustains. Thus the defendant will bear responsibility if a trivial injury is converted into a fatal one due to the failure, say, of ambulance crew to attend the victim by consequence of a subsisting strike or poor weather.[53]

A more controversial example of a subsisting condition is provided by the case of *Blaue*,[54] in which the question arose whether the accused, who had stabbed his victim, was causally responsible for that victim's death when she refused, for religious reasons, a life-saving blood transfusion. The victim's decision, motivated as it was by an existing belief system, was considered to be one of the internal characteristics of the victim, as much as a medical condition was. As such, in line with *Murton*, the defendant must take the risk. This was the position taken by the Court of Appeal, approving the principle that the defendant must take his victim as he finds him.

The decision has been criticised on a number of grounds, however. In particular, why was the victim's decision treated as a **subsisting condition** rather than a **new intervening cause**?[55] Would it have been treated in the same way, for instance, if the refusal were motivated by an irrational fear of needles, or the victim had a grudge against Blaue, or if the religious sect concerned lacked social support? It has been argued, for example, that, her decision should break the chain of causation because it was free and informed, that is, was a voluntary one. In other words it was her decision and not B's act which made the difference. Why should Blaue bear responsibility if the victim takes a moral choice to kill himself, any more than he should if, crippled by the wound, the victim took a conscientious decision to end her life with dignity rather than endure life-long humiliation?[56]

---

[47] *State* v *Frazier* 339 Mo. 96 (1936).
[48] The eponym here being the 'thin skull' principle.
[49] *Dyson* [1908] 2 KB 454, CCA; cf. *Jordan*, below.
[50] (1862) 3 F & F 492.
[51] Cf. *Hayward* (1908) 21 Cox CC 692; *Towers* (1874) 12 Cox CC 530; *Dawson* (1985) 81 Cr App Rep 150.
[52] Cf. *Mackie* (1973) 57 Cr App R 453; *Williams and Davis* [1992] 2 All ER 183, below. Cf. *Carey* [2006] EWCA Crim 17, and *Dawson* (1985) 81 Cr App R 150; *Watson* [1989] 1 WLR 684.
[53] See for example *Smith*, below.
[54] *Blaue* [1975] 1 WLR 1411.
[55] See below.
[56] There is some doctrinal support for attributing causal responsibility for suicide to the actions of the defendant who motivated it, provided that the causal sequence began with an unlawful attack to which the suicide was directly attributable. *Stephenson* v *State* 205 Ind 141 (1932); *Dhaliwal* [2006] EWCA Crim 1139. See Professor Ormerod's insightful commentary at [2006] Crim LR 925; See also J. Horder and L. McGowan, 'Manslaughter by Causing Another's Suicide' (2006) Crim LR 1035.

The explanation for *Blaue*, it is suggested, must be that we live in a world in which death is caused by wounds and blows and not by ideas, however unusual or perverse. Action is the execution of an idea, not its result.[57] The victim's decision was, no doubt, a pre-condition of her death but no more caused it than if she had foolishly decided to stay at home and nurse herself. After all, the harm which occurred (death or serious injury) was intended,[58] it was an operative cause of death (she died of loss of blood) and it was within the range of harms rendered foreseeable by the accused's unlawful act.[59] What policy or principle of fairness would not select Blaue as the cause of the victim's death? He must take his own bad luck. A simpler analysis might simply be to say that omissions cannot break the chain of causation.[60]

B Intervening acts and events

As *Blaue* and *Smith* illustrate the effect of an intervening (or supervening) act, omission, or event may be to contribute to the criminal harm.[61] Such an effect is consistent with the **continued responsibility** of the defendant. Alternatively, it may operate to divert responsibility from the defendant, in which case it is known as a 'sole' cause, a 'superseding' cause, or a new cause intervening, otherwise known as a *novus actus interveniens*.

1 Victim's conduct contributing to the occurrence or extent of injury

(a) Escape cases

Most of the case law concerned with self-inflicted injuries involves injuries contracted in the course of trying to escape from a threat posed by the accused. The general approach taken by the courts has been that such actions will not break the chain of causation between the accused's initial act of wrongdoing and the eventual injuries. It is important to note that the courts have more recently set notional limits upon this rule of practice. These limits are generally expressed in terms of foreseeability. If the victim's response to the accused's conduct was 'reasonably foreseeable' or the 'natural consequence'[62] thereof (as it normally will be), the causal chain is not interrupted. Thus in *Roberts* the accused was found causally responsible for injuries suffered when the victim jumped out of a moving car in response to a threatened sexual assault, since such a response was reasonably foreseeable. In *Mackie*, in which a child of three fell downstairs to his death attempting to escape his violent father, a similar test was used with the variation that the attempt to escape must be the natural consequence of the unlawful act. As this was a manslaughter case the attempt to escape was also to involve the reasonably foreseeable risk of some, albeit not necessarily serious, harm.

Another response stresses not so much whether the victim's response was reasonably foreseeable but rather whether it was 'reasonable' in the sense of not being completely disproportionate or 'daft'.[63] In most cases the different formulations of the test disclose no real difference. After all, if a response is daft or disproportionate, it will not be reasonably foreseeable.

---

[57] See section 6.6 on Intention, Chapter 6.
[58] Blaue was convicted of voluntary manslaughter on the ground of diminished responsibility.
[59] *R v Master* [2007] EWCA Crim 142. For criticism of this test see Moore (2010) chs 9 and 10.
[60] See discussion of *Holland*, below.
[61] See also *Dyson*, *Smith*, above.
[62] *R v Mackie* (1973) 57 Cr App R 453; *R v Corbett* [1996] Crim LR 594; *Roberts* (1971) 56 Cr App R 95; cf. *R v Beech* (1912) 76 JP 287.
[63] *R v Lewis* [2010] EWCA Crim 151 CA.

A problem with both such tests arises where the victim overreacts or suffers some unusual harm because of the kind of person he/she is. We have seen, in the section above, that such cases could be treated as subsisting conditions for which the defendant must bear the risk. However, in practice, they are not always so treated in escape cases. Confusion is added to confusion when, as is increasingly evident, judges mix the above tests with ones based upon voluntariness or free choice. Such a 'mixed' test was used in *R v Williams and Davis*.[64] The deceased, a hitch-hiker, died of injuries sustained when he jumped out of a car in response to threats against him by the appellants. The Court of Appeal held that if the conduct of the victim is treated as voluntary it is, in effect, 'uncaused' and so incompatible with the defendants' causal responsibility. However, in deciding whether an action was involuntary, the question to be asked was the surely quite separate question whether it 'was within the range of responses which might be expected from a victim placed in the situation in which he was'. One final confusion was provoked by the court ruling that, in reaching a conclusion, the jury should be asked to '**bear in mind any particular characteristic of the victim** and the fact that in the agony of the moment he may act without thought and deliberation'. The test is thus extremely ambiguous. It faces in two different directions. The first suggests that the causal link will be broken by any response which is not reasonably foreseeable, bearing in mind the context within which the victim was placed. The second suggests that the jury may perhaps ignore foreseeability if the victim's response is attributable to some 'particular characteristic' bearing on voluntariness. What is not clear, however, is whether the characteristics the judge was talking about were those which would be apparent to the accused, e.g. age, sex or size, when they performed the act in question, or whether, as in *Blaue*, they may be locked deep within the victim's psyche, for example unusual timidity or phobic disposition. What breaks the causal chain – the reasonableness/ foreseeability of the victim's reaction from the defendant's point of view, or the reasonableness/voluntariness of the victim's reaction from his own point of view? In the light of *Blaue* it must surely be the latter, and rightly so. The fairness of imposing responsibility for unforeseeable/unforeseen consequences can be accommodated by insisting on cogent *fault* requirements.

(b) *Victim's injuries contributed to or exacerbated by contributory negligence*

Two situations can be considered. The first is where, without the victim's negligence, the harm would not have been suffered at all. The second is where, subsequent to the accused's wrongful act, the victim does something which exacerbates his injury.

In both cases the contributory negligence of the victim or of a third party will not generally deflect causal responsibility from a culpable actor as long as the defendant contributed substantially to the outcome. Thus it is no answer to manslaughter that the deceased was drunk and, if not drunk, would have heeded the calls of a cart-driver to get out of the way, if the injury was still attributable to the driver's excessive speed.[65] There are very few instances where the action of the victim has been found to break a causal sequence. Where it has occurred it tends to be because it can be used to show how the defendant was not negligent or the harm was not attributable to the negligence. Thus if the driver could have done nothing to avert the accident, no responsibility would ensue.[66]

Where the victim's injuries are exacerbated by a failure to seek or act upon medical advice to which the defendant's action substantially contributes, the causal sequence is not

[64] [1992] 2 All ER 183.
[65] *Walker* (1824) 1 C & P 320.
[66] As in *Dalloway* (1847) 2 Cox CC 273, above; cf. *State v Preslar* 48 NC 421 (1856).

broken. In *Holland*, for example, the victim of a serious assault with an iron bar refused to submit to the amputation of a finger, recommended to prevent tetanus. The original assailant was held to be causally responsible for the resultant death from tetanus. A similar approach has been adopted where the victim has neglected to take reasonable precautions. Thus in *Wall's* case the causal responsibility of a prison governor for an illegal flogging was not excluded by evidence that the victim had probably precipitated his own demise by the consumption of brandy.[67]

The same principle applies where the contributory negligence is that of a third party. Thus in an American case the defendant's appeal against a conviction for manslaughter was refused when the victim had been removed from hospital by his mother against medical advice. Evidence showed that this had precipitated his demise as he had a broken neck.[68]

Under modern conditions the refusal of a victim to submit to minor medical treatment, or to take the modicum of care necessary to prevent a minor injury turning into a life-threatening injury, could arguably be considered differently. It must be remembered that the principles of causation are used, symptomatically, to ensure that the defendant is fairly selected as the cause of the criminal harm concerned. In line with the modern approach in escape cases, it might be supposed that here too the more perverse the victim's conduct is, the more appropriate it might be to hold him, rather than the defendant, responsible for his fate. Following the line taken above in connection with *Blaue*, the view taken here is that it would be better that criminal liability hinged explicitly on an assessment of the defendant's fault rather than tortured reasoning about the 'real' cause of a victim's eventual injury. A good rule of thumb in this regard which covers the case of both *Blaue* and *Holland* is that the omissions of the victim cannot break the chain of causation.

2 Third party's act contributing to the occurrence or extent of injury

(a) *Third party responds to the danger posed by A's conduct*

Earlier we referred to two obvious ways in which a causal chain maybe broken, namely the unconnected voluntary intervention of a third party (or victim), known as a *novus actus interveniens*, or some other abnormal coincidence. In this section we will consider further the relatively narrow operation of this principle. In particular, it should be noted that in the case of third party actions the chain of causation will not be broken by actions taken to avert the danger prompted by the accused's action. So for instance, if a person wrestles with a bank robber who is holding a gun, it will be the bank robber and not the third party who will be the legal cause of any subsequent harm if the gun discharges. An example which shows the (undue?) limits to which the principle can be stretched is *Pagett*.[69] The defendant was held responsible for the consequences of the police marksman's action when the latter shot the 'human shield' the defendant was using to resist arrest, even though there was evidence that this was disproportionate to the threat offered.

(b) *Medical treatment*

Medical treatment, in accordance with acceptable clinical practice, which happens to accelerate the death of the victim is not considered a cause of death nor capable of breaking the chain of causation. So in *Malcherek* the Court of Appeal ruled that it was the original

---

[67] *Holland* (1841) 2 Mood & R 351; *Wall* (1802) 28 State Tr 51; see also *Flynn* (1867) 16 WR 319.
[68] *People v Clark* 106 Cal App 2d 271.
[69] (1983) 76 Cr App Rep 279, above; cf. *Pizano v Superior Court of Tulane County* 21 Cal 3d 128 (1978) discussed in Perkins and Boyce (1982) 804–9.

attacker who was the cause of the deceased's death and not the doctor who had turned off his life support following brain death.[70]

Even where the treatment is not in accordance with acceptable clinical practice it is rare that it will supersede the causal responsibility of the initial wrongdoer. If the initial wound or injury continues to be a 'potent' or 'operative' cause.[71] In *Smith*[72] the victim died of a stab wound to the lung, but not before he had been dropped twice before reaching medical attention and had received artificial respiration. The artificial respiration was the result of a misdiagnosis and is the last thing a person with a hole in the lung needs. It very probably precipitated the death, which normal treatment would have prevented. Despite all these significant contributions the defendant's conviction for murder was upheld. The real issue was whether the defendant's contribution was still substantial and operative, rather than how bad the treatment was.

Similar conclusions were reached in *Cheshire*,[73] where the deceased died of respiratory failure. The defendant's contribution was gunshot wounds to the leg and abdomen, which had left the deceased with respiratory problems. In attempting to alleviate these problems doctors had performed a tracheotomy. It was negligently performed and subsequently treated and was the direct cause of the deceased's death. Nevertheless this did not exclude the defendant's responsibility '. . . unless the negligent treatment was so independent of his acts, and in itself so potent in causing death that [the jury] could regard the contribution made by his acts as insignificant'.[74] Given the facts of *Cheshire* it might be thought that poor medical treatment can never break the chain of causation. This is not the case although what follows is inevitably speculative.

When will inappropriate medical treatment break the chain of causation?

In *Cheshire*, Beldam LJ stated that it would only be in the most extraordinary and unusual case that the accused would not be responsible for injuries or death suffered by medical treatment 'attempting to repair the harm done'. This was not an extraordinary and unusual case, because it is in the nature of medical treatment that action directed to alleviate one medical problem may precipitate another. Moreover, using our earlier frame of reference, death occurring due to incompetent medical treatment is within the range of risks created by the defendant's action.[75] A clearer (and less rhetorical) test is to be found in the American case of *Kane*:[76] 'it is only where the death is solely attributable to the (medical staff), and not at all induced by the primary (cause), that its intervention constitutes a defence'. What the court is looking for is some 'new act' which can reasonably be said to begin a new chapter of events.

There is one rather dubious example of such a case in domestic law. In *Jordan*[77] the defendant stabbed the victim, whereupon the victim was taken to hospital. After several weeks of treatment, during which time the wound had begun to heal, the victim died after

---

[70] [1981] 2 All ER 422.
[71] The American form of this test says that the chain of causation may be broken when the 'dangerous forces' unleashed by the initial wrongdoing have 'come to rest'.
[72] *Smith* [1959] 2 QB 35.
[73] *Cheshire* [1991] 3 All ER 670; cf. *McKechnie* (1992) 94 Cr App Rep 51; *Dear* [1996] Crim LR 595; *Mellor* [1996] Crim LR 743.
[74] Per Beldam LJ at 677.
[75] *R v Warburton* [2006] EWCA Crim 267 (CA).
[76] *Kane* (1915) 213 NY 260, 107 NE 655 at 657 cited by J. Hall, *General Principles of Criminal Law,* Indianapolis: Bobbs-Merrill (1960) 263.
[77] *Jordan* (1956) 40 Cr App Rep 152.

two unfortunate medical errors, which latter evidence was not available to the jury. The first was the administration of a drug, to which it was known the deceased was intolerant. The second was the intravenous delivery of an abnormal quantity of liquid. The post-mortem examination showed that the deceased died of pneumonia as a direct result of these two medical errors. The Court of Criminal Appeal held that if this evidence had been considered by the jury they would not have been satisfied that the wound caused death, since the treatment was 'palpably wrong' and 'not normal'. The fact that the treatment is 'palpably wrong' or even 'grossly negligent' should not be, however, a relevant considera-tion given that there can be more than one substantial cause of death. This is clear from both *Smith* and *Cheshire*. At best this case could be justified on the basis of the American 'dangerous forces' principle. The original attacker was not the cause because V was no longer at risk from the wound. The autopsy would no doubt have put the cause of death as pneumonia and given the clinical reasons for this.

Jordan, notwithstanding it is submitted that inappropriate medical care will break the chain of causation only in the following cases, namely where:

(a) The treatment was not a response to the diagnosed condition but was, for example, given for ulterior reasons, including mischief, or by mistake. This would be both unusual and extraordinary, since 'ordinary' medical treatment is end-directed, the end being the recovery of the patient from the diagnosed condition, or palliative care. The Court in *Kane* gives as an example the hypothetical case of the negligent (or intentional) administration of a deadly poison by hospital staff. By extension a massive overdose of the prescribed drug would seem to discharge the defendant from responsibility for the ensuing death.[78]

(b) Although the treatment was a response to the deceased's diagnosed condition – that condition had stabilised – even though it was still subsisting, and that the treatment was so misinformed as to precipitate the death of the deceased (and possibly anybody else who would have suffered it). For example, giving a drug to which the victim had a known intolerance,[79] or transfusing blood known to be contaminated[80] would surely be considered 'extraordinary', while the defendant's act could hardly in the circum-stances be considered anything other than an insignificant causal contribution. By the same principle the position of the removal of a stabilised victim from life support would also seem to break the chain of causation if due, say, to mistaken identity, but not if due to negligent diagnosis.[81] So also, if D had damaged V's right kidney, would be the mistaken removal of the other healthy kidney.

This leaves at large problems such as death due to allergy or drug intolerance, where the intolerance is not known. On the basis of cases such as *Blaue*, such 'subsisting' conditions con-tribute to the causal sequence rather than displace the defendant's causal responsibility.

3 Intervening cause supersedes defendant's act

(a) *Intervening acts of third parties* (novus actus interveniens)

As has been seen, the general doctrinal stance taken in the field of causation is that the accused will bear causal responsibility for the consequences of an unlawful action intended

---

[78] J. Hall, op. cit. at 263.
[79] *Jordan*, above.
[80] Or perhaps performing incompetent surgery while intoxicated; Perkins and Boyce (1982) 803.
[81] J. Hall, op. cit. at 263.

or foreseen to involve the risk of harm to the victim. Counterposed to this principle is the rule that the defendant's responsibility may be blocked by an unconnected (independent) voluntary act of a third party.[82] One way of explaining this rule is that it is an example of the general principle that the defendant will only be responsible for harms occurring within the risk created by the defendant's act. Thus he will be responsible if the victim dies of negligent medical treatment (within the risk) but not if he is shot dead in his bed by a terrorist, or given poison by mistake (not within the risk).

The issue of political morality underpinning the voluntariness formulation is different from the foreseeability approach, or the 'within the risk formulation', however. The issue here, but less so in other cases of *novus actus*, is why one defendant should bear responsibility for harms voluntarily produced by another, when other options are available which more precisely reflect the harm which we attribute to that defendant. The criminal law has in place a number of different offences, the scheme behind which is to ensure that the defendant is punished according to the precise wrong for which he is responsible. This is particularly important in cases where there is a joint enterprise between two or more parties to injure V where one of the parties, D, withdraws from that enterprise and the others carry on to kill V. The rules governing this situation will be covered in detail in Chapter 19. However, for our present purposes, it suffices to say that, in certain circumstances, D will remain liable for the death on the basis of his initial participation in a fatal attack. But if the killing bears no relation to the initial joint enterprise, D may escape liability on the basis of the intervening acts of his co-attackers. So, in *Rafferty* D was a party to a joint enterprise to beat V. D withdrew from the attack after delivering some blows and kicks and left the scene. His co-attackers eventually stripped V naked, dragged him into the sea and drowned him. The Court of Appeal approved the trial judge's direction to the effect that 'the drowning of (V by the others) . . . was so completely different from the injuries for which Rafferty was responsible, that it overwhelmed those injuries and destroyed any causal connection between them and the death of V.' On slightly different facts, however, the Supreme Court of Canada preferred to apply a reasonable foresight rather than an independent voluntary act test governing whether the acts of a third party broke the chain of causation. In *R v Maybin* (ML) *et al.*[83] B was set upon in a pub by C and D, two pool players, for moving of the balls. They punched and kicked him repeatedly in the face and head rendering him unconscious. A third party, E, arrived on the scene and he then punched B and carried him outside, leaving him on his back. B died later that afternoon. The medical cause of death was bleeding in the brain which may have been caused by E. At first instance the trial judge directed the jury to acquit C and D. The British Columbia Court of Appeal, allowed the prosecutor's appeal and ordered a new trial. The Supreme Court of Canada dismissed C and D's appeal. In the circumstances of this case, it was open to the trial judge to find that C and D caused the death, notwithstanding the potentially fatal intervention of E on the basis that their initial attack rendered it not unforeseeable that further non-trivial harm would be caused by the actions of others. A similar decision was reached by the House of Lords in the *Cars* case in which a company were held responsible for causing the release of polluted matter into a river although the release was infact effected by (the voluntary action of) a trespasser. Their Lordships ruled that since such an intervention was reasonably foreseeable the company could not defend themselves

---

[82] Omissions do not begin or break chains of causation in the absence of a duty of intervention. See *R v Girdler* [2010] RTR 28; [2009] EWCA Crim 2666 (CA): 'mere tacit standing by and looking on' are insufficient to amount to causing.

[83] *R v Maybin* (ML) *et al.* 2012 SCC 24.

by saying the release was not their doing.[84] As can be seen, therefore, there is at the heart of causation doctrine a fundamental uncertainty. Do acts of third parties break the chain of causation initiated by the initial factual cause if they are **independent and voluntary** or only if they are voluntary and **unforeseeable**? Does it depend on the context? Or do judges simply toss a coin? In the next section we will see that this uncertainty has also struck doctrine where it is the victim whose acts have contributed to his harm.

(b) Intervening act by victim

A fully informed voluntary act of the victim may also break the chain of causation. An instructive case is *Dalby*[85] in which the defendant was indicted for manslaughter. Dalby had supplied controlled drugs to his friend, who had died as a consequence of injecting himself with the drugs. One of the issues dealt with was causation. Was Dalby the legal cause of death? Using a *Roberts* reasonable foresight test he was. It was reasonably foreseeable that a person, supplied with drugs for injection, would use them in this way. Using a voluntariness test he was not, since the victim is responsible for the consequences of his own action. Domestic criminal law has long treated Othello rather than Iago as the cause of Desdemona's death. Although Iago is responsible for influencing Othello to kill Desdemona, he does not cause the death, which is all Othello's own act.[86] As a corollary, if Dalby's victim had been a child (and therefore lacking the ability to make free, informed decisions), the defendant would properly be treated as the legal cause of death.[87] In *Dias*, as in *Dalby*, the Court of Appeal ruled that the supplier's initial causal contribution is supplanted by the victim's own free chosen action.

In another drug-induced homicide case, *Finlay*, however, the Court of Appeal held that the causal responsibility of the supplier of a filled syringe was not undone by the voluntary act of the donee in injecting himself. He caused it precisely because this event **was** reasonably foreseeable and so, as in *Empress*, capable of being guarded against.[88]

More recently in *Kennedy (No. 2)*, while eschewing the *Empress* approach, the Court of Appeal essayed another basis for ridding doctrine of the inconvenience posed by *Dalby* and *Dias* in cases of drug-induced homicide. The issue was whether K's own unlawful act of supplying a loaded syringe caused the death of the victim. The Court of Appeal held that it did. The problem of causation was obviated by the device of treating both supplier of the syringe and victim as parties to a single act of causing a noxious substance to be administered. Unfortunately it was not explained how D can illegally cause heroin to be taken by V by the same transaction by which V voluntarily administers it to himself. On a further appeal, the House of Lords agreed that this made no sense and allowed the appeal.

> It is possible to imagine factual scenarios in which two people could properly be regarded as acting together to administer an injection. But nothing of the kind was the case here. As in *R v Dalby* and *R v Dias* the appellant supplied the drug to the deceased, who then had a choice, knowing the facts, whether to inject himself or not. The heroin was, as the certified question correctly recognises, self-administered, not jointly administered. The appellant did not administer the drug. Nor, for reasons already given,[89] did the appellant cause the drug to be administered to or taken by the deceased.

---

[84] N. Padfield, 'Clear Water and Muddy Causation: Is Causation a Question of Law or Fact, or Just a Way of Allocating Blame?' [1995] Crim LR 683.

[85] [1982] 1 WLR 425.

[86] As Williams puts it: 'What a person does (if he has reached adult years, is of sound mind and is not acting under mistake, intimidation or other similar pressure) is his own personal responsibility and is not to be regarded as having been caused by other people.' G. Williams, *Textbook of Criminal Law* 39.

[87] G. Williams, ibid. 39. Cf. *Michael* (1840) 9 C & P 356.

[88] *Environment Agency v Empress Car Co. (Abertillery) Ltd* [1999] 2 AC 22. See further *R v Girdler* [2009] EWCA Crim 2666 (CACD), *supra*.

[89] That is, because the injection was freely chosen and fully informed.

The effect of this decision is to return the law to the position that the independent voluntary act of the victim or a third party breaks the chain of causation.[90] Foreseeability remains the test in strict liability offences, however.[91] There are, no doubt, good reasons for this. If we look at *Empress Cars*, for example, the question to be considered is the appropriateness[92] of attributing the cause of pollution to a company who profits from the pollutant's storage and transmission. It would be unfortunate if the foreseeability test was resurrected more generally.[93]

(c) *Intervening events*

Another implication of the principle that the defendant takes responsibility only for those unforeseen consequences arising within the risk created by his unlawful act is that the defendant is not liable for coincidences, or 'abnormal' events, or 'acts of God'. An example of such a coincidence is Case 3 above. A more challenging problem is posed in the following variation.

> **Case 7**
> As in Case 6 except that before he is discharged he contracts a deadly virus as a direct consequence of being in hospital.

On the one hand, Case 7 has things in common with Case 5. A's action created a specific risk of B being treated in hospital, which in turn must generate a specific risk of contracting possibly life-threatening disease. Hospitals are dangerous places. On the other hand, it is also like Cases 5 and 6. This is one of life's tragic coincidences. Common sense, which approved the application of risk theory in Case 4, now objects that the real cause of death is the virus and not the man whose actions led him to encounter it. Such authority as there is on the specific point, with the support of most commentators, supports this conclusion. Thus, in the American case of *Bush* it was held that where a wounded man contracted scarlet fever from his surgeon, the chain of causation linking the wound with the death was broken since scarlet fever was not 'the natural consequence of the wound'.[94]

5.7 CAUSATION AND SOCIAL JUSTICE

As we have seen, the moral principle which is generally held to underlie the criminal law is that the state's authority to punish requires subjects to have had the capacity or fair opportunity of conforming to the law. This principle is reflected to a limited extent in the law of defences where excuses such as duress, insanity, diminished responsibility and provocation may relieve a person from criminal responsibility. In the sphere of causation, as in the field of defences, that principle is reflected in the generally accepted doctrinal

---

[90] This does not leave the supplier entirely immune from the risk of prosecution, if death transpires from self administration. In appropriate circumstances the supplier may be under a duty to intervene to prevent death, based upon the *Miller* principle. See Chapter 4.

[91] Compare the position in Scotland in which the free and informed action of the drug taker does not necessarily break the chain of causation linking supply and death. Whether causation is established or not is 'a question of fact'. *MacAngus and Kane* v *HM Advocate* (2009) HCJAC 8.

[92] See *Evans* [2009] EWCA 650.

[93] For a different view see T. Jones, 'Causation, Homicide and the Supply of Drugs' (2006) 26 Legal Studies 139–54.

[94] *Bush* v *Commonwealth* (1880) 78 Ky. 268 at 271; *viz.* Hall, *General Principles of Criminal Law* 263; Williams, *TCL* 387.

dogma that voluntariness underpins causal agency. Causal sequences can only begin with voluntary actions and can only be interrupted by voluntary actions (or abnormal events). In practice, however, what counts as a voluntary act of the defendant is unusually flexible, whereas what counts as a voluntary act of a third party, or an unforeseeable reaction from a victim, or an abnormal event, is unusually restricted.

An implicit problem which emerges from this account, and writ large in the drug-induced homicide cases, is how cogent is the notion of voluntariness as a basis for assigning causal responsibility. Tim Jones for example has argued that English law accords voluntariness of action undue weight in the decision as to whether someone is properly held accountable for a harmful consequence. No such primacy is evident in jurisdictions such as Scotland or Australia where the focus is upon whether the outcome was to be expected.[95] Moreover, all of our behaviour is to a certain extent influenced or determined, whether by events, by other people or internal body chemistry or psychology. What decides, if not questions of policy, whether such an influence negates the voluntariness essential to the fair imputation of criminal responsibility? An increasingly influential view is that, contrary to the opinions of theorists such as Hart and Honore, the real cause of a criminal harm is often rendered invisible by the ascription of responsibility. The assignment of criminal responsibility necessarily operates in a different way from the way responsibility is assigned elsewhere in political and social life. Historians are not wont to put the cause of the Second World War down to the atavistic impulses of a single man with a toothbrush moustache. Whole books are written about its causes. Even criminologists search far beyond the narrow frame of reference provided by the criminal law for the causes of crime. Yet the criminal law wants single 'causing' actors upon whom to place the whole burden of responsibility. Is this compatible with a commitment to social justice?

If we consider the following examples, the full force of this argument may become apparent.

Case 8

A spikes the drink of B, a weak-minded paedophile with no experience of alcohol. B commits a sexual assault on a child while under the influence.

Who or what causes the assault? A? B? The alcohol? B's sexuality? Or his father who sexually abused him as a child and which experience constructed B in his sexuality?

Case 9

B, a house surgeon exhausted after having been on duty for 24 hours, commits a grave error of judgement which kills his patient.

Who do we say caused the death? The doctor? The health administrator who instituted the 24-hour roster? The health authority which decided the budget? The government minister who squeezed health service funding? The civil servants who advised the minister? The economists who advised them? Or the state of the economy which influenced their advice?

---

[95] T. Jones, 'Causation, Homicide and the Supply of Drugs' (2006) 26 Legal Studies 139–54 at 152–3.

Case 10

B, a drug addict, injects her boyfriend, V, also a drug addict and who is suffering from withdrawal symptoms, with a dose of heroin. The heroin is unusually pure and hence too strong for his system. He dies as a result.

Who do we say caused the death? B for doing the injecting? V for asking her to? X who cut the heroin and forgot to reduce its potency? Y who supplied it to her? Z who manufactured the pure heroin? S who imported it? P, the Afghan farmer who grew it? R who introduced V to heroin? Or the British Government who removed the controls on Afghan poppy production when removing the Taliban from power?[96]

The problem posed for criminal doctrine is that there appears to be no principled way of ensuring that the legal cause of these criminal harms is fairly selected. The criminal law finds it convenient to draw a veil over the causal contributions of others, however influential these may have been, if it might deflect from the retributive and other functions which punishing B maybe expected to fulfil. Moreover, it is not good enough simply to claim that B, in these examples, voluntarily committed the offence and therefore, irrespective of the causal contributions of others, is fairly selected to bear responsibility, because we can produce no authentic rule which can tell us what 'voluntary' means. In one sense the above defendants' actions were voluntary. They were not unconscious and knew what they were doing. In another sense their actions were entirely involuntary. They were operating within a context created by other people and other subsisting conditions beyond their ability to influence.[97]

On this view, the principle which holds that only free agents can be held criminally responsible is incoherent, since nobody is as free as criminal doctrine pretends to assume and as free as they need to be to justify singling them out, and not some other person or condition, to bear personal responsibility. If the basis for a causal requirement is to reflect the retributive function of moral desert, then it seems clear, as Cases 8, 9 and 10 testify, that justice is not being done if those selected as human causes are nothing more than scapegoats earmarked by context, for reasons of policy, to take responsibility for society's ills.[98] Accordingly, Alan Norrie has argued that a method of assigning responsibility should be developed which took full account of the context within which individual action takes place.[99] As he puts it: 'A fully *moral* account of the wrongdoing in cases (of horrible crime) would have to recognise both that the social and structural factors operating behind the back of the criminal were effective in causing crime, and that the criminal was also its causal agent.'[100] A system for putting on record society's recognition that responsibility for wrongdoing must be shared between the individual actor and the society which made him is already hinted at in relation to juvenile offenders. Juvenile justice involves less emphasis on young offenders shouldering the full burden of (individuated) responsibility. The context, economic, educational, and familial in which wrongdoing takes place is heavily determinative of both procedures and processes. The message broadcast is more how to put right what has gone wrong, rather than holding an individual to account for his wrongdoing.

---

[96] For discussion see W. Wilson in Clarkson and Cunningham (eds), *Criminal Liability for Non-aggressive Death*, Aldershot: Ashgate (2008).

[97] For another example of the 'slippery' notion of voluntariness consider again whether *Blaue*'s decision was voluntary (since chosen) or involuntary (since a matter of obligation). See page 110.

[98] See A. Norrie (1993) ch. 7; A. Norrie (2001) chs 1, 5; A. Norrie, 'A Critique of Criminal Causation' (1991) 54 MLR 685 at 694 ff.

[99] A. Norrie (2001) chs 9 and 10.

[100] Ibid. at 220.

It will be obvious from the attempts made here to make sense of the apparent inconsistencies in causation doctrine that I take the less radical view that there is no deep injustice in holding those who have the capacity to act as moral agents fully responsible for their actions. Although we are bound to accept the unfortunate truth that individuals exhibit relative degrees of free choice in all their dealings, this does not discredit the system of blame and punishment. The assumption underpinning the criminal law, which is that individuals have the power to choose whether to do good or to do evil and must bear moral (and criminal) responsibility when they choose the latter, not only treats individuals with respect: it is a necessary assumption for a society concerned to maintain its moral integrity. We can ensure that defendants are justly treated by refining our notions of blameworthiness or our notions of desert in punishment rather than distorting commonsense notions of cause and effect.

It is suggested, in conclusion, that while a degree of indeterminacy is inevitable in causal judgments this is not, in itself, necessarily a bad thing, as long as decisions are not arbitrary and the reasons of policy or principle underpinning the judgments are geared towards the social and moral purposes criminal law embodies.[101] In short, policies should reflect and deliver criminal justice. The problem posed by doctrine in the field of causation is that neither the principles nor the policies guiding decision-making are clearly articulated.

Criminal justice requires both substantive and formal justice. Formal justice requires like cases to be treated alike. Theoretically, criminal justice is served when all questions of criminal liability are decided by reference to rules and principles capable of distinguishing fairly and consistently between those falling within the rules and those without. Formal justice, unlike substantive justice, cannot tell us, however, whether it is a good thing for our defendants to be held criminally responsible for their actions in the first place. Substantive justice requires all morally or politically troublesome cases to be decided in accordance with policies and principles underpinning the law. What the case law under discussion tells us is that there is no explicit moral or policy foundation to the so-called principles of causation. Why did the court use a substantiality test in *Smith,* but a reasonable foresight test in *Mackie,* a 'bear the risk' test in *Blaue* but a voluntariness test in *Williams*? Again, why did the trespasser's voluntary (and unforeseen) intervention not break the chain of causation in the *Empress Cars* case, if the deceased's voluntary and foreseen intervention did have this effect in *Kennedy*? Is it really justified to adopt a different test of causation in strict liability cases simply to prevent the inconvenience of having no-one to hold to account? The only possible response to this question requires us to remember what the purpose of causation in criminal law which is to attribute responsibility for the consequences of wrongful action. This is not an analytical function but a moral one. At all times, in other words, the question seeking solution is whether it is just and appropriate to hold the defendant to account. Sometimes, as in the drug supply cases, the voluntary act test may be appropriate. Other times, as in this case or *Empress Cars,* the reasonable foresight test may be applicable. Other times as in *Blaue* or *Cheshire* the 'within the risk' test takes priority. An acknowledgement of this fact with a pragmatic solution occurred in a recent case in the Canadian Supreme Court in which the Court admitted that there could be no hard and fast rules governing when a factual chain of causation was broken. In the words of Karakatsanis J 'Both the "reasonable foreseeability" and the "intentional, independent act" approach may be useful in assessing legal causation depending on the specific factual matrix. However, neither is determinative of whether an intervening act severs the chain

---

[101] See further J.R. Lucas, *On Justice,* Oxford: Clarendon (1980) chs 4, 5.

of causation so that an accused's act is not a significant contributing cause of death. They are tools to assist in addressing the test for legal causation.'[102]

Students who visit this area may, therefore, rightly congratulate themselves on finding that the case law is a bit of a mystery. If one forgot the rhetoric of foreseeability, voluntariness, abnormality and so on, however, what would soon become clear is that there is one coherent thread underpinning the case law, which is that people should be held accountable for the consequences of their own unlawful actions unless it would clearly inappropriate, for reasons of morality, common sense or otherwise, to hold otherwise. This renders explicit the moral principle that the defendant should not pass the buck of causal responsibility onto the victim's medical carers, or his medical condition, or his belief system, or his psychic characteristics, or his wider social context. On this basis, most of the cases detailed in this chapter can be accounted for.

Summary

Where an unlawful act of the accused is the factual cause of a criminal harm it will normally also be the legal cause. The defendant will be the factual cause of a criminal harm if the harm would not have occurred, but for the defendant's act or, exceptionally, if it would have been sufficient in itself to cause the harm in the absence of another, independently operating, concurrent cause. It is generally no objection to the ascription of legal cause that the harm suffered or the manner in which it came about was unexpected, nor that the victim or others contributed to its occurrence. This general rule is subject to the following qualifications. The accused will not be the legal cause of a criminal harm if his/her causal contribution is trivial. If, subsequent to the defendant's act, another act or event occurs which is independent of this act and is a sufficient cause of the criminal harm this act or event may break the chain of causation linking the defendant's act with the ensuing harm. In the case of intervening acts of a third party the chain of causation will be broken by their voluntary action. Persons reacting to danger are not deemed to act voluntarily. In the case of intervening acts of the victim the chain of causation may also be broken by the victim's voluntary act. The victim's act will not be treated as voluntary, however, if it is by way of direct reaction to the defendant's unlawful act unless perhaps it is an abnormal reaction. Intervening events will break the chain of causation if they are abnormal, in the sense of not being such events as are rendered more likely to occur by reason of the defendant's conduct.

---

[102] *R* v *Maybin* (ML) *et al.* (2012) SCC 24; a similar view was advanced by the Court of Appeal in *R* v *Girdler* [2009] EWCA Crim 2666.

Further reading

Elliott, C.S. and de Than, C., 'Prosecuting the Drug Dealer When a Drug User Dies' (2006) 69 Modern Law Review 986–95.

Hart, H.L.A. and Honore, A., *Causation in the Law* (2nd edn) Oxford: Clarendon Press (1985).

Jones, T., 'Causation, Homicide and the Supply of Drugs' (2006) 26 Legal Studies.

Norrie, A., 'A Critique of Criminal Causation' (1994) 54 MLR 685 at 694.

Ormerod, D. and Fortson, R., 'Drug Suppliers as Manslaughterers (Again)' [2005] Crim LR 819.

Wilson, W., *Central Issues in Criminal Theory*, Oxford: Hart (2002) ch. 3.

Wilson, W., 'Dealing with Drug Induced Homicide' in C.M.V. Clarkson and S. Cunningham (eds), *Criminal Liability for Non-aggressive Deaths*, Aldershot: Ashgate (2008) 176–98, ch. 5.

6 Mens rea

Overview

The vast majority of criminal offences are constituted simply upon proof of a breach of a criminal prohibition. For other crimes, specifically those of a stigmatic character, liability depends, in addition, upon proof of fault. The most common fault terms are intention, recklessness, knowledge and negligence. In this chapter we examine the meaning of these fault terms and how they are used both to grade offences in terms of seriousness and to filter those deserving of punishment from those which are not.

6.1 INTRODUCTION

At an earlier stage in our history the notion of *mens rea* was broadly conceived as a synonym for 'guilty mind', a term loose enough to allow the conviction for, say, manslaughter of anyone thought to be blameworthy and, therefore, deserving of punishment. The modern approach conceives of *mens rea*, less expansively, as including only the state of mind expressly or impliedly referred to in the offence definition as accompanying or prompting the conduct in question.[1] The more common words used to describe this state of mind include intention, recklessness, wilfulness, knowledge and malice. Negligence, on this approach, is not, strictly speaking, a form of *mens rea* because it describes no state of mind, rather an (unacceptable) standard of conduct. Nevertheless negligence will be treated here as part of the family of *mens rea* words since, like the rest of the family, it signifies fault, albeit in a different manner from the other members of the family. Crimes of negligence are counterposed to crimes of strict liability. Such crimes, as will be seen, may be committed without the need for the prosecution to prove *mens rea* in this slightly extended sense. Even for these crimes, however, a guilty mind of sorts must be established since the prosecution must disprove any excuse or justification for which the defendant adduces evidence.

The link between blame, punishment and the notion of personal moral responsibility has not always been dominant in the criminal law. Blaming people for their conduct is a social practice. Each society devises its own practice of blaming which is, as often as not, an effect of practices of punishment rather than their cause.[2] As late as the eighteenth century the awful majesty of the criminal law was invoked to punish a pig for homicide and mice, rats and locusts for theft.[3] If we operate upon the assumption that punishment is society's mechanism for expressing blame, such a response may seem irrational, not to mention pointless and inappropriate.[4] Such a link is not essential, however, for the operation of an effective criminal justice system. It has been suggested that the full moral enormity evoked by the concept of homicide may require the most awful retribution exacted against the

---

[1] Cf. *Dodman* [1998] 2 Cr App R 338.
[2] See R.A. Duff, *Trials and Punishment*, Cambridge: CUP (1986) ch. 2.
[3] See generally E.P. Evans, *The Criminal Prosecution and Capital Punishment of Animals*, London: Faber and Faber (1987).
[4] The potency of this point is well illustrated by Julian Barnes' satire on the animals cases in *The History of the World in 10½ Chapters*, London: Jonathan Cape (1989) ch. 3.

responsible and irresponsible alike. A judge who dons a black cap to sentence a pig to a cruel and lingering death may succeed, better than mere summary execution, in satisfying the blood lust lurking beneath the skin of the retributivist justification. The execution of sentence may be just as effective as a human execution in deterring others and making the moral point that murder is wrong. It may be more so. What does it tell us about the implacable rigour of criminal justice that it will pursue, judge and execute even a dumb animal which kills an innocent?[5]

Since blame, in modern liberal society, derives from the notion of personal responsibility, in theory we do not now blame those who, like children, lunatics and animals, are not responsible for their actions. We should be careful, though, not to get too carried away with the idea that full personal responsibility is, in our 'civilised society', an invariable prerequisite for either blame or punishment. Like all social practices flexibility and ambiguity are encountered in the system of blaming. Sometimes the logic of 'no blame in the absence of responsibility' fails to record our society's true politicised response to the causing of harm. When we see the newspaper coverage of notorious murder trials involving serial killings or infant victims we may be tempted to think that where serious harm has been perpetrated, the public want blood and are not too choosy about whether it be the blood of the guilty or the innocent, of the responsible or the irresponsible. Sometimes even children, the insane and animals get short shrift from society when the harm they cause is particularly serious. Dogs are typically summarily 'put down' when they attack children; the insane are, typically, 'hospitalised' for violent killings. Children may be 'incarcerated' and demonised for serious offences. The rhetoric says that such a response is not a mark of blame and such treatment is not punishment. The reality is that those concerned would hardly know the difference.

6.2 CHOICE AND CHARACTER: TWO MODELS OF RESPONSIBILITY

There are two basic models of personal responsibility operative in the criminal law, namely choice and character theory. Both models reflect the presumption that liability, at least for serious offences, requires proof of fault. Choice theory has had its most influential expression in the work of H.L.A. Hart. It will be encountered again in the chapter on defences. It holds that 'criminal liability is unjust if the one who is liable was not able to choose effectively to act in a way that would avoid criminal liability, and because of that he violated the law'.[6] This concept of personal responsibility is one which informs the retributive aim of punishment. It reflects the generally held assumption that all citizens are free to conform to or infringe the law and must therefore take responsibility for the consequences of their own free choice.

The rival model is character theory. It will also be covered in greater detail later. It holds that a person must bear responsibility not for his choices but for his character, since it is his person and not his deeds which is in the dock. On this model, responsibility is lacking wherever deeds are not a true reflection of his (good) character. At this early stage it should be noted that character theory is a plausible basis for understanding negligence-based responsibility and certain defences such as loss of self control and duress.[7] It is less

---

[5] Cf. M. Foucault, *Discipline and Punish: the Birth of the Prison*, London: Penguin (1991) ch. 1.
[6] H. Gross, *A Theory of Criminal Justice*, New York: OUP (1979) 137.
[7] Cf. K. Huigens, 'Virtue and Criminal Negligence' 1 Buffalo Crim LR 431; J. Gardner, 'The Gist of Excuse' (1998) 1 Buffalo Crim LR 575.

plausible, however, in the context of criminal responsibility generally. As long as we hold to the view that, whatever functions it has, punishment must be deserved, it seems clear that sometimes a proper basis for deciding what is deserved is what the defendant has chosen to do could have avoided doing, rather than the kind of character his deed discloses.[8]

6.3 SUBJECTIVE AND OBJECTIVE FAULT

If **freely choosing to do wrong** is the basis for desert in punishment then one would expect liability to be predicated upon the prosecution proving the existence of some form of mental state on the part of the wrongdoer, for example intention, knowledge, or awareness, which reflects conscious choice. This mental state or attitude accompanying wrongdoing is termed subjective fault. The accused is at fault in acting with this state of mind. If **bad character** is the basis for desert in punishment, proof of an accompanying mental attitude is not so crucial. People can show bad character through their actions both by thinking and by **not** thinking of the wrongfulness of their action. So, A shows **subjective** fault by directing his car at his enemy in order to kill him. His mental state is that of intention. A shows **objective** fault by driving his car in such a way that ordinary reasonable people would realise, although he did not, that he was subjecting other road users and pedestrians to the unjustified risk of harm. We term this type of fault negligence. Negligent conduct is blameworthy not on account of the actor choosing to do wrong but on account of the fact that he fails to behave like ordinary people.

It is widely accepted that criminal responsibility should depend upon proof of subjective fault.[9] This view is not universal, however. On the one hand, it will usually be difficult to prove what was in a person's mind at the time of acting. They may not even know themselves. On the other, requiring subjective fault ignores the fact that sometimes we feel justified in blaming people lacking a criminal 'intent'. People who fail to consider the ways in which their conduct may affect others distance themselves morally from reasonable people. They exhibit a dangerous and perhaps frightening character defect. It is perhaps not surprising, therefore, that criminal doctrine reflects an uneasy tension between these two forms of fault.

Increasingly, statutes are passed comprising fault elements which do not require proof of a subjective mental element. A recent example in which objective fault suffices for criminal liability is the (statutory) offence of rape. Under the common law the fault element of rape was recklessness, which was defined so as to require subjective fault. The prosecution bore the burden of proving that the accused did not honestly believe the victim to be consenting, that is, of proving an attitude of mind. Under the new definition the prosecution task is easier since the accused's belief in the fact of consent must now be a reasonable one. The jury are entitled to discount the accused's honest belief, in other words, if the circumstances are such that reasonable people would not have formed such a belief.[10] People who do not take care to ensure others are consenting to their sexual advances or harbour unrealistic ideas about 'what women want' are blameworthy precisely because they are inexcusably out of step with society's core values of respect for others.

---

[8] Fletcher (1978) 463–5; see though R.A. Duff, 'Choice, Character and Criminal Liability' (1993) 12 Law and Philosophy 345, who denies that choice and character are separate paradigms of responsibility.

[9] For an example of judicial scepticism as to its merits see the judgment of Lord Diplock in *Caldwell* [1981] 1 All ER 961.

[10] Sexual Offences Act 2003 section 1.

It is important, therefore, when analysing individual crimes, to interpret whether the fault required by the offence is subjective or objective. As a rule of thumb, the more serious the crime the more likely it is that subjective fault will be required although, in truth, the difference between subjective and objective fault may be more apparent than real.

> **Case 1**
> Adam is observed to drive his car at full tilt towards Eve while she is crossing the road. As she moves to avoid the impending crash Adam is seen also to change direction. He hits and kills Eve. Adam claims that he did not intend to kill Eve but only to frighten her. He did not even think she might get hurt.

If Adam's claim is to be believed he cannot be guilty of murder, which is a crime of intention (subjective fault). However, can we believe him? The evidence stacks up against him. Not only was he driving at full tilt towards Eve, he changed direction just before hitting her. The prosecution may think that this is good enough evidence to show an intention to kill. The facts seem to speak for themselves. The prosecution might well therefore charge with murder, relying on the jury's good sense to infer a subjective state of mind (intention) from objective facts (manner of driving). In other words Adam may well be found guilty of murder whether the fault element in murder is objective or subjective. We tend to ignore what people say they intended or foresaw, when this is out of step with our experience.

Although subjective fault is the norm for traditional core crimes such as property crimes and crimes of violence, it should be noted that these form a tiny proportion of the overall total of criminal offences. In fact, the vast majority of criminal offences **do not** require proof of fault, objective or subjective at all. These are termed strict liability offences. Many traffic offences, for example, are constituted simply upon proof of the relevant conduct, for example parking in the wrong place or failing to display a tax disc. This is obviously completely out of step with the ethic discussed earlier that censure and punishment should be deserved and should be limited to those who are blameworthy. Indeed some hold that it undermines this ethic. The position is complicated by the fact that Parliament often will not indicate one way or the other whether an offence is one of strict liability (no fault required) or requires proof of fault. In such circumstances, as will be seen in the next chapter, the courts may nevertheless interpret the provision as requiring a fault element. So, in *B v DPP*, the accused was charged under section 1 Indecency with Children Act 1960 with inciting a girl under 14 to commit an act of gross indecency. The accused claimed that he believed the girl to be over 14. Although there is no mention in the Act of any fault element he argued that, given the gravity of the offence, the Act should be interpreted to require one. The House of Lords, quashing the conviction, agreed that Parliament should be presumed to have intended a fault element in the absence of words to the contrary. It should be noted that the (implied) fault element was subjective fault. His belief that the girl was over 14 did not have to be a reasonable one.

6.4 *MENS REA* AND THE STRUCTURE OF CRIME

Under our society's present practices of blaming, blame is a function both of the harm which conduct produces and the fault attributable to the defendant for bringing about that harm. Both harms and fault are differentiated vertically, according to an ascending scale of seriousness. An example of harms vertically differentiated are crimes of violence, ascending in seriousness from minor harm (s. 47) to serious harm (s. 20) to death (homicide). *Mens rea* also operates to structure harms vertically. For example, section 18 of the Offences Against the Person Act makes it an offence to cause someone grievous bodily harm (GBH) with intent to cause GBH. Section 20 of the same Act makes it an offence simply to inflict GBH maliciously (intentionally **or** recklessly). The former state of mind is singled out as being more culpable than the latter and the offence carries a higher maximum sentence. The *mens rea* words contained within the definition of offences generally reflect degrees of choice. They are not, strictly speaking, signifiers of villainy or bad character.[11] A person intends to kill for the purpose of the law of murder, whether she does it to get her hands on the deceased's money or, at the deceased's request, to put a stop to the pain of his terminal illness. This supports the view that people tend to be punished for their choices rather than their character. If their character is not adequately reflected in their choice, this is a reason to mitigate sentence, not to excuse entirely. Apart from the strict liability offences just mentioned, the majority of common crimes of *mens rea* have intention **and** recklessness as alternative fault elements. It is the fact of choosing to do harm which thus fixes a person with responsibility rather than the degree of commitment shown to the outcome.

Where intention is a sole mental element this will often be because having the relevant intention is constitutive of the wrongdoing prohibited by the offence rather than simply a fault element. For example, taking a person's property without permission only becomes a criminal offence if it is done with the intention of depriving the owner permanently of the property.[12] It is this intention which makes the taking *wrongful* rather than making it simply *blameworthy*. It is theft, not borrowing without permission, which the law prohibits.

6.5 THE *MENS REA* WORDS AND THEIR MEANINGS

When a jury is asked to decide whether the accused 'intended' a consequence or was 'reckless' or 'dishonest' the first problem it will face is what the relevant word means. Does the judge tell them or do they apply their own understanding? Judicial activity in the field of *mens rea* shows a somewhat schizophrenic attitude towards the *mens rea* words and their meanings. Occasionally judges insist upon a technical meaning to an everyday word.[13] On the other hand, judges and academic commentators[14] often express the preference that the *mens rea* words carry their everyday meaning. The most compelling reason for this is that by allowing words such as intention, recklessness and dishonesty to embody popular usage, citizens will be in a better position to pitch their conduct in accordance with the rules. If the meaning of dishonesty in the law of theft, for example, were to carry some arcane legal nuance, violence might be done to the reasonable expectations of ordinary citizens.

> **Case 2**
> Adam, who needs some motor oil, takes some from his mother Eve's garage, knowing that she will consent.

[11] In property crimes the fault term 'dishonesty' is an exception.

[12] J. Horder, 'Crimes of Ulterior Intent', in A. Simester and A. Smith (eds), *Harm and Culpability*, Oxford: Clarendon Press (1996) 153.

[13] Malice is an example of a word with a technical meaning. See generally A.R. White, *Misleading Cases*, Oxford: Clarendon Press (1991) ch. 1.

[14] See for example the infamous *Brutus v Cozens* [1973] AC 854 where the House of Lords insisted that non-technical words in a statute should be left, undefined, to the tribunal of fact; cf. A.R. White *Misleading Cases*, Oxford: Clarendon Press (1991).

A conviction for theft requires proof of dishonesty. This requirement protects **honest** citizens from conviction for taking things without permission if, as here, the context renders the taking perfectly socially acceptable. Dishonesty should not then carry a meaning contrary to our moral 'common sense'.

There are numerous examples of judges advocating an 'ordinary language' approach to the meaning of the *mens rea* words and then not reaching agreement upon such meaning,[15] or reaching agreement upon a meaning other than that presented in ordinary speech.[16] As we shall see, it is not always possible to discern whether the reason for disagreement is due to ambiguities of language, conceptual fallacy, or simply the understandable desire to put dangerous villains behind bars. Where a gap is opened up between popular and judicial usage it is pretty rare, however, that such a gap favours individual defendants.

6.6 INTENTION

In theory, intention is central to a cogent notion of criminal responsibility. What marks human action off from other events in the natural world, like the movement of the stars and the snarling of dogs, is that our action has meaning for us. We have intentionality. If we see a human being raise a gun to his eye, aim it at another person, and pull the trigger we (think we) know what he means by this action. We know he intends to shoot, if not kill the victim. He may fail, but we know what is in his mind. If we saw a monkey do likewise we would not know what was in the monkey's mind. We cannot plausibly assert, therefore, that the meaning to be attributed to the monkey's behaviour is the same as in the former case. We have no concept of monkey intentionality. Shooting the gun for the monkey, then, may mean nothing. It may be just an incident of 'monkeyness', like fire is an incident of volcanoes.

From one point of view, therefore, if it is intentionality which separates our actions from the behaviour of monkeys and volcanoes then it is intentionality which forms the basic building block of choice upon which criminal responsibility is founded. Intention is the obvious and clearest form of mental attitude grounding responsibility, but not necessarily the only one.[17] It would make no sense for a criminal justice system only to punish those harms which were specifically aimed at. There must be space for punishing examples of culpable risk-taking, for example.

'Intention', like other *mens rea* words, (presumptively) reflects a degree of fault. Ideally, therefore, the criminal law incorporates a meaning which does the job required, in this case supporting a rational system of blame and punishment. Such a system, as we have seen, should enable crimes involving similar harms to be differentiated consistently according to the defendant's mental element. For instance, it should enable murder (a crime of intention) to be distinguished from less serious killings. With this former crime in mind for purposes of illustration, what is it, then, to intend a consequence?

---

[15] Cf. *Cato* [1976] 1 WLR 110 and *Caldwell* [1982] AC 341.
[16] See *Hyam* v *DPP* [1974] 2 All ER 41: *R* v *Caldwell*, above.
[17] R.A. Duff, 'Acting, Trying and Criminal Liability' in Shute *et al.* (eds), *Action and Value in the Criminal Law* 77; and generally R.A. Duff, *Intention, Agency and Criminal Liability: Philosophy of Action and the Criminal Law*, Oxford: Basil Blackwell (1990); I. Kugler, *Direct and Oblique Intention in the Criminal Law*, Aldershot: Ashgate 2002.

A Everyday usage and its relevance to criminal responsibility

In everyday speech intention is used coextensively with words such as 'aim', 'reason', 'desire' and 'purpose'. A yet more common synonym is the word 'mean'. We intend whatever we mean to do. We do not intend what we do not mean to do. Every child knows this and considers it the ultimate 'knock-down' argument against a threat of punishment. This represents the core meaning of intention, commonly described as direct intention. In *Mohan*, a case on attempt, intention in this focal sense was described as 'a decision to bring about, insofar as it lies within the accused's power . . . (the relevant consequence) no matter whether the accused desired the consequence or not'.[18] Antony Duff has provided a test for characterising this state of mind. The test is whether a given actor would treat his actions as a failure if the relevant consequence did not occur.[19]

> **Case 3**
> Adam decides to kill Eve. Desiring to make her death look like an accident he creates a gas leak in her house in the expectation of causing an explosion when she lights the cooker. Eve dies in the subsequent explosion.

Adam has a direct intention to kill Eve in Case 3.[20] He wants to kill her. He has decided to kill her and would consider his actions a failure if she did not die. It should be noted that the intention exists even if Adam confidently expects his initiative not to succeed. What is important is that the death of Eve is the point of, reason for and purpose behind his action. It is what he means to achieve. Purposive action is the clearest possible case of intentional action. Compare Case 4.

> **Case 4**
> Adam and Eve are having an argument. Adam pulls out a gun and threatens to shoot her. Eve tells Adam he is a coward and would not dare. Without deliberating Adam shoots her dead.

Case 4 also involves direct intention. It might be objected that Adam's action was too impulsive to be intentional. Such a claim is fallacious. Action can be goal-directed without us requiring conscious mental orders prompting us to action.[21] What distinguishes us from monkeys is not that all our actions are calculated to achieve explicit goals. Rather, what we do expresses what we are up to. Action is the **expression** of mental activity rather than its result. Remember this the next time you 'unconsciously' swat an irritating fly.[22]

Not all instances of **direct intention involve desiring a consequence for its own sake**. Direct intention also describes the state of mind of one who decides to bring about one, possibly unwanted, consequence as a means of achieving another.

---

[18] [1975] 2 All ER 193 CA (Crim) per James LJ at 200.
[19] R.A. Duff, *Intention, Agency and Criminal Liability*, Oxford: Basil Blackwell (1990) 61.
[20] Purpose and intention are not completely interchangeable. For example, purpose is a narrower state of mind than intention. I may switch on the TV with the purpose (and intention) of watching cricket and with the intention (only) of switching off again at the fall of the first wicket: A.R. White, *Misleading Cases* 56.
[21] H. Gross (1979) 97–8; cf. A.J. Ashworth, *PCL* (2006) 158; and see Woollin (1999) Cr App R 8.
[22] Cf. *Ryan* v *R* (1967) 121 CLR 205.

Case 5

Adam's wife, Eve, is trapped in a car which is about to be engulfed by flames after an accident. She pleads with Adam, who has escaped the wreckage, to kill her before she is burnt to death. Adam does so by a gunshot through the heart.

Here Adam does not want Eve's death for its own sake but he does decide to kill her and would redouble his efforts if his first shot missed the target, so he satisfies the test of failure. Adam has a direct intention to kill. Compare the following case.

Case 6

Adam is a wicked scientist who wishes to save his wife from imminent death by heart failure. In furtherance of this he kidnaps Eve and surgically removes her heart for transplant into his wife.

Once again, it will be appreciated that Adam does not intend to kill Eve in the sense that her death is desired or aimed at or that he would consider his action a failure if Eve survived. His state of mind is rather one of indifference to Eve's fate. This seems to render him reckless (he could not care less) rather than intentional as to this consequence. On a broader view, Adam's conduct in Cases 5 and 6 is nevertheless intentional. Indifferent he may have been, but he nevertheless 'decided' or 'meant' to kill her. Killing Eve is the means to Adam's end or purpose, so he intends both means and end. This form of intention can be distinguished from what is sometimes known as oblique intention where, once again, it is appropriate to designate a consequence as intended although it was not aimed at or desired for its own sake. Oblique intention refers to those cases where an actor can only achieve his aim at the cost of causing also an inevitable side-effect and he acts accordingly.

Case 7

Adam places a bomb in the hold of an aircraft, piloted by Eve, in which his cargo is being transported. His plan is to blow up the aircraft in mid flight and claim insurance on the cargo. He knows that if his scheme goes according to plan Eve will be killed.[23]

In Case 7 Adam does not directly intend the death of Eve either for its own sake or as a means to an end. The death of Eve is but a side-effect of his plan rather than the plan itself. He would no doubt be relieved if a miracle occurred and Eve survived. Nevertheless because Eve's death is factually inseparable from the successful realisation of Adam's purpose and he knows this, it is appropriate to treat both consequences as intended. Williams has explained oblique intention as follows: 'intention includes not only desire of the consequence (purpose) but also foresight of the certainty of the consequence as a matter of legal definition'.[24]

This tendency to conflate what one knows will happen with what one desires to happen is loosely termed a consequentialist approach. It proceeds from the proposition that since the end result is the same – Adam is not prepared to forfeit Eve's death – then the morally relevant aspect of his state of mind is also the same whether he wanted it to occur or not. A significant problem with this approach is that it is not too difficult to present cases where

---

[23] An example given by Lord Hailsham in *Hyam v DPP, infra.*
[24] G. Williams, 'The *Mens Rea* for Murder: Leave it Alone' (1989) 105 LQR 397, 398.

the analysis seems to break down and its conclusions fail to correspond with our common-sense notions of intentionality.[25]

Case 8

Adam throws Eve, his baby daughter, out of a third floor window in a vain attempt to prevent her death in a raging inferno. He knows that her death is practically certain but acts in the vain hope that a miracle might occur to save the child.

If intention denotes a state of mind and that state of mind is choice, then clearly Adam does not intend to kill Eve although he may foresee her death as a virtual certainty. Having the intention to save Eve's life means that, as a matter of basic logic, Adam cannot also have the intention to kill her. Oblique intention must, at the very least, be restricted to cases where the side-effect is linked to success in the actor's plan. In Case 8, it is not. If Adam succeeds in his plan (saving Eve's life) the result (foreseen death of Eve) would not occur.

Even with this qualification, however, determining a person's intention seems to require account **sometimes to be given** to a person's reasons for acting. This is particularly obvious with oblique intention. If I pull my child's loose tooth out, knowing this cannot be done without him suffering significant pain, only a passing spaceman from Mars could reach the conclusion that I intended to hurt him. The meaning of a word, like intention, seems to require account sometimes to be given to a person's reasons for acting. Consider some further examples.

Case 9

Eve, a doctor, removes the hospital's sole life support machine from Adam who is terminally ill, and transfers it to Cain, who is not. She knows that the consequence will be that Adam dies, but determines to do it since Cain's chances of recovery are far higher.

Let us assume, for the moment, that no special defence is available here. Would we say that Eve intends to kill Adam but that she has good reason for doing so, or would we say that she intends him no harm at all but intends to do all she is able to prevent an unnecessary death? I think that most people would say the latter. Whether they would be right to do so is another matter. There is, in fact, a strong penological logic in deeming the death to be intentional and basing liability, if any, upon the quality of reasons she offers for her conduct.[26] This is apparent in the following variation of Case 7.

Case 10

Eve, a doctor, removes the hospital's sole life support machine from Adam who is terminally ill, and transfers it to Cain, who is not. She knows that the consequence will be that Adam dies, but determines to do it since she is in love with Cain.

There seems little conceptual difference between Cases 9 and 10. In both cases Adam's death can be analysed as an undesired side-effect of a course of action Eve was unwilling

---

[25] For an extensive treatment see I. Kugler, *Direct and Oblique Intention in the Criminal Law* (2002), Aldershot: Ashgate; see also A.R. White, *Misleading Cases* ch. 4.

[26] There is a possibility that the defence of necessity or duress of circumstances would be available to Eve in Case 9, although not Case 10.

to eschew.[27] Either, then, she intends his death in both cases, or in neither. The former conclusion can be made more palatable by allowing her an excuse or justification based upon the objective reasonableness of her decision.[28] As we shall see later this is not the approach adopted by domestic law, which leaves the question of Eve's intention, in both cases, to the jury.

1 Intention and risk-taking

A person's **direct** intention can be determined without reference to his likelihood of success. If A's reason for firing a gun at B is to kill B he intends to kill B, even though he is an appalling marksman and realistically assesses his chances of success as only one in a hundred. What a person intends **obliquely** is, however, only capable of being determined by reference to what he foresees. If, without desiring it, he foresees it to a lesser degree than certainty, say, as highly probable, we have less cause to designate his state of mind as intentional as to the outcome. Deliberate risk-taking of this character may be culpable – it may be recklessness – but it seems too far from intention's core meaning to count as intention. It is, then, important to understand the difference between foreseeing a consequence as (highly) probable and foreseeing it as practically certain.

Case 11

Adam is cast adrift in an open boat with Eve, hundreds of miles from land. There is enough water only for one. Adam chooses to take all the water himself and pushes Eve overboard, not for the purpose of killing her but to be rid of a visible source of moral guilt.

Case 12

Adam is cast adrift in an open boat in shark-infested waters with Eve. Just as dry land is sighted the boat springs a leak. Unless one of them leaves the boat Adam knows the boat will sink with the great likelihood that one or both will die, either eaten by the sharks or by drowning. He throws Eve over the side.

In Case 11 the death of Eve is factually (though not logically) inseparable from what Adam means to achieve. This is a case of oblique intention. Death as a side-effect is foreseen as a certainty, or rather, we should say, as a virtual/moral certainty, as nothing is certain. Adam knows Eve's death is a moral certainty since, although by a miracle she might survive, he has no (substantial) doubt that her death will follow. We would say, because of this absence of doubt, that he means to kill her. In Case 12, however, although Eve's death may be foreseen as (highly) probable it is not so inevitable that the only sensible conclusion to be drawn is that he means to kill.[29]

There is, however, an obvious moral symmetry between Cases 11 and 12.[30] Eve's death in each case is something which Adam is unwilling to forfeit in achieving a more pressing

---

[27] Would it, should it, make any difference to the question of intention if Eve was not a qualified doctor but, for example, Cain's wife?

[28] See note 26.

[29] This is not an argument for the proposition that taking risks of this character with another's life should not be murder: cf. W. Wilson, 'A Plea for Rationality in the Law of Murder' [1990] 10 LS 307; G.R. Sullivan, 'Intent, Subjective Recklessness and Culpability' [1992] OJLS 380; J. Horder, 'Varieties of Intention, Criminal Attempts and Endangerment' (1994) 14 LS 335, 341–4.

[30] And Cases 5 and 6.

ambition. By such reasoning, some have come to insist that oblique intention includes consequences foreseen as probable as well as those foreseen as (morally) certain. Accordingly, the House of Lords held in 1975 that a jealous lover who poured petrol though a letterbox, knowing that her lover's wife and children were inside the house, intended to kill them, whatever else she may have meant to achieve, if she foresaw this as likely.[31] Two obvious reasons underlie this decision. The first is the problem of proof. If we can never know for sure what Mrs Hyam's purpose was, at least we can have a pretty good idea about what she thought would probably happen. We can presume, since she is an ordinary person, that she intended whatever she thought likely to happen. The second is the question of culpability. People who deliberately court risks are often just as culpable as those who act purposively. Lord Diplock's reasoning was as follows:

> . . . no distinction is to be drawn . . . between the state of mind of one who does an act because he desires it to produce a particular evil consequence and the state of mind of one who does the act knowing full well that it is likely to produce that consequence although it may not be the object he was seeking to achieve by doing the act. What is common to both these states of mind is willingness to produce the particular consequence and this, in my view is . . . (intent).[32]

In essence this statement reduces to the following (fallacious) proposition. A person who willingly courts the risk of a consequence occurring is as blameworthy as a person who intends a consequence, since he has it in his power to prevent that harm occurring. Therefore, a person who willingly courts the risk of that consequence occurring, intends that consequence. The problem with this approach is twofold. First, it dresses up a clearly technical meaning of intention in the guise of an everyday meaning. The approach does not reflect a consistent everyday usage and, if judges were truly so interested in what intention meant in everyday speech, the easiest way to incorporate such a meaning would be to leave the meaning to the jury's own good sense. The second is that the technical meaning is inadequate for the task set, namely to ensure that people receive the appropriate criminal label for their wrongdoing. Lord Diplock was right to say that 'willingness' (or choice) to produce a particular evil consequence is central to a cogent notion of intention. However, it is also central to a cogent notion of recklessness and this must render the broad definition inadequate if a distinct line is to be maintained between crimes of intention (such as murder) and crimes of recklessness (such as manslaughter). There is a clear moral difference between deciding to kill someone and deciding to endanger their life.[33] In short, although Mrs Hyam is the kind of person we might wish to convict of murder because she is so wicked, the test adopted to 'catch her' would also 'catch' a lot of people we might prefer to hold guilty of manslaughter – the quintessential crime of risk-taking.

In one situation only is it plausible to treat deliberate risk-taking as a form of intention, namely where the analytical difference between deciding to kill someone and deciding to endanger their life breaks down.[34] Consider the following case.

---

[31] *Hyam v DPP* [1975] AC 55. Others of their lordships used different words to convey the relevant degree of risk. Viscount Dilhorne used the phrase 'highly probable' at 59; Lord Cross 'probable' at 71.

[32] Per Lord Diplock at 63.

[33] This distinction may collapse in certain circumstances (see below pp. 152 and 371–3); also W. Wilson (1990) at 315–18; cf. J. Horder, 'Varieties of Intention, Criminal Attempts and Endangerment' (1994) 14 LS 335 at 341–4.

[34] The Law Commission, LC 304 *Murder, Manslaughter and Infanticide*, have accepted this as a basis for distinguishing intention from recklessness for the purpose of the crime of murder. For discussion see W. Wilson, 'The Structure of Criminal Homicide' [2006] Crim LR 471–85; W. Wilson, 'What's Wrong with Murder?' [2006] Criminal Law and Philosophy 157–77.

Case 13

Adam and Eve, bored with Paradise, decide to play a game of Russian roulette. They load a revolver with one bullet and, in accordance with their plan, take three turns each at revolving the chamber, placing the gun to the other's head and pulling the trigger. On Eve's final 'throw' she shoots Adam dead.

Each spin of the chamber involves a one in six chance of the gun discharging. The degree of risk which Eve foresees is not even probable, let alone highly probable, yet she, unlike the archetypal reckless killers – the motorist, the arsonist, the incompetent safe blower – does more than foresee the risk. She acts for the purpose of creating that risk since, if there were no risk involved, she would not play the game. Indeed there would be no point to it. These are grounds for saying that Eve really does choose death, rather than merely, in Lord Diplock's weak approximation, her willingness to risk it.[35] Here, the everyday meaning of intention might be put under legitimate strain. This insight was picked up by a lone judge in *Hyam*. Lord Hailsham insisted that Mrs Hyam killed intentionally not because she foresaw death as likely or highly probable (although she probably did). It was because she deliberately exposed the victim 'to a serious risk of death . . .'.[36] He would not have made this distinction, one assumes, unless he was seeking to distinguish Mrs Hyam from the average fire-raiser, who takes risks with people's lives but whose purpose in acting is not to expose them to such risks.[37]

2 Summary

It may be helpful to summarise the major points so far. A consequence can be intended, it has been suggested, even where not desired for its own sake, as long as a decision has been made to bring it about. This will normally follow from the fact that a consequence is foreseen as a practically certain side-effect of what the actor is aiming to achieve. Everyday usage is not entirely cogent, however, since it is apt to take into account the reasons prompting a person to action. Where those reasons are deemed good ones, even consequences foreseen as certain maybe deemed unintended (Case 9). Where they are deemed bad ones, consequences foreseen as mere probabilities may be deemed intended (Cases 12 and 13). If transported wholesale into the legal sphere, this could lead to inconsistency and injustice in cases where the jury approve or disapprove of the agent's reasons for acting. 'Intention' in the legal sphere, as in everyday usage, has a job to perform. That job is not simply to allow juries to convict people of crimes they think deserving, but to ensure that people are convicted of the right crimes. To fulfil this job, intention must bear a meaning distinct from that conveyed by other *mens rea* words. As we shall see now the courts have made heavy weather of devising such a meaning.

B Intention in the criminal law: intention, purpose and motive

The above discussion makes clear that in everyday usage a person's motive may sometimes be taken into account in determining his intention. In theory, this should not be the

[35] For a strong challenge to this view see J. Horder, 'Varieties of Intention' at 341–4.

[36] *Hyam* at 54.

[37] He reinforces this viewpoint by distinguishing dubiously between victims who are 'aimed at' and victims who are not, at 55.

case in the criminal sphere.[38] If punishment attaches to people's **choices** rather than their **character**, the question why a person formed an intention to offend should make no difference to criminal liability. For instance, in *Lynch* v *DPP* the House of Lords held that a person who took part in a killing because his life was threatened if he did not, still intended to take part.[39] He was like the man visiting the dentist. His desire to escape from one source of agony led him to intentionally embrace another sort. Having the intention to escape his own death was quite consistent with forming the intention to take part in killing another. He intended the full package. This should be compared with a similar case in which motive and intention were **confused** by the court. In *Steane* the defendant had made broadcasts for the enemy during the Second World War.[40] He had done so under threats that, if he did not do so, his wife and children might be sent to a concentration camp. His conviction for doing acts likely to assist the enemy with intent to assist the enemy[41] was quashed by the Court of Appeal on the grounds that where a person's conduct provides evidence that he had either a lawful intention (protecting his family) or an unlawful intention (to assist the enemy), the jury should be allowed to determine the true intent. *Steane* is a puzzling decision. Having the former (lawful) intent did not, unlike Case 8, **exclude** having the latter (unlawful) intent. Rather it was really the motive for it. The defendant decided/intended to help the enemy as a means to help his family. Perhaps he did not desire it, but, like the man visiting the dentist, he nevertheless **intended** it should happen. The view is widely held that the Court of Appeal, in their anxiety to show mercy in *Steane*, confused intention with motive.[42] A better solution, then, would be for liability to be negated on the ground of duress rather than lack of the necessary intention.[43] No such mistake was made in *Cox*.[44] A doctor was found guilty of attempted murder (a crime of intention) for administering a fatal dose of drugs for the purpose of killing his patient. He did so for reasons of compassion, as the patient was suffering the intolerable pain of terminal cancer, but ultimately he acted so as to kill.

C The meaning of intention in the criminal law

The modern history of intention in the criminal law shows a tension between a purpose-based idea of intentionality and a broader meaning which includes foresight of certainty (or even probability[45]) as an alternative form. This tension reflects the difficult job the criminal law has to do, in particular deciding upon whether someone is punishable or not and, if he is punishable, for what crime. Another difficulty, as we shall see, is that the majority of statements concerning the legal meaning of intention have occurred in the context of murder cases. It may be that the meaning of intention has been slewed, as a result, to support the policy goal that all 'wicked' killers be labelled as murderers irrespective of their actual state of mind.

---

[38] A notable exception is the requirement of dishonesty in property offences. See below.

[39] *Lynch* v *DPP for Northern Ireland* [1975] AC 653.

[40] [1947] KB 997.

[41] An offence under wartime defence regulations.

[42] They showed no such confusion in *Lynch*, above.

[43] As Glanville Williams put it: 'The concept of intention cannot distinguish between the man who assists the enemy in order to save his family and the man who assists the enemy in order to earn a packet of cigarettes. It is only the law of duress that can make that distinction.' *The Mental Element in Crime* at 21; cf. Denning, *Responsibility before the Law* (1961) 27.

[44] (1992) 12 BMLR 38.

[45] See discussion of *Hyam, supra*.

In *Moloney* the trial judge, on the authority of *Hyam*, told the jury that Moloney had the necessary intention (to kill or do serious injury) 'when he foresees it will **probably** happen, whether he desires it or not'. The House of Lords allowed the appeal, disapproving the trial judge's direction and the *Hyam* test of intention. Acting in the knowledge that a consequence is probable or highly probable is not the same as intending that consequence. Quite apart from its pernicious influence on the law of homicide it was quite clear that for the quintessential crimes of intention such as attempts and wounding with intent to cause grievous bodily harm such a broad definition was inappropriate.[46] Lord Bridge said that whether a person intended a consequence or not was a matter for the jury, not a matter of definition, and only in exceptional cases (which this was not) should any guidance be given as to the meaning of intention, beyond the routine explanation that intention was different from motive. The exceptional cases referred to by Lord Bridge are cases where the evidence supports the conclusion that it was not the accused's aim to kill. In *Moloney* and a number of subsequent cases the courts have struggled to agree exactly what the jury should be told.

One version holds that it should be told that knowledge of the certainty of the outcome is intention as a matter of law.[47] The alternative version is that the jury should be told that foresight of virtual certainly is not intention as a matter of law but is a state of mind from which they may infer intention if they feel it appropriate. In *Hancock and Shankland* both these options surfaced in a case in which the defendants had thrown a lump of concrete from a bridge into the path of an oncoming car against whose occupants they had a grudge. There were two reasons why they might have done this. The first was to kill the occupants. The second was to stop them reaching their destination. The House of Lords held that, if the jury was not convinced it was their purpose to kill, it could nevertheless find intention established if they were convinced death was foreseen as a virtual certainty.[48] In *Nedrick*[49] Lord Lane CJ, synthesising the rulings in *Moloney* and *Hancock*, gave the following guidance for judges directing juries **in cases where there is insufficient evidence of a direct intent** to kill or cause serious injury:

> If he did not appreciate that death or serious injury was likely to result from his act, he cannot have intended to bring it about. If he did, but thought that the risk was (negligible), then it may be easy for the jury to conclude that he did not intend to bring about that result. On the other hand, if the jury are satisfied . . . that the defendant recognised that death or serious harm would be virtually certain (barring some unforeseen intervention) to result from his voluntary act, then that is a fact from which they might find it easy to infer that he intended to kill or do serious harm, even though he may not have had any desire to achieve that result.[50]

A tidied-up version of this direction has now been produced by the House of Lords in *Woollin*. W, having lost his temper with his baby son, threw him with much force across the room causing the infant to hit his head on a hard object. The child later died as a consequence of his injuries. W was charged with murder. Under interrogation W admitted he realised there was a risk of serious injury but denied any desire to kill or hurt the child. The prosecution case, relying on *Nedrick*, was that the necessary intention to kill or cause serious

---

[46] See R.A. Duff, 'Intention, *Mens Rea* and the Law Commission Report' [1980] Crim LR 147.
[47] 'The probability of the consequences taken to have been foreseen must be little short of overwhelming before it will suffice to establish the necessary intent', *Moloney*, per Lord Bridge.
[48] [1986] 1 All ER 641.
[49] [1986] 3 All ER 1.
[50] At 3.

injury was present if, when acting, W must have known it was virtually certain that such injury would be caused. His defence, *inter alia*, was lack of intent to cause serious injury.

At first instance the trial judge directed the jury that if they were satisfied that W appreciated when he threw the child that there was substantial risk that he would cause serious injury to it then it would be open to them to find that he intended to cause serious injury to the child. W's appealed against conviction on the basis that this direction was incorrect insofar as it used the words 'substantial risk' rather than 'virtual certainty'. The appeal eventually reached the House of Lords. The House agreed that the judge was in error. He should not have departed from the *Nedrick* model direction which was 'a tried and tested formula'[51] designed to draw a distinct line between intention and recklessness and between murder and manslaughter. Although it may sometimes be necessary for juries to be given guidance on how foresight may relate to proof of intention, this should be exceptional. Otherwise there is a danger that the jury will be confused and assume, wrongly, either that foresight of risk **constitutes** intention or that direct intention requires proof of foresight in addition to purpose.[52] When guidance is given it should be in the form of the clear statement of Lord Lane CJ in the model direction with one qualification, namely substituting for 'infer' the word 'find'. It should conclude with the rider that 'the decision is one for the jury to be reached upon a consideration of all the evidence.'

At first sight it might appear that the House of Lords have finally accepted foresight of virtual certainty as a separate form of intention. If we examine the model direction more closely, however, intention is still left undefined. The direction is couched in the conditional negative; it does not say '**you must** find intention if the defendant foresaw the consequence as certain'; rather it says 'do **not** find intention **unless** the defendant foresaw the consequence as certain'. *Woollin*, like *Nedrick*, reminds us forcefully what intention is not, namely the state of mind of someone who foresees a consequence to a lesser degree of probability than that of virtual certainty,[53] but does not tell us what it is. It seems probable that the court's failure to clarify this issue reflects an untheorised reluctance to remove a little useful ambiguity from doctrine.

1 The effect of *Woollin*

The *Woollin* direction gives the jury all the encouragement they need to convict heartless killers of murder. In *Matthews*, for example, the Court of Appeal made clear that, although foresight of certainty was evidence of, without constituting, intention, nevertheless if the jury were convinced that the defendants knew it was virtually certain that the result of throwing another boy from a bridge into a river would lead to his death then they would inescapably treat this as (indirect) intention.[54] In *Stringer* it went further, possibly too far. A youth of low IQ set fire to a staircase in the family home knowing that his family were upstairs in bed. He walked away when the staircase was ablaze. The Court of Appeal said that there was no need for independent evidence that he knew death or serious injury was virtually certain. The inference that he knew this was irresistible. Accordingly, the requisite intent for a murder charge was made out.[55]

---

[51] (1999) Cr App R 8, at 19 per Lord Steyn.
[52] The Court of Appeal in *Allen* [2005] EWCA Crim 134 reasserted the view also put forward in *Moloney* and *Hancock* that the *Nedrick* direction should be exceptional and only appropriate in cases where the prosecution do not rely/fully rely on the fact that it was the defendant's purpose to produce the consequence.
[53] This state of mind is 'recklessness'.
[54] *Matthews* [2003] 2 Crim App R 461.
[55] *R v Stringer* [2008] EWCA Crim 1222.

On the other hand the ambiguity deriving from the permissive rather than mandatory wording of the direction allows for a pragmatic response where applying the standard meaning would be counter-intuitive. Compare *Cox* with the superficially similar case of *Bodkin Adams*.[56] Here a doctor gave his patient, who was suffering excruciating pain, a dose of painkillers so large that it advanced the death of the patient. Devlin J ruled that as long as the dose was given for clinical reasons (pain relief), the doctor's action, and his intent, were lawful. This intention, in effect, would not transmute into a criminal intent simply because a quicker death was foreseen as a virtual certainty.[57]

How can we reconcile this case with the proposition that motive is irrelevant to intention? The answer is that a person's reasons for acting may help us to decide what an actor was aiming at, but they do not form a separate basis upon which to make moral sense of his actions. If a person's intention was to kill, such that he would experience a sense of failure if he did not succeed, that intention cannot be displaced by a knowledge of why he came to form that intention. On the other hand, as *Adams* shows, only by knowing why the defendant acted as he did can we know what he was trying to achieve.[58] If he was not trying to bring about the death then he was not intending it, directly at any rate. Whether he intended it indirectly is now a question for the jury, taking into account all the evidence.[59] This approach is expressly approved by the Law Commission, who recommend the codification of the existing law in the following terms:

(1) A person should be taken to intend a result if he or she acts in order to bring it about.
(2) In cases where the judge believes that justice will not be done unless an expanded understanding of intention is given, the jury should be directed as follows: an intention to bring about a result may be found if it is shown that the defendant thought that the result was a virtually certain consequence of his action.[60]

In consequence, a jury are not directed that they are bound to find that Dr Adams intended his patient's death if they are convinced he foresaw it as certain, only that they are entitled to. Needless to say most juries will prefer not to find intention established, notwithstanding the defendant's foresight of virtual certainty. In such a case it will either refuse to take the inference that the consequence was intended or seek a further direction from the judge on this point.[61] How should a judge respond to such an inquiry? The weakness of *Woollin* lies in its resounding silence on this issue. Does the judge tell the jurors simply that it is up to them to decide? Does he resort to the first version? Or does he give them some further guidance, as the judge actually did in *Adams*?[62] This is not clear. Implementing the first version (foresight of certainty = intention) would make things a lot simpler. However, it would require the creation of a defence, for example necessity, to ensure that a person who knowingly committed the *actus reus* of an offence, but for a good reason, was not automatically convicted.

---

[56] [1957] Crim LR 365.
[57] This is known as the doctrine of double effect.
[58] See also *Hancock and Shankland*, below.
[59] See *Lynch* and *Steane*, above; Devlin J himself implemented intention in its oblique sense in *Gamble v NCB* [1959] 1 QB 11 and in its direct sense in *Adams*, above. See also Chapter 18.
[60] LC 304, *Murder, Manslaughter and Infanticide* (2006) para. 3.27.
[61] W. Wilson, 'Doctrinal Rationality after *Woollin*'; V. Tadros, 'The homicide ladder' (2006) MLR 601, 604.
[62] Cf. Lord Scarman in *Gillick v West Norfolk and Wisbech AHA* [1986] AC 112, 190, 'The bona fide exercise by a doctor of his clinical judgment must be a complete negation of the guilty mind which is an essential ingredient of the criminal offence . . .'.

The Court of Appeal was of this view in a case involving the legality of separating conjoined twins.[63] The separation was needed to preserve the life of Jodie, the stronger twin with a good life and quality of life expectancy. Without the operation, both would die. With the operation, the inevitable result would be the death of Mary, the weaker twin, whose continued survival was dependent upon Jodie whose major organs she exploited. Deciding that the operation was lawful, Ward LJ and Brooke LJ were clear in holding that a surgeon operating to separate Mary and Jodie would have the criminal intention necessary to support a charge of murder and would need to avail herself of a defence.[64] However, Robert Walker LJ felt able to say that the *Woollin* direction might be inappropriate in cases of 'double effects' such as this, where a 'good motive' cancelled out a bad intention. In this context he approved the principle approach taken by the House of Lords in *Gillick*.[65]

What are trial judges to make of all this in future cases? Despite the dicta of the judges in *Re A*, the general opinion is that foresight of virtual certainly is evidence from which intention can be inferred but is not intention as a matter of law.[66] The Law Commission have recently nailed their colours to the wall on this one in the clearest possible terms. It states that intention is of one form only, namely direct intention, and that foresight of certainty is relevant only in that it provides evidence, possibly irresistible evidence, of intention. '. . . a desire [sic] to bring something about, a desire which maybe inferred from proof that the person in question foresaw that the event in question was virtually certain to come about if they acted in a certain way (which they went on to do).'[67]

D Conclusion

The foregoing discussion raises an important question. Why is it necessary to reflect 'degrees of choice' at all, given the difficulty of pinpointing a satisfactory meaning for the *mens rea* words? If all serious crimes had alternative fault elements of intention or recklessness, this would allow (bad) motivation to be taken into account, and reduce the tendency to manipulate the meanings of words, and methods of proof, so as assimilate them to the defendant's overall 'fault-profile'.[68] As it is, judges, academics and legal philosophers spend far more time than is healthy or necessary debating the nuance of meanings conjured up by the *mens rea* words,[69] particularly intention.

The important justification for retaining gradations of fault despite the above objections derives from the fact that society considers injury by risk-taking as a breach of a different basic moral obligation (to take care) than injury by attack.[70] Since the basic moral

---

[63] Of course problems will still arise in cases outside the medical arena. Cf. *Re A (Children)* 29 September 2000, the case concerning the legality of separating conjoined twins. Robert Walker LJ approved in this context the following statement of Goff LJ in *Re F* ([1993] AC 789 at 815): 'For present purposes I do not think it greatly matters whether one simply says that that is not an unlawful act, or that the doctor lacks criminal intent, or that he breaches no duty or that his act did not cause death.'

[64] See Chapter 10.

[65] Lord Scarman in this case said that a doctor who in the exercise of his clinical judgement gave contraceptive advice and treatment to a girl under 16 without her parents' consent did not (intend to assist or encourage the commission of unlawful sexual intercourse) 'because the bona fide exercise by the doctor of his clinical judgment negated the *mens rea* which was an essential ingredient of those offences'.

[66] See, for example, LC 304, *Murder, Manslaughter and Infanticide* (2006) 58; LC 305, *Participating in Crime* (2007).

[67] Ibid.

[68] Including considerations of motivation.

[69] See N. Lacey, 'A Clear Concept of Intention: Elusive or Illusory' (1993) 56 MLR 621.

[70] It is less easy to see how causing injury by deliberate risk taking is a breach of a different basic obligation than injury caused by mere carelessness.

obligations are differentiated it follows that the obligation actually broken should be precisely identified or labelled so that blame and punishment do not exceed the scope of the defendant's wrong.[71]

Much more could be done to ensure a proper fit between our notion of intentional action and the moral culpability it is thought to denote.[72] The present unacceptable degree of doctrinal ambiguity has been made necessary by

(i)   judicial reluctance to develop a general defence of necessity to entitle certain honourable motives to negative liability for crimes of intention, and
(ii) the present structure of homicide which withholds the label of 'murderer' from certain classes of wicked killer.

If these problems were sorted out, much doctrinal ambiguity could be expected to wither away.

Two reforms can be suggested which might advance doctrinal rationality.[73] The first is to replace the *Nedrick/Woollin* 'fudge' by the earlier proposals of the Law Commission in the draft Criminal Law Bill.[74] Clause 1(a) of the Bill provides:

> A person acts intentionally with respect to a result when
> (i)   it is his purpose to cause it; or
> (ii) although it is not his purpose to cause it, he knows that it would occur in the ordinary course of events if he were to succeed in some other purpose of causing some other result.

The effect of subsection (ii) is twofold. It allows the conviction of those who are doubtful of success in their main project, for example of Adam in Case 7 if he suspected the bomb might not go off. It also prevents conviction where the defendant's purpose, as in Case 8, contradicts the criminal intention alleged.[75] What it does not achieve, however, is to convict those, such as *Woollin* himself who was actuated simply by anger, who know that their action will certainly result in the relevant (prohibited) consequence but whose action is spontaneous and not calculated to achieve an ulterior purpose. To deal with such a case subsection (ii) might appropriately be reworded along the following lines:

> (ii) although it is not his purpose to cause it, he knows that it is certain to occur, barring some unforeseen circumstance, or that it would be if he were to succeed in his purpose of causing some other result.[76]

Only very rarely, then, would the jury need to apply a test other than that which they would uncomplicatedly adopt in everyday speech.

---

[71] See on this J. Gardner, 'Rationality and the Rule of Law in Offences against the Person', (1994) Camb LJ 502.
[72] See G.R. Sullivan, 'Intent, Subjective Recklessness and Culpability', (1992) OJLS 380; J. Horder, 'Varieties of Intention, Criminal Attempts and Endangerment' (1994) 14 LS 335, 341–4.
[73] See generally the debate between A. Norrie and R.A. Duff: A. Norrie, 'Oblique Intention and Legal Politics' [1989] Crim LR 793 and 'Intention: More Loose Talk' [1990] Crim LR 642; R.A. Duff, 'The Politics of Intention: a Response to Norrie' [1990] Crim LR 637.
[74] Appended to *Legislating the Criminal Code: Offences Against the Person and General Principles*. A slightly modified version of this appears in a Home Office Consultation Paper.
[75] This argument was unsuccessful in *Chandler v DPP* [1964] AC 763. A and B had agreed to demonstrate on an airfield as a protest against nuclear weapons. The issue was whether this purpose was 'prejudicial to the safety or interests of the State'. Their argument that it was the direct opposite was rejected. Their purpose was prejudicial if the judge thought it was.
[76] Professor Smith suggests the following modification: 'he knows that it will occur in the ordinary course of events, or that it would do so if he were to succeed in his purpose of causing some other result' (2002) 77.

Clause 1 fails to offer a just solution in cases of good motive such as *Adams or Re A*. It would need to be supplemented, therefore, by easing present restrictions on the development of justificatory defences so as to entitle an acquittal wherever bringing about the proscribed consequence was an undesired, unavoidable and not disproportionate side-effect of action intentionally taken in pursuance of a legal right or duty or in the prevention of harm. The second suggestion is to constitute one particular form of risk taking as equivalent to intention, at least for the crime of murder. Where a defendant's **purpose** is to create a risk of death, as opposed to foreseeing death to whatever degree of probability, this should be treated as an equivalent mental state to that of intending to kill.[77] Terrorists who plant bombs for the purpose of creating terror do not simply act **in spite of** 'knowing of the risk of death or serious injury'. They act in this way **because of** it. This conclusion is in no way diminished by the giving of warnings. If the warning is sufficient to save the public from injury, it is inevitably also sufficient to endanger the bomb disposal experts who act so as to prevent the danger. These are grounds for concluding that planting bombs is a breach of the basic obligation not to kill rather than not to act dangerously.

The advantage of such developments is that they offer to maintain a clear distinction between intention and mental attitudes of lower culpability, while affording a clear and rational basis upon which to justify the treating of certain forms of wicked risk-taking as constitutive of intention. Without them doctrine will inevitably remain unstable.

6.7 RECKLESSNESS

Recklessness sufficient to ground criminal liability may, like negligence, be as to a circumstance constitutive of the crime in question or as to a consequence. If we examine criminal damage, for example, a person can be reckless as to both consequences and circumstances. So Adam commits criminal damage **intentionally** if, in a fit of anger, he throws Eve's mobile telephone onto the floor, damaging it. He commits it recklessly **as to consequences** if, in mischief, he throws the telephone at Eve (who drops it), expecting her to catch it. He commits it recklessly **as to circumstances** if when he throws the mobile telephone he does not know whether it belongs to Eve or him.

A Recklessness in the criminal law

Many serious crimes have intention and recklessness as alternative mental attitudes grounding fault. Crimes of violence under the Offences Against the Person Act 1861 are obvious examples. Although the two fault elements are distinct, there is a small degree of convergence at the top end of recklessness. A person who unreasonably runs a risk of injuring another to a very high degree of probability is reckless as to that consequence. If the risk of injury is virtually certain and he knows it, he is presumed to intend that consequence. Although often treated as equivalents in fault terms, recklessness is, however, a different kind of *mens rea* word from intention. The latter is unequivocally 'morally neutral'. A person may display virtue and vice in equal degrees 'intentionally'. Recklessness, on the other hand, although not strictly a synonym for vice or wickedness, is a word, like dishonesty and cowardice, which can be used pejoratively to signify fault. This semantic

---

[77] See Case 13. The Law Commission, LC 304 *Murder, Manslaughter and Infanticide*, have accepted this as a fault element in murder. For discussion see W. Wilson, 'The Structure of Criminal Homicide', [2006] Crim LR; W. Wilson, 'What's Wrong with Murder?' [2006] Criminal Law and Philosophy.

ambiguity has had an unfortunate effect upon its usage in criminal doctrine.[78] Doctrine in the field of recklessness has disclosed a basic lack of consensus about what the word is doing.[79] Recklessness has been a battleground upon which opposing conceptions of criminal fault have been waged.

The legal meaning of recklessness has oscillated over the years between subjective and objective forms. In its objective form recklessness is a synonym for negligence. Supporters of the objective form argue that an unreasonable failure to attend to an obvious risk of harm provides its own moral warrant for punishment. In its subjective form recklessness means knowingly taking an unjustified risk. Here the justification for punishment is personal choice.

1 The subjectivist stance

The leading authority for the subjective approach to recklessness is *Cunningham*.[80] The defendant had removed a gas meter from an empty house so as to steal money from it. He thus left an exposed pipe with gas leaking from it. He was convicted of maliciously administering a noxious thing so as to endanger life contrary to s. 23, Offences Against the Person Act 1861. The point at issue was whether the defendant had the relevant malice. The Court of Criminal Appeal, quashing the conviction, held that malice requires no 'ill-will' towards the person injured but simply an intention to do the harm done or recklessness, in the sense that 'the accused foresees the particular harm that might be done, and yet has gone on to take the risk of it'. All crimes of malice now carry intention or recklessness as their fault elements.[81]

This approach was adopted as standard in the 1970s, largely and significantly in the field of criminal damage. This is not surprising. The Criminal Damage Act 1971 was based upon recommendations of the Law Commission[82] which itself adopted the subjective approach. The Law Commission in the Draft Criminal Law Bill 1993 endorsed such an approach.[83] Clause 1 of the Bill is a clear restatement of the subjective position:

> . . . a person acts –
> (b)   recklessly with respect to
>   (i)   a circumstance, when he is aware of a risk that it exists or will exist, and
>   (ii) a result when he is aware of a risk that it will occur, and it is, in the circumstances known to him, unreasonable to take the risk.

Two points are apparent in this definition. The first is that the prosecution must prove subjective awareness of the risk, whether that risk is as to the result or the circumstances. The second is that it contains an objective element limiting the scope of liability. The prosecution must show that the risk was, in all the circumstances, unreasonable for the defendant to take. Whether it is unreasonable or not is determined by means of a practical

---

[78] J. Gardner and H. Jung, 'Making Sense of *Mens Rea*: Antony Duff's Account' (1991) 11 OJLS 559 at 574.

[79] See for example G. Williams' response to *Caldwell* in 'Recklessness Redefined' (1981) 40 CLJ 252; J.C. Smith's commentary upon the same case in [1981] Crim LR 393.

[80] [1957] 2 QB 396.

[81] One important caveat to this is murder whose traditional fault element is malice aforethought. This means the intention to kill or cause grievous bodily harm. Reckless as to either of these consequences is insufficient. See Chapter 13.

[82] Offences of Damage to Property (Law Com. No. 29) which itself reflected the view of the then leading commentator of the day, J.W.C. Turner, the editor of *Kenny's Outlines of Criminal Law* (1966), Cambridge: CUP.

[83] Law Com. No. 218, London: HMSO (1993).

equation in which the degree of risk and gravity of the harm are balanced against the social utility of the risk-taking activity. Jumping a traffic light is likely to be deemed reckless if actuated by a desire to get home quickly for tea but not if the desire is to get a seriously ill person to hospital. This reasonableness requirement is also central to negligence as we shall see. Significantly, unlike intention, the 'unreasonableness' requirement allows for the explicit intrusion of some value judgements into prosecutorial decisions and the determination of guilt. It allows, for example, decisions to be taken not to prosecute doctors who conduct high-risk operations and, less satisfactorily, corporate enterprises which take cost-related risks with the public's safety.[84]

(a) *Problems with subjectivism*

Potential problems with the pure subjective approach became apparent in the case of *Parker*,[85] where the accused, frustrated in his attempts to use an out-of-order telephone in a public telephone box, smashed the receiver onto the cradle, so damaging it. On his account, he did so in the heat of the moment, without thinking of the consequences. He was convicted of causing criminal damage and the conviction was upheld by the Court of Appeal. In so deciding the Court of Appeal ruled that a person was reckless not only when he was **conscious of the risk** he was running but also if 'he closed his mind to the obvious fact that there is some risk of damage resulting from that act'. Such an approach might be thought inconsistent with the subjectivist stance encountered in *Cunningham*, since it seems to require no conscious appreciation of the risk courted. Indeed, the case might be thought a good advertisement for the objective test. It is difficult to deny that Parker was at fault, albeit objectively so. We blame him because he allowed himself to lose control, when people of reasonable (good) character would not have done.

The decision is, in fact, quite consistent with a subjectivist approach. The words 'closed his mind to the risk' imply that the defendant knew of the risk concerned without bothering to attend to it. This interpretation was subsequently adopted by the Court of Appeal in *R v Stephenson*.[86] A homeless vagrant suffering from schizophrenia, having made himself comfortable for the night in a haystack, lit a fire so as to keep himself warm. The haystack was damaged and the accused was convicted of arson. Medical evidence was adduced to show that his mental condition would render him less able than ordinary people to foresee the consequences of his action. The judge, echoing *Parker*, directed the jury that the mental element of recklessness was satisfied if the vagrant closed his mind to the obvious risk of harm issuing from his act and that the fact that schizophrenia had caused this closing of the mind did not affect the matter. In effect, the judge directed the jury to apply an objective test of fault. The accused was reckless if the reasonable man would have been aware of the obvious risk of damage to the stack. The Court of Appeal quashed his conviction.

Geoffrey Lane LJ stated: 'the test remains subjective, that the knowledge or appreciation of risk of some damage must have entered the defendant's mind even though he may have suppressed it or driven it out . . . (if) schizophrenia was . . . something which might have prevented the idea of danger entering the defendant's mind at all . . . then the defendant was clearly entitled to be acquitted'.[87]

---

[84] Due to the impact of the requirement that the risk taken be 'unreasonable' in the circumstances; see A. Norrie, *Crime, Reason and History* (1993) 81.

[85] [1977] 1 WLR 600.

[86] [1979] QB 695.

[87] 704.

The distinction drawn, therefore, was between a person who closes his mind (a subjective mental attitude) and someone whose mind is closed (a state of unawareness/inadvertence). The long-term problem posed by *Stephenson* was that the statement went further than necessary to ensure the blameless go free. The acquittal of the vagrant could have been achieved by requiring him to have realised the dangers attending his conduct **had he troubled to think about it**. Taken together the two statements suggest, however, that a person, whether schizophrenic or not, can never be reckless **unless** the risk first enters the mind before perhaps being forced out again by a reluctant conscience. Such a notion of recklessness reflects neither its core meaning nor a cogent notion of responsibility based upon subjective fault. In particular, it assumes that knowledge of (and therefore personal moral responsibility for) risks can only come about via a process of conscious mental deliberation. This is not so. First, as a matter of strict principle awareness should not be necessary for a person to be subjectively at fault. All that is necessary is for the person concerned to fail to measure up to her own standards of carefulness or competence. Indeed, failing to think while doing something extremely dangerous, e.g. driving, is likely to result in the actor blaming herself if harm results. Second, one can know of risks without thinking of them. Human action, as *Parker* partly acknowledges, is not constructed in this 'mentalist'[88] fashion. Most risk-avoidance strategy takes place in a different 'mental world' altogether, namely the unconscious. We **unconsciously** avoid sources of danger – at least when our own skins are on the line. Our knowledge that fire burns, that water drowns, that electricity electrocutes, that cliffs collapse is enough to keep us out of danger without the need for elaborate mental activity on our part.[89] If we substituted the telephone cradle for Parker's own top of the range smart phone suffering a temporary malfunction we can be pretty sure he would not have 'smashed the phone down without thinking'. His mind would have 'miraculously' remained open.[90]

2 *Caldwell* recklessness

In *Caldwell*[91] the House of Lords proposed a test of recklessness which did not require proof of awareness. Some have viewed the case simply as evincing a formal recognition that choosing to act dangerously may be expressed without conscious advertence to particular risks.[92] A more common view, however, is that dissatisfaction with subjectivism led the court to the other extreme of abandoning any pretence that the legal meaning of recklessness should express a defendant's choice to expose others or their property to the risk of harm.

The defendant set fire to a hotel in drunken anger after quarrelling with the owner. He was indicted on two counts of arson contrary to s. 1(1) and (2) Criminal Damage Act 1971. He pleaded guilty to the first count alleging 'simple' arson, but pleaded not guilty to the aggravated form which required proof that he had damaged property 'with intent to endanger life or being reckless whether life was endangered'. He claimed that, because he was drunk, it did not enter his mind that he might endanger life. This argument was rejected at first instance and on appeal, on the broad basis that drunkenness is no defence

---

[88] See H. Gross, (1979) 22–5; White, op. cit. 45.
[89] See J. Brady, 'Recklessness', 15 Law and Philosophy (1996) 183.
[90] A.R. White (1991) 43.
[91] [1981] 1 All ER 961.
[92] G. Syrota, 'A Radical Change in the Law of Recklessness' [1982] Crim LR 97; cf. G. Williams, 'Divergent Interpretations of Recklessness' (1982) 132 NLJ 289.

to a crime of recklessness.[93] The House of Lords went further to give an account of why it was no defence, namely that to be reckless as to a result did not require it to be established that the accused was aware that his conduct provoked the risk of that result so long as the risk was obvious. The fact that the defendant was drunk was, in other words, 'neither here nor there'.

The effect of *Caldwell* was dramatic. In effect, it changed the fault element in crimes of recklessness from (subjective) recklessness to (objective) negligence. What is important is not that the risk was foreseen but that it was obvious, that is, that it **should have been foreseen**. The defendant in *Stephenson* would have been guilty under this test as simple unawareness (failing to give thought) seems to be enough. The decision was followed in a number of subsequent case decisions, most notably a decision of Lord Diplock himself in *Lawrence*.[94] In this case a motor cyclist was indicted for causing death by reckless driving. In the course of his opinion Lord Diplock proposed a test of recklessness similar to that given in *Caldwell*. He went on to say, however, that in deciding whether the risk was obvious (and serious) the jury may apply the 'standard of the ordinary prudent motorist as represented by themselves'.[95]

(a) Caldwell *recklessness: capacity and experience*

Caldwell posed particular problems for the unknowledgeable or inexperienced and those whose inadvertence results from mental or other incapacity. If punishment is a matter the accused's desert, it is difficult to justify punishing those whose failure to conform to the relevant standards is due to the fact that they lack his capacities for foresight, skill and care. If, therefore, recklessness is to be a distinct basis of liability from negligence it makes sense that its distinctiveness should lie in a requirement that the defendant in question had both the 'capacity and a fair opportunity'[96] to have acted otherwise.[97] In *Caldwell* itself Lord Diplock seemed, at one point, to accept that such capacity was central to liability for recklessness. Insisting that the notion of fault proposed is one which is subjective to the defendant, he explained that fault is derived from the fact that a person failed to give thought to whether or not there was a risk in circumstances where, if thought **had** been given (by him), it would be obvious. With this slant *Caldwell* recklessness loses much of its capacity for injustice. It would acquit not only people, like C, who lack the mental capacity to appreciate the risks involved in their conduct, but also those whose failure to appreciate a risk was due to simple lack of knowledge. In *Elliott* v *C*[98] the Divisional Court considered this interpretation of *Caldwell* and rejected it, resulting in the conviction of a fourteen-year-old mentally subnormal girl for arson. The Queen's Bench Divisional Court held that the sole issue was whether the risk would have been obvious to the ordinary, prudent person, **not** whether it would be obvious to the accused if she had thought about it. Such a decision clearly ran contrary to the principle that punishment should be deserved.

3 The retreat from *Caldwell*

Perhaps for this latter reason *Caldwell* never resulted in a wholesale revision of the concept of recklessness in the criminal law. Its influence was largely confined to criminal damage

---

[93] The more precise basis will be examined in depth in the chapter on defences.
[94] [1981] 1 All ER 974.
[95] At 982.
[96] A principle advanced by H.L.A. Hart in *Punishment and Responsibility* (1968). For discussion see Chapter 9.
[97] [1983] 2 All ER 1005.
[98] [1983] 2 All ER 1005.

and dangerous driving, activities which, as has been explained, generate their own reasons for dispensing with a requirement of foresight. In other areas of the criminal law, in particular crimes of violence, recklessness continued to carry its *pre-Caldwell* meaning.[99] The final blow to *Caldwell* recklessness was dealt by the House of Lords in *R v G*.[100] In this case two boys, aged 11 and 12, set fire to some newspapers in the back yard of a shop and threw them under a wheelie bin before leaving. The fire spread to the bin and eventually burnt down the shop, causing over one million pounds damage. The trial judge, applying *Caldwell* instructed the jury to judge the defendants' recklessness by reference to what an ordinary reasonable bystander would have foreseen. As in *Elliott*,[101] they were told not to make allowance for the defendants' youth, lack of maturity or their own inability to assess the situation. The Lords unanimously allowed the appeal and overturned *Caldwell*. To justify departing from a previous decision, the judges did not refer to similar precedents, but instead relied on 'compelling legal considerations',[102] namely legislative intent and fairness. In agreement with Lord Edmund Davies' dissenting speech in *Caldwell*, Lord Bingham found that it was no part of the purpose behind the Criminal Damage Act 1971 to alter the meaning of the term 'reckless'.

Moreover, it was found that the *Caldwell* approach to recklessness '[. . . was] capable of leading to obvious unfairness. [. . .] It is neither moral nor just to convict a defendant (least of all a child) on the strength of what someone else would have apprehended'.[103] The case-specific approach to young defendants was highlighted by Lord Steyn in his speech when he referred to the UN Convention on the Rights of the Child.[104]

The House reaffirmed its fidelity to the principles of subjectivism, and the fact that a defendant's state of mind must be culpable in order for the courts to impose liability. One has to be aware of a risk in order to be properly blamed for it, especially with regard to a serious crime such as criminal damage. It is 'not clearly blameworthy to do something involving a risk of injury to another if [. . .] one genuinely does not perceive the risk.'[105]

Much of the criticism of the *Caldwell* direction relied on the unfairness it created when applied to children, the absent-minded and the inexperienced, in particular in cases such as *Elliott* and indeed *R v G* in the first instance. One solution would have been to adapt the *Caldwell* direction to require the failure to consider the risk to be culpable, a view which had been mooted by the House of Lords in *Reid*, or to include considerations of age and/or other relevant characteristics, in a similar manner to the then test for provocation.[106] Lord Bingham in his lead judgment acknowledged this option but decided against it, principally on the grounds that it would lead to 'difficult and contentious argument' regarding the various characteristics to be taken into account. He also claimed it was a further misinterpretation of the Parliamentary intention behind section 1 of the Criminal Damage Act 1971.

Accordingly, the *Caldwell* approach to recklessness, establishing an objective test for culpability, was well and truly abandoned by the Law Lords in *R v G*, reinstating *Cunningham*

---

[99] *Spratt* [1990] 1 WLR 1073, disapproving the use of the *Caldwell* test *in DPP* v *K (a Minor)* [1990] 1 WLR 1067; *R v Savage, DPP v Parmenter* [1991] 4 All ER 698.
[100] [2003] UKHL 50; [2004] 1 AC 341 (HL).
[101] [1983] 2 All ER 1005.
[102] Lord Steyn in *R v G* at para 53.
[103] Lord Bingham at para 29.
[104] At 53.
[105] At para 32.
[106] *R v Reid* [1992] 3 All ER 673, 690.

recklessness and subjectivism as the benchmark for criminal liability. However, both Lord Steyn and Lord Roger of Earlsferry made allowance for the enlarged notion of awareness which appeared in *Parker*, according to which 'if a defendant closes his mind to a risk, he must realise that there is a risk'. The conviction of such wrongdoers is, according to them, compatible with a subjectivist approach to recklessness and did not warrant the baby-in-the-bathwater approach which characterised *Caldwell*.

It seems therefore that after almost 30 years of criticism and despite an 'unusual degree of judicial solidarity (or stubbornness)'[107] since the early 1980s, the courts have now rejected the *Caldwell* approach and applied a single, straightforward definition of recklessness throughout the range of offences, making the *Cunningham* or subjectivist approach the only valid one. Ironically though, a few months after *R* v *G* altered the meaning of recklessness, the *fault element* of one of the most serious offences, namely rape, reverted back to objectivism. By the Sexual Offences Act 2003 it is not enough that the defendant honestly believed the victim to be consenting. His belief must now be a reasonable one, which means in effect that the *mens rea* of the crime is now closer to objective negligence than subjective recklessness. This suggests that the restated subjective definition of recklessness itself may be unduly generous. Following *R* v *G* a number of issues remain alive, in particular the cogency of an approach to recklessness which ignores the possibility that a person may be **subjectively** at fault for taking a risk of which he is unaware. As Antony Duff has explained, a failure to appreciate obvious risks or, in the case of recklessness as to circumstances, entertaining unreasonable beliefs, may display a 'seriously culpable practical indifference to the interests which the agent's actions in fact threatened'.[108] In his view, deliberately running a risk of which one is subjectively aware is but one manifestation of such an attitude of indifference.[109] Another manifestation, as *Caldwell* itself illustrates, is not attending to the risk at all. This insight is important since it seeks to pinpoint the practical sense in which inadvertent risk-taking may be (subjectively) blameworthy.[110] To fully understand this point let us examine the crime of criminal damage – a perfect exemplar of the notion of recklessness as practical indifference. Representations of criminal damage in the media and popular culture[111] conjure up a vision of a hooligan who 'mindlessly' smashes shop windows, telephone boxes and car windscreens. They offer a picture of a person who relieves personal frustrations by damaging other people's property. The word 'mindless' in this context is significant. It is suggestive of a notion of moral fault which is present **because of**, and not **in spite of**, the actor's thoughtlessness. Such thoughtlessness may be due to anger, intoxication, indifference, or lack of socialisation but not absent-mindedness, inadvertence, inexperience or incapacity which displays no such culpable indifference.[112] There is a strong case in respect of crimes of recklessness for ignoring the easy claim that 'the prospect of causing harm by doing what I did did not cross my mind.' If the boys in *R* v *G* had been 16 they would no doubt have made the same claim. At that age should such a claim avail them as a defence? Or should we punish them because they had the capacity to think about the risk but failed to? Or must we rely on the jury choosing to ignore the issue by concluding that they must have 'closed their mind to the obvious'? If so, this is tantamount to introducing an evidential fiction into the criminal law to

---

107 Cf. H. Keating, note 117.
108 'Intention, Agency and Criminal Liability' 172.
109 Since *Caldwell* also ibid. 158–62.
110 This is the slant preferred in *R* v *West London Coroner, ex parte Gray* [1988] QB 467.
111 A. Burgess, *A Clockwork Orange*, Harmondsworth: Penguin (1996).
112 R.A. Duff, *Intention, Agency and Criminal Liability*, Oxford: Basil Blackwell (1990).

accommodate a legal and moral lacuna, similar to that existing with respect to indirect intention. There is evidence already that this is happening in a manner which goes way beyond the sensible approach in *Parker*. In *Booth* v *CPS* the Magistrates found that a person who ran out into the road without thinking, causing damage to a car with which he collided, knew 'of the risks associated with running into the road, namely the risk of collision and damage to property. Aware of those risks he then deliberately put them out of his mind and, for reasons of his own, ran into the path of a car'. The Divisional Court did not interfere. Perverse the finding may be – who when thinking of running into a road considers damaging a car, rather than their own necks, as the risk to be avoided? – but significant nevertheless in showing how the 'closing the mind test' can be exploited by fact finders when faced with those who cause damage 'thoughtlessly'.[113]

B Conclusion: recklessness and the politics of social control

Throughout this section the view has been advanced that *Cunningham* recklessness is too narrow to serve society's interests and that *Caldwell* recklessness is too broad, at least as it is traditionally interpreted, since it promotes these interests at the expense of individual justice. It punishes not only those who on any account deserve punishing – those who do not think because they do not care – but also those who on any account deserve **not** to be punished – those who lack the capacity or fair opportunity to avoid taking unjustified risks.[114] What is necessary is a test of recklessness which allows society's purposes to be fulfilled without rendering morally innocent individuals instruments of those purposes.

For some, the looseness of the superficially promising 'practical indifference' test illustrates the quandary our society is in. On the one hand, the moral legitimacy of the criminal law is vouchsafed by a commitment to subjective fault. On the other hand, limiting liability to cases of *Cunningham* recklessness will make society a much more dangerous place. Western liberal society lacks the kind of moral and political consensus which makes for effective 'attitude-sensitive' social control. There are substantial numbers of people 'out there' who, without the excuse of suffering mental disorder or inexperience, have values, priorities and behavioural features unconducive to social order. Such people may cause social harms without 'evil in mind' but as *R* v *G* and *Parker* illustrate, this does not prevent the evil from occurring. The indifference test makes the pretence of justifying punishment on the basis of subjective fault, while giving power to the jury to convict simply if they consider the defendant's values to be out of line with their own.[115]

In most cases this objection can be met by basing responsibility upon a person's learned moral experience rather than his adherence to society's values.[116] Punishment is not unfair so long as the defendant has the practical knowledge and experience to enable him to understand, **even in retrospect**, that his behaviour was out of step with widely held moral values.[117] It should not be necessary to show that he agreed with such values or acted in

---

[113] Quoted from *Blackstone Criminal Practice*, Oxford: OUP (2007), 518.
[114] See discussion of *Elliott* v *C*, above.
[115] A. Norrie, *Crime, Reason and History*, London: Weidenfeld and Nicolson (1993) ch. 4.
[116] See Ghosh [1982] 2 All ER 689.
[117] For an interesting exploration of this issue in the context of an analysis of *R* v *G* see H. Keating, 'Reckless Children' [2007] Crim LR 546; cf. Tadros, 'Recklessness and the Duty to Take Care' in Shute and Simester (eds) (2002) 254–7.

conscious denial of them. Such a solution, if not perfect,[118] would do much to reconcile society's interests and purposes and the need to ensure that punishment is limited to cases where the defendant could realistically be expected to have avoided offending.

6.8 KNOWLEDGE AND BELIEF

Whereas intention is the paradigm fault element for result crimes, knowledge is the corresponding fault element for conduct crimes and also for result crimes, in respect of any circumstance it is incumbent upon the prosecution to prove. Recklessness or belief as to such circumstances are sometimes used as alternative fault terms. Examples of conduct crimes with knowledge as a fault element include knowingly allowing a person under the age of eighteen to consume intoxicating liquor on licensed premises and knowingly being concerned in the fraudulent evasion of import regulations.[119] A knowledge element also exists in relation to handling stolen goods, where there is an alternative fault element to knowledge, namely one of belief. The difference between these two states of mind is not easy to fathom.[120] Presumably one knows goods are stolen when one personally witnesses the theft. In all other cases one can only believe. It is not the case then that 'belief is simply a degree of knowledge.'[121] It is rather an alternative fault element which depends upon (often easier) proof that the defendant accepted the existence of a given state of affairs.[122]

Examples of result crimes in which knowledge or belief (or recklessness) as to circumstances may be an element include crimes of violence. A person who adduces evidence that he thought a person was consenting, say, to physical contact, will escape liability unless the prosecution can prove that he did not know or believe[123] this to be the case.[124]

Statutory crimes constituted upon proof that a particular circumstance exists often include an express requirement of knowledge as to this circumstance. This is by no means the invariable rule, however. The task of the court, where a knowledge element is not expressed, will be to construe whether Parliament intended that liability should depend upon such knowledge or whether the omission was deliberate. The presumption is that conduct is **not** to be criminalised in the absence of fault. In cases where the ascription of blame as well as the prevention of harm seems implicit in the offence, the courts have shown themselves willing to read into an offence a requirement of knowledge. Thus in *Sweet* v *Parsley* it was held that the statutory offence of being 'concerned in the management of premises which were used for the purpose of smoking cannabis'[125] was not committed in the absence of knowledge.[126]

---

[118] See A. Nome's critique (1993) 71–81.

[119] See s. 170(2) Customs and Excise Management Act 1979.

[120] See generally S. Shute, 'Knowledge and Belief in the Criminal Law' in Shute and Simester (eds), *Criminal Law Theory: Doctrines of the General Part*, Oxford: OUP (2002).

[121] I am indebted to Stephen Shute on this point for having pointed out a sloppy error in a previous edition of this book, in 'Knowledge and Belief in the Criminal Law'. See previous note. See further E. Griew, 'Consistency, Communication and Codification: Reflections on Two *Mens Rea* Words' in P. Glazebrook (ed.), *Reshaping the Criminal Law* (1978).

[122] See discussion below on 'wilful blindness'.

[123] 'Belief' since one cannot know something to be the case which is, in fact, untrue.

[124] See for example *DPP* v *Morgan* [1976] AC 182.

[125] Contrary to s. 5(b) Dangerous Drugs Act 1965, a provision since repealed.

[126] See Chapter 7.

A What counts as knowledge?[127]

There are three degrees of knowledge. The first degree is actual knowledge. A person acts knowingly in relation to a relevant circumstance when he is aware of that circumstance.

The second degree is known as 'wilful blindness' or 'shutting one's eyes to an obvious means of knowledge'.[128] This occurs where actual knowledge is absent only because, suspecting the truth, the accused turns a 'blind eye' for fear his suspicion is correct. Suspicion, even strong suspicion, does not equate to knowledge[129] but it may nevertheless constitute knowledge where it is coupled with a refusal to investigate the cogency of the suspicion. Clearly this renders the line between knowledge and 'mere suspicion' rather hard to draw. This indeterminacy may seriously compromise the cogency of the wrongdoing requirement thought central to the constitution of criminal offences.[130] An example, discussed by Professor Ormerod, is the offence of being knowingly concerned in the fraudulent evasion of income tax which threatens to criminalise the householder who pays his builder in cash suspecting the latter may fail to declare it on his tax return.[131] In *Westminster CC v Croyalgrange Ltd and Another*, on a charge of knowingly using, causing or permitting the use of any premises as a sex establishment without a licence, Lord Bridge explained the position as follows:

> (to enable effective enforcement of the provision by the council) it is always open to the tribunal of fact, when knowledge on the part of the defendant is required to be proved, to base a finding of knowledge on evidence that the defendant had deliberately shut his eyes to the obvious or refrained from inquiry because he suspected the truth but did not want to have his suspicion confirmed.[132]

The third degree of knowledge is constructive knowledge. This differs from the other two degrees of knowledge in requiring neither awareness nor even a purposive avoidance of the means for learning the truth. It is enough that the relevant knowledge would have been gained had proper and reasonable inquiries been instituted. This degree of knowledge is **not enough** for crimes where the fault element is described in terms such as 'knowing', 'believing' or being 'reckless' as to the existence of a relevant circumstance. It will be enough, however, for certain crimes of negligence where conviction depends upon proof that the accused had 'reasonable cause' to believe or suspect some relevant fact, or some such formula. It will also be enough for those strict liability crimes incorporating a no-negligence defence, where the burden of proving 'due diligence' lies on the defence.

B How extensive does knowledge have to be?

Crimes with a knowledge component often have a number of circumstances constitutive of liability. Does knowledge have to extend to all of them? In *Westminster v Croyalgrange*, for example, there were two relevant circumstances. The first was that premises were being

---

[127] See generally D.N. Husak, 'Willful Ignorance, Knowledge, and the Equal Culpability Thesis', *The Philosophy of Criminal Law: Selected Essays*, Oxford: OUP (2010).

[128] See *Roper v Taylor's Central Garages* [1951] 2 TLR 284; and generally M. Wasik and M.P. Thompson, ' "Turning a Blind Eye" as Constituting *Mens Rea*' (1981) 32 NILQ 328.

[129] *Forsyth* [1997] 2 Cr App R 299.

[130] Cf. Shute, note 120 above, and Tadros, 'Recklessness and the Duty to Take Care' in Shute and Simester (eds) (2002), 254–7.

[131] D. Ormerod, 'Summary Evasion of Income Tax' [2002] Crim LR 3 at 13.

[132] [1986] 2 All ER 353 at 359; the Law Commission favours 'belief' rather than 'suspicion' in their definition of this state of mind: Law Com. No. 177, London: HMSO (1989) cl. 18(a).

used as a sex establishment. The second was that this use was not in accordance with a licence. Was it necessary to show knowledge not only of the use but also that such use was not licensed? The House of Lords concluded that knowledge of both circumstances was necessary. Problems of proof were not likely to arise in practice because, in the normal case, suspicion that premises were being used for the unlawful purpose would amount to suspicion that they were also unlicensed. Both suspicions, unacted upon, would amount to wilful blindness. The important point of principle involved was that, without a knowledge requirement as to both circumstances, a person could be liable without proof of fault where he believed honestly and on reasonable grounds that a licence was in force.[133]

Inaccurate knowledge is still knowledge if the inaccuracy does not bear on the criminality of the accused's conduct. In *Ellis, Street and Smith*,[134] the defendants knew that they were importing prohibited goods contrary to s. 170(2). What they did not know was that the prohibited goods they were actually importing was cannabis and not the pornographic material they believed themselves to be importing. The Court of Appeal held that liability required simply that they knew they were importing prohibited goods.[135]

Inaccurate knowledge of one sort will avail the defendant, and that is mistaken knowledge as to the legal implications of one's action. If the thing the defendant thinks he is doing is legal it cannot be made illegal by a mistake of law. In *Taaffe*[136] the defendant thought he was importing currency into the country and mistakenly thought this was illegal. In fact, unknown to him, he was importing cannabis. The House of Lords held that since he did not know this and since s. 170(2) had a requirement of knowledge, the offence was not made out. It did not matter that he thought he was committing an offence similar to the one charged since (unlike in the case of *Ellis, Street and Smith*)[137] there was no such offence. On the facts as he believed them to be he was innocent of any charge.[138]

6.9 NEGLIGENCE

A Liability for risk-taking: recklessness and negligence compared

When we say that a person is 'negligent', we normally have in mind the synonym 'careless'. The word careless, however, is a word with more than one meaning. Applied to conduct, carelessness may mean:

(1) The person failed to satisfy an objective standard of care either through incompetence, as in 'he raised his glass and carelessly poured the drink down his shirt', or ignorance or thoughtlessness (inadvertence) as in 'forgetting the milk was on the stove he carelessly allowed it to boil over'.
(2) The person acts without caring, as in 'he jumped the traffic lights, careless whether he hit anyone or not'.

The first meaning corresponds with that adopted in the tort of negligence. It refers to cases where the defendant fails to satisfy an objective standard of carefulness or competence in breach of duty and in so doing causes the victim harm.

---

[133] As where for example he was unaware that a valid licence had been rescinded; see Lord Bridge at 358.
[134] (1987) 84 Cr App R 235.
[135] See also *Leeson* [2000] Cr App Rep 233.
[136] [1984] AC 539.
[137] [1987] Crim LR 44. See note 134.
[138] This is a good example of the application of the principle of legality. See Chapter 1.

The second meaning is a synonym for 'recklessness'. Recklessness suggests a state of mind in which the actor appreciates but does not care about the risks he is running, or perhaps does not care enough even to attend to them. Although recklessness may be, and usually is, characterised by negligence, as when a reckless driver drives without observing prudent safety precautions, it need not be. The reckless motor racing driver may not care about the risks to which he is subjecting himself. Nevertheless he may be an object of admiration rather than blame and his level of skill may be such as to enable him to win a *grand prix* without exposing himself or others to a socially unacceptable level of risk.

The essential semantic difference, therefore, between recklessness and negligence is that recklessness, like intention, is an attitude of mind (not caring) whereas negligence is a manner in which conduct is performed (not taking care).[139] Thus:

Case 14

Adam discharges a loaded revolver at Eve, having first checked to ensure the bullet is not opposite the firing pin, causing him to conclude, wrongly, that his action is innocuous.[140]

Case 15

James, a foolhardy shootist, thinks that he can match William Tell and shoot an apple off his son's head. He fails, and kills his son.

On the analysis so far, Case 14 is a case of negligence but not recklessness.[141] Case 15 is a case of recklessness **and** negligence.

As has been explained, since risk-taking is inherent in all human activity, both forms, to be worthy of blame or censure, require that the risk courted was unjustified. Whether it is unjustified or not depends upon such matters as the likelihood of the harm materialising, the gravity of the harm risked, and the utility of the risk-taker's act. Case 16, then, involves neither recklessness nor negligence.

Case 16

As in Case 15 except James is not foolhardy and the apple is a poisonous snake about to bite his son.

The criminal law has not always honoured this semantic distinction between negligence and recklessness. In particular, recklessness, as we have seen, was treated in *Caldwell* as a synonym for negligence. This had the result of compromising the traditional justification for punishing crimes of recklessness, namely that punishment is deserved by those, and only those, who show subjective moral fault.

B Negligence in the criminal law

The Law Commission have provided a clear and accurate restatement of the meaning of negligence. Negligence occurs where a person 'fails to exercise such care, skill or foresight

---

[139] As one commentator, explaining our usage of the word, reminds us, it makes sense to talk of 'being in a reckless mood today', but not of being in a negligent mood: A.R. White (1991) 33.

[140] These facts are based those in *Lamb* (1967) 2 QB 981.

[141] Cf. Lord Goff in *R v Reid* [1992] 3 All ER 673, 690.

as a reasonable man in his situation would exercise'.[142] From this definition it can be appreciated that negligence may inhere in

(a) not being careful;
(b) not being skilful;
(c) not foreseeing a risk attending his conduct.

Applied to the focal crime of negligence, namely careless driving, a person will drive negligently by

(a) taking one's eyes off the road to ogle a passer-by (lack of care);
(b) failing to perform an effective emergency stop (lack of skill);
(c) skidding into a ditch due to braking at normal speed on black ice (lack of foresight).

As the case of gross negligence manslaughter suggests, there may be degrees of negligence. 'Extra' negligence may be imported by the degree of incompetence shown, the objective seriousness of the risk courted, or by the relative inadequacy of any steps taken to minimise such risk. The statutory crimes of careless and dangerous driving are constituted upon this basis. Careless driving becomes dangerous driving when a driver falls 'far below' the expected standard and when such a failure brings obvious risks of danger.[143]

The latter two offences are examples of the rare statutory offences the nub of which is that the defendant acted negligently. More commonly, a crime may have negligence as the fault element attaching to one or more circumstances constituting the offence.[144] An example of a statutory offence where negligence suffices in relation to an offence element is that of insider dealing. It is committed by a person who has information as an insider if he 'encourages another person to deal in securities that are . . . price-affected securities in relation to the information, knowing or having reasonable cause to believe that the dealing would take place (on the stock market)'. The essence of this offence is then that it can be committed negligently as to this latter circumstance.[145] This is so also for the crime of rape which, by the Sexual Offences Act 2003, is committed unless the defendant's belief, if any, that the victim was consenting is a reasonable one.

Yet more commonly, a negligence requirement may infiltrate an otherwise strict liability offence by the incorporation of a no-negligence or 'due-diligence' defence. For example, by section 28 Misuse of Drugs Act 1971, a person has a defence to the otherwise strict liability crime of possessing controlled drugs if he can prove that he neither believed nor suspected nor had reason to suspect that the substance or product in question was a controlled drug.

C The justification for punishing negligence

Criminal liability for negligence is not uncontroversial. It contradicts the usual justification for punishment, namely that people who choose to do wrong choose also the punishment attached to that wrong and so deserve it. Punishment is generally justified on utilitarian

---

[142] Law Commission Working Paper No. 31: *Codification of the Criminal law: General Principles.* 'The Mental Element in Crime' 57.
[143] Road Traffic Act 1988, s. 2A (as substituted by the Road Traffic Act 1991), and Road Traffic Act 1988, s. 3.
[144] Negligence as to circumstances is sometimes admitted as the basis for liability at common law. For example, mistakes in relation to certain defences must be reasonable ones.
[145] Criminal Justice Act 1993, s. 52(2)(a) and (3); a good example of a common law crime which has negligence as a fault element with regard to one circumstance is that of constructive manslaughter.

grounds, in particular that the prospect of punishment may serve to concentrate the mind of those whose activities, when performed badly, threaten the health and welfare of others. Although plausible, the weakness in this justification is that of utilitarian justifications generally, namely that it may allow the individual to be sacrificed for the good of others.

More plausibly, negligence may denote a different form of moral fault than conscious wrongdoing. In the *Herald of Free Enterprise* ferry disaster over a hundred people lost their lives as a result of a grossly dangerous safety system. If it could be shown that with thought, care and the expenditure of a reasonable amount of money such lives would not have been lost, would the operators concerned not be fully deserving of blame, censure and punishment? Should it be an excuse that those involved did not think that the system and its operation were dangerous, when the mere description of how the disaster happened sends shivers down the spine?[146] Accordingly, Hart insists that punishment for negligence is quite consistent with retribution. The justification for blame and censure is not, then, that the accused consciously brought about a criminal harm but that having had the fair opportunity and capacity to avoid it, he failed to do so.[147]

1 Negligence and capacity

The major problem for the criminal law is to decide whether the basis for liability is simply the failure to conform to an objective standard of care; or whether it is also necessary to show that the defendant himself was personally (subjectively) at fault by having the mental and physical capacity to measure up to this standard but nevertheless failed to do so. Although there are instances of the criminal law adopting the latter approach,[148] the general stance taken is the former. So it is no excuse for a crime of negligence that the accused did his incompetent best. For careless driving it is no excuse that the defendant was a learner driver on his first lesson.[149] The flip-side to this is that those who possess a special skill, for example police officers with advanced driving qualifications, are judged against the same objective standards as everybody else.[150] As has been seen, the criminal law's insensitivity to the capacities of the individual defendant has occasionally spilled over into the neighbouring field of recklessness.[151] Even following the House of Lords overruling of *Caldwell*, the potential problems posed by the overuse of the 'closing one's mind' form of recklessness indicates that there is some way to go before a clear distinction can be drawn between the two fault elements.[152]

---

[146] Cf. Lord Hewart in *Bateman* (1925) 19 Cr App Rep 8.
[147] H.L.A. Hart, *Punishment and Responsibility* (1968) 152 ff.
[148] *Hudson* [1965] 1 All ER 721.
[149] *McCrone* v *Riding* [1938] 1 All ER 157.
[150] *R* v *Bannister* [2009] EWCA Crim 1571.
[151] *Elliott* v *C* [1983] 2 All ER 1005; see now *R* v *G* [2002].
[152] See discussion of *Parker* and *Booth* v *CPS* above.

Summary

Criminal liability depends upon responsibility. Responsibility, presumptively, depends upon proof of fault. A traditional legal synonym for 'fault' is 'guilty mind'. *Mens rea* is a synonym for 'guilty mind'. Modern usage, however, restricts the meaning of *mens rea* to the mental state provided expressly or impliedly in the definition of the offence. By convention this is held to include negligence, which is the fault requirement for some offences but is not strictly a 'mental attitude'. Responsibility may sometimes be assigned and punishment may occur in the absence of negligence or any mental attitude. In such cases liability is termed 'strict'.

The three most usual fault terms are intention, recklessness and negligence. What it is to intend a consequence is not yet settled in the criminal law. A preponderance of opinion considers that intention covers two states of mind, namely acting for the sake of a consequence (direct intention) or acting in the knowledge that a consequence is virtually certain even though that consequence may not have been desired or aimed at (indirect intention). However, it is not entirely clear whether knowledge that a consequence is virtually certain is a form of intention in itself or simply evidence from which the jury are entitled to infer intention. It is probably safe to assume that it is the latter.

In standard usage negligence means a failure to satisfy objective standards of care whether due to incompetence, or thoughtlessness or ignorance (inadvertence). Recklessness means an attitude of indifference to, or not caring about, the risks or danger attending one's conduct. Recklessness as a fault term, in common with intention and unlike negligence, denotes an attitude of mind. It is the attitude of someone who consciously runs an unjustified risk. It differs from indirect intention in that it is constituted upon proof of foresight of a lower degree of risk than 'virtual certainty'. Also, unlike indirect intention, recklessness is negated if the risk taken was objectively justified.

Where the fault element of an offence is constituted by knowledge this includes not only actual knowledge but also wilful blindness. Wilful blindness refers to the state of mind of the person who deliberately fails to make inquiries in the face of overwhelming evidence that a relevant fact exists. It is not the same as strong suspicion, which is not knowledge for this purpose. Constructive knowledge, that is the knowledge one would have had if one had made proper and reasonable inquiries, is sufficient for those crimes where negligence as to some fact is sufficient for liability.

Further reading

Duff, R.A., *Intention, Agency and Criminal Liability*, Oxford: Blackwell (1990).

Goff, R., 'The Mental Element in the Crime of Murder' (1988) 104 Law Quarterly Review 30.

Griew, E., 'States of Mind, Presumptions and Inferences' in P. Smith (ed.), *Criminal Law. Essays in Honour of J.C. Smith*, London: Butterworths (1987).

Horder, J., 'Gross Negligence and Criminal Culpability' (1997) University of Toronto Law Journal 495.

Kugler, I., *Direct and Oblique Intent in Criminal Law*, Aldershot: Ashgate Dartmouth (2002).

Lacey, N., 'A Clear Concept of Intention: Elusive or Illusory' (1993) 56 Modern Law Review 621.

Simester, A., 'Can Negligence be Culpable?' in J. Horder (ed.), *Oxford Essays in Jurisprudence*, Oxford: OUP (2000).

Smith, J.C., 'A Note on Intention' [1990] Criminal Law Review 85.

Tadros, V., 'Recklessness and the Duty to Take Care' in S. Shute and A.P. Simester (eds), *Criminal Law Theory*, Oxford: OUP (2002).

Tadros, V., *Criminal Responsibility*, Oxford: OUP (2005) ch. 8.

Wilson, W., *Central Issues in Criminal Theory*, Oxford: Hart (2002) ch. 5.

7 Strict liability

Overview

Strict liability refers to that vast raft of regulatory offences which are constituted without the need to prove fault. Whether an offence is strict liability or not is usually not specified in the enacting statute. It is for the judge to determine whether this was Parliament's intention. Corporate and vicarious liability refers to that form of (derivative) liability where a legal person, say an employer, is liable on account of the wrongdoing of another, say an employee. A corporation is a legal person for the purpose of criminal liability and so can sometimes be criminally liable for the actions or omissions of its members.

7.1 INTRODUCTION

Although the criminal law is the creature of the common law, most criminal offences are now statutory offences. These include common law offences incorporated into statute as well as originating offences. The signal characteristic of common law offences is that they are constituted as a form of wrongdoing or immoral conduct. So murder illustrates how, for the common law, the wrongfulness inheres in the attitude of mind brought to the deed rather than simply the deed itself. For obvious reasons, where a common law offence is incorporated into a statute, a mental element will normally also have been included. In the case of originating statutory offences there may or may not be an explicit mental element.[1] Where there is not, it is a question of construction as to whether a mental element was intended. Offences construed as lacking a definitional mental element are known as strict liability offences.[2]

The best-known examples of strict liability offences are from the field of road traffic offences. They include failures to comply with a traffic signal or to display a vehicle licence. Conviction for such an offence does not depend upon proof that the failure was knowing, reckless, or even negligent. That it occurs is enough.

Case 1

Adam buys a new holder for the tax disc on his car, the other having lost adherence. He mounts it on the windscreen. While parking he notices that it is still not adhering properly. He takes it off and carefully replaces it, taking care to smooth the holder down over its full surface area. He goes off to do his shopping. Despite all the care he has taken, the holder, which is defective, falls off and onto the floor. A traffic warden notices the disc is missing. Adam is charged with failing to display a tax disc.

Adam is guilty of the offence, his conscientiousness, or 'due diligence', being no defence to this strict liability offence.

---

[1] There are some common law crimes including blasphemy, public nuisance, criminal libel and contempt of court.

[2] See generally A.P. Simester (ed.), *Appraising Strict Liability*, Oxford: OUP (2006).

7.2 STRICT LIABILITY OFFENCES

A Public welfare offences

Just as murder, theft, and assault are focal cases of crimes involving a mental element, so are traffic offences, pollution, health and safety, and food regulation focal cases of strict liability.[3] To understand how this dichotomy came about, it may be beneficial to examine briefly some of the history surrounding the emergence of strict liability offences, together with the process by which an offence may come to be constituted as one lacking a definitional fault element.

Although the common law embraced fairly late the principle that criminal liability requires an accompanying guilty mind, that principle was firmly established by the mid-nineteenth century when the prototype strict liability offences began to roll off the statute book.[4] Early examples included those concerned with regulating conditions in factories in the interests of harm prevention.[5] Since the policy of the Acts was primarily to prevent harm, it was thought that the requirement of proving that individual factory owners were individually at fault for dangerous working conditions would leave too much room for manoeuvre. In effect, therefore, these Acts made a substantial contribution to the creation of a two-tier system into which subsequent enactments could be slotted according to the view taken of the policy generating the Act in question.

The Factories Acts were followed by a proliferation of strict liability offences seeking to regulate various matters relating to public welfare, some, but not all, of which were geared to the prevention of harm. These included health and safety, building, pollution and the sale and preparation of drugs, food, liquor and tobacco.[6] Such offences were not explicitly constituted as strict liability offences. They became so by dint of Parliament's failure, deliberate or otherwise, to specify a mental attitude and by the courts' interpreting this failure as a legislative decision to impose strict liability.

B Stigmatic offences

Once it became recognised that liability might be incurred for statutory offences in the absence of fault, judges showed themselves prepared to consider every enactment on its merits. These included offences attacking some form of individualised 'wrongdoing' rather than, as in the case of most early public welfare offences, entrepreneurial 'corner-cutting'. The first case in which this became evident was *Prince*.[7] The defendant was convicted of taking an unmarried girl under the age of sixteen out of the possession and against the will of her father or mother, contrary to section 55 Offences Against the Person Act (OAPA) 1861. It was held not to be of the essence of this offence that the defendant knew her to be under age. Over the years the courts have shown no consistency in their treatment of offences lacking an explicit fault element. In *Hibbert*,[8] decided six years before *Prince*, the

---

[3] F. Sayre, 'Public Welfare Offences' (1933) 33 Col LR 55; G. Williams, *CLGP* (1953) ch. 7; N. Lacey, C. Wells and O. Quick, *Reconstructing Criminal Law* (4th edn), Cambridge: CUP (2010).

[4] Earlier examples date from the eighteenth century concerned largely with the adulteration of food, liquor and tobacco and the attendant losses of public revenue. See *Woodrow* (1846) 15 M & W 404.

[5] W.G. Carson, 'White Collar Crime and the Institutionalisation of Ambiguity' in M. Fitzgerald, G. McLennan and J. Pawson (eds), *Crime and Society*, London: Routledge (1990) 134.

[6] See generally L.H. Leigh, *Strict and Vicarious Liability*, London: Sweet and Maxwell (1982).

[7] (1875) LR 2 CCR 154.

[8] *Hibbert* (1869) LR 1 CCR 184.

accused was charged under the same section. This time, however, he knew the girl to be under age but did not know her to be in the custody of her father. It was held that proof of *mens rea* as to this latter element was necessary.[9] A strict liability offence is not necessarily, therefore, an offence in which liability is strict as to all the elements of the offence. It is one where such liability exists in respect of one or more elements.

More recently, offences dealing with the possession of proscribed drugs have been construed to carry strict liability as to the fact of possession.[10] Neither of these offences, it will be appreciated, has the general character of 'public welfare offences'. They attack a form of wrongdoing rather than regulate the performance of potentially dangerous activities. This is seen most obviously in *Hibbert* and *Prince*, where it is difficult to account for the inconsistency of treatment unless the court was influenced by the greater moral 'wrong' involved in taking a girl from the known custody of her father, than simply taking a girl, of any age, 'off the streets'.[11] The modern trend is for a *mens rea* requirement to be **presumed** in the absence of cogent reasons to the contrary, particularly as regards offences of patent moral wrongdoing. This has led to the welcome marginalisation of *Prince*,[12] although recent decisions indicate that, at least in the area of sexual activity with minors, liability continues to survive the absence of *mens rea*.[13] Most recently the Supreme Court effected a robust restatement of the 'unswerving' policy of strict liability in this area in *R v Brown*.[14]

7.3 JUSTIFYING STRICT LIABILITY OFFENCES

The obvious justification for strict liability offences is that they serve society's purposes. Indeed, it has been argued that strict liability should be the norm for all offences, the idea being that state punishment can only be justified on preventive utilitarian grounds.[15] Questions of desert on this view should be relevant to sentencing, not conviction.

The advantage of this latter proposal is that it would link the resources of the criminal justice system more closely to the needs of society (what do we do with this offender?) rather than those of the individual (is he to blame?). Rather than 500 person hours spent deciding whether Mrs Hyam was guilty of murder and five hours deciding what to do with her, human and financial resources should be primarily devoted to the latter question. After all, that is where the state's primary interest is located.

Clearly such justification stands in opposition to the idea of no liability in the absence of fault, upon which the moral authority of the criminal law is premised. It assumes the operation of the criminal justice system to be at the sole disposal of society. The organising ethic underlying the operation of the criminal law opposes this, and rightly so. The main output of the system is criminal justice which requires, at least as a general principle, individual rights to trump utility rather than the other way around. This means that individuals should not be subject to state coercion except upon proof of culpable nonconformity to

---

[9] Compare also *Cundy v LeCocq* (1884) 13 QBD 207 and *Sherras v De Rutzen* [1895] 1 QB 918.

[10] *Warner v Metropolitan Police Commissioner* [1969] 2 AC 256; cf. *Sweet v Parsley* [1969] 1 All ER 347 for another example of inconsistency.

[11] In theory, this should be irrelevant for crimes of strict liability where harm prevention, rather than punishment for wrongdoing, is the accepted basis for liability; cf. A. Norrie (1993) 90–4.

[12] See for example *B (a minor) v DPP* [2000] 1 All ER 833, below.

[13] *R v G* [2008] UKHL 37. Court of Appeal ruled that strict liability for the crime of unlawful sexual intercourse with a minor was not incompatible with Article 6. See J. Stanton-Ife, 'Strict Liability: Stigma and Regret' (2007) 27 OJLS 151.

[14] [2013] UKSC 43.

[15] Lady Barbara Wootton, *Crime and the Criminal Law* (1963) 35–55.

coercive rules.[16] Such ideas have underpinned recent claims that strict liability offences are contrary to Art. 6(2) ECHR as they effectively negate the presumption of innocence.[17] Such an argument has not borne fruit in the European Court, which treats the presumption as a matter of procedural rather than substantive import.

The utilitarian justification is, however, perfectly cogent in the case of public welfare offences of a regulatory nature which have a preventive rather than a censuring function.[18] The point of strict liability for regulatory offences is to make effective enforcement possible.[19] The *mens rea* requirement is an obvious hindrance to efficient and effective social regulation for the benefit of all. In *Lim Chin Aik* v *The Queen*[20] the policy behind this was discussed:

> Where the subject-matter of the statute is the regulation for the public of welfare of a particular activity – statutes regulating the sale of food and drink are to be found among the earliest examples – it can be and frequently has been inferred that the legislature intended that such activities should be carried out under conditions of strict liability.[21] The presumption is that the statute . . . can be effectively enforced only if those in charge of the relevant activities are made responsible for seeing that they are complied with.

It is not difficult to understand how strict liability might first have been thought justifiable in cases of tobacco or liquor adulteration.[22] The associated social harm was the avoidance of excise duty. By mixing dutiable material with non-dutiable material the duty payable could be reduced. The point of strict liability is to remove the easy strategy of mixing fifty per cent tobacco with fifty per cent straw, paying duty on only the tobacco and then denying all knowledge of how the adulteration may have come about.

Associated with this justification is the presumption that the nature and degree of punishment for strict liability offences should be governed by preventive rather than blaming criteria. Fines are the obvious insignia of strict liability offences as imprisonment is of core crimes. Fines have an obvious (and effective) preventive function if they are pitched at the right level.[23] Most public welfare offences seek to regulate potentially dangerous corporate activities.[24] Fines are a cost like any other business cost. Efficient businesses ensure that unnecessary costs are not incurred to ensure maximum profitability. The highest standards of care can best be maintained where there is a refusal on the part of the legal system to take into account how the standard came to be breached. By fining, businesses can be forced not simply to be reasonably careful but to be scrupulously careful.[25] This may be

---

[16] See H.L.A. Hart, *Punishment and Responsibility* (1968) generally, and for his critique of Lady Wootton's proposals see ibid. (2nd edn) Oxford: OUP (2008), ch. 7; K. Simons, 'Criminal Law: When is Strict Liability Just?' (1997) 87 Journal of Criminal Law & Criminology 1075.

[17] *R* v *G* [2008] UKHL 37; R.A. Duff, 'Strict Liability, Legal Presumptions and the Presumption of Innocence' in A.P. Simester (ed.), *Appraising Strict Liability*, Oxford: OUP (2006).

[18] Cf. F. Sayre, 'Public Welfare Offences' (1933) 33 Col LR 55 at 80.

[19] See W.G. Carson, op. cit. generally.

[20] [1963] AC 160 PC.

[21] Cf. *Salabiaku* v *France* (1988) 13 EHRR 379.

[22] In fact a number of such regulatory measures predated the Factories Acts.

[23] In practice they are not what makes this analysis less plausible; cf. A. Hutchinson, 'Note on *Sault Ste Marie*' (1979) 17 Osgoode Hall Law Journal 415.

[24] Preventing pollution is a typical contemporary illustration of the need for heightened corporate due diligence warranting strict liability. See for example *R* v *Ezechukwu* [2012] EWCA Crim 2064; [2013] Env LR 15; *R (on the application of Thames Water Utilities Ltd)* v *Bromley Magistrates' Court* [2013] EWHC 472 (Admin) [2013] Env LR 25.

[25] See generally C. Howard, 'Strict Responsibility in the High Court of Australia' (1960) 76 LQR 547; A. Kenny, *Freewill and Responsibility*, Oxford: OUP (1978) 93.

unfair to those who do their utmost to comply, but fairness is not the point where blame is not being assigned. Their exaction is no more/no less unfair than a change of interest rates designed to damp down consumer demand.[26]

Outside the field of corporate regulation the justification for imposing strict liability on individuals, say in the field of road traffic offences, turns upon a more delicate weighing of fairness to the individual against the social benefits which attach. The balancing exercise is made easier, in theory, because no stigma attaches and by the fact that the individual's own welfare is indirectly advanced by having such a system. Where non-stigmatic forms of punishment such as fines are adopted, a form of social justice is achieved even if individual penal fairness is unavoidably forfeited. The corollary is that decisions such as *Prince* are objectionable on any grounds.[27]

While these various justifications are plausible, they are not entirely so. Even if it could be shown that strict liability keeps standards up and makes enforcement easier, it is by no means clear that other strategies might not be equally efficient and effective while ensuring a basic minimum fairness.[28] An obvious way of doing this would be for public welfare offences to involve strict liability qualified by a 'due diligence' defence. This is examined below.

7.4 THE PRESUMPTION OF *MENS REA*

Until fairly recently it seemed that the courts were operating under a presumption that, in the absence of an explicit mental element, Parliament must be presumed **not** to have intended one whatever the offence. The high-water mark of such an approach is the case of *Warner*[29] in 1968 where the House of Lords interpreted the offence of being in unauthorised possession of drugs as not requiring proof that the person knew or ought to have known that the thing he possessed was drugs. In the same year this approach was explicitly rejected by the House of Lords in *Sweet* v *Parsley*.[30] It was held that 'being concerned in the management of premises used for the purpose of smoking cannabis' could not be committed in the absence of knowledge of such use. The operative presumption in cases where Parliament does not incorporate a mental element is that one is nevertheless intended unless the statutory context provides otherwise, or unless the nature of the offence is such that it is possible to infer a contrary intention.[31]

In *Sweet* v *Parsley* Lord Reid said the presumption operated as follows.

> Our first duty is to consider the words of the Act: if they show a clear intention to create an absolute offence that is an end of the matter. But such cases are very rare. Sometimes the words of the section which creates a particular offence make it clear that *mens rea* is required in one form or another. Such cases are quite frequent. But in a very large number of cases there is no

---

[26] For discussion of the fit between forms of punishment and forms of crime see Dan Kahan, 'Punishment Incommensurability' [1998] Buffalo Crim LR 691.

[27] Recent case law indicates that this is likely to continue for the foreseeable future. Cf. *B* v *DPP*; *K* [2001] 3 All ER 897; *Brown, supra*.

[28] G.R. Sullivan, 'Strict Liability for Criminal Offences in England and Wales Following Incorporation into English Law of the European Convention on Human Rights', in Simester (ed.) (2006).

[29] *Warner* v *MPC* [1969] 2 AC 256.

[30] [1970] AC 132 at 148.

[31] A strong restatement of this principle was made by the Court of Appeal in *M* [2009] EWCA Crim 2615 concluding that bringing a prohibited article into a prison, an offence newly enacted by the Offender Management Act 2007 amending section 40C(1)(a) of the Prison Act 1952, was not a strict liability offence.

clear indication either way. In such cases there has been a presumption that Parliament did not intend to make subject to criminal liability persons who were in no way blameworthy in what they did. Whenever a section is silent as to *mens rea* there is a presumption that, in order to give effect to the will of Parliament, we must read in words appropriate to require *mens rea*.

The notable modern trend is for this presumption to be respected where the crime charged attacks a form of moral wrongdoing even where the obvious implication is that Parliament intended to impose strict liability. Most recently, in *B (a minor)* v *DPP* the appellant, aged 15, was charged under section 1 Indecency with Children Act 1960 with inciting a girl under 14 to commit an act of gross indecency with him. The question for consideration was whether the appellant's belief that she was over the age of 14 was relevant to guilt. The justices and Divisional Court held that it was not and that section 1 was an offence of strict liability. The House of Lords quashed the conviction, holding that there was nothing to displace the common law presumption that *mens rea* was required.[32] Again in *K* the House of Lords said that unless the wording of a statutory provision rules out the presumption that *mens rea* must be proved, it is implied into the provision even where it appears that Parliament intended otherwise. So, on a charge of indecent assault against a girl,[33] it was for the prosecution to prove that the accused did not honestly believe the girl to be over 16 (and knew that she was therefore incapable of giving consent). The important feature of this case is a readiness on the part of the House of Lords to ignore the intention of Parliament if this conflicts with the principle of responsibility. It is probably not coincidental that both these decisions are subsequent to the enactment of the Human Rights Act which requires judges to interpret statutory provisions in a manner which is compatible with Convention rights.[34] Nevertheless, as Professor Sir John Smith has put it, 'The snag is that we can no longer take the words of a statute at face value – even obvious face value'.[35] The passing of the Sexual Offences Act 2003 removes the need to prove fault in relation to age but these latter decisions are likely to have a continued impact upon the reasoning of courts where a statute is silent upon the matter of *mens rea*, at least with regard to offences of a stigmatic character.

7.5 REBUTTING THE PRESUMPTION

Although these cases seem to indicate that the Supreme Court has set its face against strict liability in the absence of express Parliamentary language, this is not to say that this attitude prevails across the full spectrum of criminal offences. Accordingly, it is important to understand the range of considerations the courts have historically taken into account in deciding whether the presumption of *mens rea* is rebutted. In *Sweet* v *Parsley* Lord Pearce gave the following indication: 'the nature of the crime, the punishment, the absence of social obloquy, the particular mischief and the field of activity in which it occurs and the wording of the particular section and its context, may show that Parliament intended that the Act should be prevented by punishment regardless of intent or knowledge'. These different considerations will now be discussed.

[32] [2000] 1 All ER 833. For incisive analysis of the question whether strict liability offends see 6 ECHR, R.A. Duff in Simester (ed.) (2006).

[33] In *Deyemi* [2007] the presumption was rebutted in a case involving unknowing possession of a firearm due to a preponderance of authorities.

[34] See discussion in Chapter 1 at note 142.

[35] [2001] Crim LR at 995.

A The statutory context

In deciding whether to apply the presumption the first recourse is the words of the section itself in the context of the Act as a whole. If they indicate that *mens rea* either is, or is not, required the court will determine accordingly. If they indicate nothing, the presumption will operate unless it can be displaced. The court will take into account the type of provision enacted. If it is of common law origin or bears obvious comparison to such an offence the presumption may be irresistible. The court will also take into account the context of the provision. It has been held, not always consistently, that where a statute includes an explicit *mens rea* requirement for certain provisions but not for the provision in question the presumption must be that the omission was intentional.[36] This principle informed the House of Lords decision in *R* v *G*. It was held that, by contrast with the provisions of the Sexual Offences Act 2003 in relation to sexual activity with a person **between** the ages of 13 and 16 where the presumption of *mens rea* holds, the presumption is rebutted in relation to s. 5 Sexual Offences Act 2003 in relation to sexual activity with a person **under** the age of 13. It was clear from the wording of the relevant provisions that s. 5 was intended to be a strict liability offence.[37]

The court will also take into account the words of the relevant provision. Certain words express a mental element: 'intending', 'reckless', 'knowing' are obvious examples. Others imply a mental element. Examples include 'permitting', 'suffering', or more obviously, 'wilfully'. Thus in *Sheppard*[38] it was held that the offence of wilfully neglecting a child in a manner likely to cause unnecessary suffering was only committed upon proof of a mental element as to the risks generated by the defendant's conduct. Other words have been interpreted not to imply a mental element. An example is 'cause'. In *Alphacell* v *Woodward* the defendant company was convicted of 'causing' polluted matter to enter a river contrary to section 2 Rivers (Prevention of Pollution) Act 1951.[39] The House of Lords upheld the conviction, construing the offence as one of strict liability. 'Cause' was given this unusual non-purposive meaning since the context seemed to require it. The relevant section made it an offence to 'cause or knowingly permit' pollutants to enter a river. The House of Lords, not surprisingly, considered that whatever 'cause' meant it must mean an absence of 'knowing' wrongdoing. It was a short step to interpreting it to require no fault element whatsoever.

B The social context

Whether such an interpretation is consonant with the approach taken by the House of Lords in *K* is open to question. As we shall now see, the courts are more open to finding the presumption of *mens rea* rebutted in respect of offences which are essentially preventive rather than punitive in character. A comparison of the above two cases, for example, will show that *K* was clearly a stigmatic offence and which carried a substantial prison term. *Alphacell* v *Woodward* was not, and carried a relatively minor maximum punishment. It was easy, then, to interpret *K* as a crime of *mens rea* and *Alphacell* one of strict liability. The approved structure of reasoning in determining 'Parliament's intention' in these cases was articulated by Lord Scarman in *Gammon* v *Attorney-General for Hong Kong*:[40]

---

[36] *Cundy* v *Le Cocq* (1884) 13 QBD 207; cf. *Sherras* v *De Rutzen* [1895] 1 QB 918.
[37] The Court further concluded that the provision did not breach Article 6 of the ECHR [2008] UKHL 37. See above at note 17.
[38] *Sheppard* [1981] AC 394.
[39] [1972] AC 824.
[40] [1984] 2 All ER 503 in the Privy Council.

the law . . . may be stated in the following propositions . . .

(1) there is a presumption of law that *mens rea* is required before a person can be held guilty of a criminal offence;

(2) the presumption is particularly strong where the offence is 'truly criminal' in character;

(3) the presumption applies to statutory offences, and can be displaced only if this is clearly or by necessary implication the effect of the statute;

(4) the only situation in which the presumption can be displaced is where the statute is concerned with an issue of social concern; public safety is such an issue;

(5) even where a statute is concerned with such an issue, the presumption of *mens rea* stands unless it can be shown that the creation of strict liability will be effective to promote the objects of the statute by encouraging greater vigilance to prevent the commission of the prohibited act.

In *M*[41] Rix LJ, approving *Gammon*, presented the following 'default position', namely that 'despite the absence of any express language, there is a presumption, founded in constitutional principle, that *mens rea* is an essential ingredient of the offence. Only a compelling case for implying the exclusion of such an ingredient as a matter of necessity will suffice. Therefore the absence of express language, even in the presence of express language elsewhere in the statute, is not enough to rebut the presumption unless the circumstances as a whole compel such a conclusion.'

1 Real crime and public welfare crime: a false dichotomy?

Implicit in the statement in *Gammon* is a false dichotomy which it would be beneficial to explore, namely that the concerns of 'real crimes' and regulatory offences differ fundamentally, thus accounting for the absence of the *mens rea* requirement in the latter. This is true to a large extent. Regulatory offences are there to advance society's welfare interests, most particularly but not exclusively by seeking to prevent harm. Real crimes are there however to punish culpable wrongdoing which is not to say that murder, treason, and fraud are not crimes provoking 'social concern' and involving threats to 'public safety'. Of course they are but that is not the sole rationale for them. Rather, it is that they are forms of serious moral wrongdoing which require, unlike regulatory crime, public condemnation for breach. This is the reason *mens rea is* required. The case of *PSGB* v *Storkwain* is a good illustration of how these respective concerns of prevention and blame can become muddled in the absence of clear thinking.[42] The defendant was charged under s. 58(2) of the Medicines Act 1968 with supplying specified drugs other than in accordance with a doctor's prescription. He had supplied drugs to customers who were using forged prescriptions, reasonably believing them to be genuine. The House of Lords upheld the decision of the Divisional Court to the effect that section 58(2) was an offence of strict liability. The offence was 'regulatory' in the obvious sense that it sought to regulate practices in the retail industry. The provision dealt with a matter of 'social concern', namely the danger that pharmacists might facilitate the entry of proscribed drugs onto the market. Imposing strict liability would encourage pharmacists to exercise greater diligence than if a *mens rea* requirement were insisted upon.[43] However, the offence in question carried a maximum prison sentence of two years when tried on indictment, implying a recognition that the pharmacist's default might occur for morally discreditable reasons. Imprisonment is the penalty most obviously

---

[41] At para 23. See note 31.

[42] [1985] 3 All ER 4; cf. *Blake* [1997] Crim LR 207.

[43] Although see B. Jackson, '*Storkwain*: a case study in strict liability and self-regulation' [1991] Crim LR 892.

associated with blameworthy challenges to the rule of law and it is the prospect of imprisonment which lends offences their stigmatic character. If section 58(2) was not 'truly criminal',
so justifying the absence of the normal fault requirement, what then could be the justification
for the prospective loss of liberty?[44] A similar charge can be levelled against the decision
in *Muhamad*, where the Court of Appeal ruled that, despite carrying a maximum sentence
of two years, the offence of materially contributing to bankruptcy through gambling was
a strict liability offence.[45] A safer way of distinguishing strict liability offences from core
crimes would be simply to require all offences punishable by imprisonment (a stigmatic
punishment) to be interpreted as requiring *mens rea* (moral fault).

C Penal efficacy

The final factor limiting deviations from the presumption of *mens rea* is penal efficacy.
Paraphrasing Lord Scarman's words in *Gammon*, it is not enough that the subject-matter
of the offence deals with an issue of social concern and public safety. It also has to be
shown that imposing strict liability would be effective in meeting these objects. In *Lim
Chin Aik* v *The Queen*[46] the defendant was convicted of violating immigration regulations
in that he had remained in Singapore after having been prohibited from so doing by official
ordinance. Clearly, immigration regulation is a paradigm case of regulatory provision appropriate for strict liability. It is non-stigmatic and deals with a matter of acute social concern.
Nevertheless the conviction was quashed. The prohibition order had not been brought
to the defendant's attention and there was nothing he could have done to discover that he
was the subject of the prohibition. As a result there was no point in subjecting him to state
coercion for unknowing failure to comply.[47]

7.6 DEFENCES

Crimes of strict liability are not, strictly speaking, crimes of no fault liability.

Case 2

As Case 1 except that Eve, Adam's ex-wife, removes the tax disc from the windscreen while
Adam is not looking in order to create mischief.

Here it seems that Adam will not be liable. As will be appreciated, the basis for imposing
strict liability in the first place is an interpretation of Parliament's intention. Logically,
therefore, even where the wording of a statute is interpreted as carrying strict liability, a
requirement of voluntariness of action (or omission) will usually manifest itself in the
conduct element of the offence definition. The mischievous voluntary intervention of Eve
would seem to take Adam outside the scope of the offence.[48] The absence of the tax disc is
properly interpreted not as a case of Adam 'failing' to display one but rather a case of Eve
'succeeding' in removing one.[49]

---

[44] See also *Gammon* v *A-G for Hong Kong* [1984] 2 All ER 503.
[45] [2003] EWCA Crim 1856.
[46] [1963] AC 160 PC.
[47] Cf. *Reynolds* v *GH Austin & Sons Ltd* [1951] 2 KB 135.
[48] Cf. *Spurge* [1961] 2 All ER 688 at 690 per Salmon J; *Alphacell* v *Woodward* [1972] 2 All ER 475 HL. This principle
     was confirmed by the Court of Appeal in *R v Robinson-Pierre* (2014) 158(3) SJ 37. See Chapter 4.5 at note 34.
[49] The position would be less certain if in Case 2 Eve was Adam's infant daughter.

Further that where the defence adduces evidence of duress, necessity insanity,[50] automatism or other excuse or justification, the normal presumption operates that the prosecution must disprove the defence.[51]

Other common law jurisdictions have developed, by judicial innovation, a defence particular to strict liability offences, namely a defence of due diligence. The significant feature is that the burden of proof is on the defendant. This relieves the prosecution from the burden, perhaps the impossible one, of proving lack of care on the part of another. At the same time it gives the defence the opportunity to show how the occurrence of the proscribed event was effectively unavoidable. In *R v City of Sault Ste Marie* Dickson J said, surely correctly, that to punish under such circumstances for the purpose of advancing collective interests was a basic and unnecessary violation of the principle of the values criminal law is designed to serve, namely individual autonomy.[52]

Due diligence defences are already incorporated, erratically, into a number of offences. An example appears in the Misuse of Drugs Act 1971. By section 5 it is a strict liability offence to be in possession of a controlled drug. By section 28 it is a defence if the defendant can prove that he neither believed nor suspected nor had reason to suspect that the substance in question was a controlled drug. Other strict liability offences are tempered by a 'reasonable excuse defence'.[53]

The courts have not seen fit to develop such defences and so such issues are left to the discretion of Parliament.[54] It must be pointed out, however, that the 'penal efficacy' requirement, if it is to mean anything, should carry with it an automatic due diligence defence. There have been recent suggestions that strict liability offences lacking due diligence defences are contrary to Article 3 of the ECHR. If so, this will mean that, in future, courts may feel the need to interpret strict liability offences as incorporating such defences.[55] If the point of creating strict liability is 'to promote the objects of the statute by encouraging greater vigilance to prevent the commission of the prohibited act'[56] then there is an argument that there is no warrant for creating it where negligence-based liability will be equally effective.[57]

7.7 EVALUATION

How are crimes of strict liability to be accounted for? Are they aberrations from the basic norm of common law liability, namely *actus reus non facit reum nisi mens sit rea*? Or is this latter principle, itself, an aberration from a statutory norm which is strict liability?

The operation of Western legal systems shows that the criminal law exhibits two separate paradigms of responsibility. One, where individual justice is paramount, requires proof of

---

[50] But see *DPP* v *Harper, The Times*, 2 May 1997.
[51] See most recently *Santos* v *CPS Appeals Unit* [2013] EWHC 550 (Admin); cf. *Martin* [1989] 1 All ER 652; *Pommell* [1995] 2 Cr App Rep 607; *Sheppard* [1980] 3 All ER 899; *Burns* v *Bidder* [1967] 2 QB 227; *Hill* v *Baxter* [1958] 1 QB 277, and see Chapter 8. See also T. Ward, 'Magistrates, Insanity and the Common Law' [1997] Crim LR 796.
[52] *R v City of Sault Ste Marie* (1988) 45 CCC (3d) 5; *Proudman* v *Dayman* (1941) 67 CLR 536.
[53] Cf. *R v Unah* [2011] EWCA Crim 1837; *B v DPP* [2012].
[54] See *London Borough of Harrow* v *Shah*, below.
[55] By section 3(1) Human Rights Act 1998 legislation 'must be read and given effect in a way which is compatible with Convention Rights'. Possible rights violated include Articles 3 and 6. See Mrs Justice Arden, 'Criminal Law at the Crossroads' [1999] Crim LR 439, 446, 450; cf. *Salabiaku* v *France* (1988) 13 EHRR 379, *R* v *DPP ex parte Kebilene and others* [2000] Crim LR 486.
[56] Lord Scarman, above.
[57] See G. Williams, *CLGP* (1953) 271–2.

definitional fault. One, where fairness to the individual is trumped by social utility, does not. Neither should be thought misguided or aberrational. These paradigms operate to separate law's censuring and preventive functions where rights and utility conflict. The major problem with strict liability is not the fact that it exists, but that it is not properly identified as such by Parliament and that offence elements often reflect considerations pertinent to the other paradigm.[58]

The resulting penal equation may be expressed as follows:

(i)   If the function of the offence is to express censure for wrongdoing taking the form of a challenge to the private rights and interests or public interests, then punishment must be deserved.[59] Desert in punishment requires proof of fault. At its most basic, fault is absent unless the person subject to coercion had the capacity and fair opportunity to have acted otherwise. Negligence-based liability, or strict liability tempered by a defence of due diligence, is the very least justice demands of such censuring offences whatever additional preventive function they may carry.

(ii) If the function of the offence is primarily to promote public safety/well-being (*Alphacell*), or otherwise to prevent harm to public or private interests rather than to express moral disapproval, punishment can be justified on general utilitarian grounds, whether or not in any individual instance punishment may also be deserved.[60]

Since the justification for punishment relied upon is utilitarian rather than retributive in nature, the following conditions should be met for punishment to be acceptable. The punishment concerned:

(a)   does not exceed that necessary to fulfil the preventive function;
(b)   does not signify any social disapproval of the conduct in question;
(c)   is necessary, by its tendency to ensure greater vigilance and care, to ensure the proscribed conduct does not occur, and could not be achieved in any other way;
(d)   does not carry counterbalancing harmful side-effects.

These considerations together rule out imprisonment, limiting the scope of punishment to fines. In the case of corporate activities, fines must be pitched at the level of any other economic cost. Likewise, in the case of individual activities, they must be high enough to provoke the adoption of standards of unusual carefulness and vigilance. Where a defence of due diligence would equally well secure the preventive aim advanced, it should be adopted.

It goes without saying that it should be the task of Parliament, rather than the courts, to determine the appropriate categorisation of the offence. The most straightforward way of ensuring that the functions of censure and prevention are kept separate is the enactment of a rule of interpretation that offences carry fault elements as to all the elements of an offence unless Parliament provides otherwise,[61] and in all cases where punishment may involve a prison term.[62] This way, Parliament would be required to consider explicitly in relation to every new offence the policy grounds for departing from this norm. Problems

---

[58] For an incisive elaboration of this position see A. Brudner, 'Agency and Welfare in the Penal Law' in Shute *et al.* (1993) 21–53; cf. G. Lamond, 'What is a Crime?' (2007) OJLS 18.
[59] *Prince* and *Warner* should, on this analysis, not have been construed to involve strict liability offences.
[60] See D. Kahan, 'Punishment Incommensurability' in [1998] Buffalo CLR 691.
[61] Proposed by the Law Commission: Draft Criminal Code cl. 20; cf. *K*, above.
[62] Enactment of the Human Rights Act has led judges increasingly to adopt such an approach. Cf. *A-G's Ref no. 4 of 2002* [2004] UKHL 43; and see note 55. See generally Ashworth (2013) ch. 4.

posed by cases such as *Storkwain* could most satisfactorily be dealt with by interlocking measures including both strict and fault-based liability with punishments to match.

7.8 CORPORATE AND VICARIOUS LIABILITY

It will be apparent from the foregoing that strict liability enables companies and other corporate bodies to be subjected to criminal penalties without the need to show that any individual was personally at fault. Subjecting the company to penalty, rather than any individual member of the company who may happen to bear primary responsibility, has a number of advantages. First, it may help to plug an evidential gap. In *Alphacell* v *Woodward*,[63] it could not be shown, for example, which of the company's employees had caused the river to become polluted. What was clear was that the river had become polluted through the defendant company's activities. In other words, the company had caused the river to be polluted. Strict liability, therefore, was key to holding the company accountable.

Second, it ensures that the 'bill' for activities causing social harms is picked up by the entity (the company) which benefits by those activities rather than some hapless individual who happened to be in the wrong place at the wrong time. In so doing it also prevents the company from passing the buck of responsibility, so encouraging the institution of systems and procedures designed to minimise the social harms attributable to its activities.[64]

There are a number of doctrinal mechanisms for imputing liability to the company or other employer. The traditional mechanism is that of vicarious liability. As a matter of general principle criminal liability cannot be imposed on one person for the unauthorised acts of another. The significant qualification to this 'rule' is that liability may be imposed **vicariously** on an employer if the wording of a statute on an 'extended construction'[65] allows the acts of an employee to be attributed to the employer.[66] Once again, *Alphacell* is a good example. The offence was 'causing polluted matter to enter a river'. The company's employees, acting in the course of their employment, had 'caused' polluted matter to enter a river and so the company had 'caused' polluted matter to enter a river.[67] In *Coppen* v *Moore (No. 2)*[68] the owner of a shop was held liable for selling goods (a ham) under a false description when the goods had, in fact, been sold under such description by an employee acting without authority in the owner's absence. This decision is also unexceptionable as a matter of statutory interpretation since the employee was his employer's agent for sale rather than selling in his own right. The real seller of goods can only be the owner. Also unexceptionable is *Tesco Stores Ltd* v *Brent London Borough Council*[69] where Tesco was held to have 'supplied' a video to an under-age person through the act of its employee.

Other words which have been interpreted to carry vicarious liability show the conceptually fragile, policy-driven basis to this interpretive approach to vicarious liability. In *Green* v *Burnett*[70] an employer was held vicariously liable for the actions of his employee in 'using' a vehicle with defective brakes contrary to the Motor Vehicles (Construction and

---

[63] [1972] AC 824.
[64] See also *London Borough of Harrow* v *Shah* [2000] Crim LR 692.
[65] Law Commission Consultation Paper No. 135 *Involuntary Manslaughter*, London: HMSO (1994) (hereafter Law Com. No. 135, London: HMSO (1994)).
[66] *Mousell Bros* v *London and North Western Railway* [1917] 2 KB 836.
[67] Cf. *National Rivers Authority* v *Alfred McAlpine Homes East Ltd* [1994] 4 All ER 286.
[68] [1898] 2 QB 306.
[69] [1993] 2 All ER 718.
[70] [1955] 1 QB 78.

Use) Regulations. In *Melias* v *Preston* goods in the possession of an employee were held, by virtue of that possession, also to be in the possession of the employer.[71]

The restricted scope of the qualification should be understood. If the wording of a statute indicates that the duty imposed is a personal one, vicarious liability is excluded. This may be achieved by importing an express or implied mental element on the part of the employer or by denoting a physical activity requiring, unlike 'selling' or 'supplying', the personal involvement of the employer. In *James & Son Ltd* v *Smee*[72] an employee used a van on company business. Unknown to the company, its brakes were defective. It was held that while the company could be vicariously liable for 'using the vehicle' contrary to the Motor Vehicles Regulations it could not be convicted under the same regulations of 'permitting' the offence. This would require the company to have had knowledge, including constructive knowledge, of the state of the brakes.

An example of a category of offences requiring personal involvement are driving offences. It has been held, for example, that only the driver of a motor vehicle can be guilty of careless driving.[73] It follows that an employer would not commit the strict liability offence of driving without a licence vicariously on behalf of his employee. In both the previous examples an employer may, however, be liable as accessory upon proof of the necessary *mens rea*.

As will be apparent from *James* v *Smee*, the impact of vicarious liability is limited to offences of strict liability. If an offence carries a *mens rea* or negligence requirement with respect to any of the offence elements the prosecution must show that the employer, and not merely the employee, possessed that fault element. In the corporate field, as we shall see, it may sometimes be possible to attribute the *mens rea* or negligence of individual officers of the company to the company itself. This is not a case of vicarious liability but rather of direct liability, the company being 'identified' with its controlling officers. Outwith this specialised situation there is one further case where the *mens rea* of an employee may be attributed to the employer. This is where the delegation principle applies.

7.9 THE DELEGATION PRINCIPLE

The delegation principle applies to those fairly rare statutory offences liability for which may only be incurred by persons of special status, say the owner, occupier or licensee of premises. For example, it is common for licensing provisions to place sole responsibility for satisfying the conditions of the licence on the licensee alone rather than also upon his servants or agents. If, then, such a statute makes it an offence for a person 'knowingly to sell intoxicating liquor' in breach of certain conditions of the licence, a licensee might avoid his social responsibilities by the easy device of delegating their performance to another.[74]

As a result, the rule has developed, to counter these poorly (because narrowly) drafted statutes, that a licensee who delegates the performance of his duties to another delegates also has potential liability for the other's defaults. If the delegatee breaches the terms of the licence, the delegator will be liable as if the relevant acts or omissions constituting the

---

[71] [1957] 2 QB 380.
[72] [1955] 1 QB 78.
[73] *Thornton* v *Mitchell* [1940] 1 All ER 339.
[74] The more extensive notion of delegation apparent in tort law (non-delegable duties of care) does not appear to operate in the criminal sphere.

breach, and any accompanying fault element, were his own. In *Allen* v *Whitehead*[75] the licensee of a café installed a manager, visiting the café only a couple of times a week. He had been warned by the police that prostitutes were apt to congregate in the café, it being an offence under the Metropolitan Police Act 1839 'knowingly' to 'permit or suffer' prostitutes to do so. He told his manager to refuse entry to prostitutes and placed a notice to this effect on the café wall. The manager ignored his instruction and continued to allow known prostitutes to congregate there. The licensee was convicted of the section 44 offence notwithstanding his own lack of knowledge and the steps he had taken to exclude the prostitutes. The knowledge of the manager was imputed to the licensee. It should be noted that liability was dependent here upon the manager having the relevant knowledge. It should also be noted that the decision was dependent upon delegation not employment. If the prostitutes had been allowed to congregate by the licensee's non-pay-rolled spouse, friend, or co-licensee, therefore, liability would still have been incurred as long as delegation had occurred.[76]

This begs the question, of course, as to what counts as delegation. Is a licensee in danger of incurring criminal liability for the defaults of others every time his back is turned or he asks the other to 'watch the shop'? It seems not, although the exact cut-off point between delegating control and the routine and unavoidable mere ceding of control is not at all clear. In *Vane* v *Yiannopoulos*[77] the House of Lords held that a restaurant licensee did not commit the offence of knowingly selling liquor to unauthorised persons[78] when a waitress, contrary to his instructions, sold liquor to youths who were not consuming a meal. Although the licensee was on the premises, he was in a different room on another floor of the same restaurant. At the root of the decision was a clear distaste for the idea that the *mens rea* principle could be dispensed with simply because Parliament had inadvertently required knowledge on the part of the licensee rather than the selling manager or employee.[79] The narrow basis to the decision was, however, that delegation must be complete rather than partial. A person did not delegate authority merely by turning his back or leaving another person in temporary control of a room. It would be different if the licensee absented himself from the premises. Other decisions have adopted a similar stance, although in *Howker* v *Robinson* it was held that a licensee of a pub who was serving in the public bar was liable when his barman sold alcohol to a minor in the lounge bar. It is submitted that this latter decision, in which the matter of delegation was treated as a question of fact rather than law, cannot be reconciled with *Vane*.[80]

7.10 THE SCOPE OF VICARIOUS LIABILITY

Vicarious liability, like its civil law counterpart will only be incurred where the employee or delegatee is acting within the scope of his employment/authority. In other words, the employer/delegator will be liable if the other does something he was employed to do but in an unauthorised way. He will not be liable if the employee does something he was not

---

[75] [1930] 1 KB 211.

[76] *Linnett* v *Metropolitan Police Commissioner* [1946] KB 290.

[77] [1965] AC 486.

[78] Contrary to s. 22, Licensing Act 1961.

[79] The Draft Criminal Code, by cl. 29, would allow liability to be incurred vicariously only if Parliament provided so expressly.

[80] See for example *Winson* [1969] 1 QB 371; *Bradshaw* v *Ewart-James* [1983] 1 All ER 12; *Howker* v *Robinson* [1973] QB 178.

employed to do. So, if in *Howker* v *Robinson* the pub bouncer had served the under-age customer or the barman had sold illegal 'hooch' to a legitimate customer, liability would not have been incurred by the publican.

7.11 CORPORATE LIABILITY

We have seen that an individual may, exceptionally, be liable for the crimes of another under the body of doctrine known as vicarious liability. In the usual case this will be where the crime charged is one of strict liability, the actor is an employee of the defendant and it is possible as a matter of statutory construction to attribute the former's conduct to the latter. Yet more exceptionally the *mens rea* or negligence of the employee (or other delegatee) may be imputed to the employer where delegation has occurred and the wording of the offence limits liability to persons of the status of the delegator. This body of doctrine applies to companies and other corporations as well as individual persons for the simple reason that a corporation is, for most purposes, a legal person. Companies, like individuals, can commit crimes. They can commit crimes directly. They can also commit crimes vicariously. The most obvious of such offences are those which are specifically directed towards the activities of companies and other employers such as health and safety offences.

> **Case 3**
> The board of Asbes Ltd, a manufacturer of asbestos products, passes a resolution requiring factory managers to reduce the operating level of ventilation systems, as a cost-cutting measure, in breach of statutory safety regulations which make it an offence to fail to provide adequate ventilation.

> **Case 4**
> Adam, a factory manager of Asbes Ltd, turns off the ventilation system at his factory, against company instructions and in breach of the same statutory regulations, for two hours a day at the request of the workforce who want to enjoy their lunch-breaks free from the noise of the motors.

In Case 3 Asbes Ltd will be liable directly for the breach of safety regulations. In Case 4 it will be liable vicariously for the default of Adam.[81]

Outside the realm of regulatory offences, **companies** face a broader spectrum of liability for crimes of *mens rea* than **individual employers**. This is because under the right conditions the company may incur liability for the activities of its senior officers. This is in addition to any personal liability of the officers and to any regulatory offence the company may, directly or vicariously, thereby also have committed.

The process by which the company itself, in addition to any individual member of the company, may incur liability is known as identification. This was explained by Lord Reid in *Tesco* v *Nattrass*[82] as follows:

> A living person has a mind which can have knowledge or intention or be negligent and he has hands to carry out his intentions. A corporation has none of these: it must act through living persons, though not always one and the same person. The person who acts is not speaking or acting for the company. He is acting **as the company** and his mind which directs his acts is

---

[81] *Coppen* v *Moore*, above.
[82] [1972] AC 153.

the mind **of the company** (my emphasis). There is no question of the company being vicariously liable. He is not acting as a servant, representative, agent or delegate. He is an embodiment of the company ... within his appropriate sphere, and his mind is the mind of the company. If it is a guilty mind then that guilt is the guilt of the company. It must be a question of law whether (a person) ... is to be regarded as the company or merely as the company's servant or agent.[83]

In its simplest manifestation a small company which is under the sole control of an individual may be directly identified with any offence committed by that individual in his management of the company. A good example is *Kite and OLL Ltd*.[84] Peter Kite was the managing director of a small outdoor pursuits centre run by OLL Ltd which specialised in giving canoeing instructions. He had been told by two of his instructors of inadequacies in the safety measures attending canoeing expeditions and had done nothing about it. Four youngsters were killed when a canoe capsized in heavy seas in Lyme Bay. Both Peter Kite and the company were convicted of manslaughter. Peter Kite **was** OLL Ltd to all intents and purposes. His failure to address the obvious dangers surrounding the canoeing trips was thus easy to impute to the company. Why it should be necessary to convict the company when Peter Kite's own responsibility was only too evident will be addressed later.

It should be noted that the identification principle is of a very different nature than vicarious liability. The latter, it will be remembered, imposes liability on the employer or delegator even for the deeds of minions. For the purposes of direct corporate liability, however, only the conduct and guilty minds of a company's controlling officers can be identified with the company. To be a controlling officer requires more than the exercise of managerial responsibility. It requires the person(s) concerned to represent the company's 'directing mind and will' in the control of the company's affairs.[85]

The distinction has been described as that separating the 'brains' of the company from its 'hands'.[86] In this context the 'brains' include, most obviously, the managing director, company secretary, the board of directors and those others who enjoy sufficient autonomy in the organisation and management of the company for their deeds and decisions fairly to be attributed to the company. The people who take orders from the company, even if they engage in brainwork and devolved decision-making, are its hands. On this basis, Tesco was held not liable for the error of a branch manager in breaching the Trades Description Act 1968 in the marketing of products. By section 24(1) of that Act Tesco was able to avoid liability if the default was not their own but that of 'another person' which it had exercised all 'due diligence' to avoid. The branch manager was held not to be an 'embodiment of the company' – his 'brain' was used to implement policy rather than to formulate it – and so was 'another person' for the purpose of this defence.[87]

It will be appreciated that the effect of *Tesco v Nattrass* is rather perverse. In many cases corporate responsibility will only be incurred where the wrongdoer is to all intents and purposes, like Peter Kite, the company. And in such cases, of course, this is where there is least need since individual responsibility will normally also be present. If companies are to bear responsibility for the acts of their employees such responsibility is most needed in medium to large companies where power is so diffuse as to make it impossible or impracticable to attribute any individual employee default to the conduct of the company itself.[88]

---

[83] At 170.
[84] December 1994, unreported.
[85] *HL Bolton (Engineering) Co. Ltd* v *T.J. Graham & Sons Ltd* [1957] 1 QB 159 at 172.
[86] Ibid. at 172 per Denning LJ.
[87] Cf. *Vehicle Operator Services Agency* v *FM Conway Ltd* [2012] EWHC 2930 (Admin).
[88] See generally J. Gobert 'Corporate Criminality: Four Models of Fault' [1994] 14 LS 393 at 401.

Should companies be allowed to escape responsibility for their misdeeds on the ground of the sheer sophistication of their decision-making processes?[89]

The courts have occasionally shown dissatisfaction with the restrictions on corporate liability introduced by *Tesco v Nattrass*.[90] Evidence of this dissatisfaction is a willingness to recategorise those offences for which imposing vicarious liability is thought appropriate. Indeed, it is perhaps surprising that Tesco's liability was approached via the doctrine relating to identification rather than that of vicarious liability. After all, the offence charged was a strict liability offence, albeit subject to a defence of due diligence. It would surely have made more sense to approach the issue of liability as it was in *Coppen v Moore*. In a more recent case involving Tesco the company was held liable for the acts of a checkout assistant who knowingly sold a video to an under-age customer.[91] Tesco argued that it had no means of knowing that the customer was under age and so could avail itself of the statutory defence that it had reasonable grounds for believing the customer to be over eighteen. This argument was rejected. Since the company would never be in a position to have such knowledge it was clear that liability was strict for them, the due diligence defence only availing them if such diligence could be imputed to the checkout assistant. This decision seems correct as a matter of policy. If there is to be an offence of selling videos to under-age persons, the entity most appropriately held responsible for such supply is the selling company. After all, it is the company which is in the best position to prevent such sales taking place and it is the company which profits if its 'hands' are unresponsive to the directives of its 'brains'.

A more direct broadside on the restrictive notion of identification introduced by *Tesco v Nattrass* occurred in *Meridian Global Funds Management Asia Limited v Securities Commission*.[92] Two senior fund managers employed by Meridian bought into a New Zealand company without Meridian's knowledge. By New Zealand law this placed an obligation on the owners of the shares to inform the Stock Exchange if they knew or ought to have known that their stake gave them a controlling interest. Was Meridian liable for the actions of its fund managers, it being ignorant of the same? On the basis of the *Tesco* test it would appear not. The actions of the fund managers were not the actions of the 'directing mind and will' of the company but of two 'loose cannons' acting independently of that mind and will. Nevertheless the Privy Council held that the knowledge of the fund managers should be attributed to the company and so Meridian was liable. The Privy Council said that in deciding whether to attribute the knowledge of an employee to the company, it was necessary to examine the statute to see whether from its wording and originating policy such attribution would be appropriate. In the case of the New Zealand statute it clearly would be. The whole point of the statute was for the stock exchange to know the identity of those who gain controlling interests in companies. If investment managers could buy controlling interests in companies on behalf of their company and keep silent about it, that policy would be thwarted.[93] It followed that the relevant knowledge-holders in the company would have to be not those who constitute the controlling mind of the company but those who, with the company's authority if not its knowledge, acquired the interest. This case seems to present a more flexible notion of corporate liability than that suggested by the 'directing mind and will' metaphor. One, moreover, which is more

[89] Cf. C. Wells, *Corporations and Criminal Liability* (2nd edn), Oxford: OUP (2001) 110–13.
[90] For a recent affirmation of the principle see *R v St Regis Paper Co Ltd* [2011] EWCA Crim 2527.
[91] *Tesco Stores Ltd v Brent LBC* [1993] 1 WLR 1037.
[92] [1995] 3 All ER 918.
[93] For a similar decision and analysis see *In re Supply of Ready Mixed Concrete (No. 2)* [1995] 1 AC 456.

in tune with common sense in imputing responsibility to a company for the misdeeds of its employees and officers.[94]

7.12 THE SCOPE OF CORPORATE LIABILITY

The traditional theory of the criminal law focuses, as has been seen, upon individuals and their works. Liability requires individual (harm-) causing actors who, through the choices they make, bear responsibility for their actions. This theorisation is clearly at odds with the idea that companies may be criminal subjects. Not only can responsibility not be individuated in the case of corporate wrongdoing, but also, the kind of causal processes so open to discovery and inspection in cases of individual wrongdoing are typically far more diffuse in the corporate setting. And yet it seems undeniable that companies are quite capable of causing harm for which they, distinct from any individuals which comprise them, are the proper focus for a finding of accountability. Indicative of the kind of contradictions issuing from this state of affairs is the mismatch between doctrines emerging in support of corporate liability for homicide and the general juridical context in which punishment invariably takes the form of imprisonment and its justification emphasises a rehabilitative or else spiritual and moral dimension to which companies, by their nature, are resistant. This tension hints at the need for a deeper, richer focus for the institutions of state coercion than the actions of individual 'straws in the wind', one based in institutional dynamics and processes irreducible to the decisions and motivations of individuals.[95]

The scope of corporate liability is in two respects more restricted than that of individuals. First, corporate liability will only be incurred in respect of those crimes which are punishable by a fine. It follows that a company cannot be liable for murder since this offence carries a mandatory prison sentence. One cannot incarcerate a company. If, therefore, the mandatory sentence was removed, a company might theoretically be liable if, for example, its controlling officers authorised the killing of a rival or 'whistle-blower'. Second, a company will not be liable for those actions which are quintessentially human and personal such as bigamy, rape, unlawful sexual intercourse, and incest.[96] It may yet be liable as an accessory assuming, as in the case of marriage bureaux and sex establishments, the controlling officers to be acting within the scope of their office.

A particular problem arising out of the identification doctrine is that it seems ill-disposed to impose liability for crimes of violence. Until recently this was thought to be attributable to the nature of crimes of violence themselves. They are committed by real people rather than abstract entities.[97] It is largely for this reason that corporate liability for personal injury has taken the regulatory route. Recently, however, the ability of companies to conduct their activities in flagrant disregard for the health and safety of employees and members of the public has become an object of widespread concern. A conviction under health and safety regulations just will not hit the spot in cases like the Zeebrugge ferry disaster, where safety systems instituted by P&O were found grievously wanting. In a prosecution of the company and certain employees of the company arising out of this disaster, the argument was rejected that manslaughter could only be committed by a natural person. A corporate body may now be indicted for manslaughter. At common law so long as there were persons, capable of

---

[94] See also *Seaboard Offshore Ltd* v *Secretary of State for Transport* [1994] 2 All ER 99 which suggests that direct corporate liability may be incurred for a corporate failure to take reasonable steps to prevent harmful outcomes.
[95] C. Wells, *Corporations and Criminal Responsibility* (2001).
[96] *ICR Haulage Ltd* [1944] KB 551.
[97] *Cory Bros Ltd* [1927] 1 KB 810; *Meridian Global Funds Management Asia Limited* v *Securities Commission* at 925 per Lord Hoffmann.

identification with the company, whose conduct and mental state in discharging their func-tion satisfies the offence definition, this was sufficient to impute liability to the company.[98] By the Corporate Manslaughter and Corporate Homicide Act 2007 liability for corporate manslaughter may arise, otherwise than by virtue of the doctrine of identification, if its senior management is implicated in a gross breach of a duty of care which causes death.[99]

7.13 PROBLEMS OF ATTRIBUTION

To fully understand the context of the passing of the 2007 Act it will be beneficial to look more closely at the P&O case in which, although it was conceded that a prosecution for corporate manslaughter might properly be brought, the prosecutions of both company and individuals failed. To appreciate why, it is necessary to examine more closely the general context within which the ferry capsized. The immediate cause of the sinking was that the ferry set sail with the bow doors still open. The responsibility for closing the doors was with the assistant-bosun, but he was asleep. The chief officer had the responsibility of checking to ensure the ferry did not sail without the doors being closed, which he had failed to do. Without more, this would probably mean that one or other of them, or indeed both of them, were guilty of manslaughter. The decision not to prosecute these two was taken by the prosecution on the ground that it would not have been in the public interest to do so. This would have rendered these two 'hands of the company' scapegoats for more general systemic defaults, which would have been likely to further fuel dissatisfaction against the company. Other officers of the company had pinpointed the risk of the ferry sailing with the doors open. Indeed it had happened several times before but without mishap. They had recommended a warning light be installed on the bridge so that the captain would be aware that the doors were still open. This recommendation did not reach the attention of a responsible officer or, if it did, it was not acted upon. One way or another, what, in hindsight, appears to be an arresting danger was not translated by senior manage-ment into effective safety procedures and systems. The Sheen Inquiry into the tragedy pinpointed the failure of P&O to devise a safe system for the operation of the ferries, which failure fell far below what could reasonably have been expected.[100]

Why, then, given all these various individual and systemic defaults, was **the company** not liable? The answer is straightforward and calls into question the appropriateness of derivative liability as a basis for punishing companies. First, consider the company's potential liability for the conduct of the assistant-bosun and chief officer. The company cannot be vicariously liable in manslaughter for the actions of the two crewmen since manslaughter is a crime requiring proof of fault and so fault on the part of the company must be established. Although the **actions** of an employee can be attributed to the company, his *mens rea* cannot be unless he can be identified with the company. This was not such a case: the assistant-bosun and chief officer were hands, not brains.

This leaves open the possibility that the company may be identified with the defaults of its senior management – its directing mind. However, such was the amorphous command structure of the company that no individual or number of individuals could be shown to be person(s) at fault, which fault could then be attributed to the company. It was the company's (risk-identifying and removing) system which was at fault, not the conduct of any individual within the system.

---

[98] [1991] Crim LR 695. See generally Lacey, Wells and Quick (2010) 235–50.
[99] For discussion see *infra*.
[100] *MV Herald of Free Enterprise*: Report of the Court (No. 8074), Department of Transport (1987) para. 8.50.

It might be argued that where responsibility for an event is shared amongst a number of functionaries, whether hands or minds, responsibility should be 'aggregated' such that the 'acts, omissions and mental states of more than one person within (the) company . . . be combined in order to satisfy the elements of a crime'.[101] Such an argument appears to have been rejected, by implication, in another of the judgments arising out of the Zeebrugge disaster.[102] As Smith and Hogan argue, such a conclusion is probably correct where the offence element to be proved is intention, knowledge, recklessness, belief or other **mental attitude**. Two innocent states of mind do not make one guilty state of mind. It is probably not correct where the fault element is negligence. A few trivial individual lapses combined might make one case of (corporate) negligence. And a 'series of minor failures by officers of the company might add up to a gross breach by the company of its duty of care'[103] such that liability for gross negligence manslaughter might now properly be incurred.[104] Such a possibility was not entertained in *Attorney-General's Reference (No. 2 of 1999)*, a case arising out of the Southall train disaster in which the Court of Appeal affirmed the identification doctrine as the basis for corporate liability for manslaughter.[105]

In 1996 the Law Commission proposed, in the narrow field of corporate manslaughter, the creation of an alternative offence of corporate killing which could be prosecuted in those cases, such as *P&O Ferries*, where a gross management failure of the company[106] is not fairly attributable to the defaults of individual officers or employees.[107] In 2000 the Government issued a consultation paper based on these proposals[108] which it followed up with a modified set of proposals and draft Bill in 2005. The Bill became law in July 2007.[109] The effect of the Act is to abolish gross negligence manslaughter in so far as it currently applies to companies replacing it with an offence of 'corporate manslaughter'. By section 1 of the Corporate Manslaughter and Corporate Homicide Act 2007

(1) an organisation[110] to which this section applies is guilty of an offence if the way in which its activities are managed or organised—
   (a) causes a person's death, and
   (b) amounts to a gross breach of a relevant duty of care owed by the organisation to the deceased.

Although a welcome move in the right direction it should be noted that this is a more restrictive provision that that first proposed by the Law Commission. This is because by subsection (3) the organisation is guilty 'only if the way in which its activities are managed or organised by its senior management is a substantial element in the breach referred to in

[101] J. Gobert, op. cit. at 404 and see C. Wells, *Corporations and Criminal Responsibility* (2001).
[102] *R v HM Coroner for East Kent, ex parte Spooner* (1989) 88 Cr App Rep 10 at 17 per Bingham J.
[103] Smith & Hogan (2011) at 189; cf. J. Gobert, op. cit. 403–6.
[104] This was not an option in *P&O European Ferries Ltd* since manslaughter was at this time a crime of recklessness the fault element in which could not be aggregated in the same way as negligence. For a criticism of this aspect of the decision see C. Wells, 'Law Commission on Involuntary Manslaughter' [1996] Crim LR 545 at 548–53.
[105] [2000] Crim LR 475, and see the critical commentary thereon.
[106] Defined as occurring if 'the way in which the company's activities are managed or organised fails to ensure the health and safety of persons employed in or affected by those activities': cl. 4(2)(a); *P&O European Ferries (Dover)* (1991) 93 Cr App R 72.
[107] Law Com., *Legislating the Criminal Code: Involuntary Manslaughter*, Law Com. No. 237 (1996); Draft Involuntary Homicide Bill, cl. 4(1), (2).
[108] Home Office, *Reforming the Law on Involuntary Manslaughter: the Government's Proposals*, London: HMSO (2000).
[109] Home Office, *Corporate Manslaughter: the Government's Draft Bill for Reform* Cm 6497, London: Home Office (2005).
[110] The organisations to which this section applies include corporations, local authorities, police forces; a partnership, or a trade union or employers' association, that is an employer and certain Crown Bodies listed in Schedule 1 of the Act.

subsection (1)'. Its original proposals for corporate killing referred only to 'management failure' which would include any management activity at any level of the company which was so badly performed as to result in death. As Chris Clarkson argues, this is a weakness in the new Act turning attention away from the company and back onto individuals, and also failing precisely to delineate the attributes of senior as opposed to lesser managers.[111] In short although prosecution will become easier to mount they will remain procedurally complex and less likely to be useful in the very cases where they are most needed, cases of gross organisational failure. More detailed discussion relating to the conduct and fault element of the offences will occur in Chapter 12.

7.14 WHY PUNISH COMPANIES?

It was explained earlier that corporate liability has grown up on the back of vicarious liability, itself a necessary adjunct of an effective system of strict liability regulatory offences. If, say, edicts relating to public health and safety are to work, the entity who bears responsibility for breaches of such regulations must be the employer rather than the employee whether that employer is an individual or a corporation. Within the framework of regulatory offences the point of punishing companies is to prevent harm, not to apportion blame. If individuals are to blame they can be punished separately on retributive grounds, but there still remains a purpose in punishing the company, namely effective enforcement.[112] It has been argued that effective corporate regulation can, in fact, best be achieved by a more extensive system of vicarious liability, tempered in the case of serious offences such as *P&O Ferries* by a defence of due diligence. Cases such as *Meridian* and *Tesco* v *Brent* may show the way forward in this respect. Indeed, vicarious liability may well be an improvement on the present position. The straitjacket imposed by the identification doctrine in cases where fault is required but harm prevention is still the point of the offence, is a pernicious one. *Tesco* v *Brent* makes far more sense of the point of corporate regulation than *Tesco* v *Nattrass*. A further obvious improvement, unfortunately missing from the 2007 Act, would be to allow individuals within the company to bear secondary party liability. As has been widely argued the possibility of a conviction for manslaughter would tend to concentrate the minds of company officers quite effectively.[113]

The desirability of any derivative model of corporate fault has, however, been questioned and indeed, was rejected by the Law Commission in their 1996 Report. Not only is it deficient where responsibility for wrongdoing is not capable of being identified with the company. It also fails to capture the obvious truth, particularly evident in disaster cases involving large companies, that the realities underpinning unsafe corporate practices are often not reducible to the aims, ambitions and attitudes of individuals wherever situated in the organisational hierarchy. They may reflect a culture of indifference or non-compliance for which no current member of the company is responsible.[114]

---

[111] 'Senior management', in relation to an organisation, means the persons who play significant roles in (i) the making of decisions about how the whole or a substantial part of its activities are to be managed or organised, or (ii) the actual managing or organising of the whole or a substantial part of those activities.

[112] See generally Law Commission Consultation Paper No. 195, *Criminal Liability in Regulatory Contexts*, London: TSO (2010).

[113] C.M.V. Clarkson, 'Corporate Manslaughter: Yet More Government Proposals' [2005] Crim LR 677–89; Frank Wright [2007] Crim LR.

[114] J. Gobert, op. cit. 407; cf. S. Field and N. Jorg 'Corporate Liability and Manslaughter: Should We Be Going Dutch?' [1991] Crim LR 156 at 159. Moreover, as the *Maxwell* case (see *Bishopsgate Investments Management Ltd* v *Homan* [1994] EWCA Civ 33) indicates the company may be as much a victim of the wrongdoing of its controlling mind as the public.

This is now the philosophy underpinning the Corporate Manslaughter and Corporate Homicide Act 2007, albeit tempered by an unfortunate emphasis on the activities of senior management.[115] Arguably this philosophy should stretch further than cases of corporate homicide. An ingenious and radical proposal is that companies should be liable not on the basis of the harm individual members of the company, however senior, have, through their acts or omissions, wrought but on the adequacy of the steps taken to ensure such harms do not reoccur, otherwise known as 'reactive fault'.[116] This proposal has the undeniable advantage of keeping harm prevention as the foundation upon which corporate liability is built, while leaving it open for companies to be censured and punished for the fault they evince in contradistinction to any misdeeds of its officers and employees. A better bet for future doctrinal development where censure lies at the heart of society's politicised response to corporate wrongdoing, is, it is submitted, the model provided by the Law Commission in their 1996 Report.[117]

Summary

Where a statute creates a criminal offence without specifying a fault element there is nevertheless a presumption that Parliament intended there to be one. This presumption operates most strongly with respect to offences of a stigmatic character. The presumption is rebuttable where the wording of the statute indicates otherwise or where, by virtue of the nature of the crime, strict liability would be a more effective means of addressing its mischief.

Although as a rule criminal liability cannot be imposed on one person for the unauthorised acts of another, even if that other is the former's employee, there are a number of mechanisms for imputing liability to a company or other employer. The traditional mechanism is that of vicarious liability. Liability may be imposed vicariously on the employer if the wording of a statute, on an 'extended construction',[118] allows the acts of an employee to be attributed to the employer.[119] Liability can, on rare occasions, be imputed to a person of special status, say the owner, occupier or licensee of premises, where he has delegated the performance of statutory duties personal to him, to another.

As a legal person a corporation may be guilty of a criminal offence most notably those strict liability offences which regulate its activities. Beyond this, corporations face a broader spectrum of liability for crimes of *mens rea* than individual employers. This is because under the right conditions the company may incur liability for the activities of its senior officers. This is in addition to any personal liability of the officers and to any regulatory offence the company may, directly or vicariously, thereby also have committed. The process by which the company itself, in addition to any individual member of the company, may incur liability is known as identification. By the Corporate Manslaughter and Corporate Homicide Act 2007 a corporation can be liable for (gross negligence) manslaughter in the absence of a culpable senior person(s) with whom the company can be identified. Liability is nevertheless restricted by requiring proof that the way in which its activities are managed or organised by its senior management was a substantial element in the breach which caused the death.

---

[115] See generally B. Fisse and J. Braithwaite 'The Allocation of Responsibility for Corporate Crime: Individualism, Collectivism and Accountability' (1988) 11 Sydney L Rev 468.

[116] See generally B. Fisse and J. Braithwaite, op. cit.

[117] For a rejection of this idea see G.R. Sullivan, 'The Attribution of Culpability to Limited Companies' [1996] Camb LJ 515.

[118] Law Commission Consultation Paper No. 135, *Involuntary Manslaughter*, London: HMSO (1994).

[119] *Mousell Bros v London and North Western Railway* [1917] 2 KB 836.

Further reading

Duff, R.A., *Answering for Crime*, London: Hart Publishing (2007).

Gobert, J. and Punch, M., *Rethinking Corporate Crime*, London: Butterworths (2003).

Horder, J., 'Strict Liability, Statutory Construction and the Spirit of Liberty' (2002) 118 LQR 459.

Horder, J., *Excusing Crime*, Oxford: OUP (2004) ch. 6.

Manchester, C., 'Knowledge, Due Diligence and Strict Liability in Regulatory Offences' [2006] Crim LR 213.

Reid, K.,' Strict Liability: Some Principles for Parliament' (2008) 29 Statute Law Review 173.

Simester, A. (ed.), *Appraising Strict Liability*, Oxford: OUP (2005).

Wells, C., *Corporations and Criminal Responsibility* (2nd edn) Oxford: OUP (2001).

8 Relationship between *actus reus* and *mens rea*

Overview

In theory, the *mens rea* of any crime should match the *actus reus*. This means that at the time of committing the *actus reus* of crime *x*, D should also be possessed of the *mens rea* for crime *x*. It possibly should also mean that where the accused's *mens rea* does not match the *actus reus* he should be liable only to the extent, if at all, that they do match. For example if the *actus reus* is death the *mens rea* should be intention or recklessness as to this death. Otherwise D is being punished for the wrong harm. This chapter examines these principles with a view to seeing how far they are replicated in doctrine.

8.1 INTRODUCTION

We have seen that, as a general proposition, those crimes apt to provoke the risk of imprisonment should, and as a rule do, require proof both of a harmful deed committed by the accused and also of an accompanying mental attitude sufficient to render that deed punishable. Implicit in this general proposition is a requirement that deed (*actus reus*) and mental element (*mens rea*) 'concur'. Concurrence requires *mens rea* and *actus reus* to coincide in point of time. This is known as temporal coincidence. It also seems to require that the *mens rea* matches or corresponds with the *actus reus*. This is known as the correspondence principle.

A few examples will suffice to illustrate the operation of this principle.

Case 1

Adam invites Eve, his deadly enemy, to tea. His plan is to ply her with tea and cucumber sandwiches and, having gained her confidence, to shoot her dead. The plan misfires when, shortly before Adam takes out his gun, Eve starts to choke on a sandwich. Adam, in a compassionate gesture, pats her on the back causing Eve to overbalance and fall. She hits her head and dies.

Adam intends to kill Eve. He has killed Eve. However, he did not kill her **with** the intention to kill her or to cause her any injury. *Mens rea* and *actus reus* did not coincide in point of time. As a result he is not guilty of murder, or even manslaughter.

Case 2

Adam places some poison in Eve's cocoa, intending thereby to poison her. After she has drunk the poison he immediately repents his action. He calls the ambulance, causes her to be sick and walks her round the room in an attempt to keep her alive until medical help arrives. The ambulance arrives too late to be of use and Eve dies.

Adam has the *mens rea* for murder. He has committed the *actus reus* of murder, namely a poisoning which caused Eve's death. This was accompanied by *mens rea* in the sense that the intention to kill Eve prompted the deed which caused her death. His repentance did not prevent that concurrence of *mens rea* and *actus reus* and so he is guilty of murder.

Case 3
Eve, wishing to kill her husband Adam's dog, laces the family leftovers with rat poison, and puts them in the doggy bowl. Adam, hungry after a day's golf, eats the leftovers and dies.

Case 4
Eve, wishing to kill her husband, Adam, laces his dinner with rat poison. Adam, who is not hungry, gives his dinner to Eve's dog, which dies.

The starting point for deciding the appropriate criminal charge is, in all cases, a consideration of the social harm which has been committed and the mental attitude which accompanied it. In Case 3 the social harm is a homicide. The mental attitude which accompanies it is an intention to damage property (the dog). This mental attitude does not concur with the definitional *actus reus* of homicide. Eve's liability for homicide cannot therefore be sustained. A similar analysis shows that Eve is not guilty of criminal damage in Case 4. The appropriate criminal charge in both cases would be the offence definition in which mental attitude does concur with the definitional *actus reus*. In Case 3, this is attempted criminal damage. This requires a mental attitude of intending to commit criminal damage and an *actus reus* of some more than preparatory steps towards the execution of this offence. Both elements are satisfied. In Case 4, adopting the same analysis, the appropriate criminal charge will be attempted murder.

A Temporal coincidence

Cases 1 and 2 are illustrations of the principle that there should be temporal coincidence between *actus reus* and *mens rea*. Case 2 illustrates that as long as *mens rea* and *actus reus* coincide in point of time for as long as a split second, the necessary coincidence is established.

1 Qualifications to the requirement of temporal coincidence
In certain situations the courts have shown an understandable reluctance to implement the full logic of the temporal coincidence requirement.

(a) *The rule in* Thabo Meli
In cases of homicide temporal coincidence is satisfied notwithstanding the fact that the act which causes death is **unaccompanied** by *mens rea*, if this absence is the result of the accused's believing that he has already caused death by a prior unlawful act. In *Thabo Meli* v *R* two men, acting in pursuance of a prearranged plan, plied their victim with drink and then beat him over the head with intent to kill him. They then rolled him over a cliff so as to make it appear that he had stumbled to his death. In fact the victim was not dead when they rolled him over. He died later of exposure at the foot of the cliff. The men argued that they were not guilty of murder since the act which caused death was leaving the man to the elements. This act was unaccompanied by an intention to kill since they thought the victim

was already dead. The intention to kill accompanied the previous act of beating the victim about the head, but this act did not cause death. Since the actual death was not caused by an act actuated by a mental state sufficient to convict of murder, a conviction for murder could not lie. The Privy Council rejected this argument on the basis that it was 'impossible . . . to divide up what was really one series of acts in this way'.[1]

Quite why it was impossible is not explained but it seems that the court did not like the conclusion which the mechanical application of logic compelled. The court found it difficult to resist the common-sense conclusion that a person who has the *mens rea* for the crime and is causally responsible should also bear full criminal responsibility. A different conclusion was reached in the earlier Rhodesian case of *Shorty*,[2] not cited in *Meli*, where the court accepted that since the intention to kill had evaporated by the time the act causing death occurred (putting the supposed corpse in a sewer) a murder conviction was not possible. The proper verdict was attempted murder, the *actus reus* of which did concur with the relevant *mens rea*. In *Chiswibo*[3] the Federal Supreme Court distinguished *Meli* on the tenuous ground that there was no prearranged plan to kill. It held that the proper verdict was attempted murder where death was caused by a burial rather than the blow to the head which the defendant believed to have caused death. In the later English case of *Church*, where there was also no prearranged plan to kill, *Meli* was followed, however. Homicide was the appropriate verdict if 'the appellant's behaviour (could be regarded) from the moment he first struck her to the moment when he threw her into the river as a series of acts designed to cause death or grievous bodily harm'.[4]

It has been argued that *Meli* and *Church* are inconsistent with the principle of concurrence.[5] An alternative analysis holds that it is not inconsistent as long as the **original act** is still the **legal** cause of death. In *Le Brun* D knocked his wife unconscious. He picked her up but then accidentally dropped her, resulting in her head hitting the pavement. This caused her death. The Court of Appeal ruled that the original blow was also an operative cause of death since:

(a) death would clearly not have occurred if he had not first hit her, and
(b) nothing which happened subsequently had broken the chain of causation set off by this original act and which ended with the wife's death.

The husband's later acts were thought to amount only to a 'tidying up' operation, designed to serve the interests of the husband rather than the wife, and thus incapable of interrupting a causal sequence. The upshot of this is that an act causing death was accompanied by a matching mental element. If his initial blow had directly killed her, he would have been guilty of murder if the blow was inflicted in furtherance of a decision to kill or cause grievous bodily harm. If it was not inflicted with this intention, he would have been guilty only of manslaughter. This reasoning has enjoyed some strong support by academic commentators,[6] although logically it should not matter whose interests the 'tidying up' were meant to favour as long as the event which precipitated the death was not a complete coincidence.[7]

---

[1] *Meli and others* v R [1954] 1 All ER 373 per Lord Reid at 374.
[2] *Rex* v *Shorty* 1950 Southern Rhodesia 280.
[3] (1961) 2 S. Afr. LR 714.
[4] (1965) Cr App R 206 at 210; see also *Moore* [1975] Crim LR 229.
[5] A.J. Ashworth *PCL* (2006) 164–5; G. Williams *TCL* (1983) 256.
[6] *Le Brun* [1992] QB 61; G.R. Sullivan, 'Cause and Contemporaneity of *Actus Reus* and *Mens Rea*' (1993) Camb LJ 487 at 495–500; cf. G. Marston, 'Contemporaneity of Act and Intention of Crimes' (1970) 86 LQR 208.
[7] *Smith* [1959] 2 All ER 193; *Jordan* (1956) 40 Cr App Rep 152 (see p. 115).

(b) *Continuing acts*

A quite different problem is posed where, at the inception of harm-causing conduct, *mens rea* was absent but later was formed when the positive acts constituting that conduct were (apparently) complete. Here again, the courts have sometimes sought to resist the implementation of the principle by a variety of devices. In *Fagan* the accused inadvertently parked his car on a policeman's foot. When requested to remove the car he desisted, flavouring his refusal with some salty invective. He was charged with assaulting a police officer in the execution of his duty. The problem here was that the act which led to force being applied to the policeman's foot was unaccompanied by the *mens rea* for assault, inadvertence being insufficient. On the face of it, therefore, the offence was not committed since the offence could only be committed at the earliest when the decision not to remove the car was made, and **this decision** prompted no subsequent act of assault on D's part. The court was understandably unhappy with this conclusion and decided that the act constituting the assault endured for as long as force was being applied to the policeman's foot. This meant that the act of assault continued until the car was removed, by which time *mens rea* had been formed. Although the court's reasoning is notably flimsy, it seems that it thought that this feature was sufficient to distinguish the case from those where, as in firing a gun, the 'harming act' had ended and the clock cannot be turned back.[8]

(c) *Inexcusable failures to undo excusable harms*

A variation on this theme occurs where there is no continuing act which can form the subject-matter of the offence. In such a case it appears that liability may nevertheless attach if the defendant, whether blameless or not, has caused a preventable harm which, in breach of duty, he omits to remedy.

> **Case 5**
> A is driving his car at speed, but legally, along an unlit road. B runs out into the middle of the road without warning. A is unable to avoid him. C witnesses the resulting crash. A gets out of his car to investigate but, on recognising that B is his deadly enemy whom he wishes dead, gets back into the car and drives off. C also does nothing to help. B dies later of injuries sustained in the crash, which prompt medical attention would have prevented.

On the face of it, this can be analysed like Cases 1 and 4 above. A has the *mens rea* for murder. He has committed the *actus reus* of murder by performing an act which resulted in B's death. However, the act which caused death was unaccompanied by, in the sense of not having been the result of, A's intention to kill B. The conclusion appears to be then that A is not guilty of murder. The courts have latterly resisted this conclusion by designating as the relevant murderous conduct A's failure to render assistance, rather than the initial crash. Since this failure to render assistance was accompanied by *mens rea*, the coincidence principle is not breached. The basis of A's liability is his causal responsibility. This places upon him a duty to remedy the harm unleashed by his conduct.[9] Although this reasoning neatly avoids offending the principle of concurrence, it does create its own problems.[10] In particular, it should be noted that there is relatively little moral distinction between A and

---

[8] The Law Commission have adopted the continuing act doctrine as a basis for liability. Draft Criminal Law Bill 1993 (Law Com. No. 218) cl. 31.

[9] *Miller* (above, pp. 90–1).

[10] G.R. Sullivan, op. cit. 489–95.

C in such a case and yet the fact that A and not C was the driver means that A's failure to provide assistance puts him at risk of a murder conviction and C's of nothing more than a police officer's raised eyebrow. This discrepancy is troubling and arguably should be dealt with by imposing on **all** citizens a limited duty of rescue, or making report to the appropriate authorities.[11]

B Definitional concurrence

It was seen in Cases 3 and 4 that the definitional *mens rea* must concur with the exact same definitional *actus reus*. This is subject to some important qualifications.

1 Qualifications to the requirement of definitional concurrence

(a) *Transferred malice*

A qualification of the requirement of definitional concurrence is provided by the doctrine of transferred malice. This holds, in effect, that the requirement that *actus reus* and *mens rea* concur is not breached where the **formal** requirements of the offence charged 'concur' with the result intended or foreseen by the accused, even if the accused did not intend or foresee the **actual** result which occurred. An illustration of the principle in operation is the ancient case of *Gore*.[12] A woman wanting to do away with her sick husband laced his medicine with rat poison. His condition deteriorated, as did that of his father who also took some. The obnoxious effects which followed led to the latter questioning the apothecary's competence. To vindicate his honour the apothecary took a large draft of the adulterated medicine, which killed him. The woman was held guilty of the murder of the apothecary. The murderous malice (intent) she entertained towards the husband was transferred to the *actus reus* committed against the apothecary. The general principle of transferred malice has been described as follows: 'if the defendant intends a particular consequence, he is guilty of a crime of intention even though his act takes effect upon an object (whether person or property) that was not intended.'[13] The principle probably applies to transfer recklessness as well as intention.[14] Thus A will be guilty of the consummated offence in all of the following examples, presented in order of difficulty.

Case 6

A throws a brick at B's window. It misses and breaks C's window.

Case 7

A aims and fires a gun at B, intending to kill him. It misses B but hits C, a bystander, wounding him.

Case 8

A aims and fires a gun at B, intending to kill him. C unexpectedly, wishing to protect B, pushes him out of the way, is hit by the bullet and dies.

---

[11] See above at p. 98.
[12] (1611) Co Rep 81.
[13] G. Williams, *CLGP* (2nd edn) 126.
[14] Ibid. 127.

Case 9

A throws a brick at B's window. The brick strikes and injures a passing dog.

Case 10

A throws a brick at B's window, although he can see B standing nearby and realises he may be hit. The brick is intercepted by a passing car driven by C, breaking the windscreen and seriously injuring the driver.

Case 11

A posts a letter-bomb through his neighbour B's door. B witnesses this and, although he does not know what the package contains, immediately posts it back. A's partner C, who knows nothing of A's plans, opens the package, which sets the house on fire, injuring C.

Case 12

A aims and fires a gun at B, intending to kill him. It misses B but C, a bystander, shocked by the noise, suffers a heart attack and dies.

In Case 6 A intends criminal damage on B's window. This intention is transferred to meet the *actus reus* committed against C's window. In Case 7 A is guilty of unlawful wounding. A intends to kill B by wounding and, therefore, must intend to wound. A's *mens rea* in respect of B is transferred to the *actus reus* committed against C. Case 8 is a variation on Case 7, although here A is guilty of murder. It is of no legal relevance that C pushes B out of the way. What is important is that A is the legal cause of C's death and has the *mens rea* for murder. Case 9 is a variation on Case 7. Although a dog is a different kind of property from a window, it is still property. The discrepancy is legally irrelevant. A had the *mens rea* for criminal damage and criminal damage is what occurred. In Case 10, A is guilty of unlawfully inflicting grievous bodily harm. The *mens rea* for this offence is foresight of injury. A foresaw B being hit. This foresight can be transferred to meet the *actus reus* of the crime perpetrated on C which he did not foresee. In Case 11 A is guilty of arson.[15] He will be guilty of arson with intent to endanger life or being reckless as to whether life would be endangered, depending upon his state of mind. Once again, his malice against B will be transferred over to meet the *actus reus* of the offence against C. It is legally irrelevant that B posted the package back since this action will not break the chain of causation linking A's conduct with the final outcome. As we have seen, if B knew what the package contained A would not be guilty of arson or aggravated arson since B's voluntary action would then break the chain of causation. B would be liable under those circumstances and A would be guilty only of an attempt.[16] Case 12 is the most difficult to decide. On the face of it, once again, what A intended – the death of a person – is what he got, which renders him liable for murder. Jeremy Horder, however, qualifies this conclusion by denying this result where it is too remote a consequence to be attributed to A's initial act. In his view this would be such a case since not only was the victim not intended but the manner of his death was not even foreseen.[17] With respect, remoteness is an insufficiently precise concept to justify muddying the waters of attribution in this way.

---

[15] Under s. 1(2) Criminal Damage Act 1971.
[16] See Chapter 18.
[17] J. Horder, 'Transferred Malice and the Remoteness of Unexpected Outcomes' [2006] Crim LR 383.

It should be noted that transferred malice operates only within fairly narrow limits. In particular, the doctrine cannot be used to render A guilty of a crime for which he lacked *mens rea*. It is not a form of constructive liability in which responsibility for crime A is imposed upon the accused simply to punish him for having the *mens rea* for crime B.[18]

It should also be noted that reliance on the doctrine of transferred malice is only necessary where the defendant's *mens rea* does not concur with the *actus reus* of the crime charged but does concur with the formal elements of that crime. It need not be relied upon where, although it was not A's intention to kill or wound B, or damage the relevant item of property, he nevertheless has *mens rea* sufficient to sustain liability for the crime charged. Consider the following examples.

Case 13

A throws a brick at B in a crowded room. B ducks and the brick hits C, causing him injury.

Case 14

A throws a brick at B, who is standing in front of C's shop window. B ducks and the brick breaks the window.

In Cases 13 and 14, A will be guilty of assault on C and criminal damage in respect of the window. The assault on C can be supported either by using the doctrine of transferred malice or alternatively by establishing that A was reckless in respect of the injury sustained by C. This will not be difficult in Case 13. The evidential presumption that A realised that someone else (including C) might have been injured would be difficult to counter. In Case 14, although malice cannot be transferred between the crime intended (assault) and the *actus reus* of the crime consummated (criminal damage) the prosecution should nevertheless have little difficulty persuading the jury that A was (*Cunningham*) reckless with respect to the damage sustained by the window. This reasoning was not exploited in *Pembliton*.[19] A threw a stone at B intending to hit him. The stone missed and broke a window. An intention to injure a person by throwing a stone at him was held not transferable to the crime of malicious damage when the stone broke a window.

The doctrine of transferred malice has its critics, most notably Ashworth and Glanville Williams. Ashworth questions whether it has a point to it which could not adequately be covered by other aspects of criminal doctrine, most notably outcome-liability for recklessness (Case 14) and the law of criminal attempts.[20] His argument is indebted to his general belief that people should be punished according to what they intend rather than for the accidents of fate arising from the execution of that intention.[21] The majority who are not of this persuasion find it difficult to see the desirability of punishing, say, an attempt on the life of B rather than the consummated offence against C.[22] This is in no way to condone or support constructive liability. But if A kills in furtherance of a murderous intention, what principle of morality is breached and what aim of punishment confounded if we convict

---

[18] An example being constructive manslaughter.
[19] (1874) 2 CCR 119.
[20] 'Transferred Malice and Punishment for Unforeseen Consequences' in P.R. Glazebrook (ed.), *Reshaping the Criminal Law* 77–94 at 85–7.
[21] A refinement on this view has been put forward by A. Dillof, 'Transferred Intent: An Inquiry into the Nature of Criminal Culpability' (1998) Buffalo Crim LR 501.
[22] See for example D. Husak, 'Transferred Intent' (1996) 10 Notre Dame J Law, Ethics and Public Policy 65.

him of murder? The doctrine of transferred malice seems to be demanded by general principles of liability rather than being an exception to it. In this respect it has an obvious affinity with transferred **defences**. As we shall see, if A fires a gun at B in self-defence that defence transfers to excuse the killing of C if C is the unintended recipient of the bullet.[23]

Williams also believes the doctrine contrary to principle[24] and suggests that liability should not be imposed where the defendant was not at least negligent as to the outcome occurring.[25] This would mean that at least in Cases 8, 10, 11 and 12, the doctrine would not apply. It is difficult to see any merit in this suggestion.[26] Either we embrace liability for unintended events or we do not. If we do, all we need to be convinced of is that punishing the outcome rather than the intention is morally justifiable. Since the evil outcome is formally identical to the outcome intended, it seems obvious that it is.

(b) *Definitional non-correspondence*

The reader who has followed carefully the discussion on concurrence might be forgiven for supposing that a person's conditions of liability generally require the prosecution to prove a perfect coincidence between the outcome for which it is sought to punish the accused and his mental attitude. The general message which appears is that cases such as *Thabo Meli*, *Fagan*, *Miller*, and the doctrine of transferred malice are not significant exceptions to the principle that criminal liability is incurred for **chosen** outcomes rather than for the accidents of fate which can be causally attributed to the accused's wrongful conduct. This latter form of liability is known as **constructive liability**. It is liability **imposed** on the accused rather than liability **chosen** by his decision and/or willingness to bring about the prohibited result. Liability for chosen consequences is generally assumed to be the principled norm of criminal liability, with constructive liability an unprincipled throwback to the penal excesses of less civilised times. If we examine criminal doctrine more closely, however, it is possible to discern another pattern to the construction of criminal liability – one which reflects the enduring popularity of constructive liability. In particular, criminal doctrine is full of examples appearing to confound the 'correspondence principle' which is a particular application of the requirement of definitional concurrence. The principle has been described as follows: 'If the offence is defined in terms of certain consequences and certain circumstances, the mental element ought to correspond with that by referring to those consequences or circumstances. If a mental element as to a lesser consequence were acceptable, this would amount to constructive liability'.[27]

The principle holds, in other words, that where *actus reus* and *mens rea* do not correspond, the liability of the accused should not exceed the harm actually encompassed by his own *mens rea*. The major problem which breaches of the correspondence principle are thought to engender is the risk of unfair labelling. Consider, for example, the crime of manslaughter. Compliance with the correspondence principle would require A to be guilty

---

[23] See also *Pagett* (above, p. 104). J. Horder insists that the resulting defense is an excuse rather than a justification. See J. Horder, 'Self-defence, Necessity and Duress' (1998) Can J Law and Juris 143 at 145–9; M. Bohlander, 'Transferred Malice and Transferred Defences' (2010) NCLR 555–624.

[24] G. Williams, *CLGP* (2nd edn) 135–7.

[25] Ibid. 132–4.; cf. J. Horder, 'Transferred Malice and the Remoteness of Unexpected Outcomes' [2006] Crim LR 383.

[26] Cf. Smith and Hogan, op. cit. 93–5.

[27] Ashworth and Campbell, 'Recklessness in Assault – And in General?' (1991) 107 LQR 187 at 192. For a penetrating review of the interplay of these and other principles and policies of the criminal law, see A.J. Ashworth, 'A Change of Normative Position: Determining the Contours of Culpability in Criminal Law' (2008) NCLR 232; B. Mitchell, 'Minding the Gap in Unlawful and Dangerous Act Manslaughter: A Moral Defence of One-punch Killers' (2008) 72 Journal of Criminal Law 537–47.

of a crime of **homicide** if, and only if, the mental element corresponded with its *actus reus* (conduct causing death) by 'referring to (that) consequence'.[28] In fact, liability for manslaughter does not require such correspondence. Far from requiring the *mens rea* to refer to the consequence of death, it requires not even a recognition on the accused's part that his conduct was likely to cause harm. The supposed unfairness of this is that A is labelled for the 'wrong' crime. Constructive manslaughter is, as its title suggests, the quintessential example of constructive liability. Murder, itself, seems to breach the correspondence principle. Liability does not depend upon the accused intending (or foreseeing) death as a result of his actions. Intending serious bodily harm, without more, is enough. Other examples of the principle not being followed are assault occasioning actual bodily harm[29] and the unlawful infliction of grievous bodily harm.[30] In both cases liability may be incurred where the harm intended or foreseen by the accused was less than the harm referred to in the offence definition.[31]

A strong case can be made that the correspondence principle, unlike other applications of the concurrence principle, does not, in fact, describe an ethical standard underscoring actual criminal doctrine, and it is for this reason that it is more honoured in the breach than in the observance. Non-observance is not intrinsically objectionable.[32] It only becomes so if it results in the defendant being labelled unfairly with the wrong crime. What must be sought, it has been argued, is a proper balance between the gravity of the crime charged and the gravity of the defendant's conduct in relation to the crime charged.[33]

Consider the following cases, suggested by Horder, as support for a reconsideration of our attitude to the correspondence principle.

Case 15

A, a driver, speeding home from the office to put his children to bed, knocks over and kills a pedestrian. He was aware, because of the speed he was travelling, that any crash he might have would be likely to be fatal.

Case 16

X, an evil surgeon, removes B's kidney without consent under local anaesthetic. He gives no thought to the risk that B might not survive the shock, which she does not.

It is fairly clear here that if either of these wrongdoers should be guilty of murder it should be X, and yet it is A, not X, who has a *mens rea* which corresponds with the *actus reus* of murder, X giving no thought to the possibility of death. This is reason to doubt the general value of the correspondence principle.[34] Where causal responsibility for the same

---

[28] This is basically the position adopted by the Criminal Law Revision Committee, 14th Report (1980, Cmnd 7844) (hereafter CLRC).

[29] Contrary to s. 47, Offences Against the Person Act 1861. See Chapter 11.

[30] Contrary to s. 20, Offences Against the Person Act 1861. See Chapter 11.

[31] See generally A.J. Ashworth, 'A Change of Normative Position: Determining the Contours of Culpability in Criminal Law' (2008) NCLR 232.

[32] J. Horder, 'Two Histories and Four Hidden Principles of *Mens Rea*' (1997) 113 LQR 95.

[33] See generally J. Horder, 'A Critique of the Correspondence Principle in Criminal Law' [1995] Crim LR 759; J. Gardner, 'Rationality and the Rule of Law in Offences against the Person' (1994) 53 Camb LJ 502; B. Mitchell, 'In Defence of a Principle of Correspondence' [1999] Crim LR 195; J. Horder, 'Questioning the Correspondence Principle – A Reply' [1999] Crim LR 206.

[34] Horder concedes it has value in limiting criminal liability for crimes of basic intent. For such crimes, for example unlawful infliction of grievous bodily harm, the *mens rea* should, at least, require some foresight of that consequence.

consequence (e.g. death) leads to a hierarchy of offences differentiated only by their mental elements (e.g. murder and manslaughter) the imposition of the relevant criminal label should, ideally, depend upon different degrees of moral wickedness rather than, say, different degrees of foresight.[35]

The comparable case is where the *actus reus* of the relevant crime takes the same form but has a variable degree of gravity (e.g. grievous as opposed to actual bodily harm). The correspondence principle holds that it would be wrong to hold A guilty of inflicting serious injury unless he at least foresaw the risk of causing **serious** harm. It should not be enough that he foresaw only some harm. Horder argues that the ethic of fair labelling would not require this in all cases. It should be enough that A **intends** to cause some harm which, in the circumstances of the infliction, provoked the risk that serious harm might result.

Case 17

A, a vile brute, decides he wants to injure and frighten B, his wife. He takes a knife and draws it across her cheek drawing blood, as was his intention. In fear and pain V jerks her head and the knife stabs her in the eye.

V has suffered grievous bodily harm. A's *mens rea* does not 'refer to such consequence'. He intended only a minor wound and foresaw nothing else. Would it be an error of labelling to convict him of (maliciously) inflicting/causing grievous bodily harm? The law says not.[36] In this it fails to accord with the opinion of the majority of commentators[37] who feel that we should only be held responsible for the consequences we choose.[38] The view adopted by Horder, and the one taken here, is that it is quite fair, assuming A intended B some injury, that A takes the 'bad luck' of the injury extending beyond that intended or actually foreseen.[39] The point is that we do not simply choose what we intend or willingly bring about. We also choose, in the sense of 'make', our luck, whether it is good or bad.

8.2 MISTAKE

We have seen how certain mistakes do not affect liability. If A shoots the wrong person 'by mistake' or buries and kills a live person under the mistaken belief that he has already killed him, these mistakes do not affect liability. Neither will it avail the defendant that he was mistaken as to the law applicable, even if the mistake was perfectly reasonable.[40] On the other hand, certain mistakes may operate to negate criminal liability. A person may rely on the defence of self-defence to escape liability for a crime of violence although his belief that he was the subject of an imminent attack was mistaken.[41] Again, a person is not guilty of theft if he mistakenly believes the owner to consent to his taking of the property. This conclusion is an application of the general principle that it is for the prosecution to prove *mens rea*, but begs the question as to when the prosecution bears this burden. In

---

[35] Cf. J. Horder, op. cit. 763.
[36] See *Mowatt* [1968] 1 QB 421.
[37] But not the wider public, apparently. See P.H. Robinson and J.M. Darley, 'Objectivist Versus Subjectivist Views of Criminality: A Study in the Role of Social Science in Criminal Law Theory' (1998) 18 OJLS 409.
[38] The author himself was once an advocate of this stance. See for example W. Wilson, 'A Plea for Rationality in the Crime of Murder' [1990] 10 LS at 307.
[39] W. Wilson, 'Murder and the Structure of Homicide' in A. Ashworth and B. Mitchell (eds), *Rethinking English Homicide Law*, Oxford: OUP (2000), 36–43.
[40] *Chambers* [2008] EWCA 2467.
[41] See Chapter 10.

general, a mistaken belief will only affect liability where the prosecution bears the burden of proving the truth (or untruth) of the substance of the issue mistaken. This accounts for the decision in *Ellis*[42] where the defendants were convicted for knowingly importing prohibited goods, although they were mistaken as to the nature of the goods imported. They thought they were importing pornography. In fact it was prohibited drugs. It was held that this mistaken belief was irrelevant to liability. Since the defendants intended to import pornography the prosecution were able to establish an intention which corresponded with the *actus reus* of the offence charged (importing prohibited goods), if not with all the details of the offence they thought they were committing.

The courts have shown a notable reluctance to propound the principles dictating which elements of the *actus reus* of a given crime should carry a corresponding mental element.[43] It is fairly rare, even for crimes of *mens rea*, that every element in the *actus reus* bears a corresponding mental element. For example, it is part of the *actus reus* of infanticide that the infant be under the age of two. But it is no part of the prosecution's case to prove a mental element corresponding with this element of the *actus reus*. Sometimes, in statutory crimes, this is made explicit. For example, the *actus reus* elements of sexual assault are:

(a) an intentional non-consensual touching;
(b) the circumstances or purpose which render the touching 'sexual'.[44]

However, it is not necessary for the prosecution to show that A intended the touching to be non-consensual or was reckless as to this fact.

Case 18
A, a customer at an 'Elizabethan banquet', pinches the bottom of a 'serving wench' believing the occasion to be such that the woman would consent. She does not.

The *mens rea* in sexual assault is proof of intention to touch and lack of reasonable belief that the woman would consent. Whether his belief was reasonable or not would be a matter for the jury.

Nor is it necessary for the prosecution to show that A believed his touching to be sexual.[45] So, if A thought pinching serving wenches' bottoms was not sexual because both purpose and context prevented it being so, this would also not avail A if the jury thought it was 'by its nature sexual'. Guilt in Case 18 is not uncontroversial because the mistake made (he believed she would consent) manifests no disposition to challenge the values upheld by the criminal law nor of an absence of respect for the rights and interests of the 'serving wench'. In the alternative scenario this cannot be said. A's only argument is that he did not realise society would think so badly of his anti-social behaviour, a claim which, on some accounts of moral blameworthiness, discloses the very vice (a failure to attend to society's core values) against which crimes such as indecent assault are pitted. Once again, there is no knock-down moral case against requiring a person who deliberately attacks the autonomy of another to bear the risk that society will judge him to have committed a more serious wrong than that which he knew himself to be committing.

---

[42] [1987] Crim LR 44.
[43] See Chapter 7.
[44] Sections 3 and 98(b) Sexual Offences Act 2003.
[45] Cf. *Court* [1989] AC 28.

Summary

A basic premise underpinning the common law is that *actus reus* and *mens rea* should concur. Specifically,

(1) liability should depend upon proof that the defendant had the relevant mental attitude at the moment of committing the *actus reus* of a criminal offence. This is known as temporal coincidence. A qualification, in the case of homicide, is that the premise is satisfied if *mens rea* is lacking only because of the accused's belief that he has already caused death by a prior unlawful act;

(2) Offence definitions should match any relevant consequence or circumstance with an exactly matching mental state on the part of the defendant. This is known as the correspondence principle. Without such correspondence, it is thought, the defendant will be punished for the wrong harm. This premise is satisfied if the defendant commits the formal *actus reus* of an offence with the relevant *mens rea* for that offence but the subject-matter of that *actus reus* was other than that intended or foreseen by the defendant. This qualification is known as the doctrine of transferred malice. It is not clear whether the correspondence principle does in fact accurately describe an ethic enshrined in criminal doctrine. The majority of crimes of violence, for example, bear an *actus reus* without a corresponding mental attitude.

Further reading

Ashworth, J., 'A Change of Normative Position: Determining the Contours of Culpability in Criminal Law' (2008) 11(2) New Criminal Law Review 232–56.

Bohlander, M., 'Transferred Malice and Transferred Defenses: A Critique of the Traditional Doctrine and Arguments for a Change in Paradigm' (2010) 13(3) New Criminal Law Review 555–624.

Horder, J., 'A Critique of the Correspondence Principle' [1995] Criminal Law Review 759.

Mitchell, B., 'In Defence of the Correspondence Principle' [1999] Criminal Law Review 195.

9 Defences (1)

Overview

To establish fault the prosecution bears the burden of proving not only the *mens rea*, if any, for the crime in question but also of disproving any defence in support of which evidence is adduced. In the following two chapters these general defences will be examined, evaluated and categorised.

9.1 INTRODUCTION

In everyday life it is not unusual to be blamed and censured for wrongs we have done, real or imagined. Suppose we are accused of breaking a neighbour's window. Assuming we do not deny involvement, our response is likely to involve the giving of reasons. By giving reasons we seek to deflect or reduce the blame which might otherwise have been attached to our act. This is useful both to ourselves – it may get us 'off the hook' – and to our neighbour. It allows her to make an informed judgement whether it would be right to ask for compensation, to retaliate or perhaps to move house. In making such a decision, the nature of the reasons we offer are very important. Reasons may be offered as justification, as excuse, or in mitigation.

A justificatory reason might be that we broke the window in order to extinguish a fire which was threatening to engulf the house. An exculpatory reason (excuse) might be that the ladder upon which we were standing had slipped so as to make contact with the window unavoidable. A mitigating reason might be that we did our best to avoid the window but that our skill at taking corner kicks was not as refined as we had supposed. Assuming it was accepted, if our reason was justificatory the neighbour might congratulate herself upon choosing to live next door to such a model citizen. The window was broken but the house was intact. The harm she thought to attribute to us was, in fact, a benefit in disguise. If it was exculpatory the neighbour might withdraw her initial censure but privately wish we were not so accident-prone. The harm had occurred but we were not to blame for it. If it was offered in mitigation the response might be, 'Well, don't do it again, and what about a new window?' The harm had occurred, we were to blame; but not so much as if we had done it deliberately.

The criminal law reflects this same moral basis by having a range of defences stretching from justification (e.g. necessity or self-defence) through complete excuses (e.g. automatism or duress) to partial excuses (e.g. loss of self control or diminished responsibility). Justification involves the claim that the action of the defendant was not wrong but was a permissible or even the right thing to do. Excuses involve the claim that although the action of the defendant was wrong, no blame or, in the case of partial excuses, only qualified blame attaches to him. The cogency of the distinction together with the implications, if any, of these differences will be examined in a later section.[1]

---

[1] See D. Husak, 'On the Supposed Priority of Justification to Excuse' (2005) 24 Law and Philosophy 557; J. Gardner, 'In Defence of Defences' in *Offences and Defences, Selected Essays in the Philosophy of Criminal Law*, Oxford: OUP (2007); A Simester, 'On Justifications and Excuses', in L. Zedner and J. Roberts (eds), *Principles and Values in Criminal Law and Criminal Justice: Essays in Honour of Andrew Ashworth*, Oxford: OUP (2012) 95.

The point of defences in the criminal law is to ensure that (only) the blameworthy are punished according to their degree of fault. As such they 'refine the wording of (offence definitions)'.[2] By and large, therefore, defences operate in tandem with the *mens rea* requirement to ensure that blameless people are not unjustly punished for having caused a social harm.[3] Thus, while a person who is forced at gunpoint to rob a bank cannot argue that she did not intend to do so, she may still claim to be excused on the ground of absence of fault.[4]

It is important to understand that the criminal law's attitudes to the types of reasons we might wish to offer in defence of our actions do not always shadow the wider social response. In particular, the public's disposition to censure is sensitive to the defendant's motive for acting. Thus, doctors performing euthanasia upon the terminally ill, and police officers, vigilantes and the victims of crime who resort to informal methods of crime control or self-help are, typically, lauded rather than condemned in the popular press. The public often find it baffling that such people have no defence to their crimes. What kind of system is it, the cry goes up, which punishes victims and police more than the criminals they turn upon?

The criminal law tends to restrict the impact of good motives, as we have seen. Good motive does not necessarily expunge the wrongness of a deed when it is judged from the point of view of society as a whole, rather than by what it signifies to the individual wrongdoer. Stealing dogs from vivisection units for reasons of compassion is just as wrong, from this perspective, as Cruella Deville stealing Dalmatian puppies to make fur coats. The criminal law has more functions to perform than to reflect the public's not always cogent sense of wrongdoing. Such functions include not simply punishing obvious villains who manifest their bad character by action,[5] but securing public order as well as sustaining the moral structure by which people's ideas of correct and incorrect behaviour are first learned and then maintained. Allow good motives to be defences and the law loses objectivity. In a democracy it is society, politically organised, and not, for example, the animal rights' activist (or broad public sentiment) which decides whether what one does is wrong or blameable.[6] As a result, restrictions are placed upon the development of criminal defences.

9.2 CATEGORISING DEFENCES

The law of defences catalogues the range of reasons which (from the law's point of view) can be used to expunge the wrongness of the act and/or the blameworthiness of the defendant for that act. They operate in different ways, however. Some, for example mistake and intoxication, operate by negating an element in the crime, namely *mens rea*. Some, such as insanity and diminished responsibility, exempt a person from responsibility/full responsibility due to mental incapacity. Because of this absence of capacity the court may have a dispositive discretion even where the defence is successful. Others, such as self-defence, coercion, and necessity operate by way of 'confession and avoidance', otherwise known as affirmative defences. These concede that the elements of the crime are established but deny the wrongfulness of the act, for example self-defence and necessity, or the culpability of the actor, for example, duress. These affirmative defences will be examined in the next chapter.

---

[2] P.H. Robinson, 'Criminal Law Defences: A Systematic Analysis' (1982) 82 Col L Rev 199 at 209.
[3] See generally G. Williams, 'Offences and Defences' (1982) 2 LS 233.
[4] Cf. *Steane* [1947] KB 997.
[5] See Chapter 5.
[6] J. Horder, 'On the Irrelevance of Motive in Criminal Law', in J. Horder (ed.), *Oxford Essays in Jurisprudence*, Oxford: OUP (2000).

9.3 A RATIONALE TO DEFENCES

An important question which must first be addressed is whether there is any overall rationale to our system of defences so that we can understand why some reasons for not complying with primary obligations are permissible and some are not. If there is a rationale it may enable us to evaluate the defences currently available and to predict defences which are capable of emerging.

The various rationales of criminal defences tend to vary according to whether a defence is an excuse or a justification.[7]

A Excuses

There have been various attempts made to establish some core unifying rationale to criminal excuses capable of providing a blueprint for both their development and constitutional elements.[8] Utilitarianism conceives of their essential organising characteristic as being any condition which would tend to destroy the point of, and therefore the justification for, punishment.[9] As punishment is only justified if it has utility, excuses signal cases of non-deterrable nonconformity to rules, encompassing conditions as far removed conceptually as insanity and duress. A theory of excuses more firmly located in the individual moral claim to avoid punishment is causation theory.[10] If the defendant is not the true 'author' of his conduct, say due to insanity, duress, or duress of circumstances, it is not appropriate to attribute blame to him. Over the full span of excuses, where actions are best analysed as chosen rather than caused, this is not a particularly cogent rationale. More persuasive are capacity (choice) theory and character theory. These pinpoint, more incisively, the moral claim to avoid punishment which excuses embody.[11] With choice theory, blame and punishment is predicated upon the fact that the accused voluntarily defied a legal prohibition or, in Hart's persuasive reworking of this position (capacity theory), that he failed to conform his behaviour to the relevant standards although he had the capacity and a fair opportunity to do so.[12] Excuses, partial or complete, intercede to ensure those lacking this capacity, say through insanity, or lacking opportunity, say because of coercion, escape punishment/full punishment. The other strong contender for a general rationale for criminal excuses is that they represent contexts which prompt people to act out of character, that is, otherwise than in accordance with their settled dispositions.[13] We excuse the

---

[7] This is not invariably the case: see D. Husak, 'On the Supposed Priority of Justification to Excuse' (2005) 24 Law and Philosophy 557.

[8] See, for example, J. Horder, 'Criminal Culpability: The Possibility of a General Theory' (1993) 12 Law and Philosophy 193; for general discussion see G. Fletcher, *Rethinking Criminal Law*, Boston, MA: Little, Brown (1978) ch. 10; M. Bayles, 'Character, Purpose and Criminal Responsibility' (1982) 1 L & Phil 5; R.A. Duff, 'Choice, Character and Criminal Liability' (1993) 12 L & Phil 345; V. Tadros, *Criminal Responsibility*, Oxford: OUP (2005) and 'The Characters of Excuse' (2001) 21 Oxford J Legal Stud, 495–519, at 517; K.J.M. Smith and W. Wilson, 'Impaired Voluntariness and Criminal Responsibility' (1993) 13 Oxford J Legal Stud 69; W. Wilson, 'The Filtering Role of Crisis in the Constitution of Criminal Excuses', (July 2004) XVII(2) Canadian Journal of Law and Jurisprudence.

[9] See Chapter 3.

[10] See for example Lord Goddard CJ in *Hill v Baxter* [1958] 1 QB 277 at 283. For an extended discussion of this point see pp. 193–4 and see R. Mackay, *Mental Condition Defences in the Criminal Law*, Oxford: Clarendon Press (1995) 95–7; M. Moore, 'Causation and Excuses' (1985) 73 Cal LR 1091.

[11] M. Moore, 'Causation and Excuses' (1985) 73 Cal LR 1091; P. Arenella, 'Character, Choice and Moral Agency' in E.F. Paul, F.A. Miller and J. Paul (eds), *Crime, Culpability and Remedy*, Oxford: Clarendon Press (1990).

[12] H.L.A. Hart, *Punishment and Responsibility*, Oxford: Clarendon Press (2008) ch. 2 [hereinafter Hart]; and see Kadish, 'Excusing Crime'.

[13] N. Lacey, *State Punishment* (1988) 65–8.

coerced wrongdoer because his wrongdoing was not reflective of a vicious character, rather of an unruly fate. 'There but for the grace of God . . .', as we tend to put it. Some commentators prefer to explain the relevance of character in constituting criminal excuses in another way. On this view, it is not so much that the action is out of character which excuses. How can it? There can be no gap between our global character and the character we display at a given time.[14] So it is no defence to murder that this was a one-off isolated incident which made no sense in terms of the actor's previous history; nor to gross negligence manslaughter for a surgeon to say that this was one isolated blip in an otherwise impeccably conscientious career; nor to theft that the excitement of finding a case full of fivers on a park bench subverted the finder's usual honest disposition. So, in relation to the excuse known as duress, if A robs a bank to allay a threat of death it is not that A's action **is out of character** that excuses A. Rather, it is that his action tells us nothing about bad about his character. By doing what he has done the only character displayed is that of someone who, quite reasonably and understandably, and **for this reason alone excusably**, prefers not to sacrifice himself for the sake of conformity to a criminal prohibition. Excuses, on this latter view, are distinct from defences of impaired capacity such as insanity or infancy, and like justifications although less so, occasions where the accused's motivation for infringing a legal prohibition was quite consonant with what we have come to expect of ordinary decent people of good character rather than a moral aberration.[15]

In fact, none of these accounts are entirely satisfactory as a general theory of excuses. Either, as with character theory, they do not do justice to the full range of criminal excuses and their doctrinal elements[16] or alternatively, as in Hart's capacity theory of excuses, they fail to account for the relatively few excuses on offer.[17] On the other hand, some excuses are better explained by one approach than another. Loss of self-control, for example, is best accounted for by (out of) character theory. Rather than centre the excuse in the absence of the capacity or fair opportunity to conform, or the part reasonableness of the reaction, is it not rather that certain provoking circumstances may subvert even the decent citizen's good character so that, quite abnormally for him, he follows his own personal reasons for action rather than the reasons he should be following, embodied in criminal prohibitions?[18] On the other hand some excuses, such as duress, seem to require more than one rationale. Sometimes reasonableness of reaction is stated to be of the essence, supporting the (good) character approach. This is particularly so for what is termed duress of circumstances. On other occasions it is the overwhelming nature of the crisis which excuses, particularly in cases involving direct victimisation. This can best be explained in terms of the actor's lack of fair opportunity.[19]

---

[14] J. Gardner, 'The Gist of Excuses' [1998] Buffalo Crim LR 575, 581; Fletcher (1978) 801; G.R. Sullivan, 'Making Excuses' in A.P. Simester and A.T.H. Smith (eds), *Harm and Culpability*, Oxford: Clarendon Press (1996) 131 at 135–40.

[15] For criticism of this all-encompassing view of excuses see J. Horder, *Excusing Crime* (2004); V. Tadros, *Criminal Responsibility* (2005) 286.

[16] For example the defence of voluntary withdrawal for accessorial liability requires a very different kind of organising rationale from other excuses and justifications – one based essentially in societal needs rather than fairness to the individual beset by crisis. This rationale is reflected in its distinctive elements: see K.J.M. Smith, A *Modern Treatise of the Law of Criminal Complicity*, Oxford: Clarendon Press (1991).

[17] In domestic law, for example, there is no recognised defence of involuntary intoxication, hormonal/biochemical/ environmental determinism, or brain-washing, each of which could be subsumed quite easily under Hart's theory of excuses. Cf. P. Westen, 'An Attitudinal Theory of Excuse' (2006) Law and Philosophy 28.

[18] K.J.M. Smith and W. Wilson, 'Impaired Voluntariness and Criminal Responsibility' at 96.

[19] W. Wilson, 'The Filtering Role of Crisis in the Constitution of Criminal Excuses' (2004) XVII(2) Canadian Journal of Law and Jurisprudence.

B Justificatory defences

Although sharing a common defence template – spontaneous reaction to crisis – there is good cause to analyse excuses and justifications differently. People whose action is justified need no excuse for what they do and the criminal law permits or even approves their conduct, and those who help them. Excuses are needed to ensure an escape from censure and punishment for people whose action was wrong but, realistically, unavoidable or otherwise not indicative of a character who puts his own projects before the interests of others. In this section we shall examine what makes an action legally justified, notwithstanding it embraces all the elements of a criminal offence. Before we do so, however, it will be beneficial to examine why it may be necessary to distinguish excuses from justifications given that they both result in a negation of liability.

1 The point of distinguishing between justification and excuse

As has been suggested, in everyday life the moral force of a justification is different from that of an excuse. We may accept our neighbour's excuse for breaking our window but we might still wish he lived somewhere else. If our neighbour has a justification, however, we are likely to approve his action. Is there any comparable difference between excuses and justifications in the criminal law or is the distinction simply 'theoretical'?[20] In one sense it is. The courts do not categorise defences according to whether they are excuses or defences and certainly, from the point of view of the perpetrator of an offence, little hangs on the distinction. Either a defence 'works' or it does not. If it could be shown that justificatory defences render the action of the defendant entirely lawful, a number of consequences would seem to follow, however:

(1) A person has the right to resist aggression where that aggression is excused, say because the aggressor is acting under duress or while insane, but not where it is justified. So, if the owner of the mountain hut in Case 2, below, were to prevent Eve from entering, any liability would then depend upon the tricky question whether Eve was justified or merely excused in gaining entry. If she were justified, not only should the owner be liable for an assault if he used force to repel the attack but, if Eve and Cain died of hypothermia as a result of being excluded, liability for murder might then accrue.[21] It is doubtful whether the courts would wish to implement this logic since it might, in effect, amount to recognising a duty of easy rescue – currently unacknowledged in English law.[22]

(2) Where a justification has been accepted, this effects a change in the law so as to render legal conduct which otherwise is illegal. If it is the case, then, that Eve is justified in Case 2 in breaking in and taking food this ruling will mean that other people in such circumstances are entitled to do so. If she is merely excused, no change in the law has occurred and no rights are affected.

(3) It is recognised that a person who assists someone whose action is justified cannot be guilty as an accomplice, whereas he may still be guilty if the action is only excused. Case 1 gives an example.

---

[20] P. Greenawalt, 'The Perplexing Boundaries of Justification and Excuse' (1984) Columbia Law Review 1847; P.H. Robinson, 'Criminal Law Defences: A Systematic Analysis' (1982) 82 Col LR 199; J.C. Smith, *Justification and Excuse in the Criminal Law*, London: Stevens (1989); Fletcher (1978) ch. 10.

[21] This is not necessarily so, however. See discussion on pages 200–1. See Fletcher for some other examples of the problems posed: 760–5.

[22] Not necessarily, however. See S. Uniacke, note 27 below.

> **Case 1**
>
> Adam comes across Cain fighting with Eve and about to shoot her. Adam goes to Eve's assistance by giving her a gun. Eve uses it to shoot Cain dead.

If Eve were acting reasonably in self-defence and Adam knew this, Adam would not be liable as an accomplice to criminal homicide since her conduct would be objectively lawful. If Eve were merely excused, say on the ground of diminished responsibility, insanity or duress, Adam would have no defence since her conduct would be objectively wrongful.[23] This illustrates the idea that 'acts are justified; actors are excused'.[24] Just because Eve was excused would not mean that the offence had not taken place. Since the offence had taken place, it follows that Adam could be an accessory to it.

(4) A final distinction is sometimes said to be that where a person is in fact justified in acting as he does, but is unaware of this fact, he will still be able to plead justification.[25] This proposition must be doubted in the light of the decision in *Dadson* and it would seem contrary to principle.[26] It is certainly not the case with excuses. If A, a taxi driver, goes the wrong way down a one-way street, he will be guilty of an offence even though it subsequently transpired that his 'fare' had, unknown to him, threatened him with death if he did not.

But how can we tell whether a person's claim amounts to an excuse as opposed to a justification? Consider, for example, Case 2.

> **Case 2**
>
> Eve and her child Abel are lost in freezing conditions on a mountain. Eve breaks into a mountain hut for shelter and food for herself and Abel.

Let us assume that Eve has a defence. Would one say that her action was wrong but that she was blameless? Or would one say that her action was socially permissible and so lawful? This is not a merely theoretical quandary, as has been explained. If the owner of the hut wished to use force to defend his property against Eve's intrusion, the legality of so acting might well depend upon whether Eve is justified in what she does rather than merely excused.[27] In order to answer this question it is necessary to examine what it is about justificatory defences which can render the apparently unlawful lawful.

2 Moral forfeiture

No one rationale for justification fully covers the full range of justificatory defences.[28] The plausibility of the different rationales varies according to the nature of the defence. A

---

[23] Cf. *Bourne* (1952) 36 Cr App R 125.

[24] Robinson's explanation of defences: loc. cit. 229.

[25] See the qualification to and elaboration upon this in G. Williams, 'Offences and Defences' (1982) 2(3) LS 249–52.

[26] *Dadson* (1850) 2 Den 35. See Chapter 4. John Gardner argues, surely correctly, that 'no action is justified unless it is true both that there was an applicable (guiding or moral) reason for so acting or so believing and that this corresponds with the actual (explanatory reason) why the act was performed or the belief held.' J. Gardner, 'Justifications and Reasons' in Simester and Smith (eds), *Harm and Culpability*, Oxford: Clarendon Press (1996) 103–6; cf. Tadros (2005) 284–6.

[27] See S. Uniacke, *Permissible Killing: The Self-Defence Justification of Homicide*, Cambridge: CUP (1994) 181–2. Cf. J. Horder, 'Self Defence, Necessity and Duress' (1998) Canadian Journal of Law and Jurisprudence 143, 150.

[28] See generally J. Horder, previous note.

major challenge posed by all defences, for example, is the position of third parties. In Case 2, do Eve's and Abel's needs mean the hut owner's rights are overridden? If so, this could seriously compromise the very notion of a right. This does not hold for all justificatory defences, however. A rationale commonly cited in support of self-defence, for example, is that of moral forfeiture. Force used against an aggressor is deemed lawful because, by himself acting unlawfully, the aggressor forfeits the protection of the law.[29] Such a rationale is quite plausible in standard self-defence cases, but becomes less so when the aggressor is blameless, say because he is insane or honestly but mistakenly believes the other to be attacking him.

3 Defence of autonomy

An alternative rationale does not require the forfeiture of rights. It deems action to be justifiable where it is taken in defence of the personal autonomy/physical security of the actor, or that of another, and does not use another as a means to achieve this end.[30] The fact of taking protective action does not mean that others affected forfeit their rights but rather that their interests may be overridden or advanced, incidentally, in pursuit of this lawful purpose, their rights remaining intact. This would mean, for example, that the owner of the cabin in Case 2 would be entitled to claim compensation from Eve for any harm done to his interests[31] and possibly even to resist her intrusion, although Eve would be acting lawfully.[32] Following the same analysis a defence is probably available not only to justify protective action taken against aggressors but also against any person who poses an unjust threat of harm to the actor or another.

Case 3

Adam is a passenger on a sinking ship. While attempting to climb a staircase to safety, he encounters Eve, another passenger, blocking his way. In a state of terror she is unable to move either forward or back. Adam throws her out of the way to her certain death.

Action against Eve is, as in self-defence, unavoidable because it is she who is threatening, albeit innocently, Adam's protected interest (i.e. his life). Eve is not being victimised, that is, being used as a means to an end but is simply being removed from Adam's escape route. As we saw earlier, the law of criminal omissions confirms that society does not expect us to sacrifice ourselves for the good of others. On this basis, although there is little authority on the matter, we would expect Adam's conduct to be justified and not merely excused.[33] This approach is plausible but does not provide a solution to every problem case where physical security/autonomy is under threat.

Case 4

Adam, Eve and Cain are trapped in a cave with sufficient provisions to survive for seven days. Adam, anxious to ensure his own survival, commandeers, by means of a gun, all provisions for himself. Eve and Cain, anxious to ensure their survival, overpower Adam and kill him.

---

[29] G. Fletcher (1978) 858, and see generally J. Dressler (1987) 181–2; S. Uniacke, above.
[30] See generally G. Fletcher (1978) 860–75.
[31] *Vincent* v *Lake Eyrie Trans Co.*, 109 Minn. 456, 124 N.W. 221 (1910).
[32] Cf. *Ploof* v *Putnam* 81 Vt. 471, 71A 188 (1908).
[33] Cf. J.C. Smith, *Justification and Excuse in the Criminal Law*, London: Stevens (1989) ch. 3.

Would Eve's and Cain's action be justified? After all, they are acting in furtherance of their own protected interest which is being threatened by the conduct of Adam. But is not Adam's conduct equally justifiable? And he, moreover, has done nothing more than that necessary to ensure his own survival. The autonomy route gives no easy answer to this question.

4 Balancing interests

A third rationale superficially offers greater promise in this respect. It holds action, otherwise unlawful, to be justified if the interests to be advanced by action outweigh the interests which would thereby be compromised. It is not difficult to account for a number of justificatory defences in this way, most particularly necessity and the prevention of crime.

There are two forms of this justificatory rationale, a utilitarian and a rights-based form.

(a) *Balancing outcomes*

The most straightforward (utilitarian) form holds that action is justifiable where the social harm it causes is outweighed by the harm it prevents or the good it secures. In short, action is justified if it is the lesser of two evils. On this basis the killing of Adam by Eve and Cain is justifiable since it is better for one to die than for two. Similarly, in Case 2, Eve may be treated not as having caused harm but rather as having prevented it.[34] A number of problems attach to this approach. The initial difficulty is that it can be used to justify exploiting innocent people for the benefit of others, for example, killing one or more innocent human beings if this would prevent a greater loss of life. This is compatible neither with the principle of the sanctity of human life nor with a respect for individual autonomy.

A second problem is that it may not afford a clear basis for action:

> **Case 5**
> Adam is driving down a narrow mountain road. Rounding a corner he finds a group of school-children walking towards him. In the split second available his choice is either to run through the school-children, thus killing one or more of them, or sacrifice himself by driving over the cliff.

On the present approach, Adam is justified in the former action if the harm caused is less than the harm avoided, but only excused (or worse) if the harm caused exceeds that avoided. This may be a difficult calculation where he has passengers. A more satisfactory rationale for Case 5 is the above autonomy-based justification.[35]

A final problem is that a harm-based approach may be incompatible with the rule of law. Can we all flout rules wherever some discernible advantage accrues from so doing? What are rules for, if not to give us advance warning of what we may and may not do?[36] Allowing Eve a justificatory defence effectively allows her to legislate questions of right and wrong conduct subject only to the **retrospective** ratification of politically unaccountable judges – a problem for democracy. For this reason it has been suggested that justificatory defences are limited to 'one-off emergencies where the individual is uniquely placed to grasp what has to be done and the law's coordinating function is not subverted.[37]

---

[34] Cf. P.H. Robinson, 'Criminal Law Defences: A Systematic Analysis' (1982) 82 Col LR 199 at 213.

[35] Or reliance on the doctrine of double effect. See Chapter 5.

[36] See Fletcher (1978) 792–8.

[37] J. Horder, 'On the Irrelevance of Motive', note 5 187–8; W. Wilson, 'The Structure of Criminal Defences', see note 47.

(b) *Balancing rights*

The non-utilitarian form of this rationale concentrates not upon whether the action taken is the lesser of two evils, but upon whether the action was necessary to uphold the hierarchy of rights which criminal law acts to defend. The criminal law forms a framework of rules curtailing individual freedom of action only insofar as this is necessary to support and maintain the welfare and autonomy of others. It is for this reason, for example, that doctors can take emergency action without the consent of a comatose patient to safeguard their welfare. On this view, the purpose of the law of theft is not to provide absolute protection to property, but to allow us to live our lives free from one (relatively minor) potential obstacle to living an autonomous life, namely the denial or usurpation of the fruits of ownership by others. Property crimes such as theft are, therefore, a means to an end – maximising the scope and value of human autonomy – not an end in themselves. The important implication of this is that a true maximisation of autonomy requires all inferior interests to yield to superior interests in cases of conflict.[38] For example, property rights must yield to personal rights since they are only there in the first place to make 'life worth living'.[39] This approach would not, as the harm approach would, justify sacrificing one life to save two, let alone several to save one, because the interest advanced (life) is no stronger than the interest sacrificed. It would, however, be permissible to steal, or to injure, but not kill, someone to save another. This would leave Adam without a justification in Cases 6 and 8 and thus dependent upon being able to raise an excuse. It would, however, render the mother's action justified in principle in both Cases 4 and 5. It would also appear to entitle Adam to commandeer the provisions in Case 7 but not Eve and Cain to kill Adam to recapture them – an unsatisfactory conclusion given that their conduct is morally indistinguishable.

Another weakness with this approach is that, like the outcomes approach, it is capable of justifying the victimisation of innocent people. It might justify, for example, coerced blood transfusions or kidney transplants to save a patient's life.[40] Even subject to a 'one-off' emergency qualification, then, the provisional view taken here is that the autonomy-based theory of justification is the most persuasive basis for understanding the majority of justificatory defences currently on offer[41] and to inform any subsequent doctrinal developments. The letter of the law can be broken, even if this means that third party interests are damaged, as long as the action is taken to prevent harm and the interests damaged are an unavoidable **side-effect** of that action rather than a direct attack on the autonomy of another using that other as means. These different approaches will be considered below in the section on necessity, when a final view will be taken.[42]

9.4 A COMMON DEFENCE TEMPLATE

In this and the succeeding chapter some attempt will be made to categorise defences according to whether they are excuses or justifications, although it may well be 'premature'

---

[38] For a different way of ordering interests see A. von Hirsch and N. Jareborg, 'Gauging Criminal Harms: A Living Standards Analysis' (1991) 11 OJLS 1; A. von Hirsch, *Censure and Criminal Sanctions*, Oxford: OUP (1993) 30–2.

[39] Or a right to a kidney yielding to a right to life; see A. Brudner, 'A Theory of Necessity' (1987) 7 OJLS 339 at 361–5.

[40] See A. Brudner, op. cit. 358–65. It also ignores the fact that, sometimes, less harm may be done by sacrificing the **superior** interest; cf. A. von Hirsch and N. Jareborg, op. cit.

[41] The prevention of crime is an obvious exception.

[42] Pages 258–70.

given the unwillingness of judges to make such a distinction and the undeniable difficulty of categorising certain defences.[43] Indeed, the attempt to identify such a rationale may be less helpful than simply drawing attention to those constant elements in the constitution of criminal defences which quite understandably, if erroneously, have lent support to the view there is a unified rationale rather than a collection of different claims to avoid punishment.[44] These constant elements (which I term the basic defence template) distinguish true excuses and justifications from quasi-defences rooted in the defendant's personality or psychological make-up. And, crucially, these constant elements which constitute the basic defence template support the alternative view that the various rationales of criminal defences complement, rather than compete with, each other. It creates the conditions under which it may be appropriate to justify the actor's conduct or excuse an actor for lacking the capacity or fair opportunity of conforming to the standards demanded, or which may reassure us that he did not betray the standards of character which we have come to expect of ordinary decent citizens, or was truly out of character.

The basic defence template which is common to all core defences is that in the face of an external trigger the actor reacted in such a way as to permit the usual inference to be blocked that he is a person of an anti-social character usually implicit in the fact that he has infringed a legal prohibition.[45] While the template helps structure defences according to shared moral organising themes it has nevertheless led to confusion as to what that theme is and thus to the appropriate constituent elements. For example, loss of self-control is particularly difficult to place. Is the underlying claim, like self-defence, 'because of the circumstances in which I was placed I acted reasonably/as reasonably as could be expected according to the relevant social standards applicable?' Or is it, like diminished responsibility, 'because of matters outside my control I experienced the norm as less easy to conform to than other people'?[46] The view advanced here is that this common defence template ensures that defences with **different rationales** are appropriately configured rather than being indicative of a **unifying rationale**. As we shall see in this and the following chapter, all defences whether excuses or justifications comprise three elements, namely (i) a trigger, (ii) a reaction (iii) a finding that the reaction does not disclose a dangerous or otherwise anti-social character based either in the reasonableness of the reaction (e.g. self-defence, mistake, or duress) or, alternatively, the unreasonableness of expecting the defendant to have acted any better (e.g. loss of self-control or automatism).[47]

9.5 EXCUSES

Excuses[48] 'excuse' in different ways, as has been explained. The two major models of excuses are largely consistent insofar as they proceed from agreement that the defendant's

---

[43] Robinson, op. cit. generally; cf. Smith and Hogan, op. cit. 194.

[44] The idea that there is such a unified rationale often leads, most notoriously in provocation in recent times, to inappropriate convergence in some elements of individual defences. See W. Wilson, 'The Structure of Criminal Defences' [2005] Crim LR; for criticism see J. Gardner, 'In Defence of Defences' in *Offences and Defences, Selected Essays in the Philosophy of Criminal Law*, Oxford: OUP (2007).

[45] G. Fletcher, *Rethinking Criminal Law* (1978) 799–802.

[46] J. Gardner and T. Macklem, 'Compassion Without Respect? Nine Fallacies in *R v Smith*' [2001] Crim LR 623; R. Mackay and B.J. Mitchell, 'Provoking Diminished Responsibility: Two Pleas Merging into One' [2003] Crim LR 745.

[47] W. Wilson, 'The Filtering Role of Crisis in the Constitution of Criminal Excuses' (July 2004) XVII(2) Canadian Journal of Law and Jurisprudence; W. Wilson, 'The Structure of Criminal Defences' [2005] Crim LR; P. Westen, 'An Attitudinal Theory of Excuse' (2006) Law and Philosophy 289.

[48] See generally J. Horder, *Excusing Crime* (2004); V. Tadros, *Criminal Responsibility* (2005).

claim to avoid punishment is that he lacked the bad character upon which the state's licence to punish is premised. On one account this is because his reasons for nonconformity were consistent with the values of a good citizen. On the other account, which will be emphasised here, it is because he was deprived of a realistic choice to conform his behaviour to the law whether due to internal incapacity or externally prompted crisis.[49] In the absence of capacity to conform, punishment is not only unfair, it is inappropriate; just as it is inappropriate to make animals the subject of a criminal prosecution.[50] Insanity and automatism are clear examples of this type of excuse.[51] In the absence of a fair opportunity to conform it would not be reasonable or fair (as he is only human) to expect the defendant to choose otherwise. Duress is a clear example of this type of excuse. The first excuse to be dealt with is that which represents the focal case of incapacity to conform, namely involuntary behaviour.

9.6 INVOLUNTARY BEHAVIOUR: GENERAL

Overview

A claim that one's action is involuntary amounts to a denial of authorship, that is, the capacity to have acted otherwise. It will be an excuse, therefore, that the physical cause of the *actus reus* of the offence in question was something or someone other than the accused. It will also be an excuse that, due to mental abnormality, the accused was unable to appreciate what he was doing or the significance of what he was doing. Where that mental abnormality is the result of some internal condition, for example brain damage, the excuse amounts to insanity, also termed insane automatism, for which the court retains special powers of disposition. Where the abnormality is the direct result of some external trigger, for example concussion, the excuse is termed (simple) automatism. This entitles the defendant to an unqualified acquittal.

Conduct which is 'literally' involuntary is generally treated as lacking even the hallmarks of action which, as explained earlier, is central to criminal liability.[52] If the defendant has not **acted** he can hardly be held to have **committed** the *actus reus* of any offence. Unlike standard excuses such as duress or mistake where the moral claim amounts to 'Don't blame me. I'm only human,' this defence amounts to a denial of authorship, in other words 'Don't blame me. It wasn't me that did it.'

What is the difference, then, between (punishable) **action** and (unpunishable) mere **behaviour?** An early attempt to define action describes it as a 'movement of the body which follows our volition'.[53] In other words, we are acting when the thing we do is something

---

[49] M. Bayles, 'Character, Purpose and Criminal Responsibility' (1982) 1 Law and Philosophy 5.

[50] Under the alternative model capacity-based excuses are not excuses at all but exemptions from liability. Children and the insane need no excuse for what they do. See, for example, J. Gardner, 'The Gist of Excuses' [1998] Buffalo Crim LR 575, 587–8. This may be correct as a matter of analytical propriety but it is more convenient to treat all claims to avoid punishment which do not negate the fact of wrongdoing as excusing the defendant from liability.

[51] 'As early as 1313 the Council of Vienna was responsible for a resolution to the effect that if a child, a madman or a sleeper (sleepwalker) killed or injured someone he was not to be held culpable.' Cited from N. Walker, *Crime and Insanity in England, Vol. 1: The Historical Perspective*, Edinburgh: Edinburgh University Press (1968) 166.

[52] See generally W. Wilson, 'Impaired Voluntariness: The Variable Standards' [2003] Buffalo Crim LR 1011.

[53] J. Austin, *Lectures on Jurisprudence* (3rd edn) (1869) 426.

which we will ourselves to do. Such an understanding is no longer thought illuminating since bodies, it seems, do not work like this.[54] When we comb our hair our arm lifts in response to neural impulses, not in response to any mental order to the arm to raise itself. Most action, then, is performed on 'automatic pilot', but this is not to say that such action is in any sense 'involuntary'. A more sophisticated understanding treats voluntary action as in some sense expressive of what the actor wishes to achieve. Action is behaviour with a point to it, even if, as in cases of habitual mannerisms, the point may be lost to the actor. We do not treat nervous tics and muscle spasms as action because action is conceived as something people 'do' rather than something which happens to them. Voluntariness, on this view, is an ingredient in action rather than a word qualifying it. Scratching one's nose is action if it expresses the actor's desire to relieve an itch. It is voluntary action even if the actor desperately wishes not to scratch his nose. It is not action if the finger comes into contact with the nose as a result of a neural spasm.[55] For general purposes, however, perhaps the most useful notion of voluntariness treats conduct as voluntary if it is not involuntary, and conduct is involuntary if he could not have acted otherwise than he did had he so decided.[56]

The prosecution, consonant with its general function, bears the burden of proving the defendant's conduct is voluntary in this narrow or literal sense.

Case 6

A uses B's hand against his will to punch C.

On a charge of assault, the prosecution will be unable to discharge their burden of proving the *actus reus* of assault on the part of B since it was not by B's act that C was hit. Thus absence of voluntariness strikes right at the heart of the *actus reus* requirement. On the other hand, the prosecution are under no general burden of proof in connection with what has been termed states of 'metaphorical' or 'moral' involuntariness – where free choice is compromised but not destroyed.

Case 7

A allows B, her wicked employer, to place a knife in her hand and stab C with it, feeling 'power-less' to prevent it.

Here it is no part of the prosecution's case to prove that this is what A wanted to do. Such states of 'metaphorical' or 'moral' involuntariness are only capable of negating liability if they happen to negate the *mens rea* of the crime or fit the 'template' of recognised defence, such as duress.[57] The effect and purpose of these templates is to control the quality of reasons capable of negating liability. A will only be able to rely on duress if she reasonably feared for her life or physical safety if she resisted.

If voluntary action is simply action which could have been prevented had D so willed, it follows that most action is voluntary in the narrow sense. To understand what the law

---

[54] H.L.A. Hart (1968) 90; G. Williams, *TCL* (1983) 148.
[55] H.L.A. Hart (1968) 105–6. The American Model Penal Code designates an action as voluntary if it is a product 'of the effort or determination of the actor': 1.13(3), 2.01(2)(d).
[56] See G. Williams, *TCL* 148.
[57] The term is that of S. Kadish, 'Excusing Crime' (1987) 75 Calif LR 257, 266; cf. G. Fletcher's 'Physical and Normative Involuntariness', *Rethinking Criminal Law* (1978) 803; Dickson J, *Perka et al.* v *The Queen* (1984) 13 DLR (4th) 1 at 14–15.

means by (literal) voluntariness of action, therefore, it is best to consider examples of involuntariness. To aid comprehension these will be separated into two groups – those where the actor lacks

(a) the physical capacity, or
(b) the mental capacity to act otherwise than he did.

9.7 INVOLUNTARY BEHAVIOUR (I): PHYSICAL INCAPACITY

Where the physical cause of a person's movements is an event outside the person's control that movement is involuntary and, subject to one qualification, an unqualified excuse.

Case 8

Adam suffers a heart attack at the wheel of his car which causes him to careen through a red traffic light.

Case 9

Adam trips over a loose paving stone and bumps into B, sending him sprawling onto the pavement.

In both the above cases Adam's conduct is involuntary. In Case 8 he will not be guilty of either careless/dangerous driving or failing to comply with a traffic sign since he is not the 'author' or 'cause' of the relevant behaviour. For similar reasons he will not be guilty of an assault in Case 9 although here, it should be noted, the substance of his excuse is equally an absence of *mens rea*.

The key importance of the requirement of voluntariness is seen, as in Case 8, in respect of those crimes where the prosecution do not have to prove *mens rea*, that is in crimes of negligence and strict liability. While it would be no excuse for a motorist charged with careless driving that they were on their first driving lesson and had not yet learned the rudiments, it is an excuse that, for reasons outside his control such as a heart attack, the motorist was merely behind the wheel as opposed to 'driving' the car.[58] For crimes of strict liability, including most driving offences, involuntariness of action may operate as a discrete defence superimposed upon the conditions of liability. It marks one small chink in the armour of strict liability.

Similar results follow where a person's behavioural control is compromised by other events. The author or cause is deemed to be the traumatic event which wrests physical control from a responsible actor, rather than any bodily movement which that event triggered.[59]

> Suppose a driver had a stroke or an epileptic fit, both instances of . . . Acts of God; he might well be in the driver's seat or even with his hands at the wheel, but in such a state of unconsciousness that he could not be said to be driving. A blow from a stone or an attack by a swarm of bees, I think, introduces some conception akin to a *novus actus interveniens*.[60]

---

[58] In *Cox v Rawlinson* [2010] C.L.Y. 2294 it was an excuse for a driver precipitating a car crash that this was preceded by an epileptic fit (County Court Croydon 18 January 2010).

[59] A.J. Ashworth, *PCL* (2006) 100; for an attack on the 'causation' approach to excuses see M. Moore, 'Causation and the Excuses' (1985) 73 Cal L Rev 1091.

[60] Lord Goddard CJ in *Hill v Baxter* [1958] 1 QB 277 at 283.

Allied to these instances are cases where the agent's loss of control over what he is doing is not attributable to a crisis which affects his body (or mind), but one which affects his activities, as where a car driver suffers an unexpected brake failure causing him to fail to give precedence to a pedestrian on a crossing.[61] This is the purest form of non-authorship since a runaway car cannot literally be driven.[62] The courts have not always respected this logic, possibly for reasons of expediency. For example in *Neal* v *Reynolds* the defence was unable to rely on automatism although it was accepted that the defendant was unable to avoid failing to give precedence on a crossing due to the unforeseeable action of the pedestrian.

A Prior fault

Although the conceptual basis of the excuse in cases of involuntary action is lack of author-ship, the moral claim to avoid punishment in these cases is that the responsibility for a harmful event is not **fairly attributable** to the defendant. It follows from this that a defend-ant will not have an excuse if a physical loss of control is attributable to the defendant's own prior fault.

> **Case 10**
> A points his loaded rifle at B in jest. A loud noise is heard and A pulls the trigger as a reflex action.[63] B is killed.

> **Case 11**
> On approaching a red traffic signal A applies the brakes, which fail due to poor maintenance on A's part. As a result he is unable to stop.

> **Case 12**
> A, a building labourer, is carrying a hod of bricks on a scaffold. He notices that his shoe is undone but decides not to do it up until the bricks are delivered. He trips up and the bricks fall on top of a passer-by, seriously injuring him.

In each of the above cases A's action is involuntary in the sense that the relevant conduct did not issue from a decision on his part to act in the relevant manner. Nevertheless his conduct is treated in law as voluntary since A was, in none of these cases, denied a fair opportunity of complying with the law. In each case, if he had acted responsibly, the rele-vant dangerous state of affairs would not have materialised.[64] It is reasonable to ascribe authorship to A in these cases since A is metaphorically the 'author of his own misfor-tunes'. This is not to say that A will necessarily be guilty of a criminal offence in all these cases as will now be explained. In Case 11 **A will be liable** for failing to obey a traffic signal since this is a strict liability offence and his 'I was not driving' excuse can be ignored due to his prior fault. In Cases 10 and 12, however, although A's physical behaviour will be

---

[61] *Burns* v *Bidder* [1967] 2 QB 227.
[62] Salmon J in *Spurge* [1961] 2 All ER 688, 690.
[63] *Gray* v *Barr* [1971] 2 All ER 949.
[64] *Larsonneur* (1933) 97 JP 206; *Winzar* (1983) *The Times*, 28 March above.

deemed voluntary, the prosecution must still prove the mental attitude required by whatever offence A is charged with. In Case 10 this could be gross negligence manslaughter. The prosecution will have to show that A displayed the necessary 'gross negligence' to incur liability for manslaughter. In Case 12, on a charge of maliciously inflicting grievous bodily harm, they must show that A foresaw harm befalling the passer-by. If they cannot, as is likely, A must be acquitted.

This type of analysis is adopted throughout the field of (successful) claims of involuntariness of action, whether in its literal or broader metaphorical sense. The basic idea is that it is not inappropriate to enforce a duty of rule-observance on those whose failure or incapacity could reasonably have been avoided.[65] Thus to successfully raise duress it is not enough simply for a defendant to adduce evidence of coercion. If he puts his future autonomy at risk by joining a dangerous gang, he cannot cry 'foul' later on if he is coerced into participation in a criminal venture. This corresponds directly with the position with involuntary action. If a lorry driver falls asleep at the wheel due to a failure to take sufficient rests, the imposition of liability will be justified since he chose to bring about the conditions which he is now claiming to support his defence.[66] He voluntarily traded in the promise of future autonomy for freedom now.[67]

9.8 INVOLUNTARY BEHAVIOUR (II): AUTOMATISM

As discussed above, underpinning fault generally, and defences in particular, is the idea that people should not be punished who did not freely choose to commit a criminal offence. This absence of choice is most marked in cases where the defendant's conduct is **literally** involuntary. The present discussion will concern itself with those occasions where involuntary behaviour stems from mental abnormality – cases where, in the words of Bramwell B, 'the defendant would not act differently if there were a policeman at his elbow'. Involuntary behaviour due to mental abnormality may result in an **outright acquittal** unless such abnormality amounts to insanity, in which case a **special verdict** of not guilty by reason of insanity will lie.

The general parameters of automatism are described in the following statement of Lord Denning, who, it should be noted, makes no conceptual distinction between physical and mental causes:

> No act is punishable if it is done involuntarily and an involuntary act in this context – some people prefer to speak of it as automatism – means an act which is done by the muscles without any control by the mind such as a spasm, a reflex or a convulsion; or an act done by a person who is not conscious of what he is doing, such as an act done whilst suffering from concussion, or whilst sleepwalking.[68]

Covered by this statement are the more obvious forms of involuntary behaviour, dealt with above, where, although conscious, the defendant is physically unable to control how he would like to act because he stumbles, sneezes, or is subject to a spasm or reflex action. Also covered are cases where loss of control is attributable to some mental abnormality – automatism strictly so-called. These have been held to include conduct while suffering

---

[65] P. Robinson, 'Criminal Law Defences', loc. cit. 268; cf. S. Kadish, 'Excusing Crime', loc. cit. 259.
[66] *Kay* v *Butterworth* (1945) 61 TLR 452; *Sibbles* [1959] Crim LR 660.
[67] P. Robinson, 'Causing the Conditions of One's Own Defence' (1985) 71 Virginia Law Review 1. Cf. L. Alexander, 'Causing the Conditions of One's Defense: A Theoretical Non-problem' (March 2013) Criminal Law & Philosophy [online article not yet assigned to an issue].
[68] *Bratty* v *A-G for Northern Ireland* [1963] AC 386.

concussion, diabetic hypoglycaemia,[69] post-traumatic stress syndrome, epileptic fit[70] or the side effects of medically prescribed drugs.[71]

Strictly speaking, automatism refers to conditions where the defendant's conscious mind is dissociated from that part of the mind which controls action. Since it is this conscious mind which tells us what things should and should not be done, this leaves the defendant unable to pitch his behaviour in accordance with rules. As can be appreciated, such conditions are rare and when they do occur are, as often as not, symptoms of the type of mental disorder which can render the defendant legally insane. Thus epilepsy and sleep-walking are usually treated in common law jurisdictions as examples of insanity for the purpose of criminal responsibility. Although these are cases of automatism, law designates these conditions as automatism resulting from insanity, or simply insane automatism. The remaining conditions such as concussion or hypnosis are capable of providing evidential support for a defence of simple (non-insane) automatism, entitling an outright acquittal. Since the nature of the defence of automatism invites comparison with insanity and other defences involving mental abnormalities, it is dealt with here rather than, as is more usual, in the chapter on *actus reus*.

A Automatism and crimes of *mens rea*

With respect to standard crimes requiring proof of *mens rea* successful claims of automatism do not require a total absence of consciousness. It is sufficient that, through mental abnormality, the fault normally associated with the presence of *mens rea* is absent. A subject suffering hypoglycaemia or concussion may therefore use their condition to negate the intention of foresight required for crimes of violence, theft or criminal damage.[72] An extreme example is that of *R v T*,[73] where the defendant engaged in a robbery with two other people in the course of which she stabbed the victim with a penknife. Medical evidence showed, however, that she was suffering from post-traumatic stress disorder, consequent upon having been raped. The symptoms of this condition reduce to a mixture of anxiety, depression, emotional numbness and disconnection but, unusually, it is medically identified by its cause – an external trauma.[74] The judge ruled that the defence of automatism was properly left to the jury. This is a problematic decision. On the face of it her action was purposive which ordinarily should have resulted in a conviction. Evidently, however, the judge was sensible to the ways the mind and the body can be dissociated from each other and for this reason considered that she did not necessarily intend her actions. If her story was true, she would have known what she was doing but her mind may have been insensible to the normative implications. She would have been acting as if in a dream. As in dreams, the mechanism of the mind which allows her (and us) to pitch our actions in accordance with our beliefs, knowledge and ambitions, and therefore in accordance with a system of rules, was absent.[75] Similar decisions have been reached, with more justification perhaps, in cases involving diabetics suffering hypoglycaemia, and medication which is apt to trigger mental confusion and consequent disordered behaviour.[76]

---

[69] *Quick and Paddison* [1973] QB 910; *Hennessy* [1989] 2 All ER 9 CA.
[70] *Cox* v *Rawlinson* [2010] C.L.Y. 2294 (County Court Croydon 18 January 2010).
[71] *T* [1990] Crim LR 256; *R* v *Huckerby* [2004] EWCA Crim 3251.
[72] *R* v *Clarke, infra.*
[73] [1990] Crim LR 256.
[74] M. Weller, 'Post Traumatic Stress Disorder' (1993) NLJ 878.
[75] See further W. Wilson, 'Impaired Voluntariness: The Variable Standards' (2003) Buffalo Crim LR 1011.
[76] See *Quick*, below.

B Automatism, negligence and strict liability

Automatism, as with other forms of involuntary conduct, is more fundamental than a simple denial of *mens rea* since it may also operate as a defence to crimes of negligence and strict liability, where *mens rea* is not required. Most significant in this context are driving offences. It operates in the same way as might a sudden operating defect in the car, for example, sudden brake failure.

> There does not seem to this court to be any real distinction between a man being suddenly deprived of all control of a motor car by sudden affliction of his person and being so deprived by some defect which suddenly manifests itself in the motor car. In both cases the motor car is suddenly out of control of its driver through no fault of his.[77]

However, doctrine works more harshly against the defendant than for crimes of *mens rea*. For crimes of strict liability, unlike the position seen in *R v T*,[78] the courts have generally insisted that behaviour does not cease to be voluntary simply because the defendant was deprived of the capacity to pitch his behaviour in accordance with the relevant standards. Rather, a total absence of conscious control is required.[79] Thus in *Broome v Perkins*[80] the defendant, a diabetic, was charged with driving without due care and attention. He had suffered a partial loss of consciousness, having taken insulin. His condition was such that his mind was dissociated from the mental processes necessary to drive a car responsibly. He was able to discharge the mechanical functions – accelerating, braking, swerving to avoid obstacles, changing gear and so on, but not the normative functions – driving systematically according to rules. In short, he could not have driven any better if there were a policeman at his elbow. Nevertheless the court ruled that it was not possible for him to rely on automatism since his consciousness and control were seriously impaired rather than absent. The supposed justification for this harsh result is that the offence charged was not an offence requiring proof of fault and it was fault which the evidence showed was lacking – not the capacity to drive a car or engage in other end-directed activities. This was (supposedly) evidenced by the fact that the defendant was still able to take driving decisions. This point was acknowledged in *Roberts v Ramsbottom*[81] in which Neill J conceded that the defendant 'was at no time aware of the fact that he was unfit to drive; accordingly no moral blame attaches to him'.

These decisions are clearly driven by questions of policy rather than principle. If authorship is insisted upon it can only be because, without authorship, fault is absent. And, if fault must be established, no meaningful distinction can be drawn between cases where the defendant is not driving and cases where he is driving but nevertheless is, for reasons outside his physical or mental control, deprived of the capacity or fair opportunity of complying with a driving regulation.[82] This principle is accepted with respect to other excuses where an equivalent lack of capacity or fair opportunity exists. Duress is available to careless and dangerous driving as much as it is to crimes of *mens rea*[83] which begs the question why coercion vitiates free choice while a loss of the ability to reason practically through to action does not. It is probable, then, that the real basis for restricting the availability of

---

[77] Salmon J, *Spurge* [1961] 2 All ER 688, 690.
[78] See below, footnote 81.
[79] *Stripp* (1978) 69 Cr App R 318 CA; *Budd* [1962] Crim LR 49.
[80] [1987] Crim LR 271.
[81] [1980] 1 All ER 7.
[82] Smith and Hogan, op. cit. 43.
[83] See *Conway* [1988] 3 All ER 1025; *Martin* [1989] 1 All ER 652, below.

automatism in strict liability cases is the policy implication of allowing a partial 'blackout' to excuse offences, whose own main rationale is to head off spurious excuses and other courtroom prevarications. Take, for example, *Attorney-General's Reference (No. 2 of 1992)*.[84] A lorry driver was charged with causing death by dangerous driving. He raised the defence of automatism, relying on the fact that driving for a long period on a motorway had caused him to fall into a trance, caused by the repetitive visual stimuli encountered on such journeys. This was a recognised medical condition and on this basis the jury acquitted. On appeal by the Attorney-General, the Court of Appeal ruled that the defence ought not to have been left to the jury since the condition did not entirely remove voluntary control. In this case the defendant would have been able to 'steer the vehicle and usually to react and return to full awareness when confronted by significant stimuli'.[85] However, it is difficult to see how the Court of Appeal could sensibly have reached any other decision. What motorway driver has not, on occasion, driven without awareness? Should this be a reason to acquit, or to increase sentence?[86]

C Conditions of automatism

The range of conditions which may offer support to a defence of automatism (simple) are, theoretically, any condition which renders the defendant unaware of what he is doing or otherwise unresponsive to reason.[87] Such conditions, as has been mentioned, are equally capable of supporting a defence of insanity which is distinguished from automatism only by its presenting cause as we shall see. Conditions which have or are thought to ground the defence include post-traumatic stress syndrome,[88] involuntary intoxication through drink or drugs,[89] carbon monoxide poisoning,[90] toxic shock,[91] hypnotic suggestion,[92] concussion,[93] confusional arousal,[94] epileptic fit[95] and, although there is strong authority to the contrary, sleepwalking.[96]

The most common presenting cause of simple automatic behaviour, however, is diabetes. In *Quick* a nurse attacked a patient and was convicted of assault occasioning actual bodily harm. He relied on evidence that he was a diabetic and was suffering, at the relevant time, from hypoglycaemia caused by taking insulin. At first instance the trial judge ruled that this amounted to a plea of insanity. The defendant, anxious to avoid a special verdict, thereupon changed his plea to guilty. He then appealed the judge's ruling. On appeal the Court of Appeal quashed the conviction saying that the defence should have been put to the jury. Lawton LJ described automatism as 'a malfunctioning of the mind of transitory effect, caused by the application to the body of some external factor, such as violence, drugs, including anaesthetics, alcohol and hypnotic influences'. Central to a successful plea

---

[84] [1993] 4 All ER 683.
[85] At 690 per Lord Taylor CJ.
[86] Cf. *Lawrence* [1981] 1 All ER 974.
[87] Such as post-traumatic stress syndrome. See generally R.D. Mackay, 'Non Organic Automatism: Some Recent Developments' [1980] Crim LR 350.
[88] *K* (1971) 3 CCC (2d) 84.
[89] *Quick & Paddison* [1973] QB 910, 922.
[90] *Cullum* (1973) 14 CCC (2d) 294.
[91] *King* (1961) 129 CCC 391.
[92] *Obiter* Lawton LJ in *Quick*. See below.
[93] Lord Denning in *Bratty*. See note 68.
[94] A suggestion raised in *Lowe*, Manchester Crown Court, March 2005.
[95] *Cox v Rawlinson* [2010] C.L.Y. 2294 (County Court Croydon 18 January 2010).
[96] See discussion at note 174.

of automatism, *Quick* tells us, is the fact that the condition results from some external 'trigger' which allows the 'cause' of the ensuing harm to be attributed to the event rather than defendant himself. Here that external trigger was the taking of insulin.

It is not every external event causing mental disturbance which will support a defence of automatism, however. The trigger must be in some sense extraordinary. In this respect automatism compares with other excuses such as duress and loss of self control where the cause of a criminal harm can similarly be attributed elsewhere but only if the (external) prompt is substantial enough as might make a reasonable person act as the accused did.[97] In *R* v *T* we saw that the trigger was a rape. Compare the Canadian case of *Rabey* where the trigger was the defendant's experience of having been jilted by his girlfriend.[98] Traumatised by his loss he took a pot shot at her with a rock, causing her injury. But here, the defendant was unable to rely upon his mental dissociation, even though it was effectively identical to that in *R* v *T*, namely the condition known as post-traumatic stress disorder. The court took the view that what had happened to the defendant was not so out of the ordinary as to count as an external cause. It should be noted that if the court does, as here, conclude that the external prompt is not extraordinary but the medical evidence still supports a finding of mental dissociation, the defendant's status is one of insane automatism.[99] The condition is deemed indicative of intrinsic mental fragility.

D Prior fault: self-induced automatism

As explained above, automatism has a number of features in common with other excuses. In particular, automatism, in addition to denying voluntary wrongdoing, involves the claim that the defendant was not at fault for acting as he did, lacking the capacity and fair opportunity to conform his behaviour to the standards demanded by law. Under certain circumstances this may justify punishment even where the conduct causing the harm in question was literally involuntary. Some examples of this have already been considered in the context of cases of involuntary muscle movement and accident. If A had acted responsibly in Case 12, the incident would not have occurred and he had the opportunity of so acting.[100] It would be less than A deserved to allow him to 'pass the buck' of responsibility over to the 'accidents of fate'. A similar position is encountered where mental incapacity is caused by external factors over which the defendant can be expected to exercise control. Where that external factor is voluntary intoxication, special rules apply which remove the defence from certain categories of crime[101] even though the defendant was entirely unaware of what he was doing and had no reason to know that the consequences might be dangerous. Thus in *Lipman* a defendant was unable to rely on automatism on a charge of manslaughter when, following ingestion of LSD, he suffocated his girlfriend believing himself being attacked by snakes.[102] His condition was self induced.

Where automatism does not result from the voluntary ingestion of intoxicants but the defendant is nevertheless at fault for getting himself into a dangerous condition the defence is likewise not available. In *Quick* the defendant had become violent in the course

---

[97] This supports the capacity rather than character model of responsibility as the latter tends to view excuses and absence of capacity as involving quite distinct claims to avoid punishment. And see below, Chapter 13.5.A.2.
[98] (1980) 2 SCR 513 Can SC.
[99] As the later English case of *Hennessy* [1989] 2 All ER 9 confirms.
[100] Cf. *Ryan* v *R* (1967) ALR 577.
[101] Known as crimes of basic intent (pp. 234–6 below).
[102] [1969] 3 All ER 410.

of a hypoglycaemic episode induced by a combination of diabetes and his own failure to maintain a satisfactory blood sugar level. Lawton LJ made it clear that such a failure was capable of disentitling the defendant from relying on automatism. If the jury had been so directed a conviction would have been proper:[103]

> A self-induced incapacity will not excuse . . . nor will one which could reasonably have been foreseen as a result of either doing something, as for example taking alcohol against medical advice after taking certain prescribed drugs, or failing to have regular meals while taking insulin.

In the later case of *Bailey* this proposition was qualified somewhat. Once again, the evidential foundation which the defendant raised for this defence was hypoglycaemia following ingestion of insulin with insufficient food to compensate. Griffiths LJ ruled that the defence would fail only if the accused acted (or failed to act) knowing 'that his actions or inaction are likely to make him aggressive, unpredictable or uncontrolled with the result that he may cause some injury to others'.[104] In other words, if the defendant's condition could have been prevented he will still be able to rely on automatism, unless **he was aware** that by acting in this way he was rendering himself a potential threat, that is, he discloses moral fault.[105] It should be noted that the decision in *Bailey* appears inconsistent with *Lipman* where liability was also imposed upon the basis that the defendant's condition was self-induced and not upon the basis that he foresaw he might become dangerous. Presumably in *Lipman*, the court was influenced by policy concerns absent in *Bailey*.

Although the approach in *Bailey* is to be preferred to that in *Quick* it does not always produce a kind result. A recent illustration is the case of *R v Rigby (Nigel)*[106] in which a diabetic suffered a hypoglycaemic episode while driving, after visiting his wife in hospital following her surgery for cancer. He had noticed that his blood sugar was abnormally high in the morning and so had administered an extra dose of insulin before the visit. However, he did not test himself again before leaving the hospital, but did drink a small amount of Lucozade. He did not notice any of the normal warning signs that preceded an episode and the episode culminated in him colliding and killing the victim, who was walking on the road because of icy conditions. He was convicted of causing death by careless driving. This conviction was grounded in the fact of his error of choosing to drive without rechecking his blood sugar levels, knowing that there was *some* risk of a hypoglycaemic episode. There but for the grace of God, as they say.

9.9 INVOLUNTARY BEHAVIOUR (III): INSANITY[107]

The defence of insanity is unusual in a number of ways. First, if successfully raised it will not result in an unqualified acquittal, but rather a special verdict of not guilty by reason of insanity. Upon such verdict the court has a wide-ranging dispositive discretion which includes hospital order, guardianship, absolute discharge, and supervision.[108] Before 1991 the only power available was mandatory indefinite committal to a mental hospital at the

---

[103] *Quick* [1973] 1 QB 910; the conviction was nevertheless quashed as the defence was not left to the jury.

[104] *Bailey* [1983] 2 All ER 503 at 506; cf. *Quick* above; *Bell* [1984] 3 All ER 842; *Hardie* [1984] 3 All ER 848.

[105] See generally R.D. Mackay, *Mental Condition Defences in the Criminal Law*, Oxford: Clarendon Press (1995) ch. 3.

[106] [2013] RTR 306(23), CA.

[107] See generally R. Mackay, *Mental Condition Defences in the Criminal Law*, Oxford: Clarendon Press (1995) 102–4; A. Loughnan (ed), *Manifest Madness: Mental Incapacity in the Criminal Law* (Oxford Monographs on Criminal Law & Justice), Oxford: OUP (2012).

[108] Criminal Procedure (Insanity and Unfitness to Plead) Act 1991.

Home Secretary's discretion.[109] As a result, the defence was understandably unpopular with defendants who might otherwise have wished to avail themselves of it.[110] The case law contains a number of instances of defendants relying upon non-insane automatism, who changed their plea to guilty upon the trial judge ruling that their defence was properly one of insanity.[111] Even a 'life' sentence for murder may be preferable to an indefinite committal – which might really mean life.[112] Although the defence has not gained significantly in popularity since the change in the law, it is not clear why, given the wide-ranging discretion now available.[113]

A second unusual characteristic is that, unlike other defences, it may be raised by either defence or prosecution.[114] The prosecution may raise it when the defendant puts his sanity at issue, for example by pleading diminished responsibility[115] or non-insane automatism.[116] When this occurs it seems probable, on analogy with the position on fitness to plead, that the standard of proof is the criminal standard.[117] Third, when raised by the defence, the burden of proof is with the defendant rather than, as is usual, the prosecution.[118] Fourth, a right of appeal exists against a special verdict even though technically the defendant has been found not guilty.[119]

The question of the defendant's sanity may be relevant at two other times in the course of a trial. It may be relevant upon arraignment, at which time defence, prosecution or judge may raise the issue that the accused is unfit to stand trial (unfit to plead).[120] If the court finds the defendant unfit to plead then a jury will be empanelled to determine whether the conduct element is made out. If it is not, the defendant is acquitted.[121] If it is, the judge has a dispositive discretion in all cases (including murder)[122] either to admit to hospital, or to make a supervision order, guardianship order or absolute discharge. The issue of fitness is decided by the judge as soon as it arises, considering matters such as whether the defendant understands the nature of the charges, can follow the course of the proceedings, can give evidence, and so on. The defendant's sanity may also be relevant at the time of sentencing. In this section we will consider insanity only as it is used as a defence.

---

[109] Criminal Procedure (Insanity) Act 1964, s. 5 and Sched. 1; see R.D. Mackay, op. cit. 106–8.

[110] R. Mackay, 'Fact and Fiction about the Insanity Defence' [1990] Crim LR 247.

[111] See for example *Hennessy* below.

[112] Although as Mackay's research shows, judges did not always implement the mandatory hospital order, op. cit. 254–5.

[113] R. Mackay and G. Kearns, 'The Continued Underuse of Unfitness to Plead and the Insanity Defence' [1994] Crim LR 576; plea of NGRI (not guilty by reason of insanity) used in only five cases in 1992.

[114] In *Price* [1963] 2 QB 1, Lawton J appeared to dissent from this view.

[115] *Bastian* [1958] 1 WLR 413.

[116] *Bratty* v *A-G for Northern Ireland* [1963] AC 386 at 411–12 per Lord Denning; *R v Dickie* [1984] 3 All ER 173 at 180 per Watkin LJ.

[117] Beyond reasonable doubt: *R v Podola* [1959] 3 All ER 418; *R v Robertson* [1968] 3 All ER 557; cf. though *Bratty* at 411–12 per Lord Denning.

[118] The onus is on the defence to establish such insanity on a balance of probabilities. See *R v Smith* (1911) 6 Cr App R 19; *R v Carr-Briant* [1943] KB 607.

[119] Criminal Procedure (Insanity) Act 1964, s. 2. See the fascinating account of the interplay of substantive and procedural aspects of the defence in A. Loughnan, 'Manifest Madness: Towards a New Understanding of the Insanity Defence' [2007] MLR 379.

[120] Criminal Procedure (Insanity and Unfitness to Plead) Act 1991, s. 2.

[121] In *R v Antoine* [2001] 1 AC 340 the House of Lords ruled that this conduct element did not include *mens rea*. However in *R v Burke* [2012] EWCA Crim 770 the Court of Appeal ruled that in connection with the offence of voyeurism it did include a mental element, namely that the defendant not only did the act concerned but did so for sexual gratification.

[122] Following Domestic Violence, Crime and Victims Act 2004, s. 24.

A The legal test of insanity

Overview

Insanity bears a very limited meaning for the purpose of criminal liability. A person is not excused simply because he is medically diagnosed as suffering from serious mental abnormality. A person is only excused on the ground of insanity if, at the time of acting, he was not aware of what he was doing and its significance or, if he was aware, that it was legally wrong. The lack of understanding or awareness must be due to a defect of reason caused by disease of the mind. It is this latter feature which serves to distinguish insanity from simple automatism.

The legal test of insanity is contained in a set of principles given by the judges in *M'Naghten's* case:[123]

> To establish a defence on the ground of insanity it must be clearly proved that, at the time of committing the act, the party accused was labouring under such a defect of reason, from disease of the mind, as not to know the nature and quality of the act he was doing, or if he did know it, that he did not know he was doing what was wrong.

The essence of the insanity defence is the removal of cognitive capacity (understanding and awareness) resulting from insanity rather than the condition itself. We do not excuse because the defendant was insane but because his mental condition was such as to prevent him being conscious that he was performing a wrongful act.[124]

The *M'Naghten* rules have a precise if unsatisfactory logic to them which it would be beneficial to explore. First, it must be shown that the defendant was suffering from a defect of cognition which rendered him unaware of what he was doing or the significance of what he was doing. Second, this defect of cognition must be caused by a defect of reason. Finally, this defect of reason must itself be caused by a disease of the mind. If it is not so caused, the defendant may possibly be entitled to an outright acquittal on the ground of non-insane automatism. Many of the leading authorities on insanity are, in fact, cases where the defendant sought (unsuccessfully) to raise the defence of simple automatism.[125] What counts as a disease of the mind is, then, of crucial concern to us. As will become apparent, the difference between insanity (insane automatism) and simple automatism is very much a matter of legal rather than medical definition.[126] A particular distinguishing feature, as we have seen, is that under simple automatism the condition is deemed to be prompted by **external** causes.

1 Defects of cognition

A defect of cognition is a defect of understanding or awareness. Two such defects are identified in the *M'Naghten* rules. The first is a defect which renders the accused unable to appreciate the nature and quality of his act. Such a defect may operate to negate the

---

[123] (1843) 10 Clark & Fin 200.

[124] H. Gross (1979) 298–300; the defence is not available in summary proceedings: *R v Horseferry Magistrates Court ex parte K* [1997] Crim LR 129.

[125] *Bratty* [1963] AC 386; *Kemp* [1957] 1 QB 399; *Sullivan* [1984] AC 156; *Hennessy* [1989] 2 All ER 9.

[126] Since the enactment of the Human Rights Act 1998 the courts must give priority to medical definitions at risk of contravening Article 5 ECHR. See Sutherland and Gearty, 'Insanity and the European Court of Human Rights' [1992] Crim LR 418.

definitional elements of the crime (*mens rea* and *actus reus*). It may also operate as an excuse superimposed onto the definitional elements for those whose actions may be purposive but are not, for reasons negating fault, subject to the defendant's normative control. States of dissociation are examples of these.[127] As a general rule, however, to count as legally sane a person needs to know what he is doing and the physical implications of what he is doing.[128] A person wielding a knife needs to know that knives can cause harm, that the object in front of him is a person capable of suffering injury, and that what he is doing is capable of causing that harm. A defendant charged with murder must have known that he was cutting the throat of a human being. If he is entirely unaware of acting, or unable, believing the world to be constructed in the image of cartoon adventures, to imagine the link between his act and the victim's death, the defence will lie. Similarly, if he believes that he is defending himself against a vicious animal,[129] or cutting a loaf of bread.

Little attempt has been made to assess how this limb might affect the criminal responsibility of a person for theft, but it seems reasonable to suppose that any defect of cognition which prevents the defendant realising his act is theftuous should suffice.[130] Thus a defendant charged with theft, who is unaware that objects are the subject of ownership, believing them to be 'floating around' waiting for people to avail themselves of them, should have a defence. So also should the 'Queen of England' who believes she owns all property or is entitled to appropriate it as 'tribute'.[131] Such defendants will also be protected under the second limb of the rules.

This leads to the related question of insane delusions. There are a number of conditions disposing the patient to suffer isolated delusions within long periods of lucidity. Such conditions, which include bipolar disorder[132] and schizophrenia, may result in paranoia or the sufferer hearing 'voices' which instruct them to commit a criminal harm. Are such people insane within the meaning of the *M'Naghten* rules? The *M'Naghten* rules deal specifically with insane delusions but allow them to negate responsibility only in a very restricted sense, namely where they operate to prevent the defendant from understanding the nature and quality of his act or that the act is wrong. Thus if the insane delusion causes the defendant to think a person is about to rape her, she will have a defence if she kills in self-defence, since the nature and quality of her act – an unjustified killing – is other than she thinks – a killing in self-defence. If the insane delusion causes her to think that the person **has previously** raped her and she kills in revenge, she will not have a defence since the nature and quality of her act – a revenge killing – is just as she thinks. If criminal responsibility turns on the defendant's having a free choice to conform or not to conform, the notion of choice operating here appears too narrow.[133] How free is the choice of a person instructed by God to kill,[134] or whose sense of personal identity is being destroyed by a conviction that the world is out to get them?[135] In the specific case of murder this problem is mitigated by the existence of the partial defence of diminished responsibility which covers such cases. For all other crimes, however, no such escape route beckons.

---

[127] *Rabey* above, described in S.J. Morse, 'Diminished Capacity' in Shute *et al.* (1993) 274.
[128] *Codere* (1917) 12 Cr App Rep 21.
[129] Cf. *Lipman* [1969] 3 All ER 410.
[130] Cf. *Egan* [1997] Crim LR 225.
[131] *People* v *Wetmore* 583 P.2d 1308 (1978).
[132] *R* v *M (M)* [2011] EWCA Crim 1291.
[133] It seems that juries may be sensitive to this fact; cf. R. Mackay [1990] Crim LR 247; R. Mackay and G. Kearns [1994] Crim LR 576.
[134] A limited defence of diminished responsibility may be available.
[135] *Humphreys* [1995] 4 All ER 1008.

The second defect of cognition referred to is the defendant's unawareness that what he was doing is wrong. Prior to the *M'Naghten* rules a superficially similar test had been used which required the jury to consider whether the defendant 'knew what he was doing, and was able to distinguish whether he was doing good or evil'.[136] Although a vague term, the phrase had the flexibility to allow juries to assess the defendant's moral responsibility for his action. The *M'Naghten* rules appear, on first sight, to offer a comparable degree of flexibility. The judges explained the meaning of 'knowing that what he is doing is wrong' as follows: 'if the accused was conscious that the act was one that he ought not to do, and if that act was (illegal), he is punishable'.

The requirement that the defendant be aware that his act was one 'he ought not to do' suggests commonsensically that he must be alert to some normative ground for acting otherwise, for example the standards of reasonable people at the time he is committing the act in question.[137] This is not, however, the interpretation which has been placed upon the rule. In *Windle* the defendant suffered from a strange form of insanity which allowed the suicidal obsessions of his wife to be transferred to him.[138] As a result, although he later admitted he knew what he was doing and that it was illegal, he gave her 100 aspirin tablets with fatal results. On the basis of his admission the Court of Criminal Appeal affirmed the ruling of the trial judge that there was no evidence of insanity. To know that an act is wrong, it was said, means to know that it is 'legally wrong' rather than wrong according to his own (moral) standard or the standard of others. In the earlier case of *Codere*, the Court of Criminal Appeal reached a similar conclusion but this time made clear the influence of policy rather than coherent notions of criminal responsibility: 'it is obvious that this proposition is wholly untenable and would tend to excuse crimes without number and to weaken the law to an alarming degree'.[139] Whether the anxiety of the Court of Criminal Appeal was well-founded or not is a matter of opinion, but it is clear that the application of the test misses the point of the second limb. This seems to be to ensure that those who are bereft of any standard by which to assess whether their action is properly to be pursued or not should not be found responsible. It is not to offer a defence to any Tom, Dick or Harry who claims his (distorted) morality was a higher consideration than the law.[140] Windle's utter state of moral confusion rendered him unable to reason practically about what 'he ought not to do'. Under such conditions it is difficult to see how a defendant could, in any meaningful way, be capable of being influenced by what he knew to be the legal position.

This stance seems to remove the political protection of this limb of the *M'Naghten* rules from all the mentally disordered save the few 'drooling idiots'[141] who do not know that theft and murder are illegal. Interestingly, however, research shows that the second limb of the defence is no less successful than the first even though the *Windle/Codere* test is theoretically too narrow to offer a realistic defence. The conclusion has been drawn that judges and juries and counsel are treating *Windle* with the (scant) respect it deserves.[142] Defendants who are unable, whatever their state of legal knowledge, to appreciate at the

---

[136] *Arnold* (1724) 16 St Tr 695, 765.
[137] Dixon J in *The King* v *Porter* 55 CLR 182 at 190.
[138] [1952] 2 QB 826. *Windle* was upheld in *Johnson* [2007] EWCA Crim 1978.
[139] (1917) 12 Cr App Rep 21.
[140] J. Hall, *General Principles of the Criminal Law*. See next note.
[141] J. Hall, op. cit. 481: cf. *Report of the Committee on Mentally Abnormal Offenders* Cmnd 6244, London: HMSO (1975) para. 18.8.
[142] Though see now *Johnson* [2007] EWCA Crim 1978.

time they acted that they 'ought not to have acted' in this way appear to receive a more sympathetic hearing than the strict legal position might lead one to expect.[143] Indeed, recent research shows that it is now the more popular of the two limbs.[144] While such 'principled' pragmatism is welcome it would still be more desirable 'for the law, practice and theory to be in harmony'.[145] In *Johnson* a retrograde step in this direction was taken. The defendant was a paranoid schizophrenic who had stabbed a neighbour in an unprovoked attack. The Court of Appeal, affirming *Windle*, held that if the defendant knew that what he was doing was legally wrong the second limb was inapplicable although his mental abnormality may have induced him to believe it was not morally wrong.[146]

(a) Compulsive and irrational behaviour

An excuse based upon defects of cognition has the advantage that its operation can be fairly easily controlled. It is not difficult to mistake when a person's cognitive functions are deranged or to trace such derangement to a particular mental disorder.[147] Further, when it operates, the excuse may negate a definitional element of the crime concerned, particularly the *mens rea*. Allowing a person to escape responsibility for lack of *mens rea* is not only compatible with penal policy, it is essential to it. In *R v Coley*; *R v McGhee*; *R v Harris*, the Court of Appeal explained the distinction between involuntary behaviour and irrational behaviour. To raise automatism the behaviour must be involuntary. If it is not involuntary but irrational this can only affect liability if *mens rea* is absent.[148]

> **Case 13**
> Adam adulterates Eve's coffee with alcohol as a joke. He suggests to her that she drops the cup on the floor to see if it will bounce. She does so without considering the possibility that it might break.

Eve is not in a state of automatism. Her action is irrational, not involuntary. To be acting involuntarily she would have to be unaware of what she was doing. Her liability for criminal damage is not assured, however. The prosecution will still need to prove *mens rea* for the crime, that is, that Eve intended or foresaw damage to the cup. This they will be unable to do because the facts tell us that she does not consider 'the possibility'. If she did, and dropped the cup because the alcohol unleashed her sense of 'silliness', then a conviction will be appropriate.

Apart from the crime of murder, where the partial defence of diminished responsibility may be available, for all other crimes volitional abnormalities do not bear upon criminal responsibility, since such conditions do not remove the *mens rea* or the 'action' part of the *actus reus*. Mental abnormality producing compulsive or impulsive behaviour, like other supposed determinants of behaviour such as poverty, education, upbringing and peer pressure, is treated as one of the constituent elements of the human condition which may dispose towards crime but is not deemed to excuse it.

---

[143] R. Mackay, *Mental Condition Defences in the Criminal Law*, Oxford: Clarendon Press (1995) 102–4.
[144] R. Mackay, B. Mitchell, L. Howe, 'Yet More Facts about the Insanity Defence' [2006] Crim LR 399 at 406.
[145] M. Allen, *Textbook on Criminal Law* (11th edn), Oxford: OUP (2011) 137.
[146] See note 142.
[147] This does not stop medical experts often conflating cognitive and volitional disorders. See research of Mackay *et al.* above, note 144.
[148] [2013] EWCA Crim 223.

Further, the kind of volitional defects which may be attributable to psychosis[149] or other mental disorder are less amenable to empirical verification. This has bred an understandable reluctance to allow a defence of 'irresistible' impulse, although it is recognised that some medical disorders and syndromes dispose to such a condition. Allowing such a defence, it is thought, may delay justice, offer immunity to dangerous (and blameworthy) people and encourage the invention of divisive social categories. It is also thought that allowing such a defence would threaten to subvert the notion of moral fault.[150] There is a big difference between committing a criminal harm because there is a gun to one's head and doing so because the urge to do so, if unsatisfied, would cause immense psychic pain. The latter must rely not upon our standards of acceptable behaviour but upon our compassion.[151]

On another view, volitional defects resulting from mental disorder should excuse as long as they are attributable to the disorder, rather than, for example, weak-mindedness.[152] Unfortunately medical science has not yet been able to demonstrate conclusively how mental abnormality affects volitional control. There is clearly scope for misleading expert testimony here. How can it be shown that the impulse was irresistible rather than simply too tempting to resist? Why should we accept, for example, the paedophile's claim that he could not help himself any more than we would if the temptation was a huge cache of banknotes and the temptee a very greedy person?

One response is that for the purpose of setting accountability the law should distinguish between those, such as the paedophile, who failed to resist an impulse **upon which he desired to act** and those whose condition **causes them to fail** to resist an impulse **upon which they desired not to act**.[153] Punishment of the latter, it might be thought, is inconsistent with the principle that excuses should be available where the accused lacks the capacity and fair opportunity to act otherwise than he did. Although uncontroversial examples of such conditions are hard to come by, one such is the condition known as environmental dependency syndrome. Sufferers find themselves unable to resist imitating what others around them may be doing, however hard they try. Worse, the sight of an object with a known function may cause an irresistible impulse to use it, whether the object is a comb, in which case they will comb their hair with it, or a gun, when they will fire it. Sufferers 'experience a loss of free will that is quite unlike the experience of patients with obsessive-compulsive behaviour, impulsive behaviour, manic disinhibition or any of the other conditions that might bring about superficially similar symptoms'.[154] It seems reasonable that pathological conditions affecting the mind, if they have a known cause with a known disposition to compulsive behaviour, should also operate as a defence where they disable a defendant from acting otherwise than he did.

(b) Psychopathy

The criminal law, by concentrating on the choices which people make rather than the causes or determinants of these choices, reminds us of the central significance, for criminal liability, of personal responsibility. The choice is ours, we are told, whether we are mentally,

---

[149] Severe 'disorders with loss of insight shown characteristically by delusions, hallucinations and certain forms of thought disorder'. The belief that others are manipulating one's thoughts: K.W.M. Fulford, 'Value, Action, Mental Illness, and the Law' in Shute *et al.* (1993) 307.
[150] *Kopsch* (1925) 19 Cr App R 50; *R v Sodeman* [1936] 2 All ER 1138.
[151] G. Fletcher (1978) 846.
[152] S. Kadish, 'Excusing Crime' (1987) 75 Calif LR 257.
[153] See D. Meyerson, 'Fundamental Contradictions in Critical Legal Studies' [1991] OJLS 439.
[154] D. Healy (1991), 17 May, *New Scientist* 40.

morally or economically fragile, to break rules or to conform to them and it is choice which informs our system of blame and responsibility. Consistent with this view, psychopathy is deemed to be consistent with the exercise of free will. It is defined as a 'persistent disorder or disability of the mind . . . which results in abnormally aggressive or seriously irresponsible conduct on the part of the person concerned'.[155] Even if the condition is a determinant of behaviour the psychopath is not seen as lacking the ability to choose to conform to rules. Psychopaths know what the rules are, know what they are doing and that it is wrong, and thus, typically, take pains to avoid detection. This shows that their 'rule-following mechanism' is intact, if less influential on behaviour than society considers acceptable. They are able to act purposively, that is, to put plans into operation, and understand the consequences of their actions both for themselves and for their victim. It might be argued that some form of limited defence should be available to take account of the fact that psychopaths, if responsible for their choices, are not necessarily responsible for being psychopaths in the first place.[156] Such an argument has been raised in the context of other excuses and has been rejected – with good reason [157] The condition, in theory, is in any event capable of supporting the partial defence of diminished responsibility, although juries have shown themselves reluctant to accept it.[158]

2 Defects of reason

A person who suffers a cognitive defect of the type described above will only come within the scope of the *M'Naghten* rules if the defect is the result of a defect of reason. Although many cognitive defects may result from defects of reason, they may equally stem from other sources. A search through any textbook of mental disorders will produce an impressive array of diseases, conditions, and syndromes indicative of mental abnormality and which may dispose towards unpredictable behaviour. One such condition, typically the result of brain damage, operates to remove a person's memory, both short- and long-term. This causes sufferers to be unable to remember anything for more than a few seconds. Every time the patient's doctor enters the room she will, therefore, see a complete stranger. Another condition removes the ability to see order in the world. The condition is so extreme that the sufferer can make no sense of anything he sees. In a famous example, 'a man mistook his wife for a hat'.[159]

Such abnormalities might obviously dispose the sufferer to cause harm. He might forget to turn the cooker off, thus causing a fire, or forget to pay for items at a checkout.[160] She might mistake her husband for a dartboard. The result of such cognitive deficiencies is to negate *mens rea* for any crime they are likely to be charged with. But would the lack of *mens rea* be due to a defect of reason? On one view it would not. A defect of reasoning could cause a man to mistake his wife for a hat but, arguably, a defendant suffering from a true defect of reasoning will persist with this mistake even after 'the hat' begins to speak. Commonsensically, however, the moral claim to avoid punishment is the same whether the mistake is the result of seriously disordered perception only or whether it is more deepseated. Both mistakes negate the mental ability to order the facts necessary to enable them to recognise that their conduct fell within the ambit of a prohibitory rule.

---

[155] Mental Health Act 1983, s. 1(2).
[156] See G. Williams, *TCL* (1983) 653–6.
[157] *Kingston* [1994] 3 All ER 353 HL.
[158] *Byrne* [1960] 2 QB 396.
[159] Oliver Sacks, *The Man Who Mistook his Wife for a Hat*, London: Picador (1986).
[160] Such was the subject-matter of *Clarke* [1972] 1 All ER 219 below.

A distinction is nevertheless made between a defect of reason and everyday absent-mindedness or mental confusion. In *Clarke* the appellant was charged with theft from a supermarket. She had placed some articles in her bag rather than the basket provided and had not paid for them. Her defence was that she had no intention to steal the items and that her behaviour was simply the result of absent-mindedness. To support her story she called medical evidence that she was clinically depressed, a condition which disposes to absent-mindedness. The trial judge ruled that she was raising a defence of insanity, whereupon she changed her plea to guilty. Her appeal was allowed on the basis that her powers of reasoning were unaffected by the illness. She had suffered simply a lapse of concentration.[161] In *Cox* v *Rawlinson* the Court accepted that epilepsy could ground the defence of automatism where the effect was to disable a driver from avoiding a crash, that is, where simple lack of control rather than mental confusion/dissociation was the cause of the accident.[162]

3 Disease of the mind

Clarke illustrates how a person suffering from the type of cognitive defect described above may not be legally insane. An unqualified defence is available in the relatively rare case that the mental disorder is not attributable to a 'disease of the mind'. Such a person may be entitled to an unqualified acquittal on the ground of (non-insane) automatism or simple lack of *mens rea*. As will be apparent from the discussion on automatism, the question whether a person is suffering from a disease of the mind is a question of law rather than medicine, although medical evidence may well be used in reaching that conclusion.

Two separate approaches have been taken as to what counts as a disease of the mind. The first takes a disease of the mind to be any disease which affects the ability to reason, whether a disease of the brain, a disease of the body which affects the mind, or a disease which simply affects the functioning of the mind. The leading authority for this approach is *Kemp*[163] in which an elderly man of good character attacked and killed his wife with a hammer. He was suffering from arteriosclerosis (hardening of the arteries) which caused him to black out due to congestion of blood in the brain. His defence was that his action was involuntary (automatism). Medical evidence supported the view that he did not know what he was doing when he picked up the hammer and struck his wife. Devlin J, in finding the defence to be one of insanity, rejected the argument that a disease of the mind involved a disease of the brain, despite the inconsistent conclusion reached a year earlier in *Charlson*.[164] He concluded:

> the condition of the brain is irrelevant and so is the question of whether the condition of the mind is curable or incurable, transitory or permanent . . . (In) the *M'Naghten* rules . . . the words 'from disease of the mind' . . . were put in for the purpose of limiting the effect of the words 'defect of reason' . . . The words ensure that the defect is due to disease of the mind and not simply to an untrained one . . . Hardening of the arteries is a disease which is capable of affecting the mind in such a way as to cause a defect, temporarily or permanently, of its reasoning, understanding and so on, and so is in my judgment a disease of the mind . . . within the meaning of the rules.[165]

On this basis, a disease of the mind may have an organic cause or it may involve simply a functional disturbance or psychosis. Organic causes may include

---

[161] *Clarke* [1972] 1 All ER 219.
[162] *Supra.*
[163] (1957) 1 QB 399.
[164] [1955] 1 WLR 317 in which a man suffering a brain tumour killed his son during a 'blackout'.
[165] [1957] 1 QB 399 at 407–8.

(a) diseases of the brain, e.g. senile dementia, epilepsy
(b) brain damage due to external agency, for example boxing or intoxicants,[166] and
(c) diseases of the body which have an effect upon the function of the mind, e.g. arterio-sclerosis and brain tumour.

Functional psychosis more accurately corresponds with the medical profession's assessment of 'diseases of the mind', probably since, unlike the foregoing, they 'treat' such conditions, and includes schizophrenia, bipolar disorder and psychopathy.

What is less clear is whether Devlin J would include **any** 'condition' which impaired the mind's ability to reason as a disease of the mind. This would render even concussion a disease of the mind. On the face of it he does, since the test includes conditions which can be temporary and curable.[167]

In *Bratty* a different approach was adopted but with the same purpose. The defendant was charged with murder, having strangled a girl with a stocking. Weak medical evidence was adduced to show that he may have performed the killing while unconscious, suffering from psychomotor epilepsy. The trial judge withdrew the defence of automatism from the jury on the basis that, if the jury believed the defendant's story that he had 'blacked out' and was unaware of what he was doing, his condition was one of insane, not simple automatism. This approach was approved in the House of Lords.[168] In the opinion of Lord Denning what makes a person insane within the meaning of the *M'Naghten* rules is not so much the nature or cause of the defendant's condition but that he may represent a danger to society and therefore be in need of specialised treatment, rather than an unqualified acquittal:

> any mental disorder which has manifested itself in violence and is prone to recur is a disease of the mind. At any rate it is the sort of disease for which a person would be detained in hospital rather than be given an unqualified acquittal.[169]

One advantage of this approach is that it limits the scope of *Kemp*, leaving a defence of automatism to those, like the concussed, whose condition is temporary and unlikely to manifest itself again in violence. An apparent disadvantage of *Bratty* is that the test appears restricted to crimes of violence. This may not have been practically significant at the time the statement was made since the defence was rarely raised except in cases involving serious violence. However, given the wide dispositive discretion now available to judges it promises to become more significant in the future as the popularity of the defence increases.[170]

Another disadvantage was highlighted in the case of *R v Quick* and gave rise to a second, more commonsensical approach to insanity. *Bratty*, as the above quotation indicates, appears to justify treating as insanity all conditions affecting reasoning which have a tendency to recur, as long as, on the occasion in question, the condition manifested itself in violence. Thus, the fact that violence was unlikely to recur does not seem to affect the applicability of the insanity defence, nor that the condition could be easily remedied.[171] In *Quick*, however, this latter fact is treated as central. The defendant was a diabetic who

---

[166] *R v Coley; R v McGhee; R v Harris*, 77 JCL. 194, CA (12/03/2013).
[167] On the other hand, the use of the word 'curable' suggests a condition which cannot be remedied without medical attention. This might exclude conditions such as concussion.
[168] *Bratty v A-G for NI* [1963] AC 386, 412.
[169] See previous note.
[170] See research done by Mackay *et al.* (2006), note 144.
[171] *Burgess*, below.

assaulted a patient while suffering from hypoglycaemia. Evidence showed that this was due to a combination of failing to eat and taking alcohol following taking insulin. Lawton LJ stated that the insanity defence was not appropriate for those whose conditions were transitory and caused by some external factor such as violence or drugs (such as insulin), even if the condition was likely to recur. He emphasised that the choice was not simply between an unqualified acquittal and a special verdict. There was a third option for those whose disordered condition was only likely to recur if they allowed it to. That option was a conviction and was appropriate where the automatism was self-induced or should have been prevented by the accused. The courts should hesitate to treat a condition as insanity which could be controlled by the use of drugs or other means. Rather they should aim to protect society by punishing those at fault in allowing themselves to get into a dangerous condition, but otherwise be prepared to acquit.[172]

In *Sullivan* the House of Lords adopted the *Kemp* rather than the *Bratty* or *Quick* approach. S attacked an elderly man while suffering from an epileptic seizure. His defence of automatism was refused and was put to the jury as one of insanity, whereupon he changed his plea to guilty. His appeal against conviction was rejected by the House of Lords. In the course of his opinion Lord Diplock stated, *obiter*, that a disease of the mind might not cover 'temporary impairments (of the mental faculties) resulting from an external physical factor such as a blow to the head . . . or the (therapeutic) administration of an anaesthetic'.[173] Beyond this he agreed with Devlin J:

> that 'mind' in the *M'Naghten* rules is used in the ordinary sense of the mental faculties of reason, memory, and understanding. If the effect of disease is to impair these faculties so severely as to have either of the consequences referred to in the latter part of the rules, it matters not whether the aetiology of the impairment is organic, as in epilepsy, or functional, or whether the impairment itself is permanent or is transient and intermittent. What was important was not how easily remedied the condition was, but whether it resulted from internal or external causes.

Sullivan set the stage for the current domestic approach to sleepwalking. This will be examined later in some detail, not least because it casts some light on the cogency of the external/internal test used to distinguish sane and insane automatism. In *Burgess* the defendant broke a bottle over his girlfriend, hit her with a video recorder and then tried to strangle her. The defence raised the defence of automatism with supporting evidence that it was carried out during a sleepwalking episode. The judge ruled that the evidence supported an insanity plea rather than simple automatism. The Court of Appeal dismissed the appeal on the basis of the *Sullivan* ruling. The expert medical opinion was that sleepwalking was a mental abnormality, was transmitted through heredity and hence, though there were external triggers – drugs, alcohol, excessive fatigue, sleep deprivation, tiredness and stress can all precipitate sleepwalking – the episodes were due to an internal factor, namely, the inbuilt tendency of the person to sleepwalk.[174]

(a) *Internal and external causes: the cogency of the distinction*

In some cases mental abnormality can be attributed to a combination of internal and external factors. The problem may then arise as to how to determine whether the condition

---

[172] [1973] QB 910 at 922.

[173] [1984] AC 156 at 172.

[174] See discussion at note 186 below. If the sleepwalking is precipitated by alcohol and the subject knows that alcohol is likely to precipitate an episode of sleepwalking (*Finegan v Heywood* (2000) HCJ), then the sleepwalker would be considered reckless and a conviction may be proper. See *Quick*, above, also *Bailey* [1983] 2 All ER 503.

is due to the one rather than the other. What seems clear is that external prompts can, themselves, become internal conditions once they lead to continuing pathology. For instance, if a car accident causes a defendant to commit a criminal harm while suffering from its immediate effects he may avail himself of the defence of automatism.[175] If, however, that accident causes brain damage which disposes him to commit crime, only insanity will lie. This despite both conditions resulting from the selfsame trauma.[176]

Another challenging problem was encountered in *Hennessy*. The defendant sought to attribute his failure to take insulin, and therefore his conduct, to a number of external causes, in particular marital and work problems which had caused him to suffer clinical depression. If these counted as external causes an outright acquittal would have been proper.[177] A similar argument had been successful in *R v T* where the trauma of a rape was held to conduce to a state of (non-insane) dissociation inconsistent with the presence of *mens rea*.[178] This argument was rejected at first instance and on appeal. The Court of Appeal, relying on *dicta* of Lord Diplock in *Sullivan*, drew a distinction between the type of everyday external causes (lacking 'the feature of novelty or accident') which might dispose someone to suffer stress and anxiety and those which were abnormal. A similar distinction was drawn in *Rabey*.[179] If Hennessy had been in a car accident, or had suffered a rape, and had forgotten to take his insulin he would apparently have been able to avail himself of the defence of automatism. As his depression was simply due to his susceptibility to 'normal' (whatever they are)[180] external pressures, however, he was forced to rely on insanity.[181] Hennessy's problem was that he could not show that his condition was a 'one-off'.[182]

Whether the distinction between 'normal' and 'abnormal' or 'novel' or 'accidental' external prompts holds up here is a matter of some doubt. Clearly rape is traumatic in a way that losing one's job or one's spouse, debilitating as it is, is not. Yet concentrating upon the 'abnormal' is not entirely cogent. Would a burglary or a mugging be sufficiently extraordinary to support the defence? Would a reasonable person suffering from such a temporary crisis be less or more disposed to suffer mental dissociation than a person whose spouse had died or decamped? Would it make any difference if the spouse had been murdered or kidnapped? Although common sense may be able to make a distinction between *R v T* and *Hennessy*, the test of 'novelty or accident' seems ill-equipped to deliver criminal justice.

The status of hypnotic influences, which is generally assumed to cause simple as opposed to insane automatism, may have to be reassessed in the light of this decision.[183] Not everybody is susceptible to the type of hypnotic influences which, it is claimed, may impel a person to commit crime. Is auto-suggestion 'novel' or 'accidental' or is it simply very persuasive to very suggestible people? And, for those who are susceptible, it is rare for the subject to do things, e.g. take off their clothes, which they really do not wish to do. This suggests that hypnosis acts to disinhibit rather than remove authorship. If this is correct,

---

[175] *Stripp* (1978) 69 Crim App R 318.

[176] *Stripp*, above.

[177] [1989] 2 All ER 9.

[178] See note 73.

[179] See note 101.

[180] See, for example normal/abnormal discussion in Chapter 5.

[181] Rather he disclosed, through his evidence, his propensity to suffer 'bad luck' – a mark of character.

[182] The Crown Court decision in *Thomas*, *The Times* 21 November 2009, suggests that such considerations influenced the court to consider a sleepwalking episode prompted by a recent shock to the psyche as a 'one off'.

[183] Lawton in *Quick*.

the subject still retains sufficient mental resource to comply with the law, perhaps justifying a conviction rather than acquittal whether qualified or not.[184]

The problem of principle posed by the internal/external division is that it makes illogical, hair-splitting distinctions inevitable, allowing some an outright acquittal while condemning others to plead guilty or take the risk of a special verdict. Diabetes gives a prime example of this. It may dispose to violence and other irrational behaviour where blood sugar is excessively high (hyperglycaemia) or low (hypoglycaemia). Both can be caused by external factors, such as the consumption of alcohol or insulin, or internal factors, for example lack of food or insulin deficiency. The upshot is that the person whose condition is caused by the body overproducing insulin (internal cause) may be legally insane, whereas the diabetic whose condition is caused by insulin overdose (external cause) is sane. Yet the condition of both can be 'cured' by a lump of sugar. Hardly satisfactory.

A related problem arose in the recent Crown Court case of *Lowe* in connection with sleepwalking.[185] The defendant, who had no history of violence, went out drinking with his aged father, with whom he had hitherto had a good relationship. Later that night he killed his father in the course of a violent attack. The defence case, which was fully supported by the medical testimony, was that Lowe had a history of sleepwalking and that the attack occurred while in just such a condition or, alternatively, when he was in a 'confusional arousal state', that is, when he was coming out of sleep but was still unaware of what he was doing. The medical evidence confirmed that disturbance during deep sleep may result in a sleepwalking episode. Under the *Burgess* approach this counts as an **internal factor**, as the sleepwalking would be indicative of underlying mental abnormality. Lowe has a sleepwalking tendency (internal factor) and he sleepwalks when he takes alcohol and/or is disturbed during deep sleep. The view taken was that even if an external factor was implicated, the innate mental disorder was the driving force behind the act. There was, however, another possibility, namely that a force other than the innate mental disorder was at work and that this was the sole cause of the attack. On the night in question there was a strong possibility that Lowe may have been forcibly aroused by his father into what the medical experts described as a confusional state. This state could have led to the savage assault on his father and would count as an **external factor**.[186] Such a conclusion was apparently the deciding factor in the prosecution withdrawing charges in the case of *Thomas* in which the defendant strangled his wife having awoken from a nightmare in which he was being attacked by intruders.[187]

Lowe and *Thomas* highlight the problematic nature of *Burgess*, raising questions about the function of expert medical evidence in automatism cases. In *Lowe*, in particular, the medical experts were understandably not able to confirm whether the attack was committed while sleepwalking or while in a confusional arousal state. The trial judge directed the jury that it was open to them to find the defendant not guilty if it was a reasonable possibility that the attack took place during a confusional state brought on by a forcible arousal. Otherwise, assuming the attack was indeed not volitional, it was open to deliver a special verdict if, as the defence had claimed in the alternative, they were persuaded that it may have been undertaken while sleepwalking. This direction presented the jury with a wholly

---

[184] *Kingston* [1994] 3 All ER 353 HL.
[185] Manchester Crown Court, March 2005.
[186] See W. Wilson, I. Ebrahim *et al.*, 'Violence, Sleepwalking and the Criminal Law' (parts 1 and 2) [2005] Crim LR 614; R. Mackay and B.J. Mitchell, 'Sleepwalking, Automatism and Insanity' [2006] Crim LR 901.
[187] *The Times*, 18 November 2009.

unrealistic task since they were also quite properly told that sleepwalking (insanity) had to be established by the *defence* on a balance of probability, whereas confusional arousal (simple automatism) had to be negatived by the *prosecution* to the criminal standard of proof. Even if juries can make sense of this one it is difficult to believe that they will ever find it easy to deliver an outright acquittal in cases of murderous violence. Given the necessarily abstruse nature of the direction available, it is manifestly probable that a jury will deliver a special verdict (or indeed convict), whatever view is taken of the evidence, wherever the burden of proof lies and whatever the standard. And indeed this is exactly what happened in *Lowe*. Similar problems have arisen in connection with epilepsy.[188]

In this light and, given that medical evidence of mental disorder is in any event being filtered through legal definitions, it would seem to make more sense for the court to be given specific powers of disposal in crimes of violence, whether or not mental disorder strictly so termed is the causative feature, wherever the defendant's conduct is appropriately attributable to a medically recognised determinant.[189] Alternatively, at least as a stopgap measure, it may be appropriate for the criminal law to return to the approach adopted in *Bratty* so that physical, mental, or neurological conditions which are innate rather than the product of external trauma are treated as insanity if they trigger violence, but not otherwise. As has been explained, sleepwalking is a common enough activity and sleepwalkers are known to be able to perform any number of activities while 'unconscious'. The apparent consequence of *Burgess* is that activities which would, in a conscious person, result in criminal liability, will convert an otherwise normal person who performs them while sleepwalking into a person who is legally insane. This is difficult to support on any ground, medical, legal, or practical. It would mean that a sleepwalker who dropped a cup while making a cup of fantasy midnight tea, or who urinated in a hotel cupboard, would be insane for the purpose of the law of criminal damage, a serious departure from the notion that the verdict of criminal courts communicates desert. It is noteworthy, *Hennessy* apart,[190] that where violence has not occurred, the case law is far less concerned by the external/internal distinction. For example, in cases where the defendant suffers a temporary (total) loss of consciousness due to internal causes, whether due to cerebral haemorrhage, epilepsy (*petit mal* or *grand mal*) or diabetes, they have often been afforded an excuse for crimes of 'inattention', such as driving offences.[191] And, as has been seen, in *Clarke* depression leading to mental confusion was treated as capable of negating the *mens rea* for theft without resort to the special verdict. This commonsense approach coheres with Article 5(1) ECHR which enacts that the detention of a person of unsound mind is lawful only to the extent that such detention is necessary for his or the public's safety and that his mental abnormality is established by 'objective medical expertise'.[192] This is now incorporated in domestic law. Any hospital order must be justified by medical evidence that justifies detention in hospital on grounds of a mental disorder within the Mental Health Act 1983 which in turn requires specialist treatment.[193]

---

[188] See the fascinating research done by R. Mackay and M. Reuber, 'Epilepsy and the Defence of Insanity – Time for a Change?' [2007] Crim LR 782.

[189] For a different view see Mackay and Mitchell (2006).

[190] Hennessy was charged with taking and driving away and driving while disqualified.

[191] This seems to follow from *Broome v Perkins* (1987) 8 Cr App R 321; *Cox v Rawlinson* [2010] C.L.Y. 2294 (County Court Croydon 18 January 2010). *Lewendon, The Times*, 14–16 December 1961 and generally G. Williams, *Textbook of Criminal Law* (1983) 676–7.

[192] *Winterwerp v Netherlands* (1979) 2 EHRR 387. This is required by s. 37 Mental Health Act 1983.

[193] Section 24 Domestic Violence, Crime and Victims Act 2004.

B Involuntary behaviour: evaluation[194]

By ignoring medical definitions the law of insanity is pitched in such a way as to create some apparent problems of justice. Notable in this respect is the exclusion of certain extreme cases of compulsive behaviour which may be thought to negate a free choice. Psychoses such as manic depression, paranoia or schizophrenia may provide the basis for a defence, but only where they have the effects stated in the rules.[195] If they operate simply to disinhibit or result in impulsive or even compulsive behaviour, however, they do not offer a defence,[196] even if the offence in question would not have been committed if the defendant had not suffered the condition.[197]

Quite apart from the human rights implications, common sense and a commitment to fair labelling dispose us not to consider conditions such as epilepsy, sleepwalking, and diabetes as insanity.[198] Cases such as *Sullivan* illustrate dramatically the great division sometimes existing between doctrine and the purposes doctrine is designed to serve. It is only a matter of time before English Courts are forced to reconsider *Sullivan* and all cases where there are no objective medical grounds for attributing mental malfunction to mental abnormality. In the meantime English law is bereft of a satisfactory method of dealing with defendants who, although lacking fault, have a condition which poses a potential threat to the public. In this latter case, in order to avoid a special verdict the defendant changed his plea to guilty. By their agreement and subsequent sentence (probation under medical supervision), all parties indicated that the defendant was not properly the subject of criminal proceedings. Nevertheless a formal collusion was necessary to avoid the consequences of attaching the inappropriate label of insanity to the defendant's condition. As things now stand the court has a sentencing discretion, including absolute discharge, guardianship and supervision. Coupled with restrictions now imposed on unnecessary hospitalisation,[199] this should mean that the insanity defence will become more popular and recent evidence confirms this opinion.[200]

A long-term solution would be to follow the recommendations of the Butler Committee largely reproduced in the Draft Criminal Code[201] which would tear up the *M'Naghten* rules entirely. Problems of social defence posed by conditions disposing to automatism would be dealt with by a new defence of mental disorder. This would allow the court to offer a method of disposal appropriate to the defendant's condition, in line with the 1991 Act, without the stigma which a finding of insanity generates.

---

[194] See generally The Bradley Report, a review of people with mental health problems or learning disabilities in the criminal justice system (2009) http://www.cambridgeshire.gov.uk/NR/rdonlyres/CD1F1F71-3A87-43C7-BFF7-54F0741DBA04/0/TheBradleyReport.pdf; R.D. Mackay 'Ten More Years of the Insanity Defence' [2012] Crim LR 946.

[195] Although, as we shall see, compulsive behaviour may under certain circumstances offer a partial defence to murder.

[196] Other jurisdictions, particularly Civil Law countries, allow severe mental disorder to excuse. For the history of the insanity defence in English law see N. Walker, *Crime and Insanity in English Law, Vol. 1: The Historical Perspective*, Edinburgh: Edinburgh University Press (1968).

[197] H. Gross (1979) 298–302.

[198] See for example the response to the House of Lords decision in *Sullivan* [1984] AC 156 reflected in P. Fenwick and E. Fenwick (eds), *Epilepsy and the Law: A Medical Symposium on the Current Law*, London: Royal Society of Medicine (1985); R. Mackay and M. Reuber, 'Epilepsy and the Defence of Insanity – Time for a Change?' [2007] Crim LR 782.

[199] Section 24 Domestic Violence, Crime and Victims Act 2004. See note 197.

[200] See note 192; R. Mackay and G. Kearns, 'The Continued Underuse of the Insanity Defence' [1994] Crim LR 576.

[201] Butler Report on Mentally Abnormal Offenders (Cmnd 6244, 1975) cl. 35–6; see generally E. Griew, 'Let's Implement Butler on Mental Disorder and Crime' [1984] CLP 47.

As for other forms of mental illness, the Butler Committee recommended that severe mental illness (that is, the major psychoses) or handicap should be a defence to a criminal charge, whether they produced cognitive or volitional defects. Clause 34 of the Draft Criminal Code allows only cognitive defects, including lack of *mens rea*, to sustain a defence of mental disorder. Such defects include impairment of intellectual faculties, delusions, abnormal perceptions and 'thinking so disordered as to prevent reasonable appraisal of the defendant's situation . . .'. The omission of explicit reference to volitional defects in the Code may, however, be more apparent than real. The notion of personal responsibility underpinning the criminal law is probably well served by ignoring the easy claim that the impulse to offend was irresistible. If it really was irresistible it should not be too difficult to rest the excuse in the more fundamental claim that the defendant lacked the basic rationality demanded by clause 34. As one commentator puts it: 'it must be irrational to want to produce unjustified harm so intensely that failure to satisfy that desire will create sufficient dysphoria to warrant an excuse'.[202]

The courts are showing an increased willingness to allow excuses where external events render effective rule-following impossible and where such events compromise the minimal capacities for rational action.[203] There is some scope already for treating conditions caused by psychosis in the same way, where it can be shown that the defendant's conceptual (as opposed to volitional) capacity to follow rules (rationality) has been compromised. Given the limited scope of diminished responsibility and the dispositive flexibility now open to the courts, it is perhaps surprising that defendants are not seeking to adduce such ideas.

A weakness in the proposals of both the Butler Committee and the Law Commission is the continued emphasis upon the cause of irrationality, rather than the irrationality itself. This might unfairly prejudice those who commit a criminal harm without responsibility and without a corresponding mental condition to support it.[204] A fairer approach might be to focus upon the effect of abnormality rather than its source. Under such an approach mental abnormalities falling short of *M'Naghten* would operate as a cognate excuse wherever there is evidence of interference with the defendant's rule-following processes, so as to render effective rule-following impossible and the public safety can be assured by requiring some form of dispositive control.[205]

9.10 MISTAKE

In Chapter 8 it was seen how certain mistakes do not affect liability. If A shoots the wrong person 'by mistake' or buries and kills a live person under the mistaken belief that he has already killed him, these mistakes do not affect liability. On the other hand, it was also seen how the making of a mistake may negate criminal liability. A person is not guilty of rape if he mistakenly but reasonably believes the other to be consenting, or of theft if he mistakenly believes the item appropriated to be his own property, since this belief is inconsistent with the *mens rea* requirements of the two offences. Certain mistakes operate more like

---

[202] S.J. Morse, 'Diminished Capacity' in Shute, Gardner and Horder (1993) 265; as an example of such a condition see the discussion on environmental dependency syndrome (above, p. 218). Another classic case of irrational action dressed in the clothes of compulsive behaviour is Munchausen's syndrome by proxy, the condition suffered by nurse Beverley Allitt who killed her patients as a means of drawing attention to herself.

[203] *R v T* above.

[204] See generally K. Fulford, 'Value, Action, Mental Illness and the Law' in Shute *et al.* (eds) (1993).

[205] The Law Commission published a discussion paper on insanity and automatism on 23 July 2013 [scoping paper published in July 2012 and responses informed the discussion paper]: http://lawcommission.justice.gov.uk/docs/insanity_discussion.pdf.

true defences, excusing the accused although the formal elements of the offence are established. Although acting in different ways, it is not inaccurate to designate both types of mistake as excuses since they challenge the propriety of attributing a given wrongful deed to the defendant. In this section some different mistakes will be examined with a view to assessing their potential impact on criminal liability. The general principle which emerges is that a mistake may affect liability if

(a) it negates an element in the *mens rea* which the prosecution carry the burden of proving, or
(b) the mistake was as to the existence of facts or circumstances which would have provided the defendant with a discrete defence.

A Definitional mistakes

In *DPP* v *Morgan*[206] the House of Lords ruled that where the definition of the offence incorporates a mental element and the defendant was labouring under a mistake which might preclude that mental element the only issue for the court was whether that mental element was present or not. Thus where, on a charge of rape, the defendant asserts that he mistakenly believed the victim to be consenting the prosecution would fail unless this claim can be disproved. It would fail although the defendant had no reasonable grounds for forming this belief. The Sexual Offences Act 2003 has now removed this latter feature within the constitution of the offence of rape. Reasonable grounds are of the essence.[207] However, the principle involved remains sound. A mistake which negates a mental element which the prosecution bears the burden of proving prevents liability from being incurred. If it does not, or the prosecution does not bear such a burden, it will not affect liability.

> **Case 14**
> A buys a new car. On the way home from the garage he exceeds the speed limit as the speedometer is faulty.

In Case 14, were A to be charged with a speeding offence, a crime of strict liability, it will make no difference to his liability that he quite reasonably assumed he was driving within the speed limit as the prosecution do not bear the burden of proving that the speed limit was exceeded knowingly or negligently.

For crimes of negligence, an honest though unreasonable mistake will be similarly inoperative.

> **Case 15**
> A, a doctor, injects B, an unconscious patient, with painkiller, mistakenly believing him to be receiving treatment for cancer. In fact B needs a large dose of adrenalin to prevent death from a wasp sting to which he is allergic. B dies as a result.

On a charge of manslaughter by gross negligence, A's mistake will not affect his liability if the jury are convinced that it was grossly unreasonable in all the circumstances.

[206] [1976] AC 182.
[207] By section 1(1).

Occasionally the courts have allowed mistaken beliefs to excuse from liability, although the offence is not defined so as to render the substance of the belief an offence element. In *Tolson* the Court for Crown Cases Reserved stated that a married person has a defence to bigamy if she goes through a marriage ceremony with another under the reasonable misapprehension that her husband is dead.[208] The court made clear that the defence took effect although all the elements of offence were present. It was the reasonableness of the belief rather than the fact that it was honestly held which provided the excuse.

In *DPP* v *Morgan*[209] the House of Lords ruled that on a charge of rape it is misconceived to present the issue, as it had been in *Tolson*, in terms of a defendant having a defence of (reasonable) mistake.[210] As Lord Hailsham put it, since the *actus reus* of rape was non-consensual intercourse, the *mens rea* for this crime was an intention to have **non-consensual** intercourse. It followed that that intention would inevitably be negatived by an honest (albeit unreasonable) belief that the other were consenting.[211]

This begs the question, of course, as to whether the prosecution bear the burden of proving a given mental element. As explained in Chapter 8, even offences of *mens rea* do not demand that every part of the *actus reus* has a corresponding mental element. The possibility therefore remains that a defence of reasonable mistake may sometimes be available, as it was in *Tolson*, to accommodate the culpability gap arising where an *actus reus* element carries no corresponding mental element. Significantly, with regard to crimes of moral wrongdoing at least, the House of Lords have shown an increasing willingness to construe *actus reus* elements as carrying a corresponding mental element. Thus in *B (a minor)* v *DPP*,[212] on a charge of inciting a girl under 14 to commit an act of gross indecency[213] the House of Lords ruled that the offence was one of *mens rea* and that a mistaken belief that the girl was over 14 negated that *mens rea*. There was no requirement that the appellant's mistaken belief be based on reasonable grounds.[214] It seems then that the potential scope of an excuse of reasonable mistake is extremely limited. The signs are that the courts are more likely to interpret an offence as bearing an (undisclosed) mental element than to tailor special defences of reasonable mistake to qualify the rigours of strict liability.

B Mistake as to defences

Criminal liability requires the prosecution not only to prove the definitional elements including *mens rea*, but also to **disprove** any defence (including those expressed or implied in the offence-definition) for which evidence is adduced. Mistakes may have a bearing also upon the successful raising of a defence. For example, a person who uses force to defend herself may find that she was mistaken in her view that she was being attacked and therefore in her view that the use of force was necessary. The fact that she was mistaken is not fatal to the successful raising of the defence. The general position as to the relevance of mistakes as to defences depends upon the nature of the mistake and the nature of the defence raised.

Following *Morgan*, Sexual Offences Act 2003 notwithstanding, mistakes negating a definitional element are operative whether or not the mistake is reasonable. *Morgan* did not affect the position with respect to non-definitional defences such as self-defence,

---

[208] *Tolson* (1889) 23 QBD 168.
[209] [1976] AC 182.
[210] *R v Tolson* was held to still be good law in *R v Barrett* (1981) 72 Cr App R 212; [1980] Crim LR 641.
[211] *DPP* v *Morgan* [1976] AC 182; *Kimber* [1983] 1 WLR 1118 CA.
[212] [2000] 1 All ER 833.
[213] Section 1 Indecency with Children Act 1960.
[214] See also *R v K* [2001] Crim LR at 995; *R v Kumar* [2004] EWCA Crim 3207; [2005] Crim LR 470.

consent, necessity, and duress. In *Jones* it was held that a genuinely held though mistaken belief that the victim consented to rough and undisciplined play is a defence to assault, and is a matter to be left to a jury. Again, in *Williams*[215] it was held that a defendant could avail himself of self-defence although he was mistaken in his belief that he was repelling an unjustified attack. The erstwhile requirement that the mistake made be a reasonable one[216] was abandoned in line with the position adopted in *Morgan*. This is now encapsulated in Statute. By s. 76(3) Criminal Justice and Immigration Act 2008 the question whether the degree of force used by D was reasonable in the circumstances is to be decided by reference to the circumstances as D believed them to be. If the belief is unreasonable this does not prevent the availability of the defence, unless it is induced by voluntary intoxication,[217] but it may affect the jury's assessment of the credibility of the belief.

Williams was approved in *Beckford v R*,[218] a Privy Council decision, in these terms: 'If . . . a genuine belief, albeit without reasonable grounds, is a defence to rape because it negatives the necessary intention, so also must a genuine belief in facts which if true would justify self-defence be a defence to a crime of personal violence because the belief negates the intent to act unlawfully'.[219] The same principle was later said to apply where the defendant is correct in his assessment that the use of force is justified, but mistakes the amount of force necessary to satisfy the justified object.[220] More recently this has been doubted[221] and, indeed, it seems inconsistent with the general principle that mistakes of law (here, what the law regards as reasonable force) do not exculpate unless they negate a definitional mental element.

With regard to excuses such as duress and duress of circumstances, it has remained the case that mistakes will only negate liability where they are grounded in reason. By contrast with mistakes in self-defence a person who mistakenly believes that he is being coerced, whether by a person[222] or by circumstances,[223] cannot rely on the defence unless the mistake made is a reasonable one. The clarity of this position was confused somewhat following the decision in *Martin* where, despite clear statements to the contrary by the House of Lords in *Howe* and *Graham*, this part of the test was not implemented, apparently in error. In line with the decisions on self-defence what mattered, the Court of Appeal found, was that the belief was honestly entertained, not that it was reasonable.[224] The House of Lords in *Hasan* clarified the position, insisting that for duress to exculpate wrongdoing a mistaken belief that it was necessary to avoid a threat of death or serious injury must be reasonable as well as honest. Apart from the constitutional propriety this restatement of the formal position seems, on the face of it, ill judged.[225] Differentiating between definitional and non-definitional, or justificatory or excusatory, defences is difficult to defend from the point of view of morality or general penal policy.[226] Society seems to stand more in need of protection from those who honestly, but unreasonably, believe others to be consenting to

---

[215] (1984) 78 Cr App R 276.

[216] *Albert v Lavin* [1982] AC 546.

[217] In which case it cannot be relied upon. Mistakes induced by drunkenness are automatically unreasonable. See *infra*.

[218] [1988] AC 130.

[219] Lord Griffiths at 144. Necessity is probably best analysed in the same way. A mistake here, therefore, need only be honest to be operative.

[220] In *Scarlett* (1994) 98 Cr App R 290 CA, that object was the removal of a drunk from the defendant's pub.

[221] *Owino* [1995] Crim LR 743 at 744; followed in *DPP v Armstrong-Braun* [1999] Crim LR 416.

[222] *Graham* [1982] 1 WLR 294; *Howe* [1987] 1 All ER 771.

[223] *Martin* [1989] 1 All ER 652.

[224] *Martin* [2000] 2 Cr App R 42; see also *Cairns* [1999] 2 Cr App R 137.

[225] For a different view see J. Gardner, 'The Gist of Excuses' note 37, 580–1. Cf. *Baker and Wilkins* [1997] Crim LR 497; *DPP v Rogers* [1998] Crim LR 202.

[226] See A. Simester, 'Mistakes in Defence' (1992) 12 OJLS 295; G. Williams, *TCL* (1983) 138.

their sexual advances than from those who honestly, but unreasonably, believe they will be killed or seriously injured if they do not take part in a robbery. The Sexual Offences Act 2003 confirms this. The former mistake is that of an objectively dangerous person. The latter is anything but. Would it not serve criminal justice better to distinguish between those mistakes which reflect the kind of ordinary human vulnerabilities which many excuses already attend to[227] and those which reflect, all too obviously, the viewpoint and values of an anti-social character?[228] Again, why should those who are unreasonably panicked into taking reasonable action be any more vulnerable to liability than those who are reasonably panicked into taking reasonable action?[229] It may perhaps be argued that a tendency to see threats where there are none is the kind of character defect which should not absolve a person from responsibility for their unjustified action and (socially unacceptable) behaviour. But if one takes this view it is hard to see why those relying on justificatory defences such as self-defence should be in any better position.

9.11 INTOXICATION[230]

> ### Overview
>
> Intoxication is not a true excuse.[231] Its effect on liability is limited to its potential to support a defendant's claim that he/she lacked a mental element in respect of which the prosecution bears the burden of proof. For crimes of *mens rea* involuntary intoxication can be adduced in evidence to support a claim of absence of *mens rea*. In the case of voluntary intoxication such evidence is only effective to negate *mens rea* for crimes of specific intent, defined as those which cannot be committed by recklessness. For crimes of negligence, strict liability and crimes of recklessness, adducing such evidence will be ineffective.

A Intoxication: its effect on criminal liability

Unlike cognate defences such as duress and provocation, intoxication is an excuse for no crime.[232] This is so even if the intoxication was involuntary and the defendant would not have committed the crime if sober.[233] Intoxication, like insanity and mistake, can only be relevant to criminal responsibility if it negatives an element in the definition of a crime, most obviously *mens rea*.[234] Although the defence is most typically raised in cases of drunkenness, it may arise through the ingestion or administration of either drink or drugs.

---

[227] For example automatism, insanity.

[228] V. Tadros, *Criminal Responsibility*, Oxford: OUP (2005).

[229] A. Simester, 'Mistakes in Defence' (1992) 12 OJLS 295; G. Williams, *TCL* (1983) 138.

[230] See generally J. Herring, C. Regan, D. Weinberg and P. Withington (eds), *Intoxication and Society: Problematic Pleasures of Drugs and Alcohol*, Palgrave Macmillan (2012).

[231] A. Simester, 'Intoxication Is Never a Defence' [2009] Crim LR 3.

[232] P. Handler, 'Intoxication and criminal responsibility in England, 1819–1920' (2013) 33(2) OJLS 243.

[233] See *Kingston*, below.

[234] Law Commission Consultation Paper No. 127 *Intoxication and Criminal Liability*, London: HMSO (1993) para. 1.12 (hereafter LCCP No. 127 (1993)). It may also operate to support a defence of automatism for crimes not requiring proof of intention, knowledge or belief. An example is rape where occasionally defendants have sought to escape liability on the ground that they were asleep at the time. See *R v Robertson* [2012] EWCA Crim 609 CA.

The doctrine has positive and negative aspects. The positive aspect is that evidence of intoxication may be used to displace the inference that a jury may, without being bound to,[235] take that a person foresees and intends the natural consequences of his act. Thus, where a baby's nurse got so drunk at the baby's christening party that she put the baby on the fire in mistake for a log of wood the inference that she intended to kill could be resisted.[236] If she had been sober (and sane) it would have been difficult to conclude otherwise.

The negative aspect is that if the definition of the offence does not require proof that the accused intended or foresaw a particular consequence, providing evidence of intoxication will be useless, or even worse. Thus a person charged with causing death by dangerous driving will not help his cause by raising evidence that he was blind drunk at the time, since it is no part of the prosecution's case to prove that he intended or foresaw death. He will, therefore, effectively make the prosecution's case for them if he admits his condition.

The exculpatory scope of intoxication varies according to whether the intoxication is voluntary or involuntary. While either defence is relevant only insofar as the effect is to negate *mens rea*, in the case of voluntary intoxication, the scope of *mens rea* which it is able to negate is severely limited. In simple terms, if the crime charged requires the prosecution to prove intention as to one of the elements of the offence, evidence of voluntary intoxication may be used to negate that intention.[237] If the crime requires proof only of recklessness, recklessness cannot be negated by evidence of voluntary intoxication. It is perhaps helpful, therefore, to consider voluntary intoxication not just as a defence (for crimes of intention) but also as a sort of 'anti-defence' (for crimes of recklessness), forming a self-contained body of doctrine which may relax the requirement for most crimes of recklessness that the prosecution prove foresight.

B Distinguishing voluntary and involuntary intoxication

The notion of voluntariness at work here is a relatively narrow one. It can best be appreciated by considering first what counts as involuntary intoxication. Intoxication will be deemed involuntary if it is coerced,[238] or the defendant entirely mistakes what he is consuming, for example he believes he is taking aspirin[239] when in fact he is taking LSD.[240] Some doubt exists whether self-induced mistake renders intoxication involuntary, as where the defendant accidentally drinks from the wrong glass, or whether the mistake must be induced by the 'stratagem' of another as where a person's drink is 'spiked'.[241] In principle, both causes should excuse as long as the defendant is deprived of a fair opportunity to conform.[242] Intoxication will also be treated as involuntary if the intoxicant is taken under doctor's prescription, as long as any medical regime was adhered to. In the case of drugs taken for medicinal purposes, intoxication will sometimes be deemed involuntary even if the

---

[235] The effect of s. 8 Criminal Justice Act 1967.

[236] A famous example cited in Kenny's *Outlines of the Criminal Law* (19th edn), Cambridge: CUP (1965) 69.

[237] Cf. *Fotheringham*, below.

[238] Perkins and Boyce, op. cit.; G.R. Sullivan, 'Involuntary Intoxication and Beyond' [1994] Crim LR 272: Law Com. No. 229 *Legislating the Criminal Code: Intoxication and Criminal Liability*, London: HMSO (1995).

[239] Or beer – *Ross* v *HM Advocate* 1991 SLT 564.

[240] See for example the American case of *People* v *Carlo* (1974) 46 A.D.2d 764.

[241] By Lord Mustill in *Kingston* at 370; cf. *Pearson's Case* (1835) 2 Lew 144.

[242] *Eatch* [1980] Crim LR 650; cf. Perkins and Boyce (1982) 1002, who cite the American case of *State* v *Brown*, 38 Kan 390 (1888) as authority for this proposition; G.R. Sullivan, op. cit. 275; see generally Law Com. No. 229 (1995).

drugs had not been prescribed for the defendant, as long as any intoxicating effect was unforeseen.[243]

In all other cases intoxication will be deemed voluntary. This will include cases where the defendant is addicted and unable to resist the temptation,[244] or if he misjudged the amount of alcohol he was taking or its intoxicating effect.[245] Similarly if he knowingly took an overdose of a prescribed drug or knowingly failed to follow medical advice when taking the drug.[246]

The case of involuntary intoxication is a key testing ground for the different rationales of excuses.[247] A person who offends while involuntarily intoxicated arguably discloses neither the bad character nor the quality of choice necessary to justify punishment. However, the criminal law allows responsibility to be negated only when involuntary intoxication is used to support a denial of *mens rea*.[248] In this sense the position is little different from cases of voluntary intoxication. Involuntary intoxication is a more substantial defence only insofar as it may be used in respect of a larger class of crimes. Thus:

Case 16

Eve spikes Adam's lemonade with gin at a party. At the party Adam puts his arm round Jane's shoulder, who does not consent, mistakenly believing her to be consenting, has non-consensual sexual intercourse with Ruth, mistakenly believing her to be consenting although she protests vigorously. On the way home from the party he is breathalysed by Cain, a policeman, and found to have an excess of alcohol in his bloodstream. On being informed of this, the effect of the alcohol causes Adam to lose his temper and hit Cain.

Adam can rely on his involuntary intoxication in respect of the assault on Jane because it supports his plea of lack of *mens rea* (belief in consent), but not in relation to the rape, which requires Adam's belief to be reasonable. He cannot rely upon it in connection with the drink driving offence since this offence does not require proof of *mens rea*. Neither can he rely upon it in connection with the attack on Cain since there is no suggestion that he lacks the *mens rea* for an assault (i.e. the intention to hit Cain). A distinction must be drawn between intoxication depriving the defendant of *mens rea*, and intoxication acting simply as a disinhibitor as here.

The case of *Kingston* points up this distinction. The Court of Appeal quashed the conviction of a person who had committed a serious sexual assault on a young boy after his coffee had been spiked, without his knowledge, with disinhibiting soporific drugs.[249] There was no suggestion that he lacked the *mens rea* for the crime in question. The case was argued, and won, upon the basis that he would not have committed the offence if sober. This was a remarkable decision. His excuse amounted, in effect, to one of externally

---

[243] *Hardie* [1984] 3 All ER 848, above p. 203. Law Com. No. 229 (1995) recommends the adoption of this provision in codifying legislation.

[244] However, under certain circumstances addiction may result in such mental abnormality as to bring the defendant within the scope of the *M'Naghten* rules or diminished responsibility.

[245] *R v Allen* [1988] Crim LR 698; cf. *Reg v Mary R* (1887) cited by Kenny (1965) 68.

[246] Cf. *R v Quick and Paddison* [1973] QB 910.

[247] See on this J. Horder, 'Pleading Involuntary Lack of Capacity' [1993] CLJ 298; K.J.M. Smith and W. Wilson, 'Impaired Voluntariness and Criminal Responsibility' 13 OJLS 69; G.R. Sullivan, 'Making Excuses' in A. Simester and A.T.H. Smith (eds), *Harm and Culpability*, Oxford: Clarendon Press (1996).

[248] In *R v Sheehan and Moore* (1974) 60 Cr App R 308; [1975] Crim LR 339 the Court of Appeal ruled that it was not necessary for the jury to be convinced that through drunkenness, the defendant lacked the **capacity** to form the *mens rea* for the crime concerned so long as the relevant *mens rea* was absent.

[249] [1993] 4 All ER 373 HL.

induced irresistible impulse, a claim which is not accepted in English law except within the narrow confines of diminished responsibility. It is thought that a person with his cognitive faculties intact should always resist doing what he knows to be wrong. Criminal responsibility involves taking personal responsibility for one's choices.[250] This means that a defendant is not entitled to pass the buck of either causal or moral responsibility for his choices on to someone or something else. As Sir John Smith has observed, where might its logic propel the range of excuses? Could Othello escape responsibility for the murder of Desdemona on the basis that his desire to kill her was prompted by the deceitful stratagem of Iago rather than his own free choice?[251] It is not surprising that the House of Lords reversed the Court of Appeal's decision, reasserting the rule that involuntary intoxication would only operate as a defence if it negated *mens rea*.[252] It should be noted that this still leaves room for involuntary intoxication in cases like *Kingston* where, instead of being simply disinhibited, the defendant's capacity to follow rules was temporarily disactivated. This might occur where the defendant was unused to drink and, instead of being in control, fell over his victim, in so doing touching her indecently.[253]

C Voluntary intoxication

In contrast to involuntary intoxication which is applicable to all crimes of subjective *mens rea*, voluntary intoxication can be used to support a denial of *mens rea* only for a limited category of crimes known as **crimes of specific intent**.

1 Crimes of specific intent identified

The modern law of intoxication is contained in the leading case of *Majewski*,[254] which synthesises a number of developments stemming from the case of *DPP v Beard*[255] in which the notion of 'specific intent' was first extensively canvassed. In this case, D who was drunk put his hand over his victim's mouth in order to effect rape. She died of asphyxiation. His conviction for murder was quashed on the basis that murder was a crime which required the prosecution to prove a specific intent to kill or cause grievous bodily harm. This they could not do. They could prove only an intent to rape.

In the leading case of *Majewski* the House of Lords again considered the relevance of voluntary intoxication to proof of *mens rea*. The defendant attacked a police officer in a pub while under the influence of drink and drugs. He was charged with assault on a police officer and sought to deny *mens rea*, relying upon his self-induced intoxication. The House of Lords, upholding his conviction, said that evidence of voluntary intoxication could only be used to negate *mens rea* for crimes, such as murder, which require proof of a specific intent. It was not relevant for crimes not requiring proof of *mens rea*, nor for crimes of 'basic intent'. Assault was a crime of basic intent. A number of different tests were essayed as to the identifying characteristics of a crime of specific intent. One suggestion was that a crime of specific intent was one of ulterior intent, that is, a crime where it must be shown that the accused intended something beyond satisfying the *actus reus* of the offence

---

[250] H.L.A. Hart, *Punishment and Responsibility*, Oxford: OUP (1968) 47.
[251] Commentary on Court of Appeal decision in *Kingston* [1973] Crim LR 781 at 784.
[252] [1994] 3 All ER 353.
[253] This would have the advantage of creating doctrinal consistency with other developing areas of excuse, for example post-traumatic stress syndrome, where following capacity has been compromised by external trauma: W. Wilson, 'Involuntary Intoxication: Excusing the Inexcusable' (1995) 1 Res Publico 25.
[254] *DPP v Majewski* [1977] AC 443.
[255] *DPP v Beard* [1920] AC 479.

definition.[256] The weakness in this test is that it fails to account for offences such as murder which are properly termed crimes of specific intent and where the prosecution need prove nothing more than an intention (specifically) to bring about the conduct element of the offence. Another suggestion was that a crime of basic intent is a crime which can be committed recklessly. A crime of specific intent, then, is simply a crime in which the *mens rea* element is (specifically) intention and nothing less.[257]

In *Caldwell* this latter view was preferred. *Majewski* was interpreted as authority for the proposition that 'self-induced intoxication is no defence to a crime in which recklessness[258] is enough to constitute the *mens rea*'. The upshot is that if a crime requires proof that the accused intended to bring about the *actus reus* of the offence charged or some consequence other than the *actus reus*, it is a crime of specific intent.[259] If Majewski had been charged with either wounding with intent to cause grievous bodily harm (ulterior intent) or causing grievous bodily harm with intent to cause grievous bodily harm (specific intent properly so-called)[260] his intoxication would have been relevant in deciding whether he had formed this intention.[261] As he was charged only with assault, a crime of (subjective) recklessness, intoxication was not relevant to the question of *mens rea*.

It follows that section 18 Offences Against the Person Act 1861,[262] murder,[263] attempt, burglary,[264] theft,[265,266] and robbery are crimes of specific intent. In each of these cases if A, due to intoxication, fails to form the intention referred to in the definition of the offence the prosecution will be unable to discharge its burden of proof. Crimes which can be committed recklessly, including those forms where foresight or awareness must be proved, are crimes of basic intent. Thus assault, malicious wounding, sexual assault,[267] manslaughter,[268] rape, criminal damage, taking and driving away a motor vehicle[269] are crimes of basic intent. A person who commits any such offence while intoxicated will relieve the prosecution from the burden of proving recklessness.[270] He will be taken to be aware of any matter of which he would have been aware if sober. One apparent exception to this is where the defendant harms the victim by accident, as where D falls off a railing onto the victim beneath, where the accident would not have occurred but for the defendant's intoxication.[271] In such

---

[256] A good example is burglary contrary to s. 9(1)(a) Theft Act 1968. A person commits this offence by entering premises with the intention of stealing therefrom. The prosecution must prove simply this ulterior intention to gain a conviction. It is not necessary to show the theft was actually carried out.

[257] Lord Elwyn-Jones at 474–5. Doubt has recently been cast upon this rationale in *Heard* [2007] EWCA Crim 125.

[258] Since self-induced intoxication is recklessness as denned in *Caldwell*, if it renders A oblivious.

[259] In *Heard* [2007] EWCA Crim 125 it was suggested *obiter* that a crime requiring recklessness to some consequence going beyond the *actus reus*, e.g. criminal damage, being reckless as to whether life would be endangered, is a crime of specific intent. This is not supported by the authorities, with the possible exception of the pre-*Caldwell* case of *Orpin* [1980] 2 All ER 321.

[260] Under s. 18, Offences Against the Person Act 1861.

[261] In *R v Garlick* [1981] 72 Cr App R 291; [1981] Crim LR 178 it was underlined that the issue for the jury is not whether the defendant had the **capacity** to form the intention; the question is whether he **did** have the intention.

[262] *Meakin* (1836) 7 C & P 297; *Pordage* [1975] Crim LR 575.

[263] *DPP v Beard*, above.

[264] *Durante* [1972] 3 All ER 962.

[265] *Ruse v Read* [1949] 1 KB 377.

[266] *Bennett* [1995] Crim LR 877.

[267] *Burns* (1973) 58 Cr App R 364; *Heard* [2007] EWCA Crim 127; cf. *C* [1992] Crim LR 642.

[268] *Lipman* [1970] 1 QB 152.

[269] *MacPherson* [1973] RTR 157.

[270] For a useful discussion of the grey area between intoxication and insanity and its effect on liability for crimes requiring proof of foresight (here aggravated criminal damage) see *R v Coley; R v McGhee; R v Harris*, 77 JCL 194, CA (commentary by Tony Storey).

[271] *Brady* [2006] EWCA 2413.

a case it appears the defendant's absence of *mens rea* is fatal to a charge of assault or the malicious infliction of grievous bodily harm, both crimes of basic intent. Presumably it would be also fatal to a charge of criminal damage if a drunk stumbled and knocked over a piece of pottery. Accidents are accidents, even if prompted by intoxication.

The above list of basic intent crimes is clearly not exhaustive and the status of such supportive authority as exists must, in any event, be qualified where it predates *Majewski* and *Caldwell*. One rather surprising addition to the list of basic intent crimes is s. 3(1)(a) Sexual Offences Act 2003 the meat of which is committed where a person (a) intentionally touches another person (B), and (b) the touching is sexual. This offence seems on the face of it to be a specific intent crime requiring proof that D intentionally made sexual contact with the victim. In *Heard*, the defendant while drunk had rubbed his penis against a police officer's leg. He argued that he did so in a drunken stupor and did not intend to 'touch another person' sexually. The Court of Appeal ruled that the offence was one of basic intent and so his intoxication could not have rendered him incapable of forming the *mens rea* for offence. It was enough, in other words that he intentionally did the rubbing. It was not necessary to show that he intended the rubbing to be of a sexual character.[272]

What will no doubt be obvious from these lists is that, with the exception of property offences and attempt, every specific intent crime has a basic intent counterpart of lower culpability. In practice, this means that a person who successfully raises evidence of intoxication which negates a crime of specific intent, e.g. murder, may still be convicted of a crime of basic intent, e.g. manslaughter. In so doing a neat reconciliation is achieved between the *mens rea* principle and the policy of social defence.[273]

2 The rationale for restricting the exculpatory scope of voluntary intoxication

The usual explanation as to why self-induced intoxication cannot be relied upon to negate *mens rea* is that it is itself a reckless course of conduct.[274] This argument was for a time more cogent, following *Caldwell*, than when it was first articulated by Lord Elwyn-Jones in *Majewski*. For criminal damage at least, voluntary intoxication preventing a person from appreciating the dangers attending his conduct satisfied the definitional fault element since a failure to appreciate an obvious risk was recklessness under *Caldwell*. This still left a problem for crimes of subjective recklessness, including assault, where the prosecution bear the burden of proving foresight.[275] A failure to establish foresight, albeit occasioned due to intoxication, is a failure to prove a fault element of the offence.[276]

Moreover, a requirement of foresight supplies a necessary moral connection between the harm caused and the defendant's conduct.[277] In one situation only can it be uncontroversially argued that a moral connection survives the absence of conscious wrongdoing, namely 'Dutch courage' crimes. These are cases where the defendant deliberately becomes intoxicated so as to steel himself to commit a crime for which he would lack the courage if

---

[272] The position of s. 20 Offences Against the Person Act 1861 is particularly problematic. See below.

[273] Ashworth, *PCL* (2010) 214–16.

[274] By Lord Elwyn-Jones [1977] AC 443 at 475.

[275] And also where the lacuna operates.

[276] This proposition must now be read in the light of *Richardson and Irvine* [1999] 1 Cr App R 392. The appellants, who were university students, dropped the complainant off a balcony in the course of drunken horseplay. The Court of Appeal said that the jury should not have been told to consider whether the reasonable, sober man would have realised the injury might result but whether these appellants themselves, had they not been drinking, would have realised that their actions might cause injury.

[277] An instance of this connection being ignored is the House of Lords' decision in *Kingston*. See generally A.J. Ashworth, *PCL* (2010) 213–14; P.H. Robinson, 'Causing the Conditions of One's Own Defences' (1985) 73 Virginia LR 1.

sober. In such cases the prior fault of the defendant is rightly deemed to disqualify his use of the defence.[278]

The accepted basis to the restriction is that voluntary intoxication supplies an alternative fault element for basic intent crimes. So for crimes such as unlawful wounding (a basic intent crime) the prosecution can discharge their burden of proving fault by showing the defendant

(a) intended to wound, or
(b) wounded recklessly, or
(c) wounded while (voluntarily) intoxicated.

Lord Simon's opinion in *Majewski* reflects this analysis: 'There is no juristic reason why mental incapacity (short of *M'Naghten* insanity) brought about by self-induced intoxication, to realise what one is doing or its probable consequences should not be such a state of mind stigmatised as wrongful by the criminal law, and there is every reason why it should be'.[279]

An obvious justification for extending the fault element in this way is the policy of social protection. Research indicates that voluntary intoxication is often a factor disposing some people to certain forms of criminal behaviour.[280] It may render a person insensible to the possible consequences of his action, thus disposing him/her to commit crimes of inattention and recklessness. It may provoke anger and irrational aggression, and is thus implicated in a large proportion of assault and domestic violence cases.[281] It may disinhibit and relax moral restraint, thus disposing one to sexual crimes.[282] Favouring the policy of social protection over the principle of *mens rea* might be thought quite justified in cases where the defendant's intoxication disposed to the crime committed.[283] It seems, however, that the policy is influential even where the defendant's prior fault cannot supply the moral connection.[284] In *Lipman*,[285] for example, a man killed his girlfriend by suffocating her with a length of sheet while experiencing an LSD-induced hallucination that he was being attacked by snakes. His conviction for manslaughter was upheld notwithstanding a total absence of awareness of what he was doing and of any suggestion that the drug he took disposed to the harm committed. A possible doctrinal escape route from this quagmire of confusion is advanced in the final section.

D Intoxicated mistakes

Certain mistakes induced by intoxication may negate *mens rea*. Consistent with what has been said above, such mistakes will only operate as a defence if the crime concerned is a crime of specific intent.

---

[278] *A-G for Northern Ireland* v *Gallagher* [1963] AC 349.
[279] At 455. For discussion of the interplay of, and borderline, between, intoxication and insanity see *R* v *Coley, McGhee and Harris* [2013] EWCA Crim 223, CA.
[280] J. Hodge, 'Alcohol and Violence' in P. Taylor (ed.), *Violence in Society* (1993) 129–34; cf. Blackstone 4. Commentaries *26. Lacey, Wells and Quick (2003) ch. 3.
[281] In *R* v *Asmelash* [2013] EWCA Crim 157 voluntary intoxication was ruled not to form part of the circumstances for consideration under the Coroners and Justice Act 2009 s. 54(1)(c), as amplified by s. 54(3), in the context of the partial defence of loss of control.
[282] See for example *R* v *Kingston*.
[283] See generally C. Miles, 'Intoxication and Homicide: A Context-specific Approach' (2012) 52(5) Brit J Criminol 870–88; S. Gough, 'Intoxication and Criminal Liability: The Law Commission's Proposed Reforms' (1996) 112 LQR 335.
[284] See generally J.C. Smith, 'Intoxication and the Mental Element in Crime' in P. Wallington and R. Merkin (eds), *Essays in Memory of Professor Lawson*, London: Butterworths (1986).
[285] [1970] 1 QB 152.

> **Case 17**
> Eve mistakenly takes an umbrella from the umbrella stand in a pub, believing it, due to her intoxicated condition, to be her own.

Eve will have a defence to the crime of theft. The *mens rea* elements in this crime – dishonesty and an intention to permanently deprive the owner of his property – require the prosecution to prove a specific dishonest intent, which it clearly cannot. Compare the following case.

> **Case 18**
> Adam, after a night at the pub, escorts Eve home. She invites him in for coffee. Later, upon Adam becoming amorous, Eve tells Adam that she is not interested in having sex with him. Adam, whose concentration was wandering because of the drink, understood Eve to be saying that she did want sex and proceeds, without thinking, to overcome her resistance.

Rape is a crime of negligence since it requires any belief in consent to be reasonable.[286] As Adam forms his belief that Eve is consenting while he is intoxicated, that belief cannot be relied upon. In short, intoxication supplies or at least substitutes for the *mens rea* for the crime.[287] In *Fotheringham* the defendant was not able to rely upon his intoxicated belief that the fourteen-year-old baby-sitter inhabiting the matrimonial bed was his wife and was therefore a consenting party.[288] As more than one commentator has pointed out,[289] this decision seems to miss the essence of the defendant's defence which was not that he mistakenly believed the girl to be consenting, but that he mistakenly believed her to be his wife and, therefore, he lacked the (specific) intention to have **unlawful** sexual intercourse. This decision seems to suggest that once a crime is designated a crime of basic intent, intoxication cannot be used to negate **any element** of the offence, **even** an element which requires proof of intention.

1 Intoxication and true defences

A slightly different issue is whether a defendant can rely on a **non-definitional defence** such as self-defence or duress, where the defendant, because he is intoxicated, believes wrongly that the conditions necessary for the defence to be operative are present. The position appears to be that, with one limited exception, a drunken mistake can neither excuse nor justify crime. In the case of excuses such as duress or loss of self control the reason for this is straightforward. Reasonable people do not make drunken mistakes and reasonableness of response is of the essence of loss of self control and duress. There is some old authority to the contrary[290] but it predates the new rules on intoxication and is unlikely, therefore, to have withstood the test of time.

A problem surfaces, however with respect to affirmative defences such as self-defence. Self-defence can be relied upon where D honestly believes that he is the victim of an attack or threatened attack even though this mistake is unreasonable.[291] Defendants who defend themselves against a perceived (yet non-existent) attack are able to say 'I did not intend an

---

[286] Sexual Offences Act 2003, s. 1(1).

[287] And arguably should supply it even though the mistake might still have been made if sober; cf. though *Woods* (1982) 74 Cr App R 312; *Richardson and Irvine* [1999] 1 Cr App R 392.

[288] (1989) 88 Cr App R 206 CA.

[289] See for example Clarkson and Keating (2010) 399.

[290] *Letenock* (1917) 12 Cr App R 221.

[291] See *Beckford* [1987] 3 All ER 425.

unlawful assault'. Where the mistake is induced by alcohol, consistency would seem to demand that if the mistake was induced by voluntary intoxication, it will avail the defendant for crimes of specific intent but not for crimes of basic intent. The courts, always alert to the opportunities for confounding expectations in this area, nevertheless have held in *O'Connor*[292] that a drunken mistake can only be used to negate *mens rea* (and only then for crimes of specific intent). It could not be used at all to support a cognate defence such as self-defence, even though the successful establishment of the defence seems to involve a denial of an (unlawful) intention.[293] Thus, on a charge of murder, the defendant was not entitled to rely upon his mistaken belief in the need for self-defence where this belief was formed while intoxicated. A defendant could, however, rely upon his intoxication to support a claim that he did not intend to kill or commit serious injury, for example to show that he was unaware that the gun he was wielding was loaded, or that the punches he threw were life-threatening. The common law position is now encapsulated in Statute. By section 76(4)(b) of the Criminal Justice and Immigration Act 2008, for the purpose of self defence D may not rely on any mistaken belief attributable to intoxication that was voluntarily induced.

2 Intoxication and statutory defences

To compound the confusion provoked by cases such as *O'Connor*, there is authority that, for statutory defences of mistaken belief, a mistake induced by intoxication may be operative **even for crimes of basic intent**. In *Jaggard* v *Dickinson*[294] the defendant broke into a house which, because she was drunk, she believed to belong to a friend. She was charged with criminal damage (a crime of basic intent). Under s. 5(2) and (3) of the Criminal Damage Act 1971 a person has a defence if she believes the owner would consent, **irrespective of whether the belief was justified**. Since she had this belief, and the reasonableness of it was irrelevant, the Queen's Bench Divisional Court allowed her appeal against conviction. Although the decision is consistent with the approach generally taken with regard to the exculpatory effect of mistakes of fact as embodied in *Morgan* and *Beckford*, it is difficult to reconcile with the principle which holds that intoxication is only relevant for crimes of specific intent. It is also inconsistent with *O'Connor* insofar as it prevents intoxicated mistakes being relied upon to raise even a justificatory defence.

3 Intoxication and mental disorder

Intoxication can produce cognitive defects similar to those experienced by those suffering from sane or insane automatism (insanity). Such defects, moreover, are the result of an impairment of the defendant's powers of reasoning.[295] Nevertheless the defendant is treated as responsible where his unconsciousness or lack of understanding is due to his prior fault. Voluntary intoxication counts as prior fault. Involuntary intoxication does not, and so counts as an external trigger for the purposes of automatism. A person who is involuntarily intoxicated and, not knowing what he is doing, lashes out and injures another person escapes criminal liability for assault. The fault lines between intoxication

---

[292] [1991] Crim LR 135; cf. *O'Grady* [1987] 3 All ER 420. A possible legal escape route may be to rely on the condition known as confusional arousal. See discussion on pp. 224–5.

[293] This principle was affirmed by the Court of Appeal in *Hatton* [2005] EWCA Crim 2951. Cf. *Gatnlen* (1858) 1 F and F 90 in which this argument was considered well founded. The Law Commission recommend the abrogation of this rule (Law Com. No. 229 (1995)) so that drunken mistakes can be used to support a defence for crimes of specific intent.

[294] [1980] 3 All ER 716.

[295] See *R* v *Coley, McGhee and Harris* [2013] EWCA Crim 223, CA for a consideration of the issues and interplay between insanity, automatism and voluntary intoxication in a case of attempted murder.

per se and automatism can be understood by examining *Beard*. Beard was unable to claim automatism as he was not acting involuntarily. His action was conscious and purposive. However, he was able to rely on his intoxication for the purpose of negating the specific intent necessary of murder. This intoxication did not avail him for manslaughter or rape, both of which are basic intent crimes.

Intoxication may be pertinent to liability in the following circumstances, however. First, where a pathological change in the brain has occurred due to the aggravating effects of prolonged alcohol or drug abuse. In such a case a disease of the mind may be established sufficient to satisfy the *M'Naghten* rules.[296] In principle any mental derangement should suffice, even in the absence of organic degeneration,[297] as long as it is not simply a state of intoxication. The law 'has to consider the state of mind the accused is in, not how he got there'.[298] Thus if drunkenness produces temporary insanity, for example delirium tremens (DTs), this should be sufficient to come within the rules.[299]

Mental abnormality, falling short of *M'Naghten* insanity, which results from intoxication will otherwise not affect responsibility unless the defendant's condition falls within the scope of s. 2 Homicide Act. Intoxication alone cannot support this defence unless it constituted a recognised medical condition. Alcoholism *per se* does not constitute diminished responsibility.[300]

E Conclusion

The present law on intoxication treads a fine line between social defence and the principle of responsibility.[301] If intoxication is **involuntary** the defendant will escape liability if the effect of the intoxication was to negate *mens rea*, but not otherwise. This means that the defendant is offered no excuse at all for crimes of inattention or inadvertence or for crimes of *mens rea* where the effect was merely disinhibitory. If intoxication is **voluntary** the defendant will escape liability where the effect is to negate any **intention** present in the definition of the offence. For crimes of inadvertence, including criminal damage, evidence of intoxication is irrelevant to liability and, indeed, may well supply the necessary fault element. For crimes where proof of awareness forms part of the mental element the general legal position is accurately expressed in relation to the fault elements of certain offences under the Public Order Act 1995. By section 6(5) '. . . a person whose awareness is impaired by intoxication, shall be taken to be aware of that which he would be aware if not intoxicated, unless he shows either that his intoxication was not self-induced or that it was caused solely by the taking or administration of a substance in the course of medical treatment'.[302] Although restricted to public order offences this provision is widely accepted as being an accurate description of the law's approach for all crimes.[303]

---

[296] *Davis* (1881) 14 Cox CC 563.
[297] Devlin J in *Kemp* [1957] 1 QB 399.
[298] Devlin J, ibid. at 407.
[299] *Davis*, above.
[300] *R v Wood* [2009] 1 WLR 496 Court of Appeal; *R v Stewart* [2009] 1 WLR 2507; cf. *Tandy* [1989] 1 All ER 267; *R v Dowds* [2012] EWCA Crim 281; [2012] Crim LR 612 and see M. Gibson, 'Intoxicants and Diminished Responsibility: the Impact of the Coroners and Justice Act 2009' [2011] Crim LR 909.
[301] That is, that people should not be found guilty of a crime for which they lack fault.
[302] The American Model Penal Code takes a similar position, which itself was approved in *Majewski*.
[303] Cf. A.J. Ashworth (2010) 218; Smith and Hogan op. cit. 251. This is the final conclusion of the Law Commission who recommend the codification of the existing law, including a provision similar to that appearing in s. 6(5) Law Com. No. 229 (1995). A draft Bill of 1998 incorporates a similar provision; Home Office, Violence: Reforming the Offences Against the Person Act 1861 (1998) Draft Bill cl. 19.

The principled objection to the present law on intoxication is that if getting drunk is not the *mens rea* for wounding with intent to cause grievous bodily harm, it is no more the *mens rea* for malicious wounding. Accordingly if drunken unawareness, inattention, or dangerousness is a serious policy problem (and clearly it is a widespread problem), perhaps it should be drunken unawareness, inattention or dangerousness which should be punished rather than allow the courts to continue to impose fictionalised responsibility for a crime where *mens rea* is clearly lacking.[304] The 'policy hole' could be filled by a conduct crime of 'dangerous intoxication', which was the recommended option of the Butler Committee;[305] alternatively, by a result crime of 'causing harm while intoxicated'. This was once the recommended option of the Law Commission.[306] A later recommendation followed the pragmatic line of codifying the existing law, including a provision similar to that appearing in section 6(5).[307] Since it is common knowledge that intoxication disposes people to commit crime, **voluntary** intoxication supplies the fault element which intention and recklessness normally express. It is not necessarily contrary to principle, therefore, to hold a person responsible for an unforeseen harm if both the harm and the lack of foresight were occasioned by voluntary intoxication (a mind at fault).[308] A more elegant solution would be to remove entirely the need to rely on such 'constructive recklessness'. This could be done by replacing *Cunningham* recklessness by a humanised form of *Caldwell* recklessness, requiring the risk to be foreseen unless the failure to foresee the risk was itself culpable, as the fault element in crimes of violence.[309] The desirable consequence which would follow is that voluntary intoxication would lose its capacity to excuse for all crimes of recklessness, without challenging the law's internal consistency, inadvertence due to intoxication[310] being culpable under such a test.[311]

The latest Law Commission thinking is that the specific/basic intent dichotomy fails to do the job it should be doing and should be abandoned. It proposes a substitute scheme which comprises no rigid categorisation of offences but instead concentrates on whether voluntary intoxication can, as an inherently reckless form of behaviour, be substituted for the fault element of the offence in question (as it can in arson and in most of what are currently accepted as basic intent crimes). The general rule is then that in determining whether the allegation has been proved, D is to be treated as having been aware at the material time of anything which D would then have been aware of but for the intoxication. It then lists five cases in which the general rule does not apply: in those cases, evidence of D's intoxication may be taken into account in determining whether the allegation has been proved, namely that at the material time –

(a) D intended a particular result (but this does not include merely intending to do the acts which constitute the conduct element of the offence),

---

[304] This is a solution advocated by Ashworth: also LCCP No. 127 (1993). On this see G. Virgo, 'The Law Commission Consultation Paper on Intoxication and Criminal Liability' [1993] Crim LR 415.

[305] Report of the Committee on Mentally Abnormal Offenders, Cmnd 6244 (1975).

[306] In LCCP No. 127 (1993) the Law Commission has subsequently resiled from this latter position in 'Legislating the Criminal Code' in which they recommend a 'codification' of the present law 'based upon *Majewski*'.

[307] Law Com. No. 229 (1995); for a useful review of reform suggestions see R.D. Mackay, *Mental Condition Defences in the Criminal Law*, Oxford: Clarendon Press (1995) 171–9.

[308] Cf. J. Plamenatz, 'Responsibility, Blame and Punishment' in P. Laslett and W.G. Runciman (eds), *Philosophy, Politics and Society*, 3rd Series (1989) at 182; S. Cough, 'Surviving Without *Majewski*' [2000] Crim LR 719.

[309] S. Gardner, 'The Importance of *Majewski*' (1993) 14 OJLS 279; also note at (1993) 109 LQR 21.

[310] Or anger, haste, etc.

[311] See *Reid* [1992] 3 All ER 673. This would be unlikely to have any serious detrimental effect on conviction rates for crimes of violence.

(b) D had any particular knowledge as to something (but this does not include knowledge as to a risk),

(c) D had a particular belief, amounting to certainty or near-certainty, that something was then, had been, or would in future be, the case,

(d) D acted fraudulently or dishonestly,

(e) D was reckless for the purposes of subsection (5)(a)(ii) or (b)(ii) of section 47 of the Serious Crime Act 2007 (c. 27) (concerning proof for the purposes of that section that an act is one which, if done by another person, would amount to the commission of an offence by that other person).

So, for example, in relation to theft (intention), handling (knowledge or belief), murder (intention as to the result), fraud (intention to make gain or cause loss), evidence of voluntary intoxication must be taken into account in deciding whether that fault element was present. Whether the proposals will make the law clearer is a matter for conjecture. It has been argued, for example, that for some offences, drawing the line between a person intending the act (intoxication not relevant) and intending the consequence (intoxication relevant) may cause difficulty.[312] The provisional view taken here is that the proposals are generally sound and, in so far as it seeks to place culpability at the heart of the defence, certainly better than the scheme of liability it aims to replace.

Summary

To establish fault sufficient to ground criminal liability the prosecution bears the burden of proving not only the *mens rea*, if any, for the crime in question but also of disproving any defence in support of which evidence is adduced. It is possible and helpful to categorise most defences as operating either to excuse the defendant from punishment or to justify his act. An excuse designates the defendant's conduct as wrongful but allows the defendant to escape punishment as a concession to his human frailty. A justification designates the defendant's conduct as socially permissible and/or desirable, and therefore lawful, notwithstanding the offence-definition. The courts have largely resisted such categorisation but it is implicit in certain rules qualifying the defences. Thus, a person who helps another using justified force, say in self-defence, is acting lawfully. On the other hand, a person who helps another use unjustified, but excused, force is acting unlawfully. Excuses include involuntary behaviour, denials of capacity on the ground of automatism, insanity, diminished responsibility and age, mistake, intoxication, duress and duress of circumstances. Justifications include necessity, and public and private defence.

A claim that one's action is involuntary amounts to a denial of authorship, that is, the capacity to have acted otherwise. It will be an excuse, therefore, that the physical cause of the *actus reus* of the offence in question was something or someone other than the accused. It will also be an excuse that, due to mental abnormality, the accused was unable to appreciate what he was doing or the significance of what he was doing. Where that mental abnormality is the result of some internal condition, whether organic or functional, the excuse amounts to insanity for which the court retains special powers of disposition. Where the abnormality is the direct result of some external cause, the excuse is termed automatism. This entitles the defendant to an unqualified acquittal. These excuses are available to negate

---

[312] Consider, for example, a drunk person who shoots a loaded pistol at his friend in an effort to prove he is the fastest draw.

liability even for crimes of strict liability where *mens rea* does not have to be shown. In such cases, however, the involuntariness must be total. Where involuntariness of action is self-induced or the defendant shows himself to be at fault in succumbing to the incapacity, the excuse will be unavailable.

Insanity bears a very limited meaning for the purpose of criminal liability. A person is not excused simply because he has a mental abnormality, even if its nature is such as would substantially impair his moral responsibility. A person is only excused on the ground of insanity if, at the time of acting, he was not aware of what he was doing and its significance or, if he was aware, that it was legally wrong. The defence usually amounts to a lack of *mens rea*; irresistible impulse is not insanity. The insanity defence is available even to strict liability crimes, where awareness does not otherwise have to be shown. The lack of understanding or awareness must be due to a defect of reason caused by disease of the mind. A disease of the mind includes organic or functional conditions of the mind or brain and any physical disease which affect the mind's ability to reason. Even where the condition is temporary or unlikely to recur it will be designated as insanity if it issues from internal causes. The insanity defence may be raised by either prosecution or defence. Whoever raises the defence must prove it – defence, on a balance of probabilities; prosecution, beyond reasonable doubt.

Intoxication is not a true excuse. For crimes of *mens rea* involuntary intoxication can be adduced as evidence to support a claim of absence of *mens rea*. A drunken intent is still an intent. In the case of voluntary intoxication such evidence is only effective to negate *mens rea* for crimes of specific intent, namely those which cannot be committed by recklessness. For crimes of negligence, strict liability and crimes of recklessness, adducing such evidence will be ineffective.

Mistakenly concluding that the circumstances are such that action, otherwise unlawful, is justified or excused is generally a defence unless that mistake is formed due to voluntary intoxication.

Further reading

Bean, P. *Madness and Crime*, London: Willan (2007).

Child, J., 'Drink, Drugs and Law Reform: A Review of Law Commission Report No. 314' [2009] Criminal Law Review 488.

Dingwall, G., *Alcohol and Crime*, London: Willan (2005).

Ebrahim, I., Fenwick, P., Wilson, W., Marks, R, Peacock, K.W., 'Violence, Sleepwalking and the Criminal Law: (1) The Medical Aspects' [2005] Criminal Law Review 601.

Gardner, J., 'Justifications and Reasons', in A. Simester and A. Smith (eds), *Harm and Culpability*, Oxford: Clarendon Press (1998).

Gardner, J., 'The Gist of Excuses' (1998) Buff CLR 575.

Goldstein, A., *The Insanity Defense*, New Haven: Yale University Press (1967).

Goldstein, A., Katz, J., 'Abolish the "Insanity Defense" – Why Not?' (1963) 73 Yale Law Journal 853.

Hathaway, M., 'The Moral Significance of the Insanity Defence' (2009).

Horder, J., 'Pleading Involuntary Lack of Capacity' (1993) 52 Cambridge Law Journal 298.

Horder, J., *Excusing Crime*, Oxford: OUP (2007).

Law Commission Consultation Paper (No. 197) *Unfitness to Plead*, London: TSO (2010).

Loughnan, A., '"Manifest Madness": Towards a New Understanding of the Insanity Defence' (2007) MLR 379.

Mackay, R.D., 'Fact and Fiction about the Insanity Defence' [1990] Criminal Law Review 247.

Mackay, R.D., 'Righting the Wrong? – Some Observations on the Second Limb of the M'Naghten Rules' [2009] Criminal Law Review 80.

Mackay, R.D. and Kearns, G., 'More Fact(s) about the Insanity Defence' [1999] Criminal Law Review 714.

Mackay, R.D. and Mitchell, B.J., 'Sleepwalking, Automatism and Insanity' [2006] Criminal Law Review 901.

Mackay, R.D., Mitchell, B.J. and Howe, L., 'Yet More Fact(s) about the Insanity Defence' [2006] Criminal Law Review 399.

Mackay, R.D., Mitchell, B.J. and Howe, L. 'A Continued Upturn in Unfitness to Plead – More Disability in Relation to the Trial' [2007] Criminal Law Review 530–45.

Mackay, R.D. and Reuber, M., 'Epilepsy and the Insanity Defence – Time for Change?' [2007] Criminal Law Review 782.

Tadros, V., *Criminal Responsibility*, Oxford: OUP (2005).

Wilson, W., Ebrahim, I., Fenwick, P., Marks, R., 'Violence, Sleepwalking and the Criminal Law: (2) The Legal Aspects' [2005] Criminal Law Review 614.

10 Defences (2): affirmative defences

Overview

In this chapter we examine the defences of compulsion, necessity and self-defence. These are affirmative defences. These defences negate liability although all the definitional elements of the offence are present. In each case the claim to avoid liability is that the action undertaken by the defendant was reasonably necessary to avoid the unjust threat of harm. Each defence can be differentiated, however. In duress the claim to be excused is that it is unfair to expect a person to sacrifice themselves, or a person for whom they are responsible, for the sake of conformity to the law, even where this involves the victimisation of another innocent person. Such action is excused because it is necessary from the actor's own quite reasonable point of view. In necessity the claim is that it advances society's purposes if a person breaks the law if this is the only reasonable method of preventing a greater evil. Such action is therefore justified because the action is necessary from society's, rather than the individual's, point of view. In self-defence the claim is that it is socially permissible to defend oneself or others against someone who launches an unjust attack. Such action is justified because society is organised upon the premise that those who attack other people forfeit their right to state protection, as against those they attack.

10.1 RELATIONSHIP BETWEEN THE DEFENCES

It is easy to confuse these three defences as they all reduce to the fact that the defendant's action was necessary to avoid harm befalling him/her/someone else. It is important not to confuse them, however, not least because their scope is different. Duress, for example, is not a defence to murder but self-defence is, and necessity may be. A brief outline of the usual coverage of these defences follows to show their essential points of difference.

Consider the following hypothetical case.

Case 1
D threatens V with death unless V helps him to beat up X.

(a) If V succumbs to D's threat and beats up X he may raise the defence of duress. Obedience to the criminal law does not demand a disproportionate personal sacrifice. Note the action taken by V is a wrong committed against an innocent person. D's wrong is excused as a concession to D's ordinary human frailty.

(b) If V resists the threat and attacks D, he may raise the defence of self-defence. The law permits people to protect themselves from those who would unjustly harm them. Note the action taken is not a wrong but a justified act of self-defence against the wrongdoer.

(c) If V escapes the threat by driving off at high speed the wrong way down a one-way street he may raise the defence of duress of circumstances to a charge of dangerous driving. Again, the law does not demand a disproportionate personal sacrifice. Note the action taken is a wrong but this time it involves no victim. D is excused for his wrong as a concession to his human frailty.

(d) If V pushes X to the ground to prevent D delivering the first punch on X he may raise the defence of necessity. The criminal law embraces the moral imperative that people, faced with a crisis demanding immediate action, may embrace the lesser of two evils, even if that evil is nonconformity to the law. Note the action taken is not a wrong but a justified act designed to advance the common good.

10.2 COMPULSION: INTRODUCTION

A defendant may be excused on the ground of compulsion in either of two cases. The first is where the source of the compulsion concerned is a wrongdoer who 'nominates' a crime to be committed by the defendant under threat of suffering unjustified consequences. This is known as duress by threats. The second is where the source is some imminent peril, for the purpose of averting which the defendant 'nominates' and executes their own crime. This is known as duress of circumstances. The difference between the two forms can be understood by considering the following two examples.

> **Case 2**
> A threatens to kill B's child unless B breaks the speed limit and drives him to the airport.

> **Case 3**
> B drives C, his infant child, to hospital at above the speed limit. He does so because C is dangerously ill with a burst appendix.

Case 2 involves duress by threats since A has nominated the crime to be committed by B. Case 3 involves duress of circumstances since B nominates his own crime. It should be noted that in both cases the defence requires that action be taken to evade an immediate peril; that is, a peril which only immediate action will counter.[1]

10.3 THE RATIONALE FOR EXCUSING ON GROUNDS OF COMPULSION

Duress, in either form, is not an easy defence to account for.[2] Motive and context, although generally deemed irrelevant by the criminal law, are here placed centre-stage. The acceptance of duress as an excuse has been plausibly attributed to the unique combination of a good motive operating in a penologically acceptable context. The motive is the defendant's understandable desire to avoid harm. This is a desire which is already given a strong level of doctrinal support through the defence of self-defence, leading some to view the two defences as moral equivalents.[3] The context is that punishment would serve no purpose whether as deterrent or other vehicle of social defence and would not be considered the defendant's just desert given any of the rationales underpinning excuses.

---

[1] This is the conclusion to be drawn from the case of *Cole* [1994] Crim LR 582, CA.
[2] See M. Wasik, 'Duress and Criminal Responsibility' [1977] Crim LR 453; I. Dennis, 'Duress, Murder and Criminal Responsibility' (1980) LQR 208.
[3] J. Horder, 'Autonomy, Provocation and Duress', [1992] Crim LR 706, 709; cf. D.W. Elliot, 'Necessity, Duress and Self-defence' [1989] Crim LR 611.

A question-mark hanging over the defence is whether it operates, like self-defence, as justification or, like diminished responsibility, as an excuse. A number of authorities and commentators assert that duress is a defence of justification, being a special instance of justificatory necessity.[4] The doctrinal clothes in which it is dressed support such an opinion. The defence contains a requirement of reasonableness (of reaction) which limits other defences of justification such as self-defence. Further, the defence is not available to murder and this is often explained by saying that threats of death do not justify killing,[5] which on one theory of justification, at least, is quite correct.[6]

Certainly there are occasions where duress of circumstances, at least, discloses a justificatory character, namely where (Case 4) the defendant takes a rational choice to vindicate the structure of interests which the criminal law exists to support:

Case 4

Adam, a motorist, is followed on a motorway by a lorry driven too fast and too close to be able to stop safely in case of emergency. Adam breaks the speed limit as a means of escaping the danger.

Clearly Adam's action is coerced. Whether he is the victim of duress by threats or duress of circumstances is less clear. In either form his action would appear to be justified rather than merely excused. This is a case more akin to self-defence than duress. The speed limit is in place to protect people from harm, not to place them in jeopardy. It follows that its proscriptions must give way, if reasonably necessary, for self-protection.[7]

A more complete analysis is that duress (including duress of circumstances) is a multi-faceted defence. It may operate as a justification, as above, but more usually it is an excuse. The excuse takes two forms. First, where (Case 2), through the corrosive effect of fear, the defendant's will is subjugated by that of his coercer. On this view it operates as a form of moral insanity similar to provocation in which 'the rational will is deposed from the throne of action'.[8] Duress's justificatory 'doctrinal clothes' (reasonableness of reaction is necessary) are likely to have developed to keep the excuse under control rather than as an open acknowledgement of its justificatory nature. It also operates as an excuse, where the defendant, though not overborne by fear, chooses what for him, if not for society as a whole, is the lesser of two evils (Case 5). This provides him with an imperfect justification. Imperfect because his conduct is objectively wrong, although still excusable because we cannot expect reasonable people to have chosen any differently.[9]

Case 5

Adam, a taxi driver, is instructed by Eve, an escaping bank robber, to break the speed limit or be shot dead. Adam complies.

---

[4] Cf. A. Wertheimer, *Coercion,* Princeton University Press (1987); cf. T. Honore, 'A Theory of Coercion' (1990) 10 OJLS 94; W.R. LaFave and A.W. Scott, *Criminal Law,* Minnesota: West Publishing (1972) 374.

[5] Lord Salmon in *Abbott* v *The Queen* [1977] AC 755, PC.

[6] It is not necessarily correct under the utilitarian model.

[7] This analysis appears to be supported by the reasoning in *Pommell* [1995], below. In principle, moreover, the death or serious injury limitation should not be necessary. See p. 261 below.

[8] A. Norrie, 'Free Will, Determinism and Criminal Justice' (1983) LS 60 at 63. Norrie's position is directly contrary to the position adopted here. G. Fletcher (1978) 830–1.

[9] See generally J. Gardner, 'Justifications and Reasons' and 'In Defence of Defences' in J. Gardner, *Offences and Defences, Selected Essays in the Philosophy of Criminal Law* (OUP 2007); cf. Westen, 'An Attitudinal Theory of Excuse' (2006) 25 Law and Philosophy 289 at 348.

Judges often conflate these quite different rationales. Typical is the following statement of Lord Hailsham in *Howe*: 'as a concession to human frailty . . . a reasonable man of average courage is entitled to embrace as matter of choice the alternative which a reasonable man could regard as the lesser of two evils'. If duress is a genuine excuse it should be applicable, within limits, even though the choice is not reasonably viewed as a lesser of two evils as long as it was the result of (will-sapping) fear or was a reasonable and understandable option from the defendant's point of view. If it is a justification, on the other hand, it should not be thought of as a concession to human frailty.[10]

The most plausible analysis of the doctrinal elements of duress is that they simply reflect the organisational framework common to all core excuses. The template common to all core defences is that in the face of an external crisis the actor reacted in such a way as to permit the usual inference to be blocked that he is a person of an anti-social character usually implicit in the fact that he has infringed a legal prohibition.[11]

10.4 COMPULSION (I): DURESS BY THREATS – THE LEGAL POSITION

The broad constituent elements of duress by threats are expressed in the following statement:[12] 'Threats of immediate death or serious personal violence so great as to overbear the ordinary power of human resistance should be accepted as a (personal) justification for acts which would otherwise be criminal.'[13]

A What threats are required?

The defendant must act to avert an unjust threat of serious injury or death to him/herself or another.[14] It is not enough simply to entertain a rational desire to escape from a difficult or impossible situation:

Case 6
A offers to provide B's child, who is critically ill, with life-saving medical facilities if B beats up C.

In Case 6 the defence is not available since neither B nor her child is being **unjustly** threatened with serious harm or worse for failure to comply.[15] That the threat must be of death or serious injury means that financial coercion or blackmail will not suffice.[16] This distinguishes the defence of duress from its counterparts in civil law where it is necessary only to show absence of consent, albeit often limited by requirements of reasonableness.

---

[10] Cf. *R v Rahman* [2010] EWCA Crim 235.
[11] G. Fletcher, *Rethinking Criminal Law* (1978) 799–802.
[12] Per Lord Edmund-Davies in *DPP for Northern Ireland* v *Lynch* [1975] 1 All ER 913, 917 approving the statement of Murnaghan J in *Whelan* [1934] IR 518, 526.
[13] Author's parenthesis. The use of the word *personal* indicates that although justifiable from the defendant's point of view it is not from the wider society. Similar rationales are used by the Law Commission in Law Commission No. 83 *Defences of General Application*, London: HMSO (1977) para. 2.28 (hereafter Law Com. No. 83 (1977)); also the American Model Penal Code, s. 2.09(1).
[14] The threat must be of physical harm. Acting to allay serious psychological harm, say in a person for whom one has responsibility, is not enough: *Baker* [1997] Crim LR 497. There is no obvious logic in this restriction given the rationale of the defence.
[15] Duress of circumstances may sometimes be available in cases if immediate emergency.
[16] *Singh* [1972] 1 WLR 1600; *Valderrama-Vega* [1985] Crim LR 220.

In the criminal law free choice is only deemed absent **where the harm threatened was so great as to leave the defendant with effectively no other option** (thus making punishment unjustified and pointless and therefore them not blameworthy). An obvious objection is that the requirement is too restrictive, at least if serious injury means 'grievous bodily harm'.[17] What should be important is that the harm threatened is out of proportion to the price exacted.[18] In cases not involving the victimisation of an innocent person, at least, this restriction is hard to support.[19] What reasonable person would not commit a speeding offence in order to avoid, say, a sexual assault or a very painful but nevertheless unserious blow?[20] Such an argument was rejected by the Court of Appeal in *Quayle* in which duress of circumstances was raised in answer to a charge under the Misuse of Drugs Act in which the defendant claimed he was entitled to consume cannabis to combat severe neurological pain following a leg amputation.[21] Lord Simon in *Lynch v DPP for Northern Ireland* had canvassed the possibility that a threat of imprisonment might ground the defence of duress.[22] However, in *Dao* it was held to be no answer to the charge of cultivating cannabis that the defendants had been duped into entering a cannabis factory, locked in the premises with no means of escape and told that unless they assisted in the cultivation they would not be allowed out. A credible threat of death or serious injury was also necessary.[23] In *Regina v A*, however, it was stated *obiter* that a credible threat of rape could ground the defence of duress or duress of circumstances.[24]

B Threats against third parties

No English case has decided that duress by threats is available where the threats are directed against someone other than the accused. In *Hurley and Murray*[25] the Supreme Court of Victoria held that duress would be available where the threats were directed against the accused's partner. In *Ortiz* the Court of Appeal assumed, without deciding the point, that the defence would be available where the threats were directed against the accused's wife and family.[26] There are obvious reasons for allowing the defence where there is a close emotional relationship between the accused and the people whose safety is threatened. Whether the defence should be available where it is the safety of strangers which is threatened is less clear. In *Hasan* the House of Lords stated, *obiter*, that it would extend to cover threats directed against 'a person for whose safety the defendant would reasonably regard himself as responsible',[27] but no further. The Court of Appeal in the earlier case of

---

[17] It is taken to mean this in Australia: *Hurley* [1967] VR 526. English authorities are ambiguous. It should be noted that 'grievous bodily harm' is normally defined as 'really serious injury' rather than simply 'serious injury'.

[18] See *Perka* (1984) 13 DLR (4th) 1.

[19] *Graham*; *Hudson and Taylor* [1971] 2 QB 202: *Lynch*, above; see also Law Commission Working Paper No. 55 *Defences of General Application* (1974) paras 16–17; cf. Model Penal Code s. 209(1). There is some oblique authority for a graduated response allowing minor crimes to be offset by threats of less than serious injury. See Lord Hailsham in *Howe* [1987] 1 All ER 771, 780–2.

[20] In America, which adopts a similar approach to ours in the gravity of the threat, such a situation has afforded a person an excuse. See *Commonwealth v Reffitt*, 149 Ky 300 cited in Perkins and Boyce (1982) 1061.

[21] *Quayle & Ors Attorney General's Reference [No. 2 of 2004]* [2005] EWCA Crim 1415. An argument based on Article 8 ECHR was also rejected; see also *Altham* [2006] EWCA Crim 7.

[22] [1975] AC 653 at 686, HL.

[23] [2012] EWCA Crim 1717.

[24] *(RJ)* [2012] EWCA Crim 434; [2012] WLR (D) 76.

[25] [1967] VR 526.

[26] (1986) 83 Cr App Rep 173, CA.

[27] *Hasan* [2005] UKHL 25.

Shayler said the defence of duress of circumstances was not to be available for this reason for a member of the security services who disclosed official secrets and in his defence contended 'that his disclosures were necessary to avert threat to life or limb or serious damage to property' to other members of the security services. His appeal was dismissed on the ground that he was unable to pinpoint with any degree of precision what the threats to security might involve or who was at risk. Lord Woolf limited the application of the defence to cases where 'a defendant commits an otherwise criminal act to avoid an imminent peril of danger to life or serious injury to himself or towards somebody for whom he reasonably regards himself as being responsible'. He included amongst that class not merely members of the defendant's close circle but also cases where 'he is placed in a position where he is required to make a choice whether to take or not to take the action which it is said will avoid them being injured. Thus, if the threat is to explode a bomb in a building if defendant does not accede to what is demanded the defendant owes a responsibility to those who would be in the building if the bomb exploded.'

It is clear that this class of subjects is far wider than that proposed by Lord Bingham in *Hasan*, and for the reasons given by Lord Woolf, rightly so. An emergency is no less an emergency for the fact that the individuals threatened are not known personally to the defendant. This is an example of how the existence of the common defence template has, by wrongly implying a particular defence rationale, had a distorting effect on doctrine. Here, the rationale is assumed to be a concession to human moral frailty rather than to personal moral priorities.[28]

C A part subjective and part objective test

The principles underlying the defence of duress, which are applicable to both duress by threats and duress of circumstances, were elaborated in the case of *Graham*[29] and have subsequently been approved by the House of Lords in *Howe*[30] and *Hasan*. They emphasise the fact that, although the defence is a personalised defence, and as such contains subjective elements, it is also a claim to be free of moral blame which requires, amongst other things, minimum standards of fortitude to be satisfied.[31]

The resulting test was consciously designed to mimic provocation,[32] since both operated by means of confession and avoidance. The test asks two questions of the jury, containing both subjective and objective elements. The first is (substantially) subjective and the second (substantially) objective.

(1) Was the defendant, or may he have been, impelled to act as he did because, as a result of what he reasonably believed [the coercer] had said or done, he had good cause to fear that if he did not so act [the coercer] would kill him or . . . cause him serious physical injury?

(2) If so, have the prosecution made the jury sure that a sober person of reasonable firmness, sharing the characteristics of the defendant, would not have responded to what he reasonably believed [the coercer] said or did by taking part in the [offence]?

---

[28] W. Wilson, 'The Structure of Criminal Defences' [2005] Crim LR; for further discussion see Chapter 9 at p. 202.
[29] [1982] 1 All ER 801.
[30] [1987] 1 All ER 771.
[31] In *Hasan* Lord Bingham also reiterated an underlying theme attaching to duress, namely that its operation should be strictly limited to ensure it does not confer unjustified criminal immunity on those whom society has most to fear.
[32] This common law defence is now replaced by a statutory partial defence of 'loss of self control' whose constituent elements have substantially parted company with duress.

The fact that a defendant's will to resist has been eroded by the voluntary consumption of drink or drugs . . . is not relevant to this test.'[33]

1 The first question

The jury must consider whether the defendant's participation in the crime was or may have been due to the threat. If it was not, the defence would not be available even if the threat was objectively sufficiently coercive.[34] The test in *Graham* states that the defence is not available if the fear is not reasonably entertained. The House of Lords have now confirmed the requirement that the fear of death or serious injury must be reasonably entertained.[35] The decision in *Shayler*, for example, could equally have been decided on the ground that there was no plausible case appearing in the leaked documents that members of the public were at imminent risk of death or serious injury. He may have believed they were but the belief was not held on reasonable grounds. In *R v A* (2012) the defendant was convicted of the offence of perverting the course of justice when she falsely retracted allegations of rape against her husband. She did so, apparently in the belief that she would suffer serious injury by her husband if she did not. This fear was real but not based on reasonable grounds since no threat of violence had been made to her when she made the false retractions on which her prosecution was founded.[36]

Further, even if the belief that he was being threatened was reasonable, it will not support the defence if the threat did not give the defendant good cause to fear for his life or serious injury. An example of why he might not have good cause is if the threat was unlikely to be acted upon,[37] or the defendant could have sought police protection,[38] or if the substance of the threat was unclear. Although these two requirements are difficult to justify, it is consistent with the idea that excuses should not substitute the defendant's view of what was appropriate behaviour for that of the moral community to which he belongs.[39]

2 The second question

The prosecution bears the burden of disproving the defence.[40] This means that if they fail to convince the jury that the first limb of the test is **not** satisfied, the jury must treat it as satisfied and move on to the second limb.

The second limb requires the jury to consider whether taking part in the offence was objectively reasonable, even allowing for the fact that the fear of death or serious injury was reasonably entertained. Any doubt remaining in the jury's mind as to whether the second limb is satisfied must be cast in favour of the defence. It might be argued that this objective standard is both unnecessary and inappropriate. First, of what value is a further requirement that the coercee demonstrate reasonable standards of fortitude, if the jury are already satisfied that they reasonably feared death or serious injury if they resisted the threat?[41] Surely we need one requirement or the other – a requirement of reasonable and

---

[33] *Graham* [1982] 1 All ER 801, 806 per Lord Lane CJ.
[34] *Valderrama-Vega* [1985] Crim LR 220.
[35] In *Hasan*.
[36] In *Martin* this part of the test was not implemented, apparently in error. *Martin* [2000] 2 Cr App R 42; see also *Cairns* [1999] 2 Cr App R 137; *Safi* [2003] EWCA Crim 1809.
[37] Ibid.
[38] *Hasan*, above.
[39] They are more consistent with a character-based excuse. Cf. now *Baker and Wilkins* [1997] Crim LR 497; *DPP v Rogers* [1998] Crim LR 202 and pp. 202–3 above.
[40] The defence bears an evidential burden.
[41] K.J.M. Smith, 'Duress and Steadfastness' [1999] Crim LR 363.

proportionate reaction, as in self-defence, or a requirement simply that the reaction be to a (perceived) threat of death or serious injury. Secondly, if the basis for duress is that it operates as a concession to human frailty, the frailer the person the greater perhaps should be the concession.[42] If we allow that some people may have a tendency to mistake another's intentions, why should we not also allow that people might also fall short of 'normal' standards of courage?

The argument for an objective element requires reconsideration of the nature and associated structure of criminal excuses. Duress, like all excuses, operates by denying moral blame. Moral blame is not negated by proving oneself to be 'lily-livered'. As Kadish puts it, being 'unnaturally cowardly . . . is the very ground for blaming him. It could hardly serve as an excuse. Such defences are not accorded in moral any more than in legal judgment.'[43,44] The structure of all core defences follows this route, demanding the defendant's action to be an understandable reaction to crisis. Such an analysis may fail to accord with our moral response, where the moral weakness has its source in some identifiable feature in the defendant's physical or mental make-up for which they bear no responsibility. The law takes a step in this direction by requiring the jury to consider whether, given the characteristics of the defendant, a sober person of reasonable firmness would respond as the defendant did. Thus, if the defendant was a large, muscular boxer the jury would be entitled to expect a greater standard of fortitude than from an elderly, frail ex-teacher with a heart complaint. Given the former's characteristics, more resistance can reasonably be expected whatever the degree of threat and however persuasively articulated.[45]

Like the law of provocation on which it was modelled, and with which, in this respect, the statutory defence of loss of self-control is comparable, not all characteristics can be taken into account, however. The judge will refuse to allow the jury to consider evidence that a person is unusually susceptible to coercion.[46] In *Hegarty*[47] the defendant pleaded duress to a charge of robbery and possession of a firearm. He claimed that he had been threatened with violence against his family if he refused. In support of his plea he adduced medical evidence to the effect that he was emotionally unstable and in a 'grossly elevated neurotic state', conditions which had previously been relied upon to substantiate diminished responsibility for the killing of his wife. The judge refused to admit the evidence. The Court of Appeal dismissed the appeal on the ground that the characteristics he was relying upon were inconsistent with the notion of the 'sober person of reasonable firmness' referred to in the test.

A somewhat different conclusion was reached in *Emery*.[48] The defendant had been convicted of cruelty for failing to protect her child from violence by her partner, having herself suffered from prolonged physical abuse at his hands. The Court of Appeal held that it would be right for the jury to be given medical evidence concerning her mental state since that mental state had been induced by the very violence she was now relying upon as an excuse for her cruelty to her child. On the face of it, this is quite consistent with *Hegarty*. Emery was not giving an account of why she was a coward in general but why, as a person of

---

[42] See Law Com. No. 218 (1993) para. 29.14; Draft Criminal Law Bill, cl. 25(2) Cf. J. Horder, *Excusing Crime*, Oxford: OUP (2004).

[43] J. Gardner, 'The Gist of Excuses' [1998] Buffalo Crim LR 575, 577.

[44] S. Kadish, 'Excusing Crime' (1987) 75 Calif LR 257 at 276.

[45] J. Gardner, 'In Defence of Defences' in J. Gardner (ed.), *Offences and Defences – Selected Essays in the Philosophy of Criminal Law*, Oxford: OUP (2007).

[46] *Horne* [1994] Crim LR 584.

[47] *Hegarty* [1994] Crim LR 353.

[48] *Emery* (1993) 14 Cr App R (S) 394.

reasonable firmness, she lacked the capacity to intervene in this particular type of situation. This was because, over a long period of time, her capacity to resist threats had been eroded as would, moreover, that of the reasonable woman enduring similar treatment.

In *Bowen*[49] the Court of Appeal lent a surprising interpretation to *Emery*. The defendant, a man of low IQ, was convicted of obtaining services by deception. He adduced evidence of coercion, namely that he and his family would be petrol bombed if he did not obtain goods for the coercers. The trial judge did not refer to his low IQ when directing the jury. The defendant appealed on the basis that the judge should have told them to consider whether the reasonable man sharing the defendant's characteristics might have been unable to withstand the threat. Dismissing the appeal the Court of Appeal ruled, quite reasonably, that having a low IQ did not affect a person's ability to withstand threats and that therefore reference to his IQ would have been irrelevant.

It was further held, however, that characteristics such as serious physical or mental disability which might render 'a person less able to resist pressure' than people without such characteristics might properly be relied upon, and for such purposes medical evidence was admissible. This ruling is clearly inconsistent with *Hegarty*, arguably with the law on loss of self-control[50] and, for persons with such characteristics, also with the objective test for duress. By definition, people of reasonable firmness do not suffer from psychiatric conditions which render them unreasonably timid.[51] Although inconsistent, the *Bowen* qualification is nevertheless to be welcomed since the objective test itself discriminates against some defendants lacking a 'fair opportunity' to conform to the law. Bowen is now generally recognised as correctly decided. In recent years both post-traumatic stress syndrome[52] and low IQ[53] have been held to be characteristics which are consistent with the notion of the ordinary person of reasonable firmness. A cogent test which replicates this approach appears in clause 25 of the Draft Criminal Law Bill[54] which would ask whether 'the threat is one which in all the circumstances (including any of [the defendant's] personal characteristics that affect its gravity) he cannot reasonably be expected to resist'. It should be noted that this is considerably more subjective than that necessary to exculpate the defendant in *Emery*.[55]

D Immediacy of the threat

As with self-defence duress has a requirement of immediacy.[56] As has been explained, this reflects the template common to most core criminal defences which require the defendant's action to be a **reaction to crisis**.[57] In both cases the requirement fulfils a similar function. A person should not be acquitted of a crime unless their action was unavoidable either because it was necessary (self-defence) or because they could not help themselves (duress).[58]

---

[49] [1996] Crim LR 577, CA.
[50] See *Luc Thiet Thuan* v R [1996] 2 All ER 1033; cf. *Smith (Morgan)* [2000] 4 All ER 289.
[51] See J.C. Smith's commentary on the case at 579.
[52] *Sewell* [2004] EWCA Crim 2322.
[53] *Antar* [2004] EWCA Crim 2708.
[54] Law Com. No. 218 (1993).
[55] A broadly comparable test was applied by the House of Lords in the field of provocation.
[56] Provocation also had an immediacy requirement.
[57] Chapter 9. See generally W. Wilson, 'The Filtering Role of Crisis in the Constitution of Criminal Excuses' [2004] Can J of Law and Jurisprudence 387; 'The Structure of Criminal Defences' [2005] Crim LR 108.
[58] For a full discussion see J. Horder, 'On the Irrelevance of Motive in Criminal Law' in J. Horder (ed.), *Oxford Essays in Jurisprudence*, Oxford: OUP (2000).

In both cases, however, the requirement is not absolute, being bound up with the question whether the defendant's behaviour was reasonable in the circumstances. If the threat of harm is not an immediate one, it becomes more reasonable to take avoiding action than to capitulate. In *Gill*[59] the accused was convicted of the theft of his employer's lorry. The Court of Appeal stated *obiter* that a defence of duress was not available in circumstances such as these, where the defendant had been left alone outside his employer's yard and therefore was well able to raise the alarm and escape the threat. The courts have interpreted the immediacy requirement here, as elsewhere,[60] with a degree of flexibility. In *Hudson and Taylor*[61] the defendants were teenage girls who committed perjury. A gang had threatened to 'cut them up' if they did not do so. They pleaded duress. The trial judge refused to allow the defence since the threat could hardly have been carried out immediately in open court. Nevertheless the Court of Appeal allowed the appeal, agreeing that seeking police protection was not always reasonably to be expected, particularly in cases, as here, where the defendants were young and impressionable:

> it is always open to the Crown to prove that the accused failed to avail himself of some opportunity which was reasonably open to him to render the threat ineffective, and that upon this being established the threat in question can no longer be relied upon by the defence. In deciding whether such an opportunity was reasonably open to the accused the jury should have regard to his age and circumstances, and to any risks to him which may be involved in the course of the action relied upon.[62]

A similar result occurred in *Abdul-Hussain* in which the Court of Appeal held that fear of imminent death at the hands of the Iraqi authorities could form the evidential to a plea of duress to a charge of hijacking.[63] Although it may be unreasonable to expect girls in the position of those in *Hudson and Taylor* to trust in the law enforcement agencies, it has been argued that public policy imposes a presumption that police protection should normally be sought.[64] After all it is hardly good penal policy to concede, as *Hudson and Taylor* does, that the coercive power of the villain is more implacable than that of the state. This danger seemed particularly apparent after *Hussain*[65] where the Court of Appeal allowed that the prospect of death and torture at the hands of an oppressive state could constitute duress capable of excusing the hijacking of a plane. In so deciding the Court of Appeal ruled that imminence rather than immediacy of threat was the appropriate measure. In *Baker and Ward*[66] the defendants' convictions for robbery were quashed where, although the defendants had the opportunity to seek police protection, the judge did not direct the jury to consider whether any reasonable person in their position would have done so.[67] The House of Lords in *Hasan* have now abandoned this relaxed approach to the requirement of urgency in duress. Lord Bingham, disapproving *Hudson and Taylor*, insisted that the defence was not available unless the defendant reasonably apprehended immediate or almost immediate death or serious injury for failure to comply. If this were not the case the

---

[59] [1963] 2 All ER 688.
[60] For example the crime of assault: *R v Ireland* [1997] 4 All ER 225; also the defences of provocation and self-defence.
[61] [1971] 2 QB 202.
[62] At 207 per Lord Widgery CJ; cf. *State v Green*, below, for a less realistic response.
[63] [1999] Crim LR 570.
[64] See generally J. Horder, 'Occupying the Moral High Ground: The Law Commission on Duress' [1994] Crim LR 334 at 337.
[65] [1999] Crim LR 570.
[66] [1999] 2 Cr App R 335; cf. *Heath* [2000] Crim LR 109 below.
[67] Cl. 29.6; for an effective middle course between compassion and public policy see J. Horder, loc. cit. 338.

defendant would be expected to take evasive action or, as in *Abdul-Hussain*, be disqualified from pre-emptive action.

E Prior fault

1 Intoxication

One further aspect of the *Graham* test should be noted. Duress cannot be relied upon if the defendant's will is eroded by the voluntary consumption of drink or drugs.[68] It seems that it is unavailable even where intoxication is involuntary.[69] On the other hand, if involuntary intoxication produces a mistaken belief that one is being threatened it is submitted that such a belief should avail the defendant, **even if unreasonable**, as long as the belief, if true, would be such as to make the reasonable man do as the accused did.[70]

2 Criminal organisations

The doctrine of prior fault also denies the defence to those who voluntarily place themselves at risk of coercion. In *Sharp*,[71] the defendant joined a criminal organisation. He later participated in a robbery on a post office, in which a sub-postmaster was killed. His defence to manslaughter was duress. He claimed that he had undertaken the robbery only because he had a gun to his head. The defence was rejected upon the basis that he voluntarily joined the gang, knowing that pressure might later be brought to bear to commit an offence.[72] In *Shepherd* it was made clear that the defendant should know that the gang were apt to use violence to exact compliance, although it was not necessary for the defendant to foresee the type of crime he would be forced to commit.[73] Outwith such circumstances, duress should remain available. The rule applies equally where the defendant voluntarily runs the risk of coercion outside the scope of a criminal organisation. In *Heath* a drug user who was coerced into supplying a class B drug by his own supplier, whom he had not paid, was denied the defence on the basis that he knew the risks of mixing with drug dealers.[74] In *Ali* the Court of Appeal went further, stating that it was not necessary for the coercee to be aware that the coercer was engaged in any specific criminal activity, so long as the risk of being subjected to any compulsion by threats of violence was foreseen or ought reasonably to have been foreseen.[75] In *Hasan* the House of Lords agreed, stating that the defendant is disqualified from relying on the defence not only where he actually foresees that violence may be used to exact compliance but also where he ought reasonably to know that it may be. This is surely correct if the basis for the defence, as I take it to be, is to provide an escape route for those who, through no fault of their own, are chosen under compulsion to advance the criminal purposes of others.

The rule applies equally where the defendant voluntarily runs the risk of coercion outside the scope of a criminal organisation. In *Heath* a drug user who was coerced into supplying a class B drug by his own supplier who he had not paid, was denied the defence

---

[68] See *Bowen* [1996] Crim LR 577.

[69] *Kingston* [1994] 3 All ER 353.

[70] This is possibly now the case also for voluntary intoxication in the light of *Martin*. Note 36.

[71] [1987] 3 All ER 103, CA.

[72] *PCL* (Ashworth, 2010) suggests that 'knowing' is too favourable to the accused and that it should be enough that he should have known that non-cooperation might be met by coercion, at 223.

[73] (1988) 86 Cr App R 47. Cf. *Lewis* (1992) 96 Cr App Rep 412.

[74] [2000] Crim LR 109; *R v Harmer* [2002] Crim LR 401.

[75] [2008] EWCA Crim 716.

on the basis that he should have known the risks of mixing with drug dealers. A similar decision was reached in *Mullally*.[76] On the other hand it is arguable that the prior fault rule is in this respect at least too strict. In particular, it means that a defendant who, as a youth, courts a criminal connection such as drug consumption subsequently discovered to have only transient appeal,[77] is deprived of the defence however hard they try to sever the connection and whatever, perhaps unexpected, crime they are required to commit.

F Scope of the defence

Historically duress was never a defence to murder, although it was, and is, available for the potentially graver offence of treason at least in its lesser forms.[78] For a time it appeared that duress might nevertheless be a defence to murder, at least where the defendant was a secondary party only.[79]

The House of Lords, in *Howe*,[80] formally removed the defence from accessories to murder on the ground that there is no fair and certain basis upon which to differentiate principals and accessories in terms of culpability.[81] While this may be true, it is disappointing that a more cogent ground for withdrawing the defence from murder itself was not advanced. If it is unjust to remove the defence from the principal, that injustice is hardly remedied by withdrawing it from other, possibly less culpable, participants.

The withdrawal can also be challenged on grounds of doctrinal coherence and consistency. The argument from coherence is that duress is available to a charge of causing grievous bodily harm with intent, which is in itself sufficient *mens rea* for murder. This produces the unsupportable result that the availability of the defence depends upon an accident of fate. If the victim dies, the defendant is guilty of murder. If he does not, they have an unqualified acquittal. In *Gotts*, the House implemented Lord Griffiths' 'declaration' in *Howe* that the defence was not available to attempted murder largely for this reason. As a result, the defendant's defence that he stabbed his mother only in response to his father's threat to kill him was held to be inoperative. Lord Jauncey agreed that no moral distinction could be drawn between murder and attempted murder, since the latter required proof of an intention to kill. He went so far as to doubt whether duress should be available for 'any very serious crime' since 'the highest duty of the law is to protect the freedom and lives of those who live under it'. While an extreme point of view, it is at least morally coherent, assuming the unjustified victimisation of the innocent lies at the heart of the rejection of the defence. As we have said, however, this ignores the reason why the defence developed in the first place, namely to provide an escape route – a legal one – to a person who had none. In *Wilson* the stringency of this restriction was underscored by the poignancy of the situation. The accused was a 13-year-old youth who had taken part in a killing of a neighbour under threats from his own father. His contribution was to fetch an axe and hand it to his father in the victim's home. Also upon his father's instructions, he had struck

---

[76] [2012] EWCA Crim 687.
[77] Cf. Smith and Hogan (2011) 263.
[78] *McGrowther* (1746) Foster 13. In this case tenants following their Lords in the Scottish rebellion.
[79] *DPP for Northern Ireland* v *Lynch*. The appellant had driven members of the IRA to a place where they subsequently shot a policeman. His defence of duress was refused at first instance on the ground that it was not available to murder. His appeal was allowed in the House of Lords on the narrow ground that the defence was available if, as here, the defendant was a secondary party. In *Abbot* a majority in the PC refused to allow the defence where the defendant was a principal offender to murder.
[80] [1987] 1 All ER 771.
[81] Lord Griffiths at 789.

the victim once with a metal bar and delivered a kick to her body. He claimed that he lived in fear of his father who had used violence towards him and his mother in the past. The Court of Appeal refused to qualify the scope of the defence to accommodate the youth of the accused and the relationship he had with his father.

The argument from consistency holds that if duress is thought a requirement of criminal justice to reflect our compassion for the ordinary unheroic victims of ill luck, it should operate **whatever** the accused does as long as the reasonable person, with whatever characteristics it is thought appropriate to invest them with, could not be expected to act differently. Is selfless heroism not simply something we aspire to but an expected standard of everyday behaviour? One would hardly think so, given the present state of the law on omissions liability.[82]

Again, is it fair to treat the external prompt of coercion less generously than the internal prompt of mental abnormality? Is it fair to treat the coerced killer any less favourably than a person who kills for reasons of justified loss of self-control?[83] Most of the problems which have beset the courts in this context result from confusion as to whether duress operates as a justification or an excuse.[84] If duress were acknowledged as an excuse, there should be less objection to it operating as a defence even to murder, as indeed it is treated under German law and under the Model Penal Code.[85]

The Law Commission has recently proposed that duress should operate as a complete defence to murder and attempted murder. However, the burden of proving the various elements of the defence such as the threat, the reasonableness of the reaction and the absence of prior fault lies with the defence.[86] I am not sure this is the correct approach. A strong call can be made for coercion, like provocation, to operate as a partial excuse in the usual case where another is victimised for reasons of self-preservation.[87] After all, compassion and mercy can be expressed otherwise than through an unqualified acquittal.[88] Society may justly require the defendant to expiate the guilt which many reasonable people will feel, when, to save themselves or loved ones, they deliberately kill or injure the loved ones of others. Voluntary manslaughter, or a more focused offence label, such as culpable homicide or killing under duress, more accurately reflects the wrong involved in killings as understandable as the Law Commission defines them to be.[89]

10.5 COMPULSION (II): DURESS OF CIRCUMSTANCES

The remaining defences in this chapter have a largely justificatory profile. Strictly speaking duress of circumstances is a separate defence from necessity, existing in both excuse and justificatory forms. It operates to afford a defence to a person who would otherwise be required to make an (unreasonable) personal sacrifice. Necessity, by contrast, requires no

[82] K.J.M. Smith, 'Must Heroes Behave Heroically?' [1989] Crim LR 622.
[83] This was one of the reasons why the Law Commission proposed in 2005 that duress should be available to murder as a partial defence.
[84] Not all, though. See W. Wilson, 'The Filtering Role of Crisis in the Constitution of Criminal Excuses' [2004] Can J of Law and Jurisprudence 387.
[85] MPC, s. 2.09(1). See Fletcher (1978) 831–2.
[86] Law Com. 304 (2006) ch. 6. A.J. Ashworth, 'Principles, Pragmatism and the Law Commission's Recommendations on Homicide Law Reform', Crim LR (2007) 333.
[87] This was the view of the Law Commission in the 2005 Consultation Paper, predating the final Report. See LCCP 177 (2005) *A New Homicide Act*, Part VII. See also M. Wasik, op. cit. 453; R.F. Schopp, *Justification Defenses and Just Convictions*, Cambridge: CUP (1998) ch. 5.
[88] Draft Criminal Law Bill, para. 30.20. This is the position in several American states.
[89] See generally P.H. Robinson, 'Criminal Law Defences: A Systematic Analysis' (1982) 82 Col L Rev 199 at 209.

such contingency and is available to vindicate the decision of the actor to do good by preventing harm.[90] Here duress of circumstances will be covered, for expositional reasons, in the following section on necessity, reflecting its current treatment by the judiciary as a *sub specie* of necessity.

10.6 NECESSITY

Overview

There are two forms of necessity. Necessity as an excuse, otherwise known as duress of circumstances, operates when the defendant chooses to infringe a criminal prohibition as a means of averting an imminent peril of death or serious injury to themselves or another for whom they are responsible. The defendant is excused as a concession to his human frailty. Necessity as a justification operates where the defendant chooses to infringe the law where this represents a lesser evil than the evil which would result if the defendant performed his strict legal duty. Necessity as a justification is presently recognised explicitly only in the field of medical treatment where action, otherwise unlawful, can lawfully be taken in the defence of the patient's best interests for those incapable of giving consent, or otherwise incompetent. Justificatory necessity is, in principle, far wider than this, rendering lawful any conduct, even an intentional killing, which is an inevitable and not disproportionate side-effect of action necessarily undertaken to prevent harm. Some doctrinal support for this proposition is also to be found in the medical arena.[91]

If duress is an unusual defence, necessity is perhaps more unusual. Until recently it was a defence in name only, or perhaps we should say it was recognised only in theory. Despite having no obvious doctrinal basis, however, textbooks routinely covered it[92] and learned articles were written about it.[93]

Such an unusual state of affairs reflects the enduring power of rationalism in legal development. At an earlier stage in our legal system commentators and judges were wont to accept the existence of the defence as a matter of pure reason. An early expression of this is to be found in *Reniger* v *Fogossa* (1551):

> when laws or statutes are made, yet there are certain things which are exempted and excepted out of the provisions of the same by the law of reason, although they are not expressly excepted. As the breaking of prison is a felony in the prisoner himself . . . yet if the prison be on fire and they who are in break prison to save their lives, this shall be excused by the law of reason and yet the words of the statute are against it.[94]

In the nineteenth century judges and commentators created self-imposed restrictions on their ability to develop the common law based on the conviction that law had some

---

[90] See note 103.

[91] See *Re A (conjoined twins)* below.

[92] At a time when the defence was still not acknowledged in English law, the second edition of G. Williams *TCL* (1983) contained a chapter of 25 pages. This was as long as the chapter on insanity and twice as long as the chapter on duress.

[93] The classic work, and still the best theoretical treatment, is P. Glazebrook, 'The Necessity Plea in English Criminal Law' [1972] CLJ 87.

[94] Plowden 1, quoted in P. Glazebrook, loc. cit. 93.

identifiable source and that this source was not pure reason but Parliament. More recently still, lawyers have again become sensitive to arguments that the 'moral gaps' between different defences can and, as a matter of pure reason, should be filled by a defence of necessity. Like black holes in cosmology, therefore, although we may not be able to see the defence in the universe of legal precedents using our own unaided senses, scholars nevertheless can prove its existence by its influence on (legal) reasoning and other (legal) phenomena. Thus, an influential view holds that the defence's existence is made manifest in a number of discrete, yet congruent, doctrines. It can be seen in the structure of defences. Both self-defence and duress, for example, can be viewed as particular doctrinal manifestations of a wider moral claim to avoid punishment. That claim is simply that the defendant's action was necessary.

A classic example of how that moral claim works is the case of *Bourne*.[95] The defendant was a surgeon who was charged with unlawfully procuring an abortion under s. 58 OAPA 1861, an offence which, under the relevant provision, admitted of no defence. The woman concerned was a fourteen-year-old girl who was pregnant as a result of rape. McNaghten J directed the jury that the statute required the doctor's act to be unlawful and that it would not be unlawful if the doctor acted with the honest belief that he was operating 'for the purpose of preserving the life of the mother'. Although McNaghten J at no stage stated that the doctor had a defence if his act was 'necessary' or used the word 'necessity', the only plausible basis for the direction is an implicit defence of necessity.[96] Similar outlets for the defence have been imported into the common law so that doctors, for example, are not guilty of assault if they perform emergency operations upon patients incapable of giving consent.

A The scope of necessity

A clear expression of the potential scope of necessity was given in the highly influential Canadian case of *Perka et al.* v *The Queen:*[97] 'Generally speaking the defence of necessity covers all cases where non-compliance with the law is excused by an emergency or justified by the pursuit of some greater good.'

As will be appreciated, this statement recognises the potential of necessity to excuse or to justify, although the court as a whole limited the defence's application to excuses.[98] There are two reasons why necessity has not been thought appropriate to develop as a justification. Both hinge on the utilitarian basis to the justification. Utilitarianism justifies conduct according to whether it maximises overall social welfare. Applied to the defence of necessity, the result is that no criminal harm is done where the defendant, faced with a choice of two evils one of which must occur however the accused acts, chooses the lesser evil.

The problem with a utilitarian notion of necessity is the problem attached to utilitarianism generally, namely that it is capable of supporting immoral conduct and of defeating rights without democratic accountability.[99] It would justify, for example, the killing of one innocent to save two, or the police torture of an innocent witness (e.g. the confessional priest) if this was the only way of finding a killer. The whole point of rights, however, is to

---

[95] [1939] 1 KB 687.
[96] For other examples of 'concealed defences' of necessity, see Glazebrook, ibid.
[97] (1984) 13 DLR per MacDonald J.
[98] Cf. J. Hall, *General Principles* (1960) 425–6.
[99] For full discussion see Chapter 9.

prevent individuals from being sacrificed for the public good or in the interests of others. The second problem with utilitarianism is that it appears to allow unbridled rule-breaking. If one can show that the benefits accruing from breaking the law are greater than from conformity, rule-breaking becomes a permissible option. As one judge put it, 'necessity can very easily become simply a mask for anarchy'.[100] Accordingly, cases in which defendants have sought to justify breaking rules on a greater good argument have typically received short shrift. In *Southwark LBC v Williams*, for example, necessity was held not to be a defence to trespass when the defendants sought to justify squatting in empty local authority accommodation by relying on their homelessness. Lord Denning warned of the danger that, once admitted as a defence to trespass, 'no one's house could be safe . . . it would open a door no man could shut'.[101]

Even in cases of crisis or emergency where little prospect of anarchy was apparent, the defence was consistently refused. As late as the 1970s the defence was held to be inapplicable where emergency services sought to avoid criminal responsibility for a traffic offence. In *Buckoke v GLC*,[102] Lord Denning stated that necessity was not an accepted defence and could not, therefore, avail even the driver of a fire engine who jumped a traffic light to combat a blaze, and though such conduct would properly be considered praiseworthy.[103] Such problem cases, he felt, should be accommodated by prosecutorial discretion. In *O'Toole*[104] the defence was refused an ambulance driver on a charge of driving without due care and attention. A similar fate befell a police officer in *Wood v Richards*.[105] Over the last decade, however, this blanket denial of the defence has given way to a limited recognition. Necessity has now become recognised as capable of operating as a defence.

As we shall see, necessity still has the power for further development as a justification. Even now, the case of unconsented-to therapeutic surgical intervention is probably best seen as a limited case of justificatory necessity, and may operate as a model for its further development. Generally speaking, however, necessity has crept into English law via the back door of the defence of duress.

B Necessity as an excuse – duress of circumstances

It is now a recognised defence that the defendant was faced with an emergency such that they had no choice but to break the law if they wished to avoid death or serious injury to themselves or another. The defence has been consciously constructed in the form of an excuse, in form similar to duress by threats, rather than in the justificatory form of self-defence. This restricted form of necessity is generally termed duress of circumstances, the threat of harm originating in external circumstances rather than an individual.[106]

The first two cases in which the defence was accepted were *Willer* and *Conway*.[107] In both these cases the defendants were charged with reckless driving and pleaded the necessity to escape from a threatened attack. This was disallowed by the trial judge in both

---

[100] *Southwark LBC v Williams* [1971] ch. 734, 746.
[101] [1971] ch. 734, 746.
[102] [1971] 1 ch. 655.
[103] *Southwark LBC v Williams* [1971] ch. 734 at 744.
[104] (1971) 55 Cr App R 206.
[105] [1977] Crim LR 295.
[106] An early hint that an emergency might ground such a developing excuse was given by Edmund-Davies LJ in *Southwark* at 746. See most recently *Quayle & Ors Attorney General's Reference [No. 2 of 2004]* [2005] EWCA Crim 1425.
[107] *Willer* [1987] RTR 22; *Conway* [1988] 3 All ER 1025.

cases and the resulting convictions were quashed by the Court of Appeal. In *Conway* the Court of Appeal said that there was no difference in principle between a person who was compelled to break the law as a result of unlawful coercion and a person who broke the law in order to avert a threat of unjustified harm. Duress was expressed to be an example of necessity and 'subject to the same limitations as [the] "do this or else" species of duress'. A further development occurred in the case of *Martin*.[108] The defendant was charged with driving while disqualified. His defence relied upon a credible threat by the defendant's wife that if he did not drive his son to work, she would commit suicide. It should be noted that neither the defendant nor anyone else was threatened with an **unlawful** act of violence, which he acted to avert. Rather, the defendant was faced with 'objective dangers' threatening another. Allowing the defence, Simon Brown J made clear that duress of circumstances was an application of necessity – 'it matters not whether the risk of death is murder or by suicide or indeed by accident. One can illustrate the latter by considering a disqualified driver being driven by his wife, she suffering a heart attack in remote countryside and he needing instantly to get her to hospital.'

The defence was brought into line with that of duress by threats, by requiring the defendant to be 'acting reasonably and proportionately in order to avoid a threat of death or serious injury'. In deciding whether the defence is available the jury should be directed to consider whether the accused was 'or may have been, impelled to act as he did because as a result of what he reasonably believed to be the situation he had good cause to fear that otherwise death or serious injury would result; second, if so, would a sober person of reasonable firmness, sharing the characteristics of the accused, have responded to the situation by acting as the accused did?'[109]

It should be noted that these cases involved traffic offences. This is probably not coincidental. Although having a protective function, traffic offences do not involve the deliberate victimisation of an innocent individual and are designed to safeguard the physical interests of road users, including the actor. As a result it was a relatively safe context for the development of the defence.[110] Given that the instances of rule-breaking involved no challenge to the rights of others, it is arguably unfortunate that the courts did not construct the defence along the lines of self-defence so as to exclude the death/serious injury requirement.[111]

The judiciary has extended its application to cover other 'crimes without a victim'. In *Pommell*[112] the defence was extended to quash the conviction of a defendant for possessing a firearm without a certificate. The defendant's case was that he was in possession of the gun as a result of persuading a friend to leave it with him rather than use it for a revenge killing. He had not had the opportunity of taking it to the police station before the police arrested him. The Court of Appeal held that the defence of duress of circumstances was not limited to traffic offences but extends throughout the criminal law. It should be noted, however, that this latter finding is wider than was necessary to dispose of the case. The offence Pommell was charged with was, like traffic offences, a crime without a victim. No third party rights were undone by the defendant's 'necessary action' and so no very difficult issue of principle or policy is involved in holding the excuse applicable.[113]

---

[108] [1989] 1 All ER 652.
[109] At 654 per Simon Brown J. Two recent decisions have offered to ignore the requirement that the defendant's belief be reasonable: *Baker and Wilkins* [1997] Crim LR 497; *DPP v Rogers* [1998] Crim LR 202.
[110] Cf. *Cole* [1994] Crim LR 582, above.
[111] See D.W. Elliot, 'Necessity, Duress and Self-Defence', [1989] Crim LR 611, 614–19.
[112] [1995] 2 Cr App Rep 607.
[113] Cf. *Cole*, in which no great enthusiasm for such a prospect was voiced.

Significantly, *Pommell* was not a true case of duress of circumstances but rather one of (justificatory) necessity. Pommell was not being asked to make any personal sacrifice in handing over the weapon to its owner. His moral claim to avoid punishment was, then, 'It was the right thing to do' rather than 'Would you require me to sacrifice myself or those for whom I am responsible for the sake of fidelity to law?'[114] This is indicative of the general confusion surrounding the interface of duress and circumstances, a confusion which might well be attributable to the reluctance of judges to state explicitly that necessity exists otherwise than in its excuse form.

The Court of Appeal manifested a comparable confusion as to the respective constituents of necessity and duress of circumstances in *R v S and L* (2009), but here in reverse form. The defendants deployed unlicensed guards. Their defence to a charge under the Private Security Industry Act 2001 was that this was done to address the risk of terrorist attack on their premises. They contended that there was no alternative means for protecting those who might be passing by or those who were in those premises from death or serious injury other than by protection to be afforded by the guards. So grave was the risk of death or serious injury on the dates identified in those counts that these defendants had no choice but to deploy their unlicensed employees. At a pre-trial hearing the judge refused to find that the material relied upon supported the defence of necessity. The Court of Appeal allowed the appeal. It concluded that if the material did support the conclusion that these steps were necessary to guard against an immediate or imminent threat of a major terrorist attack on a retail store and there was no other way of avoiding the risk to those in the store or passing by, then this could ground a defence of necessity. As will be apparent, the defence claim raised is necessity in its excuse form, that is, duress of circumstances. The Court of Appeal was restricting the defendant's exculpatory claim to cases where they acted to avoid the imminent threat of death or serious injury to themselves or others for whom they were responsible. It would not, as necessity is, have been available if for example the danger was less immediate and clamant although the deployment would still satisfy a 'lesser of two evils' calculation. No such mistake was made in *Pipe v DPP* where D had been convicted of speeding at over 100 mph while rushing a child with a broken leg to hospital. Owen J held that the defence of necessity was potentially available on such facts, and was not confined (as the justices had supposed) to cases in which there was a life-threatening situation. It was not obvious that the circumstances of this case actually justified such fast driving, but he could not be sure what conclusion the justices would have reached had they properly considered the available defence. This is an important recognition of the difference between necessity in its excuse form as reflected in *Conway*, and necessity as a justification where D is not relying on a threat of death or serious injury but is simply claiming the lesser of two evils.[115] On the other hand, Lord Denning's concern regarding the potential threat to the rule of law is clearly illustrated in this case.

Another difference, perhaps is that duress of circumstances, like duress by threats, requires the threat to be an immediate one or at least an imminent one. The object of the restriction is, once again, to discourage avoidable self-help but may operate unjustly. The (inhumane) extremes to which the doctrine can be pushed in the suppression of illegal 'self-help' can be seen dramatically illustrated in the American case of *State v Green*.[116] Here the defendant's conviction for jail breaking was affirmed, even though he had suffered

---

[114] J. Horder, 'Self-defence, Necessity and Duress' [1998] Can J Law and Juris 143.
[115] [2012] All ER (D) 238 (May).
[116] 470 S.W. 2d 565 (1971) (SC Missouri); cf. *Rodger* (1997), *The Times*, 30 July.

several homosexual rapes and had been warned on the day in question that if he did not submit again he would be killed or seriously injured. Although previous complaints had been ignored by the prison authorities, the court justified the decision on the basis that he was not, at the time of making the escape, being 'closely pursued' by the intending rapists, and had not sought to avert the threat by telling the prison authorities on the occasion in question.[117] In principle, in its justificatory form, at least a requirement of reasonableness of response is probably sufficient to dispatch claims amounting to unnecessary acts of self-preservation.

C Necessity as justification

A defence of necessity, extending beyond the reach of duress of circumstances, is recognised in a number of jurisdictions. The American Model Penal Code, adopted in a number of states, would render necessity a general defence:

> Conduct which the actor believes to be necessary to avoid a harm or evil to him or to another is justifiable, provided that: (a) the harm or evil sought to be avoided by such conduct is greater than that sought to be prevented by the law defining the offence charged . . .[118]

The adoption of a general defence of necessity was rejected by the Law Commission after a working party recommended the recognition of a defence comparable in scope to that of the American Model Penal Code.[119] The Law Commission's latest position recommends the adoption of necessity only in its excuse form of duress of circumstances.[120] It leaves unprovided for, cases where the defendant causes harm to vindicate a superior interest but is not acting in an emergency to avert a threat of death or serious injury.[121]

It is now clear that the common law recognises a limited version of justificatory necessity, operating primarily but not exclusively in the area of medical care. Its effect is to render lawful activities which are wrongful by no other measure than they infringe a primary criminal norm. This is implicit in cases such as *Bourne* and *Gillick*. In *Gillick*, a justificatory defence was implicit in the House of Lords conclusion that a doctor who prescribed contraceptives to an under-age girl was acting lawfully if actuated by an honest belief that it 'was necessary for the physical, mental and emotional health of his patient'.[122]

The existence of the defence was unequivocally acknowledged in *Re F* and, more recently, in *R v Bournewood Community and Mental Health NHS Trust*.[123] In *Re F*, the House of Lords held it to be lawful for doctors to sterilise a mentally incompetent (female) patient who had formed a sexual relationship with a fellow patient. It was thought to be in her overall 'best interests' for the operation to proceed[124] on a balance of all her interests,

---

[117] Cf. *Rodger and Rose* [1999] 1 Cr App R 143. Duress of circumstances requires the threat, real or otherwise, to issue from an external source. No defence to jail-breaking that the defendants otherwise, due to depression, would have committed suicide.

[118] Section 3.02(1).

[119] Law Commission Working Party on Codification: Working Paper No. 55 (1974) para. 57; *Report on Defences of General Application* (Law Com. No. 83, 1977); for a criticism of this report see G. Williams [1978] Crim LR 128.

[120] See below; Draft Criminal Law Bill 1993 (Law Com. No. 218 (1993)) cl. 26; cl. 43 Draft Code.

[121] It recommends the retention of any justificatory defence presently recognised at common law. Cf. *Pipe, supra.*

[122] Like *Bourne* (see below at note 141) this amounts to a defence of 'concealed necessity' although the case is treated as authority for a requirement of direct intention, at least for accomplice liability, at 425.

[123] [1998] 3 All ER 289.

[124] [1989] 2 All ER 545, HL, 551 per Lord Brandon.

including her interest in remaining free from the physical and psychological effects of pregnancy, abortion or childbirth[125] on the one hand, and her interest in having procreative capacity and remaining free from surgical interference on the other. The test for the legality of medical treatment, following *Re F*, is that the treatment proposed serves the patient's (best) 'interests'. In the case of incompetents this means that surgery maybe lawful though consent is absent or even withheld.[126] Otherwise the patient '(would be) deprived of medical care to which they are entitled'.[127]

In reaching his decision Lord Goff, with whom Lords Bridge and Jauncey agreed, explained that it was the 'principle of necessity' which, among other things, allowed people to assist others without their consent. Lord Goff gave some other examples of the principle in operation:

> a man who seizes another and forcibly drags him from the path of an oncoming vehicle, thereby saving him from injury or even death, commits no wrong. But there are many emanations of this principle . . . These are concerned not only with the preservation of the health or life of the assisted person, but also with the preservation of his property and even to certain conduct on his behalf in the administration of his affairs.[128]

Lord Goff stated further that it was not of the essence of necessity that there be some emergency requiring immediate action, although in many cases this would be present. In so saying, he underlined the defence's justificatory nature. Indeed, he accepted that operations and other interventions may be justified even if performed for other than clinical reasons;[129] 'these might include such humdrum matters as routine medical or dental treatment, even simple care such as dressing and undressing and putting to bed'.[130] In *Bournewood* the defence was applied to justify the detention of a patient suffering a mental disorder and whose condition posed a potential threat to himself and others. In *Pipe* the defence was held available to justify the action of a father who speeds in order to get his injured son promptly to hospital.[131]

What should be noted about all these medical cases is that no mention is made of doctors choosing the lesser of two evils.[132] Yet there is general recognition that acting in defence of the patient's interests or, in *Bournewood*, the interests of others is not only excusable, but expected. Moreover, and crucially, it limits what the doctor can do. This is made particularly clear in *Re F*. Lord Goff explains that intervention is justified only insofar as it respects and supports the interests (and rights) of the patient. Intervention is not justified, then, if it is contrary to the known wishes of the patient, whether the patient is conscious or unconscious. Thus a doctor is not justified in performing a life-saving amputation on a patient's gangrenous leg if not consented to,[133] nor in performing a life-saving caesarean section,[134] nor in giving a blood transfusion to an unconscious Jehovah's Witness.[135] Although

---

[125] Perhaps also her sexual autonomy.
[126] *Re W (A Minor) (Medical Treatment: Court's Jurisdiction)* [1993] Fam 64.
[127] Lord Brandon in *F v W Berkshire Health Authority* [1989] 2 All ER 545 at 551.
[128] At 564–5.
[129] Cf. the important Canadian decision of *Re Eve* (1986) 31 DLR (4th) 1 CSC.
[130] At 564.
[131] *Supra.*
[132] That is, the utilitarian basis of the justification.
[133] *Re C* [1994] 1 All ER 819.
[134] *St George's Healthcare NHS Trust v S* [1998] 3 All ER 673.
[135] *Malette v Shulman* (1988) 63 OR (2d) 243; cf. *Re W (a minor) (medical treatment)* [1992] 4 All ER 627; *Re T (adult: refusal of medical treatment)* [1992] 4 All ER 649; *B v Croydon HA* [1995] 1 All ER 682, for cases where the requirement has been relaxed.

such treatment may be in the patient's physical interests it confounds their rights to privacy and autonomy. Neither is a doctor justified, in the case of temporarily incompetent patients, in doing more than reasonably necessary to secure the patient's interest before they regain consciousness and are therefore capable of giving consent. A doctor could not, whilst operating upon a victim of a car crash, perform a hysterectomy for cancer.

In theory, then, necessity operating as a justification appears, paradoxically, to be anti-utilitarian, at least in the case of medical intervention. I say 'in theory' because, although the 'patient's best interests' supposedly governed the calculation as to whether intervention was justified, in both *Re F* and *Bournewood* these interests just happened to coincide also with the interests of the carers and more general public interests.[136] Both these cases involved incompetent patients and it may be that in such cases the patient's best interests are more easily subsumable within the broader network of interests by which their lives are ordered. Outside this special situation, however, the justification for action is not that the harm prevented is greater than the harm caused. If it were, a doctor could disregard absence of consent and do what is clinically necessary. The justification for action is that it serves the patient's interests and respects their rights of privacy and autonomy. Significantly this would seem to limit the ambit of justificatory necessity to cases where the rights and interests of innocent parties are not compromised.[137] If the message we gain from the above case law is that A cannot benefit (by medical intervention) B unless B consents (or is incapable of consenting), it is clear that A cannot also harm B unless he consents. By extension the same law which denies doctors the power to act against B, a patient, for 'B's own good' must deny doctors, or any other person, the power to act against B's will for C's good. It follows that necessity would not justify A injuring, or perhaps even stealing from, B to save the life of C (as in the case of coerced blood transfusion).[138]

The attraction of a 'rights-based' anti-utilitarian theory of justificatory necessity is easy to understand. If it were possible to show that the defence were 'driven', and limited, by rights then it would pre-empt much of the usual objection to justificatory necessity, namely that in its utilitarian mode it is capable of (undemocratically) second-guessing the legislature on questions of right and wrong and putting rights at risk.[139] After all, if judges are not the appropriate people to balance conflicting individual rights and interests, who is?

On the other hand, if rights limit as well as drive the defence, when can necessity ever be operative as a justification except in the exceptional case, such as traffic offences and medical 'crimes without victims', where the intended action 'offends' no one? As will now be explained, justificatory necessity has further scope for development and, indeed, in the medical field at least, such developments have already begun.[140]

---

[136] For a criticism of the balancing procedure see generally S. Cicca, 'Sterilising the Intellectually Disabled: The Approach of the High Court of Australia' in *Department of Health v JWB and SMB* (1993) Med LR 186. In *R v Bournewood Community and Mental Health NHS Trust* [1998] 3 All ER 289 the detention of a mentally incompetent patient was held lawful on grounds of necessity although the detention was not otherwise justified under the Mental Health Act 1983.

[137] See below for qualifications to this principle.

[138] Cf. Brooke LJ in *Re A (Children)* [2001] 2 WLR 480.

[139] See Dickson J in *Perka et al. v R* (1985) 13 DLR (4th) 1, 14.

[140] For further discussion see Chapter 6.

1 Necessity operating to defeat interests

(a) Conflicting duties

One potential area of development is implicit in the judgment of McNaghten J in *Bourne*, where the interests of the foetus were clearly subjugated to those of the mother. He emphasised how rights and duties are not hermetically sealed, but interrelate and inform each other:

> If a case arose where the life of the woman could be saved by performing [an abortion] and the doctor refused to perform it because of his religious opinions and the woman died, he would be in grave peril of being brought before this court on a charge of manslaughter by negligence . . . If the doctor is of the opinion, on reasonable grounds and with adequate knowledge, that the probable consequences of the continuance of the pregnancy will be to make the woman a physical or mental wreck, the jury are quite entitled to take the view that the doctor who, under those circumstances and in that honest belief, operates, is operating for the purpose of preserving the life of the mother.[141]

In short not only was a doctor acting lawfully in terminating a pregnancy which threatened the life of the mother, it was their legal duty to do so. Proof that this is so, if needed, is the fact that responsibility would arise for a failure to act so as to secure the patient's clinical interests. On this view, the necessity defence will always come into operation to provide a legal escape route for those challenged by an apparent conflict of duties. No rational, let alone just, system of law can incorporate rules which deprive a citizen of the ability to act lawfully whether they choose to act or to refrain from acting.[142] In such circumstances the assumption is that the defendant is taken outside the normal scheme of the criminal law and is required to choose to perform the 'higher' duty, that is the duty which vindicates the higher interest. In cases of doctors and their pregnant patients the crystallised interests of the mother clearly weigh more heavily than the inchoate interests of the foetus. The choice facing the doctor is very different from the choice facing the victim of duress or duress of circumstances, taking it outside the realm of excuses.[143] The latter is a coerced choice. The former is a legal requirement.[144] This argument appeared to weigh heavily with Ward LJ in *Re A (children)* in which it was held that an operation to separate conjoined twins might be lawful if it was necessary to secure the survival of the stronger twin although the inevitable consequence of the separation would be the death of the weaker twin.[145] Of key importance for all three judges was not simply that the operation was the lesser of two evils; it was not a case of the former's interests weighing heavier than the latter. Rather, the latter was doomed whatever the doctors did. Their responsibility to advance the cause of life, therefore, demanded that they choose the least worst outcome. Thus Brooke LJ stated that the defence would be limited to cases where

(1) The act is needed to avoid inevitable and irreparable evil;

(2) No more should be done than is reasonably necessary for the purpose to be achieved; and

(3) The evil inflicted must not be disproportionate to the evil avoided.[146]

---

[141] *Bourne* [1939] 1 KB 687, 693–4.

[142] For an extended analysis of the legality of 'impossible demands', see Lon L. Fuller, *The Morality of Law*, New Haven: Yale University Press (1969).

[143] Cf. Fletcher (1978) 852.

[144] Fletcher sees this as an example of necessity as excuse, 823–33.

[145] For further discussion see Chapter 6. C. Clarkson, 'Necessary Action: a New Defence' (2004) Crim LR 81.

[146] At 1052.

(b) *Advancing interest protected by defendant's duty*

A variation upon this idea was the proposal of Wilson J in the important case *of Perka*. She proposed a restricted form of justificatory necessity. The restriction she imposed was that the interest secured by the defendant's action was one which the defendant owed a (legal) duty to defend. Such a proposal could explain cases as distinct as *Gillick*, *Bourne*, *Re F*, and *Bland*.[147] It would not, however, be necessary to show that the defendant was placed in a *Bourne* type 'no win' situation as long as the duty honoured was hierarchically superior to the duty dishonoured. Consider, in this regard *Pipe*. Mr Pipe was under a duty to his son to minister to his welfare. Under Wilson J's scheme this duty affords him the **liberty of breaking the speed limit to ensure his prompt attendance at hospital** even though there is no question of him having a **duty** to do so such that liability for wilful neglect (or manslaughter) will arise for driving at the correct speed.

A major difficulty with Wilson J's analysis is that the interest to be advanced through the performance of the duty is not in itself enough to justify action taken in support of it. So if the driver of the car was Mr Pipe's neighbour who, in the absence of Mr Pipe decided that getting the child to the hospital quickly was imperative the defence would not be available, since he is under no legal duty of care.[148] And yet it might be thought that it is an irrelevance who helps the child, assuming the danger was clamant enough, as long as someone does.[149] Such a morally unsupportable distinction leads one to suppose that there is something lacking in Wilson J's analysis. We are left with the unsatisfactory state of affairs that the parent's action is deemed justified not because it is the right thing to do but because our society gives the mother, as a duty holder, the power **to decide** that it is the right thing to do.

In the final section we will consider two further plausible grounds for the general development of justificatory necessity in the specific context of the crime of murder.

D Necessity/duress of circumstances and murder

It is difficult on any theory of justification to justify intentional killings. An early attempt which failed occurred in the classic case of *Dudley and Stephens* in which the defence of necessity was held not to be available on a charge of murder to ship crew members who, following a shipwreck, had killed and eaten a cabin boy.[150] The ratio of the case is not obvious. There are three possibilities. The first is that necessity is not a defence (to any crime) recognised in English law. This was the view commonly taken until the recent formal recognition of the species of necessity known as duress of circumstances. A second possibility, embraced by a majority of their lordships in *Howe*, is that *Dudley and Stephens* is authority for the limited proposition that necessity is no defence to murder.[151] Since, moreover, duress was treated as a subspecies of necessity it followed that duress was also no defence. The third, and most plausible, view is that no one may justifiably kill an innocent, simply to preserve their own life.[152] On this view necessity might yet justify the

---

[147] *Airedale NHS Trust v Bland* [1993] 1 All ER 821. In each of these cases the doctor owed a duty to their patient to secure at least the patient's clinical interests. Walker LJ and Brooke LJ thought the existence of such a duty critical to the legality of the operation in *Re A (Children)*.

[148] A. Brudner, 'A Theory of Necessity' [1987] 7 OJLS 339.

[149] S. Gardner, 'Necessity's Newest Inventions' [1991] 11 OJLS 125, 131–3.

[150] (1884) 14 QBD 273.

[151] By implication, therefore, the House of Lords appeared to concede that it could be a defence to other crimes.

[152] Kenny, *Outlines* (1965) 68.

commission of other crimes, and might under appropriate circumstances excuse, even justify, murder.

Case 7

Following a shipwreck Adam and Eve scramble to secure the only lifebelt available. Adam gets to the belt first and defends it against Eve. Eve, on the point of sinking, hits Adam over the head and wrests the belt from his grasp. Adam drowns.

At the moment the defendants in *Dudley and Stephens* killed the boy there was a realistic prospect of the defendants dying of starvation, but not so urgent a prospect as would raise the reasonable inference that their action was morally involuntary.[153] Eve's conduct here is clearly morally involuntary in the sense that she would not have been able to resist doing what she did. This seems a reasonable ground for distinguishing *Dudley and Stephens* on grounds of duress of circumstances.[154]

There are grounds for arguing, therefore, that a form of necessity capable of acting as a defence to murder may survive *Dudley and Stephens* and *Howe*.[155] As explained above, the most that can be said about *Dudley and Stephens* is that the court explicitly accepted the primacy of individual rights against the challenge of utility. *Dudley and Stephens* did not say that a deliberate killing could not be justified, only that a person could not justifiably kill an innocent to save his own skin. Neither did it say that a deliberate killing could not be excused, only that an excuse would not be available where there was no **immediate** necessity.

1 Necessary action consented to and in the public interest

This leaves open the possibility that a deliberate killing may be justified where individual rights are not sacrificed. So, if the victim of the killing had been chosen from among consenting participants drawing lots, scope would arguably have been available to justify the killing. Although one cannot generally consent to be killed it is clear that the public interest upholds the validity of consent exceptionally.[156] Where the decision is democratically taken in the best interests of all the participants including the eventual victim it is possible that the public interest would not be compromised.[157] If the ritual of conforming to Queensberry rules can render a killing in the course of a boxing match lawful, there seems no obvious reason why the ritual of drawing lots to prevent unnecessary loss of life should be treated any differently.[158]

2 Double effects and the preservation of life

Necessity might also, in principle, justify a killing (or lesser harm) where, by analogy with self-defence, itself a defence to murder, the result is an unpurposed side-effect of action taken directly in defence of self or others.[159] Some support for this view was offered by Robert Walker LJ in *Re A*. It was the fact that the twin's death was an unavoidable side-effect of

---

[153] As Lord Coleridge CJ implied at 286–8.
[154] Suggested by Francis Bacon in 'The Elements of the Common Laws of England' (London) 630, cited in P. Glazebrook, loc. cit. 92.
[155] This would require of course an acceptance that truly involuntary actions in the urgency of the moment be a defence to murder.
[156] Cf. *Brown* [1992] 2 All ER 552.
[157] *United States* v *Holmes* 26 Fed Cas 360 (1842).
[158] See Chapter 12.
[159] This would provide a defence in Cases 6 and 8, Chapter 9.

an otherwise lawful act of life preservation that sanctified the operation. The twin was not being exploited as a means to an end, as in the case of a forced blood transfusion. She was just an unfortunate victim of the 'fall-out' from an act quite properly calculated to save the other's life. Even supposing the former could have survived, was the latter expected to sacrifice her life to make this happen? Is this not the reason why we expect rather than deplore the transfer of scarce life-support machines from patients with scant chance of survival to those with good chances? Although judges, in the area of duress, have flirted with the idea that we may owe a duty of self-sacrifice for the good of others,[160] this is clearly an idea limited to cases where the defendant's choice is (purposely) to kill or be killed. Outside this narrow situation it is clear, as we have seen, that a bystander owes no duty to subjugate their interests to those of others, for example to rescue a child or even a multitude of children drowning in a pond. The underlying message seems to be that people are entitled to put their own interests before the interests of others, even if the harm which the former will suffer is **less** than the harm threatened if the sacrifice is not met.[161] In self-defence the justification extends even to **purposed harms** as long as the harm is the unavoidable side-effect of a lawful act of self-preservation. Here the justification operating is not utilitarian. A person is justified in killing 20 to save himself if those 20 combine to attack him. It makes no difference, moreover, to the lawfulness of their action if the attackers are not at fault – his right is protected even against the insane. In this latter case, of course, the acted-against person constitutes the threat to security or autonomy in defence of which action is taken. It may well be that this represents a necessary structural limitation on the development of the defence so that action taken against a person innocent of wrongdoing is in need of a different justification.[162]

It has been suggested that such a justification might exist where such a person stands 'in the way' of the safety of others, particularly where they are doomed to die whatever course of conduct is chosen.[163] This would justify the (reasonable) action of the ship's passenger who dislodges from a staircase an innocent (or innocents) whose conduct unjustly, though without blame, threatens his life.[164] *Re A* clearly goes beyond this. The justification proposed does not require the person acted against either to constitute the threat posed or to be blocking a route to safety. It requires simply that the action taken be necessary to avoid inevitable and irreparable evil and not be disproportionate to the evil avoided[165]. Implicitly moreover it surely requires any consequent harm to be by way of side-effect rather than as a means to an end. It would not, then, justify Eve's action in Case 7 where the action taken is directed against Adam, who is being used as a resource in the struggle for survival. Neither would it justify consensual euthanasia, as the court in *Nicklinson* concluded, rejecting the submission that the defence of necessity should be potentially available to a doctor who agreed to terminate a patient's life at the patient's request.[166]

---

[160] See *Lynch*, above.

[161] Elliot, 'Necessity, Duress and Self-Defence', [1989] Crim LR 611, 617–19, seems to support this stance. He argues that duress should act like self-defence, for the same reasons as self-defence, subject to the qualification that the defendant must not **aim** at (my emphasis) personal harm to an innocent.

[162] J.C. Smith (Smith and Hogan, 2002), *Criminal Law*, London: Butterworths. Tolley, appeared to think otherwise, treating *Re A* as a case involving self-defence, at 282.

[163] See S. Uniacke, *Permissible Killing: The Self-Defence Justification of Homicide* (1994) ch. 5; J. Horder, 'Self-Defence, Necessity and Duress' [1998] Can J of Law and Juris 143, 157 ff; F. Leverick, *Killing in Self-Defence*, Oxford: OUP (2007).

[164] See J.C. Smith, *Justification and Excuse in the Criminal Law*, London: Stevens (1989) 73. Cf. Ward LJ, *Re A (Children)* [2001] 2 WLR 480.

[165] At 1052.

[166] [2012] EWHC 2381 (Admin).

It would, however, explain the apparent legality of shooting down a passenger plane which, as in the World Trade Center attack, has been hijacked for the purpose of committing mass murder. The deaths of the innocent passengers is an undesired side-effect of implementing a moral imperative, namely the preservation of life, which deaths, moreover, will occur whether or not the life-preserving action is taken.[167] Further possible extensions to the range of justificatory defences will be considered in the next section.

10.7 USE OF FORCE IN PUBLIC AND PRIVATE DEFENCE

Overview

It is a defence to any crime in which the use of force is a conduct element that the use of force was, in the circumstances that the defendant believed them to be, reasonable and necessary for the protection of public or private interests.

The use of reasonable force is justified in defence of certain public or private interests. The paradigm example of public defence is the prevention of crime. Of private defence, it is self-defence. We saw in Chapter 4 that it would not be unlawful for Eve to push Adam to his certain death if this was immediately necessary to prevent Adam from shooting to kill.[168] This case illustrates two points which it is as well to bear in mind. First, the effect of successfully raising the defence is to render an otherwise unlawful act lawful. Second, even intentional homicide may be justified if the circumstances dictate. It may therefore profit a person who has killed another to preserve their own life or that of another, to be able to present the case as one of self-defence rather than necessity or duress. In a recent Canadian case the defendant, who had hired a hitman to kill her husband who was threatening her and her child's life, failed in this endeavour. Neither defence fitted. She was not directing force against an aggressor (self-defence) and she was not being compelled by another or force of circumstances to kill her husband.[169]

10.8 PURPOSES FOR WHICH REASONABLE FORCE MAY BE USED

Reasonable force may lawfully be used in defence of self or others from unlawful force or harm, in defence of property, in the prevention of crime, in the prevention or termination of a breach of the peace, in effecting a lawful arrest and to terminate a trespass.[170] It should be noted that the source of the relevant defence rule differs according to whether force is used in defence of public interests (prevention of crime or effecting an arrest), or private interests. In the former case the law is contained in s. 3(1) of the Criminal Law Act 1977. In the latter, the common law rules prevail.[171] These are now encapsulated by statute in the

---

[167] See J. Horder, 'Self-Defence, Necessity and Duress' [1998] Can J Law and Juris 143 for a plausible analysis of how these defences are to be distinguished. See also W. Wilson, *Central Issues in Criminal Theory*, Oxford: Hart (2002) ch. 10; M. Bohlander, 'Of Shipwrecked Sailors, Unborn Children, Conjoined Twins and Hijacked Airplanes – Taking Human Life and the Defence of Necessity' (2006) JCL 147; 'Hijacked Airplanes: May They Be Shot Down?' (2007) New Crim LR 582.

[168] Ca R v *Ryan*, 290 CCC (3d) 477 se 7, ch. 4.

[169] Case 7, ch. 4.

[170] Law Com. No. 218 (1993) Draft Criminal Law Bill, cl. 27(1).

[171] Where property is damaged in the defence of other property this is governed by the Criminal Damage Act 1971.

Criminal Justice and Immigration Act 2008 as amended by the Crime and Courts Act 2013.[172] The two sets of rules are essentially similar.[173] This is fortunate since most cases of force used in private defence will, in any event, also be instances of force being used to prevent crime. In *Cousins* it was said that the statutory and common law defences were interchangeable where force or the threat of force was used to prevent an unlawful attack.[174] Use of the common law defence remains necessary where force is used to repel unlawful force where the aggressor is able to avail himself of an excuse, for example, insanity or duress.

With respect to both public and private defence, the legal burden of proof lies with the prosecution. The defence bears the evidential burden, that is the burden of adducing sufficient evidence for the jury to give credence to the idea that the defendant may have been acting in defence. Once this burden is discharged the prosecution must prove that the defendant was not so acting. For the defence, it is most important to separate evidence which puts the **offence** in doubt and evidence supporting a **defence**.

Case 8

Adam and Eve are walking on a cliff path. Adam lunges at Eve for the purpose of kissing her. Eve pushes Adam so hard that he falls over the cliff to his death.

Here, the conduct of Eve can be used to support a claim either that she lacked *mens rea* or that she acted in self-defence. Indeed she can run both defences.[175] With the former the claim would be something to the effect that she intended nothing beyond pushing him away. That he might fall to his death was not her purpose and was not foreseen. It was an accident. Let's assume this is not her story. Rather it is that in the heat of the moment she felt that pushing him over the cliff was necessary and proportionate to the threat offered by Adam. Of course, unless Adam's demeanour was particularly threatening this would be unlikely to satisfy a jury. The former claim is the stronger.

A Rules governing the use of force

For ease of exposition the wording of s. 3(1) will be taken as a starting point for the analysis of the rules relating to both public and private defence. It should not be forgotten, however, that the source of the private defence rules, for example self-defence, remains the common law. Applied generally, a person may use such force as is reasonable in the circumstances for the relevant defence purpose. Specifically, s. 3(1) provides:

> A person may use such force as is reasonable in the circumstances in the prevention of crime, or in effecting or assisting in the lawful arrest of offenders or suspected offenders or of persons unlawfully at large.

Case 9

Adam sees Eve, a burglar, enter his cellar where he has a valuable wine collection. He follows her and knocks her over the head with a baseball bat to overpower her.

---

[172] Section 43.

[173] Some common law rules, e.g. the rule that the defendant must retreat before using force, appear now to have been superseded by the Criminal Law Act; see *McInnes* [1971] 3 All ER 295.

[174] *Cousins* [1982] 2 All ER 115, 117; see also *Clegg* [1995] 1 All ER 334.

[175] *R v Dickens* [2006] Crim LR 267.

Adam is entitled to use reasonable force:

(a) in the defence of property (wine);
(b) to prevent a crime from being committed; and
(c) to effect the arrest of Eve.

The reasonableness of Adam's use of force will depend upon whether force of the type and gravity used[176] was immediately necessary to effect whichever of these purposes Adam acted to discharge. So, in *Attwater* it was held that the defendant was unable to rely on the defence of prevention of crime when the force used (dangerous driving to prevent the escape of a driver who had caused an accident) occurred after the driver's offence had already taken place.[177]

There are two separate aspects to the reasonableness requirement, reflecting the justificatory nature of the defence. First, the use of force must be necessary. Second, the degree of force used must be proportionate to the threat encountered.

1 The use of force must be necessary

The use of force in private defence is dependent upon the existence of a justifying 'trigger' – self-defence, prevention of crime and so on. It includes the prevention or termination of a trespass so that a person can use reasonable force to remove a trespasser from his land and, apparently, any moveable object such as a motor vehicle.[178] However, the right is not absolute. In *R v Burns*[179] the defendant physically ejected a prostitute from his car when, upon seeing her properly, he thought better of it. She had asked him to be returned to the pick-up spot but he refused. The Court of Appeal agreed with the trial judge that the use of force was unlawful. Although it was lawful to use force to remove a trespasser from property, including a vehicle, this was so only if no other reasonable method of terminating the trespass existed. In this case there was, namely to return the woman, as agreed, to the pick-up spot.

(a) *Other options?*

The use of force will not be reasonable if it is not immediately necessary. If, therefore, as in *Burns*, there are other defence options available the use of force may not be reasonable. In Case 9 the objective necessity for using violence requires consideration to be given to what Adam was trying to achieve and what other means were available for this purpose. If Adam wished to capture and arrest Eve, or simply prevent his wine being stolen, the use of violence would only be immediately necessary if simple restraint (locking the cellar door) was not an option.[180] However, if Eve was entering the cellar for the purpose of committing criminal damage to the wine, the use of such violence might become necessary. Whether Adam's conduct was justifiable in the light of this would depend upon whether the amount of force used was proportionate to the threat posed. This will be covered below.

---

[176] That is, violence rather than restraint.
[177] [2011] RTR 173; Cf. *R v Morris*, unreported, 16 April 2013 CA.
[178] D.J. Lanham, 'Defence of Property in Criminal Law' [1966] Crim LR 366.
[179] [2010] EWCA Crim 1023.
[180] Imprisoning Eve, under these circumstances, is independently lawful under s. 24 Police and Criminal Evidence Act 1984.

(b) *A duty of retreat?*

At common law, a duty to retreat was imposed in cases of self-defence such that failure disentitled the victim of aggression to rely on self-defence.[181] There is no longer a duty to retreat for self-defence. However, the reasonableness of a person's reaction to a threat of force might well, in appropriate circumstances, hinge upon whether the person availed himself of a reasonable opportunity to withdraw or otherwise defuse the situation.[182] There is no doubt, however, that English law supports the right of the individual to stand their ground if they are not otherwise acting unlawfully. In *R* v *Field* F was told that B was coming round to get him. F remained where he was and, in repelling B's attack, killed him. The prosecution case was that his use of force was unreasonable since he had the opportunity to retreat and seek police protection. The Court of Appeal rejected this argument and allowed the defence. Section 76 makes no change in this respect.[183]

Case 10

Cain and Abel square up to each other in a pub. Abel, in a vain attempt to avoid a fight, threatens to smash Cain's head in. Cain punches Abel on the nose.

Whether or not Cain's use of force was necessary is a matter for the jury. They will take into account any statement of Cain as to why he threw the punch rather than, say, retreat or present a non-combative demeanour. They may conclude that Cain's conduct was more suggestive of his own aggressive intentions, or a response to Abel's provocative words. On the other hand, if Cain thought it was merely a matter of time before Abel threw his own punch and did not feel able to retreat effectively or defuse the situation, they may conclude that Cain's punch was necessary from his own point of view and, particularly if it was not followed up, also proportionate.[184]

There is no rule of law which disentitles a person to rely on self-defence where he is the initial aggressor. The position was summed up in the Scottish case of *Burns* v *HM Advocate*:

> It is not accurate to say that a person who kills someone in a quarrel which he himself started, by provoking it, or entering into it willingly, cannot plead self-defence if his victim then retaliates. The question whether the plea of self-defence is available depends, in a case of that kind, on whether the retaliation is such that the accused is entitled then to defend himself. That depends on whether the violence offered by the victim was so out of proportion to the accused's own actings as to give rise to the reasonable apprehension that he was in immediate danger from which he had no other means of escape, and whether the violence which he then used was no more than was necessary to preserve his own life or protect himself from serious injury.[185]

The position is different if he deliberately provokes a fight so as to give himself an excuse for injuring or killing the victim.[186] In both private and public defence motive makes the difference between lawful and unlawful aggression.

---

[181] J.H. Beale, 'Retreat from a Murderous Assault' (1903) 16 Harv LR 567; for a useful review of the authorities on this matter see Dressler (1987) ch. 18. No such duty applied in the case in defence of public interests.

[182] See *Bird* [1985] 2 All ER 513; Draft Criminal Law Bill 1993, cl. 28(8).

[183] *Field* [1972] Crim LR 435; *Redmond-Bate* [1999] Crim LR 998. And see most recently *Duffy* v *Chief Constable of Cleveland* [2007] EWHC 3169 (Admin).

[184] Cf. *Shannon* (1980) 71 Cr App R 192.

[185] *Burns* v *HM Advocate* 1995 SLT 1090 applied in *R* v *Harvey* [2009] EWCA Crim 469; *R* v *Rashford* [2005] EWCA Crim 377.

[186] Ibid.

> **Case 11**
> Adam shoots Eve, a member of his own gang, just as she was about to shoot Cain, a police officer. He does this believing Eve to have betrayed him and in order to curry favour with the police who are about to arrest him.

The lawfulness of Adam's action depends upon whether he is using force for the purpose of repelling an unjust attack on Cain. Here it is clear that he is not and so, in principle, he should be guilty of murder.[187]

(c) *Unjust threat*

The essence of private, if not public, defence is proportionate force used to repel an unjust threat posed by another person.[188] Self-defence may not, then, be used if the threat is justified, as in the case of a lawful arrest. Private defence is available although the attacker is not at fault, say due to infancy, insanity or mistake.[189]

(d) *Mistakes*

It should be noted that in each case, the legality of the force used is determined on the basis of the facts as they appeared to the defendant.[190] In Case 9 the legality of Adam's conduct depends upon his view of the facts. So he would be entitled to rely on the defence if, in using the baseball bat, he was mistaken as to Eve's intentions, believing her intent on criminal damage rather than theft. He is also entitled to rely on the defence if he was in error that Eve was a burglar, once again even if the belief was unreasonable. For this reason it was not fatal to the defence that at the time the defendant used force against a person believing him to be in the course of committing the offence of making off without payment the offence was in fact complete. He was entitled to be judged on the facts as they appeared to him.[191]

The requirement that the defendant be judged on the basis of the facts as they believed them to be crucially qualifies the reasonableness requirement.

> **Case 12**
> Adam, a police officer, unreasonably suspects Eve, a respected member of the Women's Institute, of being a terrorist. He challenges her and demands that she puts her hands in the air. In panic Eve reaches for her asthma inhaler. Adam shoots Eve dead, believing the object to be a gun.

Adam's liability depends upon whether the force used was reasonably necessary to meet the threat which he thought Eve's gesture represented. On the facts as he saw them, Eve was about to kill him. As a result, his action, objectively unreasonable, is reasonable given his set of beliefs. It is clearly defensive action. It goes without saying that the more

---

[187] In *R* v *Dadson* (1850) 2 Den 35. See discussion at 43. See generally J. Gardner, 'Justifications and Reasons' in A.T.H. Smith and A. Simester (eds), *Harm and Culpability* (1996) 103. For a different view see G. Williams, *CLGP* 24.

[188] S. Uniacke, *Permissible Killing* ch. 5; J. Horder, 'Self-defence, Necessity and Duress' [1998] Can J of Law and Juris 143.

[189] See, for example, *R* v *(Gladstone) Williams*, *infra*.

[190] CJI Act 2008, s. 76(3) and (4); see *Beckford*; *Williams*, above.

[191] Cf. *Attwater* above, note 177.

unreasonable the defendant's belief, the less the jury are likely to credit it. Strasbourg decisions indicate that this aspect of domestic law may have to be reviewed, at least in the case of fatal killings by agents of the state. In a number of decisions under Art. 2(2), mistaken beliefs in the necessity to use (fatal) force, the Court has required beliefs to be held 'for good reason'.[192] Whether this means that domestic law is incompatible with the Convention in this respect is open to question.[193]

2 The degree of force used must be proportionate

Having concluded that the defendant was or may have been acting in self-defence rather than, say, in revenge, retaliation or in response to provocation, the jury must also consider whether the amount of force used was or may have been reasonable. In *A-G for Northern Ireland's Reference (No. 1 of 1975)* the Court of Appeal considered the application of s. 3(1), Criminal Law Act 1977 on a charge of murder. The accused was a soldier who had shot dead a member of the public, wrongly believing him to be a member of the IRA. The question for the jury was whether the soldier's conduct was 'reasonable in the circumstances' for the purpose of preventing crime. Lord Diplock said that the jury should ask themselves if they were satisfied:

> that no reasonable man
> (a) with knowledge of such factors as were known to the accused or (reasonably)[194] believed by him to exist
> (b) in the circumstances and time available to him for reflection
> (c) could be of the opinion that the prevention of the risk of harm to which others might be exposed if the suspect were allowed to escape justified exposing the suspect to the risk of harm to him that might result from the kind of force that the accused contemplated using.[195]

As will be appreciated such a generous jury direction may well explain the concern expressed by the European Court as to the prospects that police and security services may gain undue benefit from the absence of a requirement that mistakes as to the necessity of using possible murderous force should be reasonable.

3 Proportionate from whose point of view?

The question to be considered, therefore, is not how the reasonable person **should have** responded but how the reasonable person **might have** responded to the supposed threat given the circumstances and sharing the beliefs of the accused. In deciding whether the degree of force was proportionate to the threat the jury must be directed that they should not expect the reasonable person in the heat of the moment to 'weigh to a nicety the exact amount of defensive action' which may be necessary.[196] In other words, the mere fact that the defendant overreacts does not necessarily mean that the degree of force used is disproportionate, as long as it might reasonably have been thought proportionate in the exigency of the moment.

---

[192] Cf. *A v UK* (1998) 27 EHRR 611.

[193] *McCann and Others v UK* (1996) 21 EHRR 97; *Caraher v UK* (2000) EHRLR 3, 326–9, as cited by Leverick, below; cf. A.J. Ashworth, 'The European Convention and the Criminal Law' in Cambridge Centre for Public Law, *The Human Rights Act and the Criminal Justice and Regulatory Process*, Oxford: Hart (1999); R. Buxton, 'The Human Rights Act and the Substantive Criminal Law' [2000] Crim LR 331, 337; F. Leverick, 'Is English Self-Defence Law Incompatible with Article 2 of the ECHR?' (2002) Crim LR 347.

[194] The reasonable requirement has since been dispensed with.

[195] [1977] AC 105.

[196] CJI Act 2008, section 76(7)(a).

Subject only to this latter qualification, until fairly recently it was accepted that the test of proportionality was an objective one. In other words, what mattered is not whether the accused himself believed the amount of force used was reasonable, but whether it **was** reasonable. In *Palmer*[197] this test was qualified somewhat. Lord Morris indicated that a basic yardstick for the reasonableness of the accused's response was what he himself in the urgency of the moment 'honestly and instinctively thought necessary'. This would be 'the most potent evidence that only reasonable defensive action had been taken'. The 2008 Act reproduces this basic legal position. Despite the rhetoric accompanying its enactment no substantive changes were made.[198] The overall position is encapsulated as follows:

76(6) The degree of force used by D is not to be regarded as having been reasonable in the circumstances as D believed them to be if it was disproportionate in those circumstances.

76(7) In deciding the question mentioned in subsection (3) (reasonableness of degree of force used) the following considerations are to be taken into account (so far as relevant in the circumstances of the case) –

(a)   that a person acting for a legitimate purpose may not be able to weigh to a nicety the exact measure of any necessary action; and

(b)   that evidence of a person's having only done what the person honestly and instinctively thought was necessary for a legitimate purpose constitutes strong evidence that only reasonable action was taken by that person for that purpose.

An obvious problem with the 'honestly and instinctively thought' statement is that what a person might instinctively think necessary may be far from what is objectively reasonable.[199] The instincts of the pacific, well-balanced, law-abiding person may differ markedly from those whose inclinations are essentially hostile and suspicious. Such a test may allow aggressive people to 'get away with murder'. In *Scarlett*[200] the licensee of a pub 'got away with' manslaughter having used excessive force ejecting a drunk. The Court of Appeal quashed his conviction declaring that provided he believed the circumstances called for the degree of force used, 'he is not to be convicted even if his belief is unreasonable'.

This, it is submitted, goes too far. It is important to draw a distinction between two types of mistake. The first is a mistake as to the existence of circumstances which, if present, would entitle the defendant to use force to the degree adopted. This is a mistake of fact. Here, what is important is not the reasonableness of the mistake but the fact that it is honestly held.[201] The second type of mistake is a mistake as to the amount of force which it is reasonable to use. This is a mistake of law. The accused's mistake is that he believes the law of self-defence allows him to do X whereas it only allows him to do Y. As we know, mistakes of law cannot be relied upon. In *Owino* the Court of Appeal adopted this distinction and returned the law to that provided in *Williams*. This holds that a person 'may use such force as is (objectively) reasonable in the circumstances as he believes them to be'. Consider the case of *Yaman*. T along with his mother, ran the family kebab shop. One morning when driving past, he noticed that the shutter was lifted. Inside was a warrant officer, a gas engineer and a locksmith attending the premises to execute a distress warrant to disconnect the gas meter, following alleged non-payment of gas bills. T entered the premises, and hit the locksmith over the head with a hammer. He was charged, *inter alia*,

---

[197]   *Palmer* v *R* [1971] 1 All ER 1077, 1078.
[198]   Keane [2010] EWCA Crim 2514.
[199]   S. Parish, 'Self Defence: The Wrong Direction' [1997] Crim LR 201.
[200]   [1993] 4 All ER 629.
[201]   Case 11.

with wounding with intent to do grievous bodily harm. His defence was that he thought the intruders were burglars and that he acted in self-defence. He was convicted at first instance and he appealed on the basis that the trial judge had not directed the jury in accordance with section 76(7). The appeal was rejected. The Court held that, even if it was assumed that in attacking a locksmith with a hammer D had mistakenly 'done what he honestly and instinctively thought was necessary' to resist a supposed burglary, the jury must still inevitably have concluded that the force he used was excessive. The trial judge's failure to refer to s. 76(7) when directing the jury was not therefore fatal to D's conviction for wounding under the OAPA 1861, s. 18.[202]

In *Martin (Antony)* a third kind of mistake was identified. Here the defendant who shot dead a burglar used excessive force not because he made a mistake of law but because he overestimated the danger to which he was subject. He did so due to a psychiatric disorder. Would he be able to rely on his condition to show that, on the facts as he believed them to be, the force used was reasonable? In both provocation and duress such evidence may be adduced. Here it was ruled not admissible. The question of how much force is lawful is a question of law and is an objective question. Since this decision, however, the Privy Council has held, surely correctly, that since a mistake as to the danger a person is in is a mistake of fact it can be relied upon and so medical evidences may be admissible, although it is unreasonably held.[203]

To illustrate the difference between the two types of mistake and their impact on liability, let us examine again Case 9. If Adam was unaware that the cellar door had a lock or believed that Eve had a gun and could shoot her way out, his use of the baseball bat would be consistent with an intention to use **lawful** force. If, however, Adam thinks that, notwithstanding the option of locking the door, knocking Eve on the head with a baseball bat is a reasonable way of disabling her or preventing her from stealing, the genuineness of his mistake will not make his unlawful intentions (to use disproportionate force) lawful. It seems to follow that if a person believes, unreasonably, that their assailant is about to shoot them and shoots pre-emptively, the force used is consistent with an intention to use lawful, that is **defensive**, force.[204]

Both *Yaman* and *Martin* illustrate the kind of problems likely to arise when householders unexpectedly are confronted with a burglar. In 2013 the Government made another attempt to ensure the public perceptions of the scope of the defence corresponded with the legal underpinnings. This time, however, the change is one of substance rather than language. Section 43 of the Crime and Courts Act 2013 adds a new subsection (5A) to section 76 of the 2008 Act. The effect of subsection (5A) is to apply a lower standard of reasonableness of reaction to the householder, for example, Tony Martin, than for the defence generally, for example, Private Clegg, to give **householders** 'greater latitude in terrifying or extreme situations where they may not be thinking clearly about the precise level of force that is necessary to deal with the threat faced.' Section 5A provides as follows:

> In a householder case, the degree of force used by D is not to be regarded as having been reasonable in the circumstances as D believed them to be if it was grossly disproportionate in those circumstances.

---

[202] *Yaman* [2012] EWCA Crim 1075.

[203] [1995] Crim LR 743, 744; followed in *DPP* v *Armstrong-Braun* [1999] Crim LR 416; *Shaw* [2002] 1 Cr App R 10 PC; *Martin* [2002] 2 WLR 1; this position is also adopted by the Law Commission, Law Com. No. 218 (1993), cl. 27(1). *Martin* was approved in *R v Oye* [2013] EWCA Crim 1725 CA where D attacked police officers deluded that they were evil spirits. His use of force was not objectively reasonable. His defence was one of insanity not self defence.

[204] *Shaw*, above. Contra *Martin (Antony)*. See previous note.

(6) In a case other than a householder case, the degree of force used by D is not to be regarded as having been reasonable in the circumstances as D believed them to be if it was disproportionate in those circumstances.

The intended effect of subsection (5A) is that if householders act honestly and instinctively to protect themselves or their family from intruders using force that was reasonable in the circumstances as they saw them, they will not be guilty of an offence **even if** the level of force turns out to have been disproportionate in those circumstances. It is only if the force used is '**grossly disproportionate**' will the force used be deemed unlawful. As with the previous law, whether the force used was **grossly disproportionate** or simply **disproportionate** depends upon the individual facts of each case, including the personal circumstances of the householder and the threat (real or perceived) posed by the offender. There are no hard and fast rules about what types of force might be regarded as 'disproportionate' and 'grossly disproportionate'. It seems, however, that defendants such as Tony Martin and Mr Yaman might expect more generous treatment under the new provision. But one cannot help thinking that this change in the law will complicate rather than clarify an already fragile area of doctrine. The complications do not end there. Another complication is the meaning of 'householder' since this extends far beyond the cases which prompted the legislation in the first place – the predicament of the terror-struck owner-occupier – a predicament rare enough to question the motivation behind the change in the law.

If Yaman had been decided under the new law the first question for the court, therefore, would be whether this was a householder case.[205] If it was not then the issue for the court is simply whether his reaction was disproportionate, as it was in 2012. If it was a householder case, however, then the issue would be whether his action was '**grossly** disproportionate'. By subsection (8B) a 'householder case' is one where the defendant uses force in self-defence while in or partly in a building, or part of a building that is a dwelling.[206] It applies if the defendant is not a trespasser at the time the force is used, and at that time the defendant believed the victim to be in, or entering, the building or part as a trespasser (s. 76(8)). The provision covers, therefore, not only householders but also family members and their invitees. Further it covers people who live in buildings which serve a dual purpose as a place of residence and a place of work (for example, a shopkeeper and his or her family who live above the shop). In these circumstances, the 'householders' can rely on the more generous defence regardless of which part of the building they were in when they were confronted by an intruder. Assuming then that T, who was a family member, was acting in self-defence as he saw it rather than simply protecting his property, this case would probably have been decided differently. Even if the Court of Appeal was right in saying his action was 'clearly disproportionate' it was not clearly 'grossly disproportionate' given his honest belief that the men were burglars.

[205] (8A) For the purposes of this section 'a householder case' is a case where –
(a) the defence concerned is the common law defence of self defence,
(b) the force concerned is force used by D while in or partly in a building, or part of a building, that is a dwelling or is forces accommodation (or is both),
(c) D is not a trespasser at the time the force is used, and
(d) at that time D believed V to be in, or entering, the building or part as a trespasser.

(8B) Where –
(a) a part of a building is a dwelling where D dwells,
(b) another part of the building is a place of work for D or another person who dwells in the first part, and
(c) that other part is internally accessible from the first part,
that other part, and any internal means of access between the two parts, are each treated for the purposes of subsection (8A) as a part of a building that is a dwelling.

[206] The provision also applies where the premises is forces accommodation or is both.

4 What counts as force?

In the discussion of Case 9 it was suggested that a reasonable way of countering the threat, or effecting the arrest of Eve, was for Adam simply to have locked the cellar door. If this option had been available to him the use of personal violence would presumably have been unreasonable since unnecessary. A possible problem with this analysis is that Adam, assuming he took this option, does not appear to be using **any** force, let alone reasonable force. Can one rely upon public or private defence where the defensive action taken involves the commission of a crime but not a crime involving the use of force? To deal with the specific problem first, false imprisonment does involve the use of (restraining) force even if not violence. Self-defence is, then, a defence to false imprisonment.[207]

More generally, it appears that certain forms of defensive action may be taken which fall short of the commission of an offence against the person. In *Renouf*[208] it was held that forcing a car off the road for the purpose of arresting the occupants was capable of amounting to the use of reasonable force within the meaning of s. 3(1) and did not amount to reckless driving.[209] Action taken preparatory to defensive conduct which itself involves the use of force may also be defensive action for the purpose of public and private defence. Thus a person may arm themselves to protect against a specific and imminent apprehended attack if this was necessary and proportionate to the threat.[210] It will not, however, excuse habitual possession of weapons for defensive purposes.[211] On this basis, the manufacture and possession of firebombs by a shopkeeper for the purpose of repelling looters during an ongoing riot was held lawful where the relevant provision afforded a defence for a person in possession 'for a lawful object'.[212]

Consistent with this decision it was said in *Cousins* that a person may issue a threat to kill, if this is reasonably necessary as a pre-emptive defensive measure, even though it is not in itself a use of force.[213] In the course of his judgment in this case, Milmo J said that, for the purpose of s. 3(1) and generally, if the use of force is permissible 'something less, for example a threat, must also be permissible if it is reasonable in the circumstances'.[214] Taken literally this might suggest that defensive action might justify the commission of road traffic offences, offences of possession and property offences where force is not an ingredient and whose commission is not preparatory to such an offence.[215] There is authority against this proposition. In *Renouf*, it was further held that the defence would not be operative if the 'forceful' driving was incidental to the arrest as opposed to being the means adopted for effecting the arrest.[216] This produces the peculiar conclusion that if, instead of forcing the villain off the road, the driver had merely chased him to effect a later arrest, committing minor traffic offences on the way, the defence would not be available even though the commission of such offences was a reasonable and necessary precondition of that which, by s. 3(1), he was fully justified in doing.[217]

---

[207] Cf. Law Commission Draft Criminal Law Bill, cl. 44(2)(c).
[208] [1986] 2 All ER 449.
[209] Cf. *Attwater* [2011] *supra*.
[210] *Georgiades* [1989] 1 WLR 759.
[211] *Evans* v *Hughes* [1972] 3 All ER 412.
[212] *A-G's Reference (No. 2 of 1983)* [1984] 1 All ER 988; *Vegan* [1972] NI 80.
[213] *Cousins* [1982] 2 All ER 115.
[214] At 117.
[215] See for example *Pommell* above.
[216] [1986] 2 All ER 449, 451.
[217] See also *A-G's Reference (No. 2 of 1983)* [1984] 1 All ER 988; cf. *Attwater* [2011] *supra*.

Again, in *Blake* v *DPP* it was held that public or private defence cannot justify criminal damage, in the form of graffiti, where no significant force is exerted.[218] So, a person has no defence to criminal damage if they write the name of an escaped fugitive on the walls of the local police station. Sir John Smith suggested that the answer might be different if a hammer and chisel had been used since this would involve significant force.[219] In the light of *Renouf*, this seems misconceived since the chiselling process is clearly incidental to the discharge of the defensive purpose rather than in execution of it. A more plausible example of criminal damage as operative defensive action follows:

> **Case 13**
> Adam cuts the brake cable on the car of Eve, a terrorist, so as to hinder her escape by means of that car.

This would be force used to effect an arrest.[220] It should be noted that the independent defence of lawful excuse, normally available to criminal damage, is not available here because of the risk to life.[221]

5 What offences may be committed for defensive purposes?

As will be appreciated from the above discussion, defensive action does not give a person *carte blanche* to break the law. It only provides an immunity for action taken involving the use of force, included within which is certain action taken as a pre-emptive measure in advance of the use of force, such as issuing threats or arming oneself.

It seems that this limitation is indicative of yet wider restrictions on the kind of action which can lawfully be taken for defensive purposes. This was made clear in *Attorney-General's Reference (No. 2 of 1983)* which was examined above. Although it was said that the manufacture and storage of firebombs as a protective measure could negate liability for an offence amounting, in effect, to the possession of an explosive substance for an unlawful purpose,[222] it was also suggested that the possessor might remain liable for other offences arising out of such possession. In this case it seems that the defendant may have been properly convicted of the separate offence of manufacturing and storing explosives without a licence,[223] which offence bore no equivalent 'lawful object' defence. Why this should be so is puzzling? If possessing (unlicensed) explosives for defensive (forceful) purposes is a **lawful** object, how can it nevertheless be **unlawful** to possess them in contemplation of that lawful object? Smith and Hogan make the sensible and practical suggestion that 'where contravention of any law is (i) necessary to enable the right of public or private defence to be exercised, and (ii) reasonable in the circumstances, it ought to be excused'.[224]

---

[218] *Blake* v *DPP* [1993] Crim LR 586.

[219] In *Blake*.

[220] If he simply disabled Eve's car he would have an independent defence by virtue of s. 5(2) Criminal Damage Act 1971. The Law Commission propose in the Draft Criminal Law Bill that force or threats of force against property should suffice, but propose no further change in the law; cl. 27, 29.

[221] See s. 5(1), (2)(b) Criminal Damage Act 1971.

[222] Under s. 4 Explosive Substances Act 1883.

[223] Under the earlier Explosive Substances Act 1875. Cf. *Yaman, supra*, in which the Court of Appeal assumed that being in possession of a dangerous weapon could be justified for defensive purposes.

[224] If not justified. See Case 4.

6 Justifying killing

An important question still to be considered concerns the use of lethal force. Using lethal force even in self-defence is not an unquestioned right. Respect for the sanctity of life underpins the whole of our criminal law. It explains why 'mercy killing' and 'duelling to the death' are treated as murder despite the victim's consent. It explains why even sadistic murderers are imprisoned rather than executed. Under domestic law, as has been seen, there is no intrinsic doctrinal objection to killing in self-defence so long as the use of force was necessary and proportionate to the threat. Clearly it will be if the actor believes himself to be in a 'kill or be killed' dilemma. But questions of proportionality are decided more loosely than this. In time of crisis people are unable, for obvious reasons, to judge the ultimate intentions of the supposed aggressor. This they must judge for themselves. In cases of serious danger they will typically fight like for like, and then some. Questions of proportionality cannot then be decided simply by reference to the end result but rather by reference to the nature and severity of the force used to repel the attack.

Article 2 of the ECHR[225] is more restrictive than domestic law, requiring, at least in the case of killings by police and other agents of the state, the killing to be no more than 'absolutely necessary'. If it is not, there is a direct infringement of Article 2.[226] Ashworth argues, surely correctly, that this standard and the manner in which it has been interpreted by the European Court to require strict proportionality of response[227] should be replicated in English law to ensure lethal killing by state officers involves a 'last resort' rather than a 'reasonably necessary' test.[228]

10.9 JUSTIFICATORY DEFENCES: CONCLUDING REMARKS

This latter suggestion deals with the specific problem posed *by Attorney-General's Reference (No. 2 of 1983)* but leaves uncatered-for the case of defensive conduct involving non-forceful action, since the 'right to exercise' public and private defence is limited to the right to use or threaten force for such purposes, not to commit crime generally. In this concluding section we will examine this and other gaps in the structure of justificatory defences to see how far, if at all, they may be remedied.

The present state of justificatory defences allows certain 'good reasons' to render conduct, which would otherwise be unlawful, lawful. All of these reasons reduce, in effect, to a claim that the relevant action was both a necessary and proportionate reaction to crisis. In a sense, therefore, duress, duress of circumstances and self-defence are all species of necessity. Necessity itself has not been allowed to grow into a general defence because of the lawlessness which such an unfocused claim (demanding no immediate reaction to crisis) might be expected to foster.[229] Where such crisis exists or where the harm caused is by way of side-effect there is ample room for the development of the defence.

---

[225] Article 2
  Everyone's right to life shall be protected by law. No one shall be deprived of his life intentionally save in the execution of a sentence of a court following his conviction of a crime for which this penalty is provided by law. Deprivation of life shall not be regarded as inflicted in contravention of this article when it results from the use of force which is no more than absolutely necessary:
  (a) in defence of any person from unlawful violence;
  (b) in order to effect a lawful arrest or to prevent escape of a person lawfully detained;
  (c) in action lawfully taken for the purpose of quelling a riot or insurrection.
[226] *McCann and Others* v *UK* (1996) 21 EHRR 97; *Kelly* v *UK* (1993) 16 EHRR CD 20.
[227] *Andronicou and Constantinou* v *Cyprus* (1998) 25 EHRR 491.
[228] See discussion at note 199.
[229] See for example *Southwark LBC* v *Williams*, above.

So, duress/duress of circumstances avoids this particular danger by insisting that the accused acts reasonably and proportionately to avert an immediate threat of death or serious injury to themselves or another. Committing an 'offence' simply because the supposed consequences of not doing so would be markedly worse is not justified under this doctrinal escape route. Neither is it in public and private defence, by contrast, which meets the same danger by requiring the relevant reaction to be taken against wrongdoers and others who pose unjust threats.[230] This latter requirement ensures that what counts as 'good consequences' is firmly tethered to society's expressed priorities, not unpredictably to the whims of the action-taker.

As will be appreciated, the above scheme allows many morally innocent people to fall between the gaps of these various defences. Elliot gives a particularly arresting example. A driver, threatened with unlawful (non-serious) injury, has a possible defence if they drive their car at the aggressor (force used for defensive purposes) but no defence if they commit a traffic offence in attempting to escape (not a use of force, and duress of circumstances unavailable). And yet, arguably, society is better served by responsible citizens not taking the law into their own hands in this way.[231]

A strong case can be made for the courts to develop a general defence of defensive action for crimes not involving the use of force against a wrongdoer, outflanking the duress of circumstances by not requiring the threat of death or serious injury and outflanking self-defence by not requiring action to be taken against wrongdoers and others who might pose unjust threats.[232] As Elliot's example shows, the surprise is that duress of circumstances, where a non-victimising crime is committed for defensive purposes, has taken on the doctrinal clothes of duress at all. Surely, Martin, Conway and the like need only show that their conduct was reasonable and proportionate to the harm threatened to give a satisfactory justification for their conduct, and do not use others as a means to achieve their defensive purpose. What reasonable person would not jump a traffic light to prevent a motorist with road rage bumping their car, whether or not a more sinister intent was made manifest? As explained above, the threat of death or serious injury should only be a doctrinal necessity to excuse (not justify) physical harm intentionally inflicted on an innocent. And with this slant it should be capable of excusing even murder. Further, it should not be necessary to show that the harm threatened was unlawful as long as it was not exercised under lawful authority. In this respect the development represented by *Pipe* is particularly welcome.[233]

Elliot recommends the adoption of a general defence amounting to the doing of such acts as are reasonable and necessary, in the circumstances which exist or which they believe to exist, to protect themselves or others from harm and for other defensive purposes, public and private. He suggests that only statutory intervention can solve this problem since s. 3(1) is quite explicit in allowing immunity only with regard to the exercise of force. It would be 'preposterous', given the degree of overlap between public and private defence, to allow defensive action falling short of the use of force against a wrongdoer to be lawful in self-defence or defence of property but unlawful in public defence.[234]

---

[230] S. Uniacke, *Permissible Killing: The Self-Defense Justification of Homicide* (1994) ch. 5; J. Horder, 'Self-defence, Necessity and Duress' [1998] Can J of Law and Juris 143, 157 ff.

[231] D.W. Elliot, loc. cit. 616.

[232] It should be noted that specific defences are already available in the case of certain crimes, such as theft and criminal damage, if property is appropriated or destroyed for defensive (i.e. not immoral) purposes.

[233] *Supra.*

[234] See generally D.W. Elliot, loc. cit. 616–21.

While in general agreement with Elliot's recommendations, this is not the position taken here. If Parliament places limits on the power of citizens to engage in law enforcement, that is one thing. It is quite another for judges to refuse to allow citizens to do what is reasonable and proportionate in defending themselves, their fellows or their property from immediate harm, when such action involves no deliberate challenge to the autonomy or physical integrity of an innocent person. There is no obvious substantive reason why the common law defence should remain tied to its public law counterpart and there is a good reason why it should be allowed to develop its own momentum. 'It is open to the courts to move in this direction.'[235]

Summary

The constituent elements of duress are synthesised from a statement of Lord Bingham in *Hasan:*

(1) To found a plea of duress the threat relied on must be to cause death or serious injury.
(2) The threat must be directed against the defendant or his immediate family or someone close to him.
(3) The threat must be reasonably entertained and be such as would make a person of reasonable fortitude do as the accused did.
(4) The defence of duress is available only where the criminal conduct which it is sought to excuse has been directly caused by the threats which are relied upon.
(5) The defendant may excuse his criminal conduct on grounds of duress only if, placed as he was, there was no evasive action he could reasonably have been expected to take.
(6) The defendant may not rely on duress to which he has voluntarily laid himself open.
(7) Duress does not afford a defence to charges of murder (*R v Howe* [1987] AC 417), attempted murder (*R v Gotts* [1992] 2 AC 412) and, perhaps, some forms of treason.

Further, the defence is available whether the threat issues from an individual who nominates the crime to be committed, or arises from circumstances which leave the defendant with no reasonable option other than to commit the offence which they themselves nominate as a means of escaping the threat. In the former case the defence is known as duress by threats. In the latter it is known as duress of circumstances, which is a form of necessity.

There are two forms of necessity. Necessity as an excuse, otherwise known as duress of circumstances, operates when the defendant chooses to infringe a criminal prohibition as a means of averting an imminent peril of death or serious injury to themselves or another. Necessity as a justification is presently recognised explicitly only in the field of medical treatment where action, otherwise unlawful, can lawfully be taken in the defence of the patient's best interests for those incapable of giving consent, or otherwise incompetent. Justificatory necessity is, in principle, far wider than this, rendering lawful any conduct, even an intentional killing, which is an inevitable and not disproportionate side-effect of action necessarily undertaken in defence of the physical security of the actor or another. Some doctrinal support for this proposition is also to be found in the medical arena.

[235] Smith and Hogan, op. cit. 268.

It is a defence to any crime, including murder, in which the use of force is a conduct element that the use of force was, in the circumstances that the defendant believed them to be, reasonable and necessary for the protection of protected public or private interests. The defence extends to crimes in which the use of force is not a conduct element, where the action taken by the accused is preparatory to such a crime or is accompanied or characterised by defensive force.

Further reading

Bohlander, M., 'Transferred Malice and Transferred Defenses: A Critique of the Traditional Doctrine and Arguments for a Change in Paradigm' (2010) 13(3) New Criminal Law Review 555–624.

Horder, J., *Excusing Crime*, Oxford: OUP (2004).

Leverick, F., *Killing in Self-Defence*, Oxford: OUP (2008).

Loveless, J., 'Domestic violence, coercion and duress' [2010] Criminal Law Review 93.

Sangero, B., 'A New Defense for Self-Defense' (31 July 2010) 9 Buffalo Criminal Law Review 475.

Sangero, B., *Self-Defence in Criminal Law*, Oxford: Hart (2006).

Simester, A.P., 'Mistakes in Defence' (1992) 12 Oxford Journal of Legal Studies 295.

Smith, J.C., 'Justification and Excuse in the Criminal Law' (1989) Crim LR.

Tadros, V., *Criminal Responsibility*, Oxford: OUP (2005).

Westen, P., 'An Attitudinal; Theory of Excuse' (2006) Law and Philosophy 289.

Williams, G., 'The Theory of Excuses' [1982] Crim LR 732.

Wilson, W., 'The Filtering Role of Crisis in the Constitution of Criminal Excuses' [2004] Canadian Journal of Law and Jurisprudence 387.

Wilson, W., 'The Structure of Criminal Defences' [2005] Crim LR 108.

Part III
Offences against the person

11 Non-fatal offences

Overview

The crimes of violence which will be dealt with in the first part of this chapter are, starting with the most serious and ending with the least serious, wounding or causing grievous bodily harm with intent under section 18 of the Offences Against the Person Act 1861, malicious wounding or infliction of grievous bodily harm under section 20, and assault occasioning actual bodily harm under section 47. The conduct element in both section 18 and section 20 is, alternatively, a wounding or a causing/infliction of grievous (serious) bodily harm, whether by wounding or any other means. A recognised psychiatric injury of sufficient gravity counts as serious harm for the purposes of both sections. Sections 18 and 20 are differentiated by their fault element. Section 18, which is the more serious of the two offences, requires proof of an ulterior intention (to cause serious bodily harm/resist arrest, etc.). Section 20 can be committed by intention or recklessness even as to a lesser harm than serious bodily harm. The section 47 offence is constituted upon proof of an assault, whether in the form of an infliction of force or a threat of force, which results in actual bodily harm to the victim. Actual bodily harm consists of any physical harm of significance, and includes psychiatric injury. The fault element in section 47 is intention or foresight as to the assault. There is no requirement that the harm be intended or foreseen.

11.1 INTRODUCTION

Non-fatal offences against the person may be divided into two separate categories of offence – sexual and non-sexual violations. Those same categories disclose a very wide spectrum of wrongdoing. Sexual violations range from rape to sexual assault and indecent exposure. Non-sexual violations range from attempted murder to unlawful wounding to common assault. It should be noted that both categories of offence disclose a differentiated theoretical basis for criminalisation. Some offences are constituted by an invasion of autonomy or privacy. Rape, sexual assault, and common assault are prime examples. These offences do not require any harm to be suffered but do require a non-consenting victim. Others are constituted as much as an attack on fundamental social values or public safety as on individual autonomy. These latter offences maybe committed irrespective of consent. Unlawful wounding and incest are examples of such offences. The wrongdoing is not an attack on autonomy or privacy, although this will often be present, but the threat thought to be posed to society by such conduct.

11.2 OFFENCES PROTECTING PHYSICAL INTEGRITY

The Crime Survey for England and Wales estimates that there were 1.89 million violent incidents in England and Wales in the period 2012–13. This is almost half the number experienced at its peak in 1995. The pattern of offending is, however, fairly constant over the past 20 years. The vast majority of known offenders are male, and males are twice as likely as females to be victims of violence. Both offenders and victims are most likely to be between the ages of 16 and 39.[1] Under 10 per cent are categorised as serious. These include serious wounding and homicides.[2]

As with crime generally, far more crimes of violence are likely to be committed than are recorded. Research suggests that there is no obvious relationship between the seriousness of an offence measured in terms of harm/culpability and the tendency to report, investigate, and even prosecute or punish offences.[3] Many technical assaults and worse, which take place in the normal rough and tumble of everyday life in our clubs, bars, village fetes and football grounds are unlikely to enter the criminal statistics, even where they come to police attention and, when they do so, are often dealt with out of court by means of cautions or conditional cautions.[4] Crime Surveys estimate that only around 25 per cent of crimes of violence are reported. Seriously under-reported, it seems, are racial attacks and assaults taking place in a domestic context. There are obvious difficulties facing the victims of domestic violence to report acts of violence committed by a partner, parent or surrogate parent. Compounding the difficulty, numerous studies support the finding that when they do, the police are less likely to record such violence than when it occurs between strangers, despite the fact that the former is likely to be equally if not more psychologically debilitating.[5]

Until relatively recently in the history of our criminal law even the most wanton acts of physical violence were treated relatively leniently. Contrasted with the severity of homicide, which rendered all but the most fortuitous killings a (capital) felony, appalling acts of violence, whether spontaneous or arising out of a premeditated attempt at assassination', were treated only as misdemeanours.[6] So much hinged on the 'accident of death'. This position should also be contrasted with the hundred or so capital felonies arising from the Waltham Black Acts,[7] designed largely to protect deer, or more particularly landowners' ownership thereof, from the predations of poachers. Such 'remarkable contrast' in the treatment of offences against the person and property offences left even the conservative opinion-former Sir James Fitzjames Stephen unwilling 'to suggest any explanation of the fact'.[8]

The 'modern' approach to crimes of violence stems from Lord Ellenborough's Act 1803[9] which first made the attempt to systematise the worst forms of personal violence, including homicide, as felonies. Excepting the common law offences of assault and battery, the majority of such offences now issue from the Offences Against the Person Act 1861,[10] an

---

[1] Based on the 2012–13 Crime Survey for England and Wales.

[2] All statistics from Office for National Statistics (ONS) website: http://www.ons.gov.uk/ons/rel/crime-stats/crime-statistics/period-ending-september-2013.

[3] C. Clarkson, A. Cretney, G. Davis and J. Shepherd, 'Assaults: The Relationship between Seriousness, Criminalisation and Punishment' [1994] Crim LR 4. N. Padfield, 'Out of Court (Out of Sight) Disposals' [2010] Camb LJ 6.

[4] Cf. R (Guest) v DPP [2009] 1 WLR 1999.

[5] http://www.ons.gov.uk/ons/rel/crime-stats/crime-statistics/focus-on-violent-crime/stb-focus-on-violent-crime-and-sexual-offences-2011-12.html#tab-Overall-violence-volume-and-comparison.

[6] J.F. Stephen, History of the Criminal Law of England, London: Macmillan (1883) (hereafter HCL) 112; Giles 7 St Tr 1129.

[7] See generally E.P. Thompson, Whigs and Hunters: the Origin of the Black Acts, London: Allen Lane (1975).

[8] J.F. Stephen, HCL 109.

[9] 43 Geo 3 c 58.

[10] Henceforth OAPA.

Act which, from its earliest days, has enjoyed little in the way of critical acclaim.[11] The case for reform is widely acknowledged as irresistible.[12]

The offences which will be dealt with here will begin with crimes in which physical injury must be suffered. These are, in rank order of seriousness, s. 18, s. 20, and s. 47. Finally common assault will be considered and some other offences not requiring actual physical injury will be examined in outline only.

A Wounding or causing grievous bodily harm with intent

Section 18, OAPA as amended provides as follows:

> Whosoever shall unlawfully and maliciously by any means whatsoever wound or cause any GBH to any person with intent to do some grievous bodily harm to any person, or with intent to resist or prevent the lawful apprehension or detainer of any person shall be (guilty of an offence punishable by life imprisonment).

Section 18 creates, in effect, two offences, namely (1) wounding and (2) causing grievous bodily harm, with any one of three intents specified. The prosecution must specify which form of the *actus reus* it is relying on. This is because in the wounding form no grievous bodily harm need be proved. In contrast, in the GBH form no wounding need be proved. Section 18 will often have certain conduct features in common with attempted murder since both may issue from some violent attack. However, attempted murder, unlike section 18, requires no harm to be sustained so long as an act more than merely preparatory to the commission of the substantive offence can be established. The other difference is in their respective mental attitudes. The *mens rea* for the attempt is an intention to kill. Although the intention to cause grievous bodily harm is sufficient *mens rea* for murder it is not sufficient for attempted murder.[13] Section 18 will be charged when the evidence will not support an intention to kill. Life imprisonment is the maximum sentence for the section 18 offence and is limited to the most serious cases.[14] Guidelines for sentencing are produced by the sentencing council.[15]

1 *Actus reus*

(a) *Wounding*

A wound requires 'an injury to the person by which the skin is broken. If the skin is broken, and there (is) bleeding, it is a wound'.[16] The skin contains two layers, the dermis and the epidermis. Only an injury breaking both layers is a wound. An abrasion, burn or scratch, therefore, is not a wound even though blood is showing sufficient to make a scab.[17] An abrasion or scratch becomes a wound only when true bleeding occurs, that is when the second layer is broken.

The requirement that both layers of skin be broken means that an internal rupture or broken bone will not be a wound for the purpose of s. 18 even if it is accompanied by

---

[11] J.F. Stephen, *HCL* 116–18.

[12] Law Com. No. 218 (1993) paras 12.6–12.13; Home Office, *Violence: Reforming the Offences Against the Person Act 1861*, London: TSO (February 1998); E. Genders, 'Reform of the Offences Against the Person Act: Lessons from the Law in Action' [1999] Crim LR 689.

[13] J.F. Stephen, *HCL*.

[14] See for example *R v Jenkin* [2012] EWCA Crim 2557.

[15] See website: sentencingcouncil.judiciary.gov.uk

[16] *Moriarty* v *Brooks* (1834) 6 C & P 684 per Lord Lyndhurst.

[17] *McLoughlin* (1838) 8 C & P 635.

bruising or the loss of blood.[18] One exception to this is where the internal membrane ruptured has the form of skin, as in the lining of the mouth or urethra. This is thought to account for the decision in *Waltham* where the prisoner had given a policeman a violent kick in the genitals. The external skin was unbroken, but the lining membrane of the urethra was ruptured causing a small loss of blood into the urine. It was held, comfortingly, that there was a wounding for the purpose of s. 18 (and 20).[19]

Until recently it was thought that a wound requires a battery in the sense of a direct harm-delivering act such as a stabbing.[20] The present position appears to make it sufficient that the wound issues from the direct application to the body of physical force, even if not directly at the hands of the accused. This is consistent with the use of the words 'by any means whatsoever' in section 18.[21]

Case 1

Adam, intending to prevent Eve, a police officer, from effecting an arrest, sticks out his foot to trip her. She falls over and cuts her leg.

Case 1 shows how a wound may be inflicted without the use of a weapon such as a gun or knife as long as it is delivered by some form of blow. It is not crucial that Adam delivers the blow as long as his intentional action (as here) causes the blow **directly** to be delivered.[22] Notice, if Eve merely bruised or grazed her leg (no wound), Adam's offence would be section 47 Offences Against the Person Act 1861[23] for which the maximum sentence is five years. This compares with the maximum life sentence for the section 18 offence. An extravagant disparity. It is arguably the case that wounding, like 'inflicting harm' for the purpose of section 20, no longer requires any form of harm-delivering blow directly attributable to the accused.[24]

Case 2

Adam secretes razor blades within Eve's chocolate bar, intending them to be eaten and thus to cause serious injury. Eve spits the bar out but not before suffering cuts to her mouth.

Here Eve's injury is not directly attributable to Adam's act. The direct cause of her injury is not Adam's act but her own eating of the chocolate bar. This argues against a wounding and a conviction under section 18.[25] On the other hand, a commonsense interpretation of section 18, bearing in mind the unambiguous words 'by any means whatsoever', seems to support a conviction. This interpretation gains support from the House of Lords decision in *Burstow* concerning the meaning assigned to 'inflicting' grievous bodily harm for the purposes of section 20.[26]

---

[18] *C* v *Eisenhower* [1984] QB 331 (DC).
[19] (1849) 3 Cox 442.
[20] *Beasley* (1981) 73 Cr App R 44 CA.
[21] And 'with or without a weapon' in s. 20.
[22] *Morrison* (1989) 89 Cr App R 17 CA.
[23] Or assaulting a police officer under section 89 Police Act 1996.
[24] *Wilson* [1983] 1 All ER 993, but see now *R* v *Ireland and Burstow* (see below pp. 298–9).
[25] And s. 20; see *Wilson* above.
[26] See *Burstow*, below.

(b) *Causing grievous bodily harm*

Grievous bodily harm is **caused** wherever there is an unbroken causal link between some conduct of the accused and the injury concerned.

Case 3

Adam hits Eve, a police officer, over the head, intending to resist arrest. She collapses, rupturing her cartilage necessitating a surgical repair operation. The operation goes wrong, septicaemia sets in and Eve's leg has to be amputated.

Eve has sustained grievous bodily harm and, unless the surgery was so abnormal as to break the chain of causation, Adam is the legal cause of her injury.[27] As will be apparent, 'causing' covers cases where the serious injury is not the direct result of the application of force.

'Causing', unlike 'inflicting', will also cover harm attributable to an omission, as where a parent allows a child to drink a large quantity of alcohol with dire results.[28] A serious disease constitutes grievous bodily harm.[29] It follows that a person who intentionally communicates HIV to another may be guilty of the section 18 offence.[30]

It should be noted that if the injury sustained is 'grievous' without a wound the accused is liable upon proof of causal agency, but if it is a wound solely, the accused's liability probably depends upon proof of the wounder's more direct instrumentality.[31]

Case 4

As in Case 3 except that the operation is successful.

Although the operation will result in Eve sustaining a wound, and Adam has caused her to suffer it, it would be stretching language to say that Adam has wounded her. The wound is inflicted by the surgeon rather than Adam. Adam's liability in Case 4 will probably be limited, as we shall see, to a section 47 offence or to an offence under section 89 Police Act 1996.[32] It might seem odd, given their identical mental attitude, that Adam in Case 4 takes the benefit of the accident of fate which caused Eve to twist rather than, as in Case 1, cut her knee. It might also seem odd that Adam in Case 3 is prejudiced by the accident of fate which gave him an incompetent surgeon. A possible explanation is that since a wound may incur liability on a low threshold of seriousness, it is only fair to impose liability for this most serious of offences where it is directly inflicted.

Grievous bodily harm was defined in *DPP v Smith*[33] as 'really serious harm'. For some reason, unlike the rest of this ill-fated case, this rather vague test has withstood the test of time, perhaps as a mark of sympathetic respect for a proposition which, unusually for this case, was not clearly and obviously wrong. Less frivolously, it is obviously preferable to the previous test which allowed for a conviction where the 'only intent established is one to

---

[27] This does not mean that Adam is automatically guilty of the section 18 offence, however. See discussion at notes 47–48 below.

[28] Cf. *Martin* (1827) 3 C & P 211.

[29] See *Clarence* (1889) 22 QBD 23, but see *R v Burstow*, below.

[30] And guilty of inflicting it. See *Dica* [2004] 3 All ER 593 Court of Appeal and discussion at note 34.

[31] As can be seen by comparing Case 1 and Case 4. Cf. discussion of *Burstow*, below.

[32] The assumption is that Adam has not caused Eve grievous bodily harm sufficient to incur liability for the second form of the s. 18 offence.

[33] [1961] AC 290.

interfere seriously with health or comfort'.[34] Clearly a wounding may amount to grievous bodily harm but only if serious itself, say because it results in extensive damage, loss of blood or injury to an organ. It is important to remember, however, that the *actus reus* of section 18[35] is satisfied even if the wound is not serious. Other potential serious harms include broken limbs, significant loss of consciousness[36] and damage to internal organs.

Practical clarity has been lent to the notion of grievous bodily harm by the publication by the Crown Prosecution Service of charging standards for both grievous bodily harm (sections 18 and 20) and actual bodily harm (s. 47), agreed with the police. These give the following instances of grievous bodily harm:

(1) Injuries resulting in permanent disability, loss of sensory function or significant visible disfigurement.
(2) Injuries requiring extensive surgery or transfusion.
(3) Broken limbs or skull, compound fractures, broken cheek bone and jaw.
(4) Injuries involving lengthy treatment or incapacity.
(5) Psychiatric injury.

The purpose of these standards is to promote administrative efficiency, by reducing the number of aborted charges, and fairness to the defendant. In particular it prevents prosecuting authorities overcharging a defendant so as to encourage him or her to plead guilty to a lesser charge. It nevertheless remains open to the prosecution, in their discretion, to charge under s. 20 or s. 47 even in an obviously serious case of wounding or causing grievous bodily harm.[37] Doing so may avoid a troublesome not guilty plea, which will be particularly useful where the evidence of intent is doubtful. The final say, as to whether the injury caused is serious, lies with the jury. Who knows what considerations they may take into account when deciding what is 'really serious harm'?[38] It is now clear that this will vary according to the age and, one assumes, the state of physical health of the victim.[39] If not convinced that the injury is serious, or the injury intended was serious an alternative verdict under s. 20 or s. 47 can nevertheless be returned.[40]

Serious psychological harm constitutes grievous bodily harm for the purpose of sections 18 and 20.[41] This includes, for example, serious depressive illness, but not 'mere emotions such as distress or panic'.[42] A deliberate, and successful, campaign to send someone 'mad' such as occurred in Patrick Hamilton's play *Gaslight*, will accordingly now be chargeable under section 18.

2 Mens rea

The *mens rea* for both forms of the offence is identical. The wound or causing of grievous bodily harm must be done 'maliciously'. Malice in this context means intention or subjective recklessness. Further, it must be done with one of the three 'ulterior' intents specified in the section, namely

[34] *Ashman* (1858) 1 F and F 88; *Metharam* [1961] 3 All ER 200.
[35] And s. 20.
[36] *R v Hicks* [2007] EWCA Crim 1500.
[37] See the trenchant criticism of the CPS charging practices in P. Darbyshire, 'An Essay on the Importance and Neglect of the Magistracy' [1997] Crim LR 627.
[38] B. Hogan, 'The Fourteenth Report of the Criminal Law Revision Committee: (3) Non-Fatal Offences' [1980] Crim LR 542.
[39] *Bollom* [2004] 2 Cr App R 290.
[40] *Lahaye* [2006] 1 Cr App R 205; *Mandair* [1994] 2 All ER 715.
[41] *R v Ireland, R v Burstow* [1997] 4 All ER 425.
[42] *Chan-Fook* [1994] 2 All ER 552.

(a) to cause grievous bodily harm, or
(b) to resist the lawful apprehension of any person, or
(c) to prevent the lawful apprehension of any person.

It should be remembered that s. 18 is chargeable even in cases where no serious injury was either suffered or intended if a minor wound was sustained in the course of hindering an arrest so long as that wound was inflicted 'maliciously', that is, intentionally or recklessly.

(a) The ulterior intent

Intention carries the same meaning here as in the law generally. Foresight of grievous bodily harm to whatever degree of probability is not enough.[43] Where the *actus reus* relied upon is a wounding rather than a causing of grievous bodily harm it is wrong to leave the jury with the impression that an intention to wound is sufficient to ground the s. 18 offence. An intention to wound is not the same as an intention to cause grievous bodily harm. This was well illustrated in *R v Taylor*. A stabbed his victim with a kitchen knife. Faced with a number of choices of knife, A took up a relatively innocuous knife, in addition to a fork. On this basis, although the evidence of an intent to wound was clearly made out, the evidence of an intent to do serious injury with the knife was 'equivocal'.[44] The correct charge, therefore, was the section 20 offence. Moreover, in cases where the defendant has caused the victim grievous bodily harm and the evidence supports alternative possibilities that the accused specifically intended to cause such harm or had intended harm but not of the gravity resulting, the trial judge must leave both verdicts (section 20 and section 18) to the jury to ensure it is not encouraged to convict of the more serious charge for want of an alternative.[45]

However, as a matter of evidence, the more conducive to causing grievous bodily harm the defendant's action was, the more the jury will be disposed to believe that the accused intended it. In *Banton*, A smashed a bottle in V's face. A was convicted of wounding with intent to cause grievous bodily harm. The trial judge refused to allow an alternative charge under s. 20 to be put to the jury; the Court of Appeal approved this refusal. It seems to have been accepted by both trial judge and the Court of Appeal that if A smashed a bottle in V's face it could only mean one thing, namely that A intended grievous bodily harm. A strange conclusion since the jury were surely entitled to consider whether, intentional blow notwithstanding, it was done with the relevant ulterior intent.

Directing the jury

The standard direction, which will be given in the vast majority of cases, will be to instruct the jury that they may convict of the offence only if they are convinced that the defendant intended, when wounding or causing serious injury to the complainant, to cause him serious injury. Occasionally, the *Woollin* direction may be necessary in cases where the evidence of direct intention is equivocal.[46] The jury should be directed in such cases that if convinced that the accused knew that grievous bodily harm was **virtually certain** to result, this entitles them to find such an intention.[47]

---

[43] *Belfon* [1976] 1 WLR 741; *Purcell* (1986) 83 Cr App R 45.
[44] *R v Taylor* [2009] EWCA Crim 544.
[45] So held the Court of Appeal in *Hodson* [2009] EWCA 1590, quashing D's conviction for wounding with intent.
[46] *R v Phillips* [2004] EWCA Crim 112.
[47] *Banton* [2007] EWCA Crim 1847; see Chapter 5.

> **Case 5**
>
> Adam, who is not medically qualified, comes across Eve who has suffered a road accident. He finds that he cannot remove her from the car as her leg is trapped. He amputates her leg in the misguided belief that if he does not do so she will die of blood loss before medical support arrives.

On the face of it, this is a case of direct intention. Adam acts in order to amputate Eve's leg, though as a means rather than an end in itself. As such the *Woollin* special direction should not be given. The jury, if left to its own devices, might prefer not to find intention due to the good motive. The judge should, however, direct them that Adam's motive is irrelevant.[48] Note: the fact that Adam's reaction was neither necessary nor desirable should not affect the jury's decision on this matter, although it might well affect the availability of a defence.[49]

(b) *Maliciously*

The word 'maliciously' in section 18 is troublesome. In *Mowatt* it was stated that, on a charge of maliciously causing grievous bodily harm with intent to cause grievous bodily harm, 'maliciously' adds nothing to what is already present in the word 'intent'. A person who intends grievous bodily harm must, in other words, cause it maliciously.[50] A similar result must follow on a charge of wounding with intent to cause grievous bodily harm. Where the charge is maliciously wounding or causing grievous bodily harm with intent to resist/prevent arrest, however, 'maliciously' has a job of work to do. That job is to ensure that the crime is not constituted simply upon proof of an intention to prevent arrest in the absence of at least some foresight of harm. Otherwise, the risk is present that a person who accidentally injures another in the attempt to escape arrest will be guilty of an offence carrying life imprisonment as a maximum sentence. This would be carrying constructive liability a touch far. Such reasoning was not influential, at first instance, in *Morrison*.[51] The accused, on being arrested and seized by a police officer, dived through a window pane carrying the officer with him, causing wounds to the latter's face. The trial judge directed the jury that they could convict of the section 18 offences upon proof (i) of an intent to resist arrest, and (ii) *Caldwell* recklessness as to causing harm to the officer. The accused was duly convicted. The Court of Appeal quashed the conviction, holding that proof of *Cunningham* recklessness (subjective foresight) was necessary as to the causing of harm. What was not made clear was the degree of harm which must be foreseen. On a charge of section 20 it is also necessary to show foresight of harm, but it is not necessary to show that the harm foreseen matched the *actus reus*, e.g. was grievous.[52] However, the latter is an offence carrying a maximum five years' prison term. One would expect, on a charge of section 18, a requirement that the accused foresaw the very harm specified in the charge – a wounding or grievous bodily harm.[53]

---

[48] It is not unheard of, for the judge explicitly to direct the jury not to find intention due to the special reasons for which Adam acted. See *Steane*, above: cf. *Adams* [1957] Crim LR 365; Law Com. No. 218 (1993) para. 7.13.

[49] Such as that of necessity. See *Re A (conjoined twins) supra*.

[50] *Mowatt* [1968] 1 QB 421. It may be argued, however, that absence of malice is an alternative reason for an acquittal in Case 6 below.

[51] (1989) 89 Cr App R 17 CA.

[52] That is, even if the harm foreseen was less than serious injury, *Mowatt* [1968] 1 QB 421.

[53] See above discussion.

B Malicious wounding/infliction of grievous bodily harm

Section 20 provides as follows:

> Whosoever shall unlawfully and maliciously wound or inflict any grievous bodily harm upon any person, either with or without any weapon or instrument, shall be guilty of an (offence punishable with a maximum of five years' imprisonment).

A number of points of distinction may be detected between this and section 18. Some of these are linguistic, some substantive. Unfortunately it has not been easy to unravel the two.[54] Typical is the reference to 'with or without a weapon' in section 20 but 'by any means whatsoever' in section 18. Is this purely formal – an example of an untutored draftsperson flaunting his ability to say the same thing in different ways? Or is it substantive – suggesting perhaps that s. 20, with its oblique reference to a weapon, requires a direct blow whereas section 18, with its broader statement, requires merely causal agency?[55]

There are two major substantive points of difference between s. 20 and s. 18. The first is that the section 20 offence is constituted without proof of an ulterior intent. This absence accounts for the sentencing differential in the two offences. The second is that the conduct element is denoted by the word 'cause' in s. 18, whereas in s. 20 it is 'inflict'. It is generally thought that no purpose is served by the use of these different words. Perhaps, once again, the draftsperson was simply flexing his/her linguistic muscles. Evidence that this may be so is that 'inflict' also appears in s. 23 OAPA in the context of 'inflicting' grievous bodily harm by poison, when 'causing' would be the more natural word.[56] Nevertheless, in the context of sections 20 and 18, the courts traditionally saw fit to interpret the words 'cause' and 'inflict' differently on the quite reasonable basis that if the legislature had meant the same thing they would have used the same words. This approach is no longer followed, as will be seen.

1 *Actus reus*

Like s. 18, the injury in s. 20 may be a wound or grievous bodily harm. Both carry the same meanings. In practice minor woundings, without accompanying evidence of ulterior intent, tend to be charged under s. 47, which is, in any case charged under s. 20, an alternative verdict to that charge.

(a) *Infliction*

In theory, an infliction of grievous bodily harm is narrower than a causing. While all cases of inflicting are automatically cases of 'causing', not all cases of causing are cases of 'inflicting'. The first major case in which this subtle distinction was made was *Clarence*.[57] A, knowing he had venereal disease, had sexual intercourse with his wife concealing his condition from her. He was charged under sections 47 and 20, Offences Against the Person Act 1861 when his wife contracted the disease. The Court for Crown Cases Reserved, by a majority, allowed A's appeal against conviction on both counts. It was held that both crimes required proof of an assault which here was absent.[58] On the section 20 charge

---

[54] J.F. Stephen, *HCL* 117–18.

[55] J. Gardner, 'Rationality and the Rule of Law in Offences Against the Person' [1994] 53 CLJ 502 at 506, notes that the drafter of the Act accounted for the terminological difference by the fact that the Act was consolidating existing legislation, not creating a unified code of offences.

[56] See previous note.

[57] (1889) 22 QBD 23.

[58] Note that it would not have profited the prosecution to proceed under s. 18 here since they would need to have shown an intention to cause grievous bodily injury.

the conclusion was that to 'inflict harm' on someone was to assault them as a matter of definition.

Infliction and assault

To understand this decision fully, it is necessary to anticipate some of our later discussion on common assault. A common assault can take two forms. The first is an application of force to the victim, as in a punch (battery). The second is a threat (unconsummated) of immediate violence, as in a threatening gesture or brandishing a weapon (assault). Neither form is committed where the defendant's act is consented to.

Why was there no battery here? The majority held that the battery was absent because the wife had consented. This consent was real and was not vitiated by the fact that she would not have consented had she known the true state of affairs. Stephen J gave an alternative basis for finding that there had been no assault and, therefore, no infliction. This time, however, the presence or otherwise of consent was not the crucial factor. Rather, the wife's injury did not issue from a direct application of force to her, in the manner of a stabbing, shooting, punching, etc. Communicating a disease to someone was not of this type any more than a poisoning was.[59] This is not to say that a poisoning is not unlawful but that, if unlawful, it is not on account of its being an assault. On this analysis, if the husband had forced his wife to have sex with him, the section 20 offence would still not have been committed since the disease though caused was not 'inflicted' by the intercourse.[60]

Significantly, an assault of either type was not always insisted upon to support a conviction for s. 20. Most noteworthy in this respect are a number of cases in which a victim injured himself in attempting to escape from a threat. Typical of such cases is *Lewis*.[61] The accused, who had been locked out of the flat by his wife, threatened to kill her. Upon hearing his shouts his wife, fearing for her safety, jumped from the window, breaking both legs. The Court of Appeal dismissed the husband's appeal against conviction under section 20. The offence was made out even though the accused had neither hit his wife nor put her in fear of **immediate** violence such as would justify conviction for assault. In *Martin*[62] it was held that a person who, as a practical joke, had barred the doors and turned the lights out towards the end of a theatre performance, causing people to panic and injure themselves, could be guilty of s. 20. Once again, there was no suggestion of either type of assault here.[63]

The two sets of cases were at long last reconciled by the House of Lords in *Wilson*.[64] The decision upheld the requirement for an infliction acknowledged by Stephen J in *Clarence*,[65] namely that physical injury should from the application of force, but dropped the requirement of an assault. In reaching their decision the House of Lords approved and adopted the following statement of the Supreme Court of Victoria in *Salisbury*[66]

---

[59] And, of course, if a poisoning is unlawful, it is no less unlawful for the fact of being consented to (see below p. 303).

[60] The s. 47 offence would have been committed under such circumstances, since the offence requires proof of an assault which was present, and actual bodily harm resulting from that assault which was also present. *Clarence* has been disapproved by the House of Lords. See p. 298.

[61] [1970] Crim LR 647 CA.

[62] [1881] 8 QBD 54.

[63] The reasoning of Lord Coleridge puts one in mind of the tort case of *Wilkinson v Downton* [1897] 2 QB 57 in which it was held that a cause of action can be established for intentional injury in the absence of a delivering blow.

[64] [1983] 3All ER 448 HL.

[65] And also Wills J.

[66] [1976] VR 452 at 461.

. . . the word 'inflicts' does have a wider meaning than it would if it were construed so that inflicting grievous bodily harm always involved assaulting the victim . . . grievous bodily harm may be inflicted either . . . where the accused has directly and violently 'inflicted it' by assaulting the victim, or where the accused has 'inflicted' it by doing something intentionally, which, though it is not itself a direct application of force to the body of the victim, does directly result in force being applied violently to the body of the victim, so that he suffers grievous bodily harm.

In short, although it was not necessary to show that the injury issued out of an assault perpetrated by the inflicter, it was necessary to show harm was sustained **as a result of the victim receiving a blow or other application of force to the body.**[67] An infliction thus covered cases as diverse as *Martin* and *Lewis* because the victims in these cases were injured by the direct application of force to their bodies, which force directly resulted from the defendant's intentional act. It should be noted that it is no obstacle to a section 20 conviction that someone other than the accused (*Martin*) or indeed that the victim himself (*Lewis*) has inflicted the injury. Under this test, infliction also covers cases of injury resulting from the springing of booby traps and comparable cases of injuries which are 'inflicted' but without the direct instrumentality of the accused.

> **Case 6**
> Adam, a malicious joker, gives Eve, a blind person, a false set of directions across town hoping that she gets lost. Instead she suffers serious injury when she gets knocked over by a car on a road she mistook for a pavement.

Although there can be no question of an assault here, since Eve's injury has not been sustained, directly or indirectly, at Adam's hands, there is arguably an infliction within the meaning of *Salisbury*. Force has been directly applied to Eve's person as a result of something Adam has intentionally done. Assuming the chain of causation is not broken by the accident[68] and he has the required *mens rea* (foresight of injury), he is liable under section 20.

Following *Wilson* all that seems to separate cases of **causing** grievous bodily harm from cases of **inflicting** it is that an 'inflicting' requires a positive act ('doing something intentionally'), rather than an omission,[69] and also a blow/impact of some sort ('direct application of force to the body of the victim').

(b) *Infliction of psychiatric injury*

In *Burstow* the House of Lords extended the concept of grievous bodily harm to include serious psychiatric illness. In so doing they were forced to acknowledge that grievous bodily harm could be **inflicted otherwise than by way of a blow or application of force.** Assuming psychiatric harm can be 'inflicted' it is clearly not generally inflicted by way of blows. It is not that kind of harm. Rather it is inflicted by 'attacks' on the psyche. Here serious psychiatric illness issued from a long sequence of harassing conduct by a stalker,

---

[67] Some commentators believe that an assault has never been so narrowly defined as *Salisbury* assumes. On this view the *Salisbury* test simply makes explicit what has always been implicit, namely that assaults require the infliction of unlawful force but not necessarily directly at the hands of the assaulter. See for example M. Allen (2012) 377. It is also the view taken in 'Legislating the Criminal Code' para. 18.7. Doctrinally this view cannot be readily supported. See *Wilkinson* v *Downton*, note 63 above.

[68] See Chapter 5.

[69] But see p. 83, above.

including silent phone calls, hate mail and other disturbing acts.[70] The Court of Appeal, and subsequently the House of Lords, upheld the conviction deciding that, since psychological harm had in previous cases been characterised as actual bodily harm,[71] there was no obstacle to characterising a serious depressive illness as grievous bodily harm. Further, an 'infliction' did not require anything in the way of force applied to the body of the victim. The House of Lords concluded that there was no significant distinction to be drawn between 'inflicting' and 'causing' harm.[72] What is necessary is that the accused 'caused' the relevant consequence and nothing more complicated. In effect, the law has now been placed on a footing similar to that proposed by the Law Commission.[73]

(c) The impact of Burstow

Following *Burstow* it was, for a time, possible to conceive of *Clarence* as still authoritative in relation to the reckless transmission of a sexual disease. The narrow interpretation was that *Burstow* did nothing more than **necessarily** refine the meaning of 'inflict' in the case of the unlawful delivery of psychiatric harm.

However, *Burstow* was taken in *Dica* to have effectively overruled *Clarence*. The Court of Appeal concluded that the reckless transmission of a serious sexual disease, in this case HIV, counted as an infliction of grievous bodily harm.[74] To inflict grievous bodily harm means nothing more than to cause it.

What of cases other than the transmission of sexually transmitted diseases? Significantly, in *Dica*, Judge J appeared to limit the scope of the decision to the transmission of sexually transmitted diseases.[75]

> The effect of this judgment in relation to s. 20 is to remove some of the outdated restrictions against the successful prosecution of those who, knowing that they are suffering HIV or some other serious sexual disease, recklessly transmit it through consensual sexual intercourse, and inflict grievous bodily harm on a person from whom the risk is concealed and who is not consenting to it. In this context, *Clarence* has no continuing relevance.[76]

This is a welcome restriction. Criminalising the intentional or reckless transmission of gonorrhoea or HIV is one thing but, criminalising the reckless transmission of influenza and other potentially serious airborne diseases is quite another. This would render the effect of *Burstow* rather more than a minor rewriting of a legislative provision to address a new mischief (stalking).

What of harms more obviously within the intended catchment of section 20, such as cuts, breaks, and bruises? Can these be inflicted without a blow or other application of force? Consider the following cases.

---

[70] [1996] Crim LR 331; harassment such as occurred in *Burstow* is now a statutory offence; Protection from Harassment Act 1997.

[71] *Chan-Fook* [1994] 2 All ER 552 CA; followed in *Ireland* [1997] 1 All ER 112; *R v Burstow, R v Ireland* [1997] Crim LR 810. In *Dhaliwal* the Court of Appeal reiterated the point made in *Chan-Fook* that psychological injury, not amounting to an identified or recognised psychological condition, could not amount to 'bodily harm'.

[72] Cf. Smith and Hogan (13th edn, 2011) 440; G. Virgo [1997] Camb LJ; J.C. Smith [1997] Crim LR 812.

[73] In the form of the Draft Bill contained in Law Com. No. 218, London: HMSO (1993), cl. 2–4.

[74] *Dica* [2004] EWCA Crim 1103. For discussion see M. Weait, 'Criminal Law and the Sexual Transmission of HIV' (2005) MLR 121.

[75] The Home Office Draft Bill recommends that the transmission of disease should not suffer criminal sanction under the proposed reforms except where caused intentionally. London: Home Office, *Violence: Reforming the Offences Against the Person Act 1861* (1998), cf. J.R. Spencer, 'Liability for Reckless Infection' (2004) NLJ 471.

[76] *Dica*, see note 74. L Cherkassky, 'Being Informed: The Complexities of Knowledge, Deception and Consent when Transmitting HIV' (2010) 74(3) J Crim L 242.

> **Case 7**
>
> Adam laces Eve's face cream with roughly ground glass. She suffers serious injury when the resulting abrasions turn septic.

Assuming this case is charged under section 20 Adam's liability[77] depends upon establishing an infliction.[78] Under the *Wilson/Salisbury* test this does not seem to be possible since the effect of Adam's act was not a direct application of force to Eve's body. In other words, her injury was not sustained from a blow or other impact. The impact of *R v Ireland*, *R v Burstow* (below) is widely adjudged to dispense with this latter requirement and to render *Clarence* bad law. To inflict means to cause as a matter of definition. However, it is just possible that where actual physical injury, as opposed to psychiatric injury or disease, has been sustained *Wilson* still provides the authoritative definition of infliction. In short, where cuts and bruises and breaks are the harm sustained by the victim, **the only method of delivery which counts as an infliction is some form of blow/impact/application of force.** Such a tortured interpretation carries little substantive merit other perhaps the most important, namely sustaining the illusion that the House of Lords was not seeking to entirely rewrite section 20 by its decision in *Burstow*.

The only case to consider this possibility, *Brady*, gave an ambiguous response.[79] Lord Justice Hallett said *obiter* that a man who perched precariously on railings causing him to fall off and seriously injure the victim 'caused the injuries to be inflicted'. This removes any semblance of distinction between 'cause' and 'inflict' by eliding the two concepts. In the instant case liability would only attach, of course, if the initial act of 'perching' was blameworthy in the sense that danger was foreseen. If it was not then the falling would be involuntary and incapable, in law, of being either a cause or an infliction of harm.

One other distinction between 'cause' and 'inflict' may well survive *Burstow*. In that case the deciding factor as to whether one could 'inflict psychiatric injury' was whether it was correct linguistic usage. Using that same test one can clearly 'cause' serious injury by omission but can one, as a matter of correct linguistic usage, 'inflict' serious injury by omission. This, I would suggest, is doubtful. The words 'wound' and 'inflict' seem to demand some form of action. Section 20, in other words, may well be one of those offences, along with assault and unlawful act manslaughter, which cannot be committed by omission.

In *Mandair* the House of Lords held that a jury which is not convinced that the accused had the necessary intention to cause GBH for liability under section 18 can bring in the alternative verdict under section 20.[80] This decision was criticised at the time since a jury, even if it is convinced that the accused 'caused' the necessary consequence, will not have heard argument as to whether he had also 'inflicted it'.[81] In theory, then, a jury could convict of the offence without evidence having been adduced that he had committed it. In the light of *R v Burstow*, *R v Ireland*, since the meaning of 'inflict' and 'cause' has now been elided, this difficulty is largely obviated.[82]

---

[77] Case 7 may also perhaps be an offence under s. 23, Offences Against the Person Act 1861; cf. *Gillard*, below.

[78] And foresight.

[79] *R v Brady* [2006] EWCA Crim 2413. For discussion see D. Ormerod [2007] Crim LR 568.

[80] *Mandair* [1994] 2 All ER 715.

[81] This will not matter where the harm committed is a wound since 'wound' means the same under both sections.

[82] For a criticism of this case see J.C. Smith [1994] Crim LR 666. See, however, *Banton*, above.

2 *Mens rea*

The *mens rea* for s. 20, and also s. 47, is malice. Malice does not require any ill will or spite.[83] Malice is provided by proof of intention or *Cunningham* recklessness.[84] This was confirmed in *Brady*.[85] With respect to the transmission of sexually transmitted diseases it is not clear whether the accused must know he is infected or whether, for example, wilful blindness or reckless knowledge is enough.[86] Given the context within which sexual intercourse tends to take place with all participants well aware of the dangers of unprotected sex, it is submitted that actual knowledge should be necessary.[87]

It was once accepted that the intention or foresight required must be as to the 'particular kind of harm that in fact was done', here a wounding or grievous bodily harm.[88] In *Savage* and *Parmenter*,[89] however, the House of Lords, approving the earlier Court of Appeal decision of *Mowatt*,[90] stated that the prosecution need prove only that the accused intended or foresaw the risk of some physical harm. So a father who shook his child, causing it serious injury, was guilty of the section 20 offence if it could be proved that he foresaw some harm. It was not necessary to show that he intended or foresaw grievous bodily harm.[91] Lord Ackner acknowledged this breach of the correspondence principle in *Savage*[92] but concluded that the criminal law was littered with comparable examples. Depending upon your point of view, this is a depressing example of judicial complacency. Or, the view taken here, a welcome acknowledgement that those who attack other people cannot complain if the harm which materialises exceeds that expected.[93]

C Aggravated assaults

There are a number of offences whose basic ingredient is an assault but which, because committed under circumstances which aggravate the seriousness of the assault, carry a higher penalty.[94] These aggravated assaults include assault with intent to resist or prevent a lawful arrest (s. 38 OAPA) which carries a maximum two years' prison sentence, assault with intent to rob (s. 8 Theft Act 1968) which carries a maximum of life imprisonment, assaulting a police officer in the execution of his duty (s. 89 Police Act 1996) and assault occasioning actual bodily harm (s. 47 OAPA) which, if further aggravated by religious or racial hostility, raises the maximum sentence from five to seven years.[95]

---

[83] *Cunningham* [1957] 2 QB 396.
[84] That is, foresight of harm.
[85] R v *Brady* [2006] EWCA Crim 2413.
[86] At present there has been no ruling on this matter. S. Ryan, 'Reckless Transmission of HIV' [2006] Crim LR 981.
[87] For discussion see M. Weait, 'Criminal Law and the Sexual Transmission of HIV' (2005) MLR 121; S. Ryan, 'Reckless Transmission of HIV' (2006) Crim LR 981; cf. J.R. Spencer, 'Liability for Reckless Infection' (2004) NLJ 471.
[88] Kenny, *Outlines of Criminal Law* (1962) 202, on the authority of *Pembliton* (1874) LR 2 CCR 119.
[89] [1991] 4 All ER 698.
[90] [1968] 1 QB 421.
[91] DPP v *Parmenter* [1991] 4 All ER 698. As it was **not proved** that he foresaw some injury to his son a conviction for section 47 was substituted.
[92] At 721.
[93] Cf. J. Gardner in 'Rationality and the Rule of Law in Offences Against the Person' [1994] Camb LJ 502. And see pp. 188–90 above.
[94] Excluding assaulting a police officer in the execution of his duty, for which the maximum sentence is six months, the same as for common assault.
[95] Crime and Disorder Act 1998, section 28–29.

In each case the elements of an assault must be established along with the relevant aggravating feature.[96] Typically this will involve some form of racial abuse.[97] The elements of assault will be considered separately later on in the chapter. For our present purposes it is enough to remember that an assault is committed in two separate situations. First, where unlawfully and maliciously **force has been actually applied** to another person without their consent. Second, where unlawfully and maliciously another person **has been subjected to a threat of force** without their consent.[98] Thus, the offence of assault with intent to rob may be committed either by using force or by threatening to use force on the victim to effect a robbery.[99]

D Assault occasioning actual bodily harm

By section 47 OAPA 1861, assault occasioning actual bodily harm is an offence punishable with a maximum five years' imprisonment. Like s. 20 it is an offence triable either summarily or on indictment.

1 Actus reus

The conduct elements of section 47 include:

(a) a common assault – both the *actus reus* and *mens rea* of a common assault must be established;
(b) actual bodily harm;
(c) a causal link between the common assault and the actual bodily harm.

(a) Common assault

The elements of common assault are intentionally or recklessly

(i)   inflicting undesired physical force on the person of the victim (battery), or
(ii) acting so as to lead the victim to apprehend the immediate infliction of such force, whether or not it occurs (assault).[100]

(b) Actual bodily harm

Actual bodily harm was defined by Lynskey J in *Miller* as any 'hurt or injury calculated to interfere with . . . health and comfort'.[101] It seems that this definition is no longer satisfactory as it might suggest that mere mental distress, hysteria or shock is enough. This possibility was rejected in *Chan-Fook*.[102] Actual bodily harm, it was said, includes psychiatric injury but not emotions or states of mind which are not the product of an identifiable clinical condition.[103] For such psychiatric injury to be relied upon, expert evidence must be adduced by the prosecution. If it is not, the jury should not be asked to consider it.

---

[96] *R v Isitt* [2013] EWCA Crim 265 – guilty plea to racially aggravated common assault.
[97] Examples include *Niewulis* [2013] EWCA Crim 556: a sentence of 12 months' imprisonment imposed for a racially aggravated assault on a supermarket security guard was reduced to 6 months. *R v Babbs* [2007] EWCA Crim 2737; *H* [2010] EWCA Crim 1931; [2011] Crim LR 649: *DPP v McFarlane* [2002] EWHC 485.
[98] G. Williams *TCL* (1983) describes the former as a physical assault and the latter a psychic assault.
[99] 38(2) Theft Act 1968.
[100] Assault is dealt with, in detail, below.
[101] [1954] 2 All ER 529 at 534.
[102] [1994] 2 All ER 552 CA. Affirmed in *R v Ireland, R v Burstow* [1997] Crim LR 810.
[103] *R v D* [2006] EWCA Crim 1139; [2006] Crim LR 923.

Outside psychiatric injury, the prosecution's burden in proving bodily harm is not an onerous one. Any injury which is not trivial is theoretically 'bodily harm'. In practice the aggravated assault is unlikely to be charged unless the degree of injury is fairly substantial. The Crown Prosecution Service charging standards give some examples of the type of injury appropriately charged as 'actual bodily harm'. These include loss of sensory function (including loss of consciousness[104]), extensive or multiple bruising, broken nose, minor fractures, cuts likely to require stitching or other medical treatment, broken teeth, and psychiatric injury.[105] The Divisional Court have extended this range of harms to include the cutting of a woman's pony tail, interpreting 'bodily harm' to include damage pertaining to the body. Although this might appear to be an instance of 'overcharging' – a common assault is the most obvious charge here – it is submitted this is a correct decision. Cutting off a pony tail damages the hairstyle which in turn damages the integrity of the body.[106]

(c) Causal link between the assault and the actual bodily harm

The offence definition of section 47 is assault occasioning actual bodily harm. 'Occasioning' means 'causing'. In *Roberts*[107] R tried to remove the coat of a female passenger in a moving car. Fearing a sexual attack V jumped out of the car, suffering injury. R was convicted of assault occasioning actual bodily harm. The Court of Appeal upheld the conviction. The wording of section 47 was not ambiguous. There must an assault, which there was,[108] and that assault must 'cause' actual bodily harm, which it did. To establish a causal link it must be shown that what happened 'could reasonably have been foreseen as the consequence of what he was saying or doing'. This is the standard test of causation.[109]

2 Mens rea

Roberts had appealed on the ground that the jury should have been directed to consider not only whether his action had caused the woman's injury but also whether he intended or foresaw that injury. This argument was rejected by the Court of Appeal. It was not necessary to show that the harm was actually foreseen. This would be a *mens rea* test and, moreover, one not required by section 47. The only *mens rea* required was the *mens rea* for assault, namely intention or recklessness as to physical contact or the victim's apprehension thereof.

The House of Lords has approved *Roberts*, hearing a combined appeal from *Savage*; *DPP* v *Parmenter*[110] despite doubts cast on it by the conflicting Court of Appeal decision in *Spratt*.[111] In *Savage* the accused threw a pint of beer in V's face. The glass slipped, causing a cut to the victim's wrist. In *Parmenter*, P shook his young son so roughly that he suffered serious injury. The House of Lords ruled, overruling *Spratt*, that it was not necessary for

---

[104] *T* v *DPP* [2003] EWHC (Admin); [2003] Crim LR 622.
[105] CPS changing standards; unlawful wounding/infliction of grievous bodily harm: http://www.cps.gov.uk/legal/section5/chapter_c.html#10
[106] *DPP* v *Smith* [2006] EWHC 94 (Admin).
[107] (1971) 56 Cr App R 95.
[108] The actual or apprehended contact.
[109] *R* v *Lewis* [2010] EWCA Crim 151.
[110] [1992] 1 AC 699 AC.
[111] [1990] 1 WLR 1073.

the prosecution to prove actual foresight of harm to be guilty under s. 47. 'The verdict of assault occasioning actual bodily harm may be returned upon proof of an assault together with proof that actual bodily harm was occasioned by the assault'.[112]

(a) *Evaluating* Roberts *and* Savage

It is not difficult to find fault with these decisions. Section 47 is a statutory offence carrying a maximum sentence of five years. Despite the fact that the offence carries a maximum sentence which is identical to an apparently more serious offence (section 20), its *mens rea* requirement is for a lesser common law offence carrying a maximum of six months. This hardly seems the stuff of a rational system of offences against the person. Such a system, it has been argued, would graduate both punishment and offence-label according to the level of harm chosen by the accused rather than that which actually transpires.[113]

The view taken here is that justice in punishment does not require the defendant specifically to have chosen the relevant harm but for it to be morally supportable to treat him as having chosen it.[114] It is submitted that it is supportable where the harm is the outcome, foreseen or not, of a culpable attack on the victim's autonomy. In most cases where injury is occasioned as a result of an assault it will be the result either of the accused losing control of what he is doing, as in *Parmenter*, or of the victim being frightened into doing something unpredictable, as in *Roberts*. There is scant moral case for offering the accused an immunity where he chooses to create the conditions under which 'anything is possible'. Such defendants 'make their own bad luck'. Why should they not take responsibility for it?[115]

E Other offences against the person

There are a number of other offences whose purpose is to protect autonomy and safety. Two only will be mentioned briefly here to enable the student to have some overall picture of the general structure within which civil liberties and other private interests are vindicated. The offences, dealing with poisoning, are found in ss. 23 and 24 OAPA 1861. Section 24 makes it an offence for a person to 'unlawfully and maliciously administer to or cause to be administered to or taken by any other person any poison or other . . . noxious thing with intent to injure, aggrieve or annoy'. Section 23 is the aggravated offence committed where the 'poisoning is done so as to thereby endanger (the victim's) life or inflict upon him grievous bodily harm'. Both offences can be committed either by the use of a recognised poison or by the use of a substance which in the quantities ingested or administered are apt to 'injure, aggrieve or annoy'. They are committed wherever an act of the defendant causes the substance to be ingested by or administered to the victim whether by direct or by indirect means. Lacing a person's drink or food with poison, drugs, alcohol is, therefore, within the scope of the sections. So also is intravenous administration or even, in the case of gas or acid, administration directed against the body of the victim.[116]

---

[112] Per Lord Ackner.
[113] Ashworth (2009) 314; this represents the system adopted by the Law Commission, Law Com. No. 218 (1993).
[114] For a similar view articulated in connection with defence doctrine see Horder, 'Rethinking Non-fatal Offences'.
[115] See generally J. Gardner in 'Rationality and the Rule of Law' for a persuasive elaboration of this position.
[116] *Gillard* (1988) 87 Cr App R 189.

11.3 OFFENCES PROTECTING PERSONAL AUTONOMY

Overview

Common assault comprises two forms – applying unlawful force to someone, or threatening to apply unlawful force to someone. It is of the essence of both offences that the victim does not consent. The purpose of these offences is different from that of crimes of violence generally. As with rape, this purpose is to protect the individual's right to be free of unwanted interference with their autonomy. It is not necessary to show that any harm befell the victim, only that the interference was not consented to.

A Common assault

Common assault is a generic term which comprises two separate offences: assault, properly so called, and battery, otherwise known as assault by beating. In practice both offences tend to be subsumed in the term 'common assault' or simply 'assault'. The use of the word 'battery' to denote unlawful physical contact tends to be limited to civil proceedings. The offences, which do not require proof of harm, reflect the value attributed in liberal society to individual autonomy. The protection of private interests needs state support if self-help is to be the exception rather than the norm.

Assault and battery were separate common law offences which, by s. 39 Criminal Justice Act 1988, are now statutory offences.[117] As a consequence they are no longer triable on indictment, although they may be separately included as alternative counts in the indictment.[118] Triable summarily they carry a maximum six months' prison sentence. In theory, common assault will be charged wherever actual bodily harm cannot be established, or where the harm caused is relatively trivial. As they are separate offences an indictment which charges assault by beating when the evidence supports a conviction only for assault will fail, and vice versa. In *Regina* v *Nelson (Gary)* the Court of Appeal held that on a charge of battery where the fact finders are not convinced that physical contact was made a verdict of common assault is not available as an alternative verdict.[119] Section 6(3) of the Criminal Law Act 1967 provides that only if the allegation of the offence charged (battery) impliedly includes an allegation of the alternative offence (assault) would this be possible. Since a battery can occur without an assault, as where a person is punched from behind, section 6(3) does not apply. In such a case the correct alternative verdict would have been attempted battery.[120]

The Crown Prosecution Service (CPS) charging standards state that minor bruises and cuts, abrasions, swellings, broken nose, loss or breaking of teeth, and black eyes are appropriately charged as common assaults. More serious injuries, such as appear also in the charging standards, are chargeable under sections 47 and 20. As explained earlier, however, this guidance has no force of law and there is nothing to stop prosecutors from 'under-charging'.[121] Common assault is often charged in preference to section 47 even

---

[117] *DPP* v *Little* [1992] 1 All ER 299; cf. *Haystead* v *Chief Constable of Derbyshire* [2000] Crim LR 758.

[118] By s. 40 Criminal Justice Act 1988. Prosecutors are often encouraged to charge common assault in the alternative to s. 47 since, by *Mearns* (1990) 91 Cr App R 312 CA, a person charged only with s. 47 cannot be convicted of common assault.

[119] [2013] WLR (D) 1.

[120] This was not possible in *Nelson* for technical reasons.

[121] Cf. C. Clarkson *et al.*, op. cit. See note 3 of this chapter.

where quite significant injury has been sustained. The usual reason for this is that charging the common assault allows the CPS to avoid the defendant electing trial by jury. There is no particular disadvantage attached to charging the lesser offence where the magistrates' sentencing limits are unlikely to be challenged. Indeed, there are considerable advantages attaching to summary trial in terms of expense, efficiency and the likelihood of conviction.

Although statutory offences, assault and battery are not defined by statute; such definitions and principles as there are, therefore, are derived from the common law including, since assault and battery are forms of trespass to the person, the law of torts. For ease of understanding, the two forms will be denoted consistently by their technical names of assault and battery.[122]

1 Assault

An assault is committed where a person intentionally or recklessly causes another to apprehend an immediate and unlawful contact.[123] The *actus reus* of an assault is reducible not to the fact of contact but to the threat of it. The *mens rea* is intending or foreseeing that one's behaviour will lead the other to believe he is about to suffer the infliction of unlawful force.[124]

(a) Actus reus

(i) *Threats and gestures*
The threat may be of injury or simply of an unwanted contact. Making as if to hit or kiss someone, rolling up one's sleeves in a threatening manner[125] or pointing a gun are all possible assaults. It is not necessary that there should be an intention to carry the threat out. Thus it is an assault where A points a gun at B which A, but not B, knows is unloaded.[126]

A central feature of the crime at common law is that the threat apprehended must be of **immediate** force. Since the threat must be of immediate force there is no assault if the defendant lacks the means to carry the threat out. Thus in the civil case of *Thomas* v *National Union of Mineworkers*[127] it was held that there was no assault when pickets during the miners' strike made threatening gestures and shouted abuse at working miners who were passing by in buses. It should be noted that there are a number of specific crimes which cover uttering (or causing) the threat of future injury. For example threats of death are punishable with ten years' imprisonment under the Criminal Law Act 1977, Schedule 12.[128] Threats over the telephone are offences under the Telecommunications Act 1984. Bomb hoaxes are an offence contrary to the Criminal Law Act 1977 (s. 51(1)). Finally there are a number of offences under the Public Order Act 1986 to deal with violent and threatening conduct. These include, in order of seriousness, riot (s. 1), violent disorder (s. 2) and affray (s. 3).

Quite why there is a requirement of immediacy in assault is not certain. A threat of future injury or rape is as likely to arouse anxiety or excite retaliation as an immediate

---

[122] A useful alternative way of distinguishing the two forms uses the terms 'psychic' and 'physical' assault, or assault by beating. See G. Williams *TCL* (1983); also Law Com. No. 218 (1993) para. 18.1.

[123] A loose paraphrase of the definition adopted in *R* v *Savage*, *DPP* v *Parmenter* [1991] 4 All ER 698; *Ireland* [1997] 1 All ER 112 at 114. See also Criminal Law Revision Committee 14th Report, *Offences Against the Person* Cmnd 7844 (1980) para. 158.

[124] Kenny, *Outlines* (1962) 208.

[125] *Read* v *Coker* (1853) 13 CB 850.

[126] *St George* (1840) 9 C & P 483 at 490; *Logdon* v *DPP* [1976] Crim LR 121.

[127] [1985] 2 All ER 1.

[128] Section 16 OAPA 1861.

threat. A possible reason is that unless the threat was immediate it might be difficult to exert conceptual control over the range of situations such a crime might develop to cover.[129] If causing 'psychic' injury alone was the essential feature of the *actus reus* of assault, for example, the crime's parameters might develop to include 'invading a person's body space', 'invading a person's home' or 'tampering with a person's possessions' and other activities which do not involve forms of physical confrontation.[130]

(ii) *Causing psychic injury without threats of immediate injury*

The courts have, however, always interpreted the immediacy requirement with a degree of flexibility. For example, it is not fatal that the defendant was intercepted before being in a position to deliver a blow as long as the interception was immediately necessary to stop any blow which might be forthcoming. In *Stephens* v *Myers*, another civil case, there was an incident at a parish council meeting in the course of which the defendant advanced upon the chairman in a threatening attitude. He was stopped when only the churchwarden and one other stood between him and his prey. Tindal CJ directed the jury that there was an assault 'if he was so advancing that, within a second or two of time (if he had not been stopped), he would have reached the plaintiff'.[131] Recently yet more flexibility has been imported into the concept of immediacy, leading one to question whether the rationale for the offence may have changed. In *Smith* v *Superintendent of Woking Police Station* the Divisional Court considered that a Peeping Tom who terrified his victim by peering at her in her nightclothes through the window satisfied the conduct element in assault.[132] In *Constanza* the Court of Appeal held that sending threatening letters could form the subject matter of an assault. Addressing the question of 'immediacy' the Court of Appeal ruled that it sufficed that the actions of the defendant invoked a 'fear of violence at some time not excluding the immediate future'.[133] It seems that for 'immediate' we must now read 'imminent'.[134] In *Ireland* the House of Lords restated the requirement of immediacy but held that a telephone call, even a silent phone call, may amount to an assault although no threats are issued and there is no close proximity between caller and recipient.[135] It is a matter for the jury to decide whether, notwithstanding the lack of close proximity, the victim was made to 'fear the possibility of immediate personal violence'.[136] It has been suggested that a better response would be to ensure the immediacy requirement contained sufficient flexibility to ensure that only threats arising out of confrontations – those special shock-inducing contexts which assault is configured to deal with – are criminalised as assaults.[137] The recent case law opposes this view.

It has been said that, since the threat must be of immediate force, words alone cannot be an assault. There is, in fact, little authority for this proposition,[138] beyond the unreasoned statements of some academic writers, and in *R* v *Ireland, R* v *Burstow* it was rejected.[139] Normally, of course, threatening words will be accompanied by threatening gestures, in

---

[129] For a more analytical response see J. Gardner, 'On the General Part of the Criminal Law', in R.A. Duff (ed.), *Philosophy and the Criminal Law*, Cambridge: CUP (1998) 205, 213 ff, 244–9.

[130] Of course, extending the crime in this way would also create serious evidential problems.

[131] (1830) 4 C & P 349.

[132] (1983) 76 Cr App R 234.

[133] [1997] 2 Cr App R 492.

[134] Cf. C. Wells, 'Stalking: The Criminal Law Response' [1997] Crim LR 463.

[135] *R* v *Ireland* [1997] 1 All ER 112; see also *Constanza* [1997] Crim LR 576.

[136] [1997] 4 All ER 225 at 236 per Lord Steyn.

[137] A suggestion of J. Horder, 'Reconsidering Psychic Assault' [1998] Crim LR 392, 399–402.

[138] There is some insubstantial authority in the form of *dicta* of Holroyd J in *Meade and Belt* (1823) 1 Lew CC 184.

[139] Russell (1965) 653; Kenny (1965) 219.

which case the assault can be established independently of the words. In the absence of such accompanying gestures, as long as the words indicated that the victim was about to suffer immediate unlawful force, this should be enough in principle. A victim who, in a darkened room, hears the fateful words 'hands up' needs no other sensory experience to fear, quite reasonably, for his (immediate) safety.[140]

Words may certainly **negate** an assault if their effect is to nullify any threat which would otherwise issue from the accused's conduct.[141] In *Tuberville* v *Savage* it was said that a person who laid his hand on his sword would not be committing an assault when his gesture was accompanied by the words 'If it were not assize time, I would not take such language from you'.[142] Whether the words concerned are effective in nullifying the threat is a matter of inference. Orders by armed gunmen of the 'hands up or I shoot' variety, though capable of being interpreted as a (conditional) promise **not** to shoot, are generally treated as constituting the threat rather than nullifying it.[143]

Taking *Tuberville* v *Savage* as an example, the words could not have nullified the threat unless, at least, they preceded the gesture. The view apparently taken was that Tuberville's neutralising words indicated that he lacked the *mens rea* for an attack, which was why it was held that Savage was not entitled to use force against Tuberville in self-defence.[144] This would still leave the jury entitled to convict of assault in such a situation upon the basis of foresight, which is now recognised as sufficient *mens rea*.[145] The more menacing the words, the less the jury will be disposed to infer lack of foresight.[146]

(b) Mens rea

The fault element in (psychic) assault is an intention to cause the victim to apprehend immediate unlawful force or recklessness as to such apprehension.[147] In *Spratt*[148] the Court of Appeal stated that the earlier decision of the Divisional Court in *DPP* v *K*[149] that *Caldwell* recklessness sufficed was wrong. Recklessness was to be given its *Cunningham* meaning.[150] This means that the prosecution must prove that the accused foresaw the victim's reaction.[151]

2 Battery

The offence of battery (physical assault) is committed when unlawful force has been applied, intentionally or recklessly, to the body of the victim without his consent.[152] When charging a battery the correct terminology is 'assault by beating'.[153]

---

[140] G. Williams, 'Assault and Words' [1957] Crim LR 219; *TCI* (1983) 175–6; see also *Wilson* [1955] 1 All ER 744 CCA.

[141] Horder does not fully accept this: ibid. 402.

[142] (1669) 1 Mod Rep 3.

[143] *Read* v *Coker* (1853) 13 CB 850.

[144] 'The intention, as well as the act, makes an assault. Therefore if one strikes another . . . in discourse, it is not assault there being no intention to assault.' (1669) 1 Mod Rep 3. For discussion of this point see Horder, 'Reconsidering Psychic Assault', note 137 above.

[145] See below.

[146] *Light* (1857) D and B 332; G. Williams *TCL* (1983) 175 generally.

[147] *Venna* [1976] QB 421.

[148] [1991] 2 All ER 210.

[149] *DPP* v *K (A minor)* [1990] 1 All ER 331.

[150] *Spratt* [1991] 2 All ER 210, approving *Venna*.

[151] In *Savage* [1991] 4 All ER 698 HL at 713.

[152] *Savage* [1991] 4 All ER 698, approving the definition proposed in Smith and Hogan.

[153] *DPP* v *Little* (1992) 1 All ER 299.

(a) Actus reus

In practice most batteries will involve the infliction of some harm. The Charging Standards pitch the level of harm below that for s. 47, including injuries such as minor cuts and bruises, scratches, and swellings. It should be remembered that prosecutors routinely charge more serious injuries as common assaults for the convenience of avoiding trial by indictment.

In theory, however, what distinguishes the common law offence from its statutory counterparts, the aggravated assaults of ss. 47, 20 and 18 OAPA 1861, is that a battery (or assault) requires no hurt to be suffered by the victim beyond the interference with auto- nomy occasioned by an unconsented-to contact. A kiss or caress, no less than a blow, is the *actus reus* of a battery if not consented to or otherwise is not lawful.[154] Most defences to assault and battery demonstrate that common assault is constituted as an offence solely for the vindication of personal autonomy. Of these, consent is the focal example. A consented- to kiss is lawful for the very same reason that an unconsented-to kiss is not. Both legal attitudes reflect an underlying respect for individual autonomy.

Also consistent with this idea, unconsented-to contacts issuing from the ordinary rough and tumble of everyday life do not count as batteries.[155] This will include such contacts as taps on the shoulder to attract another's attention,[156] slaps on the back in greeting, jostling, knocking and bumping in queues, on trains, and while running for the bus.[157] It has been suggested, unconvincingly, that such contacts are not unlawful because they are impliedly consented to[158] or are not hostile.[159] A more cogent reason is that they are not unlawful because their lawful occurrence is consistent with a society which vigorously defends its members' interests in remaining free from undesired contacts. Autonomy, no less than its jealous possessor, does not exist in a social vacuum. It is only a meaningful human good in the context of a society in which individuals give up some privacy and autonomy the better to enjoy its full benefits. As soon as the contact exceeds what is considered 'generally acceptable in every day life'[160] the *actus reus* is established. While a police officer may tap a person on the shoulder to attract his attention,[161] he may not exercise physical restraint such as taking hold of a person's arm[162] even, apparently, if issuing a caution.[163]

Other examples of battery include restraining a person, spitting on them, cutting their hair,[164] even, it appears, cutting[165] or stroking[166] a person's clothes while on their person. In the latter case, whether it is necessary for the victim to feel the pressure of the contact is uncertain. Arguably it should not be. A person's right to be free of undesired interference logically includes a right not to have their clothes touched while they are wearing them.[167] One practical argument against this is that it might appear inconsistent with the law of

---

[154] Kenny (1965) 218.
[155] *Collins* v *Wilcock* [1984] 3 All ER 374 at 378; *F* v *West Berkshire Health Authority* [1989] 2 All ER 545 per Lord Goff; *McMillan* v *CPS* [2008] EWHC 1457.
[156] *Coward* v *Baddeley* (1859) 4 H & N 478.
[157] *Collins* v *Wilcock* [1984] 3 All ER 374; *Katsonis* v *Crown Prosecution Service* [2011] EWHC 1860 (Admin).
[158] *Coward* v *Baddeley* (1859) 4 H & N 478.
[159] Croom-Johnson LJ in *Wilson* v *Pringle* [1986] 2 All ER 440.
[160] *Collins* v *Wilcock* at 378 per Robert Goff LJ.
[161] *Donnelly* v *Jackman* [1970] 1 All ER 987.
[162] *Kenlin* v *Gardner* [1966] 3 All ER 931.
[163] *Collins* v *Wilcock*.
[164] *DPP* v *Smith* (2006) above.
[165] *Day* (1845) 1 Cox CC 207.
[166] *Thomas* (1985) 81 Cr App R 331.
[167] A.J. Ashworth (2009) 327.

robbery, in which pick-pocketing or handbag snatching has been held not be robbery since, although force is used in effecting the theft, it is not force used against 'the person' of the victim.[168]

Forms of battery

A battery may not be committed by omission.[169] So, a person who fails to remove a log from a person pinned underneath is not guilty of common assault. In general, the position is not altered if the actor is under a legal duty to assist the victim. So a police officer will not be guilty of battery, as principal, if he fails to stop a battery committed by someone else. He may, under certain circumstances, be guilty as an accessory, however.[170] One qualification to this rule is where the accused's conduct can be interpreted as a 'continuing act'.[171]

Although most batteries are committed directly, as in the case of a punch or a kiss, a requirement of some direct contact between the assailant and the victim has not always been insisted upon. Thus, it has been held that a person who provokes a stampede,[172] sets a dog on his victim, or strikes a horse so that it upsets its rider[173] commits a battery. In *Scott v Shepherd* a person who threw a lighted squib into a market-place was held liable for assault and battery even though the squib had passed through several hands before it exploded in the ultimate victim's face.[174] More recently, it was held to be an assault where a boy placed a quantity of acid in a washroom hand-drier which discharged its load into the face of a subsequent user.[175] While this case probably pushes the notion of what it is to 'batter' or 'beat' to its limits, if not beyond, the more recent decision of *Haystead* has confirmed that a battery requires no direct physical contact between assailant and victim.[176] As long as it can be shown that it was by A's act that B suffered the application of force to his body it matters not that A's act was not directed against B's person. Here A punched C, who was holding her baby B, in the face. C dropped the baby, who hit his head on the floor. The Divisional Court upheld A's conviction for battery on B.[177] Equally significant, perhaps, is the case of *DPP v Santana-Bermudez* in which it was held that a person who gave an assurance to police officers prior to a body search that his pocket did not contain 'sharps' when it, in fact, contained a hypodermic syringe, could amount to the *actus reus* of assault by beating.[178] The Divisional Court did not explain why but it seems they accepted the reasoning of prosecuting counsel at first instance that the defendant had by his act of placing the syringe in his pocket created a dangerous situation (*Miller*), had continued that act by failing to do anything to disabuse the police of the danger and had compounded the danger by give a false assurance. The Divisional Court seems intent on redefining common (physical) assault as causing an undesired contact with the person of the victim. It is perhaps surprising, in the light of some of the earlier decisions, that it was thought necessary, in *Wilson*, to 'expand' the notion of 'inflict' in section 20 OAPA beyond the supposed limits of a battery to encompass contacts directly inflicted against the

---

[168] *P v DPP* [2012] EWHC 1657 (Admin); [2013] Crim LR 151.
[169] *Fagan v MPC* [1968] 3 All ER 442.
[170] See Chapter 19.
[171] *Fagan v MPC* [1968] 3 All ER 442. See Chapters 4, 8.
[172] As in *Martin*, above.
[173] *Dodwell v Burford* (1670) 1 Mod 24.
[174] (1773) 2 WB 1892.
[175] *DPP v K (a minor)* [1990] 1 All ER 331 QBD, subsequently overruled but not on this ground.
[176] *Haystead v Chief Constable of Derbyshire* [2000] Crim LR 758.
[177] Cf. *Mitchell* [1983] QB 741; *Dodwell v Burford* (1670) 1 Mod 24, above.
[178] [2003] EWHC 2908 (Admin).

person of the victim but not directly at the hands of the accused. Battery, some commentators insist,[179] may always have been committed in such circumstances.[180] Whether or not this is so, it was important that cases such as *Martin, Halliday* and other cases of self-inflicted injury procured by others whose doctrinal base was **unclear**, should be reconciled with cases such as *Clarence* where it was **clear**. *Wilson* effectively achieved this but things have moved on apace since then.

(b) Mens rea

Like assault, the *mens rea* of battery is intention or recklessness in the *Cunningham* sense, except here the mental attitude must be directed towards the unlawful infliction of force rather than the apprehension of it.[181] It should be noted that there is no requirement that any physical injury be intended or foreseen, only the unlawful contact.

11.4 DEFENCES TO OFFENCES AGAINST THE PERSON

All the general defences are applicable, most notably in this context public and private defence. Common assault (including battery) requires proof of an unlawful contact. A contact may be rendered lawful by consent, by necessity and by proof that it is occasioned in the context of lawful punishment of an infant.

A Consent

Overview

Applying or threatening to apply force to the person of another does not form the subject-matter of assault or battery if it is consented to.[182] This is subject to three qualifications, namely:

(1) the consent must be freely given and not vitiated by fraud;
(2) the person concerned must have the legal capacity to give consent;
(3) where the infliction of bodily harm is involved, the deed consented to must be one to which consent is legally recognised as a defence where harm is thereby caused.

1 The reality of consent

Consent may be express or implied. Implied consent accounts for the legality of most everyday contacts. The law draws a distinction, in both non-sexual and sexual offences, between consent reluctantly given and mere submission. The line drawn between these two is unacceptably vague and will be examined fully later in the chapter. Matters are not helped by the notion of consent now varying according to whether the contact is sexual or non-sexual. It seems that it is for the jury to decide whether any pressure brought to bear,

---

[179] For example Ashworth (2009) 327; Kenny (1962) 209; M. Hirst, 'Assault, Battery and Indirect Violence' [1999] Crim LR 577.
[180] See Case 6 for an example of an indirect infliction of force which probably could not be interpreted as a battery. See Draft Criminal Law Bill 1993 6(1)(a).
[181] *Venna* [1976] QB 421; *Savage and Parmenter* [1991] 4 All ER 698.
[182] See generally LCCP No. 139, London: HMSO (1995).

or other inducement, was sufficient to vitiate consent.[183] This will be obvious where an explicit threat of harm is present but less obvious where, for example, there is an assertion of authority or financial pressure.[184]

Apparent consent may also be vitiated by fraud, where the effect is to deceive V as to the nature of the act apparently consented to or the identity of the actor. Most of the cases in which such a mistake has been operative are cases involving sexual assaults, but the principle holds good generally that to consent to a contact requires V to understand the true nature of the contact being consented to. It has been held, therefore, that consent is vitiated where, innocent of the facts of life, the victim submits to intercourse, believing it to be a surgical operation.[185] Also, where she submits to an intimate internal examination, mistakenly believing the other to be performing a medical examination when it is done for sexual gratification.[186]

It should be noted that consent will not be vitiated where the victim is merely deceived as to the desirability of what she is doing or the qualities of the other person concerned. This latter qualification may offer the defendant an undeserved immunity relative to the interest violated. Thus:

Case 8

Adam, an out-of-work actor, sets himself up in business as an acupuncturist although he has no qualifications or experience. He convinces Eve that she would benefit from acupuncture and tells her that he is an expert.

Eve's consent is not vitiated. She asked for acupuncture and this is what she got.[187] In *Richardson* consent to dental surgery was effective although the dentist had been struck off and had misrepresented his qualifications.[188] These are not cases[189] of mistaken identity or mistake as to the nature of the contact. The mistake is only as to expertise or status.

In *Linekar*,[190] a prostitute's consent to intercourse was not vitiated by a fraudulent promise to pay for the sexual service. A similar conclusion was reached in *Bolduc and Bird*, where the victim was deceived into believing that a witness to her medical examination was a medical student when in reality it was a friend of the examining doctor.[191] Once again, the contact the victim consented to (medical examination/sexual intercourse) was the contact she got.

Such a stance often will appear counter-intuitive in cases where informed consent as to the potential consequences of her action will make an objective difference to the desirability of the contact concerned.[192] Increasingly, the courts require consent to be fully informed

---

[183] *Olugboja* [1982] QB 320; *McAllister* [1997] Crim LR 233; see generally S. Gardner, 'Appreciating *Olugboja*' [1996] LS 275; C. Elliot and C. de Than, 'The Case for a Rational Reconstruction of Consent in Criminal Law' (2007) MLR 225.

[184] *Latter* v *Bradell* (1881) 50 LJQB 448.

[185] *Flattery* (1877) 2 QBD 410.

[186] *Pike* [1996] 1 Cr App R 4.

[187] See *Richardson* [1999] Crim LR 62. The Law Commission apparently consider that consent is not recognised as a defence to acupuncture, para. 38.3, 5. This is improbable given its social acceptability and prevalence. Law Commission Consultation Paper No. 134 *Consent and Offences Against the Person*; see R. Leng, 'Consent and Offences Against the Person' [1994] Crim LR 480.

[188] [1999] QB 444.

[189] Like *Pike*, note 186.

[190] [1995] 3 All ER 69.

[191] (1967) 63 DLR (2d) 82; *Tabassum* [2000] 2 Cr App R 328.

[192] In sexual offences this is partly achieved by the presumption that a person does not consent to a contact where she is deceived as to the nature and purpose of the act. See below pp. 339–41.

for it to be operative. In *Tabassum*, in which the defendant induced women to submit to breast examinations by misrepresenting medical qualifications, the Court of Appeal held that such mistakes could vitiate consent.[193] Although the Court of Appeal sought to distinguish *Linekar*, *Flattery* and *Richardson*, the distinction drawn was not convincing. *Tabassum* is also consistent with *Dica* and *Konzani* which, disapproving *Clarence*, held that a person's consent to intercourse must be informed if it is to act as a defence to assault. By 'informed consent' in this context we mean that the victim was aware that her partner was suffering from venereal disease.[194] The effect of these decisions is to place agents under a duty of disclosure in cases where there is a risk of transferring a disease.[195] On the face of it the balance between autonomy and protection of the public is drawn sensibly but, as a precedent, these cases have dramatic implications if extended beyond the arena of sexually transmitted diseases, and why should they not be, given that both inflicting and assault apparently no longer require any direct act on the part of the defendant?[196] Does a patient with HIV have a duty of disclosure to a dentist, for example?[197] A further problem is what degree of knowledge the defendant must have.

> **Case 9**
> Adam, a very promiscuous man, has had sexual intercourse on countless occasions over the past ten years. He knows that there is a risk that he may have contracted HIV but fears to be tested. He has intercourse with Eve, who does not know his reputation but does know the risks of unprotected sex. Three months later Eve, is diagnosed as HIV positive. Adam is charged with assault occasioning actual bodily harm under section 20.

In both cases the issue is whether Eve has consented to the act of intercourse. This depends upon whether informed consent requires Eve to be aware of Adam's sexual history. For Eve to be fully informed, does Adam need to tell Eve of his history? Can Adam, given that he himself is in the dark about his condition, not rely on Eve's own knowledge of the risks? Both *Dica* and *Konzani* are silent on this question but whatever their undoubted merits, in requiring consent to potentially dangerous contacts to be informed, it is clear that they are a substantial step in a direction which may have profound effects upon the traditional notion of sexual autonomy, and if, extended beyond sexual intercourse, autonomy generally.[198]

2 Capacity to give consent

The reality of consent may also be compromised where the victim, by virtue of youth or mental incapacity, is unable to appreciate the nature of the act[199] or where, notwithstanding

---

[193] Acceptance of the truth of this principle probably informed the decision of counsel to recommend a guilty plea in *Piper* [2007] EWCA Crim 2151 on comparable facts.

[194] *Dica* [2004] EWCA Crim 1103; *Konzani* [2005] EWCA Crim 706. The CPS have published a policy statement on prosecuting involving the intentional or reckless sexual transmission of infection: http://www.cps.gov.uk/publications/prosecution/sti.html

[195] However, awareness can arise otherwise than by such disclosure. Knowledge may be communicated by a third party, and possibly by circumstances (e.g. attendance at a special clinic), sufficient to put the victim on notice of the risk that the accused may be suffering HIV.

[196] See *Burstow* and *DPP* v *Santana-Bermudez*, above.

[197] For discussion see LCCP No. 134 *Consent and Offences Against the Person* (1994); see also LCCP No. 139, London: HMSO (1995) para. 6.80.

[198] M. Weait, 'Knowledge, Autonomy and Consent' [2005] Crim LR 763; S. Ryan, 'Reckless Transmission of HIV' [2006] Crim LR 981.

[199] *Howard* [1965] 3 All ER 684.

such appreciation, consent is otherwise inoperative.[200] This is particularly relevant in cases involving sexual activity. Even where it does not, the courts have shown a willingness to manipulate the rules governing consent in cases involving the young so as to criminalise activities which are objectively injurious. In *Burrel* v *Harmer* a tattooist tattooed two young boys, whose arms became inflamed as a consequence. The tattooist's conviction for assault occasioning actual bodily harm was upheld on the basis that the boys were too young to understand what was involved and, therefore, to give consent. Where the activity is not obviously injurious the courts have shown themselves to be more inclined to support autonomy. So, it was held in *Gillick* that a child with sufficient mental maturity and understanding could give consent to medical treatment.[201]

3 What can be consented to?

It was explained earlier that the prosecution bears the burden of proving all the definitional elements of the crime. For certain crimes absence of consent is such an element. Rape and common assault are examples. Because absence of consent is an element of the crime, the defence bears no evidential burden whatsoever. The same principle accounts for the legality of other expressions of love and affection, such as kissing, stroking, shaking hands, touching, etc.[202] These are not lawful simply because they are justified, or excused, rather because such consented-to contacts are intrinsically 'good things', being part of everyday human interaction. The 'offence' – what is offensive – in such activities is not the activity itself but the challenge to personal autonomy which occurs when the contact is undesired.

In theory, at least, absence of consent should be a definitional element in section 47 also since this requires proof of a common assault in addition to harm.[203] The problem faced by the criminal law is that certain consented-to contacts may pose public interest problems, most particularly if the contact consented to involves the infliction of pain or injury.[204] As will now be explained, victim's consent is not an unqualified answer to the infliction of physical injury.

(a) *Consent and the infliction of physical injury*

Clearly there is room, within a reasonably civilised society, for people to consent to the infliction of injury. Sometimes personal autonomy may be enhanced by the suffering of injury. Cosmetic surgery is a topical example. It is a paradigm example of enjoying the fruits of autonomy. What does having autonomy mean if not that we are entitled to participate in dangerous sports such as rugby or cricket, or spend our hard-earned cash having a nose-job or our ears or navel pierced? But there is also room for criminalising consensual harm-causing activities, for example euthanasia, or duelling, which may harm public as well as private interests. Somehow a balance must be struck between individual autonomy and public welfare. As yet the principles which would inform this balance have not been adequately weighed in the courts. As a general rule of thumb, however, it appears that the legality of actions causing physical injury varies according to whether the injury consented to is inflicted intentionally or unintentionally.

---

[200] Because of the operation of the Sexual Offences Act 1956, ss. 5, 6, 7, 14, 15, for example. The lawfulness of various sexual activities involving children and mental defectives does not hinge upon whether their consent was forthcoming. See Law Commission Report *Consent in Sex Offences*, 16 February 2000.
[201] [1984] 1 All ER 365.
[202] Cf. A.J. Ashworth (2009) 330–119.
[203] See Williams, 'Consent and Public Policy' [1962] Crim LR 75.
[204] In such circumstances the contact is, by definition, 'injurious'. Moreover, its injuriousness does not hang on the absence or otherwise of the victim's consent.

(b) *Consent to intentionally inflicted harms*

(i) *Consensual fighting*

Historically it appears that acts of consensual violence were treated as unlawful only insofar as they had a direct and explicit impact on defined public interests. It was no concern of the state that the public might beat themselves half to death as long as the state itself was not threatened. This it might be if the injuries inflicted were so disabling as to render an individual unfit for (public) combat or if the fight might provoke a breach of the peace.[205] In *Coney*[206] a prize fight was held unlawful on this basis. Stephen, by no means a champion of civil liberties, accepted the notion that consent is a defence to assault occasioning actual bodily harm 'even when considerable force is used'.[207] However, he hinted at a wider 'and more authoritarian' basis for the decision than that of his brethren, namely that gratuitously causing serious injury is wrong in itself rather than simply because it is conducive to public disorder.

It is this moral basis, that deliberately hurting people is wrong, which has gradually come to inform criminal law doctrine. In *Attorney-General's Reference (No. 6 of 1980)*[208] it was no defence to a section 47 OAPA charge that the parties to a fist fight had agreed to the fight as a means of settling an argument. The Court of Appeal rejected the argument that since absence of consent was of the essence of an assault there was no case to answer on a charge of assault occasioning actual bodily harm. The Court said that liability depended upon whether the context (fisticuffs in a public street to settle an argument) justified the use of force. This in turn depended upon whether the activity was in the public interest. The Court of Appeal concluded that it did not, and was not. It was not in the public interest 'that people should try to cause or should cause each other actual bodily harm for no good reason'.[209] Two points should be noted. First, no particular threat to the public interest was identified in criminalising a private bout of fisticuffs. In essence therefore, the decision reduced to 'we don't like it, so you don't do it'. The burden of justifying a paradigm case of self-determination (resorting to fisticuffs rather than to lawyers) was placed on the antagonists rather than the prosecution. Second, there is no requirement, in this formulation, that the activity be one **designed** to cause harm, simply that it **should** cause harm.[210] The courts have latterly adopted a more principled approach most notably in the field of sexual activity, distinguishing between intentionally and unintentionally produced injuries.

(ii) *Injuries committed for sexual gratification*

Stephen's *dicta* notwithstanding, the first real inkling that personal autonomy might be countermanded by moral principle, rather than more explicit public interests, came in the case of *R v Donovan*,[211] almost 50 years before the *Attorney-General's Reference (No. 6 of 1980)*. The accused beat the prosecutrix, a prostitute, with a cane for the purposes of sexual gratification. She suffered cuts and bruises. The main issue was whether, assuming she consented, the beating was lawful. Swift J volunteered a clear statement of principle: 'As a general rule, although it is a rule to which there are well established exceptions, it is an unlawful act to beat another person with such a degree of violence that the infliction of

---

[205] See *Coney* (1882) 8 QBD 534, below.
[206] See previous note.
[207] *A Digest of the Criminal Law*, London: Macmillan (1894).
[208] [1981] QB 715.
[209] At 719.
[210] *Boyea* [1992] Crim LR 574.
[211] *Donovan* [1934] 2 KB 498.

bodily harm is probable, and when such an act is proved consent is immaterial'. In short, hurting people was wrong unless it took place within a context already supportive of individual autonomy such as lawful sports.[212]

The fact that the injuries were suffered in the course of a sexual encounter has led commentators, quite reasonably, to conclude that the decision was more informed by a repressive attitude towards sex than a morally neutral attitude towards consensual violence. Swift J's general reasoning does not support such a conclusion, however. The overall emphasis is on the wrongfulness of injuring people ('beat') rather than the unacceptability of the sexual context.[213]

More recently, the House of Lords in *Brown*[214] was required to determine the legality of sado-masochistic sexual activity between consenting males who had demonstrated considerably more ingenuity and potential for injury than the defendant in *Donovan*. It concluded, by a majority, that such activities were unlawful. It rejected the argument that criminal liability for injuries falling short of serious bodily harm required, whether charged under s. 47 or s. 20, proof of an assault (an ingredient in both offences) and therefore, by definition, also proof of absence of consent. It rejected also the alternative argument that even if absence of consent was not a necessary ingredient in such offences, it should be a special defence to sado-masochism since it involved freedom of sexual expression. At the root of their lordships' disagreement was not simply an argument about what the law was, but about what it ought to be. The minority did not like the activities, but felt that a free society must tolerate them unless the injuries sustained were serious and/or defined public interests were threatened. The majority also did not like the activities, so much so that they concluded that freedom of sexual expression was not 'good enough reason' to justify the infliction of intentional injury.

Of the majority, Lord Templeman's is the most cogent opinion. Unlike Lords Lowry and Jauncey he showed himself able to untangle the features of violence and sexual self-expression. In his opinion, the objection to sado-masochism is not that it is a form of sexual deviance. It is not that it involves the infliction of injury *per se*. Rather it is because it involves an inhuman passion for inflicting injury rather than one sustained incidental to an all-too-human susceptibility to passion.[215] Allow people to indulge a taste for (consensual) torture, for whatever reason, and it will not be long before the taste can better be satisfied where consent is absent. Society has the right, if not duty, to protect itself from the morally corruptive potential of 'cults of violence'.[216] The activity is criminalised in other words as conducive to causing a 'remote harm'.[217]

In *Slingsby* and *Meachen* this distinction made between harm caused incidentally and harm caused for its own sake was used to distinguish *Brown*. In *Slingsby*, following some extremely vigorous consensual sexual activity resulting in cuts to V's rectum and vagina, V died of septicaemia. S was charged with constructive manslaughter, which requires proof of an unlawful and dangerous act. Judge J withdrew the case from the jury on the basis that the activities were consensual, accidental, and therefore were also lawful. They could not

---

[212] At 507.
[213] Such an analysis removes an element of tautology from the reasoning of Swift J.
[214] [1993] 2 All ER 75. Representative of the criticism levelled against it is Kell, 'Social Disutility and the Law of Consent' (1994) 14 OJLS 121; cf. W. Wilson, 'Consenting to Personal Injury: How far can you go?' (1995) 1 Contemporary Issues in Law 45.
[215] *Slingsby* [1995] Crim LR 570; *Meachen* [2006] EWCA Crim 2414.
[216] This argument was not enthusiastically received in the European Court of Human Rights which nevertheless upheld the decision on other grounds: *Laskey, Jaggard and Brown v UK* [1997] 24 EHRR 39.
[217] See Chapter 2.

be rendered unlawful simply because injury had been sustained.[218] Left undiscussed was the legal position where although the injury inflicted was not intended, it was foreseen. If Mr Slingsby had realised the risk of causing cuts to V's rectum would this have rendered the victim's consent ineffective? In *Meachen*, on similar facts but without death resulting, the Court of Appeal quashed the defendant's conviction under section 20, while hinting that consent was only operative in such cases where the harm was accidentally inflicted. In other words, if D, without intending the injury nevertheless foresaw the risk of its occurrence, his actions would be unlawful irrespective of consent. This hint occurs in the course of the following remark.

> We agree with the comments made by the late Professor Sir John Smith on this decision (*Slingsby*): 'The offence alleged was manslaughter by an unlawful and dangerous act. It was essential for the prosecution to prove that the injuries were caused by an unlawful act, a battery. Because no injury was intended (or, indeed, foreseen) and V consented to the acts done, the judge held that there was no battery. It is respectfully submitted that this is right. In *Donovan* and in *Brown* the injuries were intended and consent to the intentional infliction of injury was held to be no defence. Here there was no question of consenting to injury because the parties contemplated no injury.'

By implication, if injury **had been contemplated**, different considerations would apply. What, in principle should be the legal position in such a case? Taking a conscious risk of causing injury is not blameworthy *per se*. It becomes blameworthy only if the relevant act is performed recklessly. This requires the risk taken to be **unreasonable**.[219] In principle, given the social importance attached to sexual autonomy, engaging in consensual 'rough sex' should not be criminalised unless the risk of serious injury was substantial.[220] Only then would the risk taken be 'unreasonable'.

A different problem surfaced in *Wilson*[221] where a prosecution was brought against a married man who, in the course of consensual activities with his wife, branded her on the buttocks with a hot iron. The trial judge, on a submission of no case to answer, ruled that he was bound by the authority of *Brown* to direct the jury to convict. The Court of Appeal upheld the appeal, ruling that it was not in the public interest that the private activities of husbands and wives should be visited by the sanctions of the criminal law where, as here, the point of the activity was, like tattooing, physical adornment rather than the infliction of pain.

Wilson was not a case of sado-masochism and it was a case where the injury inflicted was intentional. As a result, although treated as a tattooing case, it reopened the question whether sado-masochism by consenting couples, of whatever sexual orientation, is unlawful.[222] At least in cases where serious injury was not involved this would be difficult to square with society's commitment to sexual autonomy, where explicit public interests are not threatened. If sexual freedom involving consensual violence is a right, it is a right for both heterosexuals and homosexuals.[223] A reasonable restriction on the *ratio* of *Brown* is that it applies to cases of group violence, where the corruptive potential is most

---

[218] [1995] Crim LR 570.

[219] See *R v G and Another* [2003] UKHL 50, [2004] AC 1034.

[220] Cf. commentary at [1995] Crim LR 572. And see now *Dica*, note 74 above, and *Konzani*, both of which support the proposition that a person may consent to the risk of infection through intercourse. In *Dica* Judge J was again adjudicating. For a useful discussion see Simester and Sullivan (2013) 408–9.

[221] [1996] 3 WLR 125.

[222] S. Cowan 'To Buy or not to Buy? Vulnerability and the Criminalisation of Commercial BDSM' (2012) 20(3) Feminist LS 263.

[223] R. Dworkin, *Taking Rights Seriously*, London: Duckworths (1977).

heightened.[224] This reasoning was resisted in *Emmett*[225] in which an unmarried couple engaged in potentially very dangerous activities, including burning and suffocation, in the course of consensual sado-masochistic sexual activity. Distinguishing *Wilson* as a tattooing case the Court of Appeal approved the following statement of the trial judge: '. . . the degree of actual and potential harm was such and also the degree of unpredictability as to injury was such as to make it a proper cause for the criminal law to intervene.' This leaves open the possibility that sado-masochism involving lesser degrees of harm may yet be deemed lawful.[226]

(c) *Categories of lawfully inflicted intentional harms*

In the *Attorney-General's Reference (No. 6 of 1980)* Lord Lane CJ suggested that the exceptional categories where bodily harm could be consented to were all categories where the activity concerned was of social benefit and thus conducive to the public interest:

> Nothing which we have said is intended to cast doubt upon the accepted legality of properly conducted games and sports, lawful chastisement or correction, reasonable surgical interference, dangerous exhibitions, etc. These apparent exceptions can be justified as involving the exercise of a legal right, in the case of chastisement or correction, or as needed in the public interest, in the other cases.[227]

Although the language used in street fighting and sado-masochism cases reflects this restrictive approach, the overall pattern of immunity reflects a more libertarian emphasis. Harmful activities as difficult to justify as tattooing, circumcision, and boxing are all deemed lawful, although it would be an unusual claim to insist that such activities were needed 'in the public interest'. It is probably more accurate to say that positive public policy reasons in favour of the activity are necessary only in the case of harms inflicted for their own sake.

(i) *Boxing*

The legality of boxing is widely thought to be an anomaly.[228] The criminal law distinguishes between violence used in the course of organised boxing and sparring, and violence in the course of an informal bout of fisticuffs[229] or other shows of violence,[230] whether these are designed to settle a private argument[231] or for the (unlawful) delectation of the public. The immunity probably came on the back of lawful sports generally, and as an accidental outcome of *Coney*, rather than because of any perceived merit in the activity itself. Here, distinct from other contact sports, the use of violence is not incidental to the activity.[232] It is constitutive of it, no less so than with disorganised fisticuffs. A heavyweight boxer who did not enter every contest wishing to cause grievous bodily harm to his opponent

---

[224] Lord Templeman in *Brown* gave no indication that state control of sado-masochism was restricted to orgies. However, it appeared to be of prime concern to Lords Lowry and Jauncey that the activities took place in the course of homosexual group activity.

[225] 18 June 1999, Internet Transcript.

[226] As the Law Commission has recommended. See below pp. 321–2. A Swedish Court ruled in 2010 that consent operates as a defence to sado-masochism: *Sydsvenskan* newspaper report, 28 September 2010. Cf. J. Tolmie, 'Consent to Harmful Assaults: The Case for Moving Away from Category-based Decision Making' [2012] Crim LR 656.

[227] [1981] QB 715 at 719 per Lord Lane CJ.

[228] See generally D.C. Ormerod and M.J. Gunn, 'The Legality of Boxing' (1995) 15 LS 181.

[229] See Law Commission Consultation Paper No. 134 *Consent and Offences Against the Person*.

[230] For example, duelling.

[231] *A-G's Reference (No. 6 of 1980)* [1981] QB 715.

[232] See *Pallante v Stadiums Pty* [1976] VR 331.

would probably not last very long, at least in the professional ring. The distinction drawn by Lord Templeman in *Brown* between incidental violence and violence which is 'its own reward' fits, therefore, uneasily with the continued legality of boxing. There appear to be double standards operating in the field of consensual violence. On the one hand violence in the course of achieving sexual fulfilment – surely a key ingredient in general human happiness – is unlawful if not incidental to a 'legitimate' sex act. On the other hand grown men can bludgeon one another to death in the course of an organised boxing match for no better reason, apparently, than that it makes a lot of spectators very happy to witness the spectacle.

The basis for distinguishing the unlawful from the lawful contact, the prize-fight or dis-organised fisticuffs from the boxing contest, is that the latter is deemed not to be contrary to the public interest. The distinguishing feature seems to be that the infliction of very serious injury takes place in the course of a 'character-building' activity structured by rules, rather than, say, an orgy[233] or street fight, where rules are subjugated to the passions.[234]

(ii) *Surgery and body alteration*

Surgery has long been recognised as a special category of lawful contact.[235] Where surgery is for therapeutic purposes it is clearly supported by the public interest. The legality of surgical mutilation, however, should, it is submitted, be analysed differently. Some surgically caused harms can only be considered lawful if, like any other harm-laden activity, individual autonomy outweighs the public interest in prohibiting the infliction of deliberate harm. Non-therapeutic surgery such as organ donation is a case in point, since obvious scope exists for the dehumanising exploitation of the poor. Accordingly, it is probably a crime at common law to extract non-regenerative organs for reward.[236] Consent is apparently a defence to gender reassignment and sterilisation. Cases of men seeking surgical castration are not unheard of. The latter are likely to be contrary to the public interest unless positive good reasons can be adduced in their support.[237]

The lawfulness of cosmetic surgery is presumably also subject to the public interest since here again there is clearly scope for irreversible surgical mutilation.[238] This is presently the position with tattooing, body-piercing, and male circumcision.[239] Such activities are intrinsically injurious; they cannot be done without the infliction of both pain and injury. The legality of the outer limits of such activities has not been fully explored, however. A performance artist in Italy is spending her life apparently remodelling her face and body with the aid of plastic surgery. Unusually the ambition is to 'uglify' rather than beautify, in the ultimate personalised artistic statement. In the United States and the UK people have undergone unnecessary limb amputations for more obscure reasons. There are clearly strong public interest arguments against such practices, as well as for restricting the legality of some tattooing or body-piercing. If we take tattooing as an instance, although it may be expressive of personal autonomy, the reality of consent may often be questionable. It is

---

[233] Inaccurately as it turns out. See Ormerod and Gunn, ibid. at 190–2.

[234] Cf. Lord Mustill, 108–9.

[235] See generally LCCP No. 139, Part VIII; D.W. Elliott, 'Body Dismorphic Disorder, Radical Surgery and the Limits of Consent' (2009) 17 Med LR 149.

[236] By statute the practice is outlawed by the Human Organs Transplant Act 1989, s. 2; and see generally G. Dworkin, 'The Law Relating to Organ Transplantation in England' (1970) 33 MLR 353; M. Brazier, *Medicine, Patients and the Law* [5th revised edition published 2011] ch. 18.

[237] For example the patient is a sex offender; see LCCP No. 139, London: HMSO (1995) para. 8.23.

[238] Cf. L. Bibbings and P. Alldridge, 'Sexual Expression, Body Alteration and the Defence of Consent' (1993) 20 J Law and Soc 356.

[239] Female circumcision being independently unlawful by the Prohibition of Female Circumcision Act 1985.

possible, for example, that many young men in the armed forces suffer tattooing simply to conform to culturally generated expectations of manliness. Not all dehumanising 'cults' necessarily involve violence for its own sake.

There may be an argument, therefore, for restricting the practice of extensive tattooing on similar or paternalistic grounds to reasonable limits. In the case of the young, in particular, it may be argued that a tolerant and civilised society has a duty to consider not only the freedom of individuals to choose to adorn themselves but also the unfreedom which will necessarily follow from exercising that freedom. In cases of facial or whole-body tattoos, for example, the consequences are a changed social identity which is effectively irreversible.

In *Wilson* branding on the buttocks was treated, by analogy with tattooing, as satisfying the public interest test. However, it was not made clear whether it would have made a difference if the branding had been on the face or chest nor whether the particular context involved – private activities between married partners – were relevant to the question of legality. As suggested earlier, if branding is not contrary to the public interest when engaged in by married couples it is difficult to mount a (non-discriminatory) public interest argument against it when engaged in by others. Assuming, as we must, that it was done for purposes of adornment, its legality could hardly be compromised by its being effected by unmarried lovers, of whatever sexual orientation, or even by the local 'branding artist'.[240]

(d) Consent to unintentional injury

(i) Contact sports, dangerous exhibitions and entertainment

Outside the field of boxing, many of the more dangerous practices which go on on our football, rugby and cricket fields are lawful, at least where injury is not intended or, where the contact is foreseen to involve the risk of injury, where the risk run is not unreasonable.[241] Following the pattern proposed by the *Attorney-General's Reference*, such practices are lawful, if consented to, because the activity from which they issue is socially beneficial, that is, is in the public interest. It is inappropriate for a free society to punish harms committed in moments of rash enthusiasm, where the harnessing and channelling of such enthusiasm is both the point of the game and the point of **playing** games. It is probably not strictly relevant that there are positive good reasons in favour of games, however. Rough horseplay and dangerous exhibitions such as knife-throwing and trapeze work may be consented to, despite the dangers they involve. No obvious public benefit is effected by such activities but a free society would surely be diminished by their criminalisation.[242]

Consent is generally implied with respect not only to those contacts which are lawful within the rules of game but also to those illegitimate contacts which are considered inevitable constituents of the game as it is played.[243] The outer limits of what is, and can be, consented to has not, as yet, been fully explored. The legality of 'eye-gouging', stiff-arm tackles and collapsing the scrum in rugby, 'over-the-top' tackles in football, and bowling bouncers and fast high full tosses in cricket, are, therefore, of questionable legality given their obvious propensity to cause harm. Clearly, retaliatory punches and kicks are unlikely to be deemed consented to or, if consented to, deemed lawful, since, unlike boxing blows, such contacts evince no respect for structured rule-following. In *Barnes* the Court of Appeal

---

[240] Cf. *Oversby* (unreported) cited in LCCP No. 139 at 122.

[241] *Bradshaw* (1878) 14 Cox CC 83.

[242] For discussion of the burgeoning occurrence of televising dangerous activities for entertainment purposes, see Cooper, S., and James, M. 'Entertainment – the Painful Process of Rethinking Consent' (2012) Crim LR 188.

[243] *Billingshurst* [1978] Crim LR 553; cf. *Bradshaw* (1878) 14 Cox CC 83; *Moore* (1898) 14 TLR 229.

made an attempt to clarify when criminal prosecutions were appropriate for injuries effected in the course of contact sports. The defendant was convicted in the course of an amateur football game of inflicting grievous bodily harm for effecting a robust tackle which broke the victim's leg. The Court concluded, quashing the conviction, that resort to the criminal courts should be exceptional and should require a sufficiently grave breach of rules that resort to criminal proceedings was appropriate rather than the game's own internal disciplinary system. In this context consent would be presumed unless what occurred had gone beyond what a player 'might reasonably be regarded as having accepted by taking part in the sport'. Context was everything, including the type of sport, the level at which it was played,[244] the nature of the act, the degree of force used, the risk of injury, and the state of mind of the defendant, in particular whether the evidence suggested misjudgement in the heat of the moment or something more violent and calculated.[245] In cases of intentional injury a player does not (and cannot reasonably be expected to) consent.[246]

By this same reasoning, the presumption is that other sports in which the intentional causing of injury do not figure such as karate, judo and wrestling are subjected to similar principles.[247] Participants in such organised contests consent only to those contacts allowed by the rules of the contest and probably also to those other contacts the risk of whose occurrence the participants are reasonably expected to assume.[248] Hitting below the belt would fall into this category. Hitting the victim while on the floor or between rounds would not.

(ii) Horseplay

Also recognised as an activity for which valid consent can be given to dangerous risk-taking is what has been termed 'horseplay'. This has been deemed lawful, even where the degree of harm to which the participants are exposed is severe. So, in *Jones and Others* the Court of Appeal ruled that a defence of consent could be raised to a charge of s. 20 where the defendants concerned were boys who had caused others a broken arm and a ruptured spleen, during the course of rough horseplay. It is important to remember what is at issue. Obviously the injuries themselves were not consented to. Moreover, in law, they **could not be** consented to. If the boys had said to the victim, 'we are going to break your arm and rupture your spleen. How about it?', the victim's consent, if he had been fool enough to grant it, would have been ineffective. The decision is, rather, that it is **nevertheless** in (or not contrary to) the public interest for people to be free to engage in certain activities which involve a risk of serious injury so long as the point of the activity is not to realise that risk.

Surprisingly perhaps, the legality of such activities is not fed by the presence of either express or implied consent.[249] Horseplay can be relied upon not only where V actually does consent expressly or impliedly but also where D genuinely believes that is the case[250] and the victim understands that the purpose is not hostile.[251] This seems implicit in the case of

---

[244] In practice prosecutions occur most often in amateur sport. When they do occur, sentences on conviction can be surprisingly harsh *Davies* [1991] Crim LR 70 (six months); *Lloyd* (1989) 11 Cr App R 36 (eighteen months); *Chapman* (1989) 11 Cr Ap R 303 (eighteen months).

[245] Ibid.

[246] *Barnes* [2004] EWCA Crim 3246 per Lord Woolf at 511.

[247] See LCCP No. 139 (1995) 165–70.

[248] See *Billingshurst* [1978] Crim LR 553.

[249] For a different view see R. Leng, note 255 below.

[250] *R v A* [2005] All ER (D) 38 (4 July 2005).

[251] *Griffin* (1869) 11 Cox CC 402.

Jones and also in *Aitken.*[252] In the former the defendants had thrown their victim into the air and failed to catch him. In *Aitken* the defendants, as a 'prank', had doused their fellow officer's flying suit with spirit and had set light to it. In neither case was there evidence of consent sufficient to, say, negate the *actus reus* of rape. In effect, the judges in both cases were saying 'you have to put up with a bit of rough and tumble if you are a "lad" ' – an unfortunate qualification of the principle of autonomy, particularly if you are thinking of joining the armed forces. Without such a qualification, however, criminal liability might be too easily sustained by the young and inexperienced. Just how dangerous were the 'bumps' I incurred on my twenty-first birthday? Fortunately I will never know.

(iii) *Sexually transmitted disease*

It is now clear that a person can consent to the risk of contracting a sexually transmitted disease, provided that that consent is informed **and** the disease was not deliberately passed on.[253] Consent, in other words is not a defence to the section 18 offence where the harm caused is a sexually transmitted disease. The Crown Prosecution Service have issued the following policy statement concerning prosecution, which seems to encapsulate the state of substantive law at the present time:

> The informed consent of the complainant (that is, knowledge of the defendant's specific infected status) to take the risk of being infected by engaging in sexual activity with a person who is infectious – in cases where the defendant cannot be shown to have intentionally passed on the infection – is a defence in cases of section 20 grievous bodily harm. This does not necessarily mean that the defendant must have disclosed his or her condition to the complainant. A complainant may be regarded as being 'informed' for the purposes of giving consent where a third party informs the complainant of the defendant's condition, and the complainant then engages in unprotected sexual activity with the defendant. Similarly, a complainant may be regarded as being 'informed' if they become aware of certain circumstances that indicate that the defendant is suffering from a sexually transmitted infection, such as visiting the defendant while he or she is undergoing treatment for the infection in hospital.
>
> Whether the complainant gave his or her informed consent is a matter for the jury.[254]

4 Consent and the Law Commission

The Law Commission has published two consultation papers on the role of consent in offences against the person. In the latest,[255] the general proposal made is that individuals should have the right to consent to any injury falling short of serious disablement.[256] This would include controversial contexts such as sado-masochism[257] as well as those already provided for under the present law. Unorganised fighting should remain unlawful as long as the activity falls clearly outside the context of 'undisciplined, consensual horseplay'.[258] In cases of sports injuries the further proposal made is that liability should be dependent

---

[252] Cf. *Aitken* (1992) 95 Cr App R 304; *Jones* (1986) 83 Cr App R 375.

[253] See *Dica, supra.*

[254] Policy for prosecuting cases involving the intentional or reckless sexual transmission of infection 2009.

[255] R. Leng, 'Consent and Offences against the Person'; Law Commission Consultation Paper No. 134 (1994) Crim LR 480; LCCP No. 139 'Consent in the Criminal Law' (1995).

[256] See generally S. Shute, 'The Second Law Commission Consultation Paper on Consent: Something Old, Something New, Something Borrowed: Three Aspects of the Project' [1996] Crim LR 684; D.C Ormerod and M.J. Gunn, 'The Second Law Commission Consultation Paper on Consent: Consent – A Second Bash' [1996] Crim LR 694.

[257] 10.52.

[258] 14.19.

upon the injury suffered being seriously disabling, the aggressor being aware of the risk of such injury and that the risk taken be an unreasonable one to take in the context of the activity taking place.

Although there is much to commend in this wide-ranging and thoughtful report, a few concerns remain, not least the imprecision of the line drawn between seriously disabling injuries and lesser injuries to which consent is a defence. The former is defined to include injuries which

(a) cause serious distress, and
(b) involve any of the following: loss of a bodily member, permanent bodily injury, permanent functional impairment, serious or permanent disfigurement, severe or prolonged pain, serious impairment of mental health, or prolonged unconsciousness. There are a number of activities, presently lawful, which might fall into this category, amongst which the most obvious are branding and tattooing. Their legality might therefore be called into question.

It is also perhaps arguable that more weight should have been attached to some of the issues of moral principle involved. On the one hand there is the question whether people should not have the right to consent to **any** degree of injury. This is particularly pertinent in view of the urgent need to provide a cogent, morally secure basis for the continued illegality of euthanasia. On the other hand, there is the quite different issue as to whether, as a general principle, a person should have the general right to consent even to the type of harm not covered by the ambit of 'seriously disabling injury'. After all, such harms may be far from trivial. As Hart, amongst others, observes, society is not a suicide club and forms of life which threaten to subvert that practical and ethical message are axiomatically within the purview of the criminal law. It may be restrictive of personal freedom, say, to outlaw cruelty, particularly where sexually motivated, but arguably it is a restriction which is consistent with the flourishing of a tolerant, non-paternalistic and humane society. Is autonomy so sacrosanct that society preserves no right to protect one of its fundamental moral building blocks, namely the social taboo against hurting people?[259]

It makes some moral and political sense, perhaps, to draw the boundaries of the socially tolerable between those activities designed to hurt and those where hurt, as in *Jones*, *Wilson* and *Slingsby*, is the unfortunate by-product of allowing individuals the tolerant society's freedom to explore the boundaries of the socially permissible. Arguably society would be better served by drawing the boundaries of permissible injury more precisely and at varying levels depending upon whether the injury was aimed at for its own sake, e.g. sadomasochism, boxing (low level); was incidental to recreational/lifestyle activity, e.g. contact sports, body alteration, sexual activity (higher level); or was incidental to therapeutic surgery (highest level).

B Necessity

Running parallel with the defence of public interest/consent is that of necessity. The general parameters of the defence have been discussed earlier. Here we will concentrate upon the interface of the defence with that of consent in relation to common assault. Necessity may render many unconsented-to contacts lawful.[260] Thus the person who drags

---

[259] See Fletcher (1978) 770–1; W. Wilson, 'Is Hurting People Wrong?' (1992) JSWFL 388.
[260] See generally Lord Goff in *Re F*. Also in Chapter 10.

another from the path of an oncoming car does no wrong since his action is necessary. As this example shows, necessary action, like consent, does not override autonomy, it is a vindication of it.[261] So surgery, or other medical intervention, is lawful where necessary in the patient's best interests and consent is not forthcoming only because the patient is incapable of giving consent.[262] Indeed the majority of fact scenarios in which necessity can be relied upon can equally be reformulated as cases of implied consent.[263] However, refusal of consent may be overridden if the patient lacks the capacity to consent within the meaning of the Mental Capacity Act. In *Re AA* this resulted in a forced caesarean section on a woman who would have died without it. A claim of necessity will not normally override an informed refusal of consent.[264] Nor will it justify a piece of officious 'do-gooding'.[265]

In cases of young children undergoing medical treatment the consent of the parent substitutes for that of the patient but in the absence or refusal of that consent doctors may nevertheless operate if this would be immediately in the patient's best interests.[266] In the case of adults lacking the capacity to consent, the extent of lawful treatment is qualified by the nature and extent of the patient's incapacity. Where a person's incapacity is only transient, say temporary unconsciousness, a doctor is entitled only to minister to a patient's immediate medical needs. Beyond this she would need to wait until the patient regained capacity. Thus remedial surgery on the temporarily comatose victim of a car accident could not extend to performing a mastectomy if breast cancer was discovered. It also seems that the interests of permanently incompetent patients are constructed differently. With competent patients what is necessary is what is clinically necessary. With incompetent patients what is necessary is apparently much broader.[267]

C Lawful chastisement

Lawful chastisement is a defence in the case of a child punished by a parent or someone *in loco parentis*. In such cases, chastisement is lawful 'provided it does not go too far and is for the purpose of correction and not the gratification of passion or rage'.[268] Where corporal punishment is administered by a teacher, it is unlawful in the case of state educated pupils[269] unless express permission from the parent is forthcoming. No such requirement exists with respect to children attending independent schools, although thresholds of acceptable punishment created by the European Convention on Human Rights are enforced by the European Court.[270] The ECHR has ruled that the common law's notion of reasonable chastisement allows for punishment which constitutes 'inhuman and degrading treatment' and as such a breach of Article 3.[271] While corporal punishment by parents is not *per se* unlawful it was until recently unclear what degree of chastisement was lawful. The Children Act 2004 has now addressed this question. Battery of a child cannot be justified if it causes

---

[261] Cf. however, *R v Bournewood Community and Mental Health NHS Trust* [1998] 3 All ER 289; *Re A (children)* [2000], above.

[262] Lord Brandon of Oakbrook in *Re F*.

[263] See Case 1, Chapter 12.

[264] Cardozo J in *Schloendorff v Society of New York Hospital* (1914) 105 NE 92–3.

[265] *R v B* (MA) [2013] 1 Cr App R 36 CA.

[266] *Re J (a Minor) (wardship: medical treatment)* [1990] 3 All ER 930.

[267] See Lord Goff in *Re F*.

[268] *Jones* (1986) at 110; see *Hopley* (1860) 2 F & F 202.

[269] Education (No. 2) Act 1986, s. 47.

[270] Art. 3.

[271] *A v UK* [1998] Crim LR 892. The application concerned a boy who had been beaten by his stepfather with a garden cane. The English court had found that this was reasonable chastisement.

actually bodily harm, nor cruelty within the meaning of section 1 Children and Young Persons Act 1933. Neither is it justified if it is unreasonable, for example for a reason which does not require correction, such as for being late home from school because the school bus was late.[272]

11.5 REFORM OF OFFENCES AGAINST THE PERSON

The majority of commentators consider that the present law on personal violence is in need of reform. Much of the responsibility is thought to lie with the archaic and imprecise language used in the Offences Against the Person Act. The general opinion is that the Act fails to differentiate between serious offences and offences less serious in the system – a failure of both rationality and fairness. Judicial uncertainty as to whether a judge's obligation is to load the provisions with the systemic rationality they fail to embody or to attempt a purely 'neutral' interpretation has, no doubt, resulted in some very haphazard decision making. The former approach is the notable recent trend.

Under a rational system of offences the criteria of differentiation would ideally be derived from a cogent and consistently applied theory of punishment. Offences would be so structured as to ensure that the conduct-choices of the accused make it politically appropriate and fair for him to bear responsibility for the relevant harm. This has been the aim of the various reform bodies which have made recommendations in this area.[273] Most recently the Law Commission in 'Legislating the Criminal Code: Offences against the Person and General Principles'[274] took what might be termed a 'broad brush' approach to ensuring such rational differentiation. The emphasis is on conceptual clarity, which is certainly achieved, rather than focus and definition, which are not. Sections 18, 20 and 47 are replaced by, respectively, sections 2, 3 and 4. The provisions are as follows: Section 2(1): a person is guilty of an offence if he intentionally causes serious injury to another. Section 3(1): a person is guilty of an offence if he recklessly causes serious injury to another. Section 4: a person is guilty of an offence if he intentionally or recklessly causes injury to another. Maximum sentence for s. 2 is life imprisonment; for ss. 3 and 4, five years and three years respectively if tried on indictment, six months and/or a fine if tried summarily. In 1998 a draft Bill was produced for comments which incorporated these proposals almost unaltered.[275]

On the face of it such proposals look attractive. Gone are the confusing distinctions between 'inflicting' and 'causing', and between 'wounding' and 'grievous bodily harm'. Either an injury is serious or it is not. If it is, it is charged under sections 2 or 3. If it is not, it is charged under section 4. Also removed is the puzzling sentencing parity for offences ostensibly of different seriousness, and the possibility of responsibility for harms in the absence of a matching mental element.

The proposals are nevertheless not supported here. It has been argued, in my view rightly, that they are underscored by the false assumption that the object of any rational code of offences against the person is to use clear terminology (to provide fair warning) and to differentiate on grounds of seriousness of harm and culpability alone (to provide fair labelling).[276]

---

[272] Children Act (CA) 2004 section 58; cf. *R v H* [2002] Cr App Rep 59.
[273] CLRC 14th Report *Offences Against the Person* Cmnd 7844 (1980); Law Commission No. 107 *A Criminal Code for England and Wales* (1989).
[274] (1993) Cm 2370 adopting earlier proposals.
[275] Home Office, *Violence: Reforming the Offences Against the Person Act 1861* (1998).
[276] J. Gardner, 'Rationality and the Rule of Law in Offences Against the Person' (1994) 53 Camb LJ 502.

On the question of terminology, the orthodox but controversial distinction is made between the culpability of causing serious injury intentionally (s. 2) and causing it recklessly (s. 3). Intended consequences include those which it is known will occur in the ordinary course of events if 'the accused were to succeed in his purpose of causing some other result'. Recklessness requires a person knowingly to take an unreasonable risk (of injury).[277] As was suggested earlier, however, a person who is reckless as to a consequence may not have 'chosen' that consequence in quite the same way as one who intends that consequence, but his susceptibility to blame may be equal or higher. A person who knowingly risks infecting her partner with HIV arguably discloses a greater indifference to the value of life than one who, in the passion of discovering a lover's infidelity, plunges a dagger through the infidel's shoulder-blade.[278] The cogency of a provision is often seen in its treatment of the non-typical rather than the focal case. Strangely the section 4 offence may be committed by either intention or recklessness. Yet more strange is the fact that the justification offered for this difference is not that the two states of mind may evince equivalent blameworthiness but that it is often difficult to tell them apart.[279] What is sauce for the goose . . .[280]

As far as differentiation is concerned, what exactly makes a harm more serious? Its nature? Its consequence? Its effect on the victim's lifestyle? The way it is administered? The context in which it is administered? No definitional distinction between serious injury and non-serious injury is made. Prosecutorial discretion would still, then, be required and systemic rationality would once again be dependent upon something outside doctrine itself in the form of extra-legal prosecutorial guidelines on charging. Obviously this would be no more conducive to fairness in punishment than the present arrangement. On the contrary, it might be thought more rational to be more focused in the wrong which we attribute to various 'criminal deeds'. If we examine the pages of a newspaper, harms are often defined by reference to moral precepts undisclosed by traditional offence definitions, let alone the suggested new ones. Offenders may be called 'baby batterers', 'wife-beaters', 'cannibals', 'torturers', 'bullies', or 'sex fiends'. If only part of the function of punishment is to allow appropriate moral condemnation, education or prevention, it might be thought more rational to have separate offence-labels for, say, baby-beating and fighting at football matches. Torturers and poisoners already have their own offence. Would it not be better to differentiate offences in this way rather than 'amorally' according to the 'amount' of injury the victim suffers?

Of course, a rational system of offences against the person must be able to conjure up a precise and consensually validated harm. Baby/wife-beating or fighting at football matches arguably would not do so. For every person who saw such labels as constituting/aggravating factors there would likely be another who saw them as exculpating/mitigating. This would serve to undermine both rationality and fairness. On the whole, though, these contextual considerations are more directly catered for in the 1861 Act[281] than in the Law Commission's proposals for reform. What matters, surely, is that the relevant words (e.g. wounding/grievous bodily harm) excite the right moral response in the audience to whom

---

[277] Clause 1(a); clause 1(b)(ii).
[278] Yet the maximum sentence for the former is five years as opposed to life imprisonment for the latter. The Government intends to exclude the reckless transmission of disease from the ambit of any future criminal liability under the reformed Offences Against the Person Act.
[279] Para. 152.
[280] Is surely sauce for ss. 2 and 3 also.
[281] And of course also the Theft Acts 1968–78.

they are addressed,[282] which they do.[283] Can we say the same about causing 'serious injury'? Again some injuries, particularly blinding, castration, and amputation, may be considered more serious than other equally severe injuries since they not only damage the victim, but destroy part of his social and economic identity and function. There is a strong argument that the commission of such injuries, along with disfigurement, should form part of the identity of offences of violence.[284] A disfiguring or disabling injury, since it changes the way society views the victim, or he views himself, is more grave than other equally serious injuries which have no significant lasting effect.[285] A rational penal code, assuming punishment expresses society's moral response to various forms of bodily violation, should take this into account, focusing on deeds rather than 'chosen' abstract harms.

Further reading

Bell, B., Harrison, K., '*R* v *Savage*, *DPP* v *Parmenter* and the Law of Assault' (1993) 56 Modern Law Review 83.

Beyleveld, D. and Brownsword, R., *Consent in the Law*, London: Hart (2007).

British Journal of Criminology (special issue), 'Moral Panics – 36 Years on' (2009) 49(1) Brit J Criminol.

Elliot, C., and de Than, C., 'A case for Rational Reconstruction of Consent in Criminal Law' (2007) 70 MLR 225.

Gardner, J., 'Rationality and the Rule of Law in Offences against the Person' (1994) 53 Cambridge Law Journal 502.

Horder, J., 'Rethinking Non-fatal Offences against the Person' (1994) 14 Oxford Journal of Legal Studies 335.

Livings, 'A Different Ball Game?' (2007) 71 J Crim L 534.

Roberts, P., 'The Philosophical Foundations of Consent in the Criminal Law' (1997) 17 Oxford Journal of Legal Studies 389.

Weait, M., 'Criminal Law and the Sexual Transmission of HIV: *R* v *Dica*' (2005) 68 Modern Law Review 121.

Weait, M., 'Knowledge, Autonomy and Consent: *R* v *Konzani*' [2005] Criminal Law Review 763.

Wilson, W., 'Is Hurting People Wrong?' (1992) JSWFL 388.

---

[282] An example of such an offence is contained in the Criminal Justice Act 1988, s. 134 which makes torture by officials or acquiesced in by officials an offence punishable with life imprisonment.

[283] For a stimulating discussion of this and related issues see J. Gardner, ibid.

[284] J. Horder, 'Rethinking Non-fatal Offences Against the Person' (1994) 14 OJLS 335; cf. A. von Hirsch and N. Jareborg, 'Gauging Criminal Harm: a Living-Standard Analysis' (1991) 11 OJLS 1.

[285] This seems to be in line with the Law Commission's most recent thinking.

12 Sexual offences

Overview[1]

There are a number of sexual offences of varying degrees of seriousness, ranging from rape to sexual assault to indecent exposure. Some offences are primarily concerned to protect the interests of the victim. Rape and sexual assault, like common assault, exist as crimes only by virtue of the absence of the victim's consent. Others are primarily concerned to enforce social morality and/or prevent offence.[2] Thus certain familial sexual offences, such as incest, are constituted irrespective of consent.[3] The field of sexual offences is structured, unusually, according to the status of the victim and defendant. Sexual assaults on children and those with a mental disorder are treated differently from sexual assaults on competent adults. Defendants under the age of 18 are typically punishable less severely than adults. Only a man can be guilty of rape, albeit the victim can be either male or female.[4]

12.1 THE SOCIAL CONTEXT

The Crime Survey data 2009–12 estimates that, on average, 2.5 per cent of females and 0.4 per cent of males are a victim of a sexual offence (including attempts) in any 12-month period. This represents, on average per year, around 473,000 adults being victims of sexual offences. Within this figure is a total of 97,000 rapes of which 12,000 are male victims. In 2012–13 17,061 rapes were recorded by the police. This gives a recording rate somewhere between 16.5 per cent and 26.1 per cent using the upper and lower boundaries. These figures should not be confused with reporting rates, since not all reports are recorded as a crime. Females who had reported being victims of the most serious sexual offences in the last year were asked, regarding the most recent incident, whether or not they had reported the incident to the police. Only 15 per cent of victims of such offences said that they had done so. Frequently cited reasons for not reporting the crime were that it was 'embarrassing', they 'didn't think the police could do much to help', that the incident was 'too trivial or not worth reporting', or that they saw it as a 'private/family matter and not police business'. Around 90 per cent of victims of the most serious sexual offences in the previous year knew the perpetrator, compared with less than half for other sexual offences.

This latter statistic may be comforting to those minded to walk home alone after a party. But it will be disturbing to those who cherish the idea that the social ties which bind us offer protection from, rather than exposure to, the menace and trauma of rape and other

---

[1] See generally P. Rook and R. Ward, *Rook and Ward on Sexual Offences: Law and Practice* (4th edn), London: Sweet & Maxwell (2010).

[2] See for example S. Ost, 'Criminalising Fabricated Images of Child Pornography: a Matter of Harm or Morality?' (2010) 30(2) Legal Studies 230.

[3] Section 64 Sexual Offences Act 2003.

[4] Section 1 Sexual Offences Act 2003; see H. Allen, 'One Law for All Reasonable Persons?' (1988) 16 International Journal of the Sociology of Law 419.

serious sexual assaults.[5] It is perhaps unsurprising, then, with sex so much under the conceptual control of men that sexual offences, traumatising as they are, are so under-reported and the sexual autonomy of women so weakly protected.[6] One good consequence of the passing of the 1994 Act, which provides that males may also be victims, is that universalising the act of rape has served to weaken this conceptual control.[7]

12.2 THE HISTORICAL CONTEXT

The form of sexual offences was until recently heavily gendered. At its core was the crime of rape, a crime which could only be committed by a man against a woman and appeared to be born primarily not of respect of the sexual autonomy of the victim so much as an historically constructed quasi-property relationship between women and their fathers and husbands. The rape of a woman, that is, involved the violation of others, if not of their bodies, then of their social identity.[8] As a result rape was traditionally defined in a sex-specific way to take account of these 'added harms' to the system of social relationships binding men and women.[9] With the gradual dissolution of these features of our social structure, the call developed to rid the law of sexual offences of its gendered nature. In 1994 a massive symbolic step was made in this direction by the Criminal Justice and Public Order Act. Henceforth rape may be committed on a man or a woman. Whether this legal change will change the **social character** of rape is open to question.[10] Rape, one suspects, will still be an offence largely conceived of and committed by men against women.[11] For some this was reason enough to retain its sex-specific character. As such it would remain a formal visible symbol of the violence done to women by men and the pernicious assumptions which underlie it – the predatory, possessive male and the passive female victim.[12] The continued requirement in rape of a penetrating penis specifically rather than an undesired penetration *per se* supports such analysis.[13] However, the Act did formally close one door linking us to our sexually divided history. Rape now labels a particular form of bodily violation rather than a particular source of social and economic affront. This and other attempts to render the law relating to sexual offences for the modern age were carried over into the Sexual Offences Act 2003. This Act aimed to reorder and restructure sexual offences, whose rationale and structure reflected their piecemeal development through the common law, the Sexual Offences Act 1956 and the later amendments thereto. The Home Office's earlier consultation document heralded this basic philosophy which was to 'provide coherent and clear sex offences which protect individuals, especially the more vulnerable, from abuse and

---

[5] M. Anderson, 'Diminishing the Legal Impact of Negative Social Attitudes Toward Acquaintance Rape Victims' (2010) 13(4) New Criminal LR 644; E. Stanko, 'Hidden Violence against Women' in M. Maguire and J. Pointing (eds), *Victims of Crime: a New Deal?* Milton Keynes: Open University Press (1998).

[6] W. Larcombe, 'Falling Rape Conviction Rates: (Some) Feminist Aims and Measures for Rape Law' (2011) 19 Feminist Legal Studies 27.

[7] P.N.S. Rumney and R.A. Fenton, 'Judicial Training and Rape' (2011) 75(6) J Crim L 473.

[8] J. Herring, 'No More Having and Holding: The Abolition of the Marital Rape Exemption' in S. Gilmore, J. Herring and S. Gilmore (eds), *Landmark Cases in Family Law*, Oxford: Hart Publishing (2011).

[9] C. Smart, 'The Woman of Legal Discourse' (1992) 1 Social and Legal Studies 29; and see N. Lacey, C. Wells and O. Quick, *Reconstructing Criminal Law*, London: Weidenfeld & Nicolson (2003) ch. 5.

[10] *R v A* [2012] EWCA Crim 1646.

[11] There were around 12,000 reported cases of rape and sexual assault by penetration of males for the period 2011–12 compared with 85,000 for women (ONS 2013).

[12] Cf. N. Naffine, *Law and the Sexes*, Sydney: Allen and Unwin (1990); N. Lacey, *Unspeakable Subjects*, Oxford: Hart Publishing (1998) ch. 4.

[13] See N. Lacey, 'Beset by Boundaries: the Home Office Review of Sex Offences' [2001] Crim LR 3; Home Office Consultation Paper, *Setting the Boundaries: Reforming the Law on Sex Offences*, London: Home Office (2000).

exploitation, enable abusers to be appropriately punished, and be fair and nondiscriminatory in accordance with the ECHR and the Human Rights Act 1998'.[14] Part 1 of the Sexual Offences Act enacts the newly constituted structure of sexual offences which includes, rape, assault by penetration, sexual assault and causing a person to engage in sexual activity without consent. It deals with the issue of consent and, in particular, seeks to simplify the process of establishing absence of consent by the use of presumptions. The Act also covers child sex offences including those taking place within a family context. Part 2 is largely a re-enactment of the Sex Offenders Act 1997 containing measures for the protection of the public.

12.3 RAPE: THE ELEMENTS

Overview

A number of terms tend to be used in relation to rape that appear to differentiate between different types of rape. For example, reference may be made to marital rape, acquaintance rape, date rape or stranger rape. None of these phrases have any legal meaning as it is not relevant what relationship, if any, a defendant has or had to a complainant. Nor is it relevant if the act complained of occurred within a relationship. Any non-consenual penetration of a person's mouth, vagina, or anus by a man's penis constitutes the wrong in rape. Penetration is 'a continuing act from entry to withdrawal';[15] the *actus reus* is therefore satisfied by a failure to withdraw following removal of consent. It is not necessary to show that force was used or threatened, only that consent was absent.[16] Consent means that the person 'agrees by choice, and has the freedom and capacity to make that choice'.[17] Lack of consent may be established by the use of presumptions set out in the Act. Certain presumptions are conclusive of the absence of consent. Some are simply (strong) evidence of this absence.[18] The fault element is that D had no reasonable grounds for believing V to be consenting. Again, certain presumptions are conclusive of the absence of reasonable grounds. Some are simply (strong) evidence of the absence of reasonable grounds.

By s. 1 Sexual Offences Act (SOA) 2003,

A person (A) commits an offence if –

He intentionally penetrates the vagina, anus or mouth of another person (B) with his penis,
B does not consent to the penetration, and
A does not reasonably believe that B consents.

Whether a belief is reasonable is to be determined having regard to all the circumstances, including any steps A has taken to ascertain whether B consents.

---

[14] Ibid. These formed the basis for the Government's recommendation in the White Paper *Protecting the Public: Strengthening Protection against Sex Offenders and Reforming the Law on Sexual Offences* (Cm 5668) in November 2002; C. McGlynn, 'Rape, Defendant Anonymity and Human Rights: Adopting a "Wider Rerspective"' [2011] Crim LR 199.

[15] Sexual Offences Act 2003, s. 79(2).

[16] *R v Malone* [1998] 2 Cr App R 447; [1998] Crim LR 834.

[17] Section 74. Whether consent is present or not is still a matter for the jury to decide, according to the definition provided in the Act. A recent case has highlighted the need for further guidance from the judge in difficult cases (here involving voluntary intoxication): *R v Bree* [2007] EWCA Crim 804.

[18] Sections 76 and 75.

Sections 75 and 76 apply to an offence under this section.

A person guilty of an offence under this section is liable, on conviction on indictment, to imprisonment for life.

There are a number of changes made to the law by these provisions. First of all, the Act abandons the term 'sexual intercourse' and introduces instead the notion of 'penetration' by the defendant's penis, hence preserving the exclusively masculine status of the defendant. Second, the *actus reus* of rape is now defined as the penetration by the defendant's penis of the complainant's vagina, anus or mouth. The addition of forcible oral sex as rape is a significant change, made to recognise the fact that such a practice can be as devastating on the victim as 'traditional' rape, and reflecting the reality of many penetrative sexual attacks whether on males or females. Third, the act introduces a definition of consent and a number of presumptions to help the prosecution prove the complainant's absence of consent and the defendant's criminal fault. The Act introduces a new *fault element* for the offence of rape, based on the lack of reasonable belief in consent which renders the fault requirement for rape akin to negligence.

A *Actus reus*

The *actus reus* elements of rape are: (i) penile penetration; (ii) of the vagina, mouth or anus;[19] and (iii) an absence of consent. The rules relating to consent are also applicable to sections 4–7 and so will be dealt with at the conclusion of these offences.

1 (Penile) penetration
The SOA 2003 shows a willingness to use, as far as possible, descriptive and easy to understand terms and definitions in order to make the law clearer. This can be seen in the use of the word 'penetration' instead of 'sexual intercourse' when defining the *actus reus* of rape. Penetration has to be with the defendant's penis.

(a) *Penetration by the penis*
Although the act is gender neutral throughout most of its provisions, the definition of rape makes clear that the offence can still only be committed by a man. A woman who pretends to be a man in order to have sexual intimacy, including penetrative sex, with a woman is therefore not guilty of this offence.[20] What exactly is it about the penetrating penis which constitutes the wrong in rape?[21] Is it the trauma constituted by the penetration, in which case it should not matter what the penetrating object is, or the gender of the penetrator, or is it the knowledge that rape as a legal concept (as constituted by the penetrating penis) has been committed and thus that one has been constituted as a victim of rape? The Act assumes the latter and so it incorporates a different offence of similar severity to cover cases of penetration by an object or another part of the defendant's body. This covers cases where the defendant could be a woman.[22] From another point of view it has been questioned why the Act's

---

[19] In cases where it is unclear whether penetration was of the vagina or of the anus, it is permissible to allege penetration of 'the vagina or the anus'. The jury will be entitled to convict if they are sure that there was non-consensual penetration of one or the other by the defendant with his penis. *R v K* [2008] EWCA Crim 1923 CA.

[20] This is more common than it might be thought. See http://whittlings.blogspot.co.uk/2013/04/chris-wilson-convicted-because-of-his.html.

[21] See J. Gardner and S. Shute, 'The Wrongness of Rape' in J. Horder (ed.), *Oxford Essays in Jurisprudence* (2000), 193; V. Tadros, 'The Distinctiveness of Domestic Abuse' in R.A. Duff and S. Green (eds), *Defining Crimes: Essays on the Special Part of the Criminal Law* (2005) 119 at 136.

[22] Sexual Offences Act 2003, s. 2.

'continued equation of rape with penile penetration [which] defines the defendant's point of view as the legal point of view'.[23] If rape is committed irrespective of the orifice why should it not be committed irrespective of the instrument or the gender of the penetrator? The assault on the victim's autonomy is hardly diminished by such a slight distinction.

(b) Of the complainant's vagina, anus or mouth
Penetration has to refer to any of these three areas.

(i)   *Vagina*: References to any parts of the body include 'references to a part surgically constructed (in particular, through gender reassignment surgery).'[24] This confirms previous jurisprudence that '*per vaginam*' covered the case of a transsexual whose vagina was surgically created.[25] In a recent Crown Court decision it has been held that it does, bringing transsexuals within the protection and coverage of the Act.

(ii) *Anus*: Anal rape was first recognised in 1994 by the Criminal Justice and Public Order Act, which finally established that both men and women could be victims of rape.

(iii) *Mouth*: The latter is an addition made by the 2003 Act, and recognises forcible oral sex as rape, the same offence as non-consensual 'sexual intercourse'. The recognition of anal rape and the obviously penetrative nature of the act made it a logical – and indeed, called for[26] – extension of the *actus reus* of rape.

The Home Office report recommended this on the basis that 'forced oral sex is as horrible, as demeaning and as traumatising as other forms of forced penile penetration'.[27] There was debate inside and outside of Parliament and objections were raised. In particular, it was argued that including forcible oral sex as rape might devalue the offence or make juries reluctant to render a guilty verdict, especially as such cases could easily be included under the new offence of assault by penetration.[28] The Home Affairs Committee rejected such claims and included penile penetration of the mouth as rape in the new Act. The fact that the Court of Appeal upheld a sentence of 10 years' imprisonment for indecent assault by means of forced oral sex[29] under the old law indicates that courts do indeed consider oral rape as a very serious crime.[30]

(c) Rape constituted by failure to withdraw
Section 78 states that penetration is 'a continuing act from entry to withdrawal', which means that if a person consents to penetration but then changes his or her mind in the course of the act, then the defendant will be guilty of rape if he fails to withdraw. This definition follows previous case law on the subject.[31] This decision is not entirely uncontroversial. One commentator objected, 'How does one "continue to penetrate"? "Penetration . . . occurs on the instant and is then finished"'.[32] To this rather formal objection one may supply the

[23] N. Lacey, 'Beset by Boundaries: the Home Office Review of Sex Offences' Crim LR [2001] 3–14, 13.
[24] Section 78(3).
[25] *Matthews*, October 1996 cited by M. Hicks and G. Branston, 'Transsexual Rape – A Loophole Closed?' [1997] Crim LR 565.
[26] J. Temkin, *Rape and the Legal Process*, London: Sweet & Maxwell (1987).
[27] Home Office, *Setting the Boundaries: Reforming the Law on Sex Offences*, vol. 1 (chair Betty Moxon), London: Home Office (2000) para. 2.8.5.
[28] Section 2 SOA 2003.
[29] *Ragusa* [1993] 14 Cr App R (S) 118.
[30] Cf. *R v Ismail (Abokar Ahmed)* [2005] EWCA Crim 397 at 11.
[31] *R v Cooper and Schaub* [1994] Crim LR 531, following the earlier Privy Council decision of *Kaitamaki* [1985] AC 147 PC.
[32] Commentary of Sir John Smith in *Cooper and Schaub* at 532.

equally formal rejoinder: just as a tunnelling 'mole' continues to penetrate every time new forward force is applied, so a man can continue to penetrate by not withdrawing. The substantive issue at the heart of this formal objection is more interesting, namely **whether rape is the right offence to charge** where there is a failure to respond to a withdrawal of consent. Is rape the awful crime it is because of the undesired and traumatic initial penetration by the man of the victim's body, in which case the loss of autonomy could perhaps be more adequately captured by the offence of sexual assault? Or is it because of the more general loss of autonomy involved in non-consensual intercourse?[33] Whatever the answer to this question, the answer given must be expected to be filtered through the gendered ideas and expectations of the answer-giver, whether male or female. It is not surprising, perhaps, that the above objection was formulated by a male. Moreover, it is a short and undesirable step between espousing this analysis and accepting that rape is never the appropriate crime to charge where it occurs within the context of a stable sexual relationship.

B *Mens rea*

The penetration must be intentional and the defendant must not reasonably believe the victim to be consenting. The latter element, which is common to other sexual offences, will be covered later. The former element is not entirely theoretical as it is possible that in the course of, say, advanced foreplay a man may, without necessarily intending to, penetrate the other person with his penis.

12.4 ASSAULT BY PENETRATION

The Sexual Offences Act 2003, s. 2 creates a new offence of assault by penetration. It reflects the view underpinning the newly defined offence of rape that the penetration by the victim by the male penis constitutes the wrong which rape involves. As has been suggested above it is questionable whether the complainant's view that he/she is raped whatever instrument effects the penetration should be overridden in this way.

The offence is defined as follows:

(1) A person (A) commits an offence if –
    (a) he intentionally penetrates the vagina or anus of another person (B) with a part of his body or anything else,
    (b) the penetration is sexual,
    (c) B does not consent to the penetration, and
    (d) A does not reasonably believe that B consents.
(2) Whether a belief is reasonable is to be determined having regard to all the circumstances, including any steps A has taken to ascertain whether B consents.

A *Actus reus*

The *actus reus* elements of this offence are: (i) penetration of the victim's vagina or anus; (ii) with a part of D's body or anything else; (iii) the penetration must be sexual; (iv) absence of consent.

---

[33] See generally M. Madden Dempsey and J. Herring, 'Why Sexual Penetration Requires Justification' (2007) 27 OJLS 467; S. Schulhofer, *Unwanted Sex: The Culture of Intimidation and the Failure of Law* (1998); S. Shute and J. Gardner, 'The Wrongness in Rape' in J. Horder (ed.), *Oxford Essays in Jurisprudence* (2000) at 205.

1 Penetration by a part of D's body or anything else

The wrong in this offence is similar to that of rape in that it involves a penetrative sexual assault. Like rape it is committed if the organ penetrated is vagina or anus. So a person commits assault by penetration where he/she penetrates the victim's vagina or anus with a finger, dildo, broomstick, carrot or a bottle. However, reflecting the seriousness of the offence label, it is not committed upon penetration of the mouth. Such a penetration, if of a sexual nature, as say penetrating the mouth with a finger, would constitute the less serious offence of sexual assault. It differs from rape in that the conduct element is satisfied by penetration by any part of the body, other than the penis, or any other object.[34] As the essential wrong involved is sexual penetration other than by a penis, it is an offence which, like most other offences in the 2003 Act, may be committed by a man or a woman. A woman who forcibly penetrates a man or woman with a strap-on dildo commits this offence and not rape, therefore, leaving the issue of labelling propriety at large.

2 A 'sexual' penetration

To constitute the offence the penetration must be sexual. This will be examined in the next section but, as an initial illustration, a proper medical examination for example will render a penetration non-sexual.

B *Mens rea*

The touching must be intentional. A reckless penetration, if one could imagine such a possibility, is not sufficient.

12.5 SEXUAL ASSAULT

The Sexual Offences Act 2003, s. 3 creates the offence of sexual assault which is defined as follows:

    (1) A person (A) commits an offence if –
        (a) he intentionally touches another person (B),
        (b) the touching is sexual,
        (c) B does not consent to the touching, and
        (d) A does not reasonably believe that B consents.

A *Actus reus*

1 The touching of another person

Penetrative sexual acts can be charged as sexual assaults as well as sexual penetration. Where the defendant performs a non-penetrative sexual assault then section 3 comes into operation. Unlike the offence it replaced, indecent assault, a touching is necessary. Causing V to apprehend a sexual contact is not sexual assault although it will be common assault, as has been explained. By section 79(8) the touching may be 'with any part of the defendant's body', with 'anything else', and 'through anything'. So a person who presses his/her body, or brief case, against that of another person in a tube train for sexual motives may commit the offence depending upon the jury's assessment of whether the touching was

---

[34] Section 2(1).

'sexual'.[35] In *R v H* it was made clear that the touching of the victim's clothing, here her tracksuit bottoms, constituted a touching for the purpose of section 3 irrespective of whether pressure was imparted to the body. So long as the touching was sexual and was not consented to, this was a sexual assault.

2 The touching is sexual

Section 78 is applicable to sections 2, 3, and 4. It requires careful consideration. For the purposes of all three sections a touching/penetration/causing to engage in an activity is sexual if a reasonable person would consider that –

(a) whatever its circumstances or any person's purpose in relation to it, it is because of its nature sexual, or

(b) because of its nature it may be sexual and because of its circumstances or the purpose of any person in relation to it (or both) it is sexual.

Subsection 1(a) tells the jurors that they can conclude that a penetration/touching, etc., is 'sexual' if a reasonable person would believe that the *nature* of the act is sexual. A touching may be sexual, in other words, although the defendant's purpose and the context in which the touching takes place renders the touching entirely innocent. So touching a person's breast, penis or vagina is presumably **of its nature** 'sexual'.[36] Liability will then depend upon whether the touching is consented to. Obvious exceptions to this are touchings/ penetration of breast, penis or vagina occurring in the course of a properly conducted examination undertaken by a doctor for clinical purposes. An enduring problem has been whether it is possible to define 'sexual', or under the old law 'indecent' contact, without reference to the defendant's motive. Could, for example, a legitimate medical examination become a sexual assault because, as in *Bolduc v Bird*, a hidden sexual motive was involved? This was the question raised in *Kumar*.[37] A GP conducted a clinically necessary breast examination for a woman who had detected a lump on her breast. On the facts, the examination was clearly of an inappropriate nature and duration. On that basis the trial judge directed the jury that they could convict if they were convinced this was prompted by a sexual motive. The doctor's appeal was dismissed. The Court of Appeal made the following statement of principle governing clinical examinations of this nature. If:

(1) K's sole intention in conducting the examination was to gain sexual gratification, he was guilty.

(2) K's sole intention in conducting was to gain clinical information, he was not guilty.

(3) K had a dual intention, using, from the outset, a legitimate examination as cover for obtaining sexual gratification, he was guilty.

(4) K had in the course of a legitimate examination gained sexual gratification, he was not guilty.

More broadly, subsection (b) refers to touchings which may (or which may not) be sexual because of their nature. In such a case, whether the touching is sexual depends upon the jury's assessment of whether a reasonable person might conclude that the penetration is sexual in light of the surrounding circumstances and/or the defendant's purpose. Kissing or stroking would presumably fall within subsection (b). It is not of its nature sexual but it may be, depending upon the circumstances and purpose.[38] In *R v H* the Court of Appeal held that it was right to put the question of whether touching the girl's tracksuit bottoms

---

[35] This will presumably depend upon whether the contact was unavoidable because the train was full in which case the act will be overtly innocent rather than contingently sexual. See below.

[36] 'Can Touching Always Be Sexual When There Is No Sexual Intent?' (2008) 73 Journal of Criminal Law 251.

[37] [2006] EWCA 1946.

[38] *R v Price* [2003] EWCA Crim 2405.

might be 'sexual' to the jury, and upheld the conviction. The jury should be asked two questions: (1) Did they consider that because of its nature the touching could be sexual? If no, the defendant is not guilty. (2) If yes, they should ask themselves whether in view of the circumstances and/or the purpose of the person in relation to the touching, or both, the touching was in fact sexual. If so, he is guilty; if not, not guilty. Presumably the jury concluded that the fact that the touching was preceded by the request 'Fancy a shag?' lent the touching the necessary sexual element.

In the pre-Act case of *Court*, the Court of Appeal had similarly concluded that where a shop assistant spanked a young girl on the buttocks while in the shop it was a matter for the jury to decide whether reasonable people might think the act was capable of being 'indecent'. Assuming the answer to that question was in the affirmative, guilt would then depend upon whether the jury believed that the context or purpose rendered that act indecent in fact. It did so, evidence having been adduced that the defendant admitted to being a buttock fetishist.

As *R v H* affirms, section 78 reproduces the previous law in that it excludes from the ambit of the offence acts which are clearly not sexual by nature. Objectively innocent acts, for example shaking hands, or performing a rescue on a drowning swimmer, cannot be brought within subsection (b) by the surrounding circumstances or the defendant's purpose. This reflects the basic principle of criminal law that criminal liability requires both wrongdoing and a guilty mind. A person should not be subject to liability for his thoughts alone. An illustration is the pre-Act case of *George*. George, a shoe fitter, obtained sexual pleasure from taking shoes off women's feet. This was held not to be an indecent assault because from the point of view of an objective observer the act was not capable of being judged indecent. In theory, *George* would be decided the same way today. However, this is not certain since whether an act is capable of being sexual is not a matter of law. It is for the jury to decide whether the reasonable person might consider its 'nature' maybe sexual. This indeterminacy is unsatisfactory given that different juries may be expected to reach different conclusions on the same or similar facts, taking into account such things as context – did the activity take place in private? – age, sex and appearance of the participants, relationship between the parties, overt reason for the removal – was the defendant an assistant in a shoe shop? – and so on.

B Mens rea

The touching must be intentional. A reckless touching, which was sufficient for indecent assault, is not sufficient.

12.6 CAUSING A PERSON TO ENGAGE IN SEXUAL ACTIVITY WITHOUT CONSENT

Section 4 creates the offence of causing a person to engage in a sexual activity without consent. The offence is defined as follows:

> (1) A person (A) commits an offence if –
>   (a) he intentionally causes another person (B) to engage in an activity,
>   (b) the activity is sexual,
>   (c) B does not consent to engaging in the activity, and
>   (d) A does not reasonably believe that B consents.
> (2) Whether a belief is reasonable is to be determined having regard to all the circumstances, including any steps A has taken to ascertain whether B consents.

This offence shares certain core elements with the offences already examined. The subject matter of the prohibition includes sexual activity, including penetrative sex,[39] that the victim did not consent to the sexual activity and the defendant did not reasonably believe that the victim consented. These questions of consent will be examined at the end of this section.

The offence of 'causing a person to engage in sexual activity without consent' is aimed at, but not exhausted by, those who force others to do sexual acts against their will. This may involve two parties, offender and victim, as where A forces V to masturbate in front of him or her, to touch him or her sexually, or engage in sexual activity with an animal. It may also involve three parties, as where A forces V1 to engage in intercourse or other sexual activity with V2, or where A procures B, a non-victim, to engage in sexual activity with V. While a section 4 offence may involve multiple parties, the offence may also occur without the defendant taking part in the sexual activity, as where A forces B to undress in front of her and masturbate. As the latter example illustrates, this offence provides a vehicle for prosecuting a woman who forces a man to engage in sexual activity or to have sex with her.

A potential difficulty with the offence is the use of the word 'causing'. We saw in Chapter 5 that A does not **cause** B to do X simply by encouraging, or providing the where-withal for, X's commission, as where A supplies B with drugs or procures B to kill C.[40] The voluntary act of B breaks the chain of causation. Do the same rules apply here? When does A 'cause' V to engage in sexual activity?

> **Case 1**
> Adam tells Eve, his student, that he will not pass her essay unless she strips in front of him. She does so.

Has Adam 'caused' Eve to engage in sexual activity? For the purposes of the general law of causation it appears not but, significantly, it seems the word may carry a different meaning for the purpose of section 4. In *Devonald* D, a man posing as a young woman, duped V into masturbating in front of a webcam in order to post the resulting film on the internet, thus humiliating V. The prosecution fought the case and won on the basis that V's consent was vitiated by the deception. However, it was accepted by both parties that subject to this one issue, the *actus reus* was made out.[41] In other words it was assumed by all parties that D had 'caused' V to masturbate. Had he? If I buy an ice cream and give it to you and you eat it have I 'caused' you to eat it?

The offence is only committed where the causing is intentional. If in Case 1 Adam had merely told Eve that he would not pass the essay unless 'she was nice to him' and she did this in supposed satisfaction of his desire, the offence would not be made out in the absence of proof that this, or something similar, was indeed the consequence intended.

---

[39] Which carries a correspondingly higher maximum sentence: life, as opposed to ten years on indictment or six months if tried summarily.

[40] See *Kennedy (No. 2)* (2008) UKHL 38.

[41] [2008] EWCA Crim 527. A. Rogers, 'Sexual Offences: Consent: See "Purpose" of Defendant' (2008) 72 Journal of Criminal Law 280.

A Summary

Offence	Relevant act
An offence under section 1 (rape)	The defendant intentionally penetrating, with his penis, the vagina, anus or mouth of another person ('the complainant')
An offence under section 2 (assault by penetration)	The defendant intentionally penetrating, with a part of his body or anything else, the vagina or anus of another person ('the complainant'), where the penetration is sexual
An offence under section 3 (sexual assault)	The defendant intentionally touching another person ('the complainant'), where the touching is sexual
An offence under section 4 (causing a person to engage in sexual activity without consent)	The defendant intentionally causing another person ('the complainant') to engage in an activity, where the activity is sexual

A summary of the basic differences between the *actus reus* of the four offences is provided in the SOA 2003, s. 77. The summary would be more useful if there was no overlap between the offences. Unfortunately there is. For example rape can be charged under sections 1, 2, 3 and 4 and sexual penetration can be charged under sections 2, 3 and 4. Choice of charge will be within the remit of prosecutor, which decision will not necessarily be calculated in terms of the appropriate offence label.

12.7 CONSENT

A Theoretical and policy considerations

Absence of consent is a (problematic) ingredient in all the above offences.[42] As a reminder of the kinds of issues which have emerged in relation to consent consider again the married man's immunity. In *R v R*[43] the judicial convention[44] that husbands were generally immune from liability for rape (or sexual assault) on the ground of the wife's implied consent was abandoned. The political morality underpinning the erstwhile judicial adherence to the immunity was clear, if crucially partisan in its application. It was dependent upon a particular (gendered) view of marriage, namely that it was a private domain whose integrity demanded immunity from public scrutiny. If society is built upon social relations by which men and women relate in a gender-specific fashion then, in constitutional theory, the task of judges is not to remodel those relations (however desirable this might be) but to facilitate their continuance.[45]

The removal of the immunity scotched the social problem while leaving the jurisprudential problem unsolved. In so doing it raised another, infinitely more daunting one, namely what it is to consent to intercourse or other sexual activity.[46] If wives, and now

---

[42] J. Elvin, 'The Concept of Consent under the Sexual Offences Act 2003' (2008) 72 Journal of Criminal Law 519.

[43] [1991] 4 All ER 481. The case concerned the removal of the husband's immunity against rape.

[44] Dating from the time of its first positive formulation by Sir Matthew Hale, PC (1736) at 629.

[45] P. de Marneffe, 'Sexual Freedom and Impersonal Value' (March 2013) Criminal Law & Philosophy [online version not yet assigned to an issue].

[46] J. Witmer-Rich, 'It's Good to be Autonomous: Prospective Consent, Retrospective Consent, and the Foundation of Consent in the Criminal Law' (2011) 5(3) Criminal Law & Philosophy 377; M. Madden Dempsey, 'Victimless Conduct and the *Volenti* Maxim: How Consent Works' (2013) 7(1) Criminal Law & Philosophy 11.

more generally, partners of either sex, do not give implied consent how do they, or any-body else, signify **lack of consent**? In the absence of some obvious indicia of involuntari-ness such as physical coercion the notion of consent is difficult to pin down with the kind of precision desirable for such a serious offence. Even the complainant may not always 'know' whether consent is present or not. This is particularly the case where the parties are already in a sexual relationship. Taking a heterosexual partnership as an example, even in the context of an ongoing sexual relationship, a person may have any number of reasons for having sex with her partner, not all of which are consistent with an uncontroversial notion of free choice. Indeed, desire may be all too often a residuary one. It may be to pre-empt a morale-sapping argument, to prevent the displacement of aggres-sion onto children, as a capitulation to moral/financial 'blackmail'. It may be because she feels she has literally 'no choice'. In such private prisons the concept of consent becomes infinitely elastic and infinitely slippery.[47] How does a person trapped in a relationship of domination and subjugation 'know' what it is to have sex freely, if she rarely has done and is resigned to the inevitability of it all?[48] The understanding that sexual relations were not consented to may have to be an interpretation which she later places on her behaviour rather than a mental attitude which she had at the time. In the light of this, it might be argued that having absence of consent as an element in rape or other sexual relations is a comforting fiction. It may make males 'feel good' about their own sexual relations but, in the light of the empirical evidence, it does little to protect women's sexual autonomy and, it has been strongly argued, will not until relations between the sexes cast off their present form.[49]

In Sweden, largely for this reason, evidence of force or threats of force is a requirement to show absence of consent. This is also the case in related areas of domestic criminal doctrine. With duress, for example, the requirement of threats of death or serious injury is not an evidential requirement so much as a refusal on the part of legal officials to do battle with those oppressive structures in society which can render the notion of voluntariness of action incoherent. For reasons such as these, and for reasons of 'fair labelling', it has been argued, largely by men it must be admitted, that the scope of rape should be limited to its paradigm form, namely forced intercourse by strangers.[50] After all, if we adopt a notion of consent reflective of a **true** respect for sexual autonomy, what are we to do with all the people, particularly men, who remain oblivious?

One reasonable compromise would have been to require, if not force or the threat of force, some form of explicit threat on the part of the accused which renders the relevant sexual activity a less unattractive choice than the alternative.[51] The existence of such a threat gives us a clear basis upon which to insist that the victim's freedom to do what she wants with her own body has been undermined. Such threats would not have to be of violence as long as it could be shown that the decision was coerced. But it would leave

---

[47] This point receives further confirmation in *McAllister* [1997] Crim LR 233, a case on indecent assault.

[48] And so decided the Court of Appeal in *R v C* [2012] EWCA Crim 2034 (CACD) upholding the conviction of a stepfather who had subjected the complainant to many years of sexual abuse prior to the offences in question committed when she had reached adulthood.

[49] M. Barrett, *Women's Oppression Today: Problems in Marxist Feminist Analysis*, London: Verso (1980).

[50] For example G. Williams, 'Rape is Rape' (1992) 142 NLJ 11; for a comparable but more reflective view see D. Dripps, 'Beyond Rape: An Essay on the Difference between the Presence of Force and the Absence of Consent' (1992) Colum LR 1780; cf. H. Fenwick, 'Marital Rights or Partial Immunity?' (1992) 142 NLJ 870; cf. F. Kaganas, 'Rape in Marriage – Law Reform in Scotland and South Africa' (1990) 4 International Journal of Law and the Family 318–27.

[51] See J. Temkin, *Rape and the Legal Process*, London: Sweet & Maxwell (2000) 90–116.

unpunished those who induce sexual relations consequent upon offers of reward, or capitulation to moral pressure.[52]

The modern rule, reflected in s. 74 SOA 2003, is that it is not necessary, in establishing lack of consent, to show that force, the threat of force or fraud was used to secure compliance.[53] Section 74 states that a person consents if 'he/she agrees by choice and has the freedom and capacity to make that choice'. The prosecution may well rely on evidence of force to show that consent was absent, but the real question is a factual one. Did this person consent to intercourse/sexual activity or not? What consent actually consists of will be explored later.

1 Relevance of fraud or force – presumptions

Along with providing a statutory definition of consent, the Government also decided to define in the Act a series of presumptions in order to explain and clarify the law, 'setting clear boundaries for society as to what is acceptable and unacceptable behaviour'.[54] Part of the objectives of the Act in general and of those provisions in particular was to support and encourage victims in reporting sex offences. Trials for rape and other sexual offences are stressful enough for the complainant without having to suffer unnecessary cross examination about his/her private life. The presumptions prevent this being necessary in many typical rape cases. For, example, if there is evidence of force being used or threatened it is presumed that consent was absent and the complainant does not have to give evidence unless D gives plausible evidence to the contrary.[55]

The Government decided on two 'sets' of presumptions, one set being conclusive and the other 'rebuttable' or evidential. The conclusive presumptions target cases where the defendant has deceived the complainant, either as to his personality or as to the act itself. The effect of this is that by proving the relevant facts the prosecution proves also as a matter of law **both** the absence of consent and the absence of a reasonable belief therein. So if A, pretending under cover of dark to be V's husband, has intercourse with her the prosecution are relieved from the burden of proving absence of consent (and lack of reasonable belief). This is conclusively presumed. The evidential presumptions, on the other hand, do not establish **as a matter of law** the absence of consent but allow this to be presumed in the absence of evidence to the contrary. So if A has intercourse with V while she is asleep it is presumed, although not conclusively, that V did not consent. If A gives no further evidence he is convicted. If, however, he raises plausible evidence suggesting the possibility of consent, for example that they were in a stable partnership and this was normal for them the burden returns to the prosecution to prove that this was not the case and that V did not consent.

2 Fraud – conclusive presumptions

Section 76 of the Act states that:

   (1) If in proceedings for an offence to which this section applies it is proved that the defendant did the relevant act and that any of the circumstances specified in subsection (2) existed, it is to be conclusively presumed –
      (a) that the complainant did not consent to the relevant act, and
      (b) that the defendant did not believe that the complainant consented to the relevant act.

---

[52] The Law Commission recommended that in the absence of deception or mistake, threats are necessary to negate genuine consent, including threats to use non-consensual force against or to cause serious harm or detriment to the person or another. Law Commission, *Consent in Sex Offences* (2000) para 6.25.

[53] *Olugboja* [1982] QB 320. Compare Sweden where force or threat of force is necessary.

[54] Report, para. 2.10.6.

[55] *Protecting the Public*, paras 30 and 32.

(2) The circumstances are that –
  (a) the defendant intentionally deceived the complainant as to the nature or purpose of the relevant act;
  (b) the defendant intentionally induced the complainant to consent to the relevant act by impersonating a person known personally to the complainant.

These presumptions present two types of situation in which the consent of the victim and the defendant's lack of reasonable belief in consent will be conclusively established. First, presumption (a) re-states and slightly extends the common law in situations where the defendant deceives the complainant as to the nature and purpose of the act.

Under the old common law, an example of a fundamental mistake being able to vitiate consent was related to deception as to the nature of the act committed. A person tricked by a singing tutor into having intercourse, on the basis that the act is an arcane method of adding resonance to her singing voice, was held not to consent to intercourse. Here the girl consented to do activity A. She in fact did activity B. Therefore she did not consent to activity B.[56] This is equivalent to deception as to the nature of the act, as stated in section 76 2(a).

The Act, however, goes further than this and extends the existing law to deception as to the purpose of the act, rather than purely its nature. This seems to be an addition made in order to cover cases such as fake medical examinations, where the defendant might claim that a sexual act has a particular medical purpose rather than a purely sexual nature. The relevant offence committed here is sexual assault whose *actus reus* requires unconsented-to touching of a sexual nature and whose mental element matches that of rape.[57]

This was already recognised to some extent in a recent case, where three women let the defendant examine their breasts in the understanding that he was medically qualified and was performing a medical examination. The Court of Appeal held that the complainants were deceived into believing that 'the touching was for a medical purpose; [and] therefore there was no true consent since the complainants were consenting to touching for medical purposes, not to indecent behaviour; that there was, accordingly, consent to the nature of the act but not to its quality.'[58] Although the court did not explicitly distinguish between deception as to the identity of the defendant (and his qualifications) and deception as to the nature or 'quality' of the act, it laid the foundation for the second part of the presumption as to the purpose of the act. In *Linekar*, a pre-Act case, it was held not to be rape for a person to trick a prostitute into having intercourse without payment.[59] In short, what she consented to was intercourse which was exactly what she got. In the first case turning on this presumption the Court of Appeal made an important point of principle, namely that whenever raised it should be the subject of 'stringent scrutiny' since, if accepted, it is **conclusive on the question of guilt.** For this reason it concluded that the presumption was not applicable where the victim had acquiesced in intercourse with the defendant believing, due to letters sent to her by the defendant but purporting to come from the police, that she would be subject to criminal conviction and punishment if she did not. D was arrested and admitted the facts. He pleaded guilty on the basis of the judge's ruling that s. 76(2)(a) was applicable. On appeal the Court of Appeal held that section 76(2)(a) was inapplicable, since C had been deceived **but not** as to the nature or purpose of the sexual intercourse. As

---

[56] *Williams* [1923] 1 KB 340; *Flattery* (1877) 2 QBD 410.
[57] Section 3.
[58] See *Tabassum* [2000] Crim LR 686. See also *R v Green* [2002] EWCA Crim 1501. Under section 3 questions of consent are covered, as they are with rape, with the sections 75 and 76 presumptions operative.
[59] *R v Linekar* [1995] Crim LR 320.

a result the prosecution should have been required to prove absence of consent in the usual way, that is by reference to section 74. Nevertheless, the appeal was dismissed since the Court of Appeal concluded, surely correctly, that the jury would properly have found that the complainant had not exercised a free choice or consent for the purposes of s. 74 of the Act. Rather she had succumbed to the pressure inspired by D's deception.

In *Devonald*, however, a case on 'causing a person to engage in sexual activity' a notably less stringent test of purpose was accepted by the Court of Appeal. D, pretending to be female and sexually enamoured of V, duped V into masturbating on camera. His purpose was to humiliate V by posting the film on the internet. On these facts the Court of Appeal concluded, 'it is difficult to see how the jury could have concluded otherwise than that the complainant was deceived into believing that he was indulging in sexual acts with, and for the sexual gratification of, a 20 year old girl' that is acts of the same nature but an entirely different purpose than that represented by D. In the light of this conclusion *Linekar* might well be decided differently today. From the prostitute's point of view the purpose of the act was gaining money, unlike the defendant whose purpose was gaining sexual satisfaction.[60]

A recent case heard in Scotland provides another possible example of the first conclusive presumption. A woman suffering from gender dysphoria syndrome pretended to be a man in order to have penetrative sexual relations with young women. She was convicted of obtaining sexual intimacy by fraud. If she had been charged in domestic law with sexual assault or sexual assault by penetration would the prosecution be able to rely on the conclusive presumption? Did she, in other words, deceive the girls as to the nature and purpose of the act. I would suggest she did. The nature of the act consented to was sexual intercourse with a man. The act suffered was sexual penetration by a woman.[61]

The second situation in which a conclusive presumption will be found is where there is deception as to the identity of the person of the defendant. Here the act provides that consent and reasonable belief in consent will be lacking if the defendant induced the complainant to consent to the relevant act by impersonating a person known personally to the defendant.

Before the 2003 Act, by statute 'a man who induced a woman to have sexual intercourse with him by impersonating her husband commit[ted] rape'.[62] At common law it was later confirmed that impersonation of the victim's partner also vitiates consent.[63] In such cases, artlessly mirroring the position in the law of contract, the mistake made was deemed fundamental.

Case 2

Eve enters into an arranged marriage with Abel. On their wedding night Cain, Abel's twin brother, gets into bed with Eve. Eve has intercourse with Cain believing him to be Abel.

Here Cain commits the *actus reus* of rape. A person who agrees to have intercourse with A when the person they actually have intercourse with is B, does not agree to have intercourse with B.

[60] See also *Piper* [2007] EWCA Crim 2131.
[61] This was not a case of deception as to the person's identity since the defendant did not impersonate 'a person known personally to' the complainant.
[62] Sexual Offences Act 1956, s. 1(3) as substituted.
[63] *Elbekkay* [1995] Crim LR 163 CA. In this case, the defendant was the brother of the complainant's boyfriend of 18 months.

The new Act extends the old rules on impersonation in that consent might be found to be lacking if the defendant impersonated anyone known to the complainant, rather than merely his/her partner or spouse. The act does specify a limitation, however, making clear that the individual impersonated must be known personally to the defendant. Hence if the defendant claimed to be Brad Pitt or some other movie star, the prosecution will not be able to rely on section 76 to establish absence of consent but will need to rely on section 74 in the same manner as *Jheeta*.

The general question as to whether consent to sexual relations is, and should be, vitiated by non-fundamental mistakes will be discussed more fully in relation to section 74.

3 Evidential presumptions

In order to pre-empt the kind of spurious defence claims which tended to accompany even the most obvious and shocking examples of rape and other sexual assaults the 2003 Act introduced a set of evidential presumptions which include, but are not limited to, threats of immediate violence.

Section 75 of the Sexual Offences Act 2003 provides that:

(1) If in proceedings for an offence to which this section applies it is proved –
    (a) that the defendant did the relevant act,
    (b) that any of the circumstances specified in subsection (2) existed, and
    (c) that the defendant knew that those circumstances existed,
    the complainant is to be taken not to have consented to the relevant act unless sufficient evidence is adduced to raise an issue as to whether he consented, and the defendant is to be taken not to have reasonably believed that the complainant consented unless sufficient evidence is adduced to raise an issue as to whether he reasonably believed it.

(2) The circumstances are that –
    (a) any person was, at the time of the relevant act or immediately before it began, using violence against the complainant or causing the complainant to fear that immediate violence would be used against him;
    (b) any person was, at the time of the relevant act or immediately before it began, causing the complainant to fear that violence was being used, or that immediate violence would be used, against another person;
    (c) the complainant was, and the defendant was not, unlawfully detained at the time of the relevant act;
    (d) the complainant was asleep or otherwise unconscious at the time of the relevant act;
    (e) because of the complainant's physical disability, the complainant would not have been able at the time of the relevant act to communicate to the defendant whether the complainant consented;
    (f) any person had administered to or caused to be taken by the complainant, without the complainant's consent, a substance which, having regard to when it was administered or taken, was capable of causing or enabling the complainant to be stupefied or overpowered at the time of the relevant act.

These presumptions concern particular situations in which it seems highly likely that the victim did not consent and that the defendant did not reasonably believe so. If a person drugged or spiked the drinks of someone without their knowledge and then proceeded to have sex with them, it is reasonable to start from the assumption that the complainant did not consent to the acts that took place and that the defendant didn't reasonably believe that he/she did. Such facts make it inappropriate in the usual case for the complainant to give evidence on the question of consent because it will usually be obvious that she did not and so such a requirement would be unnecessarily intrusive. If the defence do not then raise plausible evidence that despite these facts the complainant did actually consent then D is convicted. It is open to the defence, however, to raise evidence suggesting that, despite the drink or drugs, the violence, the unconsciousness and so on, the complainant did in fact consent and/or that the defendant did in fact reasonably believe that it was the case. A typical defence response would be that the complainant was not stupefied and that the intoxicant acted so as to disinhibit rather than incapacitate, or that the violence was ritualised and the complainant shared his taste for sado-masochistic role playing. If the trial judge considers that this evidence was plausible the burden would then return to the prosecution to prove that C truly did not consent and/or D did not reasonably believe that she consented.[64]

Circumstances in which an evidential presumption will be found include threats of immediate violence against the complainant or another person, the complainant being unlawfully detained or unable to communicate and states of unconsciousness, whether caused by sleep, involuntary intoxication (when it is to the knowledge of the defendant) or otherwise. Despite proposals made in the Home Office reports,[65] the Government decided not to include threats or fear of serious harm or 'serious detriment' to the complainant or others, claiming that such terms were too imprecise and would give rise to too much uncertainty.[66] Therefore only threats or fear of immediate violence give rise to a presumption that the complainant did not consent.

This is similar to the approach under the old law, and indeed such a 'gesture towards the principle of maximum certainty is laudable', yet it is also 'unconvincing'.[67] First of all, the 2003 Act has done away with the offences which were seen to 'catch' situations where the use of threats was not considered sufficient to vitiate the victim's consent.[68] There is no specific lesser offence in situations where a sexual act took place because of threats or fear of violence other than immediate or non-violent inducements or threats.

In such situations, the prosecution will have to rely on the definition of consent as stated in section 74 which is, as will be discussed, far from certain.[69] Moreover, concern has been expressed about the fact that it imposes a limitation which is 'not required in defences such as duress or self-defence'.[70]

In any case, all those situations only raise a rebuttable presumption as to the complainant's lack of consent and the defendant's lack of reasonable belief in consent. Section 74 will in practice be the ultimate 'catch all' disposition on questions regarding consent or lack thereof, as long as the defence manages to rebut the presumption.

B Section 74: a definition of consent?

In cases not covered by the presumptions or where a rebuttable presumption has been rebutted the jury must examine the evidence to decide whether consent is present. Consent now is given a statutory definition. The statutory definition applies to all the preceding offences. Section 74 states that 'a person consents if he agrees by choice, and has the freedom and capacity to make that choice'.

What should be immediately apparent is that the concerns considered above about the cogency of consent as a signal of the lawfulness or otherwise of sexual contact has not been

---

[64] E. Finch and M. Munro, 'Intoxicated Consent and Drug-assisted Rape Revisited' [2004] Crim LR 789.
[65] See Report, para. 2.10.9 and *Protecting the Public*, para. 31.
[66] See in particular Beverley Hughes in the House of Commons Standing Committee B, col. 053, 14 October 2003.
[67] Ibid.
[68] Section 2 of the 1956 Act made it an offence to procure intercourse by threats.
[69] 534 ff.
[70] J. Temkin and A. Ashworth, 'Rape, Sexual Assault and the Problem of Consent' [2004] Crim LR 339.

addressed.[71] Both 'freedom' and 'choice' are 'ideas which raise philosophical issues of such complexity as to be ill suited to the needs of criminal justice.[72] Clearly those words do not refer to total freedom of choice, so all the questions about how much liberty of action satisfies the "definition" remain at large.'[73] This indeterminacy has led to judges continuing to rely on a pre-Act case law to help formulate jury directions in cases where consent is an issue. In *Olugboja* it was said that 'the dividing line . . . between real consent on the one hand and mere submission on the other may not be easy to draw. Where it is to be drawn in a given case is for the jury to decide, applying their combined good sense, experience and knowledge of human nature and modern behaviour to all the relevant facts of that case'.[74] *Olugboja* underscores the fragility of the concept of consent as the basis for the legitimacy of sexual intercourse and other sexual contacts.[75] If we are not clear as to what counts as consent are we any more clear about what counts as 'submission'? With this admonition in mind we examine in the following section some of the more troublesome applications of section 74. This will be essentially speculative since there are significant issues of principle involved and a corresponding degree of uncertainty.

1 Consent or mere submission?

When does a person who engages in sexual activity as a result of pressure from the defendant or external circumstances 'agree by choice'? In *Boyle*, a case involving intercourse laced with violence between ex-partners, the Court of Appeal noted the Judicial Studies Board Specimen Direction, number 53, which embodied the direction given by Pill J, in the trial of Mohammed Zafar. 'A female partner may not particularly want sexual intercourse on a particular occasion, but because it is her husband or her partner who is asking for it, she will consent to sexual intercourse. The fact that such consent is given reluctantly or out of a sense of duty to her partner is still consent.' In cases where things are not so clear cut the Court of Appeal was content with the trial judge's decision, based on *Olugboja*, to trust the jury to 'apply your combined good sense, your experience, and your knowledge of human behaviour and modern behaviour to all the relevant facts, including, obviously, their relationship and what you have heard about that.'[76] This statement makes clear that legality is still more indebted to social norms rather than a cogent notion of individual autonomy. But without such a reliance on social norms all sex, not merely coerced sex, is reduced to the status of the incipiently unlawful.[77]

In *R v Kirk* the Court of Appeal upheld the conviction of a defendant who had made sexual intercourse the condition of a gift of money needed by the young homeless victim to buy food.[78] In so doing it approved the distinction drawn by the trial judge between consent and 'mere submission', without clarifying it, which formed the basis of the decision in *Olugboja*.[79]

---

[71] S.C. Elliott and C. De Than, 'The Case for a Rational Reconstruction of Consent in Criminal Law' (2007) 70(2) MLR 225; S. Cowan, 'Freedom and Capacity to Make a Choice: a Feminist Analysis of Consent in the Criminal Law of Rape' in V. Munro and C. Stychin (eds), *Sexuality and the Law: Feminist Engagements*, London: Routledge-Cavendish (2007) 51.

[72] P. Roberts, 'The Philosophical Foundations of Consent in the Criminal Law' (1997) 17 OJLS 389.

[73] J. Temkin and A. Ashworth, 'Rape, Sexual Assault and the Problems of Consent' [2004] Crim LR 328–46, 336.

[74] At 355. See Boyle below.

[75] See S. Gardner, 'Appreciating *Olugboja*' (1996) 16 LS 275; Elliot and de Than, 'The Case for a Rational Reconstruction of Consent in Criminal Law' (2007) MLR 225.

[76] [2010] EWCA Crim 119 at para. 23.

[77] See generally S. Brownmiller, *Against Our Will: Men, Women and Rape*, London: Seeker and Warburg (1975).

[78] [2008] EWCA 434.

[79] The very word 'submission' is problematic in its supposed opposition to consent. Cf. *R v Doyle* [2010] EWCA Crim 119.

Presumably she 'submitted' rather than consented because she had 'no choice'. It was sex or hunger. Again, consent is doing a problematic job here. Many prostitutes, possibly the majority, make this choice on a day-to-day basis but the punters are charged with soliciting or paying for sexual services rather than rape. In this case, also, there is no question the defendant wronged the complainant but is the wrong rape? Would a better label not be 'procuring intercourse through threats, intimidation or exploitation'?

2 Does a person 'agree by choice'?

Does a person who agrees to sexual activity as a result of a deception, not falling within section 75 or 76, 'agree by choice'? In principle, consent to sexual relations *per se* should not be vitiated by non-fundamental mistakes, even if induced or knowingly exploited by the other. By non-fundamental I mean mistakes which, however profound, do not result in the other forming an erroneous idea of what is actually being done, namely having intercourse or other sexual relations with the person in question, or which do not undermine the complainant's sexual life choices.[80]

> **Case 3**
> Adam, desiring to touch Eve's breasts, tells Eve, a pop groupie, that he is Bo Diddler, a successful American pop singer. In reliance on this information, although unsure who Bo Diddler is, Eve permits the contact.

Although superficially this is similar to *Elbekkay* where the defendant impersonated the complainant's boyfriend, this is not a case where the conclusive presumption applies. This means the issue of consent falls to be decided by the jury in accordance with section 74. Adam's liability for sexual assault depends on whether it considers that she 'agree(s) by choice', having 'the freedom and capacity to make that choice'. How does the jury make that decision? Presumably jurors will be told to make their decision by applying 'your combined good sense, your experience, and your knowledge of human behaviour and modern behaviour to all the relevant facts, including, obviously, their relationship and what you have heard about that'.[81]

Leaving aside here the utter indeterminacy of that instruction the issue of principle here concerns the role of the trial judge. Although questions of consent are decided by the jury applying section 74, the trial judge nevertheless has a residual role, which is to withdraw the question of consent from the jury where the evidence is such that no reasonable jury could conclude that consent was absent. Is this such a case? The Judicial Studies Board, whose function is to provide such guidance, has omitted to address cases of consent gained by fraud outside the ambit of section 76.[82] Although, it might be argued that, if she agreed, she agreed by deception rather than 'choice', this is a case, it is submitted, where the issue of consent should not be left to the jury. This is because it is of no discernible moral significance that Eve would not have consented if she had known the true facts in this particular context. She offered willingly exactly what was asked for.

If the deception is to be capable of vitiating consent, in other words, it should be of a nature extending beyond 'disingenuous blandishments' to encompass deceptions which make a morally significant difference to the choice made by the complainant. What makes

---

[80] R. Williams, 'Deception, Mistake, and the Vitiation of the Victim's Consent' (2008) 124 LQR 132. Cf. D.N. Husak, 'Rape without Rapists: Consent and Reasonable Mistake' in *The Philosophy of Criminal Law: Selected Essays*, Oxford: OUP (2010) 233; *R v Jheeta* [2007] 2 Cr App R 34, above.

[81] [2010] EWCA Crim 119 at para. 23.

[82] Crown Court *Benchbook* (2010) 371–5.

such a morally significant difference? The view taken here is a deception which under-mines the basis upon which any reasonable person with the complainant's characteristics might choose to engage in sexual relations of the form requested. This was the view taken by the Court of Appeal in *McNally*[83] in which the Court concluded that a person who had sex with another believing him to be male did not consent to the act if it transpired that she was in fact female. Consider now Case 4.

> **Case 4**
> Eve, a person of strong religious belief with no sexual experience, agrees to have intercourse with A on the basis of his false assurance that he will marry her.

It is submitted that this misrepresentation should also vitiate C's consent. The whole basis upon which C orders her sexual life choices has been undermined by this deception. Compare *Assange* v *Swedish Prosecution Authority*[84] in which the defendant knowingly had unprotected sexual intercourse with the complainant in circumstances where she had made it clear that she would not consent without it. The first question for the Court was whether section 76 applied, namely that there was deception as to the nature or purpose of the Act. The President of the Queen's Bench Division said that it did not apply. The complainant was not deceived as to the nature or purpose of the act, which was vaginal penetration. This was a case, like *Jheeta* where the question of consent could only be decided by reference to section 74. This is his conclusion:

> It would plainly be open to a jury to hold that, if AA had made clear that she would only consent to sexual intercourse if Mr Assange used a condom, then there would be no consent if, without her consent, he did not use a condom, or removed or tore the condom without her consent. His conduct in having sexual intercourse without a condom in circumstances where she had made clear she would only have sexual intercourse if he used a condom would therefore amount to an offence under the Sexual Offences Act 2003.

Presumably, if D knowingly and explicitly misrepresented his HIV status, then consent would also be vitiated.[85] As a matter of principle, however, these cases do present some-thing of a problem. Granted that the complainant in *Assange* did not consent to inter-course without a condom this does not dispense with the question as to whether the wrong committed by Assange was rape. This is not a case like *Jheeta* where the complainant was pressured into agreeing to intercourse. Nor was it a case like *R (on the application of F)* v *CPS*[86] where the defendant acted bullyingly and oppressively in deliberately ignoring his wife's explicit and robust precondition for intercourse namely that a condom would be worn. Nor was it a case where the use of the condom was designed to prevent complete physical intimacy.[87] In short, the complainant consented to sexual intercourse. What she did not consent to was the risk of pregnancy or a sexually transmitted disease. It is submit-ted, therefore, that the appropriate wrong to be charged should be an offence against the person rather than a sexual offence. This was the view taken in *EB*[88] where the Court of Appeal ruled that a failure to disclose the defendant's HIV status would vitiate consent to

---

[83] (2013) EWCA Crim 1051.
[84] [2011] EWHC 2849 (Admin).
[85] A contrary view was taken in *EB*, although here the defendant 'failed to disclose his status' rather than misrep-resented it. It is not clear whether this distinction is valid.
[86] [2013] EWHC 945 (Admin).
[87] In such a case V's sexual life choices would be overridden and so consent should certainly be vitiated.
[88] [2006] EWCA Crim 2945.

the physical contact generally but not to the act of sexual intercourse specifically.[89] Latham LJ stated that '. . . as a matter of law, the fact that the appellant may not have disclosed his HIV status is not a matter which could in any way be relevant to the issue of consent under Section 74 in relation to the sexual activity in this case'.[90] Rape, protects people from violations of their sexual autonomy specifically not from threats to their physical well-being generally. The keywords here are 'as a matter of law'. Latham LJ is confirming that having intercourse without disclosing an STD is a criminal wrong, but the wrong is not rape. Prosecutors should charge such cases under section 20. And if they do charge rape, a submission of no case to answer should succeed.

The more difficult question of principle is where, in response to V's inquiry, the defendant expressly and knowingly misrepresented his HIV status. Here again, however, the issue of principle is the same. Was there consent? Again, the answer should be 'No' but, *Assange* notwithstanding, the wrong committed in both cases is arguably an offence against the person rather than a **specifically** sexual offence.

3 When does the intoxication of the complainant vitiate consent?

Intoxication is relevant both for the purposes of section 75 and 74. By section 75 if a person by subterfuge causes the complainant to take a substance (e.g. alcohol or rohypnol) capable of stupefying or overpowering that person then an evidential presumption arises that any sexual activity attributable to that substance is non-consensual. There is no requirement that the complainant be overpowered or stupefied, only that the substance was capable of having this effect. On the other hand, the presumption can be displaced by the defendant giving evidence that the substance did not have a stupefying or overpowering effect and that the complainant actually consented to the sexual contact. If this evidence is plausible, the prosecution is back to square one and will need to prove absence of consent in the usual way.

In cases of so-called 'date rape' drugs such as rohypnol the defence will no doubt have considerable difficulty in rebutting the presumption. With respect to alcohol, however, it will not be so difficult. It is an unfortunate but accurate summary of the law that a 'drunken consent' is still a consent. Indeed the more drunk a person is the more likely it is that he/she will embrace sexual activity. The question for the jury in such a case is whether a person who has had alcohol administered to her by subterfuge can ever 'consent by choice'. Although it was not a case of causing a person to take alcohol or drugs by subterfuge, the issue of consent in a case of an intoxicated complainant was discussed in the recent case of *Bree*.[91] The court optimistically opined that the Act provided a clear definition of 'consent' for the purposes of the law of rape. However, Hallett J also conceded that problems could arise, linked with the 'infinite circumstances of human behaviour, usually taking place in private without independent evidence, and the consequent difficulties of proving this very serious offence.'[92] *Bree* illustrates one of these ongoing problem circumstances and consequent evidential difficulties.[93] The defendant was a 25-year-old man of excellent previous character. After a very heavy evening drinking together, he had sexual intercourse with a

---

[89] In *Konzani* and *Dica*, as has been explained, consent for **purposes of section 20** has to be informed to be effective in cases of sexual intercourse. See Chapter 11 note 194.

[90] Latham LJ; S. Cowan, 'Offences of Sex or Violence? Consent, Fraud & HIV Transmission' (July 2013) New Criminal LR [just accepted not assigned to issue].

[91] *R v Bree (Benjamin)* [2007] EWCA Crim 804.

[92] Ibid. at 36.

[93] C. Gunby, A. Carline and C. Beynon, 'Alcohol-related Rape Cases: Barristers' Perspectives on the Sexual Offences Act 2003 and its Impact on Practice' (2010) 74(6) J Crim L 579.

young woman aged 19 years. He was convicted of rape. The victim stated in evidence that having lost consciousness she awoke to find the defendant engaging in sex with her. The prosecution case was that she did not in fact consent to intercourse. She knew what was happening. She knew that she did not want to have sexual intercourse, and so far as she could, made that clear. However, this case got lost a little in translation leaving the jury with the possible impression that the evidence pointed to the complainant lacking the capacity to consent.[94] The Court of Appeal therefore quashed the defendant's conviction. Distilling the Court's judgment in cases involving the voluntary consumption of alcohol the position is as follows: if the alcohol renders the victim unconscious or prevents her from knowing what is happening she does not consent **due to lack of capacity**. If the effect of the alcohol prevents the victim from communicating her lack of consent she does not consent due to lack of **free choice**. If the effect of the alcohol is to disinhibit the victim, and influence the complainant to engage in sexual activity which she would not have done if sober, she does consent. In this latter case, as was stated controversially in *Dougal*, 'a drunken consent is still consent'.[95] Questions of proof will be paramount and in each case the matter is one for the jury.[96]

C Mens rea

The *mens rea* for rape, sexual assault and assault by penetration is knowledge that the (person) is not consenting **or** a lack of a reasonable belief that the person is consenting. This is a departure from the previous law, under which the *mens rea* for rape was knowledge that the person was not consenting or recklessness as to whether (s)he was consenting. An honest belief, even if unreasonable, that the person was consenting negated this intention or recklessness. However, the absence of reasonable grounds for such a belief was held to be evidence upon which the jury may properly infer that the accused did not hold such a belief.[97] In short, while the unreasonableness of a belief did not prevent it from being a defence, it would usually destroy its credibility. No reasonable jury is going to credit a preposterous belief. It has been argued that for this reason[98] this new test 'contains no real challenge to society's norms and stereotypes about the relationship between men and women or other sexual situations, and leaves open the possibility that those stereotypes will determine assessments of reasonableness.'[99] A jury of sexist men are more likely to consider the defendant's belief as reasonable (new law) or be swayed by the defendant's story that he truly believed V to be consenting (old law) than an equivalent jury of non-sexist people of either sex. It is hard to take issue with this sentiment.

The lack of a substantive requirement of reasonableness of belief was widely criticised on the ground that it tends to favour those whose quest for sexual fulfilment is so single-minded that they are oblivious to the obvious, or those who entertain groundless ideas about what women say and do when they 'really mean no'. If the notions of consent entertained by men and women are divergent, as it appears they often are, it seems important not to accept this discrepancy as a basis for exculpating the insensitive man. Rather, if the

---

[94] See generally P. Rumney and R. Fenton, 'Intoxicated Consent in Rape: *Bree* and Juror Decision-making' (2008) 71(2) MLR 279–90.
[95] For critical comment see S. Wallerstein, '"A drunken consent is still consent" – or is it? A Critical Analysis of the Law on a Drunken Consent to Sex following *Bree*' (2009) 73 JCL 318. *R v Dougal* (2005) Swansea Crown Court, 24 November.
[96] *R v Hysa* [2007] EWCA Crim 2056 CA; *R v Wright* [2007] EWCA Crim 3473.
[97] By s. 1(1)(2) Sexual Offences (Amendment) Act 1976 and see *DPP v Morgan* [1976] AC 182.
[98] Although see V. Tadros, 'Rape Without Consent', 26 OJLS 515, 534.
[99] Temkin and Ashworth, 342.

law is rooted in a concern to vindicate the autonomy of the woman, it should be the very reason for imposing upon the man an obligation of positive inquiry. It is easier for a peaceable man to inquire, 'Do you consent?' than for a terrified woman to say, 'I do not consent'. It is hardly a heavy burden, and who would it discomfort?[100]

Following this criticism of the 'honest mistake' test, the first version of the Bill initially opted for an objective reasonableness standard, based on the 'reasonable person'. However, the initial test was quite complex and concerns were expressed that it would be unfair to certain defendants who could not attain the standard of the 'reasonable person'. The test devised in section 1(2) of the 2003 Act instead refers to a general test based on what is reasonable 'having regard to all the circumstances'. The jury decides whether the defendant's belief was reasonable, although the judge may withdraw this question from the jury if there is no evidence upon which a reasonable jury could find that it was. In *R v Ciccarelli*[101] the Court of Appeal agreed with the trial judge that there was no evidence capable of permitting the jury to infer that his belief in her consent was on reasonable grounds. The relevant act was done whilst the complainant was asleep after having had too much to drink. All the evidence stacked against him. Lord Judge CJ said that although the general burden of proof was on the prosecution the defendant had to adduce some evidence 'beyond the fanciful or speculative to support the reasonableness of his belief in her consent'. A simple assertion that he thought she was consenting was not capable of providing evidence that the belief was reasonable in circumstances where a person had intercourse with a woman he hardly knew, with whom, he had never had sexual relations, and who was asleep at the time.

The overall impact of this test will depend chiefly on the interpretation that is made of the phrase 'all the circumstances' and by whom that interpretation is made. The Government's view is that it would be 'for the jury to decide whether any of the attributes of the defendant are relevant to their deliberations, subject to directions from the judge where necessary.'[102] However, much will hinge on the Specimen Directions and the approach of the Court of Appeal. In a recent case this was the very point at issue. In *R v B* [2013] the defendant obliged his partner to have intercourse with him, having a delusion that he was a healer with special powers and that this would prevent his partner taking an improper interest in other men. The Court concluded that delusional beliefs such as he undoubtedly had would not in law render reasonable a belief that his partner was consenting when in fact she was not. A delusional belief in consent is, by definition, an unreasonable one. It matters not that D thought his belief was reasonable, if it was not.

D Summary

The *actus reus* of rape is committed where there is penetration of a person's vagina, anus or mouth by a man's penis. Penetration is 'a continuing act from entry to withdrawal';[103] the *actus reus* is therefore satisfied by a failure to withdraw following removal of consent. Rape can only be committed by a man. The other three offences can be committed by a man or a woman. Assault by penetration is committed where a person's vagina or anus is penetrated by a part of a person's body or by any other object. Sexual assault requires a

---

[100] E.M. Curly, 'Excusing Rape' (1976) 5 Philosophy and Public Affairs 325; C. Wells, 'Swatting the Subjectivist Bug' [1982] Crim LR 209; J. Gardner and S. Shute, 'The Wrongness of Rape' in J. Horder (ed.), *Oxford Essays in Jurisprudence* (2000) 193.

[101] *R v Ciccarelli* [2012] 1 Cr App R 15 CA.

[102] Government reply to the fifth report from the Home Affairs Committee Session 2002–03 HC 639: Sexual Offences Bill (Cm 5986, 2003).

[103] Sexual Offences Act 2003, s. 79(2).

'touching' of a sexual nature. Some touchings are inherently sexual. Some may be, depending upon the circumstances and the defendant's purpose. Whether the touching is of such a nature is determined by the jury taking into account how the touching would be considered by reasonable people. If a touching is objectively innocent it cannot be made criminal by the improper motive of the defendant in performing the touching. It is not necessary to show that force was used or threatened, only that consent was absent. Consent means that the person 'agrees by choice, and has the freedom and capacity to make that choice'.[104] Lack of consent may be established by the use of presumptions set out in the Act, whether conclusive or evidential.[105]

The conclusive presumptions cover situations of fraud, where the defendant intentionally deceived the complainant as to the nature or purpose of the act or intentionally induced the complainant to consent by impersonating an individual known personally to the defendant. The evidential presumptions are based on the existence of certain circumstances which were known to the defendant, such as, for example, the fact that the complainant might have been asleep or otherwise unconscious at the time of the relevant act or that any person was using violence against the complainant.[106] In the course of a trial, the prosecution will almost always try to raise one of the presumptions, preferably conclusive, to prove a lack of consent and if none apply, the jury will consider the existence of consent based on the definition in the Act.

The penetration must be intentional, but the effective *mens rea* for rape and for the offences of sexual assault and assault by penetration concerns the defendant's attitude towards the existence of consent and is based on the defendant's lack of reasonable belief that the complainant consented. It seems to go further than the common law 'couldn't care less' test of recklessness as it would only require the jury to find, 'according to all the circumstances, including any steps that the defendant has taken to ascertain whether B consents' that the defendant lacked a reasonable belief.

12.8 SEXUAL OFFENCES AGAINST CHILDREN

The Sexual Offences Act 2003 creates a number of specific offences designed to protect children and other vulnerable people from sexual exploitation. The category of child victims is subdivided by age. There are offences which apply to victims over 13 but under 16, and offences which apply only to victims under 13. The age of consent is 16. This is the age at which a male or female may lawfully consent to sexual relations; or stated from a defendant's perspective, the age below which a victim's consent will not necessarily provide a defence to a charge of a sexual offence. Until 2000 the age of consent differed for male homosexual relations as against lesbian and heterosexual relations. Following the decision in *Sutherland*, the age of consent was brought into line with that for females.[107] From time to time arguments resurface as to whether 16 is now too high an age, particularly where both parties are of similar ages. Juveniles do engage routinely in sexual relations. This is widely thought regrettable but hardly abnormal. Should this be the subject of potential criminal liability? Moreover, given that different children mature at different ages, does

---

[104] Section 74. Whether consent is present or not is still a matter for the jury to decide, according to the definition provided in the Act. A recent case has highlighted the need for further guidance from the judge in difficult cases (here involving voluntary intoxication), R v Bree [2007] EWCA Crim 804.

[105] Sections 76 and 75.

[106] Section 75, subsection (2)(d) and (a).

[107] See Sexual Offences (Amendment) Act 2000, s. 1.

any fixed age of consent make sense? Would it not be better to ask in each case whether, as s. 74, the alleged victim agreed 'by choice' and had the freedom and capacity to make that choice? The younger the child, the less likely that consent could be established under s. 74 but this will not invariably be so.[108]

A Offences against a child under the age of 13

The Sexual Offences Act 2003, ss. 5–8, create four offences involving sexual offences against children under the age of 13. These are rape of a child under 13, assault of a child under 13 by penetration, sexual assault of a child under 13, and causing or inciting a child under 13 to engage in sexual activity without consent: these offences directly correspond to the equivalent offences against adults already discussed. There are differences, however. Section 8 refers to 'causing' or 'inciting' a child to engage in sexual activity. The significance of this difference is that the offence is committed irrespective of whether the child engages in the relevant activity. The key difference is that for all these offences the offence is committed irrespective of the victim's consent and irrespective of whether the defendant entertained a reasonable belief in the victim's consent. In other words, regardless of whether or not the child desires the relevant sexual activity, and regardless of whether or not the defendant honestly and reasonably believes that the child desires that activity, the defendant can be guilty of one of these offences. That these offences involve extremely serious offence-labels, that under-age sexual activity is treated as normal by the participants, if not necessarily by the adult population, and that the relative ages of defendant and victim do not affect liability or the offence-label, calls into question their consonance with the ethics of criminalisation.[109] In theory two 12-year-olds kissing and cuddling on the back seat of a cinema could attract criminal liability. The only way for criminal charges to be avoided is if the prosecution exercise its discretion and decline to charge. The CPS have issued guidelines stating that it would not be in the public interest to prosecute such cases where consensual activities between children of similar ages take place. However, these are guidelines which are not proof against the possible influence of parents who discover their child has engaged in sexual intercourse with a Facebook 'friend' and press for a prosecution. Put this fact into the pot with the fact that liability is strict on the question of the defendant's belief that the victim is over 13, and these provisions become unacceptably harsh. A salutary illustration is the case of *R v G* where this principle informed the House of Lords decision. Here a 15-year-old boy who engaged in 'consensual' intercourse with a 12-year-old girl who had misrepresented her age as 15 was found properly convicted of rape. It was clear from the fact that fault was specifically required for the equivalent offence, where the victim was over 13 but under 16, that s. 5 was intended to be a strict liability offence.[110] Further, the provision breached neither Articles 6 nor 8 of the ECHR.[111] If the offences against those under 13 are more serious and so more stigmatic than the corresponding offence against over thirteens, is this not a reason to require some form of fault, if not necessarily subjective fault in the former case?[112]

---

[108] A case-by-case approach based on the child's maturity was adopted in respect of a child's access to contraceptives in *Gillick v West Norfolk and Wisbech Health Authority* [1986] AC 112.

[109] See Chapter 2. See J.R. Spencer, 'The Sexual Offences Act 2003: Child and Family Offences' [2004] Crim LR 347.

[110] In *R v K* the House of Lords read in such a *mens rea* requirement in the context of indecent assault against a girl of 14. [2001] 3 All ER 897, House of Lords.

[111] Presumption of innocence [2008] UKHL 37.

[112] For discussion see R.A. Duff, *Answering for Crime* (2007) 260 *et seq*.

B Offences against children under 16 but over 13

The Sexual Offences Act 2003 creates a number of other offences designed to protect children from sexual abuse. Sections 9 and 10 run parallel to the provisions in sections 7 and 8. The conduct element in s. 9 is again an intentional sexual touching, and in s. 10 is intentionally causing or inciting a child to engage in sexual activity. There are no specific offences of 'rape' and 'assault by penetration' when the victim is over 13 but under 16. These offences are covered by the general prohibitions of sections 1 and 2. The key differentiating feature in these offences is that liability is strict where the victim is under 13. However, for victims over 13 there is a defence of reasonable belief that the child is over 16. These offences are also differentiated according to whether the defendant is under or over 18.[113] In the former case the maximum penalty is mitigated.

The point of differentiating in this way is the extreme seriousness of sexual activity with persons under the age of 13, particularly in the case of adults. This is no doubt true but it is not clear why there should be cut off points of such **penal** significance when the circumstances differentiating the two cases may be **morally** insignificant. Is there any reason to treat a person's belief that a child over 13 but under 16 was in fact over 16 so very differently from a defendant's belief that a child under 13 was in fact over 16? The defendant's testimony of an honest belief may be less credible in the case of the child under 13, but should the issue not be left to the jury? Again is there any reason to treat the testimony of a defendant of 18 years and one month so very differently from that of a defendant of 17 years and 11 months when the appearance of the victim, the nature of the relationship between the two and the cogency of the belief are not materially different?

Sections 11–15 create new offences relating to children. These include 'engaging in sexual activity in the presence of a child' (s. 11), 'causing a child to watch a sexual act' (s. 12), 'arranging or facilitating commission of a child sexual offence' (s. 14) and 'meeting a child following sexual grooming' (s. 15). Again these defences are differentiated according to the age of the victim and defendant. Except for section 14 where no such defence applies, for the other offences there is a defence of reasonable belief in consent where the victim is over 13 but under 16. Sections 11 and 12 mirror sections 9 and 10 in that lesser maximum penalties apply for defendants under 18. Sections 14 and 15 do not have this provision. In relation to section 15 the offence only applies to defendants over 18 and in relation to section 14, although the offence maybe committed by a person under 18, no lesser sentence applies.

C Engaging in sexual activity in the presence of a child

By section 11:

> (1) A person aged 18 or over (A) commits an offence if –
>   (a) he intentionally engages in an activity,
>   (b) the activity is sexual,
>   (c) for the purpose of obtaining sexual gratification, he engages in it –
>   (i) when another person (B) is present or is in a place from which A can be observed, and
>   (ii) knowing or believing that B is aware, or intending that B should be aware, that he is engaging in it, and

---

[113] Under the previous law there was a young man's defence. Those under the age of 24 were given one opportunity to escape liability on the basis of a claim of mistake as to victim's age.

      (d) either –
         (i) B is under 16 and A does not reasonably believe that B is 16 or over, or
         (ii) B is under 13.
  (2) A person guilty of an offence under this section is liable –
      (a) on summary conviction, to imprisonment for a term not exceeding 6 months or a fine not exceeding the statutory maximum or both;
      (b) on conviction on indictment, to imprisonment for a term not exceeding 10 years.

The rationale of this and the succeeding section is to protect children from the corruptive influence of witnessing sexual activity. However, they are pitched at defendants whose purpose is corruptive and/or exploitative. For both offences, therefore, the mere fact of engaging in or showing the activity in the presence of a child is insufficient; the defendant must have as his purpose in engaging in the activity sexual gratification derived from the presence of the child. So parents who have sex in the presence of their offspring or lovers who have sex in a public park where children are present, or teachers who show a sex education film to pupils do not commit the offence unless sexual gratification is created or enhanced by the presence of the child. The offence requires the victim's presence in the place where the activity takes place or his/her presence in a place from which the activity can be observed. It is not necessary for the victim to see the sexual activity. It is sufficient that D believes or intends that the victim is aware that he is engaging in it. The fact that the victim refuses to look therefore is not fatal to a conviction.

D Causing a child to watch a sexual act

By section 12:

  (1) A person aged 18 or over (A) commits an offence if –
      (a) for the purpose of obtaining sexual gratification, he intentionally causes another person (B) to watch a third person engaging in an activity, or to look at an image of any person engaging in an activity,
      (b) the activity is sexual, and
      (c) either –
         (i) B is under 16 and A does not reasonably believe that B is 16 or over, or
         (ii) B is under 13.

The offence in section 12 of comparable purpose to that of section 11 refers to 'causing' the child to watch a sexual act except that here there is no need for the defendant to engage in the relevant activity. The act may be live, or in photographic form, sexual activity need not take place 'live' but may be conveyed through a photograph, a pseudo-photograph, drawing or film. It may be for immediate sexual gratification as where A derives gratification from showing V pornographic films or for the purpose of gaining sexual gratification at a later stage where the causing is done to put the child 'in the mood' for sexual activity.[114]

E Arranging or facilitating commission of a child sexual offence

By Section 14:

  (1) A person commits an offence if –
      (a) he intentionally arranges or facilitates something that he intends to do, intends another person to do, or believes that another person will do, in any part of the world, and

---

[114] *R v Abullahi* [2006] EWCA Crim 2060.

(b)   doing it will involve the commission of an offence under any of sections 9 to 13.

(2)   A person does not commit an offence under this section if –

(a)   he arranges or facilitates something that he believes another person will do, but that he does not intend to do or intend another person to do, and

(b)   any offence within subsection 1(b) would be an offence against a child for whose protection he acts.

(3)   For the purposes of subsection (2), a person acts for the protection of a child if he acts for the purpose of –

(a)   protecting the child from sexually transmitted infection,

(b)   protecting the physical safety of the child,

(c)   preventing the child from becoming pregnant, or

(d)   promoting the child's emotional well-being by the giving of advice, and not for the purpose of obtaining sexual gratification or for the purpose of causing or encouraging the activity constituting the offence within subsection 1(b) or the child's participation in it.

This offence is designed to tackle child sex trafficking. The core case is where a person approaches an agency for the purpose of procuring a child for sex but extends to cover, say, more informal arrangements between like-minded paedophiles to commit sex offences against children through internet chatrooms and so on. The offence is committed irrespective of whether the offence takes place and wherever in the world the offence is to be committed.[115] A defence is available to those, e.g. police officers, who act for the purpose of protecting a child, and do not intend the offence to take place, who make arrangements for that purpose.

F Meeting a child following sexual grooming

Section 15 makes it an offence for a person (A) aged 18 or over to meet intentionally or to travel with the intention of meeting a child aged under 16, if he has met or communicated with that child on at least two earlier occasions, and intends to commit a 'relevant offence' against that child either at the time of the meeting or on a subsequent occasion. This offence is designed to address the serious social problem of sexual grooming of child victims via the internet. Targeted at paedophiles, the offence can only be committed where A is an adult and is not committed if A reasonably believes the child to be 16 or over. The offence also fills a gap in the law of criminal attempts which prevents the conviction of a would-be adult sex offender for preparing to commit an offence against a child unless his actions have gone well beyond the preparatory stage and the child, typically, is in danger.[116] The protection of s. 15 extends to offences to be committed anywhere in the world and applies to children of all nationalities, wherever they may live.

G Other offences

The Act creates further offences against the vulnerable including sexual offences against children in abuse of trust, designed to cover those such as foster parents, or children's homes who are looking after a child. Also familial child offences, child prostitution and pornography and offences against those with a mental disorder. Discussion of these offences lies outside the scope of this chapter.

---

[115] Section 4(1)(a).
[116] See *Geddes, infra* Chapter 17.

Further reading

Cowan, S., 'Freedom and Capacity to Make a Choice' in V. Munro and C. Stychin (eds), *Sexuality and the Law*, Abingdon: Routledge-Cavendish (2007).

Finch, E. and Munro, V., 'Breaking Boundaries? Sexual Consent in the Jury Room' (2006) LS 303.

Herring, J., 'Mistaken Sex' [2005] Crim LR 311.

McGlynn, C. and Munro, V.E. (eds), *Rethinking Rape Law: International and Comparative Perspectives*, London: Routledge-Cavendish (2010).

Munro, V., 'Dev'l-in Disguise?: Harm, Privacy and the Sexual Offences Act 2003', in V. Munro and C. Stychin (eds), *Sexuality and the Law*, Abingdon: Routledge-Cavendish (2007).

Power, H., 'Towards a Redefinition of the *Mens Rea* of Rape' (2003) 23 Oxford Journal of Legal Studies 379.

Spencer, J., 'The Sexual Offences Act 2003: Child and Family Offences' [2004] Criminal Law Review 347.

Stevenson, K., Davies, A. and Gunn, M., *Blackstone's Guide to the Sexual Offences Act 2003*, Oxford: OUP (2004).

Temkin, J., *Rape and the Legal Process* (2nd edn), Oxford: OUP (2002).

Temkin, J. and Ashworth, A., 'Rape, Sexual Assaults and the Problems of Consent' [2004] Criminal Law Review 328.

Weait, M., 'Criminal Law and the Sexual Transmission of HIV: *R v Dica*' (2005) 68 Modern Law Review 121.

13 Homicide

Overview

The *actus reus* of murder and manslaughter is similar in that it requires an unlawful killing of a human being. The crimes are differentiated by their respective fault elements. Murder is an unlawful killing with 'malice aforethought'. Manslaughter is an unlawful killing without 'malice aforethought'. Malice aforethought is provided by the mental element special to murder and the absence of certain mitigating circumstances, such as loss of self control, which may reduce murder to manslaughter. This chapter will first deal with the common *actus reus*. It will then examine the mental element in murder, and murder's special defences. Finally it will deal with involuntary manslaughter, which takes two forms, namely constructive and gross negligence.

13.1 INTRODUCTION

There were 552 criminal homicides recorded for the year 2012–13, a decrease of 4 per cent over the previous year.[1] The social character of homicide is fairly constant. Male victims outnumber female victims by a ratio of around 4:3.[2] The majority of female victims are killed by family or friends, in particular, partners. Males are more likely, relative to females, to be killed by a stranger.[3]

Although criminal homicide is a relatively rare occurrence, criminal law textbooks, and this is no exception, devote an apparently disproportionate amount of space to it. This can easily be explained as an unthinking convention – a throwback to the days in which all killings were presumptively murder[4] and when commentators had good reason to emphasise it.[5] When the great classical commentaries were written, murder was, statistically, of much greater significance in the general cast of capital crimes since it was more likely to be reported, detected, prosecuted and lead to conviction than other offences. The modern treatment of homicide may show academic criminal law to be a discipline with a self-perpetuating agenda, bearing little relation to the real and changing world of crime and punishment. There are obvious features within the discipline which support such a hypothesis. Homicide is of substantial conceptual interest. In-depth discussion of the mental element in murder, of provocation, and of the dividing line between acts and omissions in cases involving medical practitioners are much more fun than some of the crimes latterly treated in respectable textbooks.[6] Even students have been known to evince some passing interest.

---

[1] The statistics relied upon in this section are culled from *Office for National Statistics, Crime in England & Wales Year Ending March 2013*, London: TSO.

[2] Ibid.

[3] Ibid. ONS 'Police Recorded Violence against the Person' (2013).

[4] William Blackstone, *Commentaries on the Laws of England* (1825) 201.

[5] Foster (*Crown Cases*) is typical of such commentators, devoting two chapters to specific crimes, namely homicide and treason, and one to accomplices. See generally Fletcher, *Rethinking Criminal Law* (1978) who himself devotes 150 pages (of 900) to homicide.

[6] See Russell on *Crime* (1965) for example.

A common justification for this continued emphasis is that homicide, particularly murder, warrants attention for being the most serious of all offences,[7] or because the interest vindicated by the law of homicide is the most important human interest of all, namely life itself. Such a justification is unpersuasive in the light of the statistical evidence which shows that criminal homicides are substantially outnumbered by deaths in road accidents, and at work, whether on oil or gas rigs, at sea while fishing, or in mining accidents.[8] Such statistics do little to change the attitudes of our legislators on the question of regulating for risks at work or on the road, and textbook writers seem little interested in devoting time and research to them, for the purpose of advancing the cause of human safety.

The justification offered here for this emphasis is that since homicide involves the violation of the most important human interest and since the consequences of being found guilty of the offence are so serious, the doctrine has been subjected to greater scrutiny than in cases involving the violation of lesser interests. In this sense the person who understands the law of murder and manslaughter has the conceptual vocabulary to make sense of much of the rest of the criminal law. In the context of murder the burden of proof for the criminal law as a whole was first made manifest; the scope of most defences, whether excuses or justifications, has generally been articulated most successfully in the context of murder; causation doctrine has been formed largely in homicide cases; the meaning of the *mens rea* words, particularly intention and recklessness, has been most extensively questioned and debated in the context of homicide; most of the important cases on accessoryship are cases involving homicide, and so on. The law of homicide is then the melting-pot within which the features of the criminal law at large are fashioned.

This has a negative as well as a positive side. The law of criminal homicide is as much about what does not count as homicide as what does, and it is not simply legal rules which determine this. Many (technically) criminal homicides are not recorded as such. Over 5,000 people are killed every year on our roads and few convictions which result tend to be for causing death by dangerous driving, which do not appear in the criminal statistics for homicide. In the workplace around 40,000 people were killed between 1966 and 2009 but only 34 companies were prosecuted for homicide and only seven cases resulted in convictions. Difficulties of proving 'individual fault' may account for some of the pitifully small number of charges brought and investigations launched.[9] The former figure may well be expected to conceal a good many deaths caused by probable relaxation of safety standards but which are filtered out of the homicide statistics by prosecutorial discretion.[10]

This state of affairs suggests that the operation of the criminal justice system does not always reflect the values thought to underlie criminal doctrine, in this case the notion of the sanctity of life. Such doctrine can convict a doctor, dog-tired after being on call all night, for a fatal act of carelessness yet not even prosecute the officers of a company who cause large-scale loss of life through apparent indifference to the principle that life is sacred.[11] In differentiating in this way criminal law seems to practise double standards – punishing individual lapses of care where individuals can be pinpointed as directly causally responsible

---

[7] A.J. Ashworth *PCL* (2009) 271.

[8] M. Levi, 'Violent Crime' in M. Maguire (ed.), *Oxford Handbook of Criminology*, Oxford: OUP (2000) at 302. C. Clarkson, 'Aggravated Endangerment Offences' (2007) CLP 278.

[9] This latter figure should not necessarily provoke the conclusion that the police are 'soft' on 'enterprise' crimes since such investigations are only warranted following a verdict at inquest of unlawful killing.

[10] C. Wells, *Corporations and Criminal Responsibility*, Oxford: OUP (2003); M. Levi, op. cit. 300. See generally Health and Safety Executive, *Workplace Deaths*, London: HSE (2010).

[11] See A. Norrie (1993) 96–107.

– but not punishing the kind of conspiracy of indifference which so characterises corporate 'killing'.[12]

These comments should be considered in the light of the general evaluative ambition of the book. Doctrine is calculated to reflect the seriousness with which society views a particular form of conduct, in terms of harm caused and culpability/dangerousness of the offender. The *mens rea* and fault requirements of different forms of homicide will, in a rational system, consistently differentiate those killings considered particularly heinous from those considered less heinous or not heinous at all.[13] There is cause to question whether the notions of fault locked up in the different forms of homicide adequately perform this function. This, in turn, prompts the question whether the legislature should rethink the forms of criminal homicide, and the judiciary reconsider some of the definitions of the *mens rea* words produced in recent years.

13.2 MEANING OF HOMICIDE

Homicide means the killing of a person. Not every killing attracts criminal responsibility, since it may be justified or excused in the same way as any other crime. A person who kills accidentally or even negligently, or who kills in self-defence, or as state executioner, has committed a homicide but not a criminal homicide. Homicides may be innocent or criminal, therefore. Difficulties of categorisation may arise in cases of criminal homicide, which includes murder, manslaughter and infanticide. Suicide is not a form of homicide because, by definition, suicide (self-killing) sets itself apart from **homi**cide (person-killing).[14] For comparable reasons abortion or child-destruction is not homicide but **feti**cide. This chapter will concentrate on murder and manslaughter, dealing with infanticide in outline only.

13.3 PUNISHING HOMICIDE

Although focal cases of murder and manslaughter may be easy to distinguish, there exists a substantial moral grey area where precise categorisation is difficult. I am wont to ask criminal law students, before their minds become poisoned by knowledge, whether they think that Mrs Hyam was guilty of murder or manslaughter.[15] Although as individuals 'don't knows' tend to be the exception, as a group the students invariably tend to fall into the 'don't know' category. Some insist she commits murder. Others are equally insistent she commits manslaughter. This ambivalent response is worrying. It suggests that there may be no 'self-evident' moral test governing the distinction between murder and manslaughter.[16] Arguably, none of this would matter if judges had a complete sentencing discretion across the range of criminal homicides. They do not. The life sentence, like the death sentence which preceded it,[17] is mandatory for murder. For manslaughter, on the other hand, while

---

[12] C. Wells, *Corporations and Criminal Responsibility,* Oxford: OUP (2003); Law Commission No. 237 *Legislating the Code: Involuntary Manslaughter*, London: HMSO (1996). See now Corporate Manslaughter and Corporate Homicide Act 2007. C. Clarkson, 'Corporate Manslaughter: Yet More Government Proposals' [2005] Crim LR 677.

[13] For analysis of the ways different jurisdictions slice up the homicide 'cake' see J. Horder (ed.), *Homicide Law in Comparative Perspective*, Oxford: Hart (2007).

[14] Although suicide is no longer a criminal offence, complicity in suicide is an offence.

[15] For discussion of *Hyam v DPP* [1974] 2 All ER 41 see above, p. 134.

[16] It also seems to suggest that some people may feel sufficiently strongly that their own judgement is correct as to be potentially resistant to a judicial direction on the matter.

[17] Until the Murder (Abolition of the Death Penalty) Act 1965.

the life sentence is available for the most serious cases, the judge is not bound even to impose a custodial sentence. This differentiation is justified on a number of grounds, none particularly cogent. The most popular is that retaining the mandatory life sentence maintains murder's symbolic moral uniqueness.[18] The sentence is indicative of what we as a society think of such killings. No better denunciation (or for that matter deterrent or incapacitant) can be made than for it to be known that, whatever the circumstances, conviction for murder means the permanent loss of liberty.

Such reasoning might be more convincing if it were possible to capture in coherent and consistent doctrine exactly what it is which sets a murderous killing apart from others.[19] Even if it were possible to fashion such doctrine, it would be unlikely, as my students regularly demonstrate, to satisfy the moral judgements of a large proportion of the population.[20] A more plausible basis, given the regularity with which such arguments have been ignored by government,[21] is that the mandatory sentence is politically expedient. If it were abolished, it would play into the hands of those moral populists who advocate a return of the death penalty. Even from the point of view of practised politicians, the death penalty is morally difficult to defend. At least the mandatory life sentence can be undone if a miscarriage of justice can be established.

As things stand at present, of course, the mandatory life sentence does not mean that a person convicted of murder will remain in prison for the rest of his life. The effect of a life sentence is that, after a suitable period has elapsed, a prisoner maybe released 'on licence'. Release on licence sustains the idea that the offender has received a life sentence since the licence is revocable for breach of any conditions attached to it, for example engaging in crime or failing to submit to supervision by a probation officer. The timing of the release will be the result of a decision made by the Parole Board which takes into account the danger to the public involved in an early release. This decision cannot be taken until the 'minimum term' imposed by the trial judge has been served; this term varies according to the relative seriousness of the killing. The Criminal Justice Act 2003 provides a schedule of principles to be taken into account by trial judges in determining this term.[22] In the most serious of cases, for example serial killings and sadistic child murders, this can be a whole life minimum term, depending upon the judges' view of the case, particularly the culpability of the defendant.[23] Even here, however, such sentences must be reviewable if they are to be consistent with our obligations under the European Convention.

By and large, the substance of this chapter is little more than an application of the general principles found in the rest of the book to the particular cases of murder and manslaughter. As a result, the treatment of fundamental issues such as causation and the meaning of the relevant *mens rea* words will be dealt with fairly cursorily. The reader will, therefore, need to read this chapter in conjunction with the relevant chapters on such

---

[18] CLRC 14th Report on *Offences Against the Person* (1980) para. 15.

[19] For an empirical study which seems to confirm this view see T. Morris and L. Blom Cooper, *A Calendar of Murder* (1960); B. Mitchell, 'Distinguishing between Murder and Manslaughter' [1991] NLJ 935–7; B. Mitchell, 'Public Perceptions of Homicide and Criminal Justice' (1998) 38 BJ Crim 453; L. Blom Cooper and T. Morris, *With Malice Aforethought*, Oxford: Hart (2004).

[20] Above, and see D.A. Thomas, 'Form and Function in Criminal Law' in P.R. Glazebrook (ed.), *Reshaping the Criminal Law*, London: Stevens (1978) 21 at 25–7: B. Mitchell, above.

[21] The latest being the House of Lords Select Committee on Murder and Life Imprisonment, paras 101–18; see also M. Wasik, 'Sentencing in Homicide' in A.J. Ashworth and B. Mitchell (eds), *Rethinking English Homicide Law*, Oxford: OUP (2000) 167.

[22] Schedule 21.

[23] The case of *Vinter and Others* v *The United Kingdom* (Application Nos 66069/09, 130/10 and 3896/10) – ECHR ruling that whole-life sentences without review breach human rights law.

issues to obtain a reasonable appreciation of the scope of the topics. Where possible reference will be made to these general matters as they relate to criminal homicide.

A Criminal homicide: the *actus reus*

It is conventional to begin the analysis of criminal homicide with the following antique quotation defining the crime of murder. If we ignore the 'malice aforethought' provision, the remainder provides the basic ingredients of the *actus reus* of criminal homicide: 'when a person . . . unlawfully kills any reasonable creature in being, and under the King's Peace, with malice aforethought, either express or implied by the law'.[24]

1 Reasonable creature

The phrase 'reasonable creature' is misleading. It seems to imply that it is not homicide to kill a person devoid of rationality. It is generally interpreted to mean only that it is not homicide to kill an animal or foetus. In modern parlance the *actus reus* of manslaughter is the unlawful killing of a human being by another human being. It should be noted, however, that the possibility that human beings who lack a fundamental feature of human-being-hood (for example a brain, in the condition known as anencephalism) may not be 'reasonable creatures' has not been tested in the courts.[25] Would a parent who deliberately failed to seek medical attention for a newly-born child with such an awful condition, intending it to die, be guilty of murder? In theory she would, although it will be remembered that a doctor who takes a professional decision not to provide life-sustaining therapy may not be guilty under those same circumstances.[26] In short certain 'unreasonable' creatures may be killed by omission if not commission. Theoretically it is not their 'unreasonableness' which provides the doctor's immunity but rather the absence of a duty to 'care'. This renders the 'killing' not 'unlawful'. The careful reader will detect a hint of circularity in this reasoning.

2 Unlawful killing

It is not clear whether the use of the word 'unlawful' has any real significance. It might mean only that a killing is not a criminal homicide if the killing is justified or excused. If this is all it means, the word adds nothing to the definition since justified or excused killings cannot result in the perpetrator's liability for criminal homicide. On the other hand, it might mean that a killing is not a criminal homicide only if it is justified, so that an excused killing will still be a criminal homicide. This would have one doctrinally useful consequence. It would support that aspect of doctrine which allows a secondary party to be convicted as an accessory to homicide even though the principal, by virtue of an excuse, is entitled to an acquittal.

---

[24] 4 Blackstone at *197. Co. Inst 47, 51; until 1996 death had to take place within a year and a day. This require-ment has now been abolished by the Law Reform (Year and a Day Rule) Act 1996. For an example of the effect of this abolition see *R* v *Clift, R* v *Harrison* [2012] EWCA Crim 2750; [2013] Crim LR 506.

[25] In *Re A (children)* The Court of Appeal authorised the separation of conjoined twin neonates despite medical evidence that it would inevitably lead to the death of one who had only a primitive brain. It is not implausible that the fact that the latter had only a primitive brain and had no expectation of a long and/or reasonable quality of life in her present condition counted heavily with the court, although this clearly did not form part of the ratio of the case. Cf. C. Davis, 'Conjoined Twins as Persons that Can Be Victims of Homicide' (2011) 19 Medical LR 430.

[26] See Chapter 4.5.

In *Attorney-General's Reference (No. 3 of 1994)* the Court of Appeal considered the potential liability for murder of a medical practitioner who performed a lawful abortion when the foetus was born alive and subsequently died due to the operation.[27] The court stated *obiter*, lending the keyword a telling significance, that liability would not be incurred since the act which caused death would be 'lawful' being in accordance with the Abortion Act 1967. As J.C. Smith says in his commentary to this case, 'the doctor has no authority (justification or excuse) to kill a person in being but he does have the lawful authority of the Abortion Act for the act which, as it happens, results in the death of a person in being'.[28]

The 'King's Peace' requirement means that killing of enemy aliens in time of war and under battle conditions is not a criminal homicide. Conversely the killing of an enemy alien in conditions other than the exercise of war will be unlawful. The other items in the definition will now be considered in greater depth.

(a) *The relevance of consent*

Consent, though it renders many everyday contacts lawful, does not generally affect the unlawfulness of criminal homicide. The reason for this is probably that the criminalisation of homicide, unlike crimes such as common assault and rape, does not owe its ultimate *raison d'être* to a respect for human autonomy. An act of killing a person, unlike, say, the act of intercourse, is deemed to be inherently wrong rather than contingently wrong.[29] It is wrong because it is a negation of a value fundamental to the human condition, namely the idea that life is sacred.[30] If killing is inherently wrong, it makes sense that consent cannot make it right. In recent years the emergence of interest-based theories of right and wrong conduct have led some to argue that consent should be capable of rendering even homicide lawful, so long as sufficient safeguards are in place to ensure that voluntary 'euthanasia' is truly voluntary and is a route for leaving life with dignity rather than simply a means of escaping from an unpleasant life experience.[31] The position traditionally adopted in criminal doctrine is that individuals have the right to **refuse** consent to treatment which **prevents them dying**, but no right to implicate others in a positive **act of killing**. If respect for individual autonomy is this strong, it might be thought that little cogent objection can be made against the provision of positive assistance based in such respect, particularly for those suffering from painful and terminal illness. We saw in Chapter 4, in cases involving the withdrawal of life-sustaining therapy from those who have suffered brain death or are in the condition known as persistent vegetative state, the distinction between 'killing' and 'letting die' is becoming increasingly blurred. Nevertheless it remains the law that acts designed to kill and which do kill, however well intentioned, constitute murder. The most recent affirmation of this principle occurred in *R v Nicklinson*. Mr Nicklinson suffered from 'locked-in-syndrome', following a stroke, which rendered every muscle in his body below his eyelids paralysed. He sought a declaration that it would be lawful on grounds of necessity for his doctors or his wife to terminate his life since his condition rendered his life intolerable. He claimed that a refusal would be in violation of his human rights and his autonomy since, because of his total paralysis, he was being

---

[27] [1996] 2 All ER 10.

[28] *Quaere* the position where the authorities deliver a prisoner to a public executioner who, known to him but unknown to them, is in fact the wrong man.

[29] The distinction between inherent and contingent wrongs – *mala in se* and *mala prohibita* – is, outside these clear cases, distinctly dubious. Kenny's *Outlines* (1962) p. 25.

[30] See generally Fletcher (1978) 235–8.

[31] See for example R. Dworkin, *Life's Dominion*, London: Harper Collins (1993); J. Rachels, 'Active and Passive Euthanasia' in J. Arthur (ed.), *Morality and Moral Controversies*, New Jersey: Prentice-Hall (1986).

denied the rights of all other people to take the steps necessary. His claim was rejected by the Court of Appeal.[32] Equally problematic is now the distinction between lawful and unlawful contributions to the death of another at that person's request falling short of causing death. In *Purdy* the claimant suffered from a form of irreversible multiple sclerosis. At some stage she knew that life would become so unbearable that she would want to end her life while still physically able to do so. By that stage, however, she would be unable to do so without assistance, so she would want to travel to a country where assisted suicide was lawful. Her husband was willing to help her to make the journey, but she was concerned that he might be prosecuted for an offence under section 2(1) of the Suicide Act 1961 if he did so. She sought judicial review of his refusal to publish details of his policy as to the circumstances in which a prosecution would be brought for complicity in a suicide contrary to section 2(1) and/or of his failure to promulgate such a policy, relying on her right to respect for her private life under Article 8(1) of the European Convention for the Protection of Human Rights and Fundamental Freedoms, as scheduled to the Human Rights Act 1998. The Divisional Court of the Queen's Bench Division dismissed her claim and the Court of Appeal dismissed her appeal. The House of Lords, departing from its earlier decision in *R (Pretty) v Director of Public Prosecutions (Secretary of State for the Home Department intervening)* [2002] 1 AC 800, allowed the appeal ruling that the DPP's refusal to publish guidelines might indeed be in breach of the claimant's human rights under Article 8(1). In so ruling the House of Lords took one small step towards acknowledging that helping someone to die may be justified so long as this furthers rather than attacks the deceased's autonomy.

(b) Conduct and causation

Homicide is a result crime. This means that normally criminal responsibility will hang upon proof that the accused performed a positive act which caused the victim's death. Causation, at least in the case of positive acts, will generally be established where 'but for' the accused's act the death would not have occurred as and when it did even if other causes contributed, as long as the voluntary act of another or abnormal event has not broken the chain of causation.[33] It is necessary to show only that the time when death would otherwise have occurred has been accelerated more than an insignificant amount.[34] Whether the defendant's act caused the victim's death is a matter of fact for the jury rather than one of law for the judge, although the judge will, of course, direct the jury about issues which will or will not affect causation.[35]

Case 1
A gives B, who is terminally ill, an overdose of painkillers designed to 'put him out of his misery'. This kills B immediately. Medical evidence shows that B would have died within days from natural causes.[36]

Although the question of causation is for the jury it is proper for the judge to direct them that by intentionally accelerating the time of death in something other than a trivial fashion the actor causes it.

---

[32] *R (Nicklinson and Lamb) v Ministry of Justice and R (AM) v DPP* [2013] EWCA Civ 961. In December 2013 nine judges of the Supreme Court heard the appeal. Judgment is expected late in 2014.
[33] Above, Chapter 5.
[34] *R v Dyson* [1908] 2 KB 454.
[35] *R v Clarke and Morabir* [2013] EWCA Crim 162.
[36] Cf. *Adams* [1957] Crim LR 365; *Cox* (1992) 12 BMLR 38 and see discussion in Chapter 5.

No direct act of violence need be shown.[37] One can kill by exposing an elderly, vulnerable or sick person to the elements,[38] by frightening a person to death, by lacing food with poison, by giving a defective map, by providing an unsafe vessel, or system of work, and so on. But not, apparently, by committing perjury.[39] There is no reason in principle why one cannot kill by transmitting a fatal disease, although most conceivable cases would not involve criminal responsibility for homicide for other reasons, for example doctrinal problems relating to victim's consent,[40] proof of causation and the practical problem that most assailants would predecease their victims.[41] A person may also kill by omission where death results from a breach of a duty to act.[42] Instances of homicide by omission are rarely treated as murder.[43] It is generally thought that this is because of difficulties of proving the necessary intention, direct or indirect. More plausibly, however, this reflects an implicit recognition on the part of prosecutors that where the defendant has taken no positive action against the victim a murder conviction is an appropriate label only where there is proof of purpose.[44]

3 In being

The substance of criminal homicide is the killing of a person 'in being'.[45] Two issues must then be addressed. When does human life begin and when does it end?

(a) *The beginning of life*

In legal terms human life begins at birth. Killing a foetus *en ventre sa mere* is not defined as a criminal homicide but may represent the offence of abortion or child destruction depending upon the age of the foetus at the time of the killing. At what point does a foetus become a human being, the subject matter of a criminal homicide?

The position is that the foetus does not become a human being until completely born, that is, when there is complete separation from the mother. A child killed before leaving the birth canal is not a human being for the purpose of the law of homicide.[46] This will be the offence of child destruction. Complete separation requires merely that no part of the child remains in the birth canal. It does not require the umbilical cord to have been severed. The foetus will become a living person, if born alive. This requires as a minimum that the child is capable of breathing – it is not necessary that the child has actually begun to breathe[47] – and maintaining an independent circulation. The test, it should be noted, is not that the child is viable but whether it **is alive**.[48] A child whose breathing and circulation are so weak and erratic that it can only survive indefinitely on life support is a living person for the purpose of the law of homicide.[49]

---

[37] Above, Chapter 5.

[38] For example *The harlot's baby case* Crompton's Justice 24 and *The sick father's case* mentioned by Blackstone Y.B. 2 Edw III, cited from Kenny, *Select Cases on Criminal Law* (1922) 92.

[39] *MacDanial* (1754) 1 Leach 44, cited from Kenny. See previous note.

[40] *Dica, Konzani*.

[41] See generally S. Bronitt, 'Spreading Disease and the Criminal Law' [1994] Crim LR 24.

[42] *Pittwood* (1902) 19 TLR 37; *Gibbins and Proctor* (1918) 13 Cr App Rep 134.

[43] *Gibbins and Proctor*, previous note; W. Wilson, 'Murder by Omission' (2010) New Crim LR 1.

[44] Where there is no such proof the matter can be dealt with either by charging the defendant with gross negligence manslaughter or Section 5 Domestic Violence, Crime and Victims Act 2004 which makes it an offence of causing or allowing the death of a child or vulnerable adult.

[45] *In rerum natura*.

[46] *Poulton* (1832) 5 C & P 329.

[47] *Enoch* (1830) 5 C & P 539.

[48] *Rance v Mid-Downs Health Authority* (1991) 1 All ER 801.

[49] See generally G. Williams, *The Sanctity of Life and the Criminal Law*, London: Faber and Faber (1958) 19–23.

Serious theoretical problems arise when the act causing death occurs with the foetus still *in utero* but the death itself occurs after birth. Authority is unanimous in holding the perpetrator guilty of criminal homicide, depending upon *mens rea*. So, in *Senior*[50] a midwife was held guilty of manslaughter for so badly delivering a child that the child died soon after birth. In *West*[51] it was held that a person who performs an act with intent to procure an abortion is guilty of murder if the effect of the act is to cause the child to be born prematurely and die.

The obvious difficulty attaching to this latter decision is that criminal responsibility, as will now be appreciated, requires a congruence of mental attitude and *actus reus* which appears absent here. The mental attitude in *West* was an intention to kill an unborn child. This is not the same as the *mens rea* for murder which is an intention to kill a person 'in being'. Of more practical significance, if foetus-killing could be the *actus reus* of murder, this would render many (unlawful) abortions and child-destructions potentially homicidal since a common surgical procedure is to expel a living foetus from the womb rather than to kill it in the womb. In the case of foetuses expelled after as little as eighteen weeks the standard criteria for being born alive – blood circulation and breathing – are likely to be satisfied, however short-lived.[52] Are all such events potential criminal homicides? On the face of it the purpose of the offences of abortion and child destruction is to impose a different moral label on foetus-killing as opposed to human-killing. That purpose would be confounded if an act directed against a foetus could be interpreted as homicidal. What are such offences for if not to render an abortionist, say, immune from prosecution for murder? More problematic is the case where the death is caused as a result of rank self-abuse by the mother, say through the unsupervised use of dangerous intoxicants. In such cases the doctrine of transferred intent will not operate to render the mother guilty of either murder or manslaughter. However, in line with *Senior*, it has been suggested that there is no doctrinal reason why liability at least for manslaughter should not be incurred.[53] This would, of course, square uneasily with the common law's supposed commitment to human autonomy.

In *Attorney-General's Reference (No. 3 of 1994)*, R stabbed his girlfriend, M, knowing that she was in an advanced state of pregnancy. As a result the child was born prematurely suffering from stab-wounds. R subsequently pleaded guilty to wounding M with intent to cause grievous bodily harm. When, 120 days later, the child died he was also charged with murder of the child. The Court of Appeal held that the trial judge was wrong to withdraw the case from the jury on the murder charge. The doctrinal mechanism which accounts for its decision is that of transferred intention. If R intended to kill or seriously injure the mother (B), this intent would transfer over to feed the *mens rea* requirement of murder against the child, once the child was born.

The House of Lords, on a further reference, rejected this conclusion.[54] It said that the doctrine of transferred malice applied only to living persons. A foetus had a special status which made it inappropriate to transfer malice in this way. This did not prevent the House from holding that R was guilty of constructive manslaughter, on the ground that R had committed an unlawful and dangerous act which caused death. As Sir John Smith remarked in his commentary, if it accepted this, why was R not guilty of murder, given that

---

[50] (1832) 1 Mood 346.

[51] (1848) 2 C and K 784.

[52] *Rance v Mid-Downs Health Authority* [1991] 1 QB 587.

[53] Smith and Hogan, op. cit. 555; cf. *Izod* (1904) 20 Cox CC 690; G. Williams *TCL* (1983) 289.

[54] [1997] 3 All ER 936.

R's intention was to cause grievous bodily harm which is the *mens rea* for murder? Indeed, the House accepted that the murder conviction would be proper if R's intention was not to kill the mother, as here, but the foetus. Regrettably, the reasoning does not stand up to scrutiny.[55]

(b) *The end of life*

Life ends when a human being stops breathing, the heart stops pumping and the brain ceases to function. In the usual case all three functions will disappear simultaneously or almost simultaneously. For example, 'cardiac arrest' produces respiratory failure which rapidly produces 'brain death' where the cessation of brain function is irreversible.

Advances in medical science have rendered it possible for a form of life to continue even though one or other of these functions is lacking. A person suffering from respiratory failure may be kept alive by mechanical ventilation. The blood can also be made to circulate in the absence of effective cardiac function. Under such conditions life may not be 'worth living' but it is nevertheless a kind of life. Removing these artificial aids will precipitate the irreversible loss of brain function responsible for consciousness, sentience and everything else which distinguishes an animal from a cadaver. In short, it will 'kill' the patient in a sense we can all recognise. This condition is known as 'brain death'. This is generally described as involving the irreversible loss of all functions of the brain including the brainstem. These functions comprise breathing, circulation, responsiveness to stimuli, muscle activity and electrical brain activity. Where 'brain death' has occurred, the removal of life support will have no meaningful consequence for the patient. Under such circumstances the only interest advanced by maintaining such functions will be the possible public interest in the provision of organs for transplant. The sensible position taken at common law is that a person who has suffered brain death is legally dead. The legal consequence of this is that such a person cannot be 'killed', whether by a medical practitioner or, one must assume although there is no authority on the matter, by anyone else. Thus, in *Malcherek*[56] the actions of doctors in removing a brain-dead patient from life support was said not to be a cause of death (since it had occurred already), leaving the person who brought about this condition responsible for the homicide.

In all other cases, the removal of artificial life support **where brain death has not occurred** results in the death of a person 'in being'. Life 'of a sort' continues as long as the brain is capable of function even though there are many conditions in which that function is so attenuated as to remove any recognisably human characteristics whatsoever. An example is persistent vegetative state, an irreversible coma where the brain stem functions but little else.[57] In *Inglis* the Court of Appeal upheld the conviction for murder of a mother whose son was suffering persistent vegetative state (pvs) following a car accident and whom she had deliberately injected with heroin as an act of compassion.[58] This was a case of causing death by affirmative action. Different principles apply where death is caused by omission. The removal of life support to a person suffering pvs is lawful if performed by medical practitioners since their duty to sustain life lasts only so long as the patient's interests are being furthered. It will not, however, be lawful if performed by a stranger or member of the patient's family, however hopeless the patient's condition. Removing life support is interpreted, in the case of medical practitioners acting in accordance with their

---

[55] [1997] Crim LR 829 at 830–1.
[56] [1981] 2 All ER 422.
[57] Persistent vegetative state (pvs).
[58] [2011] 1 WLR 1110.

duty, as 'letting the patient die'. Otherwise it is an unlawful killing, just as if a lethal injection had been administered.[59]

13.4 MURDER

The *actus reus* of murder, is that of all forms of criminal homicide and has been considered above. The formal distinction between murder and manslaughter hangs on the presence or absence of malice aforethought.

A Malice aforethought: overview

'Malice aforethought' is a term of art. There is no requirement of premeditation. At most, the requirement is that 'it must not be an afterthought'.[60] Neither is there a requirement of malice if, by malice, we mean spite or ill-will. A killing prompted by sympathy and compassion carries as much 'malice' as a killing actuated by greed, hatred, or anger. Malice aforethought comprises the intention either to kill or to cause grievous bodily harm. Unrebutted evidence that the accused justifiably lost his self control or was suffering from diminished responsibility is also capable of negating malice aforethought, in which case the proper verdict is one of (voluntary) manslaughter.

1 The mental element for murder before 1957

Sometimes an understanding of the historical background can help to make sense of the present legal position. Equally importantly it may facilitate the evaluative enterprise. A bad rule is doubly bad if it results from a misreading of authority. This appears to be one of these occasions.[61] The present legal position is very different from what it was in 1956 and, in large part, is no better for it. Before the passing of the Homicide Act 1957 it was generally accepted[62] that a person had malice aforethought where, in the absence of any excusing, mitigating or justifying circumstance she killed with one of the following mental states:

(1) an intention to kill (express malice);
(2) an intention to inflict injury so serious as to put the victim's life in peril (implied malice);
(3) an intention to do an act intrinsically likely to kill but without an intention to cause any form of physical injury (implied malice);
(4) an intention to commit a felony or resist or prevent a lawful arrest, during the commission of which a killing occurs (constructive malice).

The Act was intended to change the mental element in murder in one single respect, namely to abolish constructive malice, otherwise known as the felony-murder rule. Henceforward a killing in the course of a violent felony (e.g. robbery or rape) or while resisting arrest would not amount to murder unless the accused killed 'with the same malice aforethought (express or implied) as is required for a killing to amount to murder when not done in the course of or furtherance (of such offences)'.[63] In other words it would no longer be enough to sustain liability for **murder,** for the prosecution to prove only that the accused intended to **rob** the deceased. It would also have to be shown that the accused formed the *mens rea* for murder itself (whatever that was).

[59] See Chapter 4.
[60] Perkins and Boyce (1983) 58.
[61] For an extended discussion see W.O. Russell (1965) ch. 29.
[62] See Kenny, *Outlines of Criminal Law* (1962) 153–7; Russell (1965) ch. 29.
[63] Homicide Act 1957, s. 1(1).

Except for this provision the Homicide Act was silent on the *mens rea* for murder. An issue left untouched was the status of the offence of causing grievous bodily harm with intent. Before the Act was passed this was recognised as sufficient *mens rea* for murder. What was less certain was whether it was so as a result of the felony-murder rule or because such intention was sufficient malice in itself to form the mental element. The question had not been addressed, since there was no need to address it. One way (implied malice) or another (constructive malice), a person who killed with an intention only to cause grievous bodily harm was guilty of murder. Thus:

> **Case 2**
> A, intending to teach B, a rival villain, a lesson, breaks both his legs. This causes an artery to rupture unexpectedly. B dies when he refuses a life-saving blood transfusion for religious reasons.

A was guilty of murder. Since he intended to cause really serious harm, the malice aforethought for murder was established. Until relatively recently it was assumed that this intention was constructive malice, dating from the passing of Lord Ellenborough's Act.[64] As long ago as 1834 an authoritative report on the criminal law stated that implied malice means 'the state or disposition of the offender's mind when he wilfully does an act likely to kill or wilfully intends to put life in peril'.[65] It is clear that A lacks this mental attitude since his act was not likely to kill and he did not intend to imperil B's life. B would appear to have, therefore, only **constructive** malice. Throughout the nineteenth century this sentiment was repeated in cases where the defendant was indicted for murder where the facts were such that the felony-murder rule could not be invoked.[66] Midway through the twentieth century another editor of Kenny's *Outlines* stated, without a hint of self-doubt,[67] that implied malice included either an intention to cause life-endangering injury or an intention to expose someone to the risk of death without intending to hurt them. The intention to cause grievous bodily harm alone was not implied malice. Various editors of Russell came to the same conclusion.

2 The law post-1957

No significant doubt was cast upon this proposition until after the passing of the Act. However, in *Vickers*, it was not only doubted, but effectively ignored.[68] After *Vickers*, malice aforethought in murder is established upon proof of

(a) an intention to kill (express malice), or
(b) an intention to cause grievous bodily harm (implied malice).

(a) *GBH murder*

In *Vickers* the appellant was convicted of murder which, at that time, was a capital offence. He had broken into premises to steal and had been disturbed by an elderly lady. He struck her a number of blows, which caused her death. The trial judge directed the jury that he was guilty of murder if in striking the blows he intended to cause her grievous, in the sense of

---

[64] Offences Against the Person Act 1803 (43 Geo 111 c. 58).
[65] Report of the Criminal Law Commissioners, First Report, Parl. Papers (1834).
[66] Significant amongst such cases was *Vamplew* (3 F and F 520) in which Pollock C.B. stated: 'The crimes of murder and manslaughter are, in some instances, very difficult of distinction. The distinction which seems most reasonable consists in the consciousness that the act would be one which would be likely to cause death. No one could commit murder without that consciousness.'
[67] Kenny's *Outlines of the Criminal Law*, G. Phillips (ed.) Cambridge: CUP (1944) 153–6.
[68] *Vickers* [1957] 2 QB 664.

serious, bodily harm. He further directed them that the harm intended need not be permanent or life-threatening. The Court of Criminal Appeal approved this direction and dismissed the appeal. In *DPP* v *Smith*[69] the intention to cause grievous bodily harm was accepted by the House of Lords as constituting implied malice, although here the gravity of harm denoted by 'grievous' was modified to **really** (rather than merely) serious.[70] Later, in *Hyam*,[71] Lord Diplock attempted to reinstate the old common law position but was unsuccessful. His judgment and that of Lord Hailsham are noteworthy for the depth of historical analysis brought to bear upon the question – a quality unmatched in the two previous cases. In *Cunningham*[72] the matter was finally laid to rest by the House of Lords, which concluded (almost) unanimously that the law was correctly stated in *Vickers*, as qualified in *DPP* v *Smith*.[73]

It has been suggested, after so many authoritative statements by the House of Lords, that only Parliament can now return the common law to its previous position.[74] Although the Supreme Court probably lacks the political will to overrule one of its 'own' decisions, such an initiative is not unheard of and, given that it is the judiciary rather than Parliament which is the custodian of the common law, such a view seems to underestimate the constitutional powers (and duties) of the judiciary.[75]

As things now stand a person who forms the intention to do really serious injury to another person may be guilty of murder even where, as in Case 2, it is quite clear that death was neither intended nor contemplated nor even objectively foreseeable. This is not, of course, necessarily inappropriate. There may be compelling grounds for reintroducing limited forms of constructive liability where death issues from activities disclosing an extreme indifference to life. Rather, such a conclusion seems out of kilter with the formal abandonment of constructive liability wrought by s. 1, Homicide Act 1957.[76]

(b) *Intention to kill*

There is no controversy over the intention to kill as the mental element in murder. Such controversy as there is refers to what intention comprises. Intention, whether as to death or grievous bodily harm, refers primarily to intention in its focal sense of desire, aim or purpose. Where a person shoots or stabs his victim, poisons him or subjects him to a savage beating it is an easy inference to draw that he did so with the aim of killing or at least causing grievous bodily harm, that is, really serious injury. In such cases the jury should not be directed upon the meaning of intention. It can be left to their 'good sense'.[77] When deciding whether death or serious injury was intended they will no doubt be influenced by

---

[69] [1961] AC 290.
[70] The word 'really' is not required in judicial directions. *Janjua* [1998] 1 Cr App R 91.
[71] [1974] 2 All ER 41.
[72] [1981] 2 All ER 863.
[73] Although Lord Edmund-Davies did not dissent, he gave his support with reluctance.
[74] This was the position advocated in *Cunningham* by Lord Edmund-Davies.
[75] Lord Goff has conceded that the law is settled but 'only for the time being at least': 'The Mental Element in the Crime of Murder' [1988] 104 LQR 40 at 47. See most recently Lord Mustill in *A-G's Reference (No. 3 of 1994)* at 945–6 and Lord Steyn in *R* v *Powell* [1997] 4 All ER 545 at 551–2 who appear willing to put their heads above the parapet. Criticising GBH murder, Lord Steyn said, 'the present definition of the mental element of murder results in defendants being classified as murderers who are not in truth murderers'.
[76] For a strong and compelling defence of implied malice/GBH murder see J. Horder, 'Two Histories and Four Hidden Principles of *Mens Rea*' (1997) 113 LQR 95. He views GBH murder as consistent with a general principle underlying all crimes of violence, namely that actors must take responsibility for the unexpected consequences resulting from attacks on others, subject only to a requirement that the harm punished must not be disproportionate to the harm intended.
[77] Lord Bridge, *Moloney* [1985] 1 All ER 1025, 1039.

the objective likelihood that death would be caused. It would be wrong however for the judge specifically to direct them to draw inferences of intention from such likelihood or from the fact that either consequence was foreseen by the accused.[78] This may confuse them and lead them to believe that foresight and not intention is the fault element in murder.

Only in exceptional cases should a direction on intention be given. Such cases include those where there is evidence that the accused may have acted for a purpose other than to cause death or serious injury, as in *Hyam* or *Hancock and Shankland*, or where the evidence is otherwise equivocal on the issue of intent. It is now clear that intention in murder extends beyond its focal meaning to embrace the state of mind of a person who acts in the knowledge that a consequence is (virtually) certain whether or not he desired that consequence for its own sake. The insurance fraudster who blows up a plane in mid-flight so as to claim insurance on cargo intends not only to commit the insurance fraud but also to kill any person on the plane because he knows that the one object cannot be successfully achieved without the other.[79] In such cases the House of Lords in *Woollin* approved the following direction: 'Where the charge is murder and in the rare cases where the simple direction is not enough, the jury should be told that they are not entitled to find the necessary intention, unless they feel sure that death or serious bodily harm was a virtual certainty (barring some unforeseen intervention) as a result of the defendant's actions and that the defendant appreciated that such was the case. The decision is one for the jury to be reached upon a consideration of all the evidence.'[80]

This direction removes any leeway previously available to the jury to convict of murder on the basis of foresight falling short of moral certainty. Either the prosecution must prove the accused desired to cause death or serious injury, either for its own sake or as a means to an end, or that he foresaw it as a virtual certainty as a side-effect of what he actually wanted. If it can prove only that the accused foresaw the consequence to whatever degree of probability, it establishes only recklessness. This is sufficient for a manslaughter conviction, but not a murder conviction. Both Mrs Hyam and Messrs Hancock and Shankland are guilty of manslaughter, not murder.

As explained in Chapter 6, however, if the jury are convinced that without aiming at the consequence D neverthlesless foresaw it as virtually certain it is still not **bound** to find intention proven.[81] Acting in the knowledge that death or GBH is virtually certain is evidence, possibly irresistible evidence, of intention but it is not intention as a matter of definition.[82] To decide this the jury are expected to look at all the evidence and make their conclusion accordingly. The effect is to afford the jury some flexibility not to find intention where, as in cases such as *Adams* the defendant knows for certain that his act will cause death but his reason for acting (pain relief) is morally inconsistent with the criminal intention prescribed by the crime definition. In the more usual case of utter indifference to the victim's fate, such as the bomb in the plane hypothetical, juries can be relied upon to treat foresight of virtual certainty as synonymous with intention.

3 Sample jury directions

To understand the practical ramifications of the legal principles expounded above it might be useful to consider the kind of direction a trial judge might give a jury in different kinds of murder case. These are edited versions for the sake of clarity.

---

[78] *Woollin* [1998] 4 All ER 103, 113.
[79] For discussion, see Chapter 6.
[80] At 113.
[81] See discussion at p. 129 *et seq.*
[82] *R v Mathews and Alleyne* [2003] 2 Cr App R 461.

(a) *A case in which V died following a shooting by D*

Members of the jury to find the defendant guilty of murder the question you must ask yourself is 'Did D shoot V with the intention of killing V?' If you are not sure of the answer to this question then ask yourselves, 'Did D shoot V with the intention of causing V serious injury?' If your answer to either of these questions is yes then you must find the accused guilty of murder. In deciding whether the defendant had either of these intentions you must look at all the evidence in the case, including, in particular (the fact that a gun is a lethal weapon, three shots were fired from close range, the fact that the victim was a rival gang leader, and also the defendant's own statements about his state of mind at that time).

(b) *A case in which V died following a savage beating by D*

Members of the jury to find the defendant guilty of murder the question you must ask yourself is 'Did D beat V with the intention of killing V?' If you are not sure of the answer to this question then ask yourselves. 'Did D beat V with the intention of causing V serious injury?' If your answer to either of these questions is yes then you must find the accused guilty of murder. If you are not sure that he had either of these intentions then you may find him guilty of manslaughter. In deciding whether the defendant had either of these intentions you must look at all the evidence in the case, including in particular (the nature and duration of the beating, and the defendant's own statements about his state of mind at that time).

(c) *A case in which D a gangster throws V, a rival gangster, off the roof of a three-storey house*

D is charged with murder. He claims that it was not his intention to kill or cause grievous bodily harm to V. They were rivals and he did it to 'teach him a lesson and to make him fearful of challenging D's supremacy'.

Here there is evidence that D may well have had something else in mind other than death or grievous bodily harm when he threw V off the roof. The jury will, therefore, need some guidance as to whether they are entitled to convict D of murder given the likelihood that death or serious injury would result from such an act. A *Woollin* direction must be given therefore.

Members of the jury, you have been told that it was not D's intention in throwing V off the roof to kill him or cause him serious injury but simply to teach him a lesson. You are entitled to disbelieve this but if you think that this claim may be true I am bound to direct you that you may still find the necessary intention if you are convinced that, whatever else D intended, he knew that one of these consequences would occur. If you think that, then I must also direct you that you are **not** entitled to find the necessary intention, unless you feel sure that death or serious bodily harm was a virtual certainty, barring some unforeseen intervention, as a result of the defendant's actions, and that the defendant appreciated that such was the case. In deciding whether the intention is present, however, you must make your decision on the basis of all the evidence, including, in particular, the height of the house, the nature of the relationship between D, and V, the reaction of D following the fall of V, and the defendant's own statements about his state of mind at that time.

(d) *A case in which D, pushes his three-year-old son out of the bedroom window*

In this case, D pushes his three-year-old son out of the bedroom window to escape from a fierce house fire and then jumps himself. V dies in the fall. D survives. Again there is evidence that D had something else in mind other than causing death or grievous bodily harm when he threw V out of the window. Again, therefore, the jury will need some guidance as to whether they are entitled to convict D of murder given the extreme likelihood that death or serious injury would result from such an act. Again, the *Woollin* direction must be given therefore:

Members of the jury, you have been told that it was not D's intention in throwing V out of the window to kill him or cause him serious injury. Far from it, it was to save him. If you think that this claim may be true I must tell you that you may still find the necessary intention if you are convinced that, whatever else D intended, he knew that one of these consequences would occur. If you think that, then I must also direct you that you are **not** entitled to find the necessary intention, unless you feel sure that death or serious bodily harm was a virtual certainty (barring some unforeseen intervention) as a result of the defendant's actions and that the defendant appreciated that such was the case. In deciding whether the intention is present, however, you must make your decision on the basis of all the evidence which requires you of course to consider the context within which D threw his son off the roof, the height of the window, the ferocity of the blaze, the age of the son, and the defendant's own statements about his state of mind at that time.

A jury would probably not convict of murder on the basis of such a direction although they would no doubt still consider broken bones (grievous bodily harm) **at the very least** to be a virtual certainty and be prepared to impute that knowledge to the defendant on the basis that if they know it then he knew it. They would probably not convict because of two aspects of the direction. The first, dealt with above, is that the direction does not instruct the jury that they are **bound to** find intention where there is foresight of certainty only that they are **entitled to**. The second is that the direction tells them to reach their decision on the basis of **all the evidence**. Taking into account D's motive this form of words sends a pretty clear message to the jury that 'foresight of certainty' is not conclusive. With that message the jury's natural humanity can be relied upon to reach the common-sense verdict of not guilty. Note, if D is not guilty of murder, the jury is unlikely to bring in an alternative verdict of manslaughter either, because they will have concluded that D's reason for throwing V from the window made the throwing lawful.

Of course there are other means of avoiding a conviction for murder here, namely the possibility of raising a defence of necessity, but the most straightforward mechanism is via the *mens rea* requirement. It is perhaps unfortunate, however, that D must rely on the discretion afforded to the jury not to find intention despite foresight of certainty. A far simpler solution would be a straightforward direction from the judge that if it is convinced that D's object was to save the child rather than kill it this negates the intention necessary for murder. Simpler, perhaps, but it would cause tricky problems of application.

B Conclusions: a rational *mens rea* for murder?

The merit of the present *mens rea* for murder is its relative certainty. Carrying a mandatory life sentence, it is quite appropriate that proof of guilt should require a clearly ascertainable mental element such as intention. That said, many disagree that the intention to commit grievous bodily harm *per se* should be enough and that a rational *mens rea* for murder would require an intention to cause **life threatening** harm as a minimum to ensure a proper correspondence between act and culpability. Various reform bodies have recommended this. It also seems to have the support of the judiciary. Concerning GBH murder Lord Steyn confirmed that the House of Lords were uncomfortable with GBH murder and perhaps, under appropriate circumstances, may be emboldened to make changes.[83]

---

[83] '(Murder) is a species of constructive crime . . . This feature of the law of murder may have contributed to the problems which courts have experienced with *mens rea* in murder. But unless the House of Lords or Parliament have occasion to revisit this point the sufficiency of an intent to cause serious harm is the basic assumption upon which any analysis must proceed.' *Woollin* [1998] 4 All ER 103 at 107.

This leaves unaccounted for, however, the prospect of a murder conviction where although D neither intended to kill nor to cause GBH he did, as in *Hyam*, act with 'wicked recklessness' in regard to the prospect of death. This is murder in Scottish and American law which, in addition to intentional killings, embraces 'wicked recklessness' and 'wicked and depraved heart' as instances of malice aforethought.[84] This type of approach has been disapproved in domestic law. The reasons are undeniably plausible. First, it is not possible to convey to a jury with any degree of certainty exactly what gravity of risk characterises a murderous killing as opposed to any other criminal homicide. Is Mrs Hyam a murderer or a manslaughterer? What test of foresight would consistently[85] convict or acquit her?[86] Second, this imprecision is likely to lead juries to decide upon the appropriate category using essentially non-legal criteria, for example the quality of the defendant's motive. *Hancock and Shankland* is a prime example of such jury inequity[87] and was, of course, of signal importance in setting the House of Lords against recklessness as a form of malice. A succession of different bodies has made recommendations which do not resolve this problem but simply tinker at the edges. There is little incentive to do more, given that the mandatory sentence is not up for discussion and so any major extension in coverage of murder will likely make matters worse from the sentencing point of view, rather than better. Thus, the Criminal Law Revision Committee,[88] the Law Commission[89] and the House of Lords Select Committee on Murder and Life Imprisonment[90] have simply concentrated on requiring, for GBH murder, an awareness that the harm intended put the victim at risk of death.[91]

A solution to the problem of non-intentional but nevertheless 'wicked' killings was tabled in the Law Commission's most recent report. It proposed that the most rational manner of distinguishing murder from manslaughter is not by trying to draw lines between degrees of wickedness but by characterising murder as involving **an attack**.[92] A radical new structure of homicide is created which neatly sidesteps much of the malign influence of the mandatory sentence by dividing murder into two degrees of gravity. First degree murder, which would continue to carry the mandatory sentence, encompasses (a) intentional killing; or (b) killing with an intention to cause serious injury, in the awareness that there is a serious risk of causing death. Intention carries its present meaning. An intentional killing requires that the defendant act 'in order to bring it about'. Where justice requires it the judge should direct the jury that they may also find intention to kill if D thought that his or her action would certainly (barring an unforeseen intervention) kill, even if the death was undesired. This is an admirably lucid response to the difficulties posed by the present

---

[84] The American Model Penal Code treats the intention to cause grievous bodily harm as malice only if it manifests the extreme recklessness necessary for 'depraved heart' malice, s. 210.2(1)(b). The present *mens rea* for homicide in Scottish law is encapsulated in *R v Drury* 2001 SLT 1013.

[85] That is, across a range of different juries.

[86] CLRC 14th Report, *Offences against the Person* Cmnd 7844 (1980) paras 23, 24.

[87] They convicted at first instance.

[88] CLRC 14th Report on *Offences against the Person* (1980) para. 28.

[89] Law Com. No. 177, *Draft Criminal Code Bill* (1989), cl. 54(1).

[90] (Session 1988–9), HL Paper 78 (1989) para. 71.

[91] For discussion, see W. Wilson, 'Murder and the Structure of Homicide' in A.J. Ashworth and B. Mitchell (eds), *Rethinking English Homicide Law*, Oxford: OUP (2000) 21; S. Yeo, *Fault in Homicide*, Sydney: Federation Press (1997) ch. 3.

[92] Law Com. No. 304, *Murder, Manslaughter and Infanticide*, 28 November 2006; for commentary see A.J. Ashworth, 'Principles, Pragmatism and the Law Commission's Recommendations on Homicide Law Reform' [2007] Crim LR 333; W. Wilson, 'The Structure of Criminal Homicide' (2006); W. Wilson, 'What's Wrong with Murder?' [2006] 1(2) Criminal Law and Philosophy.

law, which would do much to simplify the task of judges and juries if only it had not, as usual, been kicked into the long grass by the legislature.[93]

The strength of the package as a whole is revealed when one turns to second-degree murder. Simple GBH murder is retained but is relegated to second-degree murder where the mandatory sentence will not bite. A disappointing feature in the Law Commission's proposals is that serious injury is itself not defined, largely because of the supposed difficulties in tying down a satisfactory definition, but one assumes Case 2 will continue to be part of the law of murder. The most significant change here is the very welcome adoption of a form of killing by risk-taking which avoids the difficulty described earlier of drawing a clear line between risk-taking as murder and risk-taking as manslaughter by requiring it to involve an attack on the victim, rather than simple endangerment. The Law Commission also includes within second-degree murder an intention to cause some injury, or the fear of some injury or a risk of some injury, whilst being aware of a serious risk of causing death. Such a mental attitude would have the felicitous effect of acquitting most dangerous drivers who kill,[94] but would cover cases such as *Hyam v DPP*, and also cases such as killing in the course of torture where an intention to cause serious injury could not be proven so long as there is awareness that there is a serious risk of causing death.[95]

13.5 MALICE MITIGATED: VOLUNTARY MANSLAUGHTER

In three circumstances a 'voluntary' killing may be mitigated to manslaughter. By 'voluntary' killing in this context we mean nothing more than a killing accompanied by the relevant criminal intent (malice) for murder but for which a partial defence applies. Allied to voluntary manslaughter is the **offence** of infanticide, a 'blood sister' of the partial defence of diminished responsibility. Whether we think of these as **offences** in their own right or partial **defences** (to the core offence of murder) the substantive basis of both voluntary manslaughter and infanticide is that the killing took place under circumstances of acute mental disturbance. The effect is to reduce what would otherwise be a conviction for murder to a lesser offence in which a sentencing discretion is operative.

Until 2010 there were three murder-specific partial **defences** which had the effect reducing the **offence** from murder to manslaughter. These were provocation, diminished responsibility and suicide pact. Each were governed by the Homicide Act 1957. Following the Law Commission reports on Murder and Partial Defences to Murder the Ministry of Justice published, in 2007, a consultation paper *Murder, Manslaughter and Infanticide: Proposals for Reform of the Law*. The consequence was the reforming provisions contained in the Coroners and Justice Act 2009.[96] These took effect in October 2010. The effect of both is to set greater restrictions upon the occasions when the context is deemed to reduce a person's responsibility for an intentional killing. In order to fully understand the

---

[93] R. Taylor, 'The Nature of "Partial Defences" and the Coherence of (Second-Degree) Murder' [2007] Crim LR 345. Successive Directors of Public Prosecutions have put their weight behind the proposals for a two-tiered law of murder. See *Guardian* 8 September 2010. The package also proposes that duress should be a complete defence, albeit with the burden of proof shifted onto the defendant. For critical comment see Ashworth [2007], previous note.

[94] For full argument see W. Wilson, 'Murder and the Structure of Homicide' in A.J. Ashworth and B. Mitchell (eds), *Rethinking English Homicide Law*, Oxford: OUP (2000) 21, 39–44.

[95] The final element in second degree murder is killing with the intent for first degree murder, but where a defence of provocation, diminished responsibility, or suicide pact succeeds.

[96] Suicide pacts were left untouched.

significance of the changes effected by the 2009 Act an account of what it replaced and the reasons for it are necessary.[97]

A Provocation: history and rationale

Most jurisdictions embody some form of 'crime of passion' defence but what should such defence encompass? This depends, of course, on the underlying defence rationale. Let us examine some hypothetical cases in which it might plausibly be argued that the context so affected the defendant's willingness and/or ability to conform to the prohibition against intentional killing that his/her fault is mitigated.

> **Case 3**
> A finds his wife, V, in bed with another man. He goes berserk and, without a thought for what he is doing, shoots wife and lover dead.

> **Case 4**
> A, the victim of his wife V's incessant 'put-downs', finally snaps when V taunts him for being an incompetent lover, and strangles her.

> **Case 5**
> A has been married for 20 years. Her husband, V, has consistently oppressed her by insisting she remains a housewife, by refusing to allow her to go out with her friends or to take driving lessons, by belittling her in company, and by giving her a niggardly housekeeping allowance on the excuse that he cannot afford it. A discovers by chance that V has a secret bank account containing £100,000 and that he makes a monthly allowance of £1,000 to a secret lover. She is outraged and hatches a plot to kill V by electrocuting him in his bath the next time he takes one. This she does three weeks later.

> **Case 6**
> A is stopped by V, a policeman, for speeding. A loses control and stabs the policeman, due to pent-up frustration and anger caused by having been stuck in a traffic jam for three hours prior to being stopped.

> **Case 7**
> A, the victim of years of physical abuse by her husband, unable to continue to submit to the terrible ordeal and fearful of the consequences if she escapes, stabs him in his bed.

In each of these cases the decision to kill is ignited by an event of sufficient psychological impact to subdue A's normal disposition to obey the law. As will be apparent, the psychological mechanism for unlocking this disinhibition may take different forms.[98] The five cases can be categorised as either evincing moral 'outrage' with (Case 3) or without (Cases 5 and 7) loss of self-control. Or loss of self-control pure and simple (Cases 4 and 6). When would it make moral sense to afford a (partial) defence to A? Do we (partially)

---

[97] See generally, A. Reed and M. Bohlander (eds), *Loss of Control and Diminished Responsibility: Domestic, International and International Perspectives*, Farnham: Ashgate (2011).
[98] Cf. *R v Evans* [2009] EWCA Crim 2243.

excuse the actor because it is unfair to punish someone for murder who may not have been able to prevent himself from so acting? This would cover Cases 3, 4, and 6. Or is the act (partially) justified because, in some sense, the law recognises that retributive retaliation is a (partially) reasonable response to the unjust 'infliction' of moral outrage? This might cover Cases 3, 4, 5 and 7.

In England and Wales doctrine originally followed the second route. Uncontrollable anger, *per se*, did not excuse. Case 3 is a classic example of a case capable of affording the defence of provocation. The defence was originally available and limited to cases where the defendant (archetypally a man) killed to vindicate personal honour. This was at a time when honour was considered almost as precious a moral commodity as autonomy is today. A killing prompted by a provoking assault on self, or the discovery of a wife committing adultery or of a family member or friend suffering attack, were considered the natural response of an honourable man, and certainly not such as would justify the mandatory (capital) sentence. The essence of the defence then was that a violation of honour (partly) justifies retributive retaliatory action.[99]

Anger or loss of self-control was not at this time seen as the distinguishing characteristic of the defence. On the contrary, the vindication of honour is demanded by reason rather than compelled by passion. At a later stage, this idea of provocation being a defence of partial justification gradually became eclipsed by a requirement that the defence would not be available unless the killing was due to a loss of self-control. This form of voluntary manslaughter became a 'crime of passion'. This change in emphasis from a justificatory defence to an excuse sits more happily with the common law's presumption that reason prompts people to obey law rather than flout it. The new notion of provocation, then, was based on the fact that reason has been 'dethroned' rather than harnessed for a 'worthy' end. On the other hand, provocation as thus constituted became a doctrinally awkward defence since, as we know, criminal liability is normally blind to context. Liability for theft is not compromised by poverty, nor assault by anger. Liability for murder is not compromised by **good** motive, such as mercy-killing, let alone bad.[100] Why does **passion but** not **compassion** negate bad character?[101] Other confession and avoidance defences at least show themselves to be consistent with the maintenance of a system of rights and obligations which characterise a liberal democracy. Allowing the defence of duress, for example, does not encourage people to 'take the law into their own hands'. It merely provides a legally validated escape route for those who are unable to rely on the law to do their (self) protecting for them. It vindicates a general right to autonomy. Provocation, on the other hand, vindicates no right known to jurisprudence unless, that is, there is an unknown right for people to go bananas because someone or something has upset them. The defence seems to allow individuals to discharge a function of the state, namely the punishment of wrongdoing, and to do so without any form of democratic control.

The notion of provocation incorporated into the common law inevitably reflected, then, the doctrinal tension created between the competing notions of the 'just' and the uncontrolled reaction.[102] In order to ensure that provocation did not become a 'soft' excuse for those who were the unrepentant prisoners of their emotions, a requirement that the response of the prisoner be 'reasonable' was grafted onto the excuse. The requirement that

---

[99] Horder (1992) ch. 2.

[100] Law Com. No. 290, *Partial Defence to Murder*, London: TSO (2004); C. Wells, 'Provocation: the Case for Abolition' in Ashworth and Mitchell (eds), *Rethinking English Homicide Law*, Oxford: OUP (2000).

[101] See discussion of *Smith (Morgan)* [2000] 3 WLR 654 below, and generally Chapter 9.

[102] R. Holton and S. Shute, 'Self-control in the Modern Provocation Defence' (2007) 27 OJLS 49.

the reasonable man might have acted similarly substantiates the moral claim that the defendant's actions were not indicative of a settled homicidal disposition. Rather they were the actions of an ordinary human being who, given the right trigger, cannot always be expected to exercise self-control.[103]

In recent years, provocation expanded to cover more morally questionable behaviours. In the case of *Doughty* the incessant cries of a baby were held to be capable of provoking the reasonable man to kill. More recently the House of Lords allowed the defence although the defendant showed himself to be lacking the self-control to be expected of reasonable adults.[104] Both cases suggested that the courts were abandoning the 'out of character' rationale to the defence and embracing the idea that provocation is a defence of impaired voluntariness, in form similar to diminished responsibility, but here 'switched on' by an external trigger rather than an internal condition. If taken further this would have the potential (and alarming) effect of bringing Case 8 within the scope of the defence.[105] More recently still, under the powerful influence of the Privy Council, the courts restated the requirement that the defendant must demonstrate the self-control to be expected of reasonable adults, returning doctrine to the 'out of character' rationale discussed above. At the time of the enactment of the Coroners and Justice Act 2009 the doctrinal elements of provocation were an external trigger[106] which caused the defendant to lose self-control and kill 'in hot blood' (the subjective prong)[107] under circumstances where ordinary people with normal powers of restraint and self-control[108] but otherwise sharing the same characteristics as the defendant[109] might have reacted in a similar way (the objective prong).[110]

1 Loss of self-control: the external trigger

Replacing provocation is a partial defence of loss of self-control.[111] Like provocation the defence operates as a defence only to murder and the defence is only partial. The formal reason for this is that only murder needs this defence since only murder carries the mandatory life sentence which might justify the existence of specialised mitigating defences. This was particularly urgent when the mandatory sentence was death.[112] The nature of the defendant's right may then be strictly speaking an immunity from (full) punishment rather than a right not to be 'labelled' a murderer.[113] Such an explanation is not able to account for the persistence of such defences in those jurisdictions where there is no mandatory sentence.

---

[103] See generally W. Wilson, 'The Structure of Criminal Defences' (2005) Crim LR 108; 'The Filtering Role of Crisis in the Constitution of Criminal Excuses' (2004) Canadian Journal of Law and Jurisprudence 387.

[104] See previous footnote. See also *R v Van Dongen* [2005] EWCA Crim 1728; [2005] Crim LR 971.

[105] *Doughty* (1986) 83 Cr App R 319. Further support for such a view can be gathered from recent cases in which the courts have been willing to 'mix and match' aspects of provocation and diminished responsibility in cases involving the killing of a violent partner, below, and see Chapter 9.

[106] *Acott* ([1997] 1 All ER 706, House of Lords); *R v Grant* [2010] EWCA Crim 3339.

[107] *R v Duffy* [1949] 1 All ER 932.

[108] *R v Holley* [2005] 3 WLR 29.

[109] *Director of Public Prosecutions v Camplin* [1978] AC 705 HL.

[110] See J. Horder, *Provocation and Responsibility*, Oxford: OUP (1992) (hereafter Horder (1992)) ch. 9, to which the discussion following owes a great debt. O. Quick and C. Wells, 'Getting Tough with Defences' [2006] Crim LR 514.

[111] B. Mitchell, 'Years of Provocation, Followed by a Loss of Control' in L. Zedner and J. Roberts (eds), *Principles and Values in Criminal Law and Criminal Justice: Essays in Honour of Andrew Ashworth*, Oxford: OUP (2012) 113.

[112] Royal Commission on Capital Punishment Report (Cmnd 8932) para. 144 (1953).

[113] In cases where the trigger relied upon is particularly serious, for example the threat of serious violence, a low, possibly not even custodial, sentence may be considered appropriate. See generally A.J. Ashworth, 'Sentencing in Provocation Cases' [1975] Crim LR 553.

Like provocation the loss of self-control defence is a defence of 'confession and avoidance'. Its essence is not a denial that the definitional elements of the offence are satisfied – these are 'confessed'. But 'superimposed' onto these definitional elements is an extra element in the fault-profile of the defendant. Success requires (unrebutted) evidence that the accused may have lost his self-control and that this loss of control issued from a 'qualifying trigger'. The defence is then established unless the jury is convinced that in acting as he did the defendant's behaviour has not measured up to the standard of self-control which ought reasonably to have been expected of him.

2 The elements of the defence

Section 54 defines the defence as follows:

(1)   Where a person ('D') kills or is a party to the killing of another ('V'), D is not to be convicted of murder if –
    (a)   D's acts and omissions in doing or being a party to the killing resulted from D's loss of self-control,
    (b)   the loss of self-control had a qualifying trigger, and
    (c)   a person of D's sex and age, with a normal degree of tolerance and self-restraint and in the circumstances of D, might have reacted in the same or in a similar way to D.
(2)   For the purposes of subsection 1(a), it does not matter whether or not the loss of control was sudden.

Section 54 includes a **subjective** element, namely a requirement that the defendant lost his self-control, and an **objective** element, namely that the loss of self-control was not out of the ordinary for a person of D's sex and age, with a normal degree of tolerance and self-restraint and in the circumstances of D.

(a) The subjective element

(i) The loss of self-control

The subjective element requires evidence that the defendant lost his self-control. It is not enough that the conduct of the victim was objectively capable of causing a loss of self-control if the defendant could have killed without it. Moreover, by subsection (6) the defence cannot be relied upon if D incited the act which constitutes the 'qualifying trigger' for the purpose of providing an excuse to use violence.

Under the previous law the subjective requirement sought to draw a line between revenge killings and provoked killings. A revenge killing, by definition, is a killing sufficiently meditated to negative the element of moral **involuntariness** inherent in the notion of a provoked killing. The distinction drawn was between a killing prompted by a spontaneous release of passion and a killing prompted by a desire for revenge,[114] albeit conjured up by an initial provocative act or event.[115] In *Ibrams* the defence was held not available where two people carried out an attack on a man who had subjected them to substantial acts of violence. Since the killing took place at night a week after the last act of violence had been committed and while the man was asleep, the evidence showed that the killing was not in hot blood.[116] Devlin J explained this idea in *Duffy*, as follows:[117]

---

[114] R. Fontaine, 'The Wrongfulness of Wrongly Interpreting Wrongfulness: Provocation, Interpretational Bias, and Heat of Passion Homicide' (2009) 12 New Crim LR 69.
[115] Cf. *East* 1 PC 234.
[116] *Ibrams* (1981) 74 Cr App R 154.
[117] [1949] 1 All ER 932.

circumstances which induce a desire for revenge are inconsistent with provocation, since the conscious formulation of a desire for revenge means that a person has the time to think, to reflect, and that would negative a sudden temporary loss of self-control, which is of the essence of provocation.

This statement had an influential effect on the modern history of the provocation defence. A long-standing issue was whether the 'sudden and temporary' requirement meant that provocation may only be relied upon if the defendant was carried away 'in the first transport of passion'.[118] Or whether it could also be relied upon where, although a significant time lapse has occurred, insufficient time has elapsed for 'reason to resume its seat'.[119] Extreme provocation may trigger different kinds of response, some no less excusable than others. It all depends upon context and the psychology of and physical attributes of the individual. The same person who would lose 'self-control' and kill when taunted by an eight-stone weakling may miraculously keep his fires under control where the provoker is rather bigger and stronger than he.

The sudden and temporary requirement had one particularly unfortunate consequence, namely that it tended to reflect the characteristics of men, who are more disposed to react with violent outbursts than women. On the one hand therefore a man might successfully rely on the defence for killing his 'nagging' wife. On the other hand, a long-term victim of domestic abuse who killed her abuser would be unlikely to avail herself of the defence unless unusually she satisfied the sudden and temporary requirement.[120] Representative of such cases is *Ahluwalia*, the facts of which warrant extended treatment.[121] The defendant wife had suffered a long period of ill-treatment and savage brutality at the hands of her husband. She had tried suicide on two occasions. Despite this she remained with him for over a decade, conceiving it a matter of wifely duty supported by a cultural code of family honour. Matters came to a head when she discovered her husband was having an affair and was threatening to leave her. She pleaded with him not to desert the family. His response was to threaten to burn her with a clothes iron if she did not leave him alone. A few hours later, she collected some petrol, threw it in his room where he was sleeping and set it alight. He died a few days later from the burns. As will be apparent, there was evidence that this killing was premeditated rather than sparked off spontaneously by a provocative act. There was also a significant time lag between the last provoking act and the reaction of the defendant.[122]

The defence argued, relying on the findings of empirical research, that the 'sudden and temporary' test was inappropriate in cases such as this since it discriminated against women. Men tend to suffer sudden explosions of anger immediately consequent upon the provoking stimulus. Women, particularly in cases of cumulative violence, tend to 'slow burn'. Their anger simmers more or less constantly and then is unleashed in a sudden eruption, typically when the danger has subsided and the neutralising effect of fear has passed.[123] The Court of Appeal, while stating that only Parliament could reverse the effect

---

[118] *East* 1 PC 234.
[119] Tindall CJ in *Hayward* (1833) 6 C & P 157; cf. Hannen J, *R v Selten* (1871) 11 Cox 674; see Russell 520–33; J. Horder (1992) chs 4, 5.
[120] See Horder, 'Sex, Violence and Sentencing in Domestic Provocation Cases' [1989] Crim LR 546; Wasik, 'Cumulative Provocation and Domestic Killing' [1982] Crim LR 29.
[121] [1992] 4 All ER 889.
[122] So also in *Thornton (No. 2)* [1996] I WLR 1174.
[123] See generally D. Nicholson and R. Sanghvi, 'Battered Women and Provocation: The Implications of *R v Ahluwalia*' [1993] Crim LR 728.

of *Duffy*,[124] stated that as long as evidence remained that the defendant killed 'during a temporary and sudden loss of self-control' the time lapse was not fatal. In short, a 'cold-blooded' killing, however much provoked, cannot be mitigated.[125]

The new defence replicates this principle. While revenge killings are explicitly excluded from the coverage of the defence[126] a delay between the trigger and the reaction is not fatal so long as a loss of self-control prompted the reaction.[127] Clearly, however, the longer the period between the trigger and the reaction, the weaker the evidence will be that a loss of self-control did actually occur. In two recent cases, heard together under the new law, the defence was held not available in just such a situation where the killings, although triggered by the consequences of the break-up of relationships, were apparently premeditated and considered, rather than spontaneous.[128]

Returning to *Ahluwalia*, although this provision addresses the 'slow burn' problem the new defence is still dependent upon the fact of the defendant having lost her control.[129] This is questionable. So long as D acted to avert the threat of serious injury it arguably ought not to matter whether she suffered a loss of self-control, or, as in this case, she kills in order to **assert control**, as the victim of kidnap might, over a situation in which she consider herself powerless.[130] What is surely important is that in such situations the defendant may not, for reasons outside her control, have a fair opportunity of pitching her behaviour according to rules.

(ii) *The qualifying triggers*

In many ways the new defence of loss of self-control is a cut-down version of the old defence of provocation. Under the old law so long as something **was said or done**[131] which triggered the defendant's loss of self-control the subjective element was satisfied. Witnessing or hearing about sexual infidelity was the archetypal trigger. The Act explicitly excludes sexual jealousy from the range of qualifying triggers, which are thus substantially attenuated.[132] However, the defence is so worded as to ensure that victim provocation of some sort will continue to lie at the heart of the defence. However, typical provocation scenarios involving those who 'snap' under conditions of mental or emotional stress will now feature, if at all, at the margins of the defence rather than, as before, at its core. This reflects a significant change in the rationale of the defence. No longer is it grounded in the recognition that killing under conditions of extreme emotional/psychological stress is an expression of ordinary human frailty and thus deserving of compassion. Rather it is grounded in the moral requirement that there be good reason for any loss of self-control resulting in extreme violence.

---

[124] Cf. Kenny (1962) 180.

[125] Although the defence of provocation was unsuccessful as the judge's direction could not be faulted the Court of Appeal nevertheless quashed the conviction as evidence of diminished responsibility had not properly been left to the jury. A retrial was ordered.

[126] S. 56(4).

[127] By section 56(2).

[128] *R v Dawes; R v Hatter* [2013] EWCA Crim 322.

[129] *R v Mann* [2011] EWCA Crim 3292.

[130] See below.

[131] In *Acott* it was held that it was not enough to show simply that the accused lost his **self-control**. He must have been **provoked** to lose his self-control. In *Acott* the defendant killed his mother in an apparent frenzy. There was general evidence that the relationship between the two of them was stormy. However, no specific provoking act or words had been raised in evidence in connection with the actual killing. The House of Lords considered, therefore, that the trial judge was right not to direct the jury upon it. Cf. *R v Grant* [2010] EWCA Crim 3339.

[132] Section 55(6)(C).

For the purposes of section 54 a loss of self-control has a qualifying trigger if D's loss of self-control was attributable as follows (section 55):

(3) to D's fear of serious violence from V against D or another identified person, OR
(4) to a thing or things done or said (or both) which –
    (a) constituted circumstances of an extremely grave character, and
    (b) caused D to have a justifiable sense of being seriously wronged, OR
(5) a combination of the matters mentioned in subsections (3) and (4).

The Act specifies only two 'qualifying triggers'. Either can be relied upon and they can work in tandem. The first trigger is that D fears that V poses a threat of serious violence against D or another person. It is not necessary that the threat be actualised but it is necessary that the fear be of serious violence. Hitherto, as has been noted, self defence was an all or nothing defence. If a person killed in self-defence this was a complete defence to murder so long as the use of force was necessary and in proportion to the threat. If, however, it was out of proportion, or there was no immediate necessity, no defence was available. An intended effect of this provision is to provide a partial defence for someone unable to avail themselves of the defence of self-defence. Perhaps, as in *Ahluwalia*, there was no threat of **immediate** harm. Perhaps, as in *Clegg*, the reaction was out of proportion to the threat.[133] The defence recognises that under conditions of extreme fear people can be expected to act unreasonably, without regard to the consequences. However, it should be noted that section 55 requires D's response to the perceived threat to be directed against the person who creates the sense of fear.

Case 8

D, a lone police officer, discovers a gang breaking into a store. X, a gang member, points a gun at D. V, another gang member, steps in front of D to prevent X shooting D. Still fearful and unable to control his reaction, D shoots V dead.

D will not be able to rely on the defence, loss of self-control notwithstanding.

The second qualifying trigger is a significantly attenuated version of the provocation defence. It applies only if the acts or words relied upon as a trigger 'constituted circumstances of an extremely grave character'. Leaving aside the rather convoluted language the intention here is to rid the law of the possibility of the jury accepting, as they were wont to for provocation, trivial triggers such as 'sexual jealousy', 'nagging', a screaming baby,[134] everyday taunting, and anti-social behaviour as grounding the defence. Illustrations from the old law which would constitute such (extremely grave) circumstances include a previous rape or act of violence, whether as victim[135] or parent or close relative of victim,[136] and blackmail.[137] One assumes also that allegations of child molesting, serious criminality, professional incompetence or wrongdoing, and other shameful activities would also count. The second requirement that the trigger 'caused the defendant to have a justifiable sense of being seriously wronged' underlines the restrictive focus lent to the new defence. It is not enough that D feels seriously wronged. It must be a justifiable sense. It is unclear, however, how much it adds to the 'extremely grave character' element. In the case of words, for

[133] Cf. *Clegg* [1997] 2 Cr App R 94.
[134] *Doughty* (1986) 83 Cr App R 319.
[135] *Complin* [1978] 2 All ER 165; *R v Greening* (1913) 29 TLR 732.
[136] *Royley* (1612) Cro Jac 296.
[137] *Edwards v R* (1973) AC 648.

example an allegation of improper conduct, the obvious answer is that the trigger will only be successful if the words are untrue because only then will the sense of being 'seriously wronged' be justifiable. In the case of deeds the words carry a further punch.

Case 9

D1 is a member of an ethnic and religious grouping who generally consider an emotional attachment to someone from outside that grouping is an affront to the family honour deserving of death. He discovers that his young daughter, V1, is planning to run away with V2, who is such a person. D1 and his son D2 confront V1 and challenge her to deny the charge. She admits it and D1 and D2 in fury kill V1 and V2.

Whether V1's plan constitutes circumstances of an extremely grave character can be decided without reference to the ethnic context. Most parents would approach the prospect of their young daughter eloping with dismay, if not alarm. The second issue is whether D1 has a justifiable sense of being seriously wronged. This probably cannot be answered without consideration of whether such circumstances are to be conceived from the point of view of D1 or from that of the wider public. Unfortunately the Act is silent on this matter. If D1 was not part of this ethnic grouping it is unlikely that his sense, if he had one, of being 'seriously wronged' would be justifiable.[138] But there is at least an argument that in the context on hand this sense was justifiable, being part of D1's cultural identity. The use of the word 'justifiable' rather than 'justified' is noteworthy here, perhaps hinting that so long as the defendant's sense is culturally validated it does not have to be universally shared. D2's position as brother, rather than father, is more tenuous in this respect. The final issue is whether, assuming the defence is available with respect to V1, it is also available with respect to V2. One must assume it is. If V1 is responsible for D1's sense of being 'seriously wronged', V2 is no less responsible.

The upshot of this discussion is that introducing notions of justified response into the loss of self-control defence detracts from the *relative* certainty that the defence of provocation latterly enjoyed. It is easier for a jury to determine whether the defendant's reaction was consistent with the level of response to be expected from ordinary people than to determine whether the emotions which prompted that reaction were justifiable. That said, it is clearly incumbent upon the jury to tailor its notion of the justified response to what is morally or politically acceptable. In this regard, the judge has been given a supervisory role with the power to remove from the jury's consideration cases of alleged loss of self-control which are clearly unmeritorious,[139] that is those cases where the judge considers that no reasonable jury could conclude that the defendant's sense of being seriously wronged was justifiable or his reaction was within normal bounds of tolerance and self restraint. Presumably, therefore, a judge would withdraw the defence from the jury if of the opinion, say, that the trigger relied upon would only elicit a loss of self-control in a defendant who was racist or homophobic.

(iii) *Sexual infidelity*

Under the previous law the archetypal trigger, in line with the defence's heavily gendered nature, was sexual jealousy and possessiveness. The new law seeks to remove that bias from

---

[138] Cf. *R v Mohammed* [2005] EWCA Crim 1880.

[139] Section 54(6). See for example *R v Dawes*; *R v Hatter* [2013] EWCA Crim 322 below.

the defence and ensure that base emotions such as sexual jealousy and unjustified anger are no longer qualifying triggers. Only justified loss of self-control is covered. Indeed, to make certain that no judge is under any illusion that sexual jealousy is no longer a qualifying trigger, section 55(6) explicitly excludes it. Now a person who kills because he witnesses or hears about the sexual infidelity of his/her partner cannot use the defence. In *R v Clinton, Parker & Evans* an important qualification to section 55(6) was made by the Court of Appeal.[140] In effect *Clinton* interprets section 55(6) to mean that sexual infidelity which prompts a loss of self-control due to sexual jealousy, possessiveness, or family honour is not a qualifying trigger. However, if the sexual infidelity provides the context within which another trigger (that is, which is not jealousy, possessiveness or family honour) operates it must be considered. In this case D killed his wife having found out she was unfaithful. However, the loss of self-control was not prompted by possessiveness or jealousy but by the fact that, when asked to reconsider her wish to leave D, she abused him and made several extremely wounding remarks including that she had had enough of looking after their children. She also derided him for his weakness and for being too weak minded to execute his desire to commit suicide. Thus, taking the whole context into account, including the infidelity, D was able to claim that he was subject to things said or done which constituted circumstances of an extremely grave character which caused him to have a justifiable sense of being seriously wronged.

In *Dawes* and *Hatter*[141] the Court of Appeal, while approving the decision in *Clinton*, agreed with the trial judge that the fact of the break up of a relationship, **of itself**, will not normally constitute circumstances of an extremely grave character and entitle the aggrieved party to feel a justifiable sense of being seriously wronged. As the trial judge observed, 'To suggest that the fact of a break-up of a relationship could amount to circumstances of an extremely grave character or that it would entitle the aggrieved party to feel a justifiable sense of being seriously wronged would be to ignore the normal meaning of these words. It would also result in the defence of loss of control being left to the jury in almost every case where one partner to a relationship kills the other, which was clearly not Parliament's intention.' The judge is saying, in other words, that there must be something in addition to the usual heartache and grievances accompanying the breakdown of a relationship which renders the circumstances sufficiently grave to warrant a justifiable sense of being seriously wronged. What that added ingredient is only time will tell but *Clinton* gives us a strong indication of the kind of matters the courts are looking for.

(iv) *Self-induced loss of self-control*

In the case of most, if not all, common law defences a defendant will not be allowed to avail himself of a defence if he causes the conditions under which he subsequently seeks to rely upon it. Thus, automatism is not a defence if the defendant's condition is caused by his own lack of conscientiousness; duress is not a defence if the defendant mortgaged his autonomy (from coercion) to a dangerous gang. In the case of loss of self-control the strict wording of section 56 runs counter to this approach, as it once did for provocation. What seems to matter is whether the jury believe the defendant to have lost his self-control, not whether the defendant rendered himself vulnerable to such a loss.

---

[140] [2012] EWCA Crim 2.
[141] *R v Bowyer* [2013] EWCA Crim 322.

> **Case 10**
>
> A, a hardened bully, teases V, his victim, mercilessly by pinching and slapping him. V, to defend himself, delivers a number of very painful blows to A's shins causing A, fearful that the blows will escalate, to lose self-control and kill V.

On the general approach to excuses it seems that A should not be able to rely on the loss of self-control, as he himself was in large part its author. This was the conclusion of the Privy Council decision in *Edwards*.[142] The defendant D was a blackmailer whose demands had stung his victim V into attacking him with a knife. D killed V as a result of his own loss of self-control. The Privy Council held that it was only because V had overreacted with a knife that D was able to rely on provocation at all. If V's reaction had been a more predictable response to D's own conduct, the defence would not have been available. In *Johnson*[143] this approach was said to be misconceived – 'we find it impossible to accept that the mere fact that a defendant caused a reaction in others, which in turn led him to lose his control, should result in the issue of provocation being kept outside a jury's consideration . . .'.[144] This might be thought to be giving a defendant two bites at the cherry – not only is his responsibility reduced for an intentional killing, but also his responsibility for precipitating the conditions of his own loss of self-control are ignored. Under the new law so long as the defendant did not purposefully incite the violence of the victim so as to provide an excuse to use violence in return the defence remains available to those responsible for their own loss of self-control.[145] It is noteworthy, in this respect, that the Act refers **not** to the loss of self-control being 'caused' by a qualifying trigger, leaving room for arguments about relative responsibility, but rather that the loss of self-control 'had' a qualifying trigger.[146] On the facts of Case 10, assuming the jury are satisfied that D had a fear of serious violence, D will therefore be able to avail himself of the defence. It should be noted that if they are not so satisfied D will probably not be able to rely on the second qualifying trigger because although the blows 'constitute circumstances of an extremely grave character', D's initial responsibility may well be thought not to have caused D to have a **justifiable** sense of being **seriously** wronged.

(v) *Loss of self-control, self-defence and the burden of proof*

Although loss of self-control and self-defence are conceptually quite distinct, the same fact configuration may raise both possibilities. A person who kills in the course of a violent fight may be the aggressor and so guilty of murder upon proof of the requisite *mens rea*. On the other hand, he may be acting reasonably in self-defence, in which case he may be entitled to an outright acquittal. Alternatively, a blow by the victim may have so frightened the defendant that it caused him to cast off all restraint and kill the aggressor. As will be appreciated the appropriate interpretation will be very much a matter of evidence. Typically the defendant will wish to defend himself on the ground of self-defence, even if there is strong evidence of loss of self-control, since relying on the latter may weaken the plausibility of the former. If the defendant decides not to raise the defence of loss of self-control, whether for this reason or any other,[147] the judge is nevertheless bound to leave

---

[142] [1973] 1 All ER 152.
[143] [1989] 2 All ER 839.
[144] [1989] 2 All ER 839 at 842.
[145] *R v Bowyer* [2013] EWCA Crim 322.
[146] Section 55, above.
[147] In *Cambridge* [1994] Crim LR 690 the defence did not raise any defence, but denied that they were the assailant.

the defence to the jury if sufficient evidence is raised. This was the case for provocation and one assumes also for the new defence.[148] Where evidence of loss of self-control sufficient in the judge's opinion to justify the jury reaching the conclusion that the defence might apply, the burden is on the prosecution to disprove it rather than upon the defendant to prove it.[149]

(b) *The objective element*

Once the jury are satisfied on the existence of a loss of self-control induced by a qualifying trigger, it must then consider whether 'a person of D's sex and age, with a normal degree of tolerance and self restraint and in the circumstances of D, might have reacted in the same or in a similar way to D.' This provision upholds the corresponding provision for provocation at the time of the enactment of the 2009 Act which required the defendant to have reacted as the reasonable man might have reacted. This allowed the jury to take into account any characteristic of the defendant which may have affected the gravity of the provocation to him or her but not any characteristic, other than age or sex, which may have affected his level of self-control.[150] The idea was that reasonable people maybe in pain, impotent, sexually deviant, deformed, black, white, or have made mistakes in the past and so be particularly vulnerable to losing their self-control when abused on that matter, but otherwise have the same level of self-control as everyone else.[151] In *R v Hill* it was agreed that having been a child victim of sexual abuse would be a circumstance which the jury should take into account in deciding how a person of reasonable tolerance might react to an alleged sexual approach.[152] In *R v Asmelash* the Court of Appeal confirmed that being voluntarily intoxicated is not one of the circumstances which the jury must take into account in deciding how D might be expected to react.[153] Faced with a defendant who lost his self-control while voluntarily intoxicated the jury should consider whether a sober person of D's sex and age, with a normal degree of tolerance and self-restraint would have reacted as D did. The requirement that D's reaction should be the 'same or similar' to what we might expect of persons of reasonable tolerance arguably adds little to the requirement that the trigger be 'grave' and the reaction be in response to a justifiable sense of being 'seriously wronged'. However, where it might be expected to kick in is where, notwithstanding the existence of a qualifying trigger of sufficient gravity, the defendant completely overreacts, for example, by setting the victim on fire rather than simply hitting him/her over the head with force sufficient to kill or cause serious injury. Although the precondition for the loss of self-control might exist it is still necessary that a person of normal self-control and tolerance might have reacted as 'in the same or similar way'.

B Evaluation

The law on provocation was crying out for reform. It was created essentially with men in mind. Men 'snap' when they are attacked, or find their wife in bed with another man, or are nagged by their partner. Male judges, not surprisingly perhaps, have thus been able

---

[148] *Hopper* [1915] 2 KB 431; *Bullard* (1957) 42 Cr App R 1; *Newell* (1980) 71 Cr App R 331; *Scott* [1997] Crim LR 597.
[149] Section 54(5)(6).
[150] *Camplin* [1978] 2 All ER 165 at 175.
[151] A problem then arises if the taunt is untrue and the defendant loses control because it is untrue and he is indignant lest it be thought to be true.
[152] [2008] CWCA Crim 76.
[153] [2013] EWCA Crim 157.

to empathise with the loss of control. It is the kind of loss they can imagine themselves experiencing. Men are perhaps less able to empathise with the kind of slow-burn response discussed in relation to *Ahluwalia* for the simple reason that they are rarely placed in the kind of disempowering situations where nasty, brutal and quick reaction to provocation is not a practical possibility. As a result women who kill in response to cumulative abuse were in a worse position than men who are subject to objectively far less provocation. Women, as a result, were forced to medicalise their predicament[154] in order to obtain equal treatment with men.[155]

To rid current law of its preoccupation with loss of self-control and the reasons for it, it might have been preferable simply for the defendant to be able to raise evidence of extreme emotional disturbance[156] and that, in that context, her failure to adhere to a rule was (partially) excusable.[157] The Law Commission's proposal, upon which the legislation was based, was more radical. It required a similar trigger – gross provocation which causes the defendant to have a justifiable sense of being seriously wronged; or reaction to fear of serious violence towards the defendant or another, or a combination of the two.[138] However, it did not require the defendant to have lost self-control in response to that trigger, nor to be suffering extreme emotional disturbance.[159] The aim was to render the reasonableness of the reaction paramount rather than the state of mind of the reacting defendant.[160] The advantage of this is that it is uncontroversially available to those who overreact in self-defence[161] and also to those who, like Mrs Ahluwalia, have reached the end of their tether but do not suffer sudden and temporary loss of self-control.[162]

An arguable disadvantage of the new defence is that the mandatory sentence will not attach to those whose reaction was a one-off due to the extreme emotional disturbance the trigger provoked. Sometimes it is right to recognise the ordinary human frailty which makes reasonable people 'lose it' on occasions.[163] We cannot expect human beings with the constitutional weaknesses of ordinary human beings always to measure up in times of extreme stress, and it would be inappropriate for the state not to recognise this fact.[164] This is the preferred response of Mackay and Mitchell who have recommended combining provocation and diminished responsibility on the basis that it is no longer practical to maintain the separateness between them.[165] The defence would be available where, at the time of killing, the defendant was suffering either from extreme emotional disturbance or

---

[154] Using diminished responsibility. See O. Quick and C. Wells (2006).
[155] Nicholson and Sanghvi, op. cit. 733–7.
[156] See J. Horder, 'Reshaping the Subjective Element in Provocation' (2005) OJLS 123.
[157] See K.J.M. Smith and W. Wilson, 'Impaired Voluntariness and Criminal Responsibility' (1993) 13 OJLS 69 and J. Horder, 'Pleading Involuntary Lack of Capacity' [1993] Camb LJ 298.
[158] Law Com. 290, *Partial Defences to Murder* (2004) 3.69–3.70; Law Com. No. 304 (2006).
[159] For critical commentary see R. Taylor, 'The Nature of "Partial Defences" and the Coherence of (Second-Degree) Murder' [2007] Crim LR 345.
[160] 'We favour as the moral basis for retaining a defence of provocation that the defendant had legitimate ground to feel seriously wronged by the person at whom his or her conduct was aimed, and that this lessened the moral culpability of the defendant reacting to that outrage in the way that he or she did. It is the justification of the sense of outrage which provides a partial excuse for their responsive conduct.'
[161] See generally A. McColgan, 'In Defence of Battered Women Who Kill' (1993) 13 OJLS 508. See p. 378, above.
[162] Report No. 290. See for example J. Horder, 'Between Provocation and Diminished Responsibility' [1999] 10 Kings College LJ 143; cf. R. Mackay, 'Diminished Responsibility and Mentally Disordered Killers' in A.J. Ashworth and B. Mitchell (eds), *Rethinking English Homicide Law*, Oxford: OUP (2000); R. Mackay and B. Mitchell, 'Provoking Diminished Responsibility: Two Pleas Merging into One?' [2003] Crim LR 745.
[163] W.Wilson, 'The Structure of Criminal Defences' (2005) Crim LR 108. Cf. Quick and Wells (2006).
[164] This view forms the basis of the corresponding provision of the American Model Penal Code Clause 210.3(1)(b).
[165] 'Provoking Diminished Responsibility: Two Pleas Merging into One?' [2003] Crim LR 745.

from unsoundness of mind which affected his behaviour to such a degree that the offence ought to be reduced to manslaughter.[166] On the other hand we ignore the morally mitigating effect of duress, mercy killing, and other 'good' motives. Why should we take into account any of the reasons which prompted a person to do 'evil', let alone add to them?[167] If compassion or mercy, rather than the consistent application of moral principle, motivates our response, surely the best legislative vehicle for its delivery would be the abolition of the mandatory sentence.[168]

13.6 DIMINISHED RESPONSIBILITY: THE INTERNAL TRIGGER

A General matters

The defence of diminished responsibility is a statutory (partial) defence defined by s. 2, Homicide Act 1957 as amended by the Coroners and Justice Act 2009. Unusually, the burden of proof is upon the defendant and only the defendant can raise it.[169] All cases where the defence is raised will therefore be charged as murder. The effect of successfully raising the defence is to reduce the liability of an intentional killer from murder to manslaughter, thus removing the mandatory sentence. In 1957 this was death by hanging and it is now life imprisonment. The judge has a discretion in sentencing varying from absolute discharge to life imprisonment. In suitable cases a hospital or guardianship order maybe preferred.[170] The defence was introduced largely to counteract the narrow application of the *M'Naghten* rules, which afforded no excuse or mitigation of sentence to those who killed while suffering from severe mental illness falling short of *M'Naghten* insanity. It has been a more popular defence than insanity, largely because of the wide discretion available for sentencing. This popularity is likely to continue, since the 1991 Act leaves hospitalisation as mandatory in cases of killing while insane. The defence is not available to attempted murder.[171]

The new defence differs from its pre-2009 counterpart in a number of ways but it remains to be seen how significant these will be in practice.[172] The latter was grounded in 'mental abnormality'. Any substantial emotional or mental abnormality could ground the defence so long as it resulted from inherent rather than external causes. This indeterminate scope meant that 'jury equity' was heavily determinative of case outcomes. The scope for such discretion is now in theory much attenuated. The defence is now unavailable unless the defendant is suffering a clinically recognised mental disorder which not only accompanies but **explains** his/her participation in the killing.

Diminished responsibility has elements in common with the statutory defences of infanticide and loss of self control, insofar as it provides a partial excuse to murder upon evidence that the defendant lacked the rational capacity to order his actions according to rules. Like these, the defence serves only as a partial excuse. The defendant's responsibility

---

[166] Cf. J. Dressler, 'Battered Women Who Kill Their Sleeping Tormentors' in Simester and Shute (2002).

[167] C. Wells, 'Provocation: the Case for Abolition' in A.J. Ashworth and B. Mitchell (eds), *Rethinking English Homicide Law*, Oxford: OUP (2000) 104–6.

[168] Cf. *R v Inglis* [2010] EWCA Crim 2637; [2011] Crim LR 243.

[169] Homicide Act 1957, s. 2(2); cf. *Straw* (1995) 1 All ER 187.

[170] Mental Health Act 1983, s. 37.

[171] *Campbell* [1996] Crim LR 495.

[172] R.D. Mackay, 'The Coroners and Justice Act 2009 – Partial Defences to Murder (2) The New Diminished Responsibility Plea' [2010] Crim LR 290; L. Kennefick, 'Introducing a New Diminished Responsibility Defence for England and Wales' (2011) 74(5) MLR 750.

is deemed impaired, not extinguished, even though it is clear that the defendant lacked a normal rule-following response.

B Statutory definition

The amended section 2 provides as follows:

> s. 2(1) 'A person ("D") who kills or is a party to the killing of another is not to be convicted of murder if D was suffering from an abnormality of mental functioning which –
>
> (a) arose from a recognised medical condition,
> (b) substantially impaired D's ability to do one or more of the things mentioned in subsection (1A), and
> (c) provides an explanation for D's acts and omissions in doing or being a party to the killing.
>
> (1A) Those things are –
>
> (a) to understand the nature of D's conduct;
> (b) to form a rational judgment;
> (c) to exercise self-control.
>
> (1B) For the purposes of subsection 1(c), an abnormality of mental functioning provides an explanation for D's conduct if it causes, or is a significant contributory factor in causing, D to carry out that conduct.'

C Elements of the defence

1 Abnormality of mental functioning

The scope of diminished responsibility is far wider than the notion of mental illness captured in the *M'Naghten* rules. Indeed, it has been held that directions to the jury along the lines that diminished responsibility is a form of 'partial insanity' or lies on the borderline of insanity should be avoided.[173] A defendant may rely upon the defence even if he is aware of what he is doing and that it is wrong, as long as his condition involved a specified abnormality arising from a recognised mental condition. The phrase 'abnormality of mental functioning' replaces 'abnormality of mind', and in this respect at least is a marked improvement on the previous law, where 'abnormality of mind' had no clearly defined parameters. Here, by contrast, the parameters are clear. A person has an abnormality of mental functioning if the person's mental functions of understanding what she was doing, and/or forming a rational judgement, and/or exercising self-control were substantially impaired such that it would be inappropriate to treat her as fully responsible.[174]

2 A recognised mental condition

The abnormality of mental functioning must be grounded in a recognised mental condition. Under the previous law there was no such requirement, which lent the defence a more extensive coverage than was originally intended. For example mercy killing, psychopathy,[175] reactive depression, battered women's syndrome, morbid jealousy and

---

[173] *Seers* (1984) 79 Cr App Rep 261.
[174] *R v Baker* [2012] EWCA Crim 2843.
[175] *Byrne* [1960] 3 All ER 1.

diabetes coupled with marriage problems were all found capable of grounding the defence.[176] Although such conditions may act as behavioural triggers they exhibit no common characteristics other than their tendency to elicit jury sympathy and understanding. The recognised 'medical condition' requirement means, in theory, that such reaction will no longer be determinative. Problems will still remain, however. Some of these were raised in responses to the Ministry of Justice Consultation Paper. While the phrase 'recognised medical condition' will clearly encompass all relevant mental disorders which are officially recognised[177] it is not restricted to these. As Mackay points out, it must cover both 'psychological' and 'physical' conditions including conditions like epilepsy, sleep disorders and diabetes.[178] Recognised medical conditions can be found in authoritative classificatory lists, including the World Health Organisation's International Classification of Diseases and the American Psychiatric Association's Diagnostic and Statistical Manual of Mental Disorders. It is likely that the following conditions, which grounded the old law, will continue to be accepted as recognised mental conditions, developmental disorders: depression, *R v Gittens* (1984); bipolar, *R v Inglis* (2010) EWCA Crim 2269; paranoid schizophrenia, *R v Sutcliffe* (1981), *R v Petrolini* [2012] EWCA Crim 2055; brain damage, psychopathy, *Byrne* (1960); paranoid personality disorder, *Martin* [2002], post-natal depression, *Reynolds* (1988). One can add to these, one assumes, autism and battered women's syndrome.

The new law, therefore, will require the testimony of expert witnesses in any case where the condition relied upon by the defendant is contested or ambiguous.[179] Contested examples which were accepted a basis for the defence under the old law include battered women's syndrome (*Ahluwalia, R v Hobson* (1997) CA) and premenstrual syndrome (*R v (Sadie) Smith* 1982). Nevertheless the decision is ultimately one for the judge. In *R v Osborne* (2010) EWCA Crim 547 the Court of Appeal ruled that attention deficit hyperactivity disorder (ADHD) would not afford any ground for allowing the appeal against conviction on the basis of diminished responsibility.

(a) *Drugs and alcoholism*

A difficulty encountered under the previous law was the availability of the defence in cases of alcoholism or drug abuse, since both can be treated as causing or synonymous with mental abnormality and, for the purpose of the new defence, lead to loss of rational judgement, loss of self-control and so on. Three situations should be distinguished.[180] The first is a case involving intoxication alone. This does not support the defence under new or old law since the defendant's condition will not be due to disease or '**inherent** cause' (old law) or 'arise from a recognised medical condition' (new law).[181] The second is where the defendant is an alcoholic who commits a criminal harm attributable to the brain damage or psychosis which may be caused by this condition. In *Tandy* the Court of Appeal acknowledged that chronic alcoholism could be a cause of mental abnormality

---

[176] *TCL* 692–4. *Nichols* (1974) *The Times*, 5 October. Also *Price*, below. Compare the facts, and outcome, of this case with *Hennessy* [1989] 2 All ER 9, above.

[177] As in the Diagnostic and Statistical Manual of the American Psychiatric Association.

[178] R.D. Mackay, 'The Coroners and Justice Act 2009 – Partial Defences to Murder (2) The New Diminished Responsibility Plea' [2010] Crim LR.

[179] Though the jury are not bound to accept the medical evidence – *R v Sanders* [1991] Crim LR 781.

[180] M. Gibson, 'Intoxicants and Diminished Responsibility: The Impact of the Coroners and Justice Act 2009' [2011] Crim LR 909.

[181] *R v Dowds* [2012] 1 Cr App R 455.

within the meaning of s. 2.[182] Presumably this will continue to be the case as chronic alcoholism is a recognised medical condition. The third is where the defendant is an alcoholic who commits a criminal harm as a result of becoming intoxicated consequent upon suffering from this condition. In *Tandy*, the defence was refused on this basis, despite evidence of serious addiction. Since the basis for excusing defendants is the defendant's inability to make rational choices as to how he would like to act, tying this excuse to a specific cause is arguably an unjustifiable restriction. What is important, surely, is **whether** responsibility is lacking rather than **why** it is lacking. The apparent reason for restricting the operation of the defence to specific causes is to reduce the scope for raising spurious excuses. If so, the rationale for the restriction is here unclear. If alcoholism is a condition relevant to responsibility at all, it is, almost by definition, a condition involving reduced willpower. In *R v Stewart* the Court of Appeal clarified the position following *Tandy* indicating that alcohol dependency syndrome could be considered a mental condition capable of producing, where it caused involuntary consumption of alcohol depending upon the evidence, an abnormality of mind. This decision is presumably equally applicable to the notion of mental functioning (loss of rational judgement or self-control) under the new law.

A related problem is the position where the defendant suffers from abnormality of mind and, in this condition, becomes intoxicated. The position here is complicated, and one which demands a lot of the jury. In *Egan*[183] the Court of Appeal said that the jury should be directed to ignore the effect of the intoxication and consider whether 'the combined effect of the other matters which do fall within the section amounted to such abnormality of mind as substantially impaired the defendant's mental responsibility'.[184] In short, this requires the defendant to prove that the killing was due to his abnormality rather than the voluntary consumption of alcohol. In *Dietschmann* the House of Lords nevertheless ruled that diminished responsibility could be relied upon where a mentally abnormal man killed while intoxicated so long as the mental abnormality played a part in the killing.[185] This presumably will continue to be the case under the new law, always assuming that the mental abnormality is a recognised mental condition.

3 Substantially impaired D's ability to do one or more of the things mentioned in subsection (1A)

This provision tightens up the previous formulation which referred to 'substantial impairment of responsibility'. Whether it is a substantive improvement is a matter of opinion but it will no doubt be easier for medical experts to reach a considered opinion based upon clinical criteria. In each case it was previously a matter for the jury as to whether the defendant's condition is such as to substantially impair his responsibility and was a matter of degree.[186] In *Lloyd*[187] it was suggested that juries should be asked to approach the notion of substantial impairment in a broad common-sense way, referring to impairments which are more

---

[182] *Tandy* (1988) 87 Cr App Rep 45; cf. *Inseal* [1992] Crim LR 35.
[183] [1992] 4 All ER 470.
[184] [1992] 4 All ER 470; approving the direction in *Gittens* [1984] 3 All ER 252; also the guidance given by Professor Smith in his commentary on the case in [1984] Crim LR 553. Followed in *R v Wood* [2008] EWCA Crim 1305.
[185] *Dietschmann* [2003] UK HL 10. Followed in *R v Wood* [2008] EWCA Crim 1305 and *R v Stewart* [2009] EWCA 593. G.R Sullivan, 'Intoxicants and Diminished Responsibility' [1994] Crim LR 156.
[186] *Byrne* [1960] 3 All ER 1.
[187] [1966] 1 All ER 107.

than trivial but less than total. Clearly this left a lot to subjective moral evaluation and, as a result, had a marked influence on the overall implementation of the defence. One reason for this was the role played by expert medical evidence in the establishment of the defence. Medical evidence was used both to establish the existence of mental abnormality and the consequent degree of impairment, although why the medical expertise should extend to this latter question is difficult to fathom. Juries, no doubt often emboldened by the pragmatic benevolence of the medical experts, showed themselves wont to accept the defence where they had sympathy for the defendant in the absence of compelling medical evidence of mental abnormality, and to reject it where they have not, in the face of overwhelming evidence. Thus in *Price* a father of a mentally-handicapped son who caused his death by casting him adrift on a river succeeded with the defence. On the other hand Peter Sutcliffe – the Yorkshire Ripper – did not, despite the strong medical evidence that he suffered from paranoid schizophrenia.[188] The new formulation sets clearer parameters for the defence by specifying what consequences of abnormal mental functioning are relevant to responsibility. It is only if the abnormality is of a nature to compromise substantially the defendant's understanding of what she was doing, and/or forming a rational judgement, and/or exercising self-control that the defence is operative.[189] The space for 'jury equity' in cases of understandable mental disturbance is thus markedly attenuated. So, in *R v Osbourne* the Court of Appeal concluded that the fact that D was suffering from ADHD did not mean that the impairment was substantial. A person with ADHD can still form the necessary intention and are not thereby deprived of the ability to understand what they are doing, form a rational judgement, and exercise self-control.[190] Again, in *R v Jackson* J's conviction for murder was upheld despite the production of fresh evidence indicating that at the time of the killing the defendant had been suffering from post-traumatic stress disorder as a result of previous sexual and physical abuse. The evidence provided no reason to doubt the jury's rejection of his defence of diminished responsibility.[191]

4 Providing an explanation for the killing

Under the previous law there was no requirement of a causal link between the abnormality and the killing. A jury was entitled to conclude for example that a person suffering from, say, clinical depression was, by that fact alone, less responsible for their actions than normal people and so should not be treated as comparably blameworthy. The new provision requires that the abnormality must provide an **explanation** for the defendant's acts and omissions in doing or being a party to the killing. It must form part of the story as to why this killing took place. The actor's reason was impaired, she did not fully understand what she was doing, her self-control was lacking and so on and that is why or one of the reasons why she did what she did. Whether it does provide an explanation for the killing is a jury question which, in cases involving multiple causes, for example depression and intoxication (see *R v Gittens*) or worse, chronic alcoholism and intoxication (see *Wood* above) could prove a bit of a challenge. On the other hand, in theory, at least those suffering from an anti-social personality disorder are arguably more likely to be within the coverage of the defence on the grounds that:

---

[188] E. Griew, 'The Future of Diminished Responsibility' [1988] Crim LR 75, 84.
[189] Section 52(1)(A).
[190] [2010] EWCA Crim 547.
[191] [2013] EWCA Crim 163 D's.

(a) anti-social personality disorder is a recognised medical condition;

(b) causes an abnormality of mental functioning so as to

(c) impair the defendant's ability to exercise self-control and

(d) provides an explanation for the killing.

This is the theory. Experience tells us however that jurors are likely to be no more sympathetic towards this defence under the new as under the old law. Why, after all, should a personality trait which deprives the actor of the ability to empathise with others and which therefore explains why he kills provide him with an excuse? The majority of jurors, one suspects, will agree with this sentiment.[192] Indeed it is implicit in the approach adopted in the United States. The American Model Penal Code expressly excludes (abnormalities) 'manifested only by repeated criminal or otherwise anti-social conduct' from the ambit of the equivalent Code defence.[193]

D Overlap with loss of self-control

Prior to the passing of the 2008 Act diminished responsibility was often successfully paired with the defence of provocation in the sense that, one way or the other, a killing under circumstances of mental disturbance could be mitigated to manslaughter. The pairing was most evident in cases where loss of self-control may have been attributable to a reduced capacity to withstand external provocation due to mental abnormality. Many, but not all,[194] involved long-term physical abuse of females by their partners. A notable example is *Ahluwalia*.[195] At trial her plea of provocation and lack of *mens rea* was rejected and she was convicted of murder. The Court of Appeal quashed her conviction on the basis that new evidence had come to light. At retrial her plea of manslaughter on the ground of diminished responsibility was accepted.

Theoretically defendants such as Mrs Ahluwalia fell between three excuse stools. Provocation was unavailable unless her claim amounted to a spontaneous and complete loss of self-control. There was no evidence of such a loss. Doctrine restricted such excusing contexts to those involving 'explosions of outrage'. It takes little commitment to feminism to understand that this defence grew out of (and had outgrown) (male) judicial sympathy to masculinised responses to emotional crises such as marital infidelity. However, diminished responsibility did not fit either, since her abnormality was symptomatic rather than systemic. It disappeared when her husband disappeared. If anything, this is a case which is more akin to self-defence than either provocation or diminished responsibility.[196] And self-defence is a full rather than partial justification (or excuse) excuse.[197]

Ahluwalia illustrates the difficult task facing judges when the excuse categories are too narrow to accommodate the defendant's moral claim to be excused. And of course it extends far wider than the case of battered woman syndrome. The Coroners and Justice Act

---

[192] See *Byrne* [1960] 2 QB 396 CCA 2; cf. N. Eastman and J. Peay, 'Sentencing Psychopaths' [1998] Crim LR 93.

[193] MPC 210.3 (1) (revised edition 1980).

[194] *Ireland* (1983) *The Times*, 26 March.

[195] [1992] 4 All ER 889.

[196] See generally C. Wells, 'Battered Woman Syndrome and Defences to Homicide: Where Now?' (1994) 14 LS 266; A. McColgan, 'In Defence of Battered Women who Kill' (1993) OJLS 508.

[197] J. Dressler, 'New Thoughts about the Concept of Justification in the Criminal Law: a Critique of Fletcher's Thinking and Rethinking' [1984] 32 UCLA L Rev 61 for a notion of justified defence which could accommodate battered women's syndrome.

does not satisfactorily address the problem of those who kill their abusers. The section 54 offence is not available unless the defendant killed having lost his/her self-control under fear of serious violence. This is not usually the reason why victims kill their abusers. More plausibly the killing is an example of the victim fighting back, thus asserting rather than losing control over an hitherto uncontrollable external agent. The section 53 defence presents difficulties of another kind, namely the requirement that 'battered woman syndrome' be established as a recognised mental condition. Is it and should it be so recognised?[198] If it is, a political dimension of such recognition must be acknowledged, namely the messages communicated to the public about 'battered women'. Similar politics surround the medicalisation of conditions such as pre-menstrual syndrome, which have also been used successfully to support a plea of diminished responsibility.[199] These messages communicate the idea that battered women kill because they are victims, dehumanised and/or abnormal rather than that they take a rational choice, as a person acting in self-defence might, to put her physical safety and integrity above that of the person seeking to destroy it.[200]

E Infanticide

Infanticide is a defence to murder and, indeed, to manslaughter. The essence of the defence is that of a voluntary killing mitigated, like loss of self-control and diminished responsibility, because responsibility is impaired. Infanticide is also a crime and can be charged as such. This carries the advantage of removing from the jury the need to consider medical evidence. This the prosecution, by charging with this offence rather than murder, already accepts. In *Gore* the Court of Appeal ruled that infanticide was an alternative offence also to manslaughter.[201] This is now enshrined in statute.[202] The offence/defence is defined in the Infanticide Act 1938[203] as follows:

> Where a woman by any wilful act or omission causes the death of her child being a child under the age of twelve months, but at the time of the act or omission the balance of her mind was disturbed by reason of her not having fully recovered from the effect of giving birth to the child or by reason of the effect of lactation consequent upon the birth of the child, then, notwithstanding that the circumstances were such that but for this Act the offence would have amounted to murder, she shall be guilty of . . . infanticide, and may for such an offence be dealt with and punished as if she had been guilty of the offence of the manslaughter of the child.

The essence of the offence, then, is a voluntary killing of a child under the age of one year by its mother. It is a noteworthy example of how doctrine is constructed out of a view taken on a matter of sentencing. It had long been recognised that the death penalty was inappropriate for mothers who killed their children in the few months after childbirth. Hormonal changes after birth commonly result in temporary depression which may become clinical depression. In severe cases this may lead to the mother killing the child.

Calls have been made in recent years for the offence/defence to be reconstructed to take into account the current state of evidence surrounding the killing of newborn infants.

---

[198] Or the sufferer from PMS: see *Sadie Smith* below.

[199] *Sadie Smith* [1982] Crim LR 531.

[200] Cf. Dressler, op. cit.

[201] *R v Gore* [2007] EWCA Crim 2789. This decision is now replicated in s. 57 Coroners and Justice Act 2009, amending Infanticide Act 1938. See R. Mackay, 'The Consequences of Killing Very Young Children' [1993] Crim LR 21 at 29.

[202] Coroners and Justice Act 2009, s. 57.

[203] Section 1(1) replacing the Act of 1922.

First, it seems clear that relatively few such killings result from mental imbalance resulting from lactation or the fact of having given birth. Considerations such as the frustrations of coping with an inconsolable child, particularly in conditions of poverty and limited space, are more conducive to such a response.[204] Yet despite this the vast majority of infant killings by mothers are treated as infanticides or lesser offences rather than murder.[205] It has been concluded that infanticide is used in practice as a means of ensuring leniency of treatment to mothers who kill their very young children, whether there are cogent medical grounds for doing so or not. In this sense infanticide is a less onerous defence to murder than is diminished responsibility.[206] In the light of such evidence the Criminal Law Revision Committee recommended that the defence should be extended to include cases where the killing was prompted by environmental or other stresses.[207] The Draft Criminal Code Bill contains a comparable provision:

> A woman who, but for this section, would be guilty of murder or manslaughter of her child is not guilty of murder or manslaughter, but is guilty of infanticide, if her act is done when the child is under the age of twelve months and when the balance of her mind is disturbed by reason of the effect of giving birth or of circumstances consequent upon birth.[208]

The failure to recommend extension of the coverage of infanticide to male parents may be considered odd, given that environmental stresses are now recognised as a serious determinant of infant killings. If a child screaming at an out-of-work mother suffering sleep deprivation in a cramped flat impairs her responsibility, there is no obvious reason why it should not impair the responsibility of a male parent in like circumstances.[209] It has been concluded that this failure is representative of an invidious tendency to show mercy only to female killers of their children. This not only potentially demeans women but may be unfair to men suffering comparable stress. Indeed, outside the field of infanticide, statistics show that mothers, although equally represented as potential killers of their children, are generally treated more favourably than fathers.[210] This tendency may itself derive from untenable assumptions. Male killers are more likely to be perceived as wicked, and mothers as victims of circumstances even though the circumstances of the killing are broadly comparable.[211] Whatever the rights and wrongs of the situation, however, it is arguable that mercy and compassion are proper objects of the criminal law given the wealth of evidence concerning the stresses of childbirth and the early period of child-rearing. Opening up the defence to fathers and mothers of children above twelve months would leave one questioning the logic of restricting the defence only to natural parents.[212] If it is thought bad public policy to open up the defence so as to potentially loosen the demands of self-control in the population at large, it may nevertheless be right to afford the defence to those (mothers) socially and congenitally most in need of it.[213]

---

[204] For strong criticism of the law in this respect see Court of Appeal decision in *Kai-Whitewind* [2005] EWCA 1092.

[205] See the study by R.D. Mackay, op. cit.

[206] P.T. d'Orban, 'Women who Kill Their Children' (1979) 134 Brit J Psychiatry 560; Mackay, op. cit. 29.

[207] Para. 103.

[208] Clause 64(1).

[209] D. Maier-Katkin and R. Ogle, 'A Rationale for Infanticide Laws' [1993] Crim LR 903.

[210] A. Wilczynski and A. Morris, 'Parents who Kill their Children' [1993] Crim LR 31.

[211] Ibid. 35.

[212] Statistically, children in their first year of life are at greater risk of being the victims of homicide.

[213] Ibid. The Law Commission, No. 304 (2006), make no substantive recommendations for the reform of infanticide.

13.7 INVOLUNTARY MANSLAUGHTER

Overview

There are two main types of involuntary manslaughter, namely constructive or unlawful act manslaughter and gross negligence manslaughter or manslaughter by breach of duty. The gist of constructive manslaughter is that the actor caused death in the course of performing an unlawful and dangerous act. The gist of gross negligence manslaughter is that the death of the victim issued from conduct of the defendant, lawful or otherwise, which was so grossly negligent that it put the life of the other in peril.

A Introduction

Involuntary manslaughter, counterposed to murder or voluntary manslaughter,[214] refers to those unlawful killings which are not deemed to be 'chosen' by the accused. Until relatively recently the principles governing liability for manslaughter were largely undeveloped. Indeed it was only in 1937 that the *mens rea* suffered its first significant elaboration in *Andrews* v *DPP*.[215] In Stephen's *History of the Criminal Law of England*, manslaughter is treated simply as what is left over when murder is subtracted from lawful killings. In Stephen's *Digest*, manslaughter is dismissed in the following words: 'Manslaughter is unlawful homicide without malice aforethought'.[216] It is probably not too misleading to say that manslaughter only exists as a crime because historically there was precious little beyond the compassion of judge or jury separating a killer, whatever his degree of fault, from the gallows. Manslaughter was the common law's untheorised concession to mercy. In a very real sense, then, involuntary manslaughter is not a 'pigeon-hole' crime like murder, theft, or assault, but a 'dustbin' crime in which killings accompanied by various states of blame-worthiness are thrown together for reasons of expedience.

Now that principles of criminal responsibility are widely understood, one might expect, if we were to start all over again with a codified criminal law, that manslaughter would be replaced by crimes which accurately reflected the wrong we attribute to various forms of culpable but unintentional killings.[217] Enacting statutory crimes such as aggravated arson, 'causing death by dangerous driving', and other crimes of 'reckless endangerment' is the modern and, arguably, more reflective way of ensuring that the elements of the crime are an accurate summation of the blame we attribute to such unintentional killers.

Involuntary manslaughter takes two forms. First, a killing committed in the course of the performance of an unlawful and dangerous act, otherwise known as constructive manslaughter. Second, a killing resulting from gross negligence in breach of duty. It is now clear, at least in the case of manslaughter by breach of duty, that it is a crime which can be committed by a company or corporation as well as an individual.[218] It is appropriate where death is the result of serious management failures resulting in a gross breach of a duty of care.[219]

---

[214] That is, murder to manslaughter by virtue of diminished responsibility, loss of self-control or infanticide.
[215] [1937] AC 576.
[216] Article 228.
[217] CLRC 14th Report (1980) para. 120.
[218] The Corporate Manslaughter and Corporate Homicide Act 2007. See Chapter 7.
[219] *A-G's Reference (No. 2 of 1999)* [2000] Crim LR 475.

B Constructive manslaughter

Overview

Constructive manslaughter is committed when the accused has performed an unlawful and dangerous act resulting in the death of the victim. 'Dangerous' means apt to subject another to the risk of harm, albeit not serious harm. It is not necessary to show that the accused appreciated that the unlawful act he was committing was dangerous in this sense as long as it would be recognised as such by the sober and reasonable person.

It was explained above how, until 1957, a killing committed in the course of a dangerous felony was murder even though the defendant lacked the necessary intention to kill or endanger life. The basis of the defendant's liability was 'constructive malice', that is, malice construed by operation of law rather than proved to be existing in his mind. Constructive malice for murder was abolished by s. 1 of the Homicide Act. Left untouched by the Homicide Act was another form of constructive liability, namely constructive manslaughter. Running parallel with the unreformed law of murder, constructive manslaughter engaged liability where a person killed in the course of performing a dangerous crime **falling short of a felony**. Whereas a killing in the course of an armed robbery would have been murder, a killing which issued unexpectedly out of the commission of an ordinary assault was manslaughter. Now, assuming lack of express or implied malice, both would be constructive manslaughter.

At its simplest, the elements of constructive manslaughter are that the accused has performed an unlawful and dangerous act resulting in the death of the victim. Accordingly, constructive manslaughter covers a very wide spectrum of blameworthiness. The breadth of the spectrum can be seen by comparing two cases. In *Goodfellow*[220] the accused, wishing to be rehoused, set light to his council house which was still occupied by his wife and children. Although he managed to rescue two of his children, his son, wife, and another woman were killed in the blaze. It was clear on the facts that he intended to hurt no one but this was a case which, before *Moloney* at least, could easily have been treated as murder.[221] As it happened, of course, he could equally well have been charged with aggravated arson. In *Mitchell*[222] the accused punched a man who had accused him of queue-jumping in a post office. The man fell on top of an 89-year-old lady, which initially broke her leg and consequently caused her death from a pulmonary embolism. The accused's conviction for manslaughter was upheld on appeal even though, transferred malice and principles of causation notwithstanding, little but an accident of fate separated the accused from the other five million or so people who have had a little rough-and-tumble in a slow-moving queue.

---

[220] (1986) 83 Cr App Rep 23.
[221] *Hyam* v *DPP* [1974] 2 All ER 41; *Nedrick* [1986] 3 All ER 1.
[222] [1983] 2 All ER 427.

1 The elements of constructive manslaughter

(a) Unlawful act

(i) The unlawful act must be criminal
It is now clear that the *actus reus* of constructive manslaughter is a criminal, rather than merely an unlawful, act.

It was not always so. Until 1839 it was generally accepted that it was manslaughter where a killing resulted from the commission of a tort[223] even though the accused intended neither to cause, nor risk causing, harm to another.[224] Thus East states that it is manslaughter if a person throws a stone at a horse if it hits and kills a person.[225] The modern law dates from *R v Franklin*, in which it was held that a person who committed the tort of negligence (or trespass) against another by inadvertently dropping a box on his head was not guilty of manslaughter.

Case 11
A, as a prank, takes away the ladder of V, a roofing contractor, as he is about to descend upon it. V falls to his death.

This would not be constructive manslaughter since A's conduct is not a crime, only the tort of trespass to goods.[226] The focal case of constructive manslaughter is the 'one punch killing' that is an ordinary case of battery which goes wrong and ends in death. Such a case contains the elements of the offence at their simplest.[227] Battery is a crime and punching is dangerous in the obvious sense that physical harm is likely to result from its commission. This requirement that there should be an unlawful act , such as a battery means that, if the battery cannot be established, say because the defendant has a defence, a conviction for manslaughter cannot be supported. A good illustration is the case of *Simon Slingsby* in which the accused managed to inflict some serious internal injuries on the deceased with a signet ring in the course of violent but entirely consensual sexual activity, including buggery. She died later of septicaemia consequent upon the injuries. The Crown Court judge ruled that since the injuries were not deliberately inflicted and were an accidental by-product of consensual conduct there was no assault upon which to support a conviction for manslaughter.[228] It should be noted that a conviction could not have been supported by the (then) unlawful act of buggery, consent not being a defence to this offence, since it was not this act which caused the death.[229]

(ii) An omission cannot form the conduct element in constructive manslaughter
It seems that liability for unlawful act manslaughter requires proof of the commission of an unlawful act as opposed to an omission. Thus a distinction is made between a parent striking his child resulting in that child's death and a parent omitting to do something, say

---

[223] *Fenton* (1830) 1 Lew 179.
[224] When it was repudiated by HM Commissioners on Criminal Law, Fourth Report (1839) [168] xix–235, Articles 65–71.
[225] At 257.
[226] (1883) 15 Cox CC 163. A may well be liable for gross negligence manslaughter in such circumstances.
[227] Despite this in *Carey* a conviction for manslaughter was quashed by the Court of Appeal where death occurred after an affray which resulted in a 15-year-old girl running away and subsequently dying due to a weak heart. This, it is submitted, is the core case of manslaughter by unlawful act. Cf. *Murton* [1862] 3 F&F 492.
[228] [1995] Crim LR 570 and commentary.
[229] Consensual buggery in private has now been decriminalised by an amendment to the Sexual Offences Act 1956, s. 12(1) (s. 143 Criminal Justice and Public Order Act 1994).

calling a doctor for a poorly child, which results in death – the crime of wilful neglect.[230] It has been argued that since there is no moral distinction between acts and omissions the distinction is untenable.[231] All that should be necessary is that the omission should be a criminal offence in its own right. The obvious justification for making the distinction is that if the moral basis for incriminating the defendant is, as wilful neglect is, a breach of duty, then liability for that breach of duty should be subject to the same rule as for other breaches of duty, namely that the breach should disclose gross negligence.

(b) Dangerous act

The requirement that the act committed be 'dangerous' reflects a weak compromise between a criminal law, based in the main part on the presumption of personal moral fault, and the supposed aberration which is constructive liability. The compromise is that liability should not be too far removed from a finding that the accused bears personal moral responsibility for the death. If death was the unexpected result of a punch it was at least a consequence threatened by the accused's conduct.[232]

(i) The dangerousness of an act is assessed objectively

As late as 1962 it was stated confidently by the leading academic authority of the day[233] that liability for constructive manslaughter depended upon proof of 'foresight of possible physical harm less than fatal harm'.[234] By 1965 this requirement of foresight had been abandoned by the courts. It was enough that the accused's act was objectively dangerous: 'the unlawful act must be such as all sober and reasonable people would inevitably recognise must subject the other person to, at least, the risk of some harm resulting therefrom, albeit not serious harm'.[235] This mirrored the approach taken by the House of Lords in *DPP v Smith* four years earlier for the crime of murder. Unlike the latter, however, the passing of the Criminal Justice Act 1967 has done nothing to alter the legal position.[236]

(ii) The unlawfulness of an act must be constituted independently of its dangerousness

A good illustration of the interplay of the two elements of unlawfulness and dangerousness is the case of *Lamb*.[237] The accused and his friend were playing around with a loaded gun. Having checked that no bullet was opposite the firing pin the accused pointed the gun at his friend and pulled the trigger. To his surprise and, no doubt, horror the gun went off, killing the friend. He had forgotten, or did not know, that the chamber of a revolver 'revolves' upon firing. His conviction for constructive manslaughter was quashed on appeal. What Lamb did was undoubtedly dangerous but it was not a crime. It would only have been an assault if his friend had apprehended injury, which he did not, and if the accused had intended, or foreseen, injury or alarm to his friend, which he did not. Since it is not a criminal offence (e.g. battery) negligently to shoot someone, no other crime had

---

[230] *Lowe* [1973] QB 702.
[231] Ashworth (2006) 289.
[232] J. Horder, 'Two Histories and Four Hidden Principles of *Mens Rea*' (1997) 113 LQR 95. On the other hand, if A steals B's priceless painting which results in B suffering an unexpected fatal heart attack, we may perhaps blame A but not, surely, for the death.
[233] J.W.C. Turner in Kenny's *Outlines* at 141.
[234] Which following the then understood common law position would have sufficed for murder.
[235] *Church* [1965] 2 All ER 72 per Edmund-Davies J.
[236] Section 8 Criminal Justice Act 1967. This is because *Church* was taken to be laying down a rule of law – manslaughter does not require proof of subjective fault – rather than evidence – subjective fault can be proved by objective means.
[237] [1967] 2 QB 981.

been committed either. If the prosecution had done their homework, Lamb may well have been liable for manslaughter, but of the gross negligence rather than the constructive variety. This would have been appropriate if his folly was so great as to exhibit gross negligence. As the jury were given no direction to this effect, it was proper to quash the conviction since he had certainly not committed constructive manslaughter.

A related point is that liability can only be incurred for this type of manslaughter if the act which causes death is criminal in itself, rather than becomes criminal simply because it is performed in a negligent or dangerous fashion. Put another way, the crime out of which constructive manslaughter is constructed must (normally) be a crime requiring proof of intention or recklessness. This point is particularly important in connection with deaths arising out of road traffic offences. If the criminality of an act could be provided merely by proof of negligence it would mean that anybody who killed another in the course of speeding, drink driving, or driving carelessly would be automatically guilty of manslaughter. Such a result would be inconsistent with the fault requirement in the other form of involuntary manslaughter, namely manslaughter by gross negligence.[238]

The moral? If D kills V while speeding or driving dangerously he can be charged with constructive manslaughter if he intended or foresaw that he might hit V (since this would render the hitting a criminal battery, or worse). If, on the other hand, he neither intended nor foresaw that he might hit V but was just plain thoughtless then he can only be charged with gross negligence manslaughter, conviction for which must satisfy the elements of that offence.

It should be noted that the requirement in *Church* that the act be unlawful is separate from the requirement that the act be dangerous. This means that the prosecution need prove only that the defendant committed an unlawful act and that, objectively, that act provoked a risk of physical injury. It does not seem to be necessary, in other words, that the accused should have committed an offence against the person or any other offence which is intrinsically dangerous. This might render even as innocuous an offence as theft a dangerous act for the purpose of constructive manslaughter. Thus, if A, in Case 13, intended to keep the ladder, V's death would issue out of a crime (theft) which, in the particular context, was objectively dangerous. The illogical result is that A's liability for (constructive) manslaughter hinges on whether he wanted to keep the ladder or not, **not on whether he foresaw injury or not.**

In the case of *DPP* v *Newbury and Jones* the House of Lords confirmed that the subject-matter of constructive manslaughter did not have to be a crime of endangerment. The sole question to be considered was whether the crime, in the circumstances in which it was committed, provoked the risk of physical injury.[239] Here two youths threw a piece of paving-stone off a bridge and into the path of an oncoming train. The paving stone fell into the driver's cab, killing the guard. Ignoring the homicide for a moment, there were three possible crimes committed here, assault/aggravated assault, and criminal damage. The House of Lords made no attempt to pinpoint the precise crime committed by the boys, however. They ruled that it was not necessary to show that the boys foresaw the risk of harm as long as the risk would have been obvious to the reasonable person. But if foresight was not necessary, what was the crime the commission of which rendered them constructively liable? It could not be battery since battery requires proof of foresight. Criminal damage was then, as is now, a crime of foresight.[240] Otherwise, the only crime left, which

---

[238] *Andrews* v *DPP* [1937] AC 576; *Bateman* (1925) 19 Cr App R 8.
[239] [1976] 2 All ER 365.
[240] It would, of course, be difficult to resist the inference that the purpose behind throwing a paving-stone into the path of a train was to create at least the risk of some harm to the train or track.

was never referred to, was the arcane offence of 'endangering the safety of any person conveyed upon a railway'.[241] It is likely that the House of Lords simply presumed that the boys had committed a crime, whether criminal damage or this latter offence. That being so, the crime, whatever it was, was clearly objectively (very) dangerous and manslaughter thus established.[242]

Such an unanalytical way of constructing the unlawful act will not arise again in practice. In *Jennings* it was stated that the prosecution must specify the unlawful act relied upon, which is undoubtedly a step forward.[243] In *R v Meeking*[244] this required a little research on the part of the prosecutor. In this case the Appellant, A, was convicted of the manslaughter of her husband. They had been drinking, and had an argument as the deceased was driving at approximately 60 miles per hours on an A road. During the row, suddenly and without warning, A pulled on the handbrake. She said later that she did this to make the deceased stop. The effect of A's action was to lock the rear wheels resulting in a crash which killed the husband. Although what A did was clearly dangerous was it a criminal act? If so, what was the crime? The crime relied upon was section 22A(1)(b) Road Traffic Act 1988 which makes it an offence to intentionally interfere with a motor vehicle in circumstances that would make it obvious that to do so would be dangerous. The only issue for the Court was whether the offence was committed where, as here, the act was performed spontaneously while the car was being driven or whether it was necessary for the act to be performed prior to the car being driven. The Court of Appeal concluded that offence was made out. In *Dhaliwal* the absence of such a criminal act was fatal to the charge of constructive manslaughter, although it was conceded that the defendant's behaviour may have caused U to kill herself. The deceased committed suicide after a long period of abuse at the hands of the defendant, her husband. Although psychiatric evidence strongly supported the fact that the 'overwhelming cause' of the suicide was this period of ill treatment the Court of Appeal agreed with the trial judge that to form the *actus reus* of constructive manslaughter the prosecution had to show that the defendant had inflicted a recognised psychiatric illness such as would form the basis of a section 20 OAPA charge.[245] This they were not able to do. It was not enough in other words that he had simply made her feel that life was not worth living, which resulted in the decision to end her life.[246] *Jennings* and *Dhaliwal* aside, *DPP v Newbury* still gives cause for concern, however. Even if we give their lordships the benefit of the doubt and concede that the boys did indeed commit a criminal offence, it allows for the conviction of people, particularly the young, who when committing a crime had no suspicion that what they were doing was dangerous.

(iii) *Causation*

As with all crimes of violence the prosecution must prove that D caused the harm, here death. In addition, it has been suggested in a number of cases that the unlawful act must be directed at a person, even if not necessarily at the victim herself. Superficially this idea is quite appealing. If A discharges a rifle at a dog and it misses and kills V, the fact that it

---

[241] Contrary to s. 34, OAPA 1861.

[242] For a similar judicial sleight-of-hand where an unlawful act was presumed but not established see *Cato* [1976] 1 WLR 110.

[243] [1990] Crim LR 588.

[244] [2012] EWCA Crim 641; [2013] Crim LR 333–335.

[245] *Chan-Fook* (1994) 99 CR App R 147.

[246] Horder and McGowan suggest that a more secure basis for a conviction would be gross negligence manslaughter, in 'Manslaughter by Causing Another's Suicide' [2006] Crim LR 1035.

is a crime to shoot a dog seems a tenuous basis upon which to hold A guilty of manslaughter, assuming this act was objectively dangerous. Should there not be a requirement that the unlawful act be directed against V? In *Dalby* this idea was accepted. The accused had supplied the deceased with a drug for intravenous use. The deceased overdosed on the drug and died. It was held that the accused was not guilty of manslaughter since the act of supply was not 'directed at' the body of the victim.[247] In one important sense the 'directed at' doctrine is of fundamental importance in the context of constructive manslaughter in that it indicates, in a manner similar to murder, that the essence of this form of homicide is an attack rather than an endangerment, the subject matter of gross negligence manslaughter.

In purely doctrinal terms, however, the requirement is both unnecessary and unsustainable. It is unnecessary because the requirement is swallowed up by the causal requirements of constructive manslaughter. The obvious reason why a manslaughter conviction was inappropriate here was that the act of supply had not caused the deceased's death. The death was caused by the deceased's own voluntary act.[248] In *Goodfellow* this latter interpretation of *Dalby* was accepted by the Court of Appeal which accordingly rejected the contention that the accused's actions had to be directed against a victim.[249] A similar result occurred in *Mitchell*,[250] in which the Court of Appeal held that the only issue bearing on the liability of the accused was whether the chain of causation linking the initial act of violence to the death of the old woman was still intact. In *Lewis* L chased V into a road following an altercation. V was killed by an oncoming car. The Court of Appeal upheld the trial judge's direction to the effect that the chain of causation between L's unlawful act and V's death would remain intact if V's response of running away was one of the responses to be expected from someone who finds himself in V's position.[251] More problematic was *R v M* where a club doorman died of an aneurysm in the course of an attack on him and a fellow doorman. A conviction for manslaughter was upheld on the basis of that (dangerous) attack despite the fact that the accused had made no physical contact with the deceased at the time of the aneurysm.[252]

The 'directed-at' requirement is also unsustainable. First, if the act of supplying the drug must be directed against the person of the deceased, then why was liability incurred in *Newbury*? The boys, it will be remembered, did not direct their act against the victim, but against the train in which he was sitting. Second, if harm need not even be foreseen by the defendants, it makes little sense to require the defendants' conduct to be directed at the victim. What defendant is not going to foresee harm befalling a victim, if he directs an objectively dangerous act against him?[253] Nevertheless, as has been suggested, there is a core of good sense at the heart of the 'aiming at' doctrine. It indicates that the courts are alert to the requirement of an **attack** in constructive manslaughter.

Although occasional statements still surface suggesting that the unlawful act must be directed against a person,[254] the orthodox view is that it is necessary only to show that the

---

[247] [1982] 1 All ER 916 at 919 per Waller LJ.

[248] *R v Kennedy (No. 2)* [2007] UKHL 38. See Chapter 5.

[249] Otherwise a terrorist who blows up an uninhabited office block for publicity would not be guilty of constructive manslaughter if a passer-by is killed, because the unlawful act was directed at the office block and not the passer-by.

[250] (1983) 76 Cr App R 293.

[251] [2010] EWCA 151. See *Williams and Davis* [1992] 2 All ER 183 and generally Chapter 5.

[252] *R v M* [2012] EWCA Crim 2293; [2013] Crim LR 335.

[253] For this reason *Dalby* was first welcomed as providing a potential Trojan horse for a return of the subjective element in the *mens rea* for constructive manslaughter. J.C. Smith [1982] Crim LR 439 at 440.

[254] *Ball* [1989] Crim LR 730 CA.

accused's conduct provoked a risk of harm and that the chain of causation linking death with the initial unlawful act is unbroken.[255] It would clearly be preferable, however, if liability for constructive manslaughter required proof of an unlawful act which the defendant, rather than the reasonable man, foresaw as dangerous.

(iv) *Emotional shock*

In *Dawson* it was held that the harm foreseeable must be physical harm, however trivial, and not merely emotional shock. The victim, who had a heart condition, had died of heart failure during the course of an armed robbery. The convictions of the robbers for constructive manslaughter were quashed. The Court of Appeal held first that if emotional shock and nothing more was foreseeable this would not be sufficient 'harm' to satisfy the *Church* test. The Court of Appeal held further that the reasonable man is credited only with the factual knowledge of the accused at the time of committing the offence. In deciding what the sober and reasonable man would foresee, the judge should have directed the jury to discount the fact of the heart condition, since this was not known to the accused.[256] It would be different if the circumstances were such as to put the defendant on notice of the victim's condition, as where it was clear to a burglar that the householder was old and frail. In such a case physical harm would be foreseeable.[257]

C Manslaughter by breach of duty

The second form of involuntary manslaughter is manslaughter by breach of duty (of care), otherwise known as gross negligence manslaughter. All of the manslaughter cases dealt with in the omissions section of Chapter 4 were cases of manslaughter by breach of duty. The classic statement of Lord Hewart CJ in *Bateman* gives the essentials. '(It must be shown that) . . . the negligence of the accused went beyond a mere matter of compensation between subjects and showed such a disregard for the life and safety of others as to amount to a crime against the state and conduct deserving of punishment.'[258]

It is appropriate to charge this form where the conduct causing death was not criminally unlawful, and in cases of omission. In both these situations unlawful act manslaughter is not available. It will be appreciated that there is an overlap between the two forms since a homicide may issue from a gross breach of a duty which coincides with the commission of an unlawful act. For example, on the facts of *Goodfellow*, not only was there an unlawful and dangerous act (arson), there was also an unarguable case of gross negligence. The facts of *Church* provide a further illustration. A knocked W out with a punch. He panicked when she failed to revive. Thinking he had killed her, A threw her body into the river where she died of drowning. He was convicted of manslaughter. The obvious basis for the conviction is that he committed an unlawful act upon her (the assault) which caused her death, albeit by a roundabout route. Another basis would be gross negligence manslaughter. Throwing a recently hale-and-hearty person in a river without making exhaustive checks to ensure the person is really dead smacks of something more than mere carelessness.

Apart from a brief hiatus between 1977 and 1995 when *Caldwell* recklessness[259] was the *mens rea* for this type of manslaughter[260] the modern history of this form has required

---

[255] *Le Brun* [1992] QB 61.

[256] *Dawson* (1985) 81 Cr App R 150; *Carey* [2006] EWCA Crim 17.

[257] As it was in the case of *Watson* [1989] 1 WLR 684; cf. *R v M* [2012] EWCA Crim 2293; [2013] Crim LR 335.

[258] At 11.

[259] *R v Stone and Dobinson* [1977] 2 QB 981.

[260] *Seymour* [1983] 2 All ER 1058; *Kong Cheuk Kwan* (1985) 82 Cr App R 18.

gross negligence. The law was returned to this state in the case of *Adomako* in which the liability of a hospital anaesthetist who had failed to notice that a patient's ventilation tube had become disconnected was considered. The position after *Adomako* is that whether one kills in a motor car, in the course of treating a sick patient, or rewiring a house, the test for manslaughter is the same.

1 Elements of manslaughter by breach of duty: overview

Manslaughter is constituted upon proof of a gross breach of a duty of care resulting in death. The elements therefore are as follows:

(1) The defendant owed the victim a duty of care.
(2) The defendant breached the duty.
(3) The breach of duty caused death.
(4) The breach of duty was gross.

(a) *The duty*

The basis upon which the duty of care is imposed is the foreseeability of injury to those who might be imperilled by careless acts or omissions. As in the civil law the offence definition is satisfied, whether or not the defendant himself was subjectively aware that there was a significant risk of causing bodily harm by his conduct.[261] Some doubt exists as to whether the duty of care arises in the same way as it does in the civil law or whether it is constructed more rigorously to ensure that all those whose lives stand at risk of endangerment for failure to act with the necessary care are owed such a duty. In *Adomako*, Lord Mackay stated that the ordinary principles of negligence apply to determine whether a duty of care exists. This renders the existence of a duty of care a matter for the judge taking into account the degree of foreseeability of injury, the relationship of the parties and the justice of the case.[262] Some typical examples of situations where a duty of care has been imposed include motor and other forms of vehicular manslaughter,[263] death in the performance of an operation or medical treatment by a doctor or a surgeon,[264] shoddy workmanship in the care of a tradesperson,[265] neglect in the case of a carer,[266] failing to supervise children in dangerous situations such as baths and swimming pools,[267] and of careless treatment of a firearm.[268] Each of these cases involves the accused being in a situation in which if extreme care is not taken it will provoke socially unacceptable levels of risk. It is clear, however, that a duty of care may be held to exist in the criminal law where no such duty would exist under the civil law. In *Wacker*, for example, the driver of a lorry was held to owe a duty of care to illegal immigrants who suffocated in the lorry in which he was transporting them. In the civil law a claim for damages would probably fail because of the complicity of the immigrants in the wrongdoing which caused their deaths.[269] This same complicity was held to be irrelevant to the question whether a duty of care was owed for the purpose of manslaughter where the only relevant issue was the degree of risk of death.

---

[261] *Pike* [1961] Crim LR 547, CA.
[262] *Wacker* [2003] QB 1207.
[263] *Kong Cheuk Kwan* v *R* (1985) 82 Cr App Rep 18.
[264] *Adomako* [1994] 3 All ER 79; *Bateman*; *Markuss* (1864) 4 F and F 356.
[265] *R* v *Prentice* [1993] 4 All ER 935.
[266] *Stone and Dobinson*.
[267] *R* v *Reeves* [2013] 2 Cr App R (S) 129(21), CA.
[268] *Lamb* [1967] 2 QB 981.
[269] For another example of the court ignoring the complicity of the deceased in his own demise see *Winter* [2011] 1 Cr App R 476.

As Herring and Palser put it: 'Criminal proceedings are not about balancing the responsibility between defendant and the victim but in determining whether the activity engaged in by the defendant is sufficiently harmful and blameworthy to justify a criminal conviction.'[270] In R v *Winter and Winter* involving employees of a fireworks company, appeals against conviction for gross negligence manslaughter were rejected after a cameraman member of the fire service was killed during an explosion at the company's premises, as it was reasonably foreseeable that a civilian employee of the fire service might come on to the site of a fire in order to film or photograph it for training purposes. The fact that the cameraman had failed to comply with instructions to leave the site did not mean that he was not owed a duty of care.[271]

In *Willoughby* D was liable for gross negligence manslaughter when V was killed at D's premises in a fire which they had together started as an insurance scam. The duty of care here arose, notwithstanding the unlawful context and V's own voluntary running of the risk, because of the dangerous context which D precipitated.[272] The Corporate Manslaughter and Corporate Homicide Act 2007 explicitly enshrines these decisions on the construction of the duty of care in relation to the liability of corporations for death. A duty of care will come into existence, notwithstanding the victim may have been complicit with the duty holder in an unlawful activity and notwithstanding any assumption of the risk of death.[273] In *Evans*, upholding the conviction of the supplier of heroin for failing to seek medical attention when the deceased became comatose following injection, the Court of Appeal confirmed that the question whether a duty of care was owed was a question of law, that is, a question for the judge.[274]

(b) The standard of care

Like the civil law the appropriate standard of care is determined objectively. It does not vary with the capacities of the defendant except to impose a higher standard of care on those holding themselves out as endowed with specialist skills. Unlike the civil law, however, a mere failure to conform to the standard of care of the reasonable man is not enough to incur liability for manslaughter. The failure must be gross.

In *Adomako* Lord Mackay stated, 'The essence of the matter, which is supremely a jury question, is whether, having regard to the risk of death involved, the conduct of the defendant was so bad in all the circumstances as to amount in their judgement to a criminal act or omission.'[275] The fault inhering in such conduct may be foresight or indifference to the risk, gross inadvertence, or an appreciation of the risk coupled with such a high degree of negligence in the attempt to avoid the risk that the jury consider a conviction is justified. The obvious problem arising with such a definition is that it requires the jury to determine the point at which civil negligence becomes criminal negligence. In the civil law the standard is determined by a judge. In the criminal law the job is given to lay people who can hardly be expected to know the civil, let alone the criminal, standard. The Court of Appeal have ruled that the uncertainty thus created does not offend Article 7 ECHR which requires the criminality of an act or omission to be determined and determinable in advance.[276] In its

[270] 'The Duty of Care in Gross Negligence Manslaughter' [2007] Crim LR 24 at 37.
[271] [2010] EWCA Crim 1474.
[272] [2004] EWCA Crim 3365.
[273] Section 2(6)(a) and (b).
[274] *Phillips* [2013] EWCA Crim 358.
[275] At 87.
[276] *Misra* [2005] 1 Cr App R 328.

favour, it allows juries to acquit a person who may have objectively acted very dangerously but does so in a context of, say, inexperience, stress, mistake or confusion which allows them to conclude that his conduct was not 'bad enough' to justify punishment. So a junior doctor who had given an incorrect injection in the course of an inadequately supervised operation, with fatal results, had the conviction quashed by the Court of Appeal in *R v Prentice*.[277]

One desirable feature in Lord Mackay's circular, if 'jury-friendly', test of gross negligence is the explicit reference to 'the risk of death'. Before *Adomako* it was by no means certain that the defendant's conduct must be such as to create the risk of death. In *Stone and Dobinson* it was said to be enough that the accused's conduct provoked the risk of injury to 'health and welfare'. More recently Lord Taylor CJ spoke of the risk of injury to health. Both seem to set the standard too low, quite apart from the unacceptable vagueness characterising 'welfare' in *Stone*.[278] Most authorities provide, however, that the risk must be of death or grievous bodily harm.[279] This coheres with a notion of homicide separated only by the type of decision made by the accused. Thus intention characterises murder and culpable risk-taking, manslaughter. However, given that manslaughter does not require proof of deliberate risk-taking, it is submitted that fairness to the accused requires the risk to be of death.[280] In cases where the accused does advert to the risk of death or GBH it is submitted that liability, as in crimes of recklessness generally, is dependent upon the risk taken being unreasonable in the circumstances which obtain.

D Corporate manslaughter

1 The scope of liability

As has been explained, the scope of corporate liability for manslaughter, although far wider than that appearing under the common law, is more restrictive than that first proposed by the Law Commission, which embraced homicide liability for death caused by 'management failure', defined as any management activity at any level of the company which was inimical to the health and safety of employees or other affected persons. Under the Corporate Manslaughter and Corporate Homicide Act 2007, however, the organisation is guilty 'only if the way in which its activities are managed or organised by its **senior management** is a substantial element in the breach'.[281] This restriction has been condemned as a weakness in the new Act.[282] Although the prosecutions of companies will become easier to mount they will remain procedurally complex and less likely to be useful in the very cases where they are most needed, cases of gross organisational failure, particularly in large companies and organisations, where it may be impossible to define, let alone identify,

---

[277] [1993] 4 All ER 935, an appeal heard at the same time as *Adomako*.
[278] G. Williams *TCL* (1983) 267.
[279] *Cato* [1976] 1 WLR 110.
[280] Law Commission Consultation Paper 135 *Involuntary Manslaughter*, London: HMSO (1994) (hereafter LCCP No. 135 (1994)) para. 5.49. In *Singh* [1999] Crim LR 582 the Court of Appeal approved the judge's summing up in which he stated that the requirement was negligence as to the risk of death, 'not merely of injury or even of serious injury'.
[281] By subsection (3). In February 2011 the first conviction was obtained in *Cotswold Geotechnical Holdings* [2011] All ER (D) 100 CA following the death of an employee in a collapsed trench.
[282] Section 1(4)(c) 'senior management', in relation to an organisation, means the persons who play significant roles in (i) the making of decisions about how the whole or a substantial part of its activities are to be managed or organised, or (ii) the actual managing or organising of the whole or a substantial part of those activities.

those senior people whose conduct was largely responsible for the death.[283] Moreover, given the Act focuses on the defaults of senior managers, it is perhaps surprising that the Act does not allow those identified as substantially to blame for the outcome to be convicted of the offence, whether as principals in their own right or as accessories to an organisation as principal offender.[284]

(a) The duty of care

Although matters relating to the constitution of the duty of care are not spelt out in the new Act it is clear that the existence of a duty of care is a matter of law and is intended not to go beyond the common law as developed since *Adomako*. Indeed by sections 3–7 the duty of care of public bodies liability is circumscribed to ensure liability does not threaten to render public bodies liable for, say, matters of public policy in relation to public authorities, or operational activities in relation to the police, emergency services or military. More broadly, the civil law of negligence, which takes into account matters such as the plaintiff's own moral and legal standing in determining his worthiness for compensation, is acknowledged as inappropriate in the criminal law where public interests in setting standards of carefulness are paramount.[285] The Act provides that the organisation must owe a 'relevant duty of care' under the law of negligence in relation to any of the following duties, namely any:

(a) owed to its employees or others working for the organisation or performing services for it;
(b) owed as occupier of premises;
(c) owed in connection with (i) the supply of goods or services, (ii) the carrying on of construction or maintenance operations, (iii) the carrying on of any other activity on a commercial basis, (iv) or the use or keeping of any plant or vehicle;
(d) owed to a person, such as a person subject to criminal or medical detention or other custodial status, by reason of being a person for whose safety the organisation is responsible.[286]

(b) The standard of care

Corporate manslaughter is dependent upon the breach of duty resulting in death as being gross, namely where 'the conduct alleged to amount to a breach of that duty falls far below what can reasonably be expected of the organisation in the circumstances'.[287] It is for the jury to determine whether a breach of duty is a 'gross breach'. And to guide this decision the Act provides a number of statutory criteria to which the jury should have regard. These include the organisation's obligations under health and safety legislation, the extent to which the organisation was in breach of these and the risk to life that is involved. Section 8 also requires the jury to have regard to what has been termed the organisation's reactive fault.[288] Is the breach indicative of any deeper corporate attitude or practice possibly

---

[283] For discussion see Chapter 7. In one of the first cases successfully prosecuted, *Cotswold Geotechnical Holdings* [2012] 1 Cr App R 153, the fine was such as to propel the small firm into administration.
[284] Cf. Clarkson (2005); Frank B. Wright, 'Criminal Liability of Directors and Senior Managers for Deaths at Work', [2007] Crim LR 949.
[285] J. Herring and E. Palser, 'The Duty of Care in Gross Negligence Manslaughter', [2007] Crim LR 24.
[286] Section 2(1).
[287] Cl. 1(4)(b).
[288] See Chapter 7 and generally B. Fisse and J. Braithwaite, 'The Allocation of Responsibility for Corporate Crime: Individualism, Collectivism and Accountability' (1988) 11 Sydney L Rev 46.

suggestive of a culture of indifference? The jury has to consider the wider context in which these health and safety breaches occurred, including cultural issues within the organisation such as attitudes or accepted practices that tolerated breaches.

The restricted scope of the offence, the way in which it tends to favour the large organisation with less transparent managerial systems, the opaque nature of the duty of care, and the imprecision of 'gross' in relation to the standard of care, renders it both less likely to affect corporate behaviour and address irresponsible corporate practices than other solutions on offer. A simpler solution may have been to create an offence of corporate killing, whose elements require a death caused as a result of a statutory duty, howsoever arising. This would make a clear linkage between statutory obligations designed to ensure health and safety and corporate responsibility for fatal outcomes. The Health and Safety at Work Act, for example, has provisions specifically designed for regulating corporate conduct, which are more sensitive to the needs of the jury than the rather opaque notion of 'duty of care'.[289]

13.8 REFORMING CRIMINAL HOMICIDE

As many problems beset the law of homicide as there have been papers and reports to address them. Perhaps the most pressing is setting the higher boundary between murder and manslaughter. As with most areas of law there is a great degree of institutional inertia built into doctrine. That inertia results from the historical development of murder, and manslaughter out of murder. Although the courts may, from time to time, tinker with the mental elements of these different offences, the boundary at the upper level is both indistinct and incoherent. Suggestions for remedying this have been canvassed above.

Setting the boundary for the lower level is equally fraught with difficulty. The approach adopted by the Criminal Law Revision Committee was to recommend the abolition of constructive and gross negligence manslaughter, limiting the offence to causing death with intent to cause serious injury,[290] or being reckless as to death or serious injury. More recently, the Law Commission[291] made less radical proposals. The recommendations[292] are largely contained in *Legislating the Code: Involuntary Manslaughter*.[293] Although it recommended the abolition of constructive manslaughter[294] it leaves the offence otherwise largely intact through the creation of two offences: (subjectively) reckless killing and killing by gross carelessness.[295] In their most recent report[296] the Law Commission make no major changes to the law of manslaughter, save for a welcome modification to constructive manslaughter based on the Government's own recommendations and the designation of the more serious cases of reckless manslaughter, where they involve an intention to cause injury or a fear or risk of injury coupled with an awareness of the serious risk of causing death, as second degree murder. Under the new proposals **manslaughter would comprise two types:**

---

[289] As argued for by Chris Clarkson, 'Aggravated Endangerment Offences' (2007); S. Griffin, 'Accountability for Deaths Attributable to the Gross Negligent Act or Omission of a Police Force: The Impact of the Corporate Manslaughter and Corporate Homicide Act 2007' (2010) J Crim L 648.

[290] Which would no longer be murder.

[291] LCCP No. 135 (1994) para. 521.

[292] LCCP No. 135 (1994).

[293] Law Commission No. 237, London: HMSO (1996).

[294] Which is nevertheless retained in a purified form by s. 2(1)(c)(ii).

[295] Paragraph 5.21, following the recommendation of the Law Commission in cl. 55 of the Draft Code 1989; see H. Keating, 'Law Commission Report on Involuntary Manslaughter' [1996] Crim LR 535.

[296] Law Commission (No. 304), *Murder, Manslaughter and Infanticide* (2006).

(1) Killing through the commission of a criminal act intended to cause injury or that the defendant was aware involved a serious risk of causing some injury (criminal act manslaughter);[297]

(2) Killing through gross negligence.

A Criminal act manslaughter

At present a person can be liable for manslaughter by committing an unlawful and dangerous act which causes death, although he himself was unaware that his conduct carried a risk of injury. This would no longer be the case under these proposals. Although it is not necessary to show death resulted from a crime of violence it is necessary to show, at the least, that the person committing an offence, as where he throws concrete into the path of a train,[298] **knew** there was a risk of harm resulting therefrom. This proposal is sensible and workable. Manslaughter is an apt offence label for an unintended killing arising from a criminal action the defendant knows to be dangerous, and certainly as good as any other with which it might be replaced. The only possible qualification one might make is to require the injury intended or foreseen to be a significant one, to ensure due proportionality between mental state and offence label.

B Gross negligence manslaughter

Gross negligence manslaughter is defined as it was in the Law Commission's earlier report requiring the defendant's conduct to have caused the death of another person where 'a risk that the conduct would cause death would have been obvious to a reasonable person in the defendant's position, the defendant had the capacity to appreciate the risk, and the defendant's conduct fell far below what could reasonably be expected in the circumstances.'[299] This proposal is more satisfactory than the present law of manslaughter by breach of duty. It provides a secure basis for taking into account the capacities of different individuals, given their state of knowledge, skill and experience, to attend to risks.[300] Such a test could quite properly convict the anaesthetist in *Adomako*, acquit the junior doctor in *Prentice* and, since constructive manslaughter is abolished under this proposal, acquit the inexperienced youngster who plays around with firearms. The justification for keeping such a catch-all crime can be best appreciated by considering *Adomako*. Only the law of manslaughter stood between the defendant and outright immunity from prosecution. Retributive justice, it is suggested, could not easily suffer such a lacuna.[301] A major problem is that it continues to give the jury an extravagant role in the labelling of an offence.[302] Two further points should be noted about this form of manslaughter. First, comparable with reckless killing, gross negligence must be as to the risk of death, as required by *Adomako*. Gross negligence as to the risk of serious injury is not enough. The Law Commission's reason for restricting the fault element in this way is to keep faith with the correspondence principle, particularly necessary given the absence of a subjective fault element. The second

---

[297] Para. 2.163.

[298] *DPP* v *Newbury and Jones*.

[299] Para. 3.60.

[300] Cf. 2(2).

[301] Fletcher (1978) 474–82.

[302] Cf. C.M.V. Clarkson (2007) who argues that offence in the field of criminal homicide should be opened up to reflect more accurately the different contexts within which non-intentional killings take place by specifically legislating for crimes of 'explicit aggravated endangerment', at 295.

point is that there is no room for reckless manslaughter. The view taken by the Law Commission is that (subjective) recklessness (as to death) will either be sufficiently serious to count as murder, or it will be subsumed in gross negligence, or, if it involves recklessness as to injury falling short of death, it will generally be in the context of the commission of a criminal act and so be subsumed by constructive manslaughter. I am not sure that this reasoning is cogent. Whether the defendant's conduct fell '*far below*' the standard expected is, after all, a jury question. Where the circumstances warrant, it would be easier simply to direct the jury to find the defendant guilty if he knew his conduct provoked an unjustified risk of death (or serious injury) but they were not sure that his attitude was one of gross negligence. On a variation of the facts of *Merrick*, if an electrician left exposed a mains cable, confidently expecting the foreseen danger of electrocution not to materialise in the short time he intended to be absent, the distinction might matter. What is also left out of this scheme, and the justifications for it, is the case of someone who foresees a risk of serious injury, falling short of life-threatening injury, arising out of conduct which does not constitute a criminal offence in its own right.[303] This is not a particularly significant lacuna but it is not difficult to conceive of an example:

Case 12
As a joke, A removes a ladder leaning against a first-floor balcony on which a window cleaner is working. He knows the window cleaner will not be able to get down to ground without jumping, and that he may break a leg trying to do so, but the height is not enough to alert him nor a reasonable person in his position to a significant risk of death. The window cleaner jumps to his death.

Assuming A does not intend to keep the ladder, which would bring his conduct within constructive manslaughter, this is a case where a manslaughter conviction would, arguably, be proportionate to the seriousness of A's wrongdoing and, at the same time, in line with the gravity of the reformulated constructive manslaughter. There is no obvious reason why it should be excluded from the scope of the reformed manslaughter.

Summary

The *actus reus* of criminal homicide is conduct which unlawfully causes the death of a living person. Conduct includes actions of any kind and also omissions in breach of duty. The conduct does not have to be the sole cause of death as long as it is a substantial and operative cause. A living person does not include a foetus in the womb or a person who has suffered brain death. It does include the newly born, even where the conduct causing death preceded a live birth, unless that conduct was the execution of a lawful abortion. It includes also a person suffering from forms of irreversible coma. Conduct is unlawful for the purpose of the law of criminal homicide if it is not validated by a defence.

Murder is committed when the defendant kills the victim with malice aforethought. Malice aforethought in this context means simply that the defendant intended to kill or, if not to kill, then to cause at least serious injury to the victim. Diminished responsibility and loss of self-

[303] Cf. *R* v *Meeking* (2012), *supra*.

control are partial defences to murder which, if successful, reduce the conviction to manslaughter. Loss of self-control, which replaced provocation, is a partial defence to murder where there is (unrebutted) evidence that the accused lost his self-control and that this loss of control resulted from a qualifying trigger. The qualifying triggers are (i) a fear of serious violence to D or another person or (ii) things said and done which constitute circumstances of an extremely grave character and which caused D to have a justifiable sense of being seriously wronged. Sexual infidelity is not a qualifying trigger. The jury must then acquit and convict of voluntary manslaughter unless they are convinced that in acting as he did the defendant's behaviour has not measured up to the standards of tolerance and self-control to be expected of a person of D's age and sex in the defendant's circumstances. Diminished responsibility is a partial defence for those who kill while suffering from an abnormality of mental functioning of understanding, rational judgement and self-control which reduces the person's responsibility for the killing. This abnormality must be grounded in a recognised mental condition.

Manslaughter takes two separate forms. The first, voluntary manslaughter, occurs where all the definitional elements of murder can be established, but it is mitigated, for reasons of provocation, infanticide or diminished responsibility, to manslaughter. The second, involuntary manslaughter, occurs where the *actus reus* of murder can be established but not the *mens rea*. The *mens rea* for involuntary manslaughter is 'lower' than that for murder but 'higher' than that which would justify an acquittal. Involuntary manslaughter is differentiated from non-punishable 'accidental' killings by requiring proof either that the accused took an unacceptably high risk of death in breach of duty in the performance of a possibly otherwise lawful activity or brought about a death in the course of committing an unlawful and dangerous act.

Further reading

Ashworth, A.J., 'Reforming the Law of Murder' [1990] Criminal Law Review 75.

Ashworth, A.J. and Mitchell, B. (eds), *Rethinking English Homicide Law*, Oxford: OUP (2000).

Blom-Cooper, L. and Morris, T., *With Malice Aforethought: A Study of the Crime and Punishment for Homicide*, Oxford: Hart (2004).

Clarkson, C., 'Corporate Manslaughter: Yet More Government Proposals' [2005] Criminal Law Review 677.

Clarkson, C., 'Corporate Manslaughter: Need for a Special Offence?' in C. Clarkson and S. Cunningham (eds), *Criminal Liability for Non-Aggressive Death*, Farnham: Ashgate (2008).

Elliott, C. and de Than, C, 'Restructuring the Homicide Offences to Tackle Violence, Discrimination and Drugs in a Modern Society' (2009) 20 KLJ 69–88.

Gardner, J. and Macklem, T., 'No Provocation without Responsibility: A Reply to Mackay and Mitchell' [2004] Criminal Law Review 213.

Gobert, J., 'The Corporate Manslaughter and Corporate Homicide Act – Thirteen Years in the Making But Was it Worth the Wait? 2007' (2008) MLR 413.

Goff, R., 'The Mental Element in Murder' (1988) 104 Law Quarterly Review 30.

Griew, E., 'The Future of Diminished Responsibility' [1988] Criminal Law Review 75.

Horder, J. (ed.), *Homicide Law in Comparative Perspective*, Oxford: Hart (2007).

Mackay, R.D. and Mitchell, B.J., 'Provoking Diminished Responsibility: Two Pleas Merging into One' [2003] Criminal Law Review 745.

Mackay, R.D. and Mitchell, B.J., 'But is this Provocation? Some Thoughts on the Law Commission's Report on Partial Defences to Murder' [2005] Criminal Law Review 44.

Mitchell, B., 'Minding the Gap in Unlawful and Dangerous Act Manslaughter; A Moral Defence of One Punch Killers' [2009] Crim LR 502.

Mitchell, B., 'More Thoughts about Unlawful Act Manslaughter and the One Punch Killer' [2009] Crim LR 502.

Ormerod, D. and Taylor, R., 'The Corporate Manslaughter and Corporate Homicide Act 2007' [2008] Crim LR 589.

Wells, C., *Corporations and Criminal Responsibility* (2nd edn), Oxford: OUP (2001).

Wilson, W., 'Murder and the Structure of Homicide' in A.J. Ashworth and B.J. Mitchell (eds), *Rethinking English Homicide Law*, Oxford: OUP (2000).

Wilson, W., 'The Structure of Criminal Homicide' [2006] Criminal Law Review 471: 5.

Wilson, W., 'Murder by Omission' (2010) New Crim LR 1.

Part IV
Property offences

14 Theft

Overview

Theft is committed when a person dishonestly appropriates property belonging to another with the intention of permanently depriving the other of it. The *actus reus* of theft is the appropriation of property belonging to another. It is no less an appropriation for being consented to or authorised. An appropriation will normally involve an outright taking, but this is not necessary. Any assumption of any of the rights of ownership will suffice. The more obvious of these rights include the right to possess, dispose of, use, modify, or destroy the property. Theft is only committed where the appropriator intends at the moment of appropriation to deprive the owner permanently of the property. Dishonest borrowing is not theft. It is not necessary for there to be a permanent deprivation, but there must be the intention to deprive permanently If the appropriation is not dishonest by the standards of ordinary people, theft is not committed. It is also not committed if, although the appropriation was dishonest according to those standards, the defendant did not realise that it was.

14.1 THEFT: INTRODUCTION

In 2012–13 there were 1.8 million recorded property offences in England and Wales. This includes around 450,000 burglaries, 400,000 vehicle offences, 100,000 bicycle thefts, 100,000 thefts from the person, 300,000 shoplifting offences and 500,000 other offences.[1] The Crime Survey estimates that this figure represents under half of the real scope of property crime, in England and Wales, put at around 5 million.[2] The number of such crimes recorded is thought to be a small proportion of the level of offending. As with other forms of criminal activity the accuracy of the overall picture of criminality is dependent upon the willingness of victims to report and the police to record the offence once reported. Many victims will not report property crimes except to support an insurance claim. As a result a large proportion of minor thefts and burglaries go unreported. Those who are uninsured have little incentive to report such offences unless they have evidence as to who the culprit was. Perhaps the most significant 'black hole' in the whole statistical picture, however, concerns shoplifting, where thefts, although evidently occurring in massive numbers, are rarely reported in the absence of a detained suspect.[3]

Much of the law relating to the punishment of property offences is contained in the Theft Act of 1968 and the Fraud Act 2006, and it is the provisions in these Acts which will be concentrated upon here. It should be noted, however, that the social pattern of offences of dishonesty is not adequately represented by these Acts, whose provisions tend to conjure up a picture of property crime in which most of the villains wear striped shirts and have bags marked SWAG over their shoulders. There is good reason to believe that, in

[1] Crime Survey England and Wales 2013.
[2] Ibid.
[3] Astor, 'Shoplifting Survey', *Security World*, Vol. 8, Part 3 (1971) cited in Clarkson and Keating (1998) 738.

purely monetary terms, what is known as 'white collar crime', for example company and banking fraud, money laundering and insider dealing, dwarfs all other property crimes.[4] Little of the former crime comes to light. It is not the kind of crime which comes to the attention of the Crime Survey reporters.[5]

These more arcane, if profitable, forms of such crime are largely regulated by a number of essentially regulatory statutes[6] such as the Companies Acts, Financial Services Acts, Banking Acts and so on. The subtle message created by such compartmentalisation of offences is that somehow 'city fraud' is not 'real crime'. Real crime, it seems, involves a real-life drama with a lawless villain, a defined victim, and an explosive event rather than, say, some well-heeled smoothie making a few interesting telephone calls to some equally smooth chums. This analysis is supported by the existence of a minimum ceiling (£5 million) for investigating commercial fraud operated by the Serious Fraud Office.[7] Why is commercial fraud so less worthy of prosecution than more mundane property offences? It should be noted that a similar compartmentalisation occurs in many cases where the state is a victim and which are technically covered by the Theft Acts. Agencies such as the Inland Revenue or Department for Work and Pensions have the power, for example, to levy penalties for tax or social security fraud without criminal prosecution.

The Acts form, in effect, a code of property offences. They include theft – replacing the old offences of larceny, embezzlement and fraudulent conversion – offences of fraud, burglary, robbery, handling and certain offences of temporary deprivation such as taking and driving away a road vehicle. The Theft Act issued out of the recommendations of the Criminal Law Revision Committee which had been asked[8] to report on simplifying the law of larceny.[9] The Report of 1966 recommended the complete replacement of an outdated set of laws which had been designed essentially to protect persons in their possession of objects, rather than more generally to protect people from interference with their property rights.[10] The Criminal Law Revision Committee were soon required to offer solutions to problems issuing out of section 16 of the new Act dealing with offences of deception. The Theft Act 1978 was the outcome. This itself has largely been superseded by the Fraud Act 2006.

14.2 THEFT: THE ELEMENTS

Theft, befittingly, lies at the heart of the Theft Act 1968. Not only is it a crime in its own right, it also forms a key ingredient in a number of other crimes, for example burglary, robbery and handling. A knowledge of theft, then, is a necessary prerequisite to understanding the scope and coverage of these offences. The maximum sentence for theft is seven years. Robbery and burglary,[11] since they are to a large degree aggravated versions, carry a heavier penalty, namely life imprisonment and fourteen years respectively.[12]

Unlike the offences we have considered so far, the beauty of the codified system is that to a large extent the elements of theft receive explicit definition. The major part of the trick

---

[4] S. Ramage, *The Serious Fraud Office Fraud Law: Book 2* (2005).
[5] M. Levi, *Regulating Fraud: White Collar Crime and the Criminal Process* (1988), London: Tavistock.
[6] Except ss. 17 and 19 Theft Act 1968.
[7] See S. Ramage, *The Serious Fraud Office Fraud Law: Book 2* (2005).
[8] In 1959.
[9] CLRC 8th Report *Theft and Related Offences* Cmnd 2977 (1966) and 13th Report *Section 16 of the Theft Act 1968* Cmnd 6733 (1977).
[10] For a theoretical overview of theft see G. Fletcher, *Rethinking Criminal Law* (1978) chs 1–3.
[11] Section 9(1)(b) at least.
[12] Ten years in the latter case if the premises entered are not a dwelling.

in mastering property offences is to develop a willingness to engage in routine statutory interpretation. The elements of theft are to be found in sections 1–6 of the Theft Act 1968. By s. 1(1) of the Act, 'a person is guilty of theft if he dishonestly appropriates property belonging to another with the intention of permanently depriving the other of it'.

In each case the questions which must be asked are, then, as follows:

(1) **Was there an appropriation?** Appropriation is partially defined in section 3.
(2) **Was the thing appropriated 'property'?** Property is defined in section 4.
(3) **Did the property, at the time it was appropriated, belong to another?** Section 5 explains what 'belonging to another' comprises.

If these questions are all answered in the affirmative the *actus reus* of theft is established. The final two questions, which relate to the *mens rea* of theft, can then be asked:

(4) **Was the appropriation of the other's property dishonest?** Section 2 provides three instances of states of mind not amounting to dishonesty. Dishonesty is left undefined.
(5) **Was that appropriation, at the time it occurred, accompanied by an intention to permanently deprive the owner of the property?** Section 6 provides some special instances where such an intention is said to exist.

To illustrate how all these elements hang together, consider the following example:

Case 1

Adam, hair-stylist to the stars, is asked by his friend Demien, an artist, if Adam would be prepared to collect and sell Demien the hair of various celebrities for a future artistic composition. Adam says he will think about it. A few days later, following a visit from the famous pop-group, Brass Monkeys, Adam telephones Demien and says he will sell Demien the discarded hair of the group members for £5,000. An hour later he changes his mind and throws the hair away. Has Adam stolen the hair?

A lay person will no doubt conclude that Adam has not. After all, he has only made a phone call. To answer the question correctly, however, sections 1–6 must be precisely interpreted and applied. Question 1 – Section 3 tells us that a person appropriates property by assuming the rights of the owner. Might this not include offering to sell property? Question 2 – Only **property** can be stolen. Is hair 'property' for the purpose of section 4? Question 3 – Adam can only steal the hair if it **belongs to someone** else. Who does the hair, assuming it is property, belong to? The group members? Adam? The occupier of the salon, if not Adam? No one? Question 4 – Section 2 says, amongst other things, that a person's appropriation is not dishonest if the appropriator believes he has the legal right to do so or thinks he would have the owner's consent. If Adam may have had such a belief the jury must acquit. Question 5 – Assuming the hair belonged to the group members, did Adam manifest the intention to permanently deprive them of it by offering it for sale?

A *Actus reus*

1 The appropriation

Under the previous law some form of 'taking and carrying away' was necessary to establish the *actus reus* of theft. Under the Theft Act 1968, although theft will normally involve a taking and carrying away, section 3 indicates that this is not now necessary. By section 3(1) 'any assumption by a person of the rights of an owner amounts to an appropriation, and this includes, where he has come by the property (innocently or not) without stealing it, any later assumption of a right to it by keeping or dealing with it as owner'.

The definition of appropriation is far wider than that accorded in everyday speech. In everyday terms, we appropriate property belonging to another when we take it, or otherwise make it our own. So we would say that destroying property is a form of appropriation. As we shall see, however, there are ways of exercising dominion over property which we would hardly call an appropriation. The precise question to be asked, then, is not so much whether the accused has appropriated the property but whether he has 'assumed the rights of the owner over the property'. This in turn requires us to consider the nature of those rights of ownership and how those rights may be assumed.

(a) *Assuming rights of ownership*

In simple terms, rights of ownership are the rights to do with property what one wills. These include the right to possess, use, consume, modify, or destroy it, and the right to lend, sell, give, hire or otherwise alienate it. Any person who assumes one of these rights, therefore, appropriates property for the purposes of s. 3. It has been held that offering to sell another person's property is an appropriation of that property where the offeror is in possession or control of the property, since this is a right of ownership.[13] It seems that the appropriation may be no less present if the offeror is not in possession of, or has not even inspected, the property. It has been objected that an assumption of the rights of owner should not occur until the accused is in a position to exercise them. Until this occurs, offering goods for sale can only be so much 'hot air'. If it defrauds the offeree, it does nothing to compromise the rights of the owner.[14] 'Hot air' it may be, but it is the law.

It is in all cases necessary to pinpoint an actual act of appropriation and show that it coincides with the *mens rea*. This will generally be easy where at the time of the appropriation the property is in the possession of the owner. It will be less easy where the person comes by property 'innocently' and then decides to 'keep or deal with it as owner'.

Case 2
A lends B a book. B places the book on his bedside table. He later decides to keep the book and places it on his bookshelf.

To be guilty of theft B must, with the relevant *mens rea*, appropriate A's property. The *mens rea* for theft is here formed after B acquires the property. B cannot be guilty of theft, therefore, unless having already acquired the property innocently, he later assumes the rights of the owner over the book by keeping or dealing with it **as owner**. Has he? On the face of it he has not.[15] The *actus reus* of theft, like other result crimes, cannot be committed by omission in the absence of a duty (to render up the property). Keeping the book on his bedside table or placing it on his bookshelf is an example of B **exercising** possession rather than an example of him **assuming** (taking on) possession or any other right of ownership. No more would it be to read the book. Reading it, after it has been lent to him for this very purpose, is an example of B exercising one of the rights of borrower. In order to appropriate A's book, it might be thought therefore, that B must **do something** to assume A's

---

[13] *Pitham and Hehl* (1976) 65 Cr App R 45 CA.
[14] G. Williams *TCL* 765.
[15] D. Ormerod and D. Williams, *Smith's Law of Theft* (2007), hereafter *Smith* (2007); cf. E. Griew, *The Theft Acts*, London: Sweet & Maxwell (1995) 45 (hereafter Griew (1995)).

rights, for example selling it, or writing his name in it, or erasing A's name, or hiding it in a suitcase or disguising it in some way, or denying that A is the rightful owner, or **omitting to do something which he is under a duty to do,** say keeping it after the loan period (bailment) has ended.[16] Under such circumstances as these, at least, it is quite appropriate to conclude that by deciding to keep the book A is thereby appropriating it.

A more plausible scenario involves situations where an account holder discovers that his account has been mistakenly credited with an amount, as where an employer pays an employee twice, by mistake. It has been argued that theft must require something more than a decision simply not to repay the excess since an appropriation requires some act directed against the relevant property.[17] Griew has suggested that the appropriation could be found in some use of the bank account which was inconsistent with honouring the payee's obligation to make restoration, for example, by reducing the credit balance or overdraft facility below the amount that ought to be paid to the payer.[18]

Despite these objections it is widely thought that a simple **decision** to keep the property amounts to an appropriation whether or not D does something inconsistent with the owner's rights.[19] The key words in section 3 are 'keeping OR dealing with it as owner' not 'keeping AND dealing with it as owner'. By keeping the property under these circumstances D is saying to himself: 'Right I am keeping this book. I don't care about the owner's rights.' He is assuming for himself the owner's right to keep it and deal with it as he wills.[20]

(b) Insubstantial appropriations

The previous discussion makes clear that an appropriation may occur by dint of an objectively fairly trivial act – erasing a name or substituting a dust-jacket or, where the defendant is already in possession, simply deciding to keep it in defiance of the owner's rights. In other words, to appropriate property the appropriator does not need to assume **all the rights of owner** – that is, to assume **complete** dominion over the property. In *Morris*,[21] the act of switching a price tag on a supermarket article[22] was held to be an **appropriation**, even though it was not an act of **deprivation**. The theft was consummated as soon as this act was completed with the relevant *mens rea*. The right of the owner which the shopper had assumed was either:

(a) the right to determine the price at which the article is sold, or
(b) the right to place price tags on the article, or
(c) more simply, the right to touch the article for the purpose of changing the price tags on the article.

Whichever of these rights the shopper assumed was inconsistent with the owner's rights.

In another instance of insubstantial appropriation, it has been held that theft of the proceeds of a bank account takes place as early as presenting the forged or unauthorised

---

[16] E. Melissaris, 'The Concept of Appropriation and the Offence of Theft' (2007) 70 MLR 581; this view is supported by A.T.H. Smith, *Property Offences*, London: Sweet & Maxwell (1994) (hereafter A.T.H. Smith) 171.

[17] See above.

[18] Griew (1995) at 37.

[19] See for example Simester and Sullivan 13.6 (iii).

[20] *Broome v Crowther* (1984) 148 JP 592. Stuart Green argues that theft is an inappropriate label for those who come by property innocently, for example lost property or property which has been misdelivered. S.P. Green, 'Theft by Omission' in J. Chalmers, L. Farmer and F. Leverick (eds), *Essays in Criminal Law in Honour of Sir Gerald Gordon*, Edinburgh: Edinburgh University Press (2010).

[21] [1983] 3 All ER 288.

[22] With a view to later purchasing it at a lower price.

cheque, even though the presentation had not and legally was not capable of adversely affecting the interests of the account holder.[23] On this basis the *actus reus* of theft disappears almost to the point where an attempt would not lie. No property was touched. It could not be touched. And the act of the so-called thief was as slight as passing over a piece of paper to a counter clerk.[24]

(c) *The relevance of consent or authority*

The question arises whether it is a necessary ingredient in an appropriation that the act be inconsistent with the rights retained by the owner. In *Morris* it was said that it was, and that it was of the essence of an appropriation that the act be by way of 'adverse interference or usurpation of the owner's rights'. Taking the goods off the shelf was not an appropriation because it was authorised or consented to. But swapping price labels amounted to an appropriation because it was not authorised. Such an analysis is consistent with the earlier decision in *Eddy* v *Niman*.[25] A shopper in a supermarket placed goods from the supermarket shelves into the basket provided, although it was his ultimate intention to steal the goods. The question to be decided, given that all the other elements of the offence were present, was whether this act was an act of appropriation. The court ruled that it was not. On the face of it, this conclusion seems correct. What rights of ownership are assumed by shoppers placing articles in the very baskets provided by the supermarket for that purpose? To assume the rights of the owner it must surely be necessary to do something more than exercise the rights of the shopper.[26]

A similar result occurred in *Fritschy*. A person took possession of a consignment of krugerrands on the understanding that he was to take them to Switzerland for resale. It was held that he did not appropriate them simply by taking possession of them with the intention of keeping them for himself.[27] Central to this and other decisions[28] is that one does not commit the *actus reus* of theft unless one has done something **manifestly wrong**. Without such an overt act, it is thought, one is being punished for one's thoughts alone.

The decision in *Fritschy* raises an obvious problem, not raised in *Morris*, concerning acts designed to usurp the owner's rights but which the owner, perhaps through ignorance or mistake, nevertheless consents to. Is this not a case where, notwithstanding authorisation or consent, the essential nature of the defendant's act is nevertheless a 'rights-assuming' one? Consider the case of *McHugh*.[29] A motorist filled up his petrol tank at a self-service petrol station, having formed the intention to drive off without paying. Although what he did was consistent with his status as a consumer, it would be going too far to say that what he did was consistent with the rights of the owner. The act authorised or consented to was **the very act** by which the defendant sought to deprive the owner of his property and was thus, unlike that in *Eddy* v *Niman*, adverse to the rights of ownership retained by the owner. *McHugh*, unlike the shopper, was treating the petrol as **his own**. It seems clear that, at least in this limited sense, a person can appropriate property even by an act authorised by the owner.

---

[23] *Chan Man-sin* v *A-G of Hong Kong* [1988] 1 WLR 196; *Governor of Pentonville prison, ex parte Osman* (1990) 90 Cr App R 281.

[24] Or transmitting a fax message to the bank staff as in *Osman* note 23.

[25] (1981) 73 Cr App R 237.

[26] See Case 2.

[27] *Fritschy* [1985] Crim LR 745 CA; see also *Skipp* [1975] Crim LR 114; cf. *Meech* [1973] 3 All ER 939.

[28] See *Morris* below.

[29] (1977) 64 Cr App R 92.

In *Dobson* v *General Accident*[30] the Court of Appeal went further. A rogue bought a Rolex watch from D using a stolen, and therefore worthless, building society cheque. D claimed under his home contents insurance policy for the theft of the watch. The insurance company was only bound to pay out if D could show the watch to be stolen which, in turn, required him to show that an appropriation had occurred. It was held that there was. It was not prevented from being so by the fact that the transaction giving rise to the taking was authorised by the owner. This decision was confirmed by the House of Lords in *Gomez*,[31] concluding that it is not of the essence of an appropriation that the defendant's act be by way of adverse interference or usurpation of the owner's rights, disapproving *Morris* on this point and overruling *Fritschy*.[32] In so doing it followed the precedent set by the House of Lords in *Lawrence* v *MPC*[33] where the issue was whether a taxi-driver, who dishonestly took too much money from an Italian student's outstretched wallet, had unlawfully appropriated the money thus taken. The defence argued that the student had consented to the taking and that this prevented an appropriation from having taken place. The House of Lords rejected this argument, holding that an appropriation can occur even where the victim consents to the taking.[34] In *Gomez* D, the assistant manager of an electrical store, entered into an arrangement with a rogue by which the latter tendered a worthless cheque to the assistant manager for goods. D told the manager that the cheque was 'as good as cash' and on that basis the manager authorised the sale. D was charged with theft, rather than obtaining property by deception which, for some strange reason, the prosecutor thought fit not to charge! The House of Lords held, by a majority, that by inducing the owner to part with his property D thereby appropriated the property.[35]

(d) Charging theft or deception

The curious reader may be puzzled at why, in many of these cases, theft was charged at all, let alone supported a conviction. To answer this question let us examine, once again, *Morris* and *Eddy* v *Niman*. Why was the shopper in *Eddy* v *Niman* not apprehended when he eventually tried to conceal the article or left the store without paying? Why was the shopper in *Morris* not allowed to pay for the goods at the reduced price and then charged, say, with obtaining property by deception/fraud? For the answer to this question one must consider both the circumstances leading to the arrest, the law of theft and other crimes possibly issuing from those circumstances, and the various decisions made by the law officers prior to trial. In *Morris* there were two defendants arising out of two separate incidents.[36] D1 was arrested after paying for the goods. D2 was arrested before doing so. There might be many reasons for the store detective deciding to 'jump the gun' in this way. She might get over-excited. She might suspect the villain is about to make a run for it. Or, she may discover that the latter has seen her looking at him and so has changed his mind.

Once the rogue is arrested, the case would be investigated by the police. A choice will then be made as to whether to bring charges or not. The charge will be instituted either by the police on the advice of the Crown Prosecution Service (CPS) or by the CPS directly on the basis of the evidence presented to them by the police. The CPS would review all

[30] [1989] 3 WLR 1066.
[31] [1993] AC 442.
[32] And a number of other cases, e.g. *Skipp* [1975] Crim LR 114 CA; *Meech* [1973] 3 All ER 939.
[33] [1972] AC 626 HL.
[34] See S. Shute and J. Horder, 'Thieving and Deceiving: What is the Difference?' (1993) 56 MLR 548.
[35] Cf. Griew (1995) 50.
[36] *Morris, Anderton and Burnside.*

the evidence and decide how to proceed. The first decision the CPS would have to make in a case like *Morris* is whether to proceed against D2. So, they would need to pinpoint what offence(s), if any, D2 had committed. Perhaps the police thought to charge him with attempting to obtain property by deception. After all, as a matter of pure common sense, his intention was not to steal goods but to deceive the shop into selling him the goods at less than their value. The CPS may have disagreed with this view and charged theft. This is not as surprising as it might seem. First, there were authorities in support of the proposition that an act of interference with property, done for the purpose of stealing, is an appropriation. Second, on the law as it stood, D2's actions were only preparatory to the commission of a crime of deception,[37] and so the charge of attempted deception might well have failed. The CPS would have had the decision whether to discontinue the prosecution against D2, to charge him with theft alone or, for safety, to charge him with theft **and** attempted deception and/or attempted theft.[38]

The decision against D1 would be less complex. On the face of it, D1 has committed the offence of obtaining property by deception rather than theft. This was certainly the intention of the Criminal Law Revision Committee who were concerned to ensure that the offences of theft and obtaining property by deception covered mutually exclusive territory. The House of Lords, apparently reluctant to allow the defendant to escape conviction on the basis of the apparently sloppy work of the prosecutor, upheld the conviction of both defendants for theft on the basis of their switching of the price labels. The effect of *Gomez* is to compound this problem. Consider the following case.

Case 3

Adam, a shopper, on taking a pair of shoes to the cash desk for purchase, notices that the price tags on each shoe show different amounts. He goes back to the counter to find another to match the lower price but cannot. He chooses, therefore, a matching shoe without a price tag on it, dishonestly intending to purchase the pair at the lower price. A store detective notices all this and arrests him before he reaches the cash desk.[39]

Before *Gomez*, theft in a supermarket would only be committed by some form of concealment, interference or taking and carrying away. Adam's act in picking up the second shoe would barely be sufficient (being merely preparatory) to count as an attempt at committing that crime. Following *Gomez* that very act is now an appropriation which, since it is accompanied by the dishonest intention of facilitating the purchase of both shoes at the lower price, is sufficient to incur liability for the consummated offence itself[40] – a remarkable state of affairs given the fact that nothing had been done to the shoes which any other purchaser was not free to do, that the cash desk had not even been reached, and that he still had time to change his mind and decide to choose a different style. How would Adam commit attempted theft of the shoes – by reaching out his hand in a possessory fashion?

The other unfortunate consequence of *Gomez* was that it extends the impact of *Morris* so that almost all cases of obtaining property by deception (now fraud by false representation) are now also cases of theft. Professor Sir John Smith, who assisted the Criminal Law Revision Committee, informs us that he formulated a 'golden rule for prosecutors' in the first edition

---

[37] Or theft by taking and carrying away from the shop.
[38] Griew (1995) 47.
[39] Based on the facts of *Kaur, Dip Kaur* v *CC for Hampshire* [1981] 2 All ER 430.
[40] And possibly when he first forms the dishonest intention, on a loose reading of section 3(1).

of *Smith on Theft* which he vainly hoped would ensure good charging practice.[41] This rule was as follows: whenever D has obtained property from P by any kind of trick or false pretence, he should be charged (with fraud) and not under s. 1(1). Theft, it was thought, should be limited to cases where a rogue took possession of property which was owned by someone else without consent. It should not cover cases where, as in *Gomez*, the villain dupes the owner into passing ownership to him and then takes his own property away. This is not what we popularly think of as theft. It is fraud. Obviously not every prosecutor had read *Smith on Theft* and certainly the advice was not heeded in *Morris* or *Gomez*, following the (bad) example set by prosecutors in earlier cases.[42]

It has been plausibly objected that assimilating the offences of theft and deception in this way is not only sloppy, it is a violation of the principle of fair labelling. Thieving and deceiving attract a different moral response and that response should be reflected both in different labels and in the different punishment price tags which each offence incurs.[43] Codifying the law, it seems, does not necessarily increase the justice or certainty which its deployment is argued to advance.

(e) *The relevance of consent or authorisation where deception is not alleged*

Since *Gomez* involved a deception, it would have been sufficient for the decision to hold that consent or authority is only irrelevant where, as in such cases, the consent was defective say due to fraud. In such a case D would still be 'appropriating' property belonging to another because he would be assuming rights over property which still, to the extent that the transaction could be undone for fraud, belonged to another within the meaning of section 5(1). Such an approach was adopted in *Mazo* in which a distinction was drawn between cases where the defendant is constituted as an outright owner and those where, as in *Gomez* and *Fritschy*, he receives only a voidable title.[44] Only in the latter situation, it was said, would a (theftuous) appropriation occur.[45] It would occur there because those rights of the previous owner retained by him by consequence of the deception or terms of agreement were being assumed by the 'new owner'. But if A, without deception, dishonestly encourages B to gift her money, or sell property to her or buy property from her, the *actus reus* of theft would not occur since the entire proprietary interest is transferred.

In *Hinks* the House of Lords rejected this approach. The appellant who had befriended D encouraged him to make her gifts of money from his bank account. She was convicted of theft, although there was no evidence of duress or deception or that he had parted with the money otherwise than by gift. The defence case was that the recipient of a valid gift could not be guilty of theft. Either there is a valid transfer of title or there is an appropriation. A donee does not 'appropriate' a gift, (s)he receives it. There cannot be both.[46] Lord Steyn said that whether or not D had gifted the money the appellant, by acquiring title, had appropriated it and was guilty of theft upon proof of dishonesty. The acquisition of title, on this view, is simply the clearest possible case of 'assuming rights of ownership'.[47] The objection to this reasoning is that criminal liability requires a wrong as well as culpability. Where was

---

[41] See generally J.C. Smith, *The Law of Theft* (1993) v.
[42] Such as *Lawrence*, above.
[43] S. Shute and J. Horder, op. cit.; C. Clarkson, 'Theft and Fair Labelling' (1993) 56 MLR 554; cf. P.R. Glazebrook, 'Thief or Swindler: Who Cares?' [1991] CLJ 389 who takes the pragmatic line that swindling and stealing can be appropriately assimilated. E. Melissaris, 'The Concept of Appropriation and the Offence of Theft' (2007) MLR 581.
[44] Voidable on account of the deception.
[45] *Mazo* [1996] Crim LR 435.
[46] See Hopkins; Kendrick [1997] Crim LR 359; S. Gardner, 'Property and Theft' [1998] Crim LR 35.
[47] [2001] 1 Cr App R 252, 262–3.

the wrong here? The civil law acknowledges none. It recognises the gift. It was H's to keep. H was not legally bound to repay the gift.[48]

(f) *Appropriation and dishonesty*

Their Lordships in *Hinks* were keen to point out that the effect of holding the acquisition of a valid title by gift or contract to be an appropriation was not to automatically render the acquirer guilty of theft. This is because a person who does acquire such a title will rarely be considered dishonest by the jury. This is because of the operation of section 2 Theft Act 1968. By section 2(1)(a) a person is not to be regarded as dishonest if he believes that he has in law the right to deprive the other of it, on behalf of himself or of a third person.

> **Case 4**
> Gibbons, a philatelist, spots a rare stamp on Orlando's stamp stall at a car boot sale. Orlando, who is 12, is selling all his stamps to give to charity. Gibbons offers Orlando £5 for the stamp although he knows it is worth nearer £50,000. Orlando accepts and the deal is done.

Hinks tells us that, although Gibbons obtains perfect title to the stamp and Orlando cannot rescind the contract he has appropriated property belonging to another. However that appropriation is only theftuous if it is dishonest. Is it? Most people would say it was. However section 2 states that as a matter of law it is not dishonest if Gibbons believes he has the legal right to the property. Why would he not have such a belief? It is a perfectly valid transaction and perfectly valid transactions pass all legal rights to the purchaser. Gibbons, in Case 4 would no doubt, claim very plausibly that he had such a belief. Why, then, was Mrs Hinks not acquitted since she no doubt may have believed that she was entitled to the gifts? The answer is simple. The trial judge wrongly failed to direct the jury in accordance with section 2. He simply asked them to consider whether she was dishonest, applying their own standards, which on the basis of her clearly immoral action they were happy to confirm. The judge could equally have asked them to apply section 2(1)(b) which states that a person is not to be regarded as dishonest if he appropriates property in the belief that he would have the other's consent if the other knew of the appropriation and the circumstances of it. As Lord Hutton said in his dissenting opinion this must mean that there can never be dishonesty where there is a valid gift (or purchase) because not only is there **a belief** in the other's consent, **there is** consent. For this reason he would have allowed Mrs Hinks' appeal. With respect, I would too! Lord Steyn, with whom two other Law Lords agreed, upheld the conviction on the basis that it was safe. In the light of section 2 it is difficult to see how they reached that conclusion.

(g) *Summary*

To summarise, the legal position following *Hinks* and *Gomez* would appear to be as follows.

(1) An appropriation does not require all the rights of the owner to be assumed. It is enough for any right to be assumed, however trivial. It does seem necessary, however, for some act to have occurred by which such rights have been assumed. A person appropriates property in a supermarket simply by handling it or placing it in the trolley. A person does not appropriate it by omitting to restore it to the shelves after her child has placed it there unbidden.

---

[48] For general discussion see Law Commission Consultation Paper No. 155 *Fraud and Deception* (1999) paras 5.24–5.32 which reject an offence constituted by mental element rather than conduct.

(2) An act is no less an appropriation by the fact that it has been authorised or consented to.

(3) This is so even if the act concerned was not the act by which the accused sought to deprive the owner of his property.

(4) Even the acquisition of an indefeasible title to property amounts to an appropriation of that property since by acquiring such title the recipient must assume the (previous) owner's rights.

(5) Liability for theft nevertheless requires the appropriation to be dishonest. In theory, this will require the judge to direct the jury as per section 2(1) Theft Act 1968. If this is done it is hard to see how a conviction will be appropriate where the appropriation is not accompanied by fraud or undue influence. This logic was ignored in *Hinks*.

Professor Sir John Smith, with customary clarity, reduces these propositions to the following:

> Anyone doing anything whatever to property belonging to another, with or without the authority or consent of the owner, appropriates it; and, if he does so dishonestly and with intent, by that act or any subsequent act, permanently to deprive, he commits theft.[49]

Stated thus, it should be clear that the notion of a theftuous appropriation is drawn far too widely to command the support of common sense or advance penal logic. Many acts not involving a deception which, under the understanding of the Criminal Law Revision Committee would not even count as criminal attempts, are now constituted as consummated theft.[50] Given that most of the decisions which have brought about this wide catchment have been cases which should and could have been brought under section 15 Theft Act 1968,[51] this in itself is unacceptable. In effect to ensure swindlers get their just deserts, theft now covers some, such as the shopper in *Eddy*, whose conduct, far from having the appearance of theft, has none of the hallmarks even of wrongdoing.

(h) *Protection for the* bona fide *purchaser*

By section 3(2) 'where property or a right or interest in property is or purports to be transferred for value to a person acting in good faith, no later assumption by him of rights which he believed himself to be acquiring shall, by reason of any defect in the transferor's title, amount to theft of the property'. The effect of this provision is to provide a limited defence to a *bona fide* purchaser of goods which he later discovers are stolen. The reason for the immunity is that criminal consequences should not attend such equivocal acts of wrongdoing. The provision is necessary because, without it, section 3 designates such behaviour an appropriation.[52] Such a person would come by property 'innocently' and 'later' assume a 'right to it by keeping or dealing with it as owner'.

The defence is circumscribed in a number of ways. It is only available where the property is transferred for value, say by purchase or pledge, and the transferee acts in good faith. No appropriation occurs in such a case if he decides to keep it or sell it. If the property is a gift, however, any act which would amount to an appropriation under section 3 will be theftuous. It should also be noted that, although there will be no theft in cases of keeping or dealing following a *bona fide* purchase, the recipient may yet be guilty of a crime which does not require an appropriation, say handling. A person who sells property, having discovered it to be stolen, could, then, be guilty of either of these offences assuming the other

---

[49] It should be noted that the requirement that there be an act of appropriation reflects the view that an assumption requires more than simply a decision to assume rights.

[50] Cf. *Mazo*, above.

[51] Which is criminalised obtaining property by deception.

[52] And, of course, a decision to keep stolen property after discovering it to be stolen would generally provide the *mens rea* necessary to render the appropriation theftuous.

elements of the offence were present.[53] The safest bet for the innocent purchaser is to keep the property.

(i) *The duration of an appropriation*

One final question must now be posed in connection with the appropriation, namely how long an appropriation lasts. Does it end with the act by which the owner's rights were assumed, or does it continue until some later event? If so, what is that event? The point was relevant in *Atakpu*.[54] A and B had committed a theft of motor cars outside the jurisdiction. They brought the cars to England, intending to resell them. Such a resale is an assumption of the rights of an owner, as we have seen. It was held, however, that as the theft had already been constituted outside the jurisdiction it could not recur within it.[55] Once stolen, goods cannot be restolen by the self-same defendants. This does not answer the question when the appropriation, that is, the theft is complete. One suggestion is that this occurs when the transaction, of which it forms part, is complete.[56] Thus, the theft of an article from a house is only complete on leaving the house even though possession may have been taken some time earlier. One theoretical problem with this is that it seems inconsistent with the potentially instantaneous appropriations illustrated by *Gomez*. One practical advantage of this is that a person who disposes of the article to someone else before he leaves the house will not be guilty of theft twice.[57] If the appropriation continues until the house is left, it follows that the stealing continues until that time.

2 Property: general definition

Only 'property' can be stolen for the purpose of the law of theft. Section 4(1) provides a general definition. ' "Property" includes money and all other property, real or personal, including things in action and other intangible property.'

Most tangible objects, with the reservations issued below in relation to flora and fauna, are property as long as the relevant object can be the subject of another's ownership. So one can steal a person's money, wallet, chequebook, bank statement, pet cat, or trousers, but not her husband. He is owned by no one, not even himself.

(a) *Human body parts*

A topical problem case is human body parts, including corpses. It seems that a buried corpse is not property since property, by definition, wants no owner.[58] However, in *Kelly*, it was held that dead bodies which have become some form of artefact or been subjected to some specialised process, as upon mummification for display purposes or preparation for dissection, are property for the purposes of the law of theft whether or not they are also proper subjects of ownership.[59] So, in *Kelly* an artist who made art works out of body

---

[53] See p. 488.

[54] [1993] 4 All ER 215.

[55] Cf. G.R. Sullivan and C. Warbrick, 'Territoriality, Theft and *Atakpu* [1994] Crim LR 650, who argue that 'theft abroad' is not theft for purposes of English law and, therefore, theft did occur upon first assuming rights of ownership in England.

[56] Smith (2007) ch. 1.

[57] Moreover, neither he by disposing nor the recipient, by receiving, will be guilty of handling stolen property since both the disposition and receiving must be effected 'otherwise than in the course of stealings', s. 22(1); see Griew (1995) 256–7.

[58] Cf. Griew 21–2; A.T.H. Smith 46–9.

[59] *Doodeward* v *Spence* (1908) 6 CLR 406; *Kelly* [1998] 3 All ER 741.

parts, including limbs and torso, given to him by a Royal College of Surgeons technician was found properly guilty of theft of the parts.[60] Body products such as blood, urine,[61] semen[62], and probably DNA, are also property capable of being stolen at least when they have become a subject of ownership, say by a blood or semen bank. The position of frozen embryos is probably comparable,[63] as is human hair. Cutting a person's hair from the head will not be theft because hair, like its 'grower', is not owned and is thus not property.[64] This is an offence against the person, not against property, just as it would be if a part of the 'living body' had been severed. If that hair had been converted into a wig or cushion filling it would become property. Arguably, hair might also be property if it had fallen to the floor following cutting in a hairdressers (see Case 1).[65] Less easy to analyse is the legal position suggested by the once infamous case of the tennis star whose ejaculate, following oral sex, may have been used to impregnate the recipient. Even assuming ejaculate was capable of being property for the purpose of the Theft Acts no proprietary rights could sensibly be retained by the ejaculator given the votive nature of the process. This was not the view taken in a recent case in which a hospital negligently destroyed sperm belonging to a patient who had bailed it with them as protection against potential infertility following chemotherapy. The Court of Appeal held that a donor retains a property interest in the sperm as against those who negligently destroyed it.[66]

(b) *Things in action and other intangible property*
A thing in action (or 'chose in action'), counterposed to a thing in possession, i.e. an object, is a thing whose use-value can only be secured by means of a legal action. Examples of things in action include debts, shares, credit balances in a bank account, copyright or trademark, and a right under a trust. A cheque is not, in itself, a thing in action. It is, at the same time, a real thing (a piece of paper or valuable security). It also represents a thing in action, namely a debt owed by one person to another.[67]

(i) *Money, cheques and bank accounts*[68]
Money can, of course, be stolen but it is personal property. Money for this purpose includes actual notes and coins.

Case 5

A takes from B a cheque for £100 drawn by C and made payable to B. C has £100 in his bank account. A opens an account in the name of B and pays the cheque into the account causing a transfer of funds from C's to A's account.

---

[60] See previous note.
[61] *Welsh* [1974] RTR 478.
[62] *Yearworth v North Bristol NHS Trust* [2009] EWCA 37.
[63] A.T.H. Smith 48.
[64] See generally J.W. Harris, 'Who Owns my Body?' [1996] 16 OJLS 55.
[65] Under the principle in *Hibbert v McKiernan* [1948] 2 KB 142 (see below p. 432). However, unless it was subject to some form of process it is more plausible to consider it not to be property.
[66] See *Yearworth*, above, note 62.
[67] Compare the position with train tickets. Is a crook who buys passengers' tube tickets for resale to other passengers appropriating the tickets or the chose in action which they represent? The former, says the Court of Appeal: *Marshall* [1998] JP 488. Neither, says Professor Smith. See below, p. 426 and 'Stealing Tickets' [1998] Crim LR 723.
[68] See generally R. Heaton, 'Cheques and Balances' [2005] Crim LR 747.

This is not a theft of money *per se*. First and foremost it is theft of the cheque form, which is both a piece of paper and also a valuable security operating, like the key to a safe, as a means of obtaining money.[69] When the cheque is paid in, causing the transfer of funds, actual money still is not stolen.[70] What is 'stolen' is C's right to draw on the account (a thing in action).[71] This thing is stolen, apparently, even though the bank must recredit C's account with the funds transferred.[72] If, instead of paying it into his account, A had cashed the cheque, actual money would have been stolen.[73] This money has not been stolen from B but from the bank.[74] Compare the following case:

Case 6

C asks his building society to issue a building society cheque for £10,000 in favour of A, from whom he intends to purchase a car. The building society does so, having first debited C's account with the money. When C goes to collect the car he discovers it is faulty. He tells A he will not proceed. A surreptitiously takes the building society cheque, which he later pays into his account.

By taking the cheque, A has not stolen £10,000 (see Case 4). Neither has he stolen a thing in action. The right to sue upon the cheque is not the drawer's right but the payee's. The *chose in action* is not then 'property belonging to another'. What he has appropriated is a valuable security (the cheque) which **does** belong to another, namely C, until he delivers it.[75] By paying in the cheque A appears to be appropriating (but not obtaining) property belonging to another.[76]

Case 7

A steals a chequebook from P's briefcase. He later purchases a coat for £100, using as payment one of P's (forged) cheques.

In this case, apart from stealing the coat,[77] A appropriates a thing in action, namely the debt owed by the bank to P, represented by the cheque.[78] If P's bank account is not in credit and he has no overdraft facility, there is no debt owed to P and therefore no theft of a thing in action. In such cases the prosecution may well prefer to charge the theft of the (cheque) form itself.[79]

Case 8

A, to satisfy a debt, draws a cheque backed by a cheque guarantee card on his own account in favour of B, knowing that he has no funds to cover it and no arrangement with the bank.

---

[69] J.C. Smith [1997] Crim LR; cf. *Kohn* (1979) 69 Cr App R 395.
[70] Causing a transfer of funds is now a separate offence by virtue of the Theft Amendment Act 1996 amending the Theft Act 1968.
[71] *Kohn* (1979) 69 Cr App R 395; *Hallam* [1995] Crim LR 323; *Williams* [2001] Crim LR 253; cf. *Burke* [2000] Crim LR 413.
[72] *Chan Man-sin* v *A-G for Hong Kong* [1988] 1 All ER 1 PC; cf. *Hilton* [1997] Crim LR 761.
[73] *Davis* (1988) 88 Cr App 347.
[74] *Burke*, above.
[75] See J.C. Smith, 'Obtaining Cheques by Deception or Theft' [1997] Crim LR 396.
[76] *R* v *Preddy and others* [1996] 3 All ER 481 overruling *Duru* [1973] 3 All ER 715.
[77] Following *Gomez*.
[78] *Chan Man-sin* v *A-G for Hong Kong* [1988] 1 All ER 1 PC.
[79] Griew 20.

Here no theft is committed since he has appropriated neither money nor a thing in action. What he has done is to **create** a right of action in favour of the payee against himself. This is not the same as appropriating an existing thing in action such as a debt.[80] A's liability, if any, is limited to a possible offence under the Fraud Act 2006.

(ii) *The scope of intangible property*

The Theft Act includes within the scope of 'property' 'intangible property'. Apart from the one example of things in action, it gives no clue as to what phenomena are intended to be covered by this mysterious phrase. Clearly not all intangible things in which a person has an interest can count as property. If it were so, the law of theft would become unworkable.

> **Case 9**
> Ukridge, Bingo's jealous brother, tells Wooster, their rich uncle, a scandalous and untrue story about Bingo so that he, Wooster, will change his will, at present benefiting Bingo, and leave it elsewhere. The ruse works. Bingo is left penniless on Wooster's death.

In this case the interest forfeited is not property. It is not possible to convert what is essentially a non-property interest into a property interest by the device of calling it intangible property. Why though is it not property? The obvious answer is that the interest concerned is only an interest and not a right. Only rights can be assumed and here Bingo has none.

Perhaps the most helpful rule of thumb capable of distinguishing between 'intangible property' and non-property interests is that of marketability. In *Attorney-General of Hong Kong* v *Chan Nai-Keung (Daniel)*, A, the director of a company, sold a valuable right owned by his company to export fabrics out of Hong Kong (an export quota) to another company without authority. It was held that the quota, as it was capable of being bought and sold, was 'intangible property' within the meaning of section 4. This explains quite neatly why the arrangement in Case 9 does not involve property since the interest concerned has no market value and nobody else could profit from it. Using the marketability test it is clear that patents, copyrights, and other forms of quotas, such as milk, fish, carbon emissions and export quotas, count as intangibles since, in each case, the rights which **they represent** can be bought and sold.

It should be noted that a person does not steal a patent, copyright or quota simply by acting in breach of it. Thus:

> **Case 10**
> A borrows B's film in which C has copyright, to make pirate copies in breach of copyright.

Here no theft has occurred. A has not stolen the film since his intention is only to borrow the film. Neither has he stolen the copyright since the copyright, being a thing in action, is simply a right to take action against someone such as himself. This right clearly has not been appropriated by A. It remains with C whatever A does with the film. In short, C's (financial) interests have been damaged by an interference with his rights of exclusive user, but no property right has been appropriated. Legal redress is thus limited to the law of copyright.

---

[80] *Navvahi* [1986] 3 All ER 102.

The 'marketability' test of intangible property, although generally useful, does not always allow us to predict what intangibles will be held to count as intangible property. Two important examples are trade secrets and confidential information. It is generally thought that a person who 'steals' a trade secret by bugging a phone line or photocopying a document upon which it appears is not guilty of theft since the thing appropriated has no identity as property. This is surprising since not only can such information be bought and sold, but also the possessor's interest in the exclusivity of that information can be vindicated by an action for breach of confidence. Trade secrets and other confidential information must be something. Why not property?[81] Why is appropriating an idea considered differently from appropriating the paper upon which it is written? The clearest English authority on the matter is *Oxford v Moss*[82] in which it was held that a student who borrowed an examination paper to help along his examination revision was not guilty of theft. Whatever he had done he had not appropriated property. Of course he would have been guilty of theft if he intended not to return the examination paper but here the subject-matter of the theft would be the paper itself and not the information contained on it.

Probably the best justification for classifying information as something other than property is that it is too amorphous a concept to be satisfactorily vindicated through the law of theft.[83] If it is to be protected it should be done by an instrument designed precisely to cover the particular mischiefs thought to be involved.[84] Exploiting the law of theft for this purpose might be not only unduly oppressive, and an example of unfair labelling, but might be difficult to keep in check.[85] The contrary view taken here is that marketable information should count as intangible property. As one commentator puts it: 'the taking of confidential information is just as real a taking as the theft of tangibles. It should also attract criminal sanctions and for the same reasons.'[86]

With regard to other common intangibles, electricity is not a form of intangible property.[87] One does not steal a person's electricity, then, by surreptitiously watching his TV. Abstracting electricity is subject to its own provision.[88] Gas is property, presumably tangible.[89] The apparent distinction drawn here is not one based on marketability, but between things capable of being collected, and therefore appropriated, and things capable only of being exploited.

(c) Land

Although by section 4(1) property includes real property, the circumstances under which one may be liable for theft of any kind of real property are actually quite limited due to the operation of section 4(2) and (3).

---

[81] See L. Weinrib, 'Information and Property' (1988) 38 UTLJ 117 who argues that confidential information is property for the purposes of the civil law which explains the existence of the right of action. This was rejected by the Supreme Court of Canada in *Stewart* (1988) 50 DLR 1. A.L. Christie, 'Should the Law of Theft Extend to Information?' (2005) J Crim Law.

[82] (1978) 68 Cr App R 183.

[83] See generally J. Penner, *The Idea of Property in Law*, Oxford: OUP (1996) ch. 5.

[84] Computer 'hacking' is one such offence, committed by unlawfully entering a computer system, with a relevant intent, for example to secure access to data or to damage the system.

[85] R.G. Hammond, 'Theft of Information' (1984) 199 LQR 252; A.T.H. Smith 51–5.

[86] Weinrib, ibid. 150.

[87] *Low v Blease* [1975] Crim LR 513.

[88] Section 13 Theft Act 1968.

[89] *White* (1853) Dears 203.

Section 4(2):
a person cannot steal land, or things forming part of the land and severed from it by him or by his directions, except in the following cases . . .

(a) when he is trustee or personal representative, or is authorised by power of attorney, or as liquidator of a company, or otherwise to sell or dispose of land belonging to another, and he appropriates the land or anything forming part of it by dealing with it in breach of the confidence reposed in him;

(b) when he is not in possession of the land and appropriates anything forming part of the land by severing it or causing it to be severed, or after it has been severed; or

(c) when, being in possession of the land under a tenancy, he appropriates the whole or part of any fixture or structure let to be used with the land.

The general effect of section 4(1) and (2) is that land itself cannot be stolen, say by moving a boundary fence or squatting.

(i) Disposals by fiduciaries in breach of confidence

An exception to this is where a fiduciary with the power to sell or dispose of land sells or otherwise deals with it in breach of confidence. Thus:

Case 11

Eve is an old woman suffering from senile dementia. Adam, her son-in-law, is given a power of attorney so that all her affairs can be taken care of. He mortgages Eve's house, in breach of confidence, to raise money for his own business deal.

Adam's conduct falls within section 4(2)(a) and he will be treated as having stolen Eve's house and land, assuming *mens rea* can be established.

(ii) Appropriations of things forming part of the land

Things on the land, e.g. temporary structures, pictures, furniture, heaps of coal, sand, garden ornaments etc., are property capable of being stolen as they do not constitute land or form part of it. Things forming part of the land, e.g. buildings, parts of buildings, walls, trees, flowers, (non-accumulated) minerals, cannot be stolen, say by being sold, used, or destroyed. There are three exceptions. First, where there is a dealing in accordance with section 4(2)(a) as above. Second, by section 4(2)(b) where a person, not in possession of land, appropriates the thing by severance or after it has been severed. Typically the person concerned will be a trespasser but it may equally include a licensee who is not in possession of the land.

Case 12

Adam, Lord Snooty's butler, arranges for Eve, a friend, and Cain, Lord Snooty's farm manager who lives, under licence, in the grounds, to dig up Lord Snooty's newly-planted hedge and remove his mahogany staircase, both for resale.

Adam and Eve steal both the hedge and the staircase, Adam by **causing** them to be severed, Eve by doing the severing. Cain's liability for the hedge depends upon where it is situated. Assuming it forms part of the land licensed, liability for theft will not be incurred since, unlike Adam and Eve, he is in possession of this land. He will be guilty of theft of the staircase since he is not in possession of that part of the land from which it is severed. If the staircase was from his own house in the grounds he would not be liable.[90]

The third exception is where the appropriator is a tenant in possession. By virtue of s. 4(2)(c) a tenant in possession can steal fixtures, that is, anything which is attached to the land intended to form part of the permanent fabric of the land (e.g. fitted fireplaces), or structures (e.g. buildings or walls) let with the land or part thereof, but nothing else forming part of the land, e.g. trees, topsoil, gravel. This limited immunity is not shared by members of his family, who would therefore be liable for appropriating trees and so on.

There is no obvious reason why Cain's liability in Case 12 should depend on whether he is a licensee, rather than a tenant, in possession or whether he steals a hedge rather than a wall[91] or staircase. Section 4 is a salutary example of how, the more detail a provision contains, the more pedantic must be its interpretation.

(d) *Restrictions on liability for appropriating flora and fauna*

(i) *Flora*

Section 4(3) provides that some cases of trespassers on land appropriating, by severance, things growing on the land will not count as theft.

> A person who picks mushrooms growing wild on any land, or who picks flowers, fruit or foliage from a plant growing wild on any land, does not (although not in possession of the land) steal what he picks, unless he does it for reward or for sale or other commercial purpose.

It follows that people who go scrumping for apples, mushrooms or blackberries, or who pick bluebells or mistletoe on other people's land, do not commit theft unless such items are cultivated.[92] This is a notable example of the principle of minimal criminalisation in operation.[93] People should not be subject to state coercion in respect of trivial interferences with the interests of others. The immunity only applies to cases of 'picking'. It does not, then, allow the removal by the roots of whole flowers, trees or bushes. Even in cases of 'picking' it does not apply where the interference is done for commercial purposes. Presumably this is because such a widescale immunity would seriously threaten the autonomy and privacy of the landowners affected. The immunity does not, then, protect the professional mushroom hunters who sell wild fungi to upmarket restaurants,[94] or the mistletoe 'poachers' who supply seasonal mistletoe auctions.

(ii) *Fauna*

By section 4(4):

> wild creatures, tamed or untamed, shall be regarded as property; but a person cannot steal a wild creature not tamed nor ordinarily kept in captivity, or the carcass of any such creature, unless either it has been reduced into possession by or on behalf of another person and possession of it has not since been lost or abandoned, or another person is in the course of reducing it into possession.

By this provision wild animals which are tamed or which are ordinarily kept in captivity are deemed, like pets and domesticated animals, property capable of being stolen. Zoo animals

---

[90] As he is not a tenant. See below.
[91] A wall, unlike a hedge, is a structure. A tenant can, therefore, steal the latter but not the former.
[92] Other offences may be committed in the case of protected species under the Wildlife and Countryside Act 1981.
[93] Above, Chapter 2.
[94] Nor indeed the restaurateur who knowingly receives them (see below at p. 489).

and fish can, then, be stolen, as can fish from a fish farm. Wild animals of the field, for example game, although property, cannot be stolen since they are not the subject of ownership. It is not theft to poach wild animals, for reasons similar to the immunity available for scrumping.[95] Such animals may, however, become property capable of being stolen when they have been caught or killed, or when they are in the process of being caught or killed, if this is done with a view to possessing them. It would, therefore, be theft to remove animals dead or alive from a trap, or after being shot for the purposes of capture, unless in either case possession had been lost or abandoned by the possessor. Hunt saboteurs who remove a wounded fox to a place of safety appropriate property for the purposes of section 4(4). Whether they are also guilty of theft will depend, as we shall see, upon their *mens rea*.

3 'Belonging to another': who does property belong to?[96]

To be guilty of theft the property appropriated must, at the time of the appropriation, 'belong to another'. Since the purpose of the Theft Act is to protect interests in property as well as the ownership of property, s. 5(1) defines 'belonging to another' in a notably wide fashion. Property belongs, for the purpose of the law of theft, to 'any person having possession or control of it, or having any proprietary right or interest (not being an equitable interest arising only from an agreement to transfer or grant an interest)'. So, there may be more than one person to whom property is regarded as belonging, at any one time. In *Marshall* it was held that a passenger who bought tube tickets for resale to other passengers was guilty of theft of the tickets from London Underground since, as against him, the purchased tickets still belonged to London Underground who had retained a proprietary interest in the tickets.[97]

Property 'belongs to another', therefore, whether that other is owner or merely in control or possession of it. If I leave my car with the garage for repair, the car 'belongs to the garage' as well as to me. This means that a theft of the car can be prosecuted even if I disappear and my ownership cannot be established. As will be seen, it also means that I can be guilty of theft of my own car if I dishonestly appropriate it from the garage.

(a) *Property abandoned and lost*

In the usual situation it will be all too clear that the property belongs to another and who that other is. But theoretically property may belong to no one, in which case it cannot be stolen. In particular, it may be abandoned as where a person throws away an old bus ticket or where a golfer gives up on a golf ball, having knocked it into an adjoining field. Accordingly, the owner of the field will not commit the *actus reus* of theft if she appropriates the ball.

A distinction must be drawn between property which is abandoned and property which is only lost. A wallet which is lost still belongs to the owner for the purpose of the law of theft, even though he may have given up hopes of finding it. Theft may still be charged as long as it is clear that there is an owner, that is, the wallet has not been abandoned. In such a case the wallet maybe described as belonging to 'a person unknown'. As maybe appreciated, where property has been lost the question whether it has also been abandoned can only be answered by reference to the owner's intention. If the latter has given up 'interest' (golf ball) it is abandoned. If he has merely given up hope (wallet) it is lost.[98]

---

[95] Above.
[96] For summary, see p. 451.
[97] *Marshall* [1998] JP 488. For criticism see J.C. Smith, 'Stealing Tickets' [1998] Crim LR 723.
[98] For a well-argued discussion of whether theft is an appropriate label for someone who omits to return lost or misdirected property see S. Green, 'Theft by Omission' (2010).

It should be appreciated that the interest retained may be a very slight one, arguably insufficient to satisfy the civil law governing the rights of finders.[99] In *Williams v Phillips*[100] it was held that putting property in a dustbin did not amount to abandoning it. By putting it in a dustbin the owner showed that he wished it to be taken by the refuse collectors rather than any Tom, Dick or Harry who happened to pass by. In so doing, all control over the property had not been ceded.[101] Putting unwanted property in someone else's rubbish-skip, on the other hand, would probably be thought to denote a total ceding of interest, the skip being treated as a movable rubbish dump rather than simply a container for rubbish removal.

It should also be noted that a decision to abandon property does not have the invariable effect of stopping property belonging to another person. Rather, it may cause the property to belong to someone other than the abandoner (and the finder). For instance, in the rubbish-skip example, although the property may no longer belong to the previous owner, it arguably might still belong to whoever has control over the contents of the skip, e.g. the owners of the house or the building contractors.

This point is of particular significance in connection with property abandoned on some-one else's land. In such cases the key question is whether the property can be claimed by the finder ('finders-keepers') or belongs to the owner/occupier of the land.[102] The position depends upon whether the owner/occupier retains sufficient control over the property as against the finder.[103] If it can be shown, then, that the occupier has rights, as against the appropriator, that the property should not be taken[104] it will belong to the former for the purpose of section 5. Thus in *Hibbert v McKiernan*[105] it was held that a person who went scavenging for lost balls on a golf course committed theft of those balls. Although, *vis-à-vis* the persons who had lost them, the balls belonged to no one since they had been abandoned, the balls nevertheless belonged to the golf club. People do not have the right to trespass on land for the purpose of finding abandoned property. To this limited extent (the right to exclude trespassers), the club retained possession and control over the balls.[106] On the other hand, as against the members of the club, they did not. Such finders do not act inconsistently with the club's right to exclude others from the hidden fruits of land ownership.[107]

(b) Theft by owners

Since the concept of 'belonging' to another is drawn so widely, it means that property can be stolen by an owner from a part-owner. Obvious illustrations include the part-owner of a race horse purloining the horse for his own exclusive use, a business partner selling jointly owned property,[108] a trustee disposing of trust property, or an executor of a will dishonestly using or disposing of testamentary property.[109] A particular problem in this

---

[99] See R. Hickey, 'Stealing Abandoned Goods: Possessory Title in Proceedings for Theft' [2006] LS 584.
[100] (1957) 41 Cr App R 5.
[101] For a more recent example of this principle in operation – donated goods taken from bags and bins outside a charity shop are not abandoned by the owner – see *R (Ricketts) v Basildon Magistrates' Court* [2010] WLR (D) 186.
[102] See generally A.T.H. Smith 74–84.
[103] *Woodman* [1974] QB 754; *Parker v British Airways Board* [1982] QB 1004.
[104] As also illustrated by *Williams v Phillips* (1957) 41 Cr App Rep 5.
[105] [1948] 2 KB 142.
[106] Cf. *Rostron* [2003] EWCA Crim 2006, another case involving the purloining of abandoned golf balls. For interesting critical comment on *Rostron* and *Hibbert v McKiernan* see Hickey, 'Stealing Abandoned Goods: Possessory Title in Proceedings for Theft' [2006] LS 584.
[107] For a more practical analysis see A.T.H. Smith 85.
[108] *Bonner* (1970) 54 Cr App R 257.
[109] *Sanders* [2003] EWCA Crim 3079.

latter respect has arisen in connection with the potential scope of constructive trusts for imposing criminal responsibility. It has been held, for example, that a fiduciary, who accepts a bribe in circumstances injurious to his principal, is a constructive trustee of that bribe for the principal. If he does not account for it, this means that he has appropriated property belonging to another by virtue of section 5(1).[110] This decision runs counter to earlier failed prosecutions for theft of employees who have taken secret profits[111] or bribes in the course of their employment without accounting for them.[112] Since it seems unarguable that, as a matter of general principle, such bribes or profits are not beneficially owned by the principal,[113] it is submitted that these latter decisions are of doubtful authority. Further support for this view is afforded by *Shadrokh-Cigari* where it was held that a transferor who transfers money under a mistake of fact retains an equitable interest in the money transferred for the purpose of section 5(1).[114]

Section 5 extends beyond cases of theft by owners from part-owners. Property belongs 'to any person having possession or control of it'. This means that an owner can steal his own property from someone who, as against him, is entitled to retain possession. So a person who dishonestly withdraws money from his bank account, which shows a credit balance only because of a fraud practised against the bank, is guilty of theft of that money from the bank.[115] This will also cover cases where the bailee of property, say a pawnbroker or repairer, has a lien on the property which entitles him to exclude the owner from possession until the bill is paid.[116] On a strict interpretation of section 5, however, it seems that an owner could be guilty of theft[117] where he takes the property back from a person lawfully in possession of it where that person has no personal right of lien (a bailee at will).

Case 13

A lends B his car. Later A secretly retakes the car. When B tells A the car is stolen, A, in furtherance of his dishonest plan, pretends to be angry and insists upon B paying him compensation.

A is no doubt guilty of fraud but is he guilty of theft of the car? On a strict reading of s. 5 he is, since B is in possession under a bailment – a proprietary interest – albeit a meagre one. This conclusion seems illogical given that B had no power to prevent the bailment from being terminated unilaterally[118] and, therefore, less right to possession than A. Nevertheless, illogical as it is, this seems to be the legal position. In *Turner*[119] the owner of a car removed his car from the road outside a garage after it had been repaired, intending thereby to avoid paying for the repairs. The judge told the jury[120] that his liability for theft did not depend upon the garage proprietor having a lien over the car. The Court of Appeal upheld this direction on the basis of a strict interpretation of section 5. It is enough that people are in possession. It does not require that they hold an enforceable right to possession. In holding thus, A in Case 13 appears to be guilty of theft of **the car**,

---

[110] *Attorney-General for Hong Kong* v *Reid* [1994] 1 AC 324.
[111] See for example *Attorney-General's Reference (No. 1 of 1985)* [1986] QB 491.
[112] *Powell* v *MacRae* [1977] Crim LR 571.
[113] See *Boardman* v *Phipps* [1967] 2 AC 46.
[114] See below, p. 437.
[115] *Hendricks* [2003] EWCA Crim 1040.
[116] *Green* v *All Motors* [1917] 1 KB 625; *Rose* v *Matt* [1951] 1 KB 810.
[117] Assuming the necessary *mens rea* can be established.
[118] See G. Williams *TCL* (1983) 749–51.
[119] [1971] 1 WLR 901.
[120] Perhaps because its existence was thought unarguable and thus to avoid unnecessarily confusing them.

and not merely the compensation. It goes without saying that a future court would hesitate before applying *Turner* in such controversial situations.[121]

(c) *Special cases of belonging*

Section 5 presents four special cases where property is deemed to belong to another. We will deal with the three most common.

(i) *Section 5(2)*

Section 5(2) deals with the case of trust property. By section 5(1) trust property belongs both to the trustees (the owners in law) and the beneficiaries under the trust (by virtue of their proprietary interest). Where a person steals trust property, either trustee or beneficiary can be the person designated as the person to whom the property belongs. Section 5(2) deals with the special case of trusts lacking a beneficial owner, in particular charitable trusts. If the trustee(s) stole trust property which lacked a beneficial owner, section 5(1) would not cover the case. By section 5(2), therefore, the trust property is deemed to belong to those who 'have a right to enforce the trust'. In the case of charitable trusts this includes the Attorney-General.[122]

(ii) *Section 5(3)*

Section 5(3) is designed to deal with cases of fundholders who misappropriate money entrusted to them for a particular purpose. In such a case, even though ownership of the funds may have passed to the fund-holder, the property, or its proceeds, may still be deemed to belong to the transferor or some other person. So D may be the owner in possession, but still be liable for appropriating property belonging to another.

> Where a person receives property from or on account of another, and is under an obligation to the other to retain and deal with that property or its proceeds in a particular way, the property or proceeds shall be regarded (as against him) as belonging to the other.

The provision may come into operation in one of two circumstances. First, where O entrusts property to R for R to deal with in a specified fashion. Thus:

Case 14

R, the treasurer of a sports club, uses money, entrusted to him for club purposes by O, the members, to go on holiday to the West Indies.

Second, where a third party (T) transfers property to R the benefit of which is due to O:[123]

Case 15

T, a purchaser of land, hands the purchase money to R, the seller's solicitor, for onward transmission to S, the seller. R, in breach of his obligation to O, the estate agent, pockets that part of the moneys representing O's commission.

---

[121] And did so in *Meredith* [1973] Crim LR 253, a Crown Court decision.
[122] Charities Act 1960, s. 28. See *R v Dyke and Munro* [2002] Crim LR 153.
[123] For a controversial example see *Floyd v DPP* [2000] Crim LR 411 and commentary.

Another example of the second circumstance is where an employee, R, makes a secret profit in the course of his employment with O. Under civil law R is liable to account for that profit to O and it seems to follow that a dishonest failure to do so will be theftuous.[124]

The essence of section 5(3) is that the property is transferred under a legally enforceable obligation for the property to be dealt with in a particular way.[125] Liability for theft does not arise simply because R failed to render O his due.[126] It arises only where the (legal) obligation concerned confers an expectation that the property or its proceeds will be earmarked for that purpose. Thus in *Hall* a travel agent took deposits from clients in respect of some air trips to America which he was to arrange. He placed the deposits into his general trading account, continuing to take them even after it became clear that he was becoming insolvent. His conviction for theft was quashed on the basis that although he was under an obligation to account to the clients for the money taken, he was not under an obligation to do anything special with the deposits, for example to put them in a special clients' account or buy the tickets with the actual moneys received. This was a classic case of insolvency. Many firms continue to accept orders backed by deposits after becoming insolvent. They use these deposits to pay existing creditors. Doing so is only theft if it is understood that the transferee will earmark the deposit for the very purpose for which it has been handed over and not use it for the firm's general purposes.[127] Such an agreement as the latter is probably the exception rather than the rule. A similar decision was reached in *DPP* v *Huskinson*[128] in which it was held not to be theft to use housing benefit for purposes other than paying the recipient's rent. The legislation concerned placed a duty upon the social services to supply the benefit to the recipient, not upon the recipient to apply it directly for the purpose supplied.

It will be apparent that the question of whether a transferee is under an obligation to deal with property or its proceeds in a particular way is not capable of being resolved by the application of a general rule. The existence of the obligation is a matter of law but it will only come into existence if the facts dictate – a jury question.[129] Obvious matters to which the jury should have regard will be the terms of any agreement between the fund-holder and the person to whom the obligation is owed. In Case 15, for example, the solicitor will incur liability for theft only if there is a contractual arrangement that the estate agent will be paid out of the proceeds of the purchaser's cheque.[130] This factual question will be decided by the jury. Different solicitors may have different arrangements with different estate agents. On the basis of the jury's finding of fact the judge will direct them, assuming the other elements of theft are present, to convict if they find the arrangement to be X and to acquit if they find the arrangement to be Y.[131]

The cases of *Hall* and *Huskinson* may be compared with *Davidge* v *Bunnett*,[132] a case falling on the other side of what is, admittedly, a fairly indistinct line. A flat sharer was

---

[124] *Attorney-General for Hong Kong* v *Reid* [1994] 1 AC 324; cf. *Attorney-General's Reference (No. 1 of 1985)* (1986) 83 Cr App R 70.

[125] Even, it appears, if the property is at all times owned by the person with the obligation. *Arnold* [1997] Crim LR 833; cf. *Klineberg* [1999] 1 Cr App R 427.

[126] Cf. *Floyd* v *DPP*, above.

[127] *Hall* [1972] 2 All ER 1009; it seems to follow, from *Gomez*, that if Hall was dishonest in taking deposits a theftuous appropriation is there and then constituted – a remarkable idea.

[128] [1988] Crim LR 620.

[129] *Breaks* [1998] Crim LR 349.

[130] Cf. *R* v *Lamb* [1995] Crim LR 77.

[131] *Mainwaring and Madders* (1981) 74 Cr App R 99.

[132] [1984] Crim LR 297.

given cheques by the others in her flat to pay the gas bill. She spent the proceeds on Christmas shopping. It was held that she had appropriated property belonging to another. The money was to be regarded as still belonging to her flatmates because the obligation undertaken by her was not simply to pay the gas bill, but to pay the gas bill **with the cheques or the proceeds of the cheques** which they had given her. Other situations caught by s. 5(3) include the case of householders who pay their tradespersons money on account for a specific purpose, for example to buy materials for the job. Also charity collectors who misapply, for their own purposes, the funds collected.[133] It should be noted that in such cases as the latter, liability may also be established under s. 5(1) since the fund concerned will form trust property.

(iii) Section 5(4)

Sometimes property transferred subject to a mistake remains in the ownership of the transferor. One such case is where the transferor purports to transfer ownership but under a mistake so fundamental as to render the transaction void; for example A purports to transfer ownership in the property to B believing him to be C[134] or settles a bill for £20 with a £50 note he mistakes for a £20 note,[135] or sells B a bag of peas believing them to be beans. In each case the property still belongs to the transferor by virtue of section 5(1).[136] Any subsequent appropriation of the property[137] with the relevant *mens rea* will be theftuous since no property right of A will have been vested in B and so the property still belongs to A.

Under certain circumstances, however, the mistake made may be such as to transfer the entire ownership in property to the transferee. In such cases, liability for theft may require reliance upon section 5(4), since otherwise it appears that there is no property belonging to another.

> Where a person gets property by another's mistake, and is under an obligation to make restoration (in whole or in part) of the property or its proceeds or of the value thereof, then to the extent of that obligation the property or proceeds shall be regarded (as against him) as belonging to the person entitled to restoration, and an intention not to make restoration shall be regarded accordingly as an intention to deprive that person of the property or proceeds.

The classic case in which reliance on section 5(4) is appropriate is where money is paid to the payee under the mistaken belief that the money is, in fact, due. In such circumstances the law of quasi-contract imposes a legal obligation upon the transferee to make restoration. A dishonest appropriation is theft of property **belonging to another** by virtue of section 5(4) even though the subject-matter of the obligation is legally his. Reliance would be appropriate in cases such as *Moynes* v *Cooper*,[138] a case decided in the absence of an equivalent provision and which therefore resulted in the acquittal of the payee. A wages clerk paid D his wages not knowing that D had already received an advance payment.

---

[133] *Wain*, 12 October 1993 CA; [1994] 1 Archbold News 5 overruling *Lewis* v *Lethbridge* [1987] Crim LR 59; and see *Floyd*, above.

[134] Cf. *Middleton* (1873) LR 2 CCR 38.

[135] *Ashwell* (1885) 16 QBD 190.

[136] Since in each case the transferor lacks the intention to constitute the transferee owner of the relevant property, because of the fundamental mistake.

[137] For example by keeping it or spending it.

[138] [1956] 1 QB 439.

D realised the mistake soon after receiving his packet[139] but kept the excess. Although D was acquitted of larceny, the effect of section 5(4) is that he would now be guilty.[140] A similar result follows if the money was paid direct into his bank account or if he paid a cheque into the account, later discovering it to be excessive.[141]

It seems, however, that s. 5(4) has become, strictly speaking, redundant due to the case of *Shadrokh-Cigari*.[142] A bank, instructed to credit C's, a child's, account with £286, credited the account instead with £286,000. D, who was C's guardian, withdrew the bulk of the money by banker's drafts under C's authority. It was held that where property was transferred under a mistake of fact, although this may be successful in passing legal title, the transferor retains an equitable interest.[143] As a result D was guilty of theft, the moneys withdrawn still belonging for the sake of section 5(1) to the bank.[144] It was not necessary to rely on section 5(4).

Section 5(4) is only applicable where the payee is under a legal obligation to make restoration. Normally he will always be under such an obligation where money is paid out under a mistake of fact. One case where such an obligation will not arise is where the transaction giving rise to the overpayment is not legally enforceable, as in gambling contracts. A gambler who is mistakenly paid or overpaid is under no obligation to make restoration of the excess.[145] Liability for theft depends then upon the prosecution being able to establish that ownership in the sum did not pass to the gambler. Predictably, the courts have shown themselves unusually susceptible to such arguments.[146] The unbalanced upshot is that while the punter cannot sue the bookmaker if he fails to pay out on a winning horse, he can be guilty of theft if he keeps 'winnings' he was not morally entitled to.

4 The property must belong to another at the time of the appropriation

Many of the problems experienced in relation to the issue of appropriation result from this requirement. A person does not commit theft simply by dishonestly appropriating something which at one time belonged to someone else. Theft is only committed if, at the very time the property was dishonestly appropriated, it belonged to someone else. This is not as silly a proposition as it might sound. The law of theft distinguishes, rightly or wrongly, between people who dishonestly breach a legal obligation to render up their own property to another, and those who dishonestly appropriate property which already belongs to another. The former position is largely covered by the civil law,[147] the latter by the criminal law. So, if A, a diner in a restaurant, decides not to pay before eating her meal she will be guilty of theft, following the principle in *Lawrence*.[148] If the decision is made only after consuming the meal, no theft will occur since the property, having been consumed no longer belongs to the restaurant.[149]

---

[139] If he had realised the mistake on taking delivery of the packet he would be guilty of theft in the ordinary way since he would be assuming (*Gomez*) rights of ownership in property which, at that split second, belonged to the transferee.

[140] Note, unlike the cases of mistake detailed above, full ownership was transferred. In the former cases this did not happen. If A wants to transfer ownership in a £50 note to B he must not only give him a £50 note but intend to. In *Moynes* v *Cooper* the clerk intended to transfer exactly what he did transfer.

[141] *Attorney-General's Reference (No. 1 of 1983)* [1985] QB 182.

[142] *Shadrokh-Cigari* [1988] Crim LR 465.

[143] Following *Chase Manhattan Bank NA* v *Israel-British Bank (London) Ltd* [1981] ch. 105.

[144] Cf. *Hendricks* [2003] EWCA Crim 1040, above.

[145] *Morgan* v *Ashcroft* [1938] 1 KB 49.

[146] *Gilks* (1972) 56 Cr App R 734.

[147] Subject to qualification by the Theft Act 1978.

[148] *Lawrence* v *MPC* [1972] AC 626; *McHugh* (1977) 64 Cr App Rep 92.

[149] By virtue of s. 5(1), Theft Act 1968. She may be guilty of an offence under s. 3, Theft Act 1978.

Why this should be is not immediately obvious since in both cases the rogue has dishonestly deprived the victim of something which was rightly his. A ramification of this is that, in order to decide whether a theftuous appropriation has occurred, it may first be necessary to determine when ownership in the property passed. This, in turn, depends on the rules on the passing of ownership.[150] Clearly these rules are not understood by ordinary folk and yet their liability may hang upon them.[151]

An important consequence of *Gomez* is that people can appropriate property by dint of inducing a transfer of ownership. All that matters is that D forms *mens rea* **before** the property **ceases to belong to the other person**. In *Kaur* a shopper found a pair of shoes in a shop with two separate price tags attached to them. She handed in the shoe with the lower price tag. She was convicted of theft at first instance. Her appeal was allowed on the basis that no appropriation of the shoes had taken place until she took them away from the cash desk.[152] When this appropriation had taken place the completion of the contract of sale had transferred ownership in the shoes to her. She was then 'appropriating' her own property and not 'property belonging to another'.

Following *Gomez* the scope for avoiding liability for theft in this way is much reduced. First, the shopper would now be appropriating property as soon as she took hold of the goods and would be guilty of theft as soon as she formed the necessary dishonest intent (see Case 3). No doubt many shoppers would be surprised at this, and rightly so. She becomes a thief in law the moment she **mentally** succumbs to an obvious temptation, even though she might later allow her conscience to get the better of her. Only difficulties of proof would, at this stage, protect her from criminal proceedings. Second, she would, in any event, be held to be appropriating property by later taking them away, ownership notwithstanding, from a person who possessed them and so to whom, for the purpose of section 5(1), they still belonged.

B *Mens rea*

The mental element in theft is dishonesty and an intention permanently to deprive the owner of the property appropriated. A person's appropriation of property may be dishonest even where he has not formed the intention permanently to deprive the owner of the property. And a person's appropriation may be an honest one even though he has formed the intention permanently to deprive the owner of the property. It is the combination of both these elements which captures the moral fault inhering in theft.

1 Intention to deprive the owner permanently of his property

Theft is not committed in the absence of an intention permanently to deprive the owner of his property. A dishonest borrowing, even if the owner is seriously inconvenienced by the removal, will not generally[153] be theft.[154] Thus:

---

[150] Sale of Goods Act 1979, ss. 17 and 18.
[151] More significantly they are not always understood by the judges themselves.
[152] Apparently because no overt unauthorised act had occurred.
[153] Two exceptional cases arise by virtue of ss. 11 and 12 of the Act which make the temporary appropriation of motor vehicles, and of works of art from museums and galleries, separate offences.
[154] By s. 6 certain borrowings are treated as equivalent to an intention permanently to deprive the owner of his property.

Case 16

Eve, a shop assistant in Adam's jeweller's shop, borrows a hugely expensive diamond tiara to add lustre to her attendance at a fashionable rave that evening. Her intention is to return it the next morning before Adam discovers it to be missing. The tiara is stolen from her while at the rave and the loss is discovered.

Eve is not guilty of theft, despite the permanent loss of the tiara. It is the absence of intention, not the fact of deprivation, which matters here. The case might suggest that the law of theft is deficient in restricting liability to cases where the accused intended a permanent taking. Is Eve no less blameworthy, and a social menace, than a petty pilferer? Should it matter whether her intention was to keep the property permanently, when her dishonest intention was to advance her own interest while at the same time compromising (potentially seriously) the interests of Adam?[155]

In real life dishonest borrowers may often find that the 'paper rules' do not always protect them. A dishonest taking of property may carry a difficult-to-rebut inference that A's intention was to keep the property. If A was so dishonest as to take property without permission in the first place, the jury may reason, why should A scruple to return the property later? Such reasoning would probably not apply in Case 16. Paradoxically, given her status as an employee and the beauty and value of the tiara, her claim that she intended to return the property would be far more credible than if she had merely taken a bar of soap from the washroom.

It is important to understand that it is not necessary for the intention itself to be a permanent one. A momentary decision is enough even if the decision is instantly reversed after the appropriation.[156] If, for one fleeting moment during the rave, Eve made a settled decision to give up her job and flee the country with the tiara, the crime is constituted. The decision to keep the tiara is an appropriation by section 3(1). It is dishonest and is accompanied by an intention to keep it. At that moment all the elements of theft coincide and so she commits theft. That she repents may mitigate her fault but it does not expunge it. In practice, of course, Eve would never be charged with theft, assuming she returned the tiara, because it would be next to impossible to prove that she had ever formed the relevant intention.

(a) *Meaning of intention*

An intention permanently to deprive is not defined in the Act. It seems reasonable to assume that the meaning of intention runs counter to its usual post-*Woollin* meaning which is that foresight of virtual certainty is not intention in itself but is evidence of intention.[157] For the purpose of the law of theft, direct intention permanently to deprive will be the exception rather than the rule. When a thief appropriates property he does not do so with the aim of depriving the other of it but rather with the aim of satisfying his own needs.[158] His intention permanently to deprive exists therefore because he knows that the inevitable consequence of satisfying this aim will be that the owner will be permanently deprived of his property. **This knowledge constitutes his intention, rather than being evidence of it.**

---

[155] G. Williams, 'Temporary Appropriation Should be Theft' [1981] Crim LR 129. See also *Mitchell* [2008] EWCA Crim 850. Hijacking a car for use in a crime is not theft, where it is later abandoned.

[156] *McHugh* (1993) 97 Cr App R 335.

[157] LC 304, *Murder, Manslaughter and Infanticide* (2006) para. 3.27.

[158] J. Horder, 'Intention in the Criminal Law' (1995) 58 MLR 678.

This is so whether or not the appropriator intends to keep the property. A person who abandons property will have the intention of permanently depriving the owner of it if he knows that the circumstances under which he abandons it means that the owner will not, barring a miracle, recover it.

(b) Conditional intention

A person may dishonestly appropriate property without having formed a settled intention to keep it. For example, a person may appropriate another's handbag to see if it contains articles worth stealing. In such circumstances an intention to deprive the owner permanently of either handbag or contents cannot be made out. Until a decision to keep or dispose of the property is made, the most that may be said of the accused's conduct is that he has attempted to steal the things he would have stolen had things transpired as he hoped.[159] Clearly no such decision has been made in connection with the handbag and cannot be made in connection with its contents until those contents are first identified. A strong case has been made that the intention to permanently deprive should be dropped from the definition of theft. Not only would this solve this problem, it would also, perhaps justifiably, criminalise those dishonest borrowings which dangerously compromise the property interests of the owner (Case 16).[160] In practice the problem is dealt with by charging attempted theft drafting the indictment so as not to specify any specific items, as in 'attempting to steal articles unknown the contents of a handbag belonging to X'.[161]

(c) Special cases of intending to deprive permanently

Section 6 qualifies the meaning of intending to deprive the owner permanently of his property. It allows a conviction for theft in certain cases where, although the appropriator does not necessarily mean the owner to lose property entirely, his intention is to fundamentally compromise the owner's rights in relation to the property. In *Lloyd* it was said that prosecutors should have resort to section 6 only in the type of exceptional circumstances envisaged by section 6 as a whole.[162] It was not intended to 'water down' the general requirement to be found in section 1. As we shall see, this provides an exceptionally narrow focus, including, most obviously, cases where the appropriator intends to ransom property back to its owner or the equivalent, cases of borrowing where the appropriator intends to return another's property only after exhausting its usefulness, and cases of lending where the dishonest lender is unable to guarantee the return of the property to the owner.

(i) Section 6(1)

> a person is to be treated as having an intention to permanently deprive the owner of his property if his intention is to treat the thing as his own to dispose of regardless of the other's rights; and a borrowing or lending of it may amount to so treating it if, but only if, the borrowing or lending is for a period and in circumstances making it equivalent to an outright taking or disposal.

This tortured provision has been more than a match for commentators attempting to discern its meaning.[163] Little is clear beyond the fact that a person is sometimes deemed to

---

[159] *Easom* [1971] 2 QB 315. For further discussion see Chapter 18, below.
[160] An argument may perhaps be framed, that both states of mind of the appropriator are covered by section 6(1). This will be examined in the next section.
[161] *Attorney-General's Reference (Nos 1 and 2 of 1979)* [1980] QB 180.
[162] [1985] QB 829.
[163] See J.R. Spencer, 'The Metamorphosis of Section 6 of the Theft Act' [1977] Crim LR 653.

have an intention to permanently deprive the owner of property even if he does not mean the owner to lose the thing permanently. Since the provision is particularly confusing and not intended as a comprehensive definition, it is not put to the jury unless the facts of the case under consideration demand it.[164] Section 6(1) contains two overlapping parts, a general provision which is itself qualified by a more restrictive sub-provision for cases of borrowing or lending property owned by another.

(ii) *Part 1*

A person has a theftuous intention not only when he intends to keep the property but also when he intends to treat the thing as his to dispose of regardless of the other's rights. The occasions when this is said to occur are circumscribed[165] but it would seem that if Eve in Case 16 had hidden the tiara behind a lavatory cistern at the rave, careless whether it was ever found again, her state of mind would fall within section 6(1). She does not 'mean Adam permanently to lose the tiara itself because she does not care either way. However, she is 'treating it as her own to dispose of regardless of Adam's rights.[166] She would lack this intention if, say, she simply left it in the cloakroom, where it could later be discovered. In *Mitchell* section 6(1) was held inapplicable in a case where D had taken a motor car to make a getaway from the scene of a crime and abandoned it a few miles away with the hazard lights on.[167]

Two other cases appear to be covered by this provision. First, where the appropriator takes property, meaning the owner to be reunited with the property only by buying it back.

> **Case 17**
> Eve removes a sweater from a department store without paying for it. Her intention is to return the next day to claim a refund, having first damaged the sweater.

Although Eve does not intend permanently to deprive the store of the sweater, her intention is nevertheless covered by section 6(1). She is treating the sweater as her own to dispose of regardless of the owner's rights. She is saying 'this is my sweater, not your sweater, so you pay'.[168] The second slightly different case is where the appropriator's intention is to set a ransom for the property, that is to return the property only upon the owner fulfilling a condition, including paying for the property.

> **Case 18**
> Eve, a student, takes a priceless book from her university library during rag week. She tells the library that she will return the book if they pay £100 into the rag fund.

This case is an example of the ransom principle. Although Eve does not (necessarily) mean the owner to be deprived permanently of the book she is, by ransoming it, treating it as her own to dispose of regardless of the owner's rights.[169] A comparable case is *Marshall*.

---

[164] *Lloyd* [1985] 2 All ER 661.
[165] *Lloyd*, above.
[166] *Williams* [1981] Crim LR 129; *Ruse v Read* [1949] 1 KB 377. Cf. *Crump* (1825) 1 C & P 658.
[167] [2008] EWCA Crim 850.
[168] Cf. *Hall* (1848) 1 Den 381.
[169] It is, of course, arguable that Eve has the necessary intention without the need to rely on s. 6(1) in Case 18 since she intends to permanently deprive the present owner of its property in favour of another.

Here the Court of Appeal held that the purchaser of unexpired tube tickets from passengers who sold them on to other purchasers was treating the tickets as his own to dispose of regardless of the owner's (London Underground) rights.[170]

The qualification that it should be the appropriator's intention to treat the property as his 'own to dispose of regardless of the owner's rights' means that the intention would not be established where the appropriator was a bailee who refused to return property until it was paid for, since he would not be acting in disregard of the owner's rights. In *Cahill* the Court of Appeal approved the following explanation of its meaning:

> an intention to use the thing as one's own is not enough . . . 'dispose of' is not used in the sense in which a general might 'dispose of' his forces but rather the general meaning given by the Shorter Oxford Dictionary: 'To deal with definitely; to get rid of; to get done with, finish. To make over by way of sale or bargain, sell'.[171]

It has been held, however, that 'disposing' for the purpose of section 6 does not require the property to be altogether 'got rid of'. In *Lavender* it was said that a contractor, who dishonestly removed doors from one council property to replace damaged doors at another, intended permanently to deprive the council of the doors within the meaning of section 6(1). This may seem surprising.[172] He may have intended to treat the doors as his own, but did he intend to treat them as his own to '**dispose of**' when he merely swapped them around a little? Would the section plausibly have been satisfied if the workers had replaced a damaged door with a spare door from the same house? On the other hand, if the contractors had taken some doors off council property and told the council that they could have them back if a ransom was paid this would have been theft under the ransom principle – a straightforward application of section 6(1).[173] In effect this is what the contractors did. They sold the council their own doors but using deception rather than extortion.

Arguably, cases of conditional intent can also be treated in this way.[174] Thus, 'lifting' a bag to facilitate a later decision to steal its contents may be thought of as treating the bag as one's own to dispose of regardless of the owner's rights. Such an analysis has not found favour with the courts, as explained above.[175]

(iii) *Part 2*

The intention also exists when the accused (a) borrows or (b) lends property if the circumstances render the borrowing or lending equivalent to an outright taking. This provision is particularly abstruse. In everyday speech we tend to use 'borrow' to refer to situations where the borrower is the beneficiary of a **consensual** transfer of temporary possession for an agreed purpose. Clearly, however, a person 'borrows' property for the purpose of section 6 by taking it **without consent**, as long as there is the intention to return it. In such circumstances we might prefer to say that he has purloined rather than borrowed the property. As far as lending is concerned, this seems to refer to situations where a person who is already in possession of property belonging to another, lawfully or otherwise,[176] lends it to someone else.[177]

---

[170] [1998] 2 Cr App R 282. For critical comment see J.C. Smith, 'Stealing Tickets' [1998] Crim LR 72.
[171] Smith and Hogan, op. cit. at 557.
[172] See J.C. Smith's criticisms of the case [1994] Crim LR 298.
[173] *Coffey* [1987] Crim LR 498.
[174] *Sharp* v *McCormick* [1986] VR 869.
[175] See *Easom* [1971] 2 All ER 945; cf. *Lloyd* [1985] QB 829.
[176] A.T.H. Smith limits the scope of the provision to cases where the possession is lawful, at 214. It is not clear why.
[177] Strictly speaking, if one can appropriate property by selling it while it is still in the possession of the owner (*Pitham and Hehl*), there is no obvious reason why one cannot also lend property that one does not possess.

Such a lending (or borrowing) will evince the necessary intention permanently to deprive the owner of the property **only** if it is for a period and in circumstances making it equivalent to an outright taking. The question which must be asked, then, is when does this occur?

Case 19

Greg Norbert and Jack Bilko are golfing rivals. Greg has never won a major championship. Jack wins them all the time. On the eve of the Open Championship, Greg removes Jack's trusty hickory shafted putter from Jack's bag and hides it. He knows that Jack will not win without it. He is right. Jack comes second and Greg wins. Greg then returns the putter as he had always intended.

Is Greg Norbert's appropriation of Jack's putter for a period and in such circumstances equivalent to an outright taking? It seems not. The period is long enough to hurt; the circumstances are acute enough to matter but together they are not equivalent to an outright taking. This was the view taken in the case of *Lloyd*.[178] Here the accused 'borrowed' cinema films for the purpose of making pirate copies. He then returned them. It was held that this was not equivalent to an outright taking. The Court of Appeal took the view that section 6(1) only applied where the effect of the taking was to exhaust the value of the property. In this case the taking of the films, albeit for a fraudulent purpose, did not diminish their value at all. 'There was still virtue in the film.' On this analysis, a borrowing or lending only amounts to theft if the 'virtue' in the property is extinguished, as where a person intends a cheque to be returned only after it has been cashed,[179] or a football season ticket after the season has ended, or a library book after the borrowing period has expired. What is unclear is how much virtue needs to be retained before liability for theft is excluded. Is it theft of the season ticket where the intention is to return it with one match remaining? A related point refers to the situation where the intention is to exhaust a specialised use for the property where its general use is unaffected. For example, if Greg had snatched one of Jack's golf balls and had used it until it was too worn for use in competitive golf, this is, in one sense, equivalent to an outright taking. The ball is no use to Jack now in the sense that it has lost the use for which it was originally acquired. On the other hand, it is still a golf ball and he could use it for practice. Does this come within section 6(1)? It is submitted that it should, as it also should if Greg took the ball so as to 'doctor' it, and thus render it less accurate than a normal ball.[180]

One last problem thrown up by the unfortunate drafting of section 6 is the position of a lending which is not for a period equivalent to an outright disposal, but is in circumstances equivalent to an outright disposal. If Eve in Case 16 had lent the tiara to a complete stranger at the rave, with no confident expectation that it would be returned before the night was over, would this come within section 6(1)? If so, it would have to be because this lending, although for a temporary period, was equivalent to an outright disposal. This would appear to be a reasonable interpretation of section 6(1) even though the precise wording of the section seems to envisage that a theftuous appropriation would only be possible where the virtue in the property is diminished by the passing of time.

---

[178] [1985] QB 829.
[179] Cf. *Arnold* [1997] Crim LR 833.
[180] See generally A.T.H. Smith 223.

(iv) *Section 6(2)*

One specific example covered by section 6(1) is referred to in s. 6(2). Where a person 'having possession or control (lawfully or not) of property belonging to another, parts with the property under a condition as to its return which he may not be able to perform, this . . . amounts to treating the property as his own to dispose of regardless of the other's rights'. This is intended to cover such cases as the defendant pawning (pledging) the other's property. Arguably, pledging property in such circumstances is only treating property as one's own to dispose of regardless of the other's rights if the pledgor is uncertain as to whether he will later be in a position to redeem the pledge.

Most commentators are agreed that if the accused is certain he will be able to redeem the pledge before a specific date set for the return of the property, section 6(2) will not apply. What is not clear is whether it would be enough that A was certain that he would be able to redeem the pledge but was uncertain that this would occur **before** the time set for return, or B's demand if no time is set.[181] It is submitted that section 6(2) should apply wherever A knows that he may not be in a position to redeem the property at the time A intends to return the property to B. If he does not, then, like the borrower of the tiara, he can hardly complain if his intention is treated as sufficiently inimical to the owner's rights as to count as an intention to deprive the owner permanently.

(d) *Taking with the intention of making restoration*

In one situation a person who 'borrows' another's property intending to make restoration has a theftuous intention irrespective of the operation of section 6. This is where the appropriator intends to return not the items themselves but their equivalent. So if A takes money belonging to B intending to repay the money when he is in funds, his intention is not to borrow that money but to take it permanently.[182] The replacement notes and coins will not be the same as those taken. The principle applies wherever the thing is a fungible, that is a thing whose use value can be restored, but not the thing itself. A flatmate who 'borrows' another's milk intends to deprive the owner permanently of that milk, although he may intend to return the equivalent. Liability in such cases is not necessarily assured, however. It would depend upon the jury's view of dishonesty.

(e) *Offences of temporary deprivation*

Certain types of temporary appropriation count as offences in their own right regardless of an intention to permanently deprive. These are, by section 11, removal of display articles from places, such as museums and art galleries, open to the public, and, by section 12, taking and driving away a conveyance without authority.

The Theft Act contains two statutory offences of temporary deprivation. These will be covered here in outline only. By section 11 it is an offence to remove articles displayed or kept for display from places open to the public. The offence is committed upon proof of removal. No intention to permanently deprive the owner of the property is required. The section only applies where the building in which the articles are housed is open to the public for the purpose of viewing either the building or part of the building, or of articles housed in it. Most obviously it covers cases where works of art or museum pieces are removed from art galleries and museums. It might also cover other public buildings such as churches or libraries, but only if the article removed is on display or kept for display. Temporarily

---

[181] Smith (2007) 2–137–8; Griew 65–6. Possibly this is implicit in Smith's analysis but it is not made clear.
[182] *Velumyl* [1989] Crim LR 299.

removing a book from the shelf of a library will not be covered by section 11. Neither will the removal of a cross or candlesticks from the altar of a church.[183] If the book, cross or candlestick were removed from a display cabinet, however, section 11 would apply.

By section 12(1) it is an offence to take a conveyance (other than a pedal cycle)[184] without consent or lawful authority for one's own or another's use.[185] By section 12(1) it is also an offence to drive or allow oneself to be carried in or on a conveyance one knows to have been taken without such authority. There is a defence of claim of right to this section similar to that contained in section 2(1)(a) and (b). Conveyance includes cars, motor cycles, boats and aeroplanes, indeed anything constructed or adapted for carrying persons.[186] It is not necessary for the conveyance to be driven away as long as it is moved.[187] Placing it on a trailer for removal will be enough.[188] But the taking must be for the taker's or another's use. Moving a car so as to remove an obstruction will not, therefore, come within the mischief of the section since it is not taken for use. The offence is committed not only where the taking away is without the owner's consent but also where the owner consents to the taking but not for the journey undertaken. A person who borrows a car for the agreed purpose of driving to Liverpool will commit the offence if he in fact uses it to drive to London.[189] On the other hand if 'true' consent is obtained by fraud, for example A borrows B's car as a result of misrepresenting that his own car is out of commission, the offence is not committed.[190]

A problem case is where the fraud perpetrated by A has an impact on the nature of the journey agreed to be undertaken. For example A borrows B's car on the understanding it is to be used to ferry his pregnant wife to hospital but he uses it to go the pub. Is this a case of no consent since the journey undertaken was not the journey consented to? Common sense would seem to support such a conclusion. Or is it a case of 'true' consent, albeit obtained by fraud?[191] Given that the mischief against which the section was directed was the social mischief of non-consensual joy-riding, it might be considered oppressive for criminal liability to be incurred simply on the basis of telling someone a lie.

2 Dishonesty

Dishonesty is not defined in the Act. This reflects the working assumption of the Criminal Law Revision Committee that the elements of the offence should, as far as possible, be couched in simple language which the jury can understand without guidance.[192] At its simplest, proof of dishonesty requires proof: (a) that the defendant intended to appropriate property belonging to another; this would require the accused to know (i) that he was appropriating property and (ii) that the property belonged to another,[193] and (b) that the appropriation was immoral.[194]

---

[183] *Barr* [1978] Crim LR 244.
[184] Covered by s. 12(5).
[185] An aggravated version of this offence is now to be found in s. 12A of the Act as inserted by the Aggravated Vehicle-Taking Act 1992.
[186] Section 12(7).
[187] *Bow* [1977] RTR 6; *Pearce* [1973] Crim LR 321.
[188] *Pearce.*
[189] *McKnight* v *Davies* [1974] RTR 4; *Phipps and McGill* (1970) 54 Cr App R 300; cf. *Peart* [1970] 2 QB 672.
[190] Cf. *Whittaker* v *Campbell* (1983) 77 Cr App R 267.
[191] *Peart* [1970] 2 QB 672.
[192] Griew is doubtful on this point, at 77.
[193] Or possibly merely that he foresaw it.
[194] G. Williams 723.

(a) *What dishonesty is not: section 2*

Section 2(1) does, however, provide three instances **negativing** dishonesty, namely where a person appropriates property in the belief:

(a) that he has in law the right to deprive the other of it, on behalf of himself or of a third person; or

(b) that he would have the other's consent if the other knew of the appropriation and the circumstances of it; or

(c) . . . that the person to whom the property belongs cannot be discovered by taking reasonable steps.

In each of these cases the existence of the relevant belief negates dishonesty as a matter of law irrespective of the view taken by the jury as to the morality of the appropriation.[195] Where the defendant raises evidence that he held such a belief the burden is on the prosecution to disprove it on the criminal standard.

(i) *Paragraph (a)*

This refers to cases where the defendant believes that he has a claim of right, for example he takes an umbrella from a stand, believing it to be his own, or, believing himself to be entitled, recovers a debt by taking the due amount from his flatmate's wallet. The same principle will apply if he takes the money by force.[196] It also applies to those cases, such as *Hinks*, where D has been constituted as owner by gift or contract in circumstances of dubious morality.

Case 20

Adam has a glut of apples. A generous chap, he places them in a box outside his gate together with the message 'Please take whatever you need. But leave some for others.' Eve comes along and takes all but two apples for the purpose of selling in her greengrocer's shop.

Following *Hinks*, Eve may be guilty of theft. Her liability is dependent upon whether she is dishonest. Although she certainly appears to be dishonest in the sense that her conduct would generally be thought immoral, the application of section 2(1)(a) seems to lead to a different conclusion. She would say in answer to the charge 'I honestly believed I was legally entitled to do what I did'. If the jury believe this, and there is no logical reason why they should not, she is entitled to be acquitted.[197]

(ii) *Paragraph (b)*

People routinely appropriate other people's property without asking them. Flatmates 'borrow' each other's milk, bread or beer. A can of beer, however, once drunk, cannot be replaced.[198] This means that the other mental element in theft (intention to permanently deprive the owner of his property) is satisfied. Accordingly, only the absence of dishonesty (or the good sense of the victim) stands between such purloiners and a possible visit to the magistrates' court. It should be remembered that it is not the fact of consent which

---

[195] That is, the intention thereof.
[196] *Robinson* [1977] Crim LR 173.
[197] If they do not the jury must consider the question of dishonesty by reference to the test in *Ghosh*. See below.
[198] *Velumyl* [1989] Crim LR 299.

prevents an appropriation from being theftuous. Following *Gomez* and *Hinks*, this is irrelevant to liability for theft.[199] It is the belief that consent would be granted if the owner knew of the appropriation and the circumstances of it which has this effect. Defendants such as Mr Fritschy cannot then rely upon paragraph (b) to escape the inference of dishonesty since the owner clearly would not have consented to the taking of the Krugerrands if he had known the true circumstances. **On the other hand** appropriating property under the genuine belief the owner would consent in such circumstances is not dishonest even though it may be extremely irritating for the victim and even if the belief is unreasonable. An unreasonable belief that the owner would consent will, however, be evidence that the belief was not honestly held.[200]

(iii) *Paragraph (c)*
This covers such cases as where A finds the property and decides to keep it, or is a bailee of property for an owner who has disappeared. Assuming the property is not abandoned, making such a decision is an appropriation of another's property with the relevant intent. The appropriation will not be theftuous, however, if A genuinely formed the belief that the owner could not be found by taking reasonable steps. The question whether A has formed such a belief is a jury question which will no doubt take into account facts such as the value of the item concerned, any distinguishing or identifying characteristics, where it was found, and so on. It should be noted that the belief itself does not have to be reasonable, although, once again, an unreasonable belief will be evidence that the belief was not honestly held. The belief will be easier for a jury to credit in the case of finding a £20 note in the middle of a public park than if it were found in the middle of public bar, underneath a neighbour's chair at a dinner party, or contained in a wallet along with the owner's driving licence. A person who finds property and later discovers the identity of the true owner will be guilty of theft by virtue of section 3 if he decides to keep it. Although the initial taking of the property may be honest and therefore innocent, his subsequent decision to keep it on discovery of the true owner will be a dishonest assumption of the rights of the owner.[201]

(iv) *Willingness to pay for property*
Section 2 contains one other factor pertinent to the question of dishonesty. By section 2(2) a person's appropriation of property may be dishonest even though he is willing to pay for it. This is not to say that such willingness will always be irrelevant. For example it may be used to negate dishonesty under paragraph (b), as where a shopper in a hurry takes a bottle of milk leaving the price on the counter. Section 2(2) covers the case where paragraph (b) could not realistically be relied upon, as where a visitor to an art gallery filches an old master, leaving a cheque for the market price pinned to the wall.

Section 2 gives us three states of mind which are inconsistent with dishonesty. Where one of these states of mind is found to exist or may exist the jury **must acquit**. It is possible that the framers of the Act believed that section 2 exhausted the range of dishonesty situations.[202] It should be noted, however, that a jury may still find a defendant **not** to have acted dishonestly although section 2 cannot be relied upon. The section gives some examples of what dishonesty is not. It does not tell us what it is.

---

[199] *Gomez.*
[200] *Holden* [1991] Crim LR 478.
[201] Cf. *R* v *Thurborn* (1849) 1 Den 387.
[202] A.T.H. Smith 264.

(b) *What dishonesty is*

Historically the meaning of dishonesty was a question of law. In the absence of a 'claim of right', that is, an honest belief by the taker that he had 'the right to take the thing and keep it' the mental element was constituted.[203] Significantly the taker was dishonest even if he, the jury, and other people would think that there was nothing wrong in what he did. An employee who borrowed money from her employer's till, intending to repay it but knowing that the owner would not consent, would then be automatically dishonest even if the amount were trivial and it was repaid before the owner discovered a theft had taken place.

Soon after the Act was passed, the Court of Appeal went to the other extreme, holding, in *Gilks*, that the test of dishonesty was whether the accused thought that what he was doing was dishonest. This was a perplexing test since its effect appears to be that the looser the defendant's moral standards the harder it will be for the prosecution to prove that he was dishonest. Robin Hood, by taking from the rich to give to the poor, might have had nothing to fear under such a test.[204] In *Feely*[205] the test for dishonesty became a jury question. The defendant, against instructions, borrowed money from his employer's till, leaving an IOU. The trial judge told the jury that they should convict if he knew that he would not have the owner's consent. The Court of Appeal quashed the conviction. They said that dishonesty was an ordinary word with which the jury would be fully acquainted. The test for dishonesty was whether the conduct of the accused fell below the standards of honesty of ordinary decent people as represented by themselves.

In *Ghosh*[206] this test was slightly modified. A consultant at a hospital falsely claimed fees for operations he had not carried out. The Court of Appeal applied a two-part test. The jury must answer two questions: (1) is the conduct of the accused dishonest according to the 'ordinary standards of reasonable and honest people'? If it is not, the prosecution fails. If it is dishonest according to those standards then the jury must consider the second question: (2) did the accused realise that what he was doing was by those standards dishonest? The full scope of this test is unclear. The judge will not normally be required to put the second question to the jury unless evidence is raised that the accused might not have realised that others might find his conduct dishonest.[207] Where A steals a person's wallet from her handbag such evidence is unlikely to be raised. The problem arises over the kind of evidence which will require the second question to be put. Clearly, it will be appropriate where the accused lacks the mental capacity to realise that what he was doing was wrong. But when else?

Case 21

A visits England from Cartland where they have free public transport. He does not pay for a bus ride, believing this also to be the case in England.

A is not dishonest according to the standards of ordinary decent people. An ordinary, decent person who mistakenly believed the English transport system to be free would not

---

[203] Kenny (1962) 295.
[204] A similar test was adopted in *Boggeln* v *Williams* [1978] 1 WLR 873.
[205] [1973] 1 QB 530 CA.
[206] [1982] QB 1053.
[207] *Price* (1990) 90 Cr App R 409. It certainly should not be put where the issue of dishonesty is also argued under section 2 as it will confuse the jury to be given two tests; *Wood* [2002] EWCA Crim 832.

be considered dishonest by anybody if he failed to render payment. It should not, there-fore, be necessary to put the second question to the jury.[208]

Case 22

Huxley visits England from Euphoria, a country whose inhabitants are celebrated for their com-mitment to pleasure. Euphoria has a law of theft as we do, and with a dishonesty component. A majority of people in Euphoria consider it not to be dishonest to appropriate flowers in cultivation, if those flowers contain narcotic substances which the appropriator wishes to exploit for his own use. Huxley takes some opium poppies from Leary's flower-bed for this purpose.

What Huxley has done is potentially dishonest, assuming he does not believe the owner to consent, according to the standards of ordinary decent people. People who take other people's flowers without permission are no less likely to be censured by jury members for having ulterior hedonistic urges. But if Huxley is unaware that Euphoria's rule of honesty does not operate here, his mistake deprived him of a fair opportunity to comply with the relevant rule. Case 22 seems to be a case in which it would be appropriate for the jury to consider the second question.

Case 23

A is a member of an anti-genocide group. Thwarted in her attempts to ban the export of bombs to Buldozia, whose authorities are engaging in genocide, she breaks into a warehouse where the bombs are stored and removes from them the detonators, which she later destroys.

Case 23 shows up the *Ghosh* test in all its (unintended) radicalism. First, it allows the jury its own say as to whether A's appropriation was theftuous.[209] Irrespective of whether A's action is praiseworthy or not, the law of theft is in place to protect the ownership and possession of property. If people can lawfully be stripped of such ownership and posses-sion on the basis of a jury's assessment of the appropriator's motive, the slippery path to anarchy beckons. As jury-persons we might well wish to acquit A because we personally disapproved of the export of bombs to Buldozia. In so doing we would, no doubt, be ensur-ing that conduct which did not defy popular morality was not subject to criminalisation.[210] But should the acquittal be justified on the basis that A's conduct was not dishonest? What if the property was our own cellar of wine and the appropriation justified on the basis that the wine was rotting our liver? What if the motive behind the appropriation was detestable, for example, racism. Should we, in this latter case, be sanguine about the ability of this and every other jury to reach a decision unaffected by whether the jury members were them-selves racists?[211]

Second, *Ghosh* appears to render A's belief that the public would morally approve of the appropriation a defence. If A feels so strongly, might she not assume such approval would be forthcoming? This is not only constitutionally problematic[212] but it does not augur well

---

[208] The court in *Ghosh* assumed otherwise. See Griew (1995) 78.
[209] Of course it also involves criminal damage, which charge is likely to be preferred as there is no dishonesty requirement.
[210] See R. Tur, 'Dishonesty and the Jury', in A. Phillips Griffiths (ed.), *Philosophy and Practice* (1985) 75.
[211] D.W. Elliot, 'Law and Fact in Theft Act Cases' [1976] Crim LR 707; 'Dishonesty in Theft: a Dispensable Concept' [1982] Crim LR 395; for a different view see R. Tur, 'Dishonesty and the Jury' (1985) 75.
[212] It may infringe Art. 7 ECHR, governing retrospective legislation. For discussion see Law Commission Con-sultation Paper No. 155 *Fraud and Deception* (1999).

for the efficient disposition of criminal trials. As one commentator has argued, (the result must be that)

> claims must multiply and lengthen trials; and it must be in the interests of some defendants to introduce as much evidence as possible on the dishonesty issue in order to obfuscate it. The consequences in terms of expense and of increased difficulty for the jury, not to speak of the danger of unsatisfactory outcomes, are surely enough in themselves to raise serious doubts about the present state of the law.[213]

(c) *Reforming dishonesty*

As a fault element dishonesty is troublesome as it is too open-ended to be consistent with the rule of law. In Case 23 for example A would be uncertain as to whether her action was theftuous or not until the jury so decided. This is arguably contrary to the Article 7 right not to be convicted under retrospective laws,[214] It should be noted that both *Feely* and *Ghosh* are Court of Appeal decisions and there is no doubt that *Ghosh* currently represents the law.[215] How might the position be improved? It is open to the Supreme Court to remedy the present precarious state of affairs by introducing a legal test of dishonesty rather than leaving it to the vagaries of the jury. One solution, suggested by Sir John Smith, would be to redefine dishonesty as 'knowing that the appropriation will or maybe detrimental to the interests of the owner in a significant practical way'. This would entitle the acquittal of those who take a short-term loan from the till believing they can repay it without difficulty and without risk to the owner. It might also acquit the petty pilferer from work. It would leave vulnerable to conviction those who appropriate property for a good motive, political or otherwise.

A more satisfactory proposal, consistent with the principle of minimal criminalisation,[216] was suggested by Elliot,[217] but would require Parliament's attention. This would be to dispense with dishonesty except as provided by section 2(1) and to add another case: 'no appropriation of property belonging to another which is not detrimental to the interests of the other in a significant practical way shall amount to theft of the property'. It should be noted that the basis of such a defence, unlike that of Professor Smith, is not A's state of mind but a state of affairs, namely that the appropriation is too trivial to warrant criminal liability. One possible consequence of the proposal is that it may offer the potential for decriminalising 'unprofitable' prosecutions such as shoplifting.[218] Its most obvious application, however, is in cases where money is 'borrowed' with the intention of replacing it.[219] This intention, it should be remembered, does nothing to counter the intention to permanently deprive the owner of that money. But it is little more blameworthy than any other case of borrowing without permission. A less radical proposal is put by Glazebrook and is targeted on this latter case. He suggests that an appropriation should not be regarded as dishonest if the property is 'money, some other fungible, a thing in action or intangible property, and is appropriated with the intention of replacing it, and in the belief that it will be possible to do so without loss to the person to whom it belongs'.[220]

[213] Griew (1995) 78–9.
[214] Cf. *Hashman* v *UK* [2000] Crim LR 185.
[215] *Cornelius* [2012] EWCA Crim 500.
[216] See Chapter 2.
[217] 'Dishonesty in Theft: A Dispensable Concept' [1982] Crim LR 395 at 410.
[218] Such thefts can already be and often are dealt with by on-the-spot fines, police cautions, and anti-social behaviour orders.
[219] Cf. A.J. Ashworth (2006) 405–9.
[220] P. Glazebrook, 'Revising the Theft Acts' [1993] Camb LJ 191.

A further case which might profitably be added to section 2 is a special defence of good motive. *Ghosh* appears to sidestep the normal principle that good motive does not render the unlawful lawful. Elsewhere in English law the pertinence of claims of good motive are filtered through existing defences such as duress of circumstances and necessity. These defences are only at an early stage of development. It might not be too radical a step to incorporate such defences immediately into the law of theft, if only to head off the more troublesome implications of *Ghosh* and *Feely*. Without such a qualification to section 2 the law of theft might not command unconditional public support. Appropriations of property belonging to another would not, on this view, be dishonest if they were undertaken in the reasonable belief that they were immediately necessary to prevent harm befalling another. The woman in Case 23 would only have a defence if she reasonably believed that her actions were immediately necessary to prevent a particular threat of harm or perhaps serious harm.[221] The advantage of such proposals is that words such as 'reasonable', 'immediately necessary' and 'harm/serious harm' would filter out all cases other than those where an obvious and uncontroversial moral justification for the appropriation existed. As such it would not be open to undue manipulation as a defence of 'civil disobedience'.

Summary

Theft is committed when a person dishonestly appropriates property belonging to another with the intention of permanently depriving the other of it. The *actus reus* of theft is the appropriation of property belonging to another. An appropriation will normally involve an outright taking but this is not necessary. Any assumption of any of the rights of ownership will suffice. The more obvious of these rights include the right to possess, dispose of, use, modify, or destroy. It includes cases where a person having first come by property, whether innocently or not, then exercises such rights as if he were the owner. Assuming rights of ownership over property is no less an appropriation for that assumption being consented to even where the effect of that consent is to transfer absolute ownership of the property to the other. Becoming an owner of property is the clearest example of assuming rights of ownership over it.

Property includes any object capable of being owned, including severed body parts which have been reduced into possession or ownership. It does not include land or other real property unless such land is sold or otherwise dealt with, in breach of confidence, by a fiduciary with the power of sale or disposal. Under certain circumstances things forming part of land are property capable of being stolen if they are severed from the land by or at the behest of a trespasser or other non-possessor. There are special exemptions in this regard with respect to the picking of wild flowers, fruit and mushrooms not done for commercial purposes.

Wild animals are not property capable of being stolen unless either

(i)   they are tamed or normally captive, or
(ii)   as with game, another person has reduced either them or their carcass, or is in the process of reducing such animal or carcass, into his possession.

---

[221] See generally Griew (1995) 79; *Pommell* [1995] 2 Cr App Rep 607.

Property includes patents, copyrights, quotas, debts and other **choses in action** but these can only be stolen where the rights they represent are appropriated. They are not stolen simply by the rights being infringed. Information, as distinct from any physical medium by which it is conveyed, is not property capable of being stolen. Property belongs to another when that other owns that property, including part and equitable ownership. It belongs also to any person having possession or control of property without ownership. It follows that an owner can steal his own property. Property is also deemed to belong to someone who has divested himself of ownership under a mistake, as against another who obtains that property by virtue of that mistake, but only if the latter is under a legal obligation to restore that property or its value or proceeds to the former. Further, property is deemed to belong to a person who has divested himself of property, as against anyone who receives that property under an obligation to retain and deal with it in a particular way.

Theft cannot generally be committed in the absence of an intention permanently to deprive the owner of the property appropriated. A borrowing will not be theft, however dishonest, since a person who borrows property lacks the intention permanently to deprive the owner of it. This is subject to a number of qualifications. First, a person who borrows money (or other fungibles) will have the intention of permanently depriving the owner of it, even if he intends to repay the money/return the fungible, since his intention will be to repay different coins/notes/return different fungibles than those appropriated. Second, by section 6(1), a person who borrows property without authority nevertheless intends permanently to deprive the owner of it if he intends the borrowing to be for a period and in circumstances making it equivalent to an outright taking. Borrowing a season ticket for the duration of the season falls into this category. Lending (another's) property to someone else is also consistent with having an intention permanently to deprive the owner of it if the lending is equivalent to an outright taking, as above. Beyond cases of borrowing or lending, a person who appropriates property without meaning the other to lose it permanently is nevertheless deemed to have the intention of permanently depriving the owner of it, if his intention is to treat the property as his own to dispose of regardless of the owner's rights. Such intention will be present if the appropriator intends to ransom the property to its owner in some way. It will also be present where a person appropriates property for a temporary period intending to abandon it and being indifferent whether the owner recovers it.

Dishonesty is not fully defined by the Theft Act. By section 2(1), however, three mental states will not amount to dishonesty as a matter of law, namely a belief on the part of the appropriator that he has a legal right to deprive the owner of the property; or the owner would consent; or the owner cannot be discovered by taking reasonable steps.

In each case it is not the reasonableness of the belief which negates dishonesty but the fact that the belief is actually held. These three mental states are not conclusive on the issue of dishonesty. In any case where evidence is adduced which indicates that the defendant may not have been acting dishonestly the jury will be asked to consider whether what he did was dishonest according to the standards of ordinary decent people. If it was not, they must acquit. If it was, they will convict if they are also sure that the defendant knew that it was dishonest according to those standards.

Further reading

Ashworth, A.J., 'Robbery Re-assessed' [2002] Criminal Law Review 851.

Beatson, J. and Simester, A., 'Stealing One's Own Property' (1999) 115 Law Quarterly Review 372.

Bogg, A., Stanton-Ife, J., 'Protecting the Vulnerable: Legality, Harm and Theft' (2003) 23 Legal Studies 402.

Green, S., *Lying, Cheating and Stealing*, Oxford: OUP (2007).

Green, S., 'Theft by Omission', in J. Chalmers (ed.), *Essays in Criminal Law in Honour of Sir Gerald Gordon*, Edinburgh: Edinburgh University Press (2010).

Griew, E., 'Dishonesty: The Objections to *Feely* and *Ghosh*' [1985] Criminal Law Review 341.

Halpin, A., 'The Test for Dishonesty' [1996] Criminal Law Review 283.

Hammond, R.G., 'Theft of Information' (1984) 100 Law Quarterly Review 252, 259.

Melissaris, E., 'The Concept of Appropriation and the Offence of Theft' (2007) 70 Modern Law Review 581.

Ormerod, D.C. and Williams, D., *Smith's Law of Theft*, Oxford: OUP (2007).

Parsons, S., 'Dishonest Appropriation after *Gomez* and *Hinks*' (2004) 68 Journal of Criminal Law 520.

Shute, S., 'Appropriation and the Law of Theft' [2002] Criminal Law Review 445.

Shute, S. and Horder, J., 'Thieving and Deceiving – What is the Difference?' (1993) 56 Modern Law Review 548.

Steel, A., 'Permanent Borrowing and Lending: A New View of Section 6 Theft Act 1968' (2008) 17 Nottingham Law Review 3.

15 Fraud and making off without payment

Overview

The Fraud Act 2006 abolished a number of offences of deception under the Theft Acts 1968 and 1978. These were replaced by a general offence of fraud, which can be committed in three ways: by false representation, by failure to disclose information, or by abuse of position. If the defendant commits any one of these three wrongs, dishonestly, with intent to make a gain or cause a loss, he commits the offence. The nub of the offence is not the **gaining or causing of loss** but the dishonest intention to do so. The Fraud Act 2006 also replaces the offence of obtaining services by deception with that of obtaining services dishonestly. The gist of this offence is managing, by dishonesty, to obtain services without paying as required, with intent to avoid paying in full or in part. A deception is not of the essence but an actual obtaining is.

15.1 FRAUD: THE LAW WHICH IT REPLACES

The Fraud Act 2006 abolished a number of offences of deception under the Theft Acts 1968 and 1978 as amended, notably obtaining (1) property, (2) a money transfer, (3) services, (4) a pecuniary advantage by deception, (5) evading liability by deception, and procuring the execution of a valuable security by deception.[1] These offences had certain common elements. The first common element was the deception itself. Deceiving is inducing a person to believe that a thing is true which is false, and which the person practising the deceit knows or believes to be false. The deception could be as to fact, law, or intention. It could be express, implied or by conduct. Silence would not amount to a deception unless a duty of disclosure exists. The nub of the matter was the intentional or reckless creation of a false impression, whether by words or deeds. The second common element was that the prohibited result must be caused by the deception. It would not be so unless another person was induced to act in a particular way as a result of the deception, for example, to buy a car because of a false description. The requirement of a human 'dupe' meant that the offence would not be committed if the relevant trickery involved a machine, as in putting a foreign coin in a vending machine to obtain chocolate because machines do not have minds and therefore cannot be deceived. It would also not take place if the deception was not operative because, for example, it was not believed or not taken account of. The final element was dishonesty, the test for which was the *Ghosh* test. The provisions relating to dishonesty in Section 2 Theft Act 1968 were not applicable in deception offences and are not applicable to fraud.

---

[1] In addition the Theft Act 1968 included three offences largely designed to cover different forms of company fraud, such as false accounting (s. 17), the making of false statements by company directors (s. 19) and suppression of documents (s. 20(1)).

A The problem with the deception offences

The major problem with the scheme of liability for fraud under the Theft Acts was that it was unduly technical and complicated. At least part of the problem was that the initial offences introduced under section 16 of the Theft Act 1968, namely obtaining a pecuniary advantage by deception, were not fit for purpose, being a veritable counsel of confusion. Although the replacement offences created by the Theft Act 1978 solved some of the problems of application they tended to deal with the problems reactively, and in piecemeal fashion. They could not keep up with the increasingly complex world of fraud, for example those involving the internet.

Questions were raised at an early stage, therefore, as to whether these individual cases of fraud would be better addressed by a generalised fraud offence.[2] After all everyone knows a fraud when they see one, don't they? The problems posed by the creation of such an offence proved, however, fairly intractable. Should such an offence be constituted by conduct? If so, what should be the outcome of such conduct? Causing someone financial loss, prejudicing their financial interests, securing a financial gain? Again, is a deception of the essence? Or is it enough that there is some sort of behaviour which induces a false belief, causing the victim to act to his detriment, etc.? If the latter, how could such an offence be formulated so as to criminalise only those actions which would otherwise be regarded as serious wrongdoing? Or should it be constituted by mental element, criminalising any dishonest securing of a benefit or causing of another to act to his financial detriment? If so, how can dishonesty be defined so as to prevent stigmatising the kind of everyday sharp practice which individuals can always be expected to get up to, and their victims to guard against? The Law Commission rejected such a broad approach in their 1999 Consultation Paper on the basis that any such offence would likely be insufficiently 'certain to comply with the requirements of the European Convention on Human Rights'.

Although not without its problems, the undoubted merit of the old system was that the law addressed forms of wrongdoing which both reflected and articulated existing social norms. This ensured consistency of treatment, fair warning and fair labelling.[3] But clearly the tide was turning. In 2002 the Law Commission was recommending the enactment of a new fraud offence recognisably similar to that which has now been enacted.[4]

B The solution

By section 1 Fraud Act 2006 a general offence of fraud is created which can be committed in one of three ways, namely (a) section 2 (fraud by false representation), (b) section 3 (fraud by failing to disclose information), and (c) section 4 (fraud by abuse of position). Fraud itself is not defined in the Act but the essence of fraud, as envisaged by the new offence, appears to be nothing more than dishonest conduct designed to cause loss or

---

[2] See, for example, G.R. Sullivan, 'Fraud and the Efficacy of the Criminal Law: A Proposal for a Wide Residual Offence' [1985] Crim LR 616; Law Commission Consultation Paper No. 155 *Fraud and Deception* (1999); Law Com. 276 *Fraud* (2002).

[3] See generally Law Commission Consultation Paper No. 155 *Fraud and Deception* (1999) and the useful commentary of D.C. Ormerod, 'A Bit of a Con: The Law Commission's Consultation Paper on Fraud' [1999] Crim LR 789. Law Com. 276 *Fraud* (2002).

[4] Law Com. 276. The offence of fraud would be committed where a person dishonestly makes a false representation, or wrongfully fails to disclose information, or secretly abuses a position of trust with intent to make a gain or to cause loss or to expose another to the risk of loss.

gain. In short, it approaches the general offence of dishonesty, rightly rejected by the Law Commission in their 1999 Consultation Paper. As we shall see, it differs from the earlier Theft Acts scheme of liability in not requiring the victim to have duped or for his/her conduct to have *caused* any relevant gain or loss. It is the dishonest conduct and intentions which are criminalised, rather than the outcome. In Chapter 2 it was questioned whether, outside cases of serious non-consensual violence, there was any uncontroversial test for determining whether a given activity was suitable for criminalisation. In particular, given that both the civil and criminal law vindicate the interests of the victims of other people's wrongdoing, what determines whether the vindication takes the form of punishment or compensation? Fraud is a good illustration of the difficulty of producing a satisfactory answer to this question. It criminalises a range of conduct which, in many cases, is little more than a self-serving lie or other sharp practice.

C Fraud

1 Fraud by false representation

The core of the new offence of fraud is fraud by false representation (Section 2(1)), which is committed where a person:

(a) dishonestly makes a false representation, and
(b) intends, by making the representation –
    (i)   to make a gain for himself or another, or
    (ii) to cause loss to another or to expose another to a risk of loss.

(a) Actus reus

The *actus reus* of the offence is making a false representation. Of key concern here, as has been explained, is the fact that neither harm nor gain need actually accrue from the representation so long as this is the intention.[5] It is not even necessary that the representee is taken in, or is otherwise influenced. This is a far cry from the traditional notion of fraud which has the protection of property interests, and therefore the effectiveness of the misrepresentation, at the core of the offence. It seems almost as if the offence were designed to cope not with the heartland of traditional fraud but rather its modern and ghostly reflections, particularly in technological scams, such as 'phishing', where unseen, unseeable computer crooks try to tempt individuals into parting with sensitive information by representing themselves to be their bank or other trusted custodian of their financial interests. David Ormerod queries what the wrong is which the offence is trying to address. It clearly is not the intentional causing of harm or the risk of harm to the other, as the wrong is made out irrespective of such harm or potential. He concludes: 'the wrong seems to be the act of lying or misleading with intent to gain or cause loss: the harm might be construed as destabilising society's processes of property and financial transfers.[6] Even if this is sufficient to warrant criminalisation, is it properly called fraud?'

(i) A representation

The *actus reus* requires the defendant to have made a false representation. As with the Theft Acts which preceded it, a representation is not defined, presumably because it is a straightforward enough concept. The nearest synonym, where the representation is verbal, is 'statement'.

---

[5] See note 4.
[6] D.C. Ormerod, 'The Fraud Act 2006: Criminalising Lying' [2007] Crim LR 193.

More generally, a useful synonym is 'making out'. So if A hands a ticket inspector a senior citizen's bus pass with his name and photograph on it he is 'making out' or 'representing' that he is a pensioner and that he is entitled to the advantages conveyed by the pass. The Fraud Act assumes such meaning and concentrates on disclosing what kinds of representations are covered and what it is for such representations to be considered false.

(2) A representation is false if –
   (a) it is untrue or misleading, and
   (b) the person making it knows that it is, or might be, untrue or misleading.
(3) 'Representation' means any representation as to fact or law, including a representation as to the state of mind of –
   (a) the person making the representation, or
   (b) any other person.
(4) A representation may be express or implied.
(5) For the purposes of this section a representation may be regarded as made if it (or anything implying it) is submitted in any form to any system or device designed to receive, convey or respond to communications (with or without human intervention).

By this it is clear that there can be no fraud in the absence of a representation which is either false or misleading.

Case 1
Adam advertises his car for sale. Eve asks to see it. As the car has a nasty scratch on the side, Adam tells Eve to come at 9 pm, when it is dark. She does not notice the scratch and buys the car.

Adam does not commit fraud by false representation as he has made no representation to her, whether expressly, impliedly or by conduct. The false impression she gets of the car is due to the dark rather than anything expressed or implied by Adam. The principle applicable here, to which there are exceptions, is that silence will not generally count as a representation.

The corollary is that a false representation is practised for the purpose of the Fraud Act in any of the following situations:

Case 2
A, a 16-year-old boy, tells B, a publican, that he is 18 in order to obtain beer in a pub.

The representation is by words and as to facts, namely that A is 18. This representation is false. A's statement amounts to fraud depending on dishonesty because he makes the statement 'intending to gain for himself' (a pint of beer). Note that the fraud is made out although there is no specifically financial trickery involved and there is no financial loss to B.

Case 3
A, who is emigrating to Australia at the end of the month, needs money to pay for his flight. He asks his bank manager for an overdraft, telling him that he intends to pay off the overdraft by working for six months at his local supermarket.

Here an express representation is made as to A's 'state of mind'. This refers to his future intentions, namely to pay off his overdraft. He makes another express representation as to his state of mind, namely that he intends to stay in England. Both these representations are false and they are both made with the intention of making a gain for himself (the overdraft).[7]

> **Case 4**
> A, a crooked solicitor, tells a client that the latter is not entitled to recover his deposit when a house purchase falls through, though A knows this is his legal entitlement. A keeps the deposit.

Here the representation is express and as to the law. It is false and made with a view to making a gain for himself (keeping the deposit).

> **Case 5**
> A, a crooked car dealer, turns back the odometer reading on a car prior to selling it. B, a customer, asks him if the reading is genuine. A says that he does not know but that he thinks it is.

A makes two representations here. The first is a representation by conduct, namely his action of turning back the odometer reading. By doing this he is representing the car to have done fewer miles than it has done. It is therefore a false representation. The second is an express (or verbal) representation as to A's state of mind, namely the fact being that A **believes** the reading to be genuine. This is false.[8] He does not believe the reading to be genuine. Both representations are made with a view to making a gain for himself (making the sale).

> **Case 6**
> A, a 14-year-old boy, dons a false moustache in order to induce a shopkeeper to sell him a packet of cigarettes.

The representation is by conduct and as to facts, namely his age. The representation is false and made with the intention of gaining a packet of cigarettes.

It is important, particularly in the case of deception by conduct, to pinpoint exactly what false representation was made with intent to gain or cause loss.

> **Case 7**
> A pays for goods in a shop with a cheque backed by her own cheque guarantee card, but having lost the bank's authority to use it.

In cases involving the use of a cheque guarantee card the bank is required to honour the cheque notwithstanding the customer's abuse of authority. What representation is A making here? Quite a few, as it turns out, and not all of them are false. A is implying that

(a) She has an account with the bank on which the cheque is drawn – this is true.
(b) She is the holder of the cheque card – this is also true.
(c) She has authority to use the cheque card – this is untrue.
(d) The bank will honour the cheque – this is true.

---

[7] Note that the advantage is the obtaining of the overdraft facility rather than the actual money received.
[8] Cf. *King* [1979] Crim LR 122.

A makes only one untrue representation then, namely that she has the bank's authority to draw the cheques. By creating this false impression, she intended to obtain the goods, and increase her indebtedness to the bank.[9] Assuming dishonesty, she has committed the offence.

The representation will sometimes be difficult to discern. In *DPP* v *Ray*[10] the defendant D was a student who consumed a meal in a Chinese restaurant and then decided not to pay for it. D stayed in his seat until the waiter left the room and then made off. The House of Lords ruled that he was guilty of evading a debt by deception, which was an offence under section 16[11] of the Theft Act 1968 and is now covered by section 2 of the 2006 Act.[12] By sitting, saying nothing, the defendant had made an implied representation that his earlier honest intentions were continuing when, in fact, they were not. Using our earlier terminology, he created a false impression that he continued to be an honest customer who intended to pay for his meal even after the contrary intention was formed. *Ray* tells us that a representation may change from being true to false with a change of circumstances.

On the other hand, as Case 1 indicates, there must be a representation. It is not enough that someone is unaware of certain facts and for someone else to have conducted themselves so as to induce that state of ignorance. For comparable reasons a person does not make a false representation by remaining silent about things of which he, but not the other, is aware. He does not make a false representation by failing to inform a purchaser of his car that it is about to fall apart, for example, or that the odometer reading is inaccurate.[13] An exception is where A is under a duty to disclose the relevant information. This is specifically provided for under section 3 of the Fraud Act but also will usually be covered by section 2. Sometimes, saying nothing is the same as saying something untrue.

Case 8

A takes his friend B to A's golf club for a round of golf. Club rules require all members to inform a senior club official when guests are invited, so that they can charge a green fee. A does not do so.

The effect of the rule is to place A under a duty to the club to inform them that B is not a member. If he omits to do so he will be making a false representation by his conduct in taking his friend onto the course.[14] By not informing the golf club of the true state of affairs, A is creating a false impression. He is saying in effect to anyone who sees him either 'I have paid this chap's green fee', or, 'This chap is a member and so does not need to pay a green fee'.

A further exception is where the circumstances giving rise to a representation change so that the original representation no longer accurately describes the true state of affairs. The representor will make a false representation if he fails to apprise the representee of the change of circumstances:

[9] Cf. *MPC* v *Charles.*

[10] [1974] AC 370.

[11] Obtaining a pecuniary advantage contrary to s. 16(2)(a), now repealed.

[12] The offence of obtaining property (the meal) by deception had not been committed because the dishonest intention was only formed after the property had already been obtained. He did not, therefore, create the false impression that he intended to pay in order to get the meal.

[13] Unless he has first changed the reading.

[14] Cf. *Firth* (1990) 91 Cr App R 217.

> **Case 9**
> A truthfully tells B, a purchaser, that his car is in good working order. Subsequently, before the contract is concluded,[15] he discovers that the car is faulty. He concludes the sale without informing B.

A's failure to 'undeceive' B amounts to a false representation. This is, in effect, what happened in *DPP* v *Ray*. A's initial implied representation that he was an honest customer who intended to pay for his meal was true. When he later decided not to pay, the original representation no longer reflected the true state of affairs but he still continued to make the same representation. By continuing to sit in the restaurant, he was representing himself as the honest customer he once was. This was untrue. On the same principle it was held to be a false representation for a house owner to fail to inform his local council that his elderly mother had died so as to obtain the benefit of having a downstairs bathroom installed which had been granted for her benefit.[16]

(ii) *A false representation*
By subsection (2) a representation is false if –

(a) it is untrue or misleading, and
(b) the person making it knows that it is, or might be, untrue or misleading.

The major problem posed by this definition is that it further blurs the gap between the traditional notion of fraud and everyday sharp practice. It covers not only false statements but also misleading statements. Sellers and tradespeople traditionally exercise a great deal of ingenuity in coming up with statements which encourage people to part with money. Such statements may be exaggerations of the truth or 'half truths'. 'Making exaggerated claims and being economical with truth' in advertising a product's qualities is usually considered regrettable but rarely punishable.

> **Case 10**
> Adam goes into Virtualworld Computers and asks to see some computers. One attracts him particularly and he asks Eve, the salesperson, 'Is this the latest model?' 'Yes,' says Eve, although she knows it will be withdrawn from stock and replaced by another model next week.

It appears that Eve has made a false representation for the purpose of section 2 since her statement is misleading, although it is spot on in terms of accuracy and although it is the kind of 'half truth' which society has traditionally condoned as being part and parcel of the seller's repertoire of selling practices. The phrase *caveat emptor* – 'Buyer beware' – is still so widely used that it implies that society expects sellers to try to gull buyers and so also expects that buyers will take responsibility for their interests, as sellers do theirs. So also overenthusiastic marketing 'puffs' are covered by section 2, although few sensible people would think these are meet for criminalisation. Does anybody believe the claim that a certain type of lager is 'probably the best lager in the world'; that a particular soap powder washes whitest; that 'in tests, 9 out of 10 cats preferred' a particular kind of cat

---

[15] Logically it should also be a deception if the discovery of the true state of affairs occurs after the contract is concluded but before the contract price is handed over, but cf. *Wheeler* (1990) 92 Cr App R 279.
[16] *Rai* [2000] Crim LR 192.

food? If not, where is the harm in saying it? If so, does the claim nevertheless constitute conduct which conforms to the widely accepted criteria of criminalisation referred to in Chapter 2, namely that the conduct

(1) is generally viewed as constituting a social threat and is not condoned;
(2) is amenable to control by the criminal law;
(3) could not reasonably be dealt with by other means;
(4) if it were criminalised, will not produce any likely harmful side-effects.[17]

Even on a generous view not all of these criteria are satisfied in connection with the outer limits of section 2. In practice, and running counter to Article 7, this will mean that whether or not a person stands at risk of conviction in these kinds of cases will be largely determined by prosecutorial discretion and the common sense and fair play of individual juries in deciding questions of honesty. This should not be so. At the very least the wrong should be clearly identifiable as a matter with which the law, civil or criminal, should concern itself. Further, there is no coherent demarcation of the boundary between civil and criminal wrongs. For example, if a person obtains goods or services and then decides not to pay for them, his liability is limited to an action for breach of contract. If, however, he tries to dupe his victim into allowing him to avoid paying he is criminally liable. Why is the line between public and private wrongs drawn in this way? In both cases a person has acted dishonestly. In both cases a person's financial interests are under attack, but no rights lost. In both cases the victim retains a remedy against the wrongdoer enforceable in the civil courts, but only where there is a false representation is the activity criminalised.

Another troublesome case concerns the question of overcharging. In *Silverman* a builder who had done work over a period of several years for two elderly women put in a bill for a job which was grossly excessive.[18] He was convicted of obtaining the money by deception, the deception being that he was charging a fair and reasonable amount for the work. Although the appeal was allowed on other grounds, the Court of Appeal accepted that in the right circumstances overcharging could amount to making a false representation. Those circumstances are that the defendant is in a strong position *vis-à-vis* the other to know

(a) that the figure he is charging is grossly excessive, and
(b) that the other, through inexperience or trust, is relying upon him to supply an honest estimate or bill.

His knowledge that this is the case means that he knows that he is creating a false impression of the true value of the job when he gives his figure. It should be noted that *Silverman* is not authority for the proposition that overcharging amounts to a false representation, only that it may do if the (over)charger exploits the trust, vulnerability or inexperience of another.[19] Otherwise, tradespersons should not stand at risk of prosecution for doing to excess what most other tradespersons do less obviously. As Griew put it: 'there is a world of difference between fraud (with which this discussion is concerned) and exploitation (with which it is not)'.[20] Unfortunately this difference has been substantially attenuated by the Fraud Act 2006.

---

[17] Herbert L. Packer, *The Limits of the Criminal Sanction*, London: OUP (1969) 296.
[18] (1988) 86 Cr App R 213.
[19] This was confirmed in *Greig* [2010] EWCA Crim 1183.
[20] Griew (1995) at 155.

(iii) *Making the representation*

Under the previous law it was of the essence of deception that the false representation was acted on by the victim. There is no longer any such requirement, as has been explained. Indeed, astonishingly, there is not even a requirement that the representation be communicated to another. So if A falsely represents to B that the car he is selling is in good condition the offence is committed, although B does not hear the statement, or receive the letter which communicates this belief to B. The offence is made out as soon as the statement or other representation is made. Putting a misleading or untrue advertisement for sale on one's car windscreen while it is in the garage constitutes a 'making of a false representation' for the purpose of the Fraud Act 2006. Under the old law such conduct would probably not have even amounted to an attempt![21]

It was also not possible to make representation to a machine under the Theft Acts. The essence of the deception offences was the tricking of a human mind. Thus, no representation occurred in the case of inserting a dud coin into a chocolate machine, transferring funds in a bank account by computer hacking, or feeding in false information to an Inland Revenue computer to reduce tax liability.[22] This requirement left a significant gap in the law of fraud, but it was thought not necessary to close it due to the usual availability of other offences such as theft, making off without payment, computer misuse or, in the case of manipulating an electrically operated machine, abstraction of electricity.[23] The Fraud Act now makes it possible to commit fraud via a machine, since a representation is regarded as having been made 'if it (or anything implying it) is submitted in any form to any system or device designed to receive, convey or respond to communications, with or without human intervention.' As Ormerod remarks, this is wider than would appear absolutely necessary and desirable. It means that a person commits fraud as soon as he types the false representation into a computer for later transmission.[24] Strangely this would not even have constituted an attempt under the Theft Acts, and so would not have constituted any criminal offence, given that the representor's acts are not, at this stage, intended to induce a false belief in anyone or anything.

(b) Mens rea

There are three *mens rea* elements in section 2, namely the person making the representation must (1) know that it is, or might be, untrue or misleading; (2) intend, by making the representation, to make a gain for himself or another, or to cause loss to another or to expose another to a risk of loss; (3) the representation must be dishonestly made.

(i) *Knowledge that the representation is, or might be, untrue or misleading*

On the face of it this provision seems to mean that the defendant cannot be liable for fraud if, notwithstanding the falsity of the statement, be believes it to be true. However, it means more than this. It is clear, for example, that a person falls foul of this section if, although he believes his statement to be true, he knows it might not be:

---

[21] See discussion of *Gullever* in Chapter 18.
[22] Unless the information is first checked by an Inland Revenue official; *Moritz* 1961, unreported, cited in Arlidge and Parry at 49.
[23] See Law Commission No. 228 *Conspiracy to Defraud*, London: HMSO (1994) paras 4.40 ff.
[24] Op. cit. 200.

Case 11

Adam, an art dealer, places an inscription on the wall next to a painting stating, as this is his belief, that the painting is by Rembrandt.

Although Adam believes the painting to be a Rembrandt he makes a false representation. Attributing paintings to Rembrandt is a notoriously tricky business, and all dealers know this, given the number of copies and workshop pieces in existence. Adam, therefore, knows the painting might not be a Rembrandt. Liability here depends simply upon proof of dishonesty (and the untruth of the representation). Once again, the criminal liability of the defendant must be decided *ex post facto* by the view the jury takes as to whether this kind of practice discloses dishonesty. What if a dealer sells not a Rembrandt, but a Warhol, having bought it himself as a Warhol for a very high sum? Suppose, because attributing Warhols is less speculative than Rembrandts, he fails to make the kind of inquiries which sellers usually do on selling high-priced paintings which, like Warhols, are easily clonable. Does he have constructive knowledge of the things he would have found out if he had done so? This is unclear but, as Ormerod suggests, the courts are customarily willing to impute such knowledge to dealers.[25]

(ii) *Dishonesty*

The test for dishonesty is the *Ghosh* test.[26] Section 2 does not apply to property offences other than theft. Normally dishonesty will be easy to infer from the fact that a false representation has occurred. In some cases, however, making a false representation may be consistent with honesty. An obvious example is where it is made for the purpose of satisfying a claim of right.

Case 12

Adam owes Eve £1,000. Desirous of its return, Eve tells Adam that she needs it immediately to pay for hospital treatment for her sick husband. This is untrue.

It seems clear that Eve's claim of right is as inconsistent with dishonesty for the purpose of fraud as it is for theft.[27] The question arises as to whether, instead of the *Ghosh* test, the judge should direct the jury explicitly that dishonesty is negatived wherever a false representation is made in order to recover property to which one believes oneself entitled. Under the old law it was held that it is unnecessary for the judge to direct the jury in such terms when the substance of the defendant's case is a claim of right.[28] The implication is that both tests naturally lead to the same result. It does not. When faced with a scenario such as Case 12 the majority of my students have tended to the view that Eve is *Ghosh* dishonest due to the deceit, irrespective of her claim of right. Such a judgement is compounded where a person's deception was gross and the claim of right unimpressive. What would a jury, make of Case 12, for example, if the £1,000 was a gambling debt which Eve required to satisfy another gambling debt, and Adam was only able to satisfy by taking his child out of her (fee-paying) school? The almost unanimous view amongst my students is that this is *Ghosh* dishonesty.

[25] Op. cit. 203 citing *Roper v Taylor's Garage* [1951] 2 TLR 284.
[26] *Cornelius* [2012] EWCA Crim 500.
[27] J.C. Smith (1997) paras 4–29, 30.
[28] *Woolven* (1983) 77 Cr App R 231.

(iii) *Intention to make a gain or cause a loss*

The key difference between the old and the new notion of fraud is the replacement of an element in the *actus reus* of the old deception offences with a *mens rea* element. The offence is now constituted, not by securing the relevant gain or loss, but by forming the intention so to do. The defendant's liability hangs upon his (ulterior) intention:

(b) . . . by making the representation –
    (i)   to make a gain for himself or another, or
    (ii) to cause loss to another or to expose another to a risk of loss.

The meaning of gain and loss is denned in section 5 of the Act as follows:

(2) 'Gain' and 'loss' –
    (a)   extend only to gain or loss in money or other property;
    (b)   include any such gain or loss whether temporary or permanent;
         and 'property' means any property whether real or personal (including things in action and other intangible property).
(3) 'Gain' includes a gain by keeping what one has, as well as a gain by getting what one does not have.
(4) 'Loss' includes a loss by not getting what one might get, as well as a loss by parting with what one has.

This definition effectively covers all the mischief contained in the old deception offences, other than the obtaining of services. It is intended to cover the same ground as the notion of gain and loss contained in section 34(2)(a) Theft Act 1968. So, for example, it covers misrepresentations designed to gain money or property, real or personal. It also covers the obtaining of services if the false representation is made with a view not to pay for those services (a gain by 'keeping what one has'). Section 2(2) is applicable if the gain was a gift, loan, or other transfer of money, a gift, loan or other transfer of personal or real property. It is applicable if the gain was the keeping of money or property already in the person's possession or control whether permanently or temporarily. For example, the offence is committed where a debtor spins a creditor a false hard-luck story in order to get extra time to pay or to avoid payment entirely. Under the previous law this was an offence only if the debtor's intention was to make permanent default which, again, seems a more apt basis for criminalisation.

To see how these different elements in fraud hang together, consider the following hypothetical example:

Case 13

Adam, having eaten a meal in Fatgirls Restaurant, discovers that he has left his cash at home. When asked for payment by Eve, Adam says that he does not intend to pay because the food was so awful, although in fact he had found it delicious. Eve, in an attempt to placate Adam, tells Adam that he does not have to pay and gives him a glass of wine 'on the house' which he accepts. Adam then orders and consumes a pudding, for which he pays with a cheque backed by a guarantee card, although he knows that he has exceeded his credit limit and so does not have his bank's authority to pay by cheque.

Adam has committed fraud in relation to the bill. His false representation has enabled him to avoid paying it. Adam has not committed theft in relation to the food as his dishonest intention was formed only after consumption of the food. Has Adam committed fraud in relation to the wine? This depends upon whether he made a representation intending by **that representation** to gain it. It appears that he has not. The representation he made was intended to enable him to avoid paying the bill, not to gain the wine. In *Wakeling*,[29] a wastrel tried to avoid work by pretending he had no shoes. In fact he had two suitable pairs. A parish officer gave him some shoes to encourage him to work. It was held that he was not guilty of obtaining the shoes by false pretences because his statement was not designed to obtain shoes but to avoid work. The position arguably should be similar in relation to Case 13. It may be argued, however, by analogy with *DPP v Ray*, that his failure to tell Eve the truth about the situation was a false representation. Having created a (continuing) false impression that he was a disgruntled customer, when he was not, this representation continues until he leaves the restaurant. In order to be guilty of fraud in relation to the wine his representation must be intended to enable him to gain the wine, however. Was it? Adam will say not. He will say he accepted the wine (not to **gain** the wine but) to reassure the restaurant of his continuing good will. The counter argument is that such intention is nevertheless consistent with having an (indirect) intention to cause **loss** to the restaurant since Adam knows this will be the inevitable consequence.[30] Adam would commit fraud in relation to the pudding, which counts as a gain (of a pudding) to him, and, although the restaurant will still get paid, a loss (of a pudding) to the restaurant, as a result of a false representation made to Eve that he has the bank's authority to write cheques. Adam also commits fraud in relation to the overdraft. By falsely representing to Eve that he had authority to draw on the cheque he caused a loss to the bank.[31]

That liability hangs on the dishonest intent rather than the result is another reason to query the aptness of criminalising what may turn out to involve a deed involving imperceptible harm and questionable fault. It is true that other property offences criminalise what maybe an imperceptible harm. Section 9(1)(a) burglary, for example, is capable of extending to entering a shop with intent to shoplift. But the harm caught by section 2 Fraud Act 2006 is even further removed from what we ordinarily expect of serious stigmatic offences.

There are four possible cases of this *mens rea* requirement. The first, which will be the most usual, is the intention to make a gain for oneself by false representation. Cases 2–7 are examples of this. The second is the intention to make a gain for someone else.

Case 14

Adam secures a guarantee on Eve's bank loan by showing Eve's bank false credit references indicating that he is creditworthy.

Adam makes a false representation with intent to make a gain for Eve.

The third case is where the representor intends to cause a loss to another. It will be rare that this will occur in the absence of an intention to make a gain, either for oneself or for another.

Case 15

Adam, who dislikes Eve, recommends that she buys shares in X company, although he believes that company to be insolvent.

---

[29] Cited, with a helpful analysis, by A.T.H. Smith 17–153.
[30] It should be noted that no oblique intention existed in *Wakeling* since, at the time of making the statement, W did not foresee the obtaining of the shoes as a virtual certainty.
[31] Cf. *MPC v Charles*.

Adam intends not only to cause loss to Eve, but also, assuming indirect intention suffices for fraud, to make a gain for the company.

> **Case 16**
> Adam is the owner of Hollywood House, a stately home open to the public. Desirous of providing some interest to bored visitors he digs a well and places next to it a sign which reads, 'Ye Olde Wishing Welle. Throw a coin down the well and your wish will come true.'

This representation is obviously false and Adam knows it. In a change from the previous law of deception Adam may be guilty of fraud although no one is taken in, although he does not intend to gain, and although no one throws money down the well. This is because he intends to cause people to throw money down the well, that is, to cause them a loss. His guilt depends upon the view the jury take as to whether his action is dishonest. Although it is unlikely such conduct would provoke a criminal prosecution and unlikely the jury would find him to be dishonest, what he does is surely too trivial to even justify the risk of criminal conviction.

The fourth case is where the representor intends not to cause loss to another but to expose another to the risk of loss:

> **Case 17**
> Adam, an economic journalist, anxious to demonstrate his power over the market, writes a column urging readers to invest in a financially fragile company, stating it is a 'sure fire winner'.[32]

Adam here intends not to cause others loss but to expose others to the risk of loss and, assuming dishonesty, is guilty on this basis.

2 Fraud by failing to disclose information

Strictly speaking, this is an unnecessary provision as it is clear that a failure to disclose information which one has a duty to disclose, as in Case 8, counts as a representation for the purpose of section 2. Section 3 was included in order to simplify the proof of guilt. It does not require an untutored jury to understand how by failing to make one disclosure one can at the same time be making another (false) disclosure. Section 3 allows a conviction simply upon proof of the duty to disclose and the failure to do so with the relevant intent. It provides as follows:

> A person is in breach of this section if he –
> (a) dishonestly fails to disclose to another person information which he is under a legal duty to disclose, and
> (b) intends, by failing to disclose the information –
>   (i) to make a gain for himself or another, or
>   (ii) to cause loss to another or to expose another to a risk of loss.

The important aspect of section 3 is the requirement that the defendant be under a legal duty of disclosure. A moral duty is not enough, although the Law Commission felt that it

---

[32] The Law Commission give *Allsop* (1977) 64 Cr App R 29 as an example. The defendant deceived a finance company into accepting risky loan applications. It was no defence to fraud that the defendant expected all the money to be repaid since the defendant intentionally exposed the company to financial risk.

should be, at least in cases where the person was being trusted to make disclosure.[33] Eve, in the Virtualworld case, is not covered by section 3, as she is under no legal duty of disclosure. Her liability, if any, depends upon the notion of 'misleading' for the purpose of section 2. The question then presents as to when a legal duty of disclosure arises. The explanatory notes to the 2006 Act provide the following guidance:

> The concept of 'legal duty' is explained in the Law Commission's Report on *Fraud*, which said: '. . . Such a duty may derive from statute (such as the provisions governing company prospectuses), from the fact that the transaction in question is one of the utmost good faith (such as a contract of insurance), from the express or implied terms of a contract, from the custom of a particular trade or market, or from the existence of a fiduciary relationship between the parties (such as that of agent and principal).
>
> For this purpose there is a legal duty to disclose information not only if the defendant's failure to disclose it gives the victim a cause of action for damages, but also if the law gives the victim a right to set aside any change in his or her legal position to which he or she may consent as a result of the non-disclosure. For example, a person in a fiduciary position has a duty to disclose material information when entering into a contract with his or her beneficiary, in the sense that a failure to make such disclosure will entitle the beneficiary to rescind the contract and to reclaim any property transferred under it. For example, the failure of a solicitor to share vital information with a client within the context of their work relationship, in order to perpetrate a fraud upon that client, would be covered by this section. Similarly, an offence could be committed under this section if a person intentionally failed to disclose information relating to his heart condition when making an application for life insurance.'

Case 8, as above, would be an example of fraud by failure to disclose, the legal duty arising by virtue of Adam's membership of the club. *Firth*[34] is another example. A hospital consultant failed, in breach of his contract with the health service, to disclose to the hospital that he was using its facilities for the benefit of private patients. As a consequence they omitted to charge him or the patients.

(a) Mens rea

The *mens rea* for section 3 is as for section 2. There is no requirement that the defendant be aware that he is under a legal duty of disclosure so such lack of knowledge will not avail Adam, in Case 8, although evidence of lack of awareness will, no doubt, influence the jury's assessment of dishonesty.

3 Fraud by abuse of position

The third form of fraud is the most controversial as it is here that fraud is cast adrift from a clearly identifiable fraudulent context. The thinking behind the section is that people in positions of trust can advance their own interests or damage the interests of others without having to 'to enlist the victim's cooperation in order to secure the desired result'. The major problem with the offence is an absence of clarity as to the intended scope of the relevant 'positions of trust'. The Law Commission made clear that it was envisaging a broader coverage than traditional fiduciary duties:

---

[33] 'For example, an antique dealer calls on vulnerable people and buys their heirlooms at unrealistically low prices, making no misrepresentation as to the value of the items but exploiting the victims' trust. There may be no legal duty to disclose the truth, but there is clearly a moral duty to do so. If the dealer's failure to do so is regarded by the fact-finders as dishonest, we see no reason why he should not be guilty of fraud.' LC 276 *Fraud* (2002) para. 724.

[34] (1990) 91 Cr App R 217.

The essence of the kind of relationship which in our view should be a prerequisite of this form of the offence is that the victim has voluntarily put the defendant in a privileged position, by virtue of which the defendant is expected to safeguard the victim's financial interests or given power to damage those interests. Such an expectation to safeguard or power to damage may arise, for example, because the defendant is given authority to exercise a discretion on the victim's behalf, or is given access to the victim's assets, premises, equipment or customers. In these cases the defendant does not need to enlist the victim's *further* cooperation in order to secure the desired result, because the necessary cooperation has been given in advance. The necessary relationship will be present between trustee and beneficiary, director and company, professional person and client, agent and principal, employee and employer, or between partners. It may arise otherwise, for example within a family, or in the context of voluntary work, or in any context where the parties are not at arm's length. In nearly all cases where it arises, it will be recognised by the civil law as importing fiduciary duties, and any relationship that is so recognised will suffice. We see no reason, however, why the existence of such duties should be essential.[35]

In other words the potential coverage of the abuse of position form of fraud is extensive and capable of constituting many unlikely relationships as contexts within which fraud may be committed. Section 4 provides as follows:

(1) A person is in breach of this section if he –
    (a) occupies a position in which he is expected to safeguard, or not to act against, the financial interests of another person,
    (b) dishonestly abuses that position, and
    (c) intends, by means of the abuse of that position –
        (i) to make a gain for himself or another, or
        (ii) to cause loss to another or to expose another to a risk of loss.
(2) A person may be regarded as having abused his position even though his conduct consisted of an omission rather than an act.

The question whether a person occupies a position in which he is expected to safeguard, or not to act against, the financial interests of another person is, so the Law Commission insisted, not a matter simply for the jury. The judge will have the overall control, by directing the jury as to whether, by virtue of his position, he is expected to safeguard the interests of the other. The following constitute some scenarios, outside standard fiduciary positions such as trustee/beneficiary, lawyer/client, director/company, in which the offence might be committed:

Case 18
Adam, who lives with his mother who suffers from dementia, collects her pension weekly and uses it to defray all household expenses. He gives £5 of the money to charitable causes each week.

Case 19
Adam, Eve's father, puts £5 per week into her account to build up a nest egg for the future. After 10 years of so doing the account is worth £5,000. Being a little hard up he withdraws £500 from her account to help pay for the family holiday.

Case 20
Adam, who works for Eve, always skips off work half an hour early when Eve is out of the office.

---

[35] Para. 7.38.

Case 21

Adam, who works in Eve's pub, routinely, and against Eve's strict instructions, uses the cheapest spirits when serving friends their drinks, in order to save them money.

Case 22

Adam, who works in Eve's pub, brings in cigarettes to sell to customers at cost price because Eve refuses to stock cigarettes.[36]

Case 23

Adam, Eve's selling agent for cricket bats, also runs his own cricket school on the side. He gives preferential credit terms, within his discretion as agent, on bats to those who sign up for courses at his school.

Case 24

Adam, Eve's flatmate, has an arrangement with Cain, a friend of his, that when Eve goes away on holiday that Cain can use Eve's room. Cain pays Adam £10 for the privilege.

As can be appreciated, in each of these cases it is possible that Adam has committed fraud as in each Adam is in a position where he might be expected not to act against the financial interests of another, intending to make a gain or cause loss by means of abuse of that position. Even Case 21, where Eve suffers no real, if any, loss and Adam makes no real gain, is potentially covered. Although it is a requirement of section 4 that Adam is in a position where he is expected to safeguard the financial interests there is no requirement that the abuse of his position will lead to damage or even the risk of damage to those interests, so long as the necessary intention to make a gain or cause a loss exists. In Case 22 it does. Adam abuses his position, intending to gain the price of the cigarettes, which is a gain although he makes no profit on the transactions. Case 24 shows the full potential uncertainty attaching to section 4. Is Adam in a position where he is expected not to safeguard or not act against the financial interests of Eve? One would possibly think so, and yet this is far away from the kind of fiduciary relationship which should surely lie at the core of the offence of fraud. In each case the potential for liability is present because of the means adopted to delimit the scope of liability which indeed seems to cover, potentially, most relationships. Although the jury can be expected to filter those who deserve punishment from those who do not *via* a finding of lack of dishonesty, it is unacceptable that the wrong in fraud is so insecurely defined, so capable of stretching beyond its core meaning and so apt to criminalise the undeserving.

(a) Mens rea

The *mens rea* for section 4 is as for section 2. There is no requirement that the defendant be aware that he is under a duty to safeguard the other's financial interests, so such lack of knowledge will not avail Adam in Case 23, although evidence of lack of awareness will, no doubt, influence the jury's assessment of dishonesty.

[36] Cf. *Doukas* [1978] 1 All ER 1061.

15.2 OBTAINING SERVICES DISHONESTLY

Section 11 replaces section 2 Theft Act 1978. It differs from that section in that it is not necessary for the service to be obtained as a result of false representation. Under the old law it would not be an offence to sneak into a cinema without paying because the services obtained (being able to watch the film) were not obtained as a result of a false representation. This will be an offence under the Fraud Act, since the services are obtained dishonestly. The section would also cover cases where the services were obtained via the use of a machine. So, for example, obtaining a parking space in a pay-on-entry car park by putting a foreign coin in the slot, or using an unauthorised credit card to purchase train tickets from an automated ticket vending machine, are examples of a section 11 offence.

It differs from sections 2, 3 and 4 of the Fraud Act in requiring the benefit actually to be obtained (not merely to have been intended). There is, however, a big overlap with section 2 Fraud Act 2006, which will make it possible to proceed under either section where the relevant services were indeed obtained as a result of a false representation and with intent to avoid paying. Where section 11 will come into its own will be in those cases where the services were dishonestly obtained otherwise than by a false representation.

(1) A person is guilty of an offence under this section if he obtains services for himself or another –
    (a) by a dishonest act, and
    (b) in breach of subsection (2).
(2) A person obtains services in breach of this subsection if –
    (a) they are made available on the basis that payment has been, is being or will be made for or in respect of them,
    (b) he obtains them without any payment having been made for or in respect of them or without payment having been made in full, and
    (c) when he obtains them, he knows –
        (i) that they are being made available on the basis described in paragraph (a), or
        (ii) that they might be, but intends that payment will not be made, or will not be made in full.

The offence is punishable with a maximum five years' imprisonment on conviction on indictment and twelve months' imprisonment on summary conviction.

A Actus reus

1 Services
Not every dishonest obtaining of services is an offence. By section 2(a) the services covered are restricted to those made available on the basis that payment has been, is being or will be made for or in respect of them.

Case 25
A asks B, his neighbour, to cut his lawn for him, falsely representing that he has hurt his back. B does so.

Case 26
A, a female nurse at a local hospital, is late for work. She sticks a pillow down her trousers and hails a taxi. She tells the driver that she is pregnant and needs the hospital. The driver takes her there for free.

What the subsection means, in effect, is that the obtaining of free services dishonestly is not an offence. In none of these examples, therefore, has the section 11 offence been committed. In each case there has been a dishonest obtaining of a benefit but in each case the services were not made available on the basis that they had been or would be paid for. Quite the opposite. Case 26 is covered by section 2 of the Fraud Act 2006. Case 25 is not covered by any provision of the Fraud Act.[37] Some other examples follow:

Case 27

A induces B, a travel agent, to organise transport to and from the airport on her trip abroad, telling him, falsely, that this will be paid for on her return.

The offence is committed here since A has obtained services, namely his transportation to and from the airport, on the understanding that it would be paid for.

More broadly, the section is satisfied wherever the person is allowed to do something for free which would otherwise have to be paid for. This would cover entering and viewing a game, show or spectacle, using an automatic car wash, playing a round of golf, hiring a car or taking goods on hire purchase.[38]

B *Mens rea*

The *mens rea* elements for section 11 are dishonesty, knowledge that payment is required or might be, and an intention not pay for the service or not to pay in full. Dishonesty is established on the basis of the *Ghosh* test and is covered above.

The offence is only made out where the defendant knows that payment is required or might be. In the usual case this requirement is superfluous as such cases will generally negate dishonesty. So a person does not commit the offence, therefore, if he parks his car in a public car park believing that it is a free car park both because he is not dishonest and also because he does not know that payment is required.

Finally the offence is only made out if it is the defendant's intention not to pay or not to pay in full. It is unclear whether this means an intention never to pay the relevant amount or simply not to pay at the time. For example:

Case 28

Adam parks his car in a pay and display car park. He has no money and so resolves to pay later when he returns from his shopping, and does so.

With respect to the offence of making off without payment it seems that the offence is not committed unless the intention not to pay is a permanent one.[39] For consistency's, if not reason's, sake it is likely that such a stance should be taken here.

---

[37] The Law Commission recommended a partial extension of section 1 to meet such cases. Law Commission Consultation Paper No. 155 *Fraud and Deception* (1999).

[38] *Widdowson* [1986] Crim LR 233.

[39] *Allen* [1985] AC 1029.

15.3 MAKING OFF WITHOUT PAYMENT

Section 3 of the Theft Act 1978 provides

(1) Subject to subsection 3 below, a person who, knowing that payment on the spot for any goods supplied or service done is required or expected from him, dishonestly makes off without having paid as required or expected and with intent to avoid payment of the amount due shall be guilty of an offence.

(2) For purposes of this section 'payment on the spot' includes payment at the time of collecting the goods on which work has been done or in respect of which service has been provided.

(3) Subsection (1) above shall not apply where the supply of the goods or the doing of the service is contrary to law, or where the service done is such that payment is not legally enforceable.

The criminal law does not generally penalise dishonest breaches of contract, whether a failure to deliver goods or services contracted for, or failure to account for such benefits once received. An exception is sometimes made where a deception is involved since this mental element is thought to mark the conduct as particularly culpable. In one case a dishonest non-payment of debt is penalised even in the absence of deception. This is where the debtor dishonestly makes off, so as to evade paying the amount due. The justification for criminalisation in this circumstance is the perceived social menace of the activity known as 'bilking'. People who **consume** goods or services and then make off without paying may be difficult to trace. For this reason a power of arrest is granted to any person, for example the provider of the goods or services, who has good reason to suspect an offence is being committed.[40] Even if the bilker is traced, there may be problems of proof in establishing a **deception or dishonest intention** formed prior to the consumption of the goods or services sufficient to establish either deception or theft. The section 3 offence allows for a conviction in the absence of one or more of the elements of theft or fraud as long as it can be shown that the accused has dishonestly made off without paying. The offence is triable either way and carries a maximum sentence of two years' imprisonment and a fine of £2,000.[41]

A *Actus reus*

1 Making off

Making off takes no particular form. A person can make off by stealth, as in slipping out of a restaurant when the waiter is not looking[42] or by trumpeting his departure, as when a dishonest motorist honks his horn in triumph when driving away after filling up at a petrol station. A question surrounds the status of permitted departures, as when a customer dupes a creditor into allowing him to depart by pretending to have left his wallet at home. This is sometimes argued not to be a making off which meaning is thought restricted to cases of 'decamping or sudden or hasty departures'.[43] Probably the best view is that a departure,

---

[40] Section 3(4).
[41] Section 4(2) and (3).
[42] Cf. *DPP* v *Ray* [1974] AC 370, above.
[43] A.T.H. Smith 20–93; F. Bennion, 'Letter to the Criminal Law Review' [1980] Crim LR 670; for a contrary opinion see Griew (1995) 13–16.

consented to or otherwise, will be a making off if the manner of departure renders it diffi-cult for D to be traced, but otherwise not.[44] This ensures that the offence does not overreach itself to cover routine cases of dishonest debtors. Thus if D leaves a dud cheque as payment with his name and address on the reverse, or if D is well known to the creditor, the offence is not committed.[45]

(a) *From the spot where payment is due or expected*

To make off requires simply that D departs from the spot where payment is due or expected.[46] Two questions must be asked in each case therefore:

(i) where is the spot where payment is due?
(ii) has D made off from it?

In *McDavitt* D was apprehended in a restaurant making for the door. The spot where payment was due was held to be the restaurant. Since D had not quit the restaurant he could only be guilty of an attempt. Presumably it would be different if D had departed the restaurant for the lavatory to avoid payment since the spot where payment was due was the restaurant whence D had made off.[47] In *Moberley* v *Alsop*[48] D travelled on a train without paying for a ticket. He was apprehended having gone through the ticket barrier. The spot where payment was due was held to include not only the place where D should have paid (the departure hall ticket office) but also the spot where D should have later made good his default (the destination ticket barrier). As D had made off from this latter spot, the offence could be committed.[49] The upshot of this case is that there may be more than one spot where payment is due.

2 Payment for goods supplied or service done

The offence is constituted upon the successful completion of the creditor's part of the bargain, whether the supply of goods or the provision of services. The offence is not committed where payment would not be required or expected due to the other's breach of contract or if the supply of goods or services was contrary to law. It would not be an offence, then, for a punter to make off without paying a prostitute.[50] Further, no offence appears to be com-mitted where the relevant benefit was not 'supplied' or 'done' as where it was abstracted secretively.

Case 29

A, knowing that a green fee is required at his local 'pay and play' golf course, decides to avoid paying by climbing over the fence on the third hole and climbing back over the fence on the penultimate hole.

---

[44] J.R. Spencer, 'The Theft Act 1978' [1979] Crim LR 24.
[45] *Hammond* [1982] Crim LR 611: a submission of no case to answer succeeded on such facts although for other reasons.
[46] *McDavitt* [1981] Crim LR 843.
[47] Cf. *Brooks and Brooks* (1983) 76 Cr App R 66.
[48] (1991) *The Times*, 13 December (DC).
[49] Although not in this case, as he had a season ticket.
[50] Section 3(3).

It seems that the offence is not committed here since although A has received the benefit of fifteen holes of golf, this was not the result of any provision of services to him.[51] In short, A has not made off without having paid as required or expected since he was given nothing to pay for.

3 Without having paid as required or expected

The offence is only constituted where the defendant makes off knowing that payment on the spot is required or expected. The offence is not committed, therefore, where D deceives the creditor into agreeing to postpone payment of the bill since, deception not-withstanding, the creditor's agreement means that D is not required or expected to make payment.[52] A particular problem concerns the case where the debtor purports to pay by means of a dud cheque. It was explained above that such a practice is consistent with the debtor 'making off' even though his departure is consented to. Has a person who purports to satisfy the debt in this way 'paid' as required or expected? It may be argued that this depends upon the nature of the dud cheque. If it is forged, for example, it seems clear that no payment has been made any more than if the currency rendered was toy money. On the other hand, if the cheque is 'dud' only because it was not authorised by the debtor's bank, it is arguable that a 'payment' of sorts sufficient to satisfy section 3 has been made because rights attach to it.[53] The safest course of action for prosecutors will be to charge under section 2.[54]

B *Mens rea*

The *mens rea* for section 3 is dishonesty and an intention to avoid payment of the amount due. Significantly, the section does not state that the intention must be to make perman-ent default. Nevertheless the House of Lords held, in *Allen*, that liability required proof of an intention permanently to avoid paying the amount due. So a hotel customer who checked out without paying would not commit the offence if he was temporarily financially embarrassed and intended to pay later.[55] Given the mischief the section was designed to counter and the absence of the word 'permanently' from the definition, the decision does not appear to be a good one.

Summary

The Fraud Act 2006 replaces a number of different offences under the Theft Acts 1968 and 1978 with a general offence of fraud which can be committed in one of three ways: by false representation; by failing, in breach of legal duty, to disclose information; and by abuse of position. Dishonesty is of the essence in each case, as is an intention, by the relevant act or omission, to make a gain or cause a loss. By contrast with the previous law it is not necessary to show that the gain was made or the loss caused for the offence to be made

---

[51] Griew (1995) 213.
[52] *Vincent* [2001] Crim LR 488.
[53] G. Syrota, 'Are Cheque Frauds Covered by Section 3 of the Theft Act 1978?' [1980] Crim LR 412.
[54] Griew (1995) 216–17.
[55] *Allen* [1985] AC 1029.

out. It is only necessary to show that this was the defendant's intention in making the representation/failing to disclose the information/abusing his position. In addition the Fraud Act criminalises a number of other acts, including the offence of possessing articles for use in fraud. This replaces the offence of 'going equipped to cheat' in section 25 Theft Act 1968. The Fraud Act also incorporates an offence of obtaining services dishonestly. This replaces the previous offence of obtaining services by deception. The important difference is that any dishonest obtaining of services is covered. There is no need for any human person to be 'duped' into providing the service. Indeed it can be effected by means of a machine. Only services made available on the basis that they have been or will be paid for are covered.

By section 3 Theft Act 1978, it remains an offence for a person dishonestly to make off without paying for goods or services when he knows that payment is there and then required or expected, if he does so intending to avoid paying. This is not an offence requiring proof of a false representation. Making off can be done blatantly or by stealth but is probably not committed where the person has the creditor's consent to leave. The intention must be to make permanent default.

Further reading

Green, S., *Lying, Cheating and Stealing*, Oxford: OUP (2007).

Ormerod, D., 'The Fraud Act 2006 Criminalising Lying' (2007) Crim LR 193.

16 Other property offences

16.1 ROBBERY

Overview

Robbery is committed when force or the threat of force is used in the course of committing theft. Proof of guilt requires therefore all of the elements of theft, including dishonesty and intention, to be established.

16.2 INTRODUCTION TO ROBBERY

The Crime Survey estimates that around 200,000 robberies were committed in the year ending March 2013, a large decrease from the benchmark year of 2001.[1] Robbery is a form of aggravated theft. The aggravating factor is the use or threat of force, which feature increases the maximum sentence to one of life imprisonment. Given that the force used may be minimal, this lends an unfortunate breadth to the offence. Robbery may be as serious as the armed robbery of a bank or building society which the word typically suggests to the imagination. Or it may differ from theft only in the merest of details, as in handbag snatching. The potential reach of the offence creates both charging and sentencing problems. At the lower levels of force, or threat of force, criminal justice requires as a minimum that charging practices are consistent and measured. Sentences should also, as far as possible, be consistent across grades of seriousness of offences.[2] Theft is triable either way. Robbery is triable only on indictment.[3] This procedural difference provokes a particular risk of differentiated treatment of similar cases.[4]

By section 8(1) Theft Act 1968: 'a person is guilty of robbery if he steals, and immediately before or at the time of doing so, and in order to do so, he uses force on any person or puts or seeks to put any person in fear of being then and there subjected to force'.

The two central ingredients of the offence are, therefore, a theft and a use or threat of violence.

A Theft

If one of the elements of theft is absent, there can be no robbery. Just as much care must be taken in pinpointing these elements, therefore, as in theft proper. A non-theftuous appropriation does not become robbery simply because unlawful force is used. A person who uses force to wrest his own property from another is not guilty of robbery. Neither is

---

[1] 2013 Crime Survey.
[2] See generally A.J. Ashworth, *Sentencing and Criminal Justice*, London: Butterworths (2005) ch. 4; P. Darbyshire, 'An Essay on the Importance and Neglect of the Magistracy' [1997] Crim LR 627.
[3] Magistrates' Courts Act 1980, Sched. 1, para. 28(a).
[4] Cf. *A-G's References (Nos 4 and 7) of 2002* [2002] Crim LR 33.

he guilty if his intention is only to appropriate the property temporarily or if his appropriation of another's property is not dishonest,[5] for example he has a claim of right under section 2(1)(a) or (b).[6] In *Forrester* the Court of Appeal accepted that a person who used force to appropriate goods belonging to his ex-landlord for the purpose of extracting a deposit wrongfully withheld, is not necessarily guilty of theft even if he knows that he is not entitled to do so. The jury might still find his action to be the action of an honest man. If so, no robbery has occurred and the defendant can be guilty only of assault.

Since an appropriation does not need a 'taking and carrying away', a person commits robbery by wresting property from the grasp of the owner even if he does not succeed in making away with it. In *Corcoran* v *Anderton*[7] the accused wrenched a handbag from its owner's hands but dropped it before making off. The robbery was complete. Even the act of tugging forcibly at the property – an act of appropriation – will be robbery although the possessor may retain control of it. Where force is used but an appropriation does not take place, an attempt may be charged. Alternatively the accused may be charged with assault with intent to rob, a separate creation of the Theft Act 1968.[8] Given the possibility of charging the attempt this latter offence might appear otiose. It was apparently designed to accommodate those (surely) rare cases where, although an assault had occurred, the accused's conduct was yet preparatory to the commission of theft. Tying up a bank employee as a preliminary to telephoning the bank manager for the key to the vault might be an example of the mischief towards which this provision is addressed.

B The use or threat of force

As explained above, robbery may differ from theft only in the merest of details. In *Dawson* A and B nudged Y so he overbalanced.[9] While Y was thus disadvantaged C stole Y's wallet. The Court of Appeal approved the trial judge's approach which was to allow the jury to decide whether the nudging amounted to force sufficient to convert a theft into a robbery. It is clear, therefore, that it is not a requirement of section 8 that force or the threat of force be used so as to overpower the victim. It is enough that the force is directed against the property as long as such force translates itself into force against the person holding it. In effect this means that most cases of handbag snatching are technically forms of robbery and may be charged as such – a regrettable conclusion for the reasons explained above.[10] Fine distinctions can be made between force directed solely against the property and force directed against the person via the property. Pickpocketing or handbag 'dipping' may involve the communication of force or pressure to the victim, but commonsensically one would hesitate to say that they involve force used **on** the victim. In such cases the distinction made by Williams between 'gentle force' used to 'snatch an article by stealth or surprise . . . and tugging it away when (she) offers resistance' is probably still the best rule of thumb available.[11] Williams gives a useful summary, with examples, of force sufficient for robbery, namely force used:

---

[5] *Forrester* [1992] Crim LR 793 CA.
[6] *Robinson* [1977] Crim LR 173 CA.
[7] (1980) 71 Cr App Rep 104.
[8] Section 8(2).
[9] *Dawson* (1985) 81 Cr App R 150.
[10] *Clouden* [1987] Crim LR 56 CA.
[11] G. Williams *TCL* 825; cf. Griew (1995) para. 3.05. For a recent example of the former see *DPP* v *RP* [2013] 1 Cr App R. D snatched a cigarette from V's hand. No robbery.

(1) to prevent or overcome conscious resistance (e.g. a tug-of-war with the owner or applying a chloroform pad to the owner's nose); or

(2) to sever an article attached to its possessor (e.g. breaking a watch chain); or

(3) in such a way as to cause injury (e.g. tearing an earring from the lobe of the ear).[12]

It should be noted that robbery may also be committed where there is a threat of force. This will normally involve some form of assault, for example menacing gestures or use of a weapon. However, proof of an actual assault is not crucial as long as the thief 'puts or seeks to put the victim in fear of being **then and there** subjected to force'. An example might be passing the victim a note containing an explicit or implicit threat of violence for failure to comply with a demand to hand over property.[13] A threat of future force or any other unpleasant consequence if the victim fails to comply will not be robbery but may be blackmail.

As robbery is not committed unless the force or threat of force is used **in order** to steal, it seems that it is necessary for A to intend V to be put in fear. It would not be enough, then, for A to do an act which was not meant to alarm V but in fact did do so.

Case 1

A, intending to steal, breaks into a bank under cover of night dressed in a balaclava. He unexpectedly comes across V, a night porter, causing V to fear for his safety.

Here A will not be guilty of robbery simply upon the basis of the fear experienced by V on encountering A. If, however, A had threatened V with violence if he sounded the alarm, robbery would then have been committed.

1 On any person

As will be apparent from the above example, it is not necessary for force to be used or threatened against the person actually in possession or control of property. The victim of the robbery may therefore be someone other than the victim of the theft such as a bystander pushed out of the way in the immediate aftermath of a theft. However, where threats are made to effect a theft, the threats must be directed against the recipient of the threat. So, it will not be robbery for A to threaten V with the death of V's baby if V does not hand over his wallet. A has not used force on the baby and has not put or sought to put the baby in fear of being subjected to force. Such conduct would, however, amount to blackmail, as it would if the threat was to destroy or damage V's property.

2 Immediately before or at the time of the stealing

Once the stealing is complete any force used thereafter will not convert the stealing into robbery. Tricky questions may be posed, therefore, as to when a stealing is ended.[14] Such questions would have been unnecessary if the Act had been drafted so as to encompass cases where force was used immediately after the stealing in order to effect the theft successfully. What is clear is that the stealing is not complete simply upon the occurrence of the appropriation. Thus force used in the course of a burglary will convert the included theft into robbery, even though the force was used after the property was reduced into the burglar's possession. In *Hale* it was held that tying up the owner of a house in which the

---

[12] G. Williams ibid. 825; for an extended discussion see A.T.H. Smith 405–7.

[13] *Katrensky* (1975) 24 CCC (2d) 350 (Can.); see A.T.H. Smith 408–9. See now, however, *R v Ireland, R v Burstow* [1997] Crim LR 810.

[14] *Vinall* [2012] 1 Cr App Rep 400.

latter had found the defendants about to make off with her jewellery box was a robbery. The question as to when the theft ended was a matter for the jury.[15] A better solution would be for the duration of the theft to be a matter of law so that in cases of theft from premises, for example, force used at any time before the premises are quit should be sufficient.

3 In order to steal

As a general proposition it must be shown that the force was used or threatened in order to effect the theft. If it was used in self-defence after a murderous attack by the indignant owner, this will not be robbery.[16] Neither, moreover, will it be robbery if, having attacked V with theft not in mind, A takes V's wallet as an afterthought.

One problem raised by *Hale* is that force used after the property is reduced into the appropriator's possession may be difficult to attribute to effecting the theft. In this case the jewellery box was under the defendant's complete control when the tying up occurred. This was apparently done, moreover, in order to prevent V calling the police rather than to prevent V from attempting to retain or recapture possession. In furtherance of this object the defendants had also threatened V with harm to her child if she contacted the police within five minutes of their leaving. If the tying up was done in order to prevent her contacting the police it is hard to argue that it was also done in order to effect the theft, unless the former was a precondition of the latter which it did not seem to be. Cross-examination of the defendants on this point should have made this perfectly clear.

4 Mental element

The basic *mens rea* for robbery is the *mens rea* for the included theft. It is a defence, therefore, that force was used to effect a temporary appropriation or that the appropriation was in support of a claim of right or was otherwise not dishonest. As explained above, the use of force to effect the appropriation does not turn an otherwise honest appropriation into a dishonest one. It is probable that the *mens rea* includes a requirement that the defendant must intend not merely to steal but also intend to use force in order to steal. Where the use of force is accidental, liability for robbery would not arise (Case 1).[17]

16.3 BURGLARY

Overview

There are two forms of burglary. One is committed upon entering a building, or an inhabited vehicle or vessel, or part thereof, as a trespasser, with one of a number of intentions, including theft. The other is committed when, whatever the initial intention, a person, having entered premises as a trespasser, then commits one of a number of offences, including theft.

Burglary accounts for around a fifth of all recorded crime according to the Crime Survey – around 450,000 cases in the year ending June 2013, a decrease of about 8 per cent from

---

[15] *Hale* (1978) 68 Cr App R 415.

[16] Cf. *Forrester* [1992] Crim LR 792 and 793, and see commentary at 794. The Court of Appeal upheld the defendant's conviction for robbery while quashing his conviction for assault on the ground that the jury should have been directed on the matter of self-defence.

[17] Smith and Hogan, op. cit. 565.

the previous year.[18] The true social impact of burglary is not adequately represented by this figure. Although, statistically, an adult may expect to suffer a burglary in the home only once every 40 years,[19] studies have shown that for some parts of the population the risks are disproportionately high, particularly those living in inner city areas, council and rented accommodation and flats.[20] Burglary accounts for a large proportion of general public anxiety concerning criminal activity. This reflects the degree of trauma typically suffered by victims. Indicative of this is the telling statistic that victims of burglary accounted for around 20 per cent of all people offered Victim Support.[21]

Section 9 of the Theft Act creates two separate offences of burglary. The focal cases reduce to entering premises as a trespasser **with intent to** steal or actually stealing having first entered premises as a trespasser. The former offence is a form of inchoate offence, the latter a consummated one. As will be seen from the precise wording of section 9, however, offences other than theft may form the meat of the burglar's nefarious sandwich. By section 9:

(1) A person is guilty of burglary if –
    (a) he enters any building or part of a building as a trespasser and with intent to commit any such offence as is mentioned in subsection (2) below; or
    (b) having entered any building or part of it as a trespasser he steals or attempts to steal anything in the building or that part of it or inflicts or attempts to inflict on any person therein any grievous bodily harm.
(2) The offences referred to in subsection (1)(a) above are offences of stealing anything in the building or part of the building in question, of inflicting on any person therein any grievous bodily harm or raping any person therein, and of doing unlawful damage to the building or anything therein.

Section 10 creates an aggravated form of burglary committed where the burglar carries with him a weapon of offence (including an imitation firearm) or any explosive. This carries life imprisonment as its maximum sentence. Following an amendment by the Criminal Justice Act 1991, s. 26(2) the maximum sentence for burglary varies according to whether the premises entered are a dwelling (fourteen years) or other premises (ten years). Burglary is triable either way where the meat of the offence is theft, but on indictment where the meat of the offence is triable only on indictment.[22]

16.4 COMMON FEATURES IN BURGLARY

In order to be guilty of burglary, whether under section 9(1)(a) or (b) or section 10, it must be shown that the accused entered a building or part of a building as a trespasser. The following questions must be asked, therefore, in connection with both forms of the offence:

(a) was there an entry? if yes,
(b) did the person entering enter as a trespasser? if yes,
(c) was the entry to a building or part of a building?

---

[18] 2013 Crime Survey for England and Wales.
[19] Based upon the estimate of a 2.5 risk of being burgled in the BCS 2007.
[20] M. Maguire and T. Bennett, *Burglary in a Dwelling*, London: Heinemann (1982). C. Mirrlees-Black, P. Mayhew and A. Percy, *The 1996 British Crime Survey*, HORS 19/96 (1996) ch. 5; *The 2000 British Crime Survey* by Kershaw, Budd *et al*. HOSB 18/00; *British Crime Survey 2009–10*.
[21] Victim Support *Annual Report* 2012 London: Victim Support. Significantly, however, in line with falling rates in property crime this is only half of the proportion in 1994.
[22] For example s. 18.

A Entry

At common law entry could be effected by a part of the body, however small. It could, and can, be effected via the innocent agency of a third party, animal or instrument.[23] Entry was not defined in the Act and might therefore be thought to encapsulate the common law meaning. This seems not to be the case. In *Collins* it was ruled that entry must be 'substantial'. In the later case of *Brown* this requirement was replaced with the hardly more meaningful requirement that it be 'effective'. It seems necessary that the insertion of part of the body should be in execution of the entry proper rather than accidental or preparatory to it. A person who inserts a hand for the purpose of unlocking the window-catch with his burglarious purpose to be effected on the other side of the building, is probably too far removed from the commission of the substantive offence to count as more than an attempter. To hold otherwise might offer to reduce attempted s. 9(1)(a) burglary almost to vanishing point.[24]

Beyond this, whether an 'effective' entry has occurred is apparently a question of fact to be decided by the jury. By common consent drawing distinctions between degrees of entry is a difficult enough task without delegating them to the jury.[25] For example, would it be an effective entry for the purpose of committing rape in the building that the accused's leg was over the window-sill?[26] A better solution would be for the question of entry to be determined by the old common law rule. The desirability of such a change is particularly obvious where theft is the 'meat' of the burglary charge.[27]

> **Case 2**
> Simon, spying an apple pie on a table in front of the baker's open window, stretches his hand inside and takes the pie.

Simon is guilty of section 9(1)(b) burglary **as a matter of law**. Logically, if Simon were apprehended just prior to picking up the pie, a conviction for section 9(1)(a) burglary is no less inappropriate, since entry (by his hand) for this unsuccessful theft is no less substantial and effective than for the successful theft. In other words, if Simon has entered as a trespasser for the purpose of s. 9(1)(b) he must equally have entered as a trespasser for the purpose of s. 9(1)(a).

B Entry as a trespasser

A person enters as a trespasser in two situations. First, where he enters without legal authority. This will generally mean without having the consent, express or implied, of the occupier, and without statutory authority. Since burglary is a criminal offence of full *mens rea*, a person does not **enter as a** trespasser if he believes he has authority to enter.[28] Second, where authority is exceeded. A police officer who enters a building under authority of a search warrant is guilty of burglary if he intends to steal.

1 Entry with occupier's consent

In deciding whether a person has entered as a trespasser, the first question to be considered is whether the occupier consented, expressly or impliedly, to the entry. The occupier is the person or persons legally entitled to exclude the entry of others. For most purposes this means

[23] For example a pair of extending tongs.
[24] *Boyle and Boyle* [1987] Crim LR 111.
[25] J.C. Smith (1997) para. 11-03; Griew (1995) 103; G. Williams *TCL* 840.
[26] Possibly so in the light of *Ryan* [1996] Crim LR 320.
[27] *Brown* [1985] Crim LR 212.
[28] *Collins* [1973] 1 QB 100 at 105 per Edmund-Davies LJ.

the owner or tenant or contractual licensee. The occupier's own guests and lodgers enter with the occupier's express consent. The occupier's family and their guests and friends will be present with the occupier's implied consent. So also will those entering under an emergency or in circumstances warranting the inference that the occupier would have consented. For example a neighbour who enters premises to put a fire out will enter with the occupier's implied consent.

It will be apparent that the status of an entrant to a building will not always be obvious. A particular problem is where the entrant enters under the apparent authority of someone who is not themselves the occupier, for example the spouse, partner, child or guest of the occupier. Under such circumstances the question to be asked is whether such a person has the occupier's implied authority to authorise the entry of the person in question.

The courts have not always observed the technicalities of the tort of trespass in burglary cases. In *Collins*, for example, the court assumed that a person, invited to enter by the occupier's daughter, automatically entered by the authority of the occupier unless that authority had been expressly refused. The defendant was a young man who climbed a ladder dressed only in his socks and sat on a young woman's window-ledge. His intention was to have intercourse with the girl whether she consented or not. He had no reason to suspect that this would be welcomed but as it turned out it was. The woman helped him into the room, and into her bed thinking he was her boyfriend paying her an ardent nocturnal visit. Later, however, while they were having intercourse the woman realised she had made a big mistake and that her bed-companion was not her boyfriend. The defendant was convicted of burglary. The key issue was whether the accused had entered as a trespasser. The Court of Appeal decided that to enter as a trespasser D must (1) enter without the express or implied permission of the occupier or a member of the occupier's household; (2) must know or be reckless that he is entering without the other's consent. On that basis his conviction for burglary was quashed. Although he may have entered premises with intent to commit rape, he did not do so as a trespasser. The court considered it 'unthinkable' that burglary could be committed by a person who was invited over the threshold by a member of the occupier's family. As Griew suggests, however, it is very far from 'unthinkable'.[29] This would be clear if the inviter had been a very young member of the family, or a weekend guest or lodger. A jury would clearly be entitled to conclude that a young child would have no implied (or apparent) authority to invite into the house a potential rapist or a rogue carrying a swag-bag over his shoulder. What would be unthinkable is that liability would be incurred even where A genuinely thought he had the owner's authority to enter.

2 Entering in excess of permission

Under the law of tort a person commits trespass not only where they enter without authority but also where, having entered under the authority either of the occupier or the law, they abuse their authority or exceed their permission.[30] If this occurs, the trespass begins at the time the abuse of authority began, not from the time of original entry. The practical effect of this is that a person who enters premises with the occupier's permission cannot be sued for trespass simply because he had it in mind to compromise the occupier's interests. The trespass will only begin when any abuse of authority begins.[31]

---

[29] Griew (1995) 99; cf. G. Williams (1983) 845–6.

[30] *Hickman* v *Maisey* [1900] 1 QB 752.

[31] There is a limited exception in the case of persons entering under authority of law, such as police officers, who enter premises and then abuse their authority by conducting an illegal search. In the latter case, as a concession to civil liberties, the trespass is deemed to begin at the time of first entry (*ab initio*), thus rendering the whole search unlawful. Even here however the doctrine has been criticised as unfair, involving a form of 'backdated' illegality; *Chic Fashions* v *Jones* [1968] 2 QB 299 per Lord Denning MR.

On the basis of *Collins* it might be thought that a similar doctrine operates in the criminal law also. The Court of Appeal gave no indication that, assuming Collins did enter under the occupier's authority, this authority would be in any way vitiated by Collins's ulterior motive. This reflects a literal reading of section 9(1). Liability is only incurred where a person enters . . . **as a** trespasser. It is not incurred simply because A later **becomes** a trespasser. Nevertheless in *Jones and Smith*,[32] another 'unthinkable' thing happened. A son who stole a television set from his parents' house was found guilty of burglary and his conviction affirmed on appeal, despite the fact that the son had a general licence to enter. The position was, no doubt, complicated by the fact that he was in cahoots with a friend who, *vis-à-vis* the parents, clearly had no authority to enter the house given the circumstances of the entry. That the friend was guilty of burglary, however, did not make the son guilty, except of course as an accessory. In reaching its conclusion the Court of Appeal formulated the following rule:

> a person is a trespasser for the purpose of s. 9(1)(b) of the Theft Act 1968 if he enters premises of another knowing that he is entering in excess of the permission that has been given to him to enter, providing the facts are known to the accused which enable him to realise that he is acting in excess of the permission given or that he is acting recklessly as to whether he exceeds that permission.[33]

This proposition has been generally taken to mean that a person who enters premises intending to commit an offence within the mischief of burglary, e.g. theft, is automatically guilty of burglary. This is so whether, as in *Jones and Smith*, the entrant has an open invitation to visit, or even is actually living with the occupier at the relevant time. Similarly a person will be guilty of s. 9(1)(a) burglary simply upon entering a shop if he enters intending to steal from it. This is far from the traditional compass of burglary which required proof of some form of 'breaking (in) and entering'. Although the 'breaking in' part was no doubt done away with by section 9 it seems reasonable to assume that it was still intended that the entering should be attended by circumstances of manifest criminality.[34] In fact, the rule's scope is yet wider:

Case 3

Arthur invites Lance, his friend, to dinner. Unknown to Arthur, Lance intends to use the opportunity afforded by Arthur tending the beef Wellington to make love to Gwen, his lover and Arthur's wife. Following their lovemaking Lance, still inflamed by desire, also steals Arthur's Frank Sinatra compact disc.

Lance knows that he is entering in excess of the permission that Arthur has granted him to enter. Applying the above rule, it seems that he has committed burglary. This extends the potential scope of section 9(1)(b) beyond the commonsense understanding of burglary. At the very least, it might be thought, the impact of *Jones and Smith* should be restricted to cases where the intention which vitiates his licence to enter is the intention to commit the offence supporting the charge of burglary.

---

[32] [1976] 1 WLR 672.
[33] At 676.
[34] Fletcher, writing before *Jones and Smith* was decided, assumed that s. 9 was designed with this ethic in mind (1978) 124–8; this is also Williams' strongly held opinion, *TCL* 847–50; cf. Griew (1995) 101–3.

C Building or part of a building

By section 9(4) a 'building' includes a vehicle or vessel constructed or adapted for human habitation, but is otherwise not defined. The general meaning attributable to building is wider than a dwelling, although this is clearly its focal meaning for the purpose of section 9. A consensus holds that a building must be some form of structure with a degree of permanence capable of being entered.[35] This includes barns, churches, shops, warehouses and even portable cabins such as freezer containers.[36] It excludes tents, but probably not sheds, garages and outbuildings. When a building is in the process of being built it will be a question of fact and degree whether it yet counts as a building for the purpose of section 9.[37]

1 Burglary from part of a building

Assuming the other parts of the offences are satisfied, burglary may be committed either upon

(i)   A entering a building as a trespasser or
(ii) A entering part of a building in respect of the entry of which part he is a trespasser.

It should be noted that a person who, having entered a building lawfully, thereafter enters part of a building with an intent to steal (or commit some other crime) in that part, will enter that part in excess of his licence and will therefore be a trespasser in respect of that entry. The upshot is that a person may be guilty of burglary even though his initial entry of the building was entirely lawful. However, to be captured by section 9 the prosecution will have to show a separate entry as a trespasser to part of (a separate part of) the building.

> **Case 4**
> A enters a shop to buy some food. While there he sees a handbag in a cloakroom. He enters the cloakroom to take the handbag.

A is guilty of section 9(1)(a) burglary if he fails to take the handbag, and of both section 9(1)(a) and (b) if he succeeds. Although he does not enter the shop as a trespasser, he does enter a defined part of the shop (the cloakroom) as a trespasser. It is in respect of this entry, therefore, that the relevant intent is formed or offence committed. What counts as a part of a building is a question of fact and degree. Clearly a room is a part of a building. It has been held that the till area behind the counter in a shop from which the public are excluded is also a (separate) part.[38] A person who enters this area to steal from a till is guilty, therefore, not only of theft but of burglary. On the other hand, it is unlikely, in shops such as supermarkets, that moving from one counter to another will be treated as moving from one part of the building to another. What seems necessary is that there is some definition to the area for it to count as a part of a building. That definition may be given by the structure of the building itself or by the occupier creating some form of defined 'exclusion zone' within the building. If the supermarket counters were in separate rooms, then, entry as a trespasser might well be established.

Another problem arises where A enters one part of a building to steal in another. If A enters the communal hall of a block of flats, intending to steal from flat 1, he has committed

---

[35] A.T.H. Smith 907; Griew (1995) 105; cf. Byles J in *Stevens* v *Gourley* (1859) 7 CB (NS) 99 at 112.
[36] *B and S* v *Leathley* [1979] Crim LR 314.
[37] J.C. Smith (2007) 11–14.
[38] *Walkington* [1979] 1 WLR 1169.

burglary since he has entered a building as a trespasser with intent to steal from the building, the flat being in the same building as the entrance hall. The problem would arise where A's initial entry to the building was lawful.

> **Case 5**
>
> A is the guest of the owner of flat 1. While there he decides to steal from flat 2. In order to do so, he has to return to the entrance hall and then gain entrance to flat 2 via flat 3.

The question arises whether A would be guilty of burglary

(i)   when he entered the entrance hall?
(ii) when he entered flat 3? or
(iii) when he entered flat 2?

The answer to the question requires a precise interpretation of section 9. The argument for (i) is that since he has theft in mind his entry of the hall is a trespass. However, he did not enter **the building** of which the hall is part as a trespasser since his initial entry to the building was lawful. As a result, A only entered the (entrance hall) **part** of the building as a trespasser. This means he does not commit burglary upon entering the hall because, by section 9(2), his intention must be to steal 'anything . . . in the part of the building in question'. Since he did not intend to steal from the entrance hall he is, then, guilty at most of attempted burglary. For the same reason it seems he is not guilty of burglary upon entering flat 3. Although he enters flat 3 as a trespasser he does not enter the flat intending to steal 'anything . . . in the part of the building in question'. A is guilty of burglary, then, when he enters flat 2.[39]

2 Inhabited vessels or vehicles

The requirement that the entry should be of a building or part of a building means that a person is not a burglar if he steals from a car or a bus. By section 9(4), however, even boats or vehicles come within the definition of 'buildings' if they are inhabited. If they are, a burglary can be committed even if the occupier is temporarily absent.

> **Case 6**
>
> Adam and Eve live in London. They own an ocean-going yacht moored in Southampton. The day before they set sail for France, Cain breaks into the yacht and steals a camera. The next day Adam and Eve sail to the Isle of Wight on the first leg of their journey. While they are on dry land and the boat is moored, Abel enters the yacht and steals a wallet.

The Act does not explain what meaning to attribute to 'inhabited'. As a result it is unclear whether a vessel or vehicle designed for habitation is inhabited whenever it is in regular use, whether or not it is being presently used,[40] or whether it is inhabited only when it is in the process of being used as a habitation.[41] The straightforward analysis is that Cain commits theft but not burglary. At the time the theft occurs the yacht is uninhabited. It is a boat when not in use as a floating home. It does not therefore count as a building for the purpose of s. 9(4). A similar analysis would be suitable if it was a caravan or camper van.

---

[39] See J.C. Smith (2007) 11–17–21.
[40] This is effectively Williams' (1983) position at 841; cf. though A.T.H. Smith 909.
[41] A.T.H. Smith 909; Griew (1995) 108.

These are only 'homes' when specifically appropriated for that purpose. Abel does commit burglary, however. At the time the theft occurs the yacht is inhabited, although Adam and Eve are not there at the time.

16.5 MODES OF COMMITTING BURGLARY

A Section 9(1)(a): entering with intent to commit certain offences

The nub of the section 9(1)(a) offence is the intention formed by the accused prior to entry. Section 9(1)(a) is typically committed with an ulterior intent of stealing. However, it may be committed in two other ways, namely entry as a trespasser

(i)   with intent to inflict grievous bodily harm,
(ii) with intent to do unlawful damage.

A conditional intent is sufficient so that a person who enters a building as a trespasser with the intention of stealing only if there is something valuable is guilty of burglary.[42] Additionally, where the jury is convinced the entrant entered with burglarious intent, but is unsure which offence was intended, a conviction is still permissible.[43]

   This form of burglary is notionally an inchoate offence since what is done is in preparation for the commission of a substantive offence. In effect, it allows for a conviction of someone who has it in mind to commit criminal damage even where the conduct of the accused is still in its preparatory stages. It should be noted that this offence does not appear in section 9(1)(b). This is understandable in the case of rape, since this offence can be charged in its own right without understating the seriousness of the defendant's conduct. It is less understandable in the case of criminal damage, as will be seen.

   The criminalisation of entering premises as a trespasser with the above purposes is justified on the basis that such conduct creates its own (psychic) harm. It is largely to counter this social mischief that burglary remains as a distinct aggravated form of theft, in which a term of imprisonment is the sentencing norm rather than the exception. In this important sense burglary is more than an inchoate crime but a consummated offence in its own right – a crime of aggressive intrusion. Accordingly, the decision in *Jones and Smith*[44] to allow liability in the absence of some act of manifest criminality is doubly unfortunate. Where the entry occasions no undue psychological discomfiture to the occupier and no theft or other offence has been committed, the basis for punishment is tenuous at best.

B Section 9(1)(b): committing certain offences having first entered as a trespasser

The specified offences contained in section 9(1)(b) differ from those in section 9(1)(a). Under section 9(1)(b), burglary is committed where, having entered as a trespasser, the entrant

(a)   steals or attempts to steal, or
(b)   inflicts or attempts to inflict grievous bodily harm.

---

[42] *A-G's References (Nos 1 and 2 of 1979)* [1979] 3 All ER 143.
[43] Williams *TCL* 842.
[44] Which is applicable to section 9(1)(a).

The notional reason for this distinction is that section 9(1)(b) offers little other than an evidential advantage to the prosecution in cases where a theft, say, can easily be proved but not an intention to steal formed prior to the entry. Looked at together, however, it is hard to resist the conclusion that section 9 is somewhat of a rag-bag with little obvious system to the offences included and excluded. Why, for example, if entering a building and stealing is an aggravated form of theft, is entering a building and causing criminal damage not an aggravated form of criminal damage? Would not most householders be more traumatised by returning to find their house smashed up than their stereo missing? Why, if attempting to inflict **grievous** bodily harm is sufficient for section 9(1)(b), is entry with intent to commit **actual** bodily harm not sufficient for section 9(1)(a)? Is this not within the general mischief of burglary?[45]

16.6 HANDLING

Overview

Handling stolen goods can occur in a number of different ways. The essential forms are receiving stolen goods and dealing with them. Receiving stolen goods occurs where the handler obtains possession or control of them. Dealing with stolen goods includes arranging to receive the goods or undertaking or assisting in their removal, disposal or realisation, or arranging to do so. Goods, for this purpose, include not only the goods originally stolen but also the proceeds, if any, and any other goods bought with the proceeds or otherwise representing them.

By section 22 Theft Act 1968:

(1) A person handles stolen goods if (otherwise than in the course of stealing) knowing or believing them to be stolen goods he dishonestly receives the goods, or dishonestly undertakes or assists in their removal, disposal or realisation by or for the benefit of another person, or if he arranges to do so.

There are four preconditions for a successful prosecution:

(1) the goods must have been stolen;
(2) the defendant must handle the goods;
(3) at the time of the handling of the goods the goods must remain stolen goods;
(4) at the time of handling the stolen goods, the defendant must be acting dishonestly and know or believe the goods to be stolen.

A *Actus reus*

1 Stolen goods

By section 24(4) stolen goods include goods obtained by blackmail or by deception within the meaning of section 15 Theft Act 1968. Section 34(2)(b) defines goods, largely in accordance with the definition of property in section 4, as including money and all other property except land other than things severed from the land by stealing.[46]

---

[45] Apparently a form of burglary may be committed without *mens rea* as to the infliction: *R v Wilson and Jenkins* [1983] 1 WLR 356 CA.
[46] The status of things in action in this context is uncertain and complicated and will not be dealt with here. For a discussion see A.T.H. Smith para. 30-06. See most recently *Forsyth* [1997] Crim LR 581 and Professor Sir John Smith's commentaries at 589–91 and 755.

By section 24(2) stolen goods include not only the goods themselves but also the proceeds and things obtained with the proceeds of any disposal or realisation of the goods or part thereof. For the purpose of the law of handling, therefore, a person may be guilty of handling stolen goods even if the thing handled has never been stolen.

Case 7

A steals a suitcase containing £100. He sells the suitcase to X, who knows it is stolen, for £5. He gives the £5 to Y to satisfy a debt. Y knows that the £5 is the proceeds of the sale of the stolen suitcase. Y buys cigarettes with the £5 and gives one to T. With the £100 A buys a coat and a hat. He gives the coat to Z and the hat to W. Z but not W knows their gift has been bought with the stolen money.

For the purpose of section 22 the following goods are stolen in Case 7: (1) a suitcase, (2) £100, (3) £5, (4) cigarettes, (5) a coat, (6) a hat. A does not handle the suitcase by selling it to X unless the sale is done for the benefit of Y rather than his own benefit. X does commit handling by receiving. Y handles the £5 by receiving it. Having the *mens rea* for handling she is guilty of handling. Y does not handle the cigarettes simply by smoking them or by giving one to T.[47] T will commit the *actus reus* of handling by receiving the cigarette and will be guilty of receiving if he has *mens rea*. Z is guilty of receiving a stolen coat. W has committed the *actus reus* of receiving but, lacking *mens rea*, is not guilty of the offence.[48]

2 Handling

A considerable degree of overlap exists between handling and theft. Many cases of handling will also be cases of theft. This is most obvious in the form of handling known as receiving where the handler receives another's (now stolen) property dishonestly, typically for the purpose of resale. This overlap is not necessarily troublesome since theft carries a lesser maximum sentence (seven years) than handling (fourteen years). Prosecutors will not necessarily rush, therefore, to charge theft where handling is the more natural charge,[49] although the present prosecutorial trend is 'down charging'.

A problem could arise if cases which were naturally theft could also be treated as cases of handling. The higher maximum sentence for handling was justified on the ground that many handlers are professional 'fences' who thus serve to secure, maintain and strengthen the economy of stealing.[50] It would be unfortunate, given this justification, if common pilferers could be caught by the handling provisions. Although by section 22(1) a thief does not commit handling simply by stealing the goods he may, however, handle goods he himself has stolen where he sells or otherwise disposes of the goods for the benefit of others as well as himself, including an accomplice or 'fence'.[51]

In practice it may be impossible to prove that the accused came by the property by stealing it – only that he is in possession of it. In such circumstances the prosecution might prefer to charge handling only. Where they do so the Court of Appeal has said that it is not necessary for the jury to be sure that the accused did not come by the property through stealing it, or even to be made aware of the provision. In effect, a petty thief in possession can be charged and convicted as a handler.[52]

---

[47] See *Bloxham*, below.
[48] Cf. *A-G's Reference (No. 4 of 1979)* (1980) 71 Cr App R 341.
[49] CLRC 8th Report Cmnd 2977 (1996) para. 132. Cf. P. Darbyshire, op. cit. 628–32.
[50] CLRC 8th Report (1966); see generally J. Hall, *Theft, Law and Society*, Indianapolis: Bobbs-Merrill (1952).
[51] Below.
[52] *Cash* [1985] QB 801.

(a) Forms of handling

A quick perusal of this section will suffice to show that handling can be committed a number of ways.[53] Most of them reduce to some form of dealing with stolen goods which is converted into handling upon proof of the relevant *mens rea*. These can be broken into five sub-types:

(i)   receiving goods;
(ii) arranging to receive stolen goods;
(iii) undertaking the retention, removal, disposal or realisation of stolen goods by or for the benefit of another person;
(iv) assisting in the retention, removal, disposal or realisation of stolen goods by or for the benefit of another;
(v)   arranging to undertake or assist, as above.

(i) Receiving goods

This requires ownership, possession or control to be transferred to the receiver, as where a dishonest shopkeeper buys them for resale. A person does not receive simply by inspecting the goods or unloading them, since possession or control is not thereby transferred. Neither, it seems, is it receiving for a person to find and take possession of stolen goods since there is no 'receipt'.[54] A person is also not guilty of receiving if he takes stolen goods innocently, discovers them to be stolen and subsequently deals with them. He may, however, be guilty of a different form of handling.

> **Case 8**
> A asks B to look after his briefcase. B agrees and takes possession. A then tells B that the briefcase is stolen and asks him to hide it. B does so.

B is not guilty of handling by receiving since he lacked *mens rea* on receipt of the goods. He will, however, be guilty of handling by undertaking the retention of stolen goods for the benefit of another person.[55]

(ii) Arranging to receive stolen goods

This form of handling does not require the transfer of possession, ownership or control. It may be effected by concluding an agreement to receive, as where A offers to give (or sell) B a stolen fridge and B tells her to deliver it the next morning.

(iii) Undertaking the retention, removal, disposal or realisation of stolen goods by or for the benefit of another person

This comprises four separate forms of handling, all of which can only be committed where the relevant conduct is performed **by or for the benefit of another person**. Where the removal, disposal etc. is performed for the sole benefit of the remover or disposer, etc. (this form of) handling is not committed.

> **Case 9**
> A buys a car. Discovering later that it is stolen, he sells it on to C.

---

[53] Eighteen, apparently, but I have not counted.
[54] See *Haider* 22 March 1985 CA (unreported); cf. *Kelly* 19 November 1984 CA No. 5624/B1/83 cited in Griew (1995) 244.
[55] See below.

A does not handle stolen goods. Although A is knowingly undertaking the realisation of stolen goods he is not doing so for the benefit of another.[56] Compare the following case.

> **Case 10**
> X steals Y's car. He sells it to V, a *bona fide* purchaser, for £10,000. V sells it to D, his daughter, for £5,000. D then discovers the car is stolen and sells the car to a garage for £10,000 intending to return the extra £5,000 to V.

D is guilty of handling the car, assuming the jury find the transaction to be dishonest. She has undertaken the realisation of the car for the benefit of V. It should be noted that it seems unnecessary that the beneficiary of the realisation should himself be the thief or even the handler of the car, as long as the realisation of the car was undertaken, at least partly, to benefit him. This conclusion is demanded by a literal interpretation of the Act, although, regrettably, it runs counter to the policy of the Act not to criminalise innocent purchasers of stolen property for dealing with it after discovering it to be stolen.[57]

Retention means 'keeping possession of'. A person who undertakes to keep stolen things at his warehouse for the benefit of another undertakes their retention. The meaning of **removal** is self-evident. A person who undertakes to move stolen goods to a hiding-place or from one safe hiding-place to another undertakes the removal of stolen goods. **Disposal** means getting rid of, whether by destruction, gift, or dumping, as where a person undertakes to get rid of the (stolen) suitcase in which the property stolen was first dis-covered. **Realisation** means converting the goods into money or money's worth. A crooked auctioneer who puts stolen goods in a sale the proceeds from which will be given to the transferor undertakes their realisation.

(iv) *Assisting in the retention, removal, disposal or realisation of stolen goods by or for the benefit of another*

This form of handling will occur when the accused helps another who himself has under-taken the retention, disposal etc. in that undertaking. That other may be the thief himself or another handler or an innocent party.

In *Kanwar* the Court of Appeal defined assistance (in the context of handling by retention), as something done (intentionally and dishonestly) for the purpose of enabling the goods to be retained, etc. This was effected, in the instant case, by giving misleading information to the police about the provenance of the goods for the purpose of putting them off the scent. It would not be enough simply to use them or say nothing about them if, say, stolen goods were brought home by a family member.[58] Other examples of such conduct (in the case of retention) would be concealing or helping to conceal the goods, or doing something to make them more difficult to find or identify, giving the name of a valuer in the case of assisting in the realisation of stolen goods, and of a haulage contractor in the case of assisting in their removal.

(v) *Arranging to undertake or assist*

Compare 'arranging to receive' (above).

---

[56] Even the purchaser: *Bloxham* [1983] 1 AC 109.
[57] See also s. 3(2).
[58] *Kanwar* (1982) 75 Cr App R 87 per Cantley J; *Sanders* (1982) 75 Cr App R 84.

3 The goods must be stolen at the time that they are handled

Goods are stolen goods for the purpose of section 22 only where, having been stolen, they remain stolen at the time the handling occurs. By section 24(3) goods cease to be regarded as stolen goods in two situations:

(a) *After they have been restored to the person from whom they were stolen or to other lawful possession or custody*

Whether they have been restored may be a difficult question to answer, particularly where the police have located the goods but do not seize possession of them in the hope that they will trap the thief or handler. Merely locating the goods will not restore them to lawful possession but assuming control over them will do so. Whether such control has been assumed or not depends upon the assuming agent's intentions. Goods will remain stolen if the intention was to wait before deciding what to do with them. Goods will be restored to lawful custody if the intention was to take charge of them so that they could not be taken. Thus a police officer who removes the rotor arm from a car in which stolen goods are stored will restore the goods to lawful custody if he does so to protect the goods, but will not restore the goods to lawful custody if he removes the rotor arm merely to ensure the driver cannot get away.[59] The consequence of restoring once stolen goods to lawful possession or custody is that any further dealings with the goods by the thief or handler will not count as a handling. However, a person who takes possession of once-stolen goods may still be guilty of the substantive offence of handling where he has earlier 'arranged' to handle them.

(b) *After the person from whom they were stolen and any other person claiming through him have otherwise ceased as regards those goods to have any right to restitution in respect of the theft*

This covers the situation where B's goods are obtained by A under a contract voidable by deception. Such goods may still be 'stolen goods' even though ownership may have passed. A person who receives the goods under such circumstances may be guilty of handling with the appropriate *mens rea*. If that same contract is affirmed by B on discovery of the deception, the goods then cease to be stolen. Any further dealings with the goods cannot then amount to handling.[60] The subsection applies to any other situation where the owner loses the right to have the property restored, for example they are sold by the villain in market overt or under other circumstances which bring into play an exception to the rule *nemo dat*.[61]

B *Mens rea*

1 Knowledge or belief

A person handles stolen goods only if he knows or believes the goods to be stolen at the time of handling the goods. In the case of receiving goods, therefore, it is necessary to pinpoint exactly when the goods were reduced into A's possession.[62] A person who initially comes by stolen goods innocently will not subsequently, on discovery of the true state of affairs, be guilty of handling them unless he commits a subsequent act of handling. Retaining

---

[59] *Attorney-General's Reference (No. 1 of 1974)* [1974] 2 All ER 899.

[60] But may, if the person dealing with them believes them to be stolen, be guilty of an attempt.

[61] Quaere, whether it also applies where the goods are converted into other goods in such a way as to extinguish the original owner's rights, for example oil paints are stolen; A buys a picture painted with the stolen paint; see A.T.H. Smith 956–7.

[62] *R v Brook* [1993] Crim LR 455.

the goods for one's own use after discovering the truth will not be such an act since it is not done for the benefit of another. This may be theft, however, unless he obtained the goods by purchase and in good faith.[63] An example where a handling will occur after an initial innocent receipt is where A agrees to store goods for B, discovers that they are stolen but nevertheless helps B to move, sell or retain them,[64] since A deals with the goods for B's benefit.

The mental element is knowledge or belief that the goods are stolen. A person knows that goods are stolen only when he witnesses the theft or is told by someone with first-hand knowledge.[65] Otherwise he may believe the goods to be stolen or suspect that the goods maybe stolen. Belief as opposed to knowledge exists where the evidence supports the inference that they are stolen and the accused actually takes this inference.[66] The accused does not take this inference if his mind is open to the possibility that they might not be stolen. Suspecting that goods might well be stolen is not the same as believing that they are stolen. Even believing that there is a probability or even high probability that the goods are stolen is apparently not enough.[67] A person must believe that it is virtually certain that the goods are stolen to believe that they are stolen. Elsewhere in the criminal law such a belief is treated as equivalent to knowledge. As one commentator has remarked, this means in effect that 'knowing or believing' is being interpreted by the courts to mean 'knowing or knowing'. The belief part of the provision is thus rendered effectively redundant.[68] The reason for this restriction is presumably to ensure that trading is not inhibited by the possibility of punishment for taking a gamble on goods which one suspects might be stolen.[69]

(a) Closing one's mind to the obvious

Where the facts are such that the only reasonable conclusion is that the goods are stolen, the jury may of course refuse to credit the accused's story that he did not believe them to be stolen. Where the circumstances indicate clearly that the goods are stolen, the accused may say that he suspected the goods might be stolen but refused to consider whether they were or not – in effect closing his mind to the obvious.

> **Case 11**
> B offers to sell A a gold ingot in a pub, saying 'I could tell you where I got this but you wouldn't want to know'. A says 'I don't want to know. I don't even want to think about it.' And he does not think about it.

On the face of it, assuming the jury credit the story, A's state of mind should be enough to ground liability as it is a form of 'constructive knowledge'. The accused forms a suspicion and then stops himself from reaching any further conclusion. The only plausible reason for doing this is to prevent himself from forming the (unwelcome) positive belief which further inquiry or reflection would have produced. He would hardly have shut his mind to

---

[63] Section 3(2).
[64] *Kanwar* above.
[65] *Hall* (1985) 81 Cr App R 260 at 264.
[66] See previous note.
[67] *Reader* (1977) 66 Cr App R 33.
[68] A.T.H. Smith (1994). See below. Cf. S. Shute, 'Knowledge and Belief in the Criminal Law' in Shute and Simester (eds), *Criminal Law Theory: Doctrines of the General Part*, Oxford: OUP (2002).
[69] J.R. Spencer, 'Handling, Theft and the *Mala Fide* Purchaser' [1985] Crim LR 92, also at 440; G. Williams, 'Handling, Theft and the Purchaser Who Takes a Chance' [1985] Crim LR 432. For a general discussion see A.T.H. Smith (1994) para. 30–49–54.

the possibility that the gold was in fact brass.[70] It has been held, however,[71] that such a state of mind is only evidence from which the jury may infer the requisite belief – a puzzling conflation of 'open-minded' suspicion with a positive belief, which latter cannot be entertained by an 'open' mind.

(b) *Proving knowledge or belief*

Section 27(3) provides evidential assistance to the prosecution especially geared to counter the plausible denial of knowledge by those who make a living out of handling stolen property.[72] If the accused is in business as a legitimate trader, it will often be difficult for the prosecution to convince the jury, who know nothing about his history, that he knew or believed the goods to be stolen. He thus has a built-in immunity against conviction. The section provides, therefore, that where the accused is charged with handling, the prosecution may produce evidence for the purpose of proving knowledge or belief that the accused has previously been found in possession of stolen goods and/or has previous convictions for both handling and theft. More specifically the evidence which may be adduced is as follows:

(a) evidence that he has had in his possession, or had undertaken or assisted in the retention, removal, disposal or realisation of stolen goods from any theft taking place not earlier than twelve months before the offence charged; and
(b) provided that seven days' notice in writing has been given to him of the intention to prove the conviction, evidence that he has within the five years preceding the date of the offence charged been guilty of theft or of handling stolen goods.

It should be noted that paragraph (a) does not require evidence of a **conviction** for handling in the previous twelve months. The idea behind this is that the coincidence of being charged more than once in a twelve-month period with an offence is unusually probative. If a rat is there to be smelt the jury should be allowed to smell it. This policy is, no doubt, quite justifiable if we can assume that the accused escaped justice on the previous occasion but there may be equally plausible explanations – not least that the police are barking up the wrong tree or that they are acting oppressively. The clear danger presented by the provision is that it may not adequately differentiate the professional fence, and the honest second hand dealer who trades in an area where every other item offered maybe the proceeds of last night's robbery. Such dealers have to make a living as well as the august merchants of New Bond Street. It goes without saying that such a rule of evidence may encourage oppressive policing.

Where the defendant has a conviction for theft or handling, the prosecution may adduce evidence from the previous five years, rather than the twelve months of paragraph (a).[73] It should be noted in this context that only evidence of convictions for theft and handling are admissible. The exclusion of swindling suggests that only experience of stealing (as opposed to swindling) is thought likely to alert people to suspicious circumstances surrounding the disposal of stolen goods.

Apparently prosecutors hesitate to rely on the provisions in section 27(3) because of understandable reluctance on the part of trial judges to allow such evidence where its probative value is outweighed by its prejudicial effect.[74] It is obviously an easy inference to

---

[70] See Griew (1995) para. 15–31–33; cf. A.T.H. Smith (1994) para. 30–52.
[71] *Griffiths* (1974) 60 Cr App R 14.
[72] Commonly known as 'fences'.
[73] Section 27(3)(b).
[74] *Knott* [1973] Crim LR 36; cf. *Davies* [1953] 1 QB 489.

draw from a previous conviction for dishonesty that the defendant is a crook. Clearly it is important that judges ensure that juries use the evidence only to counterbalance what may be their natural inclination to assume that the defendant was undone by inexperience or gullibility.[75]

2 Dishonesty

The test for dishonesty in handling is the theft test as laid down in *Ghosh*. Cases where goods are deliberately handled so as to restore the goods to lawful custody are an obvious example of an honest handling.[76] Section 2 of the Theft Act does not apply to handling, which has the surprising effect of leaving the question of the honesty of the accused, who handles goods which he believes to be his own goods, to the jury. In such cases one assumes that the judge will give the jury a very pointed direction not to find the defendant dishonest. The *Ghosh* test does seem to raise some problems in the context of handling, particularly in the light of the unavailability of section 2.

> **Case 12**
> A is seeking to buy a fishing rod. He is told by B to go to the local Sunday car boot sale where there is a regular stall devoted to fishing rods. B tells A that the rods are cheap because they are all stolen. A buys a rod from the stall.

Assuming A believes B's assertion, the question of A's dishonesty is a matter for the individual jury. Even if A confidently believes, for example, that the original owner of the rod could never be located, the jury may convict if they think his conduct is dishonest and that A knew this. They might do this if they think that, as an issue of general morality, it is wrong to buy things one believes to be stolen.[77] On the other hand, the jury might well decide the case on the basis that A is not dishonest because, *vis-à-vis* the owner, A is doing nothing which he thinks can injure his interests. Or they may give A the benefit of the doubt if he says that he did not realise other people would consider his conduct dishonest. There is clearly scope for different juries to take different views of objectively similar conduct.

Summary

Robbery is committed when force or the threat of force is used in the course of committing theft. The force must be used immediately before or at the time of committing the theft and be used for the purpose of committing the theft. The courts have interpreted this to include force used immediately after the theft where this is used to effect an escape. The force does not have to be used against the possessor of the property but it must be directed against a person rather than the property concerned. However, force used against the property may suffice if it is transmitted into force experienced by the person wearing, bearing or carrying it. The *mens rea* for robbery is the *mens rea* for the included theft. It is a defence, therefore, that force was used to effect a temporary appropriation or that the appropriation was in support of a claim of right or was otherwise not dishonest.

There are two forms of burglary. Common to both forms are the following elements: the defendant must

---

[75] See generally R. Munday, 'Handling the Evidential Exception' [1988] Crim LR 345.
[76] *Matthews* [1950] 1 All ER 137.
[77] Cf. *Roberts* (1987) 84 Cr App R 117.

(a) enter a building, or an inhabited vehicle or vessel, or part thereof, and

(b) he must make the entry to the building etc. or part thereof as a trespasser.

Section 9(1)(a) burglary is committed where these elements are present and the defendant intends, at the time of entering, to steal, inflict grievous bodily harm or do criminal damage. Section 9(1)(b) is committed where, whether or not he has such intention on entry, the defendant having entered the building etc. therein steals, attempts to steal, or inflicts or attempts to inflict grievous bodily harm. Entry for the purpose of both forms must be effective. What this means is unclear and is a matter for the jury. A person enters as a trespasser if he does not have the occupier's express or implied licence to enter, and either knows or is reckless as to this fact. A person entering with the express permission of a member of the occupier's family will generally enter under the occupier's implied licence. A person entering under the express or implied licence of the occupier nevertheless enters as a trespasser if he intends to commit an offence and, possibly, even if he enters in breach of the terms upon which the licence is granted.

Handling stolen goods can occur in a number of different ways. The essential forms are receiving stolen goods and dealing with them. Receiving stolen goods occurs where the handler obtains possession or control of them. Dealing with stolen goods includes arranging to receive the goods or undertaking or assisting in their removal, disposal or realisation, or arranging to do so. Dealing with stolen goods is only handling if it is done for the benefit of some person other than the person dealing. It will not be handling by A if A sells stolen goods to B simply to make a profit for himself. Goods include not only the goods originally stolen but also the proceeds, if any, and any other goods bought with the proceeds or otherwise representing them. Goods are also stolen for the purpose of handling when they are obtained as a result of deception or blackmail. The *mens rea* for handling is knowledge or belief, at the time of receiving or dealing with the goods, that the goods are stolen. A belief that they are probably or even very probably stolen is not the same as a belief that they are stolen. Such a belief will only exist where the handler believes that it is virtually certain that the goods are, in fact, stolen. This rule effectively obliterates the distinction between knowledge and belief.

Further reading

Ashworth, A.J., 'Robbery Re-assessed' [2002] Criminal Law Review 851.

Mitchell, B., 'Multiple Wrongdoing and Offence Structure: a Plea for Consistency and Fair Labelling' (2001) MLR 393.

Ormerod, D. and Williams, D., *Smith's Law of Theft*, Oxford: OUP (2007).

17 Criminal damage

Overview

There are two offences, namely criminal damage simple and criminal damage endangering life. Criminal damage simple, which includes arson, is committed when a person intentionally or recklessly damages property belonging to another. Aggravated criminal damage is committed where a person damages property (typically by fire) either intending to endanger life or being reckless as to that prospect.

17.1 INTRODUCTION

Most offences involving the causing of damage to property are contained in the Criminal Damage Act 1971. This forms, in effect, a code complementary to that of the Theft Act and whose main concept – property belonging to another – is shared with that Act. As with the Theft Act, the codifying Act replaced a cumbersome and antiquated set of provisions[1] with a new and comprehensive reforming code. This time it was the Law Commission whose report and proposals were relied upon.[2]

There are two main offences, namely criminal damage simple and criminal damage endangering life. Where the criminal damage takes the form of arson it is charged separately as arson. In cases involving mixed charges of criminal damage and arson, juries must be specifically directed on both charges.[3] In effect, arson operates as a third offence and, like criminal damage endangering life, is punishable by a maximum of life imprisonment. Simple criminal damage is punishable by imprisonment for a maximum of ten years.[4] The offences are triable either way, although in practice only the most serious cases are dealt with on indictment.

The Crime Survey for England and Wales revealed over half million recorded cases of criminal damage and arson in the year ending March 2013.

17.2 CRIMINAL DAMAGE

The simple form of criminal damage is defined in section 1(1):

> A person who without lawful excuse destroys or damages any property belonging to another intending to destroy or damage any such property or being reckless as to whether any such property would be destroyed or damaged shall be guilty of an offence.

The constituent elements of the offence, complementing substantially that of theft, are:

(1) a destroying or damaging;
(2) the thing destroyed or damaged must be property;
(3) the property destroyed or damaged must belong to another;

---

[1] Contained in the Malicious Damage Act 1861.
[2] Law Commission No. 29 *Criminal Law: Report on Offences of Damage to Property*, London: HMSO (1970) (here after Law Com. No. 29 (1970)). The Theft Acts were the work of the Criminal Law Revision Committee.
[3] *R v Booth* [1999] Crim LR 144.
[4] Unless taking the form of arson.

(4) intention or recklessness as to the prospect of such damage or destruction;

(5) absence of lawful excuse.

A *Actus reus*

1 Destroys or damages

Used in the alternative these words indicate the potential scope of the offence. 'Destroy' adds nothing to 'damage' save to indicate its furthest reaches. Breaking the lead of a pencil 'damages' it. Demolishing a house 'destroys' (and 'damages') it. Assuming both count as property belonging to another, both deeds constitute the *actus reus* of criminal damage.

What it is to 'damage' property is not defined in the Act. In *Morphitis* v *Salmon* it was said that in each case it was a question of fact and degree.[5] This is probably wrong. While judgements of degree will be involved in determining whether a given harm counts as criminal damage, this judgement will be made by the **judge** rather than the **tribunal of fact**.[6] Trivial harms do not count as criminal damage but the amount of harm which counts as trivial depends upon the thing harmed. Adulterating milk with water is damage.[7] Writing on a parking sign is criminal damage.[8] Scratching a scaffold bar is not damage because neither value nor usefulness is affected. It would be different if the property scratched was a piece of furniture or a car.

(a) *Temporary impairment of usefulness*

Criminal damage can be of various kinds, including 'not only permanent or temporary physical harm but also permanent or temporary impairment of its value or usefulness'. On this basis it was said that the dismantling of a scaffold barrier in a road would count as criminal damage, although the individual parts were undamaged.[9] This is consistent with pre-1971 Act decisions in which machines have been held damaged by the removal of parts necessary for the machine to work.[10]

It seems that 'impairing' the value or usefulness of property requires some actual change in the property itself to be effected. In *Drake* v *DPP* it was held that immobilising a car by the use of a wheel-clamp was not damage to the car, which required 'some intrusion into the integrity of the object', whatever that might mean. Sir John Smith has argued that wheel-clamping should count as criminal damage on the ground that 'if the car can be damaged by removing something, it seems logical that it can be damaged by adding something. The effect of attaching the clamp is no less drastic than removing the rotor arm'.[11] This argument sits uneasily with the assertion in Smith and Hogan that property is not damaged merely by a denial of its use, as in the case of theft of door or ignition keys, 'even though the owner may be put to expense before he can put the house or car to their intended uses'.[12] Adopting their words, 'if a car cannot be damaged by removing the ignition key it seems logical that it cannot be damaged by adding a wheel-clamp'. It is submitted that such a denial of use should always amount to criminal damage where normal use cannot be restored without significant remedial attention, particularly where this will itself involve the commission of criminal damage:

[5] Also *Cox* v *Riley* (1986) 83 Cr App Rep 54.
[6] Smith and Hogan, op. cit. 696.
[7] *Roper* v *Knott* [1898] 1 QB 868.
[8] *Seray-Wurie* v *DPP* [2012] EWHC 208 (Admin).
[9] *Morphitis* v *Salmon* [1990] Crim LR 48 at 49.
[10] *Fisher* (1865) LR 1 CCR 7. Cf. *Tacey* (1821) Russ & Ry 452.
[11] *Lloyd* v *DPP* [1991] Crim LR 904 at 906.
[12] Cf. *Henderson and Batley* (1984) unreported.

Case 1
Adam, a practical joker, steals Eve's front door key late at night, knowing that she will not be able to enter the house without breaking a window, which she duly does.

It is suggested that Adam commits criminal damage at the earliest when he steals the key, and at the latest when Eve herself, as an innocent agent, breaks the window.[13]

Case 2
Adam, a car-park attendant, places a large sticker on Eve's front windscreen informing her that she is illegally parked. Eve can only remove the sticker by leaving an opaque, sticky residue on the windscreen.

For reasons consistent with the analysis of Case 1 it is submitted that placing the sticker on the windscreen is criminal damage since it cannot be removed without the car suffering a 'temporary impairment of its usefulness'.[14]

It is not always necessary to show some form of impairment of value or usefulness. Temporary or permanent changes of appearance or structural integrity of a more than trivial nature will suffice. In *Hardman* v *Chief Constable of Avon and Somerset Constabulary*[15] it was said that soluble pavement graffiti was criminal damage where it necessitated the expense of removal by high-pressure water jet.[16] Other cases have not insisted upon this criterion of expensive remedial action. In *Roe* v *Kingerlee*[17] mud graffiti daubed on the walls of a cell was held to be criminal damage even though it was easily removed by water. On the other hand, spitting on a policeman's uniform was not criminal damage,[18] presumably because both the degree of interference and the action necessary to remedy the interference was trivial. It would be different in the case of more refined clothing where dry-cleaning would be necessary.

(b) *Computer hacking*
By s. 3(6) Computer Misuse Act 1990: 'for the purpose of the Criminal Damage Act 1971 a modification of the contents of a computer shall not be regarded as damaging any computer or computer storage medium unless its effect on that computer or computer storage medium impairs its physical condition'. This means, for example, that computer hackers who erase or modify information held on a computer's hard or soft disks are not guilty of criminal damage.[19]

2 Property
Section 10(1) defines property in terms very similar to those in the Theft Act 1968. Where they differ reflects the different purposes of the two Acts.

In this Act 'property' means property of a tangible nature, whether real or personal, including money and –

[13] See discussion on *Bourne, Cogan and Leak* below, pp. 588–91.
[14] Cf. commentary to *Drake* v *DPP* [1994] Crim LR 855 at 856.
[15] [1986] Crim LR 330.
[16] Cf. *Blake* v *DPP* [1993] Crim LR 587.
[17] [1986] Crim LR 735; cf. *Fancy* [1980] Crim LR 171.
[18] *A (A Juvenile)* v *R* [1978] Crim LR 689.
[19] Reversing *Whitely* (1991) 93 Cr App R 25. This will be an offence under s. 3(1) of the 1990 Act. Embodied in Police and Justice Act 2006.

(a) including wild creatures which have been tamed or are ordinarily kept in captivity, and any other wild creatures or their carcasses if, but only if, they have been reduced into possession which has not been lost or abandoned or are in the course of being reduced into possession; but

(b) not including mushrooms growing wild on any land or flowers, fruit or foliage of a plant growing wild on any land. For the purposes of this section 'mushroom' includes any fungus and 'plant' includes any shrub or tree.

The significant differences between this section and the equivalent Theft Act definition is that while land cannot generally be stolen, it can be damaged or destroyed like other property. Indeed, arson is generally committed against land. On the other hand 'intangible property', which can be stolen, is not property for the purposes of criminal damage. One cannot 'destroy' or 'damage' a milk quota, say by having it cancelled. Finally, wild mushrooms, flowers, etc. cannot be the subject-matter of criminal damage. Presumably felling an entire tree, or digging up an entire shrub, will be criminal damage since it will not count as mere 'foliage' of a 'plant'[20] growing wild on the land.[21] Digging up an entire mushroom bed would also seem to count as criminal damage, but to the land itself, rather than the mushrooms.

3 Belonging to another

As with theft, only property belonging to another can be the subject-matter of simple criminal damage. A person who smashes up his car so as to defraud his insurance company commits no offence under section 1. With respect to criminal damage endangering life this requirement does not apply, as we shall see.

By section 10(2):

(2) Property shall be treated as belonging to any person –
    (a) having custody or control of it;
    (b) having in it any proprietary right or interest (not being an equitable interest arising only from an agreement to grant or transfer an interest); or
    (c) having a charge.

(3) Where property is subject to a trust, the person to whom it belongs shall be treated as including any person having a right to enforce the trust.

Once again, this definition is similar to that obtaining in theft.[22] As with theft a person with a proprietary interest in property may commit the offence if that property also 'belongs to another' for the purpose of section 10(2) or (3).

Case 3
A, a tenant in a temper, closes the glass front door of the flat let to him by B with such ferocity that the glass breaks.

Case 4
A, a landlord in a temper, closes the glass front door of a flat let to B with such ferocity that the glass breaks.

[20] A tree.
[21] G. Williams *TCL* (1983) 905–6.
[22] For elaboration see above.

> **Case 5**
> A lends B his car for a week while the latter's is being mended. One night at a party which both A and B are attending, B gets drunk. In order to prevent B from driving home, A removes the rotor arm from the car.

In each of these cases A has damaged property belonging to another. In Cases 3 and 4 the door 'belongs' to B by virtue of his proprietary interest. In Case 5 the car belongs to B by virtue of his custody of the car. This is not necessarily to say, in any of these cases, that A is guilty of criminal damage since the prosecution must prove *mens rea*[23] and the absence of a lawful excuse. This should prove difficult in Case 5.

B *Mens rea*

By section 1(1), Criminal Damage Act the *mens rea* for criminal damage is intention or recklessness. In *Smith* it was held that where intentional criminal damage is charged, intention must be established as to all the elements of the offence including the fact that the property damaged belongs to another. A person who intentionally damages property he thinks is his alone does not intentionally damage property belonging to another.[24] On the other hand it is no answer to a charge of criminal damage that D did not know that his actions constituted criminal damage. This was the unsuccessful argument of the defendant in *Seray-Wurie* v *DPP*, who claimed that he did not realise that drawing with marker pen on parking signs constituted damage to the signs.[25]

Recklessness in this context means subjective recklessness, *Caldwell* having been overruled by *R* v *G*.[26] The defendant must be shown to have been aware of a risk of causing damage and it was, in the circumstances known to him, unreasonable to take the risk.

> **Case 6**
> Adam, wishing to claim on his buildings insurance policy sets fire to his own house. The fire spreads and damages the house of his neighbour, Eve.

Adam is not guilty of criminal damage in relation to his own house. He may, however be guilty of criminal damage in relation to Eve's house if the jury are satisfied that he was aware of a risk of causing damage and that it was an unreasonable risk to take.

The problems posed by a narrow notion of subjective fault for criminal damage in particular, the quintessential crime of thoughtlessness, have been discussed above. However, in practice it is unlikely that case outcomes will differ appreciably following the overruling of *Caldwell*. If D claims that he was unaware of the risk of causing damage the jury will usually not credit this if the risk was an obvious one. In Case 6 for example the jury would be unlikely to believe Adam, if he made such a claim and his house was semi-detached or otherwise close to that of Eve. The real benefit of the change will be seen in relation to those such as the defendants in *Elliot* v *C*[27] and *Stephenson*,[28] who are young, mentally abnormal

---

[23] So A, in Case 4, could escape liability if he did not realise his tenant had a property interest. Cf. *Smith*, below.
[24] *Smith* [1974] QB 354.
[25] [2012] EWHC 208 (Admin).
[26] *Caldwell* [1982] AC 341; *R* v *G* [2004] AC 1034.
[27] (1983) 1 WLR 939.
[28] [1979] QB 695.

or of limited intelligence or experience where such a claim will carry plausibility. Moreover, the Courts will retain the flexibility to address the more obviously blameworthy examples of causing damage without awareness by directing juries that, if not satisfied that the accused was conscious of the risk, recklessness can nevertheless be established where the accused closed his 'mind to the obvious'. There are signs that such a direction may fill much of the culpability gap left exposed by G. In *Booth* v *CPS*, for example, the Magistrates found that a person who ran out into the road without thinking and caused damage to a car with which he collided was reckless because he knew 'of the risks associated with running into the road, namely the risk of collision and damage to property. Aware of those risks he then deliberately put them out of his mind and, for reasons of his own, ran into the path of a car.' The Divisional Court upheld the Magistrates' finding. Although the Magistrates' finding that the defendant 'closed his mind' to what surely would have been the last thing he should have thought about is astonishing, it does show that there is some scope for cutting subjective recklessness down to a manageable size.[29] A far better solution, of course, would have been to implement a test of recklessness which penalised culpably thoughtless behaviour while paying due regard to the capacities and experience of the defendant.

C Lawful excuse

Both simple and aggravated arson are constituted only where the defendant acted 'without lawful excuse'. Lawful excuse, in this context, refers generally to those excusing or justifying conditions which might negate liability for any other offence. A person does not commit criminal damage if he acts under duress/duress of circumstances, necessity, or public or private defence:

> **Case 7**
> One morning, after a party thrown by Eve, Adam, a guest, finds himself alone in the house with all the doors locked and no other means of egress. He breaks the kitchen window and escapes.

> **Case 8**
> Adam, after an altercation in a car park with Eve, decides to teach Eve a lesson by ramming her car. Eve, in the attempt to escape, smashes through the barrier, narrowly missing Cain, a car-park attendant.

In Case 7, although Adam commits damage with *mens rea* he will, arguably, not incur liability as he acts with a 'lawful excuse', namely necessity. As argued earlier, necessity would appear to justify action, reasonably undertaken as an act of self-preservation, where the proscribed consequence is an **inevitable and unavoidable side-effect** of that act of self-preservation.[30] Under such circumstances, it should not be necessary to show, as it is with duress of circumstances, that the threat to be avoided was of immediate death or serious injury. In Case 7, on a charge of simple criminal damage, Eve is also, arguably, acting with a 'lawful excuse'. It will be remembered that the force used in self-defence must be directed against the aggressor. Here, although force is used, it is used for the purpose of escaping

---

[29] Quoted from *Blackstone's Criminal Practice*, Oxford: OUP (2007) 518. See also H. Keating (2007) 546.
[30] Above at Chapter 10. Case 7 might also provide a statutory defence under s. 5(2)(a).

the threat, not meeting it.[31] Here the force used is against the barrier and it is clearly necessary and reasonable. It is submitted that a defence should be recognised in this situation.[32]

Section 5 provides two cases of lawful excuse, additional to the above common law excuses or justifications, which will also negate liability for simple (not aggravated) criminal damage:[33]

> (2) A person charged with an offence to which this section applies shall, whether or not he would be treated for the purposes of this Act as having a lawful excuse apart from this subsection, be treated for those purposes as having a lawful excuse –
>
> (a) if at the time of the act or acts alleged to constitute the offence he believed that the person or persons whom he believed to be entitled to consent to the destruction of or damage to the property in question had so consented, or would have consented to it if he or they had known of the destruction or damage and its circumstances; or
>
> (b) if he had destroyed or damaged . . . the property in question . . . in order to protect property belonging to himself or another or a right or interest in property which was or which he believed to be vested in himself or another, and at the time of the act or acts alleged to constitute the offence he believed –
>
> (i) that the property, right or interest was in immediate need of protection; and
>
> (ii) that the means of protection adopted or proposed to be adopted were or would be reasonable having regard to all the circumstances.
>
> (3) For the purposes of this section it is immaterial whether a belief is justified or not if it is honestly held.
>
> (4) For the purposes of subsection (2) above a right or interest in property includes any right or privilege in or over land, whether created by grant, licence or otherwise.
>
> (5) This section shall not be construed as casting doubt on any defence recognised by law as a defence to criminal charges.

Under the Theft Act 1968 liability depends upon proof of dishonesty. Section 5 of the Criminal Damage Act 1971 has certain things in common with section 2 of that Act.[34] By section 5(2)(a) a belief that a person entitled to give consent to the damaging or destruction of property had or would consent is a defence whether or not such consent has actually been given or is forthcoming. The defendant bears an evidential burden in this respect.[35] There is no requirement that a (mistaken) belief be reasonable as long as it was honestly held. Unlike the position at common law, even mistakes induced by drink maybe relied upon.[36] In *Jaggard* v *Dickinson*[37] a person who broke into a neighbour's house believing it, in her drunken state, to be her own place of abode was held able to rely on the defence that she honestly thought the owner (with whom she cohabited) would consent.

There appear to be some limits, however, on the type of mistaken belief which may avail the defendant. In *Blake* v *DPP*[38] it was held that a vicar, who believed he had God's consent

---

[31] See generally D.W. Elliot, 'Necessity, Duress and Self-defence' [1989] Crim LR 611.

[32] See Chapter 10, generally. Compare *Lloyd* v *DPP* [1992] 1 All ER 982 where it was held that damaging a wheel-clamp to free an encumbered car was not a lawful excuse.

[33] Section 5 also operates as a defence to certain other crimes under ss. 2 and 3 of the Criminal Damage Act 1971, namely issuing threats to commit, or possessing anything with intent to commit, criminal damage. In both cases the criminal damage concerned must be in its non-aggravated form for the (statutory) defence to be applicable.

[34] P. Glazebrook, 'The Necessity Plea in English Criminal Law' [1972] CLJ 87 at 103.

[35] *Hill and Hall* [1989] Crim LR 136 and see commentary at 139.

[36] Drunken mistakes may generally only be relied upon to negate *mens rea* and even then only for crimes of specific intent. See Chapter 9.

[37] [1980] 3 All ER 716.

[38] [1993] Crim LR 586.

to damage property, did not have a belief in the consent of a 'person entitled to consent to the damage of the property', presumably because God is not a person. On that basis his marker pen graffiti on the Houses of Parliament in protest against the Gulf War was held unlawful.

In principle, the 'personhood' of the consent-giver should not strictly be relevant. One assumes, for example, that if an instruction to damage property had been given from a very living religious leader, in the manner of a fatwa, the decision would have been the same. Somehow the belief must be of a nature that the say-so of the consent-giver is relevant to the legality of the act concerned. It is submitted that only a belief amounting to a conviction that damage has been or will be consented to by a person having **legal** authority to consent should suffice:

Case 9

Adam, a young car-park attendant, is told by Eve, his immediate superior, to let the air out of the tyres of any car whose owner has failed to pay the correct car-parking charge. He does so, believing Eve to have the authority to do anything in relation to 'offending vehicles'.

There are two questions here. The first is whether letting the tyres down counts as criminal damage. It would appear that it does, acting to impair temporarily the usefulness of the cars. The second is whether Adam believes that Eve was the person entitled to consent to the damage to the property. We know that Adam believed Eve to have the authority to let down the tyres. Is this the same as believing that Eve is the person entitled to consent to him letting down the tyres? Assuming it is, Adam has a defence although the belief is unreasonable and although it does not amount to a belief that Eve has any authority of the owner to consent to the damage.

Significantly, it is the belief that the owner or other authorised person would consent which negates liability, not the belief that the act is not immoral. Authority for this proposition is the case of *Denton*.[39] The defendant set fire to machinery in a mill where he was employed, in consequence whereof the machinery and mill were damaged. He was charged with arson under section 1(1). He claimed that he was acting on the instruction of the owners who wished to perpetrate an insurance fraud. The judge ruled that on these facts he could not rely on the defence of lawful excuse under section 5(2)(a). His appeal was allowed on the basis that since the act of burning down a building by its owner is lawful, it can be no less lawful if done by another at the owner's behest. Since he believed he had this consent, he had a lawful excuse for burning the building down even though the owner may have had a dishonest motive.[40]

Section 5(2)(b) covers the case of causing damage to another's property as a means of protecting one's own property. It has long been the case at common law that such activities may be lawful under the necessity principle. Thus, a person may lawfully set fire to property (or demolish a house) to prevent a fire from spreading so as to engulf the property of the former.[41] Section 5(2)(b) is more expansive than its common law counterpart since it allows action to be taken to protect property interests or rights as well as the substance thereof. In *Chamberlain* v *Lindon* the Divisional Court upheld a decision at first instance

---

[39] [1982] 1 All ER 65.
[40] The court considered that the excuse might exist independently of s. 5(2)(a).
[41] *Cope* v *Sharpe* [1912] 1 KB 496; G. Williams *CLGP* (1st edn) ch. 17; P. Glazebrook, 'The Necessity Plea in English Criminal Law' [1972] CLJ 87 at 103.

that the holder of a right of way was not guilty of criminal damage by demolishing a wall blocking that right of way. It was not necessary that the defendant had exhausted all other possible remedies such as court action.[42] More significantly, unlike the position at common law, it seems that there is no requirement that the action taken is objectively necessary. It is enough that the defendant believed that the property, right or interest was in immediate need of protection and that the means adopted were reasonable in the circumstances:[43]

Case 10

Farmer Giles, anxious lest his pregnant cow Flossie aborts, throws Farmer Fred's noisy chain-saw into a pond, damaging it.

Giles has a defence under section 5(2)(b) if he believes that the action taken was a reasonable means of avoiding the immediate spontaneous abortion of Flossie although there was no objective danger to Flossie from the noise and though a polite request to Farmer Fred to desist would have done the trick.

The courts have, however, placed limits on the applicability of the section 5(2)(b) defence, by insisting that the action taken has the **objective effect** of a property-protecting measure. It is not enough for a person to say, 'I wanted to protect property B, so I did A, which I believed reasonable in the circumstances'. For example, in *Hunt*[44] the appellant set fire to a bed in a block of old people's flats, apparently to draw attention to the fact that the fire alarms were not working. He then phoned the fire brigade. It was held that he did not, in the words of section 5(2)(b), commit the damage **in order to protect** his own or the property of another, but rather to 'draw attention to the defective state of the fire alarm'. Again, in *Hill and Hall*[45] the defendants had been separately convicted of possessing an article (a hacksaw blade) with intent to damage property, an offence under section 3 of the Act to which section 5(2)(b) is a defence. They were in possession of the blades so as to cut through the perimeter fence surrounding a US naval base. They raised the section 5(2)(b) defence, claiming that their object was to encourage the removal of the base from the area, thus reducing the risk that their nearby homes might be damaged in a future nuclear strike against the base. The trial judge[46] concluded that the action of the defendant was undertaken to encourage the removal of the naval base and not to protect property. The Court of Appeal agreed and said that it was for the trial judge to decide, as a matter of law, whether, on the facts as the defendant believed them to be, the cutting of the wire could amount to a property-protecting act.[47] The judge had concluded correctly that, while property-protection may have been the defendants' remote aim, it was not the purpose behind the wire cutting.[48] Further, the trial judge had to determine whether, on the facts stated by the defendants, there was any evidence that they believed there was an **immediate danger** which they were acting to avert. Clearly there was no such evidence and so the matter was properly not left to the jury.[49] These two decisions are quite compatible with our conclusions in relation to Case 10. Farmer Giles may well have been worrying excessively and

---

[42] [1998] 2 All ER 538.
[43] See *Jones and Others* [2004] 3 WLR 1362.
[44] (1977) 66 Cr App R 105.
[45] [1989] Crim LR 136.
[46] Following *Hunt*.
[47] Cf. *Chandler* v *DPP* [1964] AC 763.
[48] This was an additional ground for the decision in *Blake* v *DPP* [1993] Crim LR 586.
[49] Cf. *Ayliffe and Others* [2005] EWHC 684 (Admin).

have overreacted to the supposed danger but, on the facts as he believed them to be,[50] there was evidence that he thought his action to be necessary to prevent immediate damage to his property.

17.3 CRIMINAL DAMAGE ENDANGERING LIFE

By section 1(2) Criminal Damage Act 1971 it is an offence punishable with life imprisonment[51] that a person

... without lawful excuse destroys or damages any property, whether belonging to himself or another -

(a) intending to destroy or damage any property or being reckless as to whether any property would be destroyed or damaged; and

(b) intending by the destruction or damage to endanger the life of another or being reckless as to whether the life of another would be thereby endangered.

By section 1(3) where the aggravated offence takes the form of damaging or destroying property by fire, the offence is charged as arson.[52]

A *Actus reus*

The *actus reus* of aggravated criminal damage is wider than that of the simple form. Unlike section 1(1) the offence may be committed where the property damaged or destroyed does not belong to another. So if A burns down his own house to defraud his insurance company the section 1(2) offence is committed if he was reckless as to whether he was putting the lives of others in danger. In *Merrick*[53] the potential scope for injustice arising from this provision was made manifest. M, a contractor, had, with a householder's written consent, removed a television signal receiving box from the side of the latter's house. He left a live cable exposed for six minutes before rendering it safe. He was charged and convicted under section 1(2). The Court of Appeal upheld the conviction and, one must assume, would have convicted the householder had he performed the operation himself. As Sir John Smith complained, it is extraordinary that the householder (or contractor with the householder's permission) should commit a property offence under such circumstances when he is perfectly entitled to cut the cable as he sees fit. After all, he would not be liable for installing a cable and leaving it live, however long it was left in that condition. Why should he be any more subject to coercion for rendering an existing live cable exposed?[54]

B *Mens rea*

The *mens rea* for the aggravated offence is like its simple counterpart intention or (*Cunningham*) recklessness. However, it is important to note that it is not enough for the prosecution to show that simple criminal damage has occurred accompanied by intention or recklessness as to life being endangered. It has to be shown that it was by the act constituting criminal damage that A intended to endanger the other's life or was reckless as to that fact:

---

[50] Loud noises cause spontaneous abortions in cows.
[51] Section 4(1).
[52] With intent, etc.
[53] [1995] Crim LR 802.
[54] [1995] Crim LR at 803–4.

Case 11

Adam drops a paving-stone from a bridge spanning a quiet country path, intending to hit Eve who is passing underneath on a bicycle. The stone hits the front wheel and Eve is thrown off.

Adam is not guilty under section 1(2)(b). He intends to hit Eve, thereby endangering her life; not to hit the bike and thereby endanger her life. Falling off a bicycle on a quiet country path may be painful but it is not life-threatening. In *Steer*[55] S worked off a grudge against his old business partner by firing several shots with an automatic rifle at the house occupied by the latter and his wife. Two windows were hit. He was charged, *inter alia*, with criminal damage being reckless as to whether life would be endangered. The Court of Appeal quashed S's conviction, which decision was upheld by the House of Lords. What had to be shown was that there was an intentional or reckless causing of damage to the property, which there was, and also intention or recklessness as to the prospect of danger to life flowing from that damage. Here, it was the shooting which was calculated to endanger the life of the occupants, not the damage to the window. Even flying glass is not a life-endangering event. S should have been charged with an offence against the person (e.g. assault) and simple criminal damage rather than this curious hybrid of an offence.

By contrast, in *Webster*[56] the defendant dropped a heavy coping-stone onto a passing train from a bridge. Passengers were hit by flying *debris* from the roof of a carriage partly penetrated by the stone. His conviction on a count alleging an intention 'by the same damage to endanger the life of another' was quashed, following *Steer*, on the ground that he did not intend to endanger life **by the commission of criminal damage** but by the impact of the stone itself. The Court of Appeal held, however, that since it was clear that the jury, by convicting, had concluded that the appellant intended to endanger the lives of the passengers by the penetration into the carriage of the stone itself he must also have been (*Caldwell*) reckless as to the fact that the stone might cause the roof to fall in, thereby endangering the lives of the passengers. His conviction was therefore affirmed on this basis. A similar result occurred in *Warwick*,[57] heard in combination with *Webster*, where it was held that throwing stones at, and ramming, police cars were properly charged as offences under section 1(2) since both actions could cause the driver to lose control of the vehicle as a result of damage to the vehicle (flying glass, broken suspension) which the defendant had intentionally or recklessly caused. As Lord Taylor CJ acknowledges in these cases, the distinction drawn between intention or recklessness as to the outcome, and intention or recklessness as to the manner in which the outcome is produced, is a dismal one.[58]

The offence is constituted upon proof of intention/recklessness as to the endangerment of life. It does not have to be shown that the defendant's act of damage objectively did provoke such a risk. So where A threw a fire-bomb into B's house the offence was committed, even though B was quickly able to extinguish the bomb and was at no time endangered.[59] Indeed it seems that it is committed even though the defendant had convinced himself that what he was doing was safe.[60]

---

[55] [1987] 2 All ER 833. See also *Wenton* [2010] EWCA Crim 2361.
[56] [1995] 2 All ER 168.
[57] [1995] 2 All ER 168.
[58] At 173.
[59] *Dudley* [1989] Crim LR 57.
[60] *Merrick* [1995] Crim LR 802, above; see D.W. Elliot, 'Endangering Life by Destroying or Damaging Property' [1997] Crim LR 382 at 389.

Summary

There are two main offences, namely criminal damage simple and criminal damage endangering life. Criminal damage simple, which includes arson, is committed when a person intentionally or recklessly damages property belonging to another. Unlike theft, the property includes real property. Like theft, property belongs not merely to owners but to others who have rights and interests over the property. Aggravated criminal damage is committed where a person damages property (typically by fire) either intending to endanger life or being reckless as to that prospect. The aggravated form may be committed even where the property damaged belongs to the person damaging the property. It is a requirement of the offence that the risk to life is posed by the damage to property rather than the act which caused the damage.

Part V
Inchoate offences and complicity

18 Inchoate offences

Overview

There are three crimes of general application the gist of which is to proscribe activities not unlawful in their own right but because they form a step towards the commission of another offence. These are the inchoate (undeveloped) crimes of attempt, conspiracy and the statutory offences of encouraging or assisting crime.

18.1 INTRODUCTION

The criminal law does not, as a matter of principle, punish for thoughts alone. Its function, and its limiting principle, is the punishing of wrongdoing and the prevention of harm to public or private interests. Nobody is wronged; society's interests are not 'set back'[1] when its members spend their leisure hours plotting to kill their spouse, employer or prime minister, or to rob the high street bank. They are wronged; their interests are set back only when such a plan is set in motion. They are wronged; harm to public and private interests occurs most obviously when the harm plotted is executed. However, when the levels of preparation are such that a substantial threat is posed to the security of an individual and/or the wider community, it may be reasonable and necessary for law enforcement agencies to engage in pre-emptive action. The criminal law contains a number of offences designed primarily, if not exclusively, to enable such pre-emptive action. Such offences, typically, allow law enforcement authorities to intervene before a serious harm is committed by allowing arrest and conviction for acts directed towards, or preparatory to, the commission of a substantive offence. The essence of each is that liability attaches for activities which fall short of the commission of another offence. Some such offences are constituted as offences in their own right. Examples include most offences of possession, including possessing articles for use in burglary or theft and carrying an offensive weapon.[2] Some offences have an ambiguous character. Is assault, for example, an inchoate form of the crime of battery or a crime in its own right?[3] This depends upon the interests protected by the offence. As Fletcher explains: 'It is only when we have a clear idea of the interests which an offence seeks to vindicate that we can know whether the offence is inchoate or consummated'.[4] The modern approach is to treat assault as an offence in its own right since it constitutes a direct violation of individual autonomy.[5]

In this chapter we will examine the three preparatory offences of general application which are not offences in their own right, but which are constituted as an undeveloped (inchoate) form of a particular substantive offence. These are attempt, conspiracy, and encouraging or assisting crime. It should be noted at this early stage that the latter statutory offence

---

[1] See for example Section 5 'Preparation of Terrorist Acts' Terrorism Act 2006; *R (on the application of Irfan)* v *Secretary of State for the Home Department* [2012] EWHC 840 (Admin).

[2] Theft Act, s. 25(1) and (2); Prevention of Crime Act 1953, s. 1. Possessing controlled drugs contrary to s. 5 Misuse of Drugs Act 1971 is not an inchoate offence, however.

[3] At common law assault was an attempted battery; Perkins and Boyce (1982) 615; Dressler (1987) 332–3.

[4] G. Fletcher (1978) at 133.

[5] See *Nelson (Gary)* [2013] WLR (D) 10.

replaces the common law inchoate offence of incitement.[6] This offence is designed to clarify the existing law and to improve upon it in certain key areas. More significantly, however, it substantially adds to the coverage of the inchoate offences by criminalising assisting the commission of an offence in addition to its erstwhile restricted focus on inciting the commission of an offence.

18.2 CHARGING INCHOATE OFFENCES

Since inchoate offences are not crimes in their own right, the crime charged in the indictment is, with a limited exception for common law conspiracy, one which refers to the relevant consummated crime. Thus, one is indicted for attempted theft or conspiracy to murder rather than simply for an 'attempt' or a 'conspiracy'. Generally speaking, a person will not be indicted for an inchoate offence if the substantive offence has been committed. Since the passing of Part 2 of the Serious Crime Act 2007 this is liable to occur more frequently since it will often be advantageous to charge those who encourage or assist another to commit a criminal offence under that Act, rather than as an accessory to the substantive offence.[7] At present such an option will already be embraced if it is not possible to prove one of the conduct elements in the *actus reus* of the substantive offence. A fairly common problem is the proof of causation. Thus in *Cox*[8] although it could be proved that the defendant doctor intended to kill his patient and that the patient died, it was uncertain whether the doctor's conduct caused the patient's death. As a result he was indicted for attempted murder rather than the substantive offence. Where proving the conduct elements is not a problem, the proper (though not obligatory)[9] course of action is to indict the defendant(s) for the substantive offence whether as principal or secondary party.

18.3 INCHOATE OFFENCES AND ACCESSORIAL LIABILITY

The general ground covered by these three offences, and their relationship with substantive offences and accessorial liability, is described in the following set of events:

> **Case 1**
> A wants to cheat on the national lottery scratch cards. He buys a number of scratch cards and subjects them to infra-red, X-ray and ultrasonic analysis. He discovers that he is able to identify winning cards without defacing them. A goes to his local scratch card seller (B) and explains his discovery. He encourages B to lend him all his scratch cards so that the winning cards can be identified and A and B can share the proceeds. B agrees and they formulate a plan. Later B delivers all the scratch cards to A. Next day A returns all the non-winning cards to B and takes the winning cards to C, another scratch card seller, and claims his money. C smells a rat and calls the police. A and B are both arrested.

The first (inchoate) offence takes place when A makes his proposal to B. A may be indicted for intentionally encouraging B to commit a criminal offence (theft/fraud by false representation).[10] The second offence takes place when B agrees to help A. This agreement

---

[6] The Serious Crime Act 2007.
[7] See Law Com. No. 305 *Participating in Crime* (2007).
[8] Above at pp. 135–6.
[9] *Webley* v *Buxton* [1977] 2 All ER 595.
[10] Section 44 Serious Crime Act 2007.

is the subject-matter of conspiracy (to steal or defraud). The third offence (attempt to steal or commit fraud by false representation) takes place at the latest when A claims his money from C, and possibly even earlier. A will be guilty of this offence as principal, and B as accomplice. If the attempt had not failed, A and B may be charged with the substantive offence of theft and possibly fraud by false representation.[11] A will be the principal offender and B the accessory.

18.4 ATTEMPT[12]

A person can be charged with attempting any indictable offence. This includes offences triable either way. The maximum sentence mirrors that of the substantive offence. In the case of murder, life imprisonment is the maximum rather than the mandatory sentence.[13]

The law of criminal attempts covers three separate fact situations. The first, a thwarted attempt, is when the attempter does not get to the point of executing the offence. Thus:

> **Case 2**
> Eve, intending to kill Adam, lies in wait, gun at the ready, at a place it is his wont to frequent. Adam arrives with a companion and Eve's plan is thwarted.

The second, a failed attempt, is when the attempter does everything he intended to do in order to effect his criminal project but this fails to bring about the desired consequence. Thus:

> **Case 3**
> Adam, intending to shoot and kill Eve, pulls the trigger. At the same time Eve bends over, thus causing the bullet to miss its target.

The third, an impossible attempt, occurs where the course of conduct embarked upon by the attempter to achieve a supposed criminal ambition was incapable of resulting in the commission of the substantive offence. Thus:

> **Case 4**
> Adam, intending to shoot and kill Eve, fires a gun at her sleeping form. Unknown to him Eve had died five minutes earlier.

A Justification for punishing attempts

In each one of the above three situations A will be guilty of attempted murder. The justifications for criminalising and punishing such activities, even though no obvious harm has

---

[11] B may have also committed fraud by abuse of position.

[12] For indicative reading see R.A. Duff *Criminal Attempts*, Oxford: OUP (1996); G. Yaffe, *Attempts: in the Philosophy of Action and the Criminal Law*, Oxford: OUP (2012); D. Husak, 'Why Punish Attempts at All? Yaffe on "The Transfer Principle"' (2012) 6(3) Criminal Law & Philosophy 399; J. Horder, 'Criminal Attempt, the Rule of Law, and Accountability in Criminal Law' in L. Zedner and J. Roberts (eds), *Principles and Values in Criminal Law and Criminal Justice: Essays in Honour of Andrew Ashworth*, Oxford: OUP (2012) 37.

[13] By section 1(4) Criminal Attempts Act 1981 a person cannot attempt to conspire or aid and abet an offence.

occurred, follow traditional lines.[14] From the retributive point of view an attempt carries its own social harm. In Cases 2 and 3, harm is done to the interests of Eve, also her family and wider social network whose dominion and emotional well-being will be damaged by the attack on her autonomy. At a broader level collective interests in security are also harmed. This provides a general justification for criminalising attempts and would justify the punishment of Adam for his attempts, at least if Eve (or others) were aware of the attempt made upon her life. If she was not, as in Case 4, it might be argued that the social impact of Adam's conduct was too trivial to justify punishment. However, retributive denunciation would seem to be deserved as much for the 'wrongness' of the conduct as for the harm it causes.[15]

From a utilitarian point of view it is possible to justify criminalisation and punishment even in the absence of harm. Punishing attempts may act as a separate deterrent to punishing the substantive offence for those who lack confidence of success.[16] It may also enable offenders to be isolated before they have the chance to cause harm. This both incapacitates dangerous offenders and may provide the context within which they may be rehabilitated.

B The potential scope of attempts

1 Thwarted attempts: subjectivist and objectivist approaches

A significant problem faced by the criminal law, in the case of **thwarted attempts**, is how to determine when the criminal attempt actually begins. This problem does not arise with **failed attempts** where the defendant has done everything he intended to do to bring about the substantive offence. Two contrasting approaches may be adopted in determining when the attempt begins – a subjectivist and an objectivist approach.[17] Important issues of political morality inform these approaches, most particularly the balance to be struck between a proper respect for civil liberties and the need for society to prevent crime through effective, well-timed law enforcement. To a large extent they reflect the above underlying theoretical premises. The former approach holds that the essence of a criminal attempt is an act which signifies a culpable or dangerous disposition on the part of the defendant. Since he has such a disposition it is appropriate to isolate and confine him on general utilitarian (harm-preventing) grounds or punish him on denunciatory grounds.[18] At its most extreme, subjectivism can lead to some counter-intuitive conclusions.[19]

Subjectivists generally insist that the attempt begins when the defendant's *mens rea* becomes visible in the performance of some act indicating the defendant's commitment to

---

[14] G. Yaffe, *Attempts: in the Philosophy of Action and the Criminal Law*; R.A. Duff, 'Criminal Attempts' in A. Marmor (ed.), *The Routledge Companion to Philosophy of Law*, London: Routledge (2012) 191–205; D. Husak, 'Why Punish Attempts at All? Yaffe on "The Transfer Principle"'; R.A. Duff, 'Guiding Commitments and Criminal Liability for Attempts' (2012) 6(3) Criminal Law & Philosophy 411.

[15] See above, Chapter 2; A.J. Ashworth, 'Criminal Attempts and the Role of Resulting Harm under the Code, and in the Common Law' (1988) 19 Rutgers Law Journal 725.

[16] H.L.A. Hart, *Punishment and Responsibility* (1968) 128 ff.; James Brady, 'Punishing Attempts' (1980) 63 The Monist 246 at 249.

[17] See generally R.A. Duff, *Criminal Attempts*, Oxford: OUP (1996); G. Fletcher (1978) ch. 3. D. Ohana, 'Desert and Punishment for Acts Preparatory to the Commission of a Crime' (2007) Can J Law and Juris 113; See also D. Ohana, 'Responding to Acts Preparatory to the Commission of a Crime' (2006) 25 Criminal Justice Ethics 23.

[18] On retributive grounds.

[19] Such as basing criminal liability (and punishment) not on what the defendant has done but upon what he has tried to do (Ashworth, op. cit.); also 'Belief, Intent and Criminal Liability' in J. Eekelaar and J. Bell (eds), *Oxford Essays in Jurisprudence* (1987); 'Taking the Consequences' in Shute *et al.* (eds), *Action and Value in Criminal Law*, Oxford: Clarendon Press (1993) 107; cf. R.A. Duff, 'Acting, Trying and Criminal Liability' ibid. 75.

the criminal project, and thus support intervention at an early stage. The act is not important in its own right but simply as providing unequivocal evidence of the culpability/dangerous inclinations which subjectivists hold to be the cornerstone of attempt liability. If the basis upon which coercion is ordered is crime prevention or denouncing wicked inclinations, then what is really important is not what the defendant still has to do but what he has already done.[20]

Objectivists repudiate such an approach. Our membership of a free society behoves the state not to subject us to coercion unless we have done something wrong. It is easy (and harmless) to plan a criminal endeavour, far less easy to execute it. The state's warrant to punish demands at the very least, then, an act of 'manifest criminality', that is an act which 'shows criminal intent on the face of it'.[21] The objectivist position is articulated by Fletcher:

> That criminal conduct is unnerving to the community is sufficient to justify either private or official intervention. Private intervention takes the form of defensive force; public intervention or prosecution for a criminal offence. If the public feels 'apprehension' at the suspect's manifestly criminal conduct, that is a sufficient social interest to warrant suppression. The corollary is that if an act is so equivocal that it does not generate apprehension, then it should not be subject to either private or public suppression.[22]

The stance adopted in England and Wales at least is an uneasy mixture of subjectivism and objectivism. On the question of impossible attempts the stance adopted is largely subjectivist.[23] As we shall see, liability depends upon what the defendant had in mind rather than the objective wrongfulness of his conduct. The test for when the attempt begins, by contrast, is largely objectivist, emphasising how much **remained to be done** by the defendant before the offence was consummated. Subjectivist approaches tend to emphasise how much **had already been done**. Case 2 is a commonly used illustration of the differences between the approaches. If we emphasise how much still remains to be done, we might say 'everything'. Not only has no gun been taken out, cocked, aimed and fired but we do not even have a frightened victim. How can all these 'nothings' be the subject-matter of attempted murder? If we emphasise what has been done, however, the emphasis changes from whether Eve's conduct looks like the proper subject-matter of attempted murder to the question whether it gives her the appearance of an attempting murderer. She has brought a gun. She has discovered, perhaps using painstaking research, her victim's likely whereabouts. She has brought the gun to a spot where she can successfully shoot Adam. She has loaded the gun. She has done everything that was in her control. All that remains is for the victim to arrive, alone![24]

2 Failed and impossible attempts

Little of substance differentiates the approach of subjectivists and objectivists with respect to failed attempts. For both subjectivist and objectivist the case of failed attempts is a clear signal that coercion is justified. For the objectivist, the failed attempt is the visible manifestation of an act of criminality. For the subjectivist the failed attempt is the clearest possible evidence of the defendant's dangerousness/wickedness.

The differences between subjectivist and objectivist approaches to criminal attempts can be seen most clearly in the context of impossible attempts. The objectivists hold that the

---

[20] S. Garvey, 'Are Attempts like Treason' (2011) 14 New Criminal LR 173.
[21] J. Salmond, *Jurisprudence* (7th edn) London: Stevens (1924) 404. See generally Fletcher (1978) 139–57.
[22] Fletcher (1978) at 144.
[23] Fletcher considers that the common law is uniformly subjectivist in its approach, 166–7.
[24] For a variation of this problem, see *R v Tosti* [1997] Crim LR 745.

act of the defendant must manifest the criminality contained within the consummated offence. This may have the unfortunate consequence of removing the criminal sanction from someone who is clearly culpable and dangerous. Case 4 would not be a criminal attempt from this point of view. Nothing which Adam **did** shows Adam to be a potential murderer. Entering rooms inhabited by corpses and firing guns at them is a supremely innocuous activity. In Case 4, Adam's susceptibility to punishment for attempted murder would hinge simply upon his intention. For the objectivist this would amount to punishing Adam for his **intentions alone**. If the logic here seems dubious, it does not want for support. It was stated *obiter* in an American case that a person could not be guilty of the offence of attempted rape where he assaulted a man mistakenly thinking him to be a woman, the substantive offence only being possible against a woman.[25] The House of Lords once held that a defendant who took possession of a consignment of baked beans, believing them to be stolen when in fact they were not, could not be guilty of an attempt to handle stolen goods. Lord Hailsham gave reasons as follows: 'steps on the way to the doing of something which is thereafter done, and which is no crime, cannot be regarded as attempts to commit a crime'.[26]

Subjectivists reject such reasoning. As long as what the actor thought he was doing was in fact a crime, he has the necessary criminal intent for that crime. The attempt is constituted upon proof of some act sufficient to evidence such intent. In Case 4 Adam thought he was killing a live person. Killing a live person is a criminal offence. By taking a shot at Eve's recumbent body Adam demonstrated that he was trying to kill Eve. If he was trying to kill, how can it be denied that he was, in law, 'attempting' murder? As we shall see, the Criminal Attempts Act 1981 now endorses the subjectivist approach on this important matter, while maintaining an essentially objectivist stance on other issues pertinent to the *actus reus* of the offence.

C The level of punishment: retributivist and utilitarian approaches

Should an attempt be punished as the consummated offence?[27] The answer to this question depends very much on the criterion by which one seeks to justify punishment in the first place. From the utilitarian point of view it could be argued that the level of punishment appropriate would, on general utilitarian grounds, be the same as that for the completed offence since attempters show themselves as much in need of incapacitation and rehabilitation as achievers. Moreover, the deterrent function of the criminal law is arguably as well advanced by punishing attempters as achievers. Public interests are advanced if the public are aware that people will be punished whether or not they succeed with their plan.[28] On the other hand there are good utilitarian reasons for reducing punishment for a failed attempt. First, at least for thwarted attempts, there is always the possibility that the defendant would have abandoned the project. Only those who go through with their plan are clearly so dangerous as to merit sanction. This is an argument

---

[25] *People* v *Gardner* (1893) 25 NYS 1072, 1075–6.
[26] *Haughton* v *Smith* [1973] 3 All ER 1109 at 1118.
[27] See generally M. Davies, 'Why Attempts Deserve Less Punishment Than Complete Crimes' (1986) 5 Law and Philosophy 1. For a statement of the general principle that an attempt normally carries a lesser sentence than the full offence, see *R* v *Joseph* [2001] 2 Cr App R 88 CA.
[28] There should though be a defence of withdrawal so as not to act as a disincentive for those who are so far through with their crime that they might think, 'What the heck!'

for discounting the sentence for thwarted attempts, though not failed and impossible attempts.[29] Second, with respect to failed (completed) attempts, utilitarianism has a bias towards minimalism in punishment. Punishment should be no more than is necessary to fulfil society's purposes. If it appears draconian, as it will to the majority of retributivists, the institution of punishment will lose support as well as creating unnecessary suffering to the attempter.

If we favour retributivism the level of punishment again varies depending upon whether one takes a harm-centred approach or a culpability approach.[30] It may be argued that the criminal justice system should replicate the manner in which God's justice is meted out, namely upon the basis of what we try to achieve rather than what we do achieve. Whether we take the unfair advantage approach or the expressive approach, the level of punishment, arguably, should be the same.[31] An attempted murderer is as wicked as a murderer. Indeed, as we have seen he may be more so.[32]

Ashworth goes further. He suggests that the distinction between attempts and consummated offences might profitably be collapsed. It might be appropriate to distinguish between complete (Cases 3 and 4) and incomplete attempts (Case 2) rather than, as is currently the case, between complete attempts and the substantive offence. The reasoning behind this is initially plausible. There is a high degree of moral equivalence between complete (failed) attempts and the substantive crime since both involve the defendant doing everything in his power to bring the substantive offence about. If we take murder as an example, this would justify not only punishing attempters and achievers similarly, but even punishing them for the same offence since their wrong is the same, namely 'trying to kill'. It is down to good or bad luck rather than anything intrinsic to the defendant's conduct whether the actual death occurs. The defendant can only 'try'.[33] Thus murder and attempted murder could profitably, on this view, be reduced to an umbrella offence such as acting with intent to kill. At the same time he argues that there is a moral difference between complete and incomplete attempts. The latter arguably should be treated as less serious than the former since the defendant did not get to the point of 'trying' to commit the offence. This may mean that the defendant is both less culpable and less dangerous than a complete attempter, justifying less serious consequences.[34]

Although superficially plausible, the view ignores the crucial significance of harm. Just as we would consider it unjust for a person to be rewarded for trying to finish a crossword puzzle rather than succeeding, so criminal justice must redress the evil accomplished rather than undertaken. Taking murder as an example, punishing succeeder and attempter alike does not take account of the fact that the former makes the world a very different place, for which consequence he is responsible and must take responsibility. It seems

---

[29] Cf. *R v Szmyt* [2010] 1 Cr App R 69 CA.

[30] M. White, *Retributivism: Essays on Theory and Policy*, New York: OUP (2011).

[31] For a different view see M. Davies, op. cit. 28–9.

[32] A.J. Ashworth, 'Criminal Attempts and the Role of Resulting Harm under the Code and under the Common Law' (1988) 19 Rutgers LJ 725; R. Christopher, 'Does Attempted Murder Deserve Greater Punishment than Murder? Moral Luck and the Duty to Prevent Harm' (2004) 18 Notre Dame Journal of Law, Ethics & Public Policy 419.

[33] See A.J. Ashworth, 'Taking the Consequences' in Shute *et al.* (1993) 107, and R.A. Duff, ibid. 90; N. Jareborg, 'Criminal Attempts and Moral Luck' (1993) 27 Israel LR 213.

[34] The Law Commission in their consultation paper recommend a different approach, namely to distinguish between degrees of consummation of the completed offence. Failed and impossible attempts would continue to be attempts. Thwarted attempts would become a new inchoate offence of criminal preparation.

appropriate, then, to base punishment, not upon what was intended, but upon the extent of social harm actually inflicted by the attempt.[35]

D When does the attempt begin? The common law tests

The major problem in prosecuting criminal attempts is that of determining the stage at which the attempt begins. As we have already seen, the subjectivist and objectivist approaches adopt different criteria in this respect. The common law has produced a number of tests, embodying both approaches, designed to fill the conceptual void separating acts of preparation from acts of perpetration. That there are so many of them illustrates the difficulties involved in creating a test suitable for all crimes, which successfully reconciles policies of social defence and civil liberties.[36]

1 Subjectivist tests

Two subjectivist tests have been formulated, although neither has been formally adopted in England and Wales. By subjectivist is meant that the attempt is assessed by reference to what the actor had in mind rather than what he had achieved, which is the objectivist approach. The first subjectivist test, first formulated by Stephen, holds that the *actus reus* of an attempt centres upon an act 'forming part of a series of acts which would constitute actual commission of the offence if it were not interrupted'.[37] Such a test has unashamedly subjectivist credentials allowing an attempt to be constituted at a very early stage. It would convict Eve, in Case 2, for example, even if Adam had failed to arrive at the stakeout.[38]

The second subjectivist test is the substantial steps test. It is noteworthy for being the test adopted in the American Model Penal Code. Section 5.01(1)(c) of the code is as follows:

> A person is guilty of an attempt to commit a crime if, acting with the kind of culpability otherwise required for commission of the crime, he: [. . .]
>
> (c)   purposely does or omits to do anything which, under the circumstances as he believes them to be, is an act or omission constituting a substantial step in a course of conduct planned to culminate in his commission of the crime.

Such a test would incriminate those who have gone a substantial way towards achieving their goal, while leaving untouched those who had merely been involved in planning and collecting information, tools and materials. As such it was the recommended test of a Law Commission Working Party[39] but was nevertheless eventually passed over by the Law Commission in favour of the 'more than merely preparatory' test now enshrined in s. 1 of the Criminal Attempts Act 1981.[40]

2 Objectivist tests

The stance traditionally adopted by the common law is objectivist, requiring criminal attempts to be 'proximate' to the substantive offence. The classic definition of proximity

---

[35] R.A. Duff, *Criminal Attempts*, Oxford: OUP (1996) ch. 12. For a recent argument that outcome luck should not be relevant to responsibility see Larry Alexander and Kimberly Kessler Ferzan, with Stephen J. Morse, *Crime and Culpability: A Theory of Criminal Law*, Cambridge: CUP (2009).
[36] See generally G. Williams *CLGP* 143–50.
[37] Stephen's *Digest of the Criminal Law* (5th edn 1894) article 50.
[38] The courts, in applying this test, never went so far.
[39] Law Commission Working Party; Working Paper No. 50 *Inchoate Offences: Conspiracy, Attempt and Incitement* (1973) paras 78–87.
[40] Law Com. No. 102 *Attempt and Impossibility in Relation to Attempt, Conspiracy and Incitement* (1980).

states that the attempt begins with an act or acts which are 'immediately and not merely remotely connected with the completed offence'.[41] The clearest case of proximity is the last-act test. It holds that an attempt is constituted as a matter of law whenever the defendant performs the last act necessarily performed by him to constitute the offence. If a person has pulled the trigger or broken a window prior to entering a house with burglarious intent he has committed the *actus reus* of an attempt. The last-act test is clearly inappropriate as a general limiting test from both subjectivist and objectivist points of view. Most crimes manifest both dangerousness and criminality before the defendant's last act is completed. As a result, other objectivist tests have been essayed to determine whether the *actus reus* is satisfied.

A more comprehensive test is the unequivocality test which is a direct incorporation of the objectivist theory of manifest criminality. An attempt begins when the defendant performs an act(s) which unequivocally point to his intention to commit the relevant offence. Such a test was adopted in *Davey* v *Lee*,[42] in which the defendants were apprehended having cut through a perimeter fence on their way to a hut in a compound where a quantity of copper wire was stored. It was said that these acts unequivocally pointed to the intention to steal the copper. An obvious problem with the test can be seen using the facts of *Davey* v *Lee* itself. What the defendants had done no more supported a conclusion that they intended to steal the copper than that they intended to set fire to the hut or rape the inhabitant, if any,[43] of the hut. It would be contrary to common sense, to find someone guilty of attempted rape on such facts.

A related test is the 'Rubicon test' by which a person is not adjudged to be beginning his attempt until he has 'burnt his boats' such that he cannot turn back.[44] Although this test is looser than the unequivocality test, it nevertheless makes it difficult for law enforcement agencies to intervene when the defendant is 'on the job', but is not yet in a position to execute his plan, for example, because the intended victim has not arrived at the time the arrest is made, or he has not entered the building where the offence is to take place.

The underlying requirement of proximity informing all these tests resulted in a failure to secure a conviction in some singularly troublesome cases. A well-known example is *Robinson* in which a jeweller staged a fake burglary with the intention of making a fraudulent claim to his insurance company.[45] Having tied himself up and hidden some jewels, he called for help. When the police arrived they disbelieved his story and found the jewels. He was charged with attempting to obtain money by false pretences. The Court of Appeal held that his actions were insufficiently proximate to the substantive offence to count as an attempt. A similar result occurred in *Comer* v *Bloomfield* where the defendant falsely represented to the police that his van was stolen.[46] He then made inquiries of his insurance company as to whether he was covered for the theft. It was held that these acts were insufficient to count as an attempt. What more could have been required to constitute the attempt? In *Robinson* Lord Reading implied that the attempt would be constituted at the time the facts of the pretended burglary were communicated to the insurance company upon which a claim would subsequently be based.[47] Why this would manifest criminality

---

[41] *Eagleton* (1855) Dears CC 515 at 538.
[42] [1967] 2 All ER 423.
[43] A suggestion put by Smith and Hogan.
[44] *DPP* v *Stonehouse* [1977] 2 All ER 909.
[45] [1915] 2 KB 342.
[46] (1970) 55 Cr App Rep 305.
[47] See K.J.M. Smith, 'Proximity in Attempt: Lord Lane's Midway Course' [1991] Crim LR 576 at 579.

any more unequivocally than the false report to the police is anyone's guess. It was to cope with these sort of difficulties that the subjectivist substantial steps test was embraced in the American Model Penal Code. Domestic law took a different direction, namely to incorporate the requirement of proximity in a statutory definition. The definition is in effect a 'fudge'.[48] Proximity to the completed offence is required but, in order to ensure a practical marriage of prevention and retribution, the test for proximity is couched in terms which avoid specifying the degree of proximity required.[49]

18.5 ATTEMPT: THE SUBSTANTIVE LAW

The law of criminal attempts is now encapsulated in the Criminal Attempts Act 1981. Section 1(1) defines a criminal attempt as follows: 'If with intent to commit an offence to which this section applies, a person does an act which is more than merely preparatory to the commission of the offence, he is guilty of attempting to commit the offence.'[50]

In a nutshell, then, the *mens rea* for a criminal attempt is intention and the *actus reus* is an act falling somewhere between the final consummation of the offence and acts of mere preparation.

A *Actus reus*

The only clear aspect of this definition, which is itself unfortunate, is that some form of act is required. An attempt cannot be committed by omission.

> **Case 5**
> Adam comes home to find his wife Eve, apparently dying on the floor, having had a heart attack. Desiring that she should die he fails to call the emergency services. Eve recovers.

Adam will be guilty of no offence. No harm has been caused her by his omission, even were it to be found that he owed her a duty to intervene. He cannot be guilty of attempted murder either since, intention to kill notwithstanding, he commits no act.[51] The Law Commission quite properly proposes a change to the law in this regard recommending that an attempt should be capable of commission by omission so long as the substantive offence, as here, can be committed by omission.[52] Adam's liability would then depend upon whether he owed Eve a duty by virtue of being her spouse.

1 The act interpreted

Section 1(1) defines the *actus reus* of a criminal attempt as an act which is 'more than merely preparatory to the commission of the offence'. This was intended to be a reaffirmation of the common law (proximity) test which had always sought to distinguish between acts of mere preparation and acts of 'perpetration'. The formula was intended to steer a midway course. The last act and Rubicon tests were too restrictive. On the other hand, the

---

[48] Ibid.
[49] For general discussion of the problems of definition see Law Commission, *Criminal Law: Attempt, Conspiracy and Incitement* (Law Com. No. 102, 1980) 2.40; I. Dennis, 'The Criminal Attempts Act 1981' [1982] Criminal Law Review 5.
[50] Ireland, Canada, Victoria, Singapore, and Australian Capital Territory all use a similar formula.
[51] *Nevard* [2006] EWCA Crim 2896.
[52] LCCP 183 *Conspiracy and Attempts* (2007) 230.

series of acts and substantial steps tests could conceivably incriminate for mere acts of preparation.

On the face of it, however, the statutory definition is so empty of meaning that it could provide a satisfactory benchmark for intervention for both objectivist and subjectivist.[53] The official point of view is that it gives sufficient flexibility to deal with the large numbers of different fact situations which could potentially give rise to attempt liability.[54] Some crimes necessarily involve a great many steps leading up to the consummated crime. Some complicated frauds may take months to set up. Many entirely lawful transactions may be contracted in order to set the scene for the ultimate scam. Other crimes, e.g. assaults, are often spontaneous and are over almost before they are started.

The role of judge and jury in drawing the distinction between acts of preparation and acts of consummation must be defined. The jury's task is the general one of deciding whether the acts they have been invited to consider by the judge go beyond acts of mere preparation.[55] The judge's task is twofold. First, he must decide whether the acts concerned are capable of amounting to acts going beyond mere preparation. If they are not, the judge must withdraw the case from them. Failure to do so will mean that any conviction will be quashed by the appeal court. In some of the cases which follow, this is what happened. A judge allowed the jury to consider the evidence with a view to deciding whether the relevant acts were more than merely preparatory. The jury decided they were and convicted. The Court of Appeal then quashed the conviction on the ground that not only did the acts not go beyond the preparatory stage, they were incapable of being so construed. In effect, the roles of judge and appeal court in this regard mean that the decision is largely one of law. The jury only get their hands on the case if the judge finds that it would be reasonable to convict.[56] The second task of the judge is to give guidance to the jury as to the criteria to be adopted in deciding whether the relevant acts go beyond preparation. Where the 'last act' has been performed that guidance will, no doubt, be robust.

In the early years after the passing of the Act, the common law rules were routinely relied upon as a means of determining when acts of 'mere preparation' ceased.[57] Although latterly disapproving the use of common law proximity tests,[58] it appears clear that these tests still rule the judges 'from their graves'. How other than the Rubicon test can the decision in *Dagnall* be explained? Here it was held to be attempted rape where the defendant had dragged a woman by the hair and pushed her against a fence and told her he wanted to 'fuck her' and then 'rape her'.[59] If proximity is the key it seems passing strange that a person could be considered as having gone beyond preparing for intercourse, consensual or otherwise, simply by pushing a woman against a fence and stating his intentions. There is rather more to intercourse than that. Wrongful the act certainly was, but attempted rape? Would a better criminal label not be 'assault with intent to rape'?

In the leading case of *Gullefer*,[60] Lord Lane CJ expressly rejected the Rubicon test, in reaching his decision and expounded the current approach to distinguishing between acts of 'mere preparation' and true attempts. Lord Lane CJ stated that '(the attempt) begins when the merely preparatory acts come to an end and the defendant embarks upon the

---

[53] G. Williams *TCL* (1983) 418.
[54] K.J.M. Smith, loc. cit. 580–2.
[55] By s. 4(3).
[56] See the helpful discussion in Williams *TCL* (1983) 415–17.
[57] Cf. *Widdowson* [1986] Crim LR 233; *Boyle and Boyle* (1986) 84 Cr App Rep 270.
[58] *Jones* [1990] 3 All ER 886.
[59] Cf. *Attorney-General's Reference (No. 1 of 1992)* (1993) 96 Cr App R 298 (CA).
[60] [1990] 3 All ER 882.

crime proper. When that is will depend upon the facts in any particular case'.[61] A similar formulation occurred in *Moore* v *DPP*.[62] The Court of Appeal stated that for conduct by an individual to constitute an attempt, and not an act that was merely preparatory to the commission of an offence, the conduct by the individual had to be sufficiently close to the final act that it could, 'on the application of common sense, be properly regarded as part of the execution of the individual's plan to commit the intended offence'.

Disappointingly, the notion of being embarked on the 'crime proper' or being 'on the job' was interpreted in a notably restrictive way in *Gullefer* itself, reminding one of the case of *Robinson* and why the Criminal Attempts Act attempted to replace the common law tests with a new statutory test. *Gullefer* had jumped onto a greyhound track in the course of a race and waved his arms about in a vain attempt to stop the race. His reasons for doing so were to cause the race to be abandoned, which would allow him to recover his stake. He was convicted, at first instance, of attempted theft. His appeal was allowed on the grounds that what he had done had not gone 'beyond mere preparation'. If Gullefer was to be guilty of the offence, the implication is that he would have had to ask for his stake back. Being 'on the crime proper' thus seems to be asking for an act which bears the (objective) hallmarks of theft, rather than, say, a substantial (or unequivocal) step towards the commission of the consummated offence.[63]

Judges have not, then, changed their concept of an attempt with the passing of the Act. If they had done, it would have required something far more focused than the 'more than merely preparatory' formula which, as suggested above, can mean all things to all people. This analysis is borne out by other decisions decided since *Gullefer*. In *Campbell*[64] the appellant who planned to rob a post office was apprehended by police within a yard of the post office carrying an imitation gun and a written demand for cash intended for the cashier. He was convicted of attempted robbery and his appeal was allowed. In a classic example of objectivism losing touch with the preventive point behind inchoate liability, Watkins LJ insisted that 'a number of acts remained undone' and that, at least until the post office was entered, his acts were merely preparatory. No doubt the police should have disguised themselves as cashiers and waited for the demand to be made before they pounced. Even more remarkable perhaps is the case of *Geddes*. D entered school toilets as a trespasser, equipped with rope, knife and tape. Evidence pointed to the fact that he was bent on committing kidnap of a young boy. The Court of Appeal quashed the conviction on the basis that these acts could not be considered as going beyond the preparatory stage.[65,66] Although putting himself in the position to commit the offence, he had not 'actually tried' to commit it.[67] The Law Commission were so exercised by this case, in particular, that they provisionally proposed the creation of a new inchoate offence of preparing for crime to address the gap between 'preparing for' and 'trying to commit' an offence.[68] As some have pointed out, however, such a response is unnecessary so long as the judiciary hold steadfastly to the

---

[61] At 885.

[62] [2010] All ER (D) 195.

[63] A similar analysis was offered in *Rowley* (1992) 94 Cr App R 95, a case on incitement.

[64] (1991) 93 Cr App R 350; for a more realistic response see *Tosti and another* [1997] Crim LR 746.

[65] Clarkson, C, 'Attempt: the Conduct Requirement' (2009) 29(1) Oxford J Legal Studies 25–41.

[66] *Geddes* [1996] Crim LR 894.

[67] [1990] 3 All ER 886.

[68] Law Com. Consultation Paper 183 (2007) 171–3. It abandoned this approach in the final report, responding to the criticism that the solution was worse than the problem; [2010] EWHC 1822 (Admin).

principle that attempts begin when the execution of the offence begins. When that may be will, of course, depend upon the facts but a statutory list of illustrations would solve most potential problems of application.

A more pragmatic stance was evident in *Jones*.[69] The defendant bought a shotgun, shortened its barrels, put on a disguise and waited outside a school where the intended victim, his rival in love, was due to arrive to pick up his daughter. On the man's arrival the defendant jumped into his victim's car and told him to drive on. Later he told the victim to park, whereupon he pointed the gun at the victim, saying 'You are not going to like this'. The victim grabbed the gun and threw it out of the window. The defendant's conviction for attempted murder was upheld by the Court of Appeal. They rejected the appellant's submission that he had not got to the position of being able to carry out the offence – the safety catch still being on. Taylor LJ stated that the correct approach was to ignore the common law tests and to effect a simple interpretation of the words 'more than merely preparatory'.[70] Buying and preparing the gun, donning the disguise and going to the school were acts of preparation for the crime. Jumping into the car and taking out the gun went beyond such acts. As critics observed, however, we did not need a codifying Act to produce this conclusion.[71] Jones would have been guilty under any of the common law tests. The Act was intended to loosen up the proximity tests, so as to enable successful prosecutions for those who had not 'crossed the Rubicon' but who nevertheless had embarked upon the crime itself. Yet the form of words adopted allows judges to continue to decide the cases on the basis of conduct's 'manifest criminality', or 'burning their boats', rather than manifest 'dangerousness'. Neither the Law Commission nor Taylor LJ, for example, seriously considered that the attempt, in cases involving a 'stakeout', might begin when the stakeout began. Authority now confirms this.[72] Why not? If an act of attempting murder had not begun yet, was Jones nevertheless not 'on the job' when he was waiting outside the school gates? Should he be permitted to get into the car, gun at the ready, before the attempt begins?[73] One response to this is that the criminal law already has enough crimes of preparation to allow for effective law enforcement and the prevention of harm. For instance, the police could intervene at the time of the stakeout and arrest Jones on reasonable suspicion that he was about to commit an offence, thus preventing the murder, and then charge for possessing a dangerous weapon, or possessing a weapon with intent to kill.[74]

2 Evaluation

Despite the best intentions of the Law Commission the 'more than merely preparatory' formula has done little to advance rationality in this area of law. Applying the natural meaning of the words is not the answer since the natural meaning of the words is only uncovered through the conceptual filter of an objectivist or subjectivist attitude. Using the former, the words require an act bearing the hallmark of the consummated offence. Using the latter, the words require simply an act which indicates that the offence is due to take place unless it is thwarted. As Williams puts it, discussing *Jones*, 'I do not think it an abuse

---

[69] [1990] 3 All ER 886.
[70] At 889–90.
[71] G. Williams, 'Wrong Turnings on the Law of Attempt' [1991] Crim LR 416.
[72] *Campbell* (1991) 93 Cr App R 350.
[73] See *Tosti*, above, and commentary at 747.
[74] LCCP 183 (2007) 16.48. The problem with this argument is that they would be disabled if Jones, for example, intended to kill by strangulation, drowning or corporal violence.

of language to say that Kenneth Jones started his attempt as soon as he set out with his firearm, his disguise and his Spanish money, or even when he acquired the firearm and his disguise with the firm object of using it in the offence'.[75]

The problem, then, is not so much the words themselves but the conceptual resources of the judges who interpret those words. If these conceptual resources are not to thwart the avowed policy of criminalising attempts, it is necessary for that policy, whatever it is, to be articulated clearly within the definition of an attempt.[76] Whether we use a subjectivist form of words, e.g. 'substantial steps',[77] or an objectivist form, e.g. 'on the job', the furtherance of that policy probably then requires a precise blueprint of what it is which converts thought into deed in as many potential attempt scenarios as possible. Probably the best example of such a blueprint is to be found in the Model Penal Code, which takes an un-ashamedly subjectivist stance based upon proof of the defendant taking 'substantial steps' towards commission of the substantive offence.[78] 'Substantial steps' require conduct which 'strongly corroborates' the actor's criminal purpose to effect the substantive crime.[79] It continues:

> (2) The following, if strongly corroborative of the actor's criminal purpose, shall not be held insufficient as a matter of law:
> (a) lying in wait, searching for or following the contemplated victim of the crime;
> (b) enticing or seeking to entice the contemplated victim of the crime to go to the place contemplated for its commission;
> (c) reconnoitring the place contemplated for the commission of the crime;
> (d) unlawful entry of a structure, vehicle or enclosure in which it is contemplated that the crime will be committed;
> (e) possession, collection or fabrication of materials to be employed in the commission of the crime, which are specifically designed for unlawful use or which can serve no lawful purpose of the actor under the circumstances;
> (f) soliciting an innocent agent to engage in conduct constituting an element of the crime.[80]

Williams adds two further items to the list to cover cases such as *Robinson*. These are:

(g) deceiving any person for the purpose of committing the crime, and
(h) preparing a deception for the purpose of any crime involving deception or fraud.

He concludes: 'This list beautifully clarifies nearly all the matters that have been litigated in England, most of which we have either failed to settle or settled in an impolitic way'.[81]

It is hard not to agree with this endorsement. It should be noted that the above instances are not conclusively criminal attempts. First, they may only form the *actus reus* of a criminal attempt if they strongly corroborate the actor's criminal purpose. This will first have to be established independently, e.g. through confession, for the act to be even cap-able of serving as corroboration. Second, the provision leaves the question whether the relevant act is sufficient to count as an attempt to the jury. The above list contains merely examples of what the judge as a matter of law is not entitled to remove from the jury. It is, therefore, still open to them to decide that a person reconnoitring a bank with the avowed

---

[75] G. Williams, op. cit. at 422.
[76] Williams argues, it is submitted correctly, that that policy was not articulated in the Law Commission report. The resultant fudge was clear for all to see.
[77] Williams' preferred option.
[78] Section 5.01(1)(c).
[79] Section 5.01(2).
[80] Section 5.01(2).
[81] 420–1.

purpose of robbing it, is not guilty of attempted robbery because, say, the quality of the acts concerned and the mentality of the defendant left them unsure as to whether he would have had the courage to go through with his plan.

The Law Commission recognised the usefulness of statutory examples in the 2007 Consultation Paper. Rather than exploiting such examples to elucidate the notion of a criminal attempt, however, they used them for the more contentious purpose of indicating what kinds of activities count as a new back up offence of criminal preparation. Such activities, to count as the conduct element in this offence, are such as would properly be regarded as part of the execution of the plan to commit the offence as opposed to a pure attempt, which would be limited to last acts. Critics almost unanimously opposed this proposal for being undesirable, unnecessary and unnecessarily complicated. It is undesirable and unnecessary because all acts committed 'while the defendant is on the job' are properly to be regarded as part of the attempt to commit it and the criminal law should label according to the wrong a person commits rather than the precise form the wrong takes. It is unnecessarily complicated because rather than exercising itself to ensure conceptual clarity it is proposing to create a new offence tier which advances the cogency of the scheme of liability not one jot and will only serve to compromise such (small) clarity as it currently enjoys.[82] The Law Commission abandoned the proposals in the 2009 Report.[83] Due to the absence of any clear consensus as to how the conduct element should be defined it opted to recommend no change to the conduct element of the offence, nor provide a list of statutory examples by which to clarify its scope.

B Mens rea

1 Intention

Consonant with its use in everyday language the *mens rea* for attempt, both at common law and by statute, is intention.[84] To attempt is to try. We do not generally try to achieve those consequences which we do not intend to achieve.[85] Some treat the fact of this everyday use as the final 'knock-down' argument against broadening the fault element in criminal attempts to include, for example, recklessness.[86] Others, more plausibly, hold that applying the everyday meaning is the best way of ensuring that the law of criminal attempts punishes the right people. The prosecution must prove not only that the defendant intended to perform the act necessary to constitute the conduct element in the offence (e.g. pulled the trigger of a gun) but also, in the case of result crimes, intended the consequences. The important consequence of this requirement is to render a criminal attempt an offence of higher *mens rea* than the majority of substantive offences with which it may be conjoined. In *Fallon* the defendant shot a policeman in the course of resisting arrest. He was charged with attempted murder. The Court of Appeal held that there were two issues for the jury. The first was whether the shooting was deliberate. The second was whether the defendant intended to kill the policeman. The *mens rea* would not be satisfied upon proof

---

[82] C.M.V. Clarkson, 'Attempt: the Conduct Requirement' (2009) 29(1) Oxford Journal Legal Studies 25–41.

[83] Law Com. No. 318 *Conspiracy and Attempts* (2009).

[84] L. Alexander and K. Kessler, '*Mens Rea* and Inchoate Crimes' (1997) 87 Journal of Criminal Law & Criminology 1138.

[85] Unless perhaps we are trying to prove that we cannot achieve such a consequence, as in the case where a parent to teach a child a lesson about volume tries to pour a pint of liquid into a half-pint mug.

[86] See A.R. White, *Misleading Cases*, Oxford: Clarendon Press (1991) 15; cf. D. Stuart, '*Mens Rea*, Negligence and Attempts' [1968] Crim LR 647.

of an intention only to commit really serious injury although this is enough for the substantive offence.[87] The high *mens rea* requirement can be justified as a penal counterweight to the absence of a clearly defined social harm.

(a) *The meaning of intention*

The meaning of intention will now be considered. If attempt is a synonym for 'try', a plausible meaning to ascribe to intention is 'purpose'. We try to do the things we have a purpose to do. If A acts for the purpose of achieving a consequence it follows that failure to achieve that purpose will be an object of disappointment to him.[88] The authorities take a broader notion of intention than this.

The major authority on intention in the law of criminal attempts is *Mohan*. Although the decision predates the Criminal Attempts Act, the Act does not provide its own definition and, therefore, it is reasonable to assume that its common law meaning is still binding.[89]*Mohan* defines intention as 'a decision to bring about, insofar as it lies within the accused's power . . . (the relevant consequence) whether the accused desired the consequence or not'.[90] This has been interpreted as signifying that intention bears the same meaning as in the criminal law generally. Unfortunately this meaning is still not entirely clear. Does the person who puts a bomb in a cargo plane in order to claim insurance money on the destroyed cargo have the intention to kill?[91] Likewise does the parent who throws his child from the roof of a burning tower block in the attempt to save her life, but knowing her death is virtually certain, have the intention to kill? *Mohan* makes the answer clear in both cases. The bomber does intend to kill. The parent does not. A *Nedrick* direction would not make this distinction.[92]

In *Walker and Hayles*[93] the point was emphasised that it was not necessary to give any special guidance to the jury as to what intention means unless the defendant's action was capable of supporting different inferences as to what he intended. The defendants had dropped their victim from a third-floor window. They were charged with attempted murder. The trial judge told the jury that to be guilty of attempted murder they had to be sure that the accused were trying to kill. When the jury were unable to understand this direction the trial judge gave them a *Nedrick*-style direction and told them that they could infer the intention to kill from the defendants' foresight that death was a high probability. The Court of Appeal stated that giving the jury special guidance was a mistake but not a fatal one. Special guidance was only necessary in cases where the defendant claimed that he was trying to do something other than to kill.[94] A better approach, it is submitted, would be to direct the jury in accordance with *Mohan*.

---

[87] [1994] Crim LR 519; cf. *Whybrow* (1951) 35 Cr App Rep 141; *Walker and Hayles* (1990) 90 Cr App Rep 226.

[88] See R.A. Duff, *Intention, Agency and Criminal Liability* 202–3; 'Acting, Trying and Criminal Liability' in Shute *et al.* (1993) 75–106; cf. J. Hornsby, 'On What's Intentionally Done' ibid. 55–74; cf. J. Horder, 'Varieties of Intention, Criminal Attempts and Endangerment' [1994] LS 335 at 337 ff. for an account of why a criminal attempt might not require the defendant to intend to commit the completed offence; cf. V. Chiao, 'Intention and Attempt' (2010) 4 Criminal Law and Philosophy 37.

[89] This was the view taken in *Pearman* (1984) 80 Cr App R 259 (CA).

[90] [1975] 2 All ER 193 CA at 200 per James LJ.

[91] See *R v Pearman* (1984) 80 Cr App R 259; V. Chiao, 'Intention and Attempt' (2010) 4 Criminal Law and Philosophy 37.

[92] See discussion at pp. 136–40.

[93] (1990) 90 Cr App Rep 226.

[94] See the very persuasive case argued by J.C. Smith in his commentary on *Walker and Hayles* [1990] Crim LR 47–8.

2 Attempts and recklessness as to circumstances

A problem arises in respect of those crimes, part of whose mental element is directed towards the presence of material circumstances. For such crimes the Criminal Attempts Act makes no mention of the relevant mental attitude in respect of such circumstances. If we take the crime of rape as an example, the consummated crime is constituted upon proof that the accused intended to have sexual intercourse with a person (the prohibited result), that the person did not consent (the prohibited circumstance) and that he had no reasonable belief that the person was consenting.[95] The Criminal Attempts Act describes the *mens rea* for attempting this offence as 'an intention to commit rape'. Does this mean that the accused must be shown to have known the person not to be consenting (i.e. he intended to have sex with a non-consenting person)?[96] Or is negligence as to this circumstance enough (i.e. he intended to have sex and he did not reasonably believe the person to be consenting)?[97] The stance which was taken at common law was that a person intends to commit rape if he tries to have intercourse with a woman without an honest belief that she is consenting. This was clearly sensible. In a great many cases it will be next to impossible to prove that the accused positively knew the woman not to be consenting. Moreover there seems no reason in principle or logic why we should not hold a person responsible for trying to rape a person when it can be shown that his intention was to have intercourse with the woman whether she consented or not.[98] This position was confirmed in *Khan*.[99] The appellant tried to have intercourse with a woman who did not consent. The trial judge directed the jury that in relation to the circumstances (of consent) the *mens rea* to be established need only be that necessary for the consummated offence (that is recklessness). This direction was upheld on appeal. Russell LJ explained the decision as follows:

> In our judgement . . . the words 'with intent to commit an offence' to be found in s. 1 of the 1981 Act mean, when applied to rape, 'with intent to have sexual intercourse with a woman in circumstances where she does not consent and the defendant knows or could not care less about her absence of consent'. The only 'intent' . . . of the rapist is to have sexual intercourse. He commits the offence because of the circumstances in which he manifests that intent, i.e. when the woman is not consenting and he either knows it or could not care less about the absence of consent.[100]

The reasoning in *Khan* has been adopted in the context of other offences where recklessness as to circumstances needs to be established. Two problems may be identified with this approach.

The first problem is to adduce clear criteria for differentiating between *mens rea* as to consequences and *mens rea* as to circumstances. Consider the case of aggravated arson, for example. A person is guilty of this offence if he commits arson intending to endanger the life of another or being reckless as to whether another's life will be endangered. Does the latter intention or recklessness go to consequences or to circumstances? It could be either.[101]

In *Attorney-General's Reference (No. 3 of 1992)*[102] this distinction was not explored. It was held that the offence of attempted aggravated arson did not require the would-be

---

[95] Sexual Offences Act 2003, section 1(1).

[96] This was the position earlier adopted by Law Commission No. 102 *Attempt and Impossibility in Relation to Attempt, Conspiracy and Incitement*, London: HMSO (1980) (hereafter Law Com. No. 102 (1980)) para. 2.15.

[97] This is now the position adopted by the Law Commission: Law Com. No. 177 (1981) cl. 49(2) at 1406. LCCP 183 (2007) 78.

[98] R.A. Duff, 'The Circumstances of an Attempt' (1991) 50 Cambridge Law Journal 100.

[99] [1990] 2 All ER 783.

[100] At 788.

[101] D.W. Elliott, 'Endangering Life by Damaging or Destroying Property' [1997] Crim LR 382.

[102] [1994] 1 WLR 409.

arsonist to intend to endanger life. As long as arson was intended, recklessness as to the other element would suffice. This can either be explained as the court eradicating the distinction altogether,[103] or assuming that the type of recklessness involved was as to circumstances. This is the view taken by the majority of other commentators. It is unfortunate that such serious penal consequences should hang on something so imprecise and unanalysed.

A second problem derives from part of the reasoning in the decision itself which has an impact on the potential coverage of rape as discussed above. Schiemann J stated that the essence of an attempt was that the *mens rea* for the full offence was established and that in addition to this, the prosecution could show 'that the defendant intended to supply the missing physical element from the completed offence'. Thus as long as the accused intends to cause a fire (the missing physical element), he is properly convicted of attempted aggravated arson if the prosecution can establish the relevant mental attitude for the consummated offence (intention or recklessness). This is not as satisfactory as it might sound. The relevant mental attitude in this case was *Caldwell* recklessness which did not at that time require proof of foresight of the risk that his action might endanger life. This would have produced the unfortunate result that a person was liable for an offence which, in commonsense terms, can be rephrased as attempting to endanger a person's life by arson, even though he was not even conscious that his act provoked that risk.[104] Foresight of the risk is now necessary following *R v G*, and so this problem disappears, but it re-emerges elsewhere, namely rape. The statutory offence replaces recklessness with negligence as to a circumstance, namely the fact of consent. This means that a person can be guilty of rape if his belief is unreasonable, **although he genuinely would not have committed the offence if he knew the woman not to be consenting.** The effect of the *Attorney-General's Reference* renders this fact irrelevant. The attempt is constituted through the defendant's intention to perform the act of intercourse with *mens rea* for the offence (the absence of a reasonable belief that the other is consenting). This means that a person may be guilty of attempted rape although he did not in effect intend to have intercourse with a woman who did not consent, because he genuinely, if unreasonably, believed her to be consenting. It has the even more unfortunate consequence that a person may be at risk of a conviction for attempting a strict liability crime,[105] without any intention or foresight at all. In the opinion of many commentators this would be unacceptable.[106] Both these possibilities appear inconsistent with the rationale of attempts which is to punish the defendant for deliberately trying to commit a criminal wrong.[107] The Law Commission in their latest Report, while approving this case, nevertheless propose to limit its application by restricting the fault element for circumstances to recklessness, as per *Khan*: 'where D need only be reckless as to the existence of a circumstance for the substantive offence, recklessness as to that matter also suffices for attempt.'[108]

---

[103] This appears to be Ashworth's view. Ashworth treats the *A-G's Reference* as a case on recklessness as to consequences.

[104] LCCP 183, *Conspiracy and Attempts* (2007) 78–82. Cf. D.W. Elliot, 'Endangering Life by Destroying or Damaging Property' [1997] Crim LR 382 at 392–5.

[105] Cf. *Prince* (1875) LR 2 CCR 154. See above, Chapter 7.

[106] One commentator considered such a development, when it had been mooted as a possibility, as 'fantastic': Perkins and Boyce (1982) 640–1; cf. J.C. Smith, 'Two Problems in Criminal Attempts Re-examined' [1962] Crim LR 135.

[107] Thus it has been held that a person cannot be guilty of an attempted crime vicariously, even though the substantive crime can be committed vicariously: *Gardner v Akeroyd* [1952] 2 All ER 306.

[108] The Law Commission (Law Com. No. 318) *Conspiracy and Attempts* (2009) confirming the view in the 2007 Consultation Paper. See note 104.

On the face of it this is the obviously correct response. But there is another point of view. If we treat the criminal law as constituted by two distinct paradigms of criminal responsibility, one for attacks on individual autonomy (requiring proof of subjective fault), and one for the prevention of harm (requiring no such proof), there is no reason in principle why we should not punish the latter attempts in exactly the same way as the substantive offence, i.e. without proof of *mens rea*.[109] It is plausible, for example, that a person should be guilty of attempted dangerous driving (a conduct crime) if he is apprehended in the course of attempting to drive away a car, whether he knows, or simply ought to know that the car has faulty brakes.[110] With respect to **such crimes**, at least, where much social harm can be wrought by inadvertence, the gap between the (criminal) label attached to the defendant's conduct and his culpability is not, it is submitted, too wide to be tolerated. The paradigm template is useful as far as it goes but arguably it is not complete. It may be argued in relation to rape, for example, that it should also be considered in the same light,[111] despite the obvious objection that it exists to support autonomy rather than simply prevent harm. If autonomy is so important in this case that subjective fault is unnecessary concerning the existence of consent it may be thought that it should be unnecessary for the attempt, also, which exists to vindicate the same rights of a person to be free from unwanted and unreasoned interferences with her autonomy.

3 Conditional intention

One potential problem concerning the *mens rea* for criminal attempts arises where the defendant has formed a general intention to commit a crime but has not yet a specific intention as to the precise subject-matter of the crime. For example, a person breaks into the boot of a car[112] or takes a handbag[113] to see if there is anything worth stealing. In such circumstances the defendant has what is known as a conditional intent, that is, an intention which will come into existence only when a particular condition is satisfied. At one stage a defendant was not guilty of a criminal attempt upon proof of such an intention. In *Husseyn* the position was explained as follows: 'it cannot be said that one who has it in mind to steal only if what he finds is worth stealing has a present intention to steal'.[114] The position now is that the defendant can be found guilty of a criminal attempt so long as the indictment is drafted sufficiently broadly as not to refer to specific items which may or may not have been on the defendant's 'shopping list'. Thus a person caught rifling through a handbag or the boot of a car should be charged with attempted theft of 'articles unknown from a car/handbag belonging to Z', or some similar formula. If the handbag or car contained nothing of value, so that the theft was aborted, the defendant can now be convicted of an (impossible) attempt. Once again the indictment should be worded so as to reflect what the defendant has done.[115]

---

[109] A. Brudner, 'Agency and Welfare in the Penal Law' in Shute *et al.* (1993) 21, generally.

[110] J. Dressler (1987) 341; cf. Ashworth, 'Criminal Attempts and the Role of Resulting Harm' (1988) 19 Rutgers LJ 725, 755–7.

[111] This necessitates, of course, a rational division of crimes and their elements between the two paradigms – A. Brudner, op. cit. 46–53.

[112] *Husseyn* (1977) 67 Cr App R 131.

[113] *Easom* [1971] 2 QB 315.

[114] Per Lord Scarman (1977) 67 Cr App R 131 at 132.

[115] Cf. the position at common law; *Easom* [1971] 2 QB 315.

C Voluntary abandonment

Normally the constitution of a criminal attempt must embrace the possibility that the putative attempter may desist from the consummated offence. It is for this reason that the Rubicon test is initially so persuasive and why the 'more than merely preparatory' formula is, as exemplified in *Campbells*, typically interpreted restrictively. If criminal intervention is premised upon dangerousness and moral blameworthiness then until the would-be attempter shows his true colours as action man rather than mere fantasist there is no ground for linking him to the substantive offence.[116] No separate defence of withdrawal is recognised in English law.[117] A withdrawal from an attempt is treated then as relevant only in its propensity to substantiate the actor's absence of commitment and therefore the inappropriateness of pre-emptive intervention.[118] Sufficient flexibility is built into the 'more than merely preparatory' formula to allow evidence of voluntary withdrawal to colour the court's view of whether or not the attempt had actually begun. An actor's change of mind, say in desisting from killing or robbing a bank, is used to indicate that the necessary commitment to go through with the offence was never formed, reflected by the ease with which the project was ultimately abandoned.'[119] In Duff's view this does not go far enough. There will be occasions, particularly in complicated fraud and other contexts, where the attempt takes place over the course of a significant period of time, when, although the attempt has begun, the attempter changes his mind and decides it is the wrong thing to do. In such a case a defence should be available:

> conduct takes its character as a criminal attempt from its relationship to the complete offence which she intends to commit: it counts as an attempt because it is directed towards that offence. Once she abandons that attempt, though, it ceases to be one . . . she embarked on the attempt: but in the end she did not try . . . to commit it.[120]

D Impossibility

In the previous section we considered a particular problem in relation to thwarted attempts, namely how far down the path to committing the substantive offence the defendant has to travel before he can be convicted of the attempt. In this section we consider the problem posed by impossible attempts. These arise, it will be remembered, where the course of conduct adopted to achieve a criminal ambition was incapable of resulting in the commission of the substantive offence. The spectrum of impossible attempts can be illustrated as follows:

Case 6

A buys a large quantity of talcum powder at a French hypermarket. He secretes it in his car, believing erroneously that he would have to pay duty on such a large consignment. Customs officials discover the talcum powder on a routine search.

---

[116] Such a credible link is established where the accused has performed his last act or where, notwithstanding the absence of such an act, he is sufficiently close to doing so that a hypothetical observer, knowing what he does of him, would apprehend his criminal purpose.

[117] Unsurprising that in the United States, which adopts a subjectivist approach to the constitution of criminal attempts, such a defence is recognised. See *People* v *Graham* 176 APP. Div. 38, 162 NYS 334 (1916).

[118] Smith and Hogan (1996) 327; Glanville Williams, *Textbook of Criminal Law*, London: Stevens (1983) 410.

[119] As Fletcher puts it: 'Whether the actor has an intent of (the required) degree of firmness can be determined only by waiting to see whether in fact he carries out the plan.' G. Fletcher (1978) at 188; cf. R.A. Duff, *Criminal Attempts*, Oxford: OUP (1996) 65–75.

[120] Duff (1996) 395.

Case 7

A secretes a large quantity of talcum powder in his car, believing it to be heroin. The talcum powder is discovered at Customs.

Case 8

A, a pickpocket, dips his hand into the pocket of B. The pocket is empty.

Case 9

A, a burglar, uses a penknife to try to force open a householder's reinforced steel front door. The attempt fails, as it was inevitably doomed to.

Case 10

A, a witch, sticks pins into a waxen representation of her intended victim, believing this will kill him. It does not.

The question in each of these cases is whether what the defendant has done is the *actus reus* of a criminal attempt. The common law's response to this question was not entirely cogent. Case 6 is not strictly a case of an impossible attempt at all. It is an illusory crime, which both objectivists and subjectivists would be united in holding incapable of forming the subject-matter of a criminal attempt.[121] Case 7 is a case of what is known as 'legal impossibility'. These were treated at common law as akin to illusory crimes. Since what the defendant did was lawful, it could not be converted into something unlawful by the presence of an accompanying state of mind. This would impose criminal liability for intention alone. The reasoning is disclosed in the following statement of Lord Reid: 'The crime is impossible in the circumstances, so no acts could be proximate to it.'[122]

Cases 8, 9 and 10 are cases of factual impossibility. The common law's attitude towards such cases was ambiguous. Case 9 was always treated as sufficient to impose liability. The offence itself was possible. The defendant had *mens rea* and committed an act which was sufficiently proximate to the consummated offence to manifest criminality. This was a case of ineptitude rather than factual impossibility. Case 10 has not cropped up, and probably never will, given the pragmatic nature of prosecuting authorities. In practice the matter would best be disposed of by reference to questions of proximity rather than impossibility.[123] In Case 8 the absence of the subject-matter of the crime rendered the defendant's action objectively innocuous. On the other hand, what the defendant intended to do was the subject-matter of a criminal offence and, no doubt, if not stopped he would have continued until he had managed to commit it. The general stance taken by the common law was that such conduct could not form the subject-matter of a criminal attempt.[124] Latterly, however, it had been suggested that the irrationality of the rule could be obviated to a certain extent by means of various technical measures, in particular the use of a suitably vaguely worded indictment.[125]

---

[121] See Fletcher (1978) ch. 3 generally; R.A. Duff (1996) 380; *Taaffe* [1984] 1 All ER 747.
[122] Lord Reid in *Haughton v Smith* [1973] 3 All ER 1109 at 1121.
[123] At least since the Criminal Attempts Act makes such 'impossible attempts' indictable offences.
[124] *Partington and Williams* (1976) 62 Cr App Rep 220; cf. *Collins* (1864) 9 Cox CC 497.
[125] *DPP v Nock* [1978] AC 979.

1 Impossibility under the Act

In accordance with the Law Commission's recommendation,[126] the law on impossible attempts takes the subjectivist line that an attempt is constituted by reference to what the defendant thought he was doing, rather than by what objectively he was doing. Section 1(2) and (3) together render (more than merely preparatory) conduct an attempt as long as, on the facts as they appeared to the defendant, the full offence would have been constituted.

Section 1 is as follows:

> (1)   If with intent to commit a crime to which this section applies, a person does an act which is more than merely preparatory to the commission of the offence, he is guilty of attempting to commit the offence.
> (2)   A person may be guilty of attempting to commit an offence to which this section applies even though the facts are such that the commission of the offence is impossible.
> (3)   In any case where –
>   (a)   apart from this subsection a person's intention would not be regarded as having amounted to an intention to commit an offence but
>   (b)   if the facts of the case had been as he believed them to be, his intention would be so regarded, then for the purposes of subsection (1) above he shall be regarded as having an intent to commit that offence.

Applying these complicated provisions to the above cases, Cases 6, 8 and 9 are the simplest to dispose of. In Case 9, A is guilty of an attempt if (a) he intends to commit a criminal offence. He does. He intends to commit burglary; (b) his act is more than merely preparatory. It is. This being so the attempt is constituted even though it is impossible. A similar analysis can be adopted for Case 8. In Case 6, A is not guilty of a criminal offence. This would be so even if there were a relevant offence but it was not committed because the necessary import limitation had not been reached. In both cases, on the facts as he believed them to be ('I am taking 100 litres of talcum powder through customs'), he would not disclose an intention to commit a crime.

In Case 7 the defendant would be guilty of a criminal attempt to evade customs duty since, on the facts as he believed them to be ('I am taking heroin through customs'), he would evince an intention to commit a crime. Early in the Act's career the House of Lords, in *Anderton* v *Ryan*, refused to find that a criminal attempt could be established for an act which was 'objectively innocent' as this is. It was held that a person who handled goods believing them, erroneously, to be stolen, could not be guilty of attempting to handle stolen goods (a video recorder). They quickly responded to 'just criticism'[127] and, in *Shivpuri*,[128] overruled their previous decision, to the evident relief of a great many commentators. In the latter case the defendants imported what subsequently transpired to be a quantity of snuff, believing it to be a controlled drug. It was held that the criminal attempt was established. No doubt on a strict interpretation of the Act, *Anderton* v *Ryan* should have been overruled, yet there was a kernel of good sense in it. There is a clear difference in culpability between a person whose purpose **requires** the substantive crime to be committed (Shivpuri would have dumped the snuff if he had discovered its true nature) and a person who acts for the purpose of obtaining an innocuous commodity at less than market price (Ryan would have kept the video recorder whatever its status).[129] Given that in the latter case nothing manifestly criminal or even harmful had occurred, the use of the

---

[126] Law Commission No. 102 (1980) para. 2.96.
[127] Most notably that of G. Williams, 'The Lords and Impossible Attempts' [1986] Camb LJ 33.
[128] [1987] AC 1; *Anderton* v *Ryan* [1985] AC 567.
[129] See generally B. Hogan, 'The Criminal Attempts Act and Attempting the Impossible' [1984] Crim LR 584.

criminal sanction might seem more than usually oppressive where the defendant shows no unequivocal defiance of the rule of law.[130] Adopting an example of Lord Bridge in *Anderton v Ryan*, would we really feel easy punishing a youth for having sex with a girl one year his senior and one year above the age of consent, whom he erroneously believes to be under the age of consent? Or, punishing a person for taking an umbrella he wrongly supposed to belong to someone else when in fact it belonged to him? Has the criminal law not got bigger fish to fry? Nevertheless, the clear wording of s. 1(3) excluded *Anderton v Ryan* being distinguished on this ground. If such cases were to be excluded from the ambit of criminal attempts, the mental element, as defined by s. 1 of the Criminal Attempts Act, would have to be changed so that it had to be shown to be the defendant's **purpose** (not merely intent/decision) to bring about the proscribed consequence.[131] Finally we turn to Case 10. As should be apparent, if the test is whether, on the facts as A thought them to be, her intention was to bring about the substantive offence then our witch is guilty of attempted murder. To hold otherwise would be to import objectivist ideas into a test which clearly eschews them. And yet without such a limitation the stance of the criminal law would look decidedly peculiar. Does society need protection from the 'non-effects' of superstition and incantation? Clearly not if our law-makers are to be trusted upon the issue of what counts as dangerous conduct, namely conduct capable of causing serious damage to individual or collective interests.[132] But perhaps the example is too esoteric. No sensible prosecuting authority would draft an indictment in respect of such a fantastic act. However, one can imagine less obvious cases where the defendant settles on a course of conduct which lies at the margins between practical (dangerous) action and inconsequential fantasy.

Case 11

Eve, a microbiologist, is convinced, on respectable scientific grounds, that Creutzfeldt-Jakob Disease (a fatal disease) can be communicated via ingestion of beef products contaminated with BSE. She therefore starts to ply Adam, her husband, whom she wants to kill, with as many beef products as possible, convinced that, sooner or later, his number is up. It is subsequently discovered that the disease cannot be communicated in this way.

On the strict wording of s. 1 it appears that she is guilty of attempted murder. The administration of a substance capable of killing, e.g. arsenic, even if not in the quantities administered, has been held to be the *actus reus* of a criminal attempt.[133] But here we do not have arsenic. Rather we have a pound of stewing steak and a roast forerib of beef. Nevertheless, on the facts as she believed them to be, she is attempting to kill her husband. These facts were not the undisciplined figments of an over-active imagination.[134] They were reasonable inferences taken from respectable academic opinion. It seems implausible that such an objectively innocent act as cooking a beef stew will ever be held to be the subject matter of attempted murder. But how such cases could be accommodated within the Criminal Attempts Act and insulated from less controversial types of impossible attempts is difficult to gauge.[135]

---

[130] The majority of their Lordships in *Shivpuri* felt that *Anderton v Ryan* was distinguishable on this ground. For a contrary opinion see J.C. Smith [1986] Crim LR 539.

[131] See for an extended treatment of this approach G. Fletcher (1978) 152–66; R.A. Duff, *Criminal Attempts* (1996) 380 ff.

[132] See R.A. Duff (1996) above.

[133] *White* [1910] 2 KB 124.

[134] Even if they had been it seems unrealistic to suppose that this would have affected the issue of liability.

[135] For one suggestion see G. Fletcher (1978) 165–6.

18.6 CONSPIRACY

> ### Overview
>
> Criminal conspiracy takes one of two forms. Statutory conspiracy occurs when two or more people agree on a course of conduct which amounts to a criminal offence. Common law conspiracy differs from statutory conspiracy in allowing punishment where the course of conduct agreed will not necessarily amount to a criminal offence but will amount to an act involving
>
> (a) the corruption of public morals or outraging public decency, or
>
> (b) fraud.
>
> In both forms it is not necessary that each conspirator has agreed to commit the offence so long as the offence will be committed by at least one of the parties to the agreement.

A Introduction

At common law, conspiracy was an offence consisting of an 'agreement of two or more to do an unlawful act, or to do a lawful act by unlawful means'.[136] It should be noted that it was not deemed of the essence of a conspiracy that the agreement should be to commit a criminal offence.[137] The agreement could be, for example, to commit a tort.

From an historical perspective conspiracy can be viewed as one of the more obvious examples of the state using its muscle for the purpose of social control rather than to facilitate the pursuit of individual choices. In particular, it was used in the nineteenth century as a mechanism for suppressing strikes. It rendered agreements to strike a criminal offence even though the object of the agreement (the strike) was at most only a breach of contract or tort. This particular facet of the law of criminal conspiracy was abrogated by the Trade Disputes Act 1906 but the general scope of criminal conspiracies remained intact. As late as 1974 an agreement to effect a politically motivated student 'sit-in' (the tort of trespass) was successfully prosecuted as a criminal conspiracy.[138] Subsequently the Law Commission recommended that the object of a criminal conspiracy should itself be criminal. By the Criminal Law Act 1977 most criminal conspiracies are now statutory, which requires the object of the conspiracy to be itself a criminal offence. Three common law conspiracies remain, however, the object of which does not have to be a criminal offence. These are conspiracy to corrupt public morals, to outrage public decency, and to defraud (including cases where the fraud concerned would not incur criminal liability). It was intended that these should remain only until such a time as a thoroughgoing review had been made of these offences. Forty years later we are no further ahead with this process.

B Justification for punishing conspiracies[139]

There are two possible rationales for punishing conspiracies. The first is that a conspiracy is an inchoate crime. The second is that a conspiracy to act unlawfully is a particular social evil which justifies punishing it for its own sake.[140]

---

[136] Willes J in *Mulcahy* v *R* (1868) LR 3 306.
[137] Thus setting it apart from other inchoate offences.
[138] *Kamara* v *DPP* [1974] AC 104.
[139] See generally I. Dennis, 'The Rationale of Criminal Conspiracy' (1977) 93 LQR 39.
[140] D. Husak, 'The Nature and Justifiability of Nonconsummate Offences' (1995) 37 Arizona LR 151.

With regard to its inchoate nature, conspiracy, like attempt, represents more than a mere intention to commit a crime. The fact of agreement is seen as indicative of a crime at a given stage of development. As such, it is thought to represent a sufficiently significant step towards the commission of the offence as to indicate the likelihood of a substantive offence being committed unless intervention is made. Conspiracy thus facilitates the bringing to bear of effective preventive measures at a stage when, although no attempt has occurred, the danger posed for society is first made manifest in action.[141]

One objection which has been raised in this respect is that if the justificatory underpinnings of conspiracy are that it enables early crime spotting and prevention, then conspiracy does nothing that a cogent law of criminal attempts could not do more directly. Thus Williams argues that if the test for an attempt had been a 'substantial step' the case for an (inchoate) crime of conspiracy would be a weak one since agreements to commit a criminal offence may properly be considered a substantial step towards the commission of the offence.[142]

As it happens, few conspiracies are prosecuted at an early stage, largely due to the difficulty of adducing sufficient evidence. Its major significance, therefore, lies not in its preventive potential. Indeed, indicting for conspiracy is the preferred option in many cases where the substantive offence has actually been committed and where the conspirators could be charged either as principals or as accomplices depending upon their degree of involvement.[143] This outcome may be because it is often easier to establish the conspiracy than the individual elements of the offence.[144] More broadly, charging the conspiracy rather than the substantive offence may more accurately describe the real harm attributable to the defendants' conduct.

The latter possibility introduces consideration of the second justification for punishing conspiracy, namely that the evil involved is not merely reducible to the substantive offence upon which it is parasitic. In this sense criminal conspiracy is not necessarily to be considered an inchoate offence at all. This can be understood most easily by considering the nature of common law conspiracy. Agreeing collectively to damage the interests of others was deemed sufficiently injurious or destabilising to justify the criminal sanction.[145] Such conduct is the stuff of social conflict, albeit perhaps a notion of conflict filtered through the conceptual apparatus of one particular economic class.[146] It was thus the fact of agreement rather than the object of it which made the crime.[147]

In the case of large-scale conspiracies to commit a crime this justification may seem yet more compelling. Public interests generally are threatened by crime and the more so by organised crime. Conspiracies may, therefore, be viewed as an evil in themselves. One only has to think of the terror and anxiety provoked by the September 11th attacks, and not only in the United States, to be alert to some of the reasons. One is that some crimes are so inordinate that it seems to take a special form of collectively inspired fever to commit them.[148]

---

[141] Law Commission No. 76 *Conspiracy and Criminal Law Reform* London: HMSO (1976) (hereafter Law Com. No. 76 (1976)) para. 1.5; *DPP v Nock* [1978] AC 979.

[142] Op. cit. 420–4; cf. R. Card, 'Reform of the Law of Conspiracy' [1973] Crim LR 674.

[143] It is possible to charge both, but this is generally disapproved of: *Practice Direction* [1977] 1 WLR 537. The judge may require the prosecution to elect which count to prosecute; cf. *Liggins* [1995] Crim LR 45.

[144] There may also be evidential advantages since special rules of evidence relating to conspiracy allow the admissions of co-conspirators to be used as evidence against each other.

[145] Cf. D. Hodgson, 'Law Com. No. 76 – A Case Study in Criminal Law Reform' in P. Glazebrook (ed.), *Reshaping the Criminal Law* (1978).

[146] Cf. G. Williams *CLGP* (1st edn) sections 167–69.

[147] P. Johnson, 'The Unnecessary Crime of Conspiracy' (1973) 61 Calif L Rev 1137.

[148] P. Johnson, op. cit.

Another is that they signal to the wider community an inexorable inevitability absent in individual criminal activity. Such signals act to corrode general societal morale. Some of the other more common reasons include the fact that agreeing to commit an offence makes its commission more likely – a group dynamic may be created of greater moral 'steel' than the will of individual members. Also cooperation can make for the commission of more sophisticated crimes and foster the organisational basis for the commission of future crimes.[149]

On this view, then, the justification for punishing conspiracies is that group criminal activity represents a discrete social harm, not being reducible to the wrongs/harms ascribable to the individuals concerned, and should be identified and attacked as such.[150] Despite this, given its ability to punish on the basis of something as ephemeral as a chance conversation, the crime has long been recognised as capable of advancing narrow collective interests at the expense of individual freedom. Moreover judges have not always been at the ready to protect the individual against the claims of utility and public interest.[151]

18.7 STATUTORY CONSPIRACIES

A statutory conspiracy is defined by s. 1(1), Criminal Law Act 1977.

> If a person agrees with any other person that a course of conduct shall be pursued which, if the agreement is carried out in accordance with their intentions, either
> (a) will necessarily amount to or involve the commission of any offence or offences by one or more parties to the agreement, or
> (b) would do so but for the existence of facts which render the commission of the offence or any of the offences impossible, he is guilty of conspiracy to commit the offence or offences in question.

A *Actus reus*

The gist of a statutory conspiracy is, then, an agreement between two or more people that a criminal offence shall be committed by at least one of them.

1 The agreement

An agreement must be established between two or more parties. Such an agreement may be express or implied. In many cases, since conspiracies tend to be hatched in private, the agreement can only be inferred from the conduct of the defendants. Proof of conspiracy is generally 'a matter of inference deduced from certain criminal acts of the parties accused, done in pursuance of an apparent criminal purpose in common between them'.[152] It would be easier to take this inference in the case of a terrorist bomb attack than in the case of a bout of fisticuffs at a football match.

Where no overt act has taken place a major problem will be adducing sufficient evidence both of the fact of agreement and of its scope. In a number of American states some overt act, however trivial, must be shown before a conspiracy is complete. This has the

---

[149] Law Com. No. 76 (1976) para. 1.9; cf. J. Hodgson and V. Tadros, 'The Impossibility of Defining Terrorism' (July 2013) New Criminal Law Review.
[150] Compare attempts, discussion at p. 513.
[151] See for example *Shaw* v *DPP* [1962] AC 220; *Kamara* v *DPP* [1974] AC 104; cf. Russell on *Crime* (12th edn) 203 for a contrary opinion.
[152] Grose J, *Brisac* (1803) 4 East 164 at 171.

advantage of ensuring that only agreements showing the potential to become executed can be criminalised.[153]

Although it is not necessary for the prosecution to show that all the details had been agreed, it will be necessary to show that an agreement to effect a criminal purpose had been reached as opposed to being merely discussed or fantasised about.[154] So in *Goddard and Fallick* a conviction for conspiracy to rape a child under 13, was quashed as, although the prosecution were able to adduce evidence that the matter had been discussed, it was not able to prove that it was the defendants' settled intention to commit the rape.[155]

2 Constructing the agreement

Not all explicit agreements take the form of a number of people getting together and hatching a plan. It is common, for example, for people to join a conspiracy at different times. In the very 'best' conspiracies, particularly those which are politically motivated and where there is a danger of police infiltration, the parties to a conspiracy may not even meet each other.[156] This can come about in a number of ways.[157] One way is for an organiser to make contact with all the other parties to the agreement and to fix all the terms of the agreement with each party individually without the parties ever coming into contact with each other. This is popularly known as a wheel conspiracy. Using the imagery of wheels, the organiser is the hub of the wheel, the individuals are the spokes, and the rim is the agreement which their involvement brings and which ties them all together.

Case 12

Adam, a crooked gambler (the hub) 'nobbles' Cain, a boxer, bribing him to 'throw' his forthcoming fight with Abel. Adam agrees with 50 different people (the spokes) that they will, separately, place bets on Abel with different bookmakers so as to bet a large amount of money without provoking suspicion.

In Case 12 the rim of the wheel is created by the understanding and agreement of each 'spoke' that their action is part of a joint purpose. Note the importance of the 'rim'. Simply because A conspires with B, C, D and E does not always mean that B, C, D, and E conspire **with each other**. The size of the conspiracy depends upon the nature of the agreement between the various parties. The organiser has to act as a 'link-person' between all the other parties so that they can reach agreement via his/her agency. In short, if B, C, D, and E believe they are part of a 'heist', they are linked with each other in a large-scale wheel conspiracy. If they think this is a personal one-off, the conspiracy is individuated.[158]

In cases such as Case 12, the prosecution will generally try to construct a large-scale conspiracy rather than a number of individual conspiracies, which may obviate certain evidential difficulties.[159] This may not be easy, however. In the American case of *Kotteakos* v *United States* for example,[160] the organiser agreed with 31 different people, none of whom had ever met the other, to obtain fraudulent loans for them from the government. The

---

[153] See J. Dressler (1987) at 382.
[154] *R* v *Walker* [1962] Crim LR 458.
[155] *R* v *Goddard & Fallick* [2012] EWCA Crim 1756 CA.
[156] For a challenging variation on this theme see *R* v *Mehta* [2012] EWCA Crim 2824.
[157] For an informative explanation of the structure of conspiracies see J. Dressler (1987) 391–400. The American case law examples used here are his.
[158] *R* v *Shillam* [2013] EWCA Crim 160 CA.
[159] Cf. *R* v *Ali* [2011] 3 All ER 1071.
[160] 328 US 750.

question which arose is whether there was a single conspiracy involving 32 people or 31 separate conspiracies. The court concluded that the 31 people were in it for their own individual purposes and had no interest in the participation of the others, even if they may have been aware of them. As a result they had not agreed to be part of a collective 'heist'.

Another form of conspiracy is the chain conspiracy. At its simplest, A contacts B who contacts C and so on. Thus:

Case 13

Cain, a gangster, wants to kill Abel, a rival, without attracting suspicion. He tells Eve of his plan and asks her to find a trustworthy killer. Eve contacts Adam, a professional hit-man, and pays him to kill Abel 'for a client'.

Cain, Eve and Adam are part of a single (chain) conspiracy. As with wheel conspiracies it must be shown that 'the acts of (every one of the conspirators) were done in pursuance of a common purpose held in common between them', as opposed to, say, a number of individual conspiracies where no such common purpose can be discerned.[161] Once again, this may not always be easy. For example in *United States* v *Peoni*,[162] P sold some counterfeit money to R who in turn sold it to D. D then exchanged the money in a number of business transactions with innocent people. The prosecution alleged that there was a single conspiracy involving P, R and D. The defendants claimed that they were in individual conspiracies, P with R, and R with D.[163] The court concluded that the acts of each pair of conspirators were not done in pursuance of a **common** purpose. What was influential was that only a small amount of money was involved. This meant that P had no compelling reason to believe that R could not or would not 'launder' his notes without the knowing help of another conspirator. It was not part of the (implied) plan, in other words, that R would involve other conspirators.[164]

3 The parties to the agreement

The essence of an agreement is a meeting of minds between two or more people. A person cannot 'conspire with himself'. This principle is particularly pertinent where an agreement has been reached but the agreement is compromised because of the status of one of the parties to the agreement. Can a person be guilty of a conspiracy where the other party(ies) to the agreement are, for some reason, exempt from punishment? The position is unnecessarily complicated. If the co-conspirator falls within the terms of section 2(2) the answer is no. Otherwise, the answer is yes. By section 2(2) a person is not guilty of a (statutory) conspiracy:

> . . . if the only other person or persons with whom he agrees are (both initially and at all times during the currency of the agreement) persons of any one or more of the following descriptions, that is to say –
> (a) his spouse (or civil partner)[165]
> (b) a person under the age of criminal responsibility
> (c) an intended victim of that offence or of each of the offences.

---

[161] *Meyrick* (1929) 21 Cr App R 94 at 102.
[162] 100 F 2d 401 (2d Cir 1938).
[163] J. Dressler (1987) 392.
[164] Cf. *R v Scott* (1978) 68 Cr App R 164; [1979] Crim LR 456.
[165] The Law Commission recommend the abolition of the immunity of spouses and civil partners from liability for conspiracy where the conspiracy is limited to those people. LC 318, para. 5.16.

Thus, if a person agrees to have sex with his underage daughter, a conspiracy cannot be established since the daughter is the intended victim of the offence and is so even if she consents.[166] Similarly, if the agreement was between the husband, wife and daughter, a conspiracy could not be charged. Compare Case 14:

Case 14

Adam agrees with Eve, his wife, Ruth, their underage daughter, and Cain, Ruth's mature friend, to have group sex.

Here Adam, Eve and Cain could be charged with a conspiracy, though not Ruth.[167] Each of these defendants has a non-exempt party with which to construct an agreement. It might be argued, by extension, that the defendants in *Brown*,[168] assuming they were all willing 'victims' as well as perpetrators of the various offences, could not be guilty of a (statutory) conspiracy.[169] If so this seems an unintended lacuna in s. 2.[170] It is likely, however, that they would not be treated as exempt victims, the offences supporting public welfare rather than the participants' private welfare interests.

One question left untouched by this section is whether a person may be guilty of a conspiracy where the only other person or person(s) are parties who have a defence, but are not exempt by s. 2(2):

Case 15

A tells B, a witness to a murder, that if he does not perjure himself at A's trial for murder, A will kill him. B agrees to do so.

Case 16

A agrees with B to help B abduct her (B's) child from the child's other parent.

It seems that in both these cases A will be guilty of a criminal conspiracy,[171] even though in both cases B has a defence.[172] There seems no obvious reason why a conspiracy charge should not properly lie where the 'co-conspirator' is an exempt person by virtue of s. 2(2), but will lie if the exemption arises by virtue of some other rule of law.[173]

It is quite possible to indict someone for conspiracy although the co-conspirator(s) are not discovered. So long as there is evidence of the conspiracy and the part the defendant played in it, a conviction is unobjectionable. By s. 5(8) neither is it an objection that all

---

[166] By the Sexual Offences Act 1956; *Whitehouse* [1977] QB 868. The Law Commission recommend the abolition of this exemption for the non-victim: para 5.35.

[167] As by s. 2(1) a person cannot be guilty of a conspiracy if he is an intended victim of that offence. The Law Commission now recommend that the conspiracy be chargeable for the intended victim scenario but with the victim afforded a defence, but not for the underage victim scenario. LCCP 183, 144–51.

[168] [1992] 2 All ER 552. See Chapter 11.

[169] Whether they may be guilty of a common law conspiracy, e.g. to corrupt public morals, is less certain.

[170] This scenario was posited by the Supreme Court *obiter* in *Gnango* (2011) UKSC 59, para. 47. The conclusion was that the *Tyrrell* principle did not extend to such cases.

[171] Conspiracy to perjure or to pervert the course of justice; conspiracy to abduct a child contrary to s. 56, Offences Against the Person Act 1861.

[172] Duress; and parent's defence. Case 16 is based on the facts of the common law case of *Duguid* (1907) 21 Cox CC 200.

[173] The position advocated by the Law Commission, Law Com. No. 76 (1976) paras 1.50–1.58 was that conspiracy should lie in none of these circumstances; cf. G. Williams *TCL* (1983) 435.

other co-conspirators have been acquitted, whether at this or another trial, unless 'conviction is inconsistent with the acquittal of the other person or persons in question'.[174] This it will be if the evidence is presented at the same trial and is substantially the same for all co-conspirators. In such cases the judge is bound to direct the jury to convict all or none.[175] In cases where the quality of evidence against the various conspirators differs the jury may, however, quite properly return different verdicts.[176] In Case 12, for example, some of the 'betters' might be acquitted of the wheel conspiracy on the basis of insufficient evidence of a common purpose[177] while others are convicted upon proof that they embraced the 'heist'.

4 Subject-matter of the agreement

At its simplest, the subject-matter of a statutory criminal conspiracy is the commission of a criminal offence. Section 1(1) presents the position in somewhat obscure terms, however. Instead of defining the subject-matter of a conspiracy simply as an agreement to commit a crime, section 1(1)(a) refers to an agreement that 'a course of conduct will be pursued' which will 'necessarily amount to or involve the commission of an offence . . . if the agreement is carried out in accordance with (the parties') intentions'. The major reason for this verbose formulation appears to be to ensure that it is not fatal to an indictment for conspiracy that the defendant did not realise that what had been agreed would involve the commission of a crime.[178] Thus:

Case 17
Adam and Eve agree to collect and dry 'magic mushrooms' for consumption by themselves and their friends. They believe what they are proposing to be entirely lawful.

Adam and Eve's belief will not be fatal to a conspiracy charge. They have agreed upon a course of conduct which will 'necessarily amount to or involve the commission of an offence[179] . . . if the agreement is carried out in accordance with (the parties') intentions'.[180] The principle that ignorance of the law is no defence is as applicable here as elsewhere in the criminal law.

The word 'necessarily' is significant. It was incorporated to ensure that people can only be indicted for what they intend to achieve in executing the agreement.

Case 18
Adam and Eve conspire to injure Abel seriously. The plan goes wrong and Abel dies.

The correct charge will be either the substantive offence of murder or a conspiracy to commit grievous bodily harm. A charge of conspiracy to murder is inappropriate because the parties did not agree upon a course of conduct which would 'necessarily have amounted to or involve' the commission of the relevant substantive offence.[181] In simple terms they did not agree to kill anybody.

---

[174] Section 5(8). *R v Austin* [2011] EWCA Crim 345 (CACD); *R v Dyer, Lowry & Field* [1964] Crim LR 297; Cf *R v Zaman* [2010] EWCA Crim 209 (CACD).
[175] *Longman* [1981] Crim LR 38.
[176] *R v Testouri* [2004] 2 Cr App R 4; [2004] Crim LR 372.
[177] They would remain liable for the initial conspiracy with Adam and Cain.
[178] For an example see *R v Connors* [2013] EWCA Crim 324.
[179] Under the Misuse of Drugs Act 1971, s. 5(2) and Schedule 2, Part 1, paras 3, 5; *Hodder* v *DPP* [1990] Crim LR 261.
[180] To possess, produce and supply the relevant proscribed drug.
[181] *Siracusa* (1990) 90 Cr App R 340.

However, its usage is not unproblematic since, as a matter of strict interpretation, no agreed course of conduct will ever 'necessarily' amount to or involve the commission of a criminal offence. However carefully one plans one's murder or robbery, the plans may nevertheless come to naught. If so, a conspiracy charge must always fail. It is clear, then, that the interpretation of section 1(1)(a) must, as a matter of common sense, include within the meaning of the phrase 'course of conduct' the **intended consequences** of that course of conduct:

<blockquote>

Case 19

Adam and Eve agree to dig a hole for Cain to fall into so that he injures himself.

</blockquote>

Since Cain will not necessarily fall into the hole, the 'course of conduct agreed' by Adam and Eve cannot amount to a conspiracy to commit battery upon Cain, unless we interpret the course of conduct agreed upon as including not only the digging of the hole but also the intended consequence of this (Cain falling into it). Under this (very loose) interpretation, which in fact represents the accepted position, what they have agreed upon – digging a hole so that Cain will fall into it – is a criminal conspiracy because, if the plan is carried out in accordance with their **intentions**, it will necessarily amount to the commission of a criminal offence (battery).[182]

5 Agreements subject to conditions[183]

The question arises as to whether a conditional agreement to commit a crime is sufficient to satisfy section 1(1)(a). The law of criminal conspiracy distinguishes between two types of conditional agreement. The first is where A and B plan to commit a particular criminal offence but that plan is itself subject to a separate contingency plan that it will not transpire under a certain contingency. Thus:

<blockquote>

Case 20

A and B agree to rob a bank by holding it up at gunpoint. They also agree that they will abort the robbery if any security guards are on the premises.

</blockquote>

The second is where A and B plan to do something which, under a certain contingency, will necessitate the commission of a criminal offence.

<blockquote>

Case 21

Adam and Eve agree, at 7.30 am, to drive immediately from London to Edinburgh to arrive in time for the Calcutta Cup rugby game between Scotland and England, which starts at 2.30 pm. This is an agreement which can be achieved without breaking the speed limit, but only if the traffic is exceptionally light.

</blockquote>

Once again, a prime consideration in deciding whether a conspiracy has been formed in Cases 20 and 21 is the meaning of the phrase 'a course of conduct will be pursued' which

---

[182] Since Cain will fall in. The Law Commission recommend amending the law to give effect to this interpretation. LC 318, para 2.56.

[183] For a very useful analysis see D.C. Ormerod, 'Making Sense of *Mens Rea* in Criminal Conspiracies' in (2006) CLP 185, 221–6.

will 'necessarily amount to or involve the commission of an offence . . . if the agreement is carried out in accordance with (the parties') intentions'.

In Case 20 it seems that, since the object of the agreement is a successful commission of the criminal offence, a criminal conspiracy will occur since, if their agreement goes to plan (that is, is carried out in accordance with their intentions) the offence will necessarily be committed. A robbery would necessarily occur if the agreement was carried out in accordance with their intentions, since their intentions were that the robbery would take place. In Case 21 it seems that a criminal conspiracy will not occur since, if everything goes to plan, an offence will not necessarily be committed. This will not be a criminal conspiracy since the agreement is not built around an intention to speed.[184] Speeding will not necessarily take place if the agreement is carried out in accordance with their intentions. Using similar reasoning, an agreement to rob a bank, and to shoot to kill if anybody seeks to stop them, will be a conspiracy to rob but not to murder, since a killing will not necessarily take place if the agreement is carried out in accordance with their intentions.

This distinction is not unproblematic since it could be argued that in both cases two (interlocking) agreements are made, such that in each case a criminal conspiracy can be established. In the first case, there is one agreement which necessarily involves a bank robbery and another agreement which necessarily involves no bank robbery. In the second case, there is one agreement which necessarily involves a speeding offence and another agreement which necessarily does not. In each case the agreement indicted is the agreement which necessarily involves the commission of an offence.[185]

Even if we discount this argument it may be difficult in practice to discern which side of the line a particular agreed course of conduct falls. This can be illustrated by reference to the facts of *Reed*.[186] A and B agreed that A would give advice to would-be suicides. That advice was contingent upon whether A thought suicide was appropriate or not. If it was, he would give active help. If it was not, he would seek to discourage it. They were charged with conspiracy to aid and abet suicide. A and B argued that the course of conduct they had agreed upon did not necessarily involve the commission of the offence since in any given case the advice they might be disposed to give could be to discourage rather than aid and abet the suicide. A comparable problem arose in *Jackson*.[187] Here the appellants, A, B and C, agreed that C should be shot in the leg, if it transpired that he was convicted of a burglary for which he was being tried. The purpose of the enterprise was to provide mitigation for sentencing purposes. In fact, he was shot before the trial ended, leaving him permanently disabled. A, B and C were convicted of conspiracy to pervert the course of justice. On appeal it was argued that since it was not certain that C would be convicted, they had not agreed upon a course of conduct which would necessarily result in the substantive crime.

In both cases the arguments were rejected upon the basis that the plan included not only the course of conduct agreed upon, but also its intended consequence (mitigation of sentence, help in dying). In both cases they intended a course of action which necessarily involved the commission of a criminal offence. These decisions construe the word 'necessarily' in a particularly loose way. If an agreement to commit an offence but only upon the occurrence of a particular contingency is not an agreement to pursue a course of conduct which will necessarily involve the commission of an offence (Case 21), why does it suddenly

[184] Cases 20 and 21 are adaptations of examples given in *Reed* [1982] Crim LR 819 by Donaldson LJ.
[185] See generally J.R. Spencer, 'Conspiracy and Recklessness' [2005] CLJ 279.
[186] [1982] Crim LR 819.
[187] [1985] Crim LR 442.

become so in Reed?[188] The distinction drawn in *Jackson* and *Reed* is that in these cases the defendants 'went into business' to commit a specific offence. This marks them out as agreeing to commit the relevant offences, rather than simply having the offences in mind as a potential side-effect of what they had agreed to. If this is a meaningful distinction, it is a distinction which operates outside the strict wording of the Act and, in truth, it makes little penal sense. Society is as much endangered by agreements to kill upon the occurrence of a contingency as by agreements to kill 'no matter what'. For this reason, inconsistent with this analysis, a person can be **an accessory** upon a mere appreciation that the principal may commit the substantive offence even if the substantive offence requires proof of a specific intent and the substantive offence is not agreed to.[189] We will leave the last word to Williams, expressing a sentiment which commands almost universal agreement:[190] 'The line between conditional conspiracies that are criminal and those that are not seems to be too etherial (*sic*) and evanescent to be workable in the everyday world. Parliament would have done much better to have left the word "necessarily" out of the Act.'[191]

B *Mens rea*

1 Knowledge of facts and circumstances

The mental element for conspiracy must be unpacked from s. 1(1) and (2). Ormerod concludes that this leaves us with the following fault element:

> D1 and D2 have to be proved to have a direct or oblique intention, or knowledge, including wilful blindness, that the circumstances will be such that when they perform their agreed conduct in accordance with their intentions, it will necessarily involve the commission of a criminal offence.[192]

Section 1(1) seems to require proof that any conspirator knew of any facts or circumstances which would render the course of conduct agreed upon a criminal offence.[193] It is not necessary also to show that the conspirators knew this course of conduct to amount to a criminal offence.[194] One cannot **agree** upon a course of conduct which will 'necessarily involve the commission of a criminal offence' unless one knows of the facts or circumstances which will render that course of conduct a criminal offence.[195] Thus:

Case 22

Adam agrees with Eve, Joan's roommate, that Eve will vacate the room to enable Adam to have sex with Joan. Adam knows that Joan will not consent. Eve assumes that she will.

---

[188] See also *O'Hadhmaill* [1996] Crim LR 509 – an IRA agreement to continue making bombs in case the ceasefire ended was a conspiracy to cause an explosion.

[189] *Hyde* [1990] 3 All ER 892.

[190] Smith and Hogan, op. cit. 307; A.J. Ashworth (2009) 467–70.

[191] The Draft Criminal Code does so: Law Com. No. 177 (1989) cl. 48. See also Ormerod, op. cit. 226.

[192] D.C. Ormerod, 'Making Sense of *Mens Rea* in Criminal Conspiracies' (2006) CLP 185, 221.

[193] For discussion of what counts as knowledge of facts or circumstances for the purpose of section 1, including in particular whether belief in their existence or wilful blindness suffices, see Ormerod, op. cit. 206–16; See generally S. Shute, 'Knowledge and Belief in the Criminal Law' and G.R. Sullivan, 'Knowledge, Belief and Culpability' in Shute and Simester (eds), *Criminal Law Theory: Doctrines of the General Part*, Oxford: OUP (2002).

[194] *Broad and Others* [1997] Crim LR 666. A is liable for conspiracy to produce a Class A drug, notwithstanding they did not know the drugs to fall into this category.

[195] For analysis see J.R. Spencer, 'Conspiracy and Recklessness' [2005] CLJ 279. The Law Commission propose that where the substantive crime is one which can be committed by recklessness as to a circumstance, recklessness should be sufficient for the conspiracy also. Where the substantive crime requires a higher fault element the conspirator should also have that higher element. LCCP 183 (2007) 67–83.

A conspiracy to rape cannot be established here. An agreement has been reached but not an agreement that rape should take place. A conspirator would have to know that the woman was not consenting or possibly have agreed for intercourse to take place whether or not she consented. The requirement of proof of actual knowledge is made explicit only with respect to those crimes whose constituent elements require no such proof, for example crimes of negligence or strict liability. Clearly, however, it would be a perverse interpretation which would make the mental element of conspiracy to commit a strict liability offence more exacting than that for crimes of *mens rea*.[196] By s. 1(2):

> where liability for any offence may be incurred without knowledge on the part of the person committing it of any particular fact or circumstance necessary for the commission of the offence a person shall nevertheless not be guilty of conspiracy to commit that offence by virtue of subsection (1) above unless he, and at least one other person, intend or know that the fact or circumstance shall or will exist at the time when the conduct constituting the offence is to take place.

Case 23

Adam and Eve, two experienced farmers, agree to place a large manure heap near to a river. Although they know that there is a risk of pollution they agree that it is a risk worth taking. They are prosecuted before any pollution occurs.

Adam and Eve will not be liable for conspiring to pollute waterways, even though the substantive offence is one of strict liability, since, by section 1(2), only if both of them intend or know (rather than simply suspect) that the heap will pollute the river can the conspiracy be made out. The idea behind this is that strict liability offences are quintessentially crimes concerned with harm rather than wrongdoing. It would be going too far to punish in the absence either of harm or wrongdoing. In cases of drug importation the position is slightly more complicated as it is necessary not merely for one of the conspirators to know the drugs to be imported to be controlled drugs but to know also the class of drugs to be imported. The prosecution does not prove an agreement to import Class A drugs by proving an agreement (based on erroneous knowledge) to import Class B drugs.[197] It seems however that the converse is not the case, the view apparently taken being that a mistaken belief that the conspiracy was to commit a graver offence differed from where it was to commit a less serious offence.[198] In *Saik* the House of Lords confirmed that the section 1(2) requirement extends to all crimes constituted upon proof of knowledge or intention that a particular fact exists. In the absence of such knowledge (suspicion is not enough) or intention on the part of the defendant and at least one other person, the conspiracy cannot be made out.[199] So B was not guilty of conspiracy to launder money when he only suspected the money to be the proceeds of crime. The Law Commission considers that this is too favourable to the accused. For crimes of subjective fault in relation to fault element it is enough that a conspirator possesses that fault. If enacted this would mean that an agreement to have intercourse with X without caring if she consents would constitute a statutory conspiracy.

---

[196] *Ali* [2005] EWCA Crim 87; *Saik* [2006] UKHL 18.
[197] *R v Taylor* [2002] Crim LR 205.
[198] *Patel* (1991) unreported.
[199] *R v R* [2006] EWCA Crim 1974; [2007] Crim LR 79; [2006] UKHL 18.

2 Must the substantive offence be intended?

It might seem implicit in s. 1 that a conspirator must have an intention

(a) that the agreement shall be carried out, and
(b) that the substantive offence shall be committed.

The words seem to be painting a picture of conspirators who share a common purpose, and of the conspiracy as the embodiment of that purpose. If this interpretation is correct, it would leave outside the scope of a criminal conspiracy those who aid and abet a conspiracy but whose involvement is otherwise so incidental to the criminal enterprise that they can be taken neither to have agreed to its taking place nor to intend that it shall do so.

Such authority as there is on the matter suggests, however, that an intention that the substantive offence shall be committed is not central to liability for conspiracy. So, in *Anderson* a person who supplied tools designed to cut through prison bars was held properly convicted of conspiracy to effect an escape.[200] His argument that he supplied the tools with no other intention than collecting his fee was rejected by the House of Lords, despite the fact that it was open to them to uphold his conviction on the basis of being an accessory to the conspiracy. In so doing the House of Lords held that it was not necessary to show that each party to the agreement intended the agreement to be carried out.

One possible explanation for this decision is that their Lordships were over-influenced by the law of criminal complicity. If a person can be liable as an accomplice upon proof of a knowledge that one's conduct will assist another person to commit an offence but without necessarily intending or agreeing that it should happen, why should such a person not be liable as a conspirator if it fails to happen? If this is the explanation, it does no credit either to their Lordships' interpretive skills or to their willingness to protect the individual against the claims of utility. If the law of criminal conspiracy is not to be used oppressively and unduly interfere with individual choices, its laws should be used only against those who act for the sake of bringing about the proscribed event rather than despite the fact that it will or might occur. This is the rationale, after all, for the result in Case 21. Criminalisation in such cases will make a lot of ordinary people vulnerable to a criminal conviction for going about their daily business although no substantive crime has been committed. Some of the worst excesses of the law of criminal conspiracy have occurred in just such circumstances.[201] *Anderson* is a prime example of how the law of criminal conspiracy can become stretched far beyond its focal case of 'agreeing to commit a crime'. The defendant was dubbed a principal party to a conspiracy for no other apparent reason than that he intended to do something which in fact made the mischief of the crime more likely to happen. He was, then, 'roped in' for purposes of social control and to set an example, rather than because he was a (dangerous) 'plotter'.

A more charitable explanation of the decision is that their Lordships were influenced by the very specialised 'tools' which the defendant supplied, namely diamond wire. Diamond wire is as pertinent to the commission of the substantive offence as it might appear possible to get. Unlike, say, supplying a gun to be used in a murder, which can be committed in any number of ways, with any number of tools, obtainable through any number of sources, diamond wire is the quintessential tool for cutting through prison bars. It not only does the trick, it is easy to conceal, difficult to get hold of, and has few lawful applications. Given these circumstances it might be thought that little of substance separated the mental

---

[200] *Anderson* [1985] 2 All ER 961.
[201] See *Shaw v DPP* [1962] AC 220; *Knuller v DPP* [1973] AC 435.

state of someone who supplied diamond wire so that the offence could occur and someone who supplied it, knowing that without it the offence would be unlikely to occur – a form of (distorted) oblique intention.[202] Whether this intuition is correct or not, it seems clear that the proper course would have been for the judge to direct the jury that they could (though need not) infer the necessary intention that the substantive offence be committed from the fact that the supplier knew just how apt the wire was.

3 An intention to thwart the criminal purpose

If the prosecution do not have to prove that a given conspirator intended the substantive offence to occur, does this mean that a person can be guilty of conspiracy where he simply 'joined in' with the agreement and had no intention to do anything beyond perhaps making the right noises and putting a stop to it if things went too far? Two cases give support to the view that a charge cannot be successfully laid in such circumstances. In *Ashton*[203] the defendant was convicted of conspiracy to murder. He argued that he had gone along with his friend's plan to kill the supposed killer of his (friend's) son in order to be able to prevent it happening. His conviction was quashed on this basis. In *Yip Chiu-cheung v R,*[204] X, an undercover drug enforcement officer, joined in a plan to export heroin from Hong Kong, for the purpose of trapping the suppliers and receivers. One of the suppliers, Y, was charged with conspiring with X to traffic in drugs. Y argued that X could not be a co-conspirator since he lacked the necessary *mens rea*. This argument was rejected since X did intend the offence to be committed, the better to provide evidence of the other's involvement. It was no defence to a charge of conspiracy that X joined in the plan from the best of motives. This meant that Y was guilty of conspiracy. As we have seen, this guilt does not depend upon X also being found guilty. The Law Commission disagree with this decision and propose that there should be a discrete defence of acting reasonably consistent with the defence of acting reasonably in section 50 of the Serious Crime Act 2007;[205] significantly, the Privy Council also stated that if it was X's intention to **thwart the crime** rather than execute it, for example by handing Y over **before the transaction** was effected, no conspiracy would lie. Lord Griffiths stated unequivocally that the crime required 'an agreement between two or more persons to commit an unlawful act with the intention of carrying it out. It is the intention to carry out the crime that constitutes the *mens rea* for the offence'.[206] Although a Privy Council decision, it is submitted that it is to be preferred to that of *Anderson*. The logical extension of *Anderson* is that a conspiracy may lie even though none of the parties intend to carry the agreement through. This **would** be going too far!

One question remains. Can a person be guilty of a criminal conspiracy upon an agreement that an offence shall be committed without having any intention to take part in its execution? Commonsensically he can. This, after all, is a large part of what the law of criminal conspiracy is about. In large-scale criminal operations there are masterminds and there are executors. Doctrine which failed to rope in the masterminds would seem to be missing its main target. Nevertheless in *Anderson* Lord Bridge stated that a conspiracy

---

[202] For an extended treatment of this idea see R.A. Duff, '"Can I help You?" Accessorial Liability and the Intention to Assist' [1990] 10 LS 165 at 172.

[203] [1992] Crim LR 667.

[204] [1994] 2 All ER 924.

[205] LCCP 183 (2007) 123–36; LC 318 6.56.

[206] At 928. For discussion see A.J. Ashworth, 'Testing Fidelity to Legal Values: Official Involvement and Criminal Justice' in S. Shute and A. Simester (eds), *Criminal Law Theory: Doctrines of the General Part*, Oxford: OUP (2002) 299.

would not lie against a person unless he 'assented to play his part in the agreed course of conduct'. In *Siracusa* this statement was sensibly, if controversially, glossed over by a Court of Appeal apparently more attuned to the purpose of the law of conspiracy than Lord Bridge: 'We think it obvious that Lord Bridge cannot have been intending that the organiser of a crime who recruited others to carry it out would not himself be guilty of conspiracy unless it could be proved that he intended to play some active part himself thereafter'.[207]

18.8 COMMON LAW CONSPIRACIES

Three common law conspiracies survive the passing of the Criminal Law Act. They are conspiracy to defraud, conspiracy to outrage public decency, and conspiracy to corrupt public morals. It should be remembered that unlike statutory conspiracies the object of such conspiracies does not have to be the commission of a criminal offence. It was intended that these conspiracies should remain, pending a full-scale review of fraud and obscenity. A review of fraud has taken place and legislation has followed but no further consideration has been given to common law conspiracy. If ever it is, one difficulty which must be faced is whether it is necessarily of the essence of a criminal conspiracy that the object should itself be criminal.[208] As has been suggested above, this should be the case if conspiracy is regarded as an inchoate offence pure and simple. If, on the other hand, it is an offence in its own right, there is an argument for holding agreements to damage the interests of others or the public interest potentially criminal, always assuming individuals are not thereby rendered vulnerable to conviction without fair warning.

A Conspiracy to defraud

In most cases a conspiracy to defraud will be a conspiracy to commit a criminal offence. As such the conspiracy should ordinarily be charged as a statutory conspiracy,[209] though it is not fatal to charge a common law conspiracy.[210] This might be proper if, for example, it was not clear whether the course of conduct agreed upon amounted to a criminal offence.[211] An example of agreeing to defraud a person where the fraud perpetrated would not necessarily amount to a criminal offence is *Scott v MPC*.[212] S had agreed with employees of a cinema to borrow films without the permission of the cinema or copyright owners for the purpose of making pirate copies. This was a fraud on the owners of the copyright but not a criminal fraud in the absence of theft or a deception. For a deceit to have been practised the conspirators would have had to dupe the cinema owners into handing over the films, whereas in fact the latter were entirely ignorant of the plan. The major issue in the case was whether a fraud of any kind could be committed in the absence of a deception. It was held that an agreement to 'deprive a person of something which is his or to which he is or would be entitled, and an agreement by two or more by dishonesty to injure some proprietary right of his' will constitute fraud.[213]

---

[207] (1990) 90 Cr App R 340 at 349; see also *R v Chambers* [2009] EWCA Crim 2742 CACD.
[208] The Law Commission have recommended that the offence continue until the full review of dishonesty offences has been completed: Law Com. No. 228 (1994).
[209] *R v Ayers* [1984] AC 447 (HL); *R v Goldstein*; *R v Rimmington* [2005] UKHL 63.
[210] Section 12 Criminal Justice Act 1987.
[211] See A. Reed, 'Conspiracy to Defraud: The Threshold Standardisation' (2012) 76(5) Journal of Criminal Law 373.
[212] *Scott v MPC* [1974] 3 All ER 1032.
[213] Per Viscount Dilhorne at 1039.

Conspiracy to defraud does not require that loss be actually suffered or an intent on the part of the conspirators that the victim suffers loss, so long as his interests are 'imperilled'.[214] Thus, for example, if A and B agree to dupe C into lending them his car, intending to return it later, this could be charged as a conspiracy to defraud since, notwithstanding their desire not to harm C, the agreement is one which they may realise may cause C economic damage – for example, they may crash the car, or fail to return it when he needs it. Exceptionally a conspiracy to defraud may lie without even the threat of economic loss. An important example is where a public official is deceived into acting contrary to his public duty.[215] Accordingly, it is a conspiracy to defraud where an agreement is made to deceive an official into supplying confidential information[216] or an export licence.[217]

Unlike the position with statutory conspiracies, it seems that the conspiracy can be made out even where the substantive offence is to be committed by parties other than the conspirators.[218] So where A and B had sold devices designed to alter readings on electricity meters this was held to be a conspiracy to defraud electricity boards[219] even though the relevant substantive offence was not to be committed by them but third parties.[220] It should be noted also that the conspiracy was constituted even though A and B had no interest in the commission of such offences and so lacked any intention that the agreement be carried through.[221]

B Conspiracy to corrupt public morals

By s. 5(3) Criminal Law Act 1977 an agreement to corrupt public morals or outrage public decency may be the subject-matter of a criminal conspiracy. The subsection does not expressly provide that they are common law conspiracies since it was not clear at the time of the passing of the Act whether there were substantive offences of 'corrupting public morals' or 'outraging public decency'. The position seems to be, therefore, that they are statutory conspiracies if it is a crime for one person on their own 'to corrupt public morals' or 'outrage public decency', but otherwise not. The two leading cases on conspiracy to corrupt public morals are ambiguous on this point. In *Shaw v DPP*[222] the House of Lords held that an agreement between a publisher and clients for the publisher to place the clients' advertisements for (heterosexual) sexual services to the public in the publisher's magazine was a conspiracy to corrupt public morals. What is required to establish such a corruption is not clear. Lord Simon of Glaisdale stated that the 'conduct must be such which a jury might find destructive of the very fabric of society'.[223] In *Knuller v DPP*[224] a similar result occurred in a case in which the advertisers were homosexuals. Even though what was being advertised (sex) was not necessarily a criminal offence, the agreement was. In neither case was it made clear that this ruling was based upon the fact that the subject-matter of the

---

[214] *Wai Yu-Tsang v R* [1991] 4 All ER 664 PC at 670; *R v Allsop* (1977) 64 Cr App R 29.
[215] *Welham* [1960] 1 All ER 805.
[216] Cf. *DPP v Withers* [1975] AC 842.
[217] *Board of Trade v Owen* [1957] AC 602; *Terry* [1984] 1 All ER 65.
[218] Cf. *R v Majeed* [2012] EWCA Crim 1186.
[219] *Hollinshead* [1985] AC 975.
[220] *R v Kenning* [2008] EWCA Crim 1534; [2009] Crim LR 37.
[221] Oblique intention would, then, appear to be enough for this form of conspiracy; cf. *Yip Chiu-cheng* (1994) 2 All ER 924.
[222] [1962] AC 220.
[223] See Chapter 2.
[224] [1973] AC 435.

agreement (corrupting public morals) was a criminal offence and therefore, by the same token, it was a criminal conspiracy to agree to corrupt public morals. The Court of Appeal in *Shaw* assumed it was and some of the reasoning in the House of Lords leads to a similar assumption.[225]

C Conspiracy to outrage public decency

The position on outraging public decency appears to be less uncertain. In a number of cases the existence of an offence of outraging public decency has been accepted,[226] most notably in *Gibson*[227] where the defendant was found properly convicted for having displayed in an art gallery earrings made from human foetuses. Outraging public decency appears to require more than merely causing shock since we 'live in a plural society, with a tradition of tolerance towards minorities and . . . this tolerance is itself part of public decency'.[228] Whether the conduct has this tendency or not is a jury question.[229] Conviction requires the prosecution to establish that the relevant act has been witnessed by more than one person.[230]

It seems that a conspiracy to outrage public decency is a statutory conspiracy, although it will probably not be fatal to charge it as a common law conspiracy. A conspiracy to corrupt public morals appears to be a common law conspiracy unless proved to be otherwise. A conspiracy to do something immoral which is a recognised criminal offence, for example, to commit indecent exposure or other crime of indecency, is a statutory conspiracy.[231]

D Impossibility

By an amendment to section 1,[232] it is now certain that the rules on impossibility for (statutory) conspiracy are the same as for attempts.[233] This means that where two or more people agree to pursue a course of conduct which will necessarily amount to the commission of an offence but for the existence of facts which will render its commission impossible, a conspiracy will lie. So an agreement to kill an already dead man, to steal a non-existent watch, or to import heroin (which isn't) is a criminal conspiracy. The rules on impossibility for common law conspiracy are the common law rules which distressingly, at least in the case of conspiracy to defraud, render impossibility fatal in all cases other than impossibility through ineptitude.[234]

Case 24

Adam agrees with Eve, a cinema projectionist, that Eve will provide Adam with copies of all the films shown in her cinema so that he can make pirate copies of them for later resale. Unknown to Adam and Eve a new electronic 'tag' attached to all newly-released films causes them to self-destruct when placed in a copying machine.

---

[225] Law Commission No. 76 (1976) paras 3.21–24.
[226] *Knuller* v *DPP* [1973] AC 435 per Lords Simon and Kilbrandon; *Mayling* [1963] 2 QB 717; *Rowley* [1991] 4 All ER 649.
[227] [1991] 1 All ER 439.
[228] [1972] 2 All ER at 936 per Lord Simon.
[229] *Mayling* [1963] 2 QB 717. See also *R* v *Hamilton* [2007] EWCA Crim 2062 CACD.
[230] *Rose* v *DPP* [2006] EWHC 852 (Admin); [2006] Crim LR 993.
[231] *Rowley* [1991] 4 All ER 649.
[232] By s. 5 Criminal Attempts Act 1981.
[233] The 'if carried out in accordance with their intentions' provision probably made this the case anyway.
[234] *DPP* v *Nock* [1978] AC 979.

The agreement of Adam and Eve is in the nature of a common law conspiracy to defraud, not a statutory conspiracy, as the subject-matter is not a criminal offence. Since the commission of the substantive offence is factually impossible, a punishable conspiracy cannot be established.[235]

18.9 ASSISTING OR ENCOURAGING CRIME

The third general inchoate offence of incitement was replaced by statutory offences of assisting or encouraging crime created by Part 2 Serious Crime Act 2007. Existing statutory offences of incitement such as incitement to racial hatred remain unaffected.

18.10 RELATIONSHIP WITH ACCESSORIAL LIABILITY: OVERVIEW

Those who 'aid, abet, counsel or procure', the commission of an offence are, by section 8 Accessories and Abettors Act 1861, liable as accessories to the consummated offence if the offence takes place. Thus where A **encourages** B to kill C and B does so, A is an accessory to murder. Where A **assists**, without encouraging, B to kill C and B does kill C, A is also liable as an accessory to murder. The Serious Crimes Act addresses the situation where the offence, encouraged or assisted does not take place. Where A encourages or assists the commission of an offence but the offence does not take place A will be guilty of the statutory inchoate offence of encouraging or assisting the offence. The Serious Crime Act 2007 contains two other inchoate offences to deal with those who provide knowing assistance or encouragement to a person in the commission of an offence, but without intending to assist or encourage its commission.

18.11 PART 2 SERIOUS CRIME ACT 2007: OVERVIEW

By section 44 it is an offence intentionally to assist or encourage an offence. In addition there are two other sections, 45 and 46, to deal with the case of someone who provides assistance or encouragement without the intention to do so but nevertheless believing his actions will have this effect. The major effect of Part 2 is to close the loophole that a person could be guilty of an inchoate offence if he intentionally encouraged the commission of an offence but not if he intentionally assisted it, notwithstanding the fact that, in this latter case, had the offence taken place he would have been liable as an accessory to it. A problem which threatens to pose problems for prosecutors is whether the offence is charged if **in addition to** encouraging or assisting the commission of an offence **the offence is actually committed**. The Law Commission, whose recommendations these provisions embody, made its proposals as part of a package along with secondary party liability. However, the proposals governing accessorial liability have not been enacted in tandem with the coming into force of Part 2, which leaves the law in an unsatisfactory and confusing position. The prosecution are left with the choice as to whether to charge the secondary party with the inchoate or full offence in those cases where, subsequent to an act of encouragement or assistance, the offence is actually committed. Given the complexity of the new law it may well choose to continue to charge as an accessory.[236]

---

[235] But see *Fitzmaurice* [1983] 1 All ER 189.

[236] For robust criticism of this 'complexity and incoherence' see D.C. Ormerod and R. Fortson [2009] 'The Serious Crime Act 2007: the Part 2 Offences' [2009] Crim LR 389.

A Common elements

For all offences under this Act it is a requirement that the defendant does an act capable of assisting or encouraging an offence. It is not necessary for the encouragement or assistance to be communicated to the other, or indeed for it to be particularly effective or substantial.[237] If the act performed by the defendant is not so capable then he cannot be guilty of an offence under the Act, although he intends or believes that it will take place.

> **Case 25**
>
> Adam, knowing Eve has run out of drugs, leaves a package on Eve's seat in the airport lounge intending her to take possession of it. She does not do so, not knowing what the package contains. Adam is arrested on arrival in the UK.

Adam is guilty by section 44 of assisting or encouraging the commission of an offence (importation of drugs under the Misuse of Drugs Act 1971). He has done an act capable of assisting or encouraging her to commit the offence with the intention of so doing.

> **Case 26**
>
> Adam gives Eve a package at the airport which he believes contains drugs. In fact it contains talcum powder. Adam is arrested on arrival in the UK and charged with encouraging or assisting an offence (importation of drugs under section 3 Misuse of Drugs) believing it will be committed, under section 45 of the Act.

Adam is not guilty of this offence as his act was not capable of assisting or encouraging the section 3 offence. He will be guilty however of an attempt to commit the section 45 offence.[238]

To be guilty under all three of these sections for crimes requiring proof of fault the person must believe that the other will have the fault required for the crime in question (or would have that fault were he to do it himself).[239]

> **Case 27**
>
> Adam, knowing Eve not to be consenting, encourages Cain, who also knows this, to have intercourse with Eve.

Adam is guilty of encouraging the commission of rape because he encourages the commission of non-consensual sexual penetration either believing that Cain has the necessary fault for the offence or being reckless as to this fact.

> **Case 28**
>
> Adam, knowing Eve not to be consenting, encourages Cain to have intercourse with Eve. Adam tells Cain that Eve is consenting. Cain reasonably believes this because Eve is acting under Adam's coercion.

[237] Ibid.
[238] See Jones [2007] above.
[239] Section 47(5)(a)(iii). See below Case 31.

Adam is guilty of encouraging Cain to commit the offence of rape this time because, although Adam does not 'believe' that Cain will have the necessary fault for the offence of rape, Cain himself would have the necessary fault (if he were to do the act himself).[240]

By subsection (5)(b) under all three sections 44, 45 and 46 the defendant must believe or be reckless that any circumstance or consequence necessary for the offence to be established is present.

Case 29

Adam, believing Eve to be consenting, encourages Cain, who believes she is not consenting, to have intercourse with Eve. Eve does not consent.

Case 30

John supplies Janet with a baseball bat believing it is to be used to commit minor harm on Cain. Janet in fact uses the bat to kill Katy intentionally.

Adam is not guilty of intentionally encouraging the commission of rape (s. 44), although this offence may be committed by negligence on the part of Cain. Subsection (5)(b) requires that Adam believes Eve not to be consenting or is reckless as to any circumstance (here consent) or consequence. Likewise John is not guilty of assisting murder, believing it will be committed (s. 45), as he does not believe that this consequence will occur, nor is he reckless.

B Intentionally encouraging or assisting an offence

By section 44 Serious Crime Act 2007,

(1) A person commits an offence if –
   (a) he does an act capable of encouraging or assisting the commission of an offence; and
   (b) he intends to encourage or assist its commission.
(2) But he is not to be taken to have intended to encourage or assist the commission of an offence merely because such encouragement or assistance was a foreseeable consequence of his act.

To be guilty under this section D must intend to assist or encourage the commission of the offence. If he simply foresees that his action will have this effect he cannot be guilty under this section.[241] It is not made explicit whether intention in this context means direct intention or whether foresight of virtual certainty suffices either in itself, or as evidence of intention. The better view is that a purpose to assist or encourage is necessary. Cases of oblique intention are covered by section 45. It should be noted that the prosecution need prove only that D1 intended to assist or encourage D2 to commit the offence. This does not mean that D1 must intend D2 to commit the offence. For example, if D2 asks D1 for a gun with which to kill C and D1, wishing to be helpful to D2, gives him the gun as requested it is no part of the prosecution's task to show that D1 intended D2 to kill C.

Section 47 attempts to clarify further the state of mind of an assister or encourager. What is it to intend to assist or encourage P to commit an offence? By section 47(5)(a),

---

[240] Subsection (5)(a)(iii). See text at note 239.
[241] J.J. Child, 'Exploring the *Mens Rea* Requirements of the Serious Crime Act 2007 Assisting and Encouraging Offences' (2012) 76(3) J Crim L 220.

(i) D must believe or (ii) be reckless that P would have the fault element of the offence, or (iii) would have the fault element were he to commit it.[242]

> **Case 31**
> Adam, not believing Eve to be consenting, encourages Cain to have intercourse with Eve. Adam has no thoughts either way as to whether Cain believes Eve to be consenting. Eve does not consent and Cain knows this.

Adam is guilty of the section 44 offence being reckless as to Cain's fault element.

> **Case 32**
> Adam, not believing Eve to be consenting, encourages Cain to have intercourse with Eve. Adam believes that Cain believes Eve to be consenting. Eve does not consent.

Adam is guilty of the section 44 offence because by section 47(5)(a)(iii). It is enough that he, Adam, would have the fault element for rape, were he to commit it.

1 Encouraging or assisting an offence believing it will be committed

By section 45 Serious Crime Act 2007,

> A person commits an offence if –
> (a) he does an act capable of encouraging or assisting the commission of an offence; and
> (b) he believes –
>   (i) that the offence will be committed; and
>   (ii) that his act will encourage or assist its commission.

This section is designed to cover the case where the defendant encourages or assists someone to commit an offence but does this for reasons other than wanting to assist or encourage the commission of the offence or because he is indifferent.[243]

> **Case 33**
> Eve, a gunsmith, supplies a gun to Adam who tells her that he intends to kill Cain with it.

Eve commits the section 45 offence whether or not Adam commits murder because she believes the offence will be committed and that her act will assist it to be committed.

> **Case 34**
> Adam asks to purchase from Eve a gun and also a silencer. Eve supplies the gun to Adam although, because of the silencer, she strongly suspects Adam will use it to kill.

Eve does not commit the section 45 offence. To be guilty under this section it is necessary for Eve to believe Adam will commit the offence. Suspicion, even strong suspicion, is not enough.[244]

---

[242] Ibid.
[243] Ibid.
[244] *Griffiths* (1974) 60 Cr App R 14. See generally Ormerod, op. cit.; S. Shute, 'Knowledge and Belief in the Criminal Law' in Shute and Simester (eds), *Criminal Law Theory: Doctrines of the General Part*, Oxford: OUP (2002).

Section 46 deals with the problem of someone who gives assistance or encouragement to someone he knows intends to commit an offence but is unsure which offence.[245]

2 Encouraging or assisting offences believing one or more will be committed

By section 46 Serious Crime Act 2007,

(1) A person commits an offence if –
    (a) he does an act capable of encouraging or assisting the commission of one or more of a number of offences; and
    (b) he believes –
        (i) that one or more of those offences will be committed (but has no belief as to which); and
        (ii) that his act will encourage or assist the commission of one or more of them.[246]
(2) It is immaterial for the purposes of subsection (1)(b)(ii) whether the person has any belief as to which offence will be encouraged or assisted.
(3) If a person is charged with an offence under subsection (1) –
    (a) the indictment must specify the offences alleged to be the 'number of offences' mentioned in paragraph (a) of that subsection; but
    (b) nothing in paragraph (a) requires all the offences potentially comprised in that number to be specified.
(4) In relation to an offence under this section, reference in this Part to the offences specified in the indictment is to the offences specified by virtue of subsection (3)(a).

To be guilty under section 46 it is not enough that A knows that an offence is to be committed; he must know that it is one of a number of possible offences. If it is not one of those offences he cannot be guilty.

Case 35

Eve is Adam's getaway driver. Adam instructs her to drive to Cain's house. As usual he does not tell Eve what offence he intends to commit but Eve believes, from past experience, it will be burglary, with or without violence or arson.

If Adam intends to commit burglary, arson or assault occasioning actual bodily harm Eve will be guilty under section 46. If Adam intends to commit rape on Cain, Eve will not be guilty of under section 46, nor if the offence intended is kidnap.

In *R* v *Sadique and Hussain*[247] the Court of Appeal rejected the challenge that the provision was contrary to Art. 7 ECHR on the ground that it was vague and uncertain.

C Defences

There are two defences to offences under Part 2. The first, by section 50, is the defence of acting reasonably. The defence is available wherever the facts are such or his belief in those facts is such that it was reasonable for him to act as he did in the circumstances. This is intended to cover cases like *Yip Chiu-cheung* v *R*,[248] where law enforcement officers get

---

[245] For discussion see *R* v *Sadique and Hussain* [2011] EWCA Crim 2872; [2012] Crim LR 449.
[246] This provision mirrors the legal position in accessoryship where a person can be liable as an accessory to a crime although he does not know precisely which crime is to be committed but does know it is one of a number of possible crimes. See *Maxwell* v *DPP for Northern Ireland* [1978] 3 All ER 114.
[247] [2011] EWCA Crim 2872; [2012] Crim LR 449.
[248] [1994] 2 All ER 924.

involved in the commission of crimes for the purpose of detection and arrest. It would also presumably cover the following case:[249]

> **Case 36**
> Eve tells Adam, her secretary, to type a letter to Cain, her tenant, who has not paid his rent, saying that if he doesn't vacate the premises Adam will send round some men to throw him out. This he does.

Eve's action is unlawful under the Protection from Eviction Act 1997. Adam, however, may have a defence that his action is reasonable by virtue of his contract of employment which should not require him to have to 'second guess' the legality of all Eve's actions.

The second defence, by section 51, removes from the coverage of section 44–46 those who are deemed to be 'protected' by the offence encourage or assisted. So if A, aged 12, encourages B, aged 18 to have sex with him A is not guilty of the section 44 offence.

Summary

There are three crimes of general application the gist of which is to proscribe activities not unlawful in their own right but because they form a step towards the commission of another offence. These are the inchoate crimes of attempt, conspiracy and assisting or encouraging crime.

The *actus reus* of a criminal attempt is defined, by statute, as an act which is more than merely preparatory to the commission of an offence. Distinguishing between acts of mere preparation and actual attempts is a matter for the jury, although the judge must withdraw a case from the jury where the acts concerned are incapable of being more than preparatory. Failure to do so means any conviction will be quashed. A judge may make suggestions to help the jury make its decision. A number of common law tests have been designed for this purpose. Although predating the Act they remain influential on judicial thinking. It is clear that an act is more than merely preparatory if it forms the last act necessary on the defendant's part for the substantive offence to occur. Beyond this, perhaps the most influential test now operating is the 'on the job' test. The jury will be asked to consider whether the defendant has embarked 'on the crime proper' rather than be merely preparing for it. For result crimes the *mens rea* for attempt requires proof that the accused intended not only the conduct necessary to satisfy the *actus reus* of the offence, but also the harmful consequence which the offence is designed to sanction. Intended consequences, in this context, include those consequences which the defendant tried to bring about, including those consequences foreseen as virtually certain which he is unwilling to forfeit in trying to produce some other consequence. Recklessness as to consequences on any analysis is insufficient. Where a result crime is constituted upon proof of certain circumstances and the *mens rea* in respect of such circumstances includes recklessness, then, as long as intention can be established with respect to that result, liability for an attempt is incurred upon proof of recklessness as to the relevant circumstances. It is no objection to liability for an attempt that, however hard the defendant tried, what he was doing was incapable of resulting in the commission of the substantive offence. As long as he intended to commit the offence and, on the facts as he believed them to be, his acts were capable of resulting in the commission of that offence, this is sufficient to sustain liability for an attempt.

[249] For other examples see Law Com. 300, 82–91.

Criminal conspiracy takes one of two forms. Statutory conspiracy occurs when two or more people agree on a course of conduct which amounts to a criminal offence. Common law conspiracy differs from statutory conspiracy in allowing punishment where the course of conduct agreed will not necessarily amount to a criminal offence but will amount to an act involving (a) the corruption of public morals or outraging public decency, or (b) fraud. In both forms it is not necessary that each conspirator has agreed to commit the offence so long as the offence will be committed by at least one of the parties to the agreement. The mental element in conspiracy is an intention to commit the offence agreed upon. It is not necessary to show that the conspirator knew that the course of conduct agreed upon would amount to a criminal offence. It is necessary, however, to show that the conspirator knew of any facts or circumstances which would render the course of conduct agreed upon prohibited, or intended such facts or circumstances to exist. By an amendment to section 1, the rules on impossibility for (statutory) conspiracy are the same as for attempts.[250] This means that where two or more people agree to pursue a course of conduct which will necessarily amount to the commission of an offence but for the existence of facts which will render its commission impossible, a conspiracy will lie. The rules on impossibility for common law conspiracy are, by contrast, the common law rules which render impossibility fatal in all cases other than impossibility through ineptitude.[251]

Part 2 Serious Crime Act 2007 abolished the existing crime of incitement. It is replaced by section 44 which renders it an offence to intentionally assist or encourage an offence. In addition there are two other sections, 45 and 46, to deal with the case of someone who provides assistance or encouragement without the intention to do so but nevertheless believing his actions will have this effect. The major effect of Part 2 is to close the loophole that a person could be guilty of an inchoate offence if he intentionally encouraged the commission of an offence but not if he intentionally assisted it, notwithstanding the fact that, in this latter case, had the offence taken place he would have been liable as an accessory to it.

Further reading

Ashworth, A.J., 'Belief, Intent and Criminal Liability' in J. Eekelaar and J. Bell (eds), *Oxford Essays in Jurisprudence*, Oxford: OUP (1987) 16.

Ashworth, A.J., 'Criminal Attempts and the Role of Resulting Harm under the Code in the Common law' (1988) 19 Rutgers Law Journal 725.

Ashworth, A.J., 'Defining Criminal Offences without Harm' in P. Smith (ed.), *Criminal Law: Essays in Honour of J.C. Smith*, Oxford: OUP (1987).

Bohlander, M., 'The Conflict between the Serious Crime Act 2007 and Section 1(4)(b) Criminal Attempts Act 1981 – a missed repeal?' [2010] Crim LR 483.

Child, J.J., 'The Differences between Attempted Complicity and Inchoate Assisting and Encouraging – a Reply to Professor Bohlander' [2010] Crim LR 924.

Clarkson, C., 'Attempt: The Conduct Requirement' (2009) 29(1) Oxford J Legal Studies 25–41.

---

[250] The 'if carried out in accordance with their intentions' provision probably made this the case anyway.
[251] *DPP* v *Nock* [1978] AC 979.

Dennis, I., 'The Elements of Attempt' [1980] Criminal Law Review 758.

Dennis, I., 'The Rationale of Criminal Conspiracy' (1977) 93 Law Quarterly Review 39.

Duff, R.A., *Criminal Attempts*, Oxford: Clarendon Press (1996).

Duff, R.A., 'Criminalising Endangerment' in R.A. Duff and S. Green (eds), *Defining Crimes: Essays on The Special Part of the Criminal Law*, Oxford: OUP (2005) 43.

Duff, R.A., 'Structures of Crime: Attacks and Endangerment' in *Answering for Crime: Responsibility and Liability in the Criminal Law*, Oxford: Hart (2009) Chapter 7.

Fortson, R., *Blackstone's Guide to the Serious Crime Act 2007*, Oxford: OUP (2008).

Glazebrook, P., 'Should We Have a Law of Attempted Crime?' (1969) 85 Law Quarterly Review 28.

Horder, J., 'Varieties of Intention, Criminal Attempts and Endangerment' (1994) 14 Legal Studies 335.

Ormerod, D.C. and Fortson, R., 'The Serious Crime Act 2007: The Part 2 Offences' [2009] Criminal Law Review 389.

Rogers, J., 'The Codification of Attempts and the Case for "Preparation"' [2008] Criminal Law Review 937.

Wasik, M., 'Abandoning Criminal Attempt' [1980] Criminal Law Review 785.

Williams, G., 'The Lords and Impossible Attempts, or *quis custodiet ipsos custodes*' (1986) Cambridge Law Journal 33.

19 Complicity

Overview

The subject-matter of this chapter concerns the way in which people may become implicated in crimes committed by other people, typically by giving help or encouragement to the principal offender, and the principles governing their liability. Under a system which incriminates and punishes upon the criteria of culpability and wrongdoing we should expect a distinction to be drawn between those who perpetrate crime and those who help or encourage, but do not themselves perform the conduct element of an offence. However, many criminal justice systems, and ours is no exception, operate on the basis that those who help or encourage the commission of a criminal offence should be punished along with the perpetrator for that offence (which they have not committed) rather than for the wrong they have committed – helping or encouraging a person to commit a crime.[1]

19.1 INTRODUCTION

Accessorial liability is a form of derivative liability.[2] Vicarious liability is another example. In both cases A's liability **derives** from the fact of P's liability. Dressler explains the position as follows:

> A is held accountable for the conduct of P because, by intentionally assisting him, he voluntarily identifies himself with the primary party. His intentional conduct, therefore, is equivalent to manifesting consent to liability under the civil law.[3]

Significantly, therefore, both A's deed and his culpability may fall far short of that necessary to incriminate the perpetrator of either the attempt or the substantive offence. A person may be liable as an accessory to murder by dint of an act as innocuous as driving the getaway car, providing the murder weapon in the ordinary course of business supply, or, it appears, saying 'Oh goody' upon hearing the principal's lethal plan.[4]

The common law treats the accessory as if he had committed the wrong himself, for both practical and moral reasons. At the practical level there are obvious procedural and evidential advantages in collapsing the distinction between perpetrators and other participants. Section 8 of the Accessories and Abettors Act 1861 provides that (helping or encouraging) someone to commit a substantive offence **constitutes the commission of that offence**. This enables prosecutions to proceed to a conclusion against parties to a joint criminal venture without fear of collapse for want of proof as to which of two or more persons pulled the trigger, drove the car, took the money and so on.[5]

---

[1] G. Fletcher (1978) 640–5.

[2] See G. Fletcher, Chapter 8 generally.

[3] Dressler 411; and see S. Kadish, 'Complicity, Cause and Blame: A Study in the Interpretation of Doctrine', (1985) 73 Calif LR 323 at 354.

[4] *Giannetto* [1997] 1 Crim App Rep.

[5] See for example *Forman and Ford* [1988] Crim LR 677; *Giannetto* [1997] 1 Crim App Rep 1, *infra*.

At the moral level there is no necessary distinction between different forms of participation in crime. Derivative liability is clearly appropriate when the role of the secondary party is morally congruent with that of the principal. Those who instigate crimes, for example, are at least as blameworthy as those who perpetrate them and sometimes more so. Moreover they may have a direct causal impact on the world of events which cannot be subdued by the voluntary execution by another of their unlawful purposes. Those who participate in the actual commission of the crime for the purpose of bringing about the commission of that crime by another are also appropriately dubbed the authors of such crimes. Adopting this notion of authorship rather than direct causal responsibility allows us to see why it is fair for such assistance to deserve equal ranking (and punishment) with the perpetration of the offence.[6] Secondary liability thus allows a degree of flexibility in setting the parameters of accountability for criminal wrongdoing. If causal agency is the method whereby harmful events may be attributed to individual perpetrators it is by cooperative association that accountability may stretch to include those others without whose skills, efforts, dynamism or influence some criminal activity would not occur. And so domestic law holds accessories liable and punishable for the same reason, to the same extent as the other, and therefore for the same crime.

If desert alone informed the scope of accessorial liability we might expect a distinction to be drawn between certain forms of participation in crime. Some forms might indeed entail the participator to be treated on all fours with the perpetrator. Others, however, might require the participator to be charged with a lesser inchoate offence. Still others might be excluded altogether. The common law's typically pragmatic response, rather than legislate for different degrees of involvement, is to make this a matter of prosecutorial and judicial discretion. So, it allows for the kind of sentencing flexibility which can punish the (non-perpetrating) instigators of crime as severely, or more severely, than their hired hands, while also allowing the more typical accessory to be punished less severely than the perpetrator. This poses a theoretical problem, however, namely it undermines the notion that the accessory's liability derives from what the perpetrator, rather than what he himself, has done.

As a preliminary to examining the actual scope of liability for participators, therefore, we will look at some different forms of participation in crime with a view to assessing how they might be treated to reconcile theory, doctrine and policy. First, we will consider cases where the participator appears to deserve equal treatment with the perpetrator.

Case 1

W wishes her husband, H, dead. She hires a contract killer, C, to do the job and goes on holiday. H is dead on her return.

Commonsensically we would expect W and C to be charged and punished for the same crime. Although C is the actual perpetrator of the offence we might feel that there is full moral equivalence between them, both in terms of harm and culpability. We can justify this state of affairs

(1) by holding C to be the sole principal offender with W an accessory to the offence;
(2) by holding C and W to be joint principal offenders; or
(3) by holding W to be sole principal offender, with C her accessory.

---

[6] Kadish, 'Complicity, Blame and Cause: A Study in the Interpretation of Doctrine', (1985) 73 Calif LR 323 at 354–5.

A C as sole principal offender

This is the position adopted in common law jurisdictions. The principal offender is, with one exception, defined as the perpetrator of the offence, that is the person who performs the *actus reus* of the offence with the appropriate *mens rea*. C is the principal offender because it is his voluntary act which causes the offence to be committed. It is appropriate to treat W as a secondary party to that offence because of the special instigatory role she played in it. She thus has both a 'but for' causal role and a purpose, not merely to encourage C in the commission of the offence but for the offence actually to be committed. Her accessoryship is therefore justified on the basis that she acted so as to bring about the crime charged.

B C and W as joint principal offenders

One problem with the above solution is that it seems to mistake the true nature of W's role. She has the *mens rea* for the substantive offence – she acts in order to kill. But she arguably is also the legal, not merely factual, cause of H's death because of the substantiality of her but-for contribution. This argues for principal offenders to be defined so as to incriminate all those who have control over whether or not the offence takes place, whether or not they participate in its execution.[7]

C W as principal offender

Another possibility is to define the principal offender as the prime mover in any criminal activity. This would render W, but not C, the principal offender in Case 1. W is the prime mover since, although C pulled the trigger on the gun, it was W who pulled the trigger on H's life. One situation in which a perpetrator is defined in terms of prime mover in English law is where a criminal offence is performed with the use of an innocent agent, for example a child, who does not appreciate the significance of what he is doing. In the former case we have a conscious, purposive agent. In the latter we have an innocent pawn. But both involve, as executor, an agent who does his principal's bidding.[8]

We have considered some cases where the participator appears to deserve equal treatment with the perpetrator. A person who acts with the purpose of bringing about a criminal offence and who has the power to control whether or not the offence takes place, cannot easily be distinguished morally from the person who perpetrates the offence.[9] We consider now some more problematic cases where there seems to be some disparity between the culpability and/or wrongdoing of the participator.

> **Case 2**
> T and W decide to kill H, W's husband. Their plan is for W to lure H into the swimming pool and for T to throw a net over the swimming area thus fatally hindering both H's egress and breathing. Z, a friend, on hearing of T and W's plan, suggests they use a jute net which becomes heavy in water rather than one made from artificial fibres.

[7] For discussion see G.R. Sullivan, 'Participating in Crime: Law Com. No. 305' (2008) Crim LR 19.
[8] In contract law this suffices to hold the instigator liable as principal rather than as an accessory to the agent's act. See Fletcher (1978) 657–9 for an elaboration of this view.
[9] Shachar Eldar, 'Holding Organized Crime Leaders Accountable for the Crimes of Their Subordinates' (2012) 6(2) Criminal Law & Philosophy 207.

It goes without saying that Z's suggestion is culpable and wrong. But Z neither instigated the crime nor, as far as we can tell, necessarily wanted the crime to take place. Z would be liable for no crime if he had said nothing but allowed T and W to get on with their plan undisturbed since he was under no legal duty to prevent its occurrence or even inform the police.[10] It might seem, therefore, disproportionate to tie Z into the murder rather than, say, punish him for what we apprehend is his real crime, namely to give moral support, through encouragement and advice, to the real killers.[11] This is the preferred option of the Law Commission.[12]

A greater problem than that of the callous advice-giver is the case of the cynical supplier. Most commodities have the potential to be used in the course of crime. A kitchen knife can be used to kill or cut, a screwdriver can be used to gain access, pretty wallpaper can be used to make a brothel more appealing, an old school tie can facilitate the commission of a fraud.

> **Case 3**
>
> In furtherance of Z's suggestion, W and T go into X's chandlery and ask for a large jute net big enough to fit over a swimming pool. While X is out of the room he hears W and T discuss the full details of their plan but nevertheless supplies the net so as not to lose a sale. On the day of the killing, Y, at W and T's request, acts as lookout. Everything goes according to plan.

Once again X has no duty to prevent W and T killing H. But does he have other duties? For example, can it be said that he has a duty not to sell them the net such that doing so will render him responsible **as an accessory to murder**? Arguably, if the law is consistent it cannot support X's autonomy by not imposing a duty to inform the police of what he has heard and yet punish him for doing what he is in business to do, namely sell nets and ropes.[13] And yet it does. If W and T kill H, X is an accessory to murder. Once again, a better approach may be to punish X and Y and Z for the wrong they have committed – helping or encouraging a person to commit a crime – rather than for a wrong they have not committed – the crime itself.[14] As we shall see, this suggestion has the support of the Law Commission which would limit secondary party liability to those, like W but unlike X, who, along with the principal, act with the specific intention of helping X to commit the offence.

19.2 COMPLICITY: DEFINITIONS AND TERMINOLOGY[15]

As a general principle, a person will be an accomplice to a criminal offence if he intentionally helps or encourages the principal in the commission of a criminal offence. No distinction is drawn between those who instigate an offence and those who merely provide assistance or encouragement.

---

[10] Cf. Ashworth, 'The Scope of Criminal Liability for Omissions' [1989] LQR 424.

[11] Z's conduct is the inchoate offence of intentionally assisting or encouraging the commission of an offence by section 44 Serious Crime Act 2007.

[12] Law Commission No. 305 *Participating in Crime* (2007).

[13] Would he still be doing wrong if, knowing what he did, he was merely returning a net which T had previously lent him?

[14] Fletcher (1978) 640–5. Z's conduct constitutes the inchoate offence of encouraging or assisting an offence believing it will be committed; section 45 Serious Crime Act 2007. In the German system punishment for secondary parties is formally discounted to reflect the actor's participatory rather than executory status.

[15] The leading work on complicity is K.J.M. Smith, *A Modern Treatise on the Law of Criminal Complicity*, Oxford: Clarendon Press (1991). Cf. G.R. Sullivan.

A Principals

A person is termed the perpetrator or principal if he commits the crime with the relevant *mens rea*. Thus the principal offender in murder is the person who wields the knife or shoots the gun. In theft he is the person who steals. In burglary he is the person who enters premises with the intention of stealing or who commits theft having first entered. There can be more than one principal to an offence. Thus, if A and B both enter a house for the purpose of stealing they are both principals to burglary. If A and B, by their combined efforts, kill C, A by stabbing him and B by pushing him in the river, both are principals to murder. Both have the *mens rea* and both make substantial contributions to the sub sequent death. A person does not become a principal simply by having the relevant *mens rea* for the crime.

> **Case 4**
> A and B, wishing to kill C, enter his house with guns. Each intends to kill C if the other does not. B shoots C dead. A fires another shot to make sure. They make their escape in a car driven by D and supplied by E, both of whom knew of A and B's intentions and wanted to help.

A and B are guilty of burglary as principals. B is guilty of murder as principal. A, D, and E are guilty of murder as accessory.[16] At common law E was known as an accessory before the fact. A and D, because their assistance was delivered at the time the crime was committed, were termed principals in the second degree and B a principal in the first degree. Note that no distinction was drawn between A, **who wanted to kill**, and D **who wanted to help**. By the Criminal Law Act 1967 the distinction between principals in the first and second degree was abolished, as was the distinction between degrees of accessoryship. An offender is either a principal or an accessory. Other words commonly used to denote an accessory are accomplice and secondary party.

B Innocent agents

A principal is usually but not always the perpetrator of the crime, if by perpetrator we mean the person who personally executes it. A person who uses an innocent agent or instrument to commit an offence commits the offence as principal, not accessory.[17]

> **Case 5**
> W decides to kill her husband H. She instructs T, who is unaware of her plan, to pour deadly poison into the swimming pool, telling him that it is a new form of algal control.

Here there is only one principal offender, namely W, since T is effectively no more than a puppet by which W herself tipped the poison into the pool. The agent can be a human who lacks *mens rea*, as here, or one who lacks responsibility (e.g. an infant), or who can avail themselves of an excuse, e.g. duress.[18] An example of an innocent instrument might

---

[16] A is also guilty of attempted murder as principal.

[17] See generally P. Alldridge, 'The Doctrine of Innocent Agency' (1990) 2 Crim L Forum 289; P. Alldridge, 'Common Sense, Innocent Agency, and Causation' (1992) 3 Crim L Forum 299; G. Williams, 'Innocent Agency and Causation' (1992) 3 Crim L Forum 289.

[18] Cf. *Bourne* (1952) 36 Cr App Rep 125.

include an animal or robot. So, a person who programmes a robot or teaches a monkey to enter houses and take property will be guilty of burglary as principal even though he has not himself entered premises as a trespasser.[19]

C Accessories

By section 8 Accessories and Abettors Act 1861, 'whosoever shall aid, abet, counsel or procure the commission of any indictable offence, whether the same be an offence at common law or by virtue of any Act passed or to be passed, shall be liable to be tried, indicted and punished as a principal offender'.

Section 8 confirmed the common law position, namely that accessories were guilty of the substantive offence rather than merely an inchoate offence such as incitement or conspiracy.

D Charging accessories

The prosecution need not specify whether a person is indicted as principal or as an accessory since he is being indicted for the substantive offence rather than his participation in it.[20] As will be seen, this has the advantage for the prosecution of allowing a case to proceed even where it is not clear which of two or more parties was the principal and which was the accessory. It has the potential disadvantage for the defendant that he may be uncertain of the type of case against him. Prosecutors will generally specify, however, whether a person is being charged as principal or accessory.[21]

E Trial procedure

Although there is no formal difference between accessory and principal, the accused's status may nevertheless make a difference to the way in which the trial is conducted. In particular, the mental element to be established differs according to whether the accused is a principal or an accessory. An accessory need not be shown to have the *mens rea* for the substantive offence, only that he intended to assist the principal in his commission of it. So, on a trial of murder where there are co-defendants, the prosecution will need to establish that one of them has the *mens rea* for murder and that the other, if he lacks this *mens rea*, nevertheless intended to help the other commit the offence say by driving the getaway car or keeping watch.[22] This will generally mean either that the prosecution will identify both as joint principals or identify one as the principal and the other as an accessory and proceed against them accordingly.

In cases of strict liability, if not able to identify the principal, the prosecution will need to establish that all co-defendants have *mens rea*. Thus in *Smith* v *Mellors and Soar*[23] M and S were charged with a drink-driving offence, a crime of strict liability. The evidence against them seemed superficially overwhelming. Both were seen running away from a car which had been driven by one of them with the other his passenger. Both were drunk. The prosecution were, however, not able to prove who had driven the car. This proved fatal to the

---

[19] 1 Hale *Pleas of the Crown* 555–6.
[20] *Swindall and Osborne* (1846) 2 Cox CC 141.
[21] *Maxwell* v *DPP for Northern Ireland* [1979] 1 WLR 1350.
[22] *Forman and Ford* [1988] Crim LR 677.
[23] [1987] RTR 210.

conviction of either of them. It was held that while it was not necessary to show who had been driving, it was necessary to show that whoever had not been driving knew the other to be unfit to drive. This was because proving the guilt of the accessory requires it to be shown that he intended to assist the principal to commit the offence. Without proof of knowledge such intention could not be established. By convicting both, a substantial possibility arose that the passenger in the car would be punished for aiding and abetting a crime he did not know was being committed and/or was unable to prevent. Under those circumstances it was right that neither should be convicted. If it could have been shown, then, that whoever had driven the car the other must have known of his unfitness, a conviction of both would have been proper.[24]

Problems also arise in cases of *mens rea* where it is not possible to prove the respective roles of principal and accessory. If the prosecution can only establish that an offence was committed by A or B, is unable to identify which of them, and is unable to show that the other was necessarily either an accomplice or a co-principal, the prosecution must fail. This will be so even if the evidence unequivocally points to the guilt of one of them. Thus in *Lane and Lane* a child was fatally injured at an uncertain time between noon and 8.30 pm. Evidence showed that during this period one or other of the parents was with the child, sometimes together, sometimes alone. They were charged with manslaughter. A submission of no case to answer succeeded. Since it could not be shown that both parents were present throughout, the fatal injuries may have been inflicted by one while the other was absent, thus raising a reasonable doubt in the case of both parents as to whether either, as individuals, had

(a) perpetrated the offence and/or
(b) assisted or encouraged it.[25]

Where the prosecution's only problem is in establishing which defendant actually did it and which was his assistant a prosecution will succeed. In such cases the prosecution, without more, is able to show that both have committed the offence. As s. 8 makes clear, helping or encouraging someone to commit a substantive offence **constitutes the commission of that offence**. For example, in *Giannetto*,[26] G was convicted for the murder of his wife. G appealed on the ground that there was insufficient evidence to show whether it was G himself or his 'hitman' who had done the killing. The Court of Appeal said that the essential element was that the jury find either that G had killed his wife or had encouraged another to do so. If the Crown could not say which, the jury need only be agreed that G had *mens rea* and encouraged the proscribed result. A similar result occurred in *Forman and Ford*.[27] Two police officers were in a cell with a suspect. One of the officers assaulted the suspect but it could not be established who was the assailant or that they had acted in concert. It was held that both could be convicted upon proof that one of them committed the assault and that the other, in breach of duty, had neither prevented it nor had done anything to discourage it.[28]

---

[24] For example if it could have been shown that they had earlier agreed to go on a pub crawl of their favourite ten pubs and for one of them to drive both home thereafter.
[25] (1985) 82 Cr App R 5. Section 5 Domestic Violence, Crime and Victims Act 2004 – causing or allowing the death of a child or vulnerable adult – redresses this problem.
[26] [1996] Crim LR 722.
[27] [1988] Crim LR 677.
[28] See also *R v Morton* [2003] EWCA Crim 1501; [2004] Crim LR 73. Cf. *Marsh and Another v Hodgson* [1974] Crim LR 35.

19.3 THE CONDUCT ELEMENT

A 'Aid, abet, counsel or procure'

The inclusion of four separate words suggests four separate forms of participation.[29] It is clear, however, that there is a substantial degree of overlap between them and no violence to the present position would be done if the four words were reduced to two, namely 'assisting or encouraging'.[30]

Aiding and abetting tends to be used to denote activities of parties while actually present at the scene of the crime, whether by assistance or encouragement but no violence is done to charge a person with aiding and abetting if his assistance or encouragement occurred before the crime was committed.[31] Counselling tends to be used to denote similar activities taking place before the crime is committed. Giving someone advice or encouragement can be construed as 'aiding', as 'abetting' and also as 'counselling' the offence. It is aiding because advice and encouragement can be 'helpful'. It is 'abetting' because 'abetting' means giving encouragement, whether by words or by deeds. It is generally thought there is no meaningful distinction between abetting and counselling,[32] and so it is also 'counselling'.

Nevertheless, it is clear that certain forms of participation are properly denoted only by one of these words. A person may help someone (aiding) to commit an offence without any form of encouragement, for example by selling something for use in its commission or obstructing the timely intervention of the police. Again, a person who causes another to commit an offence without that party's agreement, say by deceit, stealth or coercion, will be a secondary party to that offence as a procurer, but not as an aider, abetter or counseller. In *Attorney-General's Reference (No. 1 of 1975)* a person spiked another's drink, causing him to commit a drink-driving offence.[33] This was held to be participation by procuring the commission of the offence. It was implicit that the defendant was not an aider, abetter or counseller.

In practice, a defendant is likely to be charged using all four words. This is sensible because as long as the prosecution can show the offence to have been committed in one of the ways, a conviction may be secured. If only one word is used, however, and it is clearly the wrong word, theoretically the indictment must fail. It would be dangerous, for example, to charge the seller of an item to be used in the course of committing a crime with procuring its commission. 'Procuring' suggests, as we shall see, an act which by which a person seeks to influence the commission of the offence, whether by persuasion, threats or otherwise.[34] This would be difficult to establish in a simple case of sale. Similarly if, in the *Attorney-General's Reference*, the prosecution had charged the defendant with counselling the drink-driving offence, the defence might reasonably argue that counselling required some level of communication between accessory and principal when here there was none.

1 Level of participation

A number of related questions fall to be considered concerning the level of participation it is necessary to establish for accessoryship.

---

[29] *Attorney-General's Reference (No. 1 of 1975)* [1975] 2 All ER 684.
[30] See Law Com. No. 305 *Participating in Crime* (2007) who define the proposed conduct element as 'assisting or encouraging'. Cf. G. Williams, 'Complicity, Purpose and the Draft Code' [1990] Crim LR 1, 7 who uses the term 'helping or influencing'.
[31] *Stringer* [2011] EWCA Crim 1396 CA.
[32] J.C. Smith, 'Aid, Abet, Counsel or Procure', in P.R. Glazebrook (ed.), *Reshaping the Criminal Law*, London: Stevens [1978] 130.
[33] An offence of strict liability.
[34] For example, W, in Case 1, procures the commission of murder.

(a) *How much help or influence is necessary?*

Under the theory of derivative liability an accessory is liable because a crime has been committed and he has voluntarily associated himself with the principal's criminal project. This would seem to require that some contribution to the project be established. This contribution differs depending upon whether the participation takes the form of encouragement or assistance. **Encouragement** by its nature involves some form of communication of the encouragement by words or conduct, whether directly or via an intermediary. An un-posted letter of encouragement would not be encouragement unless P chanced to discover it and read it. On the other hand the provision of **assistance** need not involve communication between D and P.[35] For example, a person who takes on the role of unsponsored lookout while P commits an offence contributes to its commission. Lookouts are helpful even if it transpires they are not needed and even if they are not known about.[36] On the other hand, contributions as trivial as applauding at, or even attending, an illegal concert or other show have been held to be sufficient, even in the absence of evidence that they made any difference to the musician's willingness to play.[37] In *Stringer* it was held sufficient contribution to justify a conviction for aiding and abetting murder that two defendants had, together with the principal offender, chased a man before he was fatally stabbed by the principal offender. Their conduct in chasing the victim amounted to conduct assisting and encouraging the principal offender.[38]

(b) *Is a causal link between the accessory's contribution and the substantive crime necessary?*

Where the substantive offence is not carried out it may be possible to charge the secondary party with assisting or encouraging the commission of an offence under the Serious Crime Act 2007, or conspiracy or attempt. It might be thought to follow from the fact that accessories are charged with **the substantive offence** rather than the inchoate offence that the prosecution must establish something more than simply an act of intentional encouragement or help, namely **causal responsibility**.[39] In the absence of a causal link the accessory would appear to be being punished for the 'wrong harm'. He is being punished for the death, injury or theft rather than his (non-influential) encouragement or assistance. Being punished for the wrong harm is not unknown in the criminal law.[40] As we have seen, both murder and section 20 OAPA may involve criminal liability for the 'wrong harm'. But in the latter two cases the harm punished has, at least, some direct association with the harm caused.[41] With accessoryship, absent a causal requirement, the harm seems entirely distinct. Largely for this reason the Law Commission in a subsequently superseded report on secondary party liability once recommended its abolition and its replacement with an inchoate offence of assisting or encouraging the commission of an offence.[42]

---

[35] Cf. *Allan* [1965] 1 QB 130.

[36] *State* v *Tally* (1894) 102 Ala 25; cf. G. Williams (1983) 337.

[37] *Wilcox* v *Jeffrey*; cf. *Giannetto* [1997] 1 Cr App R 1; for some other examples of *de minimis* contributions see Dressler (1987) 418; J.C. Smith, 'Criminal Liability of Accessories' [1997] LQR 453, 454.

[38] [2011] EWCA Crim 1396; For comment see D.C. Ormerod, 'Joint Enterprise: *R* v *Stringer* – Murder – Aider and Abettor' (case comment) [2011] Crim LR 887; see also *Robinson* v *R* [2011] UKPC 3.

[39] For discussion see Law Com. LC 305, para. 2.30–2.31.

[40] J. Gardner, 'Causality and Complicity' in *Offences and Defences, Selected Essays in the Philosophy of Criminal Law*, Oxford: OUP (2007); cf. G.R. Sullivan, 'First Degree Murder and Complicity' (2007) 1 Crim Law & Phil 271; L. Farmer, 'Complicity Beyond Causality: a Comment', (2007) Criminal Law and Philosophy 1, 151 at 153; T. Hörnle, 'Commentary to "Complicity and Causality"', (2007) Criminal Law and Philosophy 1, 143 at 147.

[41] See Chapter 8.

[42] Law Commission No. 131 *Assisting and Encouraging Crime*, London: HMSO (1993).

The legal position is generally thought to be that a causal requirement is only necessary where accessoryship takes the form of procuring the commission of an offence. The word 'procure' is usually synonymous with 'cause'. In the *Attorney-General's Reference (No. 1 of 1975)* it was held that spiking someone's drink **procured** (rather than aided and abetted) the drink-driving offence when the victim drove home not knowing of his drunken condition. The essence of procuring was held to be 'to produce by endeavour', in other words to 'cause' the offence to be committed.[43]

Since the essence of procuring is to 'produce by endeavour' it can be appreciated that, although all cases of procuring are also cases of causing the commission of the offence, the reverse is not true. Causing is a necessary but not a sufficient element in 'procuring'. Thus in *Beatty v Gillbanks*[44] it was held that the Salvation Army did not procure a breach of the peace by a rival faction when they organised a march, knowing that it would provoke the other faction. The acts perpetrated by the defendants were presumably not acts of 'endeavouring' to produce the commission of the relevant offence.[45]

With the other forms of accessoryship it seems that no causal link need be established.[46] The general reason offered to counter a causal requirement is that, in most cases other than procuring or instigation, it will be impossible to prove one. How could the prosecution prove in the case of assistance by supply, for example, that **but for** A selling B a gun the bank robbery would not have taken place when B could have got his gun from any number of other sources?[47]

The case of *Calhaem* is generally thought to support this view.[48] W was charged with counselling (by instigation) P to murder T, her rival in love.[49] There was some evidence that P, upon meeting T for this purpose, may have reached the decision to kill T independently of W's counsel. She was convicted of murder and appealed on the basis that counselling required proof of a substantial causal link between her actions and the commission of the offence, which was absent here. This argument was rejected. Parker LJ said, however, that it was enough that 'there was some connection between the counsel of the defendant and the act done and that he was acting within the scope of his authority'. Might this mean a 'causal connection'? On the face of it, whatever Parker LJ thought he was saying, the effect seemed to be to create a loose causal requirement. On the facts of *Calhaem* such a causal link could already be presumed. The crime was 'set up' by W, and P's decision to kill arose in a context in which he had been placed in furtherance of the 'set up'. W's counselling was, then, clearly a **but for** cause of the killing. H would never have met, let alone killed T, unless he had been asked to kill her.[50] Parker LJ seemed halfway to accepting this analysis in the following passage:[51]

> if the principal offender happened to be involved in a football riot in the course of which he laid about him with a weapon of some sort and killed someone who, unknown to him, was the person whom he had been counselled to kill, he would not in our view have been acting within the scope of his authority.

---

[43] [1975] 2 All ER 684 at 686 per Lord Widgery CJ.
[44] (1882) 9 QBD 308.
[45] For a different analysis see G. Williams *TCL* (1983) 338–9.
[46] See generally Law Com. 305, para 2.30–2.31; J.C. Smith, 'Aid, Abet, Counsel or Procure', in P.R. Glazebrook (ed.), *Reshaping the Criminal Law*, London: Stevens (1978) 131–4; G. Williams *TCL* (1983) 339; *CLGP* (2nd edn) 381–3.
[47] For another view see K.J.M. Smith (1991) 87–8.
[48] See also *Luffman* [2008] EWCA Crim 1739.
[49] Counselling, not procuring, because counselling requires unanimity of purpose.
[50] Cf. K.J.M. Smith (1991) at 59.
[51] [1985] 2 All ER 269.

A more plausible reason for denying the instigator's accessorial liability in these circumstances is that he would not be, unlike in *Calhaem*, a factual cause of death. In *Stringer*,[52] however, the Court reiterated the principle that although there must be some connection between the acts of assistance and encouragement of the secondary party and the commission of the offence a 'but for' causal connection was not required. Toulson LJ stated the policy as follows: 'If D provides assistance or encouragement to P, and P does that which he has been encouraged or assisted to do, there is good policy reason for treating D's conduct as materially contributing to the commission of the offence, and therefore justifying D's punishment as a person responsible for the commission of the offence, whether or not P would have acted in the same way without such encouragement or assistance.'[53]

A possibly more satisfactory way of dealing with the problem of different degrees of causal influence might be to create a structure of offences reflecting such difference.[54] It seems extraordinary that the common law, unlike, say, the German system, makes no formal distinction between a person who successfully incites another person to kill her husband and an ordinary retailer who knowingly supplies the murder weapon.[55] This could be done by drawing a distinction between causal and non-causal participation in crime, say between instigating crime, participating in crime, and lesser acts of assistance and encouragement. The latter could be punished on an inchoate basis without the need for proof of cause. The alternative approach is to base liability as a secondary party not on causation but on *mens rea*. Where the party offering intentional support to the principal does so because he intends the offence to be committed this should render him responsible as an accessory to the crime, otherwise only inchoate liability would arise.[56]

(c) Complicity by omission and inactivity

In three circumstances a person may incur accessorial liability in the absence of any positive action. The first is where the defendant is present at the scene of a crime and the circumstances are such as to generate the inference that the principal's conduct is being approved. The second is where the party is placed under a legal duty to prevent the commission of the offence. The third is where, irrespective of whether the secondary party wishes to encourage the crime or not, the party has a legal power to prevent the commission of the offence and fails to do so.

(i) Presence at the scene of the crime

It would be unusual if the criminal law vindicated a person's right not to intervene to prevent a child drowning in a puddle of water and yet punished a person for failing to intervene to prevent an attempt to kill by drowning.[57] The general position at common law confirms this.[58] Mere presence at the scene of the crime does not automatically equate to assistance or encouragement. So in a case of a spontaneous eruption of violent disorder the prosecution must provide some evidence that the person charged did something

---

[52] [2012] QB 160.
[53] At para. 50.
[54] J. Gardner, 'Causality and Complicity' in *Offences and Defences, Selected Essays in the Philosophy of Criminal Law* (2007); cf. L. Farmer, 'Complicity beyond Causality: a Comment' (2007) 1 Criminal Law and Philosophy, 151 at 153; T. Hörnle, 'Commentary to "Complicity and Causality"' (2007) 1 Criminal Law and Philosophy, 143 at 147.
[55] The Law Commission have proposed just such a change: Law Com. 305 *Participating in Crime* (2007).
[56] Law Com. 305 *Participating in Crime* (2007).
[57] Cf. Ashworth, 'The Scope of Liability for Omissions', above.
[58] Foster, *Crown Law* 350; see generally K.J.M. Smith 34–9.

beyond standing there to assist or encourage the violence and did so intending to assist or encourage.[59]

Although there is no prerequisite for the accomplice to be present by virtue of a prearranged plan, where he/she is so present, presence is easy to construe as an act of encouragement and/or assistance.[60] A good illustration is *Coney*. Here, the mere presence of spectators at an illegal prize fight was thought to be *prima facie* evidence upon which the jury might find encouragement.[61] Indeed how could attending a prize fight not be so construed? The key aspect of the decision, however, is the jury could find the necessary encouragement irrespective of whether an individual spectator joined in the applause or not. Again, in *Wilcox* v *Jeffrey*[62] a music critic met a saxophonist, a foreign national, on his arrival in Britain. He subsequently attended and paid for a ticket to a performance given by the saxophonist which was in breach of the Aliens Order 1920. He was held to have aided and abetted the offence. It will be appreciated that the line between accessoryship (*Wilcox*) and simple bad citizenship is distressingly difficult to draw. The legal position was summed up by Hughes LJ in *Robinson*: 'If D2's presence can properly be held to amount to communicating to D1 (whether expressly or by implication) that he is there to help in any way he can if the opportunity or need arises, that is perfectly capable of amounting to aiding (and abetting). It is, however, important to make clear to juries that mere approval of (i.e. "assent" to, or "concurrence" in) the offence by a bystander who gives no assistance, does not without more amount to aiding.'[63]

Such a stance can be seen to vindicate the most abject failure of social responsibility. In *Clarkson*,[64] two soldiers entered a room to find other soldiers raping a woman. The two soldiers did nothing either to stop the rape or to encourage its continuance but stood silently and watched. The Court of Appeal quashed their conviction for aiding and abetting rape, deciding the question of liability purely on the basis of *mens rea*. What was important, the court said, was not that their unprotesting presence might, in fact, have offered some encouragement to their comrades but that they should have intended it to do so. Megaw LJ, in the course of his judgment, gives an illuminating insight into how the construction of criminal fault seems more influenced by what men may expect of other men than what society expects of all of us:

> there was at least the possibility that a drunken man with his self-discipline loosened by drink, being aware that a woman was being raped, might be attracted to the scene and might stay on in . . . the capacity of voyeur; and while his presence . . . might in fact encourage the rapers . . . , he, himself, enjoying the scene might not intend that his presence should offer encouragement to rapers.[65]

Just so, but should this make a difference to his criminal responsibility? Is not the real issue that at no serious inconvenience to themselves, the soldiers could have prevented a serious wrong from being committed?[66]

---

[59] *R v Miah* [2004] EWCA Crim 63 CA; cf. R. Ellis [2008] EWCA Crim 886 – s. 20 unlawful wounding.
[60] *Mohan* v *R* [1967] 2 AC 187; *R* v *Mendez & Thompson* [2010] EWCA Crim 516; *R* v *Archer* [2011] EWCA Crim 2252; [2012] Crim LR 292 (CACD).
[61] (1882) 8 QBD 534.
[62] [1951] 1 All ER 464.
[63] *Robinson* v *R* [2011] UKPC 3.
[64] [1971] 1 WLR 1402.
[65] At 1406.
[66] In *Robinson* v *The Queen* [2011] UKPC 3 the Privy Council restated the importance of distinguishing between those present at the scene of a crime (here murder) simply as approving witnesses and those who are present to give assistance (e.g. standing guard) or encouragement.

The major obstacle to criminalising such behaviour is that the soldiers' conduct was, arguably, no more reprehensible than if they had immediately walked out, or watched the rape of an anonymous woman from the comfort of their own bedroom window. They were voyeurs. It would probably be taking things too far to hold voyeurs liable as accessories to the rape. Their wrong, which is not at present a criminal wrong, would be in not taking reasonable steps to prevent the crime, say by calling the police, rather than for contributing to its commission.[67]

Other cases in which inactivity has been held insufficient include *Bland*,[68] in which it was held that a woman who shared a room with a man whom she knew to be dealing in drugs was not an accessory unless she assisted or encouraged him to do so.[69] In *Smith* v *Baker* it was held that a person who took a lift with a person whom he discovered to be uninsured was not complicit in the offence of driving without insurance by not removing himself from the car upon making the discovery.[70] Again, in *Allan*, a person who was present at an affray who did nothing to encourage it but who intended to join in if the need arose was not thereby rendered an accessory to the affray.

In each case the question at issue is whether there is conduct

(a) amounting to encouragement or assistance,
(b) accompanied by an intention to encourage or assist.

As will be appreciated, this will be very much a question of fact and degree. If, in *Smith* v *Baker*, the facts had been that the information had been brought to the person's attention before he got into the car, it would have been easier to construe his conduct as an act of encouragement, but it would be in no way conclusive. A hitchhiker who takes a lift with a clearly drunken driver is less easy to construe as intentionally lending his support to the offence of driving while unfit than a person who takes a lift with a chum after a joint session in the pub.[71]

(ii) *Failure to execute a duty*

The basis upon which a person may be liable as principal for omitting to prevent harm is breach of a duty, whether imposed by law or voluntarily assumed. Accessorial liability may be incurred in similar ways.[72] Thus a parent who omits, in breach of parental duty, to prevent another harming her child is liable as an accessory for any crime committed by that person against the child.[73] A store detective who turns a 'blind eye' to a theft by a customer is complicit in theft. Whether the scope of the relevant duty is the same for primary and secondary offenders is, however, not certain. For example, with respect to the creating a dangerous situation category there seems to be a difference in culpability and causation between the defendant in *Miller*[74] and, say, a motorist who, having allowed petrol to escape from his car without fault, does nothing to prevent an arsonist setting it alight. It may be then that the scope of accessorial liability for this category of duty situation is more restricted.

[67] A.J. Ashworth (2009) 433. A.J. Ashworth, *Positive Obligations in the Criminal Law* (2013) ch. 2.
[68] [1988] Crim LR 41.
[69] See also *R* v *Kousar* [2009] EWCA Crim 139.
[70] [1971] RTR 350; *Allan* (1965) 1 QB 130.
[71] G.Williams (1983) 348.
[72] K.J.M. Smith (1991) 40.
[73] *Marsh and another* v *Hodgson* [1974] Crim LR 35.
[74] See page 91.

(iii) *Failure to exercise control*

The potential scope of liability for non-intervention is in one important sense greater for accessories than for principals. A duty of intervention may arise where a secondary party has the right to control the behaviour of another. Thus, in *Tuck* v *Robson* a publican was held liable for aiding and abetting breach of the licensing laws by his patrons, by not ensuring that they left the premises at the end of closing time.[75]

There are three standard cases when a right of control becomes a duty to control, namely:

(i) where the secondary party has ownership or control of property used by the principal;
(ii) where the secondary party stands in the relationship of employer and the principal is employee or independent contractor;
(iii) where the secondary party has ownership or control of premises used by the principal.

Each case can be accounted for on the ground that the secondary party's failure to exercise the power of control amounts to encouragement or assistance.

Tuck v *Robson* is an example of the third category. Its scope is unclear, however. For example, would a publican be complicit in drug dealing if he turned a blind eye to drugs deals going on in the premises or in drink-driving offences if he failed to prevent customers supplying drink to a person he knew intended to drive home? Would an ordinary house-holder be similarly complicit if, without filling anyone's glass, he failed to control the drinking of a dinner-party guest? These examples indicate the extreme conceptual fragility of accessorial liability for omissions. It offers the prospect of individuals incurring criminal liability for acting in a socially entirely normal fashion and with it a practice of 'conscripting "controllers" into the ranks of crime prevention authorities'.[76] While this may be acceptable where, as in *Tuck* v *Robson*, the power of control is coupled with clearly defined social responsibilities to ensure customers behave themselves, it is surely not acceptable in the ordinary case of householders. Householders, unlike publicans who must comply with the terms of their licence, are not an embodiment of the law and it would be inappropriate to expect them to police their home as if they were one.[77]

An example of the first category is *Rubie* v *Faulkner* in which it was held that the statutory requirement in the case of a learner driver that a qualified driver should be on hand to supervise was held to give rise to an implicit duty on the part of the instructor or qualified driver to take reasonable steps to ensure the learner drives safely and carefully.[78] Like *Tuck* v *Robson* this was an uncontroversial example of a situation where one might expect a 'controller' to act as a surrogate police officer. A more difficult case is where the owner of a motor car does nothing to prevent a **qualified** driver from driving dangerously. In *Du Cros* v *Lambourne* the owner/passenger of a car who sat beside the driver was convicted of abetting dangerous driving even though there was no evidence of positive encouragement.[79] And in *Harris* liability was extended to accessoryship in the offence of causing death by dangerous driving.[80] It is submitted that these are correct decisions. The car owner has the power to control the way the driver drives. He can say, for example, 'drive carefully or not at all'. Driving cars is a dangerous activity and society expects car owners to 'insure

---

[75] [1970] 1 WLR 741.
[76] K.J.M. Smith (1991) 46.
[77] See Law Com. No. 305 *Participating in Crime* (2007) para. 3.39.
[78] *Rubie* v *Faulkner* [1940] 1 KB 571; cf. *Harris* [1964] Crim LR 54; M. Wasik, 'A Learner's Careless Driving' [1982] Crim LR 411.
[79] [1907] 1 KB 40.
[80] [1964] Crim LR 54.

themselves' against causing harm in every sense of the word. As a result it is appropriate to expect them, unlike, say, house owners, to exercise some form of policing role in their own car.

It is arguable that most of the confusion surrounding non-action is the result of judicial failure to clarify whether inactivity is seen as punishable because culpable in itself or punishable only if it provides evidence of (tacit) 'encouragement or assistance'. If we take as an example the case of the owner/passenger who keeps his mouth shut when the driver drives too fast, there seems to be no serious objection to the former incurring liability, **but only** if silence can be taken as evidence of tacit encouragement. Without such evidence, as in the case of someone too timid to take control, it would be taking things too far to impose liability simply because the owner/passenger was in a position to 'lay down the law' and yet did not. The case of *Cassady v Reg Morris (Transport) Ltd*[81] would seem to support such an approach. Here an employer was charged with aiding and abetting his driver's offence of failing to provide his employer with details of his journey times. The employer's failure was held capable of providing evidence of encouragement but was not to be treated as sufficient in itself to incriminate the employer. Failing to prevent an offence is not always the same as seeking to encourage it. In *J.F. Alford Transport Limited*, the Court of Appeal said that such encouragement would result from turning a blind eye knowing this would encourage the continuance of the practice.[82]

19.4 THE MENTAL ELEMENT

The *mens rea* for accessoryship is an intention to assist or encourage the commission of the offence. This incorporates the following *mens rea* elements:[83]

(a) D must do an act which in fact encouraged or assisted the later commission of the offence,

(b) D must do the act deliberately realising that it was capable of assisting/encouraging the offence,

(c) D must contemplate, at the time of doing the act, the commission of the offence by A, i.e. he foresaw it as a 'real or substantial risk' or 'real possibility', and

(d) D, when doing the act, must intend to assist/encourage A in what he was doing.

Simply understood this means that A's acts of assistance or encouragement should be given with a view to encouraging or assisting the commission of an offence, and the aider or encourager should know the nature of the offence to be committed. This basic explanation is deceptively simple and so we need to consider it more closely.

> **Case 6**
> Adam, Eve's boyfriend, asks Eve to supply him with information about the comings and goings of Cain, who inhabits an identical apartment in the same block as Eve. Eve does so. Adam uses the information provided to break into Cain's apartment and steal from it.

Adam will be guilty of burglary from Cain's apartment. Is Eve guilty as his accomplice? On the face of it, it might appear that she does. She intended to help Adam by giving him

---

[81] [1975] Crim LR 398.
[82] [1997] Crim LR 745.
[83] *R v Bryce* [2004] EWCA Crim 1231; *Webster* [2006] EWCA Crim 415.

the information. Adam has not wheedled the information out of her by subterfuge. However, this is not the same as being deserving of punishment **for that offence**. After all, Eve might think that Adam is enamoured of Cain and wishes to attract his attention. For punishment to be deserved it should be necessary, then, for Eve to know, at the very least, that Adam intends to use the information for a criminal purpose and to have some idea of what that purpose is. This involves the following *mens rea* requirements if Eve is to be found complicit:

(e) She must know or believe that her act is capable of assisting or encouraging P to commit an offence. It is not enough for Eve to know that her information will be helpful to Adam. She must know or foresee that Adam might use the information to break into Cain's flat.

(f) She must also know of any circumstance necessary to convert that act into the *actus reus* of the crime charged; Eve must know, for example, that Adam would not have Cain's consent to enter the apartment.

(g) She must also know that the principal, when performing the *actus reus* of the offence, will be or may be acting with the relevant fault, if any, required for the offence. Eve must believe not merely that Adam intends to enter the apartment without Cain's consent but to do so for the purpose of committing theft.[84]

(h) She must contemplate, at the time of supplying the information, the commission of the offence by A, i.e. she foresaw it as a 'real or substantial risk' or 'real possibility' that Adam was going to commit burglary.

A An intention to aid or encourage

Until recently the authorities were equivocal as to what it is to intend to help or encourage the commission of an offence. One line of authorities suggested that liability as an accessory requires proof that the accessory assented or approved the commission of the offence by the principal and that the encouragement or assistance given was a measure of that assent. At their strongest they suggest that a purpose to assist or encourage must be proved. The other line of authorities suggested that liability requires simply that the accessory acts in such a way that his conduct gives assistance or encouragement and that he acts with knowledge that his conduct would have this tendency.[85] The clearest example of such a case is *Lynch v DPP for Northern Ireland*.[86] Members of the IRA forced the defendant, on pain of death, to drive the getaway car in the course of a murderous assault on a police officer. The House of Lords found unanimously that liability as an accomplice was not excluded by evidence that the assistance was not given with a view to lending a helping hand. It was enough that the assistance was given knowingly. Lord Lowry CJ, relying on dicta of Devlin J in *Gamble* said that 'if some positive act of assistance is voluntarily done, with knowledge of the circumstances constituting the offence, that is enough to sustain a conviction; and it is irrelevant, in the latter case, that the aid is not given with the motive or purpose of encouraging the crime'.[87] If a defence was to be available that defence must be duress, and not an absence of *mens rea*.

---

[84] Or other offences specified in s. 9 Theft Act 1968.
[85] See most recently *J.F. Alford Transport Ltd.* [1997] Crim LR 745.
[86] [1975] AC 653.
[87] I. Dennis, op. cit. at 657.

1 Assent or approval-based tests of accessorial intention

Although there are various formulations of the assent or approval test, the authorities which follow are consistent with the more general proposition that knowing assistance/ encouragement may be evidence from which the jury may infer intention, but is not intention in itself. The general effect is that, where the secondary party is able to adduce evidence of non-assent or disapproval or ulterior (inconsistent) motive for rendering assistance, the jury are entitled to find the necessary guilty mind not proven. The merit of basing liability on assent to or approval of the principal's criminal enterprise is that it is consistent with complicity's derivative nature. A purely knowledge-based test is inconsistent. An early authority is the case of *Fretwell*. A illegally supplied an abortifacient to his girlfriend P, but only in response to her threat that if he did not do so she would kill herself. P died as a result of taking the abortifacient. A was indicted as an accessory to 'self murder'.[88] It was held that his knowledge of its intended use did not make him an accessory to the offence since he evinced no assent or approval. A similar decision was reached in *Lomas*[89] in which it was held by the Court of Criminal Appeal that a person who returns a jemmy to its owner, knowing that it is to be used in a burglary, does not, by this knowledge alone, become complicit in the burglary. *Fretwell* and *Lomas* are clear examples of cases where the jury would be entitled (if not bound) to conclude that although A knew of his principal's criminal purpose he nevertheless did not assent to it and, in this sense, intend any act of assistance.

Consistent with this analysis, cases where knowledge was held not to equate to intention include *Steane* where it was held that for acts to be done 'with intent to assist the enemy' it was not sufficient to show merely that the accused knew that his acts would have this effect. A purpose to assist was necessary.[90] More recently in *Gillick*, it was held that a doctor would not evince an intention to assist a person to have unlawful sexual intercourse simply by prescribing contraceptives, if this were done to prevent an unwanted pregnancy in the course of a '*bona fide* exercise by a doctor of his clinical judgement'.[91]

Although *NCB v Gamble*[92] was cited in *Lynch* as authority for the proposition that knowing assistance equals intentional assistance *Gamble* equally supports the proposition which now holds good throughout the criminal law, namely that acting in the knowledge that a consequence will result is evidence that the consequence is intended but not intention as a matter of law. The facts warrant careful consideration. M, a lorry driver, took delivery of a load of coal at the NCB's colliery. Having done so he took the lorry to be weighed by H, an employee of the National Coal Board. Weighing served a double purpose. It passed ownership of the coal to W and afforded W a certificate of weight, allowing him to sell the coal on to a third party. It also acted as an official *exeat* for leaving the colliery. H discovered that the lorry's load exceeded the maximum permitted under the Motor Vehicles (Construction and Use) Regulations 1955. He informed the lorry driver and asked if he intended to take the load. The lorry driver said he did, whereupon H handed him the weighbridge ticket. The Coal Board were charged and convicted as accessories to the offence committed by the owners of the lorry. The appeal was dismissed. Devlin J stated that it was necessary to show an intention to assist. Acknowledging *Fretwell*,[93] knowledge that one's act was of assistance was not conclusive but it was *prima facie* evidence of an intention to

---

[88] (1862) Le & Ca 161 CCR.
[89] (1913) 9 Cr App Rep 220.
[90] [1947] KB 997.
[91] In the words of Lord Scarman at 190.
[92] [1959] 1 QB 11.
[93] And also *Steane*, above.

assist. In the absence of an alternative explanation, therefore, the jury are bound to convict. The problem with Devlin's statement was that he gave no indication of what alternative explanation might suffice. This emboldened the House of Lords in *Lynch* to rule that even a threat to kill would not affect the issue of intention. That said, Lord Lowry's assessment of the effect of *Gamble* ignores Devlin J's very clear statement that knowing that one's act was of assistance was not conclusive but it was *prima facie* evidence of an intention to assist. Following the cases of *Moloney* and *Woollin* it seems unarguable, now, that this does not represent the law.[94] In *R v McNamara* the Court of Appeal acknowledged this while rehearsing the important point that the jury should rarely be given assistance as to the meaning of intention in the context of 'intending to assist or encourage the commission of the offence'.[95] The *Nedrick* direction should in other words be limited to cases where, as in *Gamble*, *Fretwell*, *Lomas*, and *Gillick* there is no evidence of a purpose to assist. In such cases the jury will be told that they are **entitled** to find the necessary intention, without being bound to. The Law Commission supports this meaning for accessoryship in their latest report.[96] To ensure parity of culpability between principal and accessory such as would justify derivative liability it proposes that to be guilty as an accessory the act of assistance or encouragement must be done with an intention that the principal perform the conduct element of the offence.[97] Knowledge that it would have this effect would not be enough in itself but only evidence from which the jury could infer such intention.[98]

2 Evaluation

There are no doubt grounds for giving the jury this power to pick and choose whether to infer an intention in cases of murder, not least due to the pernicious effect of the mandatory sentence.[99] With accessoryship, however, matters are more nuanced because of the general conceptual difficulty of distinguishing lending support to crime from more basic cases of poor citizenship, as illustrated in *Gamble* itself. It is easy, for example, to see juries, on the basis of a *Nedrick*-style direction, acquitting defendants such as the secretary who posts a letter to the tax office on behalf of his employer which includes a fraud of which he is aware, and yet convicting a similar secretary when a letter involved a straightforward case of blackmail.[100] Logically, however, the question in both cases should be the same. Did he lend intentional support or not to his principal's criminal objective? Without a clear test juries may be encouraged to participate in making fine, unprincipled distinctions serving the public interest but not necessarily justice to the individual.

A case can be mounted, therefore, that for complicity, at least, an intention to assist or encourage should mean that it was the defendant's purpose to assist or encourage the commission of the offence.[101] This approach has the merit of simplicity and ensures the conviction only of those who purposely lend their support to the principal's criminal ambitions, thus

[94] See Chapter 5.
[95] [2009] EWCA Crim 2530.
[96] The Law Commission, Law Com. 305 (2007); for discussion see W. Wilson, 'A Rational Scheme of Liability for Participating in Crime' [2008] Crim LR 1.
[97] Cl. 1.1(a) and cl. 1(2).
[98] Cases like *Gamble* would, then, if the proposals were accepted, be excluded from accessoryship and covered by the new inchoate offence (Section 45 Serious Crime Act 2007) of assisting the commission of an offence whose fault element is belief 'that P would perpetrate the conduct element with the fault required to be convicted of the offence'.
[99] See W. Wilson, 'Murder and the Structure of Homicide' [2006] Crim LR 471.
[100] Cf. *Salford Health Authority ex parte Janaway* [1988] 2 WLR 442.
[101] G.R. Sullivan, 'Intent, Purpose and Complicity' [1988] Crim LR 641 at 643; I. Dennis, 'Intention and Complicity: A Reply' [1988] Crim LR 649 at 651–3. Wilson (2008) 15–16.

discounting the possibility of unfairly labelling 'mechanical' helpers such as Mr Gamble as substantive offenders. An alternative method of advancing doctrinal rationality in this area would be to implement the extended definition of intention which includes foresight of certainty as a matter of law, while leaving scope for an acquittal through the provision of defences such as acting in the ordinary course of business supply, acting in satisfaction of a legal duty, acting to prevent harm and so on.[102] I think the former is the most secure option, given the availability of the extended inchoate offence in cases where a purpose to assist is not proven.

B Knowledge of circumstances

The liability of an accessory turns upon knowledge of the relevant facts and circumstances constituting the offence. In *Johnson* v *Youden* the principle was stated as follows: 'if the (secondary party) knows all the facts and is assisting another to do certain things, and it turns out that the doing of these things constitutes an offence (the assister is guilty of complicity)'.[103]

Case 7

P is the managing director of a finance company. Wishing to raise extra capital to finance expansion she decides to advertise for depositors, promising to pay one per cent above standard bank rates on deposit accounts. A, her solicitor, draws up contractual documents for intending depositors and takes a deposit from D. Unknown to all of them it is a strict liability offence for non-banking enterprises to take deposits.[104]

P, D and A are guilty of the (strict liability) offence. D and A are liable for the same reason as P is, namely that they gave acts of assistance to P in an enterprise which formed the subject-matter of an offence, with full knowledge of the facts. *Johnson* v *Youden* also makes clear, however, that liability as an accessory requires the secondary party to know of any relevant fact or circumstance necessary for the offence to be made out.[105]

Case 8

T and V are engaged in a bank robbery. Unknown to them Y, a customer in the bank, is an off-duty policeman. Y runs over to them intending to make an arrest. Z, another customer, believing Y to be another robber, intentionally trips him up, thus facilitating T and V's escape.

Z, although his intentional action is helpful to T and V, does not aid and abet the robbery since the assistance was not given with knowledge that it would assist the robbery. The position would be the same had Z shouted 'Go for it', intending to encourage Y to make the arrest but the words of encouragement were thought by T and V to be for them.

Case 9

P, knowing that V will not consent, resolves to have intercourse with V. He asks A, her room mate, to be absent from the room so as to facilitate the rape. A complies, assuming V to be a willing partner.

---

[102] Cf. *Cafferata* v *Wilson* [1936] 3 All ER 149.
[103] [1950] 1 KB 544 at 546.
[104] Section 3 Banking Act 1987.
[105] *Roberts and George* [1997] Crim LR 209.

Although the conduct element in accessoryship is satisfied by A's intentional removal from the room the *mens rea* requirement is not satisfied. To be liable as an accomplice to rape it is necessary to show not merely that A intended to assist or encourage P to have intercourse with V but intended to assist or encourage **non-consensual** intercourse. This means that A 'must contemplate, at the time of doing the act, the commission of the offence by P'. This requires her to have knowledge both that V may not consent and that there is a 'real or substantial risk' or 'real possibility P may have intercourse with V, whether or not V consents'. Given A's belief, she clearly does not have this intention.

The requirement of knowledge exists even with respect to crimes of negligence and strict liability crimes. This may create unusual, if not perverse, distinctions of responsibility. In *Callow* v *Tillstone*,[106] P, a butcher, was convicted of the strict liability offence of exposing unfit meat for sale. He had done so only on the authorisation of A, a veterinary surgeon, who had negligently certified the meat as sound. A's conviction for aiding and abetting the butcher's offence was quashed on the ground that he did not know the meat was unsound and so could not intend to assist P to commit the offence. In like fashion, on a charge of aiding and abetting unlawful sexual intercourse with a minor, an accessory cannot, unlike the principal, be guilty of the crime if he believed, however unreasonably, the victim to be over the age of consent.

1 How much does an accessory need to know?

One of the great infelicities of the current law is lack of doctrinal precision in relation to the degree of fit necessary between the offence committed and the state of knowledge/intention of the secondary party. How precisely must the offence committed match A's knowledge and intentions in giving support? In cases where the secondary party is not part of a joint enterprise with the principal but provides prior advice or assistance, does the accessory have to know an offence is to be committed or is it sufficient that he (strongly) suspects that it may be, for example? For liability as an accessory to rape does A need to know that V will not consent, or is it enough that she knows she may not? Unfortunately this is not entirely clear but there is authority for the proposition that such recklessness suffices. In *Carter* v *Richardson* the liability of the supervisor of a learner driver for abetting the offence of driving with excess alcohol was said to turn on whether the former knew that it was probable that the latter was over the limit, that is, that he was *Cunningham* reckless.[107] This may stretch the embrace of accessorial liability further than expected.

Case 10

Adam, attends Eve's party where, known to Eve and with her tacit approval, he drinks some wine. Eve knows that Adam has brought his car and suspects he may drive home in it, which he does but does not know how many units he has drunk. He is later stopped by the police and found to be driving with excess alcohol.

On the basis of *Carter* v *Richardson* it seems that Eve may be complicit in Adam's offence unless she takes steps either to supervise Adam's drinking or discourage him from driving home. Unfortunately, it is not doctrinally clear one way or the other whether

---

[106] (1900) 83 LT 411.
[107] *Blakely and Sutton* [1991] RTR 405; *Carter* v *Richardson* [1974] Crim LR 190.

recklessness is sufficient or whether the assister or encourager must know the recipient will commit the offence.[108]

What of the position where D knows an offence is to be committed but does not know which one? In the ordinary case of A and B acting in concert in a joint enterprise to commit crime this problem will not normally arise. If A and P decide that P will rape (or kill) Y, both A and P will know all the relevant facts necessary to constitute the offence.[109] Problems are most likely where A supplies tools or information for a crime, or some other form of secondary assistance, but is ignorant, or mistaken, as to some particular detail of the proposed venture. In principle, liability depends upon A having actual knowledge, rather than mere suspicion, of an intended criminal venture. If A is primed to drive the getaway car for an undisclosed crime,[110] and can do no more than guess at what that crime may be, he will not be an accessory.[111] Compare the case of *Bainbridge*.[112] A supplied oxyacetylene equipment to P. It was used to break into a branch of the Midland Bank. A was convicted as an accessory and appealed on the grounds that he did not know the details of the intended illegal use of the equipment. It was held that while it would not be enough simply to know that the equipment was to be used in some illegal venture, it would be enough to know that an offence of the type in question was intended. As long as A contemplated that the equipment was to be used for the purpose of breaking into a building and stealing, this would be enough.

This is not a particularly helpful rule. It raises doubts as to whether, for example, A who helps P to take V's car is liable for theft, assuming P has the necessary intention, if A himself believed it was taken simply for joy-riding purposes, or whether, if A helps P to enter V's house for burglarious purposes, A is liable for burglary if the form taken involves rape of the occupant rather than, as A believed, theft. Does A, in both examples, 'know the type of offence to be committed?' The problems posed by *Bainbridge* are compounded by *Maxwell*: A was a member of a terrorist organisation who was given the job of driving a car for the purpose of guiding other terrorists in a second car to an inn where they were to perpetrate an offence. He knew that this car would contain weapons and that some or all of the weapons would be used in the course of an attack involving the inn. He did not know whether the weapons to be used were to be bombs or guns or incendiary devices or whether the attack was to be on the inn itself or the people in it. In other words he did not know the type of offence to be committed. The attack was by means of a pipe bomb thrown into the inn. He was convicted as an accessory to an offence under the Explosive Substances Act 1883. The House of Lords upheld his conviction, ruling that where an accessory leaves it to his principal to choose which of a number of offences to commit, he is liable 'provided the choice is made from the range of offences from which the accessory contemplates the choice will be made'.[113]

Bainbridge and *Maxwell* combined allow the conviction of an accessory where

(a) he knows the type of offence to be committed but does not know the details, for example time, place and manner of execution, or

(b) he does not know the type of offence but does know that the offence in question is on P's shopping list of possible crimes.

---

[108] For discussion see Law Com. No. 305 (2007) paras 1.16–1.17, 2.47–2.64.

[109] It has been said that a new basis for criminal liability arises in such cases, separate from aiding and abetting: *Stewart and Schofield* [1995] 1 Cr App R 441.

[110] Cf. *Patel* [1970] Crim LR 274.

[111] Cf. *Scott* (1978) 68 Cr App Rep 164.

[112] [1959] 3 All ER 200.

[113] G.R. Sullivan, 'The Law Commission Consultation Paper' [1994] Crim LR 252, 253.

The Law Commission's proposal for dealing with the injustice of A bearing liability for what P has done, although he lacks key information about what is intended, is to hive off cases such as *Bainbridge*, where B was indifferent as to P committing the offence, into the inchoate arena. The relevant provision to deal with *Maxwell* is Clause 1 of the attached Draft Bill, as enacted in the Serious Crime Act 2007, section 46, liability for which extends to those who give assistance or encouragement to persons believing that their actions will assist or encourage such person to commit one of a number of possible crimes. Maxwell had such intention, if we understand by this the state of mind of someone who signs up to (and so intends in a conditional sense) one of a number of a list of crimes, leaving it to his principal to decide which one.

Another question which arises in the particular case of accessoryship through supply of tools or information is the number of crimes the accessory can be held liable for. It has been suggested that *Bainbridge* allows liability for an indefinite series of crimes, where it can be shown that all the crimes committed with the tool or information supplied were of the type contemplated.[114] Williams suggests that to obviate this problem there should be an element of particularity in order to make a counsellor or assister a party.[115] He proposes a rule which limits accessorial liability to the situation where the perpetrator has a particular crime in mind (or one of a number of possibilities) and the secondary party knows this. It is submitted that, although such a rule appears inconsistent with *Bainbridge*, it is nevertheless necessary if only to prevent compounding the fragility of accessorial liability for a mere act of supply.[116]

C Liability for unintended consequences

Problems of application occur where P does something unexpected or the consequence is unexpected. Consider the following example

> **Case 11**
> D1 incites D2 to kill C at her home. D2 does not kill C, but instead deliberately kills X, C's husband, when X unexpectedly arrives home.

D1 will not be liable since the crime instigated is not the crime committed. This is important because, clearly, D1 is a factual cause of X's death. Moreover he knows, in the *Bainbridge* formulation, the 'type of crime' to be committed. It would not be too surprising, then, if D1 was to be held liable. The legal position is that he is not, since the crime committed lies outside the scope of the common purpose. In the case of *Saunders and Archer*, D2 wished to kill his wife. D1 advised him to use the fabled poisoned apple trick. The plan misfired when having given the apple to his wife, she gave it to their child in D2's presence. Rather than risk being found out, D2 did nothing to prevent it. D2 was held liable as perpetrator by transferred malice. D1's liability depended upon whether this was a deliberate (and substantial) variation from the common purpose. It was held that the variation was deliberate rather than accidental as D2 could have prevented it. D1 was, therefore, not guilty as an accessory. It would have been different if the apple had been

---

[114] *A-G v Able* [1984] QB 795; G. Williams *TCL* (1983) 339–40.
[115] Ibid. at 335–40.
[116] Cf. Smith and Hogan, op. cit. 158.

fed to the child in D2's **absence**.[117] This would have been a case of the plan accidentally **miscarrying**. D1 would be guilty of an inchoate offence but not as an accessory to the substantive offence. The following case is less easy:

Case 12

D2 asks D1, a gunsmith, to supply a gun to kill X. D2 does not kill X, but deliberately kills V.

In this case a strong argument can be advanced that D1 should be liable as an accessory to V's murder **despite the deliberate variation** unless D2 knew that D1's assistance was predicated upon the murder victim being X rather than V. This is unlikely to be the case where D1 is not an instigator[118] and there is no common purpose. In the case of mere supply, as opposed to giving advice, for example, the control is with the perpetrator.[119] If D1 has no control over what is done[120] D1 is in fact lending support to any of the principal's crimes which are of the type contemplated even if they do not match the details expressly agreed.[121]

D Joint enterprise liability

There are two forms of secondary participation. There are cases of joint enterprise, where two or more people share a common purpose to commit a crime. And there are cases where, without sharing any common purpose, A helps or encourages P to commit an offence. Some disagreement exists as to whether the two forms are separated by different rules or whether joint enterprise can be viewed as a particular application of secondary liability.[122] What is certainly true is the liabilities of secondary parties who are part of a joint enterprise are more difficult to pin down. In this section we shall be examining some of the problems of application associated with this form of complicity.

The core problem case of joint enterprise liability arises where D1 and D2 agree expressly or impliedly to commit one crime, crime A, and, in the course of their doing so, D1 commits a different crime, crime X.

Case 13

D1 and D2 agree to burgle C's house. While in the house they are disturbed by C. D1 takes out a gun and kills C with it.

The basic principle, which is easy to understand but less easy to apply in practice, is that D2 will be a party to crime X, although it was not agreed to, if it arose in the course of executing the joint enterprise. If it did not, and the deviation by D1 is deliberate, he or she will not be liable **unless** he/she nevertheless contemplated its commission.

---

[117] *Gordon-Butt* [2004] EWCA Crim 961.

[118] Hawkins assumes the principle only to apply to instigators, or 'commanders', 2 PC c. 29, s. 21.

[119] Cf. *Saunders and Archer*, above.

[120] Cf. K.J.M. Smith (1991) 200.

[121] Smith and Hogan disagree. Cf. *Reardon* [1999] Crim LR 392; G. Williams (1983) 350. Most commentators make no distinction between instigators and mechanical helpers. Cf. K.J.M. Smith (1991) 200–3.

[122] *R v Stringer* [2011] EWCA Crim 1396; G. Virgo, 'Joint Enterprise Liability is Dead: Long Live Accessorial Liability' [2012] Crim LR 850; cf. P. Mirfield, 'Guilt by Association: a Reply to Professor Virgo' [2013] Crim LR 577.

1 Elaboration

The following elaboration explains and discusses the kinds of liability problems which may arise when two or more people join together to commit an offence, only for something to go wrong in the execution of the enterprise or for something unexpected to occur.

(a) *Unexpected consequences: the plan miscarries*

If D2 causes an unforeseen consequence in the execution of the joint enterprise, D1 will be liable to the extent that D2 is liable so long as the consequence arises from the execution of the joint enterprise. The principle was expressed by Lord Parker in *Anderson and Morris* as follows: 'where two persons embark on a joint enterprise, each is liable for the acts done in pursuance of that joint enterprise . . . (including) liability for unusual consequences if they arise from the execution of the joint enterprise'.[123]

> **Case 14**
> D1 and D2 agree that D2 will assault C. The plan misfires when C unexpectedly dies as a result of suffering a fall consequential upon the assault.

Here both D1 and D2 will be liable for manslaughter since the death arises from the execution of a joint enterprise. This reflects the derivative liability rationale of secondary part liability. Because D2 is liable, so is D1. In *Baldessare*[124] the accomplice of a joyrider was held jointly liable with his principal for manslaughter when the joyride ended in the death of a pedestrian. Liability hinged not upon the mere fact of complicity in the joyriding but a common purpose to engage in a particularly dangerous instance of it. The principal was driving without proper lights and at an excessive speed. The Court of Criminal Appeal held, dismissing the appeal, that the jury were entitled to take the inference from all these facts that the principal did not exceed the terms upon which A agreed to accompany him on the trip.

(b) *Unintended consequences: D2 unintentionally deviates from the terms under which D1 offered encouragement or assistance*

D1 is liable for consequences outside the scope of the common purpose where the doctrine of transferred malice applies. So if D2 kills the wrong person or burgles the wrong house **by mistake**, D1 will still be liable as an accessory. This is so whether or not D1 is part of a joint enterprise. The idea is that D1 must take responsibility not only for the things that go right, but also the things that go wrong in the course of achieving the criminal purpose. It is of the essence of these situations that the deviation is accidental.[125] If they are deliberate different rules apply. Strangely, it seems there can be joint enterprise liability even where there exists no degree of cooperation between the parties and even where they are antagonists. This strange state of affairs is the result of the recent Supreme Court decision of *Gnango*.[126] D1 and D2 engaged in a gunfight in public, each intending to kill or cause serious injury to the other. One of the parties accidentally shot and killed a passerby. The Supreme Court decided (Lord Kerr dissenting) that both D1 and D2 were guilty of murder irrespective of who fired the gun. The reasoning was as follows. Whoever had killed the passerby was guilty of murder on the transferred malice principle. The other shooter is also guilty of murder,

---

[123] *Anderson and Morris* [1966] 2 QB 110 at 118.
[124] (1930) 144 LT 185.
[125] *Saunders and Archer* (1576) 2 Plowd 473.
[126] [2012] 2 WLR 17.

therefore, because he was party to a joint enterprise to commit murder. This is a very dubious decision. There are two obvious problems with the reasoning. The first is that where two people independently form the intention to kill each other, this can hardly be described as a joint enterprise to commit murder. Rather there are two independent enterprises to commit murder. If A and B decide independently to buy an ice cream from the same vendor it would be perverse to describe them as being part of a joint enterprise to buy an ice cream. Likewise, A and P just started shooting at each other. They shared no common purpose. Second, if the joint enterprise they engaged in is murder, the Supreme Court is holding in effect that one can aid and abet one's own murder. A strange idea!

(c) *Intentional deviations*

Where the principal deliberately deviates from the terms under which encouragement or assistance is advanced, such a departure, if **substantial**, will generally negate accessorial liability.[127] In a famous old case three soldiers went scrumping for pears in an orchard. One of the three stood guard with a drawn sword as the other two collected the pears. The owner's son came to remonstrate with the guard whereupon the latter stabbed him with the sword. The other two soldiers were held not to be complicit in the murder because the presumed scope of the joint enterprise involved a trivial case of theft not an act of murderous violence. The judge ruled that the decision would have been different if they had resolved to meet resistance with force. This is a fairly straightforward case in which the action of the principal was neither authorised nor even contemplated by the others.[128] No difficulty of evidence arose since on all reasonable inferences the principal was motivated by his own murderous inclinations rather than executing a contingency plan.

(i) *Foreseen variations in the course of executing a joint criminal enterprise*

Often, in the course of committing an offence, one of the parties to what is a joint criminal enterprise goes too far. The question then arises as to whether the co-adventurers are jointly responsible for the consequences. As explained above, responsibility generally turns on whether the deviation is deliberate or accidental. If it is deliberate and substantial it may be treated as a frolic of the principal's own with the result that the co-adventurers are not liable. This is the case, whether or not it is a case of joint enterprise.[129] In cases of joint criminal enterprises, however, there are special reasons of principle and policy why co-adventurers should not routinely be allowed to shelve responsibility for the actions taken by one of them in the heat of the moment.

Case 15

A, B and C agree to do a burglary with A breaking in, B doing the stealing and C driving the getaway car. They agree time, place and method of execution but discuss nothing further. In the course of breaking in they

(i) encounter a fierce dog,
(ii) suffer a murderous attack by the resident granny,
(iii) receive an unpleasant visit from the local policeman.

If A takes it into his head to kill the dog, policeman or granny, will B or C be liable?

---

[127] Not always. See below.
[128] See *English* [1997] 4 All ER 545.
[129] See discussion of *Saunders and Archer, supra.*

The legal position is that B and C are liable if the conduct of A was **contemplated** by them as a possible incident of the execution of the joint enterprise. Liability here is based in the fact of participation in a joint unlawful enterprise which carries risks of additional harms for which parties must bear responsibility.[130] It is, of course, unrealistic to assume that the scope of the joint enterprise will be articulated with any great degree of precision in the usual case. Here, for example, B and C are unlikely to admit to contemplating any of these turn of events other than the killing of the dog. The prosecution's task, therefore, will be to use such evidence as they have to persuade the jury to draw the necessary inference.[131] This may be easy if A used a weapon and B and C knew that he carried it. It is a reasonable, though rebuttable, inference from the fact that B knew that A was carrying a gun that B contemplated its use. In *Chan Wing Siu* three robbers burst into V's flat. Each carried a knife. One of the robbers murdered V's husband. The trial judge directed the jury as follows: 'You may convict of murder if you come to the conclusion that the accused contemplated that one of his companions might use the knife to cause serious bodily injury on one of the occupants'. Sir Robin Cooke, approving this direction, made it clear that in the absence of a credible alternative explanation, knowledge that a co-accused carried a knife was strong evidence that its use was contemplated: '(Where a man) lends himself to a criminal enterprise knowing that the potentially murderous weapons are to be carried, and in the event they are in fact used by his partner with an intent sufficient for murder, he should not escape the consequences by (relying on a belief that their use was unlikely)'.[132]

If, however, B and C knew that A was carrying a weapon but contemplated only that it would be used to kill the dog or frighten the granny and the jury credit this explanation, they will not be complicit in its murderous use upon the policeman.[133] *A fortiori*, if B and C did not know that A was carrying a weapon they would not be complicit in any crime in which it was used.[134] Knowledge that A was carrying the weapon must be proved.[135] On the other hand, if B and C continue to offer support and encouragement to A after A has **unexpectedly** produced the weapon they will be complicit in murder if, as is likely, the jury take the inference that they foresaw that A might use the weapon with the fault element for murder.[136] Whether such support and encouragement has been offered is a matter for the jury. In *Willett* D1 and D2 took part in a venture to steal from V's van. On being disturbed by V, D1 returned to the getaway car. D2 drove off and, on finding V blocking his way, knocked him down, killing him. The Court of Appeal found that since D1 would not have foreseen that D2 would do this until too late D1 would only be complicit in the murder if he has actively encouraged him to do so, for example by saying 'Go for it'. Simply sitting in his seat would not amount to such encouragement.[137]

The principle which renders an accessory liable for foreseen consequences applies to cases of joint enterprise but probably no further. If, as *NCB v Gamble* suggests, an intention to assist survives cases of assistance under protest, imposing liability for contemplated but unauthorised departures from the terms under which assistance was offered would be unacceptably draconian.

---

[130] A.P. Simester, 'The Mental Element in Complicity' (2006) 122 LQR 578 at 600.
[131] Cf. *Greatrex* [1999] 1 Cr App R 126.
[132] [1984] 3 All ER 877 at 882. Approved by the House of Lords in *Powell*, below, at 563.
[133] A supposition confirmed by the Court of Appeal in *A-G's Ref (No. 3 of 2004)* [2005] EWCA Crim 1882.
[134] *Davies v DPP* [1954] 1 All ER 507; *R v Parsons* [2009] EWCA Crim 64 CA.
[135] *R v Azam* [2010] EWCA Crim 226 CA.
[136] *R v Powell*, *supra* note 132.
[137] [2010] EWCA Crim 1620. Compare *Baldessare*, *supra*.

> **Case 16**
>
> P tells A, his mother, that he intends to steal some drugs from the premises of a neighbouring gang and asks to use her car. She agrees reluctantly, fearful that without a car P will be a sitting duck when the time comes to make his escape. A knows that P is carrying a gun and knows he may use it, although she hopes he will not. P kills a member of the rival gang while stealing the drugs.[138]

It is submitted that to treat A as an accessory to murder under these circumstances would be a serious 'category mistake'.[139]

(ii) Unexpected methods of executing the joint enterprise

The 'contemplated scope of the joint enterprise' test of liability for unexpected consequences may carry a further complication. What if P deviates from what is expected not in the content but in its method. For example, P shoots V when the plan was to stab him or club him around the head. In this case the position, in line with the discussion above, is that deviations from the agreed method will only exculpate the co-adventurer if substantial or, as the courts have put it recently, the method of execution is 'fundamentally different' from that contemplated by the secondary party. In *English* the plan was to attack V using wooden posts. P's fatal use of a knife was found to be fundamentally different from that envisaged by the joint enterprise. A's conviction for murder was, therefore, quashed although the parties' joint enterprise was the commission of grievous bodily harm which would ordinarily be sufficient for murder. What counts as a fundamentally different mode of attack is a question of fact and degree and is a matter for the jury. In *English*, for example, Lord Hutton said that the use of a knife rather than a gun or vice versa would not be fundamental as they were weapons of comparable dangerousness. In the earlier case of *Gamble*, which was approved in *Powell*,[140] a different distinction was drawn between what was envisaged by the joint enterprise – a punishment 'knee-capping' with a gun – and what the principal did – slit the victim's throat with a knife. Although the weapons used were of comparable dangerousness the way they were used was fundamentally different from that which the enterprise envisaged.[141] In *Greatrex* the Court of Appeal underlined the fact that whether or not the method of attack was fundamentally different was a matter for the jury.[142] In this case it was open to them to decide that an attack with an iron bar was not materially different from the agreed method of attack, namely fists and feet.[143] An important qualification to the *English* principle was made in *Uddin*. If a weapon is produced unexpectedly by D2 in the course of a concerted attack on V by D2 and D1, D1 will be complicit in its use if he **continues** with the attack, although the weapon, or the way in which it was used, was materially different from the common purpose.[144]

Given the theory is that D1's liability derives from that of the principal for having lent support to the commission of Crime A, it is not clear why a party should escape liability

---

[138] See G. Virgo, 'Joint Enterprise Liability is Dead: Long Live Accessorial Liability' [2012] Crim LR 850.

[139] In *R v Carpenter* (2011), on comparable facts, the mother accompanied her son to the scene of the crime. Her conviction for manslaughter was upheld on the basis that she contemplated the use of the weapon (knife) but not to cause serious injury.

[140] *Powell and English* [1997] 4 All ER 545; *Gamble* [1989] NI 268.

[141] The accessories might yet be guilty under section 18 depending on *mens rea*, as occurred in *English*.

[142] See also *Daniel v Trinidad and Tobago* [2007] UKPC 39.

[143] *Greatrex* [1999] 1 Cr App R 126.

[144] *Uddin* [1999] QB 431; per Beldam LJ at 134.

simply because of a deviation in method. It is the crime to which they lend support and if that crime is committed that should surely be enough to engage liability. In *Rahman* this reasoning was largely accepted.[145] The issue was whether P's act was made fundamentally different from the acts foreseen by A as part of the joint enterprise if it was performed with an intention to kill rather than, what was agreed, an intention to cause grievous bodily harm. The Court of Appeal, upholding the conviction, said that it was not. The House of Lords agreed. In reaching their decision the following statement of principle was outlined:[146]

> P's use of a weapon to kill V did not affect A's liability, even though he was unaware of it, if A participated in an attack with P knowing that P might kill or intentionally inflict GBH UNLESS (i) P produces a weapon of which A is unaware and WHICH IS MORE LETHAL than any weapon which A contemplates P or any other participant be carrying and (ii) for that reason P's act is to be regarded as fundamentally different from anything foreseen by B.

Moreover, where A did intend or foresee that P would kill with the intention to kill the 'fundamentally different rule' did not apply anyway. It was only if A did not intend or foresee that P might kill with the intention to kill that a substantial deviation in method might exculpate. David Ormerod summarises the present position, following *Rahman*, as follows:

> The killing in the course of a joint enterprise can occur with the parties having any number of different states of mind and the question is for which the *English* (fundamentally different) qualification should be available. It seems clear cut that the qualification cannot apply where: (i) D intends that V will be killed and P kills with intent. Similarly, the qualification should not avail (ii) D who foresees that P may kill with intent to kill and he does so, nor (iii) D who intends V to be caused GBH foreseeing that P may kill with intent and P does so. In each of these D has foreseen the possibility of an intentional killing, and that is what occurs. If D foresees that V will be intentionally killed and participates in the venture, it is irrelevant by what means P intentionally brings about V's death.[147]

With respect this must be right. The fundamentally different rule has recently been restated by Toulson LI in *R v Mendez*: 'In cases where the common purpose is not to kill but to cause serious harm, D is not liable for the murder of V if the direct cause of V's death was a deliberate act by P which was of a kind (a) unforeseen by D and (b) likely to be altogether more life-threatening than acts of the kind intended or foreseen by D.' As Toulson LJ concedes, the merit of this proposed jury direction is its clarity and simplicity rather than its precision but it is probably as good as any.[148] Consider in this regard *Rafferty*.[149] The defendant was a party to a brutal attack on V on a Swansea beach involving punches and kicks. D then withdrew from the attack and left the scene. His co-attackers eventually stripped V naked, dragged him into the sea and drowned him. The Court of Appeal said that despite the existence of the joint enterprise D was not party to the killing. Having withdrawn from the enterprise, the actions of the co-adventurers bearing no resemblance to the initial attack was a *novus actus interveniens*. Toulson LJ's 'simple' jury direction

---

[145] [2007] EWCA Crim 342.

[146] *Yemoh* [2009] EWCA 930 makes the important point that it is not necessary for D to identify which of the group might commit the crime provided he foresees that one might. For case comment: A. Reed, 'Joint Enterprise and Inculpation for Manslaughter' [2010] J Crim L 200.

[147] *Rahman* [2007] Crim LR 721.

[148] It explains for example why the defendant in *Gamble* is not an accessory to murder although sharing with the principal an intention to cause the victim GBH.

[149] [2007] EWCA Crim 1846.

would arguably bring greater consistency to case outcomes in cases of substantial deviation from the joint enterprise.

An ongoing problem for the courts involves cases where a common purpose to administer a beating to V occurs, as opposed to an attack using dangerous weapons, and in the course of that beating V dies. If the killer is identified and he has the *mens rea* for murder his co-adventurers will be liable for murder only if they intended or foresaw that one of their number might kill with the *mens rea* for murder. Proving this will be easy if the common purpose was to administer a severe beating, i.e. one which amounts to serious injury. If it was not, such intention or foresight will be less easy to infer. If the killer is not identified then a co-adventurer may still be guilty of murder as accessory if it was clear that he was either the principal or an accessory, for example, because the beating was of such ferocity that the only plausible inference is that this was done with the intention to cause at least serious injury. In this case, however, to be liable requires not merely that the co-adventurer foresaw the victim might die in the course of that beating. It will be dependent, once again, upon the prosecution proving his knowledge that one of their number might kill **with the intention of killing or causing serious injury.**[150]

(iii) *Accessoryship in murder, concluding remarks*

In many cases the principal and accessory will share a common purpose to kill or cause grievous bodily harm. Accessorial liability in such circumstances poses no particular problem. As has been seen, even where death issues from a spontaneous attack where no prearranged plan is being executed it may be an easy inference to draw that each attacker intended serious injury and, moreover, was encouraging other members of the group to commit serious injury or foresaw that others might kill with the intention of killing or causing serious injury. In such circumstances this will justify the conviction of each member of the group of murder although it may be unclear who was the perpetrator and who the accessories.[151]

The final issue to be discussed is the apparent mismatch between the *mens rea* required to convict the principal of murder and that required to convict the accessory where no such unanimity of purpose exists. Although the *mens rea* for murder **as principal** is an intention to kill or do serious bodily harm the above authorities indicate that to convict the accessory it is only necessary to show that he contemplated that the principal might, in executing the joint purpose, kill or cause serious injury with the fault element for murder. In this context it must be remembered that it is not enough that D1 contemplates that D2 might kill. He must contemplate that D2 might kill either with the intention to kill or the intention to cause serious injury.[152] It might be thought that the *mens rea* of the accessory should be brought into line with that of the principal. Before *Moloney*, **both** principal and accessory could be convicted of murder upon contemplation that death or serious injury might occur.[153] Although *Moloney* did not indicate that the test was intended to apply to accessories as well as individual perpetrators, the argument goes that it must have been so intended. How can it be right to convict the wielder of a knife only upon proof of an

---

[150] For discussion of the principles applicable see *R* v *A* [2010] EWCA Crim 1622. The Crown Prosecution Service issued new guidance on 20 December 2012 which explains how charging decisions are made following crimes involving joint enterprise. See http://www.crimeline.info/uploads/docs/jointenterprise.pdf.

[151] Cf. *Uddin* [1999] QB 431; see also *Greatrex* [1999] 1 Cr App R 126.

[152] *R* v *Powell*; *R* v *Rahman*; see most recently *A, B, C & D (joint enterprise)* v *The Queen* [2010] EWCA 1622.

[153] *Hyam* v *DPP* [1974] 2 All ER 41.

intention to do serious harm, but convict the driver of the getaway car upon proof of mere foresight of the possibility that the principal might use the knife with such intent?[154] At one stage it seemed the courts were sympathetic to this idea. In *Dunbar*, for example, the liability of the accessory was expressed to be dependent upon P executing a term of an agreement between A and P. If the facts were such that A could be construed to say, 'Yes I agree that you may commit serious injury if contingency X occurs', it would be fair that A takes responsibility for the consequences of that agreement. He could not meaningfully claim, 'This is not my killing.'[155]

The requirement of authorisation or tacit agreement has, however, been dispensed with. In *Hyde* Lord Lane CJ said that 'realisation' that the principal may kill or cause serious injury was enough to supply the *mens rea* for the accessory even though the accessory did not agree to such conduct being used.[156] In *Powell*, the House of Lords approved this approach, emphasising the public policy concerns which would arise if co-adventurers could escape liability for a consequence which, though not agreed to, they contemplated, their participation encouraged and perhaps made more likely to happen.[157]

(iv) *Conviction of a lesser offence*

In *English*, the fact that the method used to kill V was fundamentally different from what had been agreed was fatal to the conviction for murder of the other parties to the joint enterprise. They could be guilty only of conspiracy or, if they had landed blows themselves, an offence under the Offences Against the Person Act 1861. It might be thought that responsibility for the death should not be shelved entirely where, as in *English*, the principal's actions though not contemplated in severity or manner were nevertheless committed in furtherance of a plan to attack V. Why should the parties to the joint enterprise to attack not, at least, be guilty of manslaughter?[158] In *Stewart and Schofield* such an argument bore fruit.[159] A and P agreed to rob C's shop and to inflict moderate injury upon C with a scaffolding bar. In fact P, motivated by racial hatred, beat C to death. P was convicted of murder as principal and A, the accessory, of manslaughter. Although at odds with the derivative basis to liability, it is arguable the decision is not inconsistent with *Powell and English*. So long as A contemplates that P intends to commit a dangerous battery on C, such contemplation is enough to render A an accessory to the lesser crime if P executes this plan only too efficiently.[160] Only if P stabbed or shot his victim (outside the scope of the enterprise) should there be an outright acquittal?[161] This reasoning was accepted in *R v Carpenter* [2011]. P entered guilty pleas to the murder of the victim and the wounding of the victim's mother. A, who was P's mother, was aware that A was carrying a knife when she accompanied him to a

---

[154] In *R v Concannon* the Court of Appeal, refusing leave to appeal against conviction, rejected the defendant's argument that such a mismatch between the *mens rea* necessary to convict the principal and that necessary to convict an accessory was a breach of Article 6 ECHR.

[155] Kadish, 'Complicity, Blame and Cause: a Study in the Interpretation of Doctrine' (1984) 73 Calif LR 323 at 354–5; cf. G.R. Sullivan, 'First Degree Murder and Complicity' (2007) 1 Crim Law & Phil 271.

[156] [1990] 3 All ER 892. Although the following cases involve murder there is no reason why the principle is not applicable in all crimes.

[157] [1997] 4 All ER 545 at 563–4 per Lord Hutton. See *R v Gamble* [1989] NI 268, above; cf. *Bamborough* [1996] Crim LR 744.

[158] This possibility was rejected, on the authority of *English*, in *Mitchell* [1999] Crim LR 496. There is also authority for the proposition that A might be liable as accessory to an assault, *Lord Mohun* (1692).

[159] In *Dunbar* [1988] Crim LR 483, P launched a murderous attack on V. The Court of Appeal ruled that A, who had instigated the attack, was guilty of murder if she was party to an agreement to kill or cause serious bodily harm but otherwise guilty of nothing.

[160] And so it was decided in *Gilmour* [2000] Crim LR 763; cf. *Betty* (1963) 48 Cr App R 6.

[161] *Uddin*, above.

'fair-play fight' with the victim. In summing-up the judge had said that if the defendant knew or realised that her son intended to use the knife to cause some injury or harm she would be guilty not of murder but of manslaughter because the killing would have been unlawful and a shared intention to that extent, but not a shared intention to kill. The jury acquitted her of murder but found her guilty of manslaughter. The ground for the appeal was that, in relation to joint enterprise, the judge had erred in directing the jury that a verdict of manslaughter would be open to them if they found P not guilty of murder. Relying on *R v Mendez*[162] D2 contended that it was murder or nothing. The Court of Appeal (Criminal Division) dismissed the appeal of D2 against her conviction of manslaughter. Richards LJ said that the unavailability of manslaughter as a possible verdict in the *R v Mendez* case had to be seen in the context of that case where use of a knife was not foreseen rather than to a case where use of a knife was foreseen but the secondary party did not share or foresee the intention with which it was used. With respect this must be right.[163]

19.5 RELATIONSHIP BETWEEN LIABILITY OF THE PARTIES

Since accessorial liability is derivative in nature, it seems to follow that, in the absence of an offence committed by a principal, there should be no liability as an accessory either. This is true, but only to a limited extent. Where the *actus reus* of the offence is missing accessorial liability cannot arise, since there is no crime from which liability can derive. This can produce surprising, if quite logical, results. In *Thornton v Mitchell* a bus driver was reversing his bus relying, as is usual, on the signals of his conductor. The conductor negligently gave the all clear when, in fact, there was a pedestrian behind the bus. The bus reversed into the pedestrian injuring him. The driver was charged with careless driving with the conductor as an accessory. The charge against the driver was dismissed on the ground that he had not been careless in relying upon his conductor's signals. The conductor was, therefore, also acquitted on the ground that there was no offence to abet.[164]

A Conviction of secondary party where perpetrator is not liable

If D2 has not committed the offence D1 cannot normally be complicit.

> **Case 17**
> D1 encourages D2 to kill V. D2 asks D3 for a gun to do the killing with which D3 supplies him. D2 arrives at V's house to find V already dead, intentionally killed by D4.

D4 is guilty of murder. D1 and D3 are not complicit in that murder. D1 is liable under section 44 Serious Crime Act 2007. D3 is liable under section 45 of the same Act. D2 is guilty of conspiracy to murder.

Where the offence has been committed but it is for some reason impossible to pin it on the principal, there can be no principled objection to accessorial liability. Thus if the principal does a bunk or is acquitted for lack of evidence the accessory can still be convicted so long as there is evidence of his involvement.[165]

---

[162] [2010] EWCA Crim 516.
[163] This reasoning also bore fruit in *Yemoh* [2009] EWCA Crim 930; cf. *Gilmour*, above; *Day and Others* [2001] Crim LR 984; for criticism see J.C. Smith's commentary and also [2001] Crim LR 333.
[164] Cf. R.D. Taylor, 'Complicity and Excuses' [1983] Crim LR 656.
[165] *R v Zaman* [2010] EWCA Crim 209; [2010] Crim LR 574.

More problematic is where the *actus reus* requirement is satisfied but the principal is acquitted (or convicted of a lesser offence) because he has a defence or lacks *mens rea*. Given that liability is derivative, can the secondary party still be convicted assuming proof of the necessary *mens rea*?

> **Case 18**
> Eve, an unmarried woman, dupes Adam into marrying Rachel, his lover, by giving cogent evidence that Adam's long-lost wife is dead.

Adam will have a defence to the crime of bigamy, namely that he reasonably believed his wife to be dead. Justifying the conviction of Eve would, therefore, require some ingenuity. She is not married and so cannot be guilty of bigamy as principal and, because Adam has a defence, there is no principal. More generally, however, judges have often displayed an understandable reluctance to embrace the full implications of the derivative theory of complicity. Two approaches have been adopted, neither entirely satisfactory. First, an attempt has been made to exploit the doctrine of innocent agency. This operates to render P liable for his own crime rather than the innocent pawn's 'non-crime'.[166] The second is to allow secondary party liability where the principal has committed the *actus* of the offence and, although himself lacking fault, the fault element in the relevant offence can be supplied by the secondary party. Both approaches were essayed in the leading case of *Cogan and Leak*.[167] L encouraged C to have intercourse with L's wife. As a result of what L told him C believed the wife was consenting when in fact she was being coerced by L. C was acquitted of rape for lack of *mens rea*. Would this be fatal to L's conviction? The dominant approach in *Cogan and Leak* was that L's liability for rape was founded upon the use of Cogan as the instrument of his unlawful intention, namely for his wife to suffer non-consensual intercourse. Superficially this is quite reasonable. If he had wished his wife to die, for example, he might have duped Cogan into plying her with poisoned cakes. Leak's conviction for murder, under such circumstances, would clearly survive the acquittal of Cogan, since Leak would properly be held to be the principal offender.

There are two important objections to the use of the doctrine in this case. An initial difficulty is that rape, unlike say murder or theft, does not appear to be the kind of activity which one can perform by proxy. Consider the definition which appears in section 1 Sexual Offences Act 2003: A person commits an offence if he intentionally penetrates the vagina, anus or mouth of another person (B) with his penis (**and** B does not consent to the penetration). Did L 'intentionally penetrate the vagina, anus or mouth of W with his penis' when he duped C into doing so? Not by any stretch of the imagination or language. If we ignore this linguistic objection, yet deeper problems emerge. If a person can be convicted of rape without effecting personal penetration, it seems to usher in potential liability for rape for women as principal, not merely as accessory. This obviously flies in the face of section 1 which requires the perpetrator to be male, or at least have a penis. However, as a matter of principle, if rape can be committed by **someone other than** a penetrating perpetrator why should that someone not be a woman?[168]

---

[166] *Thornton v Mitchell* was not a case of innocent agency because the conductor himself lacked a criminal purpose.
[167] [1976] 1 QB 217.
[168] As happened in *People v Hernandez* (1971) 96 Cal Rept 71. Indeed it might mean that a man (or woman) could commit rape on another using the 'innocent instrumentality' of a broom handle (**something other than** a penetrating perpetrator); see generally Williams *TCL* (1983) 371; K.J.M. Smith (1991) 107–10.

Of course, the ramifications do not stop here. If A can be guilty of rape without putting in a personal appearance, it follows that wherever an offence is defined in terms of some personal activity entered into by the accused (rather than some event), A's failure to engage in such activity is not fatal to a conviction. Thus it seems that a person could commit unlawful sexual intercourse without congress, bigamy without entering a registry office, or dangerous driving without entering a car.[169]

The second difficulty with the 'innocent agency' basis to the conviction is that L, being W's husband, was legally incapable at that time of committing rape upon her.[170] If L cannot legally commit rape on his wife it does seem to follow that L cannot legally commit rape on his wife, whether with or without the innocent instrumentality of another. Once again, the ramifications do not stop here. It follows, for example, that it should be no objection to Eve's conviction for bigamy in Case 18 that she was an unmarried person, even though the offence is defined quite explicitly to exclude her.[171]

The alternative basis for the conviction in *Cogan* was simpler and more secure. The court held that the husband could be found guilty as accessory to rape even though the other was acquitted for lack of *mens rea*. The decision, in effect, abandons the requirement that liability derive from the liability of another. What is important is that an offence had taken place, not that C was liable for it. The offence took place when the *actus reus* was performed. Onto this *actus reus* it was possible to graft L's own undoubted *mens rea*. His liability then lies in his decision to procure the commission of the offence, not his assistance in C's commission of it. 'C had sexual intercourse with (the wife) without her consent. The fact that C was innocent of rape because he believed that she was consenting does not affect the position that she was raped.'[172]

Similar reasoning informed the earlier case of *R v Bourne*[173] in which H forced his wife W to submit to buggery with a dog. Although W was not charged with the offence, H was convicted as an accessory to buggery and his conviction was upheld on appeal. The basis of the decision was that, although the wife would have been able to avail herself of a defence and thus escape liability, the principal offence would still have been committed thus allowing the conviction of H.

Both these cases are pragmatic responses to the doctrinal gap opened up by the derivative theory of liability. As such they are arguably supportable because, as these cases illustrate, there is no substantive reason for the gap in the first place. The right approach surely is to allow liability so long as it is possible to conjoin the secondary party's *mens rea* with an (innocent) act of another but which, if performed by the former, would have incurred liability. This would be an acceptable extension of the present law of innocent agency and finds doctrinal support in the Serious Crime Act 2007.[174] The Model Penal Code follows a comparable route providing that A is accountable for the conduct of P, 'an innocent or irresponsible person' if 'acting with the kind of culpability that is sufficient for the commission of the offence', he causes (the person) to engage in such conduct.[175] The Law

[169] Cf. *Millward* [1994] Crim LR 527.
[170] This is no longer the case following *R v R*, above, Chapter 1.
[171] The offence of bigamy is constituted as follows: 'Whoever being married goes through a ceremony of marriage with (another is guilty of an offence)' paraphrasing s. 57 Offences Against the Person Act 1861.
[172] Lawton LJ at 223.
[173] (1952) 36 Cr App R 125.
[174] Section 47(5)(iii); cf. K.J.M. Smith (1991) ch. 4.
[175] Model Penal Code, 2.06(2)(a). An alternative approach would base liability not upon accessoryship but upon their intention to cause an event which the law proscribes, Draft Code: Law Com. No. 177 (1989) cl. 26(1).

Commission makes a similar recommendation.[176] The common law doctrine of innocent agency should be replaced by a statutory offence whereby D would be liable for an offence as a principal offender if he or she intentionally caused P, an innocent agent, to commit the conduct element of an offence but P does not commit the offence because P: (1) is under the age of 10 years; (2) has a defence of insanity; or (3) acts without the fault required to be convicted of the offence. This allows for liability in all the problem cases detailed above, including Case 18, notwithstanding the fact that the offence can only be committed by a person who meets a particular description and D does not fit that description.[177]

B Level of liability

We have seen that a secondary party may be convicted as accessory although the principal bears no liability, and how it is possible for an accessory to be guilty of a lesser offence than that of the principal or even avoid liability entirely, where the principal goes beyond the terms of the joint enterprise. The question now arises as to whether the accessory may be liable for an offence greater than that of the principal offender. Consider the following examples:

> **Case 19**
> A tells P that C has raped P's infant daughter X. P, as A predicted and desired, flies into a violent rage and kills C.

> **Case 20**
> A incites P to discharge a gun supposedly loaded with blanks at C, in order to give C a fright. Unknown to P, A loads the gun with live ammunition intending that C shall die, which is what transpires.

In Case 19 assuming P is guilty only of voluntary manslaughter on the grounds of loss of self-control, is this also the limit of A's liability? Likewise in Case 20 is A's liability only that of assault (the limit of P's liability)?

There is a plausible argument that the correct position should, in fact, be that **all accessories** should be treated as **incapable** of bearing greater liability than that of the principal. Accessorial liability is, after all, derivative. 'Topping up' the secondary party's liability is likely to create broader doctrinal incoherence.

> **Case 21**
> A asks P to break into a house to steal C's jewels. P manages to steal the jewels without breaking into the house by stealing them from C's person.

If P had not stolen the jewels but had gone straight to the police, A could be liable at most for encouragement under the Serious Crime Act 2007, not burglary. It seems inconsistent that A may be liable for burglary simply because **a theft** has taken place (for which P is responsible). Arguably, then, the accessory should be punished for what has happened

---

[176] LC 305 (2007) para. 154–5.
[177] LC 305 (2007) Draft Bill cl. 3 and 4. See R. Taylor [2008] 46–7.

rather than for what has not. In *Richards* W incited P and P1 to beat up H, her husband, so as to cause him serious injury.[178] They, in fact, inflicted a wound upon him not amounting to serious injury. All were charged under s. 18 OAPA with wounding with intent to cause grievous bodily harm. W was convicted but P and P1 were acquitted of this offence and convicted of the lesser offence of malicious wounding under s. 20. On appeal W's conviction was reduced to malicious wounding on the dubious ground that the only known exception to derivative liability was where the accessory was actually present at the scene of the crime (W was an accessory before the fact under the old terminology). If she had been present the conviction could have stood. In *Howe* this approach was criticised and the old distinction between different forms of accessoryship was consigned to the dustbin of legal history. Lord Mackay, in the House of Lords, ruled that it was no objection to the conviction of a secondary party for a graver offence that the secondary party had the *mens rea* only for a lesser offence.[179] The Law Commission's latest proposal would regularise this by rendering A liable in accordance with the innocent agency provisions outlined above.

19.6 LIMITS OF ACCESSORIAL LIABILITY

Under certain circumstances an informed and deliberate decision to participate in a criminal venture will not result in liability as a secondary party.

A Victim participation

Where a statute is enacted for the protection of a particular class of persons a member of that class who is the victim of the offence may not be prosecuted as an accomplice to that offence. This proposition derives from *Tyrrell*[180] in which a girl of under sixteen was convicted of aiding and abetting the commission of unlawful sexual intercourse where she was a willing participant. The conviction was quashed on the ground that the purpose of the statute was to protect immature girls from their own immaturity (and predatory males), not to punish them for it.[181] The limits of this principle should be understood. First, the class member must be the 'victim' of the offence for which she is prosecuted. Thus if A, a fifteen-year-old girl, encourages P to have unlawful sexual intercourse with V, another fifteen-year-old, she will be liable as an accessory. Second, accessorial liability will only be avoided where the statute was enacted for the explicit purpose of protecting the class member. Thus a willing participant-victim in sadomasochistic activity may be successfully prosecuted as an accessory to a s. 47 offence since the offence was enacted to stop acts of violence rather than to protect a certain class of person from such acts.[182] It may be appreciated that it may not always be easy to discern whether the legislative purpose was to protect or condemn the victim-participant. Consider for example the offence of 'living off immoral earnings'. Is this an offence designed to protect prostitutes from unscrupulous 'pimps' or an Act designed to subvert the infrastructure of prostitution?[183]

---

[178] [1974] QB 776.

[179] [1987] 1 All ER 771 at 799; Smith and Hogan, op. cit. 171–4; G. Williams *TCL* (1983) 373–4.

[180] [1894] 1 QB 710.

[181] See also *Whitehouse* [1977] QB 868.

[182] The Supreme Court in *Gnango* made a similar ruling in a case in which A and B, both intending to kill each other, had a shoot out. A was complicit in the accidental killing of a bystander by B. He could not argue that he could not be complicit in a crime (murder) in which he was the intended victim.

[183] See generally G. Williams, 'Victims and Other Exempt Persons in Crime' (1990) 10 LS 245.

Michael Bohlander has argued cogently that the Sexual Offences Act 2003 is very much at fault in this respect, having no coherent policy, as where people under 16 engage in consensual activity, as to who can be an offender and who can be a victim.[184]

B Intention to frustrate crime

It was stated above that a person who knowingly participates in the commission of an offence for the purpose of frustrating its commission will not be liable as an accessory.[185] This is either because having such a purpose is inconsistent with having the necessary intention to assist, or, as some commentators prefer, because acting under such purpose provides the secondary party with a special defence.[186] Intention under the draft Criminal Code includes both purposive and knowing assistance. The latest Law Commission proposals provide that participating for the purpose of frustrating an offence or preventing if undertaken reasonably is a discrete defence.[187] This latter proposal supports the arguments detailed earlier against the adoption of *Woollin* direction on intention.

C Withdrawal

As a general rule, where the actor repents of his wrongdoing subsequent to its commission this goes to mitigation rather than liability. A renunciation of a criminal purpose exculpates only if it occurs before sufficient steps are taken to constitute either the substantive crime, if applicable, or an attempt if it is not.

> **Case 22**
> A sends V, his intended victim, a box of poisoned chocolates. Prior to their consumption, he repents and instructs V not to eat them.

Here A will still be guilty of a criminal attempt despite his change of heart since the *actus reus* was complete before the change of heart.[188] Interestingly, accessorial liability can be avoided if the secondary party takes effective measures to withdraw his support or countermands a crime which he has instigated. This will, however, leave any inchoate liability already accruing, e.g. incitement or attempt, untouched.[189]

> **Case 23**
> A incites P to poison chocolates destined for V. A then repents and makes exceptional efforts to prevent them being eaten.

[184] 'The Sexual Offences Act 2003 – The Tyrrell Principle – Criminalising the Victims' [2005] Crim LR 701.
[185] *Clarke* (1984) 80 Cr App R 344. For discussion see A.J. Ashworth, 'Testing Fidelity to Legal Values: Official Involvement and Criminal Justice' in S. Shute and A. Simester (eds), *Criminal Law Theory: Doctrines of the General Part*, Oxford: OUP (2002) 299.
[186] See for example Ashworth (2009) 432.
[187] Law Com. No. 177 (1989) cl. 27(6). Law Com. 305 draft Bill cl. 7(1). In proceedings for an offence to which this section applies, a person is not guilty of the offence if he proves on the balance of probabilities that (a) he acted for the purpose of (i) preventing the commission of that offence or another offence, or (ii) preventing, or limiting, the occurrence of harm, and (b) it was reasonable for him to act as he did.
[188] E. Hoebel, 'The Abandonment Defense to Criminal Attempt and other Problems of Temporal Individuation', 74 Calif LR 377 (1986); M. Wasik, 'Abandoning Criminal Intent' [1980] Crim LR 785.
[189] See previous chapter.

A will be guilty of encouragement but will avoid liability as an accessory. How can this apparent inconsistency be explained?

For the reason why withdrawal is uncontroversially accepted as a defence for complicity but not for attempt or encouragement, it is necessary to isolate their distinctive features. As has been explained, the derivative nature of accessorial liability means that it is no part of the prosecution's case to prove any commitment to the criminal purpose. With attempts, by contrast, this is central to the prosecution's case. It is because (and only because) of A's commitment to the criminal outcome that his actions are deemed wrongful. The upshot is that with attempts it is far easier to subsume the defence in the wider requirement that the prosecution prove any steps taken were accompanied by a settled intention to bring about the *actus reus* of the consummated offence. As in attempts, withdrawing from a criminal enterprise may signal an initial absence of *mens rea*, most notably in cases of joint enterprise where the principal goes beyond what is agreed and the secondary party's withdrawal is circumstantial evidence of the scope of that agreed purpose.[190] Such withdrawal may equally serve to negate the *actus reus*, as where a secondary party having first proffered his support for the criminal enterprise later withdraws it before the offence is consummated or where having given practical assistance, say in the form of a weapon, this is later revoked by retaking the weapon.[191]

Beyond such cases, withdrawing from a complicitous relationship may also serve to exculpate the secondary party rather than preventing his initial inculpation. Typically this will occur where the latter has done enough with the necessary mental element to incur liability as an accessory but he then repents his action and his involvement and takes steps to renounce his complicity. As with attempts it is not immediately obvious why this should be the case, given that the elements of complicity are satisfied.[192] Withdrawal, it should be noted, cannot easily be presented as a defence in the same way as duress or self-defence can be presented. First, it cannot be decanted into one of the usual defence templates. It is not a defence of 'reasonable reaction'. Neither is it a defence of impaired voluntariness.[193] Perhaps as a consequence withdrawal is not easy to conceive in terms of its aptitude to excuse or justify what the accessory has done. The party does not claim that it would be wrong to punish him because external events or his internal constitution rendered his conduct blameless or innocuous. So what is his claim to avoid liability?

There are two obvious possibilities. The first is a claim from policy, namely that it is desirable to afford a defence to those who have committed themselves to a criminal enterprise for the purposes of discouraging crime, and for creating an incentive to withdraw.[194] If there is no incentive to withdraw why would the secondary party ever wish to do so, let alone bring the matter to the attention of the authorities? The second is that the accused's change of heart expunges the culpability and/or dangerousness which his initial involvement

---

[190] *Perman* [1996] 1 Cr App Rep 24.

[191] D. Lanham, 'Accomplices and Withdrawal' (1981) 97 LQR 575. The Law Commission No. 300 (2006) adopt similar reasoning.

[192] See generally K.J.M. Smith, 'Withdrawal in Complicity' [2001] Crim LR 769; D. Lanham, 'Accomplices and Withdrawal' (1981) 97 LQR 575.

[193] See Chapters 8 and 9.

[194] K.J.M. Smith (1991) 255; Law Commission Consultation Paper 131 *Assisting and Encouraging Crime* (1993) 4.133.

presupposes. This argument is more compelling here than in the context of attempt liability where the constitution of the attempt, unlike that of the complicitous association, seems to require something by way of manifest wrongdoing or dangerousness to have occurred before any need to rely upon a renunciation would arise. As explained earlier, complicity requires no proximity between the conduct of the secondary party and the consummated offence. It requires only an act or assistance or encouragement, perhaps entirely innocuous in itself, in an enterprise which at some later, possibly much later, stage bears fruit. The lack of any requirement of proximity or manifest dangerousness demands, it might be thought, some avenue to be open to the secondary party to turn back the clock to enable him to redeem himself, as his change of heart would suggest he deserves.

1 The case law

The failure to settle on an agreed theory of withdrawal leads to inevitable ambiguities as to the form withdrawal must take. On the one hand the derivative basis to liability might lead one to suppose that if the basis of inculpation is voluntary association with the principal through the giving of encouragement or help then factual withdrawal, possibly coupled with communication of an intention to withdraw,[195] should be sufficient to effect a dissociation. In *R v Otway* it was stated that for withdrawal to be effective it must be voluntary, real and effective, and communicated in some form in good time.[196]

This does not satisfactorily address the issue as to what withdrawal consists of. Is it simply a matter of retracting what one has offered or is it, rather, the negating of whatever that offer has produced? Case law is ambiguous, although overall it seems more supportive of the latter analysis. It tells us that the form withdrawal has to take to be effective depends upon both the form of accessoryship and how far advanced the principal's actions are. The more directly and actively involved the participation, the more direct and active the steps necessary to withdraw. Significantly, however, what counts as direct and active steps must vary according to the nature of the participation. In some cases the most direct and active participation is consistent with withdrawal by the scantiest of actions. Thus if A procures P to kill C it seems to be enough simply for A to communicate the countermanding of his instruction.[197] On the other hand if A has merely given encouragement, prior to the offence taking place A must again serve unequivocal notice that the commission of the offence is no longer assented to. In *R v Rook*, it was held that simply not turning up to participate in a planned murder was not enough to withdraw and so R remained complicit. It was said in this case 'if participation is confined to advice or encouragement (he) must at least communicate his change of mind to the other'. The Court of Appeal left it open as to whether, in view of the seriousness of the offence, more should have done such as inform the victim or the police.[198]

It is here that we are most in need of a clear theoretical rationale. Retracting assent is a fish from a different kettle from neutralising assistance. In *Grundy* A gave details to burglars concerning the premises to be burgled and the habits of the occupants.[199] Two weeks before

[195] *Beccara and Cooper* (1975) 62 Cr App R 212.
[196] [2011] EWCA Crim.
[197] *Croft* [1944] KB 295.
[198] [1993] 1 WLR 1005.
[199] [1977] Crim LR 543 CA.

the offence was due to take place A told them that he did not want the offence to take place and sought to dissuade them from proceeding. The Court of Appeal held that this was sufficient evidence of withdrawal to be put to the jury.[200] Given that the information was influential and helpful to the burglars it may be surprising that more was not required in the way of withdrawal. It seems to provide accessories with an easy and undeserved escape route from accessorial liability. The message seems to be that you can give your assistance, get paid for it, and then on the day after make an earnest plea that the offence not be committed. The decision can be supported on the ground that it may have been asking too much by way of heroism to require A to have informed the police or the householder unless, perhaps, the crime embarked upon was a very serious one or his involvement substantial. On the other hand, it may stand as the clearest possible evidence of the judiciary's understanding that the derivative theory of liability has no justified application outside accessoryship's paradigm cases of cooperative criminal enterprise. Applied to all cases of 'lending support' it is, as suggested above, a doctrinal sledgehammer to crack a pretty fragile nut, namely the inclination natural to large proportions of the citizenry to prioritise their own interests and turn a blind eye to the dubious activities of their paymaster.

In such cases it is understandable, then, that effective withdrawal requires something more than 'unequivocal notice' of an intention to abandon the common purpose. Once the mortar is set it may indeed take a sledgehammer rather than a gentle tap to bring down the wall of cooperative criminal enterprise, although what this involves will clearly vary. In *Beccara and Cooper*[201] A, B and C broke into a house in order to steal. A gave B a knife to use on anyone who interrupted them. However, when V did interrupt them A said 'Come on, let's go' and then immediately left the house. Deciding that the withdrawal was ineffective, it was stated:

> Where practicable and reasonable there must be timely communication of the intention to abandon the common purpose from those who wish to dissociate from the crime to those who desire to continue in it. What is timely communication must be determined by the facts of each case but where practicable and reasonable it ought to be such communication, verbal or otherwise, that will serve unequivocal notice upon the other party . . . that if he proceeds . . . he does so without the further aid and assistance of those who withdraw.[202]

Here, something 'vastly more effective' was necessary. Although adopting a language consonant with derivative liability one assumes the Court of Appeal were looking for some form of positive intervention to prevent the offence taking place. What else could A have said to make his withdrawal clear? Arguably the requirement of some form of positive intervention goes to show what common purpose cases already disclose, namely that the true basis of accessorial liability is not assent or authorisation but 'lending support'. Withdrawing 'support' as opposed to 'authorisation' does seem to imply a requirement of some form of counter-action. On the other hand this analysis is difficult to reconcile with the widely-held belief that complicity requires neither causation nor commitment to the criminal outcome, but simply a willingness to align oneself with the principal's project. If this is the case there are clearly arguments for differentiating accessories according to whether they are co-adventurers, where there are strong grounds for requiring accessories to take all reasonable steps to prevent the commission of the offence, and mechanical assisters, where

---

[200] See also *Whitefield* (1983) 79 Cr App R 36.
[201] (1975) 62 Cr App R 212.
[202] Per Roskill LJ at 218.

the grounds are less strong.[203] In *Otway* the Court of Appeal approved the judge's direction to the jury to the effect that, while whether A did anything to prevent a killing which he foresaw was going to happen was **relevant** to the issue of withdrawal, he was not necessarily required to actually restrain the gunman before the jury could conclude that he had withdrawn from the enterprise. In all cases to be effective the withdrawal must be voluntary, real and effective, and communicated in some form in good time.[204]

A qualification to this latter requirement must be made in cases where A's involvement is spontaneous. In *R v Mitchell (Frank)* A, B and C started a fight with a waiter outside an Indian restaurant. They repeatedly kicked and punched him. A, B and C then walked away only for C to return and hit the victim again several times with a stick. A, B and C were charged with murder. A and B claimed they had withdrawn from the joint enterprise. The trial judge directed the jury that withdrawal required communication rather than simply walking away. The jury convicted. A and B's appeals were allowed. Communication was not required in cases of spontaneous rather than pre-planned violence.[205]

One question so far left undiscussed is whether, as in attempt, a cogent withdrawal defence implies good motivation. Is a purported withdrawal prompted by fear of apprehension, for example, effective?[206] Once again, this would seem to depend upon the theoretical basis to the defence. If we allow the defence for its incentive value, good motivation seems to be beside the point. Conceived purely in terms of public policy, as long as the defendant takes effective steps to undo what he has done society profits, whatever his motivation in so doing. It may be then that the defence has a quasi-justificatory character, differing from self-defence and necessity only insofar as it is not dependent upon the defendant's (good) reasons for acting.[207] It is, however, hard to square such a poorly motivated decision with the assumption that withdrawals must have either exculpatory or justificatory significance. If the basis of the defence is to enrich the notion of culpability and dangerousness which participation in crime expresses, good motivation is arguably as important as it is in criminal attempts. Here the defendant's withdrawal serves as an indication that the values his initial action was challenging were also the explanatory reason for the renunciation. On this approach it is only where the accessory's explanatory reasons for withdrawing match the guiding reasons why he should not have become complicit in the first place that we can say that the flame of culpability and/or dangerousness has been truly doused.

Withdrawal due to fear of detection might then be effective if such fear was prompted by a prudential recognition that the wages of crime weighed heavier than its rewards, rather than externally prompted anxiety that the 'cops were closing in'. In this latter case the would-be withdrawer has his own reasons for withdrawal (fear of detection). We blame him, change of heart notwithstanding, because he should be guided not by his own reasons but by the exclusionary reasons contained within the prohibition itself. Plausible in theory, such a motive-sensitive approach is probably too impractical to be workable in practice. Not only is the cut-off point between genuine repentance and opportunistic changes of heart conceptually vague, proving that the withdrawal is prompted by the one rather than

---

[203] K.J.M. Smith [2001] 779–82; Law Commission Consultation Paper 131 *Assisting and Encouraging Crime* (1993) 4.135.

[204] *R v Otway* [2011] EWCA Crim 3; cf. *R v Mitchell* [2008] EWCA Crim 2552; [2009] Crim LR 287 CA.

[205] [1999] Crim LR 496.

[206] For general discussion see W. Wilson, *Central Issues in Criminal Theory* (2002) ch. 7.

[207] For discussion of the reasons approach to defences see Chapter 7.

the other is also likely to prove troublesome. Even if such problems could be resolved it is unlikely, moreover, that it could be done in a manner which advanced the more general reductionist goals subscribed to by a defence of withdrawal in complicity. All these factors combined probably argue in favour of a relatively generous approach to the problem of motivation by contrast with that operating in the field of criminal attempts.

Summary

The major assumption underpinning accessorial liability is that of derivative liability. It is thought right to punish a person who participates in crime as if he himself perpetrated that crime. As suggested above, while this is clearly appropriate when the role of the secondary party is morally congruent with that of the principal it is less so for those whose participation in criminal ventures shows no particular commitment to the criminal outcome.

The various problems involved in reconciling doctrine with the derivative rationale to secondary party liability were addressed by the Law Commission in their 1993 report by proposing the abandonment of accessorial liability and criminalisation on the basis of the party's own contribution. The proposed scheme expanded the existing inchoate system of liability (of incitement) to include assisting and encouraging crime.[208] The effect was to sidestep entirely the comforting part-fiction which is derivative liability, removing difficulties posed by the different levels of involvement/culpability of principal and secondary party. The disadvantage of this proposal was that it ignored the intuition that it is often appropriate to ascribe authorship of a crime to someone other than the perpetrator. The starting point of derivative liability (punishing A for something P has done) is the actuality of crime which is, in contemporary society, largely a cooperative enterprise, whether taking the form of small partnerships or gangs, or substantial criminal organisations. Responding to this actuality by limiting accountability for the crime to those who perpetrate it might show insufficient regard for these structural dynamics which render personal causal participation as much a matter of chance or functional necessity as individuated choice. As Sir John Smith argued in the context of murder, those who are instrumental in bringing about a killing should not have their responsibility set apart from those who directly perpetrate it because '. . . (we) feel strongly that D is responsible for those deaths. If we are going to punish him because he bears that responsibility, we are going to punish him for the homicide; and if we are going to punish him for the homicide, then he ought to be charged with, and convicted of, homicide.'[209] Of course, agreeing with this latter view does not commit us to a structure of offenders comprising principals, accessories and inchoate offenders. An attractive alternative, ultimately compatible with the 1993 position, is to abandon the idea that participation in crime takes the form of physical perpetration on the one hand, or secondary participation on the other. In its place we could extend the scope of principal liability to include all those such as instigators and partners, who 'cause' or otherwise control the occurrence of a criminal act, without necessarily physically perpetrating it, relegating other forms of participation to the

---

[208] Law Commission No. 131 *Assisting and Encouraging Crime*; see K.J.M. Smith, 'The Law Commission Consultation Paper on Complicity: (1) A Blueprint for Rationalism' [1994] Crim LR 239: G.R. Sullivan, ibid. 252.

[209] J.C. Smith, 'Criminal Liability of Accessories: Law and Law Reform' (1997) 113 LQR 453 at 461.

inchoate arena. This solution could engender the necessary moral and systemic clarity in relation to the imposition of liability for those who help or encourage criminal activities. And it would solve at a stroke most of the doctrinal tensions arising from the theory of derivative liability, such as those occurring in the fields of joint enterprise liability and innocent agency and related cases.[210] The Law Commission strikes a midway point in their latest proposals. It differentiates those who help or encourage because they want the offence to be committed and those who are indifferent to its commission. It does so by hanging accessorial liability upon *mens rea* rather than causal contribution or the nature of the participation.[211] I think this balanced approach is justified. While not all such individuals can properly be said to be authors of the relevant wrongdoing it is morally fair and practically appropriate to hold someone responsible for criminal outcomes which he intends to occur and which he makes efforts to ensure.

Further reading

Buxton, R., 'Joint Enterprise' [2009] Criminal Law Review 389.

Clarkson, C, 'Complicity, *Powell* and Manslaughter' [1998] Criminal Law Review 556.

Dennis, I., 'The Mental Element for Accessories' in P.F. Smith (ed.), *Essays in Honour of J.C. Smith*, Oxford: OUP (1987).

Krebs, B., 'Joint Criminal Enterprise' (2010) Modern Law Review.

Kutz, C., 'Causeless Complicity' (2007) 1(3) Criminal Law & Philosophy 289.

Smith, K.J.M., *A Modern Treatise on the Law of Criminal Complicity*, Oxford: Clarendon Press (1991).

Taylor, R., 'Complicity, Legal Scholarship and the Law of Unintended Consequences' (2009) Legal Studies 1.

Wilson, W., *Central Issues in Criminal Theory*, Oxford: Hart (2002) ch. 7.

---

[210] W. Wilson, *Central Issues in Criminal Theory* 218–22; G.R. Sullivan, 'Inchoate Liability for Assisting and Encouraging Crime' [2006] Crim LR 1047 at 1055.

[211] Cf. *Giannetto*, above.

References

Adenaes, J., 'The General Preventive Effects of Punishment' (1966) 114 U Pa LR 949.

Alexander, L., 'Causing the Conditions of One's Defense: A Theoretical Non-problem' (March 2013) Criminal Law & Philosophy [online article not yet assigned to an issue].

Alexander, L., 'Criminal Liability for Omissions' in S. Shute and A. Simester (eds), *Criminal Law Theory: Doctrines of the General Part*, Oxford: OUP (2002).

Alexander, L. and Ferzan, K.K. with Morse, S.J., *Crime and Culpability: A Theory of Criminal Law*, Cambridge: CUP (2009).

Alexander, L. and Kessler, K., '*Mens Rea* and Inchoate Crimes' (1997) 87 Journal of Criminal Law & Criminology 1138.

Alldridge, P., 'Common Sense, Innocent Agency and Causation' (1992) 3 Crim L Forum 299.

Alldridge, P., 'Making Criminal Law Known', in S. Shute and A.P. Simester (eds), *Criminal Law: Doctrines of the General Part*, Oxford: OUP (2002) 103.

Alldridge, P., *Relocating Criminal Law*, Aldershot: Ashgate (2000).

Alldridge, P., 'The Doctrine of Innocent Agency' (1990) 2 Crim L Forum 289.

Alldridge, P., 'The Moral Limits of the Crime of Criminal Money Laundering' (2001) 5 Buffalo Criminal L Rev 279.

Allen, F.A., *The Decline of the Rehabilitative Ideal: Penal Policy and Social Purpose*, New Haven: Yale University Press (1981).

Allen, H., 'One Law for All Reasonable Persons?' (1988) 16 International Journal of the Sociology of Law 419.

Allen, M., *Textbook on Criminal Law*, London: Blackstone Press (2002).

Allen, M., *Textbook on Criminal Law*, Oxford: OUP (2007).

Allen, M., *Textbook on Criminal Law* (11th edn), Oxford: OUP (2011).

American Law Institute, *Model Penal Code and Commentaries* (Part 1: General Provisions (1985); Part II: Definitions of Specific Crimes (1980).

Amirthalingam, K., 'Causation and the Medical Duty to Refer' (2012) 128 LQR 208.

Anderson, M., 'Diminishing the Legal Impact of Negative Social Attitudes Toward Acquaintance Rape Victims' (2010) 13(4) New Criminal LR 644.

Arden, Mrs Justice, 'Criminal Law at the Crossroads' [1999] Crim LR 439.

Arenella, P., 'Character, Choice and Moral Agency' in E.F. Paul, F.A. Miller and J. Paul (eds), *Crime, Culpability and Remedy*, Oxford: Clarendon Press (1990).

Ashworth, A.J., 'A Change of Normative Position: Determining the Contours of Culpability in Criminal Law' (2008) NCLR 232.

Ashworth, A.J., 'Analysing the Rise in the Prison Population' (editorial) [2013] Crim LR 367.

Ashworth, A.J., 'Belief, Intent and Criminal Liability' in J. Eekelaar and J. Bell (eds), *Oxford Essays in Jurisprudence*, Oxford: Clarendon Press (1987).

Ashworth, A.J., 'Belief, Intent; "Criminal Attempts and the Role of Resulting Harm"' (1988) 19 Rutgers LJ 725.

Ashworth, A.J., 'CAJA 2009: Sentencing Guidelines and the Sentencing Council' [2010] Crim LR 389.

Ashworth, A.J., 'Criminal Attempts and the Role of Resulting Harm under the Code and in the Common Law' (1988) 19 Rutgers Law Journal 725.

Ashworth, A.J., 'Criminal Proceedings After the Human Rights Act: The First Year' [2001] Crim LR 855.

Ashworth, A.J., 'Firearms and Justice' (editorial) [2013] Crim LR 447.

Ashworth, A.J., 'Ignorance of the Criminal Law and the Duties to Avoid it' (2011) 74 MLR 21.

Ashworth, A.J., 'Interpreting Criminal Statutes: a Crisis of Legality?' (1991) 107 LQR 419.

Ashworth, A.J., 'Is the Criminal Law a Lost Cause?' (2000) 116 LQR 225.

Ashworth, A.J., *Principles of Criminal Law*, Oxford: Clarendon Press (1999). Republished 2006.

Ashworth, A.J., 'Principles, Pragmatism and the Law Commission's Recommendations on Homicide Law Reform', (2007) Crim LR 333.

Ashworth, A.J., 'Prosecution, Police and Public: A Guide to Good Gate-keeping?' (1984) 23 Howard JCJ 65.

Ashworth, A.J., Sentencing and Criminal Justice, London: Butterworths (1995).

Ashworth, A.J., Sentencing and Criminal Justice, London: Butterworths (2005).

Ashworth, A.J., Sentencing and Criminal Justice (5th edn), Cambridge: CUP (2010).

Ashworth, A.J., 'Sentencing in Provocation Cases' [1975] Crim LR 553.

Ashworth, A.J., 'Taking the Consequences' in S. Shute et al., Action and Value in Criminal Law, Oxford: Clarendon Press (1993).

Ashworth, A.J., 'Testing Fidelity to Legal Values: Official Involvement and Criminal Justice' in S. Shute and A. Simester (eds), Criminal Law Theory: Doctrines of the General Part, Oxford: OUP (2002).

Ashworth, A.J., 'The Binding Effect of Crown Court Decisions' [1980] Crim LR 402.

Ashworth, A.J., The Criminal Process, Oxford: Clarendon Press (1998), (2005).

Ashworth, A.J., 'The European Convention and the Criminal Law' in The Human Rights Act and the Criminal Justice and Regulatory Process, Cambridge Centre for Public Law, Oxford: Hart (1999).

Ashworth, A.J., 'The Human Rights Act 1998 and Substantive Criminal Law' [2000] Crim LR 564.

Ashworth, A.J., 'The Scope of Criminal Liability for Omissions' (1989) 105 LQR 424.

Ashworth, A.J., 'The Treatment of Good Intentions' in A. Simester and A. Smith (eds), Harm and Culpability, Oxford: Clarendon Press (1996).

Ashworth, A.J., 'The Unfairness of Risk Based Possession Offences' (2011) 5(3) Criminal Law & Philosophy 237.

Ashworth, A.J., 'Transferred Malice and Punishment for Unforeseen Consequences' in P.R. Glazebrook (ed.), Reshaping the Criminal Law, London: Stevens (1978).

Ashworth, A.J. and Blake, M., 'The Presumption of Innocence in English Criminal Law' [1996] Crim LR 306.

Ashworth, A.J. and Campbell, K., 'Recklessness in Assault – And in General?' (1991) 107 LQR 187.

Ashworth, A.J. and Horder, J., Principles of Criminal Law (7th edn), Oxford: OUP (2013).

Ashworth, A.J. and Mitchell, B. (eds), Rethinking English Homicide Law, Oxford: OUP (2000).

Ashworth, A.J. and Redmayn, M., The Criminal Process (4th edn), Oxford: OUP (2010).

Ashworth, A.J. and von Hirsch, A., Principled Sentencing, Oxford: Hart Publishing (1998).

Ashworth, A.J. and Zedner, L., 'Criminalization: Justifications and Limits' (2012) 15(4) New Criminal LR 542.

Ashworth, A.J. and Zedner, L., 'Defending the Criminal Law: Reflections on the Changing Character of Crime, Procedure, and Sanctions' (2007) 2(1) Criminal Law and Philosophy 21–51.

Ashworth, A.J., Gardner, J., Morgan, R., Smith, A.T.H., von Hirsch, A. and Wasik, M., 'Neighbouring on the Oppressive: The Government's "Anti-Social Behaviour Order" Proposals' (1998) 16(1) Criminal Justice 7.

Astor, 'Shoplifting Survey' in Security World, Vol. 8, Part 3 (1971).

Auld Report, The, Review of the Criminal Courts of England and Wales, London: Stationery Office (2002).

Austin, J., Lectures on Jurisprudence (3rd edn, 1869).

Bailin, A., 'Criminalising Free Speech?' [2011] Crim LR 705.

Baker, D., 'Critical Evaluation of the Historical and Contemporary Justifications for Criminalising Begging' (2009) 73(3) J Crim L 212.

Baker, D., The Right not to be Criminalised: Demarcating Criminal Law's Authority, Aldershot: Ashgate (2011).

Baker, D.J., 'The Moral Limits of Criminalizing Remote Harms' (2007) New Criminal Law Review, 370–91.

Baldwin, J., 'Understanding Judge Ordered and Directed Acquittals' [1997] Crim LR 536.

Barnes, J., The History of the World in 10½ Chapters, London: Jonathan Cape (1989).

Barrett, M., Women's Oppression Today: Problems in Marxist Feminist Analysis, London: Verso (1980).

Bates, B., 'British Sovereignty and the European Court of Human Rights' (2012) 128 LQR 382.

Bayles, M., 'Character, Purpose and Criminal Responsibility' (1982) 1 Law and Philosophy 5.

Beale, J.H., 'Retreat from a Murderous Assault' (1903) 16 Harv LR 567.

Beale, J.H., 'The Proximate Cause of an Act' (1920) 33 Harv LR 633.

Bedi, S., 'Why a Criminal Prohibition on Sex Selective Abortions Amounts to a Thought Crime' (2011) 5(3) Criminal Law & Philosophy 349.

Bennett, C., The Apology Ritual: A Philosophical Theory of Punishment, Cambridge: CUP (2008).

Bennett, J., The Act Itself, Oxford: Clarendon Press (1995).

Bennion, F., 'Letter to the Criminal Law Review' [1980] Crim LR 670.

Bennion, F., 'Mens rea and Defendants Below the Age of Discretion' [2009] Crim LR 757.

Berman, M., 'The Justification of Punishment' in A. Marmor (ed.), The Routledge Companion to Philosophy of Law, London: Routledge (2012).

Berman, M.N., 'Rehabilitating Retributivism' (2013) 32(1) Law & Philosophy 83.

Bibbings, L., and Alldridge, P., 'Sexual Expression, Body Alteration and the Defence of Consent' (1993) 20 J Law and Soc 356.

Binder, G., 'Punishment Theory: Moral or Political?' (2002) Buffalo Crim LR 321.

Birch, D.J., 'The Foresight Saga: The Biggest Mistake of All?' [1988] Crim LR 4.

Blackstone, W., Commentaries on the Law of England, Cadell (1825).

Blackstone's Criminal Practice, Oxford: OUP (2007).

Blom Cooper, L. and T. Morris, T., With Malice Aforethought, Oxford: Hart (2004).

Bohlander, M., 'Hijacked Airplanes: May They be Shot Down?' (2007) New Crim LR 582.

Bohlander, M., 'Of Shipwrecked Sailors, Unborn Children, Conjoined Twins and Hijacked Aeroplanes – Taking Human Life in the Defence of Necessity' (2006) JCL 147.

Bohlander, M., 'Problems of Transferred Malice in Multiple-Actor Scenarios', (2010) Journal of Criminal Law, vol. 74, no. 2, 145–162.

Bohlander, M., 'Retrospective Reductions in the Severity of Substantive Criminal Law – the Lex mitior Principle and the Impact of Scoppola v Italy No. 2' [2011] Crim LR 627.

Bohlander, M., 'The Sexual Offences Act 2003 – the Tyrrell Principle – Criminalising the Victims' [2005] Crim LR 701.

Bohlander, M., 'Transferred Malice and Transferred Defences: A Critique of the Traditional Doctrine and Arguments for a Change in

Paradigm', (2010) New Criminal Law Review, vol. 13, no. 3, 555–624.

Bomann-Larsen, L., 'Revisionism and Desert' (2010) 4(1) Criminal Law & Philosophy 1.

Bottoms, A.E., 'An Introduction to the Coming Crisis' in A.E. Bottoms and R.H. Preston, The Coming Penal Crisis (1980).

Brady, J., 'Punishing Attempts' (1980) 63 The Monist 246.

Brady, J., 'Recklessness' (1996) 15 Law and Philosophy.

Braun, A., 'The English Codification Debate and the Role of Jurists in the Development of Legal Doctrines' in M. Lobban and J. Moses (eds), The Impact of Ideas on Legal Development (series of Comparative Studies of the Development of Tort Law in Europe), CUP (2012).

Brazier, M., Medicine, Patients and the Law, London: Penguin (1992). (5th revised edn, 2011)

Brody, S.R., The Effectiveness of Sentencing: A review of the literature, Home Office Research Study No. 35 (1976).

Bronitt, S., 'Spreading Disease and the Criminal Law' [1994] Crim LR 24.

Brownmiller, S., Against Our Will: Men, Women and Rape, London: Secker and Warburg (1975).

Brudner, A., 'A Theory of Necessity' (1987) 7 OJLS 339.

Brudner, A., 'Agency and Welfare in the Penal Law' in S. Shute, J. Gardner, J. Horder (eds), Action and Value in the Criminal Law, Oxford: Clarendon Press (1993).

Brudner, A., Punishment and Freedom: A Liberal Theory of Penal Justice, Oxford: OUP (2012).

Burgess, A., A Clockwork Orange, Harmondsworth: Penguin (1996).

Buxton, Sir R., 'The Human Rights Act and Substantive Criminal Law' [2000] Crim LR 335.

Canadian HIV/AIDS Legal Network, Injection Drug Use and HIV/AIDS: Legal and Ethical Issues, 24 November 1999.

Cane, P., Responsibility in Law and Morality, Oxford: Hart (2002).

Cape, E., 'The Counter-terrorism Provisions of the Protection of Freedoms Act 2012: Preventing Misuse or a Case of Smoke and Mirrors?' [2013] Crim LR 385.

Card, R., 'Reform of the Law of Conspiracy' [1973] Crim LR 674.

Card, R., Cross, R. and Jones, R., *Criminal Law*, London: Butterworths (1994).

Carson, W.G., 'White Collar Crime and the Institutionalisation of Ambiguity' in M. Fitzgerald, G. McLennan and J. Pawson (eds), *Crime and Society*, London: Routledge (1990).

Cartwright, P., 'Publicity, Punishment and Protection: The Role(s) of Adverse Publicity in Consumer Policy' (2012) 32(2) Legal Studies 179.

Carvalho, H., 'Terrorism, Punishment, and Recognition' (2012) 15(3) New Criminal LR 345.

Chalmers, J. and Leverick, F., 'Fair Labelling in Criminal Law' (2008) 71(2) Modern Law Review 217–246.

Chalmers, J., Farmer, L. and Leverick, F. (eds), *Essays in Criminal Law in Honour of Sir Gerald Gordon*, Edinburgh: Edinburgh University Press (2010).

Chau, P., 'Duff on the Legitimacy of Punishment of Socially Deprived Offenders' (2012) 6(2) Criminal Law & Philosophy 247.

Cherkassky, L., 'Being Informed: The Complexities of Knowledge, Deception and Consent when Transmitting HIV' (2010) 74(3) J Crim L 242.

Chiao, V., 'Action and Agency in the Criminal Law' (2009) 15(1) Legal Theory 1.

Chiao, V., 'Intention and Attempt' (2010) 4 Criminal Law and Philosophy 37.

Child, J.J., 'Exploring the Mens Rea Requirements of the Serious Crime Act 2007 Assisting and Encouraging Offences' (2012) 76(3) J Crim L 220.

Christie, A.L., 'Should the Law of Theft Extend to Information?' (2005) J Crim Law.

Christie, S., 'The Relevance of Harm as the Criterion for the Punishment of Impossible Attempts' (2009) 73 Journal of Criminal Law 153.

Christopher, R., 'Does Attempted Murder Deserve Greater Punishment than Murder? Moral Luck and the Duty to Prevent Harm' (2004) 18 Notre Dame Journal of Law, Ethics & Public Policy 419.

Christopher, R. (ed.), *George Fletcher's Essays on Criminal Law*, Oxford: OUP (2013).

Cicca, S., 'Sterilising the Intellectually Disabled: The Approach of the High Courts in Australia', *Department of Health* v. *JWB and SMB* (1993) Med LR 186.

Clarkson, C., 'Aggravated Endangerment Offences' (2007) CLP 278.

Clarkson, C., 'Attempt: The Conduct Requirement' (2009) Oxford J Legal Studies 29 (1):25–41.

Clarkson, C., 'Necessary Action: A New Defence' [2004] Crim LR 81.

Clarkson, C., 'Theft and Fair Labelling' (1993) 56 MLR 554.

Clarkson, C., Cretney, A., Davis, G. and Shepherd, J., 'Assaults: the Relationship between Seriousness, Criminalisation and Punishment' [1994] Crim LR 4.

Clarkson, C.M.V., 'Attempt: The Conduct Requirement' (2009) 29(1) Oxford Journal Legal Studies 25–41.

Clarkson, C.M.V., 'Context and Culpability in Involuntary Manslaughter' in *Rethinking English Homicide Law*, Oxford: OUP (2000).

Clarkson, C.M.V., 'Corporate Manslaughter: Yet More Government Proposals', [2005] Crim LR 677.

Clarkson, C.M.V. and Cunningham, S. (eds), *Criminal Liability for Non-aggressive Death*, London: Ashgate (2008).

Clarkson, C.M.V. and Keating, H.M., *Criminal Law* (6th edn) London: Sweet & Maxwell (2007).

Coggon, J. and Miola, J., 'Autonomy, Liberty, and Medical Decision-making' (2011) 70(3) CLJ 523.

Committee on Mentally Abnormal Offenders, *Report of the Committee on Mentally Abnormal Offenders*, Cmnd 6244, London: HMSO (1975).

Cooper, S., 'Culpable Driving and Issues of Causation' (2012) 76(5) J Crim L 431.

Cooper, S. and James, M., 'Entertainment – the Painful Process of Rethinking Consent' [2012] Crim LR 188.

Cough, S., 'Surviving Without *Majewski*' [2000] Crim LR 719.

Cowan, S., 'Freedom and Capacity to Make a Choice: A Feminist Analysis of Consent in the Criminal Law of Rape' in V. Munro and C. Stychin (eds), *Sexuality and the Law: Feminist Engagements*, London: Routledge-Cavendish (2007) 51.

Cowan, S., 'Offences of Sex or Violence? Consent, Fraud & HIV Transmission' (July 2013) New Criminal LR [just accepted not assigned to issue].

Cowan, S., 'To Buy or not to Buy? Vulnerability and the Criminalisation of Commercial BDSM' (2012) 20(3) Feminist LS 263.

Crawford, A., 'Governing through Anti-Social Behaviour: Regulatory Challenges to Criminal Justice' (2009) 49(6) British Journal of Criminology 810–31.

Cretney, A. and Davis, G., 'Prosecuting "Domestic" Assault' [1996] Crim LR 162.

Cromby, J., et al., 'Constructing Crime, Enacting Morality: Emotion, Crime and Anti-social Behaviour in an Inner-city Community' (2010) 50(5) Brit J Criminol 873.

Crosby, C., 'Causing Death by Faultless Driving' (2011) 75(2) J Crim L 111 (case comment).

Crosby, K., 'Controlling Devlin's Jury: What the Jury Thinks, and What the Jury Sees Online' [2012] Crim LR 15.

Criminal Law Revision Committee 8th Report, Theft and Related Offences, Cmnd 2977 (1966).

Criminal Law Revision Committee 13th Report, Section 16 of the Theft Act 1968, Cmnd 6733 (1977).

Criminal Law Revision Committee 14th Report, Offences Against the Person, Cmnd 7844 (1980).

Cross, R., 'Reports of the Criminal Law Commissioners (1833–49) and the Abortive Bills of 1853' in P.R. Glazebrook (ed.), Reshaping the Criminal Law, London: Stevens (1978).

Crown Prosecution Service, 'Changing Guidelines for the Crown Prosecution Service' (1996), London: CPS.

Crown Prosecution Service, 'Interim Guidelines on Prosecuting Cases Involving Communications Sent via Social Media' (2012), at: http://www.cps.gov.uk/consultations/social_media_consultation.html.

Crown Prosecution Service, 'Policy for Prosecutors in Respect of Cases of Encouraging or Assisting Suicide' (2010), at: http://www.cps.gov.uk/publications/prosecution/assisted_suicide_policy.html.

Cruft, R., 'Liberalism and the Changing Character of the Criminal Law: Response to Ashworth and Zedner' (2008) 2(1) Criminal Law and Philosophy 59.

Cunningham, S., 'Taking "Causing Serious Injury by Dangerous Driving" Seriously' [2012] Crim LR 261.

Curly, E.M., 'Excusing Rape' (1976) 5 Philosophy and Public Affairs 325.

Darbyshire, P., 'An Essay on the Importance and Neglect of the Magistracy' [1997] Crim LR 627.

Darbyshire, P., 'The Importance and Neglect of the Magistracy' [1997] Crim LR 627.

Davies, M., 'Why Attempts Deserve Less Punishment Than Complete Crimes' (1986) 5 Law and Philosophy 1.

Davis, C., 'Conjoined Twins as Persons that Can Be Victims of Homicide' (2011) 19 Medical LR 430.

de Marneffe, P., 'Sexual Freedom and Impersonal Value' (March 2013) Criminal Law & Philosophy [online article not assigned to issue].

Denning, Lord, Responsibility Before the Law, Jerusalem: Magnes Press (1961).

Dennis, I., 'Duress, Murder and Criminal Responsibility' (1980) LQR 208.

Dennis, I., 'Intention and Complicity: A Reply' [1988] Crim LR 649.

Dennis, I., 'Reverse Onuses and the Presumption of Innocence' [2005] LR 901.

Dennis, I., 'Sentencing, Rehabilitation and the Prison Population' [2010] Crim LR 591.

Dennis, I., 'The Criminal Attempts Act 1981' [1982] Criminal Law Review 5.

Dennis, I., 'The Rationale of Criminal Conspiracy' (1977) 93 LQR 39.

Department of Health, Protecting Children, Supporting Parents: A Consultative Document on the Physical Punishment of Children.

Department of Transport, MV Herald of Free Enterprise: Report of the Court (No. 8074) (1987).

Devlin, P., 'Judges and Law Makers' (1976) 39 MLR 1.

Dickson, B., 'The Record of the House of Lords in Strasbourg' (2012) 128 LQR 354.

Diduck, A. and Wilson, W., 'Prostitutes and Persons' [1997] JLS 504.

Dillof, A., 'Transferred Intent: An Inquiry into the Nature of Criminal Culpability' (1988) Buffalo Criminal Law Review 501.

Dine, J., Gobert, J. and Wilson, W., Cases and Materials on Criminal Law, Oxford: OUP (2005).

Dingwall, G., 'Intoxicated Mistakes About the Need for Self Defence' (2007) MLR 70, 127.

d'Orban, P.T., 'Women Who Kill their Children' (1979) 134 Brit J. Psychiatry 560.

Dressler, J., 'Battered Women Who Kill Their Sleeping Tormentors' in S. Shute and A. Simester (eds), Criminal Law Theory: Doctrines of the General Part, Oxford: Clarendon Press (2002).

Dressler, J., 'New Thoughts about the Concept of Justification in the Criminal Law: a Critique of Fletcher's Thinking and *Rethinking*' [1984] 32 UCLA L Rev 61.

Dressler, J., 'Reflections on Excusing Wrongdoers: Moral Theory, New Excuses and the Model Penal Code' (1988) 19 Rut LJ 671.

Dressler, J., *Understanding Criminal Law*, New York: Matthew Bender (1987).

Dripps, D., 'Beyond Rape: An Essay on the Difference between the Presence of Force and the Absence of Consent' (1992) Colum LR 1780.

du Bois-Pedain, A., 'Once a Sex Offender, Always a Reoffending Risk?' (2010) 69(3) CLJ 428.

du Bois-Pedain, A. (2009), 'Terrorist Possession Offences: Curiosity Killed the Cat', (2009) 68(2) Cambridge Law Journal 261–263.

du Bois-Pedain, A., 'The Wrongfulness Constraint in Criminalisation' (Sep 2012) Criminal Law & Philosophy [online article not assigned to an issue].

Dubber, M., 'The Possession Paradigm: the Special Part and the Police Power Model of the Criminal Process' in R.A. Duff and S.P. Green (eds), *Defining Crimes*, Oxford: OUP (2005).

Duff, R.A., 'Acting, Trying and Criminal Liability' in S. Shute *et al.*, *Action and Value in Criminal Law*, Oxford: Clarendon Press (1993).

Duff, R.A., *Answering for Crime*, Oxford: Hart (2007).

Duff, R.A., 'Blame, Moral Standing, and the Legitimacy of Criminal Trial' (2010) 23(2) Ratio 123–40.

Duff, R.A., ' "Can I help you?" Accessorial Liability and the Intention to Assist' [1990] 10 LS 165.

Duff, R.A., 'Choice, Character and Criminal Liability' (1993) 12 Law and Philosophy 345.

Duff, R.A., *Criminal Attempts*, Oxford: OUP (1996).

Duff, R.A., 'Criminal Attempts' in A. Marmor (ed.), *The Routledge Companion to Philosophy of Law*, London: Routledge (2012) 191–205.

Duff, R.A., 'Guiding Commitments and Criminal Liability for Attempts' (2012) 6(3) Criminal Law & Philosophy 411.

Duff, R.A., 'Harms and Wrongs' (2001) Buffalo Crim LR 13.

Duff, R.A., *Intention, Agency and Criminal Liability: Philosophy of Action and the Criminal Law*, Oxford: Basil Blackwell (1990).

Duff, R.A., 'Intention, *Mens Rea* and the Law Commission Report' [1980] Crim LR 147.

Duff, R.A. (ed.), *Philosophy and the Criminal Law*, Cambridge: CUP (1998).

Duff, R.A., 'Presuming Innocence', in L. Zedner and J.V. Roberts (eds), *Principles and Values in Criminal Law and Criminal Justice: Essays in Honour of Andrew Ashworth*, Oxford: OUP (2012) 51.

Duff, R.A., 'Rule Violations and Wrongdoings' in S. Shute and A. Simester (eds), *Criminal Law Theory: Doctrines of the General Part*, Oxford: Clarendon Press (2002).

Duff, R.A., 'Strict Liability, Legal Presumptions and the Presumption of Innocence' in A.P. Simester (ed.), *Appraising Strict Liability*, Oxford: OUP (2006).

Duff, R.A., 'The Circumstances of an Attempt' (1991) 50 Cambridge Law Journal 100.

Duff, R.A., 'The Politics of Intention: a Response to Norrie' [1990] Crim LR 637.

Duff, R.A., 'The Role of Luck and Criminal Liability for Death' (2007) unpublished paper.

Duff, R.A., 'The Role of Luck and Criminal Liability for Death' in C. Clarkson and S. Cunningham (eds), *Criminal Liability for Non-aggressive Death* (2008), Aldershot: Ashgate.

Duff, R.A., 'Towards a Modest Legal Moralism' (Oct 2012) Criminal Law & Philosophy [online article not assigned to an issue].

Duff, R.A., *Trials and Punishments*, Cambridge: CUP (1986).

Duff, R.A. and Garland, D. (eds), *A Reader on Punishment*, Oxford: OUP (1994).

Duff, R.A. and Green, S.P. (eds), *Defining Crimes: Essays on the Special Part of the Criminal Law*, Oxford: OUP (2005) 119.

Duff, R.A. and Marshall, S.C., 'How Offensive Can You Get?' in A. Hirsch and A.P. Simester (eds), *Incivilities: Regulating Offensive Behaviour*, Oxford: Hart (2006).

Duff, R.A., Farmer, L., Marshall, S. and Tadros, V., *The Trial on Trial*, Oxford: Hart (2007).

Dufner, A., 'Should the Late Stage Demented be Punished for Past Crimes?' (2013) 7(1) Criminal Law & Philosophy 137.

Durkheim, E., *The Division of Labour in Society*, London: Macmillan (1984).

Dworkin, G., 'The Law Relating to Organ Transplantation in England' (1970) 33 MLR 353.

Dworkin, R., *Life's Dominion*, London: HarperCollins (1993).

Dworkin, R., *Taking Rights Seriously*, London: Duckworth (1977).

Dzur, A.W., 'Participatory Democracy and Criminal Justice' (2012) 6(2) Criminal Law & Philosophy 115.

Eastman, N. and Peay, J., 'Sentencing Psychopaths' [1998] Crim LR 93.

Easton, S., 'Criminalising the Possession of Extreme Pornography: Sword or Shield?' (2011) 75(5) J Crim Law 391.

Easton, S. and Piper, C., *Sentencing and Punishment: The Quest for Justice* (3rd edn), Oxford: OUP (2012).

Edwards, J., 'Coming Clean About the Criminal Law' (2011) 5(3) Criminal Law & Philosophy 315.

Edwards, J., 'Justice Denied: The Criminal Law and the Ouster of the Courts' (2010) 30(4) OJLS 725.

Eldar, S., 'Holding Organized Crime Leaders Accountable for the Crimes of their Subordinates' (2012) 6(2) Criminal Law & Philosophy 207.

Elliot, D.W., 'Dishonesty in Theft: a Dispensable Concept' [1982] Crim LR 395.

Elliot, D.W., 'Endangering Life by Destroying or Damaging Property' [1997] Crim LR 382.

Elliot, D.W., 'Law and Fact in Theft Act Cases' [1976] Crim LR 707.

Elliot, D.W., 'Necessity, Duress and Self-Defence' [1989] Crim LR 611.

Elliot, T., 'Liability for Manslaughter by Omission: Don't Let the Baby Drown!' (2010) 74(2) J Crim L 163.

Elliott, D.W., 'Body Dismorphic Disorder, Radical Surgery and the Limits of Consent' (2009) 17 Med LR 149.

Elliott, C. and de Than, C., 'The Case for a Rational Reconstruction of Consent in Criminal Law' (2007) 70(2) MLR 225–249.

Elliott, C.S. and de Than, C., 'Prosecuting the Drug Dealer when a Drug User Dies', (2006) 69 Modern Law Review 986.

Elliott, T. and Ormerod, D., 'Acts and Omissions: A Distinction without a Defense?' (2008) 39 Cambrian LR 40.

Elvin, J., 'The Concept of Consent under the Sexual Offences Act 2003' (2008) 72 Journal of Criminal Law 519.

Emmerson, B. and Ashworth, A., *Human Rights and Criminal Justice*, London: Sweet & Maxwell (2001).

Evans, E.P., The *Criminal Prosecution and Capital Punishment of Animals*, London: Faber and Faber (1987).

Farmer, L., 'Complicity Beyond Causality: a Comment', (2007) 1 Criminal Law and Philosophy 151.

Farrell, D.M., 'Using Wrongdoers Rightly: Tadros on the Justification of General Deterrence' (December 2012) Criminal Law & Philosophy [online version not assigned to issue].

Feinberg, J., *Harm to Others: The Moral Limits of the Criminal Law*, New York: OUP (1984).

Feinberg, J., 'The Expressive Function of Punishment' in R.A. Duff and D. Garland (eds), *A Reader on Punishment*, Oxford: OUP (1994).

Feinberg, J., *The Moral Limits of the Criminal Law. Vol. 1, Harm to Others*, New York: OUP (1984).

Feinberg, J., *The Moral Limits of the Criminal Law. Vol. 2, Offense to Others*, New York: OUP (1985).

Feist, A., Ashe, J. et al., *Investigating and Detecting Recorded Cases of Rape*, London: Home Office (2007).

Fenwick, H., 'Marital Rights or Partial Immunity' (1992) 142 NLJ 870.

Fenwick, P. and Fenwick, E. (eds), *Epilepsy and the Law; A Medical Symposium on the Current Law*, London: Royal Society of Medicine (1985).

Ferguson, P., 'Constructing a Criminal Code', (2010) 20(1) Criminal Law Forum 139–161.

Ferguson, P., ' "Smoke gets in your eyes. . . ." The Criminalisation of Smoking in Enclosed Public Spaces, the Harm Principle and the Limits of the Criminal Sanction', (2010) 31(2) Legal Studies 259–78.

Ferguson, P. and McDiarmid, C., *Scots Criminal Law*, Dundee: Dundee University Press (2008).

Ferrante, M., (2011) 14(1) New Criminal LR 162.

Field, S. and Jorg, N., 'Corporate Liability and Manslaughter: should we be going Dutch?' [1991] Crim LR 156.

Field, S. and Lynn, M., *The Capacity for Recklessness* (1992) 12 LS 74 at 87.

Finch, E. and Munro, M., 'Intoxicated Consent and Drug-assisted Rape Revisited' [2004] Crim LR 789.

Fisse, B. and Braithwaite, J., 'The Allocation of Responsibility for Corporate Crime: Individualism, Collectivism and Accountability' (1988) 11 Sydney L Rev 468.

Flatley *et al.* (eds), *British Crime Survey 2009–10*, London: HOSB.

Fletcher, G., 'On the Moral Irrelevance of Bodily Movements' (1994) 142 U Pa L Rev 1443.

Fletcher, G., *Rethinking Criminal Law*, Boston Toronto: Little, Brown and Company (1978).

Fletcher, G., 'The Fall and Rise of Criminal Theory' [1998] Buffalo Crim LR 276.

Fontaine, R., 'The Wrongfulness of Wrongly Interpreting Wrongfulness: Provocation, Interpretational Bias, and Heat of Passion Homicide' (2009) 12 New Criminal LR 69.

Fortson, R., Blackstone's Guide to the Serious Crime Act 2007, Oxford: OUP (2008).

Foster, Sir Michael, *Crown Law*, London (1762).

Foucault, M., *Discipline and Punish: The Birth of the Prison*, Harmondsworth: Penguin (1991).

Fulford, K.W.M., 'Value, Action, Mental Illness and the Law' in S. Shute, J. Gardner, J. Horder (eds), *Action and Value in the Criminal Law*, Oxford: Clarendon Press (1993).

Fuller, L.L., *The Morality of Law*, New Haven: Yale University Press (1969).

Gardner, J., 'Causality and Complicity' in J. Gardner, *Offences and Defences, Selected Essays in the Philosophy of Criminal Law*, Oxford: OUP (2007).

Gardner, J., 'In Defence of Defences', in J. Gardner, *Offences and Defences: Selected Essays in the Philosophy of Criminal Law*, Oxford: OUP (2007).

Gardner, J., 'Justifications and Reasons' in A. Simester and A.T.H. Smith (eds), *Harm and Culpability*, Oxford: Clarendon Press (1996).

Gardner, J., *Offences and Defences: Selected Essays in the Philosophy of Criminal Law*, Oxford: OUP (2007).

Gardner, J., 'On the General Part of the Criminal Law' in R.A. Duff (ed.), *Philosophy and the Criminal Law*, Cambridge: CUP (1998).

Gardner, J., 'Prohibiting Immoralities', (2007) 28 Cardozo L Rev 2613.

Gardner, J., 'Rationality and the Rule of Law in Offences Against the Person' (1994) 53 Camb LJ 502.

Gardner, J., 'The Gist of Excuses' (1998) Buffalo Criminal Law Review 575.

Gardner, J., 'Wrongdoing by Results: Moore's Experiential Argument' (2012) 18(4) LT 459.

Gardner, J. and Jung, H., 'Making Sense of *Mens Rea*: Antony Duff's Account' (1991) OJLS 559.

Gardner, J. and Macklem, T., 'Compassion without Respect? Nine Fallacies in *R v. Smith*' [2001] Crim LR 623.

Gardner, J. and Shute, S., 'The Wrongness of Rape' in J. Horder (ed.), *Oxford Essays on Jurisprudence*, Oxford: OUP (2000).

Gardner, S., 'Appreciating *Olugboja*' [1996] 16 LS 275.

Gardner, S., 'Direct Action and the Defence of Necessity' [2005] Crim LR 371.

Gardner, S., 'Necessity's Newest Inventions' [1991] 11 OJLS 125.

Gardner, S., 'Reckless and Inconsiderate Rape' [1991] Crim LR 172.

Gardner, S., 'Recklessness Refined' (1993) 109 LQR 21.

Gardner, S., 'The Importance of *Majewski*' (1994) 14 OJLS 279.

Gargarella, R., 'Penal Coercion in Contexts of Social Injustice' (2011) 5(1) Criminal Law & Philosophy 21.

Garvey, S., 'Are Attempts like Treason' (2011) 14 New Criminal LR 173.

Garvey, S., 'Was Ellen Wronged?' (2013) 7(2) Criminal Law & Philosophy 185.

Gearty, C., 'The HRA – an academic sceptic changes his mind but not his heart' (2010) 6 EHRLR 582.

Genders, E., 'Reform of the Offences Against the Person Act: Lessons from the Law in Action' [1999] Crim LR 689.

Gibson, M., 'Intoxicants and Diminished Responsibility: The Impact of the Coroners and Justice Act 2009' [2011] Crim LR 909.

Giles, M., 'Judicial Law-Making in the Criminal Courts: the Case of Marital Rape' [1992] Crim LR 407.

Gillespie, A., 'Perverting the Course of Justice by Deleting Indecent Images' (case comment) (2012) 76(1) J Crim L 10.

Glazebrook, P.R., 'Criminal Omissions: the Duty Requirement in Offences Against the Person' (1960) 76 LQR 386.

Glazebrook, P.R., 'Revising the Theft Acts' [1993] Camb LJ 191.

Glazebrook, P.R., 'Situational Liability' in P.R. Glazebrook (ed.), *Reshaping the Criminal Law*, London: Stevens (1978).

Glazebrook, P.R., 'The Necessity Plea in English Criminal Law' [1972] CLJ 87.

Glazebrook, P.R., 'Thief or Swindler: Who Cares?' [1991] CLJ 389.

Gobert, J., 'Corporate Criminality: Four Models of Fault' [1994] 14 LS 393.

Gobert, J. and Mugnai, E., 'Coping with Corporate Criminality' (2002) Crim LR 619.

Goff, Lord, 'The Mental Element in the Crime of Murder' (1988) 104 LQR 30.

Goodall, J.K., 'Conceptualising "racism" in criminal law', (2012) Legal Studies [originally published online].

Gordon, G.H., *Criminal Law of Scotland*, Edinburgh: W Green & Son (1967).

Gough, S., 'Intoxication and Criminal Liability: The Law Commission's Proposed Reforms' (1996) 112 LQR 335.

Gough, S., 'Surviving without *Majewski*' [2000] Crim LR 719.

Green, S.P., 'Theft by Omission' in Chalmers, J., Farmer, L. and Leverick, F. (eds), *Essays in Criminal Law in Honour of Sir Gerald Gordon*, Edinburgh: Edinburgh University Press (2010).

Greenawalt, P., 'The Perplexing Boundaries of Justification and Excuse' (1984) Columbia Law Review 1847.

Griew, E., 'Consistency, Communication and Codification: Reflections on Two *Mens Rea* Words' in P.R. Glazebrook (ed.), *Reshaping the Criminal Law*, London: Stevens (1978).

Griew, E. 'Let's Implement Butler on Mental Disorder and Crime' [1984] CLP 47.

Griew, E., 'Reckless Damage and Reckless Driving: Living with *Caldwell* and *Lawrence*' [1981] Crim LR 743.

Griew, E., 'The Future of Diminished Responsibility' [1988] Crim LR 75.

Griew, E., *The Theft Acts*, London: Sweet & Maxwell (1995).

Griffin, S., 'Accountability for Deaths Attributable to the Gross Negligent Act or Omission of a Police Force: The Impact of the Corporate Manslaughter and Corporate Homicide Act 2007' (2010) J Crim L 648.

Gross, H., *A Theory of Criminal Justice*, New York: OUP (1979).

Gunby, C., Carline, A. and Beynon, C., 'Alcohol-related Rape Cases: Barristers' Perspectives on the Sexual Offences Act 2003 and its Impact on Practice' (2010) 74(6) J Crim L 579.

Hall, J., *General Principles of Criminal Law*, Indianapolis: Bobbs-Merrill (1960).

Hall, J., *Theft, Law and Society*, Indianapolis: Bobbs-Merrill (1952).

Hall, R., *Ask Any Woman, A London Inquiry into Rape and Sexual Assault*, Bristol: Falling Wall Press (1985).

Hallevy, G., *A Modern Treatise on the Principle of Legality in Criminal Law*, London: Springer (2010).

Hamer, D., 'A Dynamic Reconstruction of the Presumption of Innocence' OJLS 31 (2011) 417.

Hammond, R.G., 'Theft of Information' (1984) 199 LQR 252.

Handler, P., 'Intoxication and criminal responsibility in England, 1819–1920' (2013) 33(2) OJLS 243.

Hanna, N., 'Facing the Consequences' (April 2013) Criminal Law & Philosophy [online version not yet assigned to issue].

Harris, J.W., 'Who Owns My Body?' [1996] 16 OJLS 55.

Hart, H.L.A., *Law, Liberty and Morality*, London: OUP (1963).

Hart, H.L.A., *Punishment and Responsibility: Essays in the Philosophy of Law*, Oxford: Clarendon Press (1968). (Also revised edn, 2008.)

Hart, H.L.A. and Honore, A.M., *Causation in the Law* (2nd edn), Oxford: Clarendon Press (1985).

Hay, D., 'Property, Authority and the Criminal Law' in D. Hay *et al.*, *Albion's Fatal Tree*, London: Allen Lane (1975).

Health and Safety Executive, *Workplace Deaths*, London: HSE (2010).

Healy, D., (1991) 17 May, *New Scientist*.

Heaton, R., 'Cheques and Balances' [2005] Crim LR 747.

Henham, R., *Sentencing and the Legitimacy of Criminal Justice*, London: Routledge (2011).

Herring, J., *Criminal Law: Text, Cases and Materials*, Oxford: OUP (2007).

Herring, J., *Criminal Law: Text, Cases and Materials*, Oxford: OUP (2009).

Herring, J., 'Mistaken Sex', [2005] Crim LR 311; contra Hyman Gross in Crim LR 2005, March, 220.

Herring, J., 'No More Having and Holding: The Abolition of the Marital Rape Exemption' in S. Gilmore, J. Herring and S. Gilmore (eds), *Landmark Cases in Family Law*, Oxford: Hart Publishing (2011).

Herring, J., 'Provocation and Ethnicity' [1996] Crim LR 490.

Herring, J., 'The Duty of Care in Gross Negligence Manslaughter' (2007) Criminal Law Review 24–41.

Herring, J. and Palser, E., 'The Duty of Care in Gross Negligence Manslaughter' [2007] Crim LR 24.

Herring, J., Regan, C., Weinberg, D. and Withington, P. (eds), *Intoxication and Society: Problematic Pleasures of Drugs and Alcohol*, London: Palgrave Macmillan (2012).

Hickey, R., 'Stealing Abandoned Goods: Possessory Title in Proceedings for Theft' [2006] LS 584.

Hicks, M. and Branston, G., 'Transsexual Rape – A Loophole Closed?' [1997] Crim LR 565.

Hirsch, A. von, 'Censure and Proportionality' in R.A. Duff and D. Garland (eds), *A Reader on Punishment*, Oxford: OUP (1994).

Hirsch, A. von, *Censure and Sanctions*, Oxford: Clarendon Press (1993).

Hirsch, A. von, *Doing Justice – The Choice of Punishments*, Report of the Committee for the Study of Incarceration (1976).

Hirsch, A. von, 'Extending the Harm Principle' in A. Simester and A.T.H. Smith (eds), *Harm and Culpability*, Oxford: Clarendon Press (1996).

Hirsch, A. von, 'Harm and Wrongdoing in Criminalisation Theory' (Nov 2012) Criminal Law & Philosophy [online article not assigned to an issue].

Hirsch, A. von, *Past or Future Crimes*, Manchester: Manchester University Press (1985).

Hirsch, A. von and Jareborg, N., 'Gauging Criminal Harms: a Living Standards Analysis' (1991) 11 OJLS 1.

Hirsch, A. von and Simester, A.P. (eds), *Incivilities: Regulating Offensive Behaviour*, Oxford: Hart (2006).

Hirst, M., 'Assault, Battery and Indirect Violence' [1999] Crim LR 577.

Hirst, P.Q., 'The Concept of Punishment' in R.A. Duff and D. Garland (eds), *A Reader on Punishment*, Oxford: OUP (1994).

Hodge, J., 'Alcohol and Violence' in P. Taylor (ed.), *Violence in Society*, London: Royal College of Physicians (1993).

Hodgson, D., 'Law Com. No. 76 – A Case Study in Criminal Law Reform' in P.R. Glazebrook (ed.), *Reshaping the Criminal Law*, London: Stevens (1978).

Hodgson, J. and Tadros, V., 'The Impossibility of Defining Terrorism' (July 2013) New Criminal Law Review.

Hoebel, E., 'The Abandonment Defense to Criminal Attempt and other Problems of Temporal Individuation' 74 Calif LR 377 (1986).

Hogan, B., 'The Criminal Attempts Act and Attempting the Impossible' [1984] Crim LR 584.

Hogan, B., 'The *Dadson* Principle' [1989] Crim LR 679.

Hogan, B., 'The Fourteenth Report of the Criminal Law Revision Committee: (3) Non-Fatal Offences' [1980] Crim LR 542.

Holton, R. and Shute, S., 'Self-control in the Modern Provocation Defence' (2007) 27 OJLS 49.

Home Affairs Committee, *Sexual Offences Bill (5th report of session 2002–03)*, HC 639, London: HMSO (2003).

Home Office, *14/02 Projections of Long-term Trends in the Prison Population to 2009; 11/06 Home Office Statistical Bulletin on Prison Population Projections*. London: Home Office.

Home Office, *A Coordinated Prostitution Strategy*, London: Home Office (2006).

Home Office, *British Crime Survey 2006/07*, London: HORDS (2007).

Home Office, *British Crime Survey 2009/10*, London: HORDS (2010).

Home Office, *Corporate Manslaughter: the Government's Draft Bill for Reform*, Cm 6497, London: Home Office (2005).

Home Office, *Protecting the Public*, Cmnd 3190 (1996).

Home Office, *Rape and Sexual Assault of Women: Findings from the British Crime Survey*, London: HORS (2002).

Home Office, *Reforming the Law on Involuntary Manslaughter: the Government's Proposals*, London: HMSO (2000).

Home Office, *Setting the Boundaries: Reforming the Law on Sex Offences*, vol. 1 (chair Betty Moxon), London: Home Office (2000).

Home Office, *Violence: Reforming the Offences Against the Person Act 1861*, London: Stationery Office (1998).

Home Office Consultation Paper, *Setting the Boundaries Reforming the Law on Sex Offences*, London: Home Office (2000).

Honderich, T., *Punishment: The Supposed Justifications*, Harmondsworth: Penguin (1984).

Honore, A., 'Are Omissions Less Culpable?' in P. Cane and J. Stapleton (eds), *Essays for Patrick Atiyah*, Oxford: Clarendon Press (1991).

Honore, T., 'A Theory of Coercion' (1990) 10 OJLS 94.

Horder, J., 'A Critique of the Correspondence Principle in Criminal Law' [1995] Crim LR 759.

Horder, J., 'Autonomy, Provocation and Duress' [1992] Crim LR 706.

Horder, J., 'Between Provocation and Diminished Responsibility' [1999] 10 Kings College LJ 143.

Horder, J., 'Bribery as a Form of Criminal Wrongdoing' (2011) 127 LQR 37.

Horder, J., 'Crimes of Ulterior Intent' in A. Simester and A. Smith (eds), *Harm and Culpability*, Oxford: Clarendon Press (1996).

Horder, J., 'Criminal Attempt, the Rule of Law, and Accountability in Criminal Law' in L. Zedner and J. Roberts (eds), *Principles and Values in Criminal Law and Criminal Justice: Essays in Honour of Andrew Ashworth*, Oxford: OUP (2012) 37.

Horder, J., 'Criminal Culpability: The Possibility of a General Theory' (1993) 12 Law and Philosophy 193.

Horder, J., 'Diminished Responsibility and Provocation' (1999) Kings College Law Review.

Horder, J., *Excusing Crime*, Oxford: OUP (2004).

Horder, J. (ed.), *Homicide Law in Comparative Perspective*, Oxford: Hart (2007).

Horder, J., 'Intention in the Criminal Law' (1995) 58 MLR 678.

Horder, J., 'Occupying the Moral High Ground: The Law Commission on Duress' [1994] Crim LR 334.

Horder, J., 'On the Irrelevance of Motive in Criminal Law' in J. Horder (ed.), *Oxford Essays in Jurisprudence*, Oxford: OUP (2000).

Horder, J., 'Pleading Involuntary Lack of Capacity' [1993] CLJ 298.

Horder, J., *Provocation and Responsibility*, Oxford: OUP (1992).

Horder, J., 'Questioning the Correspondence Principle – A Reply' [1999] Crim LR 206.

Horder, J., 'Reconsidering Psychic Assault' [1998] Crim LR 392.

Horder, J., 'Reshaping the Subjective Element in Provocation' (2005) OJLS 123.

Horder, J., 'Rethinking Non-Fatal Offences Against the Person' (1994) 14 OJLS 335.

Horder, J., 'Self-defence, Necessity and Duress' (1998) Can J Law and Juris 143.

Horder, J., 'Sex, Violence and Sentencing in Domestic Provocation Cases' [1989] Crim LR 546.

Horder, J., 'Two Histories and Four Hidden Principles of *Mens Rea*' (1997) 113 LQR 95.

Horder, J., 'Transferred Malice and the Remoteness of Unexpected Outcomes' [2006] Crim LR 383.

Horder, J., 'Varieties of Intention, Criminal Attempts and Endangerment' (1994) 14 LS 335.

Horder, J. and McGowan, L., 'Manslaughter by Causing Another's Suicide' [2006] Crim LR 1035.

Hörnle, 'Commentary to "Complicity and Causality"', (2007) 1 Criminal Law and Philosophy 143.

Hörnle, T., 'Criminalizing Behaviour to Protect Human Dignity' (2012) 6(3) Criminal Law & Philosophy 307.

Hornsby, J., 'On What's Intentionally Done' in S. Shute *et al.*, *Action and Value in Criminal Law*, Oxford: Clarendon Press (1993).

Horowitz, M.J., 'The Historical Contingency of the Role of History' (1981) 90 Yale LJ 1057.

Hoskins, Z., 'Fair Play, Political Obligation, and Punishment' (2011) 5(1) Criminal Law & Philosophy 53.

Hough, M. and Mayhew, P., *The British Crime Survey*, HORS No. 76 (1983).

Howard, C., 'Strict Responsibility in the High Court of Australia' (1960) 76 LQR 547.

Howard, C., 'What Colour is the Reasonable Man?' [1961] Crim LR 41.

Howard, J., 'Punishment, Socially Deprived Offenders, and Democratic Community' (2013) 7(1) Criminal Law & Philosophy 121.

Hoyle, C., 'Victims, Victimisation and Restorative Justice' in M. Maguire, R. Morgan and R. Reiner (eds), *The Oxford Handbook of Criminology*, Oxford: OUP (2012) 398.

Hughes, G., 'Criminal Omissions' (1958) 67 Yale LJ 590.

Hughes, G., 'Morals and the Criminal Law' (1962) 71 Yale LJ 662.

Huigens, K., 'Virtue and Criminal Negligence' (1998) Buffalo Criminal Law Review 431.

Husak, D., 'Guns and Drugs: Case Studies on the Principled Limits of the Criminal Sanction' (2004) Law and Philosophy 437.

Husak, D., 'On the Supposed Priority of Justification to Excuse' (2005) Law and Philosophy 24, 557.

Husak, D., *Overcriminalization: The Limits of the Criminal Law*, Oxford: OUP (2007).

Husak, D., 'Rape without Rapists: Consent and Reasonable Mistake' in *The Philosophy of Criminal Law: Selected Essays* (OUP 2010) 233.

Husak, D., 'The Criminal Law as Last Resort' (2004) 24 Oxford Journal of Legal Studies 207–235.

Husak, D., 'The Nature and Justifiability of Non-consummate Offences' (1995) 37 Arizona LR 151.

Husak, D., 'Transferred Intent' (1996) 10 Notre Dame J Law, Ethics and Public Policy.

Husak, D., 'Why Punish Attempts at All? Yaffe on "The Transfer Principle"' (2012) 6(3) Criminal Law & Philosophy 399.

Husak, D., 'Willful Ignorance, Knowledge, and the Equal Culpability Thesis', *The Philosophy of Criminal Law: Selected Essays*, Oxford: OUP (2010).

Hutchinson, A., 'Note on *Sault Ste Marie*' (1979) 17 Osgoode Hall Law Journal 415.

Jackson, B., '*Storkwain*: A Case Study in Strict Liability and Self-regulation' [1991] Crim LR 892.

Jackson, R.M., 'Common Law Misdemeanours' (1937) 6 Camb LJ 193.

Jareborg, N., 'Criminal Attempts and Moral Luck' (1993) 27 Israel LR 213.

Jefferson, M., 'Regulation, Businesses, and Criminal Liability' (2011) 75(1) J Crim L 37.

Johnson, P., 'The Unnecessary Crime of Conspiracy' (1973) 61 Calif L Rev 1137.

Jones, T., 'Causation, Homicide and the Supply of Drugs' (2006) 26 Legal Studies 139–54.

Kadish, S., 'Complicity, Cause and Blame: A Study in the Interpretation of Doctrine' (1984) 73 Calif LR 323.

Kadish, S., 'Excusing Crime' (1987) 75 Cal L Rev 257.

Kadish, S., 'The Decline of Innocence' (1968) 26 CLJ 273.

Kafka, F., 'In the Penal Colony' in *Metamorphosis and other Stories*, Harmondsworth: Penguin (1971).

Kaganas, F., 'Rape in Marriage – Law Reform in Scotland and South Africa' (1990) 4 International Journal of Law and the Family.

Kahan, D., 'Punishment Incommensurability' [1998] Buffalo CLR 691.

Kahan, D., 'What do Alternative Sanctions Mean?' (1996) 63 U Chic LR 591.

Kahan, D., 'What's Really Wrong with Shaming Sanctions' Yale Law School, Public Law Working Paper No. 125.

Kant, I., 'The Metaphysical Elements of Justice', Indianapolis: Bobbs-Merrill (1965).

Katz, L., *Bad Acts and Guilty Minds*, London: University of Chicago Press (1987).

Katz, L., 'Why the Successful Assassin is more Wicked than the Unsuccessful One' (2000) 88 Calif LR 791.

Keating, H., 'Law Commission Report on Involuntary Manslaughter' [1996] Crim LR 535.

Keating, H., 'Reckless Children', [2007] Crim LR 546.

Kell, D., 'Social Disutility and the Law of Consent' (1994) 14 OJLS 121.

Kelman, M., 'Interpretive Construction in the Substantive Criminal Law' (1980–81) 33 Stanford LR 591.

Kennedy, I., *Treat Me Right*, Oxford: Clarendon Press (1988).

Kennefick, L., 'Introducing a New Diminished Responsibility Defence for England and Wales' (2011) 74(5) MLR 750.

Kenny, A., *Freewill and Responsibility*, Oxford: OUP (1978).

Kenny, C.S., *Outlines of the Criminal Law*, Cambridge: CUP (1944, 1962, 1965, 1966).

Keown, J., 'Restoring the Sanctity of Life and Replacing the Caricature: a Reply to David Price' (2006) 26(1) Legal Studies 109–119.

Kershaw, M. *et al.*, *The 2000 British Crime Survey*, HOSB 18/00.

Kirchengast, T., 'Proportionality in Sentencing and the Restorative Justice Paradigm: "Just Deserts" for Victims and Defendants Alike?' (2010) 4(2) Criminal Law & Philosophy 197.

Kirchheimer, O., 'Criminal Omissions' (1942) 55 Harv LR 615.

Kugler, I., *Direct and Oblique Intention in the Criminal Law*, Aldershot: Ashgate (2002).

Lacey, N., 'A Clear Concept of Intention: Elusive or Illusory' (1993) 56 MLR 621.

Lacey, N., 'Beset by Boundaries: The Home Office Review of Sex Offences' [2001] Crim LR 3.

Lacey, N., 'Contingency and Criminalisation' in I. Loveland (ed.), *The Frontiers of Criminality*, London: Sweet & Maxwell (1995).

Lacey, N., 'Partial Defences to Homicide' in A.J. Ashworth and B. Mitchell (eds), *Rethinking English Homicide Law*, Oxford: OUP (2000).

Lacey, N., 'Philosophy, History and Criminal Law Theory' (1998) 1 Buffalo Criminal Law Review 295.

Lacey, N., 'Punishment, (Neo)Liberalism and Social Democracy', in J. Simon and R. Sparks (eds), *The Sage Handbook of Punishment and Society*, London: Sage Publishing (2012) 260–80.

Lacey, N., *State Punishment*, London: Routledge (1988).

Lacey, N., *Unspeakable Subjects*, Oxford: Hart Publishing (1998).

Lacey, N. and Pickard, H., 'From the Consulting Room to the Court Room? Taking the Clinical Model of Responsibility without Blame into the Legal Realm' (2013) 33(1) OJLS 1.

Lacey, N., Wells, C. and Quick, O., *Reconstructing Criminal Law*, Butterworths (2003).

Lacey, N., Wells, C. and Quick, O., *Reconstructing Criminal Law* (4th edn), Cambridge: CUP (2010).

LaFave, W.R. and Scott, A.W., *Criminal Law*, Minnesota: West Publishing (1972).

Lamond, G., 'What is a Crime?' (2007) OJLS 18.

Lamond, G., 'What is a Crime?' (2007) 27 Oxford Journal of Legal Studies 609.

Lanham, D., 'Accomplices and Withdrawal' (1981) 97 LQR 575.

Lanham, D., 'Defence of Property in Criminal Law' [1966] Crim LR 366.

Lanham, D., '*Larsonneur* Revisited' [1976] Crim LR 276.

Larcombe, W., 'Falling Rape Conviction Rates: (Some) Feminist Aims and Measures for Rape Law' (2011) 19 Feminist Legal Studies 27.

Lavery, J., 'Codification of the Criminal Law: an Attainable Ideal?' (2010) 74(6) J Crim L 557.

Law Commission (No. 29), *Criminal Law: Report on Offences of Damage to Property*, London: HMSO (1970).

Law Commission (No. 76), *Conspiracy and Criminal Law Reform*, London: HMSO (1976).

Law Commission (No. 83), *Defences of General Application*, London: HMSO (1977).

Law Commission (No. 102), *Attempt and Impossibility in Relation to Attempt, Conspiracy and Incitement*, London: HMSO (1980).

Law Commission (No. 205), *Rape Within Marriage*, London: HMSO (1992).

Law Commission (No. 218), *Legislating the Criminal Code: Offences Against the Person and General Principles*, London: HMSO (1993).

Law Commission (No. 228), *Conspiracy to Defraud*, London: HMSO (1994).

Law Commission (No. 229), *Legislating the Criminal Code: Intoxication and Criminal Liability*, London: HMSO (1995).

Law Commission (No. 237), *Legislating the Criminal Code: Involuntary Manslaughter*, London: HMSO (1996).

Law Commission (No. 243), *Offences of Dishonesty: Money Transfers*, London: HMSO (1996).

Law Commission (No. 276), *Fraud*, London: TSO (2002).

Law Commission (No. 290), *Partial Defences to Murder*, London: TSO (2004).

Law Commission (No. 300), *Inchoate Liability for Assisting and Encouraging Crime* (2006), London: TSO.

Law Commission (No. 304), *Murder, Manslaughter and Infanticide*, London: TSO (2006).

Law Commission (No. 305), *Participating in Crime*. London: TSO (2007).

Law Commission (No. 318), *Conspiracy and Attempts*, London: HMSO (2009).

Law Commission Consultation Paper (No. 127), *Intoxication and Criminal Liability*, London: HMSO (1993).

Law Commission Consultation Paper (No. 131), *Assisting and Encouraging Crime*, London: HMSO (1993).

Law Commission Consultation Paper (No. 134), *Consent and Offences Against the Person*, London: HMSO (1994).

Law Commission Consultation Paper (No. 135), *Involuntary Manslaughter*, London: HMSO (1994).

Law Commission Consultation Paper (No. 139), *Consent in the Criminal Law*, London: HMSO (1995).

Law Commission Consultation Paper (No. 155), *Fraud and Deception*, London: Stationery Office (1999).

Law Commission Consultation Paper (No. 177), *A Criminal Code for England and Wales*, Vol. 1, London: HMSO (1989).

Law Commission Consultation Paper (No. 183), *Conspiracy and Attempts*, London: TSO (2007).

Law Commission Consultation Paper (No. 193), *Simplification of Criminal Law: Public Nuisance & Outraging Public Decency*, London: TSO (2010).

Law Commission Consultation Paper (No. 195), *Criminal Liability in Regulatory Contexts*, London: TSO (2010).

Law Commission Report, *Consent in Sex Offences*, London: Stationery Office (2000).

Law Commission Report, *Tenth Programme of Law Reform*, London: HMSO (2008).

Law Commission Working Paper (No. 31), *Codification of the Criminal Law: General Principles. The Mental Element in Crime*, London: HMSO (1965).

Law Commission Working Paper (No. 50), *Inchoate Offences: Conspiracy, Attempt and Incitement*, London: HMSO (1973).

Law Commission Working Paper (No. 55), *Defences of General Application* (1974).

Leavens, A., 'A Causation Approach to Criminal Omissions' (1988) 76 Cal LR 547.

Lee, A., 'Public Wrongs and the Criminal Law' (May 2013) Criminal Law & Philosophy [online article not assigned to an issue].

Leigh, L.H., *Strict and Vicarious Liability*, London: Sweet & Maxwell (1982).

Leng, R., 'Consent and Offences Against the Person' [1994] Crim LR 480.

Levanon, L., 'Criminal Prohibitions on Membership in Terrorist Organizations' (2012) 15(2) New Criminal LR 224.

Leverick, F., 'Is English Self-Defence Law incompatible with Article 2 of the EHCR' (2000) Crim LR 347.

Leverick, F., *Killing in Self-Defence*, Oxford: OUP (2007).

Levi, M., *Regulating Fraud: White Collar Crime and the Criminal Process*, London: Tavistock: (1988).

Levi, M., *The Investigation, Prosecution and Trial of Serious Fraud*, Research Study No. 14, London: Royal Commission on Criminal Justice (1993).

Levi, M., 'Violent Crime' in M. Maguire (ed.), *Oxford Handbook of Criminology*, Oxford: OUP (2000).

Levy, N., 'Zimmerman's *The Immorality of Punishment*: A Critical Essay' (March 2013) Criminal Law & Philosophy [online version not yet assigned to issue].

Lewis, P., 'The Human Rights Act 1998: Shifting the burden' [2000] Crim LR 667.

Lippke, R., 'Social Deprivation as Tempting Fate' (2011) 5(3) Criminal Law & Philosophy 277.

Lippke, R., 'The Prosecutor and the Presumption of Innocence' (March 2013) Criminal Law & Philosophy.

Loughnan, A., 'Manifest Madness: Towards a New Understanding of the Insanity Defence' [2007] MLR 379.

Loughnan, A. (ed.), *Manifest Madness: Mental Incapacity in the Criminal Law* (Oxford Monographs on Criminal Law & Justice), Oxford: OUP (2012).

Loveless, J., 'Women, Sentencing and the Drug Offences Definitive Guidelines' [2012] Crim LR 592.

Lucas, J.R., *On Justice*, Oxford: Clarendon Press (1980).

MacCormick, D.N., *Legal Reasoning and Legal Theory*, Oxford: Clarendon Press (1978).

Mackay, R., 'Diminished Responsibility and Mentally Disordered Killers' in A.J. Ashworth and B. Mitchell (eds), *Rethinking English Homicide Law*, Oxford: OUP (2000).

Mackay, R., 'Fact and Fiction about the Insanity Defence' [1990] Crim LR 247.

Mackay, R., *Mental Condition Defences in the Criminal Law*, Oxford: Clarendon Press (1995).

Mackay, R., 'The Consequences of Killing Very Young Children' [1993] Crim LR 21.

Mackay, R., 'The Coroners and Justice Act 2009 – Partial Defences to Murder (2) The New Diminished Responsibility Plea' [2010] Crim LR 290.

Mackay, R. and Kearns, G., 'The Continued Underuse of Unfitness to Plead and the Insanity Defence' [1994] Crim LR 576.

Mackay, R. and Mitchell, B.J., 'Provoking Diminished Responsibility: Two Pleas Merging Into One' [2003] Crim LR 745.

Mackay, R. and Mitchell, B.J., 'Sleepwalking, Automatism and Insanity' [2006] Crim LR 901.

Mackay, R. and Reuber, M., 'Epilepsy and the Defence of Insanity – Time for a Change?' [2007] Crim LR 782.

Mackay, R., Mitchell, B.J. and Howe, L., 'Yet More Facts About the Insanity Defence' [2006] Crim LR 399 at 406.

Mackay, R.D., 'Non Organic Automatism: Some recent developments' [1980] Crim LR350

Mackay, R.D., 'Ten more years of the insanity defence' [2012] Crim LR 946.

Madden Dempsey, M., 'Victimless Conduct and the *Volenti* Maxim: How Consent Works' (2013) 7(1) Criminal Law & Philosophy 11.

Madden Dempsey, M. and Herring, J., 'Why Sexual Penetration requires Justification' (2007) 27 OJLS 467.

Madhloom, L., 'Court of Appeal: Corruption and a Reverse Burden of Proof' (2011) 75(2) J Crim L 96.

Maguire, M., 'Crime Statistics, Patterns and Trends: Changing Perceptions and their Implications' in M. Maguire *et al.* (eds), *Oxford Handbook of Criminology*, Oxford: Clarendon Press (1994).

Maguire, M., 'Crime Statistics, Patterns, and Trends: Changing Perceptions and Their Implications', in *Oxford Handbook of Criminology*, Oxford: OUP (2007).

Maguire, M. and Bennett, T., *Burglary in a Dwelling*, London: Heinemann (1982).

Maguire, M., Morgan, R. and Reiner, R. (eds), *The Oxford Handbook of Criminology* (5th edn), Oxford: OUP (2012).

Maier-Katkin, D. and Ogle, R., 'A Rationale for Infanticide Laws' [1993] Crim LR 903.

Malkani, B., 'Article 8 of the European Convention on Human Rights, and the Decision to Prosecute' [2011] Crim LR 943.

Malkani, B., 'A Rights-specific Approach to Section 2 of the Human Rights Act' (2012) 5 HER LR 516.

Marmor, A. (ed.), *The Routledge Companion to Philosophy of Law*, London: Routledge (2012).

Marshall, S. and Duff, R.A., 'Criminalisation and Sharing Wrongs' (1998) XI Canadian Journal of Law and Jurisprudence 7.

Marston, G., 'Contemporaneity of Act and Intention of Crimes' (1970) 86 LQR 208.

Martinson, R., ' "What Works?" Questions and Answers about Prison Reform' (1974) Public Interest 35.

Matravers, M., 'Political Neutrality and Punishment' (2013) 7(2) Criminal Law & Philosophy 217.

McBain, G., 'Abolishing Obsolete Legislation on Crimes and Criminal Procedure' (2011) 31(1) Legal Studies 96.

McColgan, A., 'In Defence of Battered Women Who Kill' (1993) 13 OJLS 508.

McGee, A., 'Ending the Life of the Act/Omission Dispute: Causation in Withholding and Withdrawing Life-sustaining Measures' (2011) 31(3) Legal Studies 467.

McGlynn, C., 'Rape, Defendant Anonymity and Human Rights: Adopting a "Wider Rerspective" ' [2011] Crim LR 199.

McGlynn, C. and Rackley, E., 'Criminalising Extreme Pornography: a Lost Opportunity' [2009] Crim LR 245.

McGoldrick, D., 'The Limits of Freedom of Expression on Facebook and Social Networking Sites: a UK Perspective' (2013) 13 Human Rights Law Review 125.

McLaughlin, J., 'Proximate Cause' (1921) 39 Harv LR 149.

McLaughlin, J.A., 'Proximate Cause' (1921), 39 Harv LR 149, 160.

Mead, G., 'Contracting into Crime: A Theory of Criminal Omissions' (1991) 11 OJLS 147.

Melissaris, E., 'The Concept of Appropriation and the Offence of Theft' (2007) MLR 581.

Melissaris, E., 'Toward a Political Theory of Criminal Law' (2012) 15(1) New Criminal LR 122.

Meyerson, D., 'Fundamental Contradictions in Critical Legal Studies' [1991] 11 OJLS 439.

Miles, C., 'Intoxication and homicide: a context-specific approach' (2012) 52(5) Brit J Criminol 870–88.

Mill, J.S., 'On Liberty' in J. Gray (ed.), *On Liberty and Other Essays*, Oxford: OUP (1991).

Miller, J., 'Stop and Search in England: a Reformed Tactic or Business as Usual?' (2010) 50(5) Brit J Criminol 954.

Milsom, F., *The Historical Foundations of the Common Law*, London: Butterworths (1968).

Mirfield, P., 'Guilt by Association: A Reply to Professor Virgo' [2013] Crim LR 577.

Mirrlees-Black, C. *et al.*, *The 1996 British Crime Survey*, HORS 19/96 (1996).

Mitchell, B., 'A Report on a Public Survey of Murder and Mandatory Sentencing in Criminal Homicides, in Law Commission, Consultation Paper No. 177, A New Homicide Act for England and Wales?' (2005) London: TSO, Appx A.

Mitchell, B., 'Distinguishing between Murder and Manslaughter' [1991] NLJ 935–7.

Mitchell, B., 'In Defence of a Principle of Correspondence' [1999] Crim LR 195.

Mitchell, B., 'Minding the Gap in Unlawful and Dangerous Act Manslaughter: A Moral Defence of One-punch Killers' (2008) 72 Journal of Criminal Law 537–547.

Mitchell, B., 'Public Perceptions of Homicide and Criminal Justice' (1998) 38 BJ Crim 453.

Mitchell, B., 'Years of Provocation, Followed by a Loss of Control' in L. Zedner and J. Roberts (eds), *Principles and Values in Criminal Law and Criminal Justice: Essays in Honour of Andrew Ashworth*, Oxford: OUP (2012) 113.

Mitchell, B. and Roberts, J., *Exploring the Mandatory Life Sentence for Murder*, Oxford: Hart Publishing (2012).

Mitchell, J., 'Crimes of Misery and Theories of Punishment' (2012) 15(4) New Criminal LR 465.

Montgomery, C. and Ormerod, D., *Fraud: Criminal Law and Procedure*, Oxford: OUP (2008).

Moore, M., *Act and Crime*, Oxford: Clarendon Press (1993).

Moore, M., 'Causation and Excuses' (1985) 73 Cal LR 1091.

Moore, M., *Causation and Responsibility: An Essay in Law, Morals and Metaphysics*, Oxford: OUP (2010). Moore, M., 'Four Friendly Critics: A Response' (2012) 18(4) LT 491.

Moore, M., 'Foreseeing Harm Opaquely' in S. Shute, J. Gardner, J. Horder (eds), *Action and Value in the Criminal Law*, Oxford: Clarendon Press (1993).

Moore, M., *Placing Blame: A Theory of the Criminal Law*, Oxford: OUP (2010).

Moran, L.J., 'Affairs of the Heart: Hate Crime and the Politics of Crime Control', 12 Law and Critique (2001), 331–344.

Morris, H., 'Persons and Punishment' (1968) 52 The Monist 475.

Morris, T. and Blom Cooper, L., *A Calendar of Murder*, London: Michael Joseph (1964).

Morse, S.J., 'Diminished Capacity' in S. Shute, J. Gardner, J. Horder (eds), *Action and Value in the Criminal Law*, Oxford: Clarendon Press (1993).

Morse, S., 'The Moral Metaphysics of Causation and Results' (2000) 88 Calif LR 879.

Moxon, D., *Sentencing Practice in the Crown Court*, HORS No. 103, London: HMSO (1988).

Mullender, R., 'Involuntary Medical Treatment, Incapacity, and Respect' (2011) 127 LQR 167.

Munday, R., 'Handling the Evidential Exception' [1988] Crim LR 345.

Murphy, C., 'The Principle of Legality in Criminal Law under the European Convention on Human Rights' (2010) 2 EHRL 192.

Murphy, J.G., 'Marxism and Retribution', in R.A. Duff and D. Garland (eds), *A Reader on Punishment*, Oxford: OUP (1994).

Murtagh, K., 'What is Inhuman Treatment?' (2012) 6(1) Criminal Law & Philosophy 21.

Naffine, N., *Law and the Sexes*, Sydney: Allen and Unwin (1990).

Newdick, R., 'Rights to NHS Resources after the 1990 Act' [1993] Med LR 53.

Newman, C. and Rackow, P., 'Undesirable Posters and Dubious Symbols: Anglo-German Legal Solutions to the Display of Right-wing Symbolism and Propaganda' (2011) 75(2) J Crim L 142.

Nicholas, S., Kershaw, C. and Walker, A., *Crime in England and Wales 2006/2007*. London: Home Office.

Nicholson, D. and Sanghvi, R., 'Battered Women and Provocation: The Implications of *R v Ahluwalia*' [1993] Crim LR 728.

Norrie, A., 'A Critique of Criminal Causation' (1991) 54 MLR 685.

Norrie, A., *Crime, Reason and History*, London: Weidenfeld and Nicolson (1993).

Norrie, A., 'Free Will, Determinism and Criminal Justice' (1983) LS 60.

Norrie, A., 'Intention: More Loose Talk' [1990] Crim LR 642.

Norrie, A., 'Oblique Intention and Legal Politics' [1989] Crim LR 793.

Norrie, A., *Punishment, Responsibility and Justice*, Oxford: Clarendon Press (2001).

Norrie, A., 'Simulacra of Morality' in R.A. Duff (ed.), *Philosophy and the Criminal Law*, Cambridge: CUP (1998).

Norrie, A., 'Subjectivism, Objectivism and the Limits of Criminal Liability' (1992) 12 OJLS 45.

Office for National Statistics, *Crime in England & Wales Year Ending March 2013*, London: TSO.

Ogus, A., 'The Paradoxes of Legal Paternalism and How to Resolve Them' (2010) 30(1) Legal Studies 61.

Ohana, D., 'Desert and Punishment for Acts Preparatory to the Commission of a Crime' (2007) 20(1) Canadian Journal of Law and Jurisprudence.

Ohana, D., 'Responding to Acts Preparatory to the Commission of a Crime' (2006) 25 Criminal Justice Ethics 23.

Ormerod, D.C., 'A Bit of a Con: The Law Commission's Consultation Paper on Fraud' [1999] Crim LR 789.

Ormerod, D.C., 'Causation: Causing Death by Driving when Unlicensed, Disqualified or Uninsured – Construction of "Cause"' [2011] Crim LR 471 (case comment).

Ormerod, D.C., Commentary on *Dhaliwal*, (2006) Crim LR 925.

Ormerod, D.C., 'Joint Enterprise: *R v Stringer* – Murder – Aider and Abettor' (case comment) [2011] Crim LR 887.

Ormerod, D.C., 'Making Sense of *Mens Rea* in Criminal Conspiracies' (2006) CLP 185, 221–226.

Ormerod, D.C., *Smith & Hogan Criminal Law*, Oxford: OUP (2005).

Ormerod, D.C., *Smith & Hogan Criminal Law*, Oxford: OUP (2008).

Ormerod, D.C., 'Summary Evasion of Income Tax' [2002] Crim LR 3.

Ormerod, D.C., 'The Fraud Act 2006: Criminalising Lying' [2007] Crim LR 193.

Ormerod, D.C. and Fortson, R., 'Serious Crime Act 2007: The Part 2 Offences' [2009] Crim LR 389.

Ormerod, D.C. and Gunn, M.J., 'The Legality of Boxing' (1995) 15 LS 181.

Ormerod, D.C. and Gunn, M.J., 'The Second Law Commission Paper on Consent: Consent – A Second Bash' [1996] Crim LR 694.

Ormerod, D.C. and Williams, D., *Smith's Law of Theft*, Oxford: OUP (2007).

Ost, S., 'Criminalising Fabricated Images of Child Pornography: A Matter of Harm or Morality?' (2010) 30(2) Legal Studies 230.

Packer, H.L., *The Limits of the Criminal Sanction*, London: OUP (1969).

Padfield, N., 'Clear Water and Muddy Causation: Is Causation a Question of Law or Fact, or Just a Way of Allocating Blame?' [1995] Crim LR 683.

Padfield, N., 'Out of Court (Out of Sight) Disposals' (2010) 69 Cambridge Law Journal, 6–8.

Padfield, N., 'Tariffs in Murder Cases' [2002] Crim LR 192.

Painter, K., Wife *Rape, Marriage and the Law: Survey Report*, Manchester: Manchester University Press (1991).

Palmer, H., 'Dr Adams' Trial for Murder' (1957) Crim LR 365.

Parish, S., 'Self Defence: The Wrong Direction' [1997] Crim LR 201.

Paterson, A., *The Law Lords*, London: Macmillan (1982).

Paton, H.J., *The Moral Law: Kant's Groundwork of the Metaphysic of Morals*, London: Hutchinson (1948).

Penner, J., *The Idea of Property in Law*, Oxford: OUP (1996).

Perkins, R.M. and Boyce, R.N., *Criminal Law*, New York: Foundation Press (1982).

Perlmutter, M., 'Punishment and Desert' in J. Arthur (ed.), *Morality and Moral Controversies*, New Jersey: Prentice Hall (1981).

Phillips, C. and Bowling, B., 'Ethnicities, Racisim, Crime and Criminal Justice,' in M. Maguire, R. Morgan and R. Reiner (eds), *The Oxford Handbook of Criminology* (5th edn), Oxford: OUP (2012) 370.

Picton, M., 'The Effect of the Changes in Sentencing of Dangerous Offenders Brought About by the Legal Aid, Sentencing and Punishment of Offenders Act 2012 and the Mystery of Schedule 15B' [2013] Crim LR 406.

Pinto, M., 'What are Offences to Feelings Really About? A New Regulative Principle for the Multicultural Era' (2010) 30(4) OJLS 695.

Plamenatz, J., 'Responsibility, Blame and Punishment' in P. Laslett and W.G. Runciman (eds), *Philosophy, Politics and Society*, Oxford: Blackwell, 3rd series (1989).

Povey, D. *et al.*, *British Crime Survey* (2001) HOSB 19/01.

Povey, D. *et al.*, *Notifiable Offences July 1996 to June 1997*, HORS (1997).

Power, H., 'Provocation and Culture' [2006] Crim LR 871.

Price, D., 'Fairly Bland: An Alternative View' (2001) LS 618.

Price, D., 'My View of the Sanctity of Life: A Rebuttal of John Keown's critique' (2007) LS 549.

Price, D., 'What Shape to Euthanasia after Bland?' [2009] LQR 142.

Quick, O. and Wells, C., 'Getting Tough with Defences', [2006] CLR 514–525.

Quick, O.L., 'Prosecuting "Gross" Medical Negligence: Manslaughter, Discretion, and the Crown Prosecution Service' (2006) 33(3) Journal of Law and Society 421–450.

R. Leng, *Consent and Offences Against the Person*' (1994) Crim LR 430.

Rachels, J., 'Active and Passive Euthanasia' in J. Arthur (ed.), *Morality and Moral Controversies*, New Jersey: Prentice-Hall (1986).

Rackley, E. and McGlynn, C., 'Prosecuting the possession of Extreme Pornography: A Misunderstood and Mis-used Law' [2013] Crim LR 400.

Radin, M., 'Cruel Punishment and Respect for Persons: Super Due Process for Death' 53 S Cal L Rev 1143.

Ramage, S., *The Serious Fraud Office Fraud Law* (2005).

Raz, J., *From Normativity to Responsibility*, Oxford: OUP (2011).

Raz, J., *The Morality of Freedom*, Oxford: Clarendon Press (1986).

Reed, A., 'Conspiracy to Defraud: The Threshold Standardisation' (2012) 76(5) Journal of Criminal Law 373.

Reed, A., 'Joint Enterprise and Inculpation for Manslaughter' [2010] J Crim L 200.

Reed, A. and Bohlander, M. (eds), *Loss of Control and Diminished Responsibility: Domestic, International and International Perspectives*, Farnham: Ashgate (2011).

Reeves, A., 'Judicial Practical Reason: Judges in Morally Imperfect Legal Orders' (2011) 30(3) Law & Philosophy 319.

Reuter, P. and Steven, A., *An Analysis of UK Drug Policy*, London: UK Drug Policy Commission (2007).

Rice Lave, T., 'Controlling Sexually Violent Predators: Continued Incarceration at What Cost?' (2011) 14(2) New Criminal LR 213.

Richardson, J., 'Is the Criminal Appeal System Fit for Purpose? A Reflection to Mark the 750th Issue of Criminal Law Week 1997–2013'.

Roberts, J. (ed.), *Mitigation and Aggravation in Sentencing*, Cambridge: CUP (2011).

Roberts, P., 'The Philosophical Foundations of Consent in the Criminal Law' (1997) 17 OJLS 389.

Robinson, P.H., 'Causing the Conditions of One's Own Defence' (1985) 71 Virginia Law Review 1.

Robinson, P.H., *Criminal Law Defenses*, Minnesota: West Publishing (1984).

Robinson, P.H., 'Criminal Law Defences: A Systematic Analysis' (1982) 82 Col L Rev 199.

Robinson, P.H., 'Hybrid Principles for the Distribution of Criminal Sanctions' (1987) 82 Northwestern University Law Review.

Robinson, P.H., 'Rules of Conduct and Principles of Adjudication' (1990) 57 Univ of Chicago LR 729.

Robinson, P.H., 'Should the Criminal Law Abandon the *Actus Reus–Mens Rea* Distinction?' in S. Shute, J. Gardner, J. Horder (eds), *Action and Value in Criminal Law*, Oxford: Clarendon Press (1993).

Robinson, P.H., *Structure and Function in Criminal Law*, Oxford: Clarendon Press (1997).

Robinson, P.H. and Darley, J.M., 'Objectivist Versus Subjectivist View of Criminality: A Study in the Role of Social Science in Criminal Law Theory' (1998) 18 OJLS 409.

Robinson, P.H. and Dubber, M., 'The American Model Penal Code' (2007) New Crim LR 319–41.

Roebuck, G. and Wood, D., 'A Retributive Argument against Punishment' (2011) 5(1) Criminal Law & Philosophy 73.

Rogers, A., 'Sexual Offences: Consent: See "Purpose" of Defendant' (2008) 72 Journal of Criminal Law 280.

Rogers, J., 'A Criminal Lawyer's Response to Chastisement' [2002] Crim LR 98.

Rogers, J., 'Justifying the Use of Firearms by Policemen and Soldiers: a Response to the Home Office's Review of the Law on the Use of Lethal Force' (1998) 18 Legal Studies 486.

Rogers, J., 'The Law Commission's Proposed Restructuring of Homicide' (2006) 70(3) Journal of Criminal Law.

Rook, P. and Ward, R., *Rook and Ward on Sexual Offences: Law and Practice* (4th edn), London: Sweet & Maxwell (2010).

Rosebury, B., 'Moore's Moral Facts and the Gap in the Retributive Theory' (2011) 5(3) Criminal Law & Philosophy 361.

Rumney, P. and R. Fenton, R., 'Intoxicated Consent in Rape: *Bree* and Juror Decision-making' (2008) 71(2) MLR 279–90.

Rumney, P.N.S. and Fenton, R.A., 'Judicial Training and Rape' (2011) 75(6) J Crim L 473.

Russell, Sir W.O., *Crime*, London: Stevens (1965).

Ryan, S., 'Reckless Transmission of HIV' [2006] Crim LR 981.

Sacks, O., *The Man Who Mistook his Wife for a Hat*, London: Picador (1986).

Sadurski, W., 'Distributive Justice and the Theory of Punishment' (1985) OJLS 47.

Sales, P. and Ekins, R., 'Rights-consistent Interpretation and the Human Rights Act 1998' (2011) 127 LQR 217.

Salmond, J., *Jurisprudence* (7th edn), London: Stevens (1924).

Sanders, A., 'Class Bias in Prosecutions' (1985) 24 Howard JCJ 176.

Sanders, A., 'The Limits of Diversion from Prosecution' (1988) 28(4) B J Crim 513.

Sartorio, C., 'Two Wrongs Do Not Make a Right: Responsibility and Overdetermination' (2012) 18(4) LT 473.

Sayre, F., 'Public Welfare Offences' (1933) 33 Col LR 55.

Schaffer, J., 'Disconnection and Responsibility' (2012) 18(4) Legal Theory 399.

Schopp, R.F., *Justification Defenses and Just Convictions*, Cambridge: CUP (1998).

Schulhofer, S., 'Harm and Punishment: A Critique of Emphasis on the Results of Conduct in the Criminal Law' (1974) 122 University of Pennsylvania LR 1497.

Shapiro, S., *Legality*, Harvard University Press (2010).

Shapland, J., Atkinson, A. *et al.*, *Does Restorative Justice Affect Reconviction?* London: Ministry of Justice Research Series 10/08 (2008).

Shepherd, J.D., 'A Human Right not to be Punished? Punishment as Derogation of Rights' (2012) 6(1) Criminal Law & Philosophy 31.

Shute, S., 'Appropriation and the Law of Theft' [2002] Crim LR 445.

Shute, S., 'Knowledge and Belief in the Criminal Law' in S. Shute and A. Simester (eds), *Criminal Law Theory: Doctrines of the General Part*, Oxford: OUP (2002).

Shute, S., 'The Second Law Commission Consultation Paper on Consent: Something Old, Something New, Something Borrowed: Three Aspects of the Project' [1996] Crim LR 684.

Shute, S. and Gardner, J., 'The Wrongness of Rape' in J. Horder (ed.), *Oxford Essays in Jurisprudence,* Oxford: OUP (2000).

Shute, S. and Horder, J., 'Thieving and Deceiving? What is the Difference?' (1993) 56 MLR 548.

Shute, S. and Simester, A.P. (eds), *Criminal Law Theory: Doctrines of the General Part*, Oxford: OUP (2002).

Shute, S., Gardner, J. and Horder, J. (eds), *Action and Value in the Criminal Law*, Oxford: Clarendon Press (1993).

Simester, A., 'Can Negligence be Culpable?' in J. Horder (ed.), *Oxford Essays in Jurisprudence*, Oxford: OUP (2000).

Simester, A., 'Intoxication is never a defence' [2009] Crim LR 3.

Simester, A., 'Mistakes in Defences' (1992) 12 OJLS 295.

Simester, A., 'On Justifications and Excuses' In L. Zedner and J. Roberts (eds), *Principles and Values in Criminal Law and Criminal Justice: Essays in Honour of Andrew Ashworth*, Oxford: OUP (2012) 95.

Simester, A., 'On the So-called Requirement for Voluntary Action' (1998) Buffalo Criminal Law Review 403.

Simester, A. and Chan, W., 'Intention Thus Far' [1997] Crim LR 704.

Simester, A.P. (ed.), *Appraising Strict Liability*, Oxford: OUP (2006).

Simester, A.P., 'The Mental Element in Complicity' (2006) 122 LQR 578.

Simester, A.P. and Sullivan, G.R., *Criminal Law: Theory and Doctrine*, Oxford: Hart (2007).

Simester, A.P. and Von Hirsch, A., *Crimes, Harms and Wrongs: On the Principles of Criminalisation*, Oxford: Hart Publishing (2011).

Simmons, J. *et al.*, *Crime in England and Wales 2001/2*, HOSB (2002).

Simons, K., 'Criminal Law: When is Strict Liability Just?' (1997) 87 Journal of Criminal Law & Criminology 1075.

Simons, K.W., 'Is Strict Criminal Liability in the Grading of Offences Consistent with Retributive Desert?' (2012) 32(3) OJLS 445.

Singer, P., *Rethinking Life and Death*, Oxford: OUP (1995).

Slapper, G., 'Opinion: The Desirable Dozen' (2012) 76 J Crim L 99.

Slapper, G., 'Moral Voices and Market Forces' (2012) 76(5) J Crim L 359.

Smart, A., 'Criminal Responsibility for Failing to do the Impossible' (1987) 103 LQR 532.

Smart, C., 'The Woman of Legal Discourse' (1992) 1 Social and Legal Studies 29.

Smith, A.T.H., 'Can Proscribed Drugs be the Subject of Theft?' (2011) 70(2) CLJ 289 (case comment).

Smith, A.T.H., 'Judicial Law-Making in the Criminal Law' (1984) 100 LQR 46.

Smith, A.T.H., 'Legislating the Criminal Code: the Law Commission's Proposals' [1992] Crim LR 396.

Smith, A.T.H., 'On *Actus Reus* and *Mens Rea*' in P.R. Glazebrook (ed.), *Reshaping the Criminal Law*, London: Stevens (1978).

Smith, A.T.H., *Property Offences*, London: Sweet & Maxwell (1994).

Smith, A.T.H., 'The Idea of Criminal Deception' [1982] Crim LR 721.

Smith, J.C., 'Aid, Abet, Counsel or Procure' in P.R. Glazebrook (ed.), *Reshaping the Criminal Law*, London: Stevens (1978).

Smith, J.C., 'Criminal Liability of Accessories: Law and Law Reform' [1997] 113 LQR 453.

Smith, J.C., 'Intoxication and the Mental Element in Crime' in P. Wallington and R. Merkin (eds), *Essays in Memory of Professor Lawson*, London: Butterworths (1986).

Smith, J.C., *Justification and Excuse in the Criminal Law*, London: Stevens (1989).

Smith, J.C., 'Liability for Omissions in Criminal Law' (1984) 4 Legal Studies 88.

Smith, J.C., 'Obtaining Cheques by Deception or Theft' [1997] Crim LR 396.

Smith, J.C., 'Secondary Participation and Inchoate Offences' in C. Tapper (ed.), *Crime, Proof and Punishment*, London: Butterworths (1981).

Smith, J.C., 'Stealing Tickets' [1998] Crim LR 723.

Smith, J.C., *The Law of Theft*, London: Butterworths (1997).

Smith, J.C., *The Law of Theft*, London: Butterworths (1999).

Smith, J.C., 'Two Problems in Criminal Attempts Re-Examined' [1962] Crim LR 135.

Smith, J.C. and Hogan, B., *Criminal Law*, London: Butterworths (1996).

Smith, J.C. and Hogan, B., *Smith and Hogan Criminal Law*, London: Butterworths Tolley (2002); 11th edn, Ormerod (ed.) (2005).

Smith, K.J.M., *A Modern Treatise on the Law of Criminal Complicity*, Oxford: Clarendon Press (1991).

Smith, K.J.M., 'Duress and Steadfastness' [1999] Crim LR 363.

Smith, K.J.M., 'Must Heroes Behave Heroically?' [1989] Crim LR 622.

Smith, K.J.M., 'Proximity in Attempt: Lord Lane's Midway Course' [1991] Crim LR 576.

Smith, K.J.M., 'Sexual Etiquette, Public Interest and the Criminal Law' (1991) 42 NILQ 309.

Smith, K.J.M., 'The Law Commission Consultation Paper on Complicity: (1) A Blueprint for Rationalism' [1994] Crim LR 239.

Smith, K.J.M., 'Withdrawal in Complicity' [2001] Crim LR 769.

Smith, K.J.M. and Wilson, W., 'Impaired Voluntariness and Criminal Responsibility' (1993) 13 OJLS 69.

Smith, L., *Domestic Violence: An Overview of the Literature*, Home Office Research and Statistics Department, No. 107, London: HMSO (1989).

Smith, N., 'Against Court-Ordered Apologies' (2013) 16 New Criminal LR 1.

Smith, P., 'Legal Liability and Criminal Omissions' (2002) Buffalo Crim LR 69.

Søbirk Petersen, T., 'New Legal Moralism: Some Strengths and Challenges' (2010) 4(2) Criminal Law & Philosophy 215.

Spencer, J.R., 'Conspiracy and Recklessness' [2005] CLJ 279.

Spencer, J.R., 'Handling, Theft and the *Mala Fide* Purchaser' [1985] Crim LR 92.

Spencer, J.R., 'Legislate in Haste, Repent at Leisure' [2010] Camb LJ 19.

Spencer, J.R., 'Liability for Reckless Infection' (2004) NLJ 471.

Spencer, J.R., 'Motor Vehicles as Weapons of Offence' [1985] Crim LR 29.

Spencer, J.R., 'The Metamorphosis of section 6 of the Theft Act' [1977] Crim LR 653.

Spencer, J.R., 'The Sexual Offences Act 2003: Child and Family Offences' [2004] Crim LR 347.

Spencer, J.R., 'The Theft Act 1978' [1979] Crim LR 24.

Stallybrass, W.T.S., 'Public Mischief' (1933) 49 LQR 183.

Stanko, E., 'Hidden Violence against Women' in M. Maguire and J. Pointing (eds), *Victims of Crime: A New Deal?*, Milton Keynes: Open University Press (1988).

Stannard, J.S., 'Retaliation, Catharsis and the Criminal Process' (2001) NILQ 162.

Stanton-Ife, J., 'Strict Liability: Stigma and Regret' (2007) 27 OJLS 151.

Stark, F., 'It's Only Words: On Meaning and *Mens Rea*' (2013) 72 CLJ 155.

Stephen, J.F., *A Digest of the Criminal Law*, London: Macmillan (1894).

Stephen, J.F., *History of the Criminal Law of England*, London: Macmillan (1883).

Steven, P. and Steven, A., *An Analysis of UK Drug Policy: A Monograph Prepared for the UK Drug Policy Commission* (2007).

Stevenson, K. and Harris, C., 'Breaking the Thrall of Ambiguity: Simplification (of the Criminal Law) as an Emerging Human Rights Imperative' (2010) 74(6) J. Crim. L 516.

Stone, R., 'Reckless Assaults after *Savage* and *Parmenter*' (1992) 12 OJLS 578.

Stuart, D., '*Mens Rea*, Negligence and Attempts' [1968] Crim LR 647.

Stumer, A., *The Presumption of Innocence*, Oxford: Hart (2010).

Sullivan, G.R., 'Cause and Contemporaneity of *Actus Reus* and *Mens Rea*' (1993) Camb LJ 487.

Sullivan, G.R., 'First Degree Murder and Complicity' (2007) 1 Crim Law & Phil 271.

Sullivan, G.R., 'Fraud and the Efficacy of the Criminal Law: A Proposal for a Wide Residual Offence' [1985] Crim LR 616.

Sullivan, G.R., 'Inchoate Liability for Assisting and Encouraging Crime' [2006] Crim LR 1047.

Sullivan, G.R., 'Intent, Purpose and Complicity' [1988] Crim LR 641.

Sullivan, G.R., 'Intent, Subjective Recklessness and Culpability' (1992) OJLS 380.

Sullivan, G.R., 'Intoxicants and Diminished Responsibility' [1994] Crim LR 156.

Sullivan, G.R., 'Involuntary Intoxication and Beyond' [1994] Crim LR 272.

Sullivan, G.R., 'Knowledge, Belief and Culpability' in S. Shute and A. Simester (eds), *Criminal Law Theory: Doctrines of the General Part*, Oxford: OUP (2002).

Sullivan, G.R., 'Making Excuses' in A.P. Simester and A.T.H. Smith (eds), *Harm and Culpability*, Oxford: Clarendon Press (1996).

Sullivan, G.R., 'Ministering Death', (1997) 17(1) OJLS 123–136.

Sullivan, G.R., 'Participating in Crime: Law Com No. 305' (2008) Crim LR 19.

Sullivan, G.R., 'Strict Liability for Criminal Offences in England and Wales Following Incorporation into English Law of the ECHR', in A.P. Simester (ed.), *Appraising Strict Liability*, Oxford: OUP (2006).

Sullivan, G.R., 'The Attribution of Culpability to Limited Companies' [1996] Camb LJ 515.

Sullivan, G.R., 'The Law Commission Consultation Paper' [1994] Crim LR 252, 253.

Sullivan, G.R. and Warbrick, C., 'Territoriality, Theft and *Atakpu*' [1994] Crim LR 650.

Sutherland, P. and Gearty, C., 'Insanity and the European Court of Human Rights' [1992] Crim LR 418.

Sverdlik, S., 'Punishment and Reform' (April 2013) Criminal Law & Philosophy [online version not yet assigned to an issue].

Syrota, G., 'A Radical Change in the Law of Recklessness' [1982] Crim LR 97.

Syrota, G., 'Are Cheque Frauds Covered by Section 3 of the Theft Act 1978?' [1980] Crim LR 412.

Tadros, V., *Criminal Responsibility*, Oxford: OUP (2005).

Tadros, V., 'Criminalization and Regulation' in R. Duff, L. Farmer, S. Marshall, M. Renzo and V. Tadros (eds), *The Boundaries of the Criminal Law*, Oxford: OUP (2010) 163.

Tadros, V., 'Fair Labelling and Social Solidarity' in L. Zedner and J.V. Roberts (eds), *Principles and Values in Criminal Law and Criminal Justice: Essays in Honour of Andrew Ashworth*, Oxford: OUP (2012) 67.

Tadros, V., 'Harm, Sovereignty, and Prohibition' (2011) 17 Legal Theory 35.

Tadros, V., 'Rape Without Consent' 26 OJLS 515, 534.

Tadros, V., 'Recklessness and the Duty to Take Care' in Shute and Simester (eds), *Criminal Law Theory: Doctrines of the General Part*, Oxford: OUP, 2002, 254–257.

Tadros, V., 'The Characters of Excuse' (2001) 21 Oxford J Legal Stud, 495–519 at 517.

Tadros, V., 'The Distinctiveness of Domestic Abuse' in R.A. Duff and S. Green (eds), *Defining Crimes: Essays on the Special Part of the Criminal Law*, Oxford: OUP (2005) 119 at 136.

Tadros, V., *The Ends of Harm: The Moral Foundations of Criminal Law*, Oxford: OUP (2011).

Tadros, V., 'The homicide ladder' (2006) MLR 601, 604.

Tadros, V. and Tierney, S., 'The Presumption of Innocence and the Human Rights Act' (2004) 67 Modern Law Review 402–434.

Taylor, R., 'Procuring, Causation, Innocent Agency and the Law Commission' (2008) Crim LR 32.

Taylor, R., 'The Nature of "Partial Defences" and the Coherence of (Second-Degree) Murder' [2007] Crim LR 345.

Taylor, R.D., 'Complicity and Excuses' [1983] Crim LR 656.

Temkin, J., *Rape and the Legal Process*, London: Sweet & Maxwell (1987).

Temkin, J. and Ashworth, A., 'Rape, Sexual Assault and the Problems of Consent' [2004] Crim LR 328–34.

Thomas, C., 'Are Juries Fair?' (2010) Ministry of Justice Research Series 1/10 February 2010.

Thomas, D., 'R v *Jenkin*: Sentencing – Mentally Disordered Offender – Choice between Hospital Order and Life Imprisonment' (case comment) [2013] Crim LR 246.

Thomas, D.A., 'Form and Function in Criminal Law' in P.R. Glazebrook (ed.), *Reshaping the Criminal Law*, London: Stevens (1978).

Thomas, D.A., 'The Legal Aid, Sentencing and Punishment of Offenders Act 2012: The Sentencing Provisions' [2012] Crim LR 572.

Thompson, E.P., *Whigs and Hunters: The Origin of the Black Acts*, London: Allen Lane (1975).

Thomson, J., 'A Defense of Abortion' (1971) I Phil and Pub Aff 47.

Tolmie, J., 'Consent to Harmful Assaults: The Case for Moving Away from Category-based Decision Making' [2012] Crim LR 656.

Tur, R., 'Dishonesty and the Jury' in A. Phillips Griffiths (ed.), *Philosophy and Practice* (1985).

Tur, R., 'Subjectivism and Objectivism: Towards Synthesis' in S. Shute, J. Gardner, J. Horder (eds), *Action and Value in Criminal Law*, Oxford: Clarendon Press (1993).

Uniacke, S., *Permissible Killing: The Self-Defence Justification of Homicide*, Cambridge: CUP (1994).

Uniacke, S., 'Punishment as Penalty' (March 2013) Criminal Law & Philosophy [online version not yet assigned to issue].

Victim Support, *Annual Report* (1994).

Victim Support, *Annual Report 2006*, London: Victim Support.

Virgo, G., 'Joint Enterprise Liability is Dead: Long Live Accessorial Liability' [2012] Crim LR 850.

Virgo, G., 'The Law Commission Consultation Paper on Intoxication and Criminal Liability' [1993] Crim LR 415.

Waldron, J., 'How Law Protects Dignity' (2012) 71(1) CLJ 200.

Walker, N., *Crime and Insanity in England, Vol. 1 The Historical Perspective*, Edinburgh: Edinburgh University Press (1968).

Wallerstein, S., ' "A drunken consent is still consent" – or is it? A Critical Analysis of the Law on a Drunken Consent to Sex following *Bree*' (2009) 73 JCL 318.

Walmsley, R., *Personal Violence*, Home Office Research and Planning Unit Report No. 89, London: HMSO (1986).

Ward, T., 'Magistrates, Insanity and the Common Law' [1997] Crim LR 796.

Wardhaugh, B., 'A Normative Approach to the Criminalisation of Cartel Activity' (2012) 32(3) Legal Studies 369.

Wasik, M., 'A Learner's Careless Driving' [1982] Crim LR 411.

Wasik, M., 'Abandoning Criminal Intent' [1980] Crim LR 785.

Wasik, M., 'Cumulative Provocation and Domestic Killing' [1982] Crim LR 29.

Wasik, M., 'Duress and Criminal Responsibility' [1977] Crim LR 453.

Wasik, M., 'Legislating in the Shadow of the Human Rights Act: The Criminal Justice and Police Act 2001' [2001] Crim LR 931.

Wasik, M., 'Sentencing in Homicide' in A.J. Ashworth and B. Mitchell (eds), *Rethinking English Homicide Law*, Oxford: OUP (2000).

Wasik, M. and Thompson, M.P., ' "Turning a Blind Eye" as Constituting *Mens Rea*' (1981) 32 NILQ 328.

Weait, M., 'Criminal Law and the Sexual Transmission of HIV' (2005) MLR 121.

Weait, M., 'Knowledge, Autonomy and Consent' [2005] Crim LR 763.

Weber, M., *On Law in Economy and Society*, Cambridge: Harvard University Press (1954).

Weinrib, L., 'Information and Property' (1988) 38 UTLJ 117.

Weller, M., 'Post Traumatic Stress Disorder' (1993) NLJ 878.

Wells, C., 'A Quiet Revolution in Corporate Liability for Crime' (1995) NLJ 1326.

Wells, C., 'Battered Woman Syndrome and Defences to Homicide: Where Now?' (1994) 14 LS 266.

Wells, C., *Corporations and Criminal Liability* (2nd edn), Oxford: OUP (2001).

Wells, C., *Corporations and Criminal Responsibility*, Oxford: OUP (2003).

Wells, C., 'Law Commission on Involuntary Manslaughter' [1996] Crim LR 545.

Wells, C., 'Provocation: the Case for Abolition' in A.J. Ashworth and B. Mitchell (eds), *Rethinking English Homicide Law*, Oxford: OUP (2000).

Wells, C., 'Stalking: The Criminal Law Response' [1997] Crim LR 463.

Wells, C., 'Swatting the Subjectivist Bug' [1982] Crim LR 209.

Wells, C. and Levi, M., *Corporations and Criminal Responsibility*, Oxford: OUP (2003).

Wertheimer, A., *Coercion*, Princeton: Princeton University Press (1987).

Westen, P., 'An Attitudinal Theory of Excuse', (2006) Law & Philosophy 28.

Westen, P., 'Why Criminal Harms Matter: Plato's abiding insight in the Laws' (2007) Crim Law and Philos 307.

White, A.R., *Misleading Cases*, Oxford: Clarendon Press (1991).

White, M., *Retributivism: Essays on Theory and Policy*, New York: OUP (2011).

White, R.M., ' "Civil penalties": Oxymoron, Chimera and Stealth Sanction' (2010) 126 LQR 593.

Wilczynski, A. and Morris, A., 'Parents Who Kill Their Children' [1993] Crim LR 31.

Williams, B., 'Moral Responsibility and Political Freedom' (1997) Camb LJ 96.

Williams, G., 'Assault and Words' [1957] Crim LR 219.

Williams, G., 'Complicity, Purpose and the Draft Code' [1990] Crim LR 4.

Williams, G., 'Consent and Public Policy' [1962] Crim LR 75.

Williams, G., *Criminal Law: The General Part*, London: Stevens (1961; also 1953 edition).

Williams, G., 'Criminal Omissions: The Conventional View' (1991) 107 LQR 86.

Williams, G., 'Divergent Interpretations of Recklessness' (1982) 132 NLJ 289.

Williams, G., 'Gross Negligence Manslaughter and the Duty of Care in Drugs Cases' [2009] Crim LR 631.

Williams, G., 'Handling, Theft and the Purchaser Who Takes a Chance' [1985] Crim LR 432.

Williams, G., 'Innocent Agency and Causation' (1992) 3 Crim L Forum 289.

Williams, G., 'Offences and Defences' (1982) 2 LS 233.

Williams, G., 'Rape is Rape' (1992) 142 NLJ 11.

Williams, G., 'Recklessness Redefined' (1981) 40 CLJ 252.

Williams, G., 'Statute Interpretation, Prostitution and the Rule of Law' in C. Tapper (ed.), *Crime, Proof and Punishment*, London: Butterworths (1981).

Williams, G., 'Temporary Appropriation Should be Theft' [1981] Crim LR 129.

Williams, G., *Textbook of Criminal Law*, London: Stevens (1983).

Williams, G., 'The Lords and Impossible Attempts' [1986] Camb LJ 33.

Williams, G., 'The *Mens Rea* for Murder: Leave it Alone' (1989) 105 LQR 397, 398.

Williams, G., *The Mental Element in Crime*, Jerusalem: Magnes Press (1965).

Williams, G., *The Sanctity of Life and the Criminal Law*, London: Faber and Faber (1958).

Williams, G., 'Victims and Other Exempt Persons in Crime' (1990) 10 LS 245.

Williams, G., 'What Should the Code do About Omissions?' (1987) 7 LS 92.

Williams, G., 'Wrong Turnings on the Law of Attempt' [1991] Crim LR 416.

Williams, R., 'Deception, Mistake, and the Vitiation of the Victim's Consent' (2008) 124 LQR 132.

Wilson, W., 'A Plea for Rationality in the Law of Murder' [1990] 10 LS 307.

Wilson, W., 'A Rational Scheme of Liability for Participating in Crime' [2008] Crim LR 1.

Wilson, W., *Central Issues in Criminal Theory*, Oxford: Hart (2002).

Wilson, W., 'Consenting to Personal Injury: How far can you go?' (1995) Contemporary Issues in Law 45.

Wilson, W., 'Doctrinal Rationality after *Woollin*' (1999) Mod LR 447.

Wilson, W., 'Impaired Voluntariness: The Variable Standards' (2003) Buffalo Criminal Law Review.

Wilson, W., 'Involuntary Intoxication: Excusing the Inexcusable' (1995) 1 Res Publica 25.

Wilson, W., 'Is Hurting People Wrong?' (1992) JSWFL 388.

Wilson, W., 'Murder and the Structure of Homicide' [2006] Crim LR.

Wilson, W., 'Murder and the Structure of Homicide' in A.J. Ashworth and B. Mitchell (eds), *Rethinking English Homicide Law*, Oxford: OUP (2000).

Wilson, W., 'Murder by Omission' (2010) New Crim LR 1.

Wilson, W., 'The Filtering Role of Crisis in the Constitution of Criminal Excuses' (July 2004) XVII(2) Canadian Journal of Law and Jurisprudence.

Wilson, W., 'The Structure of Criminal Defences' [2005] Crim LR.

Wilson, W., 'The Structure of Criminal Homicide' [2006] Crim LR.

Wilson, W., 'What's Wrong with Murder?' [2006] Criminal Law & Philosophy.

Wilson, W. and Smith, K.J.M., 'The Doctor's Dilemma: Necessity and the Legality of Medical Intervention' (1995) 1 Medical Law International 387.

Wilson, W., Ebrahim, I. *et al.*, 'Violence, Sleep-walking and the Criminal Law', parts 1 and 2 [2005] Crim LR 614.

Wishart, H., 'Criminal Culpability, Criminal Attempts and the Erosion of Choice Theory' (2013) 77(1) J Crim L 78.

Witmer-Rich, J., 'It's Good to be Autonomous: Prospective Consent, Retrospective Consent, and the Foundation of Consent in the Criminal Law' (2011) 5(3) Criminal Law & Philosophy 377.

Wolchover, D. and Heaton-Armstrong, A., 'Reasonable Doubt' (2010) 174(32) Criminal Law & Justice Weekly 484.

Wolff, J., *Ethics and Public Policy: A Philosophical Inquiry*, London: Routledge (2011).

Wooton, B., *Crime and the Criminal Law*, London: Sweet & Maxwell (1981).

Wright, F.B., 'Criminal Liability of Directors and Senior Managers for Deaths at Work', Crim LR (2007) 949–68.

Yaffe, G., *Attempts: in the Philosophy of Action and the Criminal Law*, Oxford: OUP (2012).

Yaffe, G., 'Moore on Causing, Acting and Complicity' (2012) 18(4) LT 437.

Yaffe, G., 'The Voluntary Act Requirement' in A. Marmor (ed.), *The Routledge Companion to Philosophy of Law*, London: Routledge (2012) 174.

Yaffe, G., 'Trying, Acting and Attempted Crimes' (2009) 28 Law & Philosophy 109.

Yankah, E., 'Legal Vices and Civic Virtue: Vice Crimes, Republicanism and the Corruption of Lawfulness' (2013) 7(1) Criminal Law & Philosophy 61.

Yankah, E., 'Paradox in Overcriminalization' (2011) 14(1) New Criminal LR 1.

Yeo, S., *Fault in Homicide*, Sydney: Federation Press (1997).

Young, W., 'The Effects of Imprisonment on Offending: A Judge's Perspective' [2010] Crim LR 3.

Zaibert, L., 'The Moralist Strikes Back' (2011) 14(1) New Criminal LR 139.

Zimmerman, M., *The Immorality of Punishment*, Broadview Press (2011).

Index